JUL 1 6 2010

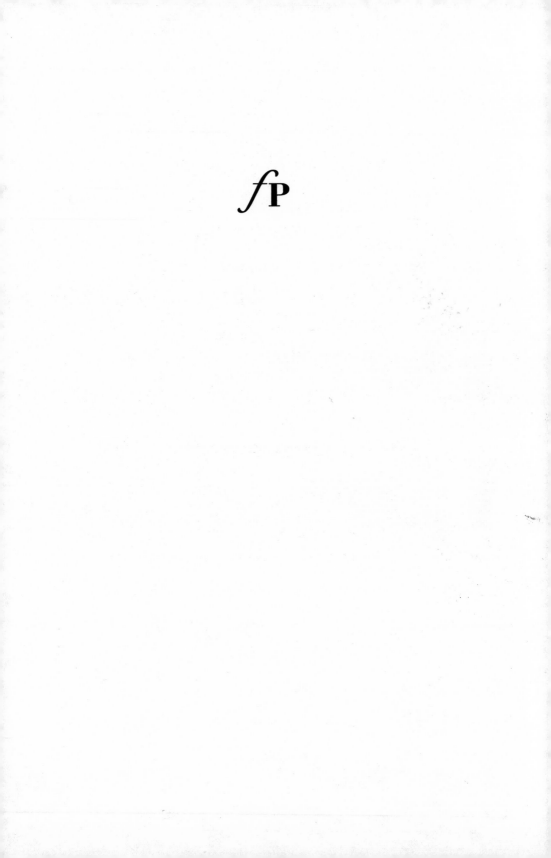

THELONIOUS MONK

*The Life and Times
of an American Original*

ROBIN D. G. KELLEY

FREE PRESS

New York London Toronto Sydney

*f*P

Free Press
A Division of Simon & Schuster, Inc.
1230 Avenue of the Americas
New York, NY 10020

First Free Press hardcover edition November 2009

FREE PRESS and colophon are trademarks of Simon & Schuster, Inc.

For information about special discounts for bulk purchases, please contact Simon & Schuster
Special Sales at 1-866-506-1949 or business@simonandschuster.com.

The Simon & Schuster Speakers Bureau can bring authors to your live event. For more
information or to book an event, contact the Simon & Schuster Speakers Bureau at
1-866-248-3049 or visit our website at www.simonspeakers.com.

Frontis photograph © Michael Ochs Archives/Getty Images

Manufactured in the United States of America

1   3   5   7   9   10   8   6   4   2

Library of Congress Control Number: 2009008526

ISBN 978-0-684-83190-9

CONTENTS

Monk: *It's the High Priest of Bebop talking.*

Nellie: (Laughing) *Oh, God!*

Monk: *The one and only Thelonious Monk. The greatest pianist in the world.*

Nellie: *Who'd you say you were?*

Monk: *The High Priest of Bebop.*

Nellie: *And?*

Monk: *The one and only great musician.*

Nellie: *And?*

Monk: *The greatest musician who ever lived.*

Nellie: *And?*

Monk: *Huh? How much other shit you want me to be?*

Nellie: *I don't know, darling, anything you want to be.*

Private recording, circa 1961

PRELUDE

I have a choice here between writing about Monk as he is, or as he seems to be, and is generally thought to be. There isn't any great difficulty about it, because both sides are fertile ground; the stories merely differ in plausibility.

Critic Paul Bacon, 1949[1]

Benetta Smith—known affectionately as "Teeny"—loved to visit her Aunt Nellie and Uncle Thelonious. For a kid growing up in the late '50s and early '60s, the Monks' tiny ground-floor apartment at 243 West 63rd Street, must have seemed almost carnivalesque. Uncle Thelonious sat at the piano turning Christmas carols into Monk originals, or holding forth with a string of friendly put-downs or challenging questions about the ways of the world. Aunt Nellie chatted away, sometimes entertaining the kids with wild and wonderful stories, sometimes cursing booking agents, managers, and anyone else who took advantage of her dear husband, sometimes gently scolding one of her nieces not to "bang" on the piano. Their two children, "Toot" (Thelonious, Jr.) and "Boo Boo" (Barbara), added to the drama and the fun; they were full of energy, and their parents encouraged them to express themselves freely. The apartment and the neighborhood became a playground for Teeny's six siblings, as well as her cousins and their family friends. Uncle "Baby," Thelonious's younger brother Thomas, lived a couple of doors down, so his four children were always in the mix.

Like all his nieces and nephews, Teeny treated her uncle as an uncle—not as some eccentric genius or celebrity. During one of her many visits in 1959 or '60, when she was about twelve years old, Teeny noticed a book of compositions by Chopin perched on her uncle's rented Steinway baby grand piano. Monk's piano was notorious for its clutter. It occupied a significant portion of the kitchen and extended into the front room. The lid remained closed, since it doubled as a temporary storage space for music, miscellaneous papers, magazines, folded laundry, dishes, and any number of stray kitchen items.

Teeny thumbed through the pages of the Chopin book, then turned to her uncle and asked, "What are you doing with that on the piano? I thought you couldn't read music? You can read that?" The challenge was on. In response, Monk sat down at the piano, turned to a very difficult piece, and started playing it at breakneck speed.

"His hands were a blur," she recalled decades later. "Then after he was through, he jumped up from the piano and just started grinning. So then I said, 'You didn't play that right.'"

"Whaaaa? What are you talking about? I played it ten times faster than anyone could!"

Teeny sassed back, "It is supposed to be played adagio and you played it allegro."[2]

Monk loved that kind of one-upmanship, the playful banter, challenges from those who weren't afraid to engage him. And he was proud of his family, including Teeny's burgeoning knowledge of music.

For well over half a century, the press and the critics have portrayed Monk as "eccentric," "mad," "childlike," "brooding," "naïve," "intuitive," "primitive," even "taciturn." As Nat Hentoff, one of the few critics who got to know Monk, observed: "Monk . . . became a stock cartoon figure for writers of Sunday-supplement pieces about the exotica of jazz. Pictures of Monk in dark glasses and goatee would usually be captioned 'Mad Monk' or 'The High Priest of Bop.' Exaggerated stories of his personal life were the 'substance' of the articles. There was no attempt to discuss the nature or seriousness of his musical intentions."[3] Journalist Lewis Lapham's sympathetic portrait of Monk for the *Saturday Evening Post* is typical of much of the writing about Monk. He described Thelonious as an "emotional and intuitive man, possessing a child's vision of the world, Monk talks, sleeps, eats, laughs, walks or dances as the spirit moves him."[4] He was said to be uncommunicative, and music was the only way he could communicate. He supposedly lived in his own little world, exiled from reality, and had no interest in anything except his music and himself. The only music that interested him was his own, or the pop tunes and old standards that he transformed into his own idiom.

Even his fans and defenders made authoritative statements about Monk's lack of interest and/or knowledge of other musical genres—especially classical music. In what was intended to be a genuine compliment, French critic André Hodeir insisted that this "true jazzman" had no interest in "serious music." He assured his readers that "no twelve-tone sirens have lured Monk away from jazz. He probably doesn't even know that such music exists. I can safely say that the gradual development of his language has been the result of intuition and intuition alone."[5] Pianist, critic, and educator John Mehegan said much the same thing in a 1963 essay. "The entire body of resources of Western man," he mused, "relating to the playing of the piano, which dates back to the sixteenth century, remains unknown to Thelonious Sphere Monk for the simple reason that Monk is not Western man. He is a Black man."[6] Even fellow jazz pianist Bill Evans famously stated that Monk's "unique and astoundingly pure music" can be explained by his lack of "exposure to the Western classical music tradition or, for that matter, comprehensive exposure to any music other than jazz and American popular music."[7]

Quincy Jones extended the myth of pure genius to Monk's entire interaction with the world, as if he were a sealed fermentation vat: "He is not familiar with many classical works, or with much life outside himself, and I think because of this he did not create on a contrived or inhibited basis."[8]

The myth is as attractive as it is absurd. The truth is, Thelonious Monk possessed an impressive knowledge of, and appreciation for, Western classical music, not to mention an encyclopedic knowledge of hymns and gospel music, American popular songs, and a variety of obscure art songs that defy easy categorization. For him, it was all music. Once in 1966, a phalanx of reporters in Helsinki pressed Monk about his thoughts on classical music and whether or not jazz and classical can come together. His drummer, Ben Riley, watched the conversation unfold: "Everyone wanted him to answer, give some type of definition between classical music and jazz . . . So he says, 'Two is one,' and that stopped the whole room. No one else said anything else."[9] Two is one, indeed. Monk loved Frédéric Chopin, Sergei Rachmaninoff, Beethoven, and Bach, and like many of his peers of the bebop generation, he took an interest in Igor Stravinsky. And his life was no more monastic than any other urban jazzman's. Indeed, it was far more colorful and interesting than a true monk's. The myths surrounding Monk have gotten in the way of the truth, and the truth about his life and music is fascinating and compli-cated—and no less original or creative than the myth.

Monk wasn't born with some kind of natural musical knowledge and ability, nor was he entirely self-taught (though he did have perfect pitch). He received a formi-dable music education and worked very hard to achieve his distinctive sound. Nor did he withdraw into an isolated musical meditation, away from the world. It took a village to raise Monk: a village populated by formal music teachers, local musicians from the San Juan Hill neighborhood of New York in which he grew up; an itinerant preacher, a range of friends and collaborators who helped facilitate his own musical studies and exploration; and a very large, extended family willing to pitch in and sacrifice a great deal so that Thelonious could pursue a life of uncompromising creativity. He drew inspiration, ideas, and lessons from family members, daily experience, joys and hard-ships, and the city itself—its sounds, its colors, its drama. Hence this book is not just about him, or his music; rather, it is an intimate story about the folks who shaped him—his hardworking and devoted mother, Barbara, his wife, Nellie, and her entire family, their children, his brother and sister and their kids, his musical kith and kin, his patron saint and friend the Baroness Nica de Koenigswarter, his childhood friends and first crushes, the people of the local community center, his ancestors and the leg-acy they bestowed upon him; not to mention the agents, managers, producers, critics, judges, cops, attorneys, and others whose actions and decisions directly affected Monk's livelihood.

Thelonious Monk was very much of the world, at least until mental and physical illness finally caused him to withdraw, making his world seem much smaller, self-con-tained, and at times impenetrable. For most of his life he remained engaged and fas-cinated with his surroundings. Politics, art, commerce, nature, architecture, history were not beyond his ken, and Monk was the kind of man who loved a good debate, despite stories of his inability to communicate. Fortunately, many of his close friends and family members have been willing to share their stories, most of which have never been told before in print. They reveal a startlingly different Thelonious Monk—witty, incredibly generous, intensely family-oriented, curious, critical, and brutally honest. In addition, Monk himself was frequently captured on tape telling stories, debating, or just shooting the breeze. The tapes were made by his friend and supporter the Baroness Nica de Koenigswarter, the photographer W. Eugene Smith (at whose loft Monk's big band often rehearsed), or by his wife, Nellie. Such tapes are a biographer's dream, for they capture impromptu conversations and ideas unmediated by interviewers or media outlets.

One of those recordings, made by W. Eugene Smith during a big-band rehearsal in June of 1964, caught Monk in a funny conversation about the power of porpoises. Overhearing soprano saxophonist Steve Lacy talk about his friend, trombonist Roswell Rudd, getting a job at the Library of Congress working for Alan Lomax organizing recorded music from around the world, Monk's ears perked up. Monk pressed Lacy for details, and Lacy in turn explained to Monk that he was listening to "Eskimo music . . . the wildest African shit you've ever heard, Chinese music . . . even the music of porpoises." Monk then explained to the room, "They say if you can ever make a tape of a porpoise and play it back, down slow enough, it's the same as the human voice. They are so close to the human species. Because they have the same box here [pointing to his throat]." After explaining that they communicate at very high frequencies, Monk performs a pretty convincing imitation of a porpoise cry. He then launches into a lecture about how man might benefit from harnessing the porpoise's ability to sense everything around them: "You know, it's an amazing thing to study the porpoises. With the study of the porpoise, they going to find out possibilities of completely obliterating a blind man's stick. Walk down the fucking street blind as a bat, and naked. They'll put a little sonar thing in his ear or something that is able to tell when you're getting up to anything, the kind of object, the texture of the object, whether it's a building or a person . . . it could tell that it's either a hard surface or cloth. Because they've checked out porpoises and they can't figure out, they hadn't been able to figure out why a porpoise can swim in dark, murky waters, so you can't see nothing at all, and they won't hit a motherfucking thing."[10]

Other tapes are more intimate, like the tapes Nellie made of Monk rehearsing at home. These tapes reveal Monk's deep and abiding love of this music, Mrs. Monk's delight in listening to her husband, and the joy they both derived from each other's company. Between and during songs, the recorder captures snippets of a love affair. Sometimes they joked with one another, or simply conversed about how to work the tape recorder; other times Nellie sang along in unison with the piano. Monk had evident trust in her knowledge and opinions about music as well as in her ability to run the tape machine, even when she was just learning how to work it. These tapes are windows into more than Monk's music. They reveal Monk as both a comic and a romantic—he had a tremendous sense of humor, and he deeply loved old songs. At the end of a tender rendition of "Tea for Two," he turned to Nellie and asked, with even greater tenderness, "Were you recording that?"[11]

The critics who interviewed him backstage or observed him dancing across the bandstand missed these sides of Monk. Like most people, he was not one to unveil himself to strangers. Sometimes Monk's eccentric public behavior was a way of salvaging whatever private life he had left. As he once told the writer Frank London Brown, "You know people have tried to put me off as being crazy. Sometimes it's to your advantage for people to think you're crazy."[12]

He got a kick out of fooling people, particularly those whom he thought were too lazy or afraid to think for themselves. One of his favorite pranks was to stare intensely at a spot on the ceiling or in the sky, either in a crowded room or on a street corner. Invariably, several people would look up with him, searching for whatever elusive object apparently fascinated him. It was an experiment in mass psychology that brought him great amusement.

But not all of Monk's bizarre actions were artifice. Thelonious suffered from bipolar disorder, the signs of which are evident as early as the 1940s. But by the early 1960s, just as he began to earn the fame and recognition that had eluded him for the first two decades of his career, various mental and physical ailments began to take an even greater toll, exacerbated by poor medical treatment, an unhealthy lifestyle, the daily stresses of a working jazz musician, and an unending financial and creative battle with the music industry. Some writers romanticize manic depression and/or schizophrenia as characteristics of creative genius, but the story of Monk's physical and mental ailments is essentially a tragedy, a story of his slow decline and the pain it caused to those closest to him. Its manifestations were episodic, so he continued to function and make incredible music up until the day of his retirement in 1976. During these nearly twenty years, his ability to lead a band and to dig out fresh interpretations of compositions he had been playing for decades, in spite of his illness and a protracted struggle with the industry, was astonishing.

Three decades ago, when I was young, messing around with piano and studying bass slightly more seriously, my new stepfather, Paul, a professional tenor sax player, had me listen to Monk and Johnny Griffin perform "Evidence." Soon I memorized everyone's solo on that record, including Roy Haynes's unaccompanied snare drum rolls, which is impossible to approximate verbally without spraying spittle on anyone standing within five feet of my mouth. I became completely obsessed with Monk's sound, his clang-clang sound of surprise, rich with deafening silences, dissonances, and harmonic ambiguities. It was that ice cream truck sound: Monk the good humor man. I worked on that sound on piano, from Monk's blues and intricate and lovely ballads to his up-tempo numbers, which nearly put me in the hospital. His sound seemed beyond my grasp, beyond my comprehension. I played more notes; I played fewer notes; I changed the chord voicings; I played in front of the beat, I danced around the beat, and finally gave up and retreated to rubato. I listened and listened some more. I even summoned him from the ancestors to help . . . and he came to me, in a dream. Decked out in divine alligator shoes, a dark green silk suit, yellow tie, bamboo sunglasses, and a cold straw hat, he snuck up behind me as I sat hunched over my stepfather's Steinway upright, looked over my shoulder, and simply mumbled, "You're making the wrong mistakes."

Here, more humbly, is an attempt to evoke his world in words, not music. Monk consistently and boldly spoke the truth, no matter whose feelings were hurt. One of his favorite mantras was "Always Know," adding that the word "Know" was Monk spelled backward with the "W" inverted. He often illustrated the point with a huge custom-made ring that had "MONK" emblazoned across the top in diamonds, turning it upside down in case you didn't get it. "Always Know!" All Ways Know!

This book is my attempt to "Know" Monk, the man behind the mystique.

1

"My Mother Didn't Want Me to Grow Up in North Carolina"

(Slavery, Freedom, Birth, Exodus)

Thelonious Monk had much to celebrate on October 10, 1957. It was his fortieth birthday, and after more than two decades of scuffling his career was on an upswing. He had a regular engagement at the Five Spot Café in New York City—his first steady gig in several years. When he opened there three months earlier, Monk had just begun to emerge from relative obscurity. Now he was the jazz world's hottest ticket, and the small East Village bar had become one of the hippest joints in the city. Adoring fans, hipsters, bohemians, and wannabes lined up outside the narrow storefront club at 5 Cooper Square, hoping to catch Monk and his legendary quartet—John Coltrane, bassist Ahmed Abdul-Malik, and drummer Shadow Wilson. That night, Monk wanted to celebrate. Friends, family, and enthusiastic fans surrounded him. His "'un' years," as his wife Nellie used to call them, were about to end.[1]

Further uptown, on West 56th Street near Fifth Avenue, another Monk—Julius Withers Monk—also had something to celebrate. On that same Thursday night, Julius Monk's latest opus, a musical comedy revue entitled "Take Five," opened at Upstairs at the Downstairs, to excellent reviews. Known to the entertainment world as a fine pianist, satirist, male model, producer, and a bit of an eccentric, Julius Monk had worked at the famed #1 Fifth Avenue Bar during the 1930s and gigged in France before becoming musical director of Le Ruban Bleu, a popular supper club, in 1943. In the 1950s, he founded the Downstairs Room and subsequently launched Upstairs at the Downstairs as a combination theater/supper club where he produced several acclaimed comic revues.[2]

Thelonious and Julius probably knew of each other. In every issue of the directory for Local 802 of the American Federation of Musicians, Thelonious's name followed Julius's in the listing of pianists.[3] They shared a lot more than the piano, the union, a reputation for eccentricity, Latinate first names, and the same surname. Both hailed from North Carolina—Julius from Salisbury in Rowan County (he was born in 1912), Thelonious from Rocky Mount in Edgecombe County (born in 1917). Their

1

geographical origins are not accidental: a century earlier, Julius's great-grandfather, Archibald Monk, had enslaved Thelonious's great-grandfather, John Jack Monk.[4]

Julius Withers Monk took great interest in studying his family's past. During the 1940s, he conducted extensive genealogical research and even commissioned a scholar to produce a detailed family tree of the Monks.[5] Yet he was only interested in the Monks who looked like him, not the nineteen slaves his great-granddaddy owned in 1860.[6] Had he known this history, he might have been inspired to head down to the Five Spot after his show and thank Thelonious personally for the privileged life he was able to enjoy. The scion of one of Salisbury's wealthiest landowners, Dr. Lawrence Monk, Sr., Julius grew up in a well-to-do family and attended the Peabody Institute in Baltimore and the Cincinnati Conservatory.[7] Julius's excellent musical education, like his father's and brother's medical school education, was partly paid for with inherited wealth, the source of which turned out to be the sweat and toil of John Jack Monk and the other African-descended people held in bondage.

While Julius grew up in affluence, Thelonious had been born into extreme poverty. His mother and grandmother spent their lives scrubbing floors for a living, and his father, Thelonious, Sr., cobbled together work as an unskilled day laborer in the railroad town of Rocky Mount. His grandfathers had lived a life of debt peonage, sharecropping for ex-slave masters and surviving pretty much from meal to meal. Yet Monk inherited more than poverty. His family passed down a rich cultural, intellectual, and political legacy—a legacy that shaped his music and his worldview in both profound and subtle ways.

The vestiges of slavery were everywhere in the Jim Crow South. More important than the memory of slavery, however, was the memory of freedom. The two generations that preceded Thelonious's lived through one of the greatest revolutions and counterrevolutions in the history of the modern world. Thelonious, his sister Marion, and brother Thomas were raised by people for whom freedom had tangible meaning. They heard first-hand stories of emancipation from their parents; stories of black men going to the polls and running for office, of former slaves founding churches and schools, and helping to build a new democracy in the Southern states. For any Southern black person living between 1865 and 1900, freedom wasn't a word taken for granted or used abstractly. As Thelonious's parents in turn passed to him, freedom meant more than breaking the "rules" of musical harmony or bending tempos. His grandparents were part of freedom's first generation of African-Americans, a generation that could dream of a good life under a hopeful democracy. Yet his parents watched that democracy—and their freedom—burn, sometimes literally, under assault by white supremacists as Jim Crow laws descended across the South. The disfranchisement of black folk and the restoration of power to the old planter class was rapid and violent. Like many families, the Monks never lost their memory of post–Civil War freedom, or their determination to possess it once again.

Thelonious Monk's music is essentially about freedom. He inherited much from those who came before him: not least a deeply felt understanding of freedom. His story begins with their song.

•   •   •

Monk's ancestors came from West Africa. The majority of slave imports into North Carolina did not come by sea directly from the African continent. Most came over land, either from South Carolina or across the northern border from Virginia. The first slaves brought to North Carolina, during the earliest days of the colony, came mostly from Barbados along with their owners. Cultural affinities and practices can help point to the African ethnic origins of slaves, but not enough is known about Monk's earliest ancestors to even speculate.[8]

We do know that all of Thelonious's people on both his mother's and father's sides ended up bound to plantations on the coastal plains of eastern North Carolina, a region renowned for its dark, rich, alluvial soil, its many rivers and tributaries, and a flat landscape as far as the eye can see. Cotton was king during the antebellum period, but its domain wasn't vast; much of the arable land in the region was used for tobacco, sweet potatoes, Indian corn, and beans. Livestock, especially pigs, was abundant.

Monk's father's people lived on both sides of the border dividing Johnston and Sampson counties. His great-grandfather, John Jack or just "Jack," was born around 1797, and it is quite possible that he was born free in West Africa.[9] In 1835, he became the property of Archibald Monk, through Monk's wife, Harriet. Harriet Monk inherited John Jack from her father, Aaron Hargrove, another prominent Sampson County planter. Eight years earlier, Hargove had given John Jack's first-born daughter, Chaney, to Harriet as a gift. Chaney was only nine years old at the time.[10] With John Jack and Chaney reunited, they, too, became "Monks," as did all the other slaves on Archibald's Newton Grove plantation.

Archibald Monk himself was never much of a planter; his heart was in sales, and in political power. Born in Sampson County around 1789, he grew up to become one of North Carolina's most prominent citizens. During the early 1820s he resided in Fayetteville and co-owned a successful dry-goods store on Hay Street. It wasn't until after he married Harriet Hargrove in 1824 that he returned to the northern district of Sampson County and took up a life as a plantation-owner and public figure.[11]

The official Monk family history leaves out one crucial story popular among the black side of the Monk clan. Around 1825 or '26—very soon after his marriage—Archibald's house slave, reputedly a beautiful young woman of mixed Indian and African heritage, bore him twin sons, Solomon and Kaplin.[12] He was still living in Fayetteville. Archibald caused quite a stir among the city fathers by bringing his mulatto children to the local Presbyterian church with him. According to the black Monk family lore, the congregation banned Archibald from coming to church, and he decided right then and there to establish his own church on his plantation where the white Monks worshipped alongside their slaves. His son, Dr. John Carr Monk, apparently inherited his father's belief that the Lord's House knows no color line (except perhaps between the floor and the gallery). Before the Civil War, John and his wife, Anne Eason Monk, attended a Methodist church in Sampson County known for admitting slaves in the galleries. They were there to mind the white children, although they were encouraged to worship. After the war, Dr. Monk was a lone dissenting voice against segregated churches for free black people. Not to be deterred, in the 1870s he converted to Catholicism, to the chagrin of his fellow white Protestant neighbors, and deeded a parcel of his land in Westbrook Township to establish "a colored school," with religious instruction being first and foremost.[13]

Even when they worshipped together, antebellum blacks and whites didn't worship the same things. Enslaved black people didn't take much stock in "massa's" God. They created their own version of Christianity and generally preferred to worship in the woods, in their poorly constructed cabins, anywhere beyond the seeing eyes of the white folks. Their sacred songs and prayers often spoke of freedom and justice, of a promised land without the lash or without toil from sunup to sundown. Their God could be forgiving, filling the master's heart with kindness; or redemptive, turning his wrath on those who continue to hold God's chosen people in Egyptland and smiting their first-born dead. Thelonious would imbibe African-American theology from this tradition, decades later.

Meanwhile the white Monks, Archibald and John, saw nothing wrong with holding other Christians in bondage, and they made a lot of money doing so. On the eve of the Civil War, Archibald Monk owned nineteen slaves and real estate valued at $10,000. Overall, his personal estate was worth $21,179, quite respectable in those days.[14]

John Jack was the oldest slave on the Monk plantation. By 1850, he was fifty-three years old and had already fathered three children, George, Isaac, and Richard, with the woman to whom he was probably married. (Slave marriages were not legally recognized, but the bonds among enslaved black people were just as deep, if not deeper, than marriage bonds recognized by the state.) She was a slave on the Monk plantation. Her name, unfortunately, is unknown, and she died before 1850. Jack subsequently married a slave on the Willis Cole plantation located in nearby Bentonville, just over the Johnston County line. Because of their proximity, slaves on the Cole and the Monk plantations had a history of social interaction. Several of the Monk slaves were wedded to Coles.[15]

We know almost nothing about "Mother Cole" except that she was part Tuscarora Indian, and proud of it. Before European colonialism, the Tuscarora occupied much of eastern North Carolina, including the coast. Between 1711–1715, the Tuscarora declared war on white settlers who were encroaching on their hunting grounds, but they were militarily decimated. Hundreds were enslaved and sold to English planters in the Caribbean. By 1754, barely 300 Tuscarora were left in the state.[16]

Though elderly by antebellum standards, John Jack and "Mother Cole" managed to have one child, Hinton, born on February 12, 1852.[17] Hinton was Thelonious, Jr.'s grandfather. Raised by his mother and other members of his extended family on the Willis Cole plantation, he spent the first thirteen years of his life in slavery. Cole's plantation wasn't huge, about 300 acres. If Hinton was anything like most slave children, by the time he was eight he was probably milking Cole's four milk cows, tending to the twenty-eight pigs, possibly digging up sweet potatoes, toting water to field hands, helping in the kitchen, and caring for infants. He was surrounded by other children; according to the 1860 Census, of the twenty Africans Willis Cole held in bondage, twelve were thirteen and younger.[18]

As Union armies marched south in the Civil War, they were confronted with waves of black men, women, and children, folks who boldly emancipated themselves with the hope that the men in blue would protect them from "massa" and the heartless "paddy rollers" (patrollers). The federal government and military called these escaped slaves "contraband," since they knew that seizing slaves, along with livestock and land, was the best way to destroy the Confederacy. But these black folk were more than contraband; they were volunteer soldiers; they were the hewers of wood and toters of water who sustained the Union army in its march to the sea; and they were candidates for citizenship in the post-war democracy.[19]

Willis Cole's "Negroes" were no different from other enslaved people caught in the whirlwind of this reluctant revolution. They traded tales of the Union army's invasion and spoke in hushed tones about President Lincoln's Proclamation that on January 1, 1863, all the black folk held as slaves in the rebellious states were henceforth free. That fateful day came and went, but nothing happened in Bentonville—no Union forces, no Lincoln, no mass exodus, no hand of God. When Hinton turned nine the following month, he was still a slave on the Cole plantation. And when the Union forces finally did arrive in Bentonville in March 1865, the Willis Cole plantation became the site of one of the most important battles in Civil War history. The Battle of Bentonville was not only the last Confederate victory of the war, it proved to be the largest military conflict ever fought on North Carolina soil, involving some 85,000 troops. It was the South's last hurrah, for once General Sherman dispatched reinforcements the Confederates withdrew. Cole had turned over his house to Confederate commanders, and he likely fled, with his twenty slaves, to Fayetteville, where most eastern North Carolina planters took refuge.[20]

A month after the Battle of Bentonville, and two weeks after Robert E. Lee surrendered to Ulysses S. Grant at Appomattox, Confederate General Joseph E. Johnston officially surrendered to General Sherman, ending both the Civil War and slavery in the state of North Carolina. For black folks it was Jubilee; for local whites, primarily those whose way of life depended on unpaid black labor, it was Armageddon. Not every planter accepted the news that all slaves were to be emancipated. Throughout the summer and fall of 1865, there were hundreds of reported incidents of African-Americans still being held in bondage. The cultural landscape for both white and black Monks changed dramatically nonetheless. A new group of black leaders emerged out of the war, many of whom fought for the Union army and saw themselves as liberators. They raised money to build churches and schools, to hire teachers, and to purchase land. Some former slaves assumed that the land of their former masters now belonged to them. Indeed, there had been some wartime distribution of land by the Union army, and the Freedmen's Bureau promised to settle former slaves on plots of their own. Not all former slaves were so bold. Tens of thousands throughout the state stuck close to their old plantations, afraid of starvation and severing deep family ties in the community. But even these families were vulnerable; there were many incidents of planters evicting their former slaves, especially those too old or weak to work.[21]

Despite these initial setbacks, black people were determined to own land, to enjoy citizenship, to exercise political power, and to live in a South where everyone would be free and equal. They remained optimistic because of the presence of federal troops and institutions such as the Freedmen's Bureau. But once Andrew Johnson was sworn in as president following Lincoln's assassination, he made his position clear: America is a "white man's nation" and white men shall rule the South. Throughout 1866, President Johnson appointed avid racists to positions of power in the Southern Provisional government. They, in turn, disarmed the majority of black federal troops while white planters formed armed terrorist organizations such as the Ku Klux Klan and the Knights of the White Camellia. In 1866, white supremacists in government passed a series of laws known as the Black Codes. The North Carolina Black Codes restricted freedom of movement of blacks, the amount of land they could own, whom they could marry (interracial marriages were outlawed), and their right to bear arms. Some of the most draconian Black Codes were the apprenticeship laws, which allowed former masters to retain control of ex-slaves under the age of twenty-one, under the pretext that they needed a guardian. Abuse of apprenticeship was rampant throughout the state, especially in Sampson County.[22]

Hinton, Thelonious's grandfather, who turned thirteen in the year of Jubilee, was ripe for such abuse. Both of his parents died, either during the war or immediately thereafter. Fortunately, Hinton's half-brother Levin Cole and his wife, Harriet, took him in. He earned his keep as a farmhand, and learned to read and write.[23] Literacy was a precious thing, especially for black people in a state where it had been a crime to teach slaves to read and write and where free blacks had been prohibited from attending public schools.

By the end of the 1860s, the prevailing political culture turned yet again. Radical Republicans in Congress overturned President Johnson's weak Reconstruction policies and passed the Fourteenth and Fifteenth amendments to the Constitution, granting black people citizenship and male suffrage, respectively. These so-called Civil War amendments marked a profound shift in constitutional history, and for a time they appeared to make the new freedom a sure thing. Former slaves not only began to vote, they ran for office and held positions in the state legislature, Congress, and even the Senate. And they insisted that free universal public education was a pillar of democracy.

For Hinton's generation, reading and writing were revolutionary acts in revolutionary times. He came of age when proud and eloquent black legislators, most of whom came up as slaves in eastern North Carolina, demanded equality under the law, the right of black people to serve on juries, a ten-hour work day, even woman's suffrage. Yet he also witnessed a reign of terror descend upon North Carolina Republicans and black voters. Through violence and intimidation, Democrats succeeded in impeaching and removing the Republican governor in 1871 and regaining control of the state legislature. Four years later, they held a constitutional convention that amended the elective county government system (mostly by gerrymandering) in order to reduce black voting power in the eastern counties. The Democrats campaigned for the amendment on overtly racial terms, arguing that allowing black majority districts was tantamount to "White Slavery in North Carolina—Degradation Worse Then Death."[24] White supremacy was given a boost during the 1876 presidential contest between Samuel Tilden and Rutherford Hayes. Tilden had won the popular vote, but both sides claimed electoral-college victory in three key states. A commission was appointed to decide the dispute and an informal compromise was struck: the Democrats were willing to cede the White House to Republican Hayes in exchange for withdrawing federal troops from the South, thus removing the last vestiges of Reconstruction.

As the post-war battle in North Carolina swung from extreme to extreme, Hinton reacted like the majority of freed people, becoming a sharecropper on John Carr Monk's land. After emancipation, Levin and Harriet Cole chose not to return to Willis Cole's place. Instead, they moved just across the county line to Newton Grove, where they worked for Monk. Hinton, working alongside his eldest brother, had returned to the same land that his daddy, John Jack, worked a generation earlier. As a free man faced with the responsibility of choosing a surname, Hinton continued to use his mother's name, "Cole."[25]

Hinton Cole proposed to a beautiful and intelligent young woman named Sarah Ann Williams some time between 1875 and 1877. Born on August 3, 1856, Sarah Ann was the eldest daughter of Friday Williams, the former slave and "mulatto" son of Blaney Williams, one of Newton Grove's richest and most prominent planters. At the time of his death in 1852, Williams owned 1,875 acres in Newton Grove, 475 acres in Duplin County, 442 acres in Greene County, and at least forty-eight slaves.[26] In 1870, Friday Williams, his second wife, Eliza, and their then eight children were renting land from Blaney's son, George Robert Williams. When Hinton and Sarah Ann met, they were practically neighbors. Ten years later, Friday's family and Hinton and Sarah Ann Cole were all working land owned by John Carr Monk's widow, Anne Eason Monk, and their children (Dr. Monk died in 1877).[27]

Like most first-generation free black Southerners, Hinton and Sarah Cole were forced into the precarious life of sharecropping. Every season they struggled to make ends meet, and still managed to raise ten children. Thelonious was the seventh in line, born in 1889.[28] At some point between 1890 and 1900, the entire family relocated to Wayne County, just east of Sampson County.[29] And yet, as residents of eastern North Carolina, they had reason to be hopeful. In 1892, while the rest of the South succumbed to white supremacy, a fusion ticket of Republicans and Populists defeated racist Democrats, winning the majority of state house and senate seats, electing dozens of African-Americans to local offices, and sending a black man, George H. White, to Congress four years later. Such interracial unity was short-lived. An appeal to white racial fears was all it took to destroy it.[30]

By the 1898 elections, Democrats swept back to power, with help from white Populists who traded interracial unity for white supremacy. And in the majority-black city of Wilmington, where Democrats could not win by vote, they took up arms and overthrew the elected government, killing scores of African-Americans and some loyal white Republicans.[31] Two years later, they succeeded in getting a constitutional amendment passed, effectively disenfranchising black voters through the use of the poll tax and literacy requirements. During the 1900 election, Alfred Moore Waddell, former congressman who led the Wilmington Insurrection, called on whites to warn any "Negro out voting" to go home immediately, and "If he refuses, kill him, shoot him down in his tracks."[32] Nonetheless, slightly over two-thirds of black voters showed up at the polls in 1900. These were scary times, but Hinton, Sarah, and their children persevered. By 1900, at least two of their sons, Jack and Alonzo, reportedly had two years of schooling and could read and write. Eventually all of their children received some level of "common schooling."[33]

It was during this period, before the turn of the century, that Hinton made the fateful decision to change his family's name from Cole to Monk. By the time a Wayne County census taker recorded his family's presence there in the spring of 1900, they were all Monks.[34] Perhaps Hinton was asserting his independence from his half-brother, or maybe he had become indebted to another landowner and had to escape without settling his debt. Whatever the reason, Hinton, Sarah, and at least one of their children eventually returned to his birthplace of Bentonville as Monks rather than Coles.[35]

Hinton and Sarah chose their children's names with imaginative flair. They picked Squire, Theodoras (also known as Theodore), Bertha—and Thelonious. "Thelonius" or "Thelonious" is the Latinized spelling of St. Tillo, a Benedictine monk renowned for his missionary work in France in the seventh century, who was kidnapped by raiders and brought to the Low Countries as a slave before he was ransomed and joined the order. In France he is called St. Theau, in Belgium he is known as Filman, and in Germany he was referred to as Hilonius.[36] It is likely that Hinton learned a bit of Catholic history—maybe even some Latin—from the school Dr. John Carr Monk established for local black children.

Born in Newton Grove on June 20, 1889, Thelonious (Sr.) began working alongside his brothers and sisters as a boy, as the family tended to livestock and picked cotton in Wayne County. He received some formal education, learning to read and write, and at some point in his young life, he picked up the harmonica and learned to play a little piano by ear. But those moments of amusement were few and far between; most of his childhood was consumed by toil.

As a young adult, he left his parents' house to join his sister and her husband in Rocky Mount. Many rural migrants were coming to the burgeoning railroad town, in search of steady employment and a decent place to raise a family. He did find Barbara Batts, another rural North Carolina migrant who carried similar hopes. But the financial opportunities the city promised proved to be elusive.

Barbara Batts, "Miss Barbara," as she was affectionately called by friends and neighbors, hailed from Edgecombe County, North Carolina's leader in cotton production, and the heart of the radical Republican Second Congressional District. Edgecombe not only had a black majority during and after Reconstruction, it developed a militant black leadership that fought tirelessly for the social, political, and economic rights of the state's freed people.[37] Barbara developed a lifelong commitment to political and civic engagement (though the Democrats would later become her party of choice), which she would pass on to her children.

Barbara's maternal grandparents, Henry and Clara (Clearly) Knight, were both slaves in Edgecombe County. Henry was born around 1830 in Deep Creek Township, on a plantation owned by Lucy Knight Batts Barlow.[38] Her family's holdings were quite extensive: She had inherited eleven slaves from her father in 1809, and by 1860 she counted thirty-eight slaves among her household of field hands and house servants.[39] Henry worked in the fields, picking cotton and foodstuffs. In 1859, Henry married Clara, a slave ten years his junior, who lived on the neighboring plantation.[40] Although their marriage was not legally recognized until 1865, they insisted that the registrar record the correct year they were wed.

Unfortunately, the couple spent most of the war apart, not only because they lived on separate plantations. Once the Union armies entered North Carolina, most slaveholding families in Edgecombe and Nash Counties fled to Warren County—but not Lucy Knight Batts Barlow. Referred to by family members as "Old Mother," Lucy was a dyed-in-the-wool Southerner who, at eighty years old, stubbornly refused to leave her property, no matter how close the Union troops came. After many efforts to persuade her to move to safer ground, the local Confederate commanders gave up, and she "was provided a detail of Infantry which was quartered in the front grove."[41] Henry and "Old Mother"'s other thirty-seven slaves had to live out the war years under constant Confederate surveillance while Clara toiled for her masters elsewhere.

It is no wonder that their first child, Georgianna (sometimes spelled Georgeanna), was not born until October 31, 1865. Georgianna Knight was Barbara Batts's mother, Thelonious Monk, Jr.'s maternal grandmother. Conceived in the last days of slavery, she was among the first generation of children born free.[42] Henry and Clara raised Georgianna and five younger children on "Old Mother"'s plantation, but after her death in 1867 much of the estate was passed down to her grandson Isaac Batts. Henry sharecropped on Batts's land, and his children helped him as soon as they were old enough. Clara "kept house" as best she could, but when hands were needed in the field they all worked. Nevertheless, Henry and Clara insisted that their children get an education. The 1880 census-taker in Deep Creek reported that three of the Knight children—Georgianna, Blunt, and Emma—had attended school that year.[43] Of course, rural schools for African-American children were rarely open more than two months out of the year, but every working minute of class was sacred.

Georgianna's formal education ended around the time that a farm laborer by the name of Speer (or Speir) Batts took an interest in her. Born in Deep Creek around 1856 to Jacob Batts and Nancy Kay, Speer spent part of his childhood as a slave and never attended school.[44] But he was reputed to be an excellent fiddler who played for dances and local community gatherings in and around Deep Creek.[45] In Scottish, "speer" means "to ask," but it was more commonly understood among the English as an old scientific term for "celestial sphere." As the word was passed down to the younger Thelonious Monk's generation, the pronunciation (and spelling) evolved into "Sphere." Thelonious eventually decided to adopt "Sphere" as his middle name, attributing it to his maternal grandfather. (He often joked that with such a name, he could never be accused of being a square.)

There were no career opportunities for black fiddlers in the rural South during the 1870s. Speer was expected to use his fingers to pick and haul coarse bolls of white cotton. When his father passed away in the mid-1870s, Speer, in his early twenties, had to take on the responsibility of caring for his aging mother and younger siblings. Between his mother's meager earnings as a domestic worker and his wages as a farmhand, they barely made ends meet. In the fall of 1878, Edgecombe farmers endured one of the worst harvests in memory, due to severe drought and global economic depression. Throughout 1879 and 1880, poor black sharecroppers and tenant farmers found themselves in deepening debt, forcing many to take to the road in search of work.[46]

Speer, his mother, and his baby brother Joshua were among them. But unlike the thousands of other African-Americans who headed to Georgia and Florida to work in the turpentine industry, or west to sharecrop in Arkansas and Mississippi, or sought refuge and opportunity in places like Kansas, Indiana, or even Liberia, the Battses stayed in the county, moving to the community of Conetoe, North Carolina. The town is only a few miles southeast of "Freedom Hill." Freedom Hill, or "Liberty Hill" as it was often called, was settled in 1865 by a group of freed slaves with the assistance of the Freedmen's Bureau. A symbol of hope and a model for political militancy for freed people throughout eastern North Carolina, Freedom Hill drew African-Americans throughout the county in search of opportunities and a safe haven against rising white violence.[47]

They did not stay in Conetoe long, and it appears that Speer's mother died there.[48] Speer decided to return to Deep Creek Township and to ask Henry Knight for his first daughter's hand in marriage. On May 8, 1884, with the Justice of the Peace presiding, Speer Batts and Georgianna Knight were married. He was twenty-eight or twenty-nine years old, she was six months shy of her eighteenth birthday.[49] It is not clear how long they stayed in Deep Creek or what they did to survive. They might have lived for a while with Henry and Clara Knight, who would remain on the Batts place for at least another twenty years.[50] But the tendency during the 1880s, especially among younger people, was to leave Edgecombe. Between 1880 and 1890, Edgecombe was one of thirty-five counties that experienced a net loss of African-Americans. By one estimate, nearly 50,000 black people left North Carolina in 1889 alone.[51]

The catalyst for the exodus was as much political as economic. The Democrats vowed to take the state back under the banner of white supremacy. Besides waging extralegal violent attacks against black civic and political organizations, in 1889 the state legislature passed the Payne Electoral Law, which gave registrars (who were predominantly Democrats) wider discretion to disqualify voters. In an effort to slow down the exodus, laws were enforced that made it illegal for a worker to break his or her contract.[52] Speer and Georgianna chose to move out of the county, but they did not go very far. In 1892, when Georgianna gave birth to Barbara, her only child, they resided in Hamilton Township just across the Martin County line, about twenty-five miles east of Deep Creek.[53] Unfortunately, Speer died soon thereafter, never having the opportunity to see his daughter grow to womanhood, or to meet his son-in-law, or to play with his three grandchildren. Whatever musical knowledge he might have passed on to little Thelonious traveled in the realm of memory and story.

Georgianna was determined to make it in Rocky Mount and to create a better life for her teenaged daughter. She wasn't alone. For many rural black folks in the region, all roads led to Rocky Mount. With the erosion of civil and political rights and the deterioration of the rural economy in North Carolina, this rapidly growing railroad and mill town represented one of the few shining beacons in a dark age.

Nestled on the Tar River where Edgecombe and Nash counties meet, Rocky Mount had blown up in just two decades, from a sleepy little mill to the largest metropolitan area in the eastern part of the state. In 1890, only 816 people resided in Rocky Mount, many of whom worked in the tobacco warehouses or the cotton mills. By 1910—three years after incorporating as a city—its population had risen to slightly over 8,000. The main catalyst was the expansion of the Wilmington and Weldon railroad, which ran along Main Street in the center of town and marked the county line between Nash and Edgecombe. The Wilmington and Weldon line had merged with several other local railroad lines to form the Atlantic Coast Line Railroad (ACLRR). In 1892, the ACLRR established repair and outfitting shops on unincorporated land just south of the town. The Emerson Shops, as they were known, attracted rural migrants looking for work.[54]

Thelonious, Sr. and Barbara were among them. They made their separate ways to the city around the same time, between 1907 and early 1909.[55] They each quickly learned that Rocky Mount was no promised land, especially for poor black people. The city was full of idle black men in search of work, as white men had exclusive access to the higher-paying skilled and semi-skilled jobs in the Emerson shops and the Rocky Mount Mills, the city's leading cotton manufacturer. The fact that both Thelonious and Barbara were literate and had some formal education did not matter.[56] Barbara and her mother, Georgianna, did what virtually all employed black women did for a living: domestic work. Georgianna took in laundry while Barbara worked as a housekeeper for a private family.[57]

The city had yet to establish a public high school for black children, so her daughter's education was informal at best.[58] Yet Georgianna's middle-class aspirations are apparent in the first photographic evidence of her and her daughter. Peering through round spectacles, Georgianna looks slightly down into the camera, lips pursed, threatening a smile. She is wearing a slightly tattered but delicate dress with a sheer bodice. Barbara stands beside her, a little distant, her bright eyes wide open. She shares her mother's high cheekbones, smooth dark-brown skin, and small stature. (As an adult, Barbara would stand at five feet, four inches.) Roughly sixteen in this picture, Barbara wears a long-sleeved virginal white dress, reminiscent of an old-time baptismal gown.

Georgianna and Barbara rented a small house on Pennsylvania Avenue in a respectable black working-class community that straddled Edgecombe and Nash counties. Respectable, but poor. Appropriately named Crosstown, the community lay adjacent to the black business district on the Edgecombe county side (or west side) of the railroad tracks. Crosstown stretched eight blocks to the east of Main Street and six blocks north from East Thomas Street to the city limits, where many residents were able to maintain gardens and keep pigs and an occasional milk cow.[59] There were a number of churches in town, and much of Rocky Mount's social life centered around its religious communities. Both women were devout Baptists.[60]

Between work and worship, and with a fairly strict mother, Barbara had very little time to socialize. But at some point, between 1910 and 1913, she met the attractive young man with the most unusual name of Thelonious. Dark-skinned with deep-set, piercing eyes and strong African features, Thelonious Monk was three years Barbara's senior and not a whole lot taller than her (contrary to later myth). According to his draft card, he was "short" and of "medium build."[61] Thelonious resided in South Rocky Mount in a black neighborhood known officially as Gibson Hill but more commonly as "Around the Y" (or "Around the Wye"), a community of mostly railroad workers and laundresses who lived in small two-room section houses. African-Americans in Crosstown and Happy Hill in the northern part of the city tended to look down upon residents in South Rocky Mount, partly because of its reputation for crime, vice, and violence, and because there were very few churches and schools in that part of town. The upstanding and pious folk from Around the Y usually went to the northside to attend church.[62]

Thelonious was one of several Monk children who left their parents' sharecropping for the promise of the city. Around 1908 or 1909, Thelonious moved into a house at 112 Dunn Street with his older sister Eulah, her husband David Whitehead, and his younger sister Hettie Fernandez Monk. A relative named Sampson Monk owned the property initially, and he later willed it to their brother Theodore "Babe."[63] In 1910, Hettie was thirteen years old and attending school, Thelonious was nineteen and worked for the railroad as a common laborer, and his brother-in-law was employed as a fireman for the ACLRR. Three years later, their youngest brother Squire joined the household, and Hettie's education came to a halt, as there was still no high school for black children in Rocky Mount. Hettie became a domestic worker.[64]

When Thelonious began courting Barbara Batts, she was young, pretty, hardworking, deeply religious, and lived in the better part of town, despite the fact that she and her mother were quite poor. They married on August 20, 1914.[65]

Thelonious moved out of the Whiteheads' place. With his new bride and mother-in-law, he rented a small house at 815 Green Avenue in the "Y," just a couple of blocks from his brother-in-law's house on Dunn Street.[66] For Barbara and her mother it was a step down. The house they moved to was not only small but, like the houses on Dunn, was so close to the railroad tracks that they had to accustom themselves to the noise of locomotives pulling in and out of the city en route to Norfolk. (Thelonious Jr. would develop a fascination with trains, and their music.) At least, at age twenty-five, Thelonious was finally independent. Despite indecently low wages, Thelonious and Barbara earned enough so that Georgianna no longer had to take in laundry.

Just a year shy of fifty, her health was already declining. Georgianna probably stopped working in the early months of 1915 when Barbara was expecting her first child. Unfortunately, the baby died soon after birth.[67] Within a couple of months of the loss, Barbara was again pregnant.

On January 18, 1916, the Monks called for Lucy Cooper, the neighborhood midwife who learned her skills in slavery, to come to the house, and that afternoon she delivered a beautiful baby girl named Marion Barbara Monk.[68] Thelonious and Barbara struggled to support their growing household. Thelonious made very little money as a non-union manual laborer for ACLRR. Whenever his services were not needed, he was out of work. Perhaps for this reason, when the Selective Service Act was passed in 1917 in preparation for the U.S.'s entry into World War I, Thelonious lied to make himself more attractive to the draft board. On his draft card, signed June 5, 1917, he recorded his birthdate as June 20, 1892, taking off three years, even though Barbara was five months pregnant with their second child, Thelonious, Jr.[69] There was significant black working-class opposition to the draft and to entry into a war for democracy abroad when African-Americans did not enjoy democracy at home. Yet many poor black men throughout the country saw the military as both a regular source of income and a means to escape the vagaries of domestic racism. Many hoped working for Uncle Sam and donning the uniform of federal authority would ensure that they would be treated like men.[70]

Despite the application, Thelonious failed to be drafted. Few black men were accepted into the segregated army. Just a couple of months after filling out his draft registration card, Thelonious lost his job with the ACLRR and began working as an "ice puller" for the Rocky Mount Fuel and Ice Company.[71]

By most accounts, this would have been an inauspicious time to have another baby. But to the superstitious or the devoutly religious, the circumstances of Thelonious, Jr.'s birth was a sign of good things to come. On October 9, Rocky Mount experienced one of the worst storms in decades.[72] By daybreak the storm had moved out to sea and the clouds cleared for a gorgeous autumn day. That evening, October 10, 1917, Miss Lucy Cooper helped deliver Barbara's first-born son.[73]

Thelonious, Sr., was happy to have a son, but the stress of work and financial instability took its toll on him; his health began to deteriorate even before he turned thirty. He suffered from asthma and related respiratory problems, and his work was irregular. Georgianna's health did not improve either, and so much of the burden of caring for the family fell on Barbara's shoulders.

During that final year of World War I, the city experienced massive food shortages due to wartime demands, not to mention a terrible outbreak of influenza during the fall of 1918. In the month of October alone, Rocky Mount reported fifty-eight deaths caused by a devastating strain of the Spanish flu.[74]

The Monks dodged the flu, but their struggles worsened. Barbara became pregnant again in the spring of 1919, and on January 11, 1920, Lucy Cooper was called over for a fourth and final time to deliver Barbara's youngest child, Thomas Monk, who would carry the nickname "Baby" his entire life.[75] A few weeks after Thomas's arrival, the

Monks moved into a slightly larger home across the street at 814 Green, presumably with a higher rent. Thelonious, Sr.'s employment had not improved, and Georgianna's kidneys began to fail. Barbara had to stop working altogether to care for the children, as well as for her ailing mother. To stay afloat, the Monks took in boarders, an employee of the Emerson shops and his wife, who also worked as a domestic.[76]

Despite these and other hardships, the Monk household was filled with laughter and plenty of music. In later years, Thelonious told interviewers that neither his mother nor his father were musicians, though his definition of musician referred strictly to those who made a living playing music. As he explained in a 1963 interview, "My parents were not musicians at all, and I am the only one in the family to have gone in this direction. . . . My mother sung in the church, but that does not count."[77] Whether it counts or not, the truth is *both* of his parents played a little piano. Barbara learned to play a few hymns by ear, and Thelonious, Sr. knew a couple of songs that he loved to play in a rollicking, ragtime style. His main instruments were the "Jew's harp" and the "blues harp," better known as the harmonica. Like most Southern harmonica players, he deftly imitated train whistles. "My father was gifted as far as music was concerned," Thomas Monk recalled. "He never had the opportunity to study, but he was gifted, really. He just had the ear for music."[78] Thelonious and his siblings also absorbed the music of the church. Besides attending church every Sunday, the kids listened to their mother—and possibly their grandmother—singing and humming hymns and gospel tunes in hushed tones around the house. Thelonious would later record some of the sacred songs he heard as a child, notably "Abide with Me," "Blessed Assurance," and "We'll Understand It Better, By and By."

Barbara, the only healthy adult in the house, faced a decision in 1921, as her mother's kidney problems advanced beyond repair. For the past decade, over one million black southerners had decided to leave their rural homes and substandard, segregated schools, heading to the urban North and its promise of freedom, opportunity, and even the right to vote. The Great Migration of African-Americans out of the South swelled the populations of New York, Chicago, Detroit, Philadelphia, and other cities.

When Georgianna Williams died on October 30, 1921, just one day before her fifty-sixth birthday, Barbara's decision loomed large. The cost of Georgianna's medical expenses left the Monks with little money for a proper burial. (Like many poor Rocky Mount residents, she was laid to rest in the city cemetery.)[79] Thelonious, Sr.'s health had worsened. His own father had died in May, leaving his mother, Sarah Ann, and brother Lorenzo, thirty-four, unmarried, and apparently unable to care for himself, at home.[80]

Finally, in the spring of 1922, Barbara contacted her cousin Louise Bryant, who had relocated to New York City several years earlier. Barbara and her three children were joining the Great Migration. On some unknown day in June of 1922, the Monks rose early and made their way to the train station, three children and overstuffed bags in tow, to catch the 6:33 a.m. "West Indian Limited" to New York. [81] Thelonious, Sr. moved whatever was left at 814 Green Avenue to a small house at 120 Dunn Street.

Thelonious Monk, Jr., age four, would not be a Southerner after all.

2

"What Is Jazz? New York, Man!"

(1922–1928)

For a woman traveling alone with three young children and their life's possessions, a twelve-hour train ride can be exhausting. For the children, however,
it was exhilarating. Four-year-old Thelonious spent much of the time with
his nose pressed against the window, watching the familiar flat countryside
fade into modern steel bridges and bustling cityscapes dotted with skyscrapers. When
the train pulled into New York's Penn Station around 7:00 on that fateful June evening,
it was still light out and the summer's heat hadn't quite subsided.

North Carolina summers were nothing like the thick, humid, dirty, congested
heat of New York City. Barbara Monk was giving up fresh country air, her house on
Green Avenue with the porch and backyard, her familiar surroundings, and her friends
and family for a tiny tenement apartment in the summer heat. It was worth it for the
schools, and for the future jobs for her children. But it wasn't easy.

With bags in tow, Barbara, Marion, Thelonious, and Thomas hopped on a streetcar
traveling along Amsterdam Avenue. As Marion remembered, "All of us fell down when
the trolley car started. The three of us, you know, we was two, four and six. And everyone was laughing and it was such a big thing. That's why I remember that. That was our
first entrance into New York."[1] Barbara's cousin from North Carolina, Louise Bryant,
met them after they disembarked from the trolley. Bryant, who was then fifty-one years
old and unmarried, had been living in the San Juan Hill neighborhood of Manhattan
for a few years and had encouraged Barbara to move north after her mother died.[2]

The Monks first moved in with Bryant, who had been living at 235 West 63rd
Street, between Amsterdam and West End Avenues, for at least three years.[3] Bryant's
building was not like the dilapidated, overcrowded tenement apartments that dominated the West 60s. Situated on the north side of West 63rd, closer to West End than
to Amsterdam, 235 was one of the relatively new buildings funded by industrialist
Henry Phipps to provide quality housing for the working poor. After he had built
the first Phipps Houses on East 31st Street in 1906 for white working class families, a
group calling itself The Citizens' Committee for the Betterment of Tenements for the
Negro People appealed to him to build similar housing for African-Americans on the
West Side.[4] Phipps purchased sixteen lots on West 63rd and West 64th Streets and

constructed six brand new buildings to house black residents. When the final structures were completed in 1911, the Phipps Houses provided 348 units of comparatively luxurious yet low-cost apartments. Designed by the noted architectural firm Whitfield and King, the Phipps Houses were one of the first model housing developments in New York City exclusively for black families. Unlike older tenements, each apartment was equipped with toilet and bath facilities, fairly spacious rooms, good ventilation, and a small courtyard in the back. Because the Phipps Houses were the most desirable housing in the neighborhood, the management selected their tenants carefully, choosing only the most "respectable" working-class families to reside there.[5]

The Monks stayed with Louise Bryant a few months, and they would eventually return to the Phipps Houses for an apartment of their own a few years later. Meanwhile, Barbara got a job working in the kitchen at the Henrietta Industrial School, right across the street at 224 West 63rd. Founded in 1892 by the Children's Aid Society exclusively for black children, the Henrietta School was referred to by residents as the "soup school" because it ran a soup kitchen for poor neighborhood kids. The pay wasn't great, but the job was convenient for a single parent. Marion recalled, "My mother got that job because she could cook. And that was good for her, because the three of us went to the nursery and we had our lunch there and everything, which made it nice."[6]

Barbara moved her family to an apartment in one of the old tenements on the same block, at 234 West 63rd, probably in the winter of 1922–23. 234 was more typical of the San Juan Hill neighborhood.[7] Activist and social worker Mary White Ovington described the tenements there as "human hives, honeycombed with little rooms thick with human beings. Bedrooms open into air shafts that admit no fresh breezes, only foul air carrying too often the germs of disease."[8] Conditions were so bad that the New York City Health Department and the Vanderbilt Clinic put out a newsletter to provide public health education to the community. Launched in 1915, the short-lived *Columbus Hill Chronicle* ran stories about tuberculosis, flies, the high infant mortality rate among blacks, and alcoholism.[9] In 1919, three years before the Monks arrived, the Woman's Municipal League of New York, along with several other civic organizations, formed the Housing Committee of the New York State Reconstruction Commission and conducted a thorough investigation of housing conditions in the West 60s. They visited the homes of 1,600 families, concluding that "in general they were old, dark, dirty and not fit for human habitation." Efforts at keeping them clean were impossible; the cellars were "full of rats," and the halls were not lighted; "the plumbing was old and often out of repair so that the air was unbreathable." Airshafts were littered with trash. There were many cases of illness attributed to the unhealthy living conditions.[10] Another survey conducted a couple of years later classified at least sixty-three percent of the housing in the neighborhood as "absolutely undesirable," and only twenty-one percent as "passable."[11]

San Juan Hill was so named in part because several black veterans of the Spanish-American War settled in the area. (San Juan Hill, near Santiago, Cuba, was the site where the legendary black cavalry known as the Buffalo Soldiers, alongside Teddy Roosevelt and his Rough Riders, waged their most ferocious battle.) But the name stuck to the neighborhood for another reason: its reputation for violence. Legend has it that the name was first used by "an on-looker who saw the policemen charging up during one of the once common race fights."[12] Between 1900 and 1917, the place was famous for its race riots. In 1905, a reporter noted that the police in the vicinity "expect at least one small riot on the Hill or in The Gut [the West End side of San Juan Hill] each week." In July of that year, what could only be described as race war overtook the entire neighborhood. Police officers from six different precincts were called in to quell the violence, but many of the officers made matters worse by ignoring white mobs and arresting and beating African-Americans. The rioting started when a group of young white men hanging out on Amsterdam attacked a black man for protecting a poor white rag peddler from physical and verbal abuse. Several black residents retaliated from the tenement rooftops, where they had stored piles of bottles and bricks ripped from dilapidated chimneys.[13]

Twelve years later, the black folks on the Hill found themselves embroiled in a series of riots. The first occurred at the end of May 1917, when a black man argued over the price of a glass of lemon and soda in a predominantly white bar on 65th and Amsterdam. The white patrons followed the man out of the bar and proceeded to jeer and slap him. He then sought refuge in a black saloon, but when the Home Defense League, a wartime outfit created to supplement the police, intervened, some members assumed the black man was the criminal rather than the victim. Men armed with guns, knives, bricks, and bottles began to stream into the streets. Over 2,000 people took part in indiscriminate fighting. When the smoke finally cleared, one black man lay dead and a thirteen-year-old black girl suffered a gunshot wound to her thigh.[14]

A little over a month later, a day after the Fourth of July, San Juan Hill erupted once again when a group of black National Guardsmen, all members of the Fifteenth Infantry of New York, ignored police orders to disperse. They had committed no crime, but apparently the sight of twenty-five black men in uniform gathered on the corner of West 61st Street was enough to arouse suspicion. Fighting began when one of the white police officers arrested Lawrence Joaquin, a black Puerto Rican guardsman who, coincidentally, had been arrested in the racial disturbances a month earlier. His comrades fought back in order to free Joaquin. As soon as whites on Amsterdam heard or saw what was happening, they came pouring out of their homes, initiating another massive melee. Several residents were injured, property was destroyed, and some of the guardsmen were arrested and jailed on Blackwells Island. African-American leaders sharply criticized the way the police handled the incident, and the commander of the Fifteenth Infantry defended his men and launched an investigation into the incident.[15] A few months later, the Fifteenth Infantry was transformed into the renowned 369th Regiment and dispatched to France, where they not only racked up an astounding combat record but, under the leadership of James Reese Europe, formed one of the greatest bands in history and introduced ragtime and early jazz to Europeans.[16]

The combination of anti-black violence, police inaction during the 1905 riots, and deteriorating housing conditions spurred a mass exodus out of San Juan Hill into the next up-and-coming black neighborhood: Harlem. In 1910, San Juan Hill was still the largest black community in Manhattan. A few years later, it would be surpassed by

Harlem, although when the Monks arrived in 1922 it was still mostly black—at least off the avenues.[17] Only whites, mostly Irish, Germans, and Italians, lived along the avenues—Amsterdam (Tenth) and West End (Eleventh)—and on certain streets. West 61st, 62nd, and 63rd Streets were all-black. Most of San Juan Hill's blacks hailed from the South or the Caribbean. On Monk's block in 1930, for example, about forty per-cent of the residents were Southern-born (primarily from Virginia, North and South Carolina, and Georgia), and about twenty percent came from the British West Indies and, to a lesser extent, Cuba and Puerto Rico. About thirty-five percent were born in New York City, a figure that also reflects the fairly large youth population in the neigh-borhood. San Juan Hill had its share of black professionals, but this was a community of porters, domestic servants, laundresses, longshoremen, cooks, chauffeurs, delivery men, truck drivers, a surprising number of musicians, and too many "general laborers" to count.[18]

With a diversity of people came a diversity of cultures. On West 63rd Street alone, the aroma of Southern-style collard greens cooked with ham hocks mixed with the dis-tinct smell of Jamaican rice and peas and fried ripe plantain. English was the main lan-guage in the community, but it came in a Carolina twang and a West Indian singsong lilt, in addition to a distinctive New York accent. Spanish and French were also spo-ken on those streets, with German and Yiddish along the white-dominated avenues. Many of the local merchants were Italian. Alberta Saunders, a long-time resident of the neighborhood, recalled: "The coal man was always Italian. Had a fish man at 62nd and Twelfth, also Italian. And they were all named 'Joe.' You had Ice Joe to get your ice, Fish Joe to get your fish, and so on and so forth."[19]

It is easy to romanticize this diversity—easy, and false. Ms. Mavis Swire (née Wilson), born and raised in the neighborhood and just three years younger than Thelonious, viv-idly remembered the tensions. "The Southern blacks called West Indians 'monkey chas-ers,' and we often referred to Southern blacks as 'possum eaters.'"[20] Thelonious was an odd exception: he reported, "They used to call me 'Monkey,' and you know what a drag that was."[21] Occasional fights broke out, and more than a few well-educated Caribbean men were known to treat their American-born counterparts with an air of superiority. But generally speaking, these communities got along—especially their New York–born offspring. "Our main fights," Ms. Swire recalled, "were with the Irish and Italians on the Avenue. . . . You have to go to the stores on the Avenue. [The whites] would not let you go by on the sidewalk. You had to walk in the street around them. So when you go up to get what you're getting, you get an empty wooden box. They're always glad to give you a box because they know you have a coal stove and you need the wood to start the fire. Once you get the box, you break up the box and everybody gets a stick. You hit anybody you can and run like mad down the street! They're not going to chase you."[22]

The daily violence young people endured in San Juan Hill haunted Thelonious for many years to come. In a 1969 interview with drummer Arthur Taylor, Monk himself responded to a question about "Black Power" with vivid memories of the kind of inter-racial and intraracial violence that permeated his neighborhood. "I did all that fighting with ofays [whites[23]] when I was a kid. We had to fight to make it so we could walk the streets. There's no reason why I should go through that Black Power shit now. I guess everybody in New York had to do that, right? Because every block is a different town. It was mean all over New York, all the boroughs. Then, besides fighting the ofays, you had to fight each other. You go in the next block and you're in another country. Don't look at a chick living in the next block and expect to be taking her home and all that; you might not make it."[24] And the police didn't help matters, as far as Monk was concerned. They epitomized racism in the city. "It looked like the order of the day was for the cops to go out and call all the kids black bastards. Anything you did, if you ran or something, they called you black bastards."[25]

Battles were not only limited to black and white, or between Caribbean and Southern blacks. African-American residents bitterly remember a Chinese restaurant on 59th and Columbus called Far East. It was notorious for not allowing African-Americans to dine inside—black customers had to come to the side or the back of the place to get takeout. Alberta Saunders remembers how she and her childhood friends would retaliate by standing outside the door and chanting, "Chinaman, Chinaman, eat dead rats." Occasionally, an employee or the owner would come out and chase them down the street with a big knife.[26]

San Juan Hill's reputation as a violent community was as strong as ever by the time the Monks settled there. About a year and a half after they arrived, San Juan Hill earned the dubious distinction of being one of the "busiest crime areas in New York City."[27] Not long after they moved into 234 West 63rd, one of their neighbors in the building, John Rose, was standing near the stoop, and suddenly drew a pistol and began shooting indiscriminately. It was a summer evening, the streets were filled with adults and children, and it is quite possible that Thelonious, Marion, and Thomas were among them. Rose managed to injure two people before police arrived. He fled into the building and barricaded himself in his apartment. After a brief standoff, the officers finally broke down the door and found him with a loaded gun and hypodermic needles.[28]

Stories of crime and violence dominated newspaper accounts of San Juan Hill. The neighborhood made great copy for voyeuristic whites fascinated by popular images of razor-toting, dice-tossing, happy-go-lucky Negroes. What the papers rarely covered was San Juan Hill's rich musical culture. Perhaps the best-known event in the neighborhood's history was the opening of the wildly successful all-black music revue "Shuffle Along" at the 63rd Street Music Hall near Broadway. Written by Flournoy Miller and Aubrey L. Lyles, with music and lyrics by Eubie Blake and Noble Sissle, "Shuffle Along" is often described as the production that launched the Harlem Renaissance in musical theater. It opened on May 23, 1921, and ran through July 15, 1922—closing just around the time the Monks moved to the neighborhood.[29]

Before the Harlem Renaissance pushed the black musical center of gravity up above 125th Street, the West Side, from the Tenderloin—also known as "Black Bohemia"—to San Juan Hill boasted the largest concentration of black musicians in the city.[30] During Mary White Ovington's six-month residence at one of the Phipps Houses in 1908, she discovered that music was a major source of income for African-Americans, even if it wasn't always their main vocation. She recalled hearing music constantly in the hallwaysand in the streets. Every household had an instrument, she wrote, "a banjo perhaps, or a guitar, a mandolin or zither, or it may be the highly prized piano. Visiting an evening in the Phipps model tenement, one hears a variety of gay tinkling sounds."[31]

The black residents of San Juan Hill also established a strong sense of community. As Thelonious's future sister-in-law, Geraldine Smith, remembers about the neighborhood, "It was like a little village. Everybody knew everybody."[32] It had a rich associational life, with well over a dozen black churches in close vicinity. The more prominent included St. Cyprian's Colored Episcopal Chapel at 171 West 63rd (the largest black Episcopalian congregation in the city) and St. Benedict the Moor Roman Catholic Church. Baptists dominated, though most of their churches were tiny storefronts. One exception was Union Baptist Church, a mainstay at 204 West 63rd until about 1930, when its pastor, the Reverend George H. Sims, decided to relocate to 145th Street in Harlem. Barbara Monk was a member of Union Baptist when she first arrived, although once it became clear the church planned to move (Sims had purchased the plot in Harlem during the summer of 1926), she switched to a small storefront Baptist church on West 61st near Amsterdam, pastored by the Reverend W. A. Johnson.[33]

Sims's departure proved a great loss to the community. He not only provided leadership on matters of race and poverty on the West Side, but he earned a reputation as a great preacher. Gordon Heath, one of Monk's childhood acquaintances, attended Union a few times with his mother. He loved the sermons delivered by Reverend Sims, who "shouted, wept, and exhorted God and the congregation to collect enough money to pay for the organ's repair, the church's roof, and the uninterrupted maintenance of his personal household. . . . Foot patting and hand clapping and rhythmic response to the minister's evangelic fervor were the order of the day."[34]

The God-fearing Barbara made sure her children went to church, but she was even more concerned about their education. At first, only Marion was old enough to attend the local elementary school, P.S. 141, located on West 58th Street just east of Tenth Avenue. By the time Thelonious turned six in the fall of 1923, he joined his sister on the five-block trek to school—a walk that often meant confronting gangs of white youths prepared to do battle with any black kids passing by. Black children necessarily traveled along Amsterdam in groups, which fostered friendship and kinship. Whites were in the minority at the school; by 1930, of the 1,104 pupils enrolled, 828 were black.[35] Although black students outnumbered whites, they were still vulnerable to racist attacks. Black children at P.S. 141, as well as P.S. 69 (the neighborhood junior high school), complained regularly of the hostility they faced from both students and teachers. (During the 1920s, the vast majority of the teachers were whites who commuted from Queens, New Jersey, or the Bronx.[36]) The word "nigger" flowed easily from the lips of many teachers, who were also quick to side with white children whenever fights broke out.[37] Saxophonist and bandleader Benny Carter, who also grew up on West 63rd Street, had vivid memories of racial discrimination during his years at P.S. 141 and P.S. 69. One incident, in particular, led to his expulsion from eighth grade during the year the Monks moved to his block. As he recalled, "We lived in a rough neighborhood and it was a rough school . . . I had a fight with a kid. A teacher intervened to help him. He kicked me from behind as I was going down the staircase, calling me a dirty nigger. I turned and punched him. I was expelled on the spot."[38]

Thelonious's formative experiences with other children did not take place at school but at summer camp. Barbara took advantage of the Fresh Air Fund, which ran a camp in Batavia, New York, a sleepy upstate town situated between Buffalo and Rochester.[39] The Fresh Air Fund goal of giving working-class city kids from all ethnic backgrounds an opportunity to spend time in the country appealed to Barbara, whose memories of rural North Carolina contrasted sharply with the claustrophobia of West Manhattan. On the stifling hot day of August 2, 1923, Barbara put her eldest son on a New York Central Railway train along with forty-six other boys, heading off on a two-week adventure. When the train arrived the next morning, the boys were given a heroes' welcome. They marched from the station to the courthouse park on Main Street, where each child was weighed, fed, and distributed to the various families to whom they were assigned. The local paper described the campers as "a motley collection of thin and cheaply-clad children. Some were pitiably pale, some had dark complexions that bespoke Italian and [H]ebrew parentage, but all aroused the sympathy and motherly instinct of the many women who watched them detrain."[40]

The same journalist took note of one kid in particular. So did the Batavia fire chief. "If any boy in the Fresh Air bunch is assured of a good time, it is Phelonius [sic] Monk, a five-year-old colored youngster, who will spend two weeks doing what every normal boy would give a gallon of ice cream and a thousand marbles to do. Little Phelonious, who may have had some hard luck when his name was picked out, was lucky enough to become the guest of the firemen stationed at fire headquarters. They have decided to make a mascot out of him and equip him with a uniform. Phelonious, who is a cunning-looking chap, was on a fire truck ringing a bell five minutes after his arrival at the station, his pearly teeth uncovered by a grin that threatened to reach his ears."[41]

The firemen were drawn to Monk on first sight. By the time he left two weeks later, he had thoroughly charmed the entire company, and he was reluctant to leave, despite bouts of homesickness. "A letter just received from his mother," reported the *Batavia Daily News*, "made him a little homesick, but he said he would like to come back and be a fireman, after he had seen his folks. He nearly cried at the station when he heard the fire trucks going to a fire this morning without him." He vowed that if he couldn't stay longer, "he will be a fireman as soon as he is old enough." He led the parade back to the train station, following the ritual weighing to see how much they gained as a result of wholesome country living. Thelonious was "strutting at the head of the line and banging away on a toy drum, his little chest proudly swelling inside his red fireman's shirt. . . ."[42]

Stretching back to the late nineteenth century, there was an established tradition of white institutions choosing "colored boys" to serve as mascots, essentially pets. Fire stations, police stations, athletic teams, did it with good humor and implicit condescension. This was the age when images of "pickaninnies" and elderly black people were used to sell products and create an atmosphere of frivolity and innocence. When Thelonious returned to camp the following year, the entire department was there to greet him at the station, despite the pouring rain. This time the local paper got his name almost right: "Before the procession started moving a member of the Batavia fire department swooped down into the crowd, singled out a tiny colored lad and hoisted him into the air. Thelonius [sic] Monk, who for two weeks last summer lived the life of Reilly as the guest of the firemen, was back again this year. Thelonius, conducting himself as becomes a veteran fresh air child, gravely shook hands with the fireman, reached for his bundle and started at once for the scene of last year's thrilling experiences." Monk was such a sensation that the *Batavia Daily News* recorded his whereabouts and adventures on a fairly regular basis. They even interviewed Fire Chief George Benedict about their favorite mascot. Noting wrongly that Thelonious hails from the "roaring 40s," known to upstate New Yorkers as the center of the Manhattan's night life, the Chief expressed admiration for his good manners and gentlemanly comportment. "He's the nicest little gentleman you'd every [sic] care to see. His mother certainly brought him up right. He played here all day long last year and got excited in the games, running around, but I never heard any bad language come from his lips. Another thing, Thelonius always says his prayers. Yes, he's brought up right."[43]

Barbara had indeed raised her children with very strong morals, but she was not a strict disciplinarian. She kept her children in line by relying on reason, faith, example, and her quiet, dignified strength. Unlike her husband, she did not believe in corporal punishment and she encouraged her children to be free-spirited, vocal, and opinionated, albeit respectful. As a child of the post-Reconstruction generation, Barbara also talked about politics. Around the time of Franklin Delano Roosevelt's bid for the presidency in 1932, she joined a local chapter of the New York Democratic Clubs, and, when she had time and her health permitted, attended a few of their forums.[44] She wanted her children to be vocal, aware, and active in the world around them. Many children in those days were expected to be seen and not heard, and dinner-table chatter was not tolerated, but Barbara Monk encouraged her children to talk, laugh, and think of dinner time as family time. "We would talk about everything that happened during the day and what was going to happen," Marion recalled. "I'd ask my mother this and that and we'd have a good conversation."[45]

Barbara did what she could to introduce her children to the city's rich cultural life. She frequently took them to Central Park in the summer to hear Edwin Franko Goldman's sixty-piece orchestra perform classic works by European and American composers. During the summer of 1923, the inaugural year of the Central Park series, Goldman's band gave sixty concerts, attracting as many as 15,000 people. Five years old, Thelonious spent many warm summer nights listening to such works as Schubert's "Serenade," Tchaikovsky's "Slavic March," Wagner's "Tannhäuser Overture," Rossini's "William Tell Overture," Strauss's "New Vienna Waltz," and plenty of Chopin and Liszt. Goldman's band continued the tradition throughout the decade, and Barbara's children frequently attended.[46] Nor did Barbara miss opportunities to make music at home, especially sacred music. As Marion recalls, "We even used to have a quartet, you know, be singing, the four of us. We used to have a good time. That was our good time at dinner time because everyone was there."[47]

Some time around late 1924 or early 1925, the quartet became a quintet when Thelonious, Sr., finally joined the family at 234 West 63rd St.[48] He still suffered from chronic bronchial problems, and the horrible conditions of the tenement houses undoubtedly aggravated his illness. Nevertheless, he managed to find work, first as an unskilled laborer on the docks, then in the boiler room of a local theater. He took a variety of odd jobs performing manual labor until he was able to secure a more permanent position as a super/maintenance man in one of the tenements. Meanwhile, Barbara left her job at the Henrietta Industrial School and found a better position as a cleaner for Children's Court located on East 22nd Street. She would remain in this job until she was forced to retire due to illness.[49]

Not long after Thelonious, Sr. arrived in New York, the family successfully applied for an apartment in one of the Phipps Houses. They moved there around 1926. Their still-new building's thirty-four units were populated with working-class families from either the South or the Caribbean—families like the Brumbertachs, the Branches, and the Ortelys from the British West Indies, or the Caldwells from North Carolina and the Atkinsons from South Carolina. They made their living by cooking, cleaning, driving, or serving mostly white folks in restaurants, cruise boats, and private homes. Some made dresses and worked in factories, and nearly one-fourth of the households supplemented their income by taking in boarders. The rent was about three dollars a week. There were many two-parent families, but there were also plenty of widowers, divorcees, single mothers, and a few single residents with no children. Everyone worked hard to make ends meet, but all were considered respectable by the Phipps management. The Monks were welcomed largely because of Barbara's kind demeanor and generosity. (The arrival of her husband probably helped her application as well.) The Southerners embraced them because they were from home, although many of the West Indians believed they had to be one of them with a name like Monk.[50]

The cultures of the West Indians and Southerners blended despite the tensions. With the music, cuisine, dialects, and manners of the Caribbean and the American South everywhere in the West 60s, virtually every kid became a kind of cultural hybrid. Thelonious absorbed Caribbean music. Through the radio and the sounds of the Victrola pouring out of his neighbors' apartments, he heard the likes of Atilla the Hun, Lord Invader, the Roaring Lion, and other prominent calypsonians of that era, and he probably heard music from the Spanish Caribbean—rumba, son, habañera, tango. Block parties on West 63rd Street became another source of cultural exchange. In the early 1930s, a philanthropist known affectionately as "Uncle Robert" used to sponsor outdoor dances on West 63rd, with live bands and free lollipops for the kids.[51] Monk was also familiar with many of the neighborhood musicians who played in local calypso or salsa bands. One can certainly hear explicit Caribbean rhythms in some of Monk's original compositions, most notably "Bye-ya" and "Bemsha Swing," which he wrote with his good friend, Barbadian-born drummer Denzil Best. The original copyrighted title was "Bimsha Swing," Bimsha (or Bim or Bimshire) being a nickname for Barbados.[52]

After a very brief stay in a small apartment one flight up, the Monks moved downstairs to apartment 20, a slightly larger ground-floor, two-bedroom flat in the rear of the building.[53] The apartment was designed around the kitchen. The front door opened into the kitchen; one bedroom was situated off to the right of it, and the living room could only be reached by walking through it. Off to the right of the living room was the other bedroom, and to the left was a tiny bathroom. The kitchen also included a hideaway bathtub. Although space was still limited, especially for a family of five, and not much sunlight found its way into their ground-floor windows, their new apartment was a giant step up from the tiny, dilapidated tenement across the street.

Once they arrived, Barbara and Thelonious, Sr. made a major acquisition that would change their middle child's life forever: "A lady gave us a piano," Thelonious recalled. "The player-piano kind. I saw how the rolls made the keys move. Very interesting. Sounded pretty good to me. I felt I did not want to waste this person's gift, so I learned to use it."[54] He wasn't the only one. His mother sat down on occasion and played the few hymns she had learned by ear. She knew just enough to earn a position as a principal pianist for the tiny storefront Baptist church she attended on West 61st Street.[55] Thelonious, Sr. tickled the ivories a bit more frequently, and if the spirit hit him he'd bang late into the night, improvising on one of the two or three songs he knew. The neighbors weren't pleased. One night some kids in the building placed a picture of a skull and crossbones on the Monks' door while he was playing. The warning worked; after that he played his music at a decent hour and a bit more pianissimo.[56]

Not long after moving into the Phipps Houses, Thelonious, Sr. was compelled, once again by health reasons, to return to North Carolina. The polluted air and cold winters had aggravated what had become a severe case of asthma. After he was hospitalized for a major asthma attack, his doctor insisted that he leave New York immediately. Marion has no recollection of her father coming back to the house to say goodbye. There might be more to the story, however: During his brief stay in New York, Thelonious also suffered a near-fatal head injury in a fight with a man wielding a baseball bat. He began experiencing bouts of memory loss that would persist for the rest of his life.[57]

After just three or four years together, Barbara and Thelonious, Sr., split once again. This time it was for good. He made at least one more trip to New York in a failed effort to convince her and the children to return to Rocky Mount, but New York was now Barbara's home. She had been doing a fine job on her own before he made the trek north, and she was determined to stay. Thelonious, Sr. moved in with his sisters, Eulah and Hettie, who still lived in the house on Dunn Street their brother Theodore ("Babe") owned, and fell right back into the life of a common laborer, securing a job at a wrecking company.[58]

Thelonious, Jr., age eleven, had lived with his father for a total of seven years, some of which were before his earliest memories. From now on, he would be raised by his mother, and by New York City.

3

"I Always Did Want to Play Piano"

(1928–1934)

66 My first musical impressions, I guess, were from listening to piano rolls," Monk once mused. "Everybody had a piano, and they used to play rolls all the time. So I had one, too. That's all people listened to, mostly piano music."[1] Thelonious began teaching himself as soon as they rolled the old upright into the door. He banged a little, listened for differences between the black and white keys, tried to mimic his father's two-fisted barrelhouse style, and in no time was picking out melodies he had heard on the radio or hymns his mother sang. But when Barbara decided that at least one of her children would receive formal lessons, that privilege was initially bestowed on big sister Marion. That didn't surprise Thelonious, who explained years later, "The girls always took [lessons] in those days."[2]

Barbara had other plans for her middle child: She envisioned Little Thelonious playing violin, like many of the West Indian boys in the Phipps Houses. But Thelonious had his own agenda. Perhaps inspired by Louis Armstrong, who was all the rage in the late twenties, or maybe his neighbor James "Bubber" Miley, a local hero and star soloist in the Duke Ellington orchestra, Thelonious wanted to play trumpet. Barbara accommodated her son and purchased a used trumpet, probably from a local pawn shop or from a musician in the neighborhood. He loved the instrument, but as Marion recalls, "The music teacher told my mother that he shouldn't play the trumpet because it was affecting . . . his blowing and he got interested in piano. So my mother said she'd give him piano lessons. But before that he was playing the piano because my father used to be banging around on the piano."[3] Thelonious himself remembered it differently. He once told writer/radio host Russ Wilson, "I started to study trumpet, but the music teacher saw me playing on the piano and he said, 'You got to take up piano.' So I took piano."[4]

Thelonious was eleven when he began taking piano lessons, although even his formal lessons began informally. He was so fascinated by the piano that he'd stay in the house during his sister's lesson and study everything she did very carefully, including the notes on the page. "I learned how to read before I took lessons, watching my sister practice her lessons, over her shoulder," Monk explained many times, in an effort to dispel persistent rumors of his musical illiteracy.[5] He also had an excellent ear.

25

According to Marion, Thelonious could "pick up any tune that came along without music. Mother said that if he was going to play he should learn how to play the right way, so the teacher who was teaching me, which I didn't like piano lessons, he started teaching my brother in my place. So, he took lessons." Marion, on the other hand, was really interested in playing the saxophone, "but they couldn't afford to buy a saxophone for me so I didn't play that."[6]

Monk's teacher was Simon Wolf. He taught a few of the neighborhood kids and was highly regarded among the parents who hired him. He wasn't cheap; Barbara paid him seventy-five cents for an hour-long lesson.[7] An Austrian-born Jew in his late thirties, Wolf was a fine classical pianist but primarily a violinist who had the distinction of studying under Alfred Megerlin, the concertmaster for the New York Philharmonic. He performed occasionally, but by the mid- to late-1920s, teaching had become his main source of income.[8] Barbara learned about Simon Wolf through her neighbors, Cyril and Harriette Heath, whose son, Seifield Gordon Heath, had been studying with him. Gordon remembered Mr. Wolf as "a soft-spoken, small, elegant, young Jewish gentleman who wore his hair just a little longer than ordinary." He was very well-trained, worldly, and "warm but impersonal, conscientious, and correct."[9] Gordon was a conscientious student, constantly working on scales, Ludwig Spohr violin studies, and Baroque pieces assigned by Wolf. But for all of his work, Gordon Heath never garnered the kind of attention Wolf lavished on his neighbor Thelonious.

Just one year older than Heath,[10] Thelonious turned out to be one of Mr. Wolf's best students. One day, Gordon's father asked Wolf for an honest assessment of his son's progress. "He works hard," Wolf confessed, "but I couldn't say if he has talent." Cyril Heath was taken aback. He then asked about Thelonious, and Wolf responded, "I don't think there will be anything I can teach him. He will go beyond me very soon."[11] Gordon remembered spending much of his junior high school years being compared with Thelonious and enduring his father's sighs of disappointment. Cyril would often say, "This boy—no father—his mother scrubs floors to pay for his music lessons and look at the progress *he* is making."[12]

Simon Wolf was not a jazz musician; he taught Thelonious works by Chopin, Beethoven, Bach, Rachmaninoff, Liszt, and Mozart. Thelonious developed an affinity for Chopin and Rachmaninoff, and he loved to work through some of the most difficult pieces. Wolf was amazed by how quickly Thelonious mastered many pieces, not to mention his curiosity about the piano's mechanics and his wide range of musical interests. Monk knew how much he impressed Wolf and was not bashful about saying so. "Didn't have to study hard—used to amaze all the teachers! No one had to make me study. I was gifted, you know—music."[13]

Wolf worked with Thelonious intermittently for about two years. By the time he turned thirteen, it was clear to Thelonious and to those around him that jazz was his first love. What Wolf could not teach him, Thelonious learned from the many jazz musicians who lived in the neighborhood. Besides saxophonist Benny Carter (who moved to Harlem after leaving his parents' house[14]), his neighbors included pianist Freddy Johnson (who would later work with Benny Carter and Coleman Hawkins[15]), reed player Russell Procope (who played with Benny Carter, Chick Webb, and eventually Duke Ellington), and the phenomenal trumpet player "Bubber" Miley, a key figure in Ellington's "Cotton Club" band in the 1920s, before he succumbed to tuberculosis in 1932 at the age of twenty-nine. The neighborhood was full of jazz sounds. When Thelonious was still in grade school, a group calling themselves the Carolina Five used to gather at the home of Percy and Theodosia Maples and hold informal rehearsals. Miley was part of that group, along with several other neighborhood musicians.[16] Even Monk's next-door neighbor, James Harrison, worked as a professional drummer in a dance band throughout the 1930s.[17]

The local jazz musician who had the greatest impact on Thelonious's early development, however, was a diminutive black woman named Alberta Simmons. She appears in no jazz dictionary or encyclopedia, and she never recorded. But for a good part of her life, she was able to make a living playing ragtime and stride piano in the tiny speakeasies in the West 30s, on 53rd and Broadway, in Flushing, Queens, and out of town when opportunities came up. Born in Virginia in 1892 (the same year as Barbara Monk), she was barely in her twenties when she started hanging out at James Reese Europe's Clef Club on West 53rd Street. There she met Eubie Blake, James P. Johnson, and Fats Waller—all pianists who would influence her style. Her career might have taken off, according to her daughter Alberta Webb, but "Things got tough back there in the 20s and she married again.... Being a woman, she got sort of sidetracked trying to raise her children. Unfortunately, things did not work out in later years." For several summers, she had a regular gig at Jack's Cabaret in Saratoga Springs, which gave her two children, Archie and Alberta, a much-needed respite from the city heat.[18]

Throughout the 1920s, she earned a little money giving piano lessons—enough, at least, to list "piano teacher" as her primary occupation in those years. During the Great Depression, she continued to teach but to survive she did domestic work.[19] Among her students was Thelonious. Simmons and her children lived with her mother, Ida Washington, at 210 West 61st Street, through the 1920s and early 1930s, before moving to 117 West 60th Street, on the east side of Amsterdam. Simmons's daughter Alberta, only two years younger than Thelonious, had vivid memories of his visits to the Simmons household. Sitting at her pristine brown Horace Waters upright, Simmons would teach him a variety of stride piano techniques and help him develop his left hand. "Thelonious used to come by and get the little rhythms that my mother had, what Fats Waller and them had. He knew about my mom."[20]

The church proved to be another critical source of Monk's musical knowledge. Barbara taught her son a few hymns on the piano, and every once in a while Thelonious would accompany her when she sang at Reverend W. A. Johnson's church on West 61st Street. Although these performances were few and far between—usually around religious holidays such as Easter or Christmas—they were memorable. When Monk reached his late teens and early 20s, he continued to accompany his mother during these holiday performances, but as soon as the song ended it was his cue to cut out. He wouldn't stay for the service. Nonetheless he became steeped in the sacred music of the black Baptist tradition. One account claims, dubiously, that Thelonious studied under "Professor" Buster Archer, Union Baptist Church's legendary organist, but this is unlikely since the church had moved uptown by the time Monk turned twelve.[21]

In any case Barbara had much to teach. She adored gospel, hymns, and old spirituals, and could be quite a taskmaster when it came to learning the music. Thelonious's nephew, Thomas Monk, Jr., remembers Easter Sundays when all the children would have to stand before the church and sing hymns with their grandmother. She'd insist on rehearsals: "We'd go to the house and she'd get on the piano. . . . And we'd be singing and she'd tell us, 'You hit the wrong note. Up, a little up, a little down.' She was like my uncle [Thelonious]. She was like a musical instructor. I'd say, 'I know how to sing it, Grandma.' She'd say, 'No, no, you got to sing with this, that, more feeling. Bring out the voice.' And we'd stay there for about two hours."[22]

Besides his mother, the most important influence on Monk's early development as a musician and as a young man wasn't a person but an institution—the Columbus Hill Neighborhood Center (renamed the Columbus Hill Community Center in 1933). Armed with a $72,000 gift from John D. Rockefeller, Jr., the Children's Aid Society transformed the old Henrietta Industrial School at 224 West 63rd Street into an elaborate after-school and summer program for children and adults. The stimulus for Rockefeller's gift grew out of a study of delinquency among black children in New York City, conducted in the fall of 1927 by a joint committee representing several social agencies. The Center, which opened its doors in October of 1928, was not to be another recreation facility but a kind of hub of community social service. It housed, for example, the Columbus Hill Health Center (AICP), the New York City Health Department's Baby Health Station, the Urban League, the Columbus Hill Day Nursery, the Child Study Association, and the Henrietta Health Center of the Children's Aid Society.[23]

It was a true center of social life for black youth in the neighborhood. Within months of its creation, about 150 girls and 320 boys were active in eighteen clubs covering a wide range of activities, including athletics, swimming, homemaking, tap dancing, and orchestra. By March of 1930, over 800 kids participated in the Center's various programs and clubs, and the staff consisted of twenty-three volunteers and twenty paid workers.[24] For the most part, the clubs were segregated by gender. Boys signed up for metal work, carpentry, and photography with Mr. Banner, and many of the girls could be found in Mrs. McIver's craft classes, where she taught advanced weaving and block printing.[25] Within each gender group, kids were divided by age. Theo Wilson remembered three distinct groups—Junior, Intermediate, and Senior—and in his view, Thelonious policed the age boundaries vigilantly. "When I was a Junior he was a Senior," Wilson mused. "And if I went into the Seniors' room to play pool, he would come in and take my stick and say I followed him there. And sometimes I would give it to him, or I wouldn't. And the last word was, I'd take a pool ball, and on the way back I'd give it to him. He was a big guy, and I didn't belong in there. But I thought, 'Who the hell is he? He doesn't run the joint.'"[26]

Thelonious would beg to differ, especially once he became a Senior. But no harsh words were exchanged; both parties knew better. Strict rules of conduct were vigilantly enforced, and fighting or other acts of misbehavior often resulted in a revoked or suspended membership. Despite San Juan Hill's reputation for violence, incidents of fighting or serious misbehavior were few and far between. Most children genuinely loved and valued the Center and its predominantly black staff. "It was the greatest thing in our lives," Mavis Swire remembered. "[The staff] had a way of making you feel like you could do great things. You can do more with your life."[27]

The Center was so popular, in fact, that when the Children's Aid Society announced in April of 1930 that it would have to close its doors due to lack of funding, angry residents organized a mass meeting and accused the Children's Aid Society of racial discrimination. Leaders of the institutions housed in the building vowed to keep the Center going. The Urban League organized a benefit performance of Marc Connelly's play "The Green Pastures" less than a month after the announcement, committing all the proceeds to the Center. The mobilization succeeded. The closing turned out to be temporary; the freshly painted and newly repaired Center was back in operation within a few weeks.[28]

For Thelonious, Marion, and Thomas, the Center became their second home. Marion remembered playing indoor games such as dominoes, checkers, ping-pong, as well as outdoor sports such as paddle ball, a miniature form of tennis. Thelonious rarely beat his big sister at paddle ball, but he excelled on the basketball court (though, contrary to popular myth, he never played for his high school basketball team), and he was a shark when it came to billiards and table tennis. "He was good in pool," Marion remembered. "He could beat everybody shooting pool, playing ping-pong. I think he won the championship with the boys in ping-pong and I won it for the girls, the championship. He was good."[29] Thelonious and Thomas, despite their two-and-a-half-year age difference, played on the same basketball team at the Center, in the "100-pound" division.[30]

Thelonious's appreciation for the Center was captured in an essay he wrote for his tenth grade English class. Titled "Stormy Days in the City and Country," it compared urban and rural lives for boys:

> On stormy days [there] is hardly anything you can do in the streets, so mostly everybody [tries] to entertain hisself at home. Some go home and read, some play checkers, etc. But I don't stay home very much on stormy days because there is a boys' club near my home called Columbus Hill Community Center. In this club there is a lot of things to entertain boys with such as basketball, pool, ping pong, checkers, craft classes and many other things. This is the way the average city boy spends his time on rainy days because there are boys' clubs all over the city.
>
> In the country it is different than in the city because there are not any boys clubs around so the boys go home and maybe invite a couple of his friends over and tell stories to each other. If the boy happens to have some game at home he and his friends play with them. A country boy can't play a game such as basketball because there is hardly any place to play such a game. If it

happen [sic] to be such a place as a boys' club in the country the boys have to travel so far to get there. This shows the life of the city boy and the country boy on stormy days.[31]

Thelonious never became a regular member of one of the Center's orchestras, but he did participate in the music program.[32] When he was about fifteen or sixteen years old, the Center held a music contest for a scholarship to the Juilliard School of Music. Thelonious entered, evidently played well, but took second place behind his friend Louis Taylor, a thirteen-year-old piano prodigy who lived a few doors down from the Monks at 227 West 63rd Street. Taylor's father delivered coal for a living and his mother worked as a domestic for a private family, but they nevertheless considered themselves among the "better classes," owing to their Barbadian origins. Nellie Monk and other members of the family believed that Taylor was chosen over Thelonious only because the administrators of the Center favored West Indians.[33] Thelonious did envy the fact that Taylor had large hands. Thomas Monk recalled, "my brother used to sort of get aggravated because he couldn't stretch like Louis or the other piano players."[34]

Taylor was enrolled in the diploma program at Juilliard from 1936 to 1940, where he studied piano under Etta C. Garcia. He also took classes in Juilliard's Extension Division and Summer School from 1946 to 1948, and he became a music teacher.[35] Years later, according to Nellie Monk, on one rainy night in 1958 during one of Monk's engagements at the Five Spot, Taylor came to the set, heard what Thelonious was doing, and passed a note to his former adversary, through club owner Joe Termini, indicating that Monk had deserved to win the scholarship that day. Monk just shrugged it off: "I'm glad I didn't go to the conservatory. Probably would've ruined me!"[36]

Monk's formal education was somewhat less successful than his informal music learning. As a junior high student, Monk appeared to be curious and engaging, but his grades were average. He graduated from P.S. 141 at the end of the winter term in 1928 and enrolled in junior high school JHS 69 on West 54th Street in the spring of 1929.[37] Junior high was no different from his elementary school in that it had a predominantly black student body and an overwhelmingly white teaching staff, except Thelonious and his friends in the West 60s had to travel a few additional blocks to get to school, crossing the great divide: Amsterdam Avenue. Battles with neighborhood white kids along the Avenue were daily occurrences, but Monk had earned a reputation as one of the kids not to mess with.

Contrary to the common lore that Monk "excelled" in mathematics and physics, his grades were never very impressive. During the seventh grade and through the fall of eighth grade at JHS 69, his math scores were successively 65, 47, and 65. In the spring term of eighth grade and fall of ninth grade, his scores rose to a respectable 80 and 75, only to plummet precipitously once he enrolled in Stuyvesant High School. Besides, he essentially failed geography in junior high, with grades ranging from 35 to 57 during the same period. He performed somewhat better in English (65 and 76 at JHS 69), he earned about a B to B+ average in spelling and drawing, and he deservedly scored a 90 for penmanship.[38] He proved quite the draftsman; his mother kept some of his junior-high school drawings for many, many years. His niece Jackie remembered seeing "a fine drawing of an old-fashioned iron. Mrs. Monk hung that drawing and others over the sink as long as I could remember."[39] For almost every other subject—physical training, science, and shop—Monk maintained about a C average. The one area in which he consistently excelled was music, earning Bs and As, which was enough for admission to the prestigious Stuyvesant High School. That, and some lobbying by Barbara.

There was no entrance examination for Stuyvesant in those days,[40] and Barbara had good reason to send her son there, even though it was very far to the east and south, at 345 East 15th Street. First, Barbara worked a few blocks from the school, as a cleaner at Children's Court on 137 East 22nd Street. She was always close to her middle child and preferred to have Thelonious closer to her, especially in light of the proliferation of crime and drugs in San Juan Hill. During the early 1930s, San Juan Hill became a leading center of the incipient heroin trade and the target of major federal drug raids.[41] Second, the then-all-boys school was one of the best high schools in the city, then as now. Ironically, though it had an outstanding orchestra and band, Thelonious never participated in the school's music programs, nor did he take any general music classes. There is no evidence that he even auditioned for the orchestra's highly coveted piano chair. Stuyvesant did not have a jazz band at the time. Some have speculated that Monk was barred from the orchestra because of his race,[42] but there were at least two black student members at the time. Solomon Moore, class of '33, held a cello chair just prior to Monk's arrival. Moore was also a star on Stuyvesant's basketball team. Thomas J. Brown, class of '35, played violin in the orchestra, performed in the school band, ran track, sang in the glee club, and was a leader in the Pan American Society.[43]

Thelonious appeared committed to school when he first entered Stuyvesant in the spring of 1932. During his first three semesters, he attended classes regularly, missing only 14 out of 285 days, and he was late only six times. He worked hard, especially for a teenaged boy who loved sports, pretty girls, and playing piano—not necessarily in that order. But in spite of his effort—and contrary to legend—Monk did not perform exceedingly well, continuing his junior-high grades. In his first semester he earned a 68 in English, a 67 in French, a 70 in math, and a dismal 40 in chemistry.[44] His best subject that semester was "Mechanic Arts," in which he scored an impressive 86. The following semester (fall 1932), his English grade dropped to a 40, French to 50, and math to 65. By the spring of 1933, although he attended classes regularly, he seems to have stopped trying. He earned "0's" in physics and French, a 50 in biology, and a surprising 20 in mechanic arts. The one course that seemed to engage him was English. He not only earned a 66, his highest grade that semester, but his English assignments dominated his composition book.

His tenth grade essays reveal his curiosity, skepticism, and wry sense of humor. Characterizing Charles Dickens's *A Tale of Two Cities* as essentially a violent conflict between rich and poor, Thelonious noted how the poor people of France were being "killed in a dreadful manner" while the nation's rulers continued their profligate lifestyle. But even amidst tragedy, Thelonious always found something amusing: The one example he cited from the text told of a young Frenchman who was sentenced by the state to be mutilated and burned alive for not properly honoring a "procession of monks" that had passed a few yards away from him.[45] In another assignment, he summarized a newspaper article about a group of University of California scientists who had invented a machine to revive patients whose hearts had stopped. The machine forced oxygen into the lungs, applied heat to the body, and rocked the patient back and forth until her/his heart began to beat. "The theory is," Monk wrote, "that the steady change in position will cause gravity to send the blood coursing through the veins and will start the heart beating. I think this will help save a lot of lives providing it does what the inventor states."[46] Another, titled "What is the Best Kind of Stove?", went for awkward deadpan:

> Before the gas stove was invented people had to hang their food over the fireplace in pots. Then after a long time of this miserable way of cooking, at last the gas stove was on the market. Of course, when it first came out it costed [sic] a lot of money but finally it was down and mostly everybody had one. And like anything else it had a bad side to it. Sometimes the people would make a mistake and leave on the gas and the result most of the time was death. Then still it was a good stove because it cooks the food quick, you can cook more of the food and it leaves a better taste to the food.
>
> According to those reasons stated above I think a gas stove is the best kind of stove.[47]

Oh, happy survivors.

It is often claimed that Monk played on his high school basketball team, but he never participated in *any* extracurricular activities at Stuyvesant. As soon as the final school bell rang, Monk rushed to the subway and headed for home. The neighborhood was the center of his social universe; here he earned the respect of his peers and developed a few deep and lasting friendships. When he wasn't playing basketball or ping-pong at the community center, Thelonious would often visit his friend Harold Francis across the street. Like a number of Monk's friends, Harold was of Caribbean descent; his parents hailed from Barbados. His father, Frederick, was a bit of a curiosity in the neighborhood because he worked as a stableman caring for horses. Harold and Monk had a lot in common. They were the same age and were known around the neighborhood as excellent pianists.[48] The pair spent many hours together taking turns playing for each other, sometimes at the Monks' house, sometimes at the community center. Occasionally they visited Alberta Simmons.

The Monks' apartment was a popular hangout not only for Harold Francis but for many of the young neighborhood musicians. Barbara's doors were always open for her children's friends, and she enjoyed the music they played. Marion remembers those impromptu jam sessions fondly. The kids would pile into the front room and "they'd be playing and the rest of us would be dancing, you know."[49] Like Thelonious, Harold

Francis was determined to become a professional musician. He would struggle until 1946, when he got his big break and replaced Ray Tunia as the pianist/arranger for the Ink Spots.[50]

Thelonious's longest-lasting friendship began inauspiciously in the summer of 1933, when he was just shy of sixteen. One day, as he was walking down his block on West 63rd Street, he saw a group of kids preparing to jump a boy who was small and slight in stature and about a year younger than Monk. The boy was desperately trying to defend himself when Thelonious intervened. "Leave that kid alone. He didn't do anything to you." Monk was calm but firm. When the gang hesitated, Monk made it clear to all that if they continued with the beating, "you're gonna have to deal with me."[51] Monk possessed the personal clout and reputation as a pugilist to persuade the kids to back off. In no time, Thelonious and the new boy became inseparable. His name was James Smith but everyone called him Sonny. Sonny wasn't a musician, but he loved music and liked to improvise on the mandolin and piano. Monk came to respect Sonny's ear, and Sonny became Monk's biggest advocate.[52]

When Sonny met Thelonious, he and his family had just moved from a tiny apartment in a Brooklyn brownstone to a tiny apartment in a five-story tenement house at 226 West 62nd Street. At the time, the Smith family consisted of Sonny, his mother, Nellie, and his two sisters—ten-year-old Nellie and eight-year-old Evelyn, who also went by "Skippy." Tuberculosis and related illnesses ravaged the rest of the family, including Evelyn's twin sister, who died soon after birth. Altogether, Mrs. Nellie Smith lost five children to "consumption." She buried her last child, fifteen-year-old Etta, on March 31, 1933.[53]

The Smiths' story is similar to that of the Monks. They, too, were part of the Southern migrant stream that settled in New York City during the early to mid-1920s. And like Barbara Monk, Nellie Smith ended up leaving her husband behind in search of a better life for her children. Born in Florida in 1899 to Harry Young and Martha Brooks, Nellie was a mere teenager when she met Elisha Bennett Smith, a tall, handsome, and debonair Pullman porter who hailed from Sumter County, Georgia.[54] Even in his old age, Smith's niece remembered him as "a wonderful physical specimen . . . who loved to dress and loved music."[55] He played a little guitar and piano, but according to family legend he only knew one song. And every chance he got he played that one song, over and over. The son of former slaves, James Riley Smith and Rosa Alger Battle, Elisha grew up alongside very successful and highly motivated siblings. His brother, James Clifton Smith, became a renowned educator and activist in St. Augustine, Florida, and his three sisters, Rosa Bell, Annie Mickens, and Lula, were all well-educated, strikingly beautiful, and famously independent. In fact, Elisha (also known as E.B.) was sort of the rebel in the family. He dropped out of school early on, loved travel and adventure, and had a weakness for pretty women. One of those pretty women, Nellie Young, was twenty-four years his junior. They married some time during World War I, settled in Jacksonville, Florida, and started a family right away. Nellie bore eight children for E.B.—the sixth child, born December 27, 1921, she named after herself. While Nellie raised his children, E.B. spent much of his time traveling up and down the eastern seaboard for the Pullman Company. He never could suppress his wandering spirit or his eye for attractive women. In 1926, Nellie Smith and her eight children left E.B. behind and made the northern trek to New York.[56]

She first moved in with her sister Elizabeth Bracy, also known as Aunt "Yank." Recently widowed, Bracy worked as a housekeeper but owned a small home on Atlantic Avenue in Brooklyn. Nellie, too, found work as a domestic, but it took four years before she was able to move out. But by the time they relocated to Albany Avenue about six blocks away, she had lost four of her children to TB and had contracted the disease herself.[57] With Etta's passing, Mrs. Smith and her three surviving children, Sonny, Nellie, and Skippy, packed their belongings and set out for Manhattan. After about a year living at 226 West 62nd Street, Nellie's health deteriorated to the point where she could no longer work and the family had to go on relief. They were forced to move again to a slightly cheaper place across the street at 237 West 62nd. Much of the burden of caring for the two girls now fell on Sonny's shoulders.

Thelonious and Sonny became a conspicuous pair at the playground and on the streets. Many of the girls in the neighborhood found them both to be particularly good-looking, and a few developed serious crushes, despite the boys' reputation for aloofness. A few of the girls, including Sonny's sister Nellie, used to gather at Monk's house to hear him play. Nellie remembered, "I was about twelve when I heard him play the piano, and that was at his house. A lot of young girls used to go to his house. His mother would let them in. Of course, a lot of girls had a crush on him. . . . All the teenage girls."[58] Nellie knew better than to expect sixteen-year-old Thelonious to take an interest in a bashful, skinny twelve-year-old. Still, after the couple was married, she recounted a far more romantic story of their first encounter: "I was playing in a playground, and we had heard about each other. One day he passed the playground, and our eyes met, and I knew him, and he knew me. We didn't speak then, and we didn't actually meet until six months later. Years later he could tell me what I wore that day."[59] Perhaps, but if Thelonious felt this way, many years would pass before he began to see little Nellie as the beautiful, intelligent, and charming brown-skinned woman with the distinctively high cheekbones and the penetrating eyes.

Meanwhile, Nellie befriended two sisters who lived just across the street, Geraldine and Edith MacMillan. The MacMillan girls, along with their older sister, Millicent Henry, moved in with their aunt Lizzie Brooks, at 238 West 62nd Street, after their mother died in 1932.[60] (Their father left when they were quite young, and was not in a position to care for his children.) "Aunt Lizzie," as she was known to practically everyone in the neighborhood, was the girls' maternal aunt—their mother's older sister. She was listed in the census as married, but her husband did not live with her and she supported the entire household on meager wages earned from domestic service. "She was everybody's aunt," Geraldine remembered. "Just a little spry lady [and] a real figurehead in the neighborhood."[61] By the time the Smiths moved to the block in 1933, Geraldine had just turned thirteen and Nellie was eleven. They all attended JHS 69 together, and Nellie and Edith became after-school playmates.

At first, Geraldine had no interest in hanging out with her little sister and her new friend. "She wanted me to come and play with them. But I said they were too young. I felt I was so big and grown. . . . She kept telling me, [the Smiths] are nice, you would like them. So then she thought she was really interesting me when she said, 'They got a cute brother.'" Geraldine had heard the buzz around the neighborhood from the other girls, and she agreed that Sonny was very good-looking, but she felt he was hard to approach and a little too cool. Nevertheless, she agreed to join Edith at the Smiths' house and in no time she and Nellie were best friends. It would be a little while before Geraldine would make Sonny's acquaintance, and even longer before she met Thelonious. Eventually, Nellie's "cute brother" began to take notice when Geraldine blossomed into a young woman.[62]

San Juan Hill was like a small town unto itself; every circle of friends seemed to overlap. While Thelonious and Sonny were still too cool, and too old, to hang out with Nellie and Geraldine, they were tight with Geraldine's cousin, Charles Stewart, who also lived with Aunt Lizzie. Stewart, a talented trumpet player and fine arranger, started jamming with Thelonious when they both were about fourteen years old (Stewart was just a few months older than Monk). In later years, Monk would praise Stewart's playing, comparing him with Clifford Brown. Stewart followed in the footsteps of his cousin (Geraldine's older brother from a different father), Clarence Brereton, who played trumpet and sometimes trombone in Noble Sissle's Orchestra during the 1930s, and in John Kirby's Orchestra in the mid-1940s.[63]

Around 1933, Monk formed his first band with Stewart and another kid from the Columbus Hill Community Center named Morris Simpson. The son of West Indian immigrants, Simpson was a fine drummer who lived a couple doors down from the Center, where his father worked as a janitor. When Morris wasn't in school, practicing drums, or playing tennis—one of his favorite pastimes—he helped his mother run a little newspaper stand on the corner of West 63rd and Amsterdam.[64] The three of them were only fifteen or sixteen, but they managed to land a few gigs in local restaurants and at dances.

There are no surviving descriptions of their music, but whatever it was, the people liked it. Monk: "They used to have what they called rent parties and they used to hire me to play when I was very young. They'd pay you about three dollars, and you'd play all night for 'em. And they'd charge admission to people who would come in and drink. That's the way some people used to get their rent together, like that."[65] Nellie wasn't old enough to attend those parties, but she heard stories from Thelonious and her brother. "Sometimes he'd get money, sometimes they'd give him a story and all that." On a good night, she said, the band could make up to ten or fifteen dollars— quite a sum at the height of the Depression. "It was always crowded. People would buy pig feet dinners and chicken dinners with potato salad, you know, a dollar a plate or fifty cents a plate." The gigs were intermittent, but when he did get paid he would always give his mother some money and use the rest to keep himself sharp. "He was earning his own money, buying his own clothes," Nellie remembered. "He was able to buy his shoes with that."[66]

The trio made a few dollars competing in "Audition Night" at the Apollo Theater. Launched early 1934, "Audition Night" took place on Mondays, the professional musicians' night off, and contestants competed for the grand prize of ten dollars. Second, third, and fourth place winners received five, three and two dollars, respectively. "Audition Night" was not the same as the more famous "Amateur Night at the Apollo" hosted by the Harlem personality Ralph Cooper. "Amateur Night" took place on Wednesdays from 11:00 to midnight, starting at the very end of 1934. Famously, unlike all the other competing amateur night competitions throughout Harlem—both the Alhambra and the Harlem Opera House hosted similar competitions in 1934— the Apollo's "Amateur Night" was broadcast live on the radio.[67] Audition Night was a quieter affair. Nellie, Monk's siblings, and other family members remember the trio bringing home the ten-dollar grand prize pretty regularly. "The three of them," Marion recalled, "would go up and they won every time they went up, so they barred them from coming up there because they were winning each time."[68] Nellie recalled in an interview that Thelonious won so many times, for five or six weeks the Apollo became a steady source of income. She, too, remembers the management telling him "Don't come back anymore."[69] Oddly, Monk's trio's victories did not lead to bigger things. Just a few years later, women vocalists were touted by the press and/or earned professional gigs as a result of winning Amateur Night contests. Thelma Carpenter, Billie Drew, and Ella Fitzgerald were all "discovered" because of their Amateur Night performances.[70] For Monk, by contrast, his legendary victories on the Apollo stage were just that— legendary.

For three young men with a little money in their pockets, there were many cheap entertainments in New York City during the Depression. Twenty or thirty cents bought a movie ticket at the Loews on 7th Avenue and 124th, or the Proctor or the Orient along 125th Street. The comedy duo Buck and Bubbles performed at the Mt. Morris Theater, and the Odeon had both movies and live acts. When Thelonious could swing it, he shelled out thirty-five to fifty cents to see some of the big bands at the Apollo, the Lafayette, or the Harlem Opera House—led by Earl Hines, Jimmie Lunceford, and Don Redmon, among others. It is very likely that he went to see Willie Lewis's band at the Lafayette in March of 1934.[71] Billed as the "year's greatest musical sensation," the Lewis band was on its way to Europe for an extended engagement beginning the following month. Some of the buzz surrounding this band had to do with its sensational new pianist, Herman Chittison. Chittison was one of Monk's favorite pianists, as Monk later acknowledged.[72] Handsome, suave, nine years Monk's senior, the Kentucky-born pianist, like Monk, had been introduced to music through hymns. At four years old, he had been able to play "Trust and Obey," and he frequently played piano at his family's church. At Kentucky State Industrial College for Colored Persons (1925–26), he became the pianist and director of the school orchestra. Two years later he hit the road with Zack Whyte and His Chocolate Beau Brummels and went on to work with Stepin Fetchit and Willie Lewis.[73] Chittison tended to play a lot of notes and possessed a demonic ability to play fast; Monk tended to play fewer notes and preferred medium tempos. But Chittison's influence is audible in recordings by the young Monk. Both loved descending runs, and "fills" (punctuation points at the ends of phrases in a tune) that were deliberately bumpy. Chittison had a strong and active left hand, which he used to create little counter-melodies. And like Monk, when Chittison backed a soloist—including a singer—he was never content to simply feed him (or her) chords in the background. He tended to be extraordinarily busy, filling in every conceivable space to the point of competing with the soloist.[74] Chittison possessed a strong melodic sense. His improvisations maintained a solid connection to each tune, and he could really swing!

Playing at the Apollo was exciting, but Monk's trio's most important gigs were the Friday night dances at the Community Center. The trio wasn't paid much, but they had a good time and always received an enthusiastic response. Sometimes they played for the fledgling tap dancers and singers in the neighborhood. Thelonious, who was himself a bit of a hoofer, enjoyed playing for tap dancers. One of the young dancers they backed up was Trotyrine Wilson, "Rita" to her friends. Born in South Carolina, she lived at the southern end of San Juan Hill, on West 55th Street. She was Alberta Webb's occasional dance partner, and they frequently rehearsed their routines at the Center. Petite and attractive, with big brown eyes and a wide sparkling smile, she was a sensation on the dance floor. And she was a triple threat: She sang and played the piano, not to mention the ukulele. "That Trotyrine was something else," Alberta mused. "She was a beautiful little gal with them feet."[75]

Thelonious thought she was beautiful, too, and he was interested in more than her feet. He was still in high school when he began to court Trotyrine in earnest; she was fifteen and Thelonious was going on seventeen. They dated for a while, but as far as Trotyrine was concerned it was nothing serious. In fact, she already held a torch for Thelonious's baby brother Thomas, who was a year younger than Trotyrine and painfully shy. (Too shy for Trotyrine, alas.) His son, Thomas Monk, Jr., had always heard that his father "was a wallflower. He wasn't flirtatious; he wasn't a womanizer. My father was always that way. Handsome guy."[76] Many of the girls in the neighborhood considered Thomas the better-looking Monk brother, though they each had their share of admirers.

While Thelonious was working hard to woo his first official girlfriend, the trio came to an untimely and unexpected end. Indomitable Aunt Lizzie Brooks had never liked the musicians' life, and she gave her nephew Clarence Brereton a hard time about it. She had her reasons. "Her youngest brother was a minstrel and he used to travel," observed her niece Geraldine. "He would write home and say how he didn't get paid, hardship, he had no carfare to come back home. . . . [H]e finally did come home after many situations like that. But he developed tuberculosis and he died. And she was finished with musicians. She thought that was the worst profession anyone could have. So here are my two brothers, both of them want to play horn and go on the road!"[77]

Aunt Lizzie was determined to keep young Charles Stewart insulated from professional music, and she did everything in her power to monitor his movements. But with four children to care for and the demands of a full-time job, she could not be everywhere. He snuck out of the house to gigs, or came up with some story to cover his tracks. But one day, while the trio was performing at a club on West 61st Street, Aunt Lizzie stormed into the place, grabbed her nephew by the ear, and literally dragged him off the bandstand. That was the end of Charles Stewart's music career. Thelonious continued to respect Aunt Lizzie, but he never forgave her for that night. Every opportunity he got, he would say to her, "Why did you stop that boy from playing? He would have been great!" She must have heard Monk say this to her many times; she lived to 105.[78]

All was not lost, however. Monk befriended another outstanding trumpet player named Denzil da Costa Best. Slight, dark-skinned, and soft-spoken, Best lived with his parents and four brothers on East 100th and Second Avenue—to some San Juan Hill residents, a universe away. Like Morris Simpson, Best was West Indian—his family immigrated in 1916, just one year before Denzil was born. His father repaired elevators for a living, but played bass and tuba in his spare time. Denzil began piano lessons at six, but then switched to trumpet against his father's wishes. He practiced surreptitiously, and after graduating from high school joined Chris Columbus's band. Once his dad heard him on the radio, all was forgiven.[79] Thelonious thought Best was the Second Coming. "[He] was one of the best trumpets I ever heard. He'd outblow everybody in the place."[80] The feeling was mutual. They were kindred spirits, not only because they lived and breathed music, but because they were willing to take chances. Best admired Thelonious for staying true to his own musical vision despite disparaging critics and musicians. "People would call his changes wrong to his face," Best later explained. "If he hadn't been so strong in his mind, he might easily have become discouraged, but he always went his own way and wouldn't change for anything."[81] Monk and Best became life-long friends. In the meantime, he was the perfect substitute for the grounded Charles Stewart.

Beginning in the fall semester of 1933, his junior year at Stuyvesant, Monk's interest in his musical education trumped any glimmer of effort in the classroom. He virtually stopped attending class, showing up only sixteen out of ninety-two days and earning 0's in all of his subjects. He made a half-hearted effort the following semester, but still only managed to make it to school thirty-one out of ninety-eight days. By April of 1934, Barbara was so concerned about Thelonious that she phoned the counselor to talk about her son's performance. Thelonious was doing so poorly that school officials had already decided to ease him out. It is not entirely accurate to say that Thelonious dropped out of school. Instead, Stuyvesant officials thought it best to transfer him to Haaren High School.[82] Located on 10th Avenue between 58th and 59th, Haaren was within walking distance from Monk's house and it catered to students who had already entered the job market. The school developed a program whereby students were allowed to create a flexible schedule combining work and school, a good thing during the Depression when few young people could afford to concentrate solely on school.[83]

Yet Thelonious chose not to enroll in Haaren High. Now that he was making a little money with his trio, he saw no reason to finish high school. He was set: Music was his life. Barbara had left North Carolina and separated from her husband in large part for her children's education, and now Thelonious had dropped out at age sixteen. He continued to live at home, play music, see Trotyrine, hang with friends, and help out with whatever cash he made. If Barbara argued with him about his schooling, there is no record of it. For a young African-American man in Depression-era New York, any income was welcome. And at least he was still at home with her.

But then the Lord called.

4

"We Played and She Healed"

(1934–1937)

For a homebody like Monk, life was good in the summer of 1934. He was sixteen, enjoyed three square meals a day, a room with a piano, unlimited time to play and write, a girlfriend, and a high level of local popularity, as a handsome, prize-winning musician. But like most Depression-era teens, his pockets were rarely full. Although Marion secured a job at the Columbus Hill Community Center,[1] the family lived mainly on Barbara's meager wages. Thelonious earned a little playing solo or trio gigs here and there, and occasional rent parties, but he did not have a union card, nor was he pounding the pavement in search of a regular job. Barbara wasn't opposed to his chosen career—as Thelonious recalled many years later, "She never figured I should do anything else. She was with me, you know. If I wanted to play music, it was all right with her."[2] But as hard as she worked, she would not allow Thelonious to just hang around the house, eating, sleeping and writing music. Working as a musician was perfectly fine, but he had to work, especially now that he decided not to attend Haaren High School in the fall.

He tried his hand at wage work, securing a job with the neighborhood ice peddler known to everyone as "Ice Joe," like his father back in Rocky Mount some sixteen years ago. "[I]t was pretty strenuous work," Thomas remembered. "He worked one day and said he'd never do that again."[3] He needed steady income from a piano stool.

Through an acquaintance of Barbara's, Thelonious landed a job that not only kept him out of the house, it took him out of the city altogether. A devout Baptist (who would soon defect to the Jehovah's Witnesses), Barbara befriended a black female evangelist and divine healer affiliated with a Pentecostal church. Some called her Reverend Graham, and she apparently earned the moniker "the Texas Warhorse," but even her name has never been confirmed.[4] She was preparing for a tour of the Midwest and Southwest in order to save souls and drive out affliction, and she desperately needed a band. She had heard Monk play, either in the family's tiny apartment or while visiting Barbara's church, so she asked him to organize a small ensemble consisting of a drummer, saxophone player, and trumpeter. As Monk later explained, the gig "wasn't through the church. [It was] through other sources, other channels."[5] Now, all he had to do was convince his mama to let him go. Barbara wanted him to work, but traveling across the country at such a young age was not what she had in mind. "She finally conceded," Thomas recalled, "'cause his heart was so bent on going. She was convinced that it was something that would be beneficial to him, 'cause he was playing the piano and that's what he wanted to do. So she let him go. And when he came back, he had changed his style of playing."[6] He packed his bags, bid farewell to his mother, sister, brother, and Trotyrine, and piled into a car with his new quartet, pulling a small trailer loaded down with luggage, a small set of drums, a battered upright piano, and a box of Bibles. It would be more than two years before he returned home to West 63rd Street.

Unfortunately, Monk left no details about the tour. He didn't talk about it with his family, and the journalists who interviewed him showed little or no interest. In 1956, he told Nat Hentoff, "While still in my teens, I went on the road with a group that played church music for an evangelist. Rock and roll or rhythm and blues. That's what we were doing. Only now they put different words to it. She preached and healed and we played. We had trumpet, saxophone, piano, and drums. And then the congregation would sing. We would play in some of the biggest churches in the towns we went through. We traveled around the country for about two years."[7] Several years later, he told journalist Pearl Gonzalez, "I once traveled with an evangelist for a couple of years. It was in the Southwest, and I was a teenager."[8] That was it. He never mentioned the evangelist's name, the names of the other musicians, or what towns they might have traveled through. Nor was he asked to describe the revivals, the music they played, or how many congregants they might attract on any given night. So why did he do it? Why abandon the center of the jazz world for the small towns and cities of Oklahoma, Kansas, Arkansas, Missouri, Indiana, and Illinois?

He didn't earn much money on the tour, and he didn't need room and board living at home. Perhaps the best explanation is Monk's own, from an interview in 1965: "It was a lot of fun!" And for him, he was essentially playing jazz. "I always did play jazz. I mean, I was playing [church] music the same way."[9]

It's also conceivable that the spirit moved Thelonious. Many years later, after his friend, the pianist Mary Lou Williams, converted to Catholicism, he occasionally joined her, Bud Powell, and her ex-husband Harold Baker for Mass at 6:00 a.m. When Mary Lou first invited him to Our Lady of Lourdes for Mass, Monk was apparently so nervous that he consumed a whole bottle of wine in advance. It only made matters worse; when he arrived that morning he was so drunk he collapsed on the floor of the church. Fortunately, they were the only two people there. Monk continued to attend Mass for a little while longer, though he never converted.[10] On the other hand, most people who knew the adult Monk remember that he rarely attended church and did not speak about religion in the most flattering terms. His brother became a Jehovah's Witness minister, and sometimes Thelonious would get into arguments with Thomas and various family members over religion. "He used to come when we were having our [Bible] study," his niece Charlotte recalls. "Daddy would say to Uncle Bubba, 'Why don't you sit down and join us?' and Uncle would say 'I'm God.' . . . He was never into religion. Religion was not his thing. He thought he was God. He never went to Kingdom Hall with my grandma. He never went to church or any of that. And his kids, he never took them to church. He said they had to have their own mind about things."[11]

When photographer and journalist Valerie Wilmer asked him in 1965 whether he was a religious man, Monk responded, "I wouldn't say so. I haven't been to church in a good while."

> Valerie W.: Do you believe in God?
> Monk: I don't know nothing. Do you?
> Valerie W.: No, I do not.
> Monk: It's a deep subject, you know, trying to think about it.
> I kinda go along with you.[12]

We will never know what the teen-aged Thelonious was feeling or experiencing at the time, but we can know what he was getting into. What was this religious movement and how did it differ from the Baptist church in which he was raised? What did these revivals look like or sound like? What kind of music was Monk expected to play? What were the conditions on the road?

Despite his silence on the subject, we can be certain of some things about his teenage tour. First, we know that his evangelist was affiliated with a "sanctified" church, most likely Pentecostal, because Monk described her as a divine "healer." Besides believing in divine or miraculous healing, what set Pentecostals apart from Baptists and other Christian denominations was their belief that speaking in tongues is the principal element of being saved or sanctified.[13] Pentecostals were even more exuberant in their style of worship than the Baptists Monk grew up with. Congregants fall to the ground as if asleep or shaking convulsively—what is referred to as "being slain in spirit." Women and men struck by the Holy Ghost make prophetic statements as if God is speaking through them. The healers, always charismatic preachers, heal the sick and infirm through prayer, special oils, a laying-on of hands, and the application of sacred cloths. They might invoke the New Testament for its references to divine healing, but their rituals closely resemble the rituals Monk's West African ancestors practiced. Consciously or not, the Pentecostals share with Africans the basic philosophical tenet that one must draw on spiritual power in the service of the believer.[14] Monk's evangelist left a deep and lasting impression on him. Despite his later skepticism, family members recall Monk occasionally referring to "miraculous" things he saw while on the road. According to his sister-in-law, Geraldine Smith, "He thought that what he was seeing was for real. He would actually see people throw away their crutches and get out of their wheelchairs and walk."[15]

Reverend Graham could have belonged to any number of churches. During the mid-1930s, the more visible Pentecostal churches included the Church of Christ (Holiness); the Church of God in Christ; House of the Lord; Church of the Living God; the Church of the Living God, the Pillar and Ground of Truth; Mt. Sinai Holy Church; and the United House of Prayer for All People, founded by the enigmatic pastor Bishop C. M. "Daddy" Grace. We can narrow down the list somewhat. The Church of Christ believed that the use of musical instruments in the sacred space of the church was sacrilegious.[16] The most likely candidates are the Church of God in Christ (COGIC) and the Church of the Living God, the Pillar and Ground of Truth. Both had a presence in New York City as well as nation-wide, and both utilized women evangelists.

The COGIC banned women from ordination, but women were known to preach as traveling evangelists. Indeed, the crucial role women played as missionaries, saving souls and preaching the gospel, drew criticism from mainline Baptist and Methodist churches, where women were largely relegated to social reform and church organization roles. This does not mean that women in the COGIC necessarily exercised more power than Baptist or Methodist women. The ban on ordination did not keep women in the Pentecostal or Holiness churches from preaching or even entering the pulpit. Lizzie Roberson, the head of the Women's Department for the Church of God in Christ from 1911 to 1940, stressed the importance of women in missionary work. Women, more so than men, built the congregations by attracting wayward sinners with their fiery street-corner and countryside sermons and divine healing abilities, even if they were not in a position to pastor churches.[17] So it is quite possible that Monk's first employer was not an ordained minister, but rather an itinerant evangelist preaching without a pulpit.

In the COGIC, music was essential for converting sinners, saving souls, and healing the afflicted. Perhaps the most famous missionary in the church's history was Sister Rosetta Tharpe, the great vocalist and guitar player who brought her brand of gospel blues to the very clubs and theaters from which sanctified churchgoers were banned. Just two years younger than Thelonious, Sister Rosetta was still a child when she accompanied her mother, the dynamic evangelist and mandolin player Katie Bell Nubin, throughout the South. Like Monk and his evangelist, Tharpe and her mother traveled from town to town, city to city, holding tent revivals, evangelizing in the streets, and even at night around places of amusement.[18]

If Monk's evangelist was an ordained minister, she was probably affiliated with the Church of the Living God, the Pillar and Ground of Truth. Unlike other Pentecostal churches, the Church of the Living God not only ordained women but was founded by a woman, the Reverend Mary Lena Lewis Tate. Established in 1903, the church grew exponentially thanks to the missionary work of dozens of primarily female evangelists. By 1918, the church had a presence in forty-eight states with headquarters in Waycross, Georgia.[19] All Pentecostal evangelists shared the same earthly mission: "preaching the Gospel (even to the poor); healing the lame, the infirm, and broken of spirit; freeing those who found themselves slaves to sin; restoring eyes that have been blinded to the truth; releasing hurting people from their oppressors; and letting the world know that now is the time of their visitation."[20]

And saving souls. This was the evangelist's *raison d'être*. Journalists and jazz critics mistakenly characterize Monk's experience on the road as if it were analogous to joining the circus, with "healing" as a kind of sideshow or spectacle, and Monk merely providing music for the show. In reality, the life of an itinerant evangelist was demanding, highly exposed, and purposeful. For one thing, whenever a "prayer band" entered a town or a city, unless the evangelist was invited to preach at a local church, they had to "fish" for souls. Sometimes that meant handing out flyers announcing a tent revival, talking to sinners on street corners, recreation centers, or standing in front of job sites or places of amusement. An evangelist often would seek out a busy corner in the black community or, if at all possible, in sections of town where black and white gathered, and preach, either unaccompanied or backed by trumpet and drums. If it wasn't convenient to roll the piano off the truck or trailer, Thelonious probably joined in on tambourine during these impromptu sessions. Once the word spread that a revival was to be held, they would set up a tent in an empty field—preferably near a river or lake and not too far from the road—and hold prayer meetings five or six nights in a week. Having access to water was important, since Pentecostals believe in baptism by immersion.[21]

As the congregants gathered, prayer bands typically opened with a familiar hymn—such as J. P. Webster's "In the Sweet By and By," or "What a Friend We Have in Jesus" by Howard Doane. The evangelist would come to the makeshift pulpit and begin to expound upon a chosen text from the Bible. No matter where the scripture led, she would find her way to the essential point of the service: sinners must be saved and accept our Lord and Savior, Jesus Christ. Her words would burn slowly at first, eliciting shouts, amens, interjections of "Preach, sister," "Bring it home," "That's right," "Lord," "Jesus," and "Heavenly Father." The congregation's "response" to her "call" was like gasoline on hot embers. The slow burn gave way to fire and brimstone, and invariably some soul would catch the Holy Ghost and begin speaking in tongues—the true language of the sanctified. At this point in the service, sermon became song, completely improvised and spontaneous, consisting of little more than a one- or two-line lyric, said to have been composed "under the spirit." They were simple, blues-inflected melodic lines made of just three or four notes, sung by the preacher in a kind of gravelly, whining voice, and repeated by the congregation. The band was expected to jump in immediately and follow the preacher's lead, punctuating at the right moments, building to a steady pulse. They had to pay attention to both the crowd and the preacher. (And it wasn't unheard-of for a band member to catch the Holy Spirit.) The pulsing, syncopated rhythms joined, bodies moving, feet stomping, hand-clapping, and chants of "Power, Power Lord/We need Your power/Holy Ghost power . . ."[22]

Monk's experience playing sacred music in the Baptist church did not fully prepare him for this. During the early 1930s, the music of the sanctified churches was more rollicking than in the black Baptist churches, possessing rhythmic elements we associate with blues, jazz, or even early rock and roll. In a 1965 interview, Monk compared the kind of gospel music he played on the road with contemporary rock and R&B. "The music I played with them," he recalled, "seems to be coming out today. They're playing a lot of it now."[23] Many of the black Baptist churches in the urban North, on the other hand, had eliminated congregational singing in lieu of the professional choir, and the hymnal had replaced the old Negro spirituals. The blues scales and chords and the heavy syncopation we tend to associate with black religious expression today were virtually absent in the mainline black churches in the North during the early part of the twentieth century. For most black Baptist and Methodist (AME) ministers at the time, those sounds, brought by southerners in the Great Migration, undermined refinement and decorum. Worse, many black clergy associated blues and jazz with the devil's music. (Ironically, Pentecostal and Holiness preachers said the same thing, despite the jazz and blues elements in their own services.) Mainline church leaders sought to remake their flock according to middle-class mores. By the 1920s, most black Baptist churches developed a rift between ecstatic shouters and congregational singing, on the one hand, and refinement, quiet, "respectful" worship, on the other.[24]

Monk hit the road at the very moment when these tensions reached what can only be described as a musical revolution in the black Baptist churches. The very growth of the Pentecostal churches in the urban North had already compelled some mainline black ministers to adapt to the Southern folkways of their congregations. But the main force behind this "revolution" was a former itinerant bluesman turned preacher named Thomas Andrew Dorsey. Perhaps best known for composing "Take My Hand, Precious Lord" (1932), Dorsey was on a mission in the early 1930s to introduce his brand of "gospel blues" to the mainline black churches. He wrote and published new songs and sold sheet music, and he emphasized improvisation and the incorporation of "trills and turns and embellishments" associated with blues piano playing.[25] Besides his own original compositions, the kind of music Dorsey hoped to introduce already existed in the sanctified churches, and some of that music had begun to circulate beyond the sacred walls of the storefront churches via radio and the phonograph machine. Such notable figures as the spectacular blind pianist Arizona Dranes, and Bessie Johnson and the Sanctified Singers, began recording on the "race record" labels in the late 1920s. Dorsey, a shrewd businessman, hired female vocalists such as Sallie Martin from the sanctified church in order to form "gospel choruses" in mainline churches.[26] In other words, black female evangelists, not unlike the woman who employed Thelonious, laid the groundwork for the rise of gospel blues in the mainline black churches.

But even more than Dorsey, Monk was drawn to another important figure behind the revolution in black sacred music: the Reverend Charles A. Tindley. Tindley (1851–1933), an African-American Methodist minister based in Philadelphia, composed more than forty-five gospel hymns, including "Leave It There," "Nothing Between," "What Are You Doing in Heaven?," "Some Day," "Stand By Me," and "I'll Overcome Someday," which, in a slightly altered form, later became the civil rights movement's best-known anthem. Tindley's gospel hymns not only had a tremendous influence on Dorsey, but they were hugely popular among Pentecostals and Baptists alike.[27]

Monk grew particularly fond of Tindley's hymn "We'll Understand It Better, By and By," which he composed around 1906. Like so many "old school" gospel musicians, Monk always referred to Tindley's composition by the first line of the chorus, "By and By When the Morning Comes," and it was under that title that he recorded it in 1959 for the soundtrack to Roger Vadim's film *Les liaisons dangereuses*.[28] The tune's medium tempo and swinging accents made it a perfect vehicle for Monk. In fact, Clark Terry and Monk's version of "One Foot in the Gutter," recorded in 1958, is based on the changes from "We'll Understand It Better, By and By."[29] It is one of those songs virtually guaranteed to move a crowd. Because it embodied the theme of salvation, the idea that the road to heaven is paved with suffering and struggle and that only by traveling on that road with faith can we truly understand God's will, Monk played it frequently at revivals. The lyrics were compelling in that setting, especially for poor souls:

We are often destitute of the things that life demands
Want of shelter and food, thirsty hills and barren lands
We are trusting in the Lord and according to His word
We will understand it better by and by.

CHORUS

By and By, when the morning comes
All the saints are gone to gathering home
We will tell the story of how we overcome
And we'll understand it better by and by.[30]

The way the music "moved" congregants may have had a direct impact on Monk's later performance style. Ecstatic expression in the sanctified churches involved the "shout step" and the "ring shout." Worshippers stood up for the Lord, sometimes rocking from side to side or hopping up and down, both feet virtually glued to the floor in the shout step. The ring shout was a holy dance whose roots can be traced directly to West Africa. Although the ring shout occurs spontaneously at first, it merges into a kind of choreographed dance of men and women moving in a circle counterclockwise, shuffling their feet and gesticulating with their arms.[31] Historian Sterling Stuckey suggested that in his mature career, when Monk left the piano bench to dance while his sidemen soloed, he was echoing the ring shout. His "dance" consisted of a peculiar spinning move, elbow pumping up and down on each turn, with an occasional stutter step allowing him to glide left and right. It was a deliberate embodiment of the rhythm of each tune: Every drummer interviewed who played with Monk said that he liked to get up to dance in order to set the rhythm; it was a form of conducting that required complete attention from the drummer. Was it also a sacred expression? Perhaps.[32] At the very least, what Monk witnessed on the road with the evangelist reinforced for him the essential relationship between music and dance—music is supposed to move the body and touch the soul.

The world west of the Appalachians was an entirely different universe from the Manhattan he grew to know and love. And travel could be quite grueling. In those days, there were virtually no hotels or motels that accommodated Negroes, so like most traveling musicians they relied on the hospitality of strangers. Every black community in every small town and city had someone who took in guests or boarders passing through. They also secured housing through the local churches. For a small fee, commensurate with Depression prices, Monk and his band enjoyed a room, a couple of hot home-cooked meals, and perhaps a good conversation that took them out of the realm of the hereafter back to the here-and-now. Because they usually worked six or seven days a week, whatever free time Monk and his fellow band members had tended to be after hours.

But where could they go? After all, Monk was working for a devout Pentecostal preacher who forbade her followers to step foot in the Devil's workshops: bars, theaters, movie houses, dances, parties, even community picnics. The Church of the Living God, like practically all Holiness and Pentecostal churches, preached total abstinence and maintained a long and detailed list of forbidden activities. Devotees had to refrain from all wines, liquors, medications that contain alcohol, "opium, morphine, cocaine, and any and all harmful drugs and habits." There was no lying, stealing, cursing, gambling, or playing any "wicked and idle games," including checkers, cards, or dominoes, nor could members attend "baseball games and horse races and all other wicked pleasures."[33]

Monk clearly was not a true believer. He might have abstained, being a teenager, and perhaps he bypassed the movies and the gambling dens, but he certainly did not abide by the rule that "ragtime songs, jazzy songs, and all jazz and wicked festivals and all places of amusement for sinners are forbidden."[34] The *only* recorded sighting of him during this period is in Kansas City in 1935. Pianist Mary Lou Williams recalled, "I met Thelonius [sic] Monk, who came to K.C. with an evangelist. . . ."[35] He wasn't just hanging out, he was sitting in and playing every chance he could. Though still a minor, he looked old enough to get past the bouncers at Kansas City's numerous nightclubs. Some of the better-known haunts included the Cherry Blossom, the Vanity Fair, the Lone Star, and the Sunset Club at 18th and Highland. The Subway Club, located just down the street at 18th and Vine, was notorious for its all-night cutting sessions. Williams, who was ten years Monk's senior and a regular member of Andy Kirk's Clouds of Joy when they met, was impressed with the new kid's keyboard skills. "While Monk was in Kaycee [Kansas City] he jammed every night, really used to blow on piano, employing a lot more technique than he does today. . . . He was one of the original modernists all right, playing pretty much the same harmonies then that he's playing now."[36] Although her last claim might be a bit of an exaggeration, especially in light of his brother Thomas's remark that he "changed his style of playing" when he returned, it is conceivable that by the time he reached Kansas City the rudiments of his new approach were already in place. He had been on the road for at least a year.

Williams wasn't the only one to discover Monk during his brief stay in K.C. Ben Webster saw Monk working with bassist Jimmy Blanton in a club, and Mary Lou hipped her boss, Andy Kirk, to Monk's talent. A few years later, Kirk would hire Monk briefly to fill in for his regular pianist but it really didn't work out since Monk was "too far out."[37] Given all the great musicians in Kansas City at the time, Monk probably made more than a few contacts. Trumpeter Hot Lips Page, who would later become one of Monk's collaborators at Minton's Playhouse in 1941, was with Bennie Moten's band in Kansas City during the summer of 1935.[38] Monk might have even run into Page's former bandmate, pianist William "Count" Basie. Basie was the master of minimalism on the keyboard. In the Kansas City tradition of "riff-style" jazz—improvising over simple repeated phrases that formed the basis for melody and harmony—Basie played just a few well-placed notes over the riffs of the horn section, and generated tremendous musical excitement. There was also a minimalism to his arrangements: Instead of writing elaborate charts, the band relied on simple arrangements whereby Basie would play the first chorus of a tune—usually a 12-bar blues or a 32-bar pop song or a variation on "I Got Rhythm"—and signal each section to come in with the appropriate riffs. Often what they played was spontaneous and improvised. The streamlined arrangements and harmonies led to a greater emphasis on the rhythmic quality—swing. The music had to be propulsive, swinging, because all of these big bands were playing for dancers.[39] After Moten died in 1935, Basie formed a new band out of Moten's alumni. Although Monk left Kansas City before the legendary tenor saxophonist Lester Young joined the Basie band, he still could have caught Young holding court at the Reno Club.[40]

Monk, like Basie, chose his notes carefully and lived by the injunction that "Less is more." He never sounded like Basie, nor did he ever identify Basie as an influence, but his travels introduced him to the Kansas City sound and the territory bands of the Southwest before most of his friends back home knew that sound. Monk had left New York thinking he was leaving the center of the jazz world, only to discover that, for the moment at least, the center had shifted. Kansas City was defining the shape of jazz to come. Pianist and band leader Jay McShann described Kansas City in those days as "a melting-pot of jazz, because you got musicians from everywhere, from the North, East, South, and West. And when cats came in . . . they'd hear different musicians. They'd hear sounds they'd never heard before."[41] Kansas City taught everyone the three principles of jazz: swing, swing, swing.

While traveling with the evangelist "was a lot of fun," for Monk, after nearly two years away from New York he was ready to come home. And he was going stir-crazy in the House of the Lord. "I had enough of church. I was in the church every night."[42] Soon after the group hit Chicago, during the winter of 1936–37, Monk bid farewell, and, with the meager earnings he had accumulated on the job and perhaps from occasional gigs along the way, he bought a train ticket for New York City.[43]

Barbara hardly recognized the man who walked through her door. Nineteen years old, still clean-shaven and baby-faced and lean, he nonetheless had assumed an air of worldly confidence. Having traveled thousands of miles, met dozens of colorful people, saved Lord knows how many souls, and played lots of music, Monk was ready to make a name and a life for himself. Just as Thelonious had changed, however, the lives of those he left behind had changed as well. His baby brother Thomas was no longer a baby. He had just turned seventeen, was incredibly handsome, and was becoming a minor sensation in the boxing ring. Though still very bashful, now he was interested in girls—one girl in particular: Trotyrine Wilson. Much to Thelonious's surprise, Trotyrine, just shy of her eighteenth birthday, was introduced as his new sister-in-law. As their son, Thomas, Jr., imagined it, "Monk was on the road for two years. She promised to wait, but after a while she said, 'Well, he's away, I don't know what he's doing.' So she started hitting on my dad."[44]

Thelonious wasn't heartbroken. He gave "Baby" his blessings and moved on.[45] They were men now. Besides, there was one unintended benefit to all this: Thomas had moved out of their tiny two-bedroom apartment, leaving more space for Thelonious,

Marion, and Barbara. Committed neighborhood people that they were, Thomas and Trotyrine moved only a couple of doors down to 239 West 63rd Street. Their apartment was also part of the Phipps Houses; Barbara had secured it for them. On December 9, 1937, Trotyrine gave birth to twins, Thomas and Marion. [46]

Sonny Smith was ecstatic to have his best friend back in the neighborhood. Sonny and his two sisters, Nellie and Skippy, had had a very difficult time during Monk's absence. Their mother's health deteriorated even further, finally succumbing to the disease that took most of her children. On July 19, 1936, Nellie Smith died at home of chronic pulmonary tuberculosis. She was thirty-seven years old. Four days later she was buried at Evergreen Cemetery in Brooklyn.[47] "Aunt" Lizzie Brooks, who had already taken on the care of her own nieces Geraldine and Edith MacMillan and Millicent Henry, insisted that the Smith children move in. She lived across the street from Nellie and had tended to her on many occasions. Aunt Lizzie not only became a second mother to the children but she protected them from being taken by child welfare authorities and placed in an orphanage.[48] Sonny was eighteen at the time of his mother's passing. Nellie and Skippy were fourteen and twelve, respectively.

Geraldine remembered how Sonny practically worshipped Monk and constantly spoke of his return as if it were the Second Coming. "Sonny was always telling me how Thelonious was very good at almost everything he did. He beat everyone at this and that, and he was smart and played the piano. He was the idol of the neighborhood." So when Geraldine finally met the legendary Thelonious Monk, playing at a Columbus Hill Community Center dance, she was expecting someone larger than life. She wasn't entirely disappointed—he *was* good at practically everything and dazzled everyone in the neighborhood with his musical skills.[49] But as she would discover over the course of their lives, he was still just a man, and often a difficult one at that.

Geraldine was more impressed with Monk's friend and champion. She always thought Sonny was cute and now that they were living together—under the watchful eye of Aunt Lizzie—she became completely enamored. The feeling was mutual, and they found sly ways to acknowledge the budding romance between them. "We lived on the top floor," she recalled, "and I would hear him play the mandolin, he would serenade me from the roof. I never knew whether to come out or just stay in and listen."[50] For the first couple of months after Monk returned, Sonny was in his element. He finally had his ace boon on hand and he was falling in love with one of the prettiest women in the neighborhood. Sadly, it came to an end when an aunt from Connecticut, one of their mother's sisters, showed up to gather the three Smith children. Sonny, Nellie, and Skippy only moved to the next state, but it might as well have been China.[51]

Meanwhile, Thelonious tried to get back into the music scene immediately. He returned rich in experience, but as broke as he was when he left. He and his old drummer Morris Simpson got together for some community center dances, but Monk needed to make some real money. Surprisingly, he didn't join the union right away, which severely limited his opportunities. Trumpeter Frank Williams remembered seeing Monk working in Albany, New York, some time around 1937.[52] It's likely that he also worked in Saratoga Springs, just thirty-five miles north of Albany, since his former mentor Alberta Simmons played there during the summers and she probably shared some of her contacts with Thelonious. Whatever the specifics, Monk ended up spending up to a week at a time outside of the city. This arrangement didn't last very long, in part because the money was never great and all the real action was back home in Manhattan. But most importantly, he developed a compelling interest to return to the city. Her name was Rubie Richardson.

5

"Why Can't You Play Music Like the Ink Spots?"

(1937–1940)

66 There were only two women in his life," is the way Nellie Monk explained it to me. "Me and Rubie."[1] No one disputes Nellie on this point. Leaving aside Monk's doting mother, Rubie Richardson was Monk's first real love, a source of joy and pride and an even greater source of heartache. He named one of his most beautiful ballads, "Ruby, My Dear," after her—although whether or not he wrote it *for* her is a source of great intra-family debate.

Beautiful and elegant, possessing smooth light-brown skin, a sparkling smile, shapely legs, and what most men in the 1930s thought of as a heavenly figure (despite a penchant for buttermilk), Rubie was undeniably one of the most desirable young women in San Juan Hill. You could identify Rubie from far away because she liked wearing a white flower in her hair, like Billie Holiday.[2] She also ran with one of the most popular cliques in the community. Rubie and her younger sister Linette were members of a social group called the "Brown Snapperettes." Mavis Swire, an acquaintance of Rubie's and decidedly not a member of the group, remembered the clique as "all of those girls in the neighborhood with shapely legs, who danced well and who the boys adored! They were the in-group. These were very attractive, very well put together, very sophisticated girls."[3] They were known for organizing socials at the community center, but they also had a reputation for being "a little snobbish."[4]

Monk's nephew, Theolonious, described Rubie as "high yellow [light-skinned]. Her family was 'up there,' they were uppity. Rubie was crazy about Thelonious."[5] Sonny's youngest sister, Skippy, was less charitable; she used to say Rubie was "such a much." On the other hand, Marion Monk and Rubie had been the best of friends since they were about seven or eight years old. Geraldine Smith described them as "two peas in a pod." Later, Rubie became godmother to Marion's son, Alonzo, and all of Thomas and Trotyrine's children grew quite fond of their "aunt." Not surprisingly, Marion was responsible for introducing Thelonious and Rubie.[6]

If anyone detected an air of superiority in Rubie's behavior, it had more to do with her Caribbean background than her actual class status. Her parents, Ackland and Florence Richardson, were born in the British West Indies, married on the eve of World War I, and immediately joined a small exodus of West Indians to Cuba seeking refuge from the British draft and work in Cuba's cane fields. Five of their six children were born in Cuba, Rubie being the second, born in 1917, and the eldest of their three daughters. They did not stay long enough to learn the language. In 1922, Ackland decided that the United States offered a brighter future, so he headed north to secure work and housing for his family. Like most Caribbean immigrants who joined the post–World War I exodus, New York City was his destination. Within a year he found a job driving a truck for a plumbing supply company, moved into a tenement apartment at 205 West 60th Street, and sent for his family. His wife, Florence, found work as a laundress.[7]

Neither Thelonious nor Rubie had expressed any romantic interest in one another prior to his tour with the evangelist's band. Although they were acquainted through Marion, they ran in completely different circles, in part because she was a grade ahead of Thelonious. However, when he returned, mature and worldly, Rubie began to look at Monk differently. The skinny kid who used to impress the neighborhood girls with his piano playing was now a confident, irresistible, ambitious, and eligible man. Once they came together (around 1937 or 1938), Rubie became a fixture in his world. She accompanied him virtually everywhere—community dances and parties, and the small dives where he worked. Frequently, Marion tagged along. "Oh, man, they could dance," recalls Alonzo White. "My mother used to tell me her and Rubie used to go out to clubs when my uncle was playing. And in those days if you were a musician you're playing to an audience who would dance. It was dance music that you played. . . . You were supposed to have some fun; they didn't come there to listen. They came there to party."[8]

Barbara adored Rubie and both of Thelonious's siblings treated her like family. The same cannot be said about the Richardsons. "Rubie's parents didn't like him at all, period," Geraldine Smith remembers. According to Nellie, Thelonious wasn't allowed in their house. "They had to meet on the corner."[9] He didn't make enough money, he was a musician, and he wasn't of Caribbean descent. Rubie's parents did not think much of Monk nor of his music, and felt that she was wasting her time waiting for him to make it. Rubie herself seemed skeptical of her boyfriend's musical path. She often asked him, in a variation of the eternal nagging question asked of all struggling artists, "Why can't you play music like the Ink Spots?"[10] In the usual version, the struggling artist recalls this question much later, when he is wildly popular. Yet those nagging questions often have a grain of truth to their assumptions. Thomas Monk, Jr., recalls that "Uncle Bubba [Thelonious] would come to my father and would say, 'I want to marry Rubie but I can't because I ain't got no money.' And my father said, 'Well, money's not everything. When Rita and I got married I didn't have a dime. I was broke and scuffling."[11]

Despite his reassurances, Thomas was less than confident in his older brother's ability to marry, settle down, and have children. Trotyrine, in particular, was thoroughly convinced it would never happen. After all, being on the road was an occupational hazard of the professional musician; it was not conducive to family life. So when Trotyrine gave birth to their third child on January 29, 1939, they decided to bestow upon him the vaunted family name of Thelonious. Someone had to continue their father's legacy. When Trotyrine filled out the birth certificate application, however, her spelling error produced "Theolonious Monk."[12]

Monk doted on his new nephew and relished the idea that they sort of shared a name, but he really wanted to marry Rubie. He also wanted to make enough money to move out of his mother's house and make a living. "I tried to find jobs," he recalled nearly twenty years later. "I worked all over town. Nonunion jobs, twenty dollars a week, seven nights a week, and then the man might fire you anytime and you never got your money. I've been on millions of those kinds of jobs. I've been on every kind of job you can think of all over New York. I really found out how to get around this city. Dance halls. Every place."[13] He took whatever jobs he could get—house parties, bar mitzvahs, local dives, even a polka band. According to Monk, these early gigs paid about seventeen dollars a week, and some were absolutely miserable. "There are a lot of things you can't remember—except the heckles."[14] He once told a friend that he had to back up singers "who sing all kinds of songs and fuck up and blame it on the musicians."[15] He desperately needed a new piano, and he needed to join the union. With help from his ever-supportive mother, he cobbled together enough cash to purchase a very fine, but used, Klein upright piano which became a fixture in his bedroom.[16] Second, he had to join the union. So in March of 1939, he paid his dues and became an official member of the American Federation of Musicians Local 802.[17]

Monk joined the union along with Eddie Heywood, Jr., a fellow pianist whom he befriended. Just two years older than Monk, Heywood had been playing professionally since he was fourteen years old. His father, Eddie Heywood, Sr., was an accomplished pianist and singer who backed several jazz and blues artists during the 1920s and 1930s, including such forgotten legends as Sippie Wallace and Butterbeans and Susie. Eddie, Jr., began working with Benny Carter immediately after obtaining his union card, and over the course of the next few years he recorded with Coleman Hawkins and Billie Holiday. He would emerge as a popular ensemble leader in his own right.[18]

Heywood really encouraged Monk as he navigated the world of professional musicians. Thanks to his father, Heywood had already gotten to know many of the older stride piano players, James P. Johnson, Willie "The Lion" Smith, Luckey Roberts, Clarence Profit, and the incomparable Art Tatum. These pianists used to get together at each other's homes for friendly jam sessions and to share ideas, and apparently Heywood brought Monk along and introduced him around. The time Monk spent among these elder statesmen and their students was as important, if not more important, to his musical development as the time he later spent with bebop greats. By Monk's account, he left a lasting impression on several of them, including Eddie Heywood, Jr. As he put it in a 1963 interview, "Every day I listen to pianists who are using my technique. If you don't know them, I know them very well. Listen to someone like Eddie Heywood, for example."[19]

Pianist Billy Taylor first met Thelonious at one of these gatherings in September of 1939. Taylor, just eighteen at the time, had come up from Washington, D.C., to hear Teddy Wilson and Charlie Christian play with Benny Goodman's band at the World's Fair in New York.[20] Much to Taylor's disappointment, Wilson had left Goodman to form his own group, but when he tried to catch the Wilson big band at a Harlem club called the Golden Gate, they had the night off. Instead, Taylor wandered into a small club managed by a friend of his father, the pianist Billy Taylor, Sr. He introduced him-self, and the manager said, "'Oh yeah! Your father tells me that you play the piano?' I said yes and he said, 'You'll have to come back and play something for me.' He takes me back there and there's a trio playing."[21]

"I proceeded to play my favorite song, 'Lullaby in Rhythm,' and I thought I was really doing something. The piano player kept looking at me funny and I didn't realize it was Clarence Profit since I'd never seen him before. So here I am, playing his compo-sition on his gig! Once I finished, Profit came up to me and said, 'Hey kid, that wasn't bad. I have some friends that would like to hear you play.'"[22] The pair proceeded to a brownstone on 140th just west of Seventh Avenue. Taylor still did not know that his escort was Clarence Profit, or that the house they were about to enter belonged to the legendary James P. Johnson. "There's some guys sitting around playing cards. He says, 'Hey fellas! I have a piano player here!' They said, 'Sit down, kid, and play something.' Now I should have known. [laughs] But I sit down and start playing 'China Boy' which was a tune I'd heard Teddy Wilson play. He was on my mind so I was doing my version of him. You know, my left hand was doing this little thing? I got about sixteen bars in when one of these guys comes over and says, 'Hmmmmm, that's nice. Let me try a little of that?' He sits down and, man . . . ! This guy has got a left hand that I didn't believe! He was just like Waller. Turns out that everybody in the room was a piano player! I mean, these guys sat down one after another and just *played*! Nobody had to say any-thing. I just sat there and thought, 'Oh shit!'"[23]

"Turned out that one of the guys was Monk! It was the first time I ever heard him. But get this! . . . The other guys were Willie 'The Lion' Smith, a guy named 'Gippy,' and James P. Johnson!" Willie "The Lion" then called Monk over to the piano bench. "Wil-lie 'The Lion' was kind of on his case. He said, 'Play your thing, man.' And he sat down and played a standard, I believe it could have been 'Tea for Two.' He was playing more like Art Tatum then. I think he really responded to the older musicians who told him to do his own thing."[24]

Monk told Billy Taylor "that 'Willie 'The Lion' and those guys that had shown him respect had . . . 'empowered' him . . . to do his own thing. That he could do it and that his thing is worth doing. It doesn't sound like Tatum. It doesn't sound like Willie 'The Lion.' It doesn't sound like anybody but Monk and this is what he wanted to do. He had the confidence. The way that he does those things is the way *he* wanted to do them."[25]

Willie "The Lion" never mentions Thelonious in his memoirs, but he described these evenings memorably: "Sometimes we got carving battles going that would last for four or five hours. Here's how these bashes worked: the Lion would pound the keys for a mess of choruses and then shout to the next in line, 'Well, all right, take it from there,' and each tickler would take his turn, trying to improve on a melody. . . . We would embroider the melodies with our own original ideas and try to develop patterns that had more originality than those played before us. Sometimes it was just a question as to who could think up the most patterns within a given tune. It was pure improvisa-tion."[26] A later generation of bebop pianists would often be accused of one-handedness;

their right hands flew along with melodies and improvisations, while their "weak" left hands just plonked chords. To the great stride players that gathered at Johnson's house and elsewhere, the left hand was just as important as the right. A weak left hand was one of Smith's pet peeves among the younger bebop piano players. "Today the big problem is that no one wants to work their left hand—modern jazz is full of single-handed piano players. It takes long hours of practice and concentration to perfect a good bass moving with the left hand and it seems as though the younger cats have figured they can reach their destination without paying their dues."[27]

Teddy Wilson, though only five years older than Monk but considered a master tickler of the swing generation, had nothing but praise for Thelonious's piano playing. "Thelonious Monk knew my playing very well, as well as that of Tatum, [Earl] Hines, and [Fats] Waller. He was exceedingly well grounded in the piano players who preceded him, adding his own originality to a very sound foundation."[28] Indeed, it was this very foundation that exposed him to techniques and aesthetic principles that would become essential qualities of his own music. He heard players "bend" notes on the piano, or turn the beat around (the bass note on the one and three might be reversed to two and four, either accidentally or deliberately), or create dissonant harmonies with "splattered notes" and chord clusters. He heard things in those parlor rooms and basement joints that, to modern ears, sounded avant-garde. They loved to disorient listeners, to displace the rhythm by playing in front or behind the beat, to produce surprising sounds that can throw listeners momentarily off track. Monk embraced these elements in his own playing and exaggerated them.[29]

What Thelonious took from the elders he shared with the young cats. He spent many afternoons jamming with his peers. Besides Denzil Best, Monk hung out with another young trumpeter named Benny Harris. Nicknamed "Little Benny" for his diminutive size, Harris was also younger than Monk and Best by two years, but he had already established a rich, clear tone on his instrument. And like Best, he, too had Caribbean roots. His father, Joe Harris, was a Kuna Indian from the San Blas Islands off the coast of Panama, and his mother, Essie, was a North Carolinian who also claimed Indian heritage. Whatever their ancestry, it is clear that one or both parents were of African descent as well. It's possible that they both emphasized their Indian heritage because, during the late 1920s and early 1930s, Joe was the live-in superintendent of an all-white building on East 18th Street. The idea that the family was "Indian" and not "Negro" might have made the tenants more comfortable.[30] But they didn't stay there long; they relocated to San Juan Hill where Little Benny became immersed in the musical community. He started out on French horn and E^b mellophone, becoming a member of the New York *Daily Mirror*'s children's band at age twelve. At age thirteen he picked up the trumpet and practiced earnestly for two years after school.[31]

Harris got to know Monk after he returned from his stint with Reverend Graham, in part because they both hung out at the Columbus Hill Community Center. Being younger than Monk, Harris looked up to him: "Monk played the piano, always dressed sharp."[32] Like Monk, Little Benny was only fifteen when he went on the road with a touring band, though they only went as far as Pennsylvania. After he returned,

Harris and Monk "played many afternoon parties together at which they not only earned money but filled up on good food, too."[33] In 1937, Harris met trumpeter Dizzy Gillespie and began to adopt his modern harmonic ideas as well as his sound. It was Dizzy who got him his first real gig with the Tiny Bradshaw band in 1939.[34]

Harris and Monk befriended a young drummer from Pittsburgh named Kenny Clarke. Kenneth Spearman Clarke (nicknamed "Klook"), born almost four years before Monk, began his musical career playing piano and organ in the church. He eventually took up the drums, toured with bands in the Midwest, and made his way to New York City with a hometown pianist named Call Cobb. In 1936, Clarke formed a short-lived trio with Cobb and his brother Frank—a bassist who played in the style of Jimmy Blanton—and he gigged with various groups in the city, landing jobs with orchestras led by Edgar Hayes and Teddy Hill (1939–1940).[35] At night he worked with veteran musicians, but by day he hung out with Thelonious and Harris, and sometimes he brought along another pianist whom he knew from Teddy Hill's band—the Panamanian-born Sonny White (*né* Ellerton Oswald).[36] Monk played with these guys and presumably worked out some of his own ideas. And he played quite a bit alone, working on new interpretations of standard tunes and composing his own songs—compositions still several years away from being recorded. As a sounding board for his own music, he always pressed his brother and sister for their opinion. Marion recalled, "He'd say: 'Say, Sis, listen to this,' and so I'd listen to it. If it was okay I'd say [so], you know?" On the other hand, if the music didn't move her, she was honest about it, and he treated her criticisms seriously.[37]

Armed with a union card and a growing number of professional contacts, especially in Harlem, Monk began working in earnest in 1939. He formed a quartet consisting of Jimmy Wright on tenor, Keg Purnell on drums, and the mysterious bass player known only as "Massapequah"—the name of a town on Long Island.[38] Each of them lived in Harlem at the time. Jimmy Wright, who would later record with Louis Jordan and distinguish himself as both a reed player and drummer on early R&B recordings, began as a Coleman Hawkins imitator.[39] Keg Purnell was a swing drummer with an easy touch who hailed from West Virginia. Though just two years older than Monk, he was a veteran of the music scene, having worked with King Oliver in 1934–35 and having led his own trio. He was only with Monk for a few months before joining Eddie Heywood, Jr., as a member of Benny Carter's band.[40]

There are no recordings of the quartet. No doubt Thelonious played in the stride style with a lot of modern dissonance thrown in. They might have played one or two of Monk's original tunes, since he had already begun writing, but most likely they played standards: "Honeysuckle Rose," "I Got Rhythm," "Indiana," "Body and Soul," and the like. As the group's leader, Monk earned a bit more than his sidemen, but not much.

America was still in the throes of the Great Depression, and African-Americans were especially hard hit. Unemployment was high and many families in New York still depended on work relief projects created by FDR's New Deal agencies. One of those agencies, the Works Progress Administration (WPA), hired musicians for various projects, but its low wages prompted Local 802 to picket their offices.[41] The union had suffered a decade of setbacks caused by the closing of venues, a dramatic decline in record sales, an increase in the number of musicians moving to New York in search of job opportunities, and the rise of sound film. Once "talkies" replaced the old silent pictures, over 3,200 New York pit musicians were suddenly out of work. The union waged a campaign culminating in a strike, to return live music and vaudeville shows to the movie theater, but it ended in utter disaster in 1937, when it became clear that the rest of the working class would not support them. In a prequel to a debate fifty years later about using acoustic synthesized music on Broadway, the union was struggling against an inevitable tide of economics and consumers. Working people not only preferred sound films but appreciated the price of the ticket, which was lower without the live talent. Freed of wages and union regulations governing musicians' hours, theater owners could show films all day long, and the jobless could escape the cold, the heat, or their general frustrations by spending their afternoons at the movies for a paltry twenty-five or fifty cents.[42] Joblessness became such a problem in New York that Local 802, with the help of leading philanthropists and patrons of the arts, launched a Musicians' Emergency Fund to provide relief for out-of-work musicians.[43]

Few black musicians uptown benefited from the Emergency Fund, and the union did little to challenge racial discrimination in the music industry. Lucrative studio jobs remained the preserve of white musicians. The union often looked the other way when unscrupulous record labels employed non-union black musicians to make "race records."[44] Despite the immense popularity of the bands led by Cab Calloway, Count Basie, Duke Ellington, Jimmie Lunceford, Lucky Millinder, Chick Webb, and others during the mid-to-late 1930s, black bands were paid significantly less than white swing bands. Throughout the 1930s and '40s, black musicians unsuccessfully challenged the union's policy of setting its pay scale considerably lower for Harlem dance halls and clubs than for venues in other parts of the city.[45] Worse, African-American bands were virtually banned from the elite hotels from which many live radio broadcasts took place. Limited radio airplay meant fewer record sales and less publicity. Absent lucrative hotel gigs and commercially-sponsored radio spots, the black bands—including the Ellington Orchestra—had to endure a grueling schedule of one-night stands to make ends meet. Having just spent two years on the road, Thelonious knew exactly what this meant: Jim Crow hotels, rooming houses in black communities, and the ever-looming possibility of racial hostility.[46]

By the time Monk turned "professional," it appeared as though the black big bands were on the verge of disappearance. In 1940, prominent music magazines as well as the black press ran several ominous articles predicting their death. In one headline, *Down Beat* magazine asked: "Are Colored Bands Doomed as Big Money Makers?"[47] African-American bands simply could not compete with the new generation of white swing bands led by the likes of Benny Goodman, the Dorsey Brothers, and Gene Krupa, who sounded more and more like the black bands and could make money much more easily. They not only adopted—or at least gestured toward—the aesthetic principles of black dance music, but they hired black arrangers to write their charts. Benny Goodman employed Fletcher Henderson, Tommy Dorsey hired Sy Oliver from Jimmie Lunceford's band, and both Paul Whiteman and Jimmy Dorsey relied on Don Redman's arrangements.

The history of American popular music is often depicted as a series of stories of white musicians imitating black innovators and getting rich, from Benny Goodman to Elvis to Eminem. Of course, the story is more complicated. Beginning with Benny Goodman, the popular white swing bands began hiring black musicians. Many critics and fans applauded Goodman's decision to bring arranger/pianist Fletcher Henderson, pianist Teddy Wilson, vibraphonist Lionel Hampton, and guitarist Charlie Christian into his band, characterizing this move as a triumph of integration. For many black musicians, however, it seemed more like "raiding" their most talented and dynamic musicians.[48]

Even if Monk had wanted to join one of the major bands in the forties, jobs were few and far between, and ultimately he lacked interest. He played briefly in bands led by Lucky Millinder, Skippy Williams, and Dizzy Gillespie, but "[The big] bands never did knock me out," he told George Simon in 1948. "I wanted to play my own chords. I wanted to create and invent on little jobs."[49] A big-band piano player was expected to provide rhythmic and harmonic support for the horn and reed sections, and occasionally take a chorus or half-chorus solo. This is not what Monk had in mind when he got his union card. And he had no intention of going back on the road again. Most of his "little jobs" were in the small bars and dives in Harlem. Bassist Red Callender recalled seeing Monk playing at Mack's in Harlem in this period. "Bedbugs would be crawling all over the joint, but Thelonious Monk was sitting at the piano. . . . Before the advent of so-called bebop, I'd hear all Monk's licks and be thrilled with it. After his sets, we walked around Harlem together."[50]

Harlem was becoming Monk's second home. Lucky for Thelonious, his best friend Sonny, along with Nellie and Skippy, returned from their aunt's house in Connecticut in 1938 and moved to Harlem. They returned to the city in part because "the aunt was really abusive, abusive in strange ways."[51] Also, Sonny made a promise to his sweetheart, Geraldine, to find his own home. Sonny rented a private house on 136th Street and Seventh Avenue. The property was sizable and well kept, and Sonny got it for a song because the owner, a notorious numbers runner named Ford, felt sorry for their having lost their mother so young. The paint on the walls was hardly dry before Sonny and Geraldine tied the knot on the 27th of June and she joined the clan uptown.[52] Eight days before Christmas, they added one more resident: their first-born daughter, whom they named Jackie. Their second-born, also a girl-child, arrived on May 4, 1940, and they named her Judith.[53]

Sonny and Geraldine were still responsible for Skippy, who was only fourteen when they returned to New York. Nellie, on the other hand, was sixteen, practical, and quite independent. With two more years of high school left, she decided her immediate future lay in dressmaking, perhaps clothing design, so she enrolled in Central Needle Trades High School, one of the city's leading industrial schools. Although it had been beset with budget issues in the mid-1930s, the school had made a remarkable comeback and almost overnight grew in popularity. By the time she started classes in 1938,

Central Needle Trades had just moved to temporary quarters on Sixth Avenue and 23rd Street with the intention of moving into a brand new multi-million-dollar, eleven-story facility on 24th between Seventh and Eighth Avenues.[54] She did not rule out college; on the contrary, Nellie was determined to further her education one way or another, but given their current financial reality, learning marketable skills and finding a decent job was paramount.

Shy little Nellie was becoming a woman now, and it seemed as though everyone noticed except Thelonious. He was far more preoccupied with having his old running buddy Sonny back in town, and the friendly uptown house was a bonus. Now he had a place to crash on late, cold nights when he didn't feel like trekking back to West 63rd Street on the IRT. Although he never moved in with Sonny and his family, he was such a frequent visitor that he might as well have changed his mailing address. Geraldine recalls too many times when Thelonious would just come through the window in the middle of the night, wanting to sleep or, worse, to talk. "At that time, I got mad at him because he would do so many outlandish things. He would come in and wake you up if you're sleeping. 'Get up!' And I would tell him, 'Thelonious, if you don't leave me alone.' And after he would get everybody awake, then he would go to sleep."[55]

Monk worked intermittently throughout 1940, and he found a hospitable community of like-minded musicians hanging out at a club inside the Cecil Hotel on 118th and St. Nicholas. The place was called Minton's Playhouse. In January of 1941, the management offered him his first regular job as the house pianist. This small Harlem club was about to become a jazz legend.

6

"They Weren't Giving Any Lectures"

(1941)

Harlem. June 1941, in the wee small hours of the morning. If you could take a stroll down 118th Street, walking west from Seventh Avenue toward St. Nicholas, passing a few brownstones and parked cars, just before you got to the end of the unusually short block, you would reach the Cecil Hotel, an elegant five-story building on the south side of the street. A large, dark blue awning extends out from the building with the words "Minton's Playhouse" emblazoned on it. You try to pass, but the faint sound of music draws you in. You climb the three small steps leading to the entrance, open the door, and suddenly you're awash in cigarette and cigar smoke, chit-chat and laughter, and swinging music. You don't see the musicians at first. To your left is a long bar, occupied by men and women whose days begin at sundown. "Togged to the bricks" in hip suits and kicks, hair conked to the roots and glistening with pomade, these are the politicians, pimps, and hustlers who run the parts of Harlem the Renaissance ignored; with them are the neighborhood regulars who found in Minton's a place to go after the day's hard work; and, of course, the musicians, dancers, and miscellaneous entertainers who make their living on stage. To your right is the coat-check room, tended by a pretty young woman with a lovely brown complexion, hair "done up," who handles your coat and "lid" with great care.

You continue past the bar, past the never-ending debates and convivial conversations, past the dazed and lonesome souls nursing twenty-cent drinks, through a set of swinging doors. Now in the club proper, all you can hear is the music. To your left is a small bandstand, about twelve inches off the floor, and an equally tiny dance floor. Behind another set of swinging doors to the right is the kitchen with its delectable scent of fried chicken, greens, and candied yams. And in the middle are over a dozen tables draped with crisp, white tablecloths, surrounded by chairs. Nearly every seat is occupied, and nearly every patron is preoccupied with the music. There are moments when the music might sound altogether foreign, by comparison to the popular swing bands of the day. But to call it "revolutionary" or "avant-garde" would be an exaggeration. These young artists joyfully jam on the familiar, retaining the head-bopping, toe-tapping, danceable quality of swing music. The drummer, Kenny "Klook-Mop" Clarke, generates sparks like a blacksmith pounding on an anvil—he maintains a driving pulse interjected with off-beat explosions on the snare and bass drum (and inter-rupted by the occasional slamming of the bathroom door, located a little too close to the bandstand). The ultimate time-keeper is the bass player, a baby-faced kid named Nick Fenton. On trumpet and occasional vocals is Joe Guy, whose full-bodied tone sounds like Roy Eldridge. He's joined by other horns: a trumpet battle with Roy Eldridge him-self, maybe, or Oran "Hot Lips" Page, or Little Benny Harris; a serenade by the great Don Byas on tenor saxophone; or the little known Sammy Davis; or the soulful Herbie Fields, one of the only white cats in the room.

The most jarring sound of all is coming from the upright piano and the kid play-ing it. Bespectacled and clean-shaven, he's just a little too thin for his gray pin-striped suit. You may not hear him at first, over the din of horns and drums, but when you do, you're startled by his broken, jagged lines and sparse, dissonant chords. They some-times sound like mistakes. The songs are familiar—"Nice Work," "Sweet Lorraine," "Stardust"—but the piano opens with strange introductions and his melodic lines compete with countermelodies that sound as if they don't fit the harmony. There are moments when he sounds a little like Teddy Wilson or Earl Hines, Herman Chittison or even Art Tatum, but these are just momentary flashes. Once he gets into his solo, he elicits winces, chuckles, and nods of approval from the audience. Some folks even shout his name: "Monk! Monk!"[1]

Welcome to Minton's: the house, legend has it, that bop built. It shares the distinc-tion, with other Harlem after-hours clubs such as Clark Monroe's Uptown House and Dan Wall's Chili Shack, of being the birthplace of modern jazz, or "bebop." Musicians who never stepped foot in Minton's speak of it as if they were there. While details are always contested and stories often exaggerated, the names, places, dates, and anecdotes surrounding Minton's are generally consistent, though frequently inaccurate. Charlie Parker and Dizzy Gillespie stood at its helm, playing circles around the old legends; Bud Powell transformed his piano into a horn at blistering tempos; Kenny Clarke, guitarist Charlie Christian, and bassist Oscar Pettiford revolutionized rhythm; pianist Tadd Dameron wrote and arranged bebop anthems; and the wacky, eccentric Theloni-ous Monk taught his peers harmony and confused the hell out of everybody. The young Turks often challenged their elders to battle on Minton's tiny bandstand, leaving idols such as Roy Eldridge and Ben Webster confused by the twists and turns of the music.

But in 1941, when Thelonious Monk became the house pianist at Minton's, most of these stories had not yet occurred. Minton's regulars tended to be unknown swing musicians, not bebop pioneers. Monk tried to correct the historical record in many subsequent interviews. "Some of those histories and articles put what happened in ten years in one year," he explained in 1956. "They put people all together in one time in this place. Over a period of time, I've seen practically everybody at Minton's, but they were just in there playing. They weren't giving any lectures."[2] Monk was one who knew; he had become a fixture there. "Monk seemed to have been there all the time," trumpeter Johnny Carisi recounted.[3] Monk's more sobering assessment of Minton's was echoed by literary giant Ralph Ellison. His oft-cited essay on Minton's Playhouse cautioned fans and scholars alike against popular romantic myths. "[T]he very effort to put the fragments together transformed them—so that in place of true memory they now summon to mind pieces of legend. They retell the stories as they have been told and written, glamorized, inflated, made neat and smooth, with all incomprehensible details vanished along with most of the wonder—not how it was as they themselves knew it."[4]

The Cecil Hotel was a beautiful building in its heyday. Built in 1895, when Harlem was the preserve of New York's white bourgeoisie, this five-story trapezoid-shaped hotel was designed to accommodate the unique corner of 118th and St. Nicholas, which runs diagonally across Manhattan's well-known grid.[5] By the 1930s, the Cecil had lost much of its luster as well as its patronage, but it was suitably located to become part of Harlem's vibrant nightlife, especially after the repeal of Prohibition on December 5, 1933. In 1938, a musician and former club owner named Monroe Henry Minton decided to transform the dining room and bar of the Cecil Hotel into a jazz club, which he named Minton's Playhouse. Minton—known by his colleagues as M.H., or just Henry—wasn't just any musician. Born in Virginia in 1884, the "old man" was a pioneer among the first generation of black jazz musicians who came up through the vaudeville circuit and made some of the genre's first recordings.[6] A tenor saxophone player, he toured with the phenomenal ragtime clarinetist, Wilbur Sweatman, whose musical imagination anticipated many of the experiments we associate with the jazz avant-garde. The only surviving recording of Minton is in a quintet made up entirely of reeds (clarinet, alto, tenor, baritone, and bass sax, led by Sweatman). The band recorded in 1917, sixty years before the founding of the World Saxophone Quartet. Sweatman himself was known to thrill audiences by playing three clarinets at once.[7]

Minton was less known for his musicianship than for his role in the musicians' union. He was the first black delegate to Local 802 and, for many years, the union's sergeant-at-arms in Harlem, making him the highest-ranking black official in the local. Despite the distrust between African-Americans and Local 802, Minton earned a reputation as a tireless advocate and a generous man, assisting fellow musicians in need of advice or a few extra dollars. And while he became an occasional thorn in the side of the union, officials appreciated his ability to "put many a dollar in the coffers of the local by getting men to become union musicians."[8] Musicians in Harlem especially respected Minton for managing the Rhythm Club, a favorite spot for serious players on 132nd and Seventh Avenue, known for its after-hours jam sessions. The Rhythm Club foreshadowed Minton's Playhouse. Willie "The Lion" Smith, who was the house pianist there for some time, remembers the club as "a hanging-out place for musicians. . . . They served food for reasonable prices and jazz men could come in at any time and play whatever they wanted without bothering with the usual singers or floor shows. It became the place where young musicians would go to learn and to be heard."[9] The union had a strict policy against jam sessions; musicians were working without pay and playing with non-union musicians. But with M. H. Minton, sergeant-at-arms, at the helm of the Rhythm Club, the policy wasn't enforced. The club had become an exception years earlier, when the previous owner/manager, trombonist Bert Hall, served as business manager for Local 802. Ultimately, Local 802 officials decided that union officers should not own or operate nightclubs, so in 1932, Minton was forced to sell off the Rhythm Club.[10]

Minton went back to performing for a few years before opening Minton's Playhouse in 1938. This time around, unencumbered by union bureaucracy, he wanted his club to embody the spirit and atmosphere of the old Rhythm Club. Initially the house band was led by Albert "Happy" Caldwell, a tenor player best known for his work a decade earlier with Louis Armstrong, Fletcher Henderson, and Jelly Roll Morton. Caldwell was a lively player, but his music was a throwback to the 1920s and failed to draw new musicians in.[11] The clientele consisted primarily of the residents of the Cecil Hotel. By 1940, Minton passed the management duties to Dewey Vanderburg, a little-known "mulatto" hustler originally from Missouri. Vanderburg was not a musician but had befriended several musicians who had lived in the Hotel Grampion with him.[12] His tenure was short-lived; Minton realized that the only way to recreate the spirit of the Rhythm Club was to hire a musician—a prominent and hip musician—to manage the club. So with the start of the new year, 1941, M. H. Minton announced that the popular bandleader Teddy Hill would be taking over as manager of the Playhouse.[13]

Hill was an ideal choice. His orchestra had become a fixture at the Savoy Ballroom, and whenever he played the Harlem Opera House, the Apollo, the Lincoln, or the Lafayette Theater, he drew crowds.[14] A Birmingham, Alabama native and product of John "Fess" Whately's renowned Industrial High School Band, Teddy Hill moved to New York in 1927, where he played tenor saxophone in George Howe's band (which was taken over by Luis Russell) and recorded with Henry Red Allen. In 1932, he formed his own orchestra and achieved some success as a bandleader, though he was never regarded as an especially distinguished player. He did have the foresight to surround himself with young, innovative players, including Dizzy Gillespie and an exciting new drummer named Kenny Clarke.[15]

That Hill should willingly disband his orchestra is unsurprising, given the shrinking opportunities for African-American bands, especially after 1940. Taking over Minton's, however, did not take him out of music. He leapt into the job with the dual intentions of entertaining the patrons and promoting young lions—musicians who might have something new to say. The first thing he did was to hire his twenty-five-year-old drummer Kenny Clarke as the club's musical director and house bandleader.[16]

Clarke's first task was to put together a house band. He hired twenty-year-old trumpeter Joe Guy—a choice likely influenced by Teddy Hill. Guy (né Joseph Luke), an alumnus of Teddy Hill's Orchestra, was a good trumpeter, a competent vocalist, and an overall entertainer. He played with exuberance and possessed a full, rich tone, though he occasionally got lost in the chord changes. He joined Coleman Hawkins's big band in 1939, but he was Hill's homeboy—born and bred in Birmingham.[17] The bass duties were handed over to another youngster named Nicholas Fenton, who had been working for Lester Young at the time of Clarke's call. The child of West Indian immigrants, Nick Fenton grew up on Manhattan Avenue and 119th—quite literally around the corner from the Cecil Hotel—and was a few months shy of his twenty-second birthday when he joined the band.[18] There was nothing innovative about his playing; he was a very good time-keeper, but often stomped his foot so hard other musicians found it distracting. Pianist Al Tinney recalled one night at the Famous Door, when Fenton began stomping to the beat: "I looked up and says, 'Where's the Indians at?' [Laughs] And nobody could play to this. I mean, he was a good bass player, but that foot."[19]

The piano chair was initially offered to another Teddy Hill Orchestra alum, Sonny White. It was an odd choice. The Panamanian-born pianist (né Ellerton Oswald) worked more in a traditional swing mode. At the time, he was accompanying Billie Holiday, and had just left Sidney Bechet to join Benny Carter's orchestra. He and Thelonious were only one month apart in age, but White had quite a bit more professional experience. With so many other gigs, White turned Clarke down.[20] So Clarke decided to go in an entirely different direction, hiring the virtually unknown Thelonious Monk.

Given Clarke's own musical inclinations, Monk was a better match. Almost a decade earlier, Clarke had developed a style of "dropping bombs," using the bass drum sparingly to add punctuation at unexpected moments, on or off the beat, instead of using it to mark time. Monk appreciated Clarke for not playing "on the bass drum too hard, which made bands sound very stiff."[21] In the wake of Jimmy Blanton's innovations with Duke Ellington, it was the bass players who had become "the instrument of tempo." Drummers were freer to place accents in unusual places. Clarke began experimenting with off-beat punctuations on the keyboard, which "proved disconcerting for the other musicians. It was also confusing for the drummers, who were playing a steady four beats to the bar; any strong, out-of-the-ordinary punctuation would throw them."[22] Monk also reveled in off-beat accents, forcing Clarke to change the way he played: "I had to change my style to play with this clique. Monk's using accents and things made me play accents more myself, on the bass drum."[23] Indeed, the way Monk "comped" behind soloists seemed as if he were "dropping bombs" on the piano; at times it sounds as if he were playing in a completely different tempo than his sidemen, yet never out of sync with the rhythm.

Clarke and Monk developed a close working relationship, and for all intents and purposes they co-led the band. The band was good, but it wasn't great. It was still a far cry from what would become known as bebop. Monk and Clarke were the true innovators among the regulars in the group, though they found ways to surround themselves with other innovative musicians (young and old). Now twenty-three years old and still living at home, Monk was ecstatic just to have a steady job in the city. Given Minton's commitment to the union and to the labor of musicians, Monk probably earned around thirty dollars a week.[24] The money wasn't great, but it was more than he had been making on intermittent club dates, and the band had Tuesdays off.[25] By late January or early February of 1941, 210 West 118th Street became Monk's second home.

Before he could begin work, however, he had to go downtown to the Police License

Division at 56 Worth Street to be photographed and fingerprinted by the NYPD in order to obtain a "cabaret identification card." The police-issued card, which had to be renewed every two years, was required of anyone who worked in establishments serving alcohol. The new requirement did not target musicians alone: chefs, barmaids, waiters and other dining workers also needed a cabaret card. This was new to Monk; the police only started requiring the cards in 1940, when the LaGuardia administration and the police chief decided that nightclub performers were potentially a bad influence and required greater monitoring and regulation. Anti-Communist and anti-labor policies proved to be the other catalyst for the new law. The city's very active Waiters' Union, which waged some militant strikes the year the cabaret card requirement was first issued, was regarded by state and federal authorities as a beehive of radical activity.[26] Although there were legal precedents for denying persons convicted of a felony or narcotics-related crime employment in bars and taverns, the city had never granted the police the power to deny performers the right to work. Monk didn't think much about it at the time. It was just another requirement for a gig. He was just happy to work.

In only three years, Henry Minton had succeeded in creating a modern version of the Rhythm Club, a space where musicians could play for and with each other. But to characterize Minton's Playhouse as a perpetual jam session would be a gross exaggeration. Although most patrons gathered around the bar in those early days, there were plenty who came to listen to the music, and on rare occasions those who could pony up the fifty-cent fee to cover the cabaret tax got up and danced.[27] The band's repertoire included arrangements of popular tunes, from ballads like "Body and Soul" and "Stardust," to swinging versions of "I Found a New Baby" or "Stompin' at the Savoy," and quite a few vocal numbers. Teddy Hill made sure there were vocalists on hand besides Joe Guy. First, he hired a pretty young singer named Betty Roché, who had come to Hill's attention after winning an amateur night contest at the Apollo. She fit right in. As her future boss, Duke Ellington, recalled, "She had a soul inflection in a bop state of intrigue, and it was presented to the listener in a most unbelievable manner by a little girl with an adult delivery. . . . She never imitated anybody, and she never sounded like anybody but Betty Roché."[28] Then Hill employed two alumni of Horace Henderson's band, Viola Jefferson and Duke Groner. All three singers worked at Minton's throughout 1941. The 35-year-old, Oklahoma-born Groner was the elder of the group, though he had only recently come to New York after the Horace Henderson band broke up. He was living in the Cecil Hotel when Minton's took off, and often came downstairs to sit in with the band or perform duets with Betty Roché. Teddy Hill liked what he heard and hired him. "We would sing cabaret style," Groner recalled, "walk around the tables and sing different ballads while the band was playing."[29]

Various musicians sat in with the band almost every night, but except for Monday nights, these were not open jam sessions. The "regulars" tended to be musicians with whom the band was familiar: guitarist Charlie Christian, trumpeters Roy Eldridge, Hot Lips Page, Rudy Williams, and Benny Harris; saxophonists Kermit Scott,

Herbie Fields, Al Sears, and Jimmy Wright, as well as more noteworthy figures: Lester Young, Ben Webster, Benny Carter, Don Byas, and Monk's future employer, the legendary Coleman Hawkins. Monk often gave up the piano stool to Eddie Heywood, Ken Kersey, and Teddy Wilson, among others.[30] Perhaps the most exciting regular addition to the band was a kid who always came on stage empty-handed: the extraordinary tap dancer and singer "Baby" Laurence Jackson. Barely twenty years old when he began hanging out at Minton's, Laurence was already renowned in jazz circles as one of the greatest hoofers alive.[31]

Monday nights were different. Monday was the off-night for the Apollo Theater, so Teddy Hill would invite the performers booked that week over to Minton's for a free buffet dinner and to hang out. Deemed "Celebrity Night," these were genuine "to-do's"—the whisky flowed, the crowds gathered, and the music didn't stop until 4:00 a.m. After the fans and regular patrons cleared out, things got interesting. "[T]here wouldn't be anyone left in the joint but musicians and entertainers," Duke Groner remembered. "And that's when it was just like one big happy Christmas party, every Monday night. You had different bands, different dancers, comedians, and all. It was just a happy-go-lucky thing. Everybody would play—if you were an instrumentalist and you felt like getting out your horn to come up, you were welcome."[32] There were as many as fifteen musicians crammed together on the bandstand, and a few others in the audience anxiously waiting their turn to jump in. Of course, the Monday night jam sessions violated Local 802 rules and union members caught playing without a contract faced fines between $100 and $500.[33] The regular union rep at the time, a man named Bob Roberts, made infrequent appearances to bring the open sessions to a premature end, but for the most part, the union looked the other way.[34]

An irregular but nevertheless important participant in the Monday night sessions was former Teddy Hill Orchestra alumnus John Birks "Dizzy" Gillespie, a young trumpeter at the forefront of the development of modern jazz. Monk had met Dizzy about two or three years earlier at the Rhythm Club, which had moved to 133rd Street, but during Minton's heyday in 1941, Dizzy barely had time to get up to 118th before 4:00 a.m. Not long after Teddy Hill took over, Gillespie was out of town a lot with Cab Calloway's orchestra, and after he was fired he worked at the Famous Door and Kelly's Stable, where the last set began at 3:00 a.m.[35] Therefore, after work Dizzy headed further uptown to the other Harlem after-hours club noted for its jam sessions: Monroe's Uptown House on 134th Street. He was joined by several Mintonians, whose muses remained restless well into daybreak. Monroe's kept its doors open until 7:00 a.m. Like Minton's, Monroe's was black-owned and operated, established a few years earlier by jazz entrepreneur Clark Monroe. The informal jam sessions began unintentionally. In 1940, Monroe hired nineteen-year-old Al Tinney to be the house pianist in a trio with trumpet player Russ "Popeye" Gillon and Ebeneezer Paul on bass. Tinney was playing what later would be considered modern harmonies,[36] which he learned from working with George Gershwin on one of his productions of *Porgy and Bess*. Tinney also befriended a number of young, innovative musicians who sat in frequently. By early 1941, the trio became a full-fledged small band that included Victor Coulsen and George Treadwell on trumpets, and Ray Abrams on tenor (drummer Max Roach joined the house band in 1942).[37] "That's where we all used to go after hours," Dizzy Gillespie recalled, "until daylight, to play."[38]

The most common story about the infamous jam sessions at both Minton's and Monroe's is that the young modernists who ran the bandstand would conspire together to keep lesser players from joining in. According to Dizzy, he and Monk would spend the afternoon together trying "to work out some complex variations on chords and the like, and we used them at night to scare away the no-talent guys."[39] Clarke remembers: "We invented tunes and chords so that people we didn't want to play with us just couldn't get up on the bandstand. . . . So when we had unwelcome sitters-in, we used to play different chords and things to discourage them. Now, in the blues, they would maybe play four chords; Monk would play twenty chords and completely lose them. Sometimes he would say to them, 'Man, get off the stand—you're not playing right.' So the guy would say, 'But I thought we were playing the blues'—and Monk would scowl and say, 'That's not the way we play the blues here; we changed all that.' Monk could be very snide when he wanted to be—nothing fazed him. He'd say anything to anybody if he thought it was right. So people were always excusing him—because he could be very outspoken. That's the way he was. If he got his face broken every time he did something like that, he would have been dead at twenty-one. Sometimes he was just plain insulting. 'Oh man,' he'd say in disgust, 'you just can't play.' That was the way he would eliminate them. It was really a joke."[40]

The employment of elaborate chord substitutions and rhythmic innovations in order to weed out the bad players, or so the story goes, ultimately contributed to the birth of bebop. Like everything else having to do with Minton's, the story is greatly exaggerated and the truth a bit more complicated. Monk always rejected this interpretation of events. As far as he was concerned, "I was playing a gig, tryin' to play music. While I was at Minton's, anybody sat in who would come up there if he could play, I never bothered anybody. It was just a job."[41] And for every musician who experienced Minton's as a cliquish, highly competitive musical culture, there are just as many who felt it was a welcoming place where good musicianship ruled. Pianist Sir Charles Thompson never experienced competition, nor had he heard about Monk and others deliberately confusing the less competent musicians. "There was just a bunch of musicians having fun together." And from his first encounter with Thelonious at Minton's, he always knew him as a "very, very, very, very nice, quiet man. Never talked too much about anything. Always smiled. I never saw a bad expression on Monk's face, ever."[42] Teddy Hill concurred: "I've never heard him in an argument seriously with anybody yet. He'd much rather take the worst of it than to argue too much about anything. I've never seen him excited except when he's playing."[43] For all of Monk's alleged critical wrath, he turned out to be a patient and sympathetic teacher to some of the young musicians who struggled on the bandstand. Bass trombonist Ted Kelly remembers sitting in one night and having a difficult time. When the tune was over, Monk pulled him aside and said, "Man, come by the house tomorrow, because you don't know what the hell you're doing." Kelly, who happened to live a few doors from Monk at 247 West 63rd, went by his house for lessons for several days in a row. When Monk thought he was ready, he brought him back up to Minton's where they rehearsed. Monk then asked Dizzy to give him a job.[44]

Even Kenny Clarke's recollections of what happened at Minton's were inconsistent. In a 1963 interview Clarke insisted that, "There's no truth to the story that we purposely played weird things to keep musicians outside the clique off the stand. All we asked was that the musician be able to handle himself."[45] Yet the legend is too popular to die. Every Minton's devotee has a tale about a guy who played poorly. Dizzy Gillespie spoke about "the Demon," a regular who would often jump on the bandstand with everyone but "couldn't play to save his life."[46] Al Tinney recalls some of the best musicians getting lost in the music during these sessions. He recounts several occasions at Monroe's when some of the guys "would go out and get a little high, and they would come back and they didn't know what they were playing some of the time. They would say, 'Where we at?' or 'What channel is it?' They forgot what tunes they were playing at particular times."[47]

Monk was less concerned with keeping poor players at bay than with achieving new sounds or working through musical problems. He'd show up at Minton's in the afternoons to practice and usually stayed well past closing time. "I've had to come back and plead with him," complained Teddy Hill, "to quit playin' the piano so I could close up the place 'cause it was against the law to keep it open any longer."[48] From Minton's, he would visit friends who had a piano, sometimes waking them up at an ungodly hour just so he could work out a problem or a new composition. He lived on about five hours of sleep and often skipped a meal or two. Thelonious was known to fall asleep at the piano.[49] On the other hand, Monk's sleepless nights and early-morning visits to friends were also early signs that something wasn't right. Monk experienced episodes of manic behavior, intense creativity, and a feverish energy, followed by a day or two of sleep.[50] These "crashes" may indicate early signs of bipolar disorder, but it is hard to say with any certainty, since no one in his family observed behavior that might be described as "depression." While recognizing the severity of his depression in later years, his sister Marion observed that as a young man, Thelonious "was very seldom, you know, depressed or anything. If he was he didn't act it around the house."[51]

Very few psychiatrists, let alone lay people, understood the causes and nature of bipolar disorder at the time, so it is not surprising that musicians, fans, and especially journalists interpreted Monk's behaviors as quirky personality traits or evidence of eccentricity. The horrible conditions under which jazz musicians labored only exacerbated his illness. The jazz club was a veritable health hazard: Alcohol was not only the clubs' primary commodity and their *raison d'être*, but club owners often encouraged musicians to "run a tab," which was then deducted from the night's pay. Narcotics and other illegal drugs were readily available, and in spite of occasional raids, the police tended to look the other way as long as they were paid off. And despite the presence of a union, jazz musicians were expected to play four sets, each over an hour. Some gigs did not end until 4:00 a.m., and during the winter months, the movement in and out of clubs can place undue strain on the body.[52]

Occasionally, Monk would disappear from the bandstand, sometimes going outside to smoke reefer. But more often than not, Teddy Hill found him sitting in the kitchen writing music.[53] His favorite spot for thinking and talking about music was the basement at Minton's, a small, diamond-shaped room with low ceilings, which Hill eventually turned into a separate after-hours club. Monk used the space to practice with other young musicians and rehearse various bands he tried to put together. It was here that he, Dizzy, Kenny Clarke, and others worked out chord substitutions, alternative voicings, and harmonic devices that could "modernize" swing music. In particular, Monk preferred descending chromatic chord progressions and dissonant, "open-voiced" chords made up of just the root and the seventh or ninth degree of the scale (See Appendix). His chords often elicited chuckles from the audience, but Monk didn't mind. He later remarked, "Anything that's very good will make you laugh in admiration, so it must be humor to make you laugh—or maybe it makes you laugh in surprise because it knocks you out."[54] Humorous, but no less serious. Monk's chords were a product of years of training, experimentation, and a solid understanding of music theory. Monk knew it, which is why he became so annoyed when critics, musicians, or fans—even the sympathetic ones—described his chords as "wrong" or "weird."[55]

Monk applied his harmonic innovations to older standards and pop songs, which formed the basic repertoire for the nightly jam sessions. They played tunes such as "Nice Work If You Can Get It," "I Found a Million Dollar Baby," "Body & Soul," "Indiana," "My Melancholy Baby," "Sweet Lorraine," "Sweet Georgia Brown," to name a few. Despite his chord substitutions, he remained surprisingly loyal to the original tunes. Indeed, not unlike pianist Al Tinney at Monroe's, Monk relished the sonorities of songs like "Nice Work" partly because Gershwin wrote these with so-called "modern" harmonic devices such as the flat ninth.[56] Of course, to Monk's ears the "flat ninth" wasn't so modern. His two years on the road playing sanctified music familiarized him with the flat ninth and other dissonant harmonies.

Minton's also provided a fertile environment for the budding composer. Legend has it that Thelonious had already composed some of his best-known tunes in the mid-1930s, while he was a teenager. Yet he did not publish or copyright anything until he started working at Minton's. Monk himself confirms this: "I started composing around 1942 when I was at Minton's."[57] His first two tunes were actually copyrighted in 1941, but he probably did not count them because they were collaborations with fellow Mintonians. The first, and most famous, was written in collaboration with Kenny Clarke and copyrighted on June 2, 1941. Initially called "Fly Rite" and then "Iambic Pentameter," Monk finally renamed it "Epistrophy." Clarke claims credit for the melodic line. He said he came up with the melody after Charlie Christian showed him a fingering while fooling around with a friend's ukulele.[58] Monk is given credit for writing the piano accompaniment, which reflects his fondness for chromaticism.[59] The title, "Epistrophy" or "Epistrophe," means "turning about" in Greek, and refers to a literary device in which a word or expression is deliberately repeated at the end of successive phrases, clauses, sentences, or verses.[60] A less common definition could be found in the 1929 edition of *Webster's New International Dictionary*: "2. *Music*. A phrase or section repeated at the end of the divisions of a cyclic composition; a refrain."[61] Combine the literary and the musical and we have a title that beautifully describes the structure of the melody. Constructed out of repeated phrases, the melodic line turns in on itself. It wasn't an easy song to improvise on—the chord changes are entirely chromatic.[62] Nevertheless, it became a Minton's favorite, and the house band used it as the opening and closing theme between sets.[63]

Less noteworthy is a forgotten jump tune called "Harlem Is Awful Messy," which Monk co-composed with Hot Lips Page and Joe Guy. Complete with humorous lyrics, "Harlem Is Awful Messy" was the trio's vain attempt at a commercial hit. "Harlem Is Awful Messy" turned out to be a bust. Page submitted the copyright application on September 16, 1941, but the song was never recorded.[64]

Although Minton's did become a kind of laboratory for new music, what was played in 1941 can hardly be called bebop. According to singer Duke Groner, Minton's "never turned out to be absolutely a bebop place, because certain guys that would come around weren't bebop musicians. So everyone was welcome. If a guy was a hard-swinging tenor man or alto man or trumpeter or trombone, whatever, he was welcome coming to play at the place."[65] For all the basement sessions, Monk never believed they were creating a completely new music; rather, they were doing what jazz musicians have always done—finding a voice, trying to play what nobody has heard before, and entertaining people. "I had no particular feeling that anything new was being built," Monk explained. "It's true modern jazz probably began to get popular there. But as for me, my mind was like it was before I worked in Minton's."[66] Kenny Clarke agreed: "You know, we hadn't really set out with the idea of developing any particular style of jazz. . . . [I]t was really unconscious."[67]

Great music is what put Minton's on the map. Monk attributed much of his own notoriety to the Monday night jam sessions: "As a result, all the different bands that played at the Apollo got to hear the original music, and it got around and talk started going about the fellows at Minton's."[68] Word certainly "got around," and so did the music, thanks to a Columbia University student named Jerry Newman. A twenty-three-year-old junior who loved jazz and played trombone in the university marching band, Newman owned a portable Wilcox-Gay Recordio "disc-cutter" that made recordings directly onto acetate discs. At first, it was just a hobby; he recorded radio shows and invited musicians over for informal recording sessions. Through those sessions he met Duke Groner, who brought him to Minton's. Newman used to entertain the audience by lip-synching to his own homemade recordings of celebrated figures, including President Franklin D. Roosevelt and Bob Hope. His act became a regular part of the floor show.[69] Newman's compensation for his comic performances was the privilege to record the music at the club and at Monroe's Uptown House. He would set up his equipment on the bandstand in the afternoon and then spend much of the night cutting 12-inch aluminum-based acetate discs.[70] The larger discs had a longer recording time than the 10-inch commercial 78s, which were limited to about three minutes per side. By recording the original 12-inch acetates at 33 ⅓, Newman was able to squeeze up to fifteen minutes of music on each side, allowing for more extended improvisations. He also cut "paper" discs, which he sold or sometimes gave to the musicians.[71] The paper discs were actually plastic-coated. They cost seven cents and were not very durable, but many musicians appreciated the opportunity to hear themselves play— particularly young artists like Monk who had yet to record professionally. Newman remembers one recording in particular, a "half-hour version of 'I Surrender Dear' that Monk made with tenor saxophonist Herbie Fields, that he [Monk] wore out playing back during intermissions. He'd say, 'it's pretty good, and that tenor boy really goes.' I still have it, but it can never be issued on account of its condition, plus the fact I ruined it by playing trombone on it."[72] When Newman decided to issue some of these recordings on the Vox label, or on his own Esoteric label years later, the musicians' excitement wore off once it became clear they would not be paid.

Nevertheless, the recordings are extraordinarily valuable because they provide the first record of Thelonious Monk. Some of these original discs are not dated, but those that are were recorded between April and June of 1941, a few months into Monk's gig. One of the earliest sessions, recorded on Wednesday, April 30, features Monk with the regular band (Guy, Fenton, Clarke), with Hot Lips Page, Benny Harris, and Herbie Fields (tenor sax) sitting in, on "Sweet Lorraine." The tempo is the kind of plodding speed Monk loved. In an eight-bar introduction, Monk playfully embellishes the melody with dissonance and humor. In the body of the tune, Monk creates a busy harmonic universe behind the soloists, sometimes creating little countermelodies using block chords, sometimes restating the melody. At the bridge, Monk takes off, much like his hero, Herman Chittison, with intricate phrases and slightly off-meter runs that dance across the entire keyboard. Monk was proud of those runs. In an interview with Les Tomkins many years later, he pointed to those passages in response to the naysayers who claimed he had no technique: "I guess those people are surprised when they hear certain things that I've done on records. They must feel awful silly about saying I don't have no technique. Because I know you've heard me make some fast runs. You can dig how stupid the statement is. I'm one of the cats that used to start them playing like lightning. We used to play like lightning all night long up at Minton's sometimes. I got tired playing fast all the time. You get so you automatically play fast. You can't play no other way."[73]

Monk might have gotten tired of playing fast, but he also tired of the criticism. For years to come, many of his sidemen bore witness to those vulnerable moments when Monk wanted to prove the critics wrong while simultaneously exposing the fallacy that lots of notes at high velocity necessarily make better music. Tenor saxophonist Johnny Griffin recalls one night in the late 1950s when Monk suddenly said to him, "'See, I can play like Art Tatum if I want.' And I said, 'Get out of here, Thelonious! Stop kidding around!' He said, 'Well, check this out.' He made a Tatumesque run on the piano and my eyeballs and my ears almost fell off of my head. He said, 'But I don't need that.' So he played what he had to play, that's all it is. He didn't need to be making flourishes and doing pianistic aerobics. He just played what he wanted to play and he did it perfectly."[74]

We can hear even more of these fast, intricate runs on "My Melancholy Baby," which the band recorded that same night, April 30.[75] Little Benny Harris sits in on trumpet and Clarke keeps more of a 2/4 swing beat on his hi-hat, giving the song a kind of vintage feel. After all, it is one of the oldest standards in the book, dating back to at least 1912.[76] Monk is the first soloist, this time taking an entire chorus. What he plays here is unmistakably Monk, but his debt to Chittison once again is apparent. Indeed, the similarities between what Monk plays and Chittison's 1938 recording of "My Melancholy Baby" are striking.[77] They both stay rooted to the melody while busily filling in space with intricate runs and other embellishments that not only exploit the entire range of the keyboard, but are deliberately jagged or uneven. The difference, however, is that Monk exaggerates all of these elements: his playing is even more jagged, more uneven, less dense in terms of providing more breathing space between notes, and he takes even greater intervallic steps. We hear the first examples of Monk's signature "whole tone" runs—scales based entirely on whole steps.

On Saturday night, May 4, Newman captured one of Monk's finest, and longest, performances—a lively version of Gershwin's "Nice Work If You Can Get It" with the regular house band.[78] Monk's mastery of "Nice Work" suggests that it was a song he played often. He would continue to play it for many years. It is a perfect vehicle for the kind of descending harmonic movement and sonorities that he loved so much. Throughout the song a listener can really *hear* Monk—not just his fingers at work, but his voice. Like a lot of pianists, he tended to sing solfeggio while he played, though a more precise description might be groaning, moaning, and humming. As he got into a song, he became louder, sometimes threatening to compete with the piano. His old mentor, Willie "The Lion" Smith, saw this as a sign of a serious player: "a pianist who growls, hums, and talks to the piano is a guy who is trying hard to create something for himself."[79]

If there is anything these recordings reveal, it is Monk trying to create something for himself. Besides employing substitute chord progressions and inventing new ways to improvise on a melody, Monk attempted to alter the structure of each song and create a new role for the piano in the rhythm section. He had no interest in "comping"— accompanying a soloist by simply feeding him chords—and if a soloist depended on the piano to provide the harmonic foundation, then working with Monk could be a challenge. As Dizzy explained, "If you're playing with Monk and you don't know the changes, shame on you. You'll never hear them from him."[80] What Monk plays behind Joe Guy on "Nice Work," for example, sounds like a solo, space filled with two-handed tremolos, jagged runs up and down the piano over several octaves, restatements of the melody, and little phrases that work as countermelodies. To Monk the piano was "orchestral" in that it had the capacity to embody all the elements of an entire band.[81]

For all of Monk's innovation and experimentation, his biggest challenge was backing singers. People came to Minton's to be entertained, and when singers like Duke Groner and Betty Roché belted out a romantic ballad, patrons expected a beautiful accompaniment. While Groner and Roché appreciated Monk's creativity, they did not think much of him as an accompanist. As Groner explained: "Well, it was a little difficult to do some vocals with Monk, because Monk was a way-out pianist, which he still is today. Betty and I both would have to tell him to play a little straighter and not put too much of his Monk stuff in there, you know. Because he would get to playing and he would get his weird chords and everything, and sometimes as a singer it would kind of throw us off. He would say all the time that he was right on the ball. But sometimes he was *off-key*."[82]

In late May, vocalist Helen Humes of Count Basie's band sat in at Minton's, and Monk backed her up without incident and apparently without complaint. The sensational Don Byas, another Basie band member, augmented the band on tenor, and Harold "Doc" West—a Minton's regular—may have occupied the drum chair in place of Kenny Clarke.[83] Monk launched a stunning rendition of Hoagy Carmichael's "Stardust" with a four-bar introduction in which the melody was barely recognizable, but then he stayed out of Humes's way, uncharacteristically. Ironically, Thelonious was never a fan of "Stardust," which he once described as "a sad song . . . if you know anything about music and harmony." He complained outright that the "music is lousy." "You have to do a lot of figuring how to play that in order to make it sound good."[84]

The recordings from Minton's, which number about twenty-three in all, prove that in 1941, Thelonious was neither a young version of Teddy Wilson nor a fully realized version of himself. He had begun to form the core of his musical conception, developed out of his own personal and collective explorations of harmony, rhythm, and the actual mechanics of the piano, as well as existing styles and musical traditions. The influence of Herman Chittison, Earl "Fatha" Hines, Art Tatum, even Count Basie is evident in many of these Minton's recordings. And they only represent a fraction of what was happening that year. Jerry Newman insisted that, "The released sides don't come anywhere near indicating how good he was in those days."[85]

By mid-summer, the jam sessions at Minton's, as well as at Monroe's Uptown House, had become renowned in New York City and beyond. Pianist and writer Herbie Nichols, one of Thelonious's first real champions, mentioned them in his weekly column for the black-owned *New York Age*: "The jam session has finally come to the attention of our swing magazines." Everyone who was anyone in the jazz world found their way to these Harlem after-hours joints, choosing to "miss their sleep" rather than miss out on an opportunity to jam with Roy Eldridge, Coleman Hawkins, and the like.[86]

Besides some publicity in the black press, Monk and the Minton's house band enjoyed some radio play, courtesy of Jerry Newman—though it was limited to Columbia University's campus. In February of that year, the Columbia University Radio Club formed and began broadcasting jazz to the dormitories. In June or July, Newman and friends from the club decided to introduce the music of Minton's to their listeners, which meant recording sets with the house band in the afternoon and running the acetates up the hill to be played on campus that evening, as if they were coming from Minton's "live."[87] The audience consisted of a few bemused day-time regulars and the Columbia students, who tried in vain to recreate the lively atmosphere of Minton's with audible chatter and enthusiastic applause after each song. With Jerry Newman and an anonymous student alternating as master of ceremonies, the Columbia crew recorded four "sets"—each one opening and closing with "Epistrophy." In order to make everything fit on the discs, the musicians tightly controlled each set, performing between four and seven songs (including the opening and closing theme), with each song running between one-and-a-half and three minutes. The emceeing duties were less than professional. At the end of one set, the anonymous emcee closed with: "This has been the Jumpin' Jive of Joe Guy and Kenny Clarke and their orchestra, featuring Nick Fenton on bass and a guy named Monk on piano. I'm sorry, I haven't found out his last name."[88] Though perhaps meant in jest, Newman reveals a lack of respect for Thelonious, who actually co-led the band with Clarke.

Despite the announcers' errors, it is a shame these recordings did not reach beyond campus. They included a few genuine jewels that did not appear on Newman's later releases. Joe Guy's "Rear Back," with its somewhat risqué lyrics, is the only surviving example of Monk playing blues in this period. His solo and accompaniment are sparse, reminiscent of Count Basie. Monk's improvisations build closely on the melody. Elsewhere, these recordings show how Monk backed vocalists—and why so many complained. Monk's many runs and his inclination to play the melody in unison threatens to overwhelm Duke Groner, who sounds as if he's singing with his hands over his ears.

Perhaps the most revelatory tune from these sessions is "Meet Dr. Christian," one of Charlie Christian's riffs on "I Got Rhythm" changes. One of Monk's later and most recorded compositions, "Rhythm-a-ning," begins with four bars that are practically identical to "Meet Dr. Christian." In turn, the first *eight* bars of Christian's tune are lifted verbatim from a horn riff Mary Lou Williams wrote for an arrangement of "Walking and Swinging," first recorded by the Andy Kirk Orchestra in 1936.[89] Monk's appropriation of Williams's phrase represents a rare example of musical "borrowing" from an artist who prided himself on originality.

The fame of Minton's house band did not translate into outside gigs or a recording contract for Monk. He continued to live at home with his mother, although now he enjoyed a bit more space since Marion married in 1939, moved into her own Phipps apartment, and gave birth to her first-born son, Alonzo, on May 31, 1940. Still, Thelonious spent most of his days and nights in Harlem, roaming from house to house playing piano, and eventually crashing at Sonny's apartment on 136th. He continued to date Rubie Richardson, but she rarely made her way uptown.[90] As Monk became more involved with his music, according to Teddy Hill, he "lost touch with everything else." Hill recalled a couple of times when Monk arrived at Minton's in the company of his girlfriend, but would forget she was there and leave without her.[91]

Monk's other obsessions, unfortunately, were gin and reefer. Drugs and alcohol were occupational hazards for jazz musicians; they worked in arenas in which alcohol was pushed and illegal drugs were readily available. There is no evidence that Monk became an addict, but he was known to drink quite a bit. Kenny Clarke recalls many nights accompanying Thelonious to the subway after a gig and "Monk would be very, very drunk." They would stand on the uptown platform, talking, until it was time to cut out, at which point an inebriated Monk would climb down from the platform, cross the tracks, and pull himself up onto the downtown platform. Clarke was always amazed he never electrocuted himself on the third rail.[92] Trumpeter Johnny Carisi, one of the few white musicians at Minton's, remembered the club as a real drinking den. "At Minton's there was a lotta getting loaded. As a matter of fact, Monk taught me how to drink. At the end of a set, he'd say, 'Come on, come to the bar.' I'd say, 'Monk, I don't drink much.' He insisted. He'd say, 'What? Call yourself a jazz player . . . ' And the next thing you know he had me drinking double gins."[93]

Whether it was the drinking or falling asleep at the piano or the occasional disappearances from the bandstand, or simply a desire for a new sound, Teddy Hill let Monk go before the end of the year was up. Monk continued to show up at Minton's and he was always welcomed, but he was no longer on the payroll.[94]

By the end of 1941, Minton's was no longer the same; the music never dulled but the crowds waned a bit, as was the case for many jazz clubs across the country.[95] Then came the attack on Pearl Harbor on December 7, 1941, and with it the sobering reality that America was at war.

7

"Since You Went Away I Missed You"

(1941–1943)

Nine days before Christmas in 1941, a card addressed to Thelonious Sphere Monk arrived in the mail. He had only recently adopted his maternal grandfather's name as his own middle name. Uncle Sam knew it, and wanted him. The return address, 155 West 65th Street, was his local draft board. He was classified 1A, available for unrestricted military service.[1]

Monk half-expected the news since registering for selective service in October 1940, and receiving a questionnaire just two months before Pearl Harbor.[2] Little over a week had passed since the attack. The United States and Britain had declared war on Japan the next day, and on December 11, Germany and Italy declared war on the United States. Hitler's troops already occupied France, Poland, Greece, Czechoslovakia, and major parts of the Soviet Union, and fighting between Allied and Axis powers spilled into North Africa. As far as Uncle Sam was concerned, Monk was an ideal candidate for service: twenty-four years old, five feet, ten and a half inches, 168 pounds, good physical condition, and unemployed.[3] Of course, there was the matter of color: The military was segregated and black troops were largely relegated to noncombat service roles.[4] But neither patriotism nor a paycheck could persuade Thelonious to don a uniform and serve his country in this fashion. He wanted to play music and take care of his mother; toting water, building bridges, and digging trenches for his fellow white troops in a Jim Crow Army simply did not appeal to him.

The letter did not include his induction papers, and Monk was able to push the draft to the back of his mind. The more immediate problem was finding work. Having lost his gig as house pianist at Minton's, Monk no longer enjoyed a steady income. Thanks to his mother, he did have a roof over his head, plenty to eat, and a decent piano at home. If it weren't for Barbara's continued support he might have had to join the world of wage work. Instead, Monk wrote music, practiced, and took whatever gigs he could find. He played in a band led by Kenny Clarke at Kelly's Stable on 52nd Street for a couple of weeks, but didn't work much more. Meanwhile, trumpeter Cootie Williams—who had formed his own orchestra late in 1941 after leaving Benny Goodman—had adopted Monk and Clarke's "Epistrophy" as the opening and closing theme for his performances. Williams's band appeared regularly at the popular Savoy

Ballroom, introducing the song to a larger audience. Williams recorded "Epistrophy" under the title "Fly Right," in Chicago on April 1, 1942, although two decades passed before it would be released. One of Monk's collaborators from Minton's, Joe Guy, was in Williams's band and participated in the recording session. The pianist was another Minton's regular—Ken Kersey. Had Monk heard Williams's version, he would have recognized the melody but not much else. The arrangement is classic Cootie—danceable and typical of the style popular at the Savoy Ballroom.[5]

Monk would have jumped at a chance to join Cootie Williams's Orchestra, or any name band at the time, but few bandleaders knew what to do with such an adventurous pianist. Ideally, Monk would have preferred to lead his own band and record his own songs, if only he could find a record label interested in his music. But even that prospect was cut short on August 1, 1942, when the American Federation of Musicians, under president James Petrillo, declared a strike against the record industry. All union musicians were banned from engaging in any recording activities. The AFM wanted the record labels to pay artists royalties every time their records were played on jukeboxes or similar devices in restaurants, clubs, bars, and anywhere else live music might be played. The union argued that "canned music" took away the musicians' livelihood. For Decca, Capitol, and many small record labels, the strike lasted a little over a year, but major labels such as RCA Victor and Columbia did not settle the dispute until November of 1944, losing quite a bit of money in the process.[6]

Things seemed to be looking up for Monk when Lucius "Lucky" Millinder hired him to replace pianist Bill Doggett during an engagement at the Savoy Ballroom in early August.[7] Dizzy Gillespie was playing with Millinder at the time and he lobbied his boss to hire Thelonious. (Monk, however, always believed Dizzy had ulterior motives: "He got me hired on piano so's he could be around me" and therefore pick up more of his ideas.[8]) Monk's old pal Nick Fenton was also in the band.[9] It was a huge gig for Monk; Millinder's orchestra was one of the hottest black dance bands in the country. Featuring Sister Rosetta Tharpe singing "spirituals in swing," the band was known for its excellent arrangements and talented players, who were expected to cut a few choreographed dance steps on the bandstand.[10] Despite the potential for long-term employment, however, the gig seemed doomed from the beginning. According to the band's drummer, Panama Francis, Millinder simply detested Monk's playing. "Monk came one night," he recalled, "and played three or four pieces with us, after which Lucky told him to shove off and never come back."[11] In truth, Monk worked for a week at the Savoy before Millinder fired Monk, without notice and without pay.

Millinder's actions prompted Monk to go to the union and file his first complaint against an employer. At a Local 802 trial board hearing on September 8, 1942, Monk testified, "I was working at the Savoy Ballroom and the defendant [Millinder] let me go. He worked at the Howard Theater. He didn't pay me for the last week at the Savoy. Sunday night another man play; he just told me I was through. The scale was $38 for six days and I worked 7 days, and they had three more days to go at the Ballroom."[12] Millinder never showed up to the hearing to testify on his own behalf, although he was in town for an engagement at the Apollo.[13] Unsurprisingly, the board sided with Monk, ruling that he was entitled to $63.33 in back wages for ten days of employment at the Savoy.[14]

During the weeks that followed, Monk was back to playing at dingy watering holes, house parties, and restaurants, though he still hung out at Minton's on Monday nights. Toward the end of September, an obscure saxophonist named John Harley hired Monk to play at a Chinese restaurant in Harlem for five dollars a night, six nights a week. Nothing about their engagement went well. After about a month of miscommunication and mutual recrimination, Harley fired Monk, initiating a series of claims and counterclaims they both brought to the union. According to Harley, Monk was habitually late and often deliberately so. He recounted one story in which Monk brought his girlfriend—Rubie Richardson—and the owner refused to give the couple a half-price discount on food. Monk stormed out of the place and did not return until 11:00, an hour after the first set was scheduled to begin. "I was looking all over for a piano player and I had to play piano until he came in," Harley testified. "I was ordered to get rid of him." Another night, Monk didn't show up at all and Harley had to hire "a blind pianist" to replace him. Harley paid the blind pianist out of Monk's measly wages. What annoyed Harley most, however, was when Monk came to work drunk or high on reefer and fell asleep at the piano. He even claimed he saw Monk smoke marijuana on the bandstand. Fed up, Harley gave Monk two weeks' notice, but as his erratic behavior only worsened the owner told Harley to let him go before the two weeks were up.[15]

Monk responded with humor, accusing Harley of being "a better liar than I am." The real issue, he claimed, was the working conditions. "The reason he got mad," Monk explained, "is because he works the musicians to death. He plays an hour and a half without stopping. I have to play every minute[.] I said we are playing too hard for this little bit of money. He was working me to death while he stood up there with his horn. The reason he fired me is because I said we were working too hard and should rest some of the time. He said to me I hope you do get off the stand so I can fire you at the end of the night and then he said you are fired and it was in the middle of the week."[16] The case was held over until November 4, at which time Harley produced two witnesses, Shadrack Dobson and Charles Lee, to attest to Monk's character and undependability. Lee, a tenor player who hung out at Monroe's and would go on to make a couple of rhythm and blues recordings with Al Tinney,[17] was openly hostile to Monk, stating, "I wouldn't want Monk on the job." Dobson, a bassist who sat in with Monk at Minton's on Monday nights, was a bit more charitable, though he agreed that Thelonious frequently fell asleep on the job. In the end, both witnesses concluded that had it not been for the owner of the restaurant, Harley probably would not have fired Monk.[18] The trial board took no action, and both parties agreed to go their separate ways. Monk was out several days' pay, and his confidence in the union began to wane. But Monk would forever be sensitive to the exploitation of musicians, especially at the hands of club owners and record labels.

Monk's inability to keep a steady job continued to dog his already suffering relationship with Rubie Richardson. She was now twenty-five years old and had established a career as a dietician. When a position opened up in Washington, D.C., toward the end of 1942, she accepted and left New York.[19] It was the end of her relationship with Thelonious, and a very difficult experience for him. "When they broke up, man, that was one of the saddest days in my uncle's life," recalled Thomas Monk, Jr., who was five at the time. "He came up to the house and talked to my mother. And he said, 'I don't know what to do. I ain't got Rubie.'"[20]

As always, Monk found some solace at Sonny's place. Sonny, Geraldine, and the children had left Harlem for the Bronx in 1942, eventually settling into a large three-bedroom apartment on Lyman Place.[21] They needed the space: on May 18, 1942, Geraldine gave birth to their third child and first son, Clifton. Thelonious now had more children to dote on and a model of family life he admired and sometimes longed for.

The only one missing was Sonny's sister Nellie. Early in the year, she had taken a job at Bridgeport Brass—an established brass works plant that was now alloying cartridge cases and manufacturing aluminum rods, nonferrous condenser tubes, and fire extinguishers for the military.[22] For several months, Nellie made the long commute to Connecticut, until she lost part of her finger in a terrible accident on the job. She was forced to take time off to recover. It was then, during the summer of 1942, that Nellie made the decision to leave New York and move back to Jacksonville, Florida, her birthplace.[23]

Elisha Smith had not seen his daughter in nearly two decades. Suddenly the sixty-six-year-old bachelor had to share his tiny house at 1304 Fairfax Street with a young woman about whom he knew next to nothing. For Nellie, who had lost her mother at a young age, reuniting with her father turned out to be a bittersweet experience. She was able to learn more about her family, and why her parents had split up. But she also found herself in the position of caregiver—"E.B." had begun to show signs of dementia.[24]

Her uncle, James Clifton Smith, a prominent educator living in nearby St. Augustine, encouraged Nellie to enroll in school rather than waste away in a low-wage job. His own daughter, Anna Lou Smith, was to begin classes that fall at Florida Normal and Industrial Memorial Institute, conveniently located in St. Augustine. An historically black college, Florida Normal had been formed the previous year, through a merger between two older schools, Florida Baptist Institute for Negroes (founded in 1879 in Live Oak) and Florida Baptist Academy (founded in Jacksonville in 1892).[25] James persuaded Nellie to move in with them and attend school with Anna Lou in the fall. Although the Smiths were raising eight children on two schoolteachers' salaries, Anna Lou had just graduated from high school at fourteen. Nellie was twenty years old and could watch out for her younger cousin.[26]

Meanwhile, Monk's own circle of friends and musical compatriots continued to grow. In 1942, he met a couple of young, talented pianists from Harlem who not only possessed facility and imagination but were open to new ideas. Earl "Bud" Powell and St. Elmo Sylvester Hope were already friends when they met Monk. And they were young: seventeen and eighteen, respectively.[27] The middle son of William and Pearl Powell, Bud grew up in one of Harlem's many extraordinary musical families. William

Powell was a stride pianist and band leader, though he made ends meet as a superintendent of apartment buildings on 140th Street and St. Nicholas and as a freelance house painter.[28] Bud's big brother, William, Jr. (Skeets), was a violinist and trumpet player, and his baby brother Richie followed their dad and Bud to the keyboards. Richie was good—good enough to one day join the Clifford Brown–Max Roach quintet. But Bud was the prodigy of the family. "By the time he was ten he could play everything he'd heard by Fats Waller and Art Tatum," his father recalled.[29] And Chopin, Debussy, Mozart, Schumann, Bach, and virtually any music his strict piano teacher placed in front of him. Like Monk, Powell attended one of the city's most distinguished public schools, DeWitt Clinton High School in the Bronx (Powell's classmates included literary giant James Baldwin), but dropped out at fifteen to play professionally. He played in his brother Skeets's band and gigged as a solo pianist around Harlem and the Village, yet one of his first regular jobs was with trumpeter Valaida Snow and her Sunset Royal Entertainers in Coney Island in 1940.[30]

Elmo Hope also had a strong classical foundation. By the time he was fourteen years old, Hope had already achieved distinction as one of Harlem's outstanding young concert pianists. Born to Caribbean immigrants Simon and Ida Gertrude Hope, Elmo attended Benjamin Franklin High School in East Harlem—renowned for its excellent music program.[31] After school, he and Powell would practice and listen to music together, though each developed his own distinctive style.[32]

Some say Hope was as talented and promising as Powell. He was fleet, inventive, possessed an exhaustive knowledge of harmony, and had aspirations to become a composer. At sixteen, he had already composed several jazz pieces, as well as modern concert works. But in the wee hours of Sunday morning, November 24, 1940, Hope suffered a tragic setback when a police officer's bullet almost ended his life. Hope and a friend had just gotten off the subway at 110th Street and were walking toward Eighth Avenue. On the way, they encountered a crowd of young men who began to scramble when someone yelled, "The cops are coming, you better run!" Elmo tried to duck into a nearby hallway on Eighth Avenue, but the officer shot him in the back. He was rushed to Sydenham Hospital in critical condition. The police charged *Hope* with felonious assault while he was in the hospital fighting for his life, but faced with no evidence and the threat of a lawsuit, they had to drop all charges.[33]

After a long, slow recovery, Elmo returned to music, though he wasn't the same. He did not return to school to complete his diploma or pursue a career as a concert pianist, choosing instead to follow Bud into the New York jazz labor market—taking gigs at taxi dance halls on 14th Street and various small dives throughout the Bronx, Brooklyn, and Coney Island.[34] But he never stopped composing. Indeed, in Monk he found a kindred spirit, a fellow composer committed to creating a new architecture for improvisational music.

Thelonious, Bud, and Elmo hit it off right away; for a while, they were inseparable. Marion recalls that once they started hanging out together, they were at Monk's mother's house "all the time."[35] But in March of 1943, Hope enlisted in the army and disappeared from the scene for several years.[36] Hope's tour of duty and his subsequent stints with R&B bands essentially led to his erasure from bebop's formative history, not to mention Monk and Powell's own musical development. Well after the war, Hope would reunite with his two friends, but in the meantime Monk became something of a big brother and mentor to Powell.

In Monk's view, Bud was a diamond in the rough just ready to be polished. "When I met him, he did not know much on the piano. He had a very distinct style, but he didn't know much about harmony, I had to teach him about it."[37] When Monk felt his young protégé was ready, he introduced Bud to the Minton's crowd in 1942. It was hardly an easy sell. Monk told Nat Hentoff later that initially Kenny Clarke opposed letting the kid on the bandstand.[38] In Clarke's version of the story, Teddy Hill was the obstacle. Evidently, the audience preferred Monk to this unknown teenager, and Hill did all he could to persuade Monk to return to the piano bench. Hill's reaction angered Monk, who threatened to walk out. By Clarke's account, Monk shouted, "Are you deaf? Don't you hear what he's doing? If you don't listen to him, I won't play any more!"[39] More than once Monk used threats to keep Bud on the bandstand. "When Bud Powell was very young," Monk recalled in a 1963 interview, "no one wanted to listen to him. When he arrived in a place where I was playing, I would leave the piano and announce 'Bud is going to play.' Everyone yelled, 'We don't want to hear him.' I said, 'Then I am not playing anymore. It's either Bud or no one.' And the audience was forced to listen to Bud."[40]

Monk was so convincing that soon Bud Powell was working regularly while Monk was still cobbling together a string of low-paying one-night stands. In 1943, Powell became the regular pianist in the Cootie Williams Orchestra.[41] Williams had to assume legal guardianship of nineteen-year-old Bud in order to take him on the road. Monk was pleased for Powell and never stopped singing his praises, but he was hurt by the turn of events: "Once again, it happened that I couldn't find a gig. Bud was getting bigger and bigger and all of a sudden some people started to believe that Bud inspired me. What a joke. When Bud would come to my house, he would ask me to show him the simplest things to teach him the harmonies that I use."[42] Pianist Mary Lou Williams also recognized the huge impact Monk's mentoring had on Powell: "Monk influenced [Bud] as a kid. He idolises Monk and can interpret Monk's compositions better than anyone I know. And the two used to be inseparable. At the piano Bud still does a few things the way Monk would do them, though he has more technique."[43]

Bud Powell could, indeed, come close to reproducing Monk, but he had his own style as well, one that placed greater emphasis on the right hand. He became famous for playing "horn-like" melodious lines with his right hand, against sparse voicings with his left—an approach he had begun to develop with Elmo Hope. When the branch of modern jazz that has come to be known as bebop took off a couple of years later, Powell's style of playing seemed more suitable than Monk's. The beboppers—Dizzy Gillespie, Charlie Parker, and their followers—reveled in speed and virtuosity. The piano was no longer essential for rhythmic support; now it joined the chorus of soloists. And Bud Powell's ability to sustain inventive and vibrant melodic lines at a blistering pace made him the most sought-after pianist of his generation. Powell was modern enough for swing bands such as the Cootie Williams Orchestra without the overwhelming dissonance that repelled so many bandleaders from hiring Monk.

In late March 1943, Monk received an "Order to Report for Induction" from Uncle Sam. He was to report to the local Army Induction Center on April 12, at 6:00 a.m. It was fifteen months since he had been classified 1-A. By now, Monk hated the Nazis and was sympathetic to the French resistance to Fascism. He was even known to show up at Minton's sporting a beret and announcing *"France libre, France libre!"*[44] Yet he was unwilling to enlist. Very few black musicians were eager to leave the music scene to fight another white man's war. Many of Monk's colleagues deliberately set out to change their status from 1A to 4F, or unfit for military service. Some ingested a mixture of benzaedrine nasal spray and coke in order to make their "heart sound defective to the draft board's doctors."[45] Others chose to "perform" for the Army psychiatrist, feigning madness, hostility, or homosexuality. Dizzy Gillespie reportedly secured his 4F status by portraying himself as a potential enemy combatant: "Well, look, at this time, at this stage in my life here in the United States whose foot has been in my ass? The white man's foot has been in my ass hole buried up to his knee in my ass hole! . . . Now you're speaking of the enemy. You're telling me the German is the enemy. At this point, I can never even remember having met a German. So if you put me out there with a gun in my hand and tell me to shoot at the enemy, I'm liable to create a case of 'mistaken identity,' of who I might shoot."[46] Jazz vocalist Babs Gonzalez painted his fingernails and toenails fire-engine red, curled his hair, and went to his neighborhood induction center in Newark wearing women's underwear. As soon as Gonzalez began to strip for his physical, the doctor immediately hustled him to the psychiatrist:

> His first question was "you look dazed. Are you drunk?" I said no. I had been smoking Marijuana. He made a notation then asked me where I got it. I told him on any corner in "Harlem" if you had the money. His next question was "did I like girls and did I have a girl friend?" I jumped out of the chair screaming never to mention girls to me. He asked why did I wear female garments. I told him I was a female impersonator on the stage and wore my attire in the street, too.
>
> He was just sitting there talking when I touched his hand saying, "You sure are an understanding man, I wish I could visit and talk with you some place after you're finished working." He snatched his hand away and promptly began stamping papers telling me to get out and wait in the next room. In fifteen minutes a guard came up and gave me a card marked "4FH" and told me to go home.[47]

Black resistance to the draft was pervasive. By late 1943, African-Americans comprised 35 percent of the nation's delinquent registrants, and between 1941 and 1946 more than two thousand black men were imprisoned for not complying with the provisions of the Selective Service Act.[48]

Monk was compliant, to a point. He made it to the induction center on time, passed his physical, but at the end of the mandatory fifteen-minute interview with the Army psychiatrist, his file was stamped "psychiatric reject" and reclassified 4F.[49] According to family lore, he went down there with Sonny Smith, who launched into a diatribe against racism and slavery in the United States, arguing that he could never be loyal to this country. Monk echoed these sentiments in his interview, and both were classified mentally unfit to serve.[50] However, given the Selective Service's track record with regard to African-American inductees, it is entirely possible that Thelonious was labeled a "psychiatric reject" without any effort on his part. Across the nation, young black men were rejected at a much higher rate than whites based on their physical and mental evaluations. The army's explanation for the disproportionate rejection rates was that black men had higher incidences of tuberculosis, cardiovascular problems, and mental illness such as "psychopathic personality," a catch-all phrase that incorporated "constitutional psychopathic inferiority, criminal records, and sexual psychopathy." The NAACP conducted its own study of local draft boards, finding that the boards were predominantly, if not completely, white, and documenting many examples of outright racial bias. Some psychiatrists on the Selective Service's Central Examining Board for Neurology and Psychiatry revealed that it was especially difficult to diagnose blacks because certain dysfunctional behaviors are "naturally" part of their character. As one doctor admitted, "The colored men offered me the greatest difficulty in diagnosis. . . . Poor cultural, occupation and educational backgrounds often made it difficult to decide whether they were defective, preschizoid, or just colored."[51]

Black men fortunate enough to avoid the draft still faced a kind of war at home. They battled a federal government seemingly indifferent to the fact that Americans were called upon to crush Nazism while white supremacy persisted in the United States. Many African-Americans believed World War II was about racial justice, and that the horrors of war provided an opportunity to demand equal treatment. Black leaders called for a "Double Victory"—a victory against fascism abroad and racism at home. The NAACP enjoyed a ten-fold increase in membership; the Nation of Islam (whose members resisted the draft) suddenly became a force to be reckoned with; and new organizations, such as the Congress of Racial Equality (CORE), came into being during the war.[52] Activists declared war over a year before Pearl Harbor when a black woman delegate to a civil rights conference proposed a march on Washington led by labor leader A. Philip Randolph. Randolph took up the challenge, warning President Roosevelt that if he did not issue an executive order banning discrimination in hiring, employment training programs, and unions, and desegregate the armed forces, 100,000 African-Americans would march on the nation's capital. While not all of the demands were met, Roosevelt averted the march by issuing Executive Order 8802 creating the Fair Employment Practice Committee (1941), which ultimately persuaded the National War Labor Board to abolish wage differentials based on race.[53]

Between black activism and the demands of the war industry, black working people fled the South in large numbers for the sprawling factories of the urban North. About 1 million African-Americans were added to the industrial labor force. Sixty percent were women who, for the most part, took the opportunity to leave domestic service for factory jobs. War-time industry proved to be a crucial battleground in the fight for racial justice. In places like Mobile, Alabama, and Philadelphia, white workers waged "hate strikes" to protest the promotion of black men and women workers, and African-Americans frequently retaliated with their own wildcat strikes to resist racism. These battles often spilled out into the city streets. Dramatic incidents of racial violence occurred in cities across the country, sometimes prompted by an act of police brutality, a shopfloor rumble, or a scuffle on a bus or a streetcar. By June of 1943, race riots had erupted in Los Angeles, Detroit, Beaumont, Texas, and Mobile, Alabama, and a black man was lynched in Marianna, Florida. Indeed, it might be said that while U. S. troops invaded Normandy and bombed Okinawa, African-Americans fought their own war at home.[54]

Although large-scale riots occurred infrequently, many African-Americans experienced small, daily skirmishes with local police. Of course, neither police harassment nor race riots were new to Thelonious. Indeed, most young black men raised in America's metropolitan areas had grown accustomed to these kinds of incidents. What was different, so it seemed, was the defiant posture of the new generation. Young black men adopted the language and sartorial style of the "hep cat," and combined it with an intellectual fervor and engagement with the world. While few went so far as to don bright-colored zoot suits with wide-brimmed hats and gold chains, they dressed sharply, and resisted not only the dominant culture and its attendant racism and patriotism, but also the rural folkways that still survived in most black urban households. They created a fast-paced, improvisational language style that sharply contrasted with the passive stereotype of the stuttering, tongue-tied Sambo. And in a world where whites commonly addressed them as "boy," young black males made a fetish of calling each other "man."[55] The police often regarded musicians as particularly defiant, if not outright criminal. Some openly dated white women, spoke back to police officers, and were involved in or associated with the drug culture that permeated the jazz scene. The very thought of able-bodied young men enjoying the stateside nightlife while others just like them were fighting and dying overseas was enough to push some cops over the edge. It was enough to render all jazz musicians suspect.

Thelonious became one of those suspects just five weeks after his induction ordeal. In mid-May, he took a brief trip to Washington, D.C., possibly to visit Rubie. On May 19, the D.C. police arrested him on suspicion of possession and use of narcotics. They held him for several hours, but he was eventually released.[56] It turned out to be the first of several arrests Monk would endure during the course of his life, but he never spoke about it publicly.

Monk hustled back to New York, and it seems his luck began to change. Minton's came calling again, this time for a fairly long-term engagement leading a quartet of some former Playhouse pals, Kermit Scott on tenor sax and drummer Harold "Doc" West. Ironically, Monk was hired to replace Sonny White (Kenny Clarke's initial choice for the house pianist at Minton's back in 1941), who had been drafted.[57] If Nick Fenton were in the band, it would have been like Minton's of two years ago, but he had enlisted in the U.S. Army in August.[58] On bass, instead, was a twenty-year-old new-comer named Oscar Pettiford. A black Indian from Okmulgee, Oklahoma, Pettiford had only recently arrived in New York with Charlie Barnet's band. He grew up per-forming in his family's band in and around Minneapolis, where he played bass and cello and proved competent on a number of other instruments.[59] Just weeks before arriving in the Big Apple, he jammed with Dizzy Gillespie and alto saxophonist Charlie Parker at the Savoy Hotel in Chicago.[60] The word "bebop" had yet to be spoken, and Parker had yet to make a name for himself, but Pettiford sensed something was happening in the music. He desperately wanted to be a part of it. At Minton's, Monk took a liking to him and found yet another student to teach. With the arrival of Pettiford, according to Monk, "We got a different way to play rhythm. Pretty soon everybody followed our example and that's the kind of rhythm section they play today."[61]

Minton's drew pretty good crowds with Monk at the helm, despite the growing com-petition from clubs in midtown, on 52nd Street, and a sudden clampdown on Harlem nightlife. City, state, and federal authorities were concerned that white servicemen on leave spent too much time uptown. Fears of crime in Harlem were greatly exaggerated, as were concerns that servicemen were contracting syphilis and gonorrhea from black prostitutes, yet these were the official explanations for what turned out to be a general-ized fear of too much interracial mingling and potential interracial violence. One of the first salvos in a new war on vice in Harlem was to close down the Savoy Ballroom on 141st and Lenox. Mayor LaGuardia gave the order to padlock the popular dance hall on April 21, 1943. Harlemites were up in arms: If vice were really the issue, the Savoy was the last place to target. It served only ginger ale, despite having a liquor license. It had eliminated its dance hostesses, and only admitted patrons over eighteen, despite the fact that the law allowed customers as young as sixteen. Closing the Savoy not only removed a major leisure outlet for black residents, it eliminated dozens of jobs.[62]

Throughout the spring and summer of 1943, it seemed as if police occupied every street corner uptown. They monitored the streets and the clubs looking for evidence of vice, and Minton's regulars were aware of the plainclothes officers occupying a table or a booth. Ascending from the IRT Station on 116th and Seventh Avenue, on Sunday night, August 1, Monk heard the faint sound of sirens and noticed a little more com-motion in the streets than usual. Plumes of smoke were blowing south from 125th Street. Uptown along Seventh Avenue, crowds of Harlem residents were gathered on street corners, fighting with police, breaking windows. A concentration of folks gath-ered in front of Sydenham Hospital on 125th Street, just east of Seventh. Monk was witnessing one of the worst civil disturbances in Harlem since the riot of 1935.

The spark that ignited the riot involved the police, who had been staking out the Hotel Braddock for illegal activities, including solicitation. Located just around the corner from the Apollo on 126th and Eighth Avenue, the Braddock was once famous for catering to show-business celebrities. It was one of Thelonious's favorite haunts. A few weeks earlier, fights had broken out in front of the hotel, prompting a permanent police presence in the lobby. The officers assigned to the Braddock barred interracial couples from entering. At about 7:30 in the evening of August 1, the police officer on duty, James Collins, arrested a black woman named Marjorie Polite, after witnessing an argument between Polite and a hotel employee. Collins intervened and charged her with disturbing the peace. When Polite resisted arrest, Collins began dragging her. A black army private, Robert Bandy, was in the lobby with his mother, Florine Roberts, and his girlfriend. Seeing a white officer attacking a black woman, he came to her defense. Bandy tried to persuade Collins to release her, but Collins threatened Bandy with his nightstick. They began fighting, and in the ensuing scuffle Collins shot Bandy in the shoulder. When word of the shooting hit the streets, Harlem blew up. Over the course of twenty-four hours, six people lay dead, nearly 700 were injured, 550 were arrested, and 1,485 stores were damaged or burned to the ground. Over thirty fires had been set, and the monetary damage came to nearly five million dollars.[63]

The insurrection dealt a severe blow to Harlem businesses, including nightclubs and bars that were already on the decline due to increased police surveillance.[64] Minton's would continue to plod along for a while, but crowds diminished and the golden age appeared more golden than ever in the memories of old-timers. More importantly, Monk was suddenly out of a job.

Despite losing the gig at Minton's, Monk spent the remaining weeks of summer in good spirits. Nellie had returned, gorgeous as ever! She still had those naturally high cheekbones and dark, deep-set eyes, and had stayed as thin as a rail—at five feet, seven inches, she barely weighed one hundred pounds. The South Florida sun gave her dark brown skin a vibrant glow, and a year in college endowed her with an air of sophistication neither Monk nor any of her friends and family had seen before. There was no mistaking the fact that she was a fully grown woman.

Although she never completed her business degree, she gained quite a lot during her year at Florida Normal and Industrial Institute. She took a range of business and liberal-arts courses with mixed results,[65] and she grew quite close to her cousin Anna Lou Smith. "Nellie was extremely generous," recalls Anna Lou, "and had a wonderful sense of humor and a wonderful way with people. I was much more introverted because I had been socially out of sync. That was a very good year for me because she kind of helped me come out of my shell."[66] Florida Normal was a strict Baptist college. Freshmen were prohibited from face-to-face dancing; daily chapel, Wednesday night prayer meetings, and vespers on Sunday were all mandatory; and three absences from any of these sacred events meant being placed on the "blue jay" list—better known as laundry duty.[67] A Baptist college just wasn't Nellie's cup of tea. And as much as she appreciated the time with her Florida family, she felt an enormous financial strain. She used to tell Anna Lou jokingly, "You know, I like living here but we're so poor. It takes ten cents to go to the movies, but to try to get that ten cents is so hard!"[68] After a year there, Nellie had had enough of Florida.

Nellie's only regret was leaving her father behind in Jacksonville. His condition worsened to the point where he could no longer live alone. He moved in with his sister,

Rosa Bell Williams, and when she could no longer handle him, he moved in with James Clifton and his family in St. Augustine. There he became a somewhat notorious character, wandering into town in search of a piano to play. He would try to break into homes or knock on the doors of strangers in his quest to play the one song he knew. At first it was charming, then an outright nuisance. His wanderings came to an abrupt end one day in 1949 when he broke into the mayor's house. He was committed to Florida State Hospital in Chattahoochee—a former correctional facility turned state mental institution notorious for mistreating patients. Fifteen days after he was admitted, he died of pneumonia. E.B. was seventy-three years old.[69]

Back in New York, Thelonious began spending more and more time at Sonny's house on Lyman Place. As devoted as he was to San Juan Hill, living there after 1942 became somewhat intolerable, because the city had begun razing all of the old tenement apartments to replace them with high-rise projects known as the Amsterdam Houses. Everything was leveled except for the Phipps Houses.[70] But escaping the noise and the dust was just part of his motivation for hanging out in the Bronx. He wanted to see Nellie. He took her out a few times for drinks, mostly to such local Bronx joints as the Band Box or a bar called Kenny's, within walking distance of Lyman Place. But Nellie soon began seeing another man known simply as "Brother Roscoe." Geraldine Smith remembered Roscoe as "a very dapper young man. He knew all the things to do and to say. He was something else." Brother Roscoe started taking Nellie out to more upscale spots, as well as museums, galleries, and occasional concerts. Monk continued to spend more time at the Smiths' place than at his own house, and one day, Brother Roscoe arrived to take Nellie boating, wearing matching shorts and shirt, cap, and carrying a large picnic basket for the trip. Roscoe was invited to sit in the living room with Monk and Sonny while Nellie finished getting ready. Thelonious broke the awkward silence. Glaring at the basket, Monk asked Brother Roscoe, "Hey, whaddya got there? What's that? We're really hungry, you think maybe you might spare some extra food?" Nervously, Roscoe relented and timidly handed over the basket. Sonny and Thelonious dug in. They didn't stop until they polished off every morsel in the basket. Roscoe was speechless and angry. When Nellie finally emerged, Brother Roscoe hustled her out of the house with his empty picnic basket. After Nellie returned from the afternoon excursion, Monk pulled her aside and said, "If you want to go out places, I can take you out. That's nothing; I can do that."[71] It was the last time Brother Roscoe came calling.

Thelonious was in love . . . again. And in Nellie he found his muse. By the end of the summer of 1943, Monk had finally completed a ballad in C minor he had been noodling around with for at least a year. He asked a friend of his, a young woman from the neighborhood named Thelma Elizabeth Murray, to pen lyrics to accompany the song's haunting melody.[72] The daughter of a Baptist minister, Murray was both a fine singer and a piano player steeped in the sacred music tradition, with a passion for popular song.[73] Like Thelonious, she wanted a "hit." Titled "I Need You So," the words could have easily referred to Monk's longing for Nellie during her year in Florida:

Since you went away I missed you,
Ev'ry hour I've wished to kiss you.
You are in my dreams, always
I need you so.

Life is incomplete without you
Don't know what it is about you
Makes my heart believe you care
I need you so!

You are my own
Still, I am all alone
Longing, waiting
I love you so darling

This is why I'll go on believing
You'll be standing by my side
Sooner than I realize
I need you so.[74]

Monk registered the composition with the U.S. Copyright Office on September 24, 1943, granting Murray full credit for her contribution. It was the first composition registered under Monk's name as the lead composer. The lyrics were never recorded, but the melody lingered on. A few months later, it was resurrected in a different key with minor alterations. He began calling it " 'Round Midnight."

8

"I'm Trying to See If It's a Hit"

(1943–1945)

By 1943, the modern jazz world's center of gravity had shifted slightly, from Harlem to West 52nd Street. Minton's was still a hot spot and some of the small clubs hung on, but the Savoy's closing sent the uptown hep cats downtown to establishments bearing names such as the Yacht Club, the Down Beat, Three Deuces, Kelly's Stable, and the Famous Door. Almost overnight, the complexion of "Swing Street" became darker (at least west of Fifth Avenue), as more and more African-Americans came downtown to listen or perform.[1]

Consequently, 52nd Street had become both a haven for cool, hip interracial communities and a racial battleground. Pianist Johnny Guarnieri reported one incident when a cop approached him and two other musicians on the sidewalk and ordered them to move along, adding "We don't want you niggers on the streets."[2] The police claimed they were merely cracking down on drugs and prostitution, but sex was often at the center of it all. White men in uniform—government-issued military and NYPD blue—harassed black men for carving with white women and fights broke out frequently. At one point, the chief of police was so fearful that 52nd Street would see a repeat of the Harlem Riot that the cops attempted to bar blacks from a popular bar called the White Rose.[3]

The Onyx Club was considered an interracial haven. Situated in the tiny, narrow basement of a brownstone, maybe sixty or seventy people could squeeze in, but not many more. One jazz writer warned that "all claustrophobes should avoid it scrupulously."[4] The Onyx regulars tended to be "musicians and singers on their time off," though tourists and celebrity seekers also found their way there.[5] It had a long illustrious history on the "strip," dating back to the late 1920s, but the venue moved, closed, and reopened several times before establishing a home at 57 West 52nd Street in 1942. Besides engaging Billie Holiday fairly regularly, the Onyx was known for presenting small swing combos, even some Dixieland groups. All that changed when Oscar Pettiford and Dizzy Gillespie persuaded the owner, Mike Westerman, to hire a small group they had just formed.

Gillespie had been champing at the bit to play some new music after several stifling weeks in Duke Ellington's trumpet section, and he wanted to put together a genuinely "modern" band that experimented with new directions in harmony and rhythm. Initially, they hired Don Byas and Budd Johnson on tenor and Max Roach on drums. Lester Young was also a frequent guest, and the band's biggest draw. They had hoped to hire Charlie Parker and Bud Powell, but Parker's union transfer from Kansas City had not come through and Powell[6] was still a minor. Cootie Williams, his employer and legal guardian, wouldn't let him out to play.[7] So when the Gillespie-Pettiford group opened in December of 1943, the piano stool became a musical chair, alternately filled by Billy Taylor and Thelonious Monk.[8]

History was being made at the Onyx Club that winter. Billy Taylor risked his regular job with Ben Webster to sit in with the Gillespie-Pettiford group: "I sat in a lot at the Onyx, during that December, and I kept getting back late to play my next set across the Street with Ben Webster, so Ben fired me. I got my job back a little later, but for a while there I was playing quite often at the Onyx, and Monk, and Monk was doing the same."[9] Monk had no job, but neither Dizzy nor Pettiford wanted to hire him as the band's regular pianist. They had a very specific concept of the piano's role in their band and Monk's style did not fit. Billy Taylor remembers Dizzy patiently teaching him specific voicings for chord changes he wanted.[10] Monk, on the other hand, would have voiced chords his own way. Less than a month into the gig, Pettiford and Gillespie found what they were looking for in Italian-born piano player Giacinto Figlia, who used the stage name George Wallington. Wallington, one of Monk's early admirers,[11] gave Dizzy the voicings he wanted, favored linear right-hand lines, and remained in the background. "We didn't need a strong piano player in there," explained Dizzy. "We needed a piano player to stay outta the way. . . . That's why George Wallington fitted in so well, because he stayed outta the way, and when he played a solo, he'd fill it up; sounded just like Bud."[12] Pettiford was less pleased, however. When Wallington missed a change and lost his place, Pettiford was often heard shouting or mumbling "White muthafucka, can't play shit!"[13]

Faced with the prospect of yet another winter without work, the fact that Monk was developing a reputation along 52nd Street as one of the most creative minds in jazz came as a small consolation. He hit the jam sessions, sat in where and when he could, wrote new compositions, and continued to drop in on his friends to use their pianos. Now that Billy Taylor had moved to New York permanently—in an apartment around the corner from Minton's—Monk had a new friend with a rented Steinway upright. Even before they started sharing the job at the Onyx, Taylor generously invited Monk to come by "any time" to play. Monk took "any time" quite literally. "I was at Minton's one night and Monk was there," Taylor remembered. "The place closed and we went around the corner to some greasy spoon to have breakfast. We were just sitting there lying to each other and talking a whole bunch of crap when Monk said that somebody told him I had a piano? I said yes. He asked me if it was a good one? I said yes. So he asked me if he could come over and practice on it some time. I said, 'Sure!' We finished breakfast and somehow we got separated. Either he ran into somebody or I did. Anyway, I went on home. I had just gotten into bed and was just about to fall asleep when somebody knocks on the door. I go to the door and it was Monk. He says, 'Can I practice now?' [laughs] . . . I said, 'Well-l-l-l. . . . It's cool with me but the people in this building work in the day. They don't start getting up until about 7:00 so that's really the earliest that I can hit it.' He says, 'Can I wait?' So I said okay and he came in. I sat in the chair and we talked. But I kept dozing off. I was just about asleep when he came and I just couldn't keep 'em open. All of a sudden I hear this little "Dee . . . dee . . . deet. . . ." I woke up and there's Monk playing!"[14]

It is too easy to caricature Monk as obsessive when it comes to the piano. Thelonious was also a practical joker with a sense of humor, and his antics were often deliberate and calculated to get a laugh or to throw someone off kilter. In Billy Taylor's view, "He was funny, man. He always had a comment about something. He was fun. I always enjoyed his company. This is one thing that really got to me from the beginning. He used to put me on from day one. And it was fun. It wasn't cruel, we used to laugh together."[15]

Monk also used to laugh quite a bit with Mary Lou Williams. Williams had been in New York off and on since 1942. By the fall of 1943, she had transferred her union membership to Local 802 and secured a regular job at Café Society downtown in Greenwich Village. Before the year was up, she moved into an apartment in Harlem on a tree-lined street called Hamilton Terrace. It became a den for musicians, artists, writers, and various political figures she met during her long engagement at Café Society.[16] Barney Josephson, an antiracist liberal, created Café Society as a kind of radical nightclub that encouraged interracial mingling. With the help of record producer and impresario John Hammond, Josephson booked a broad spectrum of jazz artists, most of whom were black. Some of the greatest piano players passed through Café Society in those days, including Meade Lux Lewis, Albert Ammons, Teddy Wilson, Hazel Scott, and Art Tatum.[17]

After hours, Williams would head uptown, check out Minton's Playhouse, and spend the early hours of the morning hanging out with other musicians, sharing ideas and shooting the breeze. Besides Monk and Bud Powell, visitors to Williams's apartment included young cats like Tadd Dameron and Kenny Dorham and established performers Lena Horne and Billy Strayhorn. Everyone who was anyone in the jazz world was "in and out of my place at all hours, and we'd really ball."[18] Thelonious and Bud usually dropped by around 4:00 a.m. Mary Lou would serve drinks, make breakfast, and everyone would "sit talk or someone would play a new composition they'd just written."[19] Monk loved to play Mary Lou's Baldwin upright, but was polite about asking. Mary Lou recalls one episode in particular:

> I had gotten very sleepy—had gotten up the previous morning to do a broadcast. Left the guys in the living room to enjoy themselves. It seems during the morning every body left. Johnnie Gary [he worked at the Café Society] being the last one to leave, left my front door open. . . . At the time I had twin beds in my bedroom.
>
> It must have been 11:30 AM when I awaken to go to the bathroom, to my surprise I saw someone stretched out on the other bed. I screamed and whoever it was ran to my bedroom door returning in disgust. I discovered it was

Monk. Immediately I asked how he got in. He said that the front door was opened & he had come to see me and discovered that I was asleep, decided not to play the piano. Thought he'd wait—ending up in the room. Well later we both laughed about this little incident.[20]

With so much free time in between jobs, Monk had begun to write more and really came to see himself as a composer. He trusted Mary Lou's ear and her frank opinions. "Usually when Monk composed a song," Williams noted, "he'd [play it] both night and day if you didn't stop him."[21] "I'm trying to see if it's a hit," Thelonious would tell her. "It'll stay with you if it's a hit."[22]

Mary Lou admired Monk for having his own original style, not just at the keyboard but in all aspects of his daily life. He didn't care what others thought about him. He wore whatever he wanted and always tried to stand out from the crowd. She credits Monk with launching the fashion craze that would come to define the bebop generation. Ever since she reunited with Thelonious in New York, she recalled seeing him "wearing a beret, with a small piano clip on it." Soon thereafter, he added a pair of custom-made shades to his ensemble. "I happened to run into Thelonious standing next door to the 802 Union building on Sixth Avenue, where I was going to pay my dues," recounted Williams. "He was looking at some heavy-framed sunglasses in a shop window, and said he was going to have a pair made similar to a pair of ladies' glasses he had seen and liked. He suggested a few improvements in the design, and I remember laughing at him. But he had them made in the Bronx, and several days later came to the house with his new glasses and, of course, a beret."[23]

Mary Lou expanded Monk's circle, introducing him to key players who would subsequently become sidemen and collaborators on his own musical journey. He grew quite fond of Art Blakey, the drummer she brought up from Pittsburgh. Diminutive, wiry, dark-skinned, friends jokingly called him a "pygmy," although the pain he experienced from color prejudice in his own community was no laughing matter. Blakey was only six months old when his mother died and his father walked out on him—by some accounts, because the child was too dark. Raised by his mother's first cousin in the bleak poverty of Pittsburgh, he began working in coal mines and steel mills at age 13. He fell in love with music and began playing piano in some of the local clubs, which offered a less dangerous alternative to the steel mills. He wasn't great on the instrument, which was a hard thing in a city that produced Earl "Fatha" Hines, Mary Lou Williams, Billy Strayhorn, Ahmad Jamal, Dodo Marmarosa, and Erroll Garner (who, according to one of Blakey's tall tales, is responsible for pushing him off the piano bench and onto the drum stool).

By the time Monk met Blakey, he had a wife and three kids back in Pittsburgh. Despite this, and the fact that the two men were separated in age only by two years and one day, Monk initially felt a little paternal toward Blakey—perhaps because he was orphaned so young. But more than anything, Monk loved Blakey because he was an extraordinarily exciting drummer who swung hard. His influences were Chick Webb, Big Sid Catlett, Sonny Greer (of Duke Ellington's orchestra), and a New Orleans drummer named Ray Bauduc—all of these drummers played in dance bands. Blakey came up, like most drummers of his generation, playing for dancers who wanted a steady beat, propulsion, breaks, and exciting moments of tension and release. Catlett took the young drummer under his wing and taught him to master the press roll, which would become Blakey's signature move. He played on and off with Fletcher Henderson until 1944, when he became the drummer in Billy Eckstine's astonishingly modern big band.[24] But before that, Monk made sure that New York heard Blakey and that the young drummer had every opportunity to develop his chops. Blakey, Bud, and Monk became a threesome on the jam session scene. "[Monk] would take Bud and I around and make the piano player get up and let Bud play, and some of the musicians would walk off, and he would say, 'Art, you play the drums.'"[25]

Early in 1944, Thelonious proposed a collaborative project with Mary Lou Williams and Bud Powell. Ideally, they would each contribute compositions that could be arranged for three pianos. Powell agreed to provide a "solo on 'Cherokee,'" whereas Williams had written an original piece titled "Bobo" and began to re-work "Scorpio," a movement in her "Zodiac Suite."[26] Monk contributed his own original piece, which he later titled "Criss Cross." (In Williams's collection, the lead sheet and the bass part, which are in her handwriting, are simply labeled "Monk.") It was an abstract piece, full of musical elements of which Monk was quite fond—chromaticism, rhythmic displacement, and dissonance. It would be another seven years before he recorded the piece with an ensemble—it was never arranged for three pianos. But once "Criss Cross" was released, critic/composer Gunther Schuller declared it "perhaps the Monk masterpiece of this period."[27]

The dream of collaboration never materialized. "Our rehearsal turned out to be the funniest," wrote Williams. "I use[d] to laugh at Bud & Monk. Monk reaching over Bud's shoulder to play his chords & Bud turning around giving Monk a mean look. This went on some time until I got sick of it—then I was never home."[28] Besides, Bud wasn't well. Still shy of his twentieth birthday, he had become a heavy drinker and, as far as Mary Lou was concerned, began showing signs of mental illness. He remained the pianist in Cootie Williams's band throughout this period, and Mary Lou found herself in the position of being Bud's third guardian, after his mother and Cootie. Between Powell's clowning and his unstable behavior, he never came through for the trio. Mary Lou lamented, "Bud was supposed to write one but I discovered he was a bit gone again."[29]

Meanwhile, Monk had no choice but to write. Powell had a regular job, and had made his first studio recordings with Cootie Williams in January of 1944. Mary Lou received a steady paycheck from Barney Josephson downtown. Monk had nothing, except for his songs. He knew that in order to get a hit, he had to do more than merely copyright his songs. Songs had to be sold, published, and played. Desperate for money, Monk began talking to Teddy McRae, a tenor player, arranger, and songwriter who had established ties to several publishing houses. Nearly ten years older than Thelonious, McRae had come out of the popular swing bands. His longest association was with Chick Webb's band, but he also played with Elmer Snowden, Stuff Smith, Lil Armstrong, recorded with Teddy Wilson and Henry "Red" Allen, and in 1941–42, was a member of Cab Calloway's band. When McRae met Monk in 1943, he had recently left Lionel Hampton to become staff arranger for Artie Shaw, through whom he established ties to major publishing firms, including Robbins Music and Regent Music Corporation. He discovered that writing and publishing music could be more lucrative than gigging. "I figured I write one good song a week, I can, you know, I can make good money, because I was getting nice advances."[30]

Thelonious shared some of his original compositions with McRae, hoping he might help him find a publisher. "The Pump" was a lively tune that represents an advanced example of rhythmic displacement.[31] He also showed McRae "You Need 'Na," a swinging number and an example of Monk's penchant for chromaticism. The title was inspired by Geraldine Smith's cousin, Charlie Beamon. A diminutive, gay black man with a rich baritone voice, Beamon struggled to make it as a singer. Monk befriended Beamon, as they were both hanging out at the Smiths' house. Beamon hired Monk to play a gig with him at a gay club in Manhattan. Before Beamon was to take the stage, a stand-up comedian offended the audience with some snide, insensitive remarks, prompting an angry brawl. Monk's niece Benetta Bines relates the story: "Thelonious grabbed him up and said 'Let's get outta here.' And Charlie is saying, 'But I haven't sung yet!'"[32] They got out intact, but it was one of those adventures Thelonious would never forget. When Monk offered to name a song after him, Charlie responded, "Well, you need not."[33]

Both compositions were entirely Monk's. McRae's only contribution was to submit the copyright registration forms and arrange for Regent Music Corporation to publish them, which he did in early February of 1944. In exchange for his services, McRae took co-composer's credits and listed himself as a claimant on both tunes.[34] McRae's actions were unscrupulous, but not uncommon. Bandleaders and arrangers, in particular, often laid claim to songs they had little or nothing to do with, or took co-composer's credit in exchange for publishing, recording, or adding a song to their repertoire. Monk had been around the business long enough to know this, but he also believed that colleagues and business partners ought to be forthright and honest in their dealings. Once Monk discovered what had happened, he severed ties with McRae and sought other routes to get his songs published and recorded. Monk was clever enough to make slight alterations to the melodies and record them a few years later under different titles: "You Need 'Na" became "Well, You Needn't," first recorded by Monk in 1947, and "The Pump" was reconstituted as "Little Rootie Tootie," retitled in honor of his first-born son. (Monk changed the melody by adding a triplet figure meant to replicate the sound of a train whistle.) McRae, on the other hand, never did anything with either song. Evidently, Artie Shaw's band wasn't interested in recording them, and if he tried to sell them to other bands there were no takers.

Monk decided to handle things on his own for the next song, a ditty based loosely on "I Got Rhythm" changes. He registered "Nameless" for a copyright as sole composer in April of 1944.[35] Although the piece was still untitled at the time, it was popular on 52nd Street as a closing theme song, and Monk was concerned about protecting his claim on the tune.[36] Music journalist and jazz producer Leonard Feather claims responsibility for giving the song the title by which it is now known. During a recording session with Dizzy Gillespie, Feather recounts, "Dizzy played a riff and said, 'Let's do this thing of Monk's.' We did it, and because we had heard it played regularly as a sign-off by the bop groups along 52nd Street, I suggested, 'Why don't we just call it "52nd Street Theme"?' "[37] Since Monk had already copyrighted the song under a different title, he earned no publishing royalties for the recording. He had also given the song an alternative name: "Bip Bop." Nearly two decades later, Thelonious tried to set the record straight during a performance/lecture at the New School for Social Research: "Well, I mean, doing a little detective work, myself, I happen to find, I found some script of a song of mine that I made up long ago that everybody used to use for signing off. All the clubs used to play it all the time. Dizzy recorded it on RCA Victor—'Fifty-second Street Theme.' The name I had at first was 'Bip Bop.' And I told the cats the name so probably that's where the name 'Bebop' came from."[38] Ironically, Thelonious never recorded "Bip Bop."

If Monk's dream of a hit eluded him in 1944, he did finally land a job—a great job. His employer happened to be one of the greatest tenor saxophonists since Adolphe Sax invented the instrument. And he was one of the few jazz musicians who had a hit. His name was Coleman Hawkins, and his hit consisted of two improvised choruses of "Body and Soul." It had been in his repertoire for years before he recorded it for RCA Victor in 1939, but to his surprise, the record sold like hotcakes—100,000 copies in the first six months, rare for an instrumental not intended for dancing. *Down Beat* anointed him "best tenor saxophonist" for that year, and from that moment on he could not play anywhere without a request for "Body and Soul."[39] Hawkins's success with "Body and Soul" was always a curiosity for Monk. "Thelonious Monk said to me," recalled Hawkins in a 1956 interview, "'You know, you never did explain to me,' he said, 'how did these people, these old folks and everybody, go for your record of 'Body and Soul'? 'Cause I've listened to the record, and I could understand if you played melody, 'cause that's what they like, those kind of people, that's what they like, they like melody. . . . They sure won't listen to anything else that's jazz!'"[40]

The call from Hawkins for Monk to join his band in March 1944 came as a pleasant surprise. Thelonious had long been an admirer of Hawkins for his musicianship, his openness to new ideas, and his ultracool style. Thirteen years Monk's elder, Hawkins came up in a very musical middle-class family in St. Joseph, Missouri. His mother, a schoolteacher and organist, began teaching her son piano from age five. By age seven, he'd taken up cello; two years later his mother gave him a tenor saxophone for his birthday. Hawkins attended the Industrial and Educational Institute in Topeka, Kansas, where he continued with cello and saxophone and advanced his knowledge of composition and harmony. Hawkins's overall intelligence earned him the nickname "Bean." A brilliant classical player on both instruments, he often found work playing in theater orchestras in Kansas City when classes were out. He toured with blues singer Mamie Smith in the early 1920s, and ended up playing with some of the great swing bands of the 1920s—from Wilbur Sweatman's band to the Fletcher Henderson Orchestra. In 1934, he left for Europe and kicked around there until 1939.[41]

Hawkins developed an appreciation for Monk's harmonic conception early on. In fact, the two musicians had much in common. (Hawkins not only employed tritone substitutions in his interpretation of "Body and Soul," but he had been experimenting with whole-tone harmony for at least a decade.[42]) Budd Johnson remembers how much Hawkins adored Monk's approach to harmony: "I don't know whether a lot of people realize that or not but he fell in love with Monk. 'Cause Hawk felt that's where it was. When he heard that playin', that piano playin' that stuff with the *changes*, he said, 'This is where it is.' . . . Hawk dug that. He said, 'Well, I want that man for a piano player.'"[43]

Hawkins sought out the freshest, most original musicians, and had little patience for those who would quibble over the difference between "modern" or "progressive," "swing" or "bebop." "I don't think about music as being new, or modern, or anything of the type," he mused. "Music doesn't go seasonable to me."[44] He dug the experiments being dubbed "bebop," and on nights off, he would catch the Gillespie-Pettiford group at the Onyx Club. Kenny Clarke was Hawkins's drummer at Kelly's Stable in 1943, and when Clarke was drafted in December, Hawkins hired Max Roach. In February of 1944, he put together a band of young lions for a recording session that would result in what critics have called Hawk's first "bebop" record: Dizzy Gillespie and Vic Coulsen on trumpet, Budd Johnson and Don Byas on tenor saxophones, and Clyde Hart on piano.[45]

Thelonious began sitting in with Hawkins as early as February, 1944.[46] By late March, Hawkins had put together his new sextet: Monk on piano, Don Byas on tenor, Little Benny Harris on trumpet, and Eddie Robinson on bass. The final addition to the band was drummer Denzil Best. Best had been working at the Three Deuces with Ben Webster, it was his first regular professional gig as a drummer since a bout with tuberculosis forced him to give up the trumpet. Although he was still finding his way on drums, Best had established a distinctive laid-back style that appealed to many musicians. When Best's job with Webster ended in mid-April, Hawkins promptly offered him the job, just in time for the band's first out-of-town gigs in Toronto and Boston.[47]

The band was set to open at the Club Top Hat in Toronto on April 19th. But at the last minute, Eddie Robinson decided he couldn't make the trip. Best proposed fellow Caribbean bassist Selwyn Warner to substitute for Robinson. Having worked with Hazel Scott and Hot Lips Page, Warner knew how to swing and had a great rapport with the drummer. The band spent two successful and restful weeks at the Club Top Hat. Conveniently situated a block from Sunnyside Beach and Amusement Park, the club was set in the middle of a popular vacation spot along Lake Ontario. Dubbed "Canada's Coney Island" and "the unemployed man's Riviera," Sunnyside Park catered to some 1.5 million beachgoers a year. It was also a center of Toronto nightlife, across the street from the open-air dance spot the Sea Breeze, and next door to the popular Palais Royale.[48] Although the weather was still a bit cool, Monk spent part of his time off strolling the boardwalk and checking out the scene. The remaining part of the day was spent rehearsing; Hawkins saw the Toronto gig as an opportunity to tighten up the band. Monk was designated the band's arranger, though Benny Harris and Denzil

Best also contributed new arrangements.[49] "We used to rehearse everyday," Hawkins recalled. "We played our arrangements. Everything we played was all written down, outside of the various solos themselves."[50] Selwyn Warner remembers playing matinees that attracted throngs of young people shouting for "Body and Soul." Hawkins would turn to the band and say, "'We'll just do a couple of choruses like the record and that'll quiet them down.'"[51]

Four or five days later, the group crossed back over the border and made their way to Boston, where they opened at the Hi-Hat Club at Columbus and Massachusetts Avenues. The Hi-Hat crowd was pretty hip; it was one of the few Boston clubs that catered to the so-called "beboppers," although no one in Hawk's band was using the phrase then. The band had great chemistry. Even during the one month bassist Selwyn Warner was with Hawkins, he observed that "the band got along with each other. Thelonious Monk was coming along in those days, getting his chops together. He was very bright, quiet and cool, but not eccentric."[52] On the stand, the band sizzled. Byas and Hawk produced a big sound, and the dynamics between them generated sparks. Monk's accompaniment encouraged flights of harmonic inventiveness on the part of all the horns. In some respects, the unison horn lines, exploring somewhat angular and complex melodies, mirrored what Gillespie, Byas, and Budd Johnson were doing at the Onyx Club. Denzil Best's drumming was understated, and laid down a strong, swinging foundation for the soloists. Hawkins was pleased.[53]

They returned to New York after a week, just in time for Selwyn Warner to give the bass job back to Eddie Robinson, and for the band to open at the Yacht Club on 52nd Street on Friday, April 28. Called "one of the largest crowds of show world luminaries," the artists who came out to greet Hawk included Duke Ellington, Count Basie, Ethel Waters, Teddy Wilson, Billy Eckstine, "and the entire cast of 'Carmen Jones.'"[54] The night was a great success, as many of these same musicians found their way on to the bandstand for a lively jam session.[55] Their engagement was extended as Monte Kay and Pete Kameran took over the space and renamed it the Down Beat Club, reopening to much fanfare on May 19.[56] Monte Kay was especially enthusiastic about Hawkins's new group, which he described as "one of the greatest combos of [Hawk's] career," despite its flaws. For him, Bean and Byas were the stars of the group, "playing those breathy, big-toned solos." He was less impressed with Monk and Harris, who, he felt, was "unable to execute what he was thinking." Nevertheless, Kay concluded that Hawkins delivered "some of the best jazz The Street ever heard."[57]

Hawkins soon found himself struggling to keep the band together. Benny Harris began drifting in and out after a few weeks, eventually leaving Hawk for Boyd Raeburn's band. Vic Coulsen, a favorite of Monk's who doubled on trumpet and cornet, sat in for Benny initially until it became his permanent gig.[58] Monk knew Vic from Minton's and Monroe's, and when jazz journalists decided Monk was print-worthy, he often gave Coulsen credit for new directions in the music. He especially loved Coulsen's phrasing, which he found more interesting than Dizzy's.[59] A native of Harlem, Coulsen was the son of an elevator operator from the Virgin Islands and a housewife from South Carolina who scraped whatever they could to give their only child music lessons.[60]

Although he appears on very few recordings, he was highly regarded among musicians in the early 1940s. Al Tinney compared him to Fats Navarro, while pianist Al Haig thought he sounded a bit like young Miles Davis—"He was a very low-key, understated type of trumpet player. He didn't have a lot of range, I don't think. His playing was rather impeccable in a way." Haig does remember Coulsen working very well with Hawkins, Monk, and Best: "he fitted that band very neatly."[61]

Stan Levey, a nineteen-year-old drummer fresh from Philly, was beside himself when he saw the band perform at the Down Beat Club. "You should have heard that rhythm section! Those guys could play! The bandstand would actually seem to levitate, these guys would cook so deeply into the beat!"[62] Thelonious attracted a number of young piano players who wanted to see what the fuss was about, but few were impressed. "One of the worst things I went through in those days was with Monk, when he was working in my group," recalled Hawkins. "I used to get it every night—'Why don't you get a piano player?' and 'What's that stuff he's playing?'"[63] When Randy Weston, an up-and-coming nineteen-year-old pianist from Brooklyn, first heard Monk at the Down Beat Club, he initially thought the same thing. He could not understand why Coleman Hawkins, his all-time musical hero, hired Monk. "He would play one note, and then another note. [I thought] I could play more piano than this." Weston was a member of the Army's Signal Corps stationed near New York City. Whenever he was granted leave or was off-duty, he made it a point to catch his hero and the strange piano player with the stranger name.[64] It turned out to be the beginning of a beautiful friendship.

Not every pianist walked away from the Down Beat Club that summer scratching his head. Herbie Nichols understood Monk right away, which is unsurprising given the similarities in their lives and careers. Two years younger than Thelonious, Nichols was born in San Juan Hill but his family made the trek to Harlem when he was seven. Their paths did not cross until they both were struggling musicians. Like Monk, Nichols was classically trained. He led a highly regarded combo in high school, and in 1937, soon after graduating, he joined the Royal Baron Orchestra. A year later Nichols became the house pianist at Monroe's and built a reputation as an excellent player with modern ideas, though he was perhaps better known for his column in the black-owned *New York Age*. He spent some time at Minton's, primarily as an observer, until he began a tour of duty in the South Pacific.[65] He returned to civilian life in August 1943, but struggled like many others to find work.

Nichols continued to write, freelancing for the short-lived *Music Dial*—the city's first black-owned jazz magazine. Monk's work with Hawk inspired Nichols to pen what proved to be the first critical notice of Monk. In a review of Oscar Pettiford's band across the street at the Onyx Club,[66] Nichols heaped lavish praise on tenor saxophonist Johnny Hartzfield, trumpeter Joe Guy, and drummer Joe Johnston. He wrote that they epitomized the best of the younger generation on their respective instruments. When it came to piano players, however, Nichols directed readers to the other side of 52nd Street. "Thelonious Monk is an oddity among piano players," he wrote. "This particular fellow is the author of the weirdest rhythmical melodies I've ever heard. They are very great too. (Don't ever praise Monk too much or he'll let you down.) But I will say that I'd rather hear him play a 'boston' [stride piano] than any other pianist. His sense of fitness is uncanny."[67]

Nichols had his reservations, however. He found Monk's use of dissonance too limiting, and compared Monk to Art Tatum and Teddy Wilson. "[W]hen Monk takes a solo, he seems to be partial to certain limited harmonies which prevent him from taking a place beside Art [Tatum] and Teddy [Wilson]. He seems to be in a vise as far as that goes and never shows any signs of being able to extricate himself."[68] Nevertheless, he concluded, "Monk, Joe Guy, Joe Johnston, Johnny Hartzfield and Pettiford would be a tough combination to beat."[69]

June 6, 1944, D-Day, is one of the most famous dates of the twentieth century. Most of America was glued to the radio. Thelonious, however, was making something other than war. The Smith family was gathered at Lincoln Hospital, where Geraldine gave birth to her fourth child, a little girl named Evelyn who would be known by her nickname "Weetee." With the house empty, Monk and Nellie enjoyed a moment of privacy and made love for the first time.[70] Thelonious was serious about Nellie and marriage probably crossed his mind, but money was an issue. Nellie and Geraldine made a little change as file clerks with the IRS,[71] and Monk was not sure how long Hawkins would keep him around.

The gig at the Down Beat Club officially ended August 17. Don Byas left the band and Hawkins took a week off. In the meantime, Clark Monroe hired Monk to fill in a week at his new establishment, the Spotlite. It was the only black-owned club on 52nd Street.[72] Monroe paired Monk with Max Roach and bassist W. O. Smith.[73] Smith, who had just been discharged from the service and was about to begin graduate school at NYU in the fall, was the same age as Thelonious. And yet, he felt like the odd man out in the trio, an old-fashioned swing bassist in a kind of bebop twilight zone. "It was a weird week. . . . I was a big-band bassist accustomed to a straight, driving, swinging four/four beat. It was unsettling to try to survive in the dislocation of the rhythmic patterns and the unsettling 'bombs' of the very experimental Max Roach. . . . This stuff was too new for me to digest."[74] Initially, he wasn't too crazy about Monk's piano playing, either, but it opened his eyes to new harmonic developments. "I thought that Thelonious was fumbling for the right notes pretty much as I would do on a piano trying to play an unfamiliar tune. I did notice some of his harmonic eccentricities, which later registered as brilliant."[75] The fact that neither Thelonious nor Max talked very much made the gig even less comfortable for Smith, though both musicians were always professional, punctual, and committed to the music. Nevertheless, it was a tough week for Smith: "I would not want the experience again."[76]

Before the week ended, Hawkins came calling again. He reconstituted the band as a quintet with the same rhythm section and Vic Coulsen, and they headed to Washington, D.C., for a two-week engagement at Club Bali, opening August 25. Club Bali had become one of the hottest jazz clubs around U Street, D.C.'s historic entertainment district known as "Black Broadway."[77]

During his stay in D.C., Thelonious hit some of the other clubs along U and T streets. At either the Crystal Caverns on 11th or Keyes restaurant on 7th and T, he heard a young tenor player named Charlie Rouse. He was still a kid, a native of D.C., just out of high school. Nap Turner witnessed Monk and Rouse's first meeting: "Just before the midnight show started, I was standing down there listening to the guys upstairs. So I happened to look over there and here's Thelonious Monk. It's night time and he got on sunglasses, you know, and a beret, and he looks weird. He's strange looking! So I'm watching him, you know what I mean? . . . While he was standing there, the band took an intermission, and Rouse comes down and Monk says to Rouse, 'What's your name?' Rouse told him his name. 'Charlie Rouse.' 'See, I'm going to put you in my bitches book. Give me your phone number.' Meaning that you are a bad, bad excellent player and I want your phone number."[78]

Monk took down Rouse's number, though it would be a while before he made that call. Not long after Monk left D.C., Rouse caught the ear of another musician—a valve trombone player turned bandleader named Billy Eckstine. Eckstine had just formed a big band chock full of all the "modern" players—Dizzy Gillespie, Charlie Parker, Budd Johnson, as well as pianist John Malachi who had played with Rouse in D. C. Eckstine needed a new tenor player, Malachi recommended Rouse, and the job was his.[79]

Hawkins returned to New York to open a week-long engagement at the Apollo on September 8. The quintet played opposite clarinetist Tommy Reynolds' big band, though Hawkins was billed as the featured artist.[80] After their set, Hawkins joined Reynolds's band for a jam session featuring Basie's "One O'Clock Jump." Critic Leonard Feather was on hand to review the show for *Metronome*, and he mentioned Monk briefly but favorably: "Thelonious Monk's piano always covers a fertile harmonic ground."[81] It would be one of the few positive reviews he'd give the pianist; Feather, a powerful voice in the jazz industry as critic, producer, promoter, and sometimes composer and arranger, would eventually become one of Monk's most vociferous detractors.

On October 10, Monk celebrated his twenty-seventh birthday doing what he loved to do best—working. (Hawkins's group had begun a three-and-a-half-month engagement at the Down Beat Club.[82]) Nine days later, Hawkins had Monk come down to Empire Studios to do a record date for the Joe Davis label. The session did not include Coulsen, just Hawkins and the band's rhythm section. In less than two hours, the quartet recorded eleven and a half minutes of quality music spread over two 78s.[83] Every tune was done in a single take. Monk, Best, and Robinson were paid scale for the date—about $30 each—while Hawkins earned a whopping $400, though no royalties were promised.[84] Given the three-minute format of 78s, Monk's presence is necessarily limited. On the two ballad selections, "Recollections" and "Drifting on a Reed," Monk does not solo, but he launches each song with concise and innovative introductions. We hear more of Thelonious on the two jump tunes, "On the Bean," based on the chord changes of "Whispering," and "Flying Hawk." His economical solos are full of Monkisms: whole-tone scales, dissonant clusters, and quotes from his own compositions.[85]

While Monk was playing and recording Hawk's music, his pal Bud Powell was playing and recording *Monk's* music in Cootie Williams's Orchestra. Two months before Monk went into the studio, Williams recorded a revised version of "I Need You So," now called " 'Round Midnight."[86] By his own account, Bud Powell had to persuade Williams to add the song to his repertoire: "When I was playing with Cootie Williams in 1944, I did most of the arrangements for the band 'cause I was the only one who could write music. I was working a lot with Thelonious then and I wanted Cootie to put 'Midnight' in the repertoire. He didn't want to, but he finally agreed on the condition that he himself would write a second part for the piece. At the time, you see, it had only the main theme."[87] Later he told his friend and patron Francis Paudras that he threatened to leave if Williams refused to put " 'Round Midnight" in the program.[88]

Powell's claim that the song lacked a bridge is actually incorrect. The original lead sheet of "I Need You So" had it. What Williams did, however, was to write a third section—an eight-bar interlude. It was played once, and never played again. Yet with that interlude, he felt justified taking co-composer's credit for the song. Williams's version of what happened differs substantially from Powell's. Williams insists that he dealt directly with Monk, who "was always around the band." It was Monk who introduced the song to Williams: "He wanted me to listen to it. And I listened to it. And I says, 'Okay, give it here. I'll put the verse to it.'" Williams liked the song, contributed "the verse," and recorded it, correctly adding, "Nobody ever did play the verse, or interlude, or whatever they call it. Nobody but me."[89]

Through Advanced Music Corporation, Williams filed for copyright on November 27, 1944, three months after the song was first recorded, with a third name on the certificate of registration in addition to Williams and Monk: lyricist Bernie Hanighen.[90] Originally from Omaha, Nebraska, Hanighen had been on the scene for a while, writing lyrics for Broadway musicals. Hanighen's lyrics typically pined on about love and longing, but in this case the dominant theme is longing and loss:

> It begins to tell 'round midnight
> 'Round midnight
> I do pretty well 'til after sundown
> Suppertime I'm feeling sad
> But it really gets bad 'round midnight
>
> Memories always start 'round midnight
> 'Round midnight
> Haven't got the heart to stand those memories
> When my heart is still with you
> And old midnight knows it too. . . .

It closes on a note of hope, the possibility of return.

Thelonious had nothing to do with these lyrics, and it's quite possible that neither he nor Thelma Murray was aware of them until they were copyrighted. It became a mainstay of Williams's repertoire, but he did not employ a vocalist, and when he did, as in the case of Ella Fitzgerald, he still played the instrumental version.[91] Moreover, Hanighen and Williams reregistered the lyric version of the song five months later under the title "Grand Finale," perhaps as a way of distinguishing the instrumental from the vocal, but it was never recorded under that title during Monk's career, nor was Hanighen's name ever removed from the original copyright. Consequently, Hanighen and his estate receive a third of the royalties from every version of " 'Round Midnight" produced. And in turn, the original composer and his estate receive only a third of the royalties—to this very day.[92]

Cootie's version of " 'Round Midnight" was released in early 1945 with "Somebody's Gotta Go," a humorous blues sung by Eddie "Cleanhead" Vinson, on the A side. "Somebody's Gotta Go" was intended as a commercial hit, though the B side drew surprising attention. The *Chicago Tribune* singled out " 'Round Midnight" as "a tour de force for Cootie, with a slow moody trumpet talking to itself. The Cootie is doing some splendid work."[93] For Monk, it was deeply ironic. On one hand, it looked as if Monk might get a hit after all. On the other, he felt completely disconnected from the composition. His protégé was at the piano, he now had to share composer's credit with two guys who contributed virtually nothing to the basic song, and it just didn't sound like Monk. To top it all off, when the sides he recorded with Hawkins were finally released in 1945, they received virtually no critical notice. Joe Davis took out a couple of ads in the black press,[94] but Hawk's overall output was so substantial that these recordings were lost in the pile.

Everywhere Monk turned, he heard other artists playing his tunes. In December 1944, Coleman Hawkins participated in a recording session led by Mary Lou Williams. They recorded an arrangement of "Lady Be Good." Monk claimed to have written the first sixteen bars of the melody; he would record them a decade later as "Hackensack."[95] Hawkins, for his part, claimed the melody as *his* own, recording it again in February of 1945 as "Rifftide."[96] Monk and Mary Lou were close and borrowed from each other on occasion, and it was customary for bandleaders to poach songs by their sidemen. While Monk did his own share of poaching, the circulation of his tunes without credit became a source of frustration.

Among musicians, however, Monk was becoming an iconic figure despite his inability to record his own music. While Hawkins and Williams were in the studio working through Monk's riff on "Lady Be Good," the men and women of the armed forces heard a hot new song by the Eddie South trio called "Mad Monk."[97] A swinging, medium-tempo, riff-based tune, it was the sort of thing folks could dance to. The A-section was based on the changes for "I Got Rhythm" and the bridge was straight from "Honeysuckle Rose." The composer, also the group's pianist, was Billy Taylor. He wrote it in tribute to Thelonious, in part because he was among the few in New York to really embrace Taylor when he first arrived. Moreover, Monk's ideas influenced and inspired Taylor to create a piece that drew on Monk's compositional ideas. "It was really the first bebop tune that I tried to write," Taylor explained. "The idea was based on [Monk's] '52nd Street Theme' . . . but I was thinking about Art Tatum, so it didn't sound like bebop. I realized that one of the devices Monk used in that song was a riff.

At the turnaround and the last couple of bars, he played what I thought was a bebop phrase. And that's what I tried to do. I tried to do my version of what Monk was trying to do."[98] In plain English, he combined swing, bebop, and stride. In that sense, it was highly appropriate as a tribute to Monk: You couldn't pin it down, but everyone liked it. In March of 1945, Taylor recorded the song with his own trio for Savoy.[99] When Thelonious heard it he was impressed. He commented to Taylor that he especially liked the idea of someone playing stride piano and bebop at the same time.[100]

The Down Beat Club engagement ended in late December when Billy Berg, a Los Angeles promoter who had recently opened a jazz club, booked Hawkins for a fairly long stay. The engagement was widely publicized, with "Delonious Monk" listed as the pianist, but by the time Berg nailed down the opening date for February 1945, Monk chose to stay behind. The versatile "Sir" Charles Thompson went in his place.[101] It was a regrettable decision. Hawk's new band recorded six sides for the Moe Asch label just before leaving for the West Coast. They played to a crowded room at Billy Berg's, recorded for Capitol Records, and played a February 12th concert organized by jazz impresario Norman Granz that Moe Asch recorded and released as *Jazz at the Philharmonic, Vol. 1*. The disc sold over 150,000 copies in the first couple of years. The band even made a cameo appearance in a movie called *The Crimson Canary* featuring Noah Berry, Jr.[102]

Talk about missed opportunities! Of course, Monk could not have anticipated any of this. All he knew was that California was at the other end of the world, far from the musical center of the universe, far from potential gigs, and far from Nellie and his aging mother. Besides, he had just spent the last eight months working for the great Coleman Hawkins. Who wouldn't hire him?

9

"Dizzy and Bird Did Nothing for Me Musically"

(1945–1947)

Thelonious found himself back in familiar territory—a struggling musician cobbling together gigs here and there. Monte Kay helped out a little, inviting Monk to participate in a series of Sunday afternoon jam sessions he sponsored at Lincoln Square. Monk performed in the first event, held January 7, 1945. He was in good company. The first band was led by Herbie Fields and included such luminaries as Buck Clayton, Don Byas, Charlie Shavers, clarinetist Buster Bailey, as well as familiar faces: Harold "Doc" West, Charlie Parker, and Baby Laurence on taps. Monk alternated with Joe Albany on piano.[1] The sessions, which were really intended for dancers, began around 4:00 in the afternoon and didn't end until 2:00 a.m. But the serious musicians and jazz fans came to listen. The Lincoln Square Sunday jam sessions left a lasting impact on Jackie McLean, then just a teenager developing his skills on the alto saxophone. "People could dance in the back if they wanted to, but most people use to take their folding chairs and move them up near the front to be near the music. That's what they were there for, not for dancing."[2]

Monk was virtually jobless until April, when Elbert "Skippy" Williams asked him to join his much-touted twenty-three-piece orchestra.[3] An underrated tenor player out of Cleveland, Williams had come up through the ranks of the big bands. Just a year older than Thelonious, he'd already served time with Eddie Cole's band in Chicago, Count Basie, Edgar Hayes, Earl Bostic, Lucky Millinder, and, most famously, Duke Ellington.[4]

Williams's band struggled to secure regular work. Meanwhile, as Thelonious scraped money together for subway fare and bummed cigarettes from friends, Dizzy and Charlie "Yardbird" Parker had become the newest sensations. "Bebop" was the word on the street, and Bird and Diz were marketed as the world's greatest purveyors of the new music. In March, they brought a quintet to the Three Deuces that included Al Haig on piano, Curley Russell on bass, and Max Roach on drums. Don Byas occasionally sat in, as well. That spring, the Three Deuces was the hottest jazz spot in New York. On Wednesday, May 16, Monte Kay and Mal Braveman hosted the first of another series of concerts, this time at Town Hall, showcasing "Modern Music." Under the auspices of the "New Jazz Foundation," the promoters headlined Gillespie, *Esquire Magazine*'s

"Top New Trumpet Star of 1945," with Charlie Parker. Leonard Feather emceed and added his own trio to the line-up in order to accompany several guest artists, including Hot Lips Page, singer Dinah Washington, violinist Stuff Smith, and Skippy Williams. Several featured guests did not show up, much to the consternation of the audience, and the Gillespie-Parker Quintet seized the spotlight.[5]

Monk was not invited to participate in this historic concert, despite the fact that his new boss was among those on stage, nor was he asked to play in the next (and last) "New Jazz Foundation" event on June 22. " 'Round Midnight" was one of the band's feature pieces, along with a tune titled "Dizzy Atmosphere," which Monk swore was derived from his ideas. To add insult to injury, Dizzy began sporting a beret with a little piano clip to accompany his heavy horn-rimmed glasses! Watching Bird and Diz catapult to fame—playing some of Monk's music—deeply wounded Thelonious. Nearly two decades later, in an interview with the French *Jazz Magazine*, he was still upset about his treatment in those days vis-à-vis Bird and Dizzy:

> I feel like I have contributed more to modern jazz than all of the other musicians combined. That's why I don't like to always hear: "Gillespie and Parker brought the revolution to Jazz," when I know most of the ideas came from me. Dizzy and Bird did nothing for me musically, they didn't teach me anything. In fact, they were the ones who came to me with questions, but they got all the credit. They're supposed to be the founders of modern jazz when most of the time they only interpreted my ideas. . . . Most musicians know this, which is why they all adopted "52nd Street Theme." It's my music: " 'Round About Midnight," "Dizzy Atmosphere." . . . It's my feeling that through playing with me, by copying my harmonies, by asking me for advice, by asking me how to get the best sound, how to write good arrangements, and relying on me to correct their music, they composed themes that came directly from me. . . . Meanwhile, I wasn't even able to find a gig. Sometimes I couldn't even enter Birdland. Do you realize what it's like to a musician to hear his own compositions and not to be even able to get inside [a club]?[6]

In all fairness, Charlie Parker did give credit to Monk in virtually every interview he conducted, calling him a true "original."[7] And the "New Jazz Foundation" concerts, despite their unequivocal historical value in legitimizing the music, were not all that well attended. But the damage was done. Skippy Williams's band managed to draw a little attention, enough to secure an engagement at the Down Beat Club playing Monday and Tuesday nights.[8] For the entire month of August, Monk was back in familiar settings. But two nights a week wasn't enough to pay the bills. Fortuitously, Coleman Hawkins returned from California in the spring and was hired to lead a quartet at the Down Beat Club. Although the club announced as early as June that he'd be appearing "nitely" opposite Billie Holiday, he apparently did not open until August 30.[9] Hawkins offered Monk the piano chair and the two were reunited with drummer Denzil Best. At the very last minute, Hawkins hired a twenty-six-year-old bass player from Detroit named Al McKibbon. His résumé included a stint with Lucky Millinder's Orchestra and Tab Smith's band, but he quit because he wasn't crazy about touring the South. When he met Hawkins, he was so broke that he had to borrow a bass to make the gig.[10]

The war officially ended on September 2, 1945. A celebratory mood pervaded the country, including The Street, where the hipsters were usually too cool to care. War-weary New Yorkers were ready to put the past behind them and embrace the promise of peace, prosperity, and productivity. It was the dawn of a new era, the "American Century," when the U.S. emerged as the leading global power. Technology became the country's obsession—the possibilities of space exploration, jet travel, the availability of cheap televisions and high-fidelity recordings. Speed was the order of the day. It was also a period of uncertainty. The atomic age had arrived, revealing an ominous side with the destruction of Hiroshima and Nagasaki, but also promising new sources of power (energy and military).

Jazz was the perfect accompaniment to the new atomic age. It had become faster and more dissonant, without losing its sense of joy and humor. Audiences were drawn to Bird's velocity and his joyous, spring-like melodies. From Hawk, Monk, and company, came hip harmonies, danceable tempos, and nostalgic references to foot-stomping swing. (Indeed, in late September 1945, Joe Davis released "Drifting on a Reed" and "Flying Hawk," selling a respectable 9,000 discs, making it the third best-selling record in his catalogue.[11]) The popularity of the clubs exploded. For anyone looking to celebrate the return of the GIs, to laugh after so many years of killing and dying, here was exuberant fun. Monk pulled listeners in because he made them laugh and wonder if he was for real. Miles Davis would rush over to the Down Beat Club to catch Hawkins and Monk while on his break from playing with Bird. "He used to come in with his horn," McKibbon recalled, "and he'd sit up on the bandstand and he'd listen to us play, watch what Monk was doing. And sometimes Monk would hit something strange . . . and he'd [Miles Davis] figure it out on his horn, but he'd never play. He would just sit and listen and laugh to himself."[12]

In Miles's version of the story, he *did* play, and Monk mentored him. "I used to ask Monk, every fucking night, to play ' 'Round About Midnight.' I'd say, 'How'd I play it?', because he wrote it, right? And he'd said, 'You didn't play it right.' Next night. 'Did I play it any better?' 'A little bit better, but that ain't the way it goes.' And one night I asked him, 'Yeah, you can play it.' . . . I [finally] got the sound. . . . It took me a long time to be able to play that song."[13] Miles had great admiration for Monk as a teacher and elder (nine years separated them), and he found his compositions brilliant and beautifully balanced. As someone who spent his days at Juilliard studying the great composers of the Western tradition, Miles believed " 'Round Midnight" was as challenging as anything Ravel, Schoenberg, or Bach had to offer. In order to play it correctly, Miles explained many years later, "You got to get all the harmonics and everything together. You have to hear the song and play it, and improvise so he [Monk] could hear the melody. . . . You have to play it so you can hear the chord changes and also hear the top. It's one of those things that you had to hear. You had to learn it and forget it."[14] Hanging out with guys like Monk ultimately convinced Miles to drop out of Juilliard. "Monk taught me more than anyone on the street when I was down there. [He's] the one who really showed me everything." He taught by demonstration rather than explanation. He would say very little, and when he did explain something he may say it once. Otherwise, you had to pay strict attention and see everything he was doing if you wanted to learn. "If you're serious you could learn from him, but if you're bullshitting you wouldn't see nothing."[15]

In November, Clark Monroe hired Hawkins's band to replace Bird's group, but the opening was delayed because police temporarily suspended the Spotlite's cabaret license. The Spotlite was one of four clubs—the others were the Down Beat, Three Deuces, and the Onyx Club—that police raided on the suspicion of drug trafficking. Dozens of people were picked up and for a couple of weeks the clubs could not serve liquor or host live music.[16] By the time the Spotlite reopened and Hawkins's band got back to work, they were ready to leave town. Norman Granz invited Hawk back to California, this time for a three-week national tour that would open in Los Angeles on November 26 and terminate in Victoria, British Columbia.[17] This time, Monk did not hesitate; he was ready for California.

On the way, they participated in an all-star concert at the Philadelphia Academy of Music. The reviewer for *Metronome* complained, "The trio was hampered not a little by pianist Thelonious Monk."[18] From there, they played a bar in Washington, D.C. The owner's explicit racism made the gig less than comfortable for the group, although Monk—always the practical joker—found ways to turn the tension into levity. As Al McKibbon remembered it, "We played in a bar where the owner was prejudiced as hell, man. He just hated Blacks, you know. He had a big easychair behind the bar that was his private chair, he sat in it. Every intermission, Monk would go and sit in that chair. [laughter] It'd break me up. He'd just sit there and smile. And steam would be coming out of the guy's ears."[19] They could laugh at the absurdity of the situation, yet it was a sign of the times. After having battled Nazis in Europe, black soldiers were returning home to the same old Jim Crow. The homefront of the Double Victory campaign had yet to be won. Even in the nation's capital, some restaurants would not serve African-Americans, hotels denied them rooms, and the police constantly harassed them. In some instances, black men in uniform were targets of hate crimes because they refused to "stay in their place." And to further exacerbate racial tensions, returning veterans and postwar demobilization meant significant shortages of jobs and housing. African-Americans suffered more than most because they were typically the "first fired, last hired."

Norman Granz empathized with the plight of black people, and viewed his Jazz at the Philharmonic series as a blow against racial prejudice. His initial vision was to take jazz out of the nightclubs and into the concert hall. He wanted to give Negro music pride of place, and in the process, convince concertgoers that the brown men and women on stage were artists—American artists. He also believed that this music could bring people together across the color line. He launched his series in the early part of 1944 with a number of concerts held at Music Town, an auditorium on the predominantly black Westside of Los Angeles. But the real catalyst for the series was a benefit concert he organized on July 2, 1944, on behalf of a group of Mexican-American teens wrongfully arrested after the "Sleepy Lagoon" murder case. Seventeen kids were rounded up after a young gang member had been found dead. Despite little or no evidence, they were convicted of second-degree murder. The case became a *cause célèbre* attracting several notable figures, including Orson Welles, Rita Hayworth, and Anthony Quinn. The concert was a huge success, drawing an enthusiastic and racially mixed crowd of more than 2,000. It was the power of jazz at work, and Granz was a true believer. He was only twenty-six years old, one year younger than Thelonious.[20]

The band opened in Los Angeles at Philharmonic Hall to a crowd of 2,600. It was the largest audience Thelonious had ever had to face, and perhaps the most enthusiastic. Hawkins's group shared the stage with pianist Meade Lux Lewis, Helen Humes, and a band fronted by tenor player Corky Corcoran.[21] Lucky Thompson was added to the group in order to re-create the dueling tenor style they had when Don Byas was in the band. As was Granz's custom, the concert culminated in a huge jam session, featuring Hawkins and combining members of both bands, including guitarist Barney Kessel, Willie Smith (alto), Vido Musso (tenor), and former Hawkins sideman Howard McGhee.[22]

The opening concert proved to be the pinnacle of the entire tour. Philo Records sponsored the tour, though their budget was limited. Philo provided a rickety bus that carried them to San Diego for a performance, but could not make it all the way up the coast to Portland, Oregon. They had to travel the last two legs of the trip by train. For Granz, who cancelled the Southern leg of the tour because of segregation, the trip became a lesson in the realities of West Coast Jim Crow. When the band arrived in Portland, fatigued and famished, they were refused service at the first restaurant they entered.[23] Although most hotels were for whites only, a few catered to black guests. Given Granz's meager budget, only the headliners like Hawk could afford a hotel anyway. So the band members did what most black jazz musicians have always done: they turned to local ministers and found lodging in private homes in the black community.[24]

The group was booked to do two shows at Portland's Mayfair Theater on a Tuesday, December 4—a matinee at 4:15 and an 8:30 show. Granz didn't fill the Mayfair, but the concert drew a pretty good crowd for a Tuesday evening, thanks to all the advance publicity he put out. Ads appeared in all the local papers, including one in the black-owned *People's Observer* that promised an "All Colored All Star 'Jazz Symphony'" that could "play everything from Brahms to Boogie!"[25] Hawkins and Eldridge were clearly the headliners, but the other artists were given equal prominence. Although the critic for the Portland *Oregonian* mistook the ad to mean that they *would* play "Brahms to Boogie," he nevertheless, found the performances satisfying, singling out Hawkins and Thompson for special praise ("Coleman Hawkins and Lucky Thompson conked them with their saxes.")[26]

The critic for the *Oregonian* never mentioned Thelonious or even made a passing reference to the pianist. But Monk did not go over well with much of the audience. According to one report, Roy Eldridge grimaced every time Monk played chords and the crowd chuckled. However, among the serious musicians who made a pilgrimage from all over the Pacific Northwest to see this concert, Monk became one of the main attractions, second only to Hawk. Eighteen-year-old Floyd Standifer, a young trumpet phenom in the making, remembers sitting in the audience completely taken with Monk: "Here was this odd-looking guy who was making this room laugh. I learned about Monk from a magazine [probably *Music Dial*]. I hitchhiked in from Gresham, where I was going to school and playing in a band. It took me a while to realize that what I first thought were mistakes and missing notes were right according to what he was trying to do. He was getting a sound and energy out of the piano that couldn't be heard any other way."[27]

The next evening, the group found themselves in more relaxed surroundings. Granz booked the band for a week-long gig at the Dude Ranch, a black-owned club on North Broadway. Located in the heart of Portland's black business and entertainment district, the Dude Ranch possessed a nice-sized dance floor, an elevated bandstand surrounded by rows of tables, and a balcony where gourmet dinners were served. The décor played on the "wild, wild west" theme, with oversized murals of black cowboys and waitresses dressed to look like Dale Evans in cowgirl get-ups. An appreciative audience filled every seat.[28]

Bill McClendon, jazz lover and editor of the Portland *People's Observer*, wrote kindly about the performance at the Dude Ranch and the larger significance of the musicians' presence in Portland. While he praised the Mayfair concert, which "knocked enthusiastic listeners to their benders," he described something magical at the Dude Ranch. That night Hawkins's band, Meade Lux Lewis, and Helen Humes "put on one of the most spectacular jam sessions that has been witnessed in this part of the country. Never before in the history of the Northwest has there been as much jazz music played per square minute by any group." He took time to heap praise upon each and every artist, including Monk, whom he described as a "fine pianist with a lot of ultra-modern ideas . . . and a lightning-like right hand."[29] But the most startling and telling commentary came not from McClendon but from pianist Meade Lux Lewis. He stood up in the club in the middle of his set and delivered a speech about the racism the band experienced in Portland: "Many people here are elated over our music, but the musicians and the guys who understand what we can do know that we have not played like ourselves throughout. When we first arrived in Portland, some of our troupe members were refused service in a restaurant because they were Negroes. I don't have to tell you the story about hotel accommodations. I hope . . . It didn't matter that our combination was an aggregation of some of the finest exponents of American jazz. Neither was there any consideration to be shown us because we performed for the utter enjoyment of Portlanders."[30] For Lewis, who spoke for the entire traveling troupe, the welcome they received from the black community at the Dude Ranch changed the whole tenor of their experience. "In the first two performances here," he concluded "we were working with a 'what the hell' attitude. Tonight the atmosphere is entirely different and I am sure you see what I mean."[31]

Thelonious certainly knew what Lewis was talking about. He thrived on this sort of hospitality, especially so far from home. On the last night of their run at the Dude Ranch, he met a young black couple named Ed and Bernice Slaughter. They reminded Monk a little of Sonny and Geraldine back home—they were hip, smart, easy to talk to, and were parents of a little boy. Ed Slaughter owned the Savoy Billiard Parlor on Williams, and was famous around these parts for having the hippest juke box in town.[32] He ordered his records through mail order companies and kept abreast of the New York jazz scene. The Slaughters were among the few who had heard about Monk before he arrived.

After the last of the customers filed out of the club, the Slaughters stayed behind with journalist Bill McClendon and Thelonious. "We sat there all night," Bernice Slaughter remembered. "They closed at 2:30, and afterwards Monk sat there and played for us. Just me and my husband and McClendon were there. And he played two or three hours. After that, he walked home with us and we sat around and talked, played some records."[33] They spoke of many topics. "Well, he was a multi-dimensional man. He was into talking about literature and politics. That's one reason he and my husband got along so well. They both liked to read and talk about what they're reading and enjoy it. . . . Monk and my husband had great rapport. The jokes and everything. They really got along well."[34]

Monk had to catch a train early in the morning, so the Slaughters stayed up with him until he left for the train station at the crack of dawn. About an hour later, there was a knock on the door: "There was Monk standing there with a bag of groceries for breakfast and three hats on his head! And a big grin. We were surprised. We opened the door and here he was with eggs and bacon. So I fixed him breakfast." Monk stayed a little while longer, eating and laughing with his adopted West Coast family, but he had to get to Seattle to meet the rest of the band to make the final gig in Victoria, Canada. The only way to get there on time would be by plane, so Ed Slaughter drove Thelonious to the airport. It was quite a spectacle—two black men, one with three hats stacked on his head, trying to purchase an airline ticket to Seattle in 1945. His son, Ed Slaughter, Jr., remembers:

> The only way my dad could get him on the plane is that he told the airline reservationist that he was a scientist and he had to go to Seattle for a meeting with the government [laughter]. The airport was very small in those days. So they paged him, "Thelonious Sphere Monk," and he's got these hats on his head and he's got his suitcase with a belt wrapped around his suitcase and a cardboard box with rope on it. When he walked across the room to board, everybody in the airport stopped what they were doing and watched him.[35]

Monk made it to Victoria, but the concert was a complete bust. The turnout was so small that Granz canceled the rest of the tour and swallowed the loss. As a parting gift, he gave each musician a first-class train ticket to their destination of choice.[36] Monk chose home.

• • •

Monk arrived home in time to spend the holidays with his family, to reunite with Nellie, and to return to work at the Spotlite with Coleman Hawkins's quartet. They played opposite trumpeter Henry "Red" Allen. A veteran of the older swing bands, Allen was linked to the burgeoning "traditionalist" movement calling for jazz musicians to reject bebop and return to their New Orleans and Chicago swing roots. Between Allen and Hawkins, Spotlite patrons were treated to the old and the new. When Allen moved to the Onyx in late January, Clark Monroe decided to go all-modern, hiring Dizzy Gillespie's sextet to fill his spot.[37]

According to Gillespie, Monroe offered him sixteen weeks—the first eight with the sextet and the second eight with a reconstructed big band. He was, after all, one of the hottest commodities in jazz at the moment. Yet Diz had had a dismal "Hepsations" big band tour of the South in 1945, thanks to Jim Crow, disorganization, and music deemed undanceable by Southern patrons. He had followed it with a booking in Los Angeles in the winter. Billy Berg hired a sextet led by Dizzy and Charlie Parker for an eight-week stint beginning on December 10.[38] It was supposed to be a kind of introduction of the 52nd Street modernists, the bebop invasion of the West Coast. The popular myth is that the music was too far out for West Coast audiences and that patrons stopped coming to the club (c.f. Clint Eastwood's *Bird*). In fact, Billy Berg's was packed every night. And it wasn't as if L.A. jazz fans were completely unfamiliar with the new music—Hawkins's group with Monk had played the L.A. Philharmonic two weeks earlier to an enthusiastic crowd. What is true is that Berg wanted more commercial music, and Dizzy and Bird tried to satisfy his demands by adding a few vocal numbers to their repertoire, but they could only compromise so much. The biggest setback for the tour, however, had nothing to do with music. Toward the end of their engagement, Parker experienced a severe mental breakdown and ended up at Camarillo State Hospital for an extended stay.[39]

Before Dizzy left California, however, he replaced Bird with Lucky Thompson (fresh from his Portland stint with Monk and Hawkins), and made a few records for Ross Russell's independent Dial label on February 7, 1946. One of the tracks was Monk's "'Round Midnight," to which he added his own eight-bar introduction and a nine-bar cadence or ending. Dizzy had originally written the introduction as the cadence to "I Can't Get Started," but it worked even better as an opening to "'Round Midnight." Both additions were so popular that Monk himself made them integral to the entire composition in his own performances.[40] The Dial version marked the second studio recording of Monk's work, but Thelonious himself had yet to record any of his own tunes.

Monk did receive publishing royalties to which he was entitled: about two cents per record to be split with Cootie Williams and Bernie Hanighen. To add insult to injury, a couple of weeks after Dizzy's band opened at the Spotlite, Leonard Feather arranged a recording session for Coleman Hawkins and did not include Monk. Billed as "Coleman Hawkins' 52nd Street All-Stars," Feather chose Jimmy Jones to play piano.[41]

Monk was grateful to have a steady job, but being passed over for another recording session was a hard pill to swallow. An even harder pill was witnessing the sensational press Dizzy received once his band took residence at the Spotlite. As soon as the sextet expanded into seventeen pieces, the big band became the headliner, while Hawkins's band was slowly pushed to the margin. While Hawk wasn't jealous of the attention Gillespie was getting, he did openly express his dislike for the big band, which he found a bit ragged and disorganized. "Dizzy sounded great with just six men," he told a reporter from *Metronome* magazine. "Now he has a big band that plays the right kind of music but sloppily."[42] And he wasn't wrong. As the band's arranger and organizer, Walter "Gil" Fuller, explained, "they wanted a big band in there, and they gave us a week or a week and a half to get it together. . . . Dizzy can't remember what happened. He didn't even know what the music was gonna sound like and never showed up for rehearsals until Friday, the opening day."[43]

When the decision was made to expand the sextet, there was only a week's time to form a band. There were no arrangements, and no budget to pay an arranger to put together some music. Gil Fuller turned to Billy Eckstine, hat in hand. The Eckstine band had broken up and Fuller knew that their arrangements were among the best of modern big band music. Eckstine generously shared what he had, which included compositions by Tadd Dameron, and both Fuller and Gillespie contributed compositions.[44]

Gillespie and Fuller recruited some of the finest young brass and reed players.[45] To Dizzy's delight, Kenny Clarke had just been discharged from the army and was ready to play again. Although Clarke had been away from the scene three years, his rhythmic conception was precisely what Gillespie wanted for the band.[46] Now all he needed was a pianist. Bud Powell was on piano, but his tenure there was short-lived. "The money was a little erratic, and Bud was super-erratic," Dizzy recalled in his memoir.[47] Gillespie began looking for Powell's replacement.

Meanwhile, Monk was playing with Hawkins, listening to Dizzy's band during his break, and giving unsolicited advice. More importantly, Gil Fuller had begun to tap Thelonious for music. "Monk was a freak for tunes," Fuller explained. "He had all kinds of strange shit going on. And we got all the things from him."[48] Fuller, like anyone else who patronized the Down Beat Club or the Spotlite, had heard Hawkins's band play some of Monk's originals. Tunes like "'Round Midnight," "I Mean You" (or "Stickball"), and "You Need 'Na" occasionally entered the band's repertoire.[49] In the fall of 1945, Fuller offered to publish some of Monk's compositions with Consolidated Music, a firm he had recently co-founded with Gillespie. Despite Monk's bad experience with Teddy McRae, he decided to try again. Although Fuller never claimed co-composer's credits, he nonetheless put himself down as a claimant on all songs, entitling him to half of what would have been a two- to five-cent royalty on each recording. In late October 1945, Fuller registered a song Monk was calling "Manhattan Moods."[50] Less than a year later, Monk was calling it "Ruby, My Dear."[51] He returned to "Ruby, My Dear," not because of any nostalgia for Ms. Richardson, but because the lyric worked. The first four notes say those three little words, and he wanted to find a lyricist someday who could transform the haunting melody into a haunting refrain.

Toward the end of February, when it became clear to Fuller that they needed more material for the band, he leaned on Monk for tunes. Thelonious came through with two more. He gave Fuller another ballad, this one tentatively titled "Feeling that Way Now."[52] At one point he'd called it "Y Don't U Try Now," then "Why Do You Evade the Facts."[53] A copy of the score found among Mary Lou Williams's papers provides a fully-elaborated composition with the voicings and left and right hand written out in Monk's handwriting. For this version Monk struggled to incorporate "Sarah" into the title: "Be Merrier Sarah," "Sarah Made the Error," and "Be Fairer Sarah."[54] (Sarah Vaughan? A pseudonym for someone else?) It didn't stick and he eventually settled on "Monk's Mood." The other tune he turned in to Fuller was called "Playhouse," dedicated to his old haunt up on 118th Street. Fuller dug "Playhouse" because it was a danceable, upbeat tune with a strong Caribbean flavor. He saw it as a vehicle for the kind of Latin/Afro-Cuban rhythms he and Dizzy would eventually explore with the big band over the next couple of years. Six years would pass before Thelonious recorded "Playhouse," and by then it would become "Bye-ya."[55]

By the time Dizzy's new big band was ready to open in April, Hawkins had left the Spotlite and joined Norman Granz's touring "Jazz at the Philharmonic."[56] It was only logical that Gillespie would hire Monk to take over for the eternally absent Bud Powell. After all, Monk knew the music, he had a long-established relationship with Kenny Clarke, and Gil Fuller had already pulled in Monk's tunes with the intention of arranging them for the band.

"I had no trouble outta Monk, not too much," Dizzy recalled, "but Monk wasn't showing up on time either. It was against the law to show up on time."[57] Gil Fuller concurred: "Monk never did show up on time. Anytime we got ready to hit, we'd hit without a piano player. 'Where's Monk . . . ?' He just wouldn't show up on time. . . . So Dizzy's mad."[58] Indeed, Monk became notorious for being late. His behavior marked a sharp contrast from his work habits under Coleman Hawkins. Hawk never complained about Monk being tardy, and he always appeared professional and focused.

Dizzy tolerated Monk's tardiness, despite pressure from Clark Monroe to fire him. But some members of the band disliked his playing. For sidemen used to pianists who copped Bud Powell's style, Monk's approach was completely unorthodox. Bassist Ray Brown complained that Monk never really "comped" properly behind the band, choosing to do his own thing. Sometimes he sat at the piano motionless and did nothing until he felt the time was right: "[M]ost piano players in most big bands sit down and they play with the band, you know. But Monk would just sit there like *this*. And all of a sudden there'd be a pause from all the trumpets and everything, and Monk would go 'plink!' like that. And everybody would go 'Yeah!'"[59]

The extant recordings from Gillespie's big band reveal just how adventurous Monk had become since his last recordings. His chords sound even more dissonant than anything documented from Minton's or in the studio with Coleman Hawkins. Of the tunes on which Monk is audible, recorded at the Spotlite in June of 1946, Monk plays fewer notes, and his comping is extremely jarring. He plays in the pauses, and what he plays sounds so harmonically disorienting that there are moments—especially on "Our Delight"—when the piano seems to overtake the entire band. Although Gillespie has never publicly criticized Monk's playing, either as a soloist or accompanist, he gave him very little solo space during these performances. But having no solo space has never stopped Monk from playing melodic lines or countermelodies beneath other soloists. There is a brilliant moment in "Groovin' High" where Monk plays flashes of his composition "Evidence" behind Dizzy Gillespie's trumpet solo. It is an interesting juxtaposition since "Groovin' High" is based on the chords from the song "Whispering" and Monk's "Evidence" (originally titled "Just Us" and then "Justice") is based on "Just You, Just Me."[60]

For all of Fuller's efforts to "get" Monk's tunes, only one made it into the band book: " 'Round Midnight." Dizzy had been playing it for a while and already had an arrangement of it from his time playing with the Hepsations. The one recording of the big band performing " 'Round Midnight" with Monk at the piano renders him virtually invisible. In nearly six and a half minutes of music, Thelonious is granted only a four-bar solo, not enough even for the master of economy to make a coherent musical statement. On June 10, the orchestra made a studio recording for Musicraft, but there is no evidence that Monk was part of it. The little piano that comes through does not sound like Monk.

Monk stayed with the band for a month, but was not having fun. He had more fun up at Club 845 on Prospect Avenue in the Bronx, just a few blocks from Sonny and Nellie's place. Club 845 hosted Sunday afternoon jam sessions with some of the big-name artists, from Ben Webster to Freddie Webster, Dexter Gordon to Gene Ammons.[61] On Monday nights, he still made his way up to Minton's Playhouse. Between Minton's and Club 845, he began playing with an outstanding bassist named Gene Ramey. Monk liked Ramey's big, plucky sound, and his grounding in the hard-swinging Kansas City style was not insignificant. Monk always wanted a rhythm section that could swing.[62]

Monk's stint with Dizzy came to an inauspicious end on the last day of June. The band opened at the Apollo on June 28 for a week-long engagement.[63] Dizzy was nervous; it was the band's Apollo debut and its first gig outside the Spotlite. Monk showed up late one time too many, but on this occasion he had company. Kenny Clarke tells the story best:

> One day Monk and I were hanging out in the Braddock Bar near the Apollo with some friends, talking about old times. It was the kind of musicians' conversation where one anecdote leads to another and everyone tries to top everyone else's story. After quite a few tastes had gone down, I looked casually at my watch and realized with a shock that the show had started and the band must already have hit. "My God," I shouted to Monk. "Come on, we're late!"
>
> We raced back to the theatre and ran right into the manager, who was furious. Dizzy wasn't too thrilled, either. He was striding about on stage and peering into the wings, looking for us. Milt Jackson had taken over on drums, but there was a conspicuous absence of a piano player.
>
> Having been house drummer at the Apollo some years before, I knew the theatre layout very well, so I sneaked around backstage, slipped through the

curtains, nudged Bags, took the sticks from him and slid on to the drum stool as he slid off. Dizzy looked over, did a double take, and said, "How in hell did you get up there?" I said, "Don't worry about it—I'm here, I'm playing and that's what counts." We had only missed the opening theme music, but Dizzy was still mad, and poor Monk got the brunt of it. There was no way he could get to the piano without being seen by Dizzy—and when he tiptoed out from the wings, Diz was waiting for him. He pointed his finger accusingly at Monk and told him right there, in front of the audience: "You're fired!" And that was the end of Monk's career with Dizzy. John Lewis was in the wings listening to the band. Dizzy beckoned him on stage and he stayed on as both pianist and arranger after that.[64]

John Lewis's presence in the wings wasn't coincidental. Clarke had been lobbying Dizzy to hire Lewis in place of Monk for some time.[65] Lewis and Clarke had been in the army, like their explorer namesakes; had served together in France; and had become fast friends. They even performed together during their three-year tour of duty. Lewis, who grew up in Albuquerque, New Mexico, had loved Dizzy's music ever since he heard a broadcast from Los Angeles of the sextet with Charlie Parker. Once he got to New York in the fall of 1945, he worked on 52nd Street for a while and began hanging out with Dizzy's big band, offering arrangements while waiting to receive his union card.[66] He had his eye on the piano chair ever since the band formed. When the opportunity finally came, Lewis was there to seize it.

Dizzy's decision to fire Monk and hire Lewis angered and disappointed Gil Fuller. "I never forgave Dizzy for that. I didn't think Monk was a piano player like Oscar Peterson, that type of thing, but he had material that we needed. And the idea was to collect as much music as possible."[67] For Fuller, that meant collect as much money as possible. As claimant on so many of Monk's tunes, he was also looking to receive a share of the royalties. Monk was only one of many writers in Fuller's stable. At one point, Fuller had so many people writing for the band and for his publishing company that he became more of a manager than an arranger, distributing writing and arranging jobs to ghost-writers, and adding his name to the scores. It was a questionable practice, but this was the nature of the business.[68] Despite Fuller's reputation, and even after Dizzy dropped Monk from the band, Thelonious continued to work with Consolidated Music.

Call it ironic, call it bittersweet, but within a couple of weeks of the Apollo fiasco, the first magazine profile ever written about Monk appeared on newsstands all over Harlem and in major black urban communities across the country. The piece appeared in *Rhythm: Music and Theatrical Magazine* in July 1946. A short-lived, black-owned periodical devoted to African-American arts and entertainment, *Rhythm* claimed a national readership in excess of 80,000.[69] The author was none other than Herbie Nichols, the pianist and writer who had championed Monk two years earlier for *Music Dial*. Titled "The Jazz Pianist–Purist," the article was accompanied by photos of Monk at Minton's Playhouse posing at the piano (by then the management had replaced the upright with a baby grand) and jamming with Max Roach and bassist Gene Ramey.

He looks dapper: jacket and tie, clean-cut and clean-shaven, and still baby-faced. He visually fits the magazine's profile—a respectable, intelligent Negro artist committed to creating uplifting and thoughtful music. Elsewhere in the same issue, Monk is pictured shooting the breeze with Art Tatum and Eddie Heywood over the caption, "Three purveyors of modern swing piano." The photo is linked to John R. Gibson's article on the history of black dance bands, where Thelonious is surrounded by celebrated musical figures such as Duke Ellington, Mary Lou Williams, Coleman Hawkins, Count Basie, Lionel Hampton, Hazel Scott, and W. C. Handy.[70] All in all, it was a sign of deep respect for Monk's talents and potential, and, even at this early stage, nomination for uptown's cultural royalty.

In the profile, Nichols is admiring. He does not hide or obscure their friendship. He describes Monk as an extraordinary musician who walks his own path, "a very rebellious person," and one of the great musical minds he's encountered. He compares Monk to Bird and Dizzy in terms of their contribution to modern music, but argues that Monk's proclivity for slower tempos makes him unique. "It almost borders on the lethargic and may well be a key to his total personality. Monk has to be in a great mood before he will swing out in a fast tempo, and he can swing as effectively as any I know." In this respect, Monk has more in common with Ellington—a younger, underdeveloped Ellington: "His expressive and soulful figures are a reminder of Duke. This is where the similarity ends as you will find. Monk's rebellious spirit through the years has not permitted him to gain the all-around experience of an Ellington and so his enterprise has suffered."[71]

Nichols was less interested in reviewing Monk's work than in presenting a more intimate portrait of the artist, his life, his work, his process, his philosophy, his frustrations. During a visit to Monk's tiny apartment on West 63rd Street, Nichols listened to Monk pour his heart out about his struggle to find work and the meager pay he earned when he did get a gig. The system is unfair, he proclaimed, and the powers that be ought to "'let everybody live. Pay a fellow a good price especially when someone can really blow.'" By "really blow," Monk means to create something original. "His eyes light up when he speaks of instrumentalists getting the right 'sounds' out of their instruments. He is forever searching for better 'sounds,' as he loves to say. He doesn't seek these effects elsewhere. He creates them at his Klein piano. This way of thinking throughout the years has resulted in the creation of a system of playing which is the strangest I have heard and may someday revolutionize the art of swing piano playing."[72]

The two continued the conversation at the piano, sharing ideas as well as original compositions. Nichols played for Monk, who in turn gave his guest a mini concert, introducing him to "You Need 'Na," "What Now" (which he later retitled "Off Minor"), and what would become "Monk's Mood" but at the time was "Y Don't U Try Now." The song that really caught Nichols's attention, however, was "Ruby, My Dear." Nichols described hearing Monk's rendition of "Ruby" as "one of the greatest pleasures I've had listening to jazz. This song could be another 'Body and Soul,' if he would only put it down on paper and let a few other people learn it." We know now that the song had already been committed to paper when Gil Fuller copyrighted it a few months back as "Manhattan Moods." But Monk wasn't ready to share—not yet, at least. Before

Nichols left, they agreed to swap music. Nichols offered to write out three of his own compositions in exchange for " 'Round Midnight," "Ruby, My Dear," and a tune Monk had yet to title. "On the day of the proposed swap," Nichols lamented, "my tunes were the only ones completed. However, I haven't given up all hope of eventually learning his tunes which I will play morning, noon, and night."[73]

Nor had Monk given up on playing his own tunes . . . morning, noon, and night. He had plenty of time to compose, now that he was out of a job and no one seemed interested in hiring him. He practiced and wrote wherever he could—at his mother's house on his precious Klein piano, at Mary Lou's place when the crowds thinned out, at Minton's in the afternoons or after hours, or at Sonny's house in the Bronx. Sonny didn't have a piano then, but Nellie was there.

Now that she and Geraldine had taken jobs at the Pioneer Ice Cream Division on Fifth Avenue and 145th Street, Monk could always count on a few sweet entice-ments. The company packed ice cream and wrapped ice cream sandwiches for Borden's and several other companies, and every once in a while Nellie and her sister-in-law brought home a few morsels to share with the kids.[74] Monk also took time away from the piano, shooting hoops on West 63rd Street with his brother Thomas and his two sons, Thomas, Jr. and Theolonious, now ages eight and seven, respectively. As long as he refrained from using profanity, he visited his brother's apartment, debating with his sister-in-law Trotyrine, listening to "Sissy," Thomas, Jr.'s, twin sister, and doting on the baby, Charlotte, who made sure her uncle "Bubba" knew she was all of six and a half.

Weeks, sometimes months, passed between gigs, and when he did work the jobs tended to be one-nighters or a weekend here and there. Things got to be so bad that toward the end of 1946 he stopped paying union dues and let his membership lapse.[75] He got tired of waiting for gigs to come his way and decided to organize a rehearsal band made up of some younger, adventurous musicians. He created something akin to a collective, not unlike what pianist Sun Ra would establish in Chicago a few years later, or the kinds of collectives jazz musicians would develop across the country in the 1960s. There was no "leader," per se, and everyone in the group was expected to contribute ideas, compositions, new directions. About twelve musicians began meet-ing in the basement of Minton's Playhouse. Among them were Bud Powell, vibist Milt Jackson from Dizzy's band, and an excellent trombonist from Indianapolis named J. J. Johnson.[76] Johnson had played with Benny Carter and Count Basie, but only became a permanent New York resident in August of 1946.[77] Mary Lou Williams was there, too, though mainly as an observer. Every band member had to contribute fifty cents to help pay for arrangements.[78] Monk, Powell, and Jackson wrote the lion's share of the arrangements, "and some of them were real tough," Williams recalled. "Even those guys couldn't always get them right."[79]

As the group's organizer, composer, and one of the principal arrangers, presumably Monk received a share of the money in the kitty. At one point this paltry bit of change might have been Monk's only source of income. But money wasn't his primary motiva-tion, according to Mary Lou Williams. She claimed he formed the band to challenge the practice of downtown musicians coming uptown and "stealing" the music. Reportedly Monk said to Mary Lou, "We are going to get a big band started. We're going to create something that they can't steal, because they can't play it."[80] Though "they" might be read as "whites," Monk rarely saw the terrain of music in such stark racial terms. He was more concerned about being ripped off by his peers—Teddy McRae, Gil Fuller, and to a lesser degree, his friend Dizzy. It seemed as though everyone but Monk benefited from the new direction in jazz. Thelonious felt it acutely when band members began to abandon the project in order to accept paying gigs. No such opportunities were forthcoming for him. Within weeks the group collapsed.

While Monk's proposal failed to produce a working band, it set a precedent that would come to define Thelonious's role in the jazz world for the rest of his life. He became a teacher. His operations moved from the basement of Minton's to his apartment on San Juan Hill, and soon all the young cats made their way over there. Although he had the run of the house, because the piano was in Thelonious's bedroom as many as five or six musicians squeezed into his tiny room to work on songs, chord progressions, arrangements, or just the everyday challenges of making music. A frequent visitor in those days was a tall, brown-skinned kid from Harlem of West Indian descent named Theodore Rollins, though his friends called him "Sonny." He was only seventeen years old, a senior at Benjamin Franklin High School, but already a brilliant tenor player. Monk helped him a great deal, encouraging Sonny to develop his own sound and, most importantly, allowing him to play what he wanted. "Every day after school I would go to Thelonious Monk's place and practice with his band. He never really told me what to play, because I guess he respected my playing."[81] Rollins appreciated these afterschool sessions because the music was challenging and he came out of each rehearsal a better musician. "Monk would have what seemed to be way-out stuff at the time and all the guys would look at it and say 'Monk, we can't play this stuff . . .' and then it would end up that everybody would be playing it by the end of the rehearsal, you know. . . . It was hard music."[82]

After he graduated in the spring of 1947, Rollins continued his "studies" with Monk, practicing with whomever showed up.[83] He also began to bring some of his uptown pals along with him. Surrounding Rollins was an entire crew of talented teenaged musicians who lived in the Sugar Hill section of Harlem. Saxophonists Jackie McLean and Andy Kirk, Jr. (a brilliant musician who tragically stopped playing before turning twenty years old), drummer Art Taylor, pianist Kenny Drew and bassists Arthur Phipps and Connie Henry all might be regarded as the original "Sugar Hill Gang." Sonny introduced McLean and Taylor to Monk, and at different points in their careers they would become Monk's sidemen. For McLean, hanging out with Monk wasn't just about the music; it represented an intellectual engagement of a very high order. "Monk is a deep person. . . . His interests vary far beyond what most people would imagine. He's very easy to know as long as you deal with him in a plain and friendly way. But if you try to be dishonest with him or play mental chess with him, then you might have trouble. His mind is something that should be respected at all times. People are too quick to think that a jazz musician knows jazz and that's it, you know."[84] Art Taylor was thoroughly impressed with Monk's encyclopedic knowledge of tunes and chord progressions, yet he saw in Thelonious a model of a thinking person engaged with the world. "He had that kind of intelligence, that kind of wit, that kind of manner, musically and socially, that was important to me."[85]

Monk's model of sage musical leadership also extended to a group of young musicians in Brooklyn. The bridge between the Brooklyn cats and Thelonious turned out to be Randy Weston, the curious young pianist whom Monk used to see at the Down Beat Club when he was with Hawkins. Soon after he was discharged from the service, Weston began visiting Monk at his apartment on West 63rd Street. "I'll never forget that first visit. He never spoke beyond basic greetings. He didn't have the Steinway in the kitchen yet, but he had a small piano in his room and a picture of Billie Holiday on the ceiling and this red light! It was incredible. He'd sit at the piano and play and I'd listen."[86] Weston grasped Monk's "simplicity and unique sense of rhythm. He can say so much with so little." What he "said," however, was hardly simple; it was unabashedly modern, grounded in the blues and yet deeply personal. Listening to Monk, Weston learned the value of having an "ethnic connection with self-expression. You're taught to play a piano in a certain way, and if you don't play it that way, it's not the correct way. Without saying a word, Monk taught me, 'Play what you feel although it may not be the way it's supposed to be.'"[87]

Weston's first visit lasted several hours, and though they hardly exchanged words, the encounter proved to be life-changing. It compelled Weston to approach his instrument differently, to find his own unique voice, and to be wary of false distinctions between "modern" and "traditional." "Later, as I read about Sufism, I came to realize what a spiritual experience I had had. Monk communicated like a Sufi priest, sending powerful vibrations musically and spiritually."[88]

As Weston's visits became more frequent and their friendship deepened, he discovered that Monk hardly lived in monastic isolation; the man's home had become a kind of village or community center for jazz musicians. He remembers going "by Monk's house and all the guys would be there. We would all sit and listen to him play. We had that tribal thing going. It wasn't planned like that, but it was something that happened. It was our culture."[89] Weston also began picking up Monk and taking him across the bridge to Brooklyn, where they might drop in at Mr. Frank Weston's restaurant for a bite to eat or head over to Randy's place on 13th Street and play piano. Through Randy, Monk met all the up-and-coming Brooklyn musicians whom he would later employ: bassists Gary Mapp, Michael Mattos, and Ahmed Abdul-Malik; drummer Willie Jones, trumpeter Ray Copeland, saxophonist Ernie Henry, to name a few. Just as Sonny Rollins became Monk's conduit to the young Harlem musicians, Weston became Monk's entrée into Brooklyn's rich jazz world.

During the first half of 1947, Monk virtually disappeared from the public record, though he never left the public view. You could find Monk up at Minton's or Club 845 in the Bronx, or on the jam session circuit. He was often with Nellie at Sonny's place. While working at Borden's, she began to experience severe bouts of nausea and abdominal pain. It became a chronic problem; she could barely hold any food down and, as skinny as she was (five feet seven and barely one hundred pounds), she began losing weight. The doctor she saw had no explanation; at one point he even suggested that it might be psychosomatic.[90] She persevered and continued to work. She really had no choice. Geraldine was pregnant again with her fifth child, who arrived too early on May 29. Her birth certificate read Benetta Smith, but because she was premature they called her "Teeny."

When Monk wasn't checking in on Nellie, he worked intermittently. One possible "sighting" was on April 14, a Monday night, at Small's Paradise. Billed as a "Battle of the Baritone Sax" featuring Leo Parker and Serge Chaloff, the flyer promoting the event listed the pianist as Earnie Washington, "Mad Genius On Piano," which has led hard-core Monk fans to believe it was a pseudonym—"earn-ing Washington(s)" or dollar bills.[91] The drummer on the date was "Art Blakely" [sic], and Miles Davis is also listed. Yet Monk had no reason to use a pseudonym; his union dues were paid up and the gig was legal. And in fact, there was a fine pianist in New York named Ernie Washington who worked with many of the same guys either at Small's or on 52nd Street.[92]

Monk maintained visibility by continuing to publish his music. Gil Fuller was still willing and eager to publish Monk with a new outfit called Monogram Music Company, and on February 21, 1947, Fuller copyrighted two more Monk tunes—"What Now," one of the songs he played for Herbie Nichols, and a swinging number titled "I Mean You."[93] The latter is especially significant because Coleman Hawkins was frequently listed as co-composer with Monk, and Hawk was the first to record the song in December of 1946. The band Hawk put together was top-heavy with young modernists, including refugees from Monk's short-lived big band—J. J. Johnson, Milt Jackson, as well as Max Roach, Curley Russell on bass, and the phenomenal trumpet player from Florida, Fats Navarro. Hank Jones was hired to play piano; evidently Monk was not even considered. When Sonora Records released the 78 several weeks later, Monk's name was not listed anywhere on the disc.[94] Yet the application to register a claim to copyright, not to mention the attached lead sheet, lists *only* Thelonious Monk as composer, not Hawkins.[95]

We can only imagine how Monk felt every time he heard "Bean and the Boys" on the radio swinging "I Mean You." Yet if hearing his own compositions on the radio wasn't surreal enough, in the spring of 1947 he also began hearing *himself* on the radio and in record shops. Jerry Newman, the Columbia University student who used to drag that slick recording device up to Minton's Playhouse, decided to cash in. In March, the Vox label released two lengthy jam sessions from May 12, 1941, spread over three 78s—"Stompin' at the Savoy" took up three sides, and the band's rendition of "Topsy," which was retitled "Charlie's Choice," occupied the remaining three sides. The personnel consists of the house band—Monk, Joe Guy, Nick Fenton, and Kenny Clarke—and guitarist Charlie Christian, who happened to be sitting in that night. The records were issued as *Vox Presents Charlie Christian*. In one fell swoop Monk was demoted from co-leader to sideman. Worse, neither Newman nor a Vox representative ever asked Monk for permission to release these recordings, and, no great surprise, he never received a dime.[96]

The guys who knew Monk from the early days at Minton's felt for him. "When I came out of the Army," pianist Allen Tinney recalled, "I was very hurt because Charlie Parker had become famous, Dizzy had become famous, Max [Roach] had become famous, and I said to myself, 'What happened to Monk?'"[97] Every time saxophonist Budd Johnson visited Monk during this period, he could see the pain, but he also witnessed an astonishing determination:

> Monk's feelings got hurt because Dizzy and Charlie were getting all the credit for this music, this style—I used to go over Monk's house with him, drink some wine with him. "Come on, I want you to hear what I'm doing," he said. "I'm gonna let them take that style and go ahead, and I'm gonna get a new style." . . . His mother would fix some food for us, and he would just play for me. All this funny-type music that he was playing. And he had gone altogether different from what he had been doing. I said, "Hey, man . . . that's outtasight! What're you doing; whaddayou call that?"
> "I don't know, man, it's just—you know." He couldn't explain it to me.[98]

Budd Johnson encouraged him. Monk concluded, "Well, I'm going on now with my new music."[99] By late summer of 1947, he had written an entire book of it. He just needed a company willing to put his ideas on wax.

10

"The George Washington of Bebop"

(September 1947–August 1948)

Mary Lou Williams first relayed the message to Thelonious. A white guy named Bill Gottlieb was looking for him. He worked for *Down Beat* magazine as a writer and photographer and he wanted to do a story on Monk. Monk was incredulous. For the past year he had been hustling for nickel-and-dime gigs. Now the nation's premier jazz periodical wanted to do a story on him? Publicity meant gigs, and Monk desperately needed both. Williams arranged the meeting for early September, 1947, and instructed Gottlieb to meet Thelonious at Mrs. Monk's apartment on West 63rd.

The bespectacled and intense Gottlieb looked more like a college professor than a typical jazz fan, but he knew his stuff. Born in Brooklyn in 1917, Gottlieb earned a bachelor's degree from Lehigh University and went on to work in the advertising department of *The Washington Post*. He began writing a weekly jazz column for the *Post* but because the paper had no budget for a photographer, he bought a Speed Graphic camera and took his own pictures. Gottlieb's reputation grew through his work with the camera. After a tour of duty in the service, he returned to New York City and started working for *Down Beat* in the spring of 1946. He covered most of the mainstream big bands and launched a feature he called "Posin'," candid shots of musicians with a sentence or two of witty commentary.[1] He had become one of bebop's more enthusiastic champions. Just prior to meeting Thelonious, he had published several photos of Dizzy Gillespie, Charlie Parker, and Miles Davis, including what would become an iconic image of Gillespie posing with a beret, glasses, and goatee—Monk-style.[2]

Why the sudden interest in Monk? Virtually every arts and entertainment magazine was scrambling for anything related to the hottest trend in music—bebop. Besides the jazz mainstays—*Down Beat*, *Metronome*, *The Record Changer*—popular magazines such as *The New Republic*, *Esquire*, and *Saturday Review* began carrying profiles, editorials, and curiosity pieces on bebop and its major players throughout 1947, a good six months to a year before debates over the new music began to really heat up.[3] The battles were fierce: bebop was great, or terrible. No one could define it musically, but that didn't matter. Musicians felt compelled to enter the debate, and some of the genre's prominent voices—Mary Lou Williams, Tadd Dameron, and Lennie Tristano—

published articles defending the new music from its detractors.[4] Of course, those musicians who came to represent the different camps continued to call music "music," and neither generational nor stylistic differences kept them from sharing the bandstand or a recording studio. But collaboration, flexibility of style, and ambiguity in genre distinctions didn't sell magazines.

Bird and Diz suddenly became the new heroes—or antiheroes, depending on one's stance—in the jazz wars. And in virtually every interview they granted, they mentioned Thelonious Monk. Monk had mastered the new harmonic developments; he was one of the pioneers at Minton's Playhouse. Suddenly Monk came across as the 1940s version of Buddy Bolden, that missing link who started it all but then disappeared. To Gottlieb, he was "the George Washington of bebop."

Gottlieb first laid eyes on Monk the previous summer at the Spotlite when Monk was still with Dizzy's big band. Gottlieb enjoyed the music but was even more fascinated by the visual spectacle: "You could recognize [Monk's] cult from his bebop uniform: goatee, beret and heavy shell glasses, only his were done half in gold."[5] From that moment on, Gottlieb wanted to have a conversation with Thelonious, but claimed he could never find him.

When Gottlieb and Monk finally did meet, they hit it off famously. They were the same age, they both really dug the Claude Thornhill band,[6] and had a thing for Billie Holiday. Gottlieb had shot some gorgeous photos of Holiday that were published in *The Record Changer* earlier that spring, and Thelonious kept a photo of Billie taped to his bedroom ceiling.[7] "In the taxi, on the way up," Gottlieb recounted, "Thelonious spoke with singular modesty. He wouldn't go on record as insisting HE started be-bop; but, as the story books have long since related, he admitted he was at least one of the originators." But Monk's interpretation of events may have been less modest than Gottlieb realized. "Be-bop wasn't developed in any deliberate way," he explained in the interview. "For my part, I'll say it was just the style of music I happened to play. We all contributed ideas . . ." Then he immodestly added, "If my own work had more importance than any other's, it's because the piano is the key instrument in music. I think all styles are built around piano developments. The piano lays the chord foundation and the rhythm foundation, too. Along with bass and piano, I was always at the spot [Minton's], and could keep working on the music. The rest, like Diz and Charlie, came in only from time to time, at first."[8]

Once they reached their destination, Monk headed straight for the piano. Former manager Teddy Hill and trumpeters Roy Eldridge and Howard McGhee just happened to drop by, though it's likely Gottlieb had tipped them off beforehand. Gottlieb took several photos of Monk at the piano—playing, posing, looking anything *but* mysterious in his slightly oversized pinstriped suit and dark glasses. Most of the shots are hatless, but Gottlieb persuaded Monk to don his famous beret for a few. Monk wasn't just posing, however. He was up there to work. Gottlieb observed how McGhee "got Thelonious to dream up some trumpet passages and then conned Thelonious into writing them down on some score sheets that happened to be in the club."[9] Then Gottlieb coaxed the men to step outside for an impromptu photo shoot. He produced one of the most widely circulated and iconic photographs in jazz history. Four pioneers of modern jazz standing abreast beneath the awning at Minton's Playhouse, the house that "bop" allegedly built. The published photo is rich with wit. Gottlieb created a Mount Rushmore of modern jazz, with Thelonious positioned on the far left in George Washington's spot.

When "Thelonius [sic] Monk—Genius of Bop" appeared in the September 24 issue of *Down Beat*, it not only revised the story of recent jazz history, but also set in motion the image of Monk as a mysterious, eccentric figure. Gottlieb made much of his "elusive" character, noting that while we've all heard stories of his "fantastic musical imagination; about his fine piano playing . . . few have ever seen him." He quoted Teddy Hill: "[Thelonious is] so absorbed in his task he's become almost mysterious. Maybe he's on the way to meet you. An idea comes to him. He begins to work on it. Mop! Two days go by and he's still at it. He's forgotten all about you and everything else but that idea." Presenting Monk to jazz audiences as a furtive and baffling figure allowed Gottlieb to make the sensational claim that he had discovered the true source for the new music. Quoting Hill again: Monk "deserves the most credit for starting be-bop. Though he won't admit it, I think he feels he got a bum break in not getting some of the glory that went to others. Rather than go out now and have people think he's just an imitator, Thelonious is thinking up new things. I believe he hopes one day to come out with something as far ahead of bop as bop is ahead of the music that went before it."[10]

That day came sooner than Hill could have imagined. Hardly a week had passed since Monk's afternoon with Bill Gottlieb when Ike Quebec, a tenor player, came knocking. He had dropped by Monk's place many times before, but this time he had a young white couple in tow, Alfred and Lorraine Lion. Alfred, somewhat small with delicate features, spoke quietly with a heavy German accent. Lorraine was tall and lean, with jet-black hair and dark eyes, and was less reserved than her husband. She talked fast and with confidence; her accent was vintage Jersey. The guests were led to Thelonious's bedroom. "Monk's room was right off the kitchen," Lorraine (now Gordon) recalled. "It was a room out of Vincent van Gogh, somehow—you know, ascetic: a bed (a cot, really) against the wall, a window, and an upright piano. That was it."[11] He also surrounded himself with photos, like the picture of Billie Holiday on his ceiling taped next to a red light bulb, a photograph of Sarah Vaughan on the wall next to his cot, and a publicity shot of Dizzy above the piano with the inscription, "To Monk, my first inspiration. Stay with it. Your boy, Dizzy Gillespie."[12] The room was relatively dark; the only window faced the alley and the lamp on his dresser gave off very little light. But it was home to his Klein piano, his woodshed and workshop, and a place to crash.

Monk knew why they were there. Alfred was the founder of Blue Note records and he ran it with Lorraine and his friend and business partner, Frank Wolff. Quebec had been one of Blue Note's recording artists since 1944. The Lions trusted Quebec's ear for new developments in jazz and made him a kind of A&R man for the label.[13] Quebec became Monk's advocate and begged Alfred and Lorraine to come check him out.[14] The Lions were hesitant until they got wind of *Down Beat*'s profile on Monk.

As Lorraine later wrote, "We all sat down on Monk's narrow bed—our legs straight out in front of us, like children. . . . The door closed. And Monk played, with his back to us."[15] He gave his guests a full-length performance, including " 'Round Midnight," "What Now," several untitled pieces, and the ballad he now called "Ruby, My Dear." Lorraine "fell in love." It wasn't the dissonant harmonies that did it; it was his commitment to stride piano. Monk, she remembered, "didn't seem so revolutionary to me. That's why I liked him so much. In those early days I couldn't listen to a lot of avant-garde musicians. I was steeped in Sidney Bechet and Duke Ellington. But Monk made the transition for me, because I was hearing his great stride piano style from James P. Johnson and the blues and his great left hand."[16]

Very few words were exchanged. By the time the Lions left, Thelonious Monk had a recording date. He had just a couple of weeks to put together a band. It was a minor miracle: After years of hustling and scraping while others put his compositions on wax, Monk finally had the chance to record his own music as a bandleader. It was a long time coming: He was just shy of his thirtieth birthday.

The Lions' enthusiastic response was a departure. The label had a reputation for signing the older generation of jazz artists, the folks young bebop fans called "moldy figs." From its origins in 1938, Blue Note focused on pianists Albert Ammons, Pete Johnson, Meade Lux Lewis, Art Hodes, and James P. Johnson; New Orleans–style reed players like Sidney Bechet and Albert Nicholas; and the resurrected trumpeter Bunk Johnson, to name a few.[17]

For two German émigrés with no previous experience in the record industry, Lion and Wolff fared pretty well. They recorded selectively during the war, and because Blue Note was an independent label, they were able to make records during the AFM recording ban. When Alfred was drafted in 1942, operations came to a virtual standstill until his discharge in November of 1943. When he returned to work, however, Lion had a new wife and dynamic business partner who helped change the face of Blue Note. Born Lorraine Stein of Newark, New Jersey, Alfred's bride had loved jazz since she was a child, especially Duke Ellington, Benny Goodman, James P. Johnson, and the classic female blues artists of the 1920s—Bessie Smith, Ma Rainey, and Mamie Smith. She and her brother Philip used to go door-to-door in Newark's black community, offering to buy their old 78s for a quarter apiece. As a teenager she helped start Newark's "Hot Club," a jazz fan/record collectors' club with chapters all over the world.[18]

Now that the war had ended, jazz was moving in new directions, and Blue Note had to keep up with the times. Because he knew all the modernists, signing Ike Quebec was a blessing. "We were very close to Ike," recalled Frank Wolff. "He knew about Monk and Bud Powell and thought they were the outstanding modern pioneers on piano."[19] Quebec was similar to Coleman Hawkins in his approach to the tenor saxophone. In the Bird era of high-velocity horn playing, Ike's preferred vehicle was the romantic ballad. Nevertheless, he hired some of the young cats for his own dates—such as bassists Oscar Pettiford and Milt Hinton—and he helped arrange Blue Note's first bebop sessions with vocalist "Babs" Gonzales and pianist Tadd Dameron. Indeed, just three weeks before Monk was scheduled to go into the studio, Tadd Dameron led a session for Blue Note with Fats Navarro on trumpet, Nelson Boyd on bass, and three future Monk sidemen—Ernie Henry (alto), Charlie Rouse (tenor), and Rossiere Vandella Wilson—better known as "Shadow"—on drums.[20] By the time the Lions "discovered" Thelonious, they had already begun to move the label into the new era.

Blue Note's gang of three completely supported their newest recording artist. They left Monk in charge of choosing his sidemen, they helped coordinate rehearsals, and, per the label's policy, they paid musicians for rehearsal time.[21] The most immediate task was to decide on the size of the ensemble and to find musicians willing and able to play Monk's music. Thelonious chose to record with a sextet and hired mostly guys he knew from Minton's or from the jam session circuit. He had been playing with Gene Ramey for the past few months, so he was the logical choice on bass. Monk's horn section consisted of all young players who had never set foot in a recording studio. On tenor he hired a Brooklyn kid named Billy Smith, and his alto player was Ike Quebec's cousin, Danny Quebec West, a seventeen-year-old saxophone prodigy.

Monk's choice for trumpet was twenty-four-year-old Idrees Dawud ibn Sulieman. When he left his hometown of St. Petersburg, Florida with the Carolina Cotton Pickers in 1941, he was known as Leonard Graham. After four years on the road, he settled in New York City, got a job with Earl Hines's band, and started hanging out at Minton's.[22] In New York Graham discovered Islam—not Elijah Muhammad's Nation of Islam, but a group calling itself the Muslim Brotherhood (not to be confused with the Egyptian group of that name). The Muslim Brotherhood identified with the Ahmadiyya movement, a radical strain of Islam founded in 1888 by an Indian Muslim, Mirza Ghulam Ahmad, who claimed to be the "Mahdi" or "Promised Messiah" and "redeemer" of the Islamic faith. The Ahmadiyyas were considered heretical by most of the Islamic world because they incorporated parts of the New Testament alongside the Qur'an, claimed that Jesus was a prophet of Islam, translated the Qur'an into languages other than Arabic, and promoted the idea that Ahmad was the Mahdi. The Ahmaddiyas established a mission in Harlem in 1920, which by the late 1940s had become a magnet for young black musicians politicized by the racism in New York.[23] For Sulieman and his fellow devotees, the Muslim Brotherhood redefined so-called Negroes from a national minority to a world majority, embracing both Africa and Asia as part of a "colored" world. It bestowed upon black American culture a sense of dignity and nobility, which appealed to the creators of the new music. Many black musicians turned to Islam not only as a rejection of the "white man's religion" but also as a means to bring a moral structure to a world suffused with drugs, alcohol, and sex.[24]

Sulieman wasn't the only Muslim on Monk's first recording date. He hired his friend and protégé Art Blakey, a recent convert to the Muslim Brotherhood. He even adopted the name Abdullah Ibn Buhaina, though he rarely used it on stage. By one account, Blakey turned to Islam after he suffered a severe beating in Albany, Georgia, for failing to address a police officer as "sir." "After that experience," he later explained, "I started searching for a philosophy, a better way of life. . . . I knew that Masonry wasn't it and that Christianity had fallen down on the job."[25] The man who showed Blakey the way was Talib Dawud (formerly Barrymore Rainey), a trumpet player who not only recruited Sulieman but who had played with Thelonious in Dizzy's big band. Not long before the Blue Note session, Blakey and Dawud had started a Muslim mission out of Blakey's apartment.[26]

Blakey, Sulieman, and fifteen other musicians had also recently formed a rehearsal band calling themselves the Seventeen Messengers, or just the Messengers. The band was not entirely Muslim, but it did attract several Ahmadiyya followers. The group's name had religious connotations—a "messenger" was a Messenger of Allah.[27] Monk not only played with the group on occasion, but the core players literally became his source for sidemen.

Muslims seemed to congregate around Monk during his Blue Note period, yet he never hired anyone for his religious affiliation. He was only interested in musicianship. Monk had always dug Blakey's drumming, and he had improved during the last couple of years traveling with Billy Eckstine's big band.[28] With fleet hands and feet and a tremendous sense of timing and coordination, Blakey's approach marked a sharp departure from both Kenny Clarke and Denzil Best. He was less interested in "dropping bombs" than using the bass drum and sock cymbal to create cross-rhythms. He rode the ride cymbal with such power and imagination that it ceased to be just a timekeeping device. And he loved to insert his signature press roll. Blakey always pushed the tempo, but because Thelonious was partial to medium tempos, almost a fox trot, he tended to rein him in. Blakey always found a way to sustain even the medium to medium-slow tempos with energy.[29] For Billy Higgins, Blakey's recordings with Monk charted a new path for modern drumming: "On the records Art made with Monk, he was playing so much stuff that it was pitiful. He was charting the course. Art was Magellan."[30]

The band rehearsed at Monk's place on West 63rd Street in quarters so close it was almost unbearable. "All the musicians were in [Monk's bedroom] with their instruments," recalled Lorraine Gordon. "All of us crammed in that room for hours, and hours, listening and planning his record dates."[31] With the session scheduled for October 15 (five days after Thelonious celebrated his thirtieth birthday), the group only had a couple of weeks to nail down the music. Lion and Wolff decided Monk would cut four sides, all original compositions. In addition to "Humph" and "Thelonious," both Monk originals, they recorded Ike Quebec's "Suburban Eyes" (based on "All God's Chillun Got Rhythm"), and "Evonce" (slang for marijuana), co-written by Quebec and Idrees Sulieman.

By the time they gathered together at WOR Studios on Broadway and West 40th, neither Sulieman, West, Smith, Ramey, nor Blakey had fully mastered the music. The band wrestled with some of the songs and the arrangements for a number of takes. Working with Thelonious was not easy. Not only was his music difficult, but like Duke Ellington, Charles Mingus, and others, he believed that his sidemen should learn to play by listening. Alfred Lion remembers, "The musicians had to learn what he was doing by ear. And even if he had written it down, he might have changed his mind fifteen times between the time a musician learned his part and the final take. You really had to have ears to play with him."[32] They started out with "Humph," one of the few songs Monk recorded only once in his career. "Humph" resembled "I Got Rhythm," except that Monk replaced the standard changes with his preferred chromatic descending chord progressions. Monk's solo was replete with stock phrases he had been playing since Minton's and that he would continue to employ for the rest of his career. Like little countermelodies he incorporated at certain points in his improvisation, he had no problem with repeating himself. It took the band three takes to produce an acceptable version of "Humph."[33]

The star of the October 15 session, however, was another Monk original. "Thelonious" was the only tune completed in one take, and melodically it sounds deceptively simple. A theme built primarily on a repeating three-note phrase, Monk arranges the horns to play descending chord changes while he bangs out the melody. Monk is the only soloist, and what he plays introduces the listener to most of the devices that would characterize his improvisations: long rests, whole-tone figures, restatements of the melody, repeating octaves and triplets, and huge intervallic leaps. He also inserts a section of stride piano full of dissonant clusters.

The Lions and Wolff were thrilled with the outcome. So thrilled, in fact, that they brought Monk back to WOR Studios nine days later to cut six more sides, this time with just Ramey and Blakey. Of the six, four were Monk originals and two were standards ("April in Paris" and "Nice Work If You Can Get It"). Following two strong versions of "Nice Work," Monk recorded "Ruby, My Dear," introduced by an elegant whole-tone run the length of the piano. Unlike all subsequent renditions, the opening melody is full of embellishments, and yet his improvisations stay fairly close to the melodic line. On "Well, You Needn't" (formerly "You Need 'Na"), Monk returns to a swinging tempo and good old chromaticism. He plays with pure joy, singing solfeggio throughout and dropping a series of locomotivelike phrases that bring his futuristic music back to early Basie and Duke.

Monk was also able to record a tune he had written some time ago. Once called "What Now," now "Off Minor," the melody was not entirely Monk's; he "borrowed" part of the A-section from his friend Elmo Hope.[34] Bud Powell had recorded it back in January of 1947 with a trio consisting of Max Roach and Curley Russell.[35] In Monk's hands, "Off Minor" is more humor than pathos. He slows the pace and allows us to hear the notes ring. There is a lot of dissonance and angularity, and Monk deliberately roughs it up. There is nothing accidental about what he plays—he sings each and every note.

Before Blue Note showed up at Monk's doorstep, he dreamed of making new music, going in a direction different from Dizzy and Bird's. These recordings represent a significant departure from bebop, the dominant paradigm for modern jazz. Ironically, the most imaginative and challenging composition he recorded during these sessions did not see the light of day for another nine years. "Introspection," which took four takes to produce an acceptable version, was unlike anything that came before it. It embodied the most radical elements of Monk's approach to composition and improvisation.[36] It was the song that could have thrown down the gauntlet to bebop artists, opening jazz to much greater harmonic and rhythmic freedom. Yet the chords and melodic line fit together so well that Monk rarely strayed from the melody when improvising. For reasons unknown, Blue Note waited until they produced an LP of Monk's music to release "Introspection." Perhaps Wolff and the Lions believed the music was too experimental to attract listeners in 1947.

Nonetheless, the Blue Note team was anxious to get Monk back into the studio yet again. As Alfred Lion explained to producer Michael Cuscuna in 1985, "Monk was so fantastically original and his compositions were so strong and new that I just wanted to record everything he had. It was so fantastic I had to record it all."[37] Less than a month later, November 21, Monk returned to the WOR Studios to record four more sides, despite the fact that Blue Note had yet to release one 78. This time, he decided to go with a quintet comprised of different personnel—the only holdover from the previous sessions was Art Blakey. In place of Sulieman, Monk hired twenty-eight-year-old George "Flip" Taitt, a pretty good swing trumpeter who was almost as obscure as Billy Smith or Danny Quebec West.[38]

Monk also hired Sahib Shihab, a twenty-two-year-old alto and baritone player from the Seventeen Messengers and Minton's Playhouse. Like Blakey, he had converted to Islam and joined the Muslim Brotherhood earlier in the year.[39] Born Edmund Gregory in Savannah, Georgia, Shihab attended classes at Boston Conservatory from 1941 to 1942, then toured with Fletcher Henderson for two years.[40] The fair-skinned, clean-cut Shihab could pass for an Ivy League student, but at the time he got the call to record with Monk he was laboring as an elevator operator.[41] Rounding out the rhythm section was bassist Bob Paige, whom Monk hired on occasion. Each band member had worked with Monk in the past and was, at least, familiar with the music.

The session generated a few jewels, but it required a lot of work and patience. On "In Walked Bud," Monk's tribute to his friend based loosely on the changes to Irving Berlin's "Blue Skies," it took four tries to produce an acceptable take. It took eight takes to create two usable versions of "Who Knows," a treacherous melody played swiftly over Monk's signature descending chromatic changes. Jumping way up and down across two octaves, Shihab had never confronted music so difficult. He told Nat Hentoff: "I had a part that was unbelievably difficult. I complained to Monk. His only answer was: 'You a musician? You got a union card? Play it!' To my surprise, I eventually did."[42] Taitt, on the other hand, never quite got it. Every take was a struggle, and each time he was a little clueless as to what to do on the bridge. He also insisted on quoting "Stranger in Paradise" on every take except for the master—perhaps an expression of how he was feeling on the date.[43]

The other two songs recorded that day were original ballads: "Monk's Mood," which endured several title changes and was first copyrighted a year and a half earlier as "Feeling that Way Now," and " 'Round Midnight." Both songs were recorded in single takes, and on both arrangements Monk used the horns as harmonic or melodic backdrops to his own improvisations. Both versions are gorgeous.

With three recording sessions over six weeks producing a grand total of fourteen releasable sides, Blue Note was ready to start pressing. Thelonious was anxious to have the fruits of his labor in record stores and on radio stations, but he had to wait for the three-person operation to manufacture the records.

In the meantime, Monk fell into his usual routine: hustling for gigs, composing, and hanging out with family and friends. He had been spending so much time up at Sonny's place that it became custom to divide Thanksgiving and Christmas between his mother's house and Lyman Place. On December 27, he was uptown to help Nellie celebrate her twenty-sixth birthday. She had recently left her gig at Borden's Ice Cream and taken a job as a waitress at Chock Full O' Nuts, all the while battling digestive and abdominal problems.[44]

Monk's first disc, with "Thelonious" on the A side and "Suburban Eyes" on the B side (Blue Note 542), was finally ready to be shipped out in early January, 1948. On Sunday, January 25, Club 845 in the Bronx became the site of an impromptu release party for Blue Note. Blakey and the Jazz Messengers, featuring Monk and Little Benny Harris, headlined the six-hour affair, which promoter Ray Pino dubbed "Variation in Modern Music."[45] The other act on the bill was Blue Note recording artist Babs Gonzalez and his "Three Bips and a Bop." The Lions and Frank Wolff could not have been more pleased. Thelonious finally had a record of his own to play on his mother's brand new console-style radio/phonograph.[46]

Lorraine Lion *was* Blue Note's marketing department. On the night of January 12, she, Alfred, and Frank took Thelonious to three different radio stations to promote the record. Although Monk wasn't always the best interviewee, he took the job seriously. He went in a dark suit and tie, with his classic gold-rimmed glasses, but no beret. Accompanying Wolff and the Lions that night was artist, critic, and amateur musician Paul Bacon, an old friend of Lorraine's from the Newark Hot Club. Just out of the service, he had begun working for Blue Note designing album covers. What Bacon thought would be a pretty routine evening turned out to be an unforgettable experience, from the moment he got in the car. "I got to ride in the back seat and Monk captivated me in thirty seconds."[47] He found Monk's performance on Fred Robbins's radio show that night particularly amusing. Robbins, host of the 120 Club Show on station WOV, was perhaps the most prominent radio personality in support of the new music. (Sir Charles Thompson had written "Robbin's Nest" for Fred.) "Robbins wasn't too deep," recalled Bacon, "and was expecting a light interview with some young musician who was hot to get his records played and make it. But Monk was incurably honest and simply couldn't engage in superficialities even if he wanted to. By the end of the show, Fred took Lorraine aside and told her in harsh terms never to bring this so-and-so up to his studio again. It was a funny scene."[48]

Lorraine knew she could not change Monk's manner or way of thinking, so she turned what she characterized as strange behavior into selling points. She also understood that even die-hard bebop fans might find Monk's music a bit challenging. She therefore set out to sell Monk the artist, and took more than a page out of William Gottlieb's *Down Beat* article. Lorraine ran with the idea that Monk was bebop's true founder. "Just as Louis Armstrong wielded the greatest influence on trumpet players and their styles and was one of the bulwarks in the development of Jazz," she opened her first press release, "so Thelonious Monk will some day be regarded as the true instigator of the modern trend in music today."[49] The laboratory for Monk's initial instigations was Minton's Playhouse. All of the serious musicians, most prominently Dizzy and Bird, headed to 118th Street to listen to Monk's "weird style on the piano" and to "assimilate his radical ideas." The larger world didn't know he existed, but the musicians did, and his champions included such distinguished figures as Mary Lou Williams, Duke Ellington, and Nat "King" Cole. "While Thelonious laid the groundwork, more commercial minds [read: Dizzy] elaborated on his strange, new harmonies and brought the music before the public. Just as Picasso established a new school of modern abstract art, so Thelonious created a new horizon of Jazz expression."[50]

Lorraine repeats Gottlieb's reportage about Monk's anonymity, adding her own hyperbole for good measure. "A shy and elusive person, Thelonious has been surrounded by an aura of mystery, but simply because he considers the piano the most important thing in his life and can become absorbed in composing that people, appointments and the world pass by unnoticed. The results of his frequent withdrawals from society are tunes whose melodies and harmonies could only come from the fantastic mind of a genius."[51] In a follow-up press release, she announced that Blue Note had "actually found the one person who was responsible for this whole new trend in music. The genius behind the whole movement—and we have had the privilege of being the first to put his radical and unorthodox ideas on wax—is an unusual and mysterious character with the more unusual name of Thelonious Monk. Among musicians, Thelonious' name is treated with respect and awe, for he is a strange person whose pianistics continue to baffle all who hear him."[52]

Lorraine wasn't just a good press agent; she was a believer. She sent copies of her press release along with cover letters to several jazz magazines and the black press. Her January 13 letter to George Hoefer, imploring him to write a piece on Thelonious for his "Hot Box" column in *Down Beat*, said more about Monk's behavior and his appearance than his music: "It's impossible to put the strangeness of his characteristics into writing," she explained, "and believe me, he's an original." She then goes on to elaborate on his "strangeness": "He's quite tall, slender build and sports a slight goatee topped by massive gold-rimmed glasses. . . . He considers it nothing to be on his feet or at the piano for a week straight, without a drop of sleep, but then makes up for it by sleeping for three days and nights, straight through. He's so loaded with ideas, that before he has time to write them down, he's thought of five others. Ninety percent of his time is spent at the piano, anybody's piano, and it takes an earthquake to pull him away from it."[53]

Hoefer took the bait, hurriedly running a short piece titled "Pianist Monk Getting Long Awaited Break," in the February 11 issue. He relied solely on Lorraine's letter and press release, taking whole passages verbatim. He emphasized Monk's obscurity, his sleep patterns, his revolutionary role at Minton's, his sartorial style, and the swing kids who mimicked him. ("You've seen his counterpart, the goateed cat with the beret and massive gold-rimmed glasses on 52nd Street for the past six years, but chances are rare that you've seen the Monk himself."[54]) Yet, Hoefer reserved very little space for Monk's record, commenting only on his "weird harmonies" and the fact that his "technique is not the greatest but his originality in improvisation is that of a genius."[55] Lion succeeded in getting Hoefer to reprint the other critical component of her press kit—that Thelonious started it all. It was Monk, he wrote, that led the "famed sessions at Minton's," but it was Diz and Bird who went on to "sell be-bop to a considerable following. They became famous in the process while the man who laid the chord foundations and inspired the harmonic progressions was forgotten, due to his own exclusiveness."[56]

Nineteen forty-eight became the year Thelonious Monk was invented. In fewer than two hundred words, Lorraine Lion—building on William Gottlieb—established the lens through which the entire world would come to see Monk. Elusive, mysterious, strange, eccentric, weird, genius—these were the foundational adjectives that formed the caricature of Monk. It was Lion who dubbed Thelonious the "High Priest of Bebop,"[57] re-presenting him to jazz audiences as a kind of mystic. His reputation for lateness, unreliability, and drunkenness only added to his image as an eccentric, as did stories of his sleeplessness and nocturnal adventures in search of someone's piano to play. Neither Lion nor Gottlieb nor anyone else seems to have considered that these episodes, or his fits of obsessive creativity, could have been early signs of manic depression. Monk's behavior was weird and made good copy. Blue Note's marketing campaign marked the beginning of Monk's iconization, his transformation into what critic Nat Hentoff called "a stock cartoon figure for writers of Sunday supplement pieces about the exotica of jazz." Monk became a novelty, marketed to the public for his strangeness—his name, his music, his bodily gestures, his famous non-verbal communication, his unpredictability. "Pictures of Monk in dark glasses and goatee," Hentoff later observed, "would usually be captioned 'Mad Monk' or 'The High Priest of Bop.' Exaggerated stories of his personal life were the 'substance' of the articles. There was no attempt to discuss the nature or seriousness of his musical intentions. Monk became part of the Sabbath sideshow of resurrected murderers, celebrated divorce cases, and Elsa Maxwell."[58]

Lion scored a huge coup when she convinced Ralph Ingersoll, the silk-stocking Communist and founding editor of the liberal newsmagazine *PM*, to run a lengthy profile of Thelonious in February of 1948.[59] Ingersoll assigned the piece to arts and culture critic Ira Peck. Peck wasn't really a jazz guy so much as a very smart dabbler in the arts. [60] As a feature writer for *PM* for the last five years, Peck had not yet encountered anyone like Monk. At their initial meeting in Monk's apartment, Thelonious said so little that Peck was ready to abandon the project, until Lorraine Lion insisted that she be present for the interview.[61] Monk eventually opened up, offering honest criticism and bold claims about his contribution to the music, but not much else. Much of Peck's story consisted of detailed descriptions of Monk's apartment, commentary from friends, acquaintances, and critics of the new music, and, unsurprisingly, Blue Note press material. Before he could talk about Monk, however, Peck had to make the case for bebop as high art, particularly for a readership more accustomed to opera, symphonies, and art museums than modern jazz. He opened with the acknowledgment that critics "have called [bebop] a kind of 'surrealist' jazz and have drawn analogies between it and the works of Picasso and Dali. Musically, it has been likened to the works of Stravinsky, whom most be-bop musicians are known to admire." After emphasizing its dissonant sonorities and the "breakneck pace" of its rhythms, he went on to quote classical pianist Eugene List, who said "Be-bop is to jazz . . . as atonality is to classical music. It uses the enlarged harmony structure of jazz but is more cerebral than emotional. I like it. Any intellectual exercise in music is fun if you want to take your mind off anything. I wish I could play first-rate be-bop."[62] Monk himself reinforced Peck and List's characterization of modern jazz by making a spirited case for experimental music in opposition to "commercial jazz." Bebop's detractors, Monk argued, "don't understand the music and in most cases never heard it. Weird means something you never heard before. It's weird until people get around to it. Then it ceases to be weird." "It's the modern music of today," he added. "It makes other musicians think—just like Picasso. It has to catch on."[63]

Without elaborating on the music, however, Peck falls back on Lion's familiar description of Monk's odd behavior. He hardly sleeps, eats when he feels like it, "wanders around from one friend's house to another, or from one club to another, working out his ideas on the piano," and still lives at home with his mother. For this part of the story, Peck reused the testimony of Teddy Hill. While acknowledging his genius, Hill described him as "undependable," adding that "Monk . . . is so absorbed in his music he appears to have lost touch with everything else." Hill claimed Monk could barely hold a conversation without his mind wandering and that he was known to forget his girlfriend in the club. Peck's portrait also relied on anonymous friends. One "friend" described a "girl that idolizes him," lighting his cigarettes and whatnot, but in whom Monk showed very little interest. "He tells me that women are a 'heckle' sometimes. He doesn't want to be tied down to anything except his music." The woman in question lived in Monk's building and dropped by "frequently to clean his room and wash his dishes."[64] The anonymous informant may have been speaking of Marion, who was still living in the Phipps Houses a couple of doors down, and came by often to help her mother by straightening up.[65] For Nellie, it must have been a difficult thing to read.

For all the anecdotes and extravagant description, the story never lost its core theme: Monk was bebop's true originator. This time Monk sheepishly accepted the idea. He told Peck that the new music "just happened. I just felt it. It came to me. Something was being created differently without my trying to." He explained that what Dizzy and Bird were playing in 1948 was not what he originally worked out at Minton's. Monk spoke candidly about not getting much recognition but admitted, "I don't get around as much. . . . I'm sort of underground in bebop." And he added that one of his biggest problems was finding musicians capable of playing his songs. Teddy Hill was quoted again: "Monk seemed more like the guy who manufactured the product rather than commercialized it. Dizzy has gotten all the exploitation because Dizzy branched out and got started. Monk stayed right in the same groove."[66]

Although it seems unlikely that Lorraine Lion or these journalists intended to pit Monk against Gillespie, some tension did exist between them, or at least some competition over their respective narratives of bebop's origins. Just a few weeks before the *PM* article appeared, Dizzy announced that he was writing a book on bebop with the assistance of Leonard Feather. The article appeared in the black-owned *California Eagle*, and it characterized Gillespie as "the creator of this newest jazz idiom."[67]

In the end, Monk and the Blue Note crew were pleased with the article. Miss Barbara was not. She was quite upset with Peck's colorful, yet degrading, description of her apartment—not to mention the accompanying photograph. He wrote about how her soot-darkened walls and worn-down linoleum "contrasted incongruously with a large new, shiny white refrigerator." As a proud, dignified Southern black woman, such language was embarrassing. Her complaints to Lorraine fell on deaf ears, largely because Lorraine could not understand the deeply ingrained sense of modesty and pride working-class black women possessed. For women who made a living cleaning other people's houses and offices, keeping a clean and orderly house of their own took on great importance.[68] Lorraine simply dismissed her concerns and practically chastised her for failing to recognize the importance of such publicity: "Look, Mrs. Monk. Your son is going to be very famous. This is just the beginning. You will have to get used to this."[69]

Lorraine Lion sent out another round of press kits just in time for the release of Monk's second 78 (Blue Note 543), with "Well, You Needn't" and "'Round Midnight." The Lions had the bright idea to invite a select group of writers to a party at their Greenwich Village apartment to listen to the test pressings of the latest disc. Among the invitees was the new managing editor of *The Record Changer*, Orrin Keepnews. He had been hired by Bill Grauer, his former Columbia University classmate, who had purchased the record collectors' newsletter in order to turn it into a first-rate, modern jazz magazine. A native New Yorker, Keepnews earned a bachelor's degree in English from Columbia in 1943, served in the Pacific theater as a radar operator on B-29 bombers, then returned to school to pursue a graduate degree. To make ends meet, he took a job as a junior editor at Simon & Schuster. When he took over the editorship of *The Record Changer*, he was still working and going to school. But he could not resist the chance to write about what he loved—jazz.[70]

The Lions had read Keepnews's first column with great interest, and they had heard about him from their friend Paul Bacon, whom Grauer had hired as the magazine's artistic director. They thought that if Keepnews could only meet Thelonious he might be persuaded to write a piece on their newest artist. "I took the bait and swallowed it whole," Keepnews confessed. "And with the arrogance of ignorance I took Monk off into a corner and proceeded to do an interview with him." He was told he couldn't get a complete sentence out of the High Priest, but he did. "I had a lovely time talking to him, frankly."[71]

The article, which appeared in the April issue of *The Record Changer*, actually focused on the music, not Monk's eccentricities or behavior. Rather than fold Monk into the bebop school, Keepnews argued that his approach to modern piano, particularly in an ensemble context, was in a class of its own. He had his own school, so to speak, anchored in a strong rhythmic style and possessed of "a sly, wry, satiric humor that has a rare maturity." He wasn't too impressed with Monk's horn players (except for Danny Quebec West), whom he found "too steeped in standard bebop; their solos sometimes fail to follow the complex pattern being established by the rhythm unit, and the ensembles tend, on occasion, to fall into standard bop cliches."[72] Nevertheless, Keepnews found more musicality and coherence in Monk's recordings than in most modern jazz. Monk's music "has a feeling of unity, warmth, and purpose that contrasts sharply with the emotionless, jittered-up pyrotechnics of Fifty-Second Street 'modernism.'" Keepnews did get a few things wrong: he places Monk at Minton's in 1938; has him recording with Hawkins in 1940 rather than 1944; and puts him on the road with Hawk for two years, "which meant that he was not on hand during the period when 'bebop' . . . was first being stylized and strongly plugged."[73] Still, for an impromptu hour-long conversation in the corner of a room with a stranger, Keepnews accomplished a lot.

Besides contacting the jazz press, Lorraine Lion made a concerted effort to reach out to the black press. Most publications turned her down, including a fairly new but widely circulated photo magazine called *Ebony*.[74] The Pittsburgh *Courier* took the bait, running virtually the entire press release with Lorraine Lion's byline (except for the paragraph describing Monk as mysterious, absorbed, and "shy and elusive").[75] Dan Burley of the *Amsterdam News* reproduced many of the same references to Monk's "aura of mystery" and his elusive behavior, while playing up the rivalry between Dizzy and Thelonious over who deserves credit for originating bebop. Burley minces no words: "Off Thelonious' groundwork, commercial-minded lads constructed a money empire and brought bebop to the public. But Thelonious has always remained in the shadows of obscurity and while others rise to fame and fortune, he has to struggle as best he can to get along."[76]

The *Chicago Defender* also bought Lion's story about Monk's eccentricity, and they accepted the claim that Thelonious was the real progenitor of bebop. Rather than run the press release verbatim, the editors sent their New York correspondent to Thelonious's house to get the scoop on the "Creator of 'Bebop.'" Remarkably, Monk talked a lot. For whatever reason, he shared his opinions fully and freely. First, he took issue with the name bebop. "I don't like to think of my music as bebop—but as modern music. I don't dig the word. It doesn't mean anything, it's just scatting like hi-de-hi-de-ho or se-bop-baty-iou." Second, he took issue with the music itself, suggesting that what often was labeled bebop lacked coherence, pretty melodies, and a strong, swinging beat—all qualities he believed were essential to good music. "I like the music to sound melodious. . . . People have to know harmony. It's harder for people to understand bebop who don't know music." He adds, "Everybody has a different conception of melody. That's why some music is prettier than other [sic]. You should always have melody in the piece." And rhythm. "I play with a swing beat. But everything's got a beat, you live by beats—the beat of your heart. If your heart stops beating that's curtains."[77] Monk was sure of the impact he'd made on modern jazz: "I hear a lot of my influence in modern music." He complained that "The public hasn't been hearing the right music," but continued to hope that "By listening and paying attention, [the public] can tell the difference between good and bad music. They'll dig. They'll learn."[78]

In many ways, it was a remarkable interview. Monk was clear, coherent, assertive, even witty. But when the issue of his love life came up, Monk was evasive once again. Perhaps protecting Nellie's privacy or his own, he was emphatic about his bachelor status, announcing that he had no plans to marry and was patiently waiting for "a beautiful millionaire woman." Whether or not Nellie laughed it off or was genuinely nervous about their future, Thelonious was suddenly getting a lot of attention and exhibited, at least on the page, a slightly inflated sense of self. And in fact there were a few millionaire women in search of their own "High Priest of Bebop." But Nellie had been waiting too long not to consider the possibility of matrimony.

Meanwhile, Monk continued to make a name for himself. On February 16, Monk's quartet (Sulieman, Blakey, and bassist Curley Russell) participated in radio station WNYC's Ninth Annual "American Music Program." Surprisingly, during the fourteen-minute broadcast, the group did not play any of Thelonious's compositions.[79] The following month, Thelonious returned to Minton's Playhouse, now as a money-earning bandleader.[80] It had been years since he was on the payroll. Teddy Hill was now the co-owner, Eddie "Lockjaw" Davis oversaw the Monday night sessions as musical director, and Monk's band—with Sahib Shihab, Al McKibbon, and Blakey—was the main attraction. Sometimes Idrees Sulieman joined the group, or Ike Quebec or Danny Quebec West showed up. These became Monk's stable of musicians, the artists who knew the music and could keep up with him.

Growing fame did not always guarantee ideal performing conditions. On April 30, he and some friends from the neighborhood, calling themselves the "San Juan Hill Association," rented the Golden Gate Ballroom on 142nd and Lenox Avenue in Harlem and organized a concert featuring Monk. The publicity billed Thelonious as "The High Priest of Be-Bop." They brought the popular "MacBeth the Great and his Calypso Serenadors" to open for Monk's group, which consisted of Sulieman, both Quebecs, Curley Russell, and Blakey. For a mere buck and a half, dancers could enjoy not only virtually nonstop music from 10:00 p.m. to 3:00 a.m., but they could meet the lovely "Miss San Juan Hill," winner of the recent neighborhood beauty pageant.[81]

The event attracted a decent turnout. Harlem and Brooklyn's West Indian community came out in droves to hear MacBeth's raucous performances of "Man Smart, Woman Smarter" and "Hold 'Em Joe." But there were glitches when Monk's group took the bandstand. Sitting at the Golden Gate's old grand piano, Monk found a dead key while the band was tuning up. No problem; he had had his share of dead keys and broken strings. But then he noticed that the pedal post was falling apart. Every time he hit the sustain pedal it jiggled uncomfortably. Once the band hit, the pedal got worse. A few choruses into the first song, Monk decided it had to go. He reached down to rip it out with one hand, while continuing to play with the other. When that didn't work, he bent down farther and applied both hands to the post. As Paul Bacon observed, "There was a slight crack, a ripping sound, and off came the whole works, to be flung aside as Monk calmly resumed playing." By the time the pianist for MacBeth returned for another set, he was a little thrown off by the sudden reconfiguration of the piano.[82] The dancers didn't care; MacBeth still rocked the house.

Monk's road to fame felt longer and more treacherous once the reviews appeared. *Down Beat*'s reviewer gave Monk's first disc only two stars each for "Thelonious" and "Suburban Eyes." He wrote, "On his own solo spots, there seem to be points at which Monk is thinking about the stock returns or the seventh at Pimlico—anything but his piano. He also has several passages where he plays straight striding Waller piano. As a modernist, this can hardly be excused. All present-day piano players have right hands with eight fingers and a rigid claw on the left hand. . . . From the Monk we expect better."[83] The reviewer for *Metronome* concurred, dismissing "Thelonious" with a letter-grade of "C," in part because he plays "an ancient piano style" (i.e., stride). "Suburban Eyes" scored a slightly higher grade of C+, largely due to the strength of Sulieman, Danny Quebec West, and Billy Smith, but "Monk's piano nullifies this capable trio's efforts."[84]

The second disc, with "Well, You Needn't" and "'Round Midnight," did not fare much better. The review in *Down Beat* said, "The Monk is undoubtedly a man of con-siderable ability both technically and harmonically but his abstractions on these sides are just too too—and I played them early in the morning and late at night. 'Needn't' doesn't require a Juilliard diploma to understand, but 'Midnight' is for the super hip alone. Why they list the personnel on a side where the whole band plays like a vibra-toless organ under the piano solo is a mystery."[85] *Billboard* proved more sympathetic, though the magazine's witty one-liners can hardly be called reviews. About "Theloni-ous," for example, this is all the reviewer wrote: "Grandaddy of the beboppers, pianist Monk turns out a controversial jazz disking worked out on one tone riff." Using a rat-ing system ranging from 0 to 100, the *Billboard* reviewer gave "Thelonious" a 68 and "Suburban Eyes" 67.[86]

The most sympathetic review to appear that spring was written by someone whose authority could have easily been questioned: Paul Bacon. Bacon, after all, was friends with the Lions and had worked for Blue Note when Monk was recording with them. And he had befriended Monk, seeing him often at Minton's Playhouse and sometimes hanging out with him a little between sets.[87] On the other hand, the jazz world was so incestuous that it wasn't uncommon for record producers to review recordings—sometimes even their own projects.[88] Bacon was a real fan and a careful listener. In a lengthy review of the second disc for *The Record Changer*, he assigns Monk a central role in shaping the direction of modern music, despite the fact that his unorthodox style had cost him jobs. Bacon believed Monk's strengths lay in his use of space, his conception of rhythmn ("Monk has a beat like ocean waves—no matter how sudden, spasmodic or obscure, his little inventions, he rocks irresistibly on"), and his ability to draw on the history of music in unpredictable ways. "He plays riffs that are older than Bunk Johnson," Bacon wrote, "but they don't sound the same; his beat is familiar but he does something strange there, too—he can make a rhythm seem almost sepa-rate, so that what he does is inside it, or outside it. He may play for a space in nothing but smooth phrases and then suddenly jump on a part and repeat it with an intensity beyond description."[89]

All the good press in the world wasn't enough to sell records. Lorraine could not sell Monk. Downtown record stores were a bust because "they thought he lacked technique."[90] She had no luck in Harlem, either. She lugged boxes of 78s uptown, but "the guys in those record stores would say, 'He can't play. He has two left hands.'"[91] She even traveled the country with her case of 78s, with little success, though she had no trouble selling other Blue Note artists. "I went to Philly, Baltimore, a whole lineup, Cleveland, Chicago. . . . I had to battle all the way to get them to buy a Monk record and listen to him."[92]

But selling records and winning converts is not the same thing. While Monk did nothing for the jazz establishment, the record collectors and *Down Beat* readers, a growing number of black musicians, writers, and artists heard in Monk's music a distillation of the modern age. Monk found a hearing early on among writers like Ralph Ellison and Langston Hughes, and his Blue Note recordings had a profound effect on a fourteen-year-old Newark kid named LeRoi Jones ("Monk was my main man"[93]), who was destined to become one of the most important poets of the postwar era. Thelonious inspired visual artists such as Romare Bearden and Norman Lewis, who spent many evenings at Minton's and heard in Monk the musical equivalent of abstract expressionism.[94] The clearest manifestation of Monk's importance for self-proclaimed black Modernists is the 1948 publication of Nard Griffin's slim volume, *To Be or Not to Bop*. A little-known Harlem writer who gained some notoriety as a jazz critic, Griffin set out to give the new music intellectual legitimacy while defusing the pitched battles between boppers and traditionalists. Rejecting the term "bebop" in favor of "the New Listen" or "the new movement in modern music," Griffin identified Monk, along with Bird and Diz, as one of its founding fathers. He called Monk "one of the more progressive minded men in music. . . . He too has contributed much to modern jazz and offers something new and different in piano work."[95] Monk and the emerging generation of modernists had created an art form that served as a metaphor for the modern age: "The next decade or so will bring about an even greater transfiguration, thus coinciding music with other developments of the period. In this day of atomic progress, jet propulsion, and many seemingly fantastic inventions and ideas, such as rockets and 'the new look' there can be no wonder that a new and dynamic idea in music is offered in the guise of BeBop."[96]

Monk probably saw Griffin's book, as it made the rounds among black musicians in Harlem. (He may have even teased Dizzy years later for stealing the title for his own memoir!) But the assessment that mattered most was beyond reach of his eyes and ears. During the summer of 1948, while Duke Ellington's band was traveling by train in the southern coast of England, trumpeter Ray Nance decided to pass the time away by listening to records on a little portable phonograph he had picked up. "I put on one of my Thelonious Monk records. Duke was passing by in the corridor, and he stopped and asked, 'Who's that playing?' I told him. 'Sounds like he's stealing some of my stuff,' he said. So he sat down and listened to my records, and he was very interested. He understood what Monk was doing."[97]

• • •

Meanwhile, 1948 was turning out to be Monk's busiest year since he left Hawkins. When his stint at Minton's ended, Monte Kay offered him a short gig at a club he was managing called the Royal Roost. In its past life, the Roost was a nondescript chicken joint on Broadway and West 47th Street, but once Monte Kay took over, it became "the Metropolitan Bopera House," or the "House that Bop Built." Bird, Dizzy, Lester Young, and Tadd Dameron were among the featured artists, and "Symphony Sid" Torin, the celebrated jazz dj, was the master of ceremonies. The Roost attracted a younger crowd (it even had a milk bar for teens) and was all about the music. Patrons not interested in drinking could pay ninety cents to sit in bleacher seats. It had no dance floor, no fancy revues, just bebop.[98] Thelonious led several sessions at the Roost during part of May and June with a band that included Milt Jackson and bassists John Simmons and Curley Russell. Dozens of musicians sat in, from Bird to tenor saxophonist Wardell Gray.[99] Although later sessions with Tadd Dameron, Dizzy Gillespie, and Bird were broadcast from the Royal Roost, none of Monk's sessions received airplay, something about which he would grumble in later years.

Many Roost regulars were still unaccustomed to Monk's style. Even some of the musicians didn't know what to do with him. Bassist John Simmons couldn't follow Monk when they first started working together. "He played between the keys, he played against the meter, and he would just play all over the piano, you know. It wasn't anything you could follow. If you didn't know the tune, you couldn't play with him. Now, if you're playing by ear, you had to listen to the melodic line. So I trained my ears to listening to Bags, you know, Milt Jackson. I'd just throw Monk out of my ear. I just closed my ears to him completely." When that didn't work, Simmons turned to cocaine, reefer, and Seagram's VO: "I was resorting to this to try to get way spaced out to keep up with Monk, and I couldn't catch him. . . ."[100]

Largely because of his association with the Roost and with Symphony Sid's "bebop all-stars," Monk was invited to play a benefit for Sydenham Hospital in Harlem held on June 9. It was the first of many benefit concerts he would participate in. Sydenham had been struggling for some time, facing severe financial shortfalls, made worse by the resignation of its director. The administration scrambled to pull together several emergency fundraisers just to keep its doors open.[101] Nat "King" Cole, one of Monk's favorite pianists, headlined the star-studded event. Besides the usual suspects (Bird, Miles Davis, Tadd Dameron, Max Roach), some of the more prominent participants included comedians Jerry Lewis, Dean Martin, and Zero Mostel, the famous dance duo the Nicholas Brothers, Jimmie Lunceford's band, and singer Thelma Carpenter. Monk brought his own sextet—Sulieman, both Quebecs, Curley Russell, and Blakey—though given the number of artists on the bill, they probably only performed a couple of tunes. Still, it was a special night for Thelonious, not because of who was there but where they played: the event was held at Central Needle Trades High School, Nellie's alma mater.[102]

On Monday, June 28, while Monk was leaving the Roost after his last Sunday night set, police rolled up on him and discovered a small bag of marijuana in his possession. He was arrested, held in the Tombs overnight, and arraigned.[103] Marijuana possession, which had been outlawed by the federal government eleven years earlier, was considered a misdemeanor in New York State.[104] Between Monk's meager income and contributions from Sonny, Geraldine, and Nellie, they were able to raise the modest bail money; he was released the next day to await a trial date. Misdemeanor or not, possession of reefer was punishable by a fine of up to $500 and/or imprisonment "not exceeding one year."[105] He also faced unemployment: The Roost never let him come back.

According to Nellie, Monk's arrest and his consequent joblessness were no accident. She insisted that the management—in this instance, Monte Kay—had set Thelonious up because they wanted to replace him.[106] Though the evidence is purely circumstantial, if the Roost wanted to get rid of Monk, his arrest came at a convenient time. Monte Kay found Monk's music interesting and had worked with him on and off since Monk's time with Hawkins at the Down Beat Club. But he still saw Monk as a "troubled guy and not too reliable."[107] Regardless of what really went down the morning of June 28, the consequences proved disastrous.

Three days following his release from jail, Monk was back in the studio for another Blue Note session, despite the current recording ban called by the AFM.[108] His commitment to the label was unshakable. Blue Note was preparing to release another 78 from the fall '47 sessions—"Off Minor" and "Evonce"—and the Lions felt he needed more music in the can. Frustrated by their inability to sell Monk's records, they decided to try something different. First, they included Milt Jackson as a featured artist on the date. Jackson had begun to gain a bit of a following as a soloist with Dizzy Gillespie and Howard McGhee, and in the spring of 1948 he briefly formed his own band with John Lewis and Kenny Clarke.[109] Jackson was a crowd favorite; his solos swung hard and seemed to lift the audience. Second, Blue Note and Monk decided to add a couple of vocal numbers. Monk hired crooner Kenny "Pancho" Hagood, whom he knew and performed with when they both were in Dizzy Gillespie's big band in 1946. Monk even changed the rhythm section, bringing John Simmons, the bassist from the Royal Roost, and drummer Rossiere "Shadow" Wilson. Neither Simmons nor Wilson was strongly identified with bebop, but both artists were incredibly versatile and had worked with swing bands representing different eras. Simmons recorded with everyone, from James P. Johnson and Big Sid Catlett to Ben Webster, Billie Holiday, and Coleman Hawkins.[110] Wilson was best known for his work with the Count Basie Orchestra, though he also played with Lionel Hampton, Benny Carter, and Earl Hines.[111] For whatever reason, Monk was looking for a change, and he put together a more mature band. Everyone in the quartet had an established reputation and a fairly long resume, although Monk was still the elder of the group.

Monk's choice of swing-era veterans and modernists paid off. The band cut six sides in nine takes, two of which were new compositions: "Evidence," based on the changes from "Just You, Just Me," was still being composed when Monk first recorded, and it's a stripped-down version of what the song will become. "Misterioso," the other new tune, was Monk's only twelve-bar blues to date. The band also updated a couple of older Monk compositions: the Minton's theme song "Epistrophy" and "I Mean You." Both songs are radical departures from earlier recordings by Cootie Williams and Coleman

Hawkins, respectively. They are more angular and dissonant, and Monk's accents on "I Mean You" are more off-center without losing a sense of swing. He brilliantly echoes Jackson's interpretation of the opening theme and plays countermelodies so jarring and unusual that they overwhelm the melody.

If Wolff and the Lions thought the addition of a couple of vocal numbers might make Monk more palatable to a popular audience, they were wrong. Monk wasn't backing a singer for a house band; he was leading his own recording session, trying to make music on his own terms. His reading of the standards "All the Things You Are" and "I Should Care" with Kenny "Pancho" Hagood were startling. Monk and Jackson create a dense chaos of lush, dissonant fills that threaten to overwhelm Hagood, who had enough trouble trying to stay in tune. The effect is as if Monk and Jackson are having a bizarre conversation behind Hagood's back, and their harmonically adventurous figures not only crash into each other but strip these songs of romanticism, investing them with humor.[112] But if Jackson and Monk had fun, Hagood did not. Always the task master, Thelonious made Hagood sing "I Should Care" out of his range, despite his protestations. According to John Simmons, "Pancho's throat was sore for a week. Couldn't get him to sing a note. He hurt himself."[113]

All the songs on the date, particularly Monk's musical dialogues with Milton Jackson, exemplify Monk's characteristic parallel voices, collective improvisation, and layering of melodic lines and countermelodies. In these and other recordings, he invents countermelodies, incorporates arpeggios (outlining chords in single notes, often emphasizing the most dissonant tonalities), and plays many different "runs" down the piano—particularly runs built on whole-tone scales. Monk, in other words, conceived of the piano as an orchestral instrument. He thought in multiple lines—two, three, even four—and played independent rhythmic lines with his left and right hands. It was a key to Monk as a composer, improviser, and arranger—three components of making music that he treated as inseparable.[114] For Monk, the composition was not just the melody but the entire performance. He had little interest in "blowing sessions." Even when musicians were improvising together, he expected a level of orchestration that would sustain the essential elements of the piece.

Thelonious left the studio on a high. It seemed like nothing could bring him down—neither the fact that he was looking at a possible drug conviction and jail time, that he was jobless, nor that his bosses at the Royal Roost chose Tadd Dameron, a pianist Monk believed "really couldn't play . . . couldn't finger nothing, hardly,"[115] to lead the house band. The feeling didn't last very long, however. A few days after the session, someone handed Thelonious a copy of the latest *New Yorker* magazine with Richard Boyer's piece on "Bop." It was a strange article—a publicity vehicle for Dizzy, a sensational and inaccurate exposé of bebop, and a provocation. The article positioned Monk and Dizzy as adversaries, labeling Gillespie the "Abraham Lincoln of jazz" (against Monk's "George Washington") for his role in freeing the music "from a weak banality" of swing and "irregular rhythm and strange new chord combinations."[116] Boyer called into question the publicity Monk received proclaiming him the progenitor of the music. "There are devotees of bebop music," he wrote, "who believe that the Monk, as Thelonious is sometimes called, had more to do with the origin of bebop than Dizzy did." He added, "There is a certain coolness between the two men, and their relations are rather formal."[117] He even raised doubts as to who between them initiated the beret, sunglasses, and goatee.

Boyer's caricature of Monk is at times flattering and at others silly or degrading. He describes Monk (who was approaching his thirty-first birthday) as "a somber, scholarly twenty-one-year-old Negro with a bebop beard, who played piano with a sacerdotal air, as if the keyboard were an altar and he an acolyte." To add to the pretensions of the portrait, Boyer attributes the following quote to Thelonious: "We liked Ravel, Stravinsky, Debussy, Prokofieff, Schoenberg . . . and maybe we were a little influenced by them."[118] If the quote is authentic, it was undoubtedly a response to a leading question—e.g., did Stravinsky or modern composers influence the development of modern jazz? Boyer even claims that Monk declared himself Arab. "Thelonious sometimes forgets that he was born on West Sixty-third Street and announces that he is a native of Damascus."[119] It's hard to imagine what questions would have elicited that one.

What hurt Monk most, however, was the reminder that for all his hard work, for all the press he had received, for all the gigs he had cobbled together, for all the recording sessions and requisite rehearsals, for all the sidemen too green or too lazy to play his music correctly, he was broke and Dizzy was rich. The article reported that Dizzy's combined income for 1948 was expected to exceed $25,000, and that over the past eight years he had earned $20,000 in royalties from recording.[120]

Monk, on the other hand, had no work. He passed the time writing, visiting friends and family—playing checkers, basketball, Ping-Pong, and double-dutch with his nieces and nephews ("He was a good turner," his niece Charlotte recalled[121])—checking in on Nellie, smoking reefer, dropping benzedrine or "bennies" every once in a while, and preparing for his court date. He also sought out places to play, sitting in wherever he could. On July 11, for example, he dropped by the Onyx Club where Charlie Parker was leading a quintet with Miles Davis, Duke Jordan (piano), Tommy Potter (bass), and Max Roach. With the High Priest in the house, Jordan gave up the piano stool so Monk and the band could blow on his original composition, "Well, You Needn't." Saxophonist and amateur audio documentarian Dean Benedetti was in the audience with his recorder and captured some of Monk and Bird's brief musical dialogue. Monk's comping is so strong and so angular that even Parker gets a little flustered toward the end of the recording.[122] But the priest wasn't trying to dethrone the prince.

On August 31, the case of The State of New York vs. Thelonious Monk finally came on the docket. Despite positive testimony from Monk's closest associates, including Alfred Lion, the judge found him guilty as charged and sentenced him to thirty days in the Tombs.[123]

11

"It's a Drag to Be in Jail"

(August 1948–August 1951)

L ike most New Yorkers, Thelonious passed by the Manhattan House of Detention at 125 White Street many times. The ominous-looking building was only seven years old in 1948, having replaced the old city jail constructed in 1902. The newer and larger facility still retained its chilling moniker "the Tombs," and for Monk the name was apt. It really didn't matter that the walls of the visiting room and the chapel had just been freshly painted "with cheerful and pleasing color schemes," or that inmates enjoyed access to a brand-new library that delivered materials to their cells.[1] He spent much of his thirty-day sentence confined to a tiny single cell in the sweltering heat of July and August, surrounded by about 900 other inmates,[2] alone, a bit shell-shocked, and without a piano. Occasionally, he played Ping-Pong in the rec room, wrote music when he could scrounge up something to write with, perhaps read a little, and spent too much of his time pacing back and forth until he could no longer stand. He slept very little because his rhythms were now determined by the regimentation of the prison system. His cycles of manic-depression probably increased as he struggled to stay sane in this unfamiliar caged world.

Frequent visits were the best antidote. Nellie came down to the Tombs as often as she could, though it sometimes meant taking precious time off from work. She had just taken a job as an elevator operator at the Taft Hotel on West 50th and Seventh Avenue.[3] Monk's siblings also came downtown to see him, along with their mother, whose health was rapidly deteriorating. These all-too-brief visits brought Thelonious a little comfort. Between visits, he had a lot of time to think and reflect—as all inmates do. In the past year he had been hailed bebop's brilliant originator and led his first recording sessions. Now he was an inmate with a criminal record. In Monk's world, reefer was almost as common as tobacco. But the world around him was changing; state and federal authorities were beginning to crack down on all narcotics, and city officials in particular set out to "clean up" 52nd Street and the Times Square area, which in their view had become a haven for crime, vice, and drug use.[4] Thelonious had been caught in the dragnet.

He apparently saw Nellie in a new light. Not long after his release, they took a brief trip. By the time they returned, Nellie Smith had become Mrs. Thelonius Monk. She was twenty-six; he was just shy of his thirty-first birthday. Where they were married, and under what circumstances, remains a mystery. Some family members seem to remember a trip to Mexico,[5] but according to Nellie's sworn testimony in Surrogate's Court, she was married in New York City in September of 1947. The month was probably correct, but she was a year off.[6]

The Smith family was ecstatic over the news. Sonny's best friend was now his brother-in-law and the kids had known their uncle Thelonious since they were born. The Monks welcomed Nellie into the family, though Marion could hardly hide her disappointment that things never worked out between Thelonious and Rubie Richardson. The other Mrs. Monk was pleased, in part because her unpredictable and special middle child had finally found someone to take care of him and give her some more grandbabies. And as a devout Christian, she would not accept anything less than holy matrimony.

The newlyweds found a place of their own at a rooming house on Kelly Street in the Bronx, just a few blocks south of Sonny and Geraldine's apartment on Lyman Place.[7] Nellie's meager wages at the Taft Hotel might have covered the rent, but Monk needed to earn a living so they could eat and get around the city. Finding work was easier said than done, however. As a result of his conviction, the NYPD revoked his cabaret card for one year,[8] which meant he could not work in establishments that served alcohol in Manhattan. The loss of his cabaret card was far worse for Monk than thirty days in jail. Lorraine Lion, who never stopped working on Monk's behalf, had already secured a gig for him in October at the Village Vanguard, a small basement club on Seventh Avenue and 11th Street. Fortunately for Monk, the Vanguard was then better known for poetry readings and folk music, and its reputation as a kind of bohemian outpost generating very little revenue kept the cops at bay. Owner Max Gordon couldn't say no to Lorraine, though he had never heard of Thelonious. It may have been her sales pitch, or possibly her outfit. "I was on Fire Island with some friends," she recalled. "I went into a little bakery there and saw a man sitting having coffee and a blueberry muffin, and I knew that he was Max Gordon. I sidled up to him in my yellow bathing suit and started to tell him about Thelonious Monk, and how Max had the club and I had the genius. He had never heard of Monk, but he said that he had a date open . . . we clinched the deal in ten minutes, with no contract, nothing."[9]

Monk's quartet opened at the Village Vanguard on October 14, 1948.[10] He brought the usual suspects—Sahib Shihab on alto, Al McKibbon on bass, and Denzil Best on drums.[11] As a precaution, Max Gordon decided to hold over pianist Billy Taylor and his trio, who had been backing a singer the previous week, to play opposite Monk just in case the audience didn't like him. Even so, hardly anyone showed up. "None of the so-called jazz critics," Lorraine remembered. "None of the so-called cognoscenti. Zilch."[12] She remembered Max having a fit. When Thelonious danced around a bit at the opening of his set and announced his tunes by addressing the audience as "human beings," Lorraine thought Gordon was going to lose it. "What did you talk me into?" he cried. "You trying to ruin my business? We're dying with this guy."[13]

Billy Taylor also remembered the empty tables and the strange looks from the audience, but he recalls Gordon defending Monk tooth and nail. "You could dance there at the Vanguard," Taylor explained, "so when the music was danceable people often got up and danced. So Monk had drums and so forth, so people assumed, well this is a quartet so they could get up and dance. But they couldn't figure out what kind of dance to do to his music. It got to be funny. People would say to Max, 'Well who is this? What's going on?' And he'd say, 'This is Thelonious Monk, he's a genius.' And they would go back and try to dance again, and they would finally give up and say, 'We can't dance to this, so let's check him out.'"[14]

Vanguard audiences had two weeks to check him out. From a commercial stand-point, the engagement turned out to be a disaster. In the long run, however, it proved to be life-changing. Thelonious found in Max Gordon a friend and champion whose club became one of Monk's most sympathetic and supportive venues. And Mrs. Lorraine Lion found in Max the romantic spark she'd been missing in her own marriage. Appar-ently the feeling became mutual. Over the course of the next year, Lorraine would leave Alfred Lion for Gordon, and the couple would become a major force in the world of modern jazz—and certainly among Monk's best allies in the cutthroat world of club owners.[15]

With virtually no regular gigs in sight, Thelonious was willing to take just about anything that came along. Sometimes he worked at the 845 Club on Prospect Avenue in the Bronx, leading an ensemble that included Art Blakey, Coleman Hawkins when he was available, and Ernie Henry on alto. When Henry wasn't available, he turned to Jackie McLean, one of the young cats from the Sugar Hill gang whom he met through Sonny Rollins. Jackie had only recently made the switch from tenor to alto, but Monk was less interested in experience than in excitement and musicality. And McLean had both. "I was young and still not sure of myself, and it was a great experience working with Monk. I was nervous, and when I would think that I was asked to play by Monk it would give me the kind of encouragement that I think young people need. . . ."[16] In McLean's young eyes, Monk was a master musician and cultural icon.

Yet, in the eyes of club owners and the industry more generally, Monk was a liability. Times were so hard that Monk once took a job as a sideman for one of *McLean's* gigs, playing background music at a cocktail sip for a measly twelve dollars. "I called up Monk and he was already there in his suit and tie and everything and he worked all night and got his twelve dollars and left."[17]

Thelonious was hungry, literally and figuratively. Sonny and Geraldine helped when they could, but they were trying to raise five kids on meager wages. Monk's siblings were not faring any better financially. Nellie and Monk lived on spaghetti and meat-balls (one of Thelonious's specialties[18]), collected bottles to return for the deposit, and bummed cigarettes from friends and acquaintances. Evelyn Smith remembers, "Nellie told a story when I was little about how they shared a cigarette. They had one cigarette that she had gotten from somebody on the job, and she smoked half of it and gave him the other half."[19] "Thelonious had trouble getting work even before he lost the [cabaret] card [a second time]," Nellie told writer Nat Hentoff. "Therefore, it wasn't a sudden total calamity. People had told so many stories about his being unreliable and eccentric that it had always been hard."[20] The irony, of course, is that the very stories circulated in the popular press and by Lorraine Lion about his so-called eccentricities and odd behavior came back to bite him. In the minds of club owners, booking agencies, and A&R men, Monk's alleged strange behavior rendered him unreliable. But so many rumors about him skipping an engagement or a recording session, as we've already seen, had more to do with the promoters using his name without his knowledge. The evidence suggests that Thelonious was indeed responsible when it came to a job. And yet, he could not change the dominant opinion. Weirdness—once a selling point—was now a source of unemployment.

One story told by Jackie McLean, and often repeated as an example of Monk's odd behavior, reveals the depths of Monk's poverty. "Monk was working up at the Audubon Ballroom, and I was working with him. During the course of the evening, I mentioned that my mother had made a chocolate pie, and Monk said that he wanted a piece of it, so I said yeah, just passing it off, like, the next time my mother makes a pie I'll call you up. But after the gig was over I went downstairs and there was Monk waiting for me. He said, 'I'll walk you home, I'm going to get that pie.' It was about four o'clock in the morning, it was weird. I was only seventeen years old, and my mother didn't really like me out late." When Jackie told Monk it was too late for company, he replied, "'I don't need to be company, I can wait for it and you can go in and get it and pass it out to me.' So he walked all the way across Harlem, up to the top of the Hill, came up to the sixth floor, and stood in the hallway while I went inside and cut a piece of chocolate pie and put it in a piece of wax paper and passed it out to him. Then he thanked me and went downstairs."[21]

His hunger manifested itself in other ways as well. He wanted a hit record, something that might generate some cash. Toward the end of 1948, a fellow San Juan Hill resident known as Frankie Alvarez approached Monk about putting a band together for a recording session with a talented crooner named Frank Paccione. Alvarez, a twenty-three-year old pop songwriter of Cuban descent whose given name was actually Frank Pelaez,[22] believed he had two potential hits and a singer who could deliver the goods. Paccione, whose stage name was Frankie Passion, was also from the neighborhood. He was only twenty-one at the time, but he had already served two years in the service and, after being discharged in 1947, tried to make it as a pop singer in Los Angeles. His style—a cross between Frank Sinatra and Perry Como—failed to make an impression on Angelenos. Within a few months he returned to New York and Alvarez approached him about two songs he'd written: one was the swinging Sinatra-esque "Nobody Know, Nobody Cares," and the other was a somewhat sappy ballad titled "Especially to You."[23] Alvarez wrote the latter hoping to interest WNEW disc jockey Martin Block, whose "Make-Believe Ballroom" had just been syndicated for a national audience. Alvarez took Block's famous sign-off phrase, "Good Night to You, and You, and Especially to You," and turned it into a song.[24] The strategy, of course, was to persuade Block to adopt "Especially to You" as the show's theme song, which would have netted a huge sum of money. (Block was already making over $22,000 a week to host the show.)

Monk readily took on the challenge, believing that if these tunes hit they could be his meal ticket. He wrote the arrangements and put together a quintet. The record-ing does not list personnel, but we do know that Monk hired Charlie Rouse on tenor, marking their recording debut, and the trumpet player might be Idrees Sulieman, since it sounds like him and Sulieman was a regular in Monk's band. He may have hired Jerry Smith on drums and bassist Michael Mattos (a Brooklynite whom he'd met through Randy Weston) since he used them fairly frequently in the early part of 1949. [25] "I can tell you that [Monk] was the MAN, the LEADER," reported Paccione, "and we gave it all we had."[26] The band was in fine form and Monk wrote innovative arrange-ments. Perhaps too innovative for a young crooner hoping for a commercial success: Monk turned the two pop songs into parodies of the genre. On "Especially to You," Monk backed Paccione's smooth tenor voice with the horns playing dissonant chro-matic obligato phrases—a technique he would employ a few years later in his hilari-ous recording of "Smoke Gets in Your Eyes." "Nobody Knows" works a little better. It swings, it showcases the whole band, and the humor is in your face. The lyrics are depressing and pitiful ("Nobody knows, nobody cares,/got their eyes closed to/just how mean she treats me") but the tempo is bouncy and upbeat. [27]

Monk, Paccione, and Alvarez had high hopes for these recordings. Alvarez released both sides on his newly launched Washington label, but nothing happened. He sent copies to WNEW hoping Martin Block might hear "Especially to You," and he hustled every available record store to carry the 78. Despite Thelonious's brief moment of fame, even his name wasn't enough to sell records. Paccione mused decades later, "I guess the bottom line is that it did not take off like we had hoped."[28]

For Thelonious and Nellie, the Bronx was temporarily home. The 845 Club became his new hangout and occasional source of income. The club paid him very little, but he could work there without a cabaret card, since enforcement was more relaxed in the outer boroughs. Bud Powell was a frequent visitor, along with pianist Elmo Hope, who had recently moved in with his mother on Lyman Place a few doors down from Sonny and Geraldine. Although Monk befriended Hope in 1942, Hope had enlisted in the service soon thereafter and after his discharge toured with Joe Morris's rhythm and blues band. His bandmates included bassist Percy Heath, drummer Philly "Joe" Jones, and a dynamic tenor saxophonist from Chicago named Johnny Griffin, whom Hope befriended and introduced to Monk and Bud. "They were like triplets, the three of them," Griffin recalled. Once Griffin joined them, the trio became a quartet, though from his perspective he felt more like a student studying with the masters. "That was my education, those three pianists. That was my university training."[29] It was also fun. Griffin remembers one memorable night, Christmas Eve 1948, at the 845 Club. "Elmo and Bud played Christmas songs together. It was pretty funny. Monk sat back with that smirk on his face."[30]

Monk and many other pianists also converged at a most unlikely spot—the back-room of a television repair shop. The proprietor, a middle-aged black man named Al Walker, was a brilliant pianist who never made it as a musician but turned his store into one of the uncharted landmarks in the history of the Bronx jazz scene. Musicians arrived in the wee hours and gathered around the grand piano he kept in the back of his shop. The jam sessions were legendary, and Monk was usually at the center of them. Clifton Smith was just a kid when his dad started bringing him to Al's shop to hear the music. "Of course when Monk came," Clifton explained, "they'd say, 'Monk is coming. Monk is coming.' Everybody flocked. I don't think they recorded his music but I was there for a few of those jam sessions. Awesome! Awesome jam sessions. And they would stay in Al's shop for a couple of days just playing music. I don't know how many TVs they were fixing, but they were definitely jamming in there."[31]

Hanging out at the 845 Club and Al Walker's shop kept Monk's spirits and his chops up, and it put him in touch with talented young players like Griffin, who later became one of his regular sidemen. Saxophonist George "Big Nick" Nicholas, who enjoyed a long-term engagement at Small's Paradise in Harlem, hired Thelonious a few times in 1949.[32] But finding work in New York just seemed impossible. Even after the Liquor Authority reinstated his cabaret card, the heart of the club scene—52nd Street—began its rapid disintegration in 1949. Many clubs closed down or became striptease joints, most of which had their liquor license revoked or suspended as part of the government's crackdown on "burlesque." The old brownstones were razed and new buildings took their place. Soon after Rockefeller Center added its new Esso building, the strip became hot investment property for various financial and commercial interests. National City Bank opened a branch on the block, Lord and Taylor announced plans late in the year to build a new store nearby, and the city acquired some corner properties on Sixth Avenue, which it sold to developers.[33]

Monk did what many musicians had to do now: find out-of-town gigs. Without the benefit of a manager or a booking agent, he secured a three-week engagement in March at the Beige Room, a small club situated in Chicago's Hotel Pershing.[34] He put together a quintet made up entirely of young, unknown New York–based musicians—alto saxophonist Freddie Douglass (clearly named after the former slave and abolitionist Frederick Douglass), trumpeter Lowell Lewis, bassist Michael Mattos, and drummer Jerry Smith.[35] One local artist who sat in at least once was a young vocalist named Frank London Brown. A second-year student at Roosevelt University, Brown sang primarily to help pay for college.[36] He loved the music and had a special affinity for Monk—even then—but in 1949 he was drifting toward more literary and political pursuits. He and Thelonious would meet again.

Monk also found work at the Hi-Hat Club in Boston, though there he tended to use local players. Bostonians did not always understand or appreciate his music, but Monk was always willing to share ideas and take younger musicians under his wing. Pianist Jaki Byard was just beginning his career when he used to see Monk at the Hi-Hat. "The cats would say, 'Is he kidding?' I'd say, 'That's Monk, man!' Every day we'd go to his house, where he was staying, and he'd walk around, he'd jot down tunes. He composed 'Off Minor' then, I remember he wrote a copy of that for me, and 'Ruby, My Dear," and a couple others."[37] Monk also met an alto player originally from Florida studying at the Boston Conservatory of Music. Quiet and studious, Gigi Gryce lived and breathed music. He wasn't a kid; just eight years younger than Thelonious, he had already spent two years in the service as a member of the celebrated Great Lakes Navy band, and he continued his formal music studies in Hartford, Connecticut after he was discharged in 1946.[38] Gryce looked to Monk as a mentor, if not a guru. Emery Smith remembered how Gigi "talked about Monk, it was like he was on cloud nine. In fact, he used to stutter when he talked about Monk's music, trying to explain what Monk's music was like. . . . He would kind of stammer because he was in awe of Thelonious."[39] Saxophonist Sam Rivers studied with Gryce in Boston. He remembered how Monk opened Gryce to greater harmonic and tonal freedom. After playing with Monk at the Hi-Hat, Gryce reported back to Rivers, "You can do anything with Monk and it comes out like it's right, you know. If you make a mistake, Monk is listening and he will make it sound right."[40]

Monk's relative absence from the New York jazz scene did not stop him from influencing a new generation of musicians, many of whom were steeped in bebop and the music of Charlie Parker but were searching for more. A couple of critics began to acknowledge that Monk, indeed, had something "more" than running substitute chord changes at breakneck speed. Once again, his pal Paul Bacon published another smart review of his latest Blue Note releases—"Epistrophy" and "In Walked Bud"— in the November 1948 issue of *The Record Changer*, comparing him with the proverbial carpenter "lustily doing everything wrong, battling his materials, and coming up with the most uniquely beautiful houses in the world."[41] Several months later, Bacon reviewed Blue Note's next release, which paired the trio version of "Ruby, My Dear" with the quartet recording of "Evidence" featuring Milt Jackson. He described "Ruby" as a "beautiful tonepoem, played with great feeling and color," and praised his solo on "Evidence" for its unity, "a result of Monk's habit of thinking of things as a whole, instead of a bar here and a bridge there."[42]

But Bacon's was a lone voice in the wilderness of North America. The only other serious critical praise Monk received that year came from across the Atlantic, in a small Swiss journal called the *Jazz-Revue*. Perhaps unbeknownst to Monk, Jean-Jacques Finsterwald and Julien-François Zbinden published a lengthy and thoughtful analysis of Monk's entire recorded output in the April 1949 edition. "His playing is simple, his style austere and sober; he uses very few melodies and concentrates all his attention on a right hand with monodic style. In spite of his audacity, Monk uses absolutely logical harmonic structures, relatively simple phrases, and the system of whole tones, a mark of Debussy that he applies at the right time." They describe moments in his music as "brilliant" and "joyous," but also suggest that when he strays too far from the basic harmonic structure it can lead to "melodic impasses."[43]

Unfortunately, the piece did nothing to stem the hostile attacks from the U.S. jazz press. *Down Beat* critics skewered Monk's latest records. Commenting on "Epistrophy," the reviewer wrote, "We have less and less patience with the far-fetched type of composition and inventiveness which are displayed by the much publicized Monk for a very simple reason. Nothing happens."[44] Similarly, the reviewer of the next release proclaimed that nothing in "Evidence" "is either interesting or exciting to us, though the Monk's whole-tone harmonies and off-cadence rhythm doubtless will appeal to the more atonally minded of the jazz gentry." "Ruby, My Dear" is merely dismissed as "abstract."[45]

Even more than *Down Beat*, the publication of Leonard Feather's much-anticipated book, *Inside Be-Bop*, dealt a devastating blow to Monk. Released in 1949, parts of it read like a response to all the press Monk received a year earlier declaring him the true founding father of bebop. Instead, Feather establishes Dizzy as the music's progenitor, with Bird in the role as junior partner. He not only dismisses Monk in a paragraph, but he suggests that his opinions have the backing of the whole community of musicians: "Monk's place in the jazz scene, according to most musicians in the bop movement, has been grossly distorted, as a result of some high-powered publicity work. He has written a few attractive tunes, but his lack of technique and continuity prevented him from accomplishing much as a pianist. In fact, Cootie Williams' original 1944 recording of ''Round Midnight,' arranged for a big band, is vastly superior to Monk's own recording as an interpretation of the theme. Monk, who has been touted as a 'genius' and a 'high priest of bebop,' would wander in and out of Minton's, often falling asleep at the piano."[46]

What Feather called "high-powered publicity work," of course, was only Lorraine Lion armed with a typewriter. While conceding that Monk "is an original thinker," Feather insists he is "not a bebop pianist, nor do his solos have any of the mystic qualities attributed to them by some non-musical admirers."[47] Feather then positions Dizzy, Kenny Clarke, and Tadd Dameron as the key figures at Minton's Playhouse, and he quotes Clarke describing how *he* wrote "Epistrophy," never once mentioning Monk.[48] In 103 pages, Feather essentially renders Monk invisible. *Inside Be-Bop* angered and upset Monk. According to family lore, Thelonious ran into Feather at Rockefeller Center one afternoon, probably in the early winter of 1949, grabbed him by the neck, and threatened to throw him over the guard rail overlooking the ice-skating rink. He was so angry, his eyes welled up as he shouted, "You're taking the bread out of my mouth!"[49]

Thelonious had more than his own mouth to worry about: Nellie was pregnant and their first child was due in December. Once she began to show, she had to quit her job as an elevator operator at the Taft Hotel. With the temporary loss of her income, Monk and Nellie had no choice but to move back to his mother's place on West 63rd Street.[50] The neighborhood had changed dramatically now that the Amsterdam Houses had been finally completed just a few months earlier. Three thirteen-story high-rise dwellings and ten six-story low-rise apartments replaced the old tenements, casting a shadow on the only prewar housing left in the community—the Phipps Houses.[51] While the daily noise from construction disappeared, the gargantuan housing project nearly doubled the population in the area.[52] The community suddenly felt crowded, but so did the Monks' tiny apartment.

The move proved mutually beneficial and timely. Not long after Nellie and Thelonious settled in, a passing bus struck Miss Barbara as she was crossing the street.[53] Although it is not clear how badly she was hurt, given that she was already frail to begin with, her recovery took quite a long time, forcing her into early retirement. Fortunately, she received a monetary settlement from the city, much of which she used to help Marion buy a house in Queens. And, of course, she helped her son and his new wife whenever she could. Now that Barbara's health had deteriorated to the point where she could no longer work, the responsibility for her care was now shared between Nellie and her new in-laws—Thomas, Trotyrine, and Marion. It wasn't easy for Nellie, especially as she entered her third trimester. Thelonious became increasingly distraught, disappearing for days at a time.

The pressure to make money, the critical dismissal of his music, and the daunting responsibility of a child were too much for Thelonious. He turned to drugs to help him forget—bennies, weed, and occasionally heroin. He started hanging out in a "shooting gallery" on East 14th Street. He was never a *bona fide* junkie; he could go weeks without a fix.[54] But Monk's sister-in-law and her kids bore witness to those times when he, Sonny, Elmo Hope, and an array of other musicians would retire to the kitchen or head to the roof to get high. And when he disappeared, he often took his brother-in-law with him.

Sonny experimented, but he was not an addict. He looked up to Thelonious and enjoyed being around him. Monk's nephew Clifton, who was seven at the time, loathed when his uncle came by the house "because he would take my father away. The building that we lived in had a courtyard and he'd come across the court and yell, 'hey, come on downstairs.' That meant we weren't going to see my father for at least two days. . . . My mother hated it. He wouldn't go to work. They would go out and party and hang out. Go to jam sessions. He'd come back and tell us about all the great musicians he heard. And she would say, 'Yeah, but what about dinner?'"[55]

The day his son was born, Thelonious was nowhere to be found. On December 27, 1949, at 7:06 p.m., Nellie met her son for the first time and called him by his father's name.[56] It should have been a doubly joyous occasion, as it was also her birthday. Yet, during the labor and delivery, she was alone in the maternity ward of City Hospital, a wretched place on infamous "Welfare Island" in the East River, once referred to as the "hell in mid-channel" because it housed asylums, quarantines, and penitentiaries for vagrants, addicts, petty thieves, and the destitute.[57] It was all she could afford. In fact, she received fine care at the hands of Dr. Fred Weissman, a young intern at City Hospital with a kind bedside manner who went on to become one of the city's most distinguished neurologists.[58]

Nellie's best friend, her sister-in-law Geraldine, came to the rescue in Monk's absence. With just enough money to pay for a cab from the hospital back to West 63rd Street, Geraldine walked all the way from the Bronx to Welfare Island in the dead of winter in order to help Nellie and the baby get home.[59] Nellie didn't even have enough money for clothes, so Geraldine went to a local Goodwill and picked up baby blankets and enough random garments to make three outfits. More importantly, she brought comfort and knowledge of childbirth and infant care. Besides having five children of her own, Geraldine was in the final stages of completing her nursing credentials.[60]

Whatever ill feelings Nellie might have harbored toward her husband disappeared when she walked in the door to the inviting arms of her mother-in-law. When Thelonious finally showed up, he was ecstatic; he adored his son and doted on the boy like most fathers, and tried to do right by his namesake. (His own father's absence may explain why he named his son Thelonious, Jr., rather than Thelonious III.) He certainly wanted to provide. His cabaret card had been reinstated, but a month after his son's birth he still owed eleven dollars in back dues to the union. He petitioned Local 802 officials for a two-week extension, which they granted, and he was finally reinstated in mid-February.[61] Jobs were still few and far between. Small's Paradise offered him some Monday night gigs, and he eked out a little cash through non-union jobs. For at least the first few weeks, Thelonious kept his promise to his son and his wife . . . and then he began to disappear again.

Nellie had to find a way to manage without depending on Monk. She moved back in with Geraldine and Sonny in early spring and took a job tailoring at Marvel Cleaners on West 35th Street. The pay was minimal: $45.00 a week plus train fare, but it gave her an opportunity to apply her considerable skills as a seamstress.[62] She was known for making incredibly stylish clothes without a pattern. Thelonious proudly wore ties, jackets, and shirts she made by hand, including a sharp herringbone number and a two-tone brown and yellow shirt of which he was particularly fond.[63]

Evelyn Smith, who was five at the time, vividly remembers Thelonious, Jr.'s, first days at Lyman Place. "Nellie said to me, 'He's going to sleep with you, OK? And if he wakes up give him this [pacifier].' . . . And I slept with him for quite some time. I don't know how long. I know I was sleeping with this little baby in my arms."[64] It wasn't too long because within weeks Thelonious reorganized the West 63rd Street apartment, at his mother's behest. She moved into the smaller bedroom and gave the larger bedroom to Thelonious, Nellie, and the baby . . . and the piano, which sat at the foot of their bed. Nellie and her son continued shuttling back and forth between Lyman Place and West 63rd Street. She did all she could to straighten Monk out, to get him off the hard drugs, and just to keep up his spirits. It wasn't an easy thing to do, given how heroin flooded black communities after World War II. "I remember Nellie being very sad," recalled Evelyn Smith.[65]

Thelonious caught a break when Norman Granz of Jazz at the Philharmonic hired him for an all-star recording session with Charlie Parker and Dizzy Gillespie. Scheduled for June 6, 1950, the rhythm section included Curley Russell on bass and Buddy Rich on drums. Using Monk on the date made perfect sense from both a musical and marketing standpoint. It was billed as a reunion of the masters of bebop. Dizzy and Bird had not been in the studio together in five years. And despite Monk's virtual disappearance from the scene, Granz still believed he was a pioneer, though he described him in the original liner notes only as "a lesser light in modern jazz but, nevertheless, an important one."[66]

To the serious boppers accustomed to the galloping tempos of Bird, Diz, and Bud, tossing Thelonious Monk into the equation might have promised something different, yet Monk was not leading the session, nor were his compositions part of the repertoire. It was Bird's session and, except for the old standard "My Melancholy Baby," all tunes on the date were Parker's. Bird was hot at the moment and Granz knew it, having just produced and released his popular "Bird with Strings" recording of 1949, and having just ended a successful JATP tour featuring Parker.[67] The session became the Bird and Diz show. Monk is practically drowned out. He makes himself heard only through some brilliant little introductions and few brief solos.[68] Nonetheless, Monk is in fine form, responding to lines tossed out by Parker and Gillespie, building on his signature whole-tone phrases, and sharpening all the smooth edges with dissonance.[69]

Most of the time, Monk comps—a lot. He abandoned minimalism in order to compensate for drummer Buddy Rich, whose rhythmic sense clashed with the bop idiom. Rich, a swing drummer critical of bebop and the new crop of drummers whom he found too "busy," was not the best choice for the session. Bird did not want him; he had unsuccessfully lobbied Granz to hire Roy Haynes.[70] Monk's on- and off-beat, dynamic comping provided the rhythmic spark lacking in Buddy Rich's heavy metronomic four-four time. It's as if Monk takes on the role of drummer, dropping accents that are as much rhythmic as harmonic. Granz's motivation for using the white, nonbebopper Rich wasn't just musical—it was political. He wanted to challenge social convention, proving to the world that jazz is the melting pot, the great unifier, bringing together artists of hitherto warring genres.[71]

Monk was happy to work again, in spite of his sideman role. Unfortunately, there were no more calls after that—no concert dates, no tours, and no other sessions. He did sit in whenever the opportunity arose. Sahib Shihab once saw Monk at Birdland, the club named after Charlie Parker located on Broadway just above 52nd Street. It had opened just before Christmas, 1949.[72] Bird and Bud Powell played there fairly regularly during the first few months of its existence. Monk angered Birdland manager Oscar Goodstein by setting his drink glass on the brand-new piano. Shihab recalls Goodstein shouting, "'Monk, Monk, remove that glass from the piano!'" Monk ignored Goodstein, launched into an unaccompanied ballad, took a sip of his drink, and then lit a cigarette and set it on the piano. By now Goodstein was fuming. "'Monk, Monk, get that cigarette off the piano!'" Monk continued unruffled before a silent and befuddled audience. The only sound besides the music was Goodstein shouting. Once the song ended and the applause died down, Monk walked over to the microphone and announced: "I wish that management would not disturb the artist when he is working!"[73] Goodstein found none of it amusing. He banned Thelonious from coming back.

By the time his son celebrated his first birthday, Monk was bottoming out. His membership in the union was finally terminated in December of 1950, after he failed to pay the 1 percent tax required of all members.[74] Nellie's recurring abdominal problems came back with a vengeance. During her pregnancy, the pain and nausea had disappeared, and when it came back, she went to a number of doctors who again dismissed her condition as psychosomatic. It wasn't until May of 1951, when she was forced to check into Roosevelt Hospital with severe stomach pain and rapid weight loss, that doctors discovered she had an advanced abdominal ulcer. She was lucky to be alive. Geraldine, now a registered nurse, attended to Nellie during the surgery that removed two-thirds of her stomach. Her recovery was long; for weeks she survived on a "sippy" diet rich in cream and milk so that she might regain her weight.[75]

Nellie's hospitalization was quite a wake-up call for Thelonious. He couldn't bear the thought of losing Nellie, nor could he imagine his son's life without her. He limited his outings and redoubled his efforts to find work. He also checked in more often on his mother, whose deteriorating health had left her largely bedridden. And if all the emotional and economic turmoil weren't enough, in the spring of 1951 he learned that Jerry Newman, who now had his own record label (Esoteric Records), released more of his Minton's recordings on an LP called *Harlem Jam Sessions*. Once again, no musician was paid.[76]

Meanwhile, Alfred Lion invited Monk back to the studio despite dismal sales of his first records. On a muggy Monday night, July 23, Monk, Milt Jackson, Sahib Shihab, Al McKibbon, and Art Blakey recorded six sides, the majority of which were new Monk originals. Indeed, the music was so new that two weeks after the session, Monk had not decided on titles for most of the songs.[77] "Four in One" is a particularly treacherous melody made up of sixteenth-note phrases.[78] "Straight, No Chaser," which Lion initially scribbled down as "Nice Piece,"[79] would eventually become one of Monk's best-known blues. "Criss Cross" (whose working title was "Sailor Cap"[80]) was a revision of Monk's contribution to the aborted collaboration with Mary Lou Williams and Bud Powell.[81]

The most noteworthy song on the date is a boppish line titled "Eronel." Its importance lay not in its musical qualities, nor is it considered one of Monk's better-known pieces. Indeed, "Eronel" is not even Monk's song, despite the initial credit he received as co-composer. It is significant for the stories behind it—stories of love and theft. Pianist Sadik Hakim, a recent convert to Islam, co-wrote it with Idrees Sulieman.[82] But it was Hakim who named it "Eronel"—Lenore spelled backwards—after an old flame of his. She was a young, attractive Jewish girl visiting from Kansas City named Lenore Gordon; he an African-American devotee of Ahmadiyya Islam. When they first met in the summer of 1944, he was still Argonne Thornton and she was but sixteen and escorted by her mother. He assumed the role of Lenore's protector in the predatory world of jazz musicians and racist police officers.[83]

Their friendship remained on the precipice of romance, but she returned to Kansas City and in an effort to assert her own independence, the following year she married a man named Joe Baroni. "Everyone knew Baroni worked for the Mafia," she recounted. She left him after a couple of months and then headed back to New York City, where she reunited with Hakim. "He said, 'You move here and marry me.' I said, 'I already made the worst decision of my life. Why would I want to marry a musician? . . . You're a great person but I don't think I'm going to make another mistake.' "[84]

It would be nearly thirty years before they saw each other again. Still, Sadik held a torch for Lenore. He penned "Eronel" five years after she turned down his proposal.[85]

The story of "Eronel" reveals the depths of Hakim's personal investment in the song. He and Sulieman believed they had something special, and tried to interest Miles Davis in recording it. He did add it to his repertoire briefly, though he disliked the bridge.[86] So Sulieman took it to Monk, who kept changing one note—the last note of the second bar. "I said, 'That's the wrong note but play it again. Leave that note in. We'll do the writers' credits three ways.'"[87] Monk did a little more than contribute one note. The chord voicings are his, as are little embellishments in both the A–section and the bridge, but the melody clearly belongs to Sulieman and Hakim. Unfortunately, when the record was released and the song copyrighted, only Monk's name appeared. Both Sulieman and Hakim were hurt, and Sulieman spent a better part of his life giving Thelonious grief about the error. Years later, while they were all in Copenhagen, he appealed to Monk: "Why don't you make a statement and tell them how it really happened?" But Thelonious would just smile and say, "They forgot it, ha ha."[88] It was only after Monk died that Thelonious Monk, Jr., restored their names as co-composers of "Eronel."

Monk left the studio early that morning buoyed, hopeful that the session was a sign of things to come. He decided to stay home more often to play with his son and to sit with his mother. She was diagnosed with cancer and was not in a condition to be left alone for long stretches of time, though Thomas and Trotyrine dropped by every day.[89] And she had her share of visitors. The beloved Miss Barbara had established a reputation in the neighborhood as a quiet caregiver, and now some of her neighbors returned the favor. Alice Crawford came often. She lived in the building and had known the Monks for many years. Alice and her sister were long-time Jehovah's Witness devotees. She would sit and talk with Barbara, share copies of *The Watchtower* and *Awake!* magazines, and occasionally persuaded her to come to Kingdom Hall, but she never aggressively proselytized. Barbara was genuinely moved by the Witness message that Jesus now rules over the Messianic Kingdom in heaven and that he will soon cleanse the earth and restore it to paradise after the Battle of Armageddon.[90] As a committed Baptist, she believed in the resurrection of Christ and knew he would come again, so the message the Crawford sisters brought did not seem too far from the Christian vision she knew. It was enough for her to convert. Thelonious was not religious at the time, but he had no choice but to accept her conversion. Although their refusal to salute any flag or participate in war probably amused him,[91] he did not like the fact that Witnesses reject any medical procedures that involve blood or artificially prolonging life. Given her weakening condition, no one knew what medical treatment she might need. But he did all he could to accommodate her, sometimes spending hours at the piano playing her favorite sacred songs.[92]

On one of those summer evenings Monk spent sitting with his mother, Bud Powell decided to pay him a visit. It was a Wednesday—August 9, 1951, to be exact—and Bud decided they might hang out a bit since Thelonious wasn't working. He was accompanied by a young woman and a man Monk had never met. Thelonious suggested they go outside and sit in the young woman's car, so as not to disturb his mother. As they talked, two uniformed officers approached the car and flashed their badge. They were from the narcotics squad. Unbeknownst to Monk, Bud tossed a small glassine envelope in Monk's direction and it landed near his feet. The officers noticed, seized it, and arrested everyone in the car without a search warrant.[93] Within minutes Monk was in the back of a squad car on his way to Central Booking.

12

"The 'Un' Years"

(August 1951–May 1953)

olice charged Thelonious Monk, Bud Powell, and Powell's two friends with violating section 422 of the New York Public Health Law—possession of narcotics. Once processed at Central Booking, it was too late to appear before a judge, so they all spent the night in the Tombs. The next morning, appearing in Felony Court, they faced a judge who transferred Powell to a psychiatric ward and released the woman on her own recognizance. Powell's male friend was held over because he was out on bail for a prior arrest for drug dealing.[1] Thelonious faced the charges by himself, insisting that the packet of heroin did not belong to him. When asked to whom it belonged, he would not say. He refused to rat out Bud Powell. (As Monk would explain years later, he did not want to go down as "a drag" or a snitch.[2]) The judge ordered that he be held on $1,500 bail—an astronomical figure considering Monk's financial situation. Unable to make bail, he was sent promptly to the work-house on Rikers Island.[3]

Nellie was beside herself. "Every day I would plead with him. . . . 'Thelonious, get yourself out of this trouble. You didn't do anything.' But he'd just say 'Nellie, I have to walk the streets when I get out. I can't talk.'"[4] She appealed to everyone she could think of for bail money. Alfred Lion didn't have enough cash, but offered to help raise the money by calling his friends. Paul Bacon was on the list. "Alfred called and said, Paul, we got a problem. You got any money? I had just gotten paid so I contributed fifty dollars, which was practically all I had at the time."[5] Despite his efforts, however, Lion came up short. Nellie also turned to Maely Dufty, a talented writer for the *New York Citizen-Call* and wife of William Dufty, who would later become the ghost-writer for Billie Holiday's memoir, *Lady Sings the Blues*. A Jewish émigré who had barely escaped German-occupied Czechoslovakia during World War II, Maely Dufty had a reputation in Harlem as a fighter for justice and a lover of jazz. (On her very first night in the United States, she headed straight to the Renaissance Ballroom in Harlem and sought out Duke Ellington![6]) Nellie was in terrible shape when she walked into Dufty's apartment. Still recovering from intestinal surgery, she was visibly underweight and completely spent. With tears rolling down her cheeks, she explained that they hardly had enough money to care for an eighteen-month-old baby, let alone enough for bail or an attorney. Dufty was quick to act, first contacting someone in the Narcotics Division of the U. S. Treasury Department to intervene on Monk's behalf. She wanted Monk transferred to a hospital and held there for seventy-two hours in order to prove he was not an addict. She argued that the absence of withdrawal symptoms would provide sufficient evidence of his innocence. In addition, she argued, the amount of heroin involved was so minuscule that it should have been clear to any judge that Monk was not dealing. The agent promised to look into it, but could not interfere in the case. Dufty then turned to the NAACP legal defense department. "Sorry, but we don't touch anything involving narcotics," she was told. But Dufty believed what happened to Monk was an obvious miscarriage of justice, and could not understand the NAACP's response. "This involves a man being prejudiced against and robbed of his civil liberties . . . He is being prevented from being able to prove his innocence in the ONLY manner it can be proven—isolation."[7] The NAACP could not be persuaded, but the staffer she spoke with suggested they turn to attorney Andrew Weinberger, who was eager to take on the case. But they still needed money.

Raising the money to pay Weinberger proved difficult, especially in the jazz world. No one seemed to believe Monk was innocent. "I went to a disk jockey," Dufty later recalled. "He laughed at me. I went to the owner of a hip jazz joint. He laughed harder. Everywhere I went for help, people would burst into gales of laughter as soon as I said: 'Thelonious Monk.'"[8] Only Alfred Lion and his circle of friends stepped up, donating the money they raised in their unsuccessful effort to make bail to pay the attorney's fees. By the time his case came to trial, he had already spent two months at Rikers. The judge elected to release him with time served.

Those sixty days were perhaps as hard on Nellie as they were on Thelonious. She continued to work every day at Marvel Cleaners, but had to supplement her income by taking on additional work as a seamstress. (Mary Lou Williams paid her the princely sum of twenty-five dollars to alter five gowns.[9]) The Department of Correction had just permitted weekend visits, making it easier for Nellie to see her husband. Monk depended on Nellie's visits to restore his spirits. He had no piano, was granted very little free time to write, and as an inmate in the workhouse he had to work. Like the other prisoners, Monk either worked in the bakery or the wrapping and shipping room.[10] These were the longest sixty days of his life.

Monk was released two days before his thirty-fourth birthday. The occasion provided an opportunity to thank all those who had supported him, especially Alfred Lion, who not only raised money for his attorney but paid his ten-dollar union fees while he was in jail.[11] But Monk had much to celebrate besides his freedom. Blue Note announced that it would reissue seven Monk recordings on one ten-inch LP titled *The Genius of Modern Music*.[12] The move certainly pleased Monk, who, like everyone, recognized that the days of 78s were numbered. He hoped it would provide a boost to his finances. These developments were tempered by the fact that the police had revoked his cabaret card—indefinitely. Monk was neither surprised nor devastated by the loss of his cabaret card. After all, it had been three years since he'd had steady work. On the other hand, he needed anything he could get, and his options were significantly limited without a cabaret card. Now that his first LP was about to hit record stores, he had to consider the possibility that club owners might begin to take an interest in him.

Lack of money did not dampen the Monks' holiday season. Christmas was always a special day for the family, and it had become tradition to extend festivities to the twenty-seventh, when Nellie and Thelonious, Jr., celebrated their birthdays. By this time, Junior answered to the nickname "Toot," the name of the main character in Hardie Gramatky's 1939 book, *Little Toot the Tugboat*, which Walt Disney turned into an animated film in 1948. "Toot" loved the book, but earned the nickname because he learned to whistle before he could talk.[13] Gifts were meager, but the family was together. During the remaining winter months, Nellie continued to work every day while Monk stayed home with Toot, keeping house, writing music, and working with the parade of musicians who would drop by the apartment. "When he wasn't working regularly," Nellie explained, "he'd be working at home, writing and rehearsing bands that didn't have the prospects of a dog. . . . In the 'un' years, as I call them, as far as he was concerned, he felt just as confident as he does now that what he was doing musically could appeal to other people if they only took the opportunity to listen."[14]

Alfred Lion and Frank Wolff still believed in Monk, and wanted to give the world one more opportunity to listen. Soon after releasing Monk's second ten-inch LP, *The Genius of Modern Music, vol. 2*, they invited him back for what would prove to be his last studio session as a leader for Blue Note. Monk led a sextet of talented musicians, most of whom were old friends: Max Roach, bassist Nelson Boyd, trumpeter Kenny Dorham, and tenor player Lucky Thompson, his old pal from the Norman Granz tour days.[15] Rounding out the ensemble on alto was a relative newcomer named Lou Donaldson. Having just recorded for Blue Note with Milt Jackson's quintet in April, Donaldson was the label's latest discovery.[16]

The group met at WOR Studios on Saturday, May 30, and laid down six usable sides—four of which were new compositions. "Skippy," based on the chord changes for "Tea for Two," was a treacherous uptempo melody named after Nellie's sister.[17] The song's dynamic and unpredictable melodic line seemed to suit Skippy, whom the family frequently described as a "live-wire."[18] "Hornin' In" and "Sixteen" (a reference to the song's 16-bar AABA structure[19]) are studies in dissonance and whole-tone harmony. Over medium tempos, the trio of horns play phrases that still cause many uninitiated listeners to wince.

After ten takes to record these three songs, Monk's "Let's Cool One" was a walk in the park. A simple melody line played over a smooth rhythm and calming tempo, it lacked the angularity of most Monk tunes but retained its Monkish characteristics. On the other hand, Monk transformed Joe Burke and Benny Davis's 1929 "Carolina Moon" into a frenetic romp in 6/4 time, producing one of the earliest successful examples of a jazz waltz. The arrangement is notable for its inventiveness and is further evidence that he was still seeking that elusive hit. Tommy Dorsey's 1938 recording of "Carolina Moon" was wildly popular and RCA-Victor released Perry Como's rendition with the Lloyd Schaffer Orchestra in 1948.[20] For Lou Donaldson, however, their recording was a family reunion of sorts, since he, Max, and Monk all hailed from North Carolina.[21] Finally, Monk rounded out the session with a very pretty version of "I'll Follow You" without the horns, rarely straying from the melody.[22]

Two weeks later, Monk participated in a concert at Town Hall honoring his longtime friend Mary Lou Williams. Organized by the Committee for the Negro in the Arts to raise funds for its various projects, Monk's band, which included Kenny Dorham and drummer Art Taylor, appeared briefly on an overcrowded program that included Eartha Kitt, the Clarence Williams trio, and Mary Lou herself.[23] Monk had not seen much of Mary Lou earlier in the year—she and Nellie had had a falling out over work Nellie had done for her. According to Nellie, Mary Lou had refused to pay her for more alterations she had done because Mary Lou claimed the clothes did not fit properly. Nellie never forgave her, and harbored an intense dislike for Williams for the rest of her life.[24] In any event, Monk's brief reunion with Mary Lou turned out to be an unexpected farewell party—she would relocate to Europe a few weeks later and remain for two years.[25]

Monk needed more than occasional concert appearances and short-term or out-of-town gigs. When Bob Weinstock approached Thelonious about signing an exclusive contract with his Prestige label, he jumped at the chance. Both Monk and Alfred Lion had realized their recording relationship had reached a dead end—it was time to move on. And Monk was familiar with Prestige since Weinstock had already recorded Sonny Rollins, Kenny Dorham, and J. J. Johnson.[26] Weinstock could afford to pay a small—but decent—advance and seemed to have a gift for selling records. Like so many entrepreneurs in the business, Weinstock started out as an avid jazz record collector, providing hard-to-find 78s for Leonard Feather's radio show, "Jazz at Its Best" on New York's WMGM. In 1948, he rented a counter at Jazzman Joe's on 47th Street between Sixth and Seventh Avenues and sold modern records.[27] As business grew, he expanded his staff, hiring an acquaintance named Ira Gitler, who worked summers while attending the University of Missouri. He eventually moved his operations to a midtown storefront on Tenth Avenue, and in 1949, launched two labels—New Jazz and Prestige. Gitler was barely out of his teens when he decided to stay put in New York City, take classes at the New School, and devote much of his free time to Prestige.[28]

Weinstock had developed an interest in Monk when he'd heard him play with Coleman Hawkins, but his budget was limited. Then in 1952, he struck gold with King Pleasure's "Moody's Mood for Love" and the profits enabled him to sign more artists. Monk signed a three-year recording contract on August 21, 1952, which the union approved three weeks later.[29] On October 15, five days after his thirty-fifth birthday, Monk walked into Beltone Studios in Manhattan, ready to work. Intent on highlighting Monk's pianistic talents, Weinstock chose a trio setting for the first sessions. Monk hired Art Blakey and Gary Mapp, a bass player renowned in Brooklyn but unknown elsewhere. Randy Weston put Mapp and Monk together. "Gary was from Barbados and he was part of a whole group of Brooklyn bass players—Sam Gill, Ahmed Abdul-Malik, etc. We had many gigs together. We played everything from Polish weddings to Italian weddings to dances, you name it. To do a jazz concert at that time was quite rare."[30] By day Mapp worked as a police officer for the New York City Transit Authority (he earned the moniker "the Hip Cop"[31]), and the sessions he recorded with Monk represent the only evidence of his playing.

Monk's experience with Weinstock contrasted sharply from that of Blue Note. Whereas Alfred Lion and Frank Wolff not only encouraged rehearsals but paid musicians for rehearsal time, Weinstock wanted his artists to show up and blow, and if one take produced sufficient results, one take was all that was needed. "We'd record it and go on to the next one. That was my style of recording. . . . Ninety percent of the time we didn't even listen to playbacks. Don't forget, these were world-class players. They knew when they were good or not."[32] The trio recorded four sides altogether, each one limited by the 78's three-minute time constraint. "Monk's Dream," a highly danceable 32-bar romp, was technically the only new composition on the date. Despite the studio's beat-up and slightly out-of-tune piano, Monk employs open chord voicings and impressive fingering technique to great effect, dancing all over the keyboard. The two other original compositions, "Little Rootie Tootie" and "Bye-ya," were pieces he had written several years earlier but never recorded. "Tootie," now a playful dedication to his son, was originally "The Pump" (see Chapter 9). Teddy McRae had quite literally stolen it from Monk in 1944 by taking co-composer's credit, and it was now Monk's turn to "steal" it back.[33] He did alter the original melody: in the introduction and the A-section, he would hit a high-register chord three times in order to mimic the sound of the train whistle. Thelonious also dusted off his composition "Playhouse," another danceable, upbeat tune but with an even stronger Latin flavor.[34] Weinstock wanted to call it "Go." Hearing the Latin/Caribbean influence, he asked George Rivera, Prestige's accountant who was in the studio that day, for the Spanish translation. Somehow "Vaya" became "Bye-ya."[35] Finally, Monk explored the ever-popular Harry Tobias standard, "Sweet and Lovely," opening with an introduction paraphrasing his own "Ask Me Now."

Monk felt alive again. All four songs were recorded in one take, and his solfeggio singing at times threatened to overwhelm the music. Monk expresses pure joy as he sings out his ideas. Buoyed by the session, Monk took his trio to Philadelphia a week later where he played a week at the Blue Note,[36] returning in time to see the Sunday edition of *The New York Times*. In the Arts section on October 26, Monk read something he had never seen before in the mainstream press: his name. John S. Wilson, a young critic who had joined the *Times* staff that year,[37] published an essay reviewing recent recordings by modern pianists. The piece featured Eddie Heywood, Erroll Garner, and Ralph Sutton, but it led off with Thelonious Monk. Concentrating on the Blue Note release of *The Genius of Modern Music*, Wilson's review was mixed. "His piano work is revealed as being neither particularly mysterious nor especially boppish," he mused. But not being "boppish" in Wilson's opinion was not necessarily a bad thing. Instead, he called Monk a "single note man, in direct descent from Count Basie." He described him as playing in a relaxed and "unmannered" fashion, but on at least two ballads he found Monk uninspired. Part of the problem, the critic acknowledged, was that some of the recordings were made four or five years earlier, and given the advancement of the music they sounded dated. Nevertheless, he concluded: "Considering the cult worship surrounding both bop and Monk when these sides were made, they hold up surprisingly well now that the furor has passed."[38] I'm not sure what Monk thought about Wilson's opinions, but a *New York Times* review was significant. Wilson was the first critic in the mainstream press to take Thelonious seriously. And while his future reviews would vary from dismissal to praise, Wilson's persistent efforts to write about Monk ultimately contributed to broadening Monk's audience and generating opportunities.

Two months later, on December 18, Monk was back in Beltone Studios again to record four more sides. Gary Mapp returned, Max Roach occupied the drum chair, and Ira Gitler, who turned twenty-four that day, produced the date.[39] Once again, the piano had not been tuned and no one seemed to notice, except Monk, who decided to milk the bad notes rather than avoid them. The repertoire was similar to that of the last session: one standard and three originals—each recorded in one take. "Trinkle Tinkle" is a magnificent display of piano technique, yet there is nothing Tatum-esque here. It is pure Monk in sound, rhythm, and fury. There are mixed stories behind the title; producer Ira Gitler believes he might have misunderstood Monk who may have said "Twinkle, Twinkle," because when Gitler asked Monk for the title he heard "Trinkle, Tinkle, like a star."[40] On the other hand, all the great stride pianists with whom Monk identified called themselves "ticklers," so it might have been a playful corruption of that word. Either way, Monk continued to use "Trinkle Tinkle" long after the 1952 recording.

Monk went back to the Caribbean with "Bemsha Swing," another danceable number with Max Roach producing counter-rhythms with brushes. Co-written with Denzil Best, the song was a tribute to Barbados, his native land. When Best and Monk submitted the copyright request form three days before the session, the paperwork included the correct title, "Bimsha Swing." Although critics have been baffled by the title ever since, both Best and fellow Barbadian Gary Mapp understood the meaning—Bimsha was the phonetic pronunciation of "Bimshire," and Barbados's nickname was "Little Bimshire."[41] Weinstock wasn't moved by the song at first, but Ira Gitler persuaded his reluctant boss of its musical value.[42]

"Reflections" (the title provided by Ira Gitler) would evolve into one of Monk's most intriguing and romantic ballads, but he debuted it here in a tempo much closer to a fox trot than a ballad—it might be described as medium slow. It possesses a strong drive, allowing the band to swing continuously, yet it is slow enough for Monk to fill the space with complex little phrases, while never leaving the melody. Last is Monk's hilarious rendition of "These Foolish Things." After opening with a quote from "Please, Mr. Sun," a syrupy pop tune recorded by both Johnny Ray and Perry Como that year,[43] Monk is all over the keyboard, making surprising harmonic choices and deliberately seeking out the "bad" notes for comic effect.

The last weeks of 1952 passed quickly. The holidays rolled around again, which meant Toot and Nellie had another birthday to celebrate. Toot turned three and was talking up a storm. But this year his daddy couldn't stick around for the evening festivities: He had go to work. Thelonious had a week-long gig backing Sarah Vaughan at the Paramount Theater.[44] Vaughan had become a sensation that year, headlining a major tour advertised as "The Biggest Show of '52."[45] Jobs were still scarce, but Monk's fortunes seemed to be improving. By the first of the year, Monk had secured a few gigs in Washington, D.C. He performed at the Howard on January 10, returned nearly two weeks later to do a five-night stint at Club Bengasi, a one-nighter at Club Kavakos, and in March he was back at the Howard Theater for a night.[46]

Meanwhile, Barbara Monk had become progressively weaker and less mobile. She occasionally found the strength to get out of bed to feed Toot and play little games with him. "Grandma always seemed to be in front of me trying to feed me," Toot recalled. "Every time I see my grandmother she's in front of me smiling with this huge smile trying to feed me. I'm in a high chair, the window's at my back, and I just remember she was crazy about me."[47] She couldn't get enough of Little Toot and prayed Thelonious and Nellie might give her one more grandchild. Her prayers were answered; by February Nellie knew she was pregnant.

At some point during the spring or summer, Nellie's sister Skippy and her son Ronnie moved in with the Monks for a few weeks. With six people living there now, their tiny apartment suddenly felt smaller than ever. Monk's niece Charlotte recalls, "It got to be so crowded, Uncle Bubba [Thelonious] wouldn't be home. He'd be on the corner every morning."[48] Skippy tried not to be a burden; she helped around the house, made sure Nellie rested, and cared for Toot. Monk enjoyed talking to his thirteen-year-old nephew, who was a smart, sweet kid and a talented artist.[49]

And Monk had time to talk. The summer months were slow and his newly released Prestige LP was not flying off the shelves.[50] Barry Ulanov's mostly negative review in the July issue of *Metronome* didn't help matters. While hearing "some progress toward pianistic proficiency," Ulanov nevertheless dismissed Thelonious "as monotonous a composer as ever . . . rooting, tooting, trinkling, tinkling and rarely emerging from a boppist Impressionist morass."[51]

As Nellie's delivery date approached, Thelonious turned down out-of-town engagements; he was not going to miss the birth of his second child. Instead, he played concerts where alcohol was not served and one-nighters in the outer boroughs. The black-owned clubs and bars in Brooklyn not only ignored the cabaret laws but genuinely embraced Monk, introducing him to the expansive world of jazz across the river. "We had more clubs in Brooklyn than they had in Harlem," Randy Weston explained. "So every night we were hanging out."[52] The more popular spots included the Putnam Central, the Baby Grand, the Wagon Wheel, or the smaller bars like Pleasant Lounge, Club 78, Kingston Lounge, and the Club Continental. For the big events, Brooklynites might head to the Paramount Theater or to the dances held at the Elks or Sonia ballrooms. As long-time Brooklyn resident and former musician Freddie Robinson told me, "The music was everywhere. Every little corner bar had jazz."[53]

During the summer of 1953, Max Roach and Charles Mingus, the brilliant yet temperamental bassist and composer, also helped shift the weight of modern jazz across the bridge by organizing a series of Friday night concerts at the Putnam Central. Determined to become more independent of the industry, Mingus and Roach had recently started their own independent label, Debut Records, and decided to launch a series of "Jazz Workshops" that would feature significant innovators and enable artists to share more of the proceeds. They both regarded Thelonious as one of their generation's most important composers and brought him as a featured artist on the third Friday in August. That night Monk teamed up with Art Blakey, Mingus, probably Miles Davis, among others.[54]

Sunday nights Monk began attending jam sessions at the Open Door in Greenwich Village. Initiated by Robert Reisner, an art history professor and avid jazz fan, these "Sunday jazz bashes" had been going on since late April. Reisner had convinced the owner of the Open Door, Sol Jaffe, to let him invite featured artists, charge admission, and pay the musicians "scale plus." At virtually every session, Charlie Parker was the featured artist. But he was joined by many of his contemporaries, including Monk, who could play these Sunday night sessions because alcohol was not served during them.[55] It is not clear when Thelonious started showing up, but we know from a photograph by Robert Parent he was there in September. And in some cases he was paid—not much, but a gig is a gig and every dollar counted.

On Saturday, September 5, just a half-hour before midnight, Thelonious and Nellie met their one and only daughter, Barbara Evelyn Monk. Unlike her brother, she was born in Woman's Hospital, a division of St. Luke's hospital, on 110th and Amsterdam.[56] They named her after her grandmother and her Aunt Skippy, but almost immediately her family began calling her "Boo Boo." And from the beginning she looked like her daddy.

Ironically, when Barbara was born, Thelonious and Nellie were in better shape financially than they had been in the months following Toot's birth, *before* he lost his cabaret card. Whereas Toot was swaddled in clothes from Goodwill, Boo Boo slept in style. "I remember very clearly my Dad and Mom went and got a crib," Toot remembered. "It was a fancy crib. I mean, you know, of course, they had middle-class aspirations from day one. So they got the *baddest* crib. And I'll never forget this crib. I remember it was a crib that had this cabinet on one end of it and something that folded over the baby. . . . I remember my sister coming home from the hospital. I can see my mother doting over the crib. And I can see my sister in the crib. My memories really begin, really begin, with my father and me and my sister being home."[57] Home is where Thelonious spent most of his time since Nellie had to return to work soon after she gave birth. Now he had a newborn daughter, an active toddler son, and a sick mother to care for. He would wake up in the morning, head to the kitchen, and fortify himself with his own energy drink—one raw egg in a glass of milk. Again, Toot recalls "Dad running around the house in a white, sleeveless t-shirt. Always seemed like it was summer time, he was always sweating, and he was changing the diapers, and he was sweeping the floors, and he was washing the dishes and we were doing this dance all day."[58]

Sometimes Thelonious had help. When his nieces could baby-sit, or Nellie was home, Monk often headed to Pat's bar on West 64th or Green Gables on West 62nd for a drink or to shoot the breeze with his neighborhood pals.[59] But it was family that kept him sane and provided an anchor. Nellie later mused, "[D]uring the worst years we didn't feel the struggle as much as other people might have because we were very close, we felt each of us was doing the best he could, and we didn't suffer for things we couldn't have. In fact, nobody talked about them."[60]

Monk still played all the time at home, and musicians came by the house to learn his tunes. But it wasn't the same as a gig. He thrived on the dynamic exchange between musicians and audiences; he needed to get paid; and he did not want to disappear. "It was torture for him not to be able to play," Nellie explained years later. "But you'd never know it from looking at him, and he didn't get bitter. Anybody with less strength would have snapped. And he was continually omitted from things—records, concerts, and the like. We'd listen to the all-night Birdland radio show, and maybe once in two months they'd play a record of his. There was no money; no place to go. A complete blank. He wasn't even included in benefits."[61]

He did have a recording contract and a label seemingly interested in his work. In November, Weinstock invited Monk back to the studio—this time under better conditions. Rather than return to Beltone and its inferior piano, they moved to the familiar surroundings of WOR Studios, where Monk had recorded for Blue Note. Realizing that the 78 was dead, Weinstock set out to make an LP, freeing Monk from the three-minute format. Monk wanted to use Sonny Rollins and trumpeter Ray Copeland on the date, but things did not work out as planned. Indeed, many things did not work out as planned, which was not altogether surprising given the date of the session: Friday November 13. Superstitions notwithstanding, the tone was set when Monk and Rollins arrived over an hour late because, they claimed, their taxi had collided with a police vehicle. Ira Gitler, who produced the session, didn't quite buy the story, but absent any other explanation he had to accept it. Losing an hour proved costly; Gitler had to generate enough music for an entire album with limited studio time. Then Copeland came down with a severe case of the flu[62] and French horn player Julius Watkins was asked to sub. The Detroit-born Watkins was an outstanding classically trained musician who, despite three years at the Manhattan School of Music, could not get an orchestra job because of his race.[63] He had spent a few years on the road playing trumpet with Ernie Fields and Milt Buckner, but his dream was to play French horn in a jazz setting. By the time Monk hired him, he had just formed his own sextet with Oscar Pettiford and Kenny Clarke.[64] Having never worked with Monk, however, Watkins faced the unenviable task of learning the music on the job.

For better or worse, Monk went with a different rhythm section. Weinstock suggested bassist Percy Heath, a relatively young but experienced player who was now part of the Prestige stable as a member of the Modern Jazz Quartet.[65] Thelonious insisted on hiring a twenty-four-year-old left-handed drummer named Willie Jones. Jones had never made a record before and critics later questioned Monk's choice. But Thelonious had a penchant for hiring young, unknown players who brought enthusiasm and drive to the music. Jones was part of the Brooklyn circle, and Randy Weston, Kenny Dorham, even Max Roach, had begun to sing his praises.[66] Monk took a chance and the result is quite good. In the remaining studio time left, they recorded three new originals. "Think of One," similar to his composition "Thelonious," draws on the ostinato form; its one-note phrase is repeated over a stop-time rhythm that releases into a swinging bridge. It served the band well as a vehicle for improvisation—though on both takes the group is hesitant in its treatment of the theme. "Let's Call This" is yet another example of Monk's unique tempos. Despite strong solos, it plods along partly because the young drummer hasn't figured out how to sustain drive in a medium-slow tempo. It's not an easy thing to do. Even the great Roy Haynes noted, "Monk played the oddest tempos."[67] "Friday the Thirteenth" was written on the spot. Its simple four-bar phrase is repeated relentlessly, although the harmonic movement is so dominant it practically overpowers the melodic line. Because it was the last song of the day and Gitler needed more material to fill out an LP, he kept gesturing to the band to keep going. "There I was in the control booth, giving signs, holding up a cardboard sign telling them not to stop. It got to be pretty comical."[68] The song exceeds ten minutes. Still, both Rollins and Watkins turn in wonderful explorations on their instrument, but ultimately it is Willie Jones who saves the day. The dynamic interchange between Jones and the rest of the band, especially toward the end, confirmed Monk's choice.

Near the end of 1953, Monk finally secured a steady gig at Tony's, a black-owned Brooklyn neighborhood joint on the corner of Grand Avenue and Dean Street. Randy Weston remembers it as "a funky, dirty bar, with a funky little kitchen." In the fall of 1953, the management sought to raise the club's profile a bit by changing its name from Tony's Bar and Grill to Tony's Club Grandean, and christening its performance space the "Fiesta Room." With the dapper Jimmy Morton as Tony's "fabulous MC," it had already become a mainstay for musicians like Gary Mapp (who led his own band), Max Roach, and Kenny Dorham, and Milt Jackson had led his own group there the same night Monk played at the Putnam Central.[69] In December, Freddie Brathwaite, a well-known local activist and promoter, and an emerging sculptor named Jimmy Gittens, organized a concert of Monk's music at Tony's. Brathwaite and Gittens were part of a circle of black Brooklyn intellectuals known as "the chessmen," because they played the game so relentlessly. In addition to using mostly Brooklyn musicians—Kenny Dorham, bassist Sam Gill, and Willie Jones—Monk brought Sonny Rollins with him. The music was swinging enough to get people on the dance floor—a rarity when Monk performed in Manhattan.[70] It proved to be a memorable event, though for most of the folks who packed into Tony's that night it wasn't the music they remembered. Randy Weston reminisced: "That evening, some gang members from Gate's End showed up and tried to break up the concert. They came in and all of a sudden they wanted to take over. Words were exchanged, fights broke out. So the cats, they were really rumbling, and the beer bottles were flying everywhere. People were trying to get to the men's room, the ladies' room, and Monk and Sonny were still playing! They didn't miss a note."[71] In spite of the ensuing chaos, the management gave Thelonious a regular weekend slot that lasted from late December 1953 to May of 1954. Monk spent every Friday, Saturday, and Sunday leading a band made up of the usual suspects: Sonny Rollins, occasionally Kenny Dorham or Ray Copeland on trumpet, Willie Jones, Michael Mattos, Sam Gill or Gary Mapp on bass, and a slew of guests.[72]

The third weekend in March, for example, Monk shared the bandstand with Miles Davis, Gigi Gryce, Charles Mingus, and Max Roach.[73] They had come together under the auspices of the Jazz Workshops that Roach and Mingus had initiated the previous summer at the Putnam Central.[74] Earlier in the week, Davis and Roach met at Thelonious's apartment to go over the music. Monk's nephew, Theolonious ("Peanut"), who just happened to come in from playing basketball, witnessed Miles, Monk, and Max crammed into the tiny front room with the upright piano. The session turned sour when Miles made disparaging remarks about Monk's playing. Monk just glared at first, but Miles would not relent and soon the dispute escalated into a shouting match. "Max didn't say nothing," recalled Theolonious, who was fourteen at the time. "Uncle Bubba stood up and towered over Miles and they were about to go to blows. And I remember thinking, 'Who is this little guy? I'll whip him myself.' Then my father [Thomas] came in the house and said, 'Miles, man, you got a problem?' And Monk said, 'This is my band, my music.' Miles said, 'But you're not playing it right, Monk.' Miles looked up at Monk and I thought he was going to hit him with the trumpet. Then Monk finally said, 'I think you better leave. This is my mother's house and I don't want no violence in here.' Then my father went over to Miles and said, 'Man, I think you better go.'"[75]

Whatever ill feelings they might have harbored did not affect the music; according to all reports, the combination of such astounding talent produced a magical night of music. The evening moved Gigi Gryce to sketch out a tune he would later call "A Night at Tony's." "I sat at the piano during intermission," Gryce later recalled, "and picked out this melody. At first I was going to call it 'The Four M's' [for Miles, Max, Mingus, and Monk].[76] Two of the "M's" appeared to have agreed to a détente, but there was one moment when Thelonious thought he might test Miles's patience. In an act of playful comeuppance, Monk left the piano, snuck up behind Miles during his solo, reached into his shirt pocket for a pack of cigarettes, and dug into his jacket pocket for matches. After he lit up, he put everything back into Davis's pockets. "It was like a vaudeville act," recalled Celia Mingus. "And Miles—Miles wasn't going to give them the satisfaction of missing a note. God, that was funny."[77] It *was* funny, but at Miles's expense. The bad blood between Monk and Miles would have a lasting effect.

Amid the sea of black faces at Tony's was a white couple from France named Henri and Ny Renaud. Henri was a fine jazz pianist, composer, and producer who had come to America to produce several recording sessions for the Vogue label. They had arrived in December 1953, and were staying with pianist George Wallington.[78] Wallington wasn't close to Monk, but he sang his praises and urged Henri and Ny to seek him out. He was easy to find; Monk was listed in the city directory, so the Renauds simply dropped by his apartment. The visits became fairly regular, and when Monk started playing at Tony's the Renauds followed dutifully. Indeed, they survived the infamous night of the brawl, awed by the realization that "there must have only been two pale faces [in the club] (my wife's and mine)."[79] Once peace was restored, he remembered, "Monk swore having noticed nothing, so caught up by his piano. Monk was a being who lived on another planet."[80] Renaud was deeply impressed with Monk's fertile musical imagination and his integrity as a human being, and Monk in turn grew fond of the French pianist. They spent good part of the winter and early spring in each other's company. One night Renaud accompanied Monk to Birdland to hear Ike Quebec and Art Blakey. Manager

Oscar Goodstein, still angry over Monk using the piano as an ashtray and a coaster four years ago, tried to bar Thelonious from the club, but Renaud rose up in his defense. Goodstein, who by now was notorious for banning musicians from the club, made an exception.[81] It would be nearly a decade before Monk set foot in Birdland again.

Meanwhile, Monk's star seemed to be rising ever so slowly. On the twenty-sixth of February, the Music Division of the New York Council of the Arts, Sciences, and Professions invited him to participate in a tribute to the "Music of Negro Composers." The event, held at the Pythian Temple on West 70th, focused on twentieth-century concert music, notably works by Nathaniel Dett, Ulysses S. Kay, William Grant Still, John Wesley Work, W. C. Handy, Harry T. Burleigh, William L. Dawson, "and others." The others were presumably Monk as well as Charles Mingus, whose compositions were also recognized. Thelonious shared the stage with jazz and classical artists alike, including pianist Alonzo Levister, vocalist Janet Thurlow, and Gloria Davy, a talented young soprano who would go on to become the first black artist to perform in *Aida* at the Metropolitan Opera House.[82]

While the world of black composers considered Thelonious a worthy voice in the musical arts, the jazz press continued to ridicule Monk's music. *Down Beat* dismissed *Thelonious Monk Blows for LP*, the "Friday the thirteenth" date Prestige released in March. The reviewer wrote, "On the seemingly endless Thirteenth almost everybody plays as if he were on the brink of tears." The reviewer blamed the producer and said Monk had "a great deal to say but needs direction. That's what a recording director is for."[83] The review didn't faze Weinstock, however, who still hoped the LP format would generate better sales. He asked Monk to come back to the studio on May 11 to record another. The studio in question was not in New York, however. It was in Hackensack, New Jersey, and it was unlike any studio Monk had seen. It was the living room of a house owned by the parents of Rudy Van Gelder, a brilliant technician. An optometrist who loved jazz, Van Gelder figured out how mic placement, acoustics, and proper levels can generate a warmer, richer sound, and it was that sound Alfred Lion loved when he first "discovered" Van Gelder in 1953. Weinstock followed suit, and soon Rudy's place in Hackensack became the first and only choice for Prestige.[84]

This time Ray Copeland made the date, but instead of Sonny Rollins, Monk hired Frank Foster, an unknown but talented 25-year-old tenor player from Cincinnati. With two young horn players on the front line, Monk made sure they were backed by seasoned rhythm musicians—bassist Curley Russell and Art Blakey on drums. In what was becoming a familiar pattern, Monk offered up three originals and a standard—the latter a humorous reading of Jerome Kern's "Smoke Gets in Your Eyes." Much like his recording of "Especially to You," he arranged the horns to play dissonant, descending chromatic obligato phrases beneath his playful and even more dissonant statement of the melody.[85] In another familiar pattern, the title "We See" was the product of another error in translation. Monk initially called it "Weetee," his niece Evelyn's nickname, but "We See" is what stuck. Like his happy, precocious, nearly ten-year-old niece, the song is joyous, boppish, and upbeat. "Locomotive," on the other hand, takes us back to the plodding tempos. For Monk it was quite deliberate; in the tradition of Count Basie and

Duke Ellington and the train-whistle guitar blues of the early century, Thelonious set out to reproduce the sound of the train. Built on an odd 20-bar chorus, it rhythmically and melodically captures the motion of the old steam engines steadily chugging, except that the slow tempo reflects what Thelonious would have heard having grown up so close to train depots in San Juan Hill and Rocky Mount. He reproduced what he knew best: the slow-moving train coming into the station.

The final song of the day, "Hackensack," was a tribute to Van Gelder and his gadgets. It has also been a source of ongoing controversy. The melody in the A-section was first recorded ten years earlier by Coleman Hawkins on a date led by Mary Lou Williams.[86] As indicated previously, the arrangement had been written by Williams, though it's not clear if the melody was hers. Either way, Hawkins added it to his repertoire and recorded it as "Rifftide," listing himself as composer.[87] Monk's version is really a variation on "Rifftide," not the same song. The A-section was significantly revised, and he wrote an entirely different bridge. Thelonious took composer's credit and Hawkins apparently never challenged him on it. And it swings, thanks in large part to Art Blakey.

With another record in the can and his weekends filled with lively performances at Tony's, Monk was ready to take on more challenges. One afternoon, while strolling along the Hudson River waterfront with Henri Renaud, he peered downriver and began to wonder aloud: "What could there be on the other side of the ocean?" he told Renaud. "How I would love to see that!" Suddenly the wheels started spinning. Renaud recounts what happened next: "I heard that Charles Delaunay and Jacques Souplet were preparing the [third Paris] Jazz festival. . . . I immediately phoned Charles, one of the rare admirers of Monk at that time."[88] It all happened so quickly, Delaunay and Souplet did not have time to include Monk's name on the roster. For Monk, it wasn't such an easy decision. He had never been out of the country. His daughter was less than a year old. Money was still incredibly tight, and since Nellie had to work, her nieces and sister-in-law had to step in and provide childcare during the day. His mother had not gotten any better and he feared she might die while he was away. Nellie reassured him that everything would be fine. She knew how badly he wanted to travel, and they both had heard that Europeans showed greater appreciation for jazz than Americans did. Perhaps he might get a few lucrative gigs? Make a record or two? Maybe the critical acclaim might help record sales, or help him get his cabaret card reinstated?

Ironically, Monk's final gig before departing happened to be a benefit sponsored by the Committee to Restore Paul Robeson's Passport. The State Department had revoked Robeson's passport in 1950 in response to his vocal opposition to U. S. foreign policy vis-à-vis the Soviet Union and anti-colonial movements, and his vociferous defense of the Communist Party's right to exist. The Truman administration and the FBI deemed him a threat to national security, following a speech he delivered at the World Peace Congress in Paris in 1949, in which he opposed war against the Soviet Union.[89] The event, billed as a "Cultural Salute to Paul Robeson," was held at Harlem's Renaissance Casino on the evening of May 26.[90] The roster included some eminent figures, including the actor and poet Beah Richards, novelist Alice Childress, Charlie Parker, Pete Seeger, Julian Mayfield, Lorraine Hansberry, and the composer Earl Robinson.[91] Monk took great pride in his participation. For one thing, the event occurred soon after the historic Supreme Court decision on Brown v. Board of Education. Thelonious could not help but notice the headline on May 17 announcing that the Supreme Court ruled that segregation was unconstitutional. Moreover, Monk was a great admirer of Paul Robeson, not only for his courageous voice for freedom and justice, but as a musician, actor, and athlete. Several years later, when critic Stanley Dance asked Thelonious, "Whom do you most admire in sports?" he answered "Paul Robeson."[92] And Robeson admired Monk: he once wrote after seeing the pianist perform, "Thelonious Monk really floored me."[93]

On Sunday, May 30, Monk made his way to Idlewild Airport in Queens, toting an old suitcase Nellie had packed with two suits, two new shirts, two ties, socks, and underwear, all wrapped neatly in cellophane, and shoes, sheet music, and his latest Prestige LP.[94] The kid from San Juan Hill was going to Paris.

13

"France Libre!"

(June 1954)

s he traveled across the Atlantic in the relative comfort of Air France's Lockheed Super Constellation,[1] Monk had quite a bit on his mind. He was going to miss home, but he knew he had to make this trip. He hungered for recognition, opportunities to play and create, and, ultimately, money. And over the years, he had developed a special fondness for France, from his high-school French class to the days at Minton's when he'd wear a beret and a "Free France" button.[2] Like most of his colleagues, Monk had heard stories of the grand treatment the French bestowed on black jazz musicians, and he knew that one of his early heroes, Herman Chittison, had made the same trip exactly twenty years before. When Chittison made his trans-Atlantic crossing to Paris, the jazz musicians' paradise was also a city in crisis. Hitler's rise to power emboldened French fascists, who rioted in the streets just months before Chittison arrived, and labor resistance to fascism generated literally hundreds of strikes and confrontations.[3] But the gardens bloomed, lovers strolled the boulevard, and intellectuals occupied the cafés to discuss the latest developments in art, literature, and the anticolonial movement. Paris proved hospitable enough for Chittison to extend his stay for four years.[4] Monk also arrived during a moment of crisis and uncertainty. Three weeks earlier, France had suffered a humiliating defeat at the hands of the Viet Minh in Dien Bien Phu. Riots erupted in France's North African colonies, and it was becoming clear the old empire could no longer hold.[5] But for many of Monk's fellow travelers, some of whom were seeking romance in the City of Light, the country's political crisis was of no real consequence.

The plane set down at Orly airport on Monday morning, May 31. Thelonious was greeted by a representative from the Paris Jazz festival ("Salon du Jazz"), who escorted him to a small hotel room on the Champs-Elysées—not far from the Blue Note on rue Artois—secured for him by Charles Delaunay.[6] The terms of his performances were hardly ideal. He was scheduled to play the following night with a French rhythm section unfamiliar with his music. And because he was a last-minute addition to the program, none of the advance publicity mentioned Monk or prepared the audience for his unique brand of jazz. His Blue Note records and recent Prestige releases received a few notices in the French jazz press, and the 1949 essay on Monk in the Swiss journal

Jazz-Revue caught the attention of hardcore fans, but Thelonious was still unknown in Paris. The festival's real headliners were Gerry Mulligan and his quartet, trumpeter Jonah Jones, pianist Lalo Schifrin, hometown favorites like pianist Martial Solal and the Claude Luter orchestra, to name a few. Fortunately, Monk's old friend Mary Lou Williams was there, having recently joined the American expatriate community in Paris. She was living at the Hotel Cristal on the Left Bank and had become a magnet for American musicians, artists, and intellectuals passing through. Unfortunately, Thelonious found Mary Lou in a particularly depressed and reclusive mood. The day Monk arrived, Williams's dear friend, pianist Garland Wilson, had died of liver failure. He was only forty-four.[7]

Nervous, sleep-deprived, and with little time to rehearse, Monk did what made sense to him: He went out to buy some reefer. He had a contact: an expatriate bluesman named Al "Fats" Edwards who resided at Trois-Maillets. Coincidentally, it was during Monk's search for weed that he first met his rhythm section, drummer Jean-Louis Viale and bassist Jean-Marie Ingrand. They were both in their early twenties and were working regularly at the Blue Note in Paris backing pianist René Urtreger. They were in the lobby of Fats's building for the same reason Monk was. As Ingrand recalls, "At eight p.m. one lovely night, we arrived as usual at the door to his apartment complex. A big Black man, his beret turned towards his ears, was in full conversation with the concierge, who did not speak a word of English. Having noticed us, he asks us if we knew Fats, and if we could take him to his apartment. He explained to us that he got Fats's address in New York and was anxious to meet him. Having recognized Monk completely by accident, we took the stairs to Fats's pad, while Monk told us that he had arrived that morning in Paris to play in the festival and was assigned a French rhythm section. At that moment, I wasn't even close to thinking that this rhythm section would include me. Later that night at Blue Note, I found out that Viale and I had been chosen to accompany Monk during his concerts."[8]

The next day, June 1, Thelonious called a rehearsal at Salle Pleyel, the huge, elegant concert hall where the festival was to be held. Monk showed up late, barely uttered a word to Ingrand and Viale, and headed immediately to the piano and began to play. Without music or direction, they wrestled with the piece the best they could until Monk finally said, "It's all right."[9] It really wasn't all right. Thelonious was not happy with his rhythm section and he said as much in an interview a few years later. "I enjoyed the visit very much," he explained to Nat Hentoff. "The only drag was I didn't have my own band with me. I couldn't find anybody to play with me that could make it."[10]

Monk's initial disappointment just added to his nervousness. By the time he returned to the Salle Pleyel that night for the concert, he was already a little tipsy. (As he would later confess, he discovered cognac in Paris and drank so much that it made him sick.[11]) Backstage, while Claude Luter's wildly popular Dixieland band performed before 3,000 enthusiastic fans, Monk continued to toss back shots of scotch. Luter completed his set, the heavy green-velvet curtain closed, and the emcee and festival organizer, Charles Delaunay, stepped on stage to introduce the Thelonious Monk trio. A smattering of diehard Monk followers showed their appreciation, but most of the folks were there to see Luter and couldn't care less about the strange American. The curtain drew back to reveal Ingrand and Viale poised to play, a lovely grand piano, and an empty bench. After a few seconds of tepid applause, Thelonious strolled onto the stage as if he hadn't a care in the world, sporting a slightly oversized blue suit with a bright blue shirt and socks to match and a bow tie. He headed straight to the microphone and spoke in a manner that would have made his French teacher proud. "*Bonsoir tout le monde. . . . Je joue* 'Well, You Needn't.'" Then he coolly walked to the piano bench and sat down, ready to play. But before he touched the keyboard he suddenly changed his mind, returned to the mic, and declared: "*Je joue* 'Off Minor.'"[12]

The audience was already restless and unforgiving, and the music did nothing to console them. Thelonious Monk was unlike anything the French had ever heard . . . or seen. He grunted and sweated, both feet flailing wildly underneath him in a macabre stationary dance. His chords were shockingly dissonant and the melody unfamiliar. When Monk would bang his elbow or forearm down on the keys, it looked contrived to fans who believed that Luter's brand of big-band swing defined jazz. Viale and Ingrand were completely bewildered. Half an hour into the set, Monk suddenly got up, Ingrand recalls, and "pointed a vengeful finger towards an unsuspecting Jean-Louis Viale. Caught off guard and not knowing what to do, Viale immediately started to play a brilliant solo. At this point a furious Monk left the stage, downed a shot of scotch, then returned and serenely sat at his piano to finish the piece still playing, as if what he had just done was absolutely normal."[13] Later in the dressing room, Monk tore into Viale, explaining that when he gets up from the piano the set is over. Hurt, dejected, and utterly confused by the evening's proceedings, Viale quit on the spot. Since they had one more show to do, Ingrand recruited drummer Gerard "Dave" Pochonnet to fill in. Pochonnet, a close friend of Mary Lou Williams, had been hanging out backstage for just such an occasion.[14]

Monk's European debut proved to be a disaster. According to the leading French jazz magazine, *Jazz Hot*, Monk was not well received that first night, and the two British critics who attended the inaugural concert, Raymond Horricks and Mike Nevard, concurred. They both took in the proceedings with a combination of fascination and disappointment, concluding independently that Monk's performance was more circus than concert. Describing him as a "kind of court jester to modern jazz," Horricks's comments were particularly harsh: "To witness a man making a fool of himself and his music as I had just done, a man committing artistic suicide, was no such pleasant sensation."[15] Nevard proved a bit more sympathetic, suggesting that while Monk might be easily dismissed "as a musical charlatan," he found the music "sometimes startling, sometimes banal," but always challenging. "You can't assess Monk because there are no set standards by which to judge him. By the normal criterion of jazz he is inferior . . . but there may be minds attuned to his weird, morse-like message."[16]

By the time the concert ended and the musicians retired to the Salle Pleyel cabaret for an informal jam session, Thelonious seemed more relaxed but was clearly inebriated. He sat in with baritone saxophonist Gerry Mulligan and his group and a few of the locals.[17] According to Horricks, Thelonious thoroughly disrupted the proceedings with his off-beat comping and strange harmonics, eliciting strange and angry looks from the other musicians. All except for Mulligan, who rose to the challenge and established a fruitful musical dialogue with Monk. The exchange ended only when Mulligan's wife, Arlyne, abruptly announced that it was late and time to go home.[18] But it wasn't late for Thelonious. Despite obvious signs of exhaustion, he made his way to Mae Mezzrow's[19] flat where she was hosting a gathering of some fifteen friends, mostly musicians. Monk arrived and dominated the piano bench. Twenty-two-year-old pianist René Urtrerger was there. "Monk played all night and eventually everyone fell asleep. When we awoke the next day, he was still at the piano."[20]

That night Monk met Joachim Berendt, an eminent German music critic and radio producer who was in Paris to record the festival for the Südwestfunk (SWF) radio network and Radiodiffusion Francaise. He was perhaps Germany's equivalent of Leonard Feather; the founding director of the jazz division at SWF, Berendt had published a tome on jazz history entitled *Das Jazzbuch* (*The Jazz Book*) the previous year.[21] Monk took a liking to Berendt and made arrangements to meet at his hotel the following evening. In Monk's mind, Berendt was a hip European who knew the music and knew Paris and might help him navigate the city. In Berendt's mind, Monk was a mystery to unravel. Monk wanted to shoot the breeze; Berendt wanted an interview. When Berendt arrived, Thelonious was sitting on his bed wearing "a fancy silk dressing gown" and ending an animated conversation with two other visitors. As soon as they left, it was the allegedly taciturn Monk who did the talking, bombarding Berendt with many specific questions about Paris. "I sensed," mused Berendt later, "that it really meant something to Monk to be in Europe and, especially so, to be in Paris."[22] Unfortunately, the German critic's limited knowledge of the city proved unhelpful. But when the tables turned and Berendt became the interrogator, Thelonious suddenly became close-lipped, if not uninterested. Berendt asked about Monk's family, racial problems in the United States, and commercialism in jazz, but his answers alternated between "okay" and "just okay." It was enough to persuade Berendt that Monk believed "that no race problem existed today."[23] Just when he thought he had exhausted all topics, Berendt casually asked about his stylish silk robe. Monk suddenly "stopped his 'just okay' attitude and even told me where he got it."[24] Thelonious wasn't interested in being an object of curiosity; he wanted to see Paris, and, if he could afford it on his minuscule budget, bring home some stylish Parisian threads.

Monk appreciated Berendt's interest in him given the generally cold reception of his music, though he did not realize at the time that Berendt was hardly his fan. Berendt agreed with certain criticisms, having found "much to criticize in Monk's harmonies, which are sometimes wrong if you accept certain harmonic rules."[25] Danny Halperin, a Canadian who worked for the *Continental Daily Mail* and had become an intimate of jazz musicians,[26] remembered hanging out with Monk the night after the first concert, listening to him complain about the audience response. "They're not really listening to what I'm playing." Overhearing their conversation, Gerry Mulligan jumped in and told Monk, "Don't bother about it . . . *I'll* be listening to you from now on. I'll be just off stage listening. If you turn a little that way you'll see me there."[27] The advice must have helped because on Thursday June 3, the second night of the festival, Monk came back swinging. Sober and focused, he ignored the "scattering of disrespectful gestures" from the audience, sat down at the piano, and took care of business. He kept the same rhythm section, having made up with Jean-Louis Viale, and this time they worked together on tunes like "We See" and "Well, You Needn't." *Jazz Hot* called Monk's performance "significantly better," and Raymond Horricks concurred.[28] "His touch was definitive, his spontaneous search for new harmonic structures successful, his rhythmic emphasis clear and direct and considerate to his supporting musicians; in short, a musician sure of himself and sure of his direction in jazz."[29] Berendt was the lone dissenting voice, insisting that both performances were poor compared to his recorded output, the only detectable difference being "he drank less before the second concert than he did before the first one."[30]

The audience seemed to concur with Berendt, for their attitude toward Monk remained unchanged. His spirits were lifted, however, when Mary Lou Williams greeted him warmly backstage. Accompanying her was an elegantly-dressed European woman of about forty years of age.[31] Her friends called her Nica, but the world knew her by a much grander name: the Baroness Pannonica de Koenigswarter. She loved jazz and believed Thelonious was one of its greatest artists. She told him that Teddy Wilson persuaded her to buy the Blue Note disc of Monk's " 'Round Midnight" during a visit to New York City in 1951. She had to catch a flight back to Mexico City, her home at the time, but once the needle hit the groove she was overwhelmed. She missed her flight and remained in New York for three more months.[32] As she later recounted to club owner Max Gordon, "The first time I heard Thelonious playing ' 'Round Midnight,' I cried."[33] Thus began what would become the most significant relationship in Monk's life outside his family.

During the course of Monk's stay in Paris, he became acquainted with Nica's stories, which succeeded in breaking down his initial detached and circumspect posture. She wasn't just any rich baroness—she was a Rothschild, one of the world's most powerful financial dynasties. Born Kathleen Annie Pannonica Rothschild in London on December 10, 1913, she was the youngest daughter of Nathaniel Charles Rothschild, a banker and amateur botanist and entymologist who loved insects more than money, and Rozsika von Wetheimstein, a beautiful and stately woman born of Hungary's Jewish elite.[34] They met during one of Charles's excursions to Hungary in search of rare butterflies. In fact, Charles named his daughter Pannonica after a *moth* he had caught in 1913, the year of her birth.[35]

Despite the loss of her father when she was ten years old, Nica thrived in the well-heeled Rothschild family.[36] She showed early promise as a painter: at age eleven she won a silver medal in an art contest held by the Royal Academy of Art.[37] She attended the best finishing schools in Paris, met with royalty, and lived a life of protected privilege. And while her mother kept her children isolated from most other kids, Nica had her two sisters, Miriam and "Liberty" (Elizabeth), and her older brother Victor, with whom she grew quite close. Victor was a fine piano player who fell in love with jazz and invited his little sister to join the affair. Teddy Wilson became his teacher, and through their relationship Nica gained entrée into the actual world of jazz—records, musicians, clubs, and the like. It would become her first love. As she once explained, "In time, I grew to feel that if the music is beautiful, the musicians must be beautiful too in some way."[38]

In the spring of 1935, Nica met Jules de Koenigswarter, a mining engineer and inspector for the Bank of Paris. Like Nica, he was from a prominent Jewish family with roots in Austria and Hungary, and a bona-fide baron to boot. They both loved to fly: When they first met in the summer of 1935, Nica had begun taking flying lessons and Jules was an accomplished pilot. As their son Shaun de Koenigswarter explained, "According to both of them, it was love at first sight ('*le coup de foudre*,' as we say in French)."[39] They spent the remaining summer months in Jules's small plane touring Europe, stopping off in Le Touquet, Deauville, Salzburg, Vienna, Budapest, Venice, and Monte Carlo. At the end of the tour, Jules popped the question. Ten years her senior and a widower with a young son, Jules was not only madly in love but quite anxious to remarry. It happened so suddenly that Nica's response was to flee. On September 19, she boarded the S.S. *Normandie*, bound for New York where her sister Liberty now lived.[40] Jules followed in hot pursuit, arriving in New York on October 7.[41] Eight days later, they were married at the New York City municipal building, to much fanfare, and set off on a honeymoon circumnavigating the globe.[42]

Now Baroness Pannonica de Koenigswarter, she joined her new husband and stepson in Paris, bore two children—Patrick and Janka—and watched in horror as fascism spread throughout Europe. On September 3, 1939, a month shy of their fourth wedding anniversary, Jules was called up by the French Army as a reservist lieutenant to assist the R.A.F. in setting up a radar network in France. Five weeks after Hitler's forces invaded France and propped up the Vichy regime, Jules managed to escape to England on June 21, 1940, where he promptly joined the Free French Army under the leadership of Général Charles de Gaulle. Five months later, he was dispatched to Brazzaville (Congo), then to Accra (Ghana), and eventually participated in the campaigns in Tunisia, Italy, and France as a member of the Première Division Française Libre (First Free French Division). By the war's end, he had been promoted to Lieutenant-Colonel and earned the highest military honors, including the Croix de la Libération, Croix de la Légion d'Honneur, and the Croix de Guerre.[43]

Meanwhile, Nica and her nanny gathered the three kids and fled France just as German tanks rolled across the border. On June 11, 1940, they boarded a ship at Liverpool en route to New York.[44] "She only stayed six months," her son Shaun recounted, "long enough to find an American family to whom she could entrust the children and to find a way of being reunited with my father."[45] But during her brief stay she became active in the France Forever Committee, founded in Philadelphia in September 1940 by chemist and French expatriate World War I hero Eugene Houdry.[46] De Gaulle himself recognized it as the official arm of the Resistance in the United States. Through France Forever, Nica volunteered to ship several tons of medical supplies to the Free French forces based in Brazzaville. She oversaw the delivery personally, boarding a Norwegian cargo ship in December 1940 and arriving in Brazzaville early in January 1941. She joined her husband in Brazzaville, then in Accra, working as a decoder and broadcasting anti-fascist messages and news of the Free French Forces into Vichy-controlled territories of French West Africa.[47] Toward the end of the year, she contracted malaria in Ghana and was granted a leave to visit her children. On New Year's Eve, 1941, Nica boarded the S.S. *Santa Paula* bound for New York City.[48] She almost didn't make it. The much-celebrated ocean liner was attacked twice by German U-boats—once off the coast of West Africa, where a torpedo came within twenty feet of the vessel, and again off the U.S. coast, where it nearly collided with another ship dodging a U-boat attack. The *Santa Paula* arrived in one piece, docking in New York harbor on January 23, 1942.[49] (Sadly, her mother-in-law did not make it; she refused to leave France and died at Auschwitz.[50]) Nica sailed back to the Gold Coast in December 1942, and three months later rejoined her husband in the First Free French Division as military driver in Cairo and later in Tunisia, Italy, and France. Holding the rank of private second-class, Nica also volunteered as a driver for the War Graves Commission, sometimes traveling close to the frontlines in Italy and Germany.[51] And like her husband, she was decorated for her service, earning the Médaille de la France Libre.[52]

Jules's military service earned him a coveted post in the diplomatic corps. He served first in Oslo (1946 to 1949) and then Mexico City, where he was counselor at the French Embassy.[53] In the meantime, Nica had had three more children, Berit (born in 1946), Shaun (1948), and Kari (1950), but quickly became bored as the wife of a diplomat. She was terribly unhappy in her marriage; she found Jules controlling and disapproving of her friends. In 1951 she began to take more frequent trips to New York to hear music and escape what had become a stifling life. For Jules, these frequent excursions and his wife's associations with black musicians became a source of embarrassment, which sometimes elicited acts of cruelty. "He used to break my records when I was late for dinner," she lamented.[54] She responded by coming home even later, extending her New York trips for weeks, months. By the time he was appointed Minister Plenipotentiary to the United States and Canada, relocating to New York City in 1953, he and Nica had separated.[55] She paid a rather dear price for her freedom. The Rothschilds did not look kindly upon her fraternizing with musicians, and separations are always messy when one is the subject of tabloids. She was not cut off entirely, but her access to the family fortune was significantly curtailed.

So when Nica first laid eyes on Monk that June night in 1954, she was essentially a free woman. She found in this unusual black man an artistic soulmate, though Thelonious did not know it at the time. Nica and Monk became fast friends, "and the rest of the time he was there we had a ball."[56] Besides Nica, Monk hung out with Mary Lou, Charles Delaunay, Henri and Ny Renaud, and some of the musicians in the festival. He spent quite a bit of time with his bassist Jean-Marie Ingrand. Despite their rough beginnings, they became friendly after the second performance, largely because Ingrand had a decent command of English. He served as Monk's unofficial guide, translator, and problem-solver, and in exchange Monk taught the young bassist his music. "One day, Monk asked me to find him a small record player," recalled Ingrand, "because he wanted me to listen to his latest disc with Sonny Rollins for Prestige. Together, we must have listened to 'Friday The 13th' a thousand times, and having studied the theme so thoroughly, I was the only one capable of playing it in Paris."[57]

The Saturday, June 5 concert featured solo piano performances by Monk and seven other pianists, including Martial Solal, Bernard Peiffer, Henri Renaud, Lalo Schifrin, and Mary Lou Williams.[58] Renaud and Delaunay found Monk's solo performance so compelling that they decided to record a radio show of Monk alone, especially since the trio performances did not seem to go over well. So Delaunay secured the studio at Radiodiffusion Française for Monday afternoon, June 7.[59]

Renaud, Delaunay, and producer André Francis never thought they would release the nine sides they recorded that afternoon.[60] After all, Monk's contract with Prestige prohibited him from recording with another label, and the circumstances that day were hardly ideal. The engineers were on strike, which meant that Francis had to man the sound board himself. But given that Monk planned to return to New York in three days, they went ahead and crossed the picket line. Monk recorded each song in one take, the repertoire consisting primarily of tunes he had recorded for Blue Note ("Off Minor," "Eronel," " 'Round Midnight," "Well, You Needn't") as well as three songs he had laid down for Prestige the previous month—"Hackensack," "Smoke Gets in Your Eyes," and "We See," which Francis originally retitled "Manganese." Perhaps he, too, couldn't understand Thelonious when he said "Weetee," or maybe Monk never told him the title, but Francis came up with "Manganese," an element from the periodic table that also doubles as a pun for "Monk at Ease."[61] Monk also included his latest composition, "Reflections," which Francis listed as "Portrait of an Eremite" (meaning hermit or recluse—*ermite* in French). Like " 'Round Midnight," Monk performed it at a kind of fox-trot tempo—slower than medium but not quite a ballad.[62]

As soon as Monk was paid, he cut out to see Paris and do a little shopping. He picked up a few berets for himself and for friends, bought some French liquor, and a few trinkets for the kids. He spent the next few days hanging out with his crew—Nica, the Renauds, Mary Lou—playing where he could, even sitting in with his new pal Jean-Marie Ingrand at the Blue Note. Ingrand, especially, found it hard to see him go. "Along with a few friends," he recalled, "I accompanied him to Orly. When he presented himself at customs, a bottle of scotch stood out from each of his pockets. This was Monk: a strange being, incomprehensible at times, but filled with kindness and simplicity at every occasion. He was a man one could easily get attached to."[63] Carrying just one piece of luggage weighing about twenty pounds, and apparently two bottles of scotch, Monk boarded Air France flight 29, headed for home.[64]

14

"Sometimes I Play Things I Never Heard Myself"

(July 1954–May 1955)

Although he had enjoyed his few days in Paris—and the money he made there—Monk was happy to be home with his family in San Juan Hill. But the excitement of his travels soon wore off and Monk had to start looking for gigs again. Without any steady bookings that summer, Thelonious continued to stay at home with his children while Nellie worked. Toot recalled, "He really did the daddy thing. And I can always see him bent over, changing Boo Boo's diapers. This is pre-Pampers, man! That was an ordeal. Putting the diapers in the bucket and changing the bucket and the whole thing and he just did it like I never heard a complaint, or a sigh, or nothing."[1]

Sometimes Thelonious dropped Boo Boo off at Thomas's house while he threw Toot on his shoulders and walked around the neighborhood. "My father would just take me out because I was older and I was always, always on his shoulders. It seemed like I was a mile up. And he loved having me on his shoulders." He'd pass by Green Gables on 62nd and Amsterdam, where his friend Baron Bennerson tended the bar, or Pat's Bar on the corner of 64th to greet his friends, then head next door to the grocery store and pick up some meat from the local butcher. Toot remembered that everyone they encountered seemed to treat his father like royalty. "At this point he wasn't 'world famous,' you know, but he sure was a somebody in the neighborhood. 'Cause everybody in the neighborhood would say hello to him and I knew something special was going on with my father. I didn't know what it was, but I knew something special was going on by the way everyone sort of dealt with him."[2]

One afternoon, Thelonious decided Toot needed a new pair of shoes. With Toot perched on his shoulders, he walked to Harry's Shoes on West 64th Street and, in what might be described as an advanced example of modern parenting, or else an astonishing act of courage, he asked his four-year-old son to pick any pair of shoes he liked. "The family was aghast because he had let them know that I picked my own shoes. I remember his argument was, 'He knows which shoes he likes. He can pick his own shoes.' His take was basically, 'I'll make sure the size is right, but in terms of the style let him wear the shoes he digs, he doesn't wear the shoes I dig.'" This was Thelonious's approach to parenting.[3] Thelonious was once asked how he would feel if his then-six-year-old son decided to become a professional musician when he grew up. Monk's answer: "The important thing is how *he* feels. How I feel don't mean nothing. He'll be the way he wants to be, the way he's supposed to be."[4] Nellie reinforced this idea. On many occasions, she reminded both Boo Boo and Toot to just "Be yourself. . . . Don't bother about what other people say, because you are you. The thing to be is just yourself."[5]

Thelonious played daddy but he also had to work. When his nieces were unavailable to baby-sit, Toot and Boo Boo often stayed with Rae McKinney, a close family friend who lived in the high-rise projects across the street. Affectionately known as "Aunt Rae," she and her husband Mac were strict disciplinarians who had no qualms about spanking their own children. "Aunt Rae was like, 'I'll kick your ass, fuck you up in a minute, boy.' She always had to temper her thing with me because she knew she had to deal with Thelonious, and Thelonious and Nellie didn't believe in hitting kids. She wonked me a few times but I just took it. I said, you know, 'If I tell Dad this'll get crazy.' He'll come over here and he'll hurt Mac and he'll hurt Aunt Rae too. But I'll never forget, Aunt Rae and Mac were so rough that they would do a tag team thing on you."[6] Despite the potential for "classic child abuse," as he put it, staying with Aunt Rae was worth the trouble because their youngest son happened to be Toot's best friend, Gregory Flowers. They remained running buddies well into their teenage years.[7]

It was a fun, relaxing summer for everyone, capped off with a celebration of Boo Boo's first birthday on September 5 and the release of Monk's latest Prestige LP recorded in May with Frank Foster and Ray Copeland. Barry Ulanov reviewed it for *Metronome*, and his opinion of Monk's work had not changed; he found most of the record "dull" and "monotonous," though he partly blamed Copeland and Foster for that.[8] But Bob Weinstock was unfazed. He called Monk back to Rudy Van Gelder's studio on September 22, along with Art Blakey and Percy Heath, to record another ten-inch LP.[9] Monk came with renewed energy and at least one new composition he titled "Work." Like "Four in One," it was one of his treacherous melodies full of strange intervallic leaps, distinctive bass counterpoint, and unique chord progressions played over a medium tempo. Thelonious also introduced his third and most famous original blues, "Blue Monk." Composed in the studio after Weinstock complained that Monk never played the blues, he borrowed part of the melody from Charlie Shavers' composition "Pastel Blue," though the sound is all Monk's.[10] The trio stretched out on "Blue Monk" for seven and a half minutes. Each successive chorus builds on the last and becomes more elaborate and playful—at one point Monk even quotes his own "Misterioso." Monk liked "Blue Monk" so much that years later he would name it as one of his all-time favorites.[11]

Still short of tunes, Thelonious came up with "Nutty." He confessed in an interview years later, "I made it up in the studio. We needed something else to record so I wrote that."[12] Much like Tadd Dameron's "Good Bait," its simple, playful melody is repeated in the bridge but modulates up to a different key. Finally, he filled in three more minutes with an unaccompanied, rubato version of "Just a Gigolo," an old, beautiful ballad by Leonello Casucci and Julius Brammer, made popular in Vienna as "Schöne Gigolo" in 1929. Irving Caesar wrote an English lyric and it was recorded by several American singers, most famously Bing Crosby and Louis Prima.[13] His introspective deconstruction of the melody drew critical acclaim and did much to establish Monk as an outstanding solo pianist.

Two days after the session, Monk had a one-night stand at Harlem's Club Baron on 132nd and Lenox Avenue. Booked without a cabaret card, he joined Sonny Rollins, Willie Jones, and an unknown bass player (perhaps Percy Heath), and the band was billed as "The Greatest in Modern Jazz."[14] Sonny Rollins was Monk's favorite saxophone player—he had wanted to hire Rollins as a permanent band member, but Rollins was destined to be a leader. Indeed, the very next month, on Monday, October 25, Thelonious returned to Van Gelder's studio as a sideman on *Rollins's* next Prestige session. (Actually, Monk was a last-minute addition, since Sonny planned to use Elmo Hope, but Hope had gotten arrested for drug possession.[15]) It was a familiar gathering—veteran bassist Tommy Potter and Sonny's pal from Sugar Hill, drummer Art Taylor—all musicians Monk liked and respected. The relaxed setting produced a real jam session atmosphere; they laid down three sides, all standards or pop tunes. Rollins, who had a penchant for old show tunes, first called Vincent Youmans' "I Want to Be Happy" at a swinging tempo. Monk threw his reputed minimalism out the window and comped busily behind Rollins, which didn't faze the saxophonist at all. They then followed with a rollicking revision of Jerome Kern's "The Way You Look Tonight." Rollins imposed a different melodic line over Kern's chord changes, prompting Weinstock to retitle the song "The Way You Blow Tonight." They closed the session with another old Broadway hit by Youmans, the romantic ballad "More Than You Know" (1929). Nearly eleven minutes in length, it is the session's masterpiece. Monk's accompaniment is more about embellishing Rollins's melodic statements than laying down a harmonic framework, producing a unique musical marriage that is at once stately and full of surprises.[16]

The two worked together again that Saturday night at a Town Hall concert produced by Bob Reisner. Monk and the other musicians knew Reisner from his infamous afternoon jazz series at the Open Door, featuring Charlie Parker. Reisner arranged the Town Hall concert as a vehicle to feature Parker, his hero, who was going through some hard times. Parker's infant daughter, Pree, had died just a few months earlier, and he had checked himself into the psychiatric ward at Bellevue Hospital less than a month before the Town Hall concert.[17] The roster of musicians appearing alongside Bird was impressive—Reisner billed the event as the "Great Moderns in Jazz . . . featuring the outstanding Jazz Groups of '54."[18] The list included Monk, Rollins, trumpeter Art Farmer and his brother Addison on bass, guitarist Jimmy Raney, Horace Silver, and Gigi Gryce, among others. (Monk's rhythm section consisted of Michael Mattos on bass and Willie Jones on drums, but it is not clear whether Rollins performed as part of Monk's band or was a featured artist in his own right.) The event was poorly publicized and badly organized, yielding just a smattering of concertgoers.[19] Despite the poor attendance, the event became an occasion for Thelonious to see old friends and make new ones. He dug hearing Gigi Gryce, whom he began seeing a bit more frequently now that Gryce was living in New York City. He also saw his friend from Paris, the Baroness Nica de

Koenigswarter. She was now living at the Stanhope Hotel on Fifth Avenue and 81st Street.[20] Monk made sure to introduce Nica to his family, especially Nellie, whom she befriended right away.

That same night Jimmy Raney's pianist, tall, white, slightly younger than Thelonious, introduced himself. His name was Hall Overton. A composer with a Juilliard degree, he had already written an opera, scored for ballet, and was completing a symphony for strings.[21] Yet, he was utterly thrilled to meet Monk, a composer whom he had admired ever since his neighbor, a college kid named Harry Colomby, gave him a copy of one of Monk's 78s from Blue Note. "[Overton] was giving me [piano] lessons," Colomby remembers, "and I couldn't pay him, so at first I gave him a free phonograph I had gotten from Sam Goody for buying records. It really didn't work too well. Then I brought him a Thelonious Monk record. And he had not heard him before. The record had 'April in Paris,' and the other side was 'Nice Work If You Can Get It.' He said, 'Whoooo' and used the phrase 'purple passages.' I remember that."[22] It made a lasting impression. That night, he told Monk that he'd recorded "'Round Midnight" with Jimmy Raney and Stan Getz the previous year[23] and expressed an interest in studying more of his compositions. Thus began a long friendship.

Monk's reputation as an innovative composer and pianist far exceeded his modest record sales, although Prestige continued to release his LPs and kept his name in circulation. By the second half of 1954, part of the jazz world had finally begun to see Thelonious as more than a sideshow. In November, Monk was invited to Columbia University's Institute of Arts and Sciences (IAS). Directed by maverick scholar Russell Potter, the IAS offered creative extension courses for the non-academic community, often devoted to music, art, politics, and controversial subjects. The Institute offered a no credit course titled "Adventures in Jazz" taught by British guitarist Sidney Gross. The gig grew out of a series of radio lectures Gross had given on WNYC. The sixty-five students were not Columbia underclassmen but New York jazz lovers—men and women willing to lay out twenty bucks for the ten-week course. The class met every Wednesday night in the School of Journalism building, in a large classroom equipped with a fancy phonograph, a grand piano, and plenty of chalkboard. A course on jazz did not go over well with some administrators and faculty, especially in the Music Department. Professor Paul H. Lang was embarrassed by it and thought the IAS had overstepped its bounds. Lang complained to the University Provost, "This sort of thing can only hurt our reputation, moreover the next morning the room looks like a stable. The piano is banged up and the phonograph which we are nursing at great cost is abused." He asked the Provost to "take action to stop this circus."[24]

For the students, "Adventures in Jazz" was hardly a circus. They were treated to a living history of the music; they met and heard Willie "The Lion" Smith, bassist George "Pops" Foster, trumpeters Henry "Red" Allen and Jonah Jones, and trombonist Jack Teagarden.[25] "Bebop" happened to be the theme the week when Gross summoned Monk to share his expertise, and his fellow invitees included Oscar Pettiford, drummer Louis Bellson, and clarinetist Jimmy Hamilton (with whom Gross had just made several recordings[26]), as well as Nat Hentoff, who talked briefly about the future of jazz, and poet Langston Hughes, who read some of his own jazz-inspired work.[27] Although Gross designated Bellson "the star performer," the nattily dressed Monk stole the show. Gross asked Thelonious to demonstrate the differences between the older swing-era harmonies and those of the modernists. A writer for the *New Yorker* observed, "Mr. Monk sat down at the piano and struck a few chords. 'Those are old-style chords,' he said. 'Now here's a new-style chord—a G seventh. . . . That's what the chords we're using nowadays sound like.'"[28] Of course, no one voiced chords like Monk, so what he played jarred the sensibilities of the uninitiated. He continued to prove his point by playing a chorus of "Just You, Just Me," followed by an ensemble rendition of the same song. Nat Hentoff remembers Gross turning to Monk and asking him to "play some of your weird chords for the class." Thelonious was taken aback by the question. "What do you mean 'weird'?" Monk replied acidly. "They're perfectly logical."[29]

On Christmas Eve, Monk was back in Van Gelder's studio, this time as a member of an "all-star" band of Prestige recording artists. Once again, Monk was a sideman, not a leader. Bob Weinstock conceived of the session as a vehicle to showcase Miles Davis, backed by Monk and three members of the Modern Jazz Quartet: Milt Jackson, Percy Heath, and Kenny Clarke. To this day, the session has been one of the most controversial in the history of jazz, and not because of the music. Evidently, Miles asked Monk to "lay out" (not play) behind him whenever he took a solo. Indignant, Monk then allegedly did various things to sabotage the session. Words were exchanged, followed by blows. Eyewitnesses like Ira Gitler and Rudy Van Gelder, not to mention Miles and Monk themselves, have tried to lay the rumors to rest.[30] In his autobiography, Miles played down any tension between the two men and explained his decision to have Monk lay out as purely musical: "Monk never did know how to play behind a horn player. . . . A trumpet player needs the rhythm section to be hot even if he is playing a ballad. You got to have that kicking thing, and most of the time that wasn't Monk's bag. So I just told him to lay out when I was playing, because I wasn't comfortable with the way he voiced his changes, and I was the only horn on that date."[31] Thelonious also deflected any suggestions of conflict. He famously told Gitler in an interview two years later, "Miles'd got killed if he hit me [chuckling]." And then he added, "I 'lay out' my own self. He got that from me. He got that 'laying out' from me."[32] In another interview a few years later, Monk's response to the ubiquitous question about the session was more sober and reasoned: "When Miles asked me to lay out during his solo on that record, I never thought nothing of it—Roy Eldridge had his piano lay out years ago."[33] And when a French jazz magazine asked him about the date, he dismissed stories about their fight as "an invention. . . . Miles and I didn't have an argument."[34]

Still, there were tensions between the two men, exacerbated in part by Monk's deteriorating relationship with Prestige. This was Monk's second sideman gig in a row; he was upset that the label had not arranged another recording session for him as a leader. Furthermore, Weinstock had no intention of including any of Monk's tunes on the date. He was the best-known composer in the room, and the exclusion of his songs was insulting, especially in an all-star session. Composers' royalties were at stake and Monk needed the money. Ira Gitler was in the studio, and, again came to Monk's defense, persuading Weinstock to include at least one of his compositions on the play-list.[35] Ironically, Monk selected "Bemsha Swing," the song Weinstock resisted at one of Monk's recording sessions two years earlier.[36] Monk was also feeling a little envious of Milt Jackson, who seemed to be thriving financially as a member of the Modern Jazz Quartet. Monk once expressed his frustrations about Jackson's success to a French jazz magazine: "Milt Jackson is like Dizzy you know. We played together plenty of times, but in the end he was the one to benefit from it. Meanwhile, I wasn't even able to find a gig."[37] And to add to the interpersonal tensions, Thelonious would have preferred to spend Christmas Eve with his family, not in Hackensack working for scale.

So when Monk arrived at Van Gelder's studio around two in the afternoon, he was already a bit agitated. And when Miles insisted that Monk lay out, Monk was in no mood to be given directives–especially from Miles Davis. On the first take of "Bag's Groove" (Milt Jackson's composition), Thelonious got up from the piano and stood next to Miles during his entire solo. An annoyed Davis asked Monk why he did it, to which Monk replied, "I don't have to sit down to lay out."[38] According to Gitler, Monk ruined another take by asking Van Gelder, "Where's the bathroom?"[39] On the other hand, there were times when the question of laying out had not been settled, causing legitimate confusion. For example, on "Swing Spring," Thelonious plays behind Miles on the melody, but on "Bag's Groove" he doesn't. When the band was about to launch into a rendition of Gershwin's "The Man I Love," Monk did not know whether to enter on the melody or not. On the first take, Milt Jackson begins his solo introduction and suddenly Monk asks, "When am I supposed to come in, man?" At which point Milt Jackson stops playing and the rest of the band lets out a collective groan. Some-one interjects, "Man, the cat's cutting hisself." Monk then repeats himself in a kind of feigned irritation, "I don't know when to come in, man. Can't I start too? Everybody else . . ." at which point Miles cuts off the conversation and says to Rudy Van Gelder, "Hey, Rudy. Put this on the record—all of it."[40]

"The Man I Love" had become a source of controversy and intrigue for other rea-sons. The song begins in a slow ballad tempo with Miles's open horn delivering a plain-tive rendering of the melody while Jackson and Monk play behind him. Then at the break, Milt Jackson leaps in to solo as the band doubles the tempo. When Monk comes in to take his solo, he decides to restate the melody, but in the original tempo while the band continues to play in double-time, as if Monk were in slow motion. Once he gets through the melody, there is a long pause—about nine measures—at which point Davis plays a phrase away from the mic, as if to remind Monk to play. Monk is spurred to action and jumps right into a short improvisation on the bridge. It was a bizarre musical moment, ripe for rumor-mongering. Some claimed Monk had fallen asleep alleging he was in a heroin-induced stupor, and Miles had to wake him up. The more common explanation is that he got lost in the music and didn't know where to go.[41] Both claims are untrue, since Monk did the same thing on the first take (released later). Miles did not come in and Monk did not pause so long, but it shows that Monk was purposely constructing his solo along these lines.

For all of the antics and the grumbling, the music itself tells a different story. Thelonious threw all he had into the session, collaborating and accompanying without compromising his own sound. A fine example is "Bemsha Swing," the one song in which Monk never lays out. Miles sounds relaxed and the two are clearly in dialogue, refuting the belief that Miles can't play over Monk's backing. But the most revealing exchanges occur on Davis's composition, "Swing Spring." Here Miles takes two solos, the second follows Milt Jackson and opens with one of his better known clichés, a quote from "Surrey with a Fringe on Top." But at the top of the third chorus, Davis lovingly slips into one of Monk's best-known signature riffs—one Thelonious had been playing over "I Got Rhythm" changes since the days at Minton's. Monk picks it up and builds his solo around the phrase, becoming more elaborate with each chorus. Then in the ninth bar of the third chorus, Monk literally takes us back to Minton's by quoting Joe Guy's "Rear Back," revealing once again Monk's wry sense of humor. The lyrics are the words of a hustler imploring his girl: "I want to sit rear back/ rear back, rear back, rear back with you."[42] All sorts of meaning could be made of this moment. Was Monk bringing a little levity to his feud with Miles? Was he suggesting, let's make up and love each other? Or was it a warning to "rear back," meaning to back off? It was meant as an inside joke, but as a musical choice, it was a slick, compact phrase that worked perfectly in his solo.

Ultimately, these and other musical interactions between Monk, Miles, and the rest of the band underscore the success of the recording date. When Ira Gitler, who left the session after about three hours of little productivity, asked Kenny Clarke that night how it went, Clarke replied "Miles sure is a beautiful cat."[43] When two French journalists essentially asked the same question of Monk almost nine years later, he remembered, "The conditions were terrible. We were tired. The producer was not in the best of moods. It was Christmas Eve, and everyone wanted to go home."[44] Monk also recalled inviting Miles back to his house where they hung out well into the early morning hours. "I even had a hard time getting rid of him that night."[45]

After the Christmas and birthday festivities, the Monks rang in the New Year of 1955 with the familiar feeling that, despite Thelonious's press and accolades, unemployment and poverty were permanent conditions. Miles Davis and the Modern Jazz Quartet had become the label's stars and Monk felt himself fading into the background. After two recording sessions as a sideman and no scheduled sessions as a leader, Thelonious let his friends know that he was ready to move on. Nat Hentoff promptly called Bill Grauer and Orrin Keepnews of Riverside Records to inform them that Monk was looking for a new label. They were ecstatic. Both men knew Monk: Grauer was the founding editor of *The Record Changer* and Keepnews had written a feature piece on Monk for the same publication in 1948. They started Riverside (so named after *The Record Changer*'s Manhattan telephone exchange) in 1953, initially reissuing classic jazz recordings by the likes of Jelly Roll Morton, Louis Armstrong, James P. Johnson, Bix Beiderbecke, Albert Ammons, and blues singers such as Blind Lemon Jefferson and Ma Rainey.[46] Their first studio sessions also reflected their predilection for the older jazz. They recorded a number of Dixieland and Chicago-style jazz bands, including

Bob Hodes's Red Onion Band, Ralph Sutton Duo, Gene Mayl's Dixieland Rhythm Kings, and clarinetist George Lewis.[47] But Grauer and Keepnews were not diehard "moldy figs"; in 1954 they signed modern jazz artist Randy Weston.

By the early summer of 1955, Weston had already recorded two LPs for Riverside and was voted "new star" pianist in *Down Beat*'s critics poll.[48] He got to know Grauer and Keepnews pretty well, in part because Weston also worked as a clerk in Riverside's shipping department. Weston became their entrée to talented modernists, the most famous being Monk. "Keepnews approached me about getting Monk," Weston remembered. "They knew I was close to Monk, so they asked me to talk to him."[49] Weston talked to Thelonious and arranged his meeting with Grauer and Keepnews.[50] Once they laid down the terms, Monk was ready to sign. But he had two matters of business to attend to: First, his contract with Prestige was not up until August, so he needed permission to be released; second, he owed Prestige $108.27 for an advance he had drawn against royalties. He could not get out of his contract unless he paid back the advance, and Thelonious was, as always, broke. Worried that Weinstock "might not turn the pianist loose quite so casually if they were aware that a rival company was standing by," Keepnews loaned Thelonious $125 to pay back the advance.[51] (The money Keepnews advanced Monk to buy out his contract was deducted from his first royalty checks.) Their sub-rosa tactics may not have been necessary, however. Weinstock was ready to release Monk and hoped another label was interested. "At the time, the money Thelonious got for recording for me was probably his only source of income. His records didn't sell then, and I recorded him often anyway, to help. . . . He had overdrawn that amount, and when he asked for his release, I was happy for him, and hoped that it would be good for him."[52] Weinstock got his money, Monk got his freedom, and Grauer and Keepnews got their man. In March 1955, Thelonious signed a three-year contract,[53] although four months would pass before they would get him into a studio.

Monk's negotiations with Prestige and Riverside were interrupted by the news that Charlie Parker had died at Nica's home in the Stanhope Hotel. On March 9, while on his way to a gig at Storyville in Boston, Parker stopped by Nica's place in terrible shape; he was weak and coughing up blood. The Baroness insisted he stay and rest. The hotel doctor diagnosed him with advanced cirrhosis and stomach ulcers and thought he should be hospitalized immediately, but Parker refused to leave. The doctor had no choice but to leave Bird in the care of Nica and her daughter. She called her own physician, Dr. Robert Freymann, to attend to Parker. He, too, believed Bird needed to be hospitalized. Three days later Bird collapsed while watching television.[54] He was only thirty-four years old.

Bird's death was a great loss to the jazz world. It turned Parker into an icon, and it pushed Nica over the precipice of an already scandalous public existence. (In fact, it proved to be the catalyst for Jules de Koenigswarter's divorce from Nica—he learned of the incident listening to Walter Winchell's gossip column on the radio.[55]) Thelonious was never really that close to Bird, but he respected him enormously. Monk attended the funeral at Abyssinian Baptist Church on March 21, and the following week headed down to Philadelphia to participate in a memorial jam session for Parker at the Blue

Note. Virtually everyone in the jazz world showed up, from Coleman Hawkins and Ben Webster to Billie Holiday and Stan Getz, providing over twelve hours of continuous music.[56] Five days later, Monk was back on stage for another Parker benefit, this time at Carnegie Hall for a crowd of 2,700. Running from midnight to 4:00 a.m., the concert was organized by Dizzy, Mary Lou Williams, Nat Hentoff, Maely Dufty, Charles Mingus, and others, and netted nearly $6,000 in proceeds in order to help defray Bird's funeral expenses and to provide for his two sons.[57]

Parker's tragic death brought the jazz community together. In particular, Monk reconnected with Charles Mingus. Mingus, *Metronome* editor Bill Coss, and Morris Eagle (an NYU grad student in clinical psychology turned producer), had launched a series of concerts at Carnegie Recital Hall and the 92nd Street YM-YWHA under the rubric "Developments of Modern Jazz." Previous concerts featured compositions by Mingus, clarinetist John La Porta, and tenor saxophonist Teo Macero, a recent Juilliard graduate and a founding member of Mingus's Jazz Composers' Workshop.[58] Workshop members were interested in fusing jazz with elements of classical music and the avant garde's forays into atonality and twelve-tone composition. While Monk's music may not have consciously incorporated these elements, the Workshop found his music worthy enough to be featured in their April 23 concert at the 92nd Street Y.[59] He was backed by Mingus, Macero, trombonist Eddie Bert, trumpeter Art Farmer, and drummer Rudy Nichols—all members of the Workshop. Hall Overton sat in when the group played compositions by Mingus and others.[60]

The concert was neither well-publicized nor well-attended, but it launched a long friendship between Monk and Mingus. Monk admired Mingus's musicianship and brutal honesty, and Mingus practically worshipped Thelonious. Just a few months after the concert Mingus wrote "Jump Monk" as a tribute to the pianist. "The reason I called it 'Jump,'" he later explained, "was because Monk was always moving around. We were working in a club in the Bronx one time and there was a revolving door. He came in and out, in and out, for about five minutes."[61] Monk would treat the Jazz Composers' Workshop as a kind of revolving door as well, but in the spring of 1955 he considered it a great source for serious, like-minded musicians. In fact, Monk hired an all-Workshop band for his next big gig—the *Tonight Show* with Steve Allen.

15

"The Greta Garbo of Jazz"

(June 1955–December 1955)

On Friday night, June 10, 1955, Monk made his television debut. The *Tonight Show* was only about eight months old but had already built a huge national following, launching the era of late-night television. It aired live from the Hudson Theater on 44th and Broadway five nights a week, but Fridays tended to attract more viewers. Monk's appearance contributed to his growing legitimacy because Steve Allen's stamp of approval carried enormous weight in America's popular culture. A pianist, prolific composer, and columnist for *Down Beat* magazine, Allen was once dubbed "the greatest friend jazz had in television" by Leonard Feather.[1] The list of musicians who appeared on the show during Allen's two-and-a-half-year reign is impressive: Louis Armstrong, Count Basie, Earl Hines, Coleman Hawkins, Teddy Wilson, Dizzy Gillespie, Sarah Vaughan, Billie Holiday, Duke Ellington, Dave Brubeck, Lester Young, to name but a few.[2] The fact that he brought on so many black artists was not lost on the African-American community, which acknowledged Allen for his contribution to civil rights. He had a reputation for treating black artists with respect, and he was not averse to addressing racial issues. The first week the show aired in September 1954, he invited singer/actress Lena Horne, even though she had been blacklisted for her associations with civil rights and left-wing organizations. At the end of her segment, Allen gave Horne a friendly peck on the cheek, which prompted hate mail from a few viewers. Rather than ignore the issue, he read one of the letters on the air and then announced to the audience, "This is an absolute bigot. If anybody knows him, he's sick. He should go to the hospital."[3]

Needless to say, Monk's appearance wasn't nearly as controversial as Horne's, but he was Allen's most unusual guest that night—the others were baritone crooner Charlie Applewhite, best-known for his frequent appearances on the Milton Berle Show, comedienne Nancy Walker, and Judy Tyler, a rising star on Broadway.[4] Besides the crew from the Jazz Composers' Workshop (Macero, Farmer, Bert, and Mingus), he had Willie Jones on drums. Allen primed the audience for Monk with a long introduction that attempted to place him in the larger pantheon of modern jazz. Calling him "a musician's musician," he described Thelonious as a man less interested in becoming famous than developing as an artist. "He doesn't have a publicity man or wear funny hats or bother to travel around much. He just sort of sits where he is and plays the kind of music he likes, and he's got a large number of rabid fans, and many of them are musicians." He spoke indirectly about Monk's role at Minton's, how Bird and Dizzy loved him, how the new music kept sorry players off the bandstand, and how the musical developments derived from bebop had profoundly shaped the current direction of jazz. "You can't stop progress," Allen mused. "Thelonious stands out because he's inconspicuous. He's the kind of a guy who thinks a lot. He doesn't say much. He just plays, and . . . here he is. I think you might like to meet him."[5] Monk came on stage, where he was greeted with applause, a warm handshake from Allen, and an invitation to have a seat, whereupon Allen proceeded to engage him in a discussion:

> Allen: Ahh Monk, you're from New York, aren't you?
> Monk: That's right.
> Allen: How did you begin playing? Did you pick it up yourself or
>   did you study?
> Monk: I took some lessons.
> Allen: Do you read now?
> Monk: Of course, sure [chuckling].

He could only laugh at the question, for if he didn't know any better he might have found it insulting. Allen then took a page from Sidney Gross's jazz class, demonstrating for the audience what standard chord progressions sound like and comparing it to Monk's modern harmonies. He then issued his grand analysis, "The basic difference I think is one of harmonics, don't you?" Monk hesitated a bit with "uhhhh" and Allen seized the moment for comic relief—at Monk's expense: "That's about what I thought you'd say there, man. I wouldn't have phrased it quite that way, you know what I mean?" Monk never lost his composure, however. Speaking with authority, he then showed Allen the first three chords of "Off Minor." "The first chord, G minor, the second chord, D flat, then F sharp 7." When Allen asked, "That's more or less it, huh?" Monk turned the comic tables with, "That's it, almost." Finally, Allen closed the interview by issuing the following warning to the audience: "Some of you aren't going to be able to make it. But don't feel bad."[6]

Monk impatiently jumped into "Off Minor" before Allen could finish his introduction. Art Farmer and Teo Macero took the first solos, followed by Monk, Mingus, and Eddie Bert—and it seems the entire group was partial to huge intervallic leaps and dissonant lines. The tonal experimentalism cherished by the Jazz Composers' Workshop dovetailed with Monk's harmonic conception and was evident here, as well as on the next number, "Well, You Needn't." Although the horn players sounded less comfortable, they went out of their way not to sound too boppish. In the end, Monk's band delivered what had to have been the most avant-garde performance of any jazz group on the *Tonight Show*.

Monk came off the bandstand feeling good. But backstage he was in for a rude awakening. Eddie Bert recalls, "[W]hen I was packing my trombone away after the broadcast, I heard Monk say to Steve 'What do you mean "scale"?' which is when I left, before the knives came out!"[7] Monk was appalled to be receiving scale for playing a nationally syndicated television show, especially as a leader. He desperately needed the money, but felt cheated and exploited. His protestations fell on deaf ears.

Once again, Monk's star was rising but his income was not. His next big gig paid very little, but the prestige and visibility it afforded more than compensated for the paltry wages. George Wein, pianist and jazz impresario, invited Thelonious to be part of an all-star band at the Newport Jazz Festival in July. Only in its second year, the brainchild of Wein and socialites Louis and Elaine Lorillard had rapidly turned the sleepy, upper-class town of Newport, Rhode Island, into one of the jazz world's most cherished events. The band to which Monk was assigned was scheduled to play a short set on the last night of the festival, Sunday July 17, following performances by the Modern Jazz Quartet and Count Basie, just before Dave Brubeck. In other words, they were an intermission band. Wein conceived of the group as a quintet consisting of Thelonious, tenor saxophonist Zoot Sims, Gerry Mulligan, and the rhythm section of the MJQ—Percy Heath and drummer Connie Kay (who had replaced Kenny Clarke). But a few weeks before the festival, Wein heard Miles Davis at Basin Street East in New York. After the set, Davis pestered Wein to include him at Newport. "You can't have a jazz festival without me," Miles said repeatedly. So Wein relented and at the last minute added Davis to the line-up as part of Monk's all-star band. He was added so late, in fact, that his name did not appear in the program.[8]

The master of ceremonies was Duke Ellington. Always eloquent and witty, Duke described the band as innovative musicians who "live in the realm that Buck Rogers is trying to reach." He gave each a separate introduction, but showed particular warmth for Monk, whom he introduced as "The High Priest of Bop, the inimitable Thelonious Monk." And Monk returned the gesture, getting up from the piano bench to personally greet one of his all-time musical heroes.[9] The band then launched into "Hackensack," playing the original melody—bridge and all—that Coleman Hawkins played when the song was known as "Rifftide." This time, Monk did not lay out when Miles soloed. But Miles made sure the audience could hear him. Aware of the faulty sound system (Wein fielded numerous complaints about the inadequate sound, calling it a "catastrophe"),[10] Davis jammed the bell of his trumpet directly into the microphone. Its full effect was clear on Thelonious Monk's " 'Round Midnight."

Like everything else having to do with Monk and Miles, this rendition of " 'Round Midnight" is shrouded in myth. Historians, critics, musicians, even Miles himself, credits this performance with launching his "comeback" from a few uneven and unproductive years under the influence of heroin addiction. Miles remembered getting "a long standing ovation. When I got off the bandstand, everybody was looking at me like I was a king or something—people were running up to me offering me record deals. All the musicians there were treating me like I was a god. . . ."[11] The aural evidence paints a very different picture, however. Miles plays tentatively during the introduction and opening melody, showing more confidence with each chorus. When he ends his solo, the audience applauds, but it is neither sustained nor overly enthusiastic.[12]

Once again, the musical exchange between Monk and Miles was marred by tension. After "'Round Midnight," Miles asked Thelonious to lay out on the third and final song: a bebop blues called "Now's the Time" by Charlie Parker. When Miles came off the bandstand, the first thing he said to George Wein was "Monk plays the wrong changes to 'Round Midnight."[13] In the car on the way back to New York, Monk complained to Miles that he had not played "'Round Midnight" correctly. Miles blew up, telling Thelonious "I didn't like what he had played behind me either, but I hadn't told him that, so why was he telling me all this shit? So then I told him that the people liked it and that's why they stood up and applauded like they did. Then I told him that he must be jealous." Miles insisted afterward that he was just kidding, but the damage was done. Angry and hurt, Thelonious had the driver stop the car. He got out and walked to the ferry.[14]

Back in the city, Orrin Keepnews had arranged a recording session for that Wednesday afternoon, July 20. He and Grauer decided on a trio setting and thought that Monk's first LPs would reach a wider audience if he did not record his original music. The theory was that Monk's unorthodox style would be more palatable interpreting popular melodies.[15] Once the public became familiar with Monk, then he could begin to introduce his original compositions. It wasn't a new theory. A growing trend emerged in the 1950s to "mainstream" or canonize jazz, particularly as the raging battles between modernists and moldy figs reached a détente and jazz had begun to achieve legitimacy as high culture.[16] Indeed, Riverside's first modern LP, *Randy Weston Plays Cole Porter In A Modern Mood*, was in essence a mainstreaming project. In Monk's case, Keepnews recalls that he and Grauer proposed an all-Ellington album.[17] Monk agreed. He obtained some sheet music and contacted two veterans for the date—Oscar Pettiford and Kenny Clarke.

The session did not go as planned. Keepnews asked the musicians to meet at Riverside's office in midtown so they could all drive out together to Van Gelder's studio in Hackensack. But Clarke never showed up. Monk suggested they use Philly Joe Jones, but Keepnews was not familiar with his music and didn't think it would be prudent. Clarke got in touch with Keepnews and explained that Thelonious had given him the wrong date. Van Gelder, possibly the busiest engineer in the jazz business, just happened to have a free slot open the next afternoon.[18] As it turned out, they needed more than an afternoon. Keepnews recalls Monk spending much of that afternoon "learning" the tunes, "as if he were seeing the material for the first time."[19] That is to say, he was playing everything slowly, determining the key of choice and transposing, figuring out the proper voicings, and familiarizing himself with each song so he could begin to play with them. For Keepnews, Monk's process was strange, tedious, and time-consuming. Clarke showed his frustration by reading the Sunday comics. The loss of precious time meant that they could record only two or three songs. They had to schedule another session the following week in order to finish the album.

In the interim, Monk headed up to the Berkshire mountains to perform at the Music Barn on July 24. Located in Stockbridge, Massachusetts, the Music Barn was a new wing of the popular Music Inn founded by Stephanie and Philip Barber. In

1950, the couple established the Inn as a kind of jazz and folk alternative to neighboring Tanglewood, where the Boston Symphony performed during the summer. They turned the grounds of the once-spectacular Wheatleigh summer cottage into a resort, performance space, and, later, the Lenox School of Jazz. The Barbers were unique, not only for establishing a "jazz" resort in a community known as the playground of New England's blue-blood elite, but for defying the neighboring resorts' unwritten code of no "Negroes or Jews" allowed. [20]

Randy Weston was responsible for Monk's invitation. Weston had been making annual pilgrimages to the Berkshires since the early 1950s, paying his upkeep by working as a dishwasher and cook at various establishments. During one of his Berkshire retreats, he wandered into the Music Inn and discovered a "Jazz Roundtable" discussion led by a bespectacled professor named Marshall Stearns. "I walk in, sit down, and heard this guy explain that jazz has West African roots. I never heard anyone say this, let alone a white scholar, but I had been interested in Africa since I was a kid, so I said, 'I have to know this guy.'"[21] Stearns was, indeed, a formidable presence. A professor of English at Hunter College and a leading authority on Chaucer, he also held a law degree from Harvard and an M. A. from Yale. He had earned a reputation as the academy's greatest champion of jazz. He founded the Institute for Jazz Studies in 1952, and the summer Monk performed there he was in the throes of completing his critically acclaimed *The Story of Jazz*.[22] Dr. Willis James, an African-American folklorist specializing in the black field holler, also made a huge impression on Weston, as did the many dynamic performances by musicians and dancers from all parts of the African diaspora. Weston approached Stephanie Barber and offered to work at the Music Inn as a dishwasher or cook just so he could be around the music and the intellectual environment. Barber hired him, but soon discovered he was more than an expert dishwasher. "He came out after everyone had gone to bed," she recalled, "I was there checking something in the office, and he played [piano]. And I thought, 'Oh my dear.'"[23] She invited Weston to perform for their guests and he put together a trio with Willie Jones and bassist Sam Gill. Soon he became a resident musician and one of professors James and Stearns's most attentive students and interlocutors.

It didn't take much to persuade the Barbers and Stearns to book Monk for the Music Barn's five-week summer concert series.[24] Stearns was ecumenical when it came to jazz styles and he respected Monk's experimentalism as well as his stride roots. He also bought into the image of Thelonious as reclusive and underground, describing him in the program as "the Greta Garbo of jazz . . . his appearance at any piano is regarded as a major event by serious followers of jazz."[25] Monk brought a quartet of old friends—bassist Michael Mattos, tenor saxophonist Charlie Rouse, with whom he had not played in several years, and Willie Jones—now a regular at the Music Inn, thanks to Randy Weston. The opening minutes did not bode well for Monk. Weston remembers it as if it were yesterday: "When the concert got ready to start, everybody's waiting . . . Stephanie's saying, 'What's happening, what's happening?' So finally, Willie Jones comes out on stage and says, 'Excuse me, ladies and gentlemen. Monk is in the toilet, so I'm going to play a drum solo.'"[26] The local critic was not pleased with the performance, singling out Jones for playing too loudly and using too many clichés. While Monk had his share of great moments, he was distracted by a summer evening of moths and flies.[27]

Monk returned to Van Gelder's studio on July 27. In the course of two sessions, the trio laid down seven sides, including swinging renditions of "Caravan," "I Let a Song Go Out of My Heart," and "It Don't Mean a Thing"; readings of "Sophisticated Lady," "I Got it Bad (and That Ain't Good)"; and a bluesy march in the form of "Black and Tan Fantasy." Monk also recorded "Solitude" as a solo piano piece. Overall, it is a tribute to Duke, yet each track is unmistakably Monk. "Mood Indigo," for example, sounds almost like a Monk original, from its medium-slow fox trot–like tempo and its rolling arpeggios to his frequent use of minor second clusters and stride piano.[28]

Some critics have described Monk's Ellington album as "restrained," at best.[29] There is some truth to this; with the exception of, perhaps, "Caravan," Kenny Clarke never lights a fire beneath Monk, and on most of the recordings he offers surprisingly monotonous brush work. The dynamics between the two men are a far cry from the Miles Davis Christmas Eve session or the halcyon days of Minton's. Nevertheless, the lack of dynamism has convinced some critics and scholars that Monk made the Ellington album with great reluctance, if not resistance.[30] On the contrary, Thelonious took great pride in the recording. "That record was a big deal," Toot remembered. "It was a big deal in the house, it was a big deal for my dad. . . . In fact, my mother told me that he was very uptight until he had gotten the word that Duke had heard the record and it was cool."[31] When Ira Gitler asked Thelonious about the album, in an interview two years after recording it, Monk replied, "I wanted to do it. I felt like playing, that's all. I know that Duke started playing some of his numbers more than he had as I recall."[32] And Thelonious admired Ellington above all other musicians. Joe Termini, owner of the Five Spot Café and Monk's future employer, remembered that "the only time I've ever seen Monk act like a little boy and looking up to somebody" was in the presence of Duke Ellington. "That was his idol."[33] On another occasion in 1959, Monk got into a little exchange with drummer Frank Butler over Duke's enduring importance. Butler, a former Ellington band member, told a reporter, "Monk grows all the time—Duke is stagnant." Thelonious overheard him, and instead of taking in the compliment he chastised his drummer. "No, he isn't—Duke is still distinctive. I know you must be kidding, or not listening."[34]

The rest of the summer was a productive time for Monk. In August he secured two weeks at the Blue Note in Philadelphia, with the same quartet he led at the Music Barn.[35] It seemed as if Monk's fortunes were beginning to change. But then a horrifying news report shattered his newfound optimism.

On August 31, the decomposed and mutilated corpse of a fourteen-year-old boy was pulled out of the Tallahatchie River not far from Money, Mississippi. The boy's name was Emmett Till. Two men, J. W. Milam and Roy Bryant, beat and shot Till several times and tied a heavy industrial fan around his neck so that he would sink to the river's bottom. His face was so badly beaten it resembled a large, bloated sponge. His mother, Mamie Till Bradley, had sent him down to Mississippi for the summer to escape the hard streets of Chicago and to visit family. His crime? He was a black city boy from up North who bragged to his friends that he had a white girlfriend and, on a dare, said "Bye-bye, baby" to the wife of a white store owner. Mamie Till Bradley decided that the world needed to see what Southern terrorism looked like, so she held an open casket funeral on September 6. Photos circulated around the world, generating outrage and anger. Less than a month after Till was kidnapped, Milam and Bryant were acquitted by an all-white jury.[36]

The murder of Emmett Till loomed in the background as the Monks tried to celebrate Boo Boo's second birthday. Like so many black families, Thelonious and Nellie could look in the face of their five-year-old son and see Emmett Till's face. The dark episode was a much-needed wake-up call for America. It tarnished the hope and possibility generated by the Supreme Court's decision on Brown v. Board of Education, and it reminded Monk that the South had been another world.

Thelonious probably talked about Till, the South, and racism with Gigi Gryce. Early that fall, Monk had agreed to do a record date with Gryce for the newly created Signal Records.[37] Between rehearsals and just hanging out, they began to spend more time together. Gryce had converted to Islam, read widely in black history and politics, and expressed concern about racial issues in the United States and across the globe. He did not give speeches or proselytize; on the contrary, he was a quiet man who generally kept to himself. And he was most animated when discussing music.

Signal Records founder Jules Colomby put together the band (Gryce, Monk, Percy Heath, and Art Blakey), organized rehearsals, and produced the session. Musicians respected Colomby—he had a good ear and was in the business but not of it. A German-Jewish émigré whose family barely escaped the Holocaust, he was eleven when his family arrived in New York in 1939. He fell in love with jazz, and eventually became a promoter, impresario, producer, musician, jack-of-all-trades jazz guy.[38] Although Gryce was officially the leader, Monk emerged as the dominant voice during the session, and of the four sides recorded, three were new Monk originals. Still, Gryce was excited to work with and learn from one of his heroes. He told Ira Gitler that it was "one of the most relaxed recording sessions" he had ever experienced.[39] Bassist Julian Euell remembers attending one rehearsal at the behest of Colomby. Gryce and Monk were going over some of Monk's difficult tunes and "Gigi never looked at a note of music." Thelonious would demonstrate something on the piano and expect Gryce to play it back. Then they would discuss it and move on to the next segment. When the rehearsal was over, "Thelonious complimented him and turned in his usual way and said: 'Now, there's a musician. . . . Now, dig it, didn't need no music, nothing. You dig? That's a musician, man.'"[40] Gryce did have trouble with some of the tunes, particularly "Gallop's Gallop," perhaps Monk's most intricate melody. "He wrote a part for me that was impossible," Gryce later explained. "I was playing melody and at the same time was playing harmony to his part. In addition, the intervals between the notes were very wide. I told him I couldn't do it. 'You have an instrument, don't you?' he said. 'Either play it or throw it away.' And he left me. Finally, I was able to play it."[41]

The session took place at Van Gelder's studio on October 15, five days after Monk's thirty-eighth birthday. They started out with the relatively easy "Brake's Sake," then jumped right into "Gallop's Gallop." It is a fine recording, despite Gigi's valiant yet failed efforts to master the melody. "Shuffle Boil," with its strong rhythmic accents and stop-time phrases, was Monk's tribute to the black hoofer tradition. The title is a corruption of "shuffle ball," a component of a tap dance combination used in certain breaks—most famously in the old vaudeville routine known as the "Shim-Sham Shimmy." The basic move—"shuffle-step, shuffle-stop, shuffle ball-change, shuffle step"—came out of African-American vernacular dance and parallels the music because it incorporates the "break," or stop-time, and the basic "time step" used a shuffled rhythm rather than lifting of the feet.[42] Monk, an old hoofer himself who loved to watch Baby Laurence dance at Minton's, knew these moves and the accompanying music. Blakey's shuffling gestures and clean breaks are essential to the song's success, along with Monk's counter bass line. Finally, they closed the session with Gryce's only contribution to the date, "Nica's Tempo." His tribute to Nica de Koenigswarter, it is an uptempo, swinging romp in a minor key.[43]

Monk's respect for Gigi Gryce extended beyond his skills as a musician and composer. Gryce pioneered jazz musicians' efforts to take control of their publishing. He could not understand why record companies were taking half of an artist's publishing royalties just to fill out paperwork. Earlier that summer, Gryce established Melotone Music, Inc., and affiliated with BMI (Broadcast Music, Inc.) in order to handle publishing rights and royalties for his own work as well as for others. (The attorney who helped him set up his corporation was future radical lawyer William M. Kunstler, who was better known at the time for writing short books on legal topics for lay audiences.[44]) Monk agreed to have Melotone Music publish the three songs he had contributed to the date. Grauer and Keepnews were not happy that Monk had just recorded and published three original songs—songs that they felt should have been released on the Riverside label. Legally, there was nothing they could do; Monk did not break his contract by recording as a sideman. More importantly, Gryce's example stuck with Monk, who, years later, would take control of his own publishing.

Thelonious was feeling pretty good. He was working and gaining more respect from fellow musicians and fans. He now walked into clubs with an air of celebrity. People stopped their conversations to stare and point, and he was sometimes approached for autographs. Throughout the fall, he began to frequent a West Village bar-turned-jazz club called Café Bohemia. Located on Barrow Street near the intersection of Seventh Avenue and Bleecker Street, the club used to be a strip joint called the Pied Piper.[45] Owner Jimmy Giarofolo opened Café Bohemia in the early spring of 1955 and hired Oscar Pettiford to lead the house band. All the major modern jazz musicians started hanging out there that summer, especially after a young, unknown alto player from Florida named Julian "Cannonball" Adderley sat in with Pettiford's band and turned the jazz world upside down.[46] Monk joined the parade of famous patrons and sat in occasionally, but he was there to listen, drink, and hang out with friends. He always ran into friends. For a brief period in November, Herbie Nichols played intermission piano at the Bohemia opposite Charles Mingus and the Jazz Composers' Workshop.[47] One night Monk noticed a young French horn player with Mingus whom he hadn't seen before. He liked his sound, his intonation, and he especially liked the way he swung with the driving rhythms of Willie Jones and Mingus. After the set, Monk asked Jones to introduce him to the cat, whose name was David Amram. "Willie said [Monk] really liked my French horn playing and I almost fainted," Amram remembered. "I said I would have been afraid to even say hello to him. So we went down and Monk said, 'I want to hang out with you, give me your number.' So he took his little address book and it had all of these papers like in all different directions, and each paper had like five different angles of stuff and I thought, 'Gosh, he's never gonna find that or remember my name.' So he wrote it down and then he called me up and came over to my place, a six-floor walk-up on East Eighth Street in the East Village. He climbed all those stairs."[48] Amram was a month shy of his twenty-fifth birthday, grew up in Washington, D. C. but had been living in Paris, playing and composing. He had returned to the States in September to study at the Manhattan School of Music and had been swept into the fold of the Jazz Composers' Workshop by Mingus himself.[49] And like Hall Overton and other emerging composers in the 1950s, he had long admired Monk's compositions. "I told him about trying to play '*Off Minor*' in Paris, so he sat down and he wrote out all of the chord changes for me. Every single chord change had indications of which were altered notes. So I saw that he had figured out exactly what he wanted, and then from there he would go off into all those amazing, endless variations. And we tried to play this and I said, 'You know, everybody seems to have a different version but none of them sound right.' And he said, 'Well, that's because they didn't ask.'" Monk taught Amram the same way he taught Gigi Gryce—to learn a song by hearing it. "When we played '*Off Minor*' he would show it to me and then he would just start playing. Then he just started playing some other stuff. I didn't even know what it was I just started playing along with him. And he really liked that. Then I found out later of course that he would do that very often anyway, and just assume that you were going to hear it and play or you'd be quiet and then play after you could hear it. He figured rather than talking about it, it would just evolve and then you could ask him later on."[50]

Monk spent the better part of the day and evening hanging out at Amram's tiny railroad flat. About a week or two later, Amram dropped by the Monks'. A bit homesick, Amram felt a sense of home with his new friends. "I met Nellie for the first time. There was this wonderful sensitivity and lovingness and these beautiful eyes that just had so much knowledge and wisdom and feeling that just when she looked at me I just felt right at home. And there I was in their place and suddenly I just felt this real warmth. And then there was this wonderful little boy, Toot, and he was already so lively and so smart and energetic and Thelonious introduced me to him and I shook his hand and he was this great little kid."[51] In the course of his visit, which lasted four or five hours, Monk also entertained a couple of unexpected guests—a young musician seeking guidance and a friend from the neighborhood. "Thelonious had a lot of people that loved him that were neighbors and friends of his family. And I just got this tremendous family sense, right in this small place in New York City of somebody that really had a home."[52]

Amram's encounter with Monk resembles Randy Weston's in 1944, or Herbie Nichols' in the early 1940s, or any number of musicians who passed through the "Monk School." Here is Monk as the mentor, father-figure, friend, and philosopher. Amram remembers:

> I was listening one time with Monk, at his house, and he had on the radio, I don't know what station it was, but for some reason they were playing some kind of country music, and it kept going on and on. . . . Finally I said, "Thelonious, do you like this kind of music too?" He paused for about a minute or so and then he said, "Listen to the drummer." So I was quiet for about another ten minutes while they played two or three songs and then he turned and he said, "Check out his brush work." So, I listened as hard as I could on that little radio with a little bit of static and somehow I could hear something so I realized, of course, what he was trying to tell me was first of all, don't be judgmental of anybody else, just listen and pay attention and look for the beauty. And then when you find the beauty, study that and don't bother with the rest of it.[53]

Amram's discussions with Monk were not limited to music. Thelonious talked philosophically about the mysteries of the world. He reflected on how pyramids were built, or how the *moai* on Easter Island came to be. He was fascinated with how animals communicated, specifically birds. "We used to talk about how the birds can do these extraordinary maneuvers where they'll all change the formation, something that even airline pilots couldn't do. . . . They just somehow knew how to do that. And it would be a mystery to us, but it was at a higher level and a lot of cultures still operate on that level, so it was almost that here we are with our wonderful mechanized U.S.A. we've lost that. And in a certain sense some of the music was trying to recapture, I guess you say, that ethos."[54]

Monk and Amram began meeting a little more frequently at a loft space on East 28th Street owned by jazz enthusiast Ken Karpe. Throughout the winter of 1955 well into spring of '56, Karpe's loft became the site for some of the city's most exciting after-hours jam sessions. The initial core of musicians included Mingus, Oscar Pettiford, Art Farmer, and Amram, who persuaded Monk to join them. Other participants included Zoot Sims, guitarist Jim Hall, Willie Jones, Art Taylor, trumpeter Thad Jones, pianist Tommy Flanagan, Chico Hamilton, and bassist Paul Chambers. At one point, the entire Max Roach–Clifford Brown quintet showed up for the jam sessions.[55] For Thelonious, who loved the jam session atmosphere, the gatherings at Karpe's place proved to be a wellspring of talented musicians, many of whom he later called on for gigs.

A few days after Thanksgiving, Thelonious left for Chicago. Sol Tannenbaum, the venerable owner of the Bee Hive Lounge, one of the larger and most popular Hyde Park jazz venues, booked Monk for a one-week engagement.[56] It was supposed to be a trio gig with the house rhythm section—bassist Wilbur Ware and drummer Wilbur Campbell—but Ware persuaded the owner to add tenor saxophonist Johnny Griffin. "I was sitting at home, watching television, and they called me and said they needed a saxo-phone player. I didn't even know Monk was in town. I went over to the club and joined the guys on the bandstand."[57] Griffin had been working around his hometown Chicago for the past couple of years after he got out of the army. He and Monk had played together in jam sessions, but this was their first actual gig. He was equally impressed with the bassist, Wilbur Ware, whose unusual harmonic sensibilities matched his own. And he could swing like nobody's business. Six years Monk's junior, the Chicago native was raised by a minister in the Sanctified church, his foster father, who happened to have a passion and gift for music. Reverend Turner played saxophone, drums, banjo, and some piano, and Wilbur picked up all these instruments and performed in the church. Then, when Wilbur was about ten years old, Reverend Turner built him a bass from veneer and real bass violin strings.[58] Ware developed quickly; he had his first pro-fessional gigs at age eleven and his first record date at fifteen. But as he drifted further away from the church and deeper into the entertainment world, he got caught up in drugs. Monk saw right away that Ware had a bad heroin habit, but he also recognized his immense talent and made sure he added Ware's name to his insanely overstuffed address book.

Thelonious had a ball in Chicago. The band played comfortably together and were able to grasp Monk's music rather quickly. "I didn't know Monk's music," Griffin recalled. "He just started playing and I had to figure out what he was doing."[59] He had no trouble. In an interview a few months later, Monk told Nat Hentoff how much he liked "the tenor I worked with in Chicago, John Griffin. He's one of the best. Also the bass player I worked with there, Wilbur Ware."[60] Joe Segal, owner of Chicago's Jazz Showcase, described the gig as "one of the Hive's all-time musical highlights in its ten-year history of presenting jazz."[61] Monk was so popular that Tannenbaum held him over, hoping he could stay through the third week of December. And according to one observer, Monk "wasn't elusive or uncooperative," contrary to his reputation.[62] On his nights off, he ventured out beyond the Bee Hive, playing in a benefit concert for patients at Vaughan Veterans Hospital hosted by the popular African-American D.J. Daddy-O-Daylie, and participating in a jam session at Roosevelt University.[63]

But the fun came to an abrupt end into the second week of December, days before he was scheduled to close.[64] Monk received a call from home. His mother was in the hospital.

16

"As Long as I Can Make a Living"

(December 1955–December 1956)

Barbara Monk was taken to St. Clare's Hospital on West 51st Street, weak, thin, and fairly unresponsive. Cancer had ravaged her entire body. Thomas, Trotyrine, Marion, Nellie, and the older kids were immediately at her bedside, but Thelonious was reluctant to see his mother—he couldn't handle seeing her in such a state. His niece Charlotte recalls, "When he finally did go to see my grandmother and saw her lying there, weak and helpless, it really messed with him."[1] To make matters worse, the family was divided over Barbara's care. Her doctor felt she needed a blood transfusion, but Barbara, a Jehovah's Witness, opposed medical procedures that involve the use of blood. Thomas, himself a convert to the religion, reluctantly agreed with his mother, adding that even if she were to receive a transfusion, it would only prolong her suffering, not her life. This merely angered Thelonious. who believed the hospital should have overruled his mother's wishes. "That's why he hated the hospital, too," Charlotte concluded. "They didn't do anything for her. They just let her die. And that just devastated him and my father, too."[2]

Barbara Monk died on Wednesday morning, December 14. She was sixty-three years old.[3] Her death sent Thelonious spiraling into depression. Indeed, he missed the wake and most of the funeral, appearing just in time to see her remains interred (she was cremated). Marion found her brother's behavior unforgivable. Thomas, Jr., who was eighteen at the time, later came to terms with his uncle's behavior. "He never believed in funerals. When my grandmother died he was devastated. My uncle never liked to be around death. He was afraid of death."[4] Barbara's absence left a huge void and a pall of sadness in the Monk household. Thelonious didn't want to be in the apartment at first, especially with the holidays, so he spent time with Sonny at Lyman Place for a little while. About a week after his mother's death, Thelonious went down to Café Bohemia to catch Art Blakey and the Jazz Messengers.[5]

That night he saw many familiar faces, including Jules Colomby's brother, Harry. They had met briefly in the fall at Mrs. Colomby's house when Jules was planning Gigi Gryce's recording date for Signal Records.[6] A devoted Monk fan since his teenage years, Harry was now a twenty-six-year-old teacher at Far Rockaway High School in Queens, still thoroughly in love with the music. He had just launched a Friday jazz concert series for his students, and Blakey and the Jazz Messengers were his inaugural act. He had come to the club to remind Blakey of the date and make sure he had directions.[7]

As the final set began winding down, Thelonious approached Harry and asked, "You've got your car? You're Jules's brother." Fortunately for Monk, Colomby did have a car and he was happy to take him up to the Bronx. And Colomby was happy to oblige. He was a huge Monk fan and considered this an opportunity to learn more about him. But before they took off uptown, Monk posed the first question—and it was a doozy.

"Do you want to be my manager?"

Colomby was taken aback. Although he loved show business and knew he would eventually give up teaching to pursue work in the industry, he never imagined managing a jazz musician—especially someone like Thelonious Monk. But as he drove along the West Side Highway listening to Monk, he began to think things through. "I totally identified with him. I knew where he was at. No job, no nothing, no police card. I had no illusion about how much money there is in jazz. But I realized that Monk was much more than a jazz musician. He was potentially a symbol. He was symbolic of strength, stick-to-it-iveness, purity, you know, beyond music, beyond jazz."[8]

For Monk's part, his rash proposal was driven by a certain logic. He had begun to develop a reputation as a major figure in the jazz world, and now needed someone to open doors for him, to make phone calls and talk to booking agents and club owners, to read contracts, and to protect him from the industry's wolves. Along came Harry Colomby, a hip schoolteacher and brother of an honest and committed promoter, producer, and musician. In Monk's mind, Colomby was ideal for the job, despite his lack of experience. Indeed, it was his lack of experience that made him trustworthy—he wasn't corrupted. As Monk said to Colomby that night, "Cool, a teacher. . . . I want you to be rich. Get rich, 'cause if you get rich I get rich." Before they exited the West Side Highway that night, Colomby decided he wanted the job. "I turned to Thelonious and said, 'I don't know how much money we're going to make, but I am going to promise you something; that in your lifetime you're going to be recognized.' And that was my mission."[9] Before Monk disappeared into Sonny's building, he offered Colomby the standard ten-percent commission.[10] Colomby agreed, sealed the deal with a handshake, and promptly set upon his very first task as manager: to print up some business cards.

Colomby had no clue as to what he was getting himself into, and given the trajectory of his life up to that point, a musician's manager was not the vocation he'd expected. A precocious child, he was only nineteen when he graduated from New York University with a B.A. in English and a philosophy minor. He wanted to teach literature at the college level so he earned a master's degree, but there were no jobs. Instead, he applied to teach high school, took a methods course at Columbia University Teachers College, and decided to take a few more postgraduate courses at Columbia's School of International Affairs. He flirted with the idea of becoming a Russian specialist and working for the FBI or the CIA, but the field was already overcrowded with a new generation of Cold Warriors anxious to defeat the Red Menace. Colomby gave up his spy dreams and settled on the even more daunting task of teaching high school students. He subbed at the predominantly black and Puerto Rican Samuel Gompers Vocational and Technical

High School in the Bronx, and taught mentally disabled girls at Bay Ridge High School before landing the job at Far Rockaway in 1954.

Students had never experienced anyone like him before. As one of his former students, Barry Zaret, recalled, "Harry was this quintessentially cool guy, always dressed well, teaching English and social studies. A bunch of us fell in love with the guy. And he just started talking about jazz. It was far-out stuff."[11] Colomby's concerts and informal talks about the music inspired Arthur Lebowitz and his classmates to form the "Gaynotes," a jazz quartet that was good enough to secure gigs in the Catskills.[12] Colomby was also fascinated with theater. Not long after joining the faculty at Far Rockaway, he formed an off-Broadway theater group called "the Arena Players" that put on a few local productions.[13]

Colomby was more dreamer than capitalist, more fan than front man. He wanted to spend time with Monk, to get to know his client. A couple of days into the job, Harry began calling Thelonious at West 63rd Street to invite him to hang out. But Nellie usually answered, and invariably her husband was asleep, or claiming to be asleep. Sometimes Colomby got through: "And Thelonious was very sweet. He would say, 'No, not today, maybe some other time.' He was being polite. He didn't want to hang out. . . . Right away I got to understand. Even when he invited me over because there was something we needed to talk about in person, sometimes I'd bang on the door and he wasn't there. . . . Eventually, I stopped showing up."[14]

It would be quite a while before Colomby would stop showing up. During the early days of their relationship, he was quick to respond to Monk's every wish. They were still getting to know one another when Monk asked if he could borrow Colomby's car to go up to the Bronx. He had just gotten his precious black-on-black two-door Ford Custom (Thelonious teasingly told Colomby that his neighbors thought he was "the Man" because he drove an undercover cop car), but he was willing to take a chance on Thelonious. Little did he know that driving—at least safe driving—wasn't Monk's strong suit. "So I stay behind with Nellie while Thelonious and Toot go off to the Bronx. Two hours go by, no Thelonious. He finally shows up and the rear bumper, which extends around to the sides of the car, is hanging off the side by several inches. It was as if he caught something. Thelonious immediately goes on the defensive. 'I didn't do that. That was there before.' Then, on the metal dashboard above the glove compartment, I see this dent, and there is Toot with a sizable lump on his forehead. That was too much for him. It was the only time in our whole relationship that he lied to me."[15]

While they did become friends, Colomby soon figured out that this was a business arrangement. He had no intention of giving up his day job—he remained a full-time teacher for the next eleven years—nor had he intended to work for free. Colomby needed to supplement his meager salary, which in 1955 was a little over $7,000. While he could foresee a bright and lucrative future, the current prospects looked bleak, especially with the cabaret card issue hanging over Monk's head. The first thing Colomby did was book Monk for a weekend in February at the Comedy Club in Baltimore. He went as a single musician, and the gig paid only $300—$100 advance and $200 at the end of the date, minus the bar tab or any other additional expenses. Monk graciously peeled off $60 of his advance—twice the agreed-upon commission—and gave it to his new manager. Colomby then set up a meeting with Jack Whittemore, the booking agent for the Shaw Agency who had booked some of Monk's earlier engagements. He wanted to know why Shaw refused to sign Thelonious as a regular client. Whittemore quipped that Monk was unreliable—he didn't always show or was chronically late to gigs, and when he did make it he was unpredictable. Colomby countered that these problems would be attended to now that Monk had a manager. Although Whittemore ended the meeting without a firm commitment to Monk, he was impressed with Colomby's chutzpah. Before he left, he told Colomby, "if you have nerve enough to manage Thelonious Monk, I guess I could have nerve to try to book him." And he did, "once in a blue moon."[16]

Meanwhile, the bookings were few and far between. He might have inherited a little bit of money from his mother, who may have stashed away some of her settlement from the bus accident. Nellie probably made just enough to cover most of the basic expenses, which included a reasonable rent of about $30 or $35 a month.[17] And when money was really tight, he could always depend on Nica. In fact, following Barbara's death, Nica offered Thelonious the most generous gift he had ever received from anyone: She bought him a car. Monk wasn't the first musician upon whom she bestowed such a gift. A year or two earlier, she bought Art Blakey a Cadillac, which stunned some in the jazz world and elicited some lighthearted teasing from Thelonious. But now it was his turn, and like a boy in a toy store he picked his favorite: a brand-new black and white 1956 Buick Special.[18] Listing for a little over $2,700, Buick promoted the Special series as "the best Buick yet" in terms of performance, power, and affordability.[19] Monk adored the car. He used to argue with Baron Bennerson, the bartender at Green Gables, over the merits of his Special versus Bennerson's Buick Roadmaster. "When Monk saw my car, he tried to tell me that his Buick Special was a better car than my Roadmaster. In fact, he said his car is the best in the world!"[20] Monk took great pleasure in driving and often recruited family and friends to ride with him. His niece Judith Smith ("Muffin") remembered how he "used to come up to the Bronx and he'd have leather driving gloves in the summer time. He would whistle up to the window and say 'Who's going south?'"[21] The kids found driving with Uncle Thelonious to be a thrilling experience. Evelyn Smith: "He was reckless! He had that Buick Special and he would take us for a ride down Third Avenue, and he would drive around each pole. Once, on the Grand Central Parkway, he crossed the island and there was oncoming traffic."[22]

Besides the car, Nica treated Thelonious to another wonderful gift. A couple of weeks into 1956, Monk accompanied her to the Steinway showroom to pick out a brand new, five-foot, seven-inch Grand M Ebony with a shimmering lacquer finish. She wanted a new piano for her apartment at the Bolivar Hotel, but she also wanted to make sure Monk always had access to a good instrument and a place away from home where he could compose. On January 30, Steinway delivered the instrument directly from the factory in Queens to her place on Central Park West and 83rd.[23] Anxious to christen the piano, Thelonious showed up that same night and jammed for hours while

Nica and friends talked and drank the night away. The usually festive atmosphere was subdued by news that Dr. Martin Luther King, Jr., the twenty-seven-year-old minister who had been leading a bus boycott in Montgomery, Alabama to end mistreatment and segregation on the city's buses, had survived an assassination attempt. King had just come to the world's attention two months earlier, after activist Rosa Parks refused to give up her bus seat to a white man. On the day Nica's piano arrived, white terrorists tossed a dynamite bomb onto Dr. King's front porch. No one was hurt, but it made clear to many observers, Monk included, that the price for social justice was high and the struggle for basic human rights in the South was little short of war. Although Monk never openly embraced nonviolence, he did admire Dr. King and the Montgomery movement's unwavering determination. Minutes after the bombing, King stood courageously upon his own porch, glass strewn everywhere, and told an agitated crowd, "I want it to be known through the length and breadth of this land that if I am stopped this movement will not stop. If I am stopped our work will not stop. For what we are doing is right. What we are doing is just. And God is with us."[24]

Monk had plenty of time to drive around in his Buick—neither Harry Colomby nor Jack Whittemore had had much luck rustling up work. Besides the Comedy Club gig in Baltimore, Monk's only other job that spring was the Easter Jazz Festival at Town Hall on March 30.[25] The concert was entirely Ken Karpe's doing, conceived as the culmination of the last five or six months of jam sessions and an opportunity to feature Monk's music. Meanwhile, Orrin Keepnews booked Van Gelder's studio for March 17 and April 3 to record Monk's next trio album—the second part of Riverside's two-pronged approach to mainstreaming Monk's music. Monk had agreed to an all-standards album using the same rhythm section he had for the Ellington sessions (Pettiford on bass and Clarke drumming). But with Kenny Clarke now living in Europe, Art Blakey sat in on drums, which proved to be an auspicious development. Blakey provided the spark, the dynamism missing from the Ellington LP. Furthermore, Monk chose several tunes that had been part of his repertoire since the 1940s—namely "Liza" and "Just You, Just Me." The uptempo "Liza" is essentially a playful, exciting conversation between Blakey and Monk, whereas the medium-tempo "Just You, Just Me" is a conversation between Monk's left and right hands.[26]

For all the humor in those two tracks, there are expressions of tenderness and introspection in two other songs. His unaccompanied rendering of Andy Razaf and Eubie Blake's "Memories of You" should be heard as his tribute to Alberta Simmons, the neighborhood piano player who took Thelonious under her wing, helped him with his stride technique, and taught him songs by the old black composers. She had befriended Blake, met Razaf, and played "Memories of You" so often it was as if it were her own composition. Thelonious thought of Miss Simmons often, and his memories of her grew in prominence as he grappled with his mother's absence. Monk also selected a tune with which he was not familiar: Rodgers and Hart's "You Are Too Beautiful," from the 1933 romantic comedy, "Hallelujah, I'm a Bum." He found it in Orrin Keepnews's copy of *The Rodgers and Hart Song Book*, which he had loaned Thelonious just prior to the recording date.[27] Monk didn't soften his dissonant sonorities, yet it contained not a hint of irony and never lost its romantic lyricism.

After the session, Keepnews rode back to Manhattan in Monk's new Buick Special. Still a relatively new driver, Monk tailed Pettiford and Blakey so he wouldn't get lost. The road was covered with snow and ice. "I was with Monk who, unsure of the route, was following them closely. Another car suddenly turned out of a side road into the space between us. Thelonious, alarmed at the thought of losing the others, swerved sharply across the highway, stopping mere inches short of smashing into a telephone pole, and then calmly informed me: 'It's a good thing I was driving. If it had been someone else, we might be dead now.'"[28] That evening, Keepnews figured out what Monk's family already knew: Ride with Thelonious at your own risk.

While Monk and Keepnews were able to find humor in their near-tragedy, the tragic events that followed a few days later were no laughing matter. A fire ravaged the Monks' tiny apartment, destroying many of their prized possessions—furniture, clothes, books, records, a large proportion of Thelonious's original music manuscripts, as well as Keepnews's copy of *The Rodgers and Hart Song Book*. Worst of all, he lost his precious Klein upright piano. The instrument had been singed badly and may have been salvageable, but the worst damage was caused by water. [29] The culprit turned out to be faulty wiring. Fortunately, no one was inside the house when the fire broke out. Thelonious, Toot, and Boo Boo happened to be visiting Geraldine and Sonny in the Bronx while Nellie was at work. Jackie, the eldest Smith child, received the call that the Monks' house was on fire.[30] Without knowing the details, he bounded down five flights of stairs, jumped in his Buick, and sped to West 63rd Street.

When Thomas Monk returned home from work and learned of the fire, he was seized with panic. Thomas Monk, Jr., witnessed the events: "My father he jumped up and I never forgot what he said. He said, 'Oh, God, don't take my brother.' He started crying, my father. My mother said, 'He's all right.' My father ran over to him."[31] By the time Thomas got there, the firemen had extinguished the blaze but were now dealing with an irate and unstable Thelonious. Having broken through the cordon of firefighters, he leaped up on the water-logged sofa and began challenging anyone who tried to enter the apartment. Again, Thomas Monk, Jr.:

> Uncle Bubba was jumping on the couch, right? The fireman says, "We can't do nothing with this guy." So my father came in there, pulled out his badge (he was still an officer, though he worked for the Transit Authority). So they let him through and he asks, "Bubba, what's wrong?"
>
> "Man, I'm not gonna let these guys in the house and chop up my piano, chop up my furniture."[32]

Thelonious's fears were not unfounded. A few years earlier, his sister Marion had a small fire in their apartment at 235 West 63rd Street. The firemen "came and messed up the whole house," recalls Monk's nephew Alonzo. Between the heavy water damage and the axes, their place looked like it had been destroyed by a hurricane.[33]

When Nellie arrived she tried her best to calm Monk down, but to no avail. Worried, she called Harry Colomby. Thelonious was desperate to leave the scene, but she feared what might happen if he left alone. As soon as Colomby showed up, the two men took off in Monk's Buick. "I was thinking, we ain't going to come out of this one," Colomby recalled. "I don't know where he was going, but he was in a dark mood. He stopped at a bar. He ordered Wild Turkey, and then we left. We drove around for a while and then he went to the Bronx, and I went home."[34]

Monk, Nellie, and the children ended up staying with Geraldine and Sonny and their seven kids—besides Jackie, Judith, Clifton, Evelyn, and Benetta, they now had four-year-old James Riley, Jr., and eighteen-month-old Gerald Pierre (born a day before Thelonious's birthday). Skippy and her son Ronnie also lived there, bringing the grand total of occupants in the Smiths' three-bedroom apartment to fifteen. Monk and Nellie slept in the living room while Skippy and the kids were distributed between two bedrooms and the den.[35]

In the fire's aftermath, where to sleep wasn't Monk's more pressing concern. He only had a few days to get ready for a concert at Town Hall scheduled for March 30—Good Friday. David Amram, who was also performing at the same event with Oscar Pettiford's band, remembers visiting Monk in the Bronx days before the concert. "His biggest concern was finding something to wear. All of his clothes got messed up in the fire, so he asked me to help him figure out something to wear to look nice."[36] Monk had a reputation for looking sharp and the loss of his hippest suits, jackets, and ties left him feeling particularly vulnerable. But when it was time to "hit it" Friday night, Monk was ready. The concert was set up as if it were one big band with interchangeable parts. Oscar Pettiford's big band opened the concert. Coincidentally, it was made up almost entirely of past and future Monk sidemen—Julius Watkins (who shared French horn duties with David Amram), Gigi Gryce, Sahib Shihab on baritone, trumpeter Ray Copeland, trombonist Jimmy Cleveland, Jerome Richardson on flute and saxophone, drummer Osie Johnson, among others. After their set, Monk came on stage and performed in a trio setting with Pettiford and Osie Johnson, while the rest of the band stayed on stage and listened. A few numbers later, Ray Copeland and Sahib Shihab joined the group to make it a quintet. For David Amram, Monk's performance proved to be one of the more important musical experiences of his life. "As Monk played, all the musicians looked at him with so much love it just about heated up the stage. The audience could feel it too, seeing all these musicians listening and looking intently and they began to pay even more attention."[37]

Although the house was small, the performers were pleased. Monk "brought down the house," according to David Amram.[38] *New York Times* critic John Wilson almost agreed. He praised all of the performances except for one: To his ears, Thelonious played "with a graceless force that occasionally was blighted by some pixyish conceptions."[39] Monk had come to expect these kinds of reviews, and if he had picked up the *Times*, he may have noticed with pleasure Riverside's ad for *Thelonious Monk Plays Duke Ellington* LP, available for $3.97.

Four days after the concert, Monk reunited with Pettiford and Blakey at Van Gelder's studio in order to complete the LP of standards that would become *The Unique Thelonious Monk*. He produced an utterly humorous rendition of "Tea for Two," and "Honeysuckle Rose," another Razaf and Blake composition, was also rich with humor and old "tickler" techniques he had mastered back in the days of hanging out with Clarence Profit and Willie "The Lion" Smith. Finally, he romanced the piano with Jimmy Van Heusen's lovely "Darn That Dream." Like his rendering of "You Are So Beautiful," Thelonious retains his uniquely dissonant voice without undermining the song's romantic quality.

Spring came and Thelonious was still waiting for Colomby to work his magic. It was tough; teaching full-time meant Colomby only had evenings and weekends to hustle gigs. He quickly discovered that there wasn't much work for any jazz artist. In 1956, most venues wanted rock and roll, with Elvis Presley dominating the airwaves with "Hound Dog" and "Don't Be Cruel." The one modern jazz group that seemed to work all the time was the phenomenal Clifford Brown–Max Roach Quintet. With Sonny Rollins, pianist Richie Powell, and bassist George Morrow rounding out the group, they were the hottest ticket in jazz at the moment. Brown, all of twenty-six years old, was hailed as the new Gabriel, the second coming on trumpet. Colomby decided to call Max Roach, a long-time friend of Thelonious, and ask for the names and numbers of club owners around the country so that he might reach out to them. Roach replied coldly, "You could find that in *Down Beat*," and hung up the phone. Colomby was taken aback. He concluded from their brief exchange that "there was no camaraderie in jazz . . . it was all very selfish, very self-involved."[40] A couple of months later, the remarkably talented Clifford Brown, along with Richie Powell and his wife Nancy Powell, were tragically killed in a car accident while driving from Philadelphia to Chicago. They were driving a Buick.[41]

Colomby knew Monk could not survive on out-of-town jobs alone. He needed his cabaret card. The first thing Colomby did that spring was apply to the New York State Liquor Authority requesting the reinstatement of Monk's cabaret card. The application required supporting letters attesting to his character. Colomby had to solicit several letters and then submit his own. "In that letter, I said I was a school teacher and I could declare that Thelonious Monk was no longer using drugs. . . . My argument was that, as a school teacher, I could not be involved with anyone who was using drugs."[42] Several others wrote on Monk's behalf, including his former producer Alfred Lion. His letter was short but direct: "Our relationship with Mr. Monk has been pleasant and satisfactory and we believe Mr. Monk to be a person of good character."[43] The request was denied.

Part of the problem was that too many powerful people in the jazz world did *not* believe Thelonious was of "good character." The old stories of his strangeness and unreliability continued to dog him, despite the positive reports about his professionalism and the growing respect for his music in high art circles. The April 1956 issue of the *British Jazz Monthly* carried a substantial article by Raymond Horricks recounting Monk's 1954 Paris Jazz Festival experience. Besides making him out to be a bit of a clown, Horricks claimed with an air of authority that "He has never been known to hold a job for very long because of his unreliable nature." He placed much of the blame for Monk's alleged irresponsibility on his *mother*, suggesting that his mother's choice to support him into adulthood meant that he could work whenever he felt like it. "Other musicians have to work unless they want to find their baggage dumped on the pavement. At least Monk has always been certain of a bed and a meal, allowing him to play the fool when he feels so inclined."[44] Horricks' words were hostile and inaccurate, but they carried weight and echoed what many club owners and booking agents believed. Colomby's strategy was to change the discourse; to "mainstream" Monk by showing the world that he was a hard-working genius. He arranged to have Nat Hentoff interview Monk for a feature article for *Down Beat*. Titled "Just Call Him Thelonious," the piece ran in the July 25 issue, alongside Hentoff's glowing review of the recently released *The Unique Thelonious Monk*. It was Monk's chance to set the record straight . . . and he did. On the strangeness and inaccessibility of his music, Monk responded, "Do I think I'm difficult to understand? Well, like what? Tell me a particular number. Some of my pieces have melodies a nitwit can understand. Like I've written one number staying on one note. A tone-deaf person could hum it."[45] Speaking to folks new to his music, Monk suggested they should "just listen to the music in the order that I've recorded it. Get the records, sit down and dig."[46] On the current state of jazz, he had little good to say. "[T]here's been nothing really original in the last six or seven years. What is an original? If it sounds original. The construction; the melody. It has to have its own sound."[47]

Not surprisingly, he devoted a good part of his commentary to responding to the kinds of claims Horricks and others continued to circulate:

I'd like to talk about the lies that have been told about me that I'm undependable on jobs and the like. I don't know how that kind of legend got around. Some fools talk a big lie, that's all. Those lies get started, and you just can't stop them. Without even investigating, people go for them, and the lies get to the booking agencies. They believe it, too, so fast and condemn you before investigating. I think the booking agents and the public should investigate if rumors are true about people before they believe them.

I have never messed up; I have never goofed a job in my life. Sometimes my *name* has been used in places that I knew nothing about, and the promoters never tried to get in touch with me. So when the public comes and I haven't shown up, the promoter blames me when he explains it to them. But I *do* have a sense of responsibility about work.[48]

He also had a consistent position on what constituted a just and fair arrangement, evident from his early grievances filed with Local 802 back in the early 1940s. Colomby understood this over time. "A lot of Monk's problems arise from the fact that he has a sharp business eye. He hates matinees, calls that an extra day. He has an uncanny ability to tell how much a club is making. Booking agencies didn't like this about him, and so a lot of strange rumors about Monk's undependability began to come out of nowhere and scare off the club owners. No one has a greater sense of business responsibility than Monk."[49]

By the end of the summer, Colomby chalked up a few successes. He got Monk two weeks at the Blue Note in Philadelphia in November with the promise of more dates in the future. But he knew all too well that trying to overturn a decade of opinion about his client required time and patience, and without a cabaret card Monk's options remained severely limited. Meanwhile, every time he visited Monk and Nellie in the Bronx, living in an overcrowded apartment with virtually nothing but a fancy sedan parked on the street, he was reminded of their struggle and his responsibility. "Nobody had a dime," he mused. "I would occasionally leave, literally, five dollars under an ashtray in the house. I had no money. I didn't want to say it to him. I just left it there. 'How does he eat?' I think Nellie was making something, you know, and gave him some money."[50]

Colomby's help was always appreciated, but the Monks' greatest fount of support continued to be family. Thomas and Trotyrine shared whatever they had with Thelonious and Nellie—clothes, money if they had it—and they kept an eye on the apartment as it was undergoing repair and renovation. The Monks even relied on "family" to renovate the apartment, hiring Helen Graham's two uncles. Graham lived on Lyman Place and was so close to the Smiths that she was considered family. The Graham brothers were expert builders, but the racism of the building trades unions limited their job opportunities. The Grahams offered Monk a considerable discount because of their longstanding friendship.[51]

For at least six months, the Smiths provided the Monks with shelter and a loving, supportive environment. Despite extremely tight quarters, the household ran efficiently and with little friction. The older children cared for the younger ones, and the adults divided the household duties.[52] The kids loved the arrangement. Toot and Barbara had become close to their cousins, and Thelonious became better acquainted with his nieces and nephews. Evelyn Smith was about twelve when the Monks moved in, and from her vantage point, "Thelonious was like a second father to all of us. He imparted certain lessons, mostly about being yourself and being truthful."[53] Monk grew especially close to sixteen-year-old Jackie because she was serious about music and she possessed a wonderful, wry sense of humor.[54] She studied violin privately, played piano, and took classes at the Bronx House School of Music. Before the fire, she loved hanging out at Monk's place and listening to her uncle play. "I sang back to Thelonious everything he played. Whatever kind of a riff it was. I don't care how complicated, I studied it myself and knew the music. . . . He would laugh." One day he asked Jackie to ride with him to Manhattan to pick up Sonny Rollins. "Before he had a chance to sit down, Thelonious said to him, 'You know, my niece can sing anything you can play? . . . Go on, sing something.'" Slightly embarrassed, she proceeded to sing "The Way You Look Tonight" the way they recorded for Prestige in 1953. A little stunned, Rollins listened respectfully; Monk beamed with pride. "See, told ya! The girl can sing anything!" Although Thelonious never gave Jackie formal lessons, his encouragement proved critical in her decision to pursue a career in music. When he finally had a chance to hear her play something she wrote on piano, he laughed. "He didn't say cut it out, so I knew that was a good sign."[55]

As much as he enjoyed his family, the Smiths' apartment sometimes felt claustrophobic. Without privacy and lacking a piano, Monk began spending more time at Nica's place, where he practiced and composed on her Steinway. Nellie often accompanied him, but sometimes he went by himself. Monk and Nica also hit the clubs together or were seen riding around in her Rolls-Royce convertible (she had yet to purchase her infamous Bentley), which generated rumors of a romantic relationship. Those close to Thelonious knew such rumors were untrue. Monk also ran with Elmo Hope, who lived with his mother near the Smiths on Lyman Place. On any given night, they might show up at a local club in the Bronx, head into Manhattan, or jam the night away at Al Walker's television repair shop.[56]

But Elmo would disappear for short periods of time. Monk had seen enough shooting galleries to know why: Elmo had a habit. Heroin use in the jazz world had reached epidemic proportions by the mid-1950s, due in part to the spectacular influx of the drug into black communities in Harlem, Brooklyn, and his own Morrisania neighborhood in the southwest Bronx. Throughout the spring and summer of 1956, it seemed as if every other musician Monk met or knew was addicted to "horse." One night in late April or May, Monk and Nica dropped in at the Embers, an exclusive supper club on East 54th Street, to check out a hot new pianist from Los Angeles named Hampton Hawes.[57] Monk dug his playing so much that he stayed until the last set and offered to take Hawes to Nica's pad for a bite to eat. Hawes recounted, "I said, okay, but first I've got to drop by this cat's house nearby to get some music. 'Don't worry about it,' he said, 'I'll wait.' I'm sure he saw through my game. I went into the alley and copped."[58] Soon thereafter, Hawes moved to New York permanently and grew close to Monk, Nellie, and Nica. Thelonious became a kind of father-figure to him, though he "never interfered in my life or put me down for being strung. . . . If he was using himself, I didn't know it, and he didn't show it, and that's what being cool is all about."[59] Monk wasn't using then, but he had in the past and knew the toll it was taking on Hawes. And he wasn't too cool to care. A few months later, when Hawes's habit left him completely broke, jobless, and virtually homeless, Monk rescued him from a bench in Central Park and brought him home. Nellie fed him, cleaned him up, and gave him a fresh change of clothes. Sonny Rollins came over that night and they had what in today's parlance is called "an intervention." Monk, Nellie, and Sonny got on his case, reminding him that he was "an important figure in jazz" and "you need to straighten yourself out before you die or something." "We're all in it together and you're too important to fuck up like this." And then Monk gave him some money to help him start over.[60]

This wasn't the first time Thelonious helped an addicted musician in need, nor would it be the last time. Just weeks after he first encountered Hawes at the Embers, Thelonious reached out to his old friend Ernie Henry. The promising alto player had all but disappeared from the jazz scene, having spent the previous few years gigging with various R&B groups and losing the battle with heroin.[61] Randy Weston, his childhood friend and army buddy, encouraged Henry to come out to the jam sessions in

Brooklyn and get his chops together.[62] Monk encouraged him as well. He promised to use Henry for his next record date and began rehearsing with him that summer.[63] To make sure Henry showed up for rehearsals, Thelonious often drove out to Brooklyn to find him. Colomby remembers accompanying Monk on one of his quests to find Henry: "I remember it was a rainy day, and we were driving around Brooklyn, not sure of his address. I said, 'Where does he live? Who is this guy?' Monk just said, 'He's a good player,' and he wanted me to find him. I remember he lived in a kind of basement apartment with his father, I think."[64] Monk did what he could to help Henry get his life back together. When Randy Weston lobbied Keepnews and Grauer to sign Henry as a Riverside recording artist, Monk concurred, stating simply, "He can play."[65] They were persuaded; Henry recorded his first album as a leader in late August 1956.[66]

For the date Henry hired Wilbur Ware, the outstanding young bassist Monk had met in Chicago. He had come to New York with Art Blakey and the Jazz Messengers that summer and settled in Brooklyn. Henry, Willie Jones, and Kenny Dorham introduced him to the local scene, and Thelonious lobbied Grauer and Keepnews to give him work.[67] Monk himself began using Ware for the few jobs he had that fall. In early September, Ware joined Monk, Gigi Gryce, and drummer Ron Jefferson, for a free concert at St. John's Recreation Center in Brooklyn sponsored by Jazz Unlimited.[68] Keepnews and Grauer infrequently used Ware for other recording sessions, but they did grant Thelonious's request to give Ware a job: They had him sleeving records and sweeping the floor at the Riverside warehouse on West 51st Street. Sometimes he slept there.[69]

Meanwhile, as Monk prepared Henry for his next Riverside record date, he and Nica went down to Café Bohemia to hear Bud Powell's trio and Miles Davis's highly touted quintet, which consisted of pianist Red Garland, tenor saxophonist John Coltrane, drummer Philly Joe Jones, and a phenomenal twenty-one-year-old bassist, Paul Laurence Dunbar Chambers, Jr.[70] Once again, the specter of the junkie arose. Sadly, this excellent band was known as much for being "a group of unreliable drinkers and junkies" as for its musicianship.[71] Ironically, the only heroin-free band member was its leader, and he was growing wary of seeing his sidemen nodding off on stage. It was a strange and sad thing for Thelonious to witness. He knew Philly Joe and had even considered him for a record date, and he recognized Chambers's and Coltrane's immense talents. He especially had his eye on Coltrane, who had been on the scene for several years, playing with Dizzy, Johnny Hodges, Earl Bostic, and a number of R&B groups before settling in with Miles.[72] Monk developed a soft spot for the quiet and self-deprecating saxophonist. A fellow homeboy born and raised in High Point, North Carolina, 'Trane in turn had long admired Monk's music ever since he recorded "'Round Midnight" with Dizzy Gillespie back in 1949. And he had recently recorded it again with Miles.[73] 'Trane sounded great most of the time, but he looked terrible. In his effort to go cold turkey, he dealt with withdrawal symptoms the way most junkies do—by drinking more. He lived on a cocktail of beer and wine and disappeared between sets. Thelonious did his best to encourage him, but Coltrane was in no shape to engage Monk—at least not yet.[74]

• • •

The Graham brothers completed the renovations on the Monks' apartment by early fall—just in time for Toot to start school. Nellie and Thelonious enrolled him in P.S. 191 on 61st and Amsterdam, where the "very old" but likable Mrs. Jampole taught his first grade class. They were all happy to be back in their new and improved home. The Graham brothers not only restored the apartment; they reconfigured it, moving closets and walls to make the space more manageable. And before closing up the walls, they had the good sense to add soundproofing material so that Monk could play without disturbing the neighbors.[75] Now all he needed was a piano.

Thelonious was as anxious as Keepnews to work on the much-anticipated third album featuring his original compositions. His first two Riverside LPs had fared relatively well with the first wave of critics; in fact, they reserved the harshest criticisms for his record label for allegedly denying Monk the opportunity to record his own music. By late summer, he began putting his band together. He knew he wanted to use Ernie Henry and Sonny Rollins, and Oscar Pettiford played well on his earlier Riverside sessions. Monk always liked Max Roach, who was now leading a quintet with Rollins dedicated to the memory of his good friend Clifford Brown. And Grauer and Keepnews knew that snagging the high-profile drummer for the date also made good commercial sense.

With no piano at home, Thelonious held informal rehearsals at the Baroness's place. Sometimes he and Sonny Rollins would work all night on one or two tunes. David Amram was on hand for some of these impromptu sessions. "That was one of the most amazing things I ever heard in my life. . . . They just kept going back and forth, stopping and starting, until they finally got to the end of the tune. Of course, Monk knew it already but he was teaching it to Sonny just very slowly, and repeating it over and over and over again."[76] Of the three new songs he had written for the album, two were tributes to Nica, who provided the space and the instrument to enable Monk to work during this difficult period. "Pannonica" is one of those strangely head-bopping ballads that swings even at the slowest tempos. Nica recorded it on her portable Wollensack reel-to-reel tape recorder some time in the summer of 1956, soon after Monk completed it. It is his spoken preamble that interests us: "It was named after this beautiful lady here. I think her father gave her that name after a butterfly that he tried to catch. I don't think he caught the butterfly."[77] He also wrote a blues referencing Nica's incessant troubles with the management at the Bolivar Hotel with the treacherous title "Ba-lue Bolivar Ba-Lues-Are." They were constantly trying to get rid of her, complaining about her late-night parties and musician friends—Thelonious included.[78] His third contribution, considered an authentic masterpiece, was called "Brilliant Corners." Full of huge intervallic leaps, the first sixteen bars of the melody and the harmonic movement are quite literally shaped like a circle while the bridge retains Monk's more characteristic descending chromatic chord progressions. In terms of tempo and rhythm, the entire first chorus is played as a slow dirge and then repeated in double-time. The solos follow the same pattern. But the biggest rhythmic challenge was the song's thirty-bar structure: He wrote a seven-bar bridge and he removed a measure from the last A-section, making it seven bars as well. For musicians used to the standard thirty-two-bar song form, "Brilliant Corners" threw them for a loop.

The *Brilliant Corners* album took three sessions and two months to complete. The first session took place the day before Monk's thirty-ninth birthday in the lavish Reeves Sound Studios in Manhattan. Grauer bid farewell to Hackensack and moved Riverside's sessions east of the Hudson. While Reeves lacked the homey feel of Rudy Van Gelder's living room, its high-end technology and massive stock of orchestral instruments made many musicians feel like kids in a candy store. Soon after Thelonious walked in he spotted a celeste, a keyboard producing bell-like sounds, and thought it would be hip to use it on the opening of "Pannonica."[79] He positioned it perpendicular to the piano, which allowed him to play it with his right hand while playing chords with his left, resulting in a strange and jarring juxtaposition of sound. The recording of "Pannonica" was not without problems, however. Despite the rehearsals at Nica's house, neither Rollins nor Henry had actually mastered the song by the time they went into the studio. There were several instances in which the band flubbed the final two-bar cadence. On one of those takes, Monk stopped the band and said, "Hold up, hold up. You messed up on that . . . tag. When you play it, keep in mind there's a tag on the song, you know?" The released version succeeds, as does their rendering of "Ba-Lue Bolivar Ba-Lues-Are," which may be Ernie Henry's finest moment on record.[80] There is a crying, human quality in his sound; his solo, with its slurred, loping notes, tells a story in the best tradition of the blues. Monk and Sonny Rollins build on Henry's sound. Rollins picks up the last few notes of Monk's solo and takes off, once again demonstrating his mastery of Monkian blues.

Compared to the subsequent sessions, the October 9 date went smoothly. Six days later, they were back at Reeves Sound Studios intent on completing the album. Four hours later, Keepnews had twenty-five incomplete takes of "Brilliant Corners" and five very frustrated and tired men—six if you include the producer.[81] The problems began when Monk would not share the music with the band. Like Duke Ellington, he genuinely believed that the best way to master a song is to learn it by ear. Despite several days of rehearsals, only Rollins had been able to master the unusual thirty-bar structure, the difficult intervals, and the shifting tempos by the time they went into the studios. (Of course, Rollins also spent a lot more time rehearsing with Thelonious at Nica's house.) Roach and Pettiford, in particular, had trouble with the song, leading Pettiford to criticize Monk's composing. "You don't have enough bars," he said at one point. Harry Colomby, who dropped by the session, remembers that Pettiford's constant needling about the song's limitations frustrated and hurt Monk. "He said to himself, 'Why is this happening to me?' That's the only time he ever uttered anything like that."[82] Keepnews concurs: "I don't remember that Sonny had any problems, but Max and Oscar Pettiford did. It almost caused a fistfight between Pettiford and Monk. Monk was a forgiving guy, but after that session he never mentioned Pettiford's name."[83] Pettiford became so angry that, on one take, he only pretended to play, strumming his fingers over the strings without producing a sound.[84]

Keepnews took the twenty-five incomplete takes and knitted together a full version.

The results are stunning. Upon listening, it becomes clear that the band had more diffi-culty playing the theme correctly and in unison than improvising. Sonny Rollins deliv-ers as near-perfect a solo as one can imagine; he takes seriously Monk's insistence on using melody as the basis for improvisation, and he is equally comfortable on the faster tempo. Monk, not surprisingly, produces a brilliant solo that might be best described as a variation on the theme. Ernie Henry's whining long-tones work beautifully against the changes, and for all of Max Roach's complaints, his judicious choices prove why he was a virtuoso of the drum solo. If the recording is marred by anything, it is the noticeable splice between the end of Roach's unaccompanied solo and the return of the ensemble playing the closing theme. For someone who had never edited multiple takes together, it wasn't bad for a first try. But Keepnews clearly recognized the problem. As he confessed thirty years later, he would have liked "to improve the editing in a couple of places."[85]

Rollins and Roach's road schedule delayed the album's completion by nearly two months. Meanwhile, Monk played a two-week engagement at the Blue Note in Phila-delphia. He led a quartet with Ernie Henry, Willie Jones, and Miles's regular bassist, Paul Chambers, who had most of November off while his boss left for Europe as part of the "Birdland '56 All-Stars."[86] Chambers was jazz's golden child. He had already recorded as a leader, was the subject of feature articles, and *Down Beat* critics were about to anoint him "New Star" on bass.[87] But with both he and Ernie Henry fight-ing their addiction and drinking heavily, Monk left for Philly feeling a little nervous. Fortunately, there were no major mishaps. Indeed, it was a good run, and Monk was unusually upbeat. According to Nellie, who accompanied Thelonious a couple of times from New York, he really engaged the audience, told "corny jokes" and made "remarks that were so timely you would have to laugh."[88]

During their engagement, he probably saw John Coltrane, who used his respite from Davis's band to move back to Philadelphia with his first wife, Naima, and their daughter Saeeda.[89] Paul Chambers was close to Coltrane, so it is conceivable that 'Trane either came out to the Blue Note to hear the band or Chambers accompanied Monk to Coltrane's house on Thirty-third Street. Whatever the case, the timing of Monk's Philadelphia gig allowed the two men to get to know each other a little better outside of New York. Here, in the City of Brotherly Love, the seeds of a longstanding friendship were sown.

Monk was back home before Thanksgiving and ready to complete *Brilliant Corners*. That Keepnews scheduled Reeves Sound Studios for December 7—the fifteenth anni-versary of the attack on Pearl Harbor—must have been a sign of things to come. Just days before the session, Ernie Henry decided to quit Monk's group and go on the road with Dizzy Gillespie.[90] This hurt Thelonious, though he really couldn't blame Henry: He needed regular work, and Monk had none. Henry's departure wasn't a total disaster. Trumpeter Clark Terry stepped in. On the other hand, there was no love lost between Monk and Oscar Pettiford, who decided not to come back . . . ever. Fortunately, Paul Chambers was available for the session and the Philly gig had prepared him well.

Anxious to finish the album, Keepnews booked the studio for 10:00—*a.m.* Not the best time for nocturnal jazz musicians, but it allowed Thelonious to bring his seven-year-old son along—though he did have to play hooky from school.[91] Only Terry and Chambers were punctual; the rest straggled in at their leisure, leaving little time to lay down two good tracks of music. And when Max Roach walked in and saw a gleaming timpani drum in the corner, he pulled a Thelonious Monk and insisted on adding it to his drum kit.[92] It was worth the time spent—on their recording of "Bemsha Swing," Roach uses the timpani to great effect, creating sudden bursts of rolling thunder. After completing "Bemsha Swing" they had about twenty minutes to vacate the studio and were still five minutes short of a completed album. Monk saved the session, filling the void with a "flawless five and a half minutes of 'I Surrender Dear.' "[93]

The session had perhaps the greatest effect on the youngest one in the recording booth. "I remember looking out into the studio at Max Roach's drums," Toot remembered, "and beautiful timpanis, kettle drums with beautiful copper bottoms. Max looked like an executive at a big desk taking care of business." When the session was over, Roach walked over to little Toot and handed him his drum sticks. From that point on, he knew exactly what he wanted to do when he grew up. He never lost those drum sticks.[94]

With *Brilliant Corners* finally in the can, Thelonious was ready for a break. Three days after the session, he was back at the Bolivar Hotel playing Nica's piano.[95] As much as he enjoyed hanging out at Nica's, he realized he desperately needed a good piano of his own. Short of cash, he and Nellie decided to rent a Steinway baby grand, not unlike Nica's. He had it delivered in time for Christmas.[96]

It had been quite a year. The fire, the dislocation, the hostile press and booking agents, the Buick, bearing witness to the ravages of heroin, bearing witness to enduring strength of family and friends, the utter frustration he felt finding musicians able to master his music, the satisfaction of composing. Monk lived in a strange limbo: feeling honored and respected, knowing his fortunes were finally rising, but also facing moments of disrespect and disappointment. He still had no cabaret card, no steady work, two children to feed, a wife dogged with health problems who had to work to pay the rent, and a guy who now took ten percent to make something happen. And suddenly, December 14—the one-year anniversary of Barbara's death—came upon Monk like a dark shadow. He had a lot to process.

Just after Christmas, Monk was driving by himself in Manhattan when he skidded on a patch of ice and careened into another vehicle. The damage was minimal, but enough for the other driver to request Monk's information. Monk got out of the car and just stood there, uncommunicative, staring into space. The frustrated driver called the police. A patrolman arrived, but Monk remained unresponsive. A fender bender is not a crime, but the officer felt compelled to take him into custody, or at least out of the freezing cold. He left a note on Monk's Buick Special: "Psycho taken to Bellevue."[97]

17

"People Have Tried to Put Me Off as Being Crazy"

(January 1957–April, 1957)

Bellevue Psychiatric Hospital might as well have been Rikers Island, as far as Monk was concerned. Surrounding the red brick building on the corner of 30th Street and East River Drive was a ten-foot-high "spear-topped, wrought-iron fence."[1] Attendants often acted like prison guards, and with 650 patients jammed into a 630-bed facility, the overcrowded conditions were reminiscent of the Tombs.[2] As soon as he was allowed access to a phone, Monk called Nellie in a panic. Nellie in turn called Colomby, Nica, and her friend Maely Dufty, who promptly contacted a lawyer in East Harlem in an unsuccessful effort to secure his release. Nica got in touch with her doctor, Robert Freymann, who immediately contacted the psychiatric ward's lead staff. In the meantime, Colomby picked up Nellie and headed straight to Bellevue.[3]

They found him, weary and anxious, yet surprisingly stoic under the circumstances.[4] No one knew what was wrong with Monk, not even the highly trained staff at Bellevue. Yet they considered him a sufficient danger to himself and others to hold him for observation. They kept him nearly three weeks. He passed the time painting pictures and taking visitors. Nellie was always there, and Nica came quite often. After almost three weeks of negotiation, Dr. Freymann secured Monk's release without a diagnosis.[5]

The absence of a diagnosis is a little surprising. One might have expected the staff psychiatrist to declare Monk a "paranoid schizophrenic," a catch-all phrase frequently applied to black patients and nonconformist artists. The list of alleged paranoid schizophrenics who passed through Bellevue in the 1950s is long and distinguished, including Bud Powell, Charles Mingus, not to mention Gregory Corso, Norman Mailer, and Allen Ginsberg.[6] Given the state of psychiatry and the overburdened staff at Bellevue, accurate diagnoses weren't always possible. Although it took nearly two more decades before doctors would correctly diagnose Monk as bipolar, he had begun to exhibit classic symptoms of the disorder—symptoms that would occur more frequently in the years to come.

Manic depression encompasses a wide range of mood disorders, and the shifts in mood tend to be episodic. Falling asleep at the piano, staring into space lost in thought, seemingly unable to recognize people around him were all indications of cyclothymia, or a depressed state. When Monk experienced hypomania, or a manic state, his moods ranged from euphoria and impatience to frenetic and volatile. Common traits of manic behavior include aimless and violent actions, a marked tendency to seek out other people, and an inability to sleep.[7] We have already seen the signs in Monk—enduring days without sleep followed by exhaustion, late-night forays in search of someone's piano to play, frenetic pacing, skipping meals. Nat Hentoff's sympathetic description of Thelonious's character reveals all the classic symptoms: "He may often stay up two or three days, and he does not eat by the clock since his periods of hunger do not always fall into regular rhythms. On a visit, if he feels like napping, he does. There are times, in his home or outside, when he doesn't feel like talking, and he may not for several hours. The latter condition usually occurs when he's worried."[8] Sahib Shihab noticed similar behavior as soon as they began working together in the late 1940s. "He wouldn't come out of his house for two weeks at a time. He wouldn't come out of his room for two weeks at a time."[9]

As we have already seen, friends, colleagues, critics, and the press were quick to interpret most of these behaviors as examples of his trademark eccentricities. When the possibility of mental illness was finally acknowledged, some of the same friends, colleagues, critics, and the press began kicking around the idea that madness may be the source of his genius.[10] Whether or not Monk produced his best work during a "manic phase" is less important than the overall impact his illness had on his ability to work and on his social relationships. The fact is, his bipolar disorder often made it difficult to work, lost him jobs, and put undue stress on his family—especially Nellie. For someone so family-oriented who did not begin to make a decent living until he was over forty, there is nothing romantic or desirable about playing the tortured artist.

Bipolar disorder and a variety of mental disorders are hereditary and scientists were just beginning to figure this out in the mid-1950s. Thelonious did not know that his own father had been living in a mental asylum for the past fifteen years. In the summer of 1941, while his son starred at Minton's Playhouse, Thelonious Monk, Sr., was committed to the State Hospital for the Colored Insane in Goldsboro, North Carolina.[11] He was fifty-two years old at the time, but the first severe signs of his illness occurred about ten years earlier, not long after he returned to North Carolina. He was known to have angry outbursts, fueled by excessive drinking, followed by bouts of deep depression and withdrawal. The episodes made it impossible for him to hold a job. Hettie and Eulah, his two sisters with whom he lived on Dunn Street, watched over him for a while, but when it became too difficult their brother, Theodore "Babe" Monk, took him in.[12]

Theodore owned land in Newton Grove, the same pocket of Bentonville where their father, Hinton Monk, had settled. He raised prize hogs, maintained three hundred acres of fruit trees, grapes, and a variety of crops, and provided for and educated six children. He was admired in the Newton Grove community. A God-fearing, devout Baptist, he was known for his generosity and honesty.[13] His wife, Mamie Lofton Monk, protested his decision to care for his difficult brother. Olivia Monk, Babe's daughter-in-law, recounted stories of Thelonious's worst episodes. "His yelling and carrying on got to be so bad, they used to put him in the mule stable. Nothing but just hay and old junk. He'd get to kicking and beating on things and you can hear him for about a mile around the place. . . . He wanted to be with his family [in New York]." After a while, Mamie could take it no longer. She called the authorities and had him committed.[14]

The State Hospital for the Colored Insane was a far cry from Bellevue. African-Americans did not check into Southern Jim Crow asylums on their own volition, and they were certainly not institutions one turned to for proper mental health care. The nearly 3,000 residents of the hospital were called "inmates" for a reason; most were there in lieu of prison—although, as one reporter put it, "this writer would prefer the jails to the hospital."[15] The hospital had a reputation for using inmates as cheap labor for construction and maintenance, child care, and agriculture, and the staff offered no therapeutic activities besides work. The institution was notorious for murders, suicides, and frequent escape attempts, and the staff did not separate children from adults.[16] In 1949, conditions improved slightly with the appointment of Drs. Mintaute and Edite Vitols, two distinguished psychiatrists from Latvia who turned the hospital into their own laboratory for the study of race and mental disorders.[17]

For eight years, Babe visited his brother in Goldsboro regularly. He kept Thelonious abreast of family news and became his brother's advocate at the hospital, making sure he was not abused or mistreated. Then in 1949, just two weeks before Thanksgiving, Babe Monk was found shot to death in the very mule stable he had used to restrain his brother. The police and coroner's offices ruled his death a suicide, with the unlikely story that he rigged a complicated scaffolding to hold a shotgun in place, tied a piece of rope to the trigger, and pulled.[18] The police never conducted an investigation, in part because Babe's widow, Mamie Lofton Monk, believed the story, though she was virtually the only family member who did, along with her daughter and son-in-law, Isabelle and Leroy Cole.[19]

With Babe's sudden death, Thelonious, Sr.'s links to family and the outside world quickly dissolved. Babe's youngest son, Conley Monk, and his wife, Olivia, continued visiting Thelonious, but once they moved to Connecticut they lost contact. Olivia vividly remembers one of their last visits. "I used to take my baby Pam to see Thelonious in the hospital. He used to play with her. He was a very pleasant old man. Good-looking. Short and heavyset, dark-brown-skinned. Oh, he just laughed and talked and had a lot of jolly. Very fun. I don't know how they could have kept him down there. But if I had some place to put him I would have brought him home with me. He didn't seem like nobody out of their mind. He never acted like he wanted to fight or drive somebody away from him or nothing like that."[20] It is likely that he suffered from bipolar disorder like his son, thus his condition was episodic. With proper medication and therapy, he might have been able to live independently, but the lack of scientific knowledge compounded by racism made it unlikely that Thelonious Monk, Sr. would ever see the world beyond the asylum grounds.

His son fared much better; he was out in less than three weeks' time. Nellie brought Thelonious home in a cab and Harry and Jules Colomby were there to greet him. Harry recalled, "When he walked in he was so queer in the face. He was happy to be home. I'll never forget, he hugged us both and said, 'Nothing should break us up.'"[21] They began working right away. He had only been out a few days when Harry took him to Ira Gitler's parents' house to be interviewed for *Metronome* magazine.[22] Monk looked quite sharp, sporting a glen-plaid suit, a grey felt hat, and draped in a salt and pepper overcoat. He confided that he was relieved to be out of the hospital and anxious to be outside, despite the freezing weather. "You see, being in the hospital, indoors so much, it gets on my nerves. I have to go and ride around a little while and then I'll go home and practice." More than anything, he wanted to "make some money." He told Gitler that he was anxious to start working again and that he hoped to put together a sextet with three horns, "the right amount of horns."[23]

Colomby got Monk six nights at the Blue Note with the house rhythm section, bassist Jimmy Bond and a phenomenal seventeen-year-old drummer Albert "Tootie" Heath—Percy Heath's baby brother. "He'd come in with his coat and hat still on," Heath remembered, "sit at the piano and just start playing. He never told us what he was playing, never gave us music or direction. He never said a single word to us for six nights. We'd have to figure out the music on our own. Fortunately, we'd been listening to Monk for a while and knew his music, but we had to find our own way."[24] Bond and Heath succeeded admirably, in spite of the fact that Thelonious dropped a brand new song into the mix he called "Light Blue"—a loping sixteen-bar theme played at a slow, plodding tempo. Monk was still struggling with his depression and feeling the aftershock of his hospitalization. Nellie, Nica, and Colomby agreed that he should not be left alone, so Nica drove him to Philly every night, stayed until the final set, and drove him home. "During the break, he would go out and sit in the Bentley with Nica," Heath observed. "He didn't interact with anyone. I thought that was strange."[25]

Monk spent the rest of the winter and spring in the city hanging out with his kids and *practicing*. Although Monk was proud of his baby grand, it quickly became an extension of the kitchen countertop and a storage space for household clutter. When he sat down to play, his back stood just a few inches from the dishwasher. Monk wanted to hear himself, so like Nica he purchased a portable reel-to-reel tape recorder and taught Nellie how to work it.[26] Some of those tapes survive, providing remarkable opportunities to eavesdrop on Monk's creative process as well as his daily life. They reveal something of Nellie's delight in listening to her husband, and the joy they both derived from each other's company. Between and during songs, the recorder captured snippets of a life-long love affair. Following a tender rendition of "Tea for Two," he asked Nellie in a surprised but gentle voice, "Were you recording that?"[27] Other times Nellie sings along in perfect unison with the piano. "My mother knew the music," Toot recalled. "She could sing all the solos, when I was little she could sing all the solos on all the records. All the tunes that I learned to sing I learned to sing them from my mother. . . . [M]y mother was singing the tunes and humming the melodies alllll the time."[28]

Whether reconstructing an old standard or working through his own originals, the tapes demonstrate that Monk's distinct sound was a product of unceasing discipline, practice, and hard work. Achieving the harmonic and rhythmic language recognized as Monk's did not come easy to him—playing "straight" was easier than playing "Monk."

Perhaps the finest surviving example of Monk playing at home is an eighty-four-minute recording of him working through one tune: Ned Washington and George Bassman's "I'm Getting Sentimental Over You" (1932). Best known as the theme song for Tommy Dorsey's Orchestra, "Sentimental" became one of Monk's favorites—he recorded it more than any other standard. Nellie made the recording some time in late March or early April 1957, just before he took it into the studio. The first take is painstaking; in five minutes, he gets through just one chorus of the melody. As he wrestles with each measure, every note in his reinterpretation of the melody is carefully placed. By the second take, played rubato (out of tempo), there are more alterations to the melody and increasingly dissonant harmonies. Toward the end of this take, Thelonious begins to integrate stride piano and improvises for the first time. Here he has reached a comfort zone, singing solfeggio and audibly enjoying himself. The fourth, fifth, and sixth takes, which together add up to a little over an hour of continuous playing, are an exercise in discovery. Monk works through a wide range of improvised figures in a fairly systematic way. He repeats certain phrases, making small rhythmic and tonal alterations each time to see how they sound. Each take is successively more adventurous; while still playing stride piano in tempo, his right hand is more off beat, his lines increasingly angular. What is most surprising to serious listeners is that this master of space and economy leaves very little silence between notes and plays nonstop for long stretches. He's listening for different possibilities to construct a tight, "edited" performance.[29]

These eighty-four minutes represents a fraction of what it took to transform "I'm Getting Sentimental Over You" into a Monk original. He rehearsed mostly at Nica's, who had recently moved from the Bolivar to the Algonquin Hotel on West 44th Street. (She also picked up some new wheels to go with her new digs, trading in her '53 Rolls Royce for a silver 1957 Bentley S1 Continental drophead coupe.[30]) Besides Monk, a parade of pianists dropped by constantly, notably Elmo Hope, Bud Powell, Kenny Drew, Horace Silver, Hampton Hawes, Dick Katz, and Sonny Clark. Art Blakey was always there, and "Philly" Joe Jones came by on occasion, as did Charles Mingus and Wilbur Ware. Sonny Rollins and John Coltrane also spent a great deal of time at the Algonquin. Coltrane and Monk had grown quite close, the latter assuming the role of mentor. Coltrane had been playing Monk's tunes as part of Miles Davis's band but wanted to learn more—in particular, "Monk's Mood." So, one night at the Algonquin, Thelonious sat down with 'Trane and taught him "Monk's Mood."[31] Hungry to know more, Coltrane made what became an almost daily pilgrimage to West 63rd Street. He recounted these visits to critic August Blume a year later: "I'd go by [Monk's] house, you know. By his apartment, and get him out of bed maybe. And he'd wake up and go over to the piano and start playing, you know. He'd play anything, like one of his tunes or whatever. He starts playing it, and he'd look at me. I'd get my horn and start trying to find what he's playing, and he tended to play over and over and over and over, and I'd get this far. Next time we'd go over it I'd get another part. He would stop when we came to parts that were pretty difficult. And if I had a lot of trouble, he'd get his portfolio out and I'd see the music, that music, he's got all of them written. And I'd read it and learn. He [believed] a guy learned without music. That way you feel it better. You feel it quicker when you memorize it and you learn it by heart, by ear. . . . When I almost had the tune down, then he would leave, leave me with it to fight with it alone. And he'd go out somewhere, maybe go to the store, or go to bed or something. And I'd just stay there and run over it until I had it pretty well and I'd call him and we'd put it down together. Sometimes we'd just get one tune a day."[32]

All of Monk's work at this point, from his solo explorations at home to his sessions with Coltrane, turned out to be rehearsals for his next Riverside recording sessions. Inspired by Monk's impromptu version of "I Surrender Dear" from the *Brilliant Corners* session, Keepnews proposed a solo piano LP titled *Thelonious Himself*. The entire album was recorded at Reeves Sound Studios in two sessions—April 5 and April 16, 1957. During the first session Monk recorded a few takes of "I Don't Stand a Ghost of a Chance with You," a popular standard from the 1930s made famous by Bing Crosby, and a few takes of "I Should Care," a tune he had recorded for Blue Note almost a decade earlier. Monk closes the session with " 'Round Midnight." Despite having played it countless times, even recording an unaccompanied version three years earlier, he approached the song as if it were a new composition. The result is a probing twenty-two-minute rubato rumination on the theme, full of false starts, unresolved cadences, and unfinished creative journeys. At one point, after failing to execute a difficult passage in the bridge, he stops and says, "Mmmm, I can't do that right, I have to practice that."[33] The master take of " 'Round Midnight" is a distillation of Monk's wanderings and one of his finest examples of solo piano on record.

Two days before returning to Reeves Studios to complete the solo album, Monk drove out to Hackensack to record with Sonny Rollins for Blue Note. It ended up being a wonderful little reunion—Alfred Lion was there and Monk had not seen Van Gelder since Riverside moved its operations to Manhattan. J. J. Johnson was on the date, along with Paul Chambers, Blakey, and pianist Horace Silver. Of the six tracks they recorded that Sunday afternoon, Monk played on two—"Reflections" and "Misterioso." He had previously recorded "Reflections" at a kind of fox trot tempo, but with Rollins Monk transformed it into a sweet ballad. The dynamic interplay between the two artists is striking; they listened to each other with such intensity that they pick up each other's riffs and play back variations. "Misterioso" was a playful experiment. Monk and Silver share piano duties, with Monk backing Rollins and Silver comping behind J. J. Johnson. As they slip on and off the piano bench, neither artist skips a beat.[34]

On Tuesday the 16th, Monk returned to Reeves Studios to finish his album, but this time he invited a couple of guests—John Coltrane and Wilbur Ware, who brought along their instruments. Though it was supposed to be a solo album, Monk invited them for one reason: to record "Monk's Mood." Thelonious liked Coltrane's interpretation enough to put it on record, and Ware's backing was icing on the cake. Monk rounded out the album with four more solo pieces, including a carefully crafted rendition of "I'm Getting Sentimental Over You." He explores Irving Berlin's "All Alone" and revisits "April in Paris." Finally, he includes another new original—a nearly ten-minute, slow, stride blues he called "Functional," about which he famously remarked, "I sound like James P. Johnson."[35] And to a certain degree, he did. He threw in many of the old tickler techniques, reminding listeners that Monk's bent notes, right-hand flourishes, and even clashing harmonies were characteristics of Harlem stride piano—and especially of James P. Johnson's playing.[36]

A few days later, Monk was back at the Café Bohemia with Nica to check out Art Blakey's Jazz Messengers and the Miles Davis quintet. It should have been a joyous evening with friends—his old protégé Jackie McLean was with Blakey, and of course 'Trane, Philly Joe Jones, and Paul Chambers were there, too. But much to Miles's consternation, Philly Joe was nodding off on the bandstand and Coltrane was wrestling with terrible withdrawal symptoms. Coltrane's struggle to break his addiction to junk left him sick, disoriented, sleep-deprived, and thirsty for liquor to ease the pain. By this time Miles was fed up. He not only fired his drummer and saxophonist after the last set but he reportedly punched and slapped Coltrane in a fit of anger. Monk witnessed the assault and tried to intervene. He turned to Coltrane and said, "As much saxophone as you play, you don't have to take that. Why don't you come work for me?"[37]

A generous gesture to be sure, but Monk didn't have a job to offer besides another recording session tentatively scheduled for late June. He still lacked a cabaret card. So Coltrane headed back to Philly to get himself together and play local gigs while Monk continued to scuffle. Bob Reisner, who used to run the Sunday afternoon jam sessions at the Open Door, established another funky spot on Seventh Avenue in the Village called "The Pad." He invited Monk to play solo piano for a night and offered him the "door"—whatever they collected in entrance fees.[38] The place was tiny and the upright piano was in shambles. David Amram, who accompanied Thelonious that night, remembers "the whole middle register [of the piano] was completely shot. . . . It wasn't that it didn't sound good. You pushed the keys down and nothing would happen except a 'clunk,' 'clunk' and no tone. So he played the entire evening with his left hand down at the very bottom of the piano and his right hand up at the very top of the piano, and played a whole incredible night."[39] Because the event was alcohol-free, the room was filled with young people, including a group of high school students from Newark. They approached Monk during the break in total awe, going on about how much they enjoyed his playing and how their parents were fans. Monk dug their energy. In the middle of the conversation, he suddenly said, "C'mon with me," and proceeded to lead the entire group to a little diner up the street and treated them to ice cream.[40] He might have blown a quarter of his take that night.

On the 14th and 15th of May, Monk did a recording date as a sideman with Art Blakey and the Jazz Messengers for Atlantic Records. Thelonious was clearly returning a favor because he did it for scale, which sent Colomby through the roof. Besides the low pay, Colomby was concerned about Monk's contract with Riverside and that no one had made the proper arrangements with the union or with Bill Grauer.[41] Besides helping out an old friend, Monk had good reasons to do the session. It was a chance to reunite with Johnny Griffin and Wilbur Ware, and all but one tune was a Monk composition. Here was another opportunity for the world to hear Thelonious's music, presumably played well.

If the first day of recording was any indication, the session seemed doomed from the start. They attempted to record two songs—"Blue Monk" and "Evidence"—and nearly every take was unsalvageable. Johnny Griffin and trumpeter Bill Hardman struggled with the music. Initially, Thelonious gave them the music, but became so frustrated with their performance that he took it away. According to Blakey, as Monk snatched the lead sheets back he told the band "They would play far better without them because they could hardly play worse."[42] At the same time, Wilbur Ware showed up to the studio stone cold drunk. He never had a chance to play: "We got down to the studio, I go in the bathroom and pass out."[43] Fortunately, James "Spanky" DeBrest, a twenty-year-old bassist out of Philadelphia, was available to fill in.

Things went infinitely better the next day. Monk showed Griffin and Hardman how to play the music, though his criticisms were unremitting. When Hardman asked Monk how he sounded after a particular take, he replied, "You played a whole lot of trumpet to be playin' nothin'."[44] Still, the band completed the album, revisiting "Blue Monk" and "Evidence," and producing strong versions of "I Mean You," "Rhythm-a-ning," and "In Walked Bud." Monk took "Blue Monk" and "I Mean You" at slower than usual tempos, partly as a test of wills between himself and Blakey, whom he sometimes accused of pushing the tempo. (Half-jokingly, Monk told Hardman at the end of the session, "We made a good record—but the drummer couldn't keep time."[45])

In the meantime, Nellie faced a new set of health challenges. She contracted a low-grade fever that persisted for weeks; she lacked energy and could barely keep her weight up. She checked in to Roosevelt Hospital, where she was diagnosed with a thyroid condition that required the removal of her thyroid gland. Geraldine attended to Nellie during her hospital stay, and she remembers the time being particularly stressful. "They were going through a lot of changes then, financial and otherwise. Nellie was on the verge of a nervous breakdown."[46] And so was Monk. Harry Colomby recalled, "Thelonious acted very badly during that period. He wanted to literally take her out of the hospital, take her out of bed and all that stuff. He was just going crazy. He was walking around drunk and dangerous."[47]

Monk had started composing a piece for Nellie just when she fell ill. He worked on it throughout the month of May between home and the Algonquin, and Nica captured a "draft" of it on tape during one of Coltrane's visits.[48] He wanted to call it "Twilight with Nellie," but the Baroness promptly suggested he use the French word for twilight: *crépuscule*. It became his obsession. He conceived of it as a through-composed piece—there would be no improvisation, no variation, just a concise arrangement. "Crepuscule with Nellie" was to be his concerto and he wanted it to be perfect. Driven to mania, he stayed up many nights wrestling with the song's middle or bridge.[49] He was desperate to finish the song because he feared he might lose his precious wife.

A thyroidectomy was no small matter, though the procedure had become a fairly routine treatment for cancer and hyperthyroidism.[50] Perhaps the most disturbing aspect of Nellie's illness was the impact it had on her psychological state. Thyroid dysfunction can produce chronic depression, and the removal of the thyroid tends to worsen matters, causing labile mood swings, confusion, and bouts of melancholy.[51] Nellie went into the hospital on the verge of a breakdown and she came out even more depressed. Instead of returning home, she checked herself into Burke Rehabilitation Hospital in White Plains, New York.[52]

Monk kept tinkering with "Crepuscule" right up to his Riverside record date on June 25. He had stayed up several nights prior stressing over the music and out of sorts in Nellie's absence. He was especially anxious about the session not only because it was to be "Crepuscule"'s debut but because he had recruited his old mentor and hero Coleman Hawkins for the date. Monk and Hawk had not played together in over ten years, though they had remained close.[53] Thelonious also hired Coltrane (as promised), trumpeter Ray Copeland, and Gigi Gryce, who also doubled as arranger for the band. The rhythm section consisted of two of his favorite cats: Blakey and Wilbur Ware. With Blakey showing up over an hour late, Monk's anxiety level was nearing its breaking point. They managed to lay down a complete version of "Crepuscule with Nellie," but at a slightly faster clip than on subsequent recordings, with Blakey's busy drumming overwhelming the sound. The next take begins much like the first, with just Monk and the rhythm section, but it breaks down after the first eight bars, followed by a rapid loss of momentum. Overcome with fatigue, Monk called it quits for the day.[54] Not one to waste precious studio time, Orrin Keepnews asked the band to record an impromptu blues without the pianist. Gryce hastily composed a Basie-ish blues riff, and the result was a thirteen-and-a-half-minute jam session titled "Blues for Tomorrow" that Riverside later issued under Hawkins's name.[55]

Monk returned the next evening rested and ready to play. He brought an arrangement of a song he'd learned as a kid: "Abide with Me." Thelonious adored the melody, which was originally titled "Eventide" by William Henry Monk (no relation). But after Henry Francis Lyte wrote his poem "Abide with Me" from his deathbed in 1847, his words were adapted to William Monk's melody. Thelonious did not know this history, but given his recent scare with Nellie's health, the lyrics resonated with him:

> The darkness deepens; Lord with me abide.
> When other helpers fail and comforts flee,
> Help of the helpless, O abide with me.[56]

He had arranged it for horns only, and the result was fifty-five seconds of pure majesty.

It was a long night of recording for some of Monk's sidemen. The music challenged the musicians, and Thelonious vacillated between being an unforgiving taskmaster and a patient teacher. He warned Ray Copeland that his elaborate runs in the upper register were "impractical" since they did not give him a chance to breathe. He explained to Copeland that a musician "should be flexible on all ranges of his horn."[57] He chastised Gryce for not writing out the horn parts exactly as he had requested. "I felt the musicians would look at the score and figure it was impossible to play. [Monk] was very angry, and he finally got exactly what he wanted."[58] But before he got it, both Hawkins and Coltrane were having trouble reconciling what Monk demanded with what Gryce had written out. When Hawkins asked for some explanation, he got an earful. Art Blakey remembers, "Monk said to Hawk, 'You're the great Coleman Hawkins, right? You're the guy who invented the tenor saxophone, right?' Hawk agreed. Then Monk said to Trane, 'You're the great John Coltrane, right?' Trane blushed, and mumbled, 'Aw . . . I'm not so great.' Then Monk said to both of them, 'You both play saxophone, right?' They nodded. 'Well, the music is on the horn. Between the two of you, you should be able to find it.'"[59]

While the disc has its share of ragged moments, it is nevertheless a display of virtuosity, musicianship, and collaboration. Monk had the band revisit some old gems, including an extended exploration of "Epistrophy," as well as "Off Minor" and "Well, You Needn't," compositions he had not recorded with an ensemble in ten years.[60] Blakey, who was on the original Blue Note recordings, brings even greater fire than he had in 1947. Both songs swing hard, but the eleven-and-a-half-minute "Well, You Needn't" stands out for the way each soloist asserts his individual voice. The master take is infamous for another reason: Monk shouts "Coltrane! Coltrane!" just before his sax solo. Ray Copeland convinced himself years later that 'Trane was nodding off, high on junk, and Monk had to wake him up.[61] The truth is a little more mundane. Monk had not planned out the sequence of soloists, so he was merely letting 'Trane know that he was next. And the recording is evidence that he was poised to play.[62]

Finally, all of Monk's fretting over "Crepuscule with Nellie" paid off. Every part of the song is carefully orchestrated, from the bass counterpoint figures to the voicings to the little fills thrown in at various points. He plays a chorus and a half with just the rhythm section and then adds the horns for the next chorus and a half. The horns are not always together and sound somewhat tentative, but it does not detract from the composition's haunting melody, descending harmonies, rhythmic displacements, and its odd thirty-three-bar structure and five-bar coda. When Nellie finally heard it on record, she smiled.

Keepnews and Grauer knew they had something special. Just a couple of weeks earlier, both *Down Beat* and *Metronome* ran glowing reviews of *Brilliant Corners*, which was released in May. *Down Beat*'s Nat Hentoff not only gave it five stars but called it "Riverside's most important modern LP to date."[63] With *Monk's Music* now in the can, Keepnews and Grauer wanted to strike while the iron was hot, so they turned to their newly established art/marketing department to come up with the right album cover. The staff consisted of designers Harris Lewine and Ken Braren, photographer Paul Weller, and Monk's old friend from his Blue Note days, Paul Bacon. Their first idea was meant to be a wacky play on his name: "They wanted me to pose in a monk's habit, on a pulpit, holding a glass of whiskey," Monk explained. "I told them no. . . . Monks don't even stand in pulpits. Then they wanted to dress me in evening clothes, white tie and all."[64] Monk's refusal took Bacon and his crew by surprise. "It never occurred to us that he would have any objection to it," recalled Bacon. "He was seriously pissed off. It was the only time he was ever mad at me. And he walked away. So Paul Weller and Harris and I looked at each other and said 'What are we going to do?' Not only does he not want to do it, but now he's mad."[65] Monk walked away to another part of the studio where Weller's props lay. He saw a little red wagon and decided to park there for a moment. The image was striking. There was Monk, sporting a clean dark three-button suit, dark tie, crisp white shirt, handkerchief, bamboo-framed sunglasses, and plaid driving cap. Bacon reluctantly asked Monk if it was OK to shoot him sitting in the wagon. Thelonious agreed.[66] "I told them I would pose in a wagon, because I have actually composed while sitting in my kid's wagon on the front sidewalk."[67] To further underscore the point, Thelonious added his own props—his brief case, a sheet of staff paper, and a long pencil.

Even if the designers sought to deliberately play on representations of Monk as "child-like" (reinforced by the lettering chosen to evoke a child's handwriting), Thelonious was too cool, too masculine, and too angry to convey anything but black manhood. The wagon simply became a performance piece, an avant-garde twist. Monk didn't know it, but he was about to become an icon for a new generation of artists, intellectuals, activists, bohemians, and free spirits. Armed with a couple of new albums of original music and a flurry of press, Thelonious was as ready as ever to find his audience. And he found them, gathered together in a tiny bar in the East Village called the Five Spot. Now all he needed was a cabaret card.

18

"My Time for Fame Will Come"

(May 1957–December 1957)

Ⅰn the late spring of 1957, Harry Colomby appealed to the State Liquor Authority once again in an effort to restore Monk's cabaret card. Both Nica and Maely Dufty offered to retain legal assistance, and the lawyer Nica hired succeeded in getting a police hearing. But it was Colomby who filled out the paperwork required by the Liquor Authority.[1] He argued that Thelonious was a drug-free, law-abiding citizen, whose productivity and growing popularity as a recording artist demonstrates his standing as a responsible working musician. Colomby banked on his own position as a white, clean-cut high school teacher, managing him, to turn the tide in Monk's favor. Again, Colomby asked Monk's prominent friends and acquaintances to submit character letters on his behalf. In May 1957, the State Liquor Authority agreed to grant Thelonious a hearing, but only on the condition that a club owner commit to hire him.

"I wanted to find a place that was small," Colomby explained. "I once drove past this place in the Village and there was a bar and I heard music. I went into it and it was the Five Spot. A place where poets hung out." The place was a nondescript Bowery bar at 5 Cooper Square, and the owners were two brothers, Joe and Iggy Termini. "Monk was brought to us by Harry Colomby," Joe Termini concurred. They not only agreed to give Monk a gig, but Joe willingly testified on Monk's behalf at the police hearing.[2] It worked. Once approved, Monk promptly headed down to 56 Worth Street, the Police License Division, where he was fingerprinted, photographed, and relieved of two bucks (the fees went to a retirement fund for cops). He walked out with card number G7321, a license to work, and a job.[3]

On the 4th of July, 1957, Monk began what turned out to be a six-month stay at the Five Spot Café. Working six nights a week, four sets a night, Monk earned $600 a week, $225 of which he kept for himself and the rest he paid his three sidemen.[4] It was his first long-term engagement as a leader and it was his first regular paycheck since working for Coleman Hawkins over a decade earlier. He was now thirty-nine years old.[5]

The story of how Monk came to the Five Spot involves more than a business transaction or Harry Colomby's serendipitous drive through the East Village.[6] The common lore is that Monk single-handedly put the tiny Bowery bar on New York's jazz map. But in truth, the Five Spot had already established its own presence in New York's artistic and cultural landscape. The Terminis' bar had become a gathering place for emerging modern artists and writers, from leading abstract expressionists to the so-called Beat Generation literati, before Monk ever stepped foot on the club's sawdust-covered floors. Rather, it was this world of experimental arts and letters that put *Monk* on a much larger cultural map. They found in Monk's angular sounds and startling sense of freedom a musical parallel or complement to their own experiments on canvas and in verse. In order to understand how this incredible marriage came to be, we need to know how a nondescript Bowery bar became the hangout for America's cultural avant-garde.

For one thing, it wasn't always called the Five Spot. When Salvatore Termini, an enterprising Sicilian born in 1884, purchased the bar in 1937, patrons knew it as the Bowery Café.[7] Situated between East 4th and East 5th Streets, where the Bowery ends and splits off into Third Avenue and Cooper Square, the Bowery Café was one of several small bars hidden in the shadows of the elevated train line known to natives as the Third Avenue El. Salvatore had no illusions about the clientele, a smattering of street drunks and thirsty vagabonds mixed with respectable working-class locals and occasional outlaws.[8] He knew the area well. In 1930, Salvatore lived in a tenement house just off the Bowery, with his wife, Angelina, and five of their six children.[9]

This watering hole was no gold mine, but it enabled Salvatore to put food on the table, purchase a modest home in Brooklyn, and launch a family-run printing business.[10] His two eldest sons, John and Frank, took on financial and administrative responsibilities for both businesses, while Ignatze ("Iggy" for short[11]) worked briefly as a linotype and monotype operator until he enlisted in the U.S. Army Air Force in May 1942. Ten months later, his nineteen-year-old brother Joe followed suit.[12]

Joe and Iggy returned home in 1946 and helped their father run the Bowery Café. Five years later, they assumed ownership of the establishment, now called No. 5 Bar. It continued to thrive as a neighborhood joint, serving the regular drunks who could pay their tab and providing a haven from the winter cold for homeless men. "It was a busy place," Iggy Termini remembered. "We were making a lot of money and it was a busy place. But all people were doing was drinking. . . . I was buying one hundred cases of wine, in gallon bottles, a month, and about thirty barrels of beer a week."[13] Then, in the latter part of 1955, the city decided that the Third Avenue El had seen its last days and embarked on a massive demolition and redevelopment project. The removal of the El brought fresh air, quiet, sunlight, a commitment to "clean up" the Bowery, and a wave of artists and musicians in search of loft spaces and cheaper rents.[14] The Termini brothers responded accordingly, transforming the drab bar into a haven for the new clientele, adorning the walls with posters from various art exhibitions.[15] The bar also attracted some neighborhood musicians, including a pianist and merchant marine named Don Shoemaker. When Shoemaker wasn't at sea, he organized jam sessions in his upstairs studio at 1 Cooper Square, next door to the bar. "They'd be coming down and buying a pitcher, a beer or whatever," Joe Termini recalled. "They were running up and down and all that, so Don Shoemaker says to me, 'Why don't you get a piano and we'll come play here.'"[16] The Terminis liked the idea, so they purchased an old upright and applied for a cabaret license. They received the license August 30, 1956, and a week later opened for business as the Five Spot, the newest jazz club in the Village. Shoemaker and a bass trumpet player named William Dale Wales simply moved the jam sessions downstairs and invited their friends to play.[17] Within weeks of the club's reincarnation, the Five Spot earned a reputation as *the* local place for cheap beer and good music.[18]

Painter Herman Cherry and sculptor David Smith were among the first wave of artist-regulars. They couldn't resist the music, or the seventy-five-cent pitchers of beer. Neither starving nor young, both artists were approaching fifty when they became part of the emerging "East Village" scene. The two men were both early proponents of abstract expressionism and widely respected in the art world. Smith, who split his time between Bolton Landing, New York, and the city, was already in the planning stages of a major retrospective of his work at the Museum of Modern Art.[19] Cherry, who had only recently moved to abstraction and mixed media works, set up a studio on the Bowery just across the street from the Five Spot.[20] They told their friends about the place, and soon the little bar became a coveted gathering spot for New York artists. The regulars included painters Willem de Kooning, Franz Kline, Joan Mitchell, Alfred Leslie, Larry Rivers, Grace Hartigan, Jack Tworkov, Mike Goldberg, Roy Newell, Howard Kanovitz, and writers Jack Kerouac, Ted Joans, Gregory Corso, Allen Ginsberg, Frank O'Hara, among others.[21] Occasionally poets read and artists with musical proficiency seized the bandstand.[22] Helen Tworkov, the club's hat-check girl and daughter of painter Jack Tworkov, put it best: "The Terminis didn't know who the artists or musicians were—the scene was self-made. It wasn't like some entrepreneur said, 'Let's start a jazz club.' It was all underground word of mouth."[23]

During the Five Spot's formative stage, the scene was nearly all-white and mostly male. Amiri Baraka was an early patron when he was still LeRoi Jones, but he didn't arrive in the Village until 1957, not long before Monk started playing there.[24] Ted Joans, an extraordinary poet, painter, sometimes jazz vocalist, sometimes jazz trumpeter, was probably the first black Five Spot regular. While he found the Five Spot friendly and hospitable, the neighborhood was not. "It was dangerous. The Italians did not want any 'spades' in their territory, so we had to be careful. Don't let them catch you with a white woman! I used to carry a blackjack and a napkin filled with hot pepper to throw in their eyes in case I was attacked."[25] When Amiri Baraka joined the community, Joans hipped him to the state of race relations. Baraka took to carrying "a lead pipe in a manila envelope, the envelope under my arm like a good messenger, not intimidated but nevertheless ready."[26] While most working-class residents were hostile to all bohemian artists, "the general resentment the locals felt toward the white bohemians," mused Jones, "was quadrupled at the sight of the black species."[27] There were very few African-Americans in the Village in 1956, though the affordable rents and the rise of the downtown jazz scene paved the way for a substantial migration of black artists.[28]

The Five Spot crowd became a little more diverse soon after David Amram joined the group. He sat in on French horn and began inviting musician friends, many of whom were African-American. One evening in November 1956, he brought a pianist named

Cecil Taylor.[29] Rather small and wiry, bespectacled, all of twenty-seven, Taylor challenged the image of the Negro jazz musician held by much of white bohemia. Raised in a middle-class family on Long Island by a mother who was a classically trained pianist, Taylor was also a poet who read widely in all the arts. He grew up listening to the black dance bands of Ellington, Basie, and Jimmie Lunceford, but, as a student at the New England Conservatory, he studied the works of Schoenberg, Webern, Berg, Bartók, and Stravinsky. His role models were Duke Ellington, Horace Silver, and Thelonious Monk (he recorded "Bemsha Swing" on his first LP), as well as Dave Brubeck and Lennie Tristano.[30] Taylor could hold his own in a conversation, but when he touched the keyboard he had the room under his spell.

"So Cecil sat down and started playing by himself," Amram recalled, "started playing all this incredible stuff—and all the painters, the artists who were sitting there, just suddenly got quiet. Instinctively they knew that this was some other stuff happening, and they were really into it."[31] Taylor's music touched a nerve. It was abstract expressionism in sound. He played with a kind of kinetic energy that can't be contained within a steady beat. Unfortunately, the Terminis' old upright piano wasn't ready for Taylor's brand of freedom. "Joe had a piano that at tops was worth $20," Taylor recounted. "It had no front on it, and the ivory was off some of the keys, but naturally when I played one of the keys broke and one of the hammers flew out and Joe got very upset. That piano was one of the weakest, worst pianos ever conceived by man."[32] According to Amram, when Joe Termini saw keys and hammers flying out of the instrument, he blew up. "He said, 'Don't you bring that guy back, he's going to break my piano! I don't want him ever to play here!' . . . And then the painters said, 'Listen, if you don't let him come back we're not going to come back here anymore.' "[33]

Needless to say, Joe changed his mind. He hired Taylor's trio—bassist Buell Neidlinger and drummer Dennis Charles—to accompany multi-instrumentalist Dick Whitmore, but Whitmore quit after three nights.[34] In turn, the Terminis gave Taylor the gig. He added soprano saxophonist Steve Lackritz (who would soon change his name to Steve Lacy) to the group and they stayed from November 29 through January 3, 1957.[35] The music was dense, complex, dissonant, and thoroughly avant-garde. Three years before Ornette Coleman opened at the Five Spot and shook up the jazz world with his free improvisations, Cecil Taylor introduced the "New Thing" to an appreciative audience. And an appreciative management: for the first time in the sleepy little bar's history, there were lines outside the door. Even the naysayers showed up, if only to offer a critique. And so it was in the winter of 1956 that Cecil Taylor, there only by the insistence of the artists, turned the Five Spot into the city's leading venue for experimental jazz.[36]

In January 1957, David Amram brought a subdued but experimental energy on French horn. He kept drummer Dennis Charles from Taylor's group and hired pianist Valdo Williams.[37] A month into the gig they added John Ore, a twenty-three-year-old bassist from Philly whose résumé included stints with Lester Young, Tiny Grimes, Bud Powell, Elmo Hope, Coleman Hawkins, and a year at Juilliard.[38] For eleven straight weeks, the Terminis kept Amram's band on the payroll, though on most nights the bandstand swelled with guests. Jack Kerouac read with the group every once in a while, and a parade of musicians sat in, including Zoot Sims, Gerry Mulligan, and fellow French hornist Julius Watkins. One night, the entire Woody Herman band showed up to play.[39] When Amram's run ended on March 20, Dale Wales, his wife, singer Jenny McKenzie, and a host of his friends returned for a month. It was the last time the original neighborhood clan would take the stage at the Five Spot. By mid-April Joe Termini, the club's front man in charge of music, decided to limit bookings to noteworthy artists. On April 18, Randy Weston opened with baritone saxophonist Cecil Payne, followed by Charles Mingus and his Jazz Workshop in May, and pianists Mal Waldron and Freddie Redd through June.[40] The Five Spot suddenly attracted nationwide attention. In June photographer Burt Glinn shot a photo spread there for *Esquire* magazine[41]; Steve Allen ran a short segment on the club for the *Tonight Show*[42]; and the patrons who typically hit Café Bohemia and the Vanguard now ventured farther east. In other words, as Amiri Baraka put it, "By the time Monk and Trane got there, The Five Spot was the center of the jazz world!"[43]

Monk's Five Spot gig coincided with the reissue of his Prestige and Blue Note recordings on twelve-inch LPs,[44] as well as the release of *Brilliant Corners*, which earned a glowing review in *Down Beat*.[45] The *Metronome* reviewer was only slightly more reserved, praising *Brilliant Corners* for capturing Monk's unique balance of complexity and simplicity. "This is real Monk; full of all the sometimes incongruous and often primitiveness that is so distinctly his own."[46]

Monk opened on July 4, playing opposite the Cecil Payne/Duke Jordan quartet. In fact, during the first two weeks of the date, Monk used Payne's bassist Michael Mattos, with whom he'd worked before, and a young drummer named Mack Simpkins.[47] While it wasn't his band, Monk was pleased with the results. "I was there for Thelonious's opening night," David Amram remembered, "and he was so excited and so happy, and so full of energy."[48] Nellie, Nica, and Harry Colomby, too, were excited and happy, but given the uncertainty of Monk's condition, they were also cautious and a bit nervous. Thelonious insisted that Nellie accompany him for the first couple of weeks in case he became restless and emotionally off-balance.[49] Colomby was worried more about Thelonious getting caught with drugs and losing his cabaret card again. He also worried about his own reputation: "I could just see the headlines— 'School Teacher Linked to Narcotics Case.' If anything like that happened, I'd be out of a job for good."[50]

On Tuesday night, July 16, Monk brought in his own quartet. Keeping his promise, he hired John Coltrane and called on his favorite bassist Wilbur Ware.[51] His choice on drums was a relative newcomer named Frankie Dunlop. A few weeks earlier, he'd heard Dunlop at a jam session at Connie's in Harlem and loved his sense of swing, his strong and solid backbeat, and the little shuffle rhythms that would become his trademark. Dunlop wasn't exactly a kid. The twenty-eight-year-old had worked with Skippy Williams and toured with Big Jay MacNeely's R&B band, but was based in his hometown of Buffalo. He was drafted by the Army and served some time in Korea, but immediately after his discharge he moved to New York City.[52] When Monk offered Dunlop the job, he had not completed his three-month waiting period and thus, by union rules, wasn't eligible to work except for one-nighters. A couple of days into the gig, the Local 802 union rep showed up and pulled Dunlop off the job. Incensed, Monk asked the union rep, "Can *you* play drums, man?" The rep replied, "What do you mean? I'm not even a drummer. I'm a trumpet player. I haven't touched my horn in 20 years." This only made Thelonious angrier. "Oh, that's a drag, man. You come and mess up my group. Can you swing like he can? . . . You're going to pull the man off who can play drums. *You* can't play. You can't find me anybody who *can* play. Now, who looks stupid? You or me?"[53]

So Monk turned to his old friend Shadow Wilson, who could swing hard with just a snare, bass drum, hi-hat, and ride cymbal.[54] He loved Wilson's drumming, but worried about his heroin addiction. When Monk used him for the early Blue Note sessions, Wilson was clean, but now he had a very bad habit exacerbated by poor health. So Monk's dream band consisted of two heroin addicts—Ware and Wilson—and a recovering addict—Coltrane. Luckily, Shadow's addiction evidently did not affect his work. As Harry Colomby put it, Shadow Wilson was "a very controlled addict. You would have never known he was an addict from his behavior. Always the consummate professional."[55]

Word of Monk's new quartet spread fast. Joe Termini: "Once we hired Monk, all of a sudden the place was crowded every night. And frankly, in the beginning, I just didn't understand what was happening. Of course, after two, three weeks, I was there nodding my head like everybody else. But in the beginning I didn't understand any of it."[56] On weekends, long lines stretched down the block and would-be patrons were turned away because the club could officially seat only seventy-six people—though barring a visit from the fire marshal, they could squeeze in another dozen or so. The Terminis quickly realized that the upright piano they had gotten at the behest of Don Shoemaker was inadequate for an artist of Monk's stature. Joe Termini acknowledged the piano's sad condition: "Hammers were flying off, strings would break." So he asked Thelonious to help them find a new instrument; he chose a Baldwin baby grand.[57]

Critic Dom Cerulli, who was on hand during the second week of the gig, wrote a glowing review for *Down Beat* in which he called Monk's musical ideas "astounding" and praised Coltrane and Ware's solo- and ensemble-playing. More importantly, he noticed the great pride Monk had for his band: "Thelonious was quite excited about his group. . . . They appear to be digging each other, and to be quite intent on building something with the group."[58] "Building" is an apt metaphor. It took a while for the quartet to become a cohesive unit, especially because Monk literally rehearsed on the bandstand. Amiri Baraka, who was there practically every night, is one of the few critics to admit that "opening night [Coltrane] was struggling with *all* the tunes."[59] For Coltrane, every song with Monk was a challenge, even after he felt he had a handle on the music. "You have to be awake all the time. You never know exactly what's going to happen. Rhythmically, for example, Monk creates such tension that it makes horn players *think* instead of falling into regular patterns. He may start a phrase from somewhere you don't expect, and you have to know what to do. And harmonically, he'll go different ways than you'd anticipate. One thing above all that Monk has taught me is not to be afraid to try anything so long as I feel it."[60]

By early August, the band really came together. Nellie's homemade recording of their performance of "Ruby, My Dear" bears this out. Shadow Wilson's brush work is exquisite and Monk plays sparse enough to allow Wilbur Ware's bass to come through. Over Monk's insistent statement of the theme, Coltrane invents a completely different countermelody to produce a beautiful duet.[61] Monk was so pleased with his band, Dom Cerulli observed, "he was out front leading or spurring the soloists fully as often as he was at the keyboard."[62] At first he just moved with the music, his attention focused on the band. His movements eventually became more elaborate, evolving into a peculiar little spinning dance, elbow pumping up and down on each turn, with an occasional stutter step allowing him to glide left and right. He'd danced before—in the recording studio or in private among friends—and in a sense he always danced at the keyboard, stomping his right foot to establish tempo and accenting off-beat phrases with his body. But this was different, and according to both Nellie and Coltrane, it was new.[63] Monk told Coltrane that he got up from the piano because "he wanted to hear the band,"[64] and he couldn't help dancing to his own music. Sometimes he'd dance to the bar, order a drink, and shuffle his way back to the bandstand.

Monk's dancing indirectly affected the music in surprising ways. "He'd leave the stand for a drink or to do his dance," Coltrane explained, "and I could just improvise by myself for fifteen or twenty minutes before he returned."[65] Monk's absence from the piano allowed for experimentation within the ensemble, opening the door for various kinds of collective improvisation. Ware's inventive playing challenged Coltrane in different ways, particularly without Monk leading. "[Ware] plays things that are foreign," Coltrane remarked. "[I]f you didn't know the song, you wouldn't be able to find it. Because he's superimposing things. He's playing around, and under, and over—building tension, so when he comes back to it you feel everything sets in. But usually I know the tunes—I know the changes anyway. So we manage to come out at the end together anyway." [66] Ware found incredible freedom in his pianoless interactions with 'Trane and Wilson. "Monk would get up and we could . . . go outside and inside. . . . [W]e'd take it out [of the song's harmonic structure] as far as we wanted to take it out. . . . Monk come back in, boom. We knew where he's at. We had one chord and we was right back into the thing. . . . The cats would say, 'Man, you play avant-garde.' . . . I didn't look at it like that. I didn't even know the meaning of the word 'avant-garde.'"[67]

The writers and artists in the audience did know its meaning, and they declared virtually every aspect of Monk's performance "avant-garde." Monk's dance, for example, was seen as a spectacular example of modern performance art in an age when expressions of bodily pleasure and excess became central to conceptual art.[68] Fans lined up outside the Five Spot for the music as well as a chance to catch Monk dance and whatever "eccentric" behavior he was rumored to exhibit. Because he perspired profusely, Nellie made huge handkerchiefs out of white sheets, which he used to wipe his face and neck. Sometimes he unfurled the sweat-drenched cloth to air out while he danced.[69]

To Monk as well as to his sidemen, there was nothing strange or eccentric about dancing to music. Nearly all of the musicians who played with him described the dance as his way of letting the band know it was swinging. For Gigi Gryce, dancing was Monk's way of "conducting. It's the way he gets what he wants. At one record date, some of the musicians were laughing as he danced without realizing that meanwhile, by following his rhythmic pulse, they were moving into the rhythm he wanted."[70] "It wasn't a stage presentation," Charlie Rouse explained, "it was how he felt at that moment. . . . When he danced, it meant the thing was swinging, and it made him do that. It was never a 'routine' where someone said, 'Keep that in, it looks good.' It was spontaneous, he often didn't do it."[71] Drummer Ben Riley knew that when Monk did not dance, it often meant the music wasn't happening. When he got up from the piano bench, it meant that "he was feeling good and he knew you knew where you were and the music was swinging and that's what he wanted."[72]

Monk's reasons for dancing were clear and unequivocal: "I get tired sitting down at the piano! That way I can dig the rhythm better."[73] Having grown up in the church and witnessed ecstatic expressions during his travels with an evangelist, dancing was a natural response to the music. He told David Amram as much: "He talked about how the music came from the dance and from the church and being able to dance to it. And of course he did that, he didn't say that in interviews, but I think assumed that by doing that people would understand that this wasn't just something coming out of a bottle of formaldehyde."[74]

The bohemian artists and, especially, the Beat Generation writers and their followers began looking at Monk as a sort of religious or sacred figure, due in part to his evangelical stage presence. Monk's image as a mystic or diviner—the "High Priest of Bebop"—appealed to the Beats. With the death of their musical guru, Charlie Parker, just two years before Monk's "return" to the New York club scene, many of these writers regarded Monk as a towering figure in jazz, akin to being a spiritual leader. In *The Subterraneans* (1958), Jack Kerouac described Monk "sweating leading the generation with his elbow chords, eying the band madly to lead them on, *the monk the saint of bop. . . .*"[75] Several years later, writer Barry Farrell mused that "Monk's name and his mystic utterances . . . made him seem like the ideal Dharma Bum to an audience of hipsters."[76]

The Beats' reverence for Monk and black jazz musicians also partly reflects a larger crisis of masculinity during the 1950s. As Norman Mailer wrote in his controversial essay, "The White Negro" (published in *Dissent* five months after Monk opened at the Five Spot), black men—particularly the hipster and the jazz musician—offered an alternative model of masculinity in the age of the gray flannel suit, suburbia, and other sterile forces. Beat writers often characterized jazz musicians as emotionally driven, uninhibited, strong black men reaching into their souls to create a pure Negro sound.[77] For many, Monk embodied this combination of abstract qualities and unbridled, authentic Negro sound (and an extremely stylish wardrobe to boot). Moreover, even musicians and critics at the time interpreted his dissonant harmonies, startling rhythmic displacements, and swinging tempos as distinctively "masculine."[78] And some critics attributed his music to racial bloodlines rather than intelligence and hard work. Listen to Albert Goldman's paean to Monk: "Monk's brand of thinking comes from the soul and the blood rather than the mind, tapping into a well of racial memory that keeps the music pure, authentic, and black. [N]o matter how gone he gets with his atonal jazz, he never loses a strong racial sound. You see, most of the modern cats are pretty well hung up between jazz and the classical stuff. They all took a little vacation up at Juilliard after the war, and before they got away they were hooked on Bach and Debussy. Now, a man like Monk is good for these cats. He's like some old oil well that keeps pumping up the good black stuff, when all the new rigs have gone dry."[79]

But Monk wasn't always playing the eccentric Negro banging at the keyboard. Monk often surprised. Between sets, he held court in the kitchen, engaging in lively conversations with band members, friends, or the staff. He discussed politics, art, culture, and expressed an interest in jazz poetry readings at the Five Spot.[80] And, despite his reputation for being taciturn or uncommunicative, he occasionally engaged the audience. In one well-worn anecdote, after Monk finished playing an entire set without Coltrane, an audience member shouted, "We wanna hear Coltrane!" Monk replied simply, "Coltrane bust up his horn." After the break, the same heckler repeated his demand to hear Coltrane. Monk, in turn, repeated his reply, at which point the heckler asked, "What do you mean, 'he bust up his horn'?" At which point Monk launched into a full-blown lecture, rising slowly from the piano bench and explaining, "Mr. Coltrane plays a wind instrument. The sound is produced by blowing into it and opening different holes to let air out. Over some of these holes is a felt pad. One of Mr. Coltrane's felt pads has fallen off, and in order for him to get the sound he wants, so that we can make better music for you, he is in the back making a new one. . . . You dig?"[81]

Monk tended to approach the bohemian art world with a sense of humor and curiosity. The regulars remember Monk's hijinks and the laughter. Hettie Jones, writer and wife of LeRoi Jones/Amiri Baraka, once witnessed Monk toting a "furled umbrella, and then laughing at us when we gasped as he pulled out a sword!"[82] Poet-painter Ted Joans used to carry jars of tempera and a pad of drawing paper when he went to the Five Spot. One night, he painted a small portrait of Monk on the bandstand. When Thelonious saw it, he asked, "What's this?"

"That's a portrait of you," Joans replied as he handed the picture to Monk to study. "He was taken by the painting. His eyes were very happy, wonderful." Thelonious then thanked Joans for the painting and proceeded to walk away with it.

"No, no. I'm not giving it to you," Joans said, panicked. Monk turned around, pointed to the image, and asked, "Who is this?"

"It's you."

"You just gave it to me."

"Yes, but I gave it to you just to look at." A bemused look suddenly came over Monk.

"You gave it to me to look at and that's *me* and it's not mine?" This dance went on for a while, until Monk reluctantly returned the painting after Joans promised to do another portrait of him to keep. Joe Termini stepped in and offered to buy the painting as long as *Monk* signed it. Monk agreed and Termini promised never to sell it. Two years later, it ended up in the hands of Ted Wilentz, owner of the Eighth Street Bookshop.[83]

The Termini brothers did not always understand Monk's humor or appreciate his sense of *joie de vivre*. He had the annoying habit of setting his lit cigarette on the piano, and too often he would doze off at the keyboard. Iggy Termini found Monk's onstage dancing strange though harmless. "But sometimes after he was through dancing, he'd wander into the kitchen and start talking to the dishwasher about God knows what."[84] And occasionally he'd wander right out the door. One night, Joe Termini found him a few blocks away staring at the moon. He asked Monk if he was lost. "No, I ain't lost. I'm here," he replied matter-of-factly. "The Five Spot's lost."[85] Despite these behaviors, the Terminis were genuinely fond of Monk. "There was a certain aura about Monk, in those days especially," recalled Joe Termini, "he's supposed to be weird, before he played the piano he faced the East and all that. . . . When I start to tell [people] that Thelonious was a very normal man, loved his family, it turns them around . . . He's a man of dignity. He carried himself well. . . . He wasn't an oddball. . . . All the musicians looked up to him. When he was playing at the Five Spot, almost everybody came to the Five Spot to see him."[86]

The Terminis and Monk did bump heads over one issue: his chronic lateness. Monk would often show up to work two, sometimes three hours late.[87] Nica usually drove him to work, and occasionally Joe Termini had to fetch him from West 63rd Street. "There was a time when I would run up and go get him," Termini explained. "I'd have a full house waiting for him. And they'd all be sitting there waiting. Nobody would walk out."[88] Monk depended on others to drive him because by the summer of 1957, he had abandoned his prized Buick. According to Harry Colomby, Thelonious lost his license after he allegedly nicked a young girl crossing the street. She suffered no injuries, but he was so distraught that he picked her up and drove her to the hospital.[89] Toot tells a very different story. He remembers the car was stolen, but when the police finally retrieved the car, Monk refused to drive it. "He said the vibe changed. There was nothing wrong with that car. . . . Like he forgot about it. Just threw it out of his mind."[90] I cannot confirm either story, but everyone agrees that at some point in the late winter, early spring of 1957, Thelonious parked the car in a lot near the West Side Highway and never drove it again. It was eventually towed away.

When Nica was unavailable, Monk caught a cab or accepted a ride from an adoring fan. One fan who became Monk's accidental chauffeur was eighteen-year-old Bob Lemkowitz. He was in awe of Monk and Coltrane, whom he likened to "Moses and Jesus walking around on that bandstand."[91] He and his friends had joined the faithful, showing up nearly every night and staying through the last set. "Then one night," Lemkowitz recalled, "I'm walking over to my car. It was late, of course. Everything is shut down. And who's standing there, off to the side in front of the Five Spot? It's Monk. I walked over to him and I said, 'Mr. Monk, can I take you somewhere?'" Monk hesitated at first, surprised by the question. But once he saw Lemkowitz's car, Monk agreed and they took off to the upper West Side. When they got to Monk's neighborhood, he asked to be dropped off on the corner. As he was getting out the car, Monk graciously thanked Lemkowitz for the ride and asked if he will see them again. "You bet!" shouted Lemkowitz. For the next few weeks, Lemkowitz began to look for Monk after the final set and drove him home when Nica wasn't there. Monk began calling Lemkowitz "my wheel man" and thanking him with quirky gifts. One night Monk slipped him a green ballpoint pen, another night a yellow crayon. Once he handed Lemkowitz what appeared to be a "carte de visite," or a small photograph on cardstock with two images of William McKinley, with the added explanation: "That's one of our presidents." Perhaps the funniest gift was a miniature replica of a trolley car, adding, "Now you know this isn't a real trolley car. It's a toy trolley car. See, look at the wheels."[92] For Lemkowitz, these small gifts were precious acts of affection and grace infused with a dose of humor. "He didn't appear to be a crazy guy. He was as straight as can be. He had these great one-liners." He once asked Lemkowitz if he had a girlfriend, to which he answered, "No, not really." Befuddled, Monk shot back: "Then who stays in your car when you get out to buy cigarettes?"[93]

Nellie had not seen Monk this happy in quite a while. He enjoyed working, loved his band, finally had money in his pocket, and relished the attention. The Terminis made sure customers knew they were in Monk's house: By the end of the summer, during intermission they played only Monk's LPs.[94] The Five Spot became a big family affair. Monk sometimes brought his underage nieces and nephews to the club and defied anyone to ask them to leave. "Thelonious would come in the middle of the night at Lyman Place and wake up the whole house," Evelyn Smith remembered, "and sometimes we would go to the Five Spot. I remember going with him and Nica. I was about twelve."[95] As soon as they walked in the door, the kids were given the royal treatment. Evelyn's sister Jackie loved how Monk introduced the kids in the family to his colleagues. "He'd bring Coltrane over and say, 'Coltrane, this is my niece Jackie, you need to know her,' or 'Meet my son, Toot. He's an important cat.' It was as if we were the celebrities. Never, 'here is the great John Coltrane' or 'you need to meet the great Bud Powell.' None of that. Imagine how that made us feel."[96] Charlotte Washington remembers feeling very comfortable at the Five Spot. So comfortable that one night she noticed her uncle dozing off at the piano. "So I just walked up to the bandstand, sat right down next to him and put my arm around him. He woke up and started to play again and I just eased my way back to my seat."[97]

Thelonious was in such a good mood that one night in July he snuck out between sets to check out Miles Davis at Café Bohemia and ended up sitting in. Thelonious had Miles in stitches when he started playing with his elbows.[98]

Monk was anxious to record his new band, as was Keepnews who arranged a studio date for late July, possibly early August. The band laid down three incredible tracks—"Nutty," "Ruby, My Dear," and the now-legendary "Trinkle, Tinkle." As brilliant as the session was, it would be four years before these recordings would see the light of day.[99] Coltrane was still under contract with Prestige and Bob Weinstock would not grant him permission to record unless Monk agreed to return the favor. Monk refused. He wanted no dealings with his old label.

Monk returned to Reeves Sound Studios on August 12 and 13 to do another Riverside LP, but not as a leader. When Orrin Keepnews found out that Monk and Gerry Mulligan were tight, he thought a meeting of these two minds would yield great music. Both men originally planned to use Monk's regular rhythm section and record one side with a quartet and the other side with a larger band, but after the first day of recording "I Mean You," "Straight, No Chaser," and an unusually fast version of "Rhythm-a-ning," both artists decided to stick with the quartet format for the rest of the album. Mulligan was anxious to sink his teeth into " 'Round Midnight" and feared that other soloists might get in his way. They rounded out the session with an ethereal version of one of Monk's preferred standards, "Sweet and Lovely," and Mulligan's original "Decidedly," a rather old-fashioned swing tune based on Charlie Shavers's "Undecided."[100]

The date ended on a positive note. Both principals appreciated the chance to play together and felt good about the outcome. And they completed the session in time for Monk and his band to get to the Five Spot.[101] Wilbur Ware arrived early to drop off his bass and pick up a bite to eat, but when it was time to go on, he was nowhere to be found. The Terminis grumbled and Colomby panicked. Knowing Ware's history with drug addiction and remembering the Blakey session where he showed up incapacitated, Colomby didn't expect him to return.[102] And he didn't, but by Ware's account the problem was neither drugs nor alcohol: "I got a tunafish salad [sandwich], ate it, and oh boy, it ate the pit of my stomach and I was sick; so sick I was afraid and I just took a taxi [home]."[103] Ware says that he called a bass player he knew to fill in; Colomby says they found a substitute on their own. Whatever the case, there was a bass player on the stand and he held his own that night. He was a familiar face among the old Five Spot crowd, having performed with both Valdo Williams and Randy Weston before Monk ever stepped foot in the place. Impressed, Monk hired him as his regular bass player. His name was Ahmed Abdul-Malik.[104]

A childhood friend of Randy Weston's, Abdul-Malik first met Monk at a Brooklyn jam session in 1949, the same year he converted to Ahmadiyya Islam and changed his name from Jonathan Timm, Jr. Although he claimed his father was Sudanese, both of his parents hailed from St. Vincent.[105] His father was a fine violinist and started his son on the instrument at age seven. Abdul-Malik went on to study piano, cello, and bass, and after graduating from the High School of Music and Art in Manhattan, he began his professional career as a jazz bassist in 1944 with Fess Williams. Over the next decade he worked with a range of artists, including Art Blakey, Don Byas, Jutta Hipp, Zoot Simms, Coleman Hawkins, and Randy Weston.[106] Weston and Abdul-Malik shared a fascination with the music of North Africa. The two of them would listen to North African musicians play on Atlantic Avenue in Brooklyn and try to play what they heard at local jam sessions. He would instruct Weston to play scales rather than chords and to lay out during his solo so that he could explore pitches on his bass that fall outside the Western tempered scale. "For this we were called rebels," Weston recalled. "We used to catch hell. They thought we were far out."[107] Abdul-Malik studied at the Cairo Oriental Institute of Music in New York, and added the kanoon (72-stringed zither) and the oud (a lute consisting of five double strings) to his repertoire of instruments.[108] When he joined Monk's band, he had just formed his own group dedicated to fusing jazz and North African music.[109]

Because of Abdul-Malik's devotion to Islam and his forays into non-Western music, he and Ware couldn't have been more different. He did not drink or smoke, showed up to work on time, was quiet and focused, and worked extremely hard. He had to learn the music on the bandstand. It took him at least a week to figure out what Monk wanted. Sometimes Monk would stop him in the middle of a song or would play the same song over again in a different tempo until Abdul-Malik got it. "Monk would ask me, 'Are you sure about such and such a tune?' And I'd say, 'Yeah, I'm sure. You know I know, I've been doing this for years.' But when we started playing, I went some place else. He looked at me and said, 'you sure you know [the] number?' I said, 'Well, I really need to check that out.'"[110] Within a couple of weeks, Abdul-Malik sounded as if he had been playing with Monk all of his life.

The summer ended on another high note. On August 25, John S. Wilson published a glowing review of *Brilliant Corners* in the *New York Times*. He called it "one of the clearest expositions of Monkism that we have had. The quirksome dissonances and eccentric rhythms that color his piano work are frequently even more expressive on the quintet's expanded palette. . . . Monk's harmonies sag top-heavily but the disk is strong evidence that this man who was once viewed as an inscrutable eccentric is slowly developing into one of the most valid jazz voices of this decade."[111] Four days later, on August 29, he took a well-deserved, week-long vacation, returning to work on September 5 to a new eight-week contract.[112] That night, Monk celebrated his daughter's fourth birthday, and the following month the Terminis celebrated Monk's fortieth. On Friday night, October 11, they surprised Monk with an impromptu birthday party and a cake big enough to share with the entire audience. Oscar Pettiford, who had since made up with Monk after the trying *Brilliant Corners* session, emceed the event.[113] The usual suspects were there—Nellie, Nica, Colomby—and the house was packed, as usual.

Monk looked forward to a slightly longer break beginning the second week of November. He took the first week off, then headed to Montreal where he and Cecil Payne played a week at Café André with the house rhythm section, bassist Neil Michaund and drummer Billy Graham.[114] He returned to New York just before Thanksgiving and prepared for a concert Ken Karpe was producing at Carnegie Hall on November 29, a fundraiser for the Morningside Community Center. The event was special in many ways; it was Monk's first concert performance since Karpe's Easter Jazz Festival in Town Hall a year and a half earlier; and it was his band's debut on the big stage. The occasion was also gratifying for Monk. The Morningside Community Center in West Harlem reminded him of the community center he grew up in; it served some 4,000 low-income youth, providing a range of social and recreational programs.[115] Monk shared the bill with Billie Holiday, Dizzy Gillespie and his orchestra, Chet Baker and Zoot Sims, and "the brilliant Sonny Rollins." The headliner was Ray Charles, who took great pleasure in revisiting his roots as a jazz musician.[116]

The concert started twenty-five minutes late, which did not augur well for such a full program. Dizzy Gillespie struck up his band before the curtain opened in an effort to calm the restless crowd.[117] Once things got under way, the concert was well worth the wait. Voice of America recorded the show for broadcast, and the tapes reveal just how tight Monk's quartet had become after eighteen weeks of steady work.[118] The group's rapport is astonishing, and Thelonious's playing is full of surprises. "Monk's Mood" is a startlingly beautiful dialogue, with Monk playing sensuous arpeggios underneath Coltrane's interpretation of the theme. The dynamism Shadow Wilson creates for the band is most evident on "Nutty," "Epistrophy," and "Bye-Ya"—in which he demonstrates his ability to evoke Caribbean rhythms. The only standard the band performs is "Sweet and Lovely," and their rendition is like an abstract expressionist painting—Monk paints swirls of color around descending chord progressions. The band played for less than an hour, and Monk was having such a good time at the piano that he hardly got up from the bench. There was no dancing around while Coltrane "strolled" with the rhythm section. Thelonious remained in constant dialogue with the band.

Even if Ray Charles garnered the lion's share of attention that night, Monk came away from Carnegie Hall enormously happy and proud of his band. He returned "home" to the Five Spot triumphant and prepared for the latest challenge—a television appearance on the popular CBS show *The Seven Lively Arts,* to air live on Sunday afternoon, December 8.[119] Organized by critics Whitney Balliett and Nat Hentoff at the behest of producer Robert Herridge, the episode was called "The Sound of Jazz," and it featured Count Basie with an all-star band, Louis Armstrong, Earl "Fatha" Hines, and Billie Holiday. The supporting cast of characters included the most distinguished names in jazz: Coleman Hawkins, Ben Webster, Lester Young, Jo Jones, Roy Eldridge, to name a few. And Monk, of course, was invited to perform in a trio with Ahmed Abdul-Malik and Osie Johnson, the versatile veteran drummer who also backed Billie Holiday in her performance. Three days before the show aired, CBS recorded the various bands at a rehearsal. Monk never made it. According to Hentoff, Monk had lost so much sleep fretting over his performance that he collapsed in a state of exhaustion.[120] We will never know what happened. Mal Waldron, Billie Holiday's accompanist, filled in for Monk with a frenetic solo piano piece appropriately titled "Nervous."[121]

But when it came time to "hit" for the cameras, Thelonious arrived at the Town Theater, aka CBS Studio 58, on 55th Street and Ninth Avenue on time and ready to play. And, as usual, he made a sartorial statement few viewers could forget: He donned a hip plaid jacket, white shirt and tie, a sporty driving cap, bamboo sunglasses, and a pair of Hush Puppies that never stayed still as he pounded out a characteristically angular yet swinging rendition of "Blue Monk." The music was great, but by the time Thelonious got up from the piano he was seething. The producers sat Count Basie against the piano right across from him, and Monk found it distracting. Colomby recalled, "While Monk was doodling around with the piano during a coffee break, the stagehands, cameramen, and everybody who could hear him wandered over to the piano. Then in came Count Basie and Billie Holiday, and Lester Young—all the stars! They gathered around the piano and stared as though they'd been hypnotized, as though it was the first time they'd ever heard anything like that. The director was so impressed by the expressions on their faces that he had Billie and Count and the rest of them stand at the piano when the show went on the air, just so he could televise their reactions while Monk played."[122] On the way home, Monk vowed that the next time Basie had a gig in town, he was going to "sit across the piano and stare at him the whole time."[123]

Besides his three minutes and thirty seconds of fame on "The Sound of Jazz," Monk appeared later that night on "The World of Jazz," John S. Wilson's half-hour radio show on WQXR.[124] Then it was off to work. Monk knew his nights at the Five Spot were numbered. Customers still came but began clamoring for new acts. And the Terminis were growing weary of Monk's regular tardiness. He also worried about his band. Shadow Wilson's health was failing, and he began missing dates.[125] Coltrane was also ready to move on. Miles wanted him back and 'Trane himself was considering a solo career. But the last days of December were not without its highlights, like the night Nat Adderley sat in, or when Monk's brother Thomas showed up with Thomas, Jr., to celebrate his twenty-first birthday.[126] His brother's appearance was unexpected; he was now studying for the ministry as a Jehovah's Witness and avoided nightclubs on principle. "My dad made me drink ginger ale," recalled Thomas, Jr. "I remember standing in the kitchen with Uncle Bubba and my dad, and he was giving Coltrane some kind of lessons. He had a chalkboard and he was writing down music. And then before he walked out on stage, Uncle Bubba turned to my dad and said, "Why don't you go preach to these cats 'cause they don't know what's happening, give them a little boost, a little spirit!"[127]

Perhaps Monk didn't realize that he'd already spent the last half-year preaching to these cats himself and giving them more than a little spirit. With the assistance of brothers Coltrane, Wilson, Ware, and Abdul-Malik, Monk had turned the Five Spot into the hippest monastery in the Western world. But it worked both ways: This tiny little bar in the East Village gave him the boost he needed. It raised his spirit, helped provide sustenance, and positioned him in a community that truly dug his music. The "un" years seemed to be behind him and Nellie, whose health improved, though he'd gladly turn down all the gigs in the world to keep Nellie around.

On December 16, Kenny Dennis took over for Shadow Wilson, whose deteriorating health put him out of commission. Monk himself did not stay much longer; his last night was the day after Christmas. The band continued to work together until New Year's, with Red Garland at the piano in place of Monk.[128] With Monk no longer employed, he was free to celebrate Nellie's and Toot's birthdays on the 27th of December. Nellie turned thirty-seven and Toot was eight years old. And this year Thelonious had money to shower them with gifts. He even treated himself to a new piece of jewelry—a black onyx ring of his own design with the letters MO above NK divided by two medium-sized diamonds. The ring was clunky and it only fit properly when he gained weight, but he adored that ring. He liked pointing out that from his vantage point it read "MONK" but from someone else's vantage point, the letters were upside down and backward and thus spelled KNOW.[129]

It was a fitting conclusion to what turned out to be a very good year. But on December 29, Monk received some terrible news: his friend and former sideman Ernie Henry was dead at forty-one. He had been clean for a year and thought he'd kicked the habit, but then he ran into a couple of old friends coming home on the subway who persuaded him to shoot up. Henry overdosed. Rather than take him to a hospital, the two guys dropped him off at his mother's house, where she found him dead the next morning.[130]

19

"The Police Just Mess with You . . . for Nothing"

(1958)

Monk rang in the New Year without a band, without a job, and without his friend Ernie Henry. He took advantage of his much-needed respite to relax, spend time with the family, and compose. That same month, Nica bid farewell to hotel life and purchased a home of her own at 63 Kingswood Road in Weehawken, New Jersey. Located across the Hudson River just off the Lincoln Tunnel, the modern two-story house had been built in the 1940s by the maverick film director Josef von Sternberg. Known for his collaborations with Marlene Dietrich and for influencing a generation of *film noir* directors, Sternberg also had a long fascination with architecture.[1] In 1935, he had Richard Neutra, one of the pioneers of modernist architecture, build his "mini-mansion" in California's San Fernando Valley, and it remains one of Neutra's most acclaimed works.[2] Although Sternberg's Weehawken house never earned such praise, it possessed a number of impressive features, including huge picture windows on each floor to showcase the spectacular view of the Manhattan skyline. Nica furnished her new home with Thelonious in mind: She put the Steinway upstairs in a large room with a brick fireplace and set up a Ping-Pong table downstairs in the dining room. Monk could rehearse and write in peace and take time out for one of his favorite pastimes. He also had to share the space with her feline friends, which began as a pair of Siamese cats but quickly became a veritable cat colony made up of offspring and rescued strays. At one point the cat population at 63 Kingswood numbered over one hundred, earning Nica's place the title the "Cat House" or the "Cat Pad."[3]

The Cat House became Monk's second home. Sometimes he and Nellie would spend the whole day hanging out there, often in the company of other musicians and friends. During one of his early visits, Nica asked Monk, "If you were given three wishes, to be instantly granted, what would they be?" He gave the question a lot of thought, pacing back and forth in front of the picture window, stopping long enough to gaze out across the river to the New York skyline. A few minutes later, he gave his answer: "To be successful musically"; "To have a happy family"; "To have a crazy friend like you!" Nica replied that he already had these things, but Monk just looked at her and smiled.[4] His point was clear: He was satisfied with life. The critical tide had turned in his favor, and he'd survived those difficult times with his family intact. During his three-and-a-half-year friendship with Nica, both she and Monk remained in each other's corner. He encouraged her to return to her childhood love of painting, and he dared her to enter the annual art contest hosted by ACA Gallery in New York. Her work was selected, along with that of 124 aspiring artists, to be exhibited in a group show.[5] When the show opened in June at ACA on East 57th Street, Thelonious was there to lend his support and good humor.

Monk christened Nica's pad with a composition paying tribute to the breathtaking view. Titled "Coming on the Hudson," it was the first thing he wrote at her Weehawken house. An oddly structured, eighteen-and-a-half-bar theme, it was classic Monk, from the medium/slow tempo and the chromatic harmonic progressions to the three-and-a-half-bar bridge. And its sound was evocative of the movement of boats slowly making their way up and down the Hudson. He recorded "Coming on the Hudson" for Riverside on February 25, soon after he had written it, with a sextet consisting of Johnny Griffin, trumpeter Donald Byrd, baritone saxophonist Pepper Adams, and a rhythm section made up of Wilbur Ware and Philly Joe Jones. This was not the lineup Keepnews and Monk had agreed upon. Blakey was the intended drummer and they planned to pair Sonny Rollins and Griffin, but Keepnews blamed Monk for not contacting them. At the last minute, he called Adams and Jones to substitute. The session turned out to be a near disaster. "Coming on the Hudson" proved to be incredibly challenging for the musicians: Ware complained that the bass part was "impossible to play."[6] Frustrated, Monk called it quits after a couple of takes.[7] Monk was doubly disappointed because he had hoped to hire Rollins as his new tenor player. Rollins had even begun rehearsing with Monk at Nica's house, generating rumors that the pair planned to open at the Five Spot in May.[8]

Thelonious opened at the Village Vanguard in April *without* Rollins. For the first couple of weeks, he led a quintet made up of tenor saxophonist Hank Mobley, Kenny Dorham, Wilbur Ware, and Shadow Wilson. After a two-week hiatus, he returned the first week of May with a quartet playing opposite the Kingston Trio.[9] It was only his second appearance at the Vanguard, his first in ten years. He was supposed to open on April 1, but a dispute between owner Max Gordon and Monk delayed the opening by a day.[10] Monk resisted the Vanguard's policy of Sunday matinees from 4:30 to 7:00 in addition to the regular Sunday night gig. He told Gordon, "Man, I ain't gonna work no seven nights a week—not me."[11] Gordon pushed back, insisting that it was club policy and there were customers who could only make the matinees. In the end, they came up with a compromise: Monk's group played the afternoon and Gordon hired a guest for the evening.[12] The gig turned out to be a real family affair. Nellie showed up and sometimes brought the kids. And it was at the Vanguard that Boo Boo made her debut as a dancer. Toot remembers, "She was dancing on the bandstand at the Vanguard when she was four years old! She was dancing . . . my sister and my father were so in tune it was truly crazy."[13]

Meanwhile, Monk's contract with Riverside was up and had to be renegotiated. That task fell to Colomby, who distrusted Bill Grauer and the label's accounting methods. "I always suspected that something was going on [because] it was so simple to cheat. All you needed was a bunch of pressing plants and different parts and God knows it's like the weapons of mass destruction."[14] He couldn't prove it at the time, but Monk's brisk record sales did not produce what he believed were comparable royalties. On the other hand, Keepnews approached Colomby with suspicion, and when Monk insisted that his manager negotiate on his behalf, Keepnews sometimes turned cold.[15] Nevertheless, the two parties came to an agreement and Colomby's efforts paid off: Monk's advances doubled and his royalty percentage slightly increased.[16]

Before signing the new contract, Monk made one more record for Riverside, but as a sideman for Clark Terry.[17] Also included were Philly Joe Jones and bassist Sam Jones,[18] and the session took place over two days—May 7 and May 12. "I was surprised when he agreed to do the gig with me," Terry reflected. "I thought he would probably say no, but he was happy to, and he was very easy to work with. He had his moments, but he was a beautiful person and I loved him very much. I wrote most of the pieces for the session and when they reissued it some years later, they retitled one of my pieces."[19] Actually, two pieces: "Pea-Eye," a swinging blues Terry originally titled "Zip Co-Ed" as a pun on college women and sex, and the uptempo "In Orbit," the title track Terry had initially called "Globetrotter." With the launching of Sputnik having occurred just a few months earlier, Keepnews and Grauer thought *In Orbit* had more market appeal.[20] The music was happy and incredibly warm, in part because Terry had recently adopted the flugelhorn—an instrument known for its rich, warm tone. Monk left his mark on nearly every tune. Besides recording one of his own compositions, "Let's Cool One," they took the changes from Monk's favorite hymn, "We'll Understand it Better, By and By," and turned it into Terry's "One Foot in the Gutter," enabling Monk to return to his church roots. In his review of the album later that year, John S. Wilson took note of the "rollicking, straightforward manner [Monk] has rarely shown before, giving Mr. Terry close, sympathetic support and galloping off on exuberant solos of his own."[21] Monk's impact was so great, in fact, that it eventually became known as Monk's album—a development that understandably irked Clark Terry: "When Monk died they brought the record out as by Monk with me as a sideman!"[22]

The Terminis offered Thelonious an eight-week engagement at the Five Spot to open on June 12.[23] They were in need of guaranteed revenue, having just opened a second Five Spot in Water Mill, Long Island, to cater to their original clientele of artists who also had studios and homes in the Hamptons.[24] Monk still hoped to hire Rollins, though it seemed unlikely. Rollins had earned critical acclaim for his recent recordings as a leader, including an astounding pianoless trio LP with Wilbur Ware, *Live at the Village Vanguard*, and he had just recorded his much anticipated *Freedom Suite* for Riverside. But Rollins's reverence for Monk was such that he continued to keep the door open in case his schedule freed up. In the meantime, Monk hired another favored tenor player, Johnny Griffin, backed by Ahmed Abdul-Malik and the fabulous Roy Haynes on drums.[25]

Monk had put together another dream band, and while Coltrane wasn't part of it, the group played to a full house most weekend nights.[26] Although Griffin had performed with Monk many times, he never had the opportunity to learn his entire repertoire. His first few weeks on the job were reminiscent of Coltrane's. "We rehearsed on the bandstand," Griffin explained. "[Monk] wouldn't pull his music out, and the joint would be loaded, every night. He had it in his briefcase, but he said it would be better if I heard it. So he would play the melody and I'm supposed to retain the melody after he played the first chorus, and I was supposed to play the second chorus coming in with the melody! So you can imagine what happened. I'd mess up, and he'd say 'No, no, no, let's do it again.' And the people loved it. You know what? I never felt embarrassed."[27] He may not have been embarrassed, but by the end of the night he was thoroughly exhausted. "I found it difficult at times, I mean, DIFFICULT. I enjoyed playing with him, enjoying playing his music, but when I'm playing my solos, for instance, the way his comping is so strong, playing his own music, that it's almost like you're in a padded cell. I mean, trying to express yourself, because his music, with him comping, is so overwhelming, like it's almost like you're trying to break out of a room made of marshmallows."[28] Like Coltrane, Griffin enjoyed those long moments when Monk left the piano to dance around or air out his gigantic, sweat-soaked handkerchiefs, or rambled to the bar for a drink. Sometimes he would even encourage Monk to leave the piano by calling "strollers." He thrived on the space and found that when he soloed over Monk's accompaniment he felt too confined. "Any deviation, one note off, and you sound like you're playing another tune, and you're not paying attention to what's going on. And it's so evident. . . . There's no space."[29] Once they mastered the repertoire and the band really jelled, however, Thelonious occasionally called familiar standards, such as Dizzy Gillespie's "A Night in Tunisia," in order to change things up and give Griffin a respite.[30]

Keepnews captured the quartet live at the Five Spot, recording two separate nights of music. On July 9, Keepnews recorded two sets of music, which included a version of "Bye-Ya" with Art Blakey sitting in, a funky little blues Monk composed in honor of the club titled "Blues Five Spot," and an unaccompanied original Monk would call "Dreamland." "Dreamland" is a bit of a mystery. It is an old-fashioned ballad that sounds as though it could have been written in the 1920s. Monk never copyrighted it, rarely performed it, and only recorded it once thirteen years later.[31] He never spoke about it nor explained whether it was just an old song or his own composition. In the end, Monk wasn't satisfied with the recording and refused to grant Riverside permission to release it.[32] (Keepnews eventually released these recordings after Monk died.[33]) Keepnews returned on August 7 and recorded enough music to make up two albums. Subsequently released as *Thelonious in Action* and *Misterioso*, the music was lively and exciting. Haynes set rather swift tempos compared to most other Monk outings, and once Griffin achieved mastery over a tune, he played with a kind of revelry that belied his complaints. Monk complemented Griffin's lengthy improvised excursions with concise, well-balanced solos.

That summer the Terminis promoted the original Five Spot as the "home of Thelonious Monk." The jazz world knew this implicitly, and anyone who wanted a glimpse of the man made his or her way to Cooper Square. One man's pilgrimage began in Africa by way of Chicago. On an especially warm night in July, a handsome, stately black man in his mid-thirties approached Thelonious for an autograph as he was sitting at the bar between sets. The man had a slight accent and sported a West African kofi hat and dark shades. "I'm one of your admirers," he said. After Thelonious signed his book, the man quietly withdrew to his seat. The next day, the man called Orrin Keepnews to request a meeting with Monk so that he could present him with a gift he had brought from his native country of Ghana. Keepnews was a bit skeptical at first, but when he called the Monk household and explained that a Mr. Guy Warren from Ghana would like to pay a visit, Nellie replied, "Oh, Thelonious knows about him and wants to meet him."[34]

Monk had been hearing about Guy Warren from Wilbur Ware and Johnny Griffin for a couple of years now. In fact, Monk and Warren played the same benefit for Chicago's Vaughan Hospital back in December of 1955, though they never met. Warren arrived in Chicago around December of 1954, and in a matter of months had become a sensation. The Windy City had never experienced anything like him: a bona fide West African who played a mean drum kit but also mastered traditional instruments like the "talking drum" and the djembe. Lionel Hampton wanted to take him on tour. Duke Ellington hired him for a few gigs. He even played with Dizzy. More importantly, Warren had gained some notoriety with his debut LP, *Africa Speaks, America Answers!* Released on the Decca label in 1957, it was the first serious effort to fuse jazz and traditional African music.[35] Born in Accra, Ghana, in 1923 (back when it was still a British colony known as the Gold Coast), Warren fell in love with jazz as a small child and learned to play drums in school. At fifteen, he began playing highlife (popular West African dance music) in local bands, and earned a scholarship to Achimota College—the colony's prestigious performing arts school. During the 1940s, he traveled briefly to the United States and spent nearly three years in England, where he became a principal member of Kenny Graham and the Afro-Cubists, playing calypso, highlife, mambo, as well as jazz.[36]

After almost three years in Chicago, he set out for the Big Apple in the early part of 1958. He put together a trio playing his own original compositions and performed regularly at the African Room on Third Avenue. Then in May, just weeks before he caught Monk at the Five Spot, he recorded his second LP, this time for RCA/Victor. Called *Themes for African Drums*, the album featured the great trombonist Lawrence Brown from Ellington's band, vibist Earl Griffith, and the sensational African-American percussionist Chief Bey.[37] The album includes a piece titled "The Talking Drum Looks Ahead," in which he improvises a blues using the talking drum (an instrument whereby a player can change the pitch by squeezing the sides of the drum and striking it with a bent stick). Warren dedicated the song "to my idol Thelonious Monk."[38]

Guy showed up on Monk's doorstep loaded down with gifts. He carried an elegant carving of Sasabonsam, the Ashanti god of the forest, a copy of *Africa Speaks, America Answers*, and an early pressing of his latest recording, *Themes for African Drums*. Monk and Warren talked quite a bit about music, but Monk would not put on Guy's record at first. He read the liner notes and expressed some skepticism. Warren recalled, "He wanted me to feel that there was nothing new. That everything in jazz had been said."[39] Once Monk did listen to Warren's music, he let him know right away that he "realized the new contribution I was bringing to jazz." In fact, according to Warren, Monk liked his music so much that he borrowed the melody from "The Talking Drum Looks Ahead" and recorded a slightly altered, slower version as a solo piano piece less than a year later. He titled it "Bluehawk," as a tribute to Coleman Hawkins and the Blackhawk club in San Francisco, but it could also be heard as a sly nod to the Ghanaian drummer.[40]

Monk and Nellie once visited Guy at his apartment on 110th Street. He had an old battered piano and they jammed together, but Monk was challenged by Warren's rhythmic approach. "I was playing my rhythms, but he said he would lose his concentration because my rhythm would dominate what he was doing," recalled Warren.[41] The music never jelled, and Warren's dream of performing with his idol never happened, but Monk did come to admire him as a musician and a friend. Warren called Monk "his Grace," and Nellie became "Nelly-O," and young Barbara became obsessed with *Themes for African Drums*. When Warren announced that he was returning home in August—he had not visited Ghana since it won independence the previous year—he offered to take Thelonious with him. "His Grace wanted to go. At one time he told Nelly-O that he was coming to live with me and he would stop running around and going on tours and all that. And Nelly-O talked to me and I said, sure he can come and stay with me. But then again Nelly-O says, 'You know how he is. I have to take care of him. His clothing, his food, his this and that. And you are a single man and you can't do that so let's not work on that.'"[42] A couple of years later, Warren sent Monk another gift: a beautiful, wide-brimmed straw hat from Northern Ghana. Observers would mistakenly call it Monk's "Chinese" hat, but Thelonious took special delight in the fact that it was from Africa. "I'll never forget when he got that package," Toot recalled. "You have to understand, Thelonious never opened mail. My mother opened mail, then me or my sister, but never my dad. But when that package came from Africa, he opened it himself, and I'll never forget the smell. It smelled like Africa; it was so fresh and clean and pure. The hat was beautiful."[43]

The summer of 1958 was busier than ever. Besides his regular Five Spot gig, Monk performed at the Newport Jazz Festival during the Fourth of July weekend. While it was the first time George Wein had invited Monk to Newport since his 1955 performance with Miles Davis, and his first appearance as a leader, Thelonious was still considered small potatoes. Monk's name was not mentioned in print ads promoting the festival, and he was granted a fifteen-minute Sunday afternoon slot. The festival paid only for a trio, and rather than employ Ahmed Abdul-Malik they assigned a talented twenty-three-year-old bassist from Philadelphia named Henry Grimes. Grimes served as the unofficial house bassist for the festival, performing that weekend with Benny Goodman's big band, Sonny Rollins, Lee Konitz, and Tony Scott. Monk used his fifteen minutes to great effect, playing renditions of "Just You, Just Me," "Blue Monk," "Well, You Needn't," and " 'Round Midnight"—as if to remind Newport fans who really owned that song.[44]

Thanks to fashion photographer-turned-filmmaker Bert Stern, a brief segment of Monk's already brief performance was caught on the highly acclaimed documentary

Jazz on a Summer's Day. Although it would be nearly two years before its theatrical release, the film not only radically altered the look of concert films, with its rich color, candid shots of audiences and scenery, avant-garde editing, and utter rejection of narration and interviews, it contributed to the iconization of certain musicians, notably Anita O'Day, Mahalia Jackson, and one Thelonious Sphere Monk.[45] Monk appears on screen for about thirty seconds wailing away on "Blue Monk," then suddenly the camera cuts away to shots of sailboats in the bay competing in the 1958 America's Cup Trials. Even the announcer's voice cuts into the performance, temporarily turning Monk's piano into background music for the yacht race.[46] And yet, it is precisely the quirkiness of the scene that reinforced for an international audience the image of Monk as an eccentric figure. Monk had no clue the film would become a runaway success, but he was pleased to know that Stern planned to pay him a couple of hundred bucks for his appearance.[47]

The following month, Monk was invited to play the New York Jazz Festival at Randall's Island. The festival, which took place August 22 and 23 at Downing Stadium in the middle of the East River, was in its third year of existence. Monk's name was included in the ads and press releases, but as the featured artist with Art Blakey's Jazz Messengers.[48] Monk did share the billing with Blakey, as well as Miles Davis, Chris Connor, the Modern Jazz Quartet, Dave Brubeck, Anita O'Day, Jimmy Giuffre, and Sonny Rollins, but Monk brought his own quartet: Griffin, Haynes, and Abdul-Malik. *New York Times* critic John S. Wilson was there and found Monk in a particularly "jaunty" mood, praising the pianist for achieving "a high level of outgoing, communicative playing that was a far cry from the widely held conception of Mr. Monk as a dour, brooding musician. Still, this is part of what one may normally expect from Mr. Monk . . ."[49]

Two major concerts, a nice run at the Vanguard, and a long engagement at the Five Spot, and no reports of the "dour" Monk. Wilson's observations were prescient; audiences began to expect the "jaunty" Monk, the joyous and humorous Monk. Real or imagined, there was a perceived shift in Monk's mood. He was getting the recognition that had eluded him for so long. In fact, several days before the Randalls Island gig, the latest issue of *Down Beat* appeared, announcing the winners of the annual International Critics Poll. There, in the "Best Pianist" category, perched above Erroll Garner, Oscar Peterson, and Earl Hines, was the High Priest of Bebop himself.[50] Winning a *Down Beat* poll, or any magazine poll for that matter, was certainly a first for Monk. And it proved to be quite an upset. The happy and upbeat Garner had been a long-time favorite among musicians and critics, noted for his melodic style and ability to swing. Peterson's astounding facility earned him the imprimatur as Art Tatum's heir apparent. Monk's rise marked a sea change in how the critics *heard* his music—the music he had been playing for the last fifteen years.

The poll results had hardly registered when Monk received a call from Bob Altschuler, the publicity director for Riverside Records, asking him to participate in an historic photo shoot for *Esquire* magazine. The magazine wanted Art Kane to produce a photograph to illustrate a special issue devoted to "The Golden Age of Jazz." Kane ambitiously called together all the major jazz musicians he could think of to pose for a group picture in Harlem. The musicians were instructed to show up on 126th Street by 10:00 a.m. Knowing Monk's reputation for lateness, Altschuler decided to personally pick him up the morning of the shoot. Altschuler arrived by cab with Gigi Gryce and sat outside Monk's apartment waiting for him. "I was not on a big generous expense account. The meter kept running, of course. . . . And we kept waiting and waiting, and finally, after about an hour and ten minutes—I was concerned we were going to miss the photograph."[51] When Monk finally emerged, he was sporting a bright yellow sports jacket, a sharp brim, and his signature bamboo-frame sunglasses. He politely apologized for being late but never explained what took so long. Later, Altschuler pulled Gryce aside to find out what happened and learned that "Monk wanted to ensure that he would be seen, and he had to think about what he was going to wear." Realizing that most musicians would wear dark suits, he decided on a light-colored jacket in order to stand out in the crowd.[52]

And crowd it was: fifty-six other musicians showed up, many of whom were genuine living legends: Basie, Roy Eldridge, Luckey Roberts, Lester Young, Jimmy Rushing. For Monk and everyone else, the photo shoot was more like an old family reunion. Besides seeing his old boss Coleman Hawkins and his long-time pal Mary Lou Williams, Monk stood with Blakey, Dizzy, Wilbur Ware, Mingus, Rollins, Sahib Shihab, Johnny Griffin, and Gerry Mulligan, among others. Taking stock of the scene, Monk took one extra precaution to make sure the wandering eye can find him in the picture. He parked himself next to the only two women in the photo besides Maxine Sullivan: fellow pianists Mary Lou Williams and Marian McPartland.[53]

Suddenly, everyone wanted a piece of Monk. Harry Colomby received a telegram in August that sent shivers down his spine: "INTERESTED IN THELONIOUS MONK MUSIC. STOP. FOR MOVIE . . ."[54] It was from Marcel Romano, the music director for celebrated filmmaker Roger Vadim. Known for the controversial and highly acclaimed *And God Created Woman* (1956), launching the film career of Brigitte Bardot (whom he'd recently divorced), Vadim had just agreed to adapt the once-scandalous eighteenth-century novel, *Les liaisons dangereuses*, to the big screen. Romano was responsible for the soundtrack and he wanted Monk.[55] He first met Thelonious at the Five Spot in the late summer of 1957, during one of his sojourns to New York.[56] Colomby was thrilled. He knew that scoring films offered a good source of income and could provide a broader audience for Monk's music. And Romano had a reputation for working with jazz musicians, having just hired Miles Davis to score Louis Malle's *Ascenseur pour l'échafaud*.[57] They wanted him to come to France to record the soundtrack, so Colomby began talking to booking agents to see if they could arrange a European tour for October. Colomby didn't get very far, but the rumor mill did: In late August *Down Beat* reported that Monk was scheduled to tour Europe with Sonny Rollins and Johnny Griffin.[58]

Colomby decided it was time to hire a publicist, so he approached Ivan Black, a Five Spot regular who also wrote press releases for the club. Black was a veteran, having begun his career as the publicist for Café Society. Before that, the Harvard graduate wrote art and theater criticism and had done some corporate publicity work, but the radical-at-heart decided to devote his energies to promoting jazz musicians and other struggling artists. Besides Monk, Ivan Black's stable of clients would include Sonny Rollins, Ornette Coleman, Charles Mingus, Herbie Mann, Miriam Makeba, and Odetta.[59]

Ivan Black had barely begun the job when *Down Beat* magazine came knocking on Monk's door hoping to do a feature on their latest poll winner. The idea for the piece initially came from Frank London Brown, the young singer who had sat in with Monk at Chicago's Beige Room nine years earlier. Now a thirty-year-old writer, Brown wasn't your typical jazz critic or journalist. He had just won the prestigious John Hay Whitney Award for creative writing and had completed a novel titled *Trumbull Park*, about several black families who integrated an all-white public housing project in a Chicago suburb.[60] Slated for publication in 1959, Brown's novel focused on the struggle for community, solidarity, even dignity in the midst of physical and psychological terror. It was a story Brown knew well, having been part of the group of black activists who desegregated Trumbull Park. Indeed, Brown's writing was an extension of his activism. Born in Kansas City but raised on Chicago's Southside, after graduating from Roosevelt University in 1951, Brown worked as a machinist, unionized textile workers, was active in the NAACP, and traveled to Sumner, Mississippi, to cover the Emmett Till trial as a reporter for the *Chicago Defender*.[61]

Brown was passionate about Monk's music. He had told *Sepia* magazine that listening to Monk influenced his writing. "[Monk] shows a daring in execution in his work that I have admired since I was 17. I try to emulate his music by writing in a jazz-oriented language."[62] And in a letter to Ivan Black, he explained that he had been writing "lyrics and short stories to be accompanied by the compositions of Thelonious Monk" and hoped he might collaborate with Monk at the Five Spot.[63] (Brown had established a weekly "Readings in Jazz" series at the Gate of Horn that summer, where he read short stories to live jazz, and he had even sent Ivan Black a taped recording of one of his readings.[64]) Unfortunately, the proposed collaboration never happened.

Brown and his new bride, Evelyn, arrived in New York in early September. He spent several days speaking with Nellie, Harry Colomby, friends, neighbors, the local bartender, and of course Monk himself. Perhaps because they knew each other, Monk felt comfortable enough to conduct part of the interview lying in bed.[65] Brown's manner was disarming, and elicited some surprisingly personal reflections. He impressed Monk as a regular, honest cat, not the fawning type but someone who was self-possessed and not afraid to speak his mind. Brown's sensitivity and attention to detail resulted in the most thorough profile on the pianist published to date. Monk comes across as proud, hard-working, family-oriented, and fair-minded. His stoic persona and allegedly reclusive personality is presented as little more than a performance—at best, an act of self-protection. As Monk famously put it to Brown, "You know people have tried to put me off as being crazy. Sometimes it's to your advantage for people to think you're crazy."[66] Nellie made a point of Monk's pride and sense of humor, dimensions of Monk that the public never saw. For his part, Colomby demolished the myth that Monk was undependable by pointing out that his insistence on fair pay and decent working conditions had resulted in a subtle kind of blacklisting.

Overall, Monk appreciated the article and found it to be truthful, though years later he complained about one quote in particular. At one point in their conversation, he tells Brown, "My music is not a social comment on discrimination or poverty or the like. I would have written the same way even if I had not been a Negro."[67] While the veracity of the statement is beyond doubt, Monk is clearly responding to a question or set of questions dear to Brown. As a black writer and activist committed to social justice at a critical juncture in the black freedom movement, Brown wanted to know Monk's thoughts about the plight of the Negro. It wasn't an unreasonable question, especially in light of the proliferation of political statements by jazz musicians during the era. Unfortunately, Monk's words would come back to haunt him, turning what was clearly a defense of artistry into a complete rejection of politics.

Meanwhile, Bill Grauer and Orrin Keepnews sensed that Monk's star was rising. In 1958, they decided to rerelease some of Monk's earlier LPs in stereo, but with radically different album covers. Beginning with *The Unique Thelonious Monk*, the first trio sessions Riverside put out in 1955, they decided to create a Thelonious Monk postage stamp as a way of recognizing his importance while poking fun at hero worship. They converted the photo to make it look like an engraving, and the price of thirty-three and one-third cents was a clever reference to the LP.[68] As a publicity stunt, however, Riverside printed faux stamps to promote the album, but when customers mistakenly (or deliberately) used them for postage, the U.S. Postal Service issued a restraining order against Riverside.[69] Most of the redesigns, however, replaced Monk's image with twentieth-century works of art—a deliberate effort to reach the kind of bohemian, intellectual audiences that patronized places like the Five Spot.[70] For the rerelease of *Monk Plays Ellington*, designers Paul Bacon and Harris Lewine selected Henri Rousseau's painting *Repast of the Lion,* because it reminded them of Ellington and his "jungle music" in the 1930s.[71] Later in the year, they released the first of Monk's live recordings from the Five Spot with Giorgio de Chirico's *The Seer* gracing the cover.[72] It was an ideal choice. *The Seer* paid tribute to poet and Surrealist icon Arthur Rimbaud, who called on the artist to be a seer in order to plumb the depths of the unconscious in the quest for clairvoyance. The one-eyed figure represented the visionary; the architectural forms and the placement of the chalkboard evoked the unity of art and science—a perfect symbol for an artist whose music has been called "mathematical."[73]

To many of the young patrons who lined up outside the Five Spot six nights a week, Monk was indeed the "Seer." When Monk was on the stand, the club was holy ground. He got to be so popular that the Terminis sometimes had to turn away customers. Of course, not every patron was a fan. His growing celebrity status and mainstream appeal produced a backlash from some of the self-appointed jazz police. One night, critic Robert A. Perlongo overheard a conversation between a rather belligerent guy and a young woman whom he was trying to impress:

"He's had it," a man behind us announced.

"The pianist, you mean?" said the girl with him.

"Yah, Monk. He went out with bebop, that stuff."

"Really?"

"Sure," said the man. "He hasn't done anything in years. Not since with Bird."[74]

While it is true that his repertoire rarely strayed beyond a dozen or so songs, patrons were treated to more than a few surprises. Like the night after the Randall's Island festival when Sahib Shihab substituted for Griffin, or Thursday, September 11, when John Coltrane did the same. Fortunately, 'Trane's wife, Naima, brought the family tape recorder to the club.[75] Only five tunes survive, however, and they were Monk chestnuts Coltrane knew in his sleep, such as "In Walked Bud," "I Mean You," and the treacherous "Trinkle Tinkle." Coltrane sounds like he never left the band, though this might be expected since he continued to rehearse with Monk at Nica's house throughout the spring and summer.[76] His playing here is strong, confident, and particularly bold when Monk "strolls" from the piano. Roy Haynes, with his signature snare and hi-hat, lights a fire under him, generating a level of frenetic energy missing from Shadow Wilson's accompaniment.[77]

One of the biggest surprises, however, occurred about a week later when Johnny Griffin left the band permanently and Sonny Rollins stepped in. Griffin enjoyed the gig but he couldn't make ends meet. "I had to make some money," he explained to me, "and I couldn't make no money at the Five Spot. The only one making money at the Five Spot was Thelonious. It wasn't a large club, it was small, so there wasn't that much money to go around. And I had a family, I had to see about them."[78] Griffin had arranged for Rollins to take his place—a dream come true for Thelonious. Rollins accepted the sideman gig only because he loved playing with Thelonious.[79] They spent twelve beautiful nights together at the Five Spot and performed one benefit concert at Carnegie Hall to help launch Mary Lou Williams's Bel Canto Foundation, founded to assist struggling, mainly drug-addicted musicians.[80] A varied group of artists came out in support of Williams's efforts, ranging from Randy Weston and Henry Red Allen to Lambert, Hendricks, and Ross. Coincidentally, Les Jazz Modes was also on the roster, giving Monk yet another chance to hear and see Charlie Rouse. It was a fortuitous encounter. Rollins had already given notice, having committed to playing the inaugural Monterey Jazz Festival the weekend of October 3, and he had suggested Rouse as a possible replacement.[81]

Monk's choice of Rouse surprised some, and disappointed many young saxophonists gunning for the slot. Nellie recalls fielding dozens of phone calls from players interested in working for her husband, including one call from a talented newcomer named Wayne Shorter.[82] But Rouse was the ideal choice for a number of reasons. Monk and Rouse had worked together before and had been acquainted for over a decade. Rouse was not only an excellent musician but he had the kind of personality Monk liked. David Amram described him as "kind of like Ernie Henry—very warm, devoted, and loving person. He loved music, and was also a consummate player."[83] He also came with a long résumé, having played with Billy Eckstine, Dizzy Gillespie, Tadd Dameron, Fats Navarro, Duke Ellington, and Count Basie—all before he turned twenty-six! Throughout the 1950s, he was everybody's sideman and played on dozens of record dates—from Clifford Brown to Eddie Cleanhead Vinson, Bennie Green to Bull Moose Jackson.[84] By the time he joined Monk, Rouse was a seasoned veteran familiar with a wide range of styles and approaches to music.

There was another way in which he resembled Henry, and for that matter Shadow Wilson: Rouse had a habit. He was using heroin when he joined the band, but he kept it under control and rarely did his addiction affect his work. Rouse was never comfortable with his condition, and he had already begun to make strides to break his habit. It would be a few years before he completely quit.[85] His manager, Princess Orelia Benskina, was instrumental in Rouse's efforts to redirect his life. The Panamanian-born dancer was eight years Rouse's senior, and had established a name as a leading proponent of African and Afro-Cuban dance. She worked in a duo with "Cuban Pete" or Pedro, and in the 1940s was a member of Asadata Dafora's dance troupe. More significantly, she was a practitioner of West African divination. In 1956 she was ordained into the "Spiritual Healers Fellowship" and owned and operated a *botanica*. Despite a life in nightclubs and theaters, she found a way to be spiritually grounded and to help others in need— including Rouse. She tried to "heal" Rouse of his drug addiction and keep him centered, and whenever he needed money or a place to stay, she was always generous.[86]

The sacred and spiritual worlds were not new to Rouse. Like Monk, he had North Carolina roots. Although he was born in West Virginia on April 6, 1924, both of his parents, William and Mary Bell Rouse, hailed from the furniture-manufacturing town of Lenoir, North Carolina.[87] Childhood sweethearts, they married young, and William worked in a sawmill for a couple of years before becoming a coal miner in West Virginia. By the late 1920s, the family headed to Washington, D.C., where Williams secured a federal job and Mary Bell took in laundry. By the time Charlie was six years old, the Rouses owned their home in a stable black working-class neighborhood.[88] Charlie's neighborhood running buddy was a boy named Warren Hester, the son of Bill Hester, a musician and leader of the popular local dance band called the Bluebirds. Charlie, who lived a couple of doors down from the Hesters, loved to sit beneath their window with Warren and listen to the Bluebirds rehearse. When Bill was out at his day job as a chauffeur, Warren and Charlie used to sneak into their band room and try to play the instruments. They were eventually caught and punished, but Charlie was already hooked. He started on saxophone in junior high school, played drums in various neighborhood bands, fooled around with a clarinet his mother bought him, and tried his hand at trumpet ("I liked Louis Armstrong").[89] By the time he enrolled in high school, he excelled in music and athletics—like Monk. During his senior year, he starred on the football team, went to school, and began playing regularly at the Crystal Cavern in D.C. with pianist John Malachi, bassist Tommy Potter, and Osie Johnson on drums. It got to be too much, so he quit football and focused solely on music, joining the Eckstine band not long after graduation.[90]

Despite having played with Monk before, Rouse was a bit overwhelmed at first. He opened the night of October 2 with very little rehearsal time. They had practiced briefly at Nica's house, but most of those rehearsals took place a couple of days into the gig, usually after the last set, and lasted until late the next morning.[91] "We rehearsed when Thelonious felt like rehearsing," Rouse explained. "He would teach me one or two tunes a night, usually just one. He would play it for me, then get up and walk around the house while I practiced it. It might seem that he wasn't listening, but he was, and when I got the melody down and started to turn it around, he come upstairs and say, 'Okay, let's play it.'"[92] As was Monk's custom, Rouse had to learn the music by ear, though he did write out some of the more difficult songs such as "Trinkle Tinkle" or "Four in One." "Sometimes he might say or write out the chord changes but on some tunes he wanted you to figure them out."[93] And just like all the tenor players before Rouse, he had to figure the songs out on the bandstand. Monk had no playlist, and Rouse never knew what his new boss was going to play until he started playing it: "The first chorus might sound like spaghetti until I got it. He didn't stop though, he just kept going."[94] He quickly learned how to simultaneously take direction from Monk while being self-directed. "Playing with Thelonious you can't wait and let him guide you; you got to be there yourself. Or he'll throw you off just like that. You have to realize that when he comps he's playing with the rhythm section, and playing with you too. During a tune, if he feels he wants you to play more, he won't tell you, he'll do a certain thing that'll drop you right in, so you got to take another chorus!"[95] And each chorus had to be strong. He let Rouse know right away that "you're not playing with a French horn now. You're out there alone."[96]

Thelonious really wanted to hear what the band sounded like, so on Rouse's first or second night he had Nica bring her portable reel-to-reel to the club. The surviving tapes not only reveal a somewhat nervous but energetic Rouse struggling with the music, they provide early evidence of the kind of rapport he and Monk would establish over the coming years.[97] On "Rhythm-a-ning," which Haynes sets at a fairly swift tempo, Rouse seems comfortable playing off the changes of "I Got Rhythm," especially after Monk leaves the piano. When Monk returns, he picks up on the last phrase Rouse plays and builds on it, turning it upside down, extending it further, until it becomes his own phrase and he takes off into his characteristic Monkian solo. Monk's elaboration of Rouse's final phrases would become a common characteristic of their uncanny musical relationship. Rouse struggles with "Epistrophy." He navigates the chromatic chord movement by borrowing a few licks from Coltrane. Rouse, like everyone else, had been listening to the way Coltrane developed a vertical approach to Monk's music, elaborating and extending chords rather than building a solo off the melody. He does the same thing on "Off Minor," once again taking a page from the book of John Coltrane. Rouse tries to match the drummer's fast tempo with a blur of eighth and sixteenth notes outlining the chords. He ends up repeating a few phrases, as if he were short of ideas, while Monk constantly restates the theme behind him. In fact, Monk steps away from the piano for only fourteen bars—less than half a chorus—and when he comes back to solo, he reinforces the melody with deliberately incomplete phrases and abstract lines.

After the set, Monk probably gave Rouse the same advice he'd given other sidemen: "If you know the melody you can make a better solo." Later Rouse related the lesson that Monk composed with the idea that musicians build on the melody, not the chord changes. "He thought if you practiced the changes themselves, you'd play the chords as such and he didn't want to hear that. He wanted you to experiment. He wanted you to be as free as possible and not be boxed in by playing from the chords."[98]

Thelonious was pleased with his new acquisition, and Rouse was happy to have steady work. Rouse not only had his habit to deal with, he had a young son from his marriage to Esperanza Rouse—a marriage that had nearly dissolved by the time he joined Monk. But his personal battles did not seem to affect his performance. Within a couple of weeks, the band had settled into a nice groove and demonstrated to the skeptics that they lost none of their luster without Coltrane, Rollins, or Griffin. Monk worked his birthday weekend and then took a week off from the Five Spot to play the Comedy Club in Baltimore. The band was scheduled to open Tuesday night, October 15. Nellie had planned to drive down to Baltimore with Monk but had to cancel at the last minute, so Nica volunteered. Just before noon, she picked up Monk and Rouse in the Bentley and headed south. "Thelonious was having one of his bad days—silent, sweating, and miserable. Finally he spoke up. 'Could we stop somewhere for a cold drink, a beer, a glass of water, anything?'"[99] Having just crossed the Delaware Memorial Bridge on Route 40, Nica decided to stop at the Park Plaza Motel in New Castle, Delaware.[100] Around 1:00, they pulled up in front of the motel and Thelonious went inside to get something to drink. Rouse was asleep in the backseat and Nica sat behind the wheel. "As Thelonious walked towards the entrance, it occurred to me that maybe I should have gone with him."[101]

Her presence would not have made matters better. It never occurred to her that Jim Crow still prevailed in Delaware.[102] No one was behind the front desk when Thelonious entered the motel. He noticed the kitchen off to the side and saw a woman washing dishes, so by his own account he walked in and asked her for some water. The woman turned out to be Mrs. Tonge, the owner's wife. She claimed he simply stared at her and said nothing.[103] Startled, she demanded that Monk leave immediately. She never actually said they don't serve Negroes, but it was clear in her response that they had no intention of catering to him. In the meantime, Mr. Harold Tonge called the police, who arrived in minutes.[104] "As I got out of the car to find out what happened," Nica reported years later, "a jeep drove up, ground to a halt, and two cops dashed up the steps."[105] There are conflicting reports as to what happened next. According to court documents the state troopers tried to question Monk, but he refused to speak. Nica intervened and explained to the officers that he was sick, so they physically escorted Monk out without arresting him. By this time, Rouse was wide awake and taking everything in. A white woman and two black men driving around in a $19,000 Bentley was enough to pique the troopers' suspicions. As soon as they left the parking lot and headed toward Route 40, the same state troopers pulled them over and ordered Thelonious out of the car. Again, Monk refused, but this time he spoke, asking Officer H. Thomas Little, "Why the hell should I?" Little had called for backup, so now several troopers "appeared in patrol cars with handcuffs and weapons."[106] According to Nica, "Thelonious was so mad, he wouldn't move. He took hold of the car door . . . and couldn't be budged until one cop started beating on his hands with a billy club, his pianist's hands."[107] Nica jumped out of the car and pleaded with the police not to hit Thelonious because he was ill, but her protests were ignored and they proceeded to beat him mercilessly with night sticks. He was finally dragged to the ground, handcuffed behind his back, and thrown on the floor of a patrol car. Monk kept fighting back by pushing the door open with his feet, so several officers continued to pummel him while he lay handcuffed. They beat him severely, ripping his red tie off his neck in the fracas.[108]

The troopers placed Monk in custody and ordered Nica and Rouse to follow them to the magistrate's office, though they had not been arrested for anything. They were held for questioning and detained for quite a while without charge. Indeed, over two hours had passed before the police searched Nica's pocketbook and the trunk of the car, where they allegedly found a bottle of pills and a small amount of marijuana in her luggage. They never obtained a search warrant, nor had they read Nica her rights. The trace amount of reefer was all they needed to charge both Nica and Rouse with possession of narcotics. Thus with Magistrate Samuel J. Hatton presiding, all three were brought into the courtroom to be indicted. Thelonious was extremely agitated and, though still handcuffed, hit the officer who held him in custody. He also refused to cooperate. "Monk didn't back down," observed Rouse. "If he thinks he's right, he sticks by what he thinks. He stood there and defied the judge. If they told him to sit down, he stood up. If they told him to say something, he said nothing."[109] Hatton angrily called for order and then added a second count of assault and battery on a police officer, along with the charges of breach of the peace, resisting arrest, and narcotics possession. Bail was set at $5,300, and he had to pay a $14.50 fine for breach of the peace. Nica and Rouse were also fined for breach of the peace and charged with narcotics possession, and bail was set at $5,000 each. Nica had to post $15,300 for their release.[110]

They never made it to Baltimore.[111] Instead, they high-tailed it back to New York City. The *New York Post* carried a story about the arrest the very next day,[112] and the police did not hesitate to suspend Thelonious's cabaret card, even though he had not been convicted of anything and had yet to stand trial. The whole ordeal sent him spiraling into a deep depression. For days, he couldn't sleep and he lost his appetite. He, Rouse, and Nica were scheduled to return to New Castle on October 21 to face charges, but Thelonious had a severe breakdown at Penn Station and was taken to Rivercrest Sanitarium in Long Island City for psychiatric treatment.[113] Attorneys Joseph Delaney and Dudley Warren represented Nica, while Monk and Rouse retained the distinguished attorney Theophilus Nix—only the second African-American lawyer to be admitted to the Delaware bar.[114] Judge Hatton was patently hostile to Nix. Because no court stenographer was assigned to the hearing, Nix asked to use a recording device. Hatton tried to block it, but Nix had already received permission from a higher court. They clashed over other issues as well. Both attorneys wanted to bar the press, but the judge refused. Most importantly, Nix wanted the narcotics charge dismissed because the police conducted an illegal search and seizure of the car. He wanted all charges against his clients dropped, including the two counts of assault and battery, and saw no reason for Monk to appear in court. Hatton refused to drop the charges and ordered the case be bound over to the Court of Common Pleas.[115] Monk eventually pleaded guilty to breach of peace and assault and battery, and was fined $123.50, but the possession charges against him and Rouse were dropped.[116] Nica, however, remained free on bail while she waited for a trial date. She felt that her future hung in the balance.[117]

Meanwhile, Monk stayed in the hospital throughout much of November.[118] Ironically, while he struggled to come to terms with his treatment at the hands of the Delaware police, a flurry of articles appeared celebrating his international importance. Frank London Brown's feature article for *Down Beat* hit the stands just days after Monk's arrest, and a few weeks later, *Down Beat* critics selected Thelonious's LP *Monk's Music* one of the five best albums of the year.[119] Jazz Standard Music Publishing Company released a book of transcribed Monk piano solos under the title, *Thelonious Monk's Piano Originals: Revealing Instincts of the Genius of Jazz.*[120] And in the November issue of *Jazz Review*, critic and composer Gunther Schuller published an extraordinary essay evaluating Monk's complete recorded works, from the Minton's tapes to his most recent Riverside discs. He concluded his lengthy essay praising Monk's originality. "[I]n these times of standardization and bland conformism we should be grateful that there are still talents such as Thelonious Monk who remain slightly enigmatic and wonderful to some of us."[121]

But under the circumstances, no tribute album, book, article, or critics poll in the world could help him. The NYPD stripped him of his right to work for a *third* time.[122] Nellie could not handle caring for Thelonious, working, and taking care of the kids, so she sent them off to stay with their aunt Marion in Queens. Marion had just bought a house in a new subdivision—so new, in fact, that there were only three completed homes on the block. Toot, who was entering third grade, remembers the neighborhood being so small that "they didn't have a school building." Instead, he and Boo Boo attended a kind of parochial "one-room schoolhouse" with a heavy emphasis on religious instruction.[123]

Monk got out of the hospital in time to play Town Hall just after Thanksgiving, one year after his triumphant concert with 'Trane at Carnegie Hall.[124] Sharing the bill with Miles Davis, Gerry Mulligan, and Jimmy Giuffre, Monk's quartet had lost some of its luster as far as critic John S. Wilson was concerned. He praised Monk for being "the most individual" of all the leaders, though he placed the blame for the quartet's failings squarely on Rouse's shoulders. Describing Rouse as "a far less exhilarating performer than his predecessor, Johnny Griffin," he suggested that his lack of a strong musical personality rendered the group "more placid . . . than it once was."[125]

Monk had to wonder if his moment in the sun was over. If so, his fears were quickly allayed when Colomby called with the news that the CBS television show *The Twentieth Century* wanted to film Monk's band at the Five Spot. Hosted by Walter Cronkite, *The Twentieth Century* was a prime-time half-hour documentary program that aired on Sunday nights. Relying mostly on archival footage, the program was designed to examine important historical events, but twice a year it aired a one-hour special meant to examine more contemporary issues. These one-hour specials were produced by Stephen Fleischman, a former Communist still sympathetic to the Left who somehow dodged the worst of McCarthyism. Fleischman had already produced a couple of controversial episodes, including an exposé of prison conditions in America.[126] Now he set out to explore the culture and attitude of college students—the generation narrator Walter Cronkite labeled "the most baffling in our history." Calling it "Generation Without a Cause," the bulk of the segment was devoted to interviews with white students at Rutgers University who described themselves as conformists concerned about marriage, family, home ownership, and obtaining a good job. Fleischman then wanted to juxtapose the "typical" college student with the "Beat generation," young people whose posture was one of political detachment but engagement with matters of art and culture. Jazz was their music and the Five Spot their hangout.[127]

Monk must have found the filming itself rather baffling. CBS bused in about eighty-odd students from Rutgers who filed into the Five Spot around 8:00 a.m.[128] They were almost entirely white and very preppy—indeed, when the camera pans the room the first time all we see are white faces. As Harry Colomby put it, "They looked like an advertising agent put them together. All white. They politely applauded. It was like the beginning of political correctness."[129] Although the students sat attentively, smoking cigarettes, drinking beer, nodding their heads silently to Monk's "Rhythm-a-ning," they did not look like the usual Five Spot crowd. Missing was the club's famous diversity of race, age, and status.[130] The band looked exhausted if not uninterested, probably because they had been up all night. At one point, the director had a young man come on the bandstand and read some bad poetry ("Sometimes, I'm really convinced/we are sterile dishes/watching with ever beginning patience/ germs/to see if they will grow") while Monk played a rather somber rendition of "Pannonica."[131]

Monk had gone six years without a cabaret card after being prosecuted for a crime he did not commit. And now the NYPD held him hostage again, but this time for what they considered an especially egregious violation: assaulting a fellow officer. As the holiday season approached, the future felt uncertain. He didn't work in December and had nothing lined up for January. Then Harry Colomby and his brother Jules approached Monk with an enticing proposition: a concert at Town Hall featuring Monk's music for big band. Jules, along with promoter Marc Smilow, would produce the concert and Riverside could record it. Thelonious loved the idea. He had not heard his music in a big band context since his days with Dizzy Gillespie's band. But before he could do anything, he needed the right arrangements and a band good enough to play them.

20

"Make Sure Them Tempos Are Right"

(January 1959–October 1959)

"As for writing for full orchestra," Monk confessed in 1956, "I've done that years back for all kinds of pieces. I haven't been doing it because I'm not the kind of person who likes to arrange, and they don't pay enough for arrangements anyway."[1] So he needed to find an arranger. He wanted someone who not only possessed a deep knowledge of his music, but who knew how to make a big band sound like a small ensemble. Jules and Thelonious both agreed that Hall Overton, now a Juilliard faculty member, was the best man for the job. During their nearly five-year acquaintance, Monk had grown especially fond of Overton, in part because he considered Hall one of the few people who genuinely understood his music. In 1957, when Ira Gitler suggested that some musicians found Monk's music too difficult to play, Monk replied, "It's not hard. Ask Hall Overton, he'll tell you."[2] When Jules approached Overton about the project, he was delighted to accept.

They began meeting in late January, early February at Overton's loft on Sixth Avenue, near the corner of 28th Street in the heart of New York City's flower district.[3] Monk knew the place well; the dilapidated fifth-floor walk-up had been a popular musicians' hangout since the mid-1950s. Hall, painter David X. Young, and pianist-arranger Dick Cary had moved into the building in 1954.[4] Young transformed the fifth floor into an artist's studio, Cary leased the third floor and installed his own Steinway, and Overton occupied the fourth floor and added two upright pianos he placed side by side.[5] Soon Overton and Cary began hosting impromptu jam sessions that attracted musicians from around the city, in spite of the building's squalid conditions. Harry Colomby still remembers the startling transition from Sixth Avenue, where the fragrance of flowers overwhelmed the senses, to the smell of "cat piss and dead rats . . . the odor was just horrific."[6] As Young recalled when he first moved in, "There were mice, rats, and cockroaches all over. You had to keep cats around to help fend them off. Conditions were beyond miserable."[7] Like Ken Karpe's loft space on the East Side, Young's place had become legendary for its early morning jam sessions.[8] Virtually everyone passed through there: Charles Mingus, Zoot Sims, Teddy Charles, Jimmy Giuffre, Roy Haynes, Gerry Mulligan, Bill Evans, Bob Brookmeyer, Stan Getz, Art Blakey, Miles Davis, Art Farmer, Gigi Gryce, Oscar Pettiford, Sonny Rollins, Lee Konitz—among others.

Early in 1957, Overton sublet part of his sublet to photographer W. Eugene Smith.[9] He was a celebrated photographer who had recently left *Life* magazine in order to create a massive photo essay of his hometown of Pittsburgh. With the support of grants, he took some 13,000 images and selected the very best for the essay, but failed to come to an agreement with either *Life* or *Look* magazines. Broke, dejected, and suffering from manic depression exacerbated by heavy drinking and benzedrine, Smith took refuge in the loft and its musical culture.[10] Like David X. Young, Smith loved jazz. He was also an audiophile as obsessed with capturing life and history on tape as he was with celluloid. He wired the place with microphones and constantly ran his reel-to-reel recorder. As a result, he not only documented these incredible jam sessions at the loft but the entire scoring and rehearsal process leading up to Monk's Town Hall concert.[11] Thanks to Smith, we can eavesdrop on Monk and Hall's process of collaboration, and destroy the myth that Hall single-handedly arranged the music while Monk spun around in his own world.

The earliest meetings proved both productive and painstaking. Monk insisted that Overton transcribe his songs directly from the piano. They would sit together at the two instruments and Monk would patiently teach Overton each song, bar by bar, note by note. Monk had lead sheets, but would not share them. Sometimes, he would play just the chords with the specific voicings and bass lines, all the while indicating what instrument should play which phrases or notes. On "Thelonious," Monk provided Hall with a precise delineation of his harmonies, movement, and rhythm. They spent at least fifteen minutes on the first two bars alone, all the while explaining how the song should sound, what notes ought to be there and how the overtones are meant to suggest the key of B$^\flat$ throughout the song.[12] On "Monk's Mood," for example, it took Overton— an excellent pianist in his own right—forty minutes to get through one chorus. Monk was exacting. He even showed Overton how to create a "ringing" note, in this case D natural, by holding down the key until it fades out while playing other notes. When he finally got through the song, he indirectly paid Overton a compliment: "I don't think I ever heard anybody play it, you know. You don't hear a song, you know, like you like to hear somebody else play it. Hear how it sound, you know."[13] Once Overton got the basics, Monk often got up from the piano bench and either paced or danced around, barking out instructions and answering questions, often into the wee hours of the morning.[14]

What becomes clear from all these tapes is that Monk is in charge. He knows what he wants and feels quite comfortable directing, if not actually teaching, Professor Hall Overton. And Monk could wax philosophical. He expounded upon the use of the introduction: "[Y]ou gotta have an introduction? Sometime it sound better when you just start right out. Just start swinging right away. Then you don't bring no lull. Introduction could put you in one kinda mood, you dig? Then you get in another kinda mood when you come on the melody."[15] He talked about how he projects harmony in the melodic line: "When I'm playing the piano, I'm not playing no chords there. I play the melody within them." And he gave little lessons in fingering, composition, structure, sound, how to reach an audience, and how to tell a story with music. Overton, for his part, listened patiently and respectfully.[16]

The work was hard and some sessions were especially difficult. One night, Overton proposed writing background lines in order to get more instruments involved and this seemed to annoy Thelonious, who wanted less harmonic density and more emphasis on rhythm.

> Monk: I do things according to what the drummer, what they're doing
> at the time.
> Hall: I know you do . . .
> Monk: The horn is blowing according to what the drummer's playing,
> you know?
> Hall: Are you opposed to that? In other words, to . . .
> Monk: No, I'm not opposed to that. I've done it many times myself.
> Hall: If you like the idea, I'd like to get some things down.

Hall continued to talk, asking Monk for ideas about the order of solos, which ultimately pushed Monk to the point of silence. Finally, Monk responded, "My mind ain't working tonight. I can't think of shit. . . . Next time we get together, it might be working. I just woke up."[17]

Most of the sessions were relaxed and full of humor. Thelonious, in particular, cracked everyone up with one-liners and colorful remarks. Listen:

> Monk: On "Crepuscule with Nellie," all we need is about two choruses on
> that, and we'll end up everything on that or something. End the set
> with that. There ain't too much you can do with that.
> Hall: How do you want to do that Monk?
> Monk: I'll play the first chorus, let the band come in for the second cho-
> rus. Then we get up and get our bread and quit. [LAUGHTER][18]

On another occasion, while working on the bridge to "Thelonious," Monk sang along as Overton voiced the chords. Suddenly Monk stopped and said, "You threw a funny note in there, you didn't mean it."

> Hall: I didn't mean it, it was a goof.
> Monk: It sound all right, though.

The room broke up in laughter.[19]

The most exciting sessions, however, were those in which either Monk or Overton had an epiphany or a musical breakthrough—like the night they decided to have Overton transcribe Monk's entire piano solo on his 1952 version of "Little Rootie Tootie" and score it for the band. It would prove to be the big band's best performance and

Overton's best-known Monk arrangement. The story begins at the keyboard, with Hall struggling with "Little Rootie Tootie" and Thelonious suggesting that he listen to the record to get it right. Overton puts the record on and they listen intently. When the song ends, Monk suddenly declares, "Have the band play the whole thing, you know. The whole thing like it is!" Hall agrees, fueling Monk's enthusiasm. Thelonious then goes on to tell Overton to "take off the solo just like that. And the places where there is harmony, you put harmony. And unison, you know? Put harmony in those little places. You know. It gives it that free sound, sounds free. I'll tell you, playing harmony all the way through makes it sound stiff."[20]

As soon as they had three solid arrangements and sketches of other pieces together, Monk decided it was time to rehearse. Overton made suggestions for band members, but the final decision was Monk's. The rhythm section was comprised of his new quartet—drummer Art Taylor, whom Monk mentored when he was still a kid in Harlem, and bassist Sam Jones. Of course, Charlie Rouse himself was part of the band, and his fellow saxophonists included alto player Phil Woods and Pepper Adams on baritone. In fact, Monk favored low-toned instruments for the ensemble, a decision for which he would be criticized.[21] The brass section consisted of trombonist Eddie Bert, Donald Byrd on trumpet, and Jay McAllister on tuba. David Amram was originally tapped to play French horn, but he had an out-of-town commitment. "It broke my heart," Amram reported. "I believe I was doing a film score, one of my few, and I couldn't get back."[22] Instead he suggested twenty-four-year-old Bob Northern. When Monk and Overton hired him, he had just completed his studies at the Vienna Academy of Music and was beating the pavement for a symphony orchestra gig. "It was hard for black musicians just to find out about auditions," he recalled. He welcomed the call from Overton.[23] "I didn't hesitate. . . . This was an occasion that nobody wanted to miss."[24]

Except for McAllister, Northern, and Woods, Monk had performed or recorded with every other member of the band. Although Thelonious respected the band, he also knew the music was difficult and he planned for two weeks of rehearsal to prepare for the Town Hall concert, scheduled for February 28. He believed they needed to learn only one song a day. "Don't make no sense working on a gang of songs if you don't play nothing right," he told Overton. "I've seen cats bring a whole group down and they run the book down like they playing on a job, and they still don't know shit. Nobody still can't play nothing. Now if they take one arrangement and run that down and learn that. One a day. . . . Let everyone take their time to learn it. Everybody don't have to be showing how fast they can read. Sight read. Take one bar."[25]

Before rehearsals began in earnest, Monk was scheduled to perform at the Chicago Civic Opera House on Valentine's Day. His new quartet—Rouse, Sam Jones, and Art Taylor—shared the stage with Sarah Vaughan, Gerry Mulligan's quartet, and Miles Davis's sextet as part of "New Jazz at the Opera House." Ken Joffe and Don Friedman, co-producers of the New York Jazz Festival, put the package together and planned for a national tour. Whatever the prospects, it was much-needed work for Monk, a much-needed break from his work with Overton, and an opportunity to hear his new band on a concert stage.[26] Nellie came along, allowing them at least a few moments to cel-ebrate Valentine's Day. The concert was a success, drawing about 3,000 people between the two scheduled shows.[27]

Monk wasn't anxious to return. When Frank London Brown, who was working on another story about Monk for *Ebony* magazine, invited Thelonious and Nellie to extend their stay in Chicago as his house guests, they readily agreed. "We were living in the projects, in the Lowden Homes, on West 95th Street," recalled Brown's widow, Eve-lyn Colbert. "But they didn't mind. We gave up our bedroom and Monk stayed in bed just about the whole time. He didn't come out. I would make dinner and breakfast and Nellie would bring him his food. So for two days or so, we didn't see him." Frank would go in and sit with Monk and shoot the breeze or gather more material for his article. Nellie rarely left him alone in the room. When she did come out to get his food, Nellie would make polite conversation with Evelyn. "She was very, very nice, very friendly."[28]

Monk started rehearsing the big band as soon as he returned. As he had promised, they worked on one tune a day, sometimes taking an hour or so to master the first few bars of a song. "It was tremendous, tedious rehearsing," Art Taylor recalled. "By the time I finished rehearsing, I forgot everything I did. . . . Nothing came easy." He was not alone. He remembered that just about everyone in the band struggled with the music.[29] Eddie Bert thought the arrangements "really captured Monk's sound" but were "hard to play at that time . . . unorthodox. I mean, you were playing piano music on your instrument. . . . But it came out."[30] The rehearsal schedule was pretty grueling, sometimes beginning around 3:00 a.m. and continuing until 7:00 a.m. Robert North-ern often went straight from rehearsal to his job as a school teacher in the Bronx.[31] The musicians were willing to put in time on the promise that a three-week tour would follow the concert. Pepper Adams was told that a concert tour "in fact was part of the package that I was approached with initially, when I was asked to play in this band for Town Hall."[32] Jules Colomby and Marc Smilow were supposed to organize it and Riv-erside Records, rumor had it, committed to underwrite the tour.

Monk proved to be a relentless taskmaster with a very clear sense of what he wanted. On "Crepuscule with Nellie," for example, he insisted that the band pay attention to dynamics. In the fifth measure of the B-section, Monk tells them, "the last two notes are louder still, until the last one is loud as you can blow." But on the next take, he chided trumpeter Donald Byrd for going a little overboard. He said, "Eh, uh, Donald Byrd, don't play too loud, you dig? Don't play it so loud so it sounds like you're play-ing by yourself."[33] He was especially hard on Byrd, who was only twenty-six at the time. On the last day of rehearsal, after playing through "Friday the Thirteenth," Monk criticized Byrd for soloing just on the chord changes. Slightly annoyed, Byrd wanted to know what he should be playing. Monk gently berated him: "You forgot all about the melody. Forgot how the melody went." He essentially repeated his oft-cited mantra: If you know the melody, you make a better solo.[34]

Most of the tapes capture Monk at the piano playing with the band. Although they were still trying to tighten up sections of "Off Minor" and "Little Rootie Tootie" the day before the concert, Monk sounded as if he really enjoyed playing with and against the band.[35] He did not simply go through the motions; rather, he crafted innovative solos and found ways to comp behind the band that propelled the rhythm. Often he got up from the bench and danced while Overton played piano and gave directions. Band members might have thought he was disengaged from the process, but those who knew him well knew that dancing was his way to feel and even display the rhythm. Northern remembered struggling with "Little Rootie Tootie" until Monk called a five-minute break, "walked into the corner of the loft and danced my whole part, note by note. . . . I watched his feet. . . . He called us back together and I played it perfectly after I watched him. That's the kind of teacher he was."[36] Eddie Bert recalled how Monk would "be dancing half the time. Hall would say, 'Well, when do you want to play the piano?' Hall would be playing the piano and Monk would be dancing in the other room saying, 'Make sure them tempos are right.'"[37] By the time the last rehearsal ended on the 27th, the band wasn't perfect but they got the tempos right.

The night of the concert was electric. Signs adorned the area around Town Hall, Broadway and 43rd Street, bright orange, black, and blue posters projecting Monk's silhouette—slick driving cap, bamboo glasses, goatee. Eight-thirty arrived and about 1,100 of Town Hall's 1,500 seats had been filled. Billed as "An Evening with Thelonious Monk," all of the major jazz critics, writers, and musicians were there, along with "a goodly crowd of young adults of both sexes, all of serious mien."[38] Photographers were everywhere. The folks who mattered most to Monk were there, too—Nellie, Sonny and Geraldine, Thomas, Marion, and some of his nieces and nephews—many of them now young adults. Monk was ready to hit, right at 8:30, but before the band could come out, critic Martin Williams, co-editor of *Jazz Review*, gave a few pre-concert remarks. He spoke longer than Monk would have liked, but the audience remained patient, attentive, and quite serious.[39]

When it was time, Monk and his quartet appeared on stage impeccably dressed in dark suits, crisp white shirts, and ties. The folks who had not seen him since the Five Spot may have noticed that he had gained a little weight and his hair was beginning to thin. The quartet opened the concert with a swinging, loping version of "Blue Monk," followed by "Straight, No Chaser," "In Walked Bud," " 'Round Midnight," and closing the set with "Rhythm-a-ning." It was standard Monk fare, tried-and-true songs that had been in circulation several years. While the band jelled pretty well, the piano was the dominant force, the glue that held everything together.[40] The audience greeted each number with enthusiastic applause. Following a short intermission, Monk appeared with the entire ten-piece band. Here was the *pièce-de-résistance*. Opening with "Thelonious," featuring Monk as the only soloist, they then slid into a nine-and-a-half-minute version of "Friday the Thirteenth." Given how the critics bashed it five years earlier for being long and monotonous, it was a challenge to resurrect it for the band. They added a counter-melody underneath that enlivened the song, and Phil Woods took off on what would turn out to be his best solo of the night. "Monk's Mood" is beautifully orchestrated; the harmonies are neither dense nor cluttered.

As Monk expected, "Little Rootie Tootie" proved to be the evening's highlight. Pure adrenaline pushed the horn section through Monk's most intricate and exacting passages. The tempo was unusually fast, and Pepper Adams and Donald Byrd delivered very boppish solos. Monk didn't seem to mind, however, because he was having so much fun. On his own solo he even quoted himself from the original 1952 recording, knowing full well that the band would follow with its own "quote" of his entire original solo. When the moment came, the band invariably flubbed the near-impossible passages but ultimately astounded the audience with virtuosity, fervor, and energy. The crowd roared. Unfortunately, Thelonious forgot to look for Keepnews's cue and, as luck would have it, they had launched into "Tootie" while Ray Fowler was changing the reel. Always a man of unvarnished honesty, he confessed to the audience that they were going to repeat the number because "the recording engineers had 'loused up.'"[41] After the final number, as the audience stood, shouting their approval, stamping their feet, and calling for an encore, Thelonious used the occasion to play "Little Rootie Tootie" again. Thelonious was moved by the evening. He received two standing ovations, and when he came out for an encore, he walked to the center stage mic and gave a heartfelt "Thank you," and then said it again into the microphone situated inside the piano.[42] His gratitude was palpable. But so was the audience's.

Thelonious left Town Hall that night feeling triumphant. Few jazz musicians are granted full concerts devoted entirely to their compositions. A few months earlier, he had been beaten in Delaware by police; now he took his place among a very tiny pantheon of artists that included Duke Ellington and Fats Waller.[43] Keepnews and Bill Grauer were also happy with the results, and could not help noticing the warm reception Monk's big band received. They knew they had a strong disc on their hands and they looked forward to the upcoming tour.

Monk went home that night exhausted. He had been going nonstop for a month. He did wake up in time to catch his band's brief appearance on Prudential's *The Twentieth Century* on Sunday night. Of course, Monk knew nothing of the show's content when they filmed him. What he saw that evening as he lay in bed with Nellie and the kids must have surprised him. As Thelonious and his band wailed away in the opening clip, Walter Cronkite described the current generation of youth as "silent, tranquil, beat." For the next fifteen minutes, they listened to academic experts and students describe the new generation as materialistic and selfish, before returning to the Five Spot to meet the "Beats" and hear Monk.[44] (Unless one noticed the sign over the bar, the un-hip would not have known who was playing since Monk's name is never mentioned.) The scene was surreal; the camera pans from the bandstand to the bar where we "eavesdrop" on a conversation between a young woman defending modern jazz and a young man criticizing it: "I think it's going too far. I enjoy something like Turk Murphy, Louis Armstrong, Duke Ellington, Johnny Smith Quartet—something I can relax and enjoy." They asked the poet who had just performed what he thought jazz meant for his generation. "To me it means something interesting, a different kind of sound." And then the camera cuts to Monk jamming away, arms crossed, lips pursed, intensely focused. The next shot pans the Five Spot, capturing a sea of white faces and their expressions as they contemplate the music. Walter Cronkite concludes: "Nowhere have we found any indication of this generation having a new movement or cause of its own." Senator J. William Fulbright of Arkansas has the last word, criticizing youth for "conformity, self-centeredness, and complacency."

Now Thelonious was neither a news hound nor an activist, but he and Nellie were well aware of the changing political world around them. They knew, for example, that young people in Fulbright's own home state faced mobs in order to integrate Little Rock's Central High School, and that the distinguished Senator had opposed Brown v. Board of Education and participated in filibustering the Civil Rights Act of 1957. And most African-Americans were aware of the Youth March for Integrated Schools in Washington, D.C. Led by Harry Belafonte, Jackie Robinson, and A. Philip Randolph, the organizers drew over 10,000 young people who rallied at the Lincoln Memorial. The march took place just a few weeks before Monk taped the segment at the Five Spot.[45] There was, indeed, a generation with a cause; they just didn't look like the kids CBS portrayed at the Five Spot.

Monk's triumphant night at Town Hall was followed by a reality check when the reviews started to appear. John S. Wilson, one of Monk's champions, acknowledged the man's genius, pointed out how rare it was for jazz musicians to have such a concert, praised the quartet, and then proceeded to criticize the big band's "bland, workaday performances." He blamed the arrangements, which "smoothed out the characteristically Monkian humps and bumps, diluted his tartness and robbed the works of their zest. It was a pipe-and-slippers version of music that is naturally querulous."[46] *Billboard* critic Bob Rolontz felt Monk "let the audience down" because he played so little, and what he played lacked "the inventiveness or the compelling quality of which he is capable." He faulted the venue, concluding that the high priest needed the "clink of glasses and hum of conversation that goes on when jazz is played in clubs like the Five Spot, where jazz sounds better—and Monk plays better."[47] *Metronome*'s Robert Perlongo appreciated Monk's individual performance, which he delivered "with an energy and dedication that was almost tiring to watch." That energy was evident in the quartet performances but missing in the orchestra, which "tended occasionally to bog down with a little too much intellectual serenity." For Perlongo, the problem wasn't the venue or the arrangements but the band's format—Monk's music worked better in a small band. It was only on "Little Rootie Tootie" that the orchestra achieved "a standard of Monkishness" equal to that of the quartet.[48]

No one wanted to blame Monk, certainly not *New Yorker* jazz critic Whitney Balliett. Balliett's essay started out as a kind of love letter to Thelonious, whose work "represents possibly the most intense and single-minded exploration of the possibilities of jazz yet made by one man." He praised how Monk takes singular phrases and reworks them until they become something else, something profound. "When he is finished, one has the impression of having viewed the restless, exciting, surprising aerie that only a handful of jazz musicians have inhabited." This didn't happen at Town Hall, Balliett complained. For one thing, Martin Williams's introductory remarks gave the event an air of pomposity that didn't sit well with Balliett (though one might detect a bit of professional jealousy since he wasn't invited on stage). The "evening," he wrote, "never seemed to fully disentangle itself from Significance; one kept waiting for the speeches to blow away, as it were, and the fun to begin."[49] And when the fun finally began, the big band fell short. While Monk was "remarkably consistent," Rouse was "dull," Art Taylor "monotonous," and the arrangements (sans "Little Rootie Tootie") were "pale, conventional small-band scorings—unison passages sprinkled with mild counter-point—in which almost no effort was made to strengthen the various competent but second-rate soloists, who needed it."[50] Even the later, more extensive reviews by Monk's champions drew similar conclusions. Gunther Schuller, for example, thought the large ensemble performances were "bland and thoroughly conventional," failing dismally to "achieve the earthy richness and propulsive swing of Monk at his best."[51]

Thelonious rarely paid attention to reviews, but the Riverside executives did. What-ever plans they might have had to sponsor a three-week tour of the big band were squelched once the reviews rolled in. The decision devastated Monk. Without a cabaret card, a concert tour would have been an ideal way to earn some money. "The Town Hall concert was really the kick-off for what was going to be a tour," Toot explained. "I think it was an eight-city tour, that never occurred because the reviews were so bad Riverside got scared. And so it's funny how that record turns out to be a classic and probably the most important record that he did during his tenure at Riverside. But at the time the company—I don't think it was Orrin or anything like that—just got cold feet because that concert did not get good reviews."[52]

Monk's relationship with Riverside cooled. But he still had to make money. Harry Colomby took more aggressive measures to protect Monk's long-term financial inter-ests. He started a publishing company, Bar-Thel Music (named for Monk's children), and affiliated with Broadcast Music Inc. (BMI), which collects royalties and license fees on behalf of its songwriters, composers, and music publishers.[53] He had also retained the Shaw Booking agency to secure a few out-of-town gigs and New York City concert appearances. In mid-March, the quartet was booked at the Apollo Theater for a week. Billed as the "wizard of the eighty-eights," Monk shared the marquee with Miles Davis and R&B singer Ruth Brown.[54] Monk had not set foot on the Apollo's stage in thirteen years, not since the night Dizzy Gillespie fired him for being late. He didn't miss it. In those days, working at the Apollo meant playing five shows a day, which for a non-headlining major band meant thirty-minute sets. The Apollo's famous revolving stage kept the show moving without delay. Monk sometimes disrupted the show's rhythms, sending Apollo owner Bobby Schiffman into paroxysms of rage. Just minutes before his Friday matinee appearance, Monk disappeared. "It was time for him to go onstage, and I'm running around frantically trying to find him. I see him standing up on the fire escape backstage, outside the building in the middle of winter with an overcoat on and his hat pulled down over his head."[55] Despite the drawing power of Miles's sextet featuring Coltrane and Cannonball Adderley, uptown audiences came mainly to see Ruth Brown, whose Atlantic recordings sold well among black consumers. During the matinees, the theater stayed pretty empty, and at night the house was a little over half full—a foreboding of things to come for jazz artists.[56]

On March 28, Monk returned to Town Hall, this time opposite singers Chris Con-nor and Dakota Staton and Dizzy Gillespie's band. John S. Wilson described the concert as a mediocre stage show complete with pop singers and a comedian (in the form of Gillespie). While Monk alone committed to an authentic "jazz program," he "was in a drab and lumbering mood."[57] Wilson's assessment may have been more of an unwitting diagnosis than a music review. April arrived and Monk began showing signs of manic behavior. The quartet was scheduled to open at Storyville in Boston on Tuesday, April 28. Having gone three nights without sleep, he arrived at the Copley Square Hotel (where Storyville was located) early that evening in terrible shape. Slightly drunk and holding a glass of liquor, he paced around in the lobby examining the walls. His band was staying about a mile away at the Hotel Bostonian on Boylston Street, but Monk preferred the luxury and convenience of the Copley. When he tried to get a room, he was refused.[58] Angry and frustrated, he wandered around the neighborhood, missing the first set and sending club owner George Wein into a panic. Wein recalls how "the audience stayed put for two solid hours without complaint."[59] (Not everyone stayed. My own mother and father went to Storyville that night and stayed for about an hour and forty-five minutes before giving up.[60]) Monk finally appeared at 10:00 and joined the rest of his group on the bandstand. But after two songs, he got up from the piano bench and "wandered aimlessly around the room, picking imaginary flies off the walls. The audience watched him in silent bewilderment."[61] Wein eventually persuaded Monk to come back to the stage for the next set at 11:30, but he did the same thing—after two songs he was through. Instead of walking around, however, he "sat motionless at the piano for what seemed like half an hour."[62] Wein tried talking to him but he remained unresponsive. After a while, Rouse, Sam Jones, and Art Taylor decided to leave; the gig was over.

Thelonious reluctantly withdrew to the Bostonian, but he so disliked the accommodations that he took a cab to the Hotel Statler-Hilton (which the night before had hosted Cuba's new president Fidel Castro and his entourage[63]) in an effort to get a room there. Again he was denied. Bitter, he decided to go home and fetch Nellie. He hopped a cab to Logan Airport, but arrived too late to catch a flight to New York. By this time Thelonious had become quite agitated. A state trooper at the airport noticed his behavior and began to question him, but when Monk would not respond, the trooper took him into custody and drove him directly to Grafton State Hospital, an insane asylum located near Worcester, in central Massachusetts.[64]

It may have seemed like déjà vu, but Grafton State was a far cry from Bellevue. Situated on 1,200 sprawling acres of farm land, the facility was divided into four distinct "colonies" meant to isolate groups of patients by gender and by diagnosis—i.e., stable patients versus "excited" patients. Monk, in his manic state, was deemed "excited" and confined to "Elms" colony, with its masonry buildings and wood-frame dormitories. The landscape was stunning: rolling hills, woodlands, a dairy farm, two- and three-story Craftsman-style brick buildings, as well as small cottages housing some 1,500 patients. The grounds bore a closer resemblance to the Music Inn or Tanglewood than a mental institution.[65]

Monk was held there for observation but not allowed to contact anyone—though the staff claimed they sent a letter to Nellie Monk. Meanwhile, no one besides the hospital staff and the state trooper knew Monk was there. The next day, Wein called Harry Colomby to ask if he had heard from Thelonious. Colomby, who knew nothing of the previous night's performance, promptly called Nellie. For a week, everyone was in a panic. Colomby hired a private investigator and Nellie and other family members made frantic phone calls to the police, hospitals, and friends in the area. The Boston police department had no record of Monk's whereabouts and the officer on duty never thought to contact the state police. They finally tracked him down after a local newscast identified Monk as a patient at Grafton State Hospital. Nellie flew to Boston immediately and brought him home.[66]

While it is not clear if the medical staff came up with a diagnosis, they did administer chlorpromazine—better known by its trade name, Thorazine. Introduced in the early 1950s as an anti-psychotic drug, it had become the drug of choice for managing manic behavior and schizophrenia. State hospitals, in particular, gravitated toward the drug because it worked quickly—sometimes in a matter of hours—and was cost-effective. There are significant side effects, including blurred vision, dizziness, drowsiness, sensitivity to light, nasal congestion, rigid muscles, and dry lips and mouth. The side effects took their toll on Monk: While taking the drug he frequently complained of stiff fingers and those closest to him noticed his dry lips.[67] "His lips were always very dry," recalled his nephew Clifton Smith. "And he put an excessive amount of Chapstick on his lips and the Chapstick would peel and he would lick his lips rapidly."[68] Since Thorazine contains a sedative, it slows movement and can dull cerebral functions. Patients on Thorazine have often compared it to having a "blanket on the brain." One of the more severe visible side effects is that it can cause abnormal and involuntary movements—traits similar to those of Parkinson's disease.[69]

The medical profession was still learning about the impact of anti-psychotic drugs in 1959, but Thorazine seemed to work fast and effectively. Dr. Robert Freymann, who had taken Thelonious on as a regular patient, agreed. He prescribed Thorazine but supplemented the drug with "vitamin shots" to counteract its sedative effects and boost energy. His infamous vitamin shots attracted a clientele of celebrities, elites, and drug-addicted jazz musicians referred by the Baroness. Harry Colomby, who occasionally took Monk to Dr. Freymann's office on the Upper East Side, would sit "in his waiting room and see dowagers from Park Avenue and then musicians because he was 'Dr. Feelgood,' you know."[70] Dr. Feelgood would go on to publish a best-selling book titled *What's So Bad About Feeling Good?* on how he treated addiction, depression, obesity, and a range of minor ailments using vitamin shots.[71] What neither Monk nor most of Dr. Freymann's patients knew at the time was that the shots were laced with amphetamines. In 1968, the New York State board suspended his medical license for administering narcotics to known addicts.[72]

None of this surprised Toot, who often accompanied his father to Dr. Freymann's office. From what he observed, the good doctor merely catered to the whims and desires of the wealthy. "A brilliant guy, very nice man, but an enabler. So, he would give Nica anything she wanted, including bennies [benzedrine pills]. So they were taking bennies, smoking, drinking Chivas Regal and Dr. Freymann was giving everybody vitamin shots of every kind. . . . Thelonious didn't need any of that stuff. But I can't completely blame Dr. Freymann because Thelonious was his own man. . . . I think it exacerbated the coming storm."[73] Irrespective of Dr. Freymann's motives, we now know that combining Thorazine and amphetamines has a deleterious effect on the patient, and that chlorpromazine inhibits the central stimulating affects of amphetamines.[74] To make matters worse, Monk's frequent drinking and occasional recreational drug use—marijuana, cocaine, uppers—meant that the impact and efficacy of the Thorazine was never consistent.

There is very little evidence that Thorazine reduced the frequency or intensity of his manic episodes. On the contrary, the combination of drugs and lifestyle choices may have exacerbated his condition. Once again, Nellie, Nica, Colomby, and even Monk decided that he should no longer travel alone. If Nellie or Nica could not accompany him, they called on Jules Colomby. (Harry was still teaching full-time.) Of course, Monk's condition had a profound effect on the family. The kids had moved back from Marion's in the late spring, early summer, but it soon became clear that Monk needed Nellie on the road. They decided to send Toot and Boo Boo to live with Nellie's sister Skippy and her son Ronnie, who was now nineteen years old. Because Skippy lived on 1304 Bristow Street, just a few blocks from Geraldine and Sonny, the kids attended P. S. 61 in the neighborhood and Evelyn was able to baby-sit after school.[75] Thelonious and Nellie knew their children were well-protected; they had most of their cousins, not to mention the entire neighborhood, looking out for them.

Fortunately, the next few gigs were nearby—a short stint at Hank's Club Evergreen near Morristown, New Jersey, about forty minutes' drive from home, and then a return engagement at the Apollo opposite Dinah Washington and the Gil Evans Orchestra.[76] Between these two engagements, Monk returned to the studio on June 1 to cut another album for Riverside. It had been over a year since he set foot in a recording studio, and nearly two years since his last studio recording session *as a leader*.[77] Monk and Keepnews decided to change things up by adding Thad Jones on cornet. A scion of Detroit's most famous jazz family (his brothers were drummer Elvin Jones and pianist Hank Jones), Thad was the star trumpeter in Count Basie's band and, in Monk's estimation, one of the most underrated musicians in the business.[78] He once said, "I think Thad Jones is a much better trumpet player [than Miles Davis]."[79]

Keepnews anticipated an easy session. He was mistaken. Thelonious introduced a new composition titled "Played Twice," the title referring to the song's structure. It is a rhythmically complex, sixteen-bar theme based on a series of repeated phrases or "echoes" that fall in different places in the meter. After several false starts and three complete takes, they finally laid down a version satisfying to Monk, but then ran out of time. They returned the next day to presumably finish the disc, recording well-established pieces—"Straight, No Chaser," "I Mean You," and a gorgeous, nearly eleven-minute rendition of his ballad "Ask Me Now." Everything went smoothly and Jones showed just how adventurous he could be, especially on "I Mean You." But it wasn't enough for an album; Keepnews wanted one more tune.

Between West 63rd Street and Nica's house, Monk began sketching out a new song, a stately sixteen-bar theme anchored in B♭ Lydian mode and delivered as a dynamic, processional march.[80] Once past the melody, the processional turns into an all-out, head-nodding, swinging dance party. He called it "Jackie-ing" for his niece. Now nineteen and committed to studying music, Jackie Smith was thrilled with the idea that her uncle would name a song after her. "Then he showed me this little half piece of paper. I was a little disappointed; the song was so short and simple. But when I heard it, it reminded me of the beginning of a song. I said to Thelonious, 'It's like an entrance, an opening. It's like a royal statement,' and he said, as if it were some kind of epiphany, 'That's what it is.'"[81] No surprise that he used it as the opening theme to his concerts.

Armed with a new composition, he and the band returned to Reeves Studios on June 4 to record it. There was one problem: Monk left the music on Nica's piano. He thought he could teach them by ear. "After he struck a few notes and sang a few more," Keepnews recalled, "there was a rebellion. The musicians insisted on having it in writing, and I quickly agreed to the delay." Monk returned with the music an hour later, but what appeared on the page to be a simple sixteen-bar theme was difficult, especially for Thad Jones. They wrestled through a couple of takes and finally produced a master they were proud of. Rouse delivered one of the best recorded solos since he had joined Monk's band. Indeed, all the solos on "Jackie-ing" were memorable, including Art Taylor's swinging introduction.[82]

With two albums in the can, Monk faced a fairly busy summer of concerts and out-of-town engagements, and he had a film score to write. He was supposed to record the soundtrack for *Les liaisons dangereuses* in Paris that spring. In fact, Colomby and Marcel Romano, the film's music director, had arranged for a short run at Club Saint-Germain and a concert at the Olympia, but the trip was cancelled. Instead, Romano and director Roger Vadim decided to come to New York to supervise the recording.[83] They arrived in May but soon discovered that pinning Monk down to a date was nearly impossible.

Meanwhile, Monk had to attend to his other obligations. On June 17, he and Nellie were back in Chicago for a two-week stay at the Sutherland Hotel and Lounge. The club was packed opening night.[84] Accompanied by his regular crew—Rouse, Taylor, and Jones—Monk's band was nevertheless billed as a quintet with "special guest stars." Who the guest or guests were is not clear; perhaps Johnny Griffin, who led his own group at the Sutherland on Monk's off night.[85] But Monk had a difficult row with the management toward the end of his engagement. Around the 27th and 28th of June, Chicago experienced a short heatwave. To the management's chagrin, Monk showed up to work one night in short pants. The Sutherland, after all, was a classy place known for its crystal chandeliers, plush mauve carpet, and white Hyde Park clientele. Although "Monk's crowd was probably the most 'way out' group," according to ex-bartender Artie Frazier, the club maintained a fairly conservative atmosphere.[86] Monk lost the battle, but their verbal exchange got back to the Shaw Agency.[87]

Monk was only home a few days before he had to play Newport on the 3rd of July. George Wein added Monk to the program just four weeks before the festival.[88] He arrived a little late due to heavy traffic and in his haste to get on the road he forgot his security pass, but one would not have known the moment he walked on stage. For one thing, he looked well-rested, happy, and was characteristically well-dressed, "wearing a neat conservative blue suit, a white shirt and a plain tie." But that's not all. Monk accessorized with a "blue fedora with a high crown and a narrow brim." Although we now associate Monk with hats, before 1959 he almost always performed hatless. George Wein couldn't believe his eyes. "You going to wear your hat, Thelonious?" he asked. Monk's reply: "I'm cold."[89] That might have been true; Newport was known for its occasional cool July evenings. He was also losing his hair and his nieces and nephews began to tease him about it.[90] Whether it was vanity or the climate, an element of Monk's trademark style was born that evening.

Once the quartet launched into the music, the hat suddenly seemed unimportant. And though they performed well-worn Monk standards, the band was on fire and the audience—the largest to date[91]—was warm and receptive. Charlie Rouse displayed a mastery of the repertoire and proved that he really was an appropriate choice for the coveted spot as Monk's horn. He quieted the naysayers—at least for the time being. And Monk had as much fun comping as he did soloing, especially on "In Walked Bud" and "Blue Monk."[92] Except for Art Taylor's occasional tendency to push the tempo, the set was close to flawless. "That night, Monk was inspired," wrote critic Dan Morgenstern. So was Morgenstern, who declared Monk's forty-minute set "the greatest performance I have heard him give" and "perhaps the most moving experience of the festival."[93]

Monk's triumphant showing at Newport was quickly overshadowed by the news that his friend and former drummer Shadow Wilson had died. A rumor circulated that he had been killed over gambling debts, but the truth was that he died of meningitis exacerbated by years of addiction and poor health. He was thirty-nine.[94] According to David Amram, "Shadow's death had an effect on Monk, certainly. He loved Shadow and always worried about him."[95] A week later, Billie Holiday died of cirrhosis of the liver. She was forty-four. Monk was never close to her personally, but he loved her artistry, her phrasing, her musical choices, and for so many years as a young man, he would wake up to Billie Holiday gazing down at him from his bedroom ceiling. She spent her final days at Metropolitan Hospital under house arrest for possession of heroin that had been planted on her. Both Shadow and Billie died too young, their lives shortened immeasurably by addiction.

Two deaths back to back put Monk in a somber mood, making it difficult to focus on the soundtrack for *Les liaisons dangereuses*. Roger Vadim and Marcel Romano stayed in New York for several weeks in an effort to coax some music from Monk, but they could not even get him to sign a contract. Vadim had to return, but Romano stayed behind to try to seal the deal. Meanwhile, as a precautionary measure, Romano commissioned pianist Duke Jordan to write some original music. If Thelonious fell through, at least they would have something.[96]

Monk thought it might help if he could see the film, so Vadim expedited a freshly edited print late June or early July, knowing that he needed the soundtrack no later than July 31. Romano arranged a screening for the 23rd of July, but Monk didn't show. The next night, however, he succeeded in corralling Thelonious, Nellie, their two children, Harry Colomby, and Nica. The film starred a young Jeanne Moreau as Juliette de Merteuil, a cunning bourgeois socialite who dares the Vicomte de Valmont (Gerard Philipe) to seduce the unwitting Marianne Tourvel, a beautiful young bride (played, incidentally, by the director's young bride, Danish actress Annette [Stroyberg] Vadim[97]). Merteuil wins her wager as Valmont and Marianne fall in love, much to his dismay. They all liked the film, according to Romano.[98] But it was Monk's opinion that mattered most, and he appreciated how Romano had already begun to insert his recordings into the working soundtrack. On the other hand, Monk may have been disappointed to see a quintet made up of Kenny Clarke, Kenny Dorham, Duke Jordan, saxophonist Barney Wilen, and bassist Paul Rovere perform in the nightclub scene.[99] Monk knew that had the European tour not been cancelled, his quartet would have been in that scene. After screening the film, he still wasn't ready to sign a contract.[100]

After the screening, Nica invited the whole entourage to her house to talk about the film and to urge Thelonious to begin working. It was already 10:00 p.m., but Thelonious was in no mood to talk business. Instead, he challenged Romano to a game of Ping-Pong. Midway into the match, Romano recounted, Monk suddenly "darted to the second floor, and sat at the piano and began to improvise. Nica timidly handed him the contract. He escaped to the living room, where he sat for only a minute in front of the TV. The kids were hungry, and being the considerate father, Monk went to the kitchen to cook them dinner. After sitting down with them for dinner, Monk played Ping-Pong again, then some piano, more TV, Ping-Pong . . . Still, at dawn, the contract had yet to be signed."[101] The next day, Monk did go to the studio, ostensibly to work on the score, but he produced nothing and still refused to sign the contract. Again, he took refuge at Nica's house, spent the night with his family partying, sleeping, playing, and eating, until finally he relented. He signed the nine-page contract on July 26 and called Rouse, Sam Jones, and Art Taylor over to Nica's house to rehearse.[102]

It took three nights in the studio—July 27 to 29—to record the soundtrack. Monk completed most of his part on the first night, Blakey's group finished the following two nights. After all the hand-wringing and stalling, Monk did not write anything new, nor did he give the musical demands of the film much thought. He added French tenor saxophonist Barney Wilen, who had just made his American debut at Newport a few weeks earlier,[103] and simply recorded his usual repertoire—"Off Minor," "Crepuscule with Nellie," "Let's Cool One," "Rhythm-a-ning," "Pannonica," "Ba-lue Bolivar Ba-lues-Are," and "Epistrophy." The one exception was a solo piano rendition of Charles A. Tindley's gospel hymn, "We'll Understand it Better, By and By."[104] It was an intelligent, if not ironic, choice to underscore the film's theme of seduction and innocence. Romano and Vadim used it to great effect during a scene where the innocent Marianne and the scheming Valmont meet up in a church. In the end, Romano flew back to Paris immediately after the session with the music secure in his suitcase. He and Vadim were happy with the results. Between Monk's contribution and the music provided by Art Blakey and the Jazz Messengers, Vadim had more than enough for an adequate soundtrack.

On July 31, Monk was supposed to travel to French Lick, Indiana, for the Second Annual French Lick Jazz Festival (a George Wein production held on the grounds of the old Sheraton Hotel there), but he pulled out at the last minute.[105] Monk may have wanted to focus on getting his ten-piece band into shape. Although the fabled tour never happened, Jules and Harry Colomby succeeded in booking the band at the New York Jazz Festival on Randall's Island for Saturday, August 22. And thanks to the generosity of club owner Art D'Lugoff, the band gave a preview concert the preceding Sunday at the Village Gate. D'Lugoff circumvented the cabaret card business by holding the event in the afternoon and providing no food or drinks. Instead, he charged admission and gave the band the door.[106]

On Friday, August 21, Monk and his quartet had to put in an appearance at the Boston Jazz Festival—another George Wein production—and returned to New York in time for the Randall's Island Festival the next evening.[107] The format was the same as Town Hall—the small group would perform a few numbers followed by the ten-piece band. Thelonious was a little nervous; after all, this was his chance to prove the critics wrong. So it didn't help matters when he and Nellie were held up in traffic and arrived a little late. The band was already beginning to warm up backstage when he realized that he'd forgotten all the charts! Without telling anyone, he jumped in the car and headed home to retrieve the music. Nellie noticed Monk rushing off and set out after him. With the two of them dashing to the parking area just before Monk's group was scheduled to perform, Peter Long, the festival's assistant producer, started chasing after the both of them. It looked like a scene from Keystone Cops: Two more festival employees chased down Long, which piqued the attention of the police. Eventually, the cops overtook Monk on the bridge with sirens blaring. Once he explained the situation, the pursuing patrolman provided a police escort, enabling him to make it home in time to gather the music and go on as scheduled.[108] When he hit the stage, however, he showed no signs of stress. Indeed, according to John S. Wilson, the band "appeared looser and more at home in the arrangements" than they did at Town Hall. But he still thought the band failed to capture Monk's "distinctive quality" on all but one number—"an exuberant piece that smacked strongly of the more ribald rhythmic side of Duke Ellington." He never identified the composition (though he's probably referring to "Little Rootie Tootie"), but believed that "it was the only time when there seemed to be a satisfactory meeting of minds among composer, arranger and band."[109]

Monk was pleased with the performance, which only heightened his disappointment over the band's prospects. He had to move on. A couple of days later, he and Nellie headed to Washington, D.C. for a week-long gig at the Caverns on Eleventh and U Street.[110] They camped out at the elegant Hotel 2400, a renovated turn-of-the-century apartment building on 16th Street, spending part of the day walking the city and taking in the nation's capital.[111] It turned out to be a short-lived working vacation. They returned home long enough to celebrate Boo Boo's sixth birthday on September 5, then were off again on a grueling nine-city tour as part of George Wein's "Newport Jazz Festival Presents." The package included Anita O'Day, George Shearing's big band, Cannonball Adderley, Lennie Tristano, British trumpeter Humphrey Lyttleton and his

Octet, and, of course, Monk's quartet. Starting in Indianapolis on September 7, the groups traveled by bus to Louisville, Chicago, Detroit, Boston, New York, Pittsburgh, Washington, D.C., ending in Philadelphia on the 20th of September.[112] Monk made every venue except Pittsburgh's Syria Mosque. The night before, the group performed at New York's Town Hall, so Monk took advantage of being home in order to rest. He rested a little too much, missing the bus in the process.[113] Monk ended up missing the Pittsburgh concert, but making the remaining gigs in Washington, D.C., and Philadelphia's Academy of Music.[114]

The tour proved to be both a musical triumph and a financial disaster. Wein and Newport Productions lost money,[115] but Monk's quartet received accolades in every city. Humphrey Lyttelton, whose band was on its first U.S. tour, was so taken with Monk that he published his musings in the British jazz journal *Melody Maker*. He initially found Monk's performance rather humorous, if not eccentric, notably the way he positioned "his elbows in an odd flapping movement like some huge, ungainly crow trying to take off from the piano stool." And he took note of Monk's newfound obsession with hats. During the first part of the tour, the hat he wore reminded Lyttelton of "some weird modernistic lampshade." "He wore this hat day in, day out—visitors to his room found him wearing it in bed."[116] (The headgear was hardly "modernistic"; on the contrary, he was sporting the farmer's hat from Northern Ghana given to him by Guy Warren!) Nevertheless, Lyttelton warned readers not to confuse his "façade" with musicianship. He confessed that he enjoyed listening to Monk "more than the rest of the package put together." Critics who believe he is a "simpleton," Lyttleton cautioned, are dead wrong. Indeed, Monk was a model of professionalism. Although he rarely talked to anyone besides Nellie, his behavior was impeccable, contradicting the "legendary tales of buffoonery" that circulated among club owners, promoters, and some musicians. His "sets were models of decorum," and he possessed a better stage manner than Lennie Tristano's group, whose performances were marred by lengthy pauses between songs and "a unanimously cool front to the audience."[117] In every city, audiences greeted Thelonious warmly and enthusiastically, and he "responded by treating them with respect, even to the extent of bowing solemnly when his solos were applauded."[118]

It was a great tour, but it ended on a sour note. As soon as they returned to New York, both Sam Jones and Art Taylor gave notice. Although Jones found working with Monk "enjoyable," and considered it a dream come true, he later said he had to leave because of "personality problems."[119] Jones joined Cannonball Adderely's band. Taylor was simply tired of touring and ready to move on. He decided to stay put in New York for a while, freelancing with different artists.[120] The timing was terrible for Monk, who was scheduled to open at Club 12 in Detroit two days later. He and Rouse played with a local rhythm section—bassist Alvin Jackson (brother of Milt Jackson) and the club's house drummer, Frank Gant. Both were fine musicians with a genuine local following, but they were not up to Monk's standards. According to Prophet Jennings, then a Detroit-based journalist, artist, and photographer, Monk "was mad every night. He was especially mad 'cause Sam Jones had left him to join Cannonball."[121] He was also mad at the club's management. Formerly Klein's Show Bar, the club was situated on 12th Street, a historically Jewish neighborhood that had recently become predominantly black. In April of 1959, Al Mendelson had bought the property from George Klein, and in an effort to boost the bar's national profile, began booking big names, such as Miles Davis, Sonny Stitt, and Monk.[122] Unfortunately, when Monk opened on September 22, the house piano was deplorable. Poor, out-of-tune pianos had long been Monk's number-one pet peeve, and at this stage in his career he saw no need to accept it.[123] Thelonious threw a fit, vowing not to return unless it was replaced. "The following evening," reported one observer, "a new baby grand piano awaited the finger tips of the genius."[124]

The audience wasn't too pleased with the genius. He played the same songs over and over again, sometimes twice in a row. For Five Spot patrons, this wasn't unusual; he was rehearsing on the bandstand, teaching his new sidemen the music. But for Detroiters whose knowledge of Monk derived from records, radio, and reputation, they thought he was putting them on. When the people started complaining, Monk shot back. "So Monk got on the stage one night," Jennings remembered, "and said of Alvin Jackson, 'This man here can't play no motherfuckin' way. So fuck all y'all. And you, too, Prophet.'" He had been drinking a lot and smoking reefer, which only accelerated his emotional descent. Nellie did her best to calm him down but he could not sleep for a couple of days. At one point, Monk decided he wanted to buy a car, so he, Nellie, and Prophet went to a local Cadillac dealer. According to Prophet, "Thelonious was looking but he didn't speak. The salesman got suspicious, you know, and wouldn't deal with him." Eventually, he crashed. "Just before he closed [at Club 12], I woke up one morning and somebody's beating on my door, and there's Monk coming up to where I was living at. I let him in. . . . He just came in and went to sleep on the floor with his clothes on."[125]

On September 28, he and Nellie headed west for the first annual Los Angeles Jazz Festival at the famed Hollywood Bowl. It was Thelonious's first trip to L.A. since he worked for Coleman Hawkins. Now he shared the limelight with Count Basie, Sarah Vaughan, and pop singer Bobby Darin.[126] He had just won the *Down Beat* International Critics Poll for best pianist a second year in a row, and was second choice in the *Down Beat* Readers' Poll. Leonard Bernstein had recently declared Monk "the most original and creative pianist in the world of jazz today."[127] And yet, Monk still felt underappreciated. Despite having surpassed piano virtuosos like Oscar Peterson for the top spot in the critics' poll, Monk complained, "Oscar Peterson never gives me any credit." He also had choice words for his concert-mate. "George Shearing copies so much jive from me," yet never mentions Monk. "I don't care who I mention, 'cause I don't envy anybody—it seems they go out of their way not to mention who they dig."[128] The Los Angeles press did not help matters, either. The early press releases prepared the ground for Monk's visit, describing him as "controversial" and "eccentric."[129]

Given Monk's state of mind and the state of his band, he wasn't thrilled about the trip. Once again, he had to hire a local rhythm section with almost no time to rehearse, and unlike a club engagement where bands had several opportunities to learn to play together, the Hollywood Bowl was a one-shot deal. Fortunately, Sam Jones happened to be in California with Cannonball and was able to make the date, but Monk still needed a drummer. Thelonious sought help from his pal Elmo Hope, who was now living and working in Los Angeles (he had come west with Chet Baker's group and decided to stay because work was plentiful).[130] Hope recommended drummer Frank Butler. Hope had worked with him in Harold Land's quintet, and Monk liked the fact that Butler was once Duke Ellington's drummer.[131]

Nellie, on the other hand, looked forward to Los Angeles. She was anxious to see her cousin and former college classmate Anna Lou Smith. Smith had recently completed her medical degree and residency and was now a practicing psychiatrist at L.A. Metropolitan Hospital.[132] Nellie also needed a break. She and Monk were exhausted from the nonstop traveling. Thelonious continued to take Thorazine, though he still experienced cycles of manic behavior and depression—made worse by sleep deprivation and intermittent dosage. Unfamiliar with the drug, Nellie sometimes doubled his dosage if he skipped a day, exacerbating the side effects.[133] Moreover, Nellie still battled stomach and intestinal problems. By the time they checked into their hotel, Nellie was experiencing severe bouts of nausea while Monk was becoming more agitated. When he took the stage on opening night, he was already showing signs of manic behavior. He performed poorly. Critic John Tynan: "Monk fumbled confusedly through 'Misterioso,' in the course of which he abruptly slammed his entire forearm across the keys. . . . As the applause faded at the close of the number, Monk suddenly rose and faced the audience. Then he lurched, staggered to regain his equilibrium and sat down again without saying a word."[134] By most accounts, when Monk had gotten up to dance he tore his pants![135] Not everyone caught it, but Thelonious was embarrassed and out of sync. Thelonious wrestled with one more tune and then walked off the stage to tepid applause. He was not called back. "What should have been the night's highlight," wrote *Los Angeles Times* columnist Mimi Clar, "a rare appearance by Thelonious Monk—was the biggest disappointment of all."[136] Another critic called Monk's performance "the biggest blunder since the man who said that Mississippi was better than California for Negroes opened his big yap."[137]

Monk headed back to the hotel as soon as the set ended. While Nellie was holed up in the room vomiting, Thelonious roamed the hallways and lobby, eventually getting into a physical confrontation with someone. The hotel staff called the police, who arrested Monk for assault to do bodily harm.[138] Fortunately, hotel management elected to drop the charges and asked the Monks to leave. Nellie packed up their things and they caught a cab to Anna Lou Smith's home on Victoria Avenue. Dr. Smith still has vivid memories of that night: "The thing that struck me, was when I opened the door, she was throwing up, but she had the suitcases! We got the suitcases away from her and got her in to see what was going on. She was so sick. She was having not only the vomiting but pain. So I called a surgeon for an emergency visit and he saw her and said she was obstructed. She went into the hospital and had surgery, for which she never forgave me."[139] Dr. Smith saved her life. Nellie remained in the hospital for nearly two weeks recovering from surgery while Thelonious traveled back and forth between the hospital and Anna Lou's home. "Thelonious was kind of in his own world," she recalled, "but he was anxious. He would get out and walk early in the morning."[140]

Monk felt very much alone and out of sorts. He spent most of his birthday in the hospital, pacing and brooding over Nellie. He did reach out to Elmo Hope, whose friendship became a source of comfort. Hope himself was wrestling with his own drug problem and had been clean for over a year, encouraged by a beautiful young piano player named Bertha Rosemond. Daughter of actor Clinton Rosemond and dancer Corine Rosemond, legends such as Nat "King" Cole, Art Tatum, and Fats Waller used to drop by their home and play the family piano. Seeing and hearing these great ticklers inspired young Bertha to take up the instrument. She had studied briefly with Richie Powell, Bud's brother, not long before he perished in the terrible car accident that claimed the life of Clifford Brown. She finally met Hope one night in October 1958 at the Hillcrest Club, where he was playing with Sonny Rollins. At the end of the set, she shyly approached Hope to tell him that she was learning his music. "He didn't believe me. He introduced me to Sonny and said, 'You know this young lady *says* she's learning my music!' I really wanted him to hear me play so I invited him over to my house for coffee and to play for him. Only then did he believe me."[141] Elmo was soon writing songs for her.[142] Monk was pleased to see Elmo and to learn that he was well and happy. Hearing Elmo talk of Bertha reminded him of Nellie, reinforcing his abiding commitment to her while providing Monk with the reassurance and comfort he needed.

Nellie was still hospitalized when Thelonious left for San Francisco, where he was scheduled to open at the Blackhawk Club on October 20.[143] He could not bear leaving her like this, so on his first day off (Monday) he flew back to L.A. to check on her. Her doctors still insisted that she remain under observation a few more days, which worried Monk even more. But he never lost his sense of humor. He turned to his wife and said, "Nellie, I hope you're not going to kick it. I can't find my socks!"[144]

Besides Nellie, Thelonious had other things to worry about. Rouse had returned to New York to find work and couldn't get back in time. And Monk still didn't have a rhythm section. He called Nica to help and she promptly contacted George Morrow, the former bassist for the Clifford Brown–Max Roach group. He agreed but at the last minute was arrested for failing to make alimony payments so he called Eddie Kahn to substitute.[145] Monk had already arranged to use Frank Butler, but he missed the opening set. And so on opening night, Monk was the *only* member of his band to show up on time. He ended up using local subs—Brew Moore on tenor, Dean Riley on bass, and drummer/percussionist Willie Bobo.[146] The next night Butler, Kahn, and Rouse were in place and things began to feel normal. The band came to life.

Monk's two-week engagement at the Blackhawk proved to be quite successful, much to the surprise of club owner Guido Cacianti. Stories of his undependability and eccentric behavior had kept Cacianti from booking Monk. "Listen, I heard about this Felonious [sic] guy—he's some kinda nut. He'll come into the club and stare at a wall."[147] Cacianti quickly changed his tune when Monk arrived on time, behaved in a professional manner, and most importantly, filled the club. Nearly all the major jazz musicians in the area came to see him, including Erroll Garner, who welcomed Monk

277 / THELONIOUS MONK

warmly. "He's playing beautifully now," Garner told writer Gover Sales, "he must feel like playing—not like that Hollywood Bowl gig." Monk, whose admiration for Garner was mutual, felt comforted by his presence. "[E]very time I get up to go he comes out from somewhere and yells, 'Is my boy still out there?' and I answer, 'Yes, Monk, I'm still here!' and sit back down again!"[148]

Monk arrived in San Francisco just three weeks after the Monterey Jazz Festival, where a twenty-nine-year-old alto player named Ornette Coleman made his first big concert debut. The Texas-born saxophonist had been on the scene for a while, playing in R&B and blues bands in the Southwest before settling in Los Angeles, where he met trumpeter Don Cherry and other like-minded young musicians interested in pushing the limits of harmony and rhythm. Coleman and Cherry had already released one album and recorded enough music for three more LPs.[149] Pianist John Lewis and critic and composer Gunther Schuller championed their music, inviting them to the Lenox School of Jazz in August of 1959, where Coleman's free-form improvisation caused a stir among students, faculty, and assorted visitors.[150] Lewis was also musical director for the Monterey Jazz Festival, and chose to add him to the roster, though he only played a couple of numbers. While the full dimensions of Coleman's style did not come through in this context, his performance set the jazz world abuzz, and Coleman and his funny-looking plastic saxophone quickly became the talk of the town.[151]

Monk had not yet confronted Coleman and his music, but he knew that a small group of younger musicians were moving in the direction of greater dissonance and experimentation. As far as he was concerned, the jury was still out on the new music. But that did not stop Canadian jazz critic Helen McNamara from associating Monk with the emerging avant-garde. She offered *The Thelonious Monk Orchestra at Town Hall* LP as an example of "the harsh protesting air that more and more is becoming the cry of the modern jazzman."[152] Increasingly, dissonance had come to mean "protest," and protest eventually became synonymous with "anger." And, as we shall see, the shifting meanings of dissonance had more to do with the political background noise—the "protesting air" of the black freedom movement—than the music itself. For the moment, Monk was well aware that change was in the air and a younger "avant-garde" was pushing jazz in new directions. Some of it he liked, much of it he disliked, and felt uncomfortable when his own music was lumped in the same category.

By sheer coincidence, Orrin Keepnews was in town to record Cannonball Adderley's quintet at the Jazz Workshop the same week Monk opened at the Blackhawk.[153] Keepnews wanted to make the best use of his stay so he proposed recording another solo piano album as a follow-up to *Thelonious Alone*. For the session, Keepnews secured Fugazi Hall, a 400-seat auditorium originally built in 1912 as a meeting hall for San Francisco's North Beach community. The acoustics were spectacular, and the huge crystal chandeliers gave it an "old school" quality. Thelonious did the rest—he came prepared with a repertoire of ten songs and recorded all but one in a single take. Each tune is a throwback to a bygone era. In the course of two unusually relaxing sessions, he performed four of his older compositions ("Pannonica," "Blue Monk," "Ruby, My Dear," and "Reflections"), four standards, and two new compositions. Among the standards, he revisits "Everything Happens to Me" and "You Took the Words Right Out of My Heart"—he began playing the latter at the Five Spot. He rediscovers Irving Berlin's "Remember," rendering it as a kind of humorous cakewalk, and exhumes Harry Richman's "There's Danger in Your Eyes, Cherie," from the 1930 musical *Puttin' on the Ritz*. The two originals are classic blues. "Round Lights," named for the Fugazi's chandeliers, takes us back to the 1920s, evoking the old jook joints and late-night rent parties.[154] "Bluehawk," as mentioned earlier, paid tribute to the club he was playing, was a clear nod to tenor saxophone giant Coleman Hawkins, and may have been borrowed from Guy Warren's talking drum.[155] If so, that would make "Bluehawk" the most ancient, and certainly the most "African," of all Monk's blues.

From the beginning of his musical life, Thelonious had always epitomized the Janus-faced musician, looking simultaneously at the future and the past. He had assiduously promoted the modern while taking pride in his ability to sound like James P. Johnson. But these recordings are deliberately and urgently nostalgic. They return us to an older day, to the generation that believed the old musicals, found comfort in radio, and sang the blues without electricity. True, when Monk plays unaccompanied, there is always a nostalgic turn. Stride is inevitable, as is his exploration of old standards. But this album felt a little more prescient, if not prophetic. A revolution in music had been declared, and Monk was staking out a position.

21

"Hell, I Did That Twenty-Five Years Ago"

(November 1959–February 1961)

After three weeks of uninterrupted rest, Nellie felt well enough to catch Monk's last weekend at the Blackhawk, and they flew back together that Monday, November 2, 1959. They were anxious to go home. It had been two months since they had slept in their own bed or seen their children. With two weeks off, Monk brought the kids home to West 63rd Street and spent time with them, mostly in bed, playing cards, board games, watching television, and sleeping. He got up to play piano, take long walks around the neighborhood, and if the spirit hit him, prove to the younger cats that this slightly overweight forty-two-year-old could still handle his business on the basketball court. He dropped in on his brother and Trotyrine, Sonny and Geraldine and their kids, or he and Nellie headed across the Hudson to Nica's house. Vacation ended on Tuesday the 17th, when he and Rouse went to Washington, D.C., to play at the Village Note through the weekend.[1]

When Monk returned, Ornette Coleman had become the New York jazz world's latest obsession. Martin Williams and the Termini brothers had arranged a special press preview at the Five Spot on November 17 to introduce Coleman and his band—Don Cherry, bassist Charlie Haden, and drummer Billy Higgins. It was meant as advance publicity for what was supposed to be a short engagement, and it worked better than anyone could have imagined. Critics and musicians who attended either hated or loved the group. Critic George Hoefer documented many of the responses: "'He'll change the entire course of jazz,' 'He's a fake,' 'He's a genius,' 'He swings like HELL,' 'I'm going to listen to my Benny Goodman trios and quartets,' 'He's out, real far out,' 'I like him, but I don't have any idea of what he is doing.'"[2] Bob Reisner, writing for the *Village Voice*, said the group "sounded their barbaric yawps to the great delight of many who are eagerly awaiting a new sound."[3]

What was this new sound? What made Coleman's music so controversial? For one thing, Coleman set out to free jazz improvisation from predetermined chord changes. He wanted to break with the traditional song form and develop a spontaneous, collective interplay where musicians could move wherever their musical phrases, gestures, note choices took them. Free improvisation did not mean playing anything any time, but it required intense listening and ensemble work. To critics listening for chord progressions and structure, what Coleman's group did might have lost them or opened them up to new possibilities. Yet, for those listening to the entire shape of the music, or Coleman's phrasing and tone, they might have concluded that he was just playing some old-fashioned blues with extended harmonies or "bad notes"—depending on one's perspective.[4]

For the next couple of weeks, the city's most eminent names in music, from Miles Davis to Leonard Bernstein, slipped into the Five Spot to hear the latest curiosity.[5] Monk was no exception. He showed up with Charles Mingus. "It was very funny. I walked in with Monk. I said, 'It's a new guy, better than Bird.' Monk walks in, spun around, says, 'Hell, I did that twenty-five years ago, but I didn't do it on every tune,' and he walked out."[6] He didn't walk out right away. He dug Billy Higgins, the young, smiling drummer from Los Angeles who never stopped swinging, no matter how far out the band went. That night, Monk put Higgins on his favored list of potential sidemen. A week later, Monk and Coleman were part of a huge Town Hall concert that included Count Basie, John Coltrane, Lee Konitz, the Art Farmer–Benny Golson "Jazztet," and the Cecil Taylor Unit. Monk fronted a quartet with Rouse, a twenty-three-year-old bassist named Scott LaFaro, and drummer Elvin Jones—younger brother of cornetist Thad Jones. With both Cecil Taylor and Coleman also on the bill, Monk was cast as one of the old men, a role he shared with Basie. John Wilson wrote, "Mr. Monk, who is normally the 'far out' element on any program on which he appears, found himself in the unusual position of being a definite conservative on a bill that included Mr. Coleman and Cecil Taylor."[7]

Ironically, Monk's own rhythm section would soon be associated with the new music—LaFaro as a member of Ornette Coleman's group and Jones as Coltrane's drummer. *New Yorker* critic Whitney Balliett described the entire concert as "a vest-pocket history of most of the radical changes in jazz improvisation during the past couple of decades." He was especially taken with Coleman, to whom he devoted nearly half of his review. But he did save some ink for Monk, praising his "slow, hymn-like rendering of 'Crepuscule with Nellie'," and singling out LaFaro and Jones for special recognition. Jones, he wrote, "proved that he is the only drummer besides Art Blakey who can manage Monk's jarring rhythmic peregrinations."[8]

Monk did not appear threatened by these "radical changes" in the music. On the contrary, he embraced his newly appointed position as a jazz elder, a swinging conservative in an age of chaos and cacophony. And Wilson was not alone in identifying Monk as one of the deans of the jazz establishment. A couple of months earlier, Dan Morgenstern declared Monk "no longer a far out cat whom some worshiped and others laughed at, but an acknowledged genius of whom his people could now all be proud."[9] French critic André Hodeir, one of Monk's more enthusiastic champions, mused, "The musician who once terrified us all no longer seems to disturb a soul. He has been tamed, classified, and given his niche in that eclectic Museum of Great Jazzmen which admits such a variety of species, from Fats Domino to Stan Kenton."[10] It's not as if Monk's music had changed or suddenly become old-fashioned; rather, the ground had shifted under his feet. The press could not stop writing about Coleman (and to a lesser degree, Cecil Taylor) and this annoyed Monk—understandable for an artist who could not work for lack of a cabaret card. One night, Nica and Nat Hentoff were sitting around listening to Coleman's records when Thelonious walked in. "Suddenly he interrupted a record. 'That's nothing new. I did it years ago.' Monk got up and started to go through the piles of Nica's records, without envelopes, stacked on the floor. He found what he wanted, played his old performance, which made his point, and said, 'I think he has a gang of potential though. But he's not all they say he is right now. After all, what has he contributed?'"[11]

Whereas Monk viewed Coleman and the new wave as upstarts, the emerging jazz avant-garde regarded Thelonious as their forefather. Coleman expressed his musical debt to Monk in his composition "Monk and the Nun," recorded in May of 1959 for *The Shape of Jazz to Come*.[12] In interviews, Coleman frequently praised Monk as an exemplar of the kind of freedom he hoped to achieve. As he explained to critic A. B. Spellman, "Rhythm patterns should be more or less like natural breathing patterns. I would like the rhythm section to be as free as I'm trying to get, but very few players, rhythm or horns, can do this yet. Thelonious Monk can. He sometimes plays one note, and because he plays it in exactly the right pitch, he carries more music in it than if he had filled out the chord. I'd say Monk has the most complete harmonic ear in jazz."[13] When Don Cherry recorded a pianoless quartet album with John Coltrane just a few months after the Five Spot debut, the only non-Coleman composition they included was Monk and Denzil Best's "Bemsha Swing."[14] Cherry considered Monk's compositions ideal vehicles for Coleman's harmolodic approach because "when you improvise [on Monk tunes] you play phrases where you can hear the harmonies too."[15]

Coleman and Cherry took a lot from Monk, but their views on freedom diverged dramatically. Monk believed his own freedom, and that of the bass and horn, depended on the drummer's ability to swing constantly. He liked expressive drummers who kept good time, avoided clutter, and never stopped swinging. On the other hand, Coleman and Monk had more in common musically than perhaps both artists realized: They both had firm roots in traditional jazz and black vernacular music. Coleman came out of a heavy blues tradition and folk idioms. His sense of rhythm is propulsive, his searching notes bend, cry, wail like the human voice. Whereas Monk held fast to a Harlem stride sensibility, Coleman never fully abandoned his rural, southern, and southwestern roots. Most critics missed these lingering traditional elements in Coleman's music because they were caught up in the hype about the New Thing.[16]

More than Coleman, Cecil Taylor aligned himself with Monk, insisting that they both worked out of a much longer, deeper tradition. Indeed, Monk's music was an early tool for Taylor's own system of composition and improvisation—what he called "constructivist principles." The basic idea was to compose, learn, and perform music by ear, to produce structured music that was not written down. A musical score, Taylor argued, "is subjugated to the feeling of jazz—they swung, 'swing' meaning the traditional coloring of the energy that moves the music." At the time Taylor developed his constructivist principles, "We used a lot of Monk's tunes. We used to take the Monk tunes out of themselves into the area in which I was going."[17]

Monk didn't worry about being overshadowed by Coleman or Taylor, and any significant ruptures caused by the so-called avant-garde were still a couple of years away. Meanwhile, Thelonious enjoyed being back in New York for the holidays. Four days before Christmas, during one of his visits to Nica's house, he unveiled a new tune. It had all the typical Monkish elements—angular phrasing, intervallic leaps, dissonant harmonies, chromatic movement, and humor. But he threw in something most of his songs did not have—lyrics:

Now it is Christmas time, hear the bell ring pretty sounds.
Ting ting ting ting ting ting ting tong.
So we'll make this Christmas better than the ones gone by.
We'll have a merrier Christmas.
Yes, it is Christmas time, hear the bell ring pretty sounds.
Ting ting ting ting ting ting ting tong.[18]

Monk was no lyricist, but his words were heartfelt. He had had some rough holidays in the past and now looked forward to a "Christmas better than the ones gone by." And he hoped the song might be a hit, giving him the wherewithal to make his family's life merrier. After all, Irving Berlin did pretty well for himself with "White Christmas." But, in the end, the quirky little 13-bar tune was inspired less by the prospect of financial security than the festive atmosphere and the strong family connection he felt being back home with the kids.

Thelonious and Nellie spent New Year's Eve with Nica and friends for a raucous night of music and drinking. When the clock struck midnight, Monk was at the piano, accompanied by Donald Byrd and Hank Mobley on tenor, playing the only thing he could play at that moment: " 'Round Midnight."[19] Whether it was the prospect of a new year, a new beginning, the stimulating atmosphere, or the double shots of Old Grand-Dad bourbon with Coke chasers, Monk was inspired. That night, he composed yet another new song, which he called "Classified Information."[20]

Monk and Rouse were back on the road the second week of January for a return engagement at Boston's Storyville. For Monk, it was an opportunity for redemption after the debacle last spring that landed him in the state mental hospital. He hired bassist Scott LaFaro again, hoping he might become a permanent band member.[21] Monk liked the way LaFaro broke up the rhythm and came up with inventive harmonies without ever losing his sense of swing. He still needed a drummer, however, so LaFaro suggested Paul Motian, a twenty-eight-year-old graduate of the Manhattan School of Music. The pair first recorded together with Tony Scott and Bill Evans in October 1959. Recognizing their wonderful rapport and chemistry, Bill Evans decided to hire both of them for his new trio in December.[22] And with Evans now one of Riverside Record's rising stars, Monk had no hope of keeping LaFaro and Motian permanently, even if he wanted to.

Much to the relief of George Wein, Monk's quartet played the week without incident. He was on time, professional, and focused. But Boston jazz critic John McLellan didn't think much of the music. Despite brilliant performances at Newport and the Boston Jazz festival the previous summer, Monk appeared uninterested, sounding "like an entirely different person" who "seemed to go through the paces in a perfunctory manner." McLellan was equally unimpressed with Rouse, whom he found "competent and sympathetic" but lacking the excitement of a Sonny Rollins or Johnny Griffin. On the other hand, he was into Scott LaFaro's inventive phrasing, though he admitted that he couldn't hear the bass! And the fact that Monk never granted LaFaro a solo disappointed McLellan.[23] However, for both LaFaro and Motian, the week-long gig was hardly a disappointment. On the contrary, Monk gave them both a clinic they would never forget. LaFaro told Martin Williams, "I learned more about rhythm when I played with Monk . . . a great experience. With Monk, rhythmically, it's just there, always."[24] The drummer also got a lesson in rhythm—specifically, where he might place his accents: "I remember Monk asked me to sing him my ride beat. He said, 'Sing me what you're playing on the cymbal.' So I sang, 'ding DING-a ding, DING-a ding, DING-a ding, DING-a ding.' He said, "The next time you play, play 'ding din GA-ding, din GA-ding, din GA-ding.' " So that's what I did. And that helped my feel and the way I felt, the way my time is my beat. That helped me grow in how I play time. To try to think of all the notes, man, all the notes that you're playing on the cymbal, and the quality of the notes."[25]

Meanwhile, Harry Colomby began working with Joe Glaser's Associated Booking Corporation in an effort to keep Thelonious working while he, Joe Termini, and Termini's attorney Benjamin Gollay worked behind the scenes to restore Monk's cabaret card.[26] Among other things, Colomby booked Monk on a television special called "I Love a Piano." Part of the ABC series *Music for a Spring Night,* the episode was set to air on March 16 and feature performances by Eugene List, Dorothy Donegan, and Cy Walter, as well as Monk.[27] Monk was also included in the "Jazz Profiles" series held at the Circle in the Square Theater. Located in the gorgeously renovated Amato Opera House on Bleecker Street in Greenwich Village, the theater was a performer's dream: the acoustics were nearly perfect and the large rectangular floor-level stage surrounded on all sides by banks of seats created a uniquely intimate environment.[28] Monk planned to use his old rhythm section of Art Taylor and Sam Jones, but Jones came down with the flu and sent twenty-two-year-old Ron Carter in his place. The Detroit-bred bassist was a recent graduate of the Eastman School of Music but had spent the previous year recording and gigging with several different artists in and around New York.[29]

Held on Monday night, February 8, the "Jazz Profiles" concert was billed as a celebration of "thirty years of Monk's creativity." It was a kind of Monk retrospective, presented in an unusually respectful manner—no emcee, no warm-up acts, no flash. Almost *too* respectful, for John S. Wilson, who was ready to relegate Monk's music to the museum. Monk, he wrote, "has created a body of pieces that have seeped into the bloodstream of jazz, which bear the unmistakable stamp of his extremely personal view of melody and structure and which in the brief span of ten years, have lost their original jarring, eccentric sound to take on the comfortable familiarity of a pair of old shoes."[30] Whitney Balliett found the performance flawless. He praised Rouse and Taylor for their individual creativity and focused ensemble playing, but saved his strongest veneration for Monk, "a combined chairman of the board, puppeteer, and power behind his own throne, ceaselessly challenged his musicians. He never lost and he never will." More than anything, the poetry of Monk's motion inspired Balliett's poetic descriptions. He loved how Monk would "wind his body sinuously from side to side in half time to the beat and, his arms horizontally crooked, slowly snap his fingers—a dancer gracefully illustrating a difficult step in delayed motion." The dance continued, even at the keyboard where he might "suddenly bend backward, bring his elbows in, shoot out his forearms, and pluck handfuls of notes from either end of the keyboard, as if he were catching trout with his bare hands."[31] Dan Morgenstern enjoyed watching and listening to Monk that evening, but what he witnessed on stage dispelled the idea that Monk was eccentric or strange or out of it. Instead, he came across as self-possessed, knowledgeable, assured: "Monk knows where he is at, and so does the listener. . . . This knowing," Morgenstern continues, "gives Monk's music that dimension of balance and structure which is so clearly lacking in much contemporary jazz. You can enjoy Monk's music, and absorb its message, because it is whole." In other words, in the era of "freedom" when some jazz renegades were trying to break with structure altogether, Monk offered a corrective. [32] For all of these critics, Monk's remarkable concert struck a cautionary note: Don't abandon tradition.

The day after Valentine's Day, Monk's group opened at Pep's Musical Bar in Philadelphia, a popular black nightclub at Broad and South Streets.[33] Every night for a week, Nica drove Monk, Rouse, and Ron Carter to Philadelphia and returned that night after the last set.[34] This time Taylor couldn't make it, so Monk hired drummer Charles "Specs" Wright, a veteran on the Philadelphia scene.[35] A fine drummer influenced by Max Roach, Wright could swing the way Monk liked, but he was an inveterate junkie with a terrible reputation. He was known for visiting clubs during the day and convincing the owners that the resident bass player or the drummer had asked him to come by and pick up their instrument (it was common for musicians with more than one-night engagements to leave their bass or drums in the club). He would then hock the instrument for drug money.[36] Monk was warned, but he was never one to shy away from hiring addicts, as long as they could play and showed up to work on time. "Specs" worked well with the quartet, prompting Monk to hire him for his next engagement at the Minor Key, Detroit's first jazz coffee house.[37]

But just when Monk thought he had found a drummer, he lost his bassist. Ron Carter had many more opportunities to play in New York than Monk could give him, so he respectfully gave notice after the Pep's gig. Several friends suggested Monk reach out to another Philadelphian, John Ore. Ore had played with David Amram's group at the Five Spot and also recorded with Elmo Hope and Willie Jones, so Monk was already familiar with him. Nica was most adamant, and, in fact, formally introduced Ore to Monk. Monk had him come over to Nica's place on March 4, during a terrible blizzard, to rehearse with the band.[38] The fact that he even made it over to Jersey in such bad weather put him in good stead with Thelonious, though it was his big sound and time-keeping that won him the job.

On March 7, Monk went to ABC-TV studios to rehearse his number, "April in Paris," for the taping of *Music for a Spring Night*, and the next morning he (and probably Nellie) headed to the airport to catch a flight to Detroit. When it was time to go on at the Minor Key, everyone was ready to hit except his drummer. Specs Wright was nowhere to be found. A few days earlier, he had gotten an advance from Associated Booking for his plane fare, but instead squandered it on a fix.[39] Monk had no choice but to employ a local drummer. That was the last time he would use Wright. The drugs finally caught up with him. Wright died three years later, at thirty-five years of age.[40]

Thelonious did the best he could under the circumstances, but between the stress of Specs taking his advance and never showing up (for which Monk was docked $500!) and the weather (Detroit remained in the teens and twenties throughout the week[41]), Thelonious came down with a very bad cold. He flew back to New York the day he was supposed to tape the ABC program *Music for a Spring Night*, but bowed out at the last minute. A potential disaster became an opportunity for twenty-nine-year-old Phineas Newborn, Jr., who substituted for Monk with a florid, Tatumesque version of "It's All Right with Me."[42]

March 26, Monk was back at Town Hall, sharing the bill with Max Roach, Kenny Dorham, Jackie McLean, and the phenomenal Nina Simone, whose memorable debut concert at Town Hall six months earlier had catapulted her to the national stage.[43] Unfortunately, this evening was memorable more for its problems than its performances. The mic malfunctioned and the line-up had to be shuffled because Simone was late. When she finally took the stage, critic John S. Wilson was not impressed with her piano playing, which in his words proved "that if one note is repeated often enough a jazz concert audience will eventually applaud."[44] Wilson was ready to go home, until Thelonious Monk rode in on his black Steinway and saved the day. "Finally," he sighed, "Thelonious Monk's Quartet brought a brief note of individuality and jazz authenticity to an otherwise routine bill."[45]

Monk and Nellie spent the next few days preparing for another trip out west. Guido Cacianti gladly invited Monk back to the Blackhawk for a three-week stint in April. Because his gig at the Blackhawk coincided somewhat with Toot and Boo Boo's spring break, they decided to turn the trip into a family vacation. The only significant challenge facing Thelonious was finding a drummer. He disliked using pick-up drummers only vaguely familiar with his music, and the Specs Wright incident underscored why he needed to establish a permanent band. Just days before he was scheduled to depart, Monk found a temporary solution. On April 5, Billy Higgins had to leave Ornette Coleman's band because he lost his cabaret card due to previous drug arrests. Learning of Higgins's impending return to California, Monk promptly hired him for the Blackhawk date, which not only allowed Higgins to work but pay his passage west.[46]

While Monk and Nellie were preoccupied with work and travel arrangements, Nica was facing one of the biggest challenges of her life. Her trial date for the Delaware arrest was set to begin the last week of March. The forty-six-year-old mother of five children, scion of one of the world's wealthiest families, guardian angel for dozens of jazz musicians, faced a possible prison term. She could survive the shame, since the

Rothschilds had long treated her as the black sheep of the family, but she genuinely feared the penitentiary. On March 23, the day before her trial was to begin, she spent a cold afternoon sitting outside of St. Martin's Episcopal Church on the corner of 122nd and Lenox Avenue in Harlem. After about two hours of intense reflection, she finally went in and lit a candle to St. Martin. As she pondered her future, she penned an emotional note to Mary Lou Williams, characterizing the moment as "a chance to start afresh, with a clean slate . . . or the onset of inevitable catastrophe." Except for her attorneys, her daughter Janka, and a handful of close friends—Sonny Rollins, and, of course, Mary Lou—she kept her ordeal a secret. In fact, she did not mention the trial to Monk or Nellie. As she explained to Mary Lou, "his protection is the root of the whole business . . . I have never discussed it with him . . . I do not believe he is really aware of it . . . I do not want him to be . . . He & Nellie have enough worries, as it is. . . ." Still, she wondered if anyone remembered that her long-awaited judgment day had come.[47]

The cards were stacked against Nica from the outset. She was tried in Wilmington's Court of Common Pleas without a jury, and the judge apparently wanted to make an example of her. Her team of excellent attorneys argued that the ten dollars' worth of marijuana had been illegally seized.[48] There was no search warrant issued, she was never informed of her rights, and the police detained her without charge until they found evidence to charge her. These were all violations of state law, her lawyers argued. But it didn't matter. On April 22, the Baroness was convicted of unauthorized possession of narcotics and sentenced to three years in prison and a $3,000 fine. She immediately appealed the decision and was released on $10,000 bail. It wasn't over, but at least she was free to go. Now she had to wait for the case to wind its way to the Delaware Superior Court docket.[49]

Monk was already in San Francisco when Nica's conviction was handed down. It is not clear if he had known about the trial or if he and Nellie had been in touch with Nica. We do know that Monk had his own troubles to contend with, beginning with his travels. Given the opening night debacle the last time he played the Blackhawk, he had begun to think the club might be jinxed. They were scheduled to open on April 12, but this time the band made it on time but Monk did not. On their way to LaGuardia Airport, the car blew a tire on the Triborough Bridge. Monk explained, "It took the man from the AAA a while to get there and in all the heavy traffic he had a time doing the job. We missed our plane, of course. Couldn't get another one until today [April 13]. It sure bugged me, you know." To make matters worse, the hotel cancelled his reservation, forcing Monk and his family to find alternative quarters.[50]

Guido Cacianti could not afford to send the capacity crowd home on opening night, so he called local pianist Vince Guaraldi, who was then living in Daly City, to substitute. Guaraldi's availability and willingness calmed Cacianti's nerves momentarily . . . until he discovered that Billy Higgins's drums had not arrived from New York. But before the venerable owner burst a blood vessel, Higgins was able to borrow a drum set and the show went on.[51] Monk made it the following night, but Higgins's drums did not, and no one in the city could loan him a set of drums. The band had no other choice but to perform as a drum-less trio. As Monk explained to Bay Area critic Russ Wilson, "I was kind of worried. . . . We're not used to playing without drums so it's hard to do. I hope we didn't disappoint anyone."[52] Luckily, the drums arrived by the end of the second set.

The quartet played to a full house practically every night.[53] Monk dug Billy Higgins, whose uncanny ability to play freely while never losing his sense of swing reminded him a little of Roy Haynes. And the feeling was mutual. Higgins echoed the sentiments of so many young musicians who described working with Thelonious as an education. Though Higgins was only twenty-three, his work with Ornette Coleman had won him international acclaim as a leading innovator on his instrument. But as Monk reminded him, he still had a lot to learn, notably knowing "when *not* to play. . . . Monk can really hip a drummer to that, if he listens to him. He is a school within himself and in the little time I worked with him, I really learned a lot."[54] They did not hang out much off the bandstand, largely because Monk and Nellie focused their attention on the kids.

Thelonious was upbeat throughout most of the trip. He enjoyed sightseeing with his family, riding the cable cars up and down the city's hilly terrain, or just staying in the hotel room sleeping or playing games. On Easter Sunday, April 17, he appeared on Russ Wilson's radio show *Jazz Audition* sounding relaxed and contented. Anyone who thought of Thelonious as taciturn and uncommunicative would have been surprised. He greeted Wilson warmly and graciously, talked about how his children are "a lot of fun," spoke fondly (though briefly) about his early musical training, and answered Wilson's questions honestly and directly. Sometimes his directness and humor flustered his host, like when Wilson asked, "Do you have any feelings or ideas about the use of the violin in jazz?" Monk didn't miss a beat: "Well, I like all instruments, played right." Wilson: "That's true, of course, played right makes quite a difference."[55]

Everything went smoothly up until the last few days of the gig, when Orrin Keepnews showed up to produce a recording session with Monk's quartet featuring drummer Shelly Manne. It was Bill Grauer's idea. He hatched the plan with Lester Koenig, whose Contemporary label had made a killing with Manne and André Previn's LP *My Fair Lady*. They believed a Monk/Manne meeting could produce enough music for two LPs, one for Riverside and the other for Contemporary. While it seemed to be a financial no-brainer, the collaboration proved an artistic disaster—especially since Thelonious wasn't interested. Keepnews expanded the band by adding tenor saxophonist Harold Land and trumpeter Joe Gordon, who was a member of Manne's ensemble. He saved money on studio space by recording at the Blackhawk in the afternoon. The session was scheduled for the 28th of April. Monk showed up tired and irritable, suffering from a bad cold. The repertoire was entirely Monk's, and from the first take Manne deferred to Thelonious on every decision. This further irritated Monk, who believed that if he had to do the work of a leader, he ought to get top billing. The group got through two songs, "Just You, Just Me" and the new song he had composed at Nica's, initially called "Classified Information." Now he called it "Worry Later" because he couldn't think of a better title. In any event, both recordings were pretty lackluster. They tried again the next morning, producing a rather boring rendition of " 'Round

Midnight." By this point, Monk had closed himself off and Manne was uninspired, perhaps even embarrassed. According to Keepnews, "Shelly asked to be excused. He knew it wasn't happening well enough, and thought the proper thing to do was to stop."[56]

Keepnews came away angry, blaming Thelonious for the session's failure. "I felt totally frustrated. My engineer and I had traveled cross-country, worked hard, and would have absolutely nothing to show for it. . . . [H]e had kept the date from happening properly by not even trying to compromise with his co-leader; more than that, he must have known all along that he really didn't want to do it, so why hadn't he spoken up and vetoed the project months ago?"[57] Of course, in Monk's thirteen years as a recording artist he rarely had the opportunity to "veto" anything. Besides, he had begun to feel overshadowed by other Riverside recording artists, notably Cannonball Adderley and Bill Evans. Harry Colomby had grown distrustful of both Grauer and Keepnews, and Monk noticed. But neither Keepnews nor Monk wanted to end the trip without an album. Thelonious agreed to a live recording that night with Land and Gordon added to the ensemble. With Higgins in the drum seat, he felt confident that the band could really swing, even if the two horn players did not know all the intricacies of his music. Monk did not make it easy for his sidemen. He resurrected a couple of older compositions—"Let's Call This" and the treacherous "Four in One" (whose melody even Rouse had trouble navigating). With the exception of their rendition of "Evidence," Monk chose to stay at the keyboard and use the piano rather than his feet to lead the band. The results are mixed, but there are some extraordinary highlights— notably the debut of "Worry Later." Everyone sounds bright and joyful, and Monk's flurry of whole tone runs sounds reminiscent of his earlier Blue Note recordings. He later changed the title to "San Francisco Holiday," a fitting tribute to his working family vacation.[58]

The Monks flew back home on May 2. Because Thelonious had no out-of-town gigs lined up, Toot and Boo Boo spent more time at West 63rd Street, although they continued to live with their Aunt Skippy and attend P. S. 61 in the Bronx. Colomby had not booked any more out-of-town engagements because he, Joe Termini, and Benjamin Gollay were in final negotiations to have Monk's cabaret card restored. Termini promised Monk a long engagement at their new club called the Jazz Gallery. Located at 80 St. Marks Place, just a few blocks from the Five Spot, the Jazz Gallery opened around Christmas of 1959. A large square room with low ceilings, the new club was about three times the size of the Five Spot; it could seat up to 250 and the adjoining oval bar could accommodate nearly 100 more customers. The size of the space alone meant that the Terminis could afford more expensive acts, even big bands. The club earned its moniker for displaying work by mostly downtown artists.[59] The Terminis expected the State Liquor Authority to issue Monk a replacement card by the end of May, allowing him to open in June.[60]

On May 17, composer Gunther Schuller paid homage to Thelonious by presenting a new work at the Circle in the Square Theater called "Variants on a Theme by Thelonious Monk (Criss Cross)." Schuller had an intense attraction to Monk's "Criss

Cross" ever since he declared it a "masterpiece" in *Jazz Review* two years earlier.[61] Schuller drew on the composition's abstract qualities and constructed four different variants or, literally, *abstractions* of the melody. Ironically, Schuller viewed "Criss Cross" as the perfect vehicle for "Third Stream" music and the experiments of the emerging jazz avant-garde—directions for which Monk had little or no sympathy. Schuller employed strings and a full ensemble of fairly diverse musicians, ranging from Bill Evans on piano, Eric Dolphy on bass clarinet, to Ornette Coleman on alto. In fact, Coleman and Dolphy were the featured soloists. Both impressed the usually skeptical John S. Wilson with their "furious melee of urgent, discordant sounds."[62] I don't know if Monk actually attended the concert, though the meaning of Gunther Schuller presenting his work as "serious music" wasn't lost on him.

For Monk himself, the month of May proved relatively quiet. He did have one engagement—one that was particularly meaningful. He was invited to perform at the United Nations under the auspices of the U.N. Jazz Society. Barely a year old, the U. N. Jazz Society was founded by two African-American men: trumpeter/composer Bill Dixon and a former alto player named Richard Jennings. They initially considered forming a U.N. jazz ensemble, but instead organized Friday lunchtime lectures and performances. In the first year alone, the Society hosted composer George Russell, Cecil Taylor, Gunther Schuller, critic Martin Williams, Benny Golson, Art Farmer, Ornette Coleman, and Randy Weston.[63] Like many African-Americans, Thelonious admired the United Nations and felt a certain urgency to support its work. The U.N. had declared 1960 "The Year of Africa," inspired largely by the wave of nations achieving independence. But what was conceived as a year of celebration turned into a year of protest when South African police massacred unarmed blacks demonstrating peacefully against apartheid laws. On March 21, nearly 7,000 people led by the Pan Africanist Congress converged on a police station in the township of Sharpeville. Some burned their pass books, others simply showed up without passes and offered themselves up for arrest. The police opened fire on the demonstrators, killing at least sixty-nine people including eight women and ten children, though the unofficial count was much higher. The massacre sparked more protests, strikes and violent uprisings all across the country. Nine days later the ruling Nationalist Party declared a state of emergency and detained over 18,000 people. The United Nations responded immediately, condemning the violence and the South African government.[64]

Thelonious thought about Sharpeville. The incident garnered extensive news coverage, and many people close to him—his brother-in-law Sonny, Randy Weston, Max Roach—commented frequently on events in South Africa. At the time both Weston and Roach were working independently on compositions inspired by the African freedom movement. Weston, in collaboration with trombonist/arranger Melba Liston and poet Langston Hughes, was completing a four-part suite he called *Uhuru Afrika*, a paean to the new African nations, and Roach was preparing to record his *We Insist: Freedom Now Suite*, which celebrated a century of the black freedom movement and the continuing struggle for African liberation. His "Tears for Johannesburg" commemorated all who died in the anti-apartheid movement.[65] Besides, Monk's beloved New

York City had become an outpost for African liberation. Organizations such as the United African Nationalist Movement, the Universal African Nationalist Movement, the United Sons and Daughters of Africa, the African Nationalist Pioneer Movement, as well as the Liberation Committee for Africa, appeared all over the streets of Harlem, Brooklyn, and the Bronx, condemning state violence in South Africa, demanding freedom and aid for emerging African nations, and calling for an end to America's apartheid system—segregation.[66]

When Monk led his quartet—Rouse, John Ore, and drummer Al Dreares—into the U.N. Secretariat building, he felt he was entering history in the making. So did the 125 people in the audience, many of whom believed that seeing Monk perform in New York in such an intimate setting was itself historic. Besides the society's regular membership (diplomats and U.N. staff representing twenty-one countries), the event drew journalists and a few prominent musicians, including Ornette Coleman, Don Cherry, tenor saxophonist Booker Ervin, composers Earle Brown and Luciano Berio, and Monk's dear friend Randy Weston.[67] Most of the attendees came to hear Monk, but a few were there to check out multi-reed player Jimmy Giuffre's quartet, with Steve Lacy (soprano sax), Buell Neidlinger (bass), and Dennis Charles (drums). Actually, a more accurate description would be Steve Lacy's trio featuring Jimmy Giuffre: "Giuffre took my trio and called it a quartet," Lacy explained. "At the time, he didn't know what to do and found my trio interesting, but it didn't work out very well. He fired me after two weeks. . . ."[68] Giuffre's avant-garde outfit opened the concert with a couple of his original compositions and then audaciously played two Monk tunes.[69]

Monk's group performed five songs before a mesmerized, though unusually subdued, crowd. They were subdued for good reason: Bill Dixon had to ask the audience and the musicians to be "as quiet as possible" because U. N. General Secretary Dag Hammarskjøld was hosting dinner for the King of Nepal three floors below.[70] Afterward Monk complimented Lacy, who in turn invited him to come check out the group at the Five Spot, where they were opening for Ornette Coleman's quartet.[71] Lacy remembers Monk digging the band's interpretation of his music. Neidlinger remembered otherwise: "Thelonious hated the way we played his music. . . . [T]he Baroness would drive him over. She'd sit in the car while he came into the kitchen to get a hamburger and a whiskey and storm around. There was a big, metal firedoor that he used to slam during our numbers. Of course, when Giuffre played Monk's music, the chords were all wrong."[72] Still, he liked what Lacy was doing and told him so.

Monk was already familiar with Lacy's music. In late 1958, Lacy recorded *Reflections: Steve Lacy Plays Thelonious Monk*, the first LP devoted entirely to Monk's music by another artist. As soon as Lacy got his hands on a test pressing he personally delivered a copy to Thelonious. It was his way of formally introducing himself. "He appreciated [the album] a lot."[73] The twenty-six-year-old soprano saxophonist had been a Monk devotee since at least 1955, though his path to the High Priest was unusual. Born Steven Norman Lackritz to Russian immigrants in New York City, Lacy started on piano, played clarinet, and then switched to soprano saxophone after discovering the music of Sidney Bechet. As a teenager, he studied with Cecil Scott and played with several Dixieland and Chicago Jazz revival bands. He did not come up through bebop like most "modern" musicians. [74] And then he met Cecil Taylor. It was Taylor who literally took Lacy and his entire band to hear Monk, and it was Taylor who added a few Monk tunes to their repertoire.[75] By the time Lacy went into the studio to record *Reflections*, he had learned about thirty Monk tunes and "listened to Monk's records hundreds of times."[76]

So when Monk asked Lacy to join his new quintet scheduled to open at the Jazz Gallery in a couple of weeks, the young saxophonist was ecstatic—and ready.

It was as if they were waiting for the resurrection. The crowd started filing in around 8:00. By 9:00, the cavernous Jazz Gallery was packed. Fans were four deep at the bar and every seat was occupied. The air was thick with cigarette smoke and anticipation. As one excited observer put it, Monk's return to the club scene was "the most momentous thing to happen in jazz in the 'Apple' in the last eighteen months."[77] Nine-thirty, no Monk. No problem. Monk's group was playing opposite John Coltrane's astounding new quartet (McCoy Tyner, Jimmy Garrison, and Elvin Jones), so there was plenty of music to be had.[78] Besides, the real aficionados did not expect Thelonious to show up on time. They knew he wouldn't let them down, so they just drank a little more, smoked a little more, and listened to 'Trane. Then around 10:15, in walked Monk. The whole room let out a collective sigh, followed by a round of applause as he made his way to the bandstand, coat, hat, and all (despite the June weather). Reunited with Joe and Iggy Termini, surrounded by friends and enthusiastic fans, accompanied by Nellie and Nica, the night of June 14, 1960, could only be described as a "homecoming." When asked how he felt, he was at a loss for words: "Yes, I like, you know, to be back, it's nice."[79]

Nice indeed. He finally had some steady bread coming in, which allowed him to stay put in New York for a while. And he had a band. Rouse and Ore knew the music, and Lacy was eager to play and even more eager to listen to the master. Best of all, Monk found a drummer. Not just any drummer, the inimitable Roy Haynes. Haynes always had a way of lighting a fire under Monk's band, no matter what the tempo. He knew he couldn't keep Haynes forever, but he stayed for the length of the gig, which turned out to be sixteen weeks.[80] For Lacy, it was like being in school, or as he put it, "like about five schools rolled up into one."[81] "He had a way of teaching you without saying anything. . . . I had like slick tendencies. I wanted to be really modern and sharp and hip. . . . And he would correct me."[82] By "slick tendencies," he meant that he would play a lot of complicated phrases that allowed him to show off his virtuosity on the horn, but he would stray from the melody as well as the rhythm. Monk's injunctions were clear: "Don't play all that bullshit, play the melody! Pat your foot and sing the melody in your head, or play off the rhythm of the melody, never mind the so-called chord changes. . . . Don't pick up from me, I'm accompanying *you*!" He taught Lacy valuable lessons about composing and improvising: "The *inside* of the tune [the bridge] is what makes the *outside* sound good. . . . You've got to know the importance of discrimination, also the value of what you *don't* play. . . . A note can be as big as a mountain, or small as a pin. It only depends on a musician's imagination." And always "*Make the drummer sound good*!"[83] Above all, Monk taught Lacy to think independently, stretch out, even make mistakes. Learning to make mistakes, to listen, to tell a story with his horn, were not things he could have gotten from copying records or studying transcriptions of Monk's music. These were "ideological, philosophical, and political" lessons. He even described his experience with Monk as "spiritual." "He was a teacher, a prophet, a visionary."[84]

And a shrewd arranger. Monk knew exactly what he wanted from his band. He didn't want the horns to play harmony. "He had us play unisons and octaves only," Lacy explained, "because he said that that's the hardest thing to do. . . . And he was right. It took us weeks to get a good sound. And finally when Rouse and I got our lines hooked up like that it was a beautiful sound. Monk would add the harmonies on the piano."[85] Unfortunately, Riverside never recorded the quintet, and the only audio record we have was taken from a CBS radio broadcast of the Quaker City Jazz Festival in Philadelphia. Performing on August 26, 1960, about ten weeks into their stint together, Lacy sounds comfortable, and he and Rouse demonstrate just how "hooked up" their unison lines really are. Despite the poor audio quality (a symptom of performing outdoors at the huge Connie Mack Stadium), Haynes and Monk can be heard driving the beat forward. As a result, Lacy is much stronger rhythmically, more direct, and more "swinging" than most of his recorded work prior to joining Monk.[86]

Monk was perennially late, but Joe Termini tolerated it since they always hired two groups. Coltrane's quartet stayed for another week, then Joe Turner, followed by Gigi Gryce.[87] Termini couldn't complain too much because Monk drew crowds, and when it was time to take the bandstand, he went to *work*. Most nights were pretty uneventful, though there were a few memorable exceptions. Like the night Harry Colomby picked Thelonious up to take him to work. When Colomby arrived at West 63rd Street, Ike Quebec was there visiting. Both men looked a little dazed, but Colomby thought nothing of it. Quebec asked for a ride to the 14th Street subway station and Colomby obliged. "As we near downtown, a cop pulls us over. Ike has this paper bag in his hands, which he slipped under a blanket in the back of the car. The cop asks what's under the blanket? And Thelonious starts telling the cop that he's late for work, he has to get to his gig, and so forth. So the cop lets us go and I drop Monk off in front of the Jazz Gallery." He then took Quebec to the 14th Street station and before heading back to the Jazz Gallery he stopped off at a record store. "When I pull up to the Jazz Gallery, I see Thelonious out front pacing back and forth, nervous as hell. He lit in to me: 'Where were you? What took you so long?' Turns out, Ike did have something in the bag—heroin and needles, what Thelonious called 'the works.' I was shaken. I mean, I just imagined the headlines: 'Schoolteacher and two musicians arrested for heroin possession!' And we had just gotten his cabaret card back!"[88]

In addition to the six nights a week Monk put in at the Jazz Gallery, his quintet made a few concert appearances. Besides the Quaker City Jazz Festival, they performed three days at the Apollo (July 29–31) as part of the Apollo Theater Summer Jazz Festival.[89] And despite inclement weather, Monk made a return appearance at the Randall's Island Jazz Festival on Saturday, August 20, and in September performed three nights at Brooklyn's Plaza Theater.[90] Surprisingly, Monk did *not* play the Newport Jazz Festival. Perhaps it was a blessing in disguise. On the second day of the festival, thousands of young fans eager to get into a sold-out concert featuring Ray Charles launched into a pitched battled with police. A full-scale riot broke out, as cops deployed tear gas and ducked flying beer bottles. The violence that night forced George Wein and Newport organizers to close down the festival.[91] Meanwhile, Charles Mingus and Max Roach decided to boycott the proceedings and hold their own "Newport Rebels Festival" at Cliff Walk Manor, not far from Freebody Park. The musician-run alternative event openly protested George Wein's inclusion of pop singers, the commercialization of the festival, racial inequality in the music business, and the general exploitative conditions jazz musicians endured. As Max Roach explained to the press, the proceeds from the Rebels Festival "will go to fight injustices that are plaguing the musician such as the cabaret-card fight, the unemployment tax . . . we are also trying to prove that the musician can produce, present, and participate himself."[92] The list of participants cut across generation and style (though the vast majority were black). They included Coleman Hawkins, Eric Dolphy, Roy Eldridge, Randy Weston, Gigi Gryce, Teddy Charles, Kenny Dorham, Ornette Coleman and his group, Jo Jones, dancer Baby Laurence, among others. Thelonious Monk's name was invoked as a possible participant, but he never made it up there.[93]

However, Monk did make it to another, more urgent event in the name of social justice. On Sunday afternoon, August 7, the New York chapter of the Congress of Racial Equality (CORE) organized "Jazz Sits In," a fundraiser in support of the Southern student movement. Besides Monk's quintet, CORE recruited the Clark Terry quintet, singer Bill Henderson, and Jimmy Giuffre's group.[94] It is fitting that the Village Gate would host the event; its owners, Art and Burt D'Lugoff, had a long association with radical and anti-racist causes dating back to the late 1940s.[95] "Jazz Sits In" was the first of several civil rights benefits in which Monk would take part. Like the recent events in South Africa, the sit-in movement in the South deeply affected Thelonious. The movement was still in its infancy, having begun seven weeks before the Sharpeville massacre. On February 1, four black students walked into the local Woolworth's in Greensboro, North Carolina, and sat down at a whites-only lunch counter. Jim Crow laws prohibited blacks from sitting at the counter; they could only stand and eat. The young men, all of whom attended North Carolina A&T, were refused service, but would not move. The next day they were joined by twenty-three classmates, and by the third day three hundred African-American students packed into Woolworth's and occupied every seat available. Within days the movement had spread across the country, with CORE emerging as the principal organizer. The New York chapter of CORE moved swiftly in support of the students, organizing sympathy boycotts and pickets of Woolworth's and other dime stores in the city and raising money for bail and related expenses. Two and a half months later, the Student Non-Violent Coordinating Committee (SNCC) was born.[96] The benefit afforded Thelonious an opportunity to meet CORE members, learn more about events in the South, and contribute to the movement he had come to admire.[97]

Monk played one more benefit before the summer ended, this one for a cause much closer to him in both proximity and personal experience. Woodsmen Enterprises, a new, black-run nonprofit organization, sponsored a jazz concert at the Bedford YMCA in Brooklyn, to raise money to renovate the Y's dilapidated buildings. The Bedford YMCA served local youth, much like Monk's precious Columbus Hill Neighborhood Center and Harlem's Morningside Community Center. The area near Bedford Avenue and Monroe Street was considered a neighborhood "in the latest stages of racial transition." As more and more working-class black families moved into what had previously been a largely Jewish neighborhood, the Bedford Y's new leaders hoped that athletics and social services might be a way to bring kids together, ease tensions, and improve the life chances of poor black youth.[98]

The Jazz Gallery gig closed on October 2, giving Thelonious a much-needed and well-deserved hiatus. He took some time to rest on his laurels, which included best pianist in the *Down Beat* International Critics Poll, for a third year in a row, and the first annual Edison International Award, the Netherlands' most prestigious music award—an honor he shared with Frank Sinatra.[99] Meanwhile, Roy Haynes gave notice. He was already one of the most sought-after drummers on the scene even during the Jazz Gallery gig, so he had no shortage of work.[100]

The Terminis signed Monk on for another extended engagement at the Jazz Gallery, starting November 15. They agreed to a quartet this time, partly for financial reasons. Rouse and Ore were ready to work again, but Monk had yet to permanently fill the drum chair. When he heard that Frankie Dunlop was available, he immediately offered him the job.[101] It had been three years since they last worked together at the Five Spot—the gig ending prematurely when the union rep pulled the young drummer off the job for failing to fulfill Local 802's residency requirement. Now, just shy of his thirty-second birthday, Frankie Dunlop had built up his resume. Since those two nights with Monk, he had worked with Charles Mingus, Sonny Rollins, Maynard Ferguson, Duke Ellington, Lena Horne, and most recently Gigi Gryce.[102] But Monk knew that he still had a lot to learn. As Dunlop recalled, school began promptly on opening night. Before taking the bandstand, Monk pulled him aside and said, "You want to solo and play fast all the time. All drummers are that way. When you're playing fast, soloing, and throwing your sticks, you think you're really playing. In your estimation, that's the hardest. Well, you know, it's really harder to play slow than it is to play fast, and to swing and create something while you're doing it." Dunlop nodded. Then when it was time to play, Monk counted out an extremely slow tempo. Every measure felt like a lifetime. Dunlop struggled to make something happen and maintain the tempo against Monk's off-meter phrases. Then Monk suddenly got up from the piano to dance, leaving Dunlop and Ore alone to support Rouse's solo. Monk sidled up alongside Dunlop and began cajoling him. "Okay. Get to me now. Swing it, pal. . . . Okay Frankie, come on now. Let me see you swing now. *Shit.* I told you it ain't easy to swing when you're playing slow. I told you that, didn't I? Come on."[103] Just when he thought it couldn't get any worse, Monk shouts, "Drum solo," Dunlop recalled. "'Let me hear something Frank. Don't be *bullshittin*'.' I was trying to do things that I couldn't do. Monk said, 'And keep the time. Here's the tempo. Don't play some shit that you don't know nothing about.'

I didn't even know how to put a paradiddle in there, because I'd never played a para-diddle that slow. And whatever I played, Monk said that he wanted it to make sense. I couldn't do any of my rudiments."[104] A trial by fire, but Dunlop survived. During the break, Thelonious underscored his point, giving his drummer advice he would never forget: "[Monk] said that, if you were swinging in jazz, it could go with any tempo, even a ballad."[105]

Monk could now say that he had a band. They rehearsed a little at Nica's, but the Jazz Gallery became their rehearsal space, the place to hone their sound and find their groove. Joe Termini happily retained Monk's band until New Year's Day. For nearly seven weeks they were the Jazz Gallery's mainstay while Gil Evans Big Band, Dizzy Gil-lespie's quintet, and Dave Brubeck's quartet passed through.[106]

In the meantime, Rouse cut an album for the Epic label, his second as a leader since joining Monk.[107] Several months earlier, Orrin Keepnews produced Rouse's first LP, *Takin' Care of Business*, for the Jazzland label, an off-shoot of Riverside Records.[108] Monk encouraged Rouse to pursue his own music, but he must have also been a little envious. It had been almost a year and a half since he set foot in a recording studio. Riverside now had a stable of artists and Cannonball Adderley was the main attraction. Feeling slighted, Monk's relationship with Orrin Keepnews deteriorated. "Whenever Orrin Keepnews called," Toot remembered, "my father would whisper, 'Tell him I'm not here.' Orrin was always the one person my dad did not want to talk to."[109] Chris Albertson, who joined Riverside's staff in October of 1960, observed a marked chill between Monk and Keepnews. In fact, Albertson found Keepnews egotistical and dif-ficult to work with. "Orrin had this grumpy look on his face. He doesn't have much of an ear for music. He can't tell when something is good or not so good, so he likes to remain neutral. He stands there stonefaced, cigarette dangling from his mouth, which made a lot of musicians uptight. . . . When I saw Orrin work, it was really the musicians producing the record."[110] Randy Weston felt the same way. "The guy thought he knew everything. He talked all the time and never listened."[111]

Occasionally Monk would drop by the office, located on West 46th in the Para-mount Hotel, and just hang out. Once he plopped down in Chris Albertson's office to check out the new guy. He was, after all, a curiosity; a jazz and blues lover born in Iceland, raised in Denmark, Albertson had been in the country only three years before landing the Riverside job.[112] "Monk just sat there for a while. After about fifteen min-utes, he said out of the blue, 'I wrote a kiddie song.' So I say, sort of jokingly, 'You think you might want to record it for us?' He said, 'Maybe.' And he walked out."[113]

Albertson's observations were on the mark—relations between Monk and River-side had soured. During the summer, Harry Colomby initiated an audit of Riverside on the suspicion that Monk was not receiving his full share of royalties. He found their accounting methods questionable, especially when Monk's record sales began to top 20,000. "When I got the auditor's report back, the very first thing that I saw on the first page was that 'We accept their internal accounting methods.' What was the point of that? I still saw a lot of 'Oops, I forgot this, oops I'. . . . knew he would never get [his money] back."[114] The audit found no wrongdoing, but three years later, when

Grauer died of a heart attack in Switzerland, Colomby alleges that Grauer had "a letter to Orrin, referring to me looking into [the finances] and being on to the fact that they had two or three sets of books."[115] Although Colomby never saw the letter, he is convinced of its veracity. And so was Thelonious, who left the company feeling that Riverside cheated him. In an interview three years later, Monk said of Riverside: "Some companies only think about making money. At least, they should give you the money they owe you."[116] Absent Riverside's accounting records, it is impossible to prove that the company underpaid Monk, but other sources reveal that Grauer engaged in questionable business practices. For example, he convinced creditors to loan him large sums of money by inflating sales figures. The company printed many more LPs than they needed and shipped them out even when they did not have orders for all of them. This gave the false impression that sales were high, but it also meant a warehouse filled with returns—which they ended up dumping at discount record stores. The company went bankrupt the year after Grauer's death.[117]

But by the end of 1960, Colomby had already seen the handwriting on the wall. He and Monk agreed that it was time to look for a new label. The only thing keeping Monk there was his contract: he owed Riverside two more LPs. And he had no real desire to work with Keepnews, not even to record a "kiddie song."

The Jazz Gallery gig ended on an upswing. Monk and his crew rang in the New Year, 1961, and Nica and Nellie were on hand to celebrate. Thelonious had just learned that George Wein was planning his first European tour and wanted to include him. Harry Colomby was hard at work trying to either renegotiate Monk's contract with Riverside or find a more appreciative label. And Monk . . . well, he was healthy and feeling good about the future. He had gone quite a while without a major breakdown and it felt good to be back at work in his home town.

Nica was also in a good mood. Reputedly a stingy tipper, she broke tradition and left the waiter a check for $100. His name was Ran Blake, and while waiting tables was not his forte (a few weeks earlier he was fired and then rehired after spilling drinks on James Baldwin and Sidney Poitier), he knew she liked her Chivas Regal with no ice, and, more importantly, he was a hell of a pianist and a Thelonious Monk devotee. A recent graduate of Bard College, Blake had been following Monk's music since 1955, studying with Gunther Schuller at the Lenox School of Jazz, catching Monk and 'Trane at the Five Spot, incorporating Monkish harmonies in his own music. He had even written to Monk inviting him to participate on his college review. He worshipped Monk almost to a fault: Once, during a wedding gig in Boston, he played some Monk "tone clusters" to disastrous effect. "The bride was getting nauseated, and someone politely asked me to leave," he recalled. But now he was in seventh heaven, having just moved to New York to study with Schuller and Bill Russo, he had some access to the Man himself. Blake will never forget the first words Monk uttered to him: "Kid, let me get some more of that fried rice." He tried on several occasions to reach out to Monk for private lessons or conversation, but Thelonious politely put him off at first. But on New Year's Eve, perhaps inspired by the festive atmosphere and overall good mood,

Monk warmed up a bit and invited Ran to drop by the house. Clearly, he liked the kid, and Nica adored him.[118]

Monk spent the next few weeks at home, writing new music, practicing, and hanging out with Nellie and the children. The city experienced one of the most severe winters in modern history. The temperature remained below freezing for three weeks, and at times the snow reached waist-high. During the first weekend in February alone, eighteen inches of snow fell on Manhattan.[119] That Saturday night, February 4, Thelonious ventured out to get some cigarettes and fresh air. He returned home around 11:00 p.m. and began kicking the snow off of his shoes when seven-year-old Boo Boo told her father that smoke was coming out the kids' bedroom closet. When he opened the closet door he discovered the clothes on fire.[120] Toot and Nellie were in the master bedroom watching television. "I remember my father came running in the room," Toot explained, "and he said, 'Get up, get up, get up, we gotta get out! We gotta get out!' And I remember him rushing my sister and me out the door and my mother looking. . . . My mother had some kind of animal coat—not alpaca—but something that cost a lot of money. She wanted it and it was burning. And I'll never forget, she ran in to grab it out of the closet . . . and I remember my father saying, 'Fuck the coat, Nellie. Get out of here,' and he threw the coat back and just pushed us all out the door."[121]

The Monks ran across the street to "Aunt" Rae McKinney's apartment in the projects and called the fire department. The heavy snow caused a delay, but the crew arrived in time to extinguish the blaze before it spread. Monk was relieved no one was hurt. It could have been a lot worse. The fire in 1956 engulfed much of the apartment, but this seemed more contained. Or so he thought. When the axe-wielding firemen finished the job and headed back to the station, Thelonious went back in to inspect the damage. Suddenly it got very, very cold.

22

"Bebopens Oversteprast"

(February–May 1961)

It was after midnight before the firemen finally left. The culprit turned out to be old or faulty wiring. With no functioning electricity, Thelonious had to wait until daylight to inspect the damage. The next morning, while the kids slept over at the McKinneys' place, he and Nellie slogged through a couple of inches of water to assess their losses. The place was a wreck. As with the last fire, the firefighters did more damage than the smoke and flames. "The firemen came and tore the place to shreds with their axes," Toot recalled. "That was in the days when you know firemen, they just did their thing, just destroying and stealing and all kinds of wild stuff. Soaked everything, absolutely everything." Most of their clothes were lost, along with tapes and records (including studio session tapes he had gotten from Riverside), and some important papers—including the charts from the 1959 Town Hall concert. Worst of all, Monk's rented Steinway piano was burned beyond repair. He had had it just over four years—nearly long enough to take ownership. Fortunately, his sheet music was spared this time, as well as his precious Edison International Award.[1]

The water eventually subsided, and later in the afternoon Toot and Boo Boo joined their parents in an effort to salvage what was left. The snow came down even harder. As the four of them tried to cope with the losses, a rather tall, thin white man suddenly walked in. It was Ran Blake, the young pianist-cum-waiter whom Nica befriended at the Jazz Gallery. Monk had forgotten that he invited Ran over for a visit: "I rang the bell and walked in, and I think the four of them were sitting on a large bed—Toot and Nellie, Thelonious and Barbara. I can almost see the piano in ashes. . . . The place was in shambles. There was water all over the place, but outside there were no visible signs that there had been a fire. I didn't know what had happened until I walked in. Evidently, the door must have been ajar."[2] For Blake, the entire experience was surreal. Here was his very first visit to his hero's house and he walked right into the aftermath of a tragedy. He tried to make himself useful. First he called Nica in Weehawken, who gave him a list of contacts to call. She would have already been with the Monks if not for the snow. Blake braved the weather and picked up some dinner, and then reached out to other musicians and Nica's contacts to rustle up supplies—second-hand clothes, blankets, food, and assorted sundry items. Blake's kind gesture, however, made Thelonious and Nellie uncomfortable. "I remember embarrassing the Monks because I was calling around to places like the Vanguard, asking if I could get takeout food, and the Monks had more money than I did." Nellie ended up returning most of these generous donations.[3]

Blake was most helpful caring for the kids while Monk and Nellie and the extended family tried to put their life back together. He took them out to restaurants and to buy clothes with money provided by the Baroness, and sometimes brought them uptown to his place on 113th and Amsterdam. Toot's buddy Gregory Flowers frequently tagged along. His fondness for Toot and Boo Boo evolved into a warm friendship; a couple of times a year he would take them out for a meal and catch up. Nellie and Monk appreciated the role he played in the kids' lives. Several years later, Blake ran into Nellie in the lobby of the Parker House Hotel in Boston and she shoved a couple of hundred dollars in his hand. "You did a lot for us," she said.[4]

Monk and Nellie moved in with Skippy, whose apartment on Bristow Street in the Bronx had become a second home for Toot and Boo Boo. The kids were already enrolled in school there and Sonny, Geraldine, and their kids were only three blocks away.[5] While the Graham brothers—the contractors who worked on the last renovation— performed their magic on 243 West 63rd Street, the Monks settled in for an indefinite stay. Skippy's place was big enough for Nellie and Thelonious and Boo Boo and Toot to have two separate bedrooms, though quarters were tight nonetheless. Skippy and her partner, Tony Brown, had a fifteen-month-old baby they named Pannonica, and Ronnie still lived at home, although at twenty years old he preferred to be out and about.[6] Monk's work and travel schedule eased the pressure; he had engagements in Chicago and Boston in March and early April, and then it was off to Europe.

The immediate aftermath of the fire must have been surreal. Losing so much so quickly left Monk incredibly vulnerable, and yet the jazz world treated him like a god. Two days after the fire, Johnny Griffin and Eddie "Lockjaw" Davis were in the studio with Orrin Keepnews recording an LP dedicated entirely to Monk's compositions. Thelonious could not make the session. Griffin remembers hearing of the fire, which ultimately gave the session a greater poignancy and urgency.[7] Monk did make it to Nola Studios on Wednesday night, February 22, for Abbey Lincoln's record date. Max Roach, Lincoln's fiancé and drummer on the session, invited Monk because she had written lyrics to "Blue Monk" and they wanted to get the composer's blessings. She cast "Blue Monk" as a sage and "monkery" meant "the act of self-searching, like a monk does."[8]

Most importantly, the band was swinging: besides Roach, she had Mal Waldron on piano, Coleman Hawkins, Eric Dolphy, Julian Priester on trombone, Art Davis on bass, and a twenty-two-year-old phenom on trumpet named Booker Little. Over Waldron's slow, bluesy arrangement, and Little's dazzling yet understated trumpet obligato, Lincoln belted out lyrics with which Monk could identify:

Going alone
Life is your own
But the cost sometimes is dear

Being complete
Knowing defeat
Keeping on from year to year
It takes some doing
Monkery's the blues, you hear
Keeping on from year to year

According to producer Nat Hentoff, Monk was quite "pleased."[9] He stuck around for most of the session, enjoying Lincoln's vibrant interpretation of Randy Weston's "African Lady," her lyrical plea for reparations for slavery in 5/4 time titled "Retribution," her swinging reading of Paul Laurence Dunbar's poem "When Malindy Sings," and her poignant rendition of "Left Alone"—a lovely ballad Mal Waldron wrote as a vehicle for Billie Holiday. Monk listened intently and danced to at least one number. According to Ran Blake, who was also among twelve or fifteen spectators at Nola Studios that evening, "Monk was thrilled by Abbey's voice. That smile. I don't think he looked at me. His eyes were riveted on Abbey."[10] After the session, Thelonious went over to Lincoln and said, "I like the way you stand."[11] Then he leaned in a little closer and offered her some advice. As Lincoln tells it, "he whispered in my ear, 'Don't be so perfect.' He meant, don't be afraid to make a mistake."[12]

The next night, Monk's quartet played a concert at the Museum of Modern Art as part of its Jazz Profiles series. His first performance since New Year's Eve at the Jazz Gallery, Monk showed up on time and the band kicked off at exactly 9:00 p.m. Besides his original compositions, he included four standards: "I'm Getting Sentimental Over You," "Sweet Georgia Brown," "Sweet and Lovely," and an unaccompanied version of "Just a Gigolo." As John S. Wilson observed, Monk played these tunes fairly straight without sacrificing his style: "the melody was never obliterated and the rhythmic attack was toe-tapping swinging." It was as if he wanted to remind listeners that he was a traditionalist in the era where "modern art" was increasingly associated with the avant-garde. The audience dug the music, and he stuck close to the printed program until the end. Anxious to end the concert, Monk dropped a song from the repertoire, played the final tune as an encore, and hastily led his band off stage ten minutes early.[13] Whatever his motivations, the audience left the museum "bewitched, bothered, and bewildered walking the streets, wandering quo vadis at 9:50."[14]

Harry Colomby booked Monk's quartet for a two-week run in mid-March at the Birdhouse in Chicago, a fairly new club on the Northside that served no alcohol[15] and held afternoon press conferences for young writers from high school and college newspapers to interview the resident artists. Monk arrived early, and graciously fielded questions from a roomful of nervous teens. In response to one kid's query into what he thought about Lawrence Welk, Monk broke up the room with his characteristically pithy and honest response: "I think he's got a good gig."[16] The more telling interview was granted to professional jazz critic and columnist for the Chicago *Sun-Times* Gabriel Favoino. Monk was uncharacteristically talkative, but he also seemed to have an agenda. He wanted to establish two points: first, that he, in fact, pioneered modern jazz in the 1940s, and two, the "new thing" in jazz has nothing new to offer. "It's been 20 years since any important changes have been made," Monk explained. "The harmony didn't do justice to the melody in those days. We had a different conception of phrasing and figuration. Nobody was writing much then. But we were game enough to make up our minds to go write this stuff." While Monk waxed philosophically about his contribution to modern music, a group of skeptical young men playing chess overheard the exchange and chimed in. One asked, "When was the change of the '40s complete?" Monk ignored the question. But then the young man followed up with, "What about Ornette Coleman, is that anything new?" "I haven't listened to him that good," Monk replied. "Like something was always happenin'. But I don't think it's going to revolutionize jazz." Favoino, who found the whole exchange telling, concluded with a prescient remark: "And so it is always. Today's trailblazers are tomorrow's conservatives."[17]

Chicagoans who packed the Birdhouse just about every night didn't think of Monk as a conservative—not just yet. It had been nearly two years since he last played the Windy City, so the jazz community was out in full force to see the "eccentric" pianist and his new band—especially Frankie Dunlop, whose hard-driving rhythms and big sound electrified audiences.[18] From Chicago, they flew to Boston for a week-long engagement at Storyville, returning home just long enough to pack for Europe.

It is startling to think that, at the age forty-three, the internationally acclaimed Thelonious Monk had only crossed the Atlantic once before, and that was seven years earlier. He felt excited, partly because he was to see more than Paris, and partly because impresario George Wein was paying him "as much or more than he would receive in a week at a night club."[19] But mostly because he was taking Nellie.

The European tour was a landmark event in Monk's career, as well as George Wein's. Unbeknownst to most artists on the tour, Wein was in dire financial straits. The year before he was forced to abandon Storyville (which had been resurrected by Ralph Snyder in name only at the Hotel Bradford), and the "riots" at Newport in 1960 forced Wein to abandon the festival the following year.[20] The future of the Newport Jazz Festival was uncertain, and so was Wein's income. Indeed, money was so tight that his wife, Joyce, had to take a job at Columbia Medical School just so they could make ends meet. This tour had to be a financial success, otherwise it might mean the end of Wein's career as a concert promoter.[21]

In truth, Wein was juggling two separate tours. A week before Monk's quartet was scheduled to arrive, Wein had already begun touring with the Newport Jazz Festival All-Stars, a traditional Chicago-style jazz outfit with the impresario himself on piano.[22] They performed in Berlin on April 8 and were to appear at the Fourth Annual Essen (Germany) Jazz Festival on the 14th, along with Monk's quartet, Bud Powell, and others.[23] Monk's entourage arrived the day they performed. Jet lag notwithstanding, the crowd's enthusiasm energized Monk, and the presence of his old friend on the same bill thrilled him. Powell had been living in Paris a little over two years now.[24] Since he was lined up to join the tour later, that night in Essen was just the beginning of a bittersweet reunion. Bittersweet because Powell looked terrible; he was visibly depressed, over-weight, drinking heavily (which, for Powell, could mean one or two glasses of wine), and taking Largactyl—an anti-psychotic barbiturate prescribed for schizophrenia that left him lethargic and caused his hands to swell. He was miserable, living at the Hotel La Louisiane under what some observers perceived to be the iron rule of his wife, Alte-via "Buttercup" Powell. She monitored his every move, kept him on Largactyl, and often locked him in his room when he wasn't working.[25] It was a delicate situation. Nellie and Buttercup were friends. Before they left for Paris in 1959, Buttercup and Bud visited the Monks' apartment with their son Johnny, who was four at the time. Although Johnny was prone to tantrums and raised by a mother who disrespected and abused his father, Thelonious adored him and Toot and Boo Boo sometimes enter-tained him.[26] From Nellie's perspective, Buttercup was caring for Bud and handling his business affairs because she had a young son to raise. Bud, after all, was her sole source of income.[27]

The reunion was short-lived; the next morning Monk and company were off to Amsterdam for the next performance. But before the concert that night, Monk's quar-tet had to head out to the town of Bussum to tape a show for Dutch television. Thijs Chanowski, the program's director, found the whole affair challenging. The musicians simply walked into the studio and started playing without saying a word. He wasn't sure how to shoot them, or how long they planned to play. All he knew was that he had fifteen minutes to fill and a small audience of young people he wanted to incorporate in the shot. As soon as the band took off, he started improvising with the cameras, using a series of wide shots and close-ups. "But just when I thought I had succeeded in getting Monk the way I wanted him," Chanowski later recounted, "he stopped right in the middle of a number and walked out. It took quite some effort to talk him into continuing, but when he finally gave in and started to play, again, he never stopped."[28] He was pleased with the results. In the surviving clip, they play a sparkling version of "Rhythm-a-ning," though the band appears tired and uninterested—all but Frankie Dunlop, who self-consciously smiles at the camera and revels in the attention. Theloni-ous stands up during the bass and drum solos and makes a half-hearted stutter step but he apparently did not feel like dancing.[29]

Fatigue did not stop the band from playing a full hour that evening in Amster-dam's Concertgebouw auditorium. The place was packed with admiring fans grateful to see the great Thelonious Monk in person. And judging from the broadcast made by a Dutch radio station, Monk was energized by the crowd and wanted to deliver a great show. The quartet opened with "Jackie-ing," and moved through the better-known compositions—including "Crepuscule with Nellie," "Straight, No Chaser," "Evi-dence," "Bemsha Swing," "Well, You Needn't," "'Round Midnight," "I Mean You," and always closing with "Epistrophy."[30] Despite what proved to be a limited repertoire of about fifteen to twenty songs, Monk's sets were never pre-planned, and, except for the opening and closing, the band never knew what was next until Monk began. But a couple of things distinguished the Amsterdam concert from the rest. First, he got up from the piano only twice—on "Straight, No Chaser" and "Evidence." If he did dance,

Thelonious Monk, Sr., 1930s.
Courtesy Thelonious Monk Estate.

Georgianna Batts and daughter Barbara,
Rocky Mount, North Carolina, circa 1910.
Courtesy Thelonious Monk Estate.

Left to right: Thomas, Marion, and
Thelonious in New York City, circa
1922. *Courtesy Thelonious Monk Estate.*

Neighborhood children lined up outside the Columbus Hill Community Center on West 63rd Street, circa 1933–1934. *Used courtesy of the Children's Aid Society.*

A page from Monk's tenth grade composition book for Mr. Marks's English Class, 1933: "My Favorite Magazine." *Courtesy Thelonious Monk Estate.*

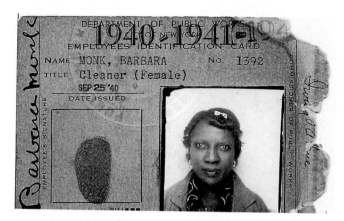

Barbara Monk's city employee identification card. She was a
cleaner for Children's Court on East 22nd Street in Manhattan.
Courtesy Thelonious Monk Estate.

Thomas, Marion, and Thelonious, circa
1940–1942. *Courtesy Thelonious Monk Estate.*

With Rubie Richardson, Monk's first serious
love. *Courtesy Thelonious Monk Estate.*

Twenty-one-year-old Thelonious Monk holds his infant nephew Theolonious. The photo was taken early spring 1939. *Courtesy Thelonious Monk Estate.*

Nellie Monk. *Courtesy Thelonious Monk Estate.*

Thomas Monk and his family at a neighborhood park outside Amsterdam Houses, circa 1948. *Left to right:* Theolonious, Charlotte, Thomas Monk, Sr., Trotyrine, Marion ("Sissy"), and Thomas, Jr. *Courtesy Thelonious Monk Estate.*

Nellie's sister Evelyn "Skippy" Smith. *Courtesy Evelyn Smith and Benetta Smith-Bines.*

Monk's first-born, "Toot," at the basketball court on West 63rd Street, circa 1953. *Courtesy Thelonious Monk Estate.*

Nellie helps "Boo Boo" (Barbara) with her homework in their kitchen at the Phipps Houses. This photo was taken not long before their second fire in 1961. *Courtesy Thelonious Monk Estate.*

Nellie's brother and Monk's best friend, James "Sonny" Smith, with his wife, Geraldine. *Courtesy Geraldine Smith.*

Nellie and Thelonious's nieces and nephews on the Smith side of the family. *Top, left to right:* Jackie Smith Bonneau, Pannonica Val-Hackett, Gerald Pierre Smith, Benetta Smith-Bines, Judith Smith. *Bottom left to right:* James Riley Smith, Jr., Evelyn Smith, Clifton Bennett Smith. *Courtesy Evelyn Smith and Benetta Smith-Bines.*

Thelonious with his nephew Ronnie Newkirk in the mid-1950s. *Courtesy of Clifton Smith.*

Monk at a Blue Note recording session, July 23, 1951. *Photograph by Francis Wolff © Mosaic Images LLC. All Rights Reserved.*

Idrees Sulieman (trumpet) and Monk at a Blue Note recording session, WOR Studios, October 15, 1947. *Photograph by Francis Wolff © Mosaic Images LLC. All Rights Reserved.*

Monk jamming with Charles Mingus (bass), Roy Haynes (drums), and Charlie Parker (saxophone) at the Open Door in Greenwich Village, September 1953. *Photograph by Robert Parent. Courtesy Getty Images. All Rights Reserved.*

Monk with an all-star band at Tony's in Brooklyn, March 1954. *Left to right:* Thelonious Monk, Miles Davis (trumpet), Gigi Gryce (saxophone), and Max Roach (drums). *Not pictured:* bassist Charles Mingus. *Photograph by Jimmy Morton. Courtesy Jimmy Morton and Fred Brathwaite, Jr., from Fred Brathwaite, Sr., Archives. All Rights Reserved.*

Monk's band at Tony's in Brooklyn, December 1953. *Left to right:* Thelonious Monk, Sam Gill (bass), Willie Jones (drums), and Kenny Dorham (trumpet). *Photograph by Jimmy Morton. Courtesy Jimmy Morton and Fred Brathwaite, Jr., from Fred Brathwaite, Sr., Archives.*

Charles Delaunay attends to Monk backstage at the Salle Pleyel, Paris, June 1954. *Photograph by Marcel Fleiss. Used courtesy of Marcel Fleiss.*

Monk and pianist Rene Urtreger, Paris, June 1954. *Photograph by Marcel Fleiss. Used courtesy of Marcel Fleiss. All Rights Reserved.*

Baroness Pannonica de Koenigswarter at the Village Vanguard. *Photograph by Raymond Ross. © Raymond Ross Archives/ CTSIMAGES.COM.*

Monk performs at the Salle Pleyel for the Paris Jazz Festival ("Salon du Jazz"), June 1954. *Photograph by Marcel Fleiss. Used courtesy of Marcel Fleiss. All Rights Reserved.*

Thelonious Monk with Sonny Rollins (tenor saxophone), Roy Haynes (drums), and Ahmed Abdul-Malik (bass), at the Five Spot Café, September 1958. *Photograph by Marvin Oppenberg. Music Division, The New York Public Library for the Performing Arts, Astor, Lenox and Tilden Foundations. All Rights Reserved.*

Thelonious lounging with Nellie before his Royal Festival Hall Concert, London, April 29, 1961. *Photograph by Erich Auerbach. Hulton Archive/Getty Images. All Rights Reserved.*

Hall Overton and Thelonious Monk look over a score during rehearsal at Eugene Smith and Overton's loft on Sixth Avenue, November 1963. Frankie Dunlop is at the drums and Butch Warren is on bass. *Photograph by Ivan Black. Music Division, The New York Public Library for the Performing Arts, Astor, Lenox and Tilden Foundations. All Rights Reserved.*

Thelonious and his nephew
Alonzo White on Monk's
first European tour, May
1961. *Courtesy Alonzo White.*

With host Reiko Hoshino during Monk's first tour of Japan,
May 1963. Ms. Hoshino owned and operated a jazz café in
Kyoto. *Courtesy Thelonious Monk Estate.*

Harry Colomby, Thelonious Monk, and Teo Macero enjoy a couple of beers and ham sandwiches between takes at a recording session, 30th Street Studios. *Photograph by Doug Quackenbush. Used by permission. Courtesy Olga Quackenbush. All Rights Reserved.*

Monk backstage at the Village Gate, 1962. *Photograph by Eddie Locke. Used by permission. All Rights Reserved.*

Monk with Dizzy Gillespie, Amsterdam Airport Schiphol, October 25, 1972. *Photograph by Nellie Monk. Courtesy Thelonious Monk Estate.*

Thelonious Monk, Jr., on drums, 1972.
Photograph by Raymond Ross. © Raymond Ross Archives/CTSIMAGES.COM.

Charlie Rouse performing with Monk not long before he left the band, 1969.
Photograph by Raymond Ross. © Raymond Ross Archives/CTSIMAGES.COM.

Boo Boo Monk in rehearsal, circa 1978–1979. *Courtesy Thelonious Monk Estate.*

Monk at the 30th Street Studios for a Columbia recording
session, 1964. *Photograph by Doug Quackenbush. Used by permission.*

this would have been his chance. On most numbers he comped unceasingly, generating a dynamic interchange between the piano and the band. Second, unlike subsequent concerts, he did not grant John Ore a solo and Dunlop was featured only on the introduction to "Jackie-ing." Over time, this would change, as Monk imposed a standard solo pattern of sax followed by piano, bass, and then drums. And yet, each performance was fresh because Monk refused to repeat himself, either in his comping or his solos. Thelonious had an uncanny ability to build an entire solo on Rouse's last phrase, while finding ways to restate the melody. Just listening to half a dozen live versions of the same tune proves the point.[31]

The next night they played in Hilversum, a bucolic town just southeast of Amsterdam, and then on to Paris for a much-anticipated concert scheduled for Tuesday the 18th. Arriving in Paris on Monday, Monk took advantage of his night off to explore the City of Light with Nellie. After dinner, they met up with the rest of his quartet and paid a surprise visit to Bud Powell, who was playing at the Blue Note with Kenny Clarke and J. J. Johnson. What happened that night tells us something of the depths of love and admiration these two artists felt for one another. A young British writer named Alan Groves saw the memorable meeting unfold. Before Monk and his entourage arrived, Powell "sat virtually motionless, and it was only his hands that moved when he did play. He appeared to have no interest in his surroundings, and little interest in his music." But when Monk walked in, "Suddenly he came alive, alert and animated. . . . The aloof and detached Monk, complete with dark glasses and hat, was suddenly as excited as Powell. Bud finished his set, and went over to sit with [them]. He and Monk chatted and giggled like children while Monk's sidemen smiled indulgently." A little later, Monk sat at the piano and played a solo piece.[32] Thelonious and Nellie left, knowing Bud would be joining them again in a couple days on the Italian leg of the tour.

The next night, Monk and his band played two shows at the Olympia Theatre. [33] The Parisians who had treated him with such hostility and disdain seven years earlier were now screaming in delight. French jazz critic Jean Tronchot bore witness: "[W]hen Thelonious finally appeared, in black shades and hat, the hall was ready to explode. He received a huge, triumphant ovation before he could even reach his piano!"[34] The music fulfilled, if not surpassed, all expectations. "Like other great pianists," waxed Tronchot, "Monk makes his instrument sound flamboyant, similar to Fats Waller. His playing, which would make a classical pianist tremble, evokes a sensational impression of power." Tronchot declared Monk's performance "probably the best [concert] of recent years."[35] It also established what would become a regular pattern for subsequent concerts on the tour. Besides opening with "Jackie-ing," and including some of his best known tunes, he consistently played three or four standards, notably "I'm Getting Sentimental Over You," "Just a Gigolo," and "Body and Soul"—the last two for solo piano. Of course, he could not leave out "April in Paris."[36]

Thelonious shared his triumphant moment with some old friends. Besides Powell, who showed up at the Olympia accompanied by his friend Francis Paudras,[37] Henri Renaud stood backstage the entire time overcome with delight.[38] As the man responsible for bringing Monk to Paris in 1954, the concert served as sweet redemption. Thelonious, Nellie, Henri, and his wife Ny enjoyed a warm reunion after the concert.

Thelonious could not have made it without his wife, to whom he paid tribute at *every* concert with a loving rendition of "Crepuscule with Nellie." If anything, the trip brought the couple closer together and further defined her roles as personal manager, business consultant, and first line of defense. Although it was Nellie's first trip to Europe, it could hardly be called a vacation. She packed and unpacked, picked out Monk's clothes, collected the money and paid Monk's sidemen, made sure the pianist was fed, rested, and on time, administered medications, dealt with hotel personnel, and employed her limited French whenever she could. Like Thelonious, she drank and indulged in some reefer, but she also did her best to keep away "well-wishers" carrying harder drugs.[39] She also possessed a shrewd business sense. Knowing the importance of publicity, she was always on hand during interviews to help elaborate on Monk's trademark one-word responses to journalists' questions. And she was always looking out for bootleggers, who seemed to be everywhere in Europe. During their Paris stay, for instance, they had gone to a party in Monk's honor at the home of a wealthy admirer. As soon as they walked in the door, Monk made a beeline to the baby grand. A few choruses into his song, Nellie suddenly heard a "click" that sounded like a recording device. She promptly whispered to Monk to stop playing and then explained to their host, "Thelonious is under an exclusive contract. . . . I hope you're not going to tape this?" To which their host responded, "*Juste pour un souvenir.*" Nellie insisted that he shut off the machine and graciously offered to send him an album instead.[40]

Nellie and Monk did find some time to relax. After the Olympia concert, they enjoyed a free day in Paris and then traveled with Bud Powell and his working trio—bassist Jacques Hess and former Monk sideman Art Taylor—to Marseille for two performances at the historic Alcazar Theatre.[41] Marseille was a sight to behold, both for its rolling hills and stunning seascape and its multi-ethnic, cosmopolitan population. It had long attracted Arab, African, and Afro-Caribbean migrants; in fact, the African quarter earned the nickname "little Harlem of Marseille." The port city also was headquarters for the movement to end the French colonial war in Algeria—a war that had just begun when Thelonious first visited in 1954.[42]

From Marseille, the tour traveled by train on April 21 to Milan, Italy, where the quartet was scheduled to tape another television program and perform that night at the Teatro Lirico, the city's oldest opera house built in the late eighteenth century.[43] Much to Monk's surprise, Bill Grauer from Riverside Records happened to be there. Grauer told Monk that he had flown in from London just to see Monk perform, but failed to mention that he and Giuseppe Barazzetta, the head of Riverside's Italian distribution, had planned to record the concert. The idea was Alan Bates's, Riverside's British distributor, who thought a European release of Monk's music would do well following the concert tour.[44] But Grauer also saw the writing on the wall; he knew Thelonious was anxious to leave the label and was not inclined to go back to the studio with Keepnews. And he knew Riverside was in deep financial trouble. Recording a couple of "live" LPs could bring in much-needed revenue. In the long run, Grauer did Thelonious a favor by helping him fulfill his contractual obligations to Riverside, but the way he went about it only heightened Monk's suspicions.

They were scheduled to play three cities in three days—Milan, Bologna, and Rome—from April 21 to 23. During those three days, Monk rarely left Bud's sight . . . nor did Buttercup. Her presence seemed to have a dampening effect on Powell. Thelonious and Bud sat across from each other on the train, rarely uttering a word. The giggles and banter they shared at the Blue Note all but disappeared, and according to Hess his mood affected his playing. During the Milan concert, "Bud would have these blanks, like he didn't remember where he was. Suddenly, in the middle of a piece, he would stop playing at the end of a chorus. I would take a chorus, then two or three, Art Taylor would take a couple and Bud was still absent. He'd be looking at his watch that he'd put on the piano, as if he didn't know he was on stage."[45]

Thelonious, on the other hand, knew exactly where he was. Buoyed by a week of strong performances and supportive audiences, Monk's quartet came out swinging in Milan. From the opening chorus of "Jackie-ing" to the closing theme of "Epistrophy," it sounds as if Thelonious is actually having a ball, reveling in Dunlop's licks, echoing and countering Rouse's phrasing, and making sure to leave space to hear John Ore's bass. The Bologna and Rome concerts were more of the same, and the Italian critics loved it. Arrigo Arrigoni proclaimed that Monk "has destroyed every kind of pre-existing piano playing, opening unexplored horizons, and making a new potential of the instrument accessible. . . . What he has forged is a style that, beyond being unrepeatable, has no equal in its lucid expression of the human spirit."[46] Arrigo Polillo, the editor of Italy's leading jazz magazine, *Musica Jazz*, saw all three performances. "In one concert they were slow taking off . . . but in another the understanding among the four was ideal, the punctuation of the effects was perfect even though not one note had been rehearsed and, on the contrary, it was improvised."[47] Polillo was equally impressed with Monk, the man, to whom he enjoyed unusual access. Of course, Nellie was on hand to run interference and translate, "rendering intelligible his spare and frugal mumbling."[48] She also gave her own assessment of her husband's career, reminding her interlocutor that in spite of his recent popularity and critical acclaim, "it's twenty-five years that he's played the same way as today."[49] But Monk's relative silence and dislike for interviews led Polillo to repeat the stereotype that he is "a giant child, full of good will and occasional whims. One is surprised when he acts like the rest of us. He lives only in his music which is a kind of halo, a personal radiation or environment."[50]

The people closest to Monk knew better. He loved to live in the world, especially the world of the upper class. He never left the house unless he was nattily dressed, and as Charlie Rouse put it, "Thelonious wanted to be in the best restaurants and the best hotels, he was really first class."[51] George Wein quickly learned that a really good meal was one way to get Monk's attention and break through his protective veneer. The veneer began to crumble when Wein introduced Thelonious to fettuccine Alfredo and Northern Italian cuisine. But for Monk's money, nothing he devoured compared with the grand pêche Melba—a dessert consisting of peaches and vanilla ice cream smothered in a sweet sauce made from raspberries, redcurrant jelly, sugar, and cornstarch.[52] He dug the fact that it was inspired by the great Australian soprano, Dame Nellie Melba, back in the 1890s when Auguste Escoffier, chef at London's swanky Savoy Hotel, saw her perform at Covent Garden. Monk paid a price, however: Halfway into the tour *his* Nellie had to let out his suits to accommodate his indulgences.[53]

Between the Rome concert and the English leg of the tour, Monk's quartet enjoyed nearly a week off. Wein, whose Newport All-Stars performed at the Olympia the night Monk and his group played Bologna, met up with Thelonious and Nellie in London and took them around the city in a rented Rolls-Royce. "T. loved grandeur," as Wein put it. He also loved clowning. When people on the streets or in passing cars stared in awe at this elegantly dressed black man riding in the back of a Rolls Royce—chauffered by a white man, no less—he gazed back and "blessed them much as would the pope from his pope-mobile."[54] The long drives and meals in exotic restaurants really deepened their friendship, allowing Wein to see a side of Thelonious the jazz press had never seen.

In the wake of his triumphs in Germany, Amsterdam, France, and Italy, Thelonious was more than ready to take on England. He was rested, having had a week off in London, and Art Blakey's group had joined the tour. (Monk's twenty-year-old nephew, Alonzo, also joined them in London. He had just enlisted in the service and wanted to travel to Europe with the band before reporting to boot camp.[55]) But England wasn't quite ready for Monk. For the first time since he arrived in Europe, he faced hostile criticism. Perhaps he should have expected it; a year earlier, British critic Michael Gibson published a lengthy piece on "Modern Jazz Piano" describing Monk as "technically suspect" and "pretentious," ultimately concluding that he was a charlatan of sorts who had contributed little to modern jazz.[56]

Even critics sympathetic to Monk's music thought the first two concerts at Royal Festival Hall (April 29) and Gaumont Hammersmith (April 30) were failures, less for the music than for his alleged "antics." Writing for *Melody Maker*, Bob Dawbarn did not appreciate Monk's dancing, which he executed "with all the grace of a captive hippo." As he shuffled across the stage, spinning, his elbows churning, he "lit a cigarette, handing it to a startled member of the audience before resuming his seat at the piano." When he did return to the keyboard, he entertained the audience by leaning forward on the piano bench almost to the point of falling over. Every time the crowd responded with "ooohs," he did it again. At the end of the set, Dawbarn saw him "stumble into the arms of George Wein."[57] Historian and occasional jazz critic Eric Hobsbawm was also at Royal Festival Hall that night. He observed that many audience members dismissed the High Priest as a "clumsy bore" and walked out. Still, Hobsbawm praised Monk as one of the few original composers the jazz world has ever produced, though he didn't think much of him as a pianist. He wrote in the *New Statesman*, "the line between planned experiment and artistic abdication or incompetence is hazy, as in modern painting; and Monk has neither the technical mastery nor the staying power which enables an Ellington or John Lewis to maintain a steady level. Nor has he the orchestral sense."[58]

Monk bears some responsibility for the evening. Before the concert, he had had

a little too much to drink. He divulged as much to Max Jones in an exclusive interview a couple of days later, though he also confessed to having thoroughly enjoyed
the evening. "You get out there and you play music in that fine auditorium. . . . that's
not work, it's a ball. I mean playing and drinking. It ain't a drag." What was a drag was
when people began walking out halfway through the second set. He noticed and it
hurt, interfering with his "vibrations" is how he described it. "But the majority stayed;
that's what matters."[59] Indeed, the majority did stay, because the band was tight and
the music swung. There were no real complaints about the music, besides the sets being
too short. Ronald Atkins would have liked to hear more, but "the musical intensity
upheld throughout the five or six numbers performed, with minimal delay between
each, left me quite satisfied." He was particularly satisfied with Dunlop, who was
always "tasteful and alert, using all his kit and quick to spot when special interpolations
were required."[60]

The rest of the tour was mixed. On May Day, Monk and Blakey played Liverpool's
Philharmonic Hall to a lukewarm audience, appeared at Leicester's De Montfort Hall
the next evening before an overflow crowd of 1,800, and performed one concert in
Birmingham on the 4th of May because slow ticket sales forced the cancellation of the
first show. Attendance at the Sheffield concert the following night wasn't much better.[61] Wein had high hopes for Manchester, the next stop on the tour. Manchester was
known as a real jazz town, and several months earlier Miles Davis had been warmly
received for his performance at Free Trade Hall.[62] And the people came, nearly filling
the hall for the first concert. Art Blakey and the Jazz Messengers performed first, electrifying the audience. When it was Monk's turn to come out, there was a slight delay and
the crowd became a little restless. Thelonious finally appeared, opened with "I'm Getting Sentimental Over You" and proceeded to play his usual repertoire, but with little
energy or interest. He got up from the piano several times and danced or disappeared
off stage. Thirty-five minutes into the set, he asked Dunlop to play a long drum solo.[63]
The crowd wasn't having any of it. According to one observer, Thelonious was "jeered
off the stage for his histrionics as much as for his music."[64] *Manchester Guardian* critic
Harold Jackson admired Monk's music on disc, but upon seeing him concluded that
"his concert manner is his worst enemy. How can you concentrate on form, development, and so on when its originator is wandering unpredictably about the stage?"[65]

So what happened? George Wein's recollections of that night sheds light on both the
performance and the performer. The story begins before the curtain rose. Thelonious
was in the dressing room drinking brandy with some friends and holding forth. By this
time, Wein knew Monk well enough to know that "when he felt like talking, it was difficult to get him to stop." A flight of stairs separated the dressing room from the stage,
so Wein came down to tell Monk that it was time to go on stage. He returned to stage
level expecting the pianist to be behind him ready to go. The rest of the band waited in
the wings while Wein made a repeat trip to the dressing room. "After running up and
down the stairs several times, I finally lost my cool and went to his dressing room and
yelled, 'Thelonious, get the hell on the stage!'" Taken aback, Thelonious glared at Wein
and without uttering a single word "walked up the stairs, sat at the piano, played a cho-

rus of one of his songs and proceeded to feature the drummer for approximately forty-five minutes of the sixty-minute performance. As he was returning to his dressing room with little or no response from the crowd, he had the defiant expressions on his face of a sulking Little Leaguer who purposely struck out because his coach yelled at him." Wein confronted him: "'What was that all about?'

"With his teeth clenched even harder than usual he said, 'You hadn't oughta yelled at me.'

"I replied, 'Thelonious, I had to run up and down those stairs six times to get you on stage and I'm getting too old and fat to do that.' . . .

"'You mean you ran up and down those stairs six or seven times?'

"'Yes.'

"'Then I don't blame you for yelling at me.'"[66]

Now the audiotape proves that Dunlop's "forty-five minute" drum solo lasted only about three minutes, but for Wein it must have felt like an eternity.[67] Nevertheless, the backstage story tells us that Monk was in no mood to play. He felt disrespected and embarrassed, especially since Wein probably dressed him down in front of Nellie, his nephew Alonzo, and friends. At the same time, their confrontation marked a breakthrough in their relationship. Thelonious was willing to admit he was wrong and respected Wein for doing the right thing. Thelonious firmly believed in fairness and mutual respect. It didn't happen again.

They finished the English leg of the tour with concerts in London and Bristol before crossing the Channel to play Zurich and Berne, Switzerland. In Berne, despite an out-of-tune piano, the quartet delivered a superb concert for an energized and appreciative audience. Besides the usual repertoire, Thelonious added a stripped-down version of Maceo Pinkard's "Sweet Georgia Brown," a tune he had introduced at his Museum of Modern Art concert a couple of months earlier. He boiled down the melodic line to a few staccato phrases, much the same way he transformed "Just You, Just Me" into "Evidence." I suspect that George Wein might have inspired Monk to return to "Sweet Georgia Brown" since his own Newport Jazz Festival All-Stars played it regularly.[68] Whatever the inspiration, we know that Thelonious altered the melody while on tour but continued to call it "Sweet Georgia Brown." Oddly, he never played it again during the rest of the tour, and a year and a half would pass before he recorded it.

After Berne, they had a three-day respite in Switzerland before embarking on the final leg of the tour. Between May 14 and the 21st, the quartet played Munich (Deutsches Museum), Stockholm, Copenhagen, returned to the Netherlands for two concerts, and closed the tour with concerts at the German Jazz-Salon in Dortmund and Kongresshalle in Berlin. Although Thelonious was anxious to return to New York—after all, they had been living in hotels for over a month—the last few concerts raised his spirits. The Scandinavians, Danish, and Germans greeted the band warmly, and they responded in kind. Indeed, the quartet's two Stockholm concerts may be arguably their best (recorded) performances of the tour.[69] The Swedish jazz press had been covering "Bebopens Oversteprast" (the High Priest of Bebop) for a decade,[70] making his first visit to the country one of the most anticipated events in recent years. Writing for *Orkester Journalen*, Bertil Sundin and Lars Werner flatly pronounced both performances, "One of our greatest jazz experiences." Sundin observed Monk's "complete control of his instrument," adding that "'I'm Getting Sentimental Over You' . . . swung so much that one could hardly sit still." Werner found his improvisations astounding: "Everything Monk played was meaningful and thematic, never any loose ends."[71] Writing for *Estrad*, another Swedish jazz magazine, Carl-Erik Lindgren was completely taken by Monk's "majestic dominance on stage," which was so overwhelming he "almost [forgot] to say how beautifully he plays."[72]

Monk's majesty was a matter of stagecraft. He came out in a slick plaid jacket, white shirt, dark tie, and one of his favorite driving caps. For the second concert that evening he sported a thick ski-bonnet—and not because he was cold. His antics and his music turned off at least one critic. *Estrad*'s Lars Resberg chose to boycott the concerts because Monk, in his view, exemplified a "crippled, sick, comical jazz." Instead, he listened to the radio broadcast and wrote a nasty, hostile review that not only criticized Monk but his colleagues who praised him. "Here, we still cultivate a kind of degeneration of music, allowing each and all of us to experience and enjoy any kind of musical presentation."[73]

In spite of the British critics, Monk left Europe on a triumphant note. George Wein was particularly pleased. He needed a success and he got one. Although he hardly got rich on his first European tour, "the facts that Thelonious acted so professionally and that the promoters showed a profit on the concerts helped serve to establish me as someone that European impresarios could work with and trust." Thelonious also had much to be pleased about. He built up his international fan base, made decent money, had fun, and gave his lovely wife an adventure she would not soon forget. On the way home, Monk and Wein had already begun to talk about the next tour.

23

"Maybe I'm a Major Influence"

(May 1961–October 1962)

Trodbackdrop to the New York City skyline as their Boeing 707 jet made its final approach to Idlewild Airport. Thelonious adored the monumental skyscrapers all clustered together; it reminded him that he was home. In the airport, Nellie picked up the latest *New York Times*, dated Monday, May 22. The headlines read, "MONTGOMERY UNDER MARTIAL LAW; TROOPS CALLED AFTER NEW RIOT; MARSHALS AND POLICE FIGHT MOB—TEAR GAS IS USED—Crowd Menaces Rally at Negro Church—Klan Enjoined."[1] She learned that the violence began a couple of days earlier when a group of Freedom Riders were beaten by racist mobs in Montgomery, Alabama. They were a multiracial group of mainly CORE activists who were traveling through the South on Greyhound and Trailways buses to test a Supreme Court ruling banning segregation in interstate travel.[2] Having just come from Berlin, the Monks had to have been struck by Dr. Martin Luther King, Jr.'s characterization of Alabama as having "sunk to the level of barbarity comparable to the tragic days of Hitler's Germany."[3] They were home, indeed.

The Monks' homecoming was tempered by another sobering reality: Their West 63rd Street apartment was still uninhabitable. The Graham brothers were hard at work on the repairs and renovations, but it would be a few months before they could reclaim their home. Meanwhile, Skippy gave the Monks a home, doing all she could to care for Toot and Boo Boo and ensure that Thelonious and her sister were comfortable. The kids were ecstatic to see their parents again, especially as Nellie unpacked a gang of strange and wonderful gifts from Europe and regaled them with tales of their travels.

Thelonious was pleasantly surprised to learn that Elmo Hope had returned from Los Angeles. He and his new wife, Bertha, and their baby daughter, Monica, moved in with Elmo's mother, Mrs. Gertrude Hope, on Lyman Place, just a few doors down from Sonny and Geraldine.[4] The Smiths immediately embraced Bertha as part of their extended family, and sometimes she, Elmo, and Monica stayed at their place. Nellie, too, welcomed Bertha into the fold. She impressed Bertha with her boundless energy, creativity, and patience—qualities needed to deal with a complicated and demanding figure like Thelonious. "Nellie was so gifted," Bertha observed. "She was the kind of person who makes you believe there wasn't anything she couldn't do, if she really wanted to. . . . She had the ability to understand what needed to be done and to take it to the next level."[5] Thelonious, on the other hand, was neither warm nor very generous—at least not at first. "I remember going to his house once and asking him to help me with 'Off Minor.' I sat down at the piano and started playing the first few bars, then he gets up and says 'It's wrong,' and just walks off. He never helped me."[6]

Thelonious was kinder to Bertha's husband. Although they did not talk much, Monk was happy to have the company of an old compatriot. He filled Elmo in on Bud Powell's condition, did what he could to help him find work, but mostly they hung out together—dropping by the 845 Club, Al Walker's TV repair shop for late-night cutting sessions, sitting out on the stoop at Lyman Place shooting the breeze on a warm night, or sharing a bottle of wine.[7] But it wasn't like old times. Now Monk was more inclined to go to Nica's than to stay up in the Bronx. He missed not having his home base, his own lair where musicians dropped by in search of knowledge, fellowship, fun, or all three. Nica's house had become his second home and his primary work studio. Toot called 63 Kingswood Road "Monkville II," though he noticed a marked difference. "A lot of individual relationships at West 63rd Street were more or less group relationships in Jersey. There'd be a whole bunch of them. He'd be forcing everybody to play ping pong all night and stuff like that, and Nica's taking a hundred million pictures of everybody and there's three thousand cats running every place all day and night."[8]

Thelonious even kept his music at Nica's, usually in a briefcase next to the piano. Fire was his main concern; he never worried about theft. That is, until he heard Jackie McLean's LP, *A Fickle Sonance*, released later in the year. One of the cuts on the album, "Five Will Get You Ten," was credited to Sonny Clark, the pianist on the date. The song was actually one of Monk's compositions, "Two Timer." He had written it at Nica's but had not recorded it. Monk may have shared the lead sheet with Clark; he may have even played it for him. But Clark was a frequent visitor to the "Cat House," and he even lived there off and on.[9] His heroin habit was out of control, and like most junkies he resorted to stealing for a fix. Neither McLean nor any of his sidemen suspected that the song had been stolen. To my knowledge, Thelonious never confronted Clark about it or mentioned it to anyone. He just let it go.[10]

As soon as Monk and Nellie got back from Europe, they headed straight for Weehawken. In fact, during the last week of May, they were there practically every day, and invariably Nica would run the tape recorder.[11] The tapes are invaluable, for they tell us something about Monk's thoughts and reveal a little more about his life. On May 25, after warming up with "Body and Soul," he decided to try something new. At first we hear him shuffle some papers and then say, "Now let me see how me make out with this now. Mmmmm!" He then proceeds to work through an arrangement of Gus Kahn and Bronislau Kaper's "All God's Chillun Got Rhythm" he had gotten from Mary Lou Williams back in the 1940s.[12] He begins playing it almost as written, with ascending arpeggios in the bass and her distinctive rephrasing of the melody, but by the second and third take he transforms the song into his own idiom—incorporating stride piano, dissonant voicings, humorous phrases in the upper register. Perhaps as a tribute to Mary Lou, he drops in a couple of "boogie-woogie" left-hand figures she was famous for. By the time he returns to the melody in the third take, Nellie adds her singing voice and Thelonious closes with a tag similar to what he liked to play at the end of Gershwin's "Nice Work if You Can Get It."[13]

Perhaps he was thinking about adding "Chillun" to his repertoire? Maybe he wanted to arrange it for the quartet, or introduce it as a solo piano piece? Or maybe he was thinking about Mary Lou? She had been away from the jazz scene for a couple of years, devoting her life to charity work and to the Catholic Church. But by mid-1961, she was preparing to return. (Her official comeback occurred in October, when her trio opened at Wells Restaurant and Music Bar.[14]) And since Nica and Mary Lou were dear friends and fairly regular correspondents, he probably knew this. Whatever the motivation, it is clear from this encounter that Monk was in the mood for old songs. He wanted to move forward by looking back, which explains why "Body and Soul" became a more prominent feature of his show, or why halfway through his European tour he began opening with a long version of "I'm Getting Sentimental Over You" instead of the customary "Jackie-ing."

Monk's nostalgic turn, if you will, was deliberate, and as we've already noted, American critics had picked up on it. Back in England, Thelonious's former touring partner and consistent champion, Humphrey Lyttelton, also recognized Monk's search for beauty and truth in tradition. In an article for *Melody Maker* published the day of Monk's Royal Festival Hall concert, Lyttelton characterized Monk as "a pianist and composer of depth, wit and iron consistency . . . who rescued modern jazz piano from a technical dead-end whose culmination is Oscar Peterson. That he does so not by flirting with Bach or Bartok but by reverting to the indigenously jazz approach of the turpentine camp blues men, should encourage rather than dismay jazz traditionalists."[15] Lyttelton wasn't just giving his expert opinion. He was staking out a position in what had become an increasingly heated war between traditionalists and the so-called avant-garde. Ornette Coleman endured significant critical backlash in 1961, and both defenders and detractors of the New Thing sharpened their daggers, ready to rumble at the slightest provocation. Two days after Monk's brief flirtation with "All God's Chillun," columnist Jesse H. Walker of the *Amsterdam News* told his readers, "If you want to hear some way out jazz, dig Cecil Taylor. . . . He makes Thelonious Monk sound like he's playing a minuet."[16]

Monk's quartet opened at the Jazz Gallery on June 1.[17] Despite it being a Thursday night, the 250-seat club was packed with adoring fans willing to forgive him for strolling in two hours late! Critic Leonard Harris believed it was well worth the wait, for Monk "was in top form. With a hint of an abstracted smile on his bearded, beatific face, he went to work developing his own interesting piano thoughts."[18] The Terminis were miffed, but they eventually forgave Monk, too. They sold a lot of drinks that night, and there were no serious complaints.

Well, maybe one.

Later that night, an inebriated Norman Mailer walked over to the Five Spot to catch Cecil Taylor. As Taylor's bassist, Buell Neidlinger, tells it, "Norman Mailer sat down for a while and all of a sudden jumped up and said, 'I've just come from the Jazz Gallery and listening to Monk, and this guy Cecil Taylor is much better than Monk and all the people at the Gallery ought to be over here listening to him.'" Neidlinger claims that Mailer's pronouncement cost them their job. At the end of the night, Iggy Termini "came over and said, 'You guys are through Sunday.' That was a Thursday."[19]

The Terminis were dedicated to Monk; they continued to tolerate his tardiness because they knew he drew crowds. Monk knew it too, which is why he hounded Joe Termini to hire a band led by Philly Joe Jones with Elmo Hope on piano. His ulterior motive, of course, was to get Elmo a gig. Termini went for it. On June 22, the Philly Joe Jones quintet opened opposite Monk at the Jazz Gallery.[20] June 22 was also Hope's first record date for Riverside since he moved back to New York. Leading a sextet that included Philly Joe, he recorded all original tunes—among them two compositions he had written for Bertha: a lovely ballad called "Eyes so Beautiful as Yours" and the boppish "A Kiss for My Love."[21]

The pairing of Monk and Philly Joe Jones turned out to be a bad idea. The two men had a volatile friendship; one night Philly Joe threw a chair at Thelonious and they almost exchanged blows.[22] And neither one respected the clock. On Saturday, July 1, Jones's group took the stand at 10:20 and played their forty-minute set. Monk's quartet was supposed to follow immediately at 11:00, but only Rouse, Ore, and Dunlop were there. Thelonious finally appeared just after 1:00 a.m., but only played for twenty-five minutes before leaving the stand to make way for Philly Joe—who was nowhere to be found. Incensed, Joe Termini implored Monk to return to the bandstand but he refused, arguing that it was Jones's shift and he had not fulfilled his responsibility. It was all too much for Termini to take; he promptly fired Monk and Jones and filed a complaint with Local 802. The Jazz Gallery went without live music until Tuesday, the Fourth of July, when Art Blakey and the Jazz Messengers filled in for a week, followed by Barry Harris's trio.[23]

Thelonious could hardly believe it. For the last four years, the Terminis had been like family. They gave Monk a chance when most club owners dismissed him as an irresponsible kook. He knew he let them down, but he was Thelonious Sphere Monk, "the one and only great musician" as he once described himself. At the time of his firing, he had just been selected number-one pianist, again, by *Down Beat*'s International Critics Poll (beating out Bill Evans and Oscar Peterson); the film *Les liaisons dangereuses*, with his score, broke box office records in France; and *Harper's Magazine* was planning a feature story on Monk.[24] Suddenly, he and Elmo were unemployed.

Between the Bronx and Jersey, Thelonious stayed busy—practicing, writing, playing with his children, and hanging out. Sometimes he, Sonny, Elmo, and various friends just gathered on the stoop on Lyman Place and talked music, politics, women, food, space travel . . . any topic that came to mind. The Smiths' youngest daughter, Teeny (Benetta) found the whole spectacle fascinating. "It was very funny. These guys would stand out there on their soap boxes and talk politics of the day. And we would stand around and listen to some of it because it was some pretty heavy stuff sometimes, sometimes very abstract. Those guys had no money, but they always had on a coat and tie. And their shoes were shined. They had a thing about being dignified, being able to speak eloquently, and who could use the most flowery language."[25] On one excruciatingly hot August day, Thelonious, Elmo, Sonny, tenor saxophonist Tina Brooks, and trumpeter Oliver Beener were holding court when suddenly the stoop collapsed into a giant sinkhole. "I happened to be looking out the window at those guys," recalled Geraldine Smith, "and out of nowhere there is this loud rumble, almost like an earthquake, and then there is a cloud of dust where the men and the stoop used to be."[26] Fifteen-year-old Evelyn Smith was outside when it happened. "It was just incredible. Oliver Beener had just stepped off when the whole stoop gave way and collapsed right into the basement. Thelonious was the first one out. He flew out of the hole and started brushing himself off, still cool. But Tina Brooks broke his arm, I believe."[27]

Brooks was taken to a hospital while the rest convened at the Hopes' apartment. Sonny and Elmo came out unscathed, but Thelonious complained of pain in his hands. A local Bronx reporter got wind of the incident and showed up at Gertrude Hope's door. By now the Smiths were there, including some of their children. Benetta recounts what happened next: "Elmo's mother was so impressed that the press was there in her house. They wanted to see if Thelonious was hurt. They asked him, 'So Thelonious, how do you feel?' No response. Mrs. Hope had gotten him a big bowl of water, propped it up on the table and told him to 'stick your hands in the bowl.' And they're taking pictures and he's saying 'aaaaaaggghhh.' Then they ask, 'Do your hands hurt?' And he's not responding to the questions. Mrs. Hope is annoyed that he's not answering the questions. She's feeling his fingers and everything. The reporter is getting a little exasperated. Finally, he asks, 'Well, is there anything you want to say?' And Monk pauses for a moment and without looking up says, 'Elmo Hope is the greatest pianist on the planet!' That was the only thing that came out of his mouth."[28] It was one of those non sequiturs that caught everyone off guard. After the reporter left—without a story, no less—Evelyn asked him why he said that, of all things. "Because they need to know who Elmo is," he replied.[29]

Three months passed before Thelonious worked again. He was not invited to either the Newport Jazz Festival, or the New York Jazz Festival on Randall's Island, and the absence of work put his whole band in limbo. Rouse used the opportunity to record another LP under his own name, John Ore started hanging out with Sun Ra and his Arkestra, while Frankie Dunlop worked where he could and spent time with his young daughter.[30] The Shaw Booking Agency got Monk another gig at the Birdhouse in Chicago—this one for two weeks. Opening October 11—the day after his forty-fourth birthday—he drew near sellout crowds.[31] Nellie was there, of course, as were Chicago's jazz heavies and curiosity-seekers who came out to hear "Weird Thelonious Monk" and see his "Monk-ey-shine antics," so wrote *Chicago Defender* columnist Al Monroe.[32]

Old friends and acquaintances also dropped by the Birdhouse. Frank London Brown, whose birthday was three days before Monk's, showed up on opening night to celebrate with his friend. It was a bittersweet reunion, because Brown was dying of leukemia. Although he appeared thin and more fragile than usual, it is doubtful he told

Monk or Nellie about his condition. Instead, he probably chose to talk music, politics, and reminisce about old times. Despite his condition, he had recently participated in a "wade-in" challenging segregation at Chicago's public beaches, and protested housing discrimination on the Southside.[33] But he was most excited about his novel-in-progress, *The Myth-Maker*. The protagonist is haunted by a sage-like monk who comes to him in a dream, and it is by listening to Thelonious Monk's recording of "Jackie-ing" that he has an epiphany about freedom, about how to break the social, psychological, and political constrictions he faces as a black man in America: "Ernest laughed at the sounds, the impossible sounds that Thelonious Monk made possible. That was it! That was his appeal, his attraction. He was free, loose, weightless, yet not in need of wings! In need of nothing but his will to be free. If . . . Monk could defy the form, frame and boundaries of musical construction, so could he, Ernest, defy the form, frame and constrictions of a most unmusical life."[34]

Frank London Brown would be dead in five months.[35]

Monk opened at the Village Vanguard on November 7, playing opposite Clark Terry.[36] Max Gordon booked Monk for an entire month, his longest engagement yet at the Vanguard. Unlike his last stay there in 1958, Gordon and Monk had no major tussles, and this time he drew a full house. The critic for *Variety* praised the quartet, singling out Ore and Dunlop for their "superb and highly imaginative" work, and Rouse for finding "the intellect and emotion of the original compositions."[37] With Monk in the house, gossip columnist Dorothy Kilgallen declared the Vanguard, "The maddest musical scene in town these days."[38] When the popular Clara Ward and the World Famous Ward Singers replaced Terry's group with their rousing brand of gospel music, the scene became even wilder. Their presence may have reminded Monk of his own gospel days, perhaps inspiring a hymn or two from the pianist.[39]

There is a scene in the film "Straight, No Chaser" in which Monk's road manager, Bob Jones, reads an encyclopedia entry on Thelonious and tells him he is famous. Monk responds as if it's news to him: "I'm famous? Ain't that a bitch!" It was feigned incredulity. He had known he was famous for some time, and he surely knew it in November of 1961. He was headlining at the Vanguard. Big-time gossip columnists found him worthy of print.[40] Robert Kotlowitz's much-anticipated article on Monk for *Harper's* had just hit newsstands.[41] The legendary Benny Goodman had just selected Monk's Town Hall Concert LP as one of the "60 Greatest Jazz Records of All Time."[42] On November 17, his quartet performed at the U.N. Correspondents Association banquet at the Hotel Pierre in honor of the president of the General Assembly, Mongi Slim, and the late Dag Hammarskjøld, the secretary general who had perished in a plane crash two months earlier. Thelonious rubbed elbows with impresario Ed Sullivan, opera diva Eleanor Steber, and a host of global movers and shakers.[43] And, to top it all off, Monk's quartet spent New Year's Eve playing Carnegie Hall.[44]

Thelonious knew he was famous, not for his hats or his dancing or his alleged "weirdness," but because of his contribution to the music. As much as Kotlowitz tried to render Monk the eccentric he had been marketed to be, Thelonious slipped in a few profound words to explain why the world should listen to him: "Jazz is America musically. It's all jazz, everywhere. . . . When I was a kid, I felt something had to be done about all that jazz. So I've been doing it for twenty years. Maybe I've turned jazz another way. Maybe I'm a major influence. I don't know. Anyway, my music is my music, on piano, too. That's a criterion or something. Jazz is my adventure. I'm after new chords, new ways of syncopating, new figures, new runs. How to use notes differently. That's it. Just using notes differently."[45]

Monk was beginning to achieve some notoriety, but stories of his eccentricity and strangeness prevailed. One exception was Stanley Dance's "A Quiz for Jazz Musicians" column in *Metronome*, a regular feature in which he asks various musicians the same set of twenty questions. Dance queried Monk for the April 1961 issue, and his answers are not those of an eccentric genius. Instead, he comes across as humorous, thoughtful, and politically and culturally engaged. He declared George Washington Carver, the great Tuskegee scientist, "one of the greatest Americans of the century," and chose *Paul Robeson* as his favorite athlete. In 1961, Robeson had been completely vilified by the Red Scare, and few remembered his athletic prowess as a star football player for Rutgers University. If anything, Monk was attempting to resurrect a fallen hero—a bold political move to be sure. He was an avid television watcher, and it shouldn't surprise us that acting was his "favorite art form." What is surprising is Monk's choice for favorite classical composer or musician—José Iturbi, the renowned Spanish conductor, composer, and pianist who appeared in several Hollywood movies in the 1940s, and was best known as a popularizer of classical music (though his solo piano recordings of Mozart and Chopin are considered small masterpieces).[46] He could have chosen Rachmaninoff, Stravinsky, Bartók, even Chopin, whom he liked, but instead picked someone whom critics have often deemed a lightweight. On the other hand, Monk could have been jiving. When asked to name his "favorite brand," he replied: "A brand-new automobile of the best kind made."[47]

We also learn from Monk's answers that he loved New York so much that he preferred the moon to any other American city. He admired all great songwriters, was influenced by "everybody and everything," believed the music industry needs "better listeners and better performers," and his greatest ambitions were to "play better" and ultimately become "a millionaire and do nothing—but have fun." And Thelonious did not believe in false modesty. His greatest single achievement?: "To have had a big hand in improving jazz."[48]

If only his finances were commensurate with his contributions.

In 1961, Colomby, Thelonious, and Nellie agreed it was time to find a new record label and get the family's general finances in order. They hired Morris Zuckerman, a prominent partner in the accounting firm Urovsky and Zuckerman, to take care of the Monks' taxes and to go after unpaid royalties where BMI could not.[49] Colomby also established a trust fund for Toot and Boo Boo. But his main task that year and the next was to negotiate a deal with a big label, a task he undertook while teaching full-time and changing jobs from Far Rockaway High School to Plainview–Old Bethpage High School on Long Island.[50]

It began with a conversation between Colomby and Teo Macero in the spring of 1961. Macero, who had been a producer at Columbia since 1957,[51] and a Monk admirer since the Jazz Composer's Workshop days in the mid-1950s, jumped when Colomby told him that his client was looking to leave Riverside. Macero immediately shot off a letter to Walter Dean in the business department, proposing that they sign Monk right away. He believed that Monk could easily sell 30,000 to 40,000 discs, and through the Columbia Record Club that figure would rise to 60,000. He made a strong case that Monk could become "as big as Miles Davis. In his own way, he shaped the modern jazz scene. He, along with Charlie Parker, has shaped American jazz to what it is today. At the moment MONK is breaking all records in Europe as an attraction. He is a strong contender for the MILES DAVIS–BRUBECK category as regards sales."[52] Macero was also confident that they could afford him. Columbia was rolling in dough in 1961, thanks to the steady profits generated by established pop artists like Tony Bennett, Doris Day, and Johnny Mathis. In fact, their pop department practically subsidized other divisions, notably the jazz division—though even jazz had its share of big sellers: Dave Brubeck, Erroll Garner, and Miles Davis.[53]

Walter Dean was persuaded. He assigned a fellow lawyer named Clive J. Davis to look into the matter and they began drafting a contract. The terms were decent enough: They proposed a two-year contract with three one-year options; a minimum obligation of one album a year; a union scale advance against 5% royalty, less production costs—scale for musicians, arrangers, copying, piano tuning, etc. These costs would also be treated as an advance against royalties. He would be guaranteed gross royalties of $15,000 over two years, though in the first draft they had planned to include a provision limiting the total royalty payment Monk could receive in any given year.[54] Colomby wasn't crazy about the terms, and he was in a strong negotiating position because RCA Victor was also interested in signing Monk. Colomby was also worried because Monk was still under contract with Riverside and owed them records. But Walter Dean was anxious to sign Monk and willing to do whatever it took to make it happen.[55] In January, Colomby's negotiating position improved when Dean was promoted to vice-president in charge of business affairs.[56] With Clive Davis's assistance, he continued to oversee the negotiations until Monk signed the contract on July 30, 1962—a full year after negotiations began. The key differences in the final contract are as follows:

- Instead of one album per year, Monk's minimum obligation would be three albums per year.
- His advance was increased to $10,000 per album, but with the standard royalty of 5 percent less deductions (paying for sidemen, arranging, copying, and other costs related to production).
- Composer's royalty for Monk's music would be two cents per composition rather than the standard one-and-a-half cents.
- Total payments during the year would not exceed $30,000. "In the event that there is any excess, this will be accounted for and paid to him after the termination of the contract."

- Monk's LPs would be included as part of the Columbia Record Club, but the downside was that if sales did not reach 50,000 units in two years, Columbia had the right to terminate the contract.[57]

Still, one stumbling block remained: Riverside Records.[58] Grauer insisted that Thelonious fulfill his obligation to record a couple more albums, but realizing that Monk would not cooperate, they mined the tapes made during Monk's European tour. Keepnews later wrote that Grauer "learned of the existence of tapes professionally recorded,"[59] but as we now know this is only half true. Grauer had already secretly recorded Monk's Milan concert, and he obtained the tapes made by the Office de Radiodiffusion-Télévision Française (ORTF) of the Paris concert. From these tapes, Riverside released a two-LP set titled *Two Hours with Thelonious*.[60] As a result of these protracted negotiations, Monk's first Columbia recording session did not occur until the late fall of 1962.

Meanwhile, Colomby wanted to get Monk's publishing in order. Prestige and Blue Note still controlled the copyright for several compositions, including "Blue Monk," "Criss Cross," and "Skippy." Colomby's goal was to repossess as much of Monk's music as possible and make Bar-Thel, Inc. the claimant. Most of Monk's former producers cooperated, including Prestige's Bob Weinstock, who "just handed over everything, lead sheets, everything they published." Colomby also discovered that a few songs had never been published or copyrighted. Thelonious wasn't willing to share his own lead sheets—at least the ones that survived the fires—so Colomby hired a copyist who transcribed some of the tunes from the record. He ended up registering eleven songs under Bar-Thel in the spring of 1962, but without Monk's cooperation he missed a few, leaving them unprotected for several years.[61]

Colomby's "help" sometimes irritated Thelonious. Once, after Nellie commended Colomby for getting his tunes back from Prestige, Thelonious replied, "What do I owe him, my life?"[62] Thelonious did not like feeling dependent on others, and he especially resented the idea that he needed some white guy to save his life. From Monk's point of view, he was the one making the music and making the money to advance his own career. Colomby worked for him, not the other way around. But we have to put these moments of anger and tension in context. Colomby felt it most palpably during Thelonious's "episodes," and given the stress Monk had endured—from changing his record label to losing his job at the Jazz Gallery to the stoop incident—his manic episodes came more frequently. In one particularly bad case, an agitated and paranoid Thelonious accused Colomby of turning Nellie on to heroin—a drug neither Nellie nor Colomby ever touched.[63]

Increased stress and age only partly explains the slow deterioration of Monk's mental health. Dr. Robert Freymann's amphetamine-laced "vitamin shots" took their toll. Monk's condition worsened, in part, because Freymann stepped up his dosage in an effort to manage his condition and boost his energy—though I suspect that Monk's rising income also enabled him to purchase more shots, as he grew more dependent on them. The treatment was not cheap: In 1963, he had given Freymann nearly $1,300 for "vitamin shots" and spent close to $500 on various prescription drugs.[64] Little wonder Monk composed so few tunes during this period.

The holidays were relatively quiet. Aside from the New Year's Eve concert at Carnegie Hall, Monk did not work for most of December and January. He and his family finally moved back to 243 West 63rd Street just in time for Christmas, but with no piano in the house he had little incentive to stay there. So he and Nellie and the children spent a good deal of time in Weehawken, where Thelonious played a lot of Ping-Pong and piano, and watched a lot of television. And celebrated: on January 19, the Delaware Superior Court overturned Nica's conviction for drug possession after she, Monk, and Rouse had been arrested in 1958. Judge Andrew Christie ruled that the marijuana seized by the state police was inadmissible. The officers had illegally detained Nica and her two passengers, failed to inform her of her constitutional rights, and obtained permission to search her suitcase under coercion.[65] Nica was both relieved by the decision and a little bitter. After hiring a team of top lawyers who spent over three years "filing legal papers, conferences, probationary reports, letters from my brother and from the agent Joe Glaser, and from Nat Hentoff, the judge concluded I wasn't an addict or a pusher and dismissed me. It cost me a fortune."[66] But in the end, justice prevailed.

Monk had justice on his mind when, exactly a week after celebrating Nica's exoneration, he and his quartet participated in a gala benefit for the Negro American Labor Council, held at the Apollo Theater. With Maeley Dufty coordinating the event and Tadd Dameron and Clark Terry serving as musical directors, they drew virtually every jazz musician in the city to 125th Street. And then there were those outside the jazz world Thelonious really admired, such as world-champion boxer Archie Moore, who emceed the event, and NALC founding president A. Philip Randolph.[67] Like Paul Robeson, Randolph had long been a hero of Monk's. A stalwart of both the civil rights and labor movements, Randolph led the fight for the integration of the armed services, federal laws against workplace discrimination, and organized the all-black Brotherhood of Sleeping Car Porters.[68]

It is fitting that on the heels of the NALC gala, Monk would begin a month-long engagement at the Village Gate—that den of radical culture and politics. Although Monk's association with the Village Gate dates back to 1959, his "work" there only amounts to a benefit and an afternoon concert. But now that Monk had fallen out with the Termini brothers, he needed a new venue that might afford him the kind of freedom he enjoyed at the Five Spot or the Jazz Gallery. Art D'Lugoff jumped at the chance despite the $2,500 a week price tag. He didn't mind; he knew Thelonious was one of the hottest tickets in town. (Of course, the fact that the Gate's publicist happened to be Ivan Black is not insignificant.[69]) Opening night, February 20, nearly five hundred people packed the club, including several of Monk's nieces and nephews. They loved seeing their uncle, but truth be told they also came to hear the young singer who shared the bill—her name was Aretha Franklin.[70]

On April 3, Monk and Nellie were off to the airport again, this time headed for the West Coast. The quartet had a two-week engagement at the Jazz Workshop in

San Francisco, followed by another two weeks at the Club Renaissance in West Hollywood.[71] It was Monk's first L.A. club appearance, not to mention his first trip back in almost three years. He preferred to forget his last visit to L.A., marred by his disastrous Hollywood Bowl performance, his emotional breakdown, and Nellie's emergency surgery. This time, there were no incidents.

Monk was warmly received at the Club Renaissance, a popular little joint on the Sunset Strip. *Los Angeles Times* critic Mimi Clar was prepared for a repeat of the Hollywood Bowl, but Monk surprised her. "The clarity and logic of his work might have been compared with the craft of an architect. Each phrase, each fragment, each plump chord had its exact place in his musical structure." He was aware of everything that went on musically. "He echoed, supported and counteracted every move made by his partners. Much of the time his immobile countenance resembled that of a priest at devotion. Indeed, the piano was his whole self, the receptacle into which he poured the contents of his soul."[72] The musicians came out en masse, including David Amram, who happened to be in L.A. on a job. Because Amram had recently grown a beard, he was surprised that Monk recognized him immediately. Monk explained, in his typical laconic fashion, "Man, that hair on your face doesn't have anything to do with who *you* are."[73] Amram also remembered that a young comedian named Hugh Romney opened for Monk that night. Romney would later adopt the moniker "Wavy Gravy" and make a name for himself as a countercultural humorist, hippie, and social activist. But in April 1962, he was a struggling comedian in Hollywood, perhaps a little ahead of his time. "He was so abstract," Amram recalled, "you were just more or less listening to somebody give a big philosophical discussion. So, the whole audience was sitting there waiting to hear Monk and in order to be polite, everybody just kinda pretended like he wasn't there. They weren't giving him the freeze or putting him down; they just completely tuned out. So at the very end, he did a version of Lenny Bruce's famous routine about the English hall entertainer. He started mentioning the names of all the great jazz musicians who had died that were up in heaven and the big jam session in the sky. By the time he got to about the thirtieth musician who had passed away, the audience was cheering. It ended up like a revival meeting. Then he closed with, 'And now we have the man who's alive for us all . . . the legendary Thelonious Monk.'"[74]

The gig ended on April 29, but the Monks stayed in L.A. for a few days visiting Nellie's cousin, Anna Lou Smith. Unlike their last stay, the atmosphere was not only pleasant, but celebratory. Besides Monk's success at the Club Renaissance, Dr. Smith had just accepted a highly coveted staff appointment with the newly created Mental Health Department at Norwalk's Metropolitan State Hospital.[75] Dr. Smith thoroughly enjoyed catching up with Nellie and discovering her husband's gentle side. "My youngest son was banging on the piano," she recalled, "and all the women in the house were shrieking 'Stop, stop, stop!' Thelonious was in his revelry, said, without looking at anybody, 'Let the boy play. Just let him play.'"[76]

Monk got out of the house one night to see Dizzy Gillespie, who was leading an eighteen-piece band at the Summit.[77] Monk caused quite a disturbance when he walked into the room, pushing past tables and waiters to get to the bandstand. As the two men embraced, all eyes were on Thelonious. He would not take a seat, choosing instead to investigate a couple of giant candy canes flanking the end of the stage, décor left over from a recent "twist" contest. Then he stood behind pianist Lalo Schifrin waiting impatiently for him to get the hint. When he did, Monk took over the piano and launched into " 'Round Midnight," taking Dizzy on a nostalgic trip to the early days of bebop. Again, Mimi Clar was there to bear witness. "Afterward, he grandly retired to a table near us, still performing even as a spectator. Gillespie resumed the course of his set, but we took little notice. We were too busy watching Monk."[78]

Thelonious was back in New York in time to play a benefit cocktail party for Jazz Arts Society on May 20. The proceeds were to fund a jazz scholarship program.[79] Held in an exclusive New York City penthouse apartment, the event and all of its elite trappings hardly reflected the goals of the Society, which was to introduce jazz music and education to urban youth as a way to "combat juvenile delinquency." With trumpeter Bill Dixon (founder of the U.N. Jazz Society) serving as its community program director, the Jazz Arts Society held many events in schools, churches, and community centers.[80]

On June 2, the quartet participated in the first federal government–sponsored jazz concert. Fans and musicians called it "Jazz at the Coliseum," but the official title for this colossal four-day event was the "First International Jazz Festival."[81] Although the organizers tried to emphasize the festival's international character by adding a few foreign artists like the Wreckers from Warsaw, Poland, and British saxophonist Tubby Hayes, the vast majority of participants were American artists—Duke Ellington, Horace Silver, Oscar Peterson, Herbie Mann, Roy Eldridge, Dave Brubeck, Clara Ward, Dinah Washington, to name a few.[82] Monk's Saturday night performance was well-received. Dan Morgenstern declared that Monk had given one of the few "worthwhile performances."[83] But the real star of the show was Duke Ellington. Duke was the toast of the town that weekend, and he played just about every day of the festival—with his own orchestra, in a small combo, even with the National Symphony Orchestra.[84] As he was being feted, he found a moment to share a word or two with Thelonious. They had much to talk about. George Wein and Duke had hatched a plan to have Monk perform with the Ellington Orchestra at the Newport Jazz Festival in July. Thelonious embraced the idea, not surprisingly, and rumors quickly spread that Monk was planning to write a special piece for the occasion to be orchestrated by Hall Overton.[85] Not so. By the time Thelonious and Duke saw each other in D.C., Billy Strayhorn had already begun writing arrangements in anticipation of Monk's appearance with the band. Strayhorn, Ellington's long-time collaborator and a Monk follower since the 1940s,[86] composed a blues he entitled "Frère Monk," replete with dissonant riffs and a flatted-fifth chord in the final chorus, and prepared a special arrangement of "Monk's Dream"—a tune Thelonious recorded ten years earlier but virtually dropped from his repertoire.[87] Ellington, Strayhorn, and Monk may have exchanged notes on the upcoming performance, knowing that their respective schedules prohibited any kind of rehearsal. They would just have to meet on the bandstand.

Meanwhile, Monk had a few jobs before Newport. The third weekend in June, his quartet returned to the Apollo for a week-long engagement. Hosted by Symphony Sid, the show also featured the Latin jazz of Tito Puente and Mongo Santamaria, the calypsonian sounds of Tommy Rey and his Steel Limbo Twisters, and the crooning vocals of Arthur Prysock.[88] Such an eclectic mix of music should have attracted a large and diverse audience, but they ended up playing to a half-empty theater. Poor ticket sales had less to do with the music than with what was happening outside the theater. On Saturday, June 23, the second day of the show, a large group of picketers appeared in front of the Apollo. Organized by the Harlem Consumers Committee, the Harlem Tenants Council, and the United African Nationalist Movement, the protesters were attempting to stop Sol Singer, a Jewish entrepreneur, from opening a restaurant next door to the theater. They targeted Apollo owner Frank Schiffman, who had leased the space to Singer, arguing that they were conspiring to drive the only black-owned establishment on the block (Lloyd's Restaurant) out of business. Schiffman responded by placing a sign in the window calling the protestors "Communist Agitators" and informing potential patrons that there were "No Labor Problems" and "These Demonstrators are ill-advised by a selfish restaurant owner who fears normal competition."[89] Thelonious was not inclined to cross picket lines, and he disliked Frank Schiffman and the entire Apollo outfit, but he had little sympathy for the protesters or their anti-Semitic slogans. Monk believed in the principle that if you want to keep black business, then patronize the black cat and don't buy from the white cat. Besides, his quartet was making $3,000 on the gig,[90] and he had just gone nearly two months without working.

The quartet began a week-long gig at the Village Vanguard during the last two days of the Apollo engagement, and then settled in for a summer-long stay at the Village Gate beginning the first week of July.[91] Before he had the chance to get comfortable, it was time to head up to the Newport Jazz Festival and face the music. He, Nellie, Nica, and Colomby arrived late Sunday afternoon, July 8, the last day of the Festival. Thus far, it had been a success, and with George Wein back in charge fans expected something extraordinary—and for many, the pairing of Thelonious Monk and the Duke Ellington Orchestra was it. At 8:00 p.m., Duke's musicians took the bandstand and played several Ellington classics, including "Rockin' in Rhythm," "Things Ain't What They Used to Be," and "Do Nothin' Till You Hear from Me."[92] Halfway into the program, Duke warmly introduced the special guest, and they launched into Strayhorn's arrangement of "Monk's Dream." The horns opened with an eight-bar introduction and then went directly to the theme. Monk found his way against the heavily syncopated accent riffs in the background, but he never changed his style to accommodate the band. Despite having a big band behind him, Monk's piano was the dominant voice throughout, and Duke was gracious enough to give him plenty of space. Indeed, most of the song consisted of Monk playing alone with the rhythm section—the band did not come in until the final cadence. And Duke was digging it, shouting, hand-clapping, exuberant from beginning to end.

The next song, Strayhorn's "Frère Monk," was less successful. Duke himself seemed only minimally familiar with the song, introducing it as "Aaaahhh 'Monk Frère.' 'Frère'? Or 'Frère Monk'? Encore." Either no one gave Thelonious the charts or he chose to ignore them, because he started out playing "Ba-lue Bolivar Ba-lues-Are." After a chorus, the band jumped in with "Frère Monk" while Monk improvised on a B♭ blues. They employed Strayhorn riffs to great effect as support for Monk's piano solo—and perhaps this was what Strayhorn had intended all along? Although Thelonious and the band were not always in sync, Duke seemed to love it anyway. Once again, his urgings and shouts of encouragement are quite audible.[93]

Duke wasn't the only one who loved it. According to John S. Wilson, "Monk proved himself to be a pianist ideally suited to Duke Ellington's band."[94] Most critics and fans, however, came to the event with high expectations but left with mixed feelings. George Wein, who always believed that "Monk's admiration for Duke was unlimited, and quite obvious," nevertheless described the collaboration as little more than "an interesting experiment."[95] And critic Bill Coss thought, "It was a wonderful idea, and was successful up to a point, though it never hit the high hoped for."[96] Thelonious never commented publicly on the performance, nor had the musicians much to say—though some members of Duke's band found Monk's refusal to remove his hat while he played extraordinarily disrespectful.[97] The real question is how did Monk's appearance measure up to the other "interesting experiment" on stage that night: the pairing of Aretha Franklin and the Ellington Orchestra?[98]

Two days later, Monk was back in New York, holding forth at his new "summer home" on the corner of Bleecker and Thompson streets.[99] He had a terrific run at the Village Gate. By all accounts, he came to work happy and healthy; except for one night, when Bobby Timmons substituted because his hands were swollen, Thelonious did not miss a set.[100] We know the band sounded great because Richard Alderson, a latter-day Jerry Newman or Dean Benedetti with a jones for jazz and a geeky interest in technology, recorded one of Monk's sets probably in August or early September.[101] He rigged an elaborate recording set-up using a single microphone he designed wired to a tape recorder located at Edward "Chip" Monck's basement apartment, next door to the Gate.[102] Monk's repertoire isn't surprising, but the band is spirited and in sync like a well-oiled machine. Alderson captured two very different renditions of "Body and Soul," which may have had a particularly poignant meaning since Monk and Coleman Hawkins played opposite one another at the Gate for little over two weeks.[103] Hawkins's mere presence inspired Monk. Eddie Locke, Hawkins's drummer at the time, recalled how Thelonious would "play little things in his solos that Hawk recognized from arrangements they'd played years before. Hawk would listen and laugh and say to me, 'Listen to that, he's trying to tempt me to get up on the bandstand and blow with him.'"[104] Hawkins never took the bait, but they did hang out together quite a bit. Sometimes they'd head over to Beefsteak Charlie's after the gig, or go uptown to Hawkins's apartment and tell stories, listen to music (often classical or opera), and have a little taste. Again, Eddie Locke was there: "I'd see Monk at the Village Gate doing all this wild shit, dancing and passing around, but when he got to Coleman's house, he didn't do that. He'd be talking just like we'd be talking about stuff. 'How do you like my suit?' 'What do you think about these shoes?' They'd be talking about stuff like that."[105]

Monk continued to do what he could for the civil rights movement. On August 11, the quartet participated in a star-studded benefit concert at the Apollo organized by the U.S. National Student Association. All proceeds went to the Southern Student Freedom Fund, a fund created to assist student activists who had been expelled from school or jailed for participating in desegregation campaigns and voter registration drives.[106]

Ironically, as Monk supported black student struggles in the South, his own son was battling racism at his public school in the Bronx. The troubles began in the seventh grade when he enrolled in Walter J. Damrosch Junior High School (JHS 136) during the 1961–62 academic year. The school was conveniently located in the Bronx not far from Skippy, Sonny, and Geraldine, and it specialized in music. Toot had already begun taking trumpet lessons with Oliver Beener and was prepared to play in the school band. Like virtually all of the students at JHS 136, he didn't own a trumpet; he and his family expected to borrow one from school. No one expected politics. "The head of the trumpet department," Toot explained, "had a beef because my father was getting a little name and he wasn't so he couldn't find an instrument for me. So I ended up in the chorus under the direction of Mrs. Jeffries." He survived the snub, though he realized that even if his parents bought him a trumpet he was going to have a hard time in the band. But the trumpet teacher wasn't the worst of his problems. One day Toot's homeroom teacher admonished him for having metal taps on his shoes. "My father wanted to go up to the school and kick his ass, but my mother suggested we send Harry Colomby to talk to him. Colomby sat down with they guy who said, 'Well, I can talk to you. You know, these goddam niggas. I can't afford the goddam shoes and then who's this black kid? You know what I mean, doncha Harry?' Harry came from that meeting, he said, 'Thelonious, you gotta get your boy out of this school.'"[107] They all agreed that a private boarding school was their best option. With the Columbia contract on the verge of being finalized, steady gigs, and more international tours on the horizon, they could afford the tuition.

Colomby was charged with the task of finding an appropriate school. He selected Cherry Lawn, a small, nonsectarian, progressive co-ed school in Darien, Connecticut. Originally founded in 1922, Cherry Lawn was exclusive, but a far cry from the blue-blood WASP culture characteristic of East Coast boarding schools—except, perhaps, for the price tag: annual tuition in 1962 ran $5,000.[108] The student population was predominantly Jewish, somewhat bohemian, artistic and intellectual, although most were scions of upper middle-class families from New England, Long Island, upstate New York, and Manhattan's Upper East Side.[109] A significant number of students hailed from Connecticut's historic Jewish communities in and around Stamford and Norwalk.[110] Toot was the only black kid in his eighth-grade class.[111] Nevertheless, its director, Anthony A. Medved, was a bit of a maverick: in his 1963 commencement address, he cautioned students against "conformity."[112] At least on the surface, the school embraced a radical ethos. Among the student essays and poems published in the 1963 yearbook, one made a compelling case for rebellion: "When the conscience is denied its freedom; when the workings of society hamper the artist, the poet, the philosopher, the musician, in short, the thinker, it is time for the 'instinct of rebellion' to declare a state of war."[113] This was Monk's type of school.

Toot was not happy about the impending move. Before they made any final decisions, however, Nellie took him to visit the campus. "It looked like something out of *Mary Poppins*. At the time I didn't know Cherry Lawn was a predominantly Jewish school, very liberal, very progressive, very cutting edge. The headmaster knew who my father was . . . so I left feeling it was cool."[114] In late August, 1962, Nellie packed up Toot and delivered him to his new school. Because she had no car, they traveled to Darien, Connecticut, by taxi. The forty-mile journey seemed extravagant at first, until the cab arrived on campus alongside limousines and various luxury cars. "This was ritzy, ritzy shit, and we come rolling through the gates in a yellow cab! We roll up in front of the main house and a kid stuck his head through the window and said, 'Hi. I'm Ronnie Greenberg. Welcome to Cherry Lawn School.' . . . I was embarrassed at first because I didn't realize that, as far as they were concerned, this was as eccentric as it gets—it's what stars do."[115] And Toot quickly learned that his father was a bona-fide star. Kids who loved jazz befriended him and jockeyed over spending the Christmas holiday over at his house. Even his first roommate, Dana Liberman, was a thirteen-year-old alto player who adorned his wall with a picture of Charlie Parker. "Dana could name every recording by Charlie Parker, John Coltrane, Miles Davis, and Thelonious Monk. He was the biggest jazz freak. He told me, 'I can't wait to celebrate your daddy's birthday.'"[116]

Nellie and Thelonious decided to send Boo Boo to boarding school the following year. Because Cherry Lawn covered sixth through twelfth grade, Colomby had to find an alternative for Boo Boo, who was slated to enter fifth grade in the fall of 1963. He settled on Green Chimneys, an experimental pre-K through elementary school situated on a beautiful seventy-five-acre farm in Putnam County, New York. Launched in 1948 as the "Green Chimneys Farm for Little Folk," its founder, S. Bernard Ross, M.D., set out to create a learning environment in which small children interact with farm animals and the natural world. By the time Boo Boo enrolled, the school had begun to attract international students from Latin America and Canada, and had expanded to eighth grade. While the student body might have grown considerably—they had about 100 students in residence—the campus had not changed. The original farm buildings remained intact. Students were exposed to a rigorous yet progressive curriculum and devoted considerable time to caring for the animals and other outdoor activities. And the tuition—ranging from $1,905 to $2,800—was significantly less expensive than Cherry Lawn.[117]

Whereas the Monk name automatically put Toot in good stead with Cherry Lawn's hippest crew, it did not carry the same weight at Green Chimneys. Headmaster Sam Ross, Jr., knew little of the jazz world; running a school occupied enough of his time. The day he received Boo Boo's tuition check, he shared with friends over dinner the unusual name of the signatory. "Everybody at the table said, 'Thelonious Sphere Monk? Do you know who he is?' And I said, 'I don't know, but this is the first time in my life that I ever received a full year's tuition in advance.'" Like her brother, Boo Boo moved into her dorm in classic Monk style, though she arrived a little too late for a welcoming party. Sam Ross recalled, "The Baroness de Koenigswarter drove Nellie, Monk, and

Barbara and dropped her off in the middle of the night—between midnight and 4:00 in the morning. I had been up waiting in my office. Barbara had all new suitcases, all new clothes. Thelonious came into my office and—still not grasping who he was—I said, 'You know, Mr. Monk, I understand you're a musician. You should try to give a concert for our children.' He replied, 'That'll open up new horizons.' And then Nellie said, 'I'll translate that for you: he'll be glad to do that.'"[118]

In the meantime, this pretty, brown-skinned ten-year-old city girl had to navigate a new curriculum, adapt to life on a farm, and make new friends in an integrated but predominantly white environment. From her very first semester, she excelled in the classroom and became a bit of a social magnet. Myra Ross, her teacher and the head-master's wife, remembered Barbara as "a really well-adjusted, popular, bright student who just did well. She was a beautiful, smart, lovely, lovely girl. Lots of friends." There wasn't a subject she couldn't handle as long as she applied herself, and she especially loved the ballet class. Her only problem was attendance. Myra Ross: "The kids would go on weekend visits or they'd go on a week's vacation. But Barbara wouldn't come back at the designated time, so I would start making phone calls. I'd finally get a hold of Nellie and I'd ask, 'Nellie, where's Barbara?' 'Oh, she was on tour with her father.' She'd be in Europe somewhere. Now, by law she was supposed to be attending a certain number of days of school, and I'd get a little frustrated, but I remember Nellie saying, 'Well, what she's doing is certainly educational.'" Mrs. Ross had her make up the lost days by writing essays about her travels. Boo Boo worked dutifully for the most part, but had her share of lapses. Once, when she and another girl in the class failed to turn in their homework, Mrs. Ross expressed her disappointment. "So they went out and got an old milk can that farmers used to use to move fresh milk from the cows to the dairy. They took one of those old milk cans and painted it with beautiful flowers."[119]

As the summer of 1962 gave way to autumn, Monk was in a bit of a financial crunch. With the added burden of private school tuition and virtually no savings, Monk needed money. He was eager to finalize the Columbia contract and get back into the studio. He even sketched out a new tune he started calling "Everything Begins Here and Everything Ends Here."[120] But now he was waiting on Riverside and Columbia to come to an agreement, and for the union to approve the contract. Finally, on September 19, the contract was approved and Teo Macero reserved the 30th Street Studio for Monk's first Columbia recording session. The earliest available date was Halloween.

24

"Everything Begins Here and Everything Ends Here"

(November 1962–September 1963)

Columbia's 30th Street Studio was a pretty extraordinary place. Located just east of Third Avenue, the former Greek Orthodox Church was purchased by Columbia in 1949 and turned into one of the finest recording studios in the city. When senior engineer Harold Chapman discovered the abandoned church, he insisted that Columbia executives leave it untouched. He was afraid that any renovations, including painting or sanding, would ruin the delicate acoustics. With 10,000 square feet of floor space and enormous ceilings, it was big enough to accommodate a full orchestra, but through the strategic use of drapes, dividers, and a little reverb, Columbia's veteran engineers could also create a more intimate sound environment.[1] The pianos were in near-perfect condition. Monk had his pick of pristine seven-foot Steinways, carefully maintained and freshly tuned before each session—the cost for which, Monk would later discover, came out of his advance.[2] Macero tried to make the studio as inviting as possible. He introduced the band to his engineer, the legendary Frank Laico. Having worked there since its inception, Laico shepherded some of the greats—Barbra Streisand, Tony Bennett, Johnny Mathis, Miles Davis, and now Thelonious Monk.[3] Macero also had the good manners to know that an afternoon session fell around lunch time (or in some cases breakfast), and he'd hung out with Monk long enough to know that the man loved to eat. So he provided a stack of ham sandwiches to munch on between takes. Macero bragged to *Down Beat* magazine that the sandwiches were the "secret" to keeping him happy and productive.[4] He neglected to mention that the sandwiches were also deducted from Monk's advance.

Thelonious may have been a little anxious about his first Columbia date, but Macero was downright nervous. A year and a half had passed since Monk had come under Columbia's aegis, and corporate expectations had only grown. The jazz press fanned the flames with stories of Monk's reputedly lucrative contract, and Macero and Columbia executives were inundated with requests and advice. George Wein unsuccessfully tried to get the label to underwrite Monk's next European tour in March.[5] Nica lobbied to write liner notes and for Columbia to use some of her art work for Monk's album covers.[6] Critics offered unsolicited advice on how to market and record Monk. Speaking for what he called "the consensus," Martin Williams strongly suggested Monk focus on his earliest work, and he even proposed a repertoire. "The general feeling is that Monk's best single piece is 'Criss Cross', followed by 'Misterioso', 'Epistrophy', 'Four in One', 'Evidence', 'Eronel', 'Gallop's Gallop', 'Skippy', 'Trinkle Tinkle', 'Crepuscule with Nellie', 'Brilliant Corners', and 'Let's Call This.'" He slyly hinted that a change in personnel might be in order, praising Monk's earlier collaborations with Milt Jackson and Art Blakey.[7] Macero had some ideas of his own. Like Orrin Keepnews before him, he thought that Thelonious still needed to be made palatable to a broader audience. The solution? An album of Monk tunes by *other* Columbia recording artists. He had already approached jazz flutist Paul Horn and classical pianist André Previn before the plan was mercifully aborted.[8]

Then there was Monk. His plan was simple, the same plan he always followed when he walked into a studio: make a good record for the people and collect your bread. He agreed that he needed to change up his repertoire rather than rerecord what he'd been performing. Besides, Riverside's impending release of his live concert LP, *Two Hours with Thelonious,* already covered that ground. On the first day, he pulled out "Bye-Ya," a tune he had not recorded in four years and rarely played after Rouse joined the band.[9] Thelonious spent the rest of the session laboring over "Body and Soul." He did at least four takes before leaving the studio, and returned the next day to work on a few more. All in all, Macero preserved three solo piano renditions of "Body and Soul," each one unique. Sometimes Monk played rubato, other times he'd swing it stride style, but he never sounded tortured or frustrated. Every take is melodic, joyful, and focused—as reflected by his audible solfeggio singing and moments when his own phrases seemed to surprise him.[10]

The second three-hour session produced only two other tracks besides "Body and Soul." The quartet delivered a lively, bluesy rendition of "Ba-lue Bolivar Ba-lues-are" and then revisited Monk's revision of "Sweet Georgia Brown" which he had introduced briefly in Europe a year and a half earlier. Monk had already abandoned the original melody in Europe, and since then had made further alterations, but even the day of the recording he still referred to the tune as "Sweet Georgia Brown." A few days later, he gave it a title: "Bright Mississippi" in honor of the civil rights struggle in the South.[11] On both songs, Monk never leaves the piano. His comping is humorous and his solo, especially on "Bright Mississippi," is downright frenetic. The band returned to 30th Street Studio the very next day, November 2, and again recorded three songs— "Monk's Dream" and two old standards, "Sweet and Lovely" and a solo version of "Just a Gigolo." "Gigolo" he had played in Europe, "Sweet and Lovely" he last played regularly with Coltrane in 1957, but "Monk's Dream" had just undergone a resurrection, thanks to Billy Strayhorn and Duke Ellington. Monk's Newport performance with the Ellington Orchestra inspired him to revisit the tune. Macero preserved two takes of "Monk's Dream," one with Rouse accompanying Monk on the melody, the other with Monk and the rhythm section alone and Rouse coming in to solo. Thelonious wasn't satisfied with Rouse's handling of the melody, so he selected the latter version for the album.[12]

Still short of a complete album after three consecutive days of recording, Macero booked 30th Street for one more session on November 6. Depending on what time Monk arrived, he might have caught a glimpse of the great Russian pianist Vladimir Horowitz, who had recorded earlier the same day. Monk admired Horowitz, whose Columbia recordings of Chopin, Schumann, Rachmaninoff, and Liszt would become part of his own personal collection.[13] I don't know if they actually met, but it is curious that amidst intense performances of works by Schuman, Schubert, Scarlatti, and Beethoven, Horowitz threw in an incomplete version of "Tea for Two"![14] A sly tribute to the High Priest?

Thelonious came prepared to work. They finished the day with a cleaner version of "Sweet and Lovely," fresh cuts at the familiar "Rhythm-a-ning" and "Hackensack," and a revisiting of "Coming on the Hudson" and "Blues Five Spot" (retitled "Five Spot Blues"). With enough music in the can, Thelonious collected his first advance. Minus scale for his sidemen and other production costs, he received a check for $8,627.53— just in time for Christmas and Nellie and Toot's birthdays.[15] Gifts were plentiful, though it was Thelonious who bought himself the most extravagant present of all—a new piano. It had been almost two years since he had lost his rented Steinway in the fire, and as much as he liked hanging out at Nica's, he needed a piano at home. Harry Colomby went to several piano companies and offered his client's endorsement in exchange for a significant discount. Steinway snubbed Monk, but Baldwin came through with a deal, although Colomby's negotiations brought the price down by a mere 20 percent. On January 10, Thelonious accompanied Colomby to the D. H. Baldwin showroom on East 54th Street, selected the right piano, and forked over $2,986.70 in cash.[16] A couple of days later, a new Baldwin M Grand occupied part of the kitchen and living room.

The tiny apartment started to look like home again. Like old times, except they weren't broke. Thelonious earned enough to be the sole breadwinner, though now he had more than his immediate family to be concerned about. Skippy wasn't earning a living, and she had two children to care for—three-year-old Nica and twenty-three-year-old Ronnie, who still lived at home but spent much of his time in the streets in search of a fix. Like so many neighborhood kids, he fell victim to heroin. His habit became a major emotional and financial burden on the family. Skippy turned to the Monks for help; she and her children were listed as dependents on their 1963 income tax return.[17] Thelonious never complained, especially since Skippy had cared for Toot and Boo Boo for so long and gave them all a place to stay after the last fire. But even the rise in income did not shield Monk from financial trouble. No sooner had he gotten his Baldwin home than his accountant, Morris Zuckerman, informed him that they owed the IRS a hefty sum of money. He had to ask Columbia for a $5,000 advance against his next album, which they granted as "long as Monk is recording his new album within the next couple of weeks."[18]

Monk didn't work at all in January, and his next gig was gratis. On Friday, February 1, he headed over to Carnegie Hall to participate in "A Salute to Southern Students," a huge benefit concert for the Student Non-Violent Coordinating Committee (SNCC). The New York-based Friends of SNCC sponsored the concert to commemorate the third anniversary of the sit-in movement and to raise money for SNCC's ongoing work in Mississippi, southwest Georgia, Alabama, Arkansas, and South Carolina. Over 4,000 organizers had been arrested on spurious or trumped-up charges, and a greater number of activists and community residents were beaten, intimidated, even fired from their jobs for fighting for basic constitutional rights. During the bitter winter of 1962–63, Mississippi authorities retaliated against the voter registration drive by cutting off the distribution of federal food surpluses to LeFlore and Sunflower counties.[19] Lacking financial resources, hundreds of young people languished in Southern jails. The concert's organizers hoped to acknowledge the activists' courage while highlighting the desperate conditions under which civil rights activists worked.[20]

The event's sponsors were some of the biggest names in entertainment and literary circles—notably Shelley Winters, Harry Belafonte, Diahann Carroll, Theodore Bikel, writers James Baldwin and Lorraine Hansberry, and musicians Nina Simone, Pete Seeger, and Cannonball Adderley.[21] The real organizers were SNCC leader Bill Mahoney and Friends of SNCC founders Alice Wright and Joanne Grant.[22] They had begun reaching out to artists in the fall of 1962, though few would commit, citing previous engagements or other conflicts.[23] Charles Mingus agreed, and so did Herbie Mann, but the biggest coup was pop singer Tony Bennett.[24] Monk received an invitation just weeks before the event, though he did not hesitate. "Monk was glad to participate and to be of some use," Alice Wright recalled. "I think he was really glad to be doing it for the kids."[25]

Carnegie Hall sold out that night, and at least 1,000 people were turned away.[26] Ossie Davis and John Henry Faulk[27] emceed the event, and Tony Bennett was billed as the main attraction. But the SNCC Freedom Singers stole the show. Besides being talented vocalists, they were SNCC field secretaries who had been active in Albany, Georgia—Bernice Johnson, Cordell Reagon, Charles Neblett, Carver Neblett, and Rutha M. Harris. They moved the crowd with freedom songs and harrowing stories of organizing in the Deep South, and they shared the stage with other activists who spoke about the violence faced by students as well as poor sharecroppers attempting to register to vote. There wasn't a dry eye in the house when they read the "Honor Roll Call"—a list of SNCC organizers currently in jail.[28]

Thelonious was deeply moved by the event. He and a bass player (probably John Ore) "played only one tune and he was very subdued as he performed."[29] No one expected a subdued performance, let alone a short one. "We were told to put him on at a certain point," Wright remembered, "because once he got on and warmed up you couldn't get him off."[30] And yet, his brevity was no indication that he was anxious to leave. He stuck around for the entire concert and afterward went to a nearby restaurant with a group of SNCC activists. Freedom Singer Bernice Johnson [Reagon] sat across from Monk that night. "I was sort of scared of him. And he said, 'That stuff, it's not going to work. That stuff you all are talking about—it's not gonna [work]. I mean, it's important and I'm here.' And it was the nonviolence, the 'redeeming your enemy through love' kind of part. He was basically saying, 'You all are gonna get yourselves killed walkin' out here in these streets in front of these crazy white people, your local crazy white people who've got guns.' He just shook his head at that."[31] Skepticism notwithstanding, he accepted an invitation to join the Friends of SNCC's Sponsoring Artists' Committee.[32]

Monk had been thinking quite a lot about death, which may explain his "subdued" mood. A couple of weeks before the concert, he lost two friends who died prematurely. On January 13, thirty-one-year-old Sonny Clark overdosed on heroin, and three days later tenor saxophonist Ike Quebec succumbed to lung cancer at the age of forty-five.[33] Monk was indebted to Quebec for helping him get his first record date with Blue Note. Clark was another matter. Monk treated him like a troubled younger brother. He not only forgave Clark for stealing his music, but he and Nellie gave him money and a place to stay when he needed it.[34] Nica also felt responsible for Clark. For the past few months, she had been paying Dr. Robert Freymann to treat him for drug addiction with a combination of vitamin shots and methadone. After a week in Bellevue Hospital, Clark left feeling as if he had broken his habit. The next day a friend gave him a bag of heroin that killed him.[35] On February 4, Monk appeared at the Village Gate for a benefit that Nica had organized to raise money for Sonny Clark's widow and two children.[36]

Monk did not realize it, but he suffered yet another loss that week. On February 7, his father died of a heart attack. He was seventy-two years old and still a resident of North Carolina's segregated state mental institution, now called Cherry Hospital.[37] He may have heard stories of his famous son and someone might have slipped him a clipping or two, but by the time his progeny began to receive significant national press, the elder Monk had become a virtual pariah. The family that cared most about him, the children of his late brother "Babe" Monk, had moved to Connecticut. He probably knew nothing about Thomas or Marion, or that his wife had been dead for over seven years. Thelonious Monk, Sr. died alone. There was no one to claim him, no one to memorialize him, no one to bury him. His remains were sent to Duke University Hospital "to be used by the anatomical board."[38]

For the younger Monk, February 7 was significant for other reasons. That night he opened at Birdland, his first performance there since December 1949, when owner Oscar Goodstein screamed at him for placing his drink and lit cigarette on their new piano.[39] Monk had no real desire to work at Birdland. Like many other musicians, he believed owner Oscar Goodstein was vindictive and disrespectful of musicians, and more than once he had barred Thelonious from the premises.[40] But Monk needed work and Goodstein needed Monk. The club was in financial trouble and Thelonious was now a draw.[41] The two-week booking turned out well. Radio station WJZ hosted a live broadcast from Birdland on Saturday nights, which gave the quartet even wider exposure.[42] One of those broadcasts reveals Monk in an especially playful mood. On "Evidence," after comping briefly behind Rouse's solo, Thelonious hits a couple of forearm bangs and then gets up from the piano, followed by muted laughter and expressions of astonishment. The crowd is clearly digging it, and Monk is digging being dug. He might have been competing for laughs with the young comedian Flip Wilson, who shared the bill with Monk.[43]

Thelonious was in good spirits, partly because he stayed so busy. On Saturday, February 23, he played an evening concert at Queensboro Community College before rushing off to Birdland for another radio broadcast.[44] He also returned to the studio to complete another album before heading off for his second European tour. The quartet was scheduled to fly on the 28th of February, so Macero booked 30th Street Studio for three consecutive afternoons, from February 25 to 27. The first day only yielded a trio recording of "Tea for Two."[45] He had been practicing it at home and decided to dust off the same arrangement he used for his Riverside trio version eight years earlier, right down to Oscar Pettiford's bass introduction (which John Ore played pizzicato rather than arco). The following day the quartet recorded a virtually forgotten Monk original, "Think of One," which had not seen the light of day in ten years. Although the song is based primarily on one note, it probably required some rehearsal time, which may explain why the session produced no other tunes. On the last day they produced four excellent tracks, none of which were part of Monk's regular repertoire—another trio version of "Tea for Two," "Criss Cross," "Eronel," and a couple of gorgeous solo piano renditions of the standard "Don't Blame Me." "Criss Cross" had been given new life by Gunther Schuller's "Variants on a Theme of Thelonious Monk (Criss Cross)," which he had recorded and performed all across the country. Monk reclaims it here, emphasizing its minor tonalities and angular shape that had come to define "Criss Cross." "Eronel," with its boppish lines, was the odd song out. Once again, Monk took full composer's credit without acknowledging Sadik Hakim and Idrees Sulieman.

Five exceptional tracks recorded over three days still fell short of a complete album, but Monk and his band had a European tour to attend to. Monk didn't leave without taking care of one important piece of business: He and the Termini brothers finally reconciled in late February, and Monk agreed to a long engagement at the Five Spot. This time it wasn't Colomby coming to the Terminis with hat in hand; quite the opposite. Joe and Iggy were in dire financial straits, and they knew Thelonious was an instant attraction. The Jazz Gallery had gone out of business the previous summer, and the Five Spot was forced to move after developers demolished 5 Cooper Square to make way for a new apartment building. The Terminis acquired 2 St. Mark's Place a few blocks away (the corner of Third Avenue and St. Mark's Place) and transformed an old cafeteria and tobacco shop into the new Five Spot. When it opened in January, patrons discovered a very different club. The new Five Spot was larger (its legal capacity was 223 patrons), but the Terminis retained the older club's character by adorning its richly painted red walls with the same posters, photos, and works of art.[46] They also installed a new grand piano, selected by none other than Monk himself.[47] All they needed now was their cabaret license. In fact, Joe Termini wanted to hire Monk's group earlier, but no license meant that neither horns nor percussion instruments could be used in the club.[48] Instead, all parties agreed that Monk's quartet would open during the second week of April (pending approval of the cabaret license). The terms of the contract reveal much about their difficult finances, their strong desire to bring Monk back, and Monk's own personal commitment to Joe and Iggy. The Terminis could not afford his regular floor of $2,000 a week, so they offered $1,000 plus half of what the house earned over and above $3,000. They also agreed to a minimum seven-month contract that could be broken "if circumstances warrant," but Monk agreed not to accept any other club engagements in New York City. He could travel, but he had to inform the Terminis four weeks in advance.[49]

Monk happily signed the contract before flying to Europe. He looked forward to the day when the Five Spot would be known again as the home of Thelonious Monk.

George Wein had to miss the first leg of the tour, so Jules Colomby traveled with the group along with Joyce Wein.[50] Thelonious almost missed the flight. Joyce went by the Monks' apartment to make sure they were packed, only to find Monk in bed in an agitated state. Nellie explained that he wasn't feeling well and wanted to cancel the trip. Joyce asked what was wrong. "My hand hurts," Monk replied. Sensing that he needed some mothering, she offered to "kiss it and make it better." Joyce kissed both hands and said "I think you can go to Europe now, Thelonious." He got up, Nellie packed, and they made their plane.[51]

Frankfurt, Hamburg, Baden-Baden, Munich, Berlin, Bremen, Düsseldorf, Stockholm, Copenhagen, Helsinki, Paris, and Brussels—twelve cities in seventeen days and practically every concert hall sold out.[52] With very few breaks between performances, this tour was more grueling than the last, especially for Nellie, who suffered from a bad cold she could not shake. Still, she made sure her husband was well-dressed, and shopped when she was up to it. In Hamburg, she purchased a fancy new tape recorder and enough neckties to fill a small suitcase. (Regrettably, in their rush to get to the next destination—Paris—they left the neckties in their hotel room.)[53] Thelonious, on the other hand, was in his glory. The Germans went wild for him and he reciprocated. Monk said of the Rhineland's jazz fans: "These cats are with it!"[54] In Baden-Baden, a bourgeois resort town in the southwest famous for its spas and gambling casinos, Monk reunited with Joachim-Ernst Berendt, the writer/critic who had interviewed him in Paris in 1954. Berendt now hosted a television show called "Jazz—Heard and Seen" (*Jazz Gehört und Gesehen*), and he booked Thelonious as a special guest.[55] Much to everyone's surprise, Monk departed slightly from the basic repertoire after Berendt asked him, "What would you say, Thelonious, is your favorite tune, or one of your favorite tunes?" Monk replied, "Well, there's a favorite hymn that I like a lot. We recorded it for a French picture. 'By and By, When the Morning Comes.' "[56] And he proceeded to play a short yet soulful solo rendition of Charles Tindley's classic. Following a rather pious verse, he irreverently switched to stride piano during the chorus, collapsing sacred and secular, veneration and humor. Another reminder that in an avant-garde world Thelonious was still old-school, and yet his German listeners might have thought his harmonies were akin to science fiction.

Monk's first tour introduced him to Europe; by this time, he was famous. Adoring fans greeted him at the airport, lined up for autographs, and applauded appreciatively as soon as he walked on stage. Columbia helped his promotion by releasing his first LP, *Monk's Dream*, to coincide with the tour, and Thelonious made sure he played tunes from the album—"Criss Cross," "Bye-Ya," "Bright Mississippi," and of course, the title track. The marketing department at Columbia enlisted major critics to contribute liner notes—Nat Hentoff, Martin Williams, Ralph Gleason, Voice of America jazz host Willis Conover, and Macero himself. Each of these men proclaimed Monk's unparalleled genius, declared him a "virtuoso" and an "original," and placed him alongside Duke Ellington in the pantheon of jazz legends.[57] The European press produced a flood of articles and pounced on Monk for interviews, especially the Parisians.[58] And the reputedly taciturn musician not only obliged but gave generously of his time. On March 9, the day of his scheduled concert at the Olympia Theatre, an uncharacteristically loquacious Thelonious sat for two long interviews.

Jazz Hot critic François Postif spent six hours with Monk in his room at the Hôtel Prince de Galles. He expected to find a difficult, "unapproachable" man but instead found Monk to be "charming," "gentle," "sociable," and possessed of "great kindness."[59] Thelonious spoke openly about his childhood, his technique, the days of Minton's Playhouse, his favorite compositions ("Blue Monk" and "'Round Midnight"), the titles of his songs, why he loves dancing to his own music, his ideas about accompaniment and improvisation, among other things. He was witty: when asked if he came from a family of musicians, he mused, "Of course, I come from a family of musicians, like all of us, since my family is the world." But he also spoke frankly about issues dear to him. He suggested that history had been unkind to him, failing to give him due credit for his role in creating bebop. And when Postif asked him about his statement in Frank London Brown's *Down Beat* profile, where he said his music is not a social commentary and that he "would have written the same way even if I had not been a Negro," Monk vehemently denied "ever saying anything so insane."[60] Whether or not Monk misremembered the quote, in 1963 as civil rights dominated the world stage, he did not want to come across as uninterested or disloyal to the black freedom movement.

After the concert, he and Nellie returned to their hotel room and met with two more journalists, Jean Clouzet and Michel Delorme of *Jazz Magazine*. Monk's playfulness with Postif contrasted sharply with what seemed like a more combative conversation with Clouzet and Delorme. Some of their questions annoyed Monk because they accepted the common stories about his behavior. The first thing they wanted to know, for example, was why he gave so few interviews. "I never refuse to talk with someone," he replied. "If I don't give more interviews, it may be because I never had the chance. . . . In fact, the real reason is that critics seem to avoid me. I don't know why. Probably because of the nonsense that has been spread about me."[61] The "nonsense," i.e., stories of his unreliability and eccentric behavior, he added, had made it difficult for him to find work. When asked if most people understand his music, he scoffed, arguing that the people have understood it but the critics have not, which only contributed to his marginalization since "they are the ones who decide what should be heard and what should not."[62] Indeed, he took the critics to task for giving Dizzy and Bird credit for his contributions to modern jazz, and he made the case that a lot of modern piano players copy his technique.[63] When Clouzet and Delorme suggested that Duke Ellington might have influenced him, Thelonious emphatically denied it, to the point of stretching the truth. "I never listen to Ellington. As I said, I haven't heard him for years. If there is an influence, it could have only happened the other way around."[64] He railed against Ornette Coleman and the avant-garde for creating music that is "illogical" and "incoherent." "Even [Sonny] Rollins seems to be affected," Monk lamented. "That's the reason why I haven't listened to him lately. He is such a wonderful musician that I can't bear the idea that he might be going in the same direction." Finally, though not surprisingly, his interviewers brought up racial issues, allowing Thelonious to give a more measured response to the frequently asked question: What role does art play in the movement for racial justice? Monk revised what he had told Postif, insisting that he doesn't think about race but rather sees himself as an American. But being an American, he added, "doesn't prevent me from being aware of all the progress that still needs to be made. . . . I know my music can help bring people together, and that's what is important. I think that jazz is the thing that has contributed the most to the idea that one day the word 'friendship' may really mean something in the United States."[65]

The quartet gave their final performance in Düsseldorf on March 17 and the next day they headed home. Anxious to complete his next album, Macero reserved 30th Street Studio for March 29, where he knocked out two more tracks—"Pannonica" and "Crepuscule with Nellie."[66] With the LP completed, Macero moved swiftly to package it and prepare for distribution. Unlike Orrin Keepnews, who kept a tight rein on everything and insisted on writing all of Monk's liner notes, Macero agreed to let those closest to Thelonious comment on his music and significance—a decision helped along by the many letters and phone calls he received from Thelonious's inner circle. He finally succumbed to Nica's requests to write the notes, though he nixed her art work for the cover. Calling the second LP *Criss Cross*,[67] Columbia's marketing department (and perhaps Macero) substantially revised Nica's original notes. The published notes still border on the hagiographic, and they were toned down from the original. But it is the latter, carefully crafted and adorned with a variety of colored pencils, that deserves our attention, for it is a rare and beautiful example of Nica baring her soul and expressing a deep love and admiration for the man and his work:

> *COLUMBIA* has acquired a star of the first magnitude. . . . probably the greatest star
> ever to dawn on the jazz horizon. . . .
> To attempt to analyze, describe, or explain the music of *THELONIOUS MONK* would not only be pretentious, but superfluous. . . .
> Thelonious's greatness lies in the very fact that he transcends all accepted formulae. . . . all well-worn adjectives and cliches. . . . A new vocabulary, alone, would suffice. . . .
> For those who have already heard him, no words are necessary. . . . and for those who are as yet ignorant the message is very simple. . . .
>
> *LISTEN. . . . . . .* [68]

In an addendum she titled "some thoughts about Thelonious," she likened him to Bartok, compared his stability and consistency to that of the Rock of Gibraltar, described him as a "one-man renaissance," insisted on the inevitability of his newfound success, and proclaimed that he "cannot HELP being original! . . . any more than he can help sounding right, whatever he does. . . . and swinging with every breath he takes. . . . !" And he's a philosopher extraordinaire and a true legend in his own time, whom she placed on par with "Professor Einstein, Charlie Parker, [and] General de Gaulle."[69]

Nica may have been Monk's most passionate champion, but she was not alone. Praise came from all corners of the European and American press. *Down Beat* critic Peter Welding practically fawned over *Monk's Dream*, and Martin Williams published a major essay in the *Saturday Review* celebrating Monk's work and long-overdue recognition. Thelonious appreciated Williams's piece because he put the question of Monk's technique to rest. He writes, "far from being an inept technician, Monk is a virtuoso—a virtuoso of the specific techniques of jazz, in challengingly original uses of accent, rhythm, meter, time and of musically expressive space, rest, and silence."[70]

Monk did not let all the press go to his head. His commitments to his community remained a high priority, even if it meant performing in the House of the Lord. On April 7, Monk and his quartet performed at the Presbyterian Church of the Master in Harlem as the featured artist in their Sunday evening jazz workshop series.[71] The Reverend Eugene Callender, a relatively young and dynamic minister, community activist, and consummate jazz lover, had just inaugurated the series in hopes of reaching a younger, hipper generation. Monk had enormous respect for Reverend Callender because of his leadership in the Harlem Neighborhood Associations and the Harlem Youth Opportunities Unlimited (HARYOU), but especially for his ongoing work with the Morningside Community Center.[72]

Three Sundays later, on April 28, Monk played another benefit—a fundraiser for his son's school, Cherry Lawn. Held at Staples High School in Westport, Connecticut, the concert drew a full house, attracting students, faculty, parents, as well as jazz fans in the area.[73] For Toot, who went by "T.J." among his classmates, seeing his peers hold his father in such esteem impressed him. The quartet played two outstanding forty-minute sets and an encore. But more than the concert itself, Toot remembered what his father said to him on the way to Westport that afternoon. "I remember getting in the limo with my father to go and during the ride over he said, 'You'll be straight after this. . . . Once I do this concert you're untouchable.' And I realize now that he knew how this private school thing worked and it was really about who you are. I knew how the white kids operated, the students whose parents donated a few dollars and all of a sudden they didn't get thrown out, they only got suspended."[74] In other words, Monk believed the concert and his name would put his son in the school's good graces. At least he hoped it would.

Monk planned to open at the Five Spot on April 14, but the Termini brothers still had no cabaret license and it became clear that the issue would not be resolved before the band left for Japan on May 9. In the interim, Colomby went back to Birdland owner Oscar Goodstein, who offered the quartet another two-week engagement. Neither Monk nor his bandmates were happy about it, least of all John Ore. Several days into the gig he and Goodstein had a heated exchange, which led Ore to quit, leaving

Monk without a bass player just days before their tour.[75] Sam Jones stepped in temporarily, and then suggested a more permanent replacement: twenty-three-year-old Edward "Butch" Warren, Jr. Thelonious didn't need convincing. He had heard Warren play before, most recently at the memorial benefit for Sonny Clark where they met. For the past two years, the Washington, D.C., native functioned as the unofficial house bassist at Blue Note, having recorded with Donald Byrd, Dexter Gordon, Herbie Hancock, Sonny Clark, and Jackie McLean.[76]

Warren's relative youth belied his experience. Monk liked the big sound Warren got from the lower register and his inventive choice of notes—characteristics he appreciated in Wilbur Ware's playing. Like so many other Monk sidemen, joining the band was like baptism by fire for Warren. "Working with Monk was pretty hard. . . . I had heard Thelonious Monk so many times at home, you know, it wasn't hard to learn his songs. We had one rehearsal, we went over the songs one time, but we did our rehearsing right there on the job." He never told Warren how to play; he simply told him to "make my music sound better."[77] Just to make sure Warren jelled with the band, Thelonious had Nellie bring the tape recorder they had bought in Hamburg down to Birdland. The tape reveals a surprisingly comfortable Warren, playing confidently on tunes like "Evidence," "Blue Monk," "Rhythm-a-ning," and "Epistrophy." Thelonious gives Warren plenty of solo space, which he uses to great effect. Unlike Ore, who rarely strayed from walking bass lines, Warren breaks up the rhythm and creates more interpretive and thematic lines. On "Light Blue," whose slow and plodding tempo tested all musicians, Warren delivers a compelling solo building on the theme—a difficult act following Monk's own stunning solo. Judging from the applause, Warren won the crowd over.[78] Thelonious hired Warren the next day. He was going to Japan.[79]

Monk had a longstanding interest in Japan. In 1955, he told David Amram that a time would come in the near future when we will have "Japanese jazz," so long as people around the world find their own path. "They shouldn't copy us," he warned. "They should have their own."[80] Art Blakey's visit to Japan in January of 1961 further piqued his interest. Blakey and the Jazz Messengers' tour marked the first wave in what would become a veritable tsunami of American jazz artists to cross the Pacific. Indeed, the locals dubbed the period from 1961 to 1964 as the "rainichi" rush, which literally means "come to Japan."[81] But even before the rainichi rush, Monk had become a giant among Japan's many jazz aficionados. In 1958, *Swing Journal*, Japan's leading jazz publication, selected *Brilliant Corners* as the number-one album in the country.[82] Critic Jiro Kubota deemed it a genuine "masterpiece," and Yui Shoichi called it a "perfect group expression." "Monk's music is like a moving canvas," Yui continues, "on which he paints wonderful sketches and provides brilliant color to the sketch in a flowing manner."[83] Jinichi Uekusa contributed a few pieces on Monk, praising his music as "a treat for the senses" and "mind-broadening," but wondering aloud if he would ever enjoy mainstream acceptance.[84] Interestingly, the Japanese jazz press, unlike the American press, focused almost exclusively on music and avoided speculations about his eccentricity or behavior.

Monk's greatest champion in Japan was not a critic but a pianist named Yagi Masao.[85] In 1959, the twenty-six-year-old pianist formed his own group featuring several Monk tunes in their repertoire, culminating in his debut LP, *Masao Yagi Plays Thelonious Monk,* recorded in the summer of 1960.[86] It was the first all-Monk LP outside the United States. Yagi brings his own boppish style to the music, but occasionally incorporates Monk licks and voicings. He is most original on "'Round Midnight," which he does as a duet with bassist Harada Masanaga, and "Off Minor." Yagi avoided songs that were too difficult; three of the eight cuts are blues and they included the ever-popular "Rhythm-a-ning."[87] Overall, the LP is fairly derivative, with Yagi's sidemen copying licks verbatim from popular American jazz musicians, and their arrangement of "Evidence" is based entirely on Blakey's Atlantic recording from 1957. Yagi made sure his hero received a copy of the album, either by post or in person during the tour, though one wonders what Monk thought about it, especially given his injunction that "they shouldn't copy us."[88]

On May 9, Thelonious and his quartet, Nellie, and Nica boarded a Japan Air Lines flight, first to Honolulu for a couple of days and then on to Tokyo. George and Joyce Wein accompanied them, along with singer Jimmy Rushing—the opening act.[89] They arrived May 12, in time to give a brief press conference at the Akasaka Prince Hotel, catch a little shut-eye, and perform the next night before a sell-out crowd at Tokyo's Sankei Hall. The remainder of the tour was much the same: they played full houses in Sendai City, Nagoya, Kokura, Sapporo, Osaka, Kyoto, and two more concerts in Tokyo—all cities with an established jazz culture.[90] During part of the tour, the Monks were accompanied by Reiko Hoshino, owner of a "kissu" or jazz café in Kyoto. She introduced them to the culture, welcomed them into her home, and became their closest friend and liaison in Japan.

Their grueling schedule left only two free days out of two weeks, but the fans made it worthwhile. Japanese audiences were among the most appreciative and enthusiastic Monk had ever encountered. They tended to applaud as soon as they recognized the opening bars of a song, the overwhelming crowd favorite being "Blue Monk." The band rarely strayed from its usual repertoire, but they played well and Monk infused even his well-worn songs with new life. For the majority of Japanese who had never seen Monk live or on film, his performance was immensely entertaining. He danced, he lurched, he sucked in his jaws and at times looked like he was in a trance, and yet he never lost his place. He knew exactly when to come back in, responded musically to his sidemen's phrases, and always directed the band—sometimes with comical results. When Monk thought Warren's solo on "Blue Monk" had gone on long enough, he signaled him by slamming his forearm on the keys, generating chuckles from the crowd.[91]

On the 23rd, the day before their departure, the quartet taped a television program for the Tokyo Broadcasting System (TBS), giving Japanese fans a chance to see Monk at work. He came on stage wearing a hat and a long overcoat draped over what appeared to be a silk suit and a light-colored thin tie with vertical stripes. He had lost a considerable amount of weight, so nothing fit him well; even his precious ring could not stay up on his finger, so every few bars or so he can be seen adjusting it. He appeared slightly inebriated but in control, attacking the keyboard like a boxer and leaping from the piano bench during Rouse's solos to dance. Monk's movements were so compelling that during Rouse's solo on "Blue Monk," the camera cuts the saxophonist out of the frame to pursue Thelonious. Even when he performed "Just a Gigolo" unaccompanied, his entire body was electric.[92]

Off stage, he met several local musicians, including Yagi Masao and a talented saxophonist named Hidehiko "Sleepy" Matsumoto, visited a couple of "kissu" or jazz cafes, and went shopping with his two best friends—Nellie and Nica. He picked up a hip silk skullcap in Tokyo, a couple of miniature Japanese Geisha dolls for Boo Boo, and his prize possession—a stunning silk smoking jacket with gold embroidery.[93] But wherever he went, someone invariably asked him or Nellie about the racial situation in the states. Days before the tour's arrival, the Japanese were bombarded with television and newspaper accounts of Birmingham, Alabama, where the nonviolent demonstrations involving black school children were met by savage force under the direction of Police Chief Eugene "Bull" Connor. They witnessed shocking scenes of black people kneeling in prayer dragged and beaten by police, teenagers sliding across the pavement from the force of fire hoses capable of taking bark off trees, children packed into paddywagons on their way to the city jail. On May 11, full-scale rioting broke out, causing President John F. Kennedy to dispatch federal troops to Birmingham to keep the peace.[94] A new civil war was breaking out in the United States, and the Monks were on the other side of the globe.

They arrived home on May 26, giving Monk and his band just two days to rest before opening at the Five Spot. With the cabaret license settled, the Terminis got the club together while Ivan Black put out a flurry of press releases announcing Monk's historic homecoming to the "new Five Spot Café." Playing opposite guitarist Kenny Burrell's trio, Monk's quartet opened to a packed house, and it remained packed the entire week.[95] As the Third Avenue space was considerably bigger than the old Five Spot, this certainly pleased the Terminis, who did everything to accommodate Thelonious. Indeed, they even revised his contract making his start time 10:15 rather than 9:30, knowing that he would probably arrive at the club closer to 11:00.[96] Hardcore fans made their pilgrimage alongside curiosity-seekers, Beat generation stragglers, tourists, and a variety of downtown celebs. The *Daily News* took note of the fact that Leonard Bernstein showed up on occasion. When asked what he thought about Monk, he replied, "He's a crude pianist . . . but he's so creative, so individual that he's a genius."[97] Playwright Brendan Behan actually climbed on stage with the resident genius after he had had a little too much to drink. As *Down Beat* reported, "While Behan sang some Welsh airs, one hand holding his pants up because of unhooked suspenders, the other draped around Monk's shoulder, Monk never gave any indication that he was aware of Behan's presence. Finally, Behan was escorted to his ringside table and dug Monk for an hour."[98]

But for an emerging avant-garde experimenting in conceptual and performance art, Monk's spontaneous dance, combined with his drinking during and between sets, embodied the perfect expression of pleasure and excess. Dance historian Sally Banes traces what she calls the rise of avant-garde performance and the "effervescent body" to Greenwich Village in 1963.[99] I suspect that Monk's own "effervescent body" spinning and lurching nightly at the Five Spot contributed to downtown artists' search for bodily freedom. The club's culture and reputation contributed as well, for at the Five Spot performance could just as easily erupt from the audience as on stage. For example, one night Monk was so late getting to the gig that a young man in the audience got up on stage, "whipped out a cordless electric shaver and gave himself a full barbering."[100]

A trip to the Five Spot to see Monk was mandatory for any self-respecting young, hip New York intellectual back then. For those who couldn't make it that summer of 1963, Monk came to them, courtesy of Jules Colomby and the New School for Social Research. Jules produced the series of Saturday evening concerts/lectures and Hall Overton served as host and interlocutor. Overton's job was to explain the music, place it in some context, and interview the musicians on stage. Held outdoors in the school's elegant gardens, the first hour of the program was broadcast on public television. The program was well-publicized and the first few concerts featuring Art Farmer, Al Cohn and Zoot Sims, and the Horace Silver Quintet, drew good crowds.[101] When Monk's quartet appeared on June 22, students, fans, and critics filled the garden.[102] To everyone's surprise—everyone close enough to the stage to hear him—Monk not only talked but was gracious, funny, and charming. Following Overton's warm introduction and a tight performance of "Criss Cross," the interview began. Monk spoke briefly but rather eloquently about his childhood, piano lessons, and how he learned harmony on his own. Then in response to a question about the origins of bebop, he took the opportunity to repeat his revision of popular jazz history. Although he explained the genesis of the name, the main point of the story is that he was bebop's true originator. He spoke about how he had originally titled his very popular tune "52nd Street Theme," "Bip Bop." "And I told the cats the name so probably that's where the name 'Bebop' came from."[103]

The staid, professorial Overton played straight man to Monk, whose humor was disarming but never naïve:

> Hall: Now, I know you have some very strong convictions about your
>   music, about what it should be and who you want to reach with your
>   music. Could you say something about that?
> Monk: Say it again please. [LAUGHTER]

Overton repeats the question.

> Monk: I'd like to reach everybody, the public plus the musicians. And that's
>   the standard that I've set for my songs. Something that will get to the
>   people's ear, plus no criticisms from the musicians. [LAUGHTER][104]

The band performed "Nutty," followed by Overton's musicological analysis, accompanied by projections of lead sheets he transcribed himself. One can imagine the collective yawn as Overton droned on about Monk's use of the second and sixth intervals and the way he creates an "interesting formal effect out of 32 bars." Several minutes passed before Overton turned to Monk and asked him to play "Trinkle Tinkle" unaccompanied. Having not played the tune in years, he made a mistake in the last measure. "I missed that," he declared, as he played the passage over, at which the audience laughed and applauded. This gesture of humility both endeared him to the crowd and conveyed just how precise and difficult his compositions are. Hall broke character when he replied, "That's all right, Monk. I've been trying for years to play it. I can't come anywhere near it."[105]

Monk had a way of undercutting the academic tenor of the lecture while maintaining his innocence. Following performances of " 'Round Midnight" and "I'm Getting Sentimental Over You," Overton delivered a gracious summary: "Monk's sense of time and his rhythmic virtuosity, his use of space are the product of a completely original and powerful musical mind. As I mentioned earlier, the truly original geniuses are rare in music, and are often unappreciated during their lifetime. I think it's a hopeful sign that Thelonious Monk is now getting the kind of acceptance he deserves, and this is happening without compromise through the music itself." But before Overton arrived at the final word, Thelonious interrupted, reminding everyone "And we're working at the Five Spot!"[106] He broke up the room. Critic John S. Wilson was there, and while he complained that he couldn't hear much of what Monk actually said from where he sat, "he did speak, and that in itself was an event."[107]

Thelonious spent the Fourth of July at Newport. It was the tenth anniversary of the venerable festival and George Wein invited just about everyone to join the party. The roster was impressive: Miles, Coltrane, Hawk, Dizzy, Duke, Cannonball, Rollins, Mulligan, Brubeck, Jimmy Smith, Nina Simone, Nancy Wilson—a veritable history of the music.[108] Wein also wanted to disrupt the performance-as-usual by putting together artists who didn't usually play together. One idea was to have clarinetist Pee Wee Russell join up with Monk's quartet. Wein thought it would be a successful pairing because they had the "same feeling for intervals" and they "both play what to many people are dischords, they are both always looking for that note—that note that is right yet different."[109] When Wein proposed the meeting a week before the festival, Russell agreed. He was already moving away from the old Chicago-style jazz. The year before he had formed a modern band with trombonist Marshall Brown, whose repertoire included Monk, Tadd Dameron, John Coltrane, and Ornette Coleman. He had also played duets with Jimmy Giuffre, whose experimental music he admired. He even went to the Five Spot to hear Monk's band a few days before Newport and chose two songs he thought were appropriate for the range and sound of the clarinet—"Blue Monk" and "Nutty."[110] Monk liked the idea, too, but he wasn't willing to rehearse, and it showed. On "Nutty," Russell goes out of his way to sound abstract, to play deliberately dissonant phrases that have no relation to the melody. For Monk, abandoning the melody was a no-no, which is why he continuously returned to the melodic line while comping behind Russell. After a while, Monk gave up and strolled, leaving Butch Warren and Frankie Dunlop to support him. On "Blue Monk," Thelonious hardly played at all behind Russell. He later complained that Monk strolled too much, leaving him hanging. When Russell heard the recording played during a blindfold test a year later, he turned cold: "No rehearsal, just pushed onto the stage, and I didn't fit into that group. Anyway, I don't like that kind of music."[111]

Judging from the applause, the fans seemed to enjoy the meeting, but critics and keen observers came away with differing opinions. Ira Gitler and Dan Morgenstern thought both artists exhibited great rapport and mutual respect.[112] John S. Wilson begged to differ. "Mr. Monk did not play while Mr. Russell was playing and Mr. Russell did not play while Mr. Monk was playing, so that the meeting amounted to little more than their presence on the same platform at the same time. If the purpose of such an arrangement is to see what sort of fire can be struck when two disparate jazz musicians are rubbed together, this meeting failed because they never got close enough to make contact."[113] Wein was ambivalent. He observed some interesting moments but blamed Monk's "strolling" for squandering what might have been an exciting musical exchange.[114] The only truly satisfied party was Columbia Records; they recorded the concert and got half an LP out of it. They pressed Miles Davis's 1958 Newport performance on the other half and released it the following year as *Miles and Monk at Newport*.[115] Originally conceived as *Monk and Miles and Newport*, Mr. Davis and some company execs would have none of it. It taught Thelonious a valuable lesson about his place in the Columbia hierarchy.[116]

Outside the Columbia matrix, Monk's star status was rising. During the summer, Harry Colomby received a call from a *Time* magazine writer named Barry Farrell. "We're interested in doing a cover story on Monk for *Time*," he announced nonchalantly. Colomby's emotions ricocheted between shock, glee, and finally dread. "I thought . . . How is he going to act? What condition is he in? From that moment on, my stomach was in knots."[117] Colomby found out soon enough. During their first meeting, Monk paced around Farrell's office in the Time-Life building, staring out the window the whole time.[118] He may have been on the verge of an episode, but he also may have been expressing his general impatience with journalists. But Farrell was indifferent to his behavior. A long-time Monk follower, he described himself as "a jazz fan in a way I am not a fan of anything else," and he took the music seriously.[119]

The Monk story came about entirely through Farrell's initiative. Recently hired as the magazine's music writer, the editors wanted him to write a cover story featuring George Szell of the Cleveland Symphony Orchestra, which Farrell wasn't keen to do. He negotiated: he would write it in exchange for a major cover story on a jazz musician.[120] The editors initially proposed Ray Charles and then Miles Davis, but nixed Charles because of his drug problems and Miles Davis was just too incorrigible.[121] To Farrell's great pleasure, they settled on Thelonious Monk—always his first choice. Farrell was one of the regulars at the Five Spot, and had just penned a piece in *Time* casting a critical eye on the folks who populated the "Home of Thelonious Monk." He noted rather disdainfully how Monk "will spend a whole night horsing around on his piano while his sidemen accompany him with all the enthusiasm of cops frisking drunks. On other nights he plays brilliantly and the sidemen follow with insight and devotion—but the applause is just the same, Monk's audience is far too devoted to him to worry about his music."[122] Once his managing editor gave him the green light, Farrell approached Monk every chance he got, "mostly walking around outside the Five Spot . . . or sitting in some dark bar at 2 a.m."[123] In time, Thelonious and Nellie came to trust Farrell. He visited the Monks' home a couple of times and learned that he and Thelonious shared some things in common besides a sense of style and a devotion to the music. Farrell loved basketball, had visited Japan, and enjoyed a hit of reefer every so often.[124] And the man was hip—twenty-eight, tall, handsome, strawberry-blond hair, he smoked Gauloise cigarettes and, like his subject, dressed stylishly. "Women loved him," proclaimed writer John Gregory Dunne. "He was that rare writer who looked the way a writer should look."[125] For the next two or three months, he would become Monk's shadow.

On August 23, Monk appeared at the Apollo for another midnight benefit concert sponsored by the Negro American Labor Council. The purpose was to honor A. Philip Randolph and raise money in support of a massive "March on Washington for Jobs and Freedom" scheduled to take place the following week. The proceeds were earmarked to pay transportation costs for thousands of unemployed workers, black and white, who wanted to attend the march. Many stars turned out: Tony Bennett, Joanne Woodward, Sidney Poitier, Paul Newman, Ossie Davis, and Ruby Dee. Even the sensational "Little Stevie Wonder" was flown out from Detroit for the event.[126] Thelonious was proud of his contribution, though a little ambivalent about not participating in the March on Washington. He did watch the march on television as he lay in bed. Harry Colomby visited that day and remembers Thelonious suddenly announcing, "I think I made a contribution to the movement without having to be there to march."[127]

Whatever guilt Thelonious may have carried for not being on the frontlines of the movement evaporated a week later when his nephew Ronnie, Skippy's son, was found dead of a heroin overdose.[128] Ronnie's death sent shockwaves through both the Monk and Smith families. For Toot and Boo Boo (who just turned ten three days earlier), Ronnie had been like a big brother. Toot recalled that when they lived together on Bristow Street and briefly on West 63rd, "Ronnie was the one that was sort of looking after me, you know?"[129] Clifton Smith felt the same way. "He was like my big brother and he taught me all kinds of stuff. Taught me how to talk to girls. Then when he got involved with drugs, I couldn't follow him around. He used to tell me, 'Don't do what I'm doing.'"[130] Ronnie's death dealt a huge blow to the family because he was so promising, talented, and beloved. Skippy suffered something of a nervous breakdown and for months could not function. She went into seclusion.

Thelonious took Ronnie's death especially hard; most family members say it had a greater emotional impact on him than the loss of his mother. He was overcome more by anger than grief. "I'll never forget the funeral," his nephew Theolonious recalled, "because Uncle Bubba was mad. Services were held at a church in Harlem and the minister kept saying that Ronnie was the nephew of Thelonious Monk and all that. It made him angry. He said, "They're mentioning my name more than they're mentioning his.'"[131] He stayed silent, seething through much of the service. When it was time to observe the body and pay respects, Thelonious leaned over the casket and began to trace crosses on Ronnie's forehead with his finger.[132] During the interment, he could no longer hold back his emotions. For all of Monk's nieces and nephews, it was one of the most unforgettable moments of their lives. Benetta recounts the story: "We were all standing around crying our eyes out. And Thelonious walked up to the grave and turned around and looked at us and he said, 'All of you! You better not be so stupid as this!' And he pointed to the grave and stormed away. I don't know how anyone else felt, but I was really, really angry. He knew that we were hurting and I didn't like him calling Ronnie stupid. He just died. It was the cruelest, hardest way to do it, but I tell you, it left an impression."[133]

Ronnie's death sent Monk into a deep depression. He eventually came out of it, but Nellie said he wasn't the same after that. Never one to mince words, Toot put it this way: "Thelonious didn't handle death very well. He got nutty when his mom died. He got nutty when Ronnie died."[134] And as if he needed another sign of how unjust the world suddenly seemed, just days after Toot and Boo Boo returned to their exclusive boarding schools, white terrorists bombed Birmingham's Sixteenth Street Baptist Church on a quiet Sunday morning, killing eleven-year-old Denise McNair and fourteen-year-olds Addie Mae Collins, Carole Robertson, and Cynthia Wesley. They were attending Sunday school. Several hours later, Birmingham's finest fatally wounded sixteen-year-old Johnny Robinson for throwing rocks at a passing car full of white teens yelling racial epithets and celebrating the church bombing. "NEGROES GO BACK TO AFRICA" was scrawled on one side of the car in shoe polish, and a Confederate flag draped the other side.[135] It was enough to make anyone go nutty.

25

"That's a Drag Picture They're Paintin' of Me"

(September 1963–August 1964)

Thelonious worked the day Ronnie died and the day of the funeral. Fans who crowded into the Five Spot each night had no clue how much their hero was suffering. Many came to see the eccentric genius do his thing, so if he danced to the bar and drank himself numb, or spun himself into a kind of mental seclusion, most would chalk it up to his performance. It wasn't that hard for Monk to mentally and emotionally withdraw before the audience's eyes because his shows had become routine. So routine, in fact, that even the critics who once adored Monk had begun to complain. Thelonious typically breezed in around 11:00 p.m., made a beeline for the kitchen to drop off his coat and maybe get a quick bite, ambled to the bar to pick up his doubleshot of Old Grand-Dad bourbon, arriving finally at the piano, where he'd launch in to an unaccompanied piece such as "Don't Blame Me." He would then turn the proceedings over to Frankie Dunlop for what impatient Monk fans regarded as an interminably long drum solo, returning to the bandstand long enough to announce "Butch Warren will play a bass solo." Meanwhile, Thelonious would disappear to the back or head straight to the bar. Finally, he'd call the quartet together and they would play four or five tunes, closing out what usually amounted to a forty- or fifty-minute set with "Epistrophy." And during these tunes he'd often lay out, dancing near the piano or in the alcove behind the bandstand. He'd repeat the same routine over the course of four sets each night.[1]

The repertoire might have been limited, but he knew how to make the same songs sound fresh each time. The fans kept coming because Thelonious always created excitement and the band always swung. But the routine sometimes dulled the sense of adventure that had come to define Monk's music. Critic/poet Amiri Baraka worried that Thelonious was playing himself into a cul-de-sac, suggesting that his sudden fame and the backing of a big record label might be the culprits. He warned, "once [an artist] had made it safely to the 'top', [he] either stopped putting out or began to imitate himself so dreadfully that early records began to have more value than new records or in-person appearances. . . . So Monk, someone might think taking a quick glance, has really been set up for something bad to happen to his playing." To some degree, Baraka thought this was already happening, and he placed much of the blame on his sidemen. "[S]ometimes," he conceded, "one wishes Monk's group wasn't so polished and impeccable, and that he had some musicians with him who would be willing to extend themselves a little further, dig a little deeper into the music and get out there somewhere near where Monk is, and where his compositions always point to." [2]

Baraka wasn't entirely off. Thelonious worked with an excellent group of musicians, but he hardly had a "great" band. The days of great bands were long gone, because all the greats had become leaders. Monk often lamented the lack of musicians who could really master his music, which partly explains the limited repertoire. But the band's problems were not exclusively musical. Frankie Dunlop had grown bored and felt he was underpaid. He also had his sights on possibly leaving music and becoming an actor. Butch Warren, who had drug problems when he joined the band, also suffered from sudden mood swings he couldn't understand.[3] Charlie Rouse was dealing with a number of personal issues. He was still battling his drug demons, despite the loving efforts of his friend Orelia Benskina. They collaborated together on the song "Un Dia," which he recorded on his 1963 release *Bossa Nova Bacchanal*, and later that year he performed in her stage show, "Princess Orelia's Afro-Pot Purée." As Rouse began contemplating leaving Monk and possibly becoming a leader, the former Les Jazz Modes manager had begun overseeing his own career.[4] Around the same time, Rouse's marriage to Esperanza deteriorated and he became romantically involved with a young woman named Sandra Capello. When they met, Rouse was on the verge of making a clean break from heroin, though from her account she gave him the boost he needed. Early in their relationship, she often accompanied him to Dr. Robert Freymann's office for methadone treatment. Within a year he had freed himself from the drug completely. "He was a different person. . . . We started going to church together in the Village."[5]

For Monk, coping with Ronnie's death proved exceedingly difficult. His illness grew worse, his bipolar episodes became more frequent, and so did his drinking and drug use. His income increased, but so did the demands on his time and the pressure to create something new. Friends and handlers such as Nica, Macero, the Colomby brothers, the Termini brothers, the critics bold enough to speak their mind, and family members bombarded him with suggestions—hire this person, fire that person, put together another big band, record another solo LP, reunite with Coltrane, ad infinitum. . . . And all the while, he had to submit to more interviews and live under greater press scrutiny. Barry Farrell of *Time* had finished conducting some thirty interviews by early fall, and as he spent the next few weeks distilling his observations into a 5,000-word essay, Thelonious had to take time out to sit for his cover portrait. The artist, Russian painter Boris Chaliapin, grew frustrated with Monk because during the course of four sittings he always fell asleep.[6] Chaliapin called it strange; I would call it exhaustion.

The third weekend in September, Monk made his debut appearance at the Sixth Annual Monterey Jazz Festival. It had taken him six years to get an invitation, and it came at the last minute. The quartet was scheduled to play Saturday the 21st, and then Monk was to perform the following afternoon with the Monterey Festival Orchestra, but for unknown reasons Monk's big-band appearance was canceled.[7] Instead, the quartet played another set on Sunday. Judging from the spirited applause, the audience didn't seem to mind. Monk stuck with his standard repertoire, but raised the bandstand with a few thrilling moments. During his unaccompanied introduction to "Sweet and Lovely," he played little stride passages at breakneck speed, à la Art Tatum, to the shock and delight of the crowd.[8] Critic Ralph Gleason later declared Monk's appearance the festival's "outstanding musical performance."[9]

Thelonious and Nellie came home to the alarming news that Bud Powell had been hospitalized for tuberculosis. Monk last saw Powell when he passed through Paris on tour, and even then he looked terrible. When he learned that Bud had to be confined to a sanatorium for several weeks with medical bills mounting, Thelonious sent money.[10] On Sunday afternoon, October 27, Oscar Goodstein held a benefit at Birdland to raise funds for Powell's medical expenses.[11] Musicians rallied to the cause. Monk made a brief appearance on his way back from the Five Spot, where he played a benefit for the Congress of Racial Equality (CORE) that had been scheduled at the exact same time as the Powell fundraiser. It was a follow-up to the "Sit In for Freedom" concert held at the Five Spot the previous Sunday.[12] Still haunted by the four black girls killed in Birmingham, Monk did not want to miss this event. Three weeks later, he was the featured artist at a "Cocktail Sip" sponsored by the Bronx chapter of CORE. Held at Goodson's Town Cabaret just a few blocks from Lyman Place, the event raised money for Sara Collins, who had lost her eyesight and her sister, Addie Mae Collins, in the bombing of Sixteenth Street Baptist Church.[13]

Early in the fall, Jules Colomby and Marc Smilow arranged another big-band collaboration with Monk and Hall Overton, this time at the newly completed Philharmonic Hall at Lincoln Center. Jules secured the hall for November 29, Overton and Monk began working on new arrangements and assembling a band, and Teo Macero prepared to record the event.[14] Thelonious agreed with Hall that the last big band was too bottom heavy tonally, so they replaced the tuba and French horn with soprano saxophone and cornet. They hired Steve Lacy and Thad Jones, as well as Eddie Bert (trombone) and Phil Woods (alto saxophone) from the original Town Hall concert, and a relative newcomer named "Dizzy" Reece on trumpet. The Jamaican-born Reece had cut his professional teeth in London in the 1950s and moved to New York in 1959. He had made a few LPs for Blue Note; one included an original composition he titled "Variations on Monk."[15] After a difficult search for a suitable baritone player, they settled on Gene Allen, a big band veteran whose resume included Louis Prima, Claude Thornhill, and Gerry Mulligan's Concert Jazz Band.[16]

Overton completed the charts some time in November and they began rehearsing at his loft on Sixth Avenue. Then, on November 22, President John F. Kennedy was fatally shot in Dallas, sending shockwaves throughout the nation and the world. But his death had an even more immediate effect on Monk's life and work. First, the Philharmonic concert was postponed until December 30. Second, Barry Farrell's *Time* magazine cover story, slated to run on November 29, was pushed back. The magazine substituted a color portrait of the newly sworn-in President Lyndon Baines Johnson, reportedly destroying the three million copies they had already printed bearing Chaliapin's por-trait of Monk.[17] The unexpected delay turned out to be a blessing in disguise. Judging from the rehearsal tapes made at Overton's loft in December, the band wasn't ready. A week before the concert, the musicians were still wrestling with Overton's arrangement of "Four in One" and Monk had just decided to include "Light Blue."[18] Overton went so far as to request an extra rehearsal at the end of the week and a serious dress rehearsal the morning of the concert (Monday, December 30).[19] To complicate matters, Dizzy Reece couldn't make the new date so they brought in trumpeter Nick Travis, a friend and bandmate of Gene Allen in Mulligan's Concert Jazz Band.

The Philharmonic concert was one of the year's most anticipated events in the jazz world. Jules Colomby and Smilow flooded the city with publicity and marshaled the press to cover the event.[20] John S. Wilson published a rather long profile on Monk and Overton the day before the concert. Following the obligatory descriptions of his eccen-tric behavior and colorfully "cluttered" apartment, Wilson relays Monk's thoughts on the concert. "It will be different music . . . different personnel and a different place." What wasn't different was his aesthetic vision—to make a big band swing like a small ensemble with more power. "A lot of people notice this free sound and don't know that they notice it," Monk explained. "That's why I like the small group—it flows with so much freedom. You get the bigger band to flow the same way by the way you write the music and the way you play it."[21]

Close to 1,500 people filed into Philharmonic Hall—short of a sell-out crowd, but a decent showing nonetheless. Critics and players came out in force, since December 30 fell on a Monday (musicians' night off), and few went home disappointed. It was not Town Hall redux. For one thing, the evening was divided into three parts with two intermissions, beginning with the big band, then an interlude with just the quartet, and finishing with the big band.[22] The ten-piece band not only performed more songs this time but Overton wrote all new charts. His arrangement of "Evidence," in which he had the band restate the melody underneath the soloists, offered a brilliant example of contrapuntal writing. The brighter instrumentation, supported by Frankie Dunlop's driving rhythm, gave compositions like "Bye-Ya" and "I Mean You" greater power and clarity. Moreover, Thelonious debuted a brand new composition he titled "Oska T," a corruption of "ask for T" (or "tea") spoken in a British accent. A simple sixteen-bar tune made up of two repeating eight-bar phrases, Monk had written it to be arranged for big band.[23] He also surprised everyone with an unaccompanied rendering of "When It's Darkness on the Delta," an old paean to the South written by New Yorkers Jerry Livington, Marty Symes, and Al Neiberg. Some jazz and Dixieland groups performed it in the 1950s after it was resurrected for the film "South of Dixie," but otherwise the song was destined for obscurity.[24] The audience responded to Monk's five-minute rumination on the melody with thunderous applause. The big finale (before the clos-ing theme of "Epistrophy"), was a nearly fifteen-minute romp through the intricate "Four in One." Reminiscent of his take on "Little Rootie Tootie," Overton arranged Monk's solo from the original Blue Note recording for the entire horn section.[25] The crowd loved it. Before the night was over, the Schaefer Brewing Company presented

Monk with an award for "his extraordinary achievement as an innovator, composer, and leader of modern jazz." Too bad they misspelled his name.[26]

Most critics effused over the concert, declaring the evening an unqualified success and singling out "Four in One" as the evening's masterpiece.[27] "Joy returned to jazz last night in Philharmonic Hall" is how George Simon opened his review for the *Herald-Tribune*. The unspoken foil, of course, was the angry political noise of the avant-garde. By contrast, "this was a swinging affair, full of the basic foot-tapping feeling that was there when jazz began." He praised Overton's charts, compared Monk's playing with that of Ellington, and described the evening as a party: "everybody, including the musicians, had a good time. . . . Jazz evenings like that are a joy indeed."[28]

A triumphant concert was the perfect capstone to an incredible year. Monk had his share of setbacks, but he also enjoyed international critical acclaim and made more money than ever before. His gross receipts for engagements amounted to $53,832, and royalties came to $22,850. An impressive figure, to be sure, but we must remember that a band is a business. After deducting what he paid in salaries, hotels, travel, supplies, union dues, commissions (both to Harry Colomby and Jack Whittemore of Shaw Booking Agency), and taxes, the Monks ended up with $33,055.[29] The press exaggerated Monk's earnings, attributing most of his newfound wealth to his Columbia contract.[30] But Columbia's accounting books tell a different story. About $1,400 of Monk's advance for *Criss Cross* went to sidemen's salaries, piano tunings, instrument rental, and miscellaneous costs.[31] Although the quartet was recorded live several times throughout the year, Monk was not always entitled to an advance because (during his lifetime, at least) these recordings were released as individual tracks on compilation records. He received a token advance of $500 for his Tokyo recording, but Columbia actually charged him $844 for his recorded performance at Newport.[32] The most egregious example of how the label did business is illustrated in Columbia's handling of the Philharmonic concert. All costs were deducted from Monk's advance: stagehands ($525), sidemen ($970.71), copyists ($90.52), Hall Overton's arranging fee ($1,400), and unnamed "costs" (mainly recording expenses and fees charged by the Philharmonic) amounting to $2,689.39. The charges whittled Monk's $10,000 advance to $4,324.38.[33] Columbia initially failed to deduct Jules Colomby's $2,000 producer's fee, so they took it from Monk's future advances in four $500 installments.[34]

Thelonious had other problems to contend with. As soon as his seven-month engagement at the Five Spot ended the last week of January,[35] Frankie Dunlop gave notice. It came as a surprise; the quartet had been preparing for another European tour in February. After nearly two years, he was ready to move on. As Monk explained it, "He wants to be an actor. He wants to do pantomime or something."[35] By "pantomime" he meant impressions, and Dunlop was a master at it. His ability to capture Monk's gestures, voice, and cadences left most people in stitches. He teamed up with Leo Morris and a dancer named Maretta to create a stage show he called "Jazz Pantomime." A mélange of music, dance, and comedic impressions of famous jazz artists, Dunlop mounted the show off-Broadway and performed it at benefits.[37]

Monk desperately needed a drummer. Besides his forthcoming tour, he had record dates lined up for January 29 and 30. Fortunately, he had someone in mind. From the end of December through January, Joe Termini had booked a series of piano trios to play opposite Monk. The pianists changed—Bobby Timmons, Junior Mance, and Walter Bishop, Jr.—but the drummer remained the same. His name was Ben Riley. A tall, quiet, handsome fellow all of thirty years old, he kept good time, had a strong sense of swing, and had a penchant for the ride cymbal and snare. During his break, Riley sat at the bar checking out Monk, but when Riley was on the bandstand, Monk usually retired to the kitchen. Weeks passed before Monk spoke to Riley, and his first words were, "Who the hell are you, the house drummer?"[38] So when Harry Colomby called him on January 29 to come down to the 30th Street Studio to record with Monk, Riley thought it was a joke and hung up. Colomby called back to reassure him that he was genuine and to say that they were waiting for him at the studio. "We never rehearsed," Riley recalled. "Monk just came out and started playing. He knew I would listen. He saw me sitting there every night at the Five Spot when his band came on. . . . He knew I was onto what he was doing, because I was listening. I heard him when he played with 'Trane, Shadow Wilson, and Wilbur Ware." [39]

Riley didn't realize that the first session *was* rehearsal. They spent the entire three hours in the studio working on various pieces but recorded only one track—"Shuffle Boil"—and it was rejected. Monk last recorded it with Gigi Gryce nearly a decade ago, so the whole band came to it cold. Because he had written it with an alto saxophone in mind, the high notes were beyond the range of the tenor. He refused to change it and Rouse rebelled: "'What are you trying to make me do?' [Monk] just said, 'It's on the horn.' Then when I heard it back, this strange sounding stuff came out, right and pretty. He said, 'You see how it sounds? The tenor is *full* up there—fuller than a soprano.'"[40] Butch Warren also had to learn a tricky bass line that was part of the melody, and Thelonious decided to take it at a swifter tempo than what he originally recorded. The only usable track from the session was an unaccompanied version of "Nice Work If You Can Get It."[41]

The next day yielded better results. They remade "Shuffle Boil," although Rouse faltered on the melody and sounded tentative throughout, and Riley was still finding his bearings. They also recorded a respectable version of "Epistrophy." Riley knew the melody and the rhythms, but he sometimes overwhelmed the band with the steady splash of his ride cymbal.[42] Before their three hours were up, however, the group delivered one fine version of "Stuffy Turkey." Based on "Rhythm" changes, the A-section is from a riff tune Coleman Hawkins made famous back in the 1940s titled "Stuffy." Hawkins claimed composer's credit for it, but pianist Sir Charles Thompson claimed *he* coauthored. Others have insisted that the tune originated with Monk.[43] Whoever wrote it, Thelonious associated the tune with Hawkins, and, given their resurgent friendship during this period, he probably recorded it as a tribute to him. He certainly made it his own, writing an entirely different bridge and arranging the melody so that the piano echoes the tenor's voicing of the melody.[44]

The band returned to the studio on February 10. Determined to complete an album,

Macero booked *two* three-hour sessions, but even with six hours of studio time they came away with only two usable tracks.[45] Once again, Monk mined his musical archive for "new" material, resurrecting the old Harry Warren-Al Dubin tune "Lulu's Back in Town," and pulling out his own "Brake's Sake," another song from the record he made with Gigi Gryce. Needless to say, Macero was disappointed; he was under enormous pressure to turn in an LP before Monk left for Europe. Thelonious wasn't happy, either, because it meant his $10,000 advance had to wait.[46] He was pleased with his new drummer, however. Riley recalled, "After we finished the session, he said, 'Do you need any money? I don't want anybody in my band being broke.' I said, "Excuse me?" He repeated himself and asked, 'Do you have a passport? You better go get it because we're leaving for Europe on Friday.' That's how I knew I got the gig."[47]

Riley got his passport, and on Friday, Valentine's Day 1964, boarded a plane with Charlie Rouse, Butch Warren, Thelonious and Nellie, and George and Joyce Wein for a seventeen-day tour that took them to Amsterdam, Stockholm, Copenhagen, Paris, Milan, Zurich, Marseilles, Brussels, and Solingen, West Germany. The trip gave Thelonious and Nellie a chance to get to know the newest member of the band. They learned that he was born in Savannah, Georgia, but grew up in Harlem's Sugar Hill. As a kid he studied with anyone who would teach him, hung out with other young drummers like Jimmy Cobb and Phil Wright, and sat in with Cecil Scott at the Club Sudan. He also attended jam sessions organized by Art Blakey and sat in wherever he could. In 1954, he enlisted in the army, served as a paratrooper, and played in the army band. When he got out in 1956, he was ready to turn professional and quickly developed a reputation as a solid yet versatile hard bop drummer. He worked with a number of artists, including Randy Weston, Mary Lou Williams, Sonny Rollins, Stan Getz, Nina Simone, Johnny Griffin, Eddie "Lockjaw" Davis, and Woody Herman.[48]

Yet, for all of Riley's experience, filling Frankie Dunlop's shoes wasn't easy, and some people in Monk's inner circle did not think he was up to the task. Nica, for one, initially opposed Riley and lobbied for Billy Higgins, but Monk was unequivocal. He explained, "This is my band and I know who I want in my band."[49] Monk not only wanted someone who could swing all the time, but a drummer willing to listen—listen to the band and listen to advice. Thelonious helped Riley become the drummer he needed, and in so doing he made him a better musician. Early on, Monk told him, "You can't always like every song the best. Another player might like the song more than you, and *his* beat might be better than *your* beat." In other words, the drummer need not always establish the beat but may follow others who swing more, and doing that required a more conversational style. Monk would often play little figures that demanded a response from Riley.[50] Monk also instructed him not to be so busy "playing that Roy Haynes shit" and to just swing. "Just learn how to swing and make everybody move to certain places and then the rest will take care of itself."[51]

When Riley asked Monk about rehearsing, he replied, "Why do you want to do that, so you can learn how to cheat? You already know how to play. Now play wrong and make *that* right."[52] As with every musician who played with Monk, it was trial by fire. During the band's first performance at Amsterdam's Concertgebouw, midway into the set Monk walked to the mic and announced, "Now, ladies and gentle-men, thank you very much. Now, Ben Riley will play a drum solo for you."[53] For a moment, Riley was caught off-guard, but he composed himself and delivered a fine unaccompanied solo. Later in the dressing room, Thelonious pulled him aside and said proudly, "How many people do you think could do what you just did? You didn't know all of the different songs, but you swung through all of that. . . . Why would you want to rehearse?"[54] Riley proved to be a good student and a loyal band member; he would go on to spend five years with Monk. "'[T]hat was like going to the univer-sity. I mean, you had your highest, you had one of the highest points of your musical career working with him."[55]

But during the tour Riley was still just a freshman at the University of Monk, and the existing recordings reveal him finding his way to the material. The audiences seemed pleased with the band, even though Monk's repertoire had changed little since his last European tour. He added "Brake's Sake" and "Stuffy Turkey" from the LP in progress, and occasionally played "Four in One," but stuck mostly with the songbook of the last two years. Nevertheless, he played to sell-out crowds who responded most enthu-siastically when they recognized a tune. He did have some trouble in Paris, where the quartet was booked to play two concerts back-to-back: the Alhambra on Saturday, Feb-ruary 22, and La Maison de l'ORTF (Office de Radiodiffusion-Télévision Française) the following night. The band arrived on the 22nd with little time for a decent sound check. The piano was poorly tuned, tinny, and the action inadequate. The condition of the instrument compromised the band's dynamics and compelled Monk to play even fewer notes than normal.[56] In an interview the next day with *Jazz Magazine's* Michel Delorme, Monk complained, "The piano is no good at [the Alhambra]. What a sad piano they got on the stage. . . . They should be able to hear the piano is no good."[57] Delorme thought Thelonious and his band played well under the circumstances, but he was less concerned with the condition of the piano than what he perceived to be a growing staleness in the band's makeup and repertoire. He politely suggested that Monk break out of the quartet format and record with a sextet, big band, or other com-bos. He also asked Monk if he planned a different repertoire for the Maison de l'ORTF concert. The question annoyed him, so he turned it back to Delorme:

> Monk: I don't know, I probably will. [Pause] What you saying? What. You
> saying I should play the same tunes or what?
> Delorme: Mmm. I don't know. I don't mind anyway.
> Monk: You saying something. You ought to know. I mean, what would be
> the hippest? Play the same songs or play something else?[58]

He did play the same songs, though the longer program allowed him to add a few more tunes such as "Four in One" and "Hackensack."[59] But there were no surprises. This disappointed critic Michel-Claude Jalard, who wrote one of the few bad reviews of the tour. He felt Monk had fallen into a routine, essentially imitating himself and draw-ing on his "memory of past improvisations" rather than generating the kinds of fresh ideas he was known for. The problem lay less with the material than with his approach to improvisation.[60] Jalard's critique was a glimpse of what was to come.

Despite the substandard piano and critical responses, Paris turned out to be one of the highlights of the trip. Bud Powell, Francis Paudras, and his wife, Nichole, surprised Monk and Nellie at the airport when they arrived Saturday afternoon. Thelonious hugged Bud and looked him over. Journalists surrounded Thelonious, peppering him with questions, but Monk ignored them. They never took their eyes off each other.[61] Powell and Paudras attended the concert that night. Paudras found Monk's performance "electrifying" and Powell was delighted. Powell had been anticipating Monk's visit for some time: A week earlier he sat at the piano in Paudras's flat (where he now resided) and belted out half a dozen Monk tunes, including "Stuffy Turkey."[62] After the concert, Nellie and Thelonious invited Francis and Bud to dinner at Gaby and Haynes in Montmarte, Paris's first soul-food restaurant and musicians' hangout. "[Thelonious] sat opposite Bud and took care of him all night, mobilizing all the waiters to make sure Bud had everything he wanted," Paudras remembered. "When we got back home, Bud asked me to put on a record by Thelonious and started dancing to it the way Monk had done while the musicians took their choruses."[63]

They moved on to Milan. Monk filled the Teatro dell'Arte, drawing one of the largest crowds for a jazz concert in the theater's history. Hardcore Monkians filled the house. Just a few months earlier, Italian Monk fans almost caused a riot after they purchased their copies of *Criss Cross*, only to discover that both sides of the disc were identical—there was no side B.[64] Monk vindicated his label by giving a terrific show. Critics Giancarlo Testoni and Arrigo Polillo found Monk's performance intelligent—"neither polemical nor pompous" but "concentrated and luscious." Their praise extended to his sidemen, including Ben Riley, who was singled out for being "free of smugness and [possessing] a sensitive attention to tone." In the end, they proclaimed the evening "one of the best jazz shows of the season."[65]

Two nights later, they were at Kongresshaus in Zurich where Monk gave another successful concert. After the show, a tall, lanky black man with a heavy accent came backstage and introduced himself as Dollar Brand—one of those unusual names Monk dug. He told Monk that he was a piano player from South Africa who had just arrived in Switzerland with his wife, singer Bea Benjamin, and his band, bassist Johnny Gertze and drummer Makaya Ntshoko. They had fled their country in the aftermath of the Sharpeville Massacre in 1960. The trio had a regular gig at the Café Africana and he invited Monk and Nellie to come hear them if they had the time. He didn't stay very long, but before he left, "[I] thanked him for the inspiration. He looked at me for a time and then said: 'You're the first piano player to tell me that.'"[66]

Inspiration might be an understatement. The twenty-nine-year-old Brand (who would soon change his name to Abdullah Ibrahim) earned the nickname "South Africa's Monk."[67] A founding member of the short-lived "Jazz Epistles," South Africa's most influential modern jazz ensemble, Brand was introduced to Monk's music by his bandmate, alto saxophonist Kippie Moeketsi. "Kippie would talk to me about Monk before I'd heard of any of his records. I was saying: 'Monk? What's this Monk thing?'

And then, man, I heard the music and I said 'aaaaaah! I can dig this . . . so this is Monk!' Kippie would be screaming about how Monk was playing the same type of sound you could hear in so-called tribal music up in the Northern Transvaal."[68] Brand's first LP as a leader, recorded in 1960, was titled *Dollar Brand Plays Sphere Jazz* and included "Misterioso," and "Just You, Just Me"—a favorite Monk standard.[69] In 1963, Duke Ellington recorded Brand's trio in Paris and he was about to release the LP. He had composed all but one song on the album, and that song was Monk's "Brilliant Corners." And even his original pieces possessed strong Monk influences. "Ubu Suku" knits together phrases from two standards Monk played: the first bar of "I'm Getting Sentimental Over You" and the second bar of "You Are Too Beautiful." It shares some similarities with "Crepuscule with Nellie," including the bass figure in the fifth measure of the melody.[70] Whether or not Monk ever grasped the impact he had had on Brand, he did discover that night in Zurich just how far his music had traveled.

The real extent of his fame hit home a couple of days later when someone handed Monk the latest edition of *Time*. There, on the cover of the February 28, 1964 edition, his painted image stared back at him. It was his image, all right, but was it his story? Barry Farrell described a strange, reclusive genius, with an eccentric taste for hats, little connection to reality, a childlike demeanor, who depends on women to care for him (Nellie and Nica), and, often in the same breath, portrays a family man, honest and pure, deserving of his long-awaited recognition. The writing was eloquent but somewhat schizophrenic. He quoted Monk vehemently protesting the "mad genius" label, and then he went on to reproduce it by recounting incidents in which he had been confined to mental institutions or speculating on his drug use. If Thelonious, Nellie, and Harry Colomby had hoped the article would help mainstream Monk's image, they were disappointed. In one particularly damaging passage, Farrell wrote: "Every day is a brand-new pharmaceutical event for Monk: alcohol, Dexedrine, sleeping potions, whatever is at hand, charge through his bloodstream in baffling combinations."[71]

By the end of the piece, Farrell took an interesting turn, suggesting that Monk isn't so colorful or controversial after all, especially compared to the brooding Miles Davis, the mystical Sonny Rollins, or the volatile Charles Mingus.[72] Here he hit on one of the main points of the piece: Monk is a good guy because he is not caught up in the "racial woes [that] are at the heart of much bad behavior in jazz."[73] Invoking a recent *Time* magazine editorial on "Crow Jim" in jazz (Farrell may have even written it), Farrell was referring to black artists who criticized whites like Dave Brubeck and Stan Kenton for exploiting "their music," and who employed jazz as a vehicle for black protest. Like most white liberals uncomfortable with rising black militancy, Farrell felt betrayed by the strident racial politics of Max Roach's *Freedom Now Suite* or the "angry" sounds of the "New Thing."[74] Monk, much to Farrell's relief, was above the fray.

In some respects, Farrell had little new to say. Most stories about Monk dating back to the late 1940s dwelled on his strange behavior, childlike aura, late-night wanderings, uncompromising attitude, the women in his life, even narcotics. What is different, however, is that Farrell pushed racial politics to the foreground. Monk's story isn't just about Monk. For some he was the symbol of black genius; for others he was the last bastion of color-blindness in an increasingly polarized world. One reader, self-identified as "an aspiring young Negro artist raised in a ghetto, and a member of the Negro blues school," praised the article for its "authenticity" and for illuminating the "forces that shape the Monk-type personality." Another reader challenged the article's characterization of Monk's stage behavior, arguing that it "is vital to the dignity, humor and discipline of his music."[75] Still others read it as classic racial stereotyping. Critic Ralph J. Gleason called the piece "revolting" and "libelous to jazz," and castigated *Time* for turning Monk into "the symbol of the native genius . . . sweaty and bizarre, so as not to ruffle the preconceptions of *Time*-thought."[76] While praising Farrell for writing "an accurate, well-rounded portrait in depth of a complex personality," Leonard Feather nevertheless concluded that the essay might actually harm jazz and race relations. To middle America, the Negro jazz musician comes across as both drug-addicted and a clownish buffoon donning a funny hat. "Not too long ago such verbs as shuffle and grin were part of the Southern white's primitive concept of the Negro. Are we to return to that also?" Feather implicitly placed some of the blame on Monk for the way he behaved in public, suggesting that more deserving musicians were overlooked because they have "never enjoyed what is presumably *Time's* idea of a rich, full, adventurous, newsworthy life. [Art] Tatum and [Jack] Teagarden never wore funny hats; [Erroll] Garner, [Count] Basie, and [Oscar] Peterson do not get up and dance in the middle of their performances; Gillespie does not arrive every day at a brand-new pharmaceutical discovery."[77]

To black nationalists and other radicals, the *Time* article constituted an attack on one of their heroes. Writer Theodore Pontiflet published a sharply worded salvo in the Harlem-based *Liberator* magazine criticizing what he considered Farrell's obsession with Monk's relationship with the baroness. The implications of the *Time* piece, he argued, not only rendered black women to "the background reduced to the domestic chores" but "warns white America that in these days of talking integration and on the fatal eve of passing a watered-down civil rights bill, they should remember that it could mean more of their daughters will be bringing home an occasional black genius." Pontiflet suggested that Monk was unaware of his own exploitation, thus unwittingly reinforcing the dominant image of him as naïve and child-like. Throughout the entire ordeal—he writes, "Thelonious Monk and his wife Nellie remain as pure as honey. The patron baroness? She was part of the deal—the bitter part of the sweet."[78]

Ironically, the left-wing Pontiflet shared much in common with the right-wing *National Review* critic Ralph de Toledano. They both treated Monk as a kind of idiot savant, unaware of the world around him, and they both believed he embodied their political position. De Toledano praised Monk for not confusing music with politics. "Like most of the best jazzmen . . . he doesn't believe that he must make his art a sledge hammer to pound away at political themes."[79] And yet, in spite of de Toledano's plea for color-blindness in jazz, he nonetheless embraced a racialized construction of jazz as more physical and emotional than cerebral. He chided Monk for being *too cerebral*, for not tapping into his "soul," and for removing any sense of "dance" from his music![80] In other words, while Monk is not too black politically, musically de Toledano finds he's not black enough.

Meanwhile, Columbia's executives were ecstatic about the *Time* feature and made sure copies were sent to all of their affiliates.[81] No one there seemed concerned with Monk's portrayal or the substance of the piece. The piece also had a positive impact on Monk's children. Boo Boo and Toot basked in their father's fame, becoming local celebrities themselves at their respective boarding schools. Because Toot was older, he felt the effects more immediately. "Remember, the cover of *Time* magazine was reserved for the likes of Dag Hammarskjöld, Winston Churchill, Robert Frost, Bertrand Russell, those kind of people. So Thelonious Monk shows up on the cover of *Time* magazine and suddenly, everybody was inviting me to dinner all the time."[82] Boo Boo's world was also affected. Green Chimneys headmaster Sam B. Ross, Jr., wrote a brief letter to *Time* thanking the magazine for its rich accounting of Monk's "long musical career," adding "his daughter attends our boarding school."[83] That letter was all a young Belgian man named Geert de Meulenaere needed to fulfill a dream of his. He had attended Monk's concert in Antwerp on February 29, but failed to get the pianist's autograph, so he sent a letter to the school in care of "Miss Barbara Monk." It was a cute gesture and it could not have come at a better moment. Ross and other administrators and faculty at Green Chimneys were planning to feature Monk in a benefit concert for the school in neighboring Danbury, Connecticut, on April 14.[84] Thus alongside a flurry of articles about Monk's impending concert, the local press published the Green Chimneys press release about the endearing letter from Antwerp. It was yet another reminder why Thelonious Monk was not to be missed.[85]

The banner emblazoned across the *Time* cover—"Jazz: Bebop and Beyond"—became the concert's theme. They mimeographed hundreds of flyers with Monk's likeness drawn by a student modeled on the *Time* cover, and offered patrons the opportunity to have their name listed in the program for a small donation of $2.00.[86] Monk's quartet nearly filled Danbury's Palace Theater, delivering two exciting sets. While Charlie Rouse "had little to say that night," according to the town's local critic, Monk put on a piano clinic. "At one time or another, Monk emulated with his piano each of the instruments on the stage with him much like a teacher shows his young pupil what to work toward."[87] During intermission, Mayor J. Thayer Bowman reminded Thelonious that his beloved Danbury was known as "the Hat City," and in a gesture of goodwill and good humor, he presented Monk with "an 'LBJ' hat." Mayor Bowman's gesture was not lost on Thelonious, for it was President Lyndon Baines Johnson's visage that displaced his on the cover of *Time* magazine. Monk graciously thanked him and promptly replaced the lamb's wool chapeau he was wearing with the white felt ten-gallon.[88]

And what about Monk? What did he think about Farrell's story? According to Ben Riley, the article "made Thelonious feel very good about himself because I think finally he understood that there were a number of people very interested in what he was playing and what he was doing."[89] He didn't change, Riley said. If anything, the attention made him want to play more, and fortunately there was no shortage of work—at least for the time being. But he did have complaints and used the occasion of another major profile, by Lewis Lapham for the *Saturday Evening Post,* to challenge Farrell and other journalists who had painted him as a crazy eccentric. "That's a drag picture they're paintin' of me, man," he told Lapham just a couple of weeks after the *Time* story appeared. "A lot of people still think I'm nuts or somethin' . . . but I dig it, man; I can feel the draft."[90] He even hinted that his sudden fame may have more to do with his image than his music. "I was playing the same stuff twenty years ago, man . . . and nobody was painting any portrait."[91] Harry Colomby also used the occasion to do some damage control. Besides emphasizing the fact that Monk wasn't one of those angry musicians who hated whitey, he portrayed his client as a hardworking musician who went straight home to Nellie every night and cared for his family. Colomby told Lapham, "He's so straight, it makes you nervous."[92] Lapham himself even took a swipe at Farrell, insisting that Monk was neither crazy nor eccentric but rather "an honest man in a not-so-honest world. . . . Monk never learned to tell the convenient lies or make the customary compromises. That he should have been proclaimed the complete and perfect hipster is an absurd irony."[93] And yet, for all his defense of Monk's sanity, Lapham fell for the oldest myth of all: "An emotional and intuitive man, possessing a child's vision of the world, Monk talks, sleeps, eats, laughs, walks or dances as the spirit moves him."[94]

For a so-called "child," Monk was tactful and shrewd enough to keep his criticisms of *Time* oblique. He understood the importance of publicity and did not want to burn any bridges. He did have one complaint about the piece that he was willing to share with the public: he insisted that Nellie never called him "Melodius Thunk." "That's a lie, man. I never heard my wife call me that. It's those reporters, man, you can't trust them."[95]

Monk returned to the studio on March 9 to finally finish his next LP, wittily titled *It's Monk's Time.* After two weeks of "rehearsal" on tour, the band found its groove. The three-hour session yielded a third and final version of "Shuffle Boil" and a brilliant solo rendition of "Memories of You" to complete the album. They also had time to record a track for the next LP. A new composition titled "Teo," it was Monk's small gift to his patient producer.[96] Based on Eddie Durham's "Topsy," a favorite of Monk's back in the days of Minton's, it was an ideal vehicle for Rouse, who still sounded a bit tentative on "Shuffle Boil."

The band had no immediate club dates, so they rehearsed in preparation for a second big band concert at Carnegie Hall scheduled for March 30—another Jules Colomby, Marc Smilow, Hall Overton collaboration. Except for Ben Riley and Jerome Richardson on baritone (he replaced Gene Allen), Monk kept the band he used at the Philharmonic. He and Overton changed the music, however. The only tune they retained from the Philharmonic concert was "Four in One." Instead, they decided to revisit the original Town Hall repertoire. Unfortunately, the charts had perished in the 1961 fire and Overton had to reconstruct them.[97] The day before the concert, Carnegie Hall administrators decided to bump Monk to June so they could give the booking to Duke Ellington for his Easter Sunday concert. Jules Colomby and Smilow had a fit.[98] They had already spent money on advertising and were still reeling from poor ticket sales from the last concert. Monk shrugged it off. He didn't think the band was ready and he appreciated having some time off. He also appreciated the great review *Life* magazine had given him for his newly released *Monk: Big Band and Quartet in Concert.* The writer Chris Welles called it "interesting and exhilarating," and "a surprisingly successful attempt to adapt his ideas to a large 10-piece band."[99] But more than anything, he appreciated finally receiving his advance check for completing *It's Monk's Time,* which came to $7,292 after all the deductions.[100]

Monk and the band were back on the road in early April, first for an engagement at Le Jazz Hot in Montreal, and then back across the border to play the first annual Cornell University Jazz Festival on April 18.[101] They returned to Canada on the 26th for a concert at Toronto's legendary Massey Hall. Eleven years earlier, a quintet made up of Charlie Parker, Dizzy Gillespie, Bud Powell, Charles Mingus, and Max Roach gave, by some counts, the greatest modern jazz concert . . . ever. While Monk wasn't about to wrest that distinction away from his old pals, he earned high praise from most of the local critics and the 1,000 fans who turned out to hear them, despite showing up an hour late. Of course, sharing the bill with a mediocre Canadian band made Monk's group sound even better. Critic Patrick Scott noted that whereas Monk played with "great beauty, rhythmic compulsion and warmth," the thirteen-piece Don Thompson band was "so utterly dreadful that I found myself wishing someone would reactivate the custom of booing and hissing an offensive performance."[102] The lone dissenting voice was long-time Monk detractor Helen McNamara. She called Monk's improvisations "ponderous," the order of solos "monotonous," and concluded that the band "never seemed to get off the ground." Not surprisingly, she praised Don Thompson's band for its "exuberance" and, in a direct inversion of Scott, presumed the audience "must have felt that they had been compensated [for Monk's poor performance] by hearing some first class musicians."[103]

From Toronto they flew to Washington, D.C., for a two-week engagement at the Bohemian Caverns. Opening night, Monk was three hours late because he and Nellie couldn't get a cab to stop for them.[104] Aside from the opening night mishap, the band had a good run at the Caverns and Rouse and Warren enjoyed being home again. Warren especially missed D.C., and he was "growing tired of making records." By the end of the gig, he'd decided to leave the band. He stayed with Monk through the next two gigs—a week at the Jazz Workshop in Boston and two concerts in Southern California. Typically, most jazz groups couldn't afford to travel cross-country for two days' worth of work, but Monk's quartet flew out to L.A. to open for the newest folk music sensation, Peter, Paul, and Mary. The trio had just won a Grammy for "Blowin' in the Wind" and achieved enough clout to select their own opening acts.[105] They chose Monk and no one else. The quartet performed before a huge crowd at the Long Beach Arena on Friday, May 22, and to an even larger audience at the Hollywood Bowl the next night. The Hollywood Bowl concert alone drew 13,500 people.[106]

When the band returned East, Warren promptly moved back to Washington into what amounted to a musical and social void. He worked briefly on a local television show and made at least one record with Bobby Timmons,[107] but then he literally disappeared—broke, homeless, drug-addicted, and sick. He eventually checked himself in to St. Elizabeth's Hospital, the district's psychiatric facility, where he was diagnosed with schizophrenia.[108] Meanwhile, Monk had to scramble to find a bass player, especially since the Carnegie Hall concert was just two weeks away. Overton initially called Richard Davis, an excellent, classically trained bassist originally out of Chicago, but Monk preferred someone with whom he was familiar—James "Spanky" DeBrest.[109] They had recorded together with Blakey in 1957 and Monk always appreciated his big tone.

They rehearsed at Overton's loft and, once again, Eugene Smith had the foresight to tape some of those sessions. The band sounded less polished than in previous rehearsals, and both Monk and Overton knew it. Listening to the tapes, one senses a kind of panic seizing both leaders, while most of the band members appear relaxed and confident. Having participated in the Town Hall concert, Phil Woods and Charlie Rouse thought they could master the material fairly easily, but two days before the concert they had difficulty with the phrasing on "Monk's Mood." At one point Hall genuinely asks, "Is there something wrong with your part there, on the A-section?" Likewise, throughout the rehearsal Monk interjects, corrects, and makes demands on the band.[110] By the final rehearsal on Saturday, June 6, just hours before the concert, the band still had not mastered all of the music—particularly "Four in One" and "Little Rootie Tootie." But by the end of the session, Thelonious seemed satisfied with the results. Long after the rehearsal ended, Overton could be heard saying to someone over the phone, "I'm not too worried about it, Monk seems to be in good spirits, playing."[111]

He was in good spirits when he walked on stage that night sporting a clean gray suit and the white cowboy hat given to him by the Mayor of Danbury.[112] Unfortunately, Carnegie Hall was half empty and the event was strangely put together. During the first half of the program featuring the quartet, the stage director decided to put a spotlight on Monk whenever he got up from the piano and danced or wandered about.[113] The reviews were mostly bad. John S. Wilson liked Monk's playing but thought the quartet "was weighted down by a heavy-handed, monotonous rhythm section." He also felt the big band was underutilized, preferring shorter solos and more ensemble playing.[114] Dan Morgenstern in *Down Beat* also blamed the rhythm section for the band's problems. He forgave Spanky DeBrest, knowing he was a last-minute replacement, and lamented the loss of Frankie Dunlop, dismissing Riley's playing as "leaden and clumsy." Monk, however, was "in brilliant form, venturing some dazzling, Tatumesque runs" during his solo rendition of "Don't Blame Me." Still, Morgenstern saw the potential and considered the Monk-Overton collaborations to be of immense historical value. "The band had a sound and texture all its own," he concluded, "and one would venture to say Overton and Monk have come up with the first truly original approach to big band writing in more than a decade."[115]

Monk survived Carnegie Hall and headed back on the road to play concerts in Minneapolis, Cleveland, and Pittsburgh, though he was still without a permanent bass player.[116] For the Newport Jazz Festival, the first weekend in July, Bob Cranshaw took over the bass duties. An extremely versatile musician, at age thirty-one he had played with just about everyone, from Teddy Wilson and Coleman Hawkins to Carmen McCrae and Lee Morgan.[117] When the quartet took the stand at Freebody Park Saturday night, July 3, Cranshaw knew the music and was ready to play his heart out. But no one else on the bandstand seemed to share his enthusiasm. "It was kind of strange," he said later. "The band didn't seem very happy. It's like no one had any energy."[118] The quartet sounded good, but by this time they could play a set in their sleep.[119] Thelonious generated excitement as usual, though his real shining hour occurred earlier in the afternoon when he participated in a piano workshop featuring solo performances by Joe Sullivan, Willie "The Lion" Smith, Dave Brubeck, Oscar Peterson, Toshiko Akiyoshi, and Billy Taylor. The event, a capsule history of jazz piano narrated by Taylor, drew a crowd of 2,000 despite intermittent downpours. (Most workshops typically attracted between three and four hundred.) Brubeck was given top billing, but Willie "the Lion" and his protégé Thelonious stole the show. They both picked "Tea for Two" as their vehicle of choice and turned the workshop into a veritable clinic. In John S. Wilson's words, in a matter of minutes the two men "summarized half a century of piano jazz."[120] Monk might have been reminiscing about Meade Lux Lewis, the wonderful pianist he'd met on the JATP tour when he worked with Coleman Hawkins nearly two decades earlier. Just two weeks before the workshop, Lewis died in a terrible car accident in Minneapolis.[121]

The band had a three-week hiatus before the next gig—the Ravinia Festival in Chicago. The huge summer-long outdoor arts festival was held every year in Ravinia Park, a bucolic, privately owned and operated park on Chicago's North Shore. The annual festival offered a wide range of music, dance, and theater experiences, though it was best known for Shakespeare. The quartet performed two much-anticipated concerts, July 29 and 31, drawing excellent crowds.[122] The new bassist wasn't feeling it, however. "Ravinia wasn't fun for me," Cranshaw recalled. "I was still young and I was ready to play, ready to hit! But I felt like I was surrounded by a bunch of grumpy old men. Of course, they'd been traveling a lot and were probably tired and I can understand that, but that's not where I was at."[123] He quit the band as soon as they returned to New York.

Thelonious was none too pleased. The quartet was scheduled to begin a month-long engagement at the Village Gate in four days.[124] Out of desperation, he hired Don Moore, a bassist ironically associated with the jazz avant-garde. He had toured with Bill Dixon and Archie Shepp as a member of their pianoless quartet, and then moved to Copenhagen in 1963, where he joined the experimental band, the New York Contemporary Five. The group recorded several Monk compositions, including "Crepuscule with Nellie," "Monk's Moods," and "Epistrophy."[125] Moore had also worked with Steve Lacy and Roswell Rudd, whose quartet focused almost exclusively on Monk's music.[126] Thus while Moore may have been familiar with Monk's work, the bands with whom he played were all pianoless and treated Monk's music as a point of departure for greater freedom. Now Moore had to play Monk with Monk.

The quartet opened on August 4 to rave reviews, though none of the critics paid attention to the new bassist.[127] Flip Wilson warmed up the crowd, and percussionist Mongo Santamaria's band and Gerry Mulligan's quartet shared the bill, but the evening was all about Monk, since it had been two years since he last played the Village Gate and six months since his last club date. Nellie and Nica were there, and so were Harry Colomby and his younger brother Bobby. A student at City College, Bobby was also an aspiring drummer who, like his brothers, fell in love with Monk's music. That night he helped a bemused critic understand the changes to "Bright Mississippi."[128]

Doug Quackenbush, a thirty-four-year-old photographer with an almost obsessive fascination with Monk, was also in attendance that week. He had been a diehard Monk fan ever since he first heard his Blue Note recordings as an aspiring teenage trumpet player growing up in Detroit. Quackenbush moved to New York and camped out at the Five Spot to see Monk and 'Trane, but by then he was carrying a Nikon alongside his trumpet case. He worked as a fashion photographer, but spent much of his free time shooting musicians, building a stunning portfolio that included memorable shots of Billie Holiday. But one night at the Five Spot, with the violence in Birmingham weighing heavily on his conscience, he found in Thelonious a reassuring and compelling subject. "Here was a man 'being himself,'" he observed, "not just in his music, but in his whole being. He looked the way he sounded, whether he was playing or dancing. I decided that I wanted to make pictures of what that looked like."[129]

When the set was over, he introduced himself and followed up with phone calls to Nellie. He eventually eased whatever suspicions she had, but nothing really happened . . . until that night Quackenbush showed up at the Village Gate. He took some pictures of Monk's band from a distance and a few shots of the empty dressing room. He stayed through the last set and fortuitously ended up sharing a cab with Don Moore, who told Quackenbush that the next day—Sunday, August 9—the band had a gig at the Music Barn in Lenox, Massachusetts. Moore told him, "if I really wanted to go, I should show up in front of Monk's West 63rd Street apartment and hope for the best—a ride."[130] He showed up and got better than he had hoped for: a ride with Thelonious and Nellie in the black Cadillac limousine sent to shuttle them to Lenox. Nellie remembered Doug and greeted him warmly, inviting him to sit up front with the chauffeur.[131] Seated across from Monk and Nellie were Charlie Rouse and Sandra Capello. As they sped along the Taconic Parkway, Thelonious praised the Cadillac for its comfort and ranted on about his ongoing ordeal to find an adequate replacement for Butch Warren. Without naming Don Moore, he "asked why bass players couldn't play their instrument" and then lamented the premature passing of Oscar Pettiford (he had died four years earlier in Copenhagen).[132]

After the Music Barn concert, he fired Moore. Quackenbush stuck around, however. For the next three months, he and his Nikon became the eye on the wall. He took over six hundred shots of Thelonious, in black-and-white and color, creating one of the most comprehensive and compelling visual portraits of the man—second only to Nica's collection of Polaroids taken over the course of two decades.[133] In those three months with Thelonious, Quackenbush learned that the secret to who Monk was and how he was able to create such imaginative art stood outside the frame of his viewfinder: "Nellie was Thelonious' anchor to reality," he observed. "She handled all the practical matters; finances, booked tickets for their tours. Laid out his clothes each day. I nicknamed her 'General Backup.' She once told me that she wouldn't even let him hammer a nail into the wall to hang a picture. She realized that his hands were essential to the family's income. She took care of the practical so he could concentrate on the creative."[134] Nellie had always been his personal assistant. Now, for all practical purposes, she had become the road manager.

On Sunday, August 16, the quartet took a day off from the Gate to play the Ohio Valley Jazz Festival in Cincinnati. Still without a permanent bassist, Monk hired Alvin Jackson out of Detroit. Jackson was a peculiar choice. He struggled with the music when he worked for Monk in 1959 at Detroit's Club 12, and he struggled with the music now. According to one eyewitness account, Jackson was "bewildered by the changes."[135] After the gig, Ben Riley suggested they call Larry Gales, whom he knew from his days with Eddie "Lockjaw" Davis and Johnny Griffin. In fact, Gales and Riley were the rhythm section for the Davis-Griffin LP, *Lookin' at Monk*.[136] Rouse also knew Gales; he'd used him before for one of his own record dates.[137] A native New Yorker, Gales began studying privately with George Duvivier at age eleven and spent two years at the Manhattan School of Music. Before that, however, he sang with the doo-wop group the Twilighters, earning a reputation as one of the most talented falsettos in the Bronx.[138] At twenty-eight, the wiry and bespectacled Gales may have been the quartet's youngest member, but he had an impressive résumé.[139] And he had the big, rich tone Monk liked, a good sense of time, and he was dependable. When the quartet returned to the Gate the third week of August, Gales was on the stand every night learning the tunes. By the end of the month, the quartet had become a band.

Monk was pleased with his new bassist and relieved that his frustrating summer had finally come to a close. He had much to look forward to: a month-long gig at the Vanguard, a couple of trips to California, another round of recording sessions. But all of this paled compared to the news that Bud Powell was coming home.

26

"Sometimes I Don't Feel Like Talking"

(August 1964–January 1967)

Bud Powell had barely walked through the door before Birdland exploded with applause. As he made his way to the bandstand, holding fast to Francis Paudras's arm and greeting well-wishers and old friends, the whole room was on its feet clapping and shouting. Birdland's diminutive emcee, Pee Wee Marquette, held the microphone and attempted to introduce "the Amazing Bud Powell" but the ovation lasted seventeen minutes. Clearly, Powell needed no introduction. When the applause finally subsided, Bud threw his head back, counted out the tempo, and took off on Irving Berlin's "The Best Thing for You Would Be Me."[1] Supporting him was drummer Horace Arnold and John Ore, who had not set foot in Birdland since his row with Oscar Goodstein forced him to leave Monk's band. But tonight, August 25, all was forgiven. New Yorkers packed Birdland to see this living legend after nearly six years in absentia. Powell restored Birdland's jazz legitimacy, and it was Goodstein's way of recovering all the money "that Bud owed me."[2]

Bud's return was the biggest jazz event of the season. Given the stories of how he barely escaped death by TB, his mental illness and emotional breakdowns, his drinking binges and bouts with poverty, those who knew Bud were just happy to see him alive. Not surprisingly, critics found Powell to be below peak and at times "moody and detached," but he had lost nothing in terms of style, imagination, or fans. As one writer put it, "his audience vociferously agreed that he was still a master, his performance a giant step up from limbo."[3] Musicians came out in force, including Monk—who slipped away from the Village Gate between sets just to catch a glimpse of him. They couldn't talk that night, but Powell sent him greetings in the form of sparkling renditions of "Bemsha Swing" and "Epistrophy."[4]

Bud was anxious to visit Thelonious, but making contact was easier said than done. Both men were working every night, and during the first weekend in September Monk had to jet up to Montreal for a short engagement at Le Jazz Hot.[5] And given Bud's delicate condition, he and Paudras did not venture out too often when they first arrived in New York. After a couple of weeks, however, Bud could wait no longer. Since Paudras had no phone number for Monk (he never thought to look in the phone book; in 1964 it was still listed), they dropped by his house one afternoon. Thelonious answered the door. Both men stood there, staring at each other and not saying a word. Paudras was about to break the silence when Monk suddenly declared, "Come on in, I'll do the airplane!" It was all incomprehensible to Paudras, but he knew enough not to try to analyze everything. Thelonious led them to the piano and, using a combination of keys, pedals, and his entire body, reproduced the sound of airplanes flying overhead. The quivering stack of dishes on the piano added to the effect. The trick sent Powell into hysterics.[6]

Now that they were reunited, Monk and Powell started hanging out together in the afternoons, often gathering at Ornette Coleman's flat in the Village where they would listen to tapes Paudras made of Powell's nightly sets.[7] Spending time with Powell brought back a rush of memories, causing Monk to wax nostalgic. When Nica invited Bud and Francis to the Village Vanguard to catch Monk's quartet (they opened September 10 for a three-week stay[8]), Thelonious launched into "In Walked Bud" as soon as he spotted his friend across the room. "I had never seen Monk look so happy at the piano," recalled Paudras. Other times, when Monk reminisced about his former "student," he betrayed a sense of sadness, loss, and nostalgia for Bud's healthier days. He told Paudras, "Yeah, I'd play him my tunes and he could retain them right off. Bud was brilliant from very early on. I showed him a lot of chords, new combinations, reversed harmonies. . . . Bud was a genius, but you know, he was so sick, and now he's fragile."[9]

The road interrupted the men's reunion. Monk left for the Monterey Jazz Festival on September 19, but without a bass player: Larry Gales was nursing a deep gash to his hand.[10] Steve Swallow proved an able substitute.[11] Thelonious was billed as one of the stars of the Festival, and promoter/emcee Jimmy Lyons planned to follow through on the previous year's failed project—to have Monk play a few numbers with a larger band.[12] The Los Angeles–based, multireed player Buddy Collette was charged with putting a larger band together for Charles Mingus, so Lyons asked Collette to augment Monk's group using the same personnel and to arrange four of his tunes for octet. Collette agreed and brought a group of fine musicians from Los Angeles: trombonist Lou Blackburn, baritone saxophonist Jack Nimitz, trumpeters Bobby Bryant and Melvin Moore, and Collette played alto and flute. Thelonious reluctantly showed up to the afternoon rehearsal but remained aloof at first. "We kept running over his music and Monk wouldn't sit at the piano," Collette remembered, "he just kept standing around, looking a little confused and unhappy." Charlie Rouse tactfully explained the problem to Collette: "Monk likes everything short." Collette understood and called for "a more staccato approach." Suddenly Monk perked up. "As we got into it, Monk smiled and went over to the piano and played with a lot of feeling . . . Charlie saved us, and we went on stage and broke it up."[13]

Indeed. The quartet went on first after Mingus's rousing performance, delivering exciting versions of "Blue Monk," "Evidence," "Bright Mississippi," and "Rhythm-a-ning."[14] Then the Festival Workshop Ensemble joined Monk's crew on Buddy Collette's "Sketches of Monk"—what was supposed to be an ambitious arrangement of four Monk tunes now limited to two. On "Think of One," set at a tempo slower than usual, the ensemble work was dynamic and solos fairly short—as rehearsed. Bobby

Bryant stole the show with a brilliant solo full of huge octave leaps and rhythmic drive. "Straight, No Chaser" is even stronger. Collette's arrangement is worthy of Hall Overton's work, and as a soloist he swings hard on alto saxophone. Monk demonstrated his mastery of the blues, opening with simple, earthy lines that become more complex as he tells his story.[15]

The octet was a big hit, and Monk an even bigger hit. He was deemed one of the festival's real stars "making the masses happy."[16] His "subdued" manner and "soft, harmonious rhythms and orderly transitions" surprised the critic for *Ebony* magazine: "Wearing a Dallas-style hat, Monk put together surprising, light-hearted combinations, making him appear more the gentle humorist than the remote eccentric."[17] Writing for the black-owned Los Angeles *Sentinel*, Les Carter found "humor, beauty and gentleness" in his music, as opposed to the new wave of artists who have been busy "subjecting the jazz audience to experimentation and pretentious intellectualism."[18] Monk also caught the ear and eye of another *Sentinel* writer, Eunice Pye, and not only for his "splendid performance," but by virtue of the fact that he came with Nellie. In what might be better characterized as social commentary than music criticism, she wryly noted: "The Negro entertainers outnumbered the whites appearing at the festival. However, the white female companions evened the score."[19]

Monk was home little more than a week before he headed out again to play at Penn State University.[20] Because the campus is inconveniently located in the very center of Pennsylvania, far from a major airport, Colomby decided to charter a bus for the band (including Larry Gales, who had recovered from his injuries) and their families. Doug Quackenbush hitched a ride, and Nellie kindly loaned him Toot's Nikon camera. She noticed how Quackenbush constantly switched from color to black-and-white film and thought two cameras would make things easier. He was appreciative, both for the use of the camera and for the entire trip, which felt like an extended picnic. Everyone was in good spirits, and "at the concert, Monk played with the intensity of a madman."[21]

Thelonious carried that intensity to 30th Street Studios a couple of days later. In three sessions over three days (October 6 to 8), the quartet revisited "Pannonica," as well as several old standards he had recorded before. On "April in Paris," he adopted what had become a standard arrangement—an unaccompanied rubato chorus followed by the whole ensemble swinging. Except for the addition of the tenor saxophone, Monk's high-spirited take on "Liza" doesn't stray too far from his Riverside trio recordings, and "Just You, Just Me" had never completely left Monk's repertoire. He did add two new pieces, though "new" is really a misnomer.[22] He recorded two unaccompanied takes of "I Love You, I Love You, I Love You (Sweetheart of All My Dreams)," and adapted the ancient nursery rhyme "This Old Man," inverting some of the melodic phrases and adding some of his own to come up with the ultra-hip "That Old Man."[23]

Macero was pleased. Six tunes plus "Teo," which he had recorded back in March, completed the album. But Columbia's brass worried about Monk's poor productivity; according to his contract, he owed the studio three LPs a year. Macero decided that if he couldn't get Monk into the studio, he'd bring the studio to Monk: he made arrangements to record him during his upcoming tour of California.[24] Thelonious was relieved to finally finish the album, which Columbia simply called *Monk,* because it meant he'd get paid. Although it took a couple of weeks for Columbia to cut his advance check for $8,176.35, it was close enough to his birthday to merit a celebration.[25] He spent October 10 at the Village Vanguard, surrounded by friends, family, and patrons. But the night turned bad when Monk found out that Bud Powell never made it to his gig at Birdland that night. Two days later, he turned up at a friend's house in Brooklyn in terrible shape. The following week, he attended a party at Nica's house and then left, unaccompanied and undetected. This time he was gone for five days. A sympathetic black police officer found him laid out on a stoop in Greenwich Village begging for a drink. Nica took him in for a while, and Francis Paudras expected to take him back to Paris, but Powell refused.[26] Bud was unraveling and Thelonious feared for his life, but he couldn't stick around to watch over him. On October 16, he was back on the West Coast for nearly a month.

From the moment Monk disembarked from the plane at San Francisco International Airport, something wasn't right. That night the band was scheduled to play at the Masonic Auditorium at 8:00 sharp, but they did not take the stage until 9:15.[27] The emcee, saxophonist Kermit Scott, an old friend from the Minton's era now living in the Bay area, tried to calm the restless crowd with a warm, effusive introduction, but after forty minutes of music, "Monk walked off stage leaving his associates in apparent bewilderment." The audience applauded and shouted for Monk to return. He obliged, played one tune, and then took a forty-minute intermission. During the second half of the concert, Monk hardly touched the piano. Well over half an hour was given to bass and drum solos. "While all this was taking place," Russ Wilson reported, "Monk was pacing the stage, looking at the audience, smoking cigarettes, and occasionally doing a stomping dance."[28] The concert ended around midnight, after the crowd had thinned out considerably. At least one angry audience member shouted, "Good riddance, Monk," while the hardcore fans stomped and whistled for more. Monk ignored the commotion and slipped into the audience to speak with a couple whose child had fallen asleep. Meanwhile, Kermit Scott returned to the stage and announced that Monk's band would return for an encore. Thelonious played " 'Round Midnight" beautifully, but by then the damage was done.[29]

The next night, Saturday, October 17, the band played UCLA's Royce Hall. They were late again, but Monk redeemed himself with a "delightful and completely absorbing" performance.[30] Two days later, the band played without incident at the newly opened Valley Music Theater in Woodland Hills, California, where Monk shared the bill with John Coltrane and Jon Hendricks, and then began a two-week engagement at the It Club on Friday, October 23.[31] Between gigs, Thelonious and Nellie stayed at Gene Autry's Continental Hotel, a new, modern facility on the Sunset Strip.[32] Soon after checking in, Monk drifted into the hotel bar and began twirling around. The hotel staff repeatedly asked him to leave and the bartender refused to serve him, but this only incensed Thelonious, who stood his ground. Finally, a staff person called Ben Riley to deal with Monk. "So I went downstairs and he's in his LBJ hat and his robe and he's got his tie and stuff on." Thelonious escorted him to the bar and told the bartender to give Riley a double Old Grand-Dad since he would not serve him. Riley tried to coax Monk back upstairs, but he stubbornly insisted on confronting the bartender. Riley downed one drink, but when Monk ordered another Riley resisted. "I said, 'Just because they won't serve you doesn't mean I'm gonna stay down here and act like a fool . . . If you want something to drink, come on up to my room.'"[33] He chose to stay. Over the course of two weeks, Monk broke a sliding glass door, damaged the ceiling in his room, and roamed the lobby staring at guests. Consequently, he was banned indefinitely from Gene Autry's Continental Hotel.[34]

Monk's odd behavior was not limited to the hotel. Hampton Hawes, who had not seen Monk since he and Nellie helped him out in New York, came by the It Club one night to check him out. When Hawes approached Thelonious at the bar during a break, "he didn't seem to recognize me. Looked over my shoulder, his elbow on the bar, staring into space the way he sometimes does . . . I said, 'Monk, it's me, Hampton.' He kept staring past my shoulder as if he hadn't heard, then turned his back and went into a little shuffling dance; danced a couple of quick circles around me, danced right up to me and said, 'Your sunglasses is at my New York pad.' And danced away."[35] Rose Robertson, a young pianist whom Larry Gales had recently met in the Bay Area, showed up at the It Club with high expectations. "The band was ready to go on, but Monk was nowhere to be found. Turned out, he was next door at the pool hall shooting pool. He finally came back, but when he noticed that someone had put a glass on the piano, he threw it down on the floor. That was so strange. So they start playing, but after a while Monk gets up and walks away, leaving the rhythm section to continue. He never came back. I remember being so disappointed because I paid to see him."[36]

It Club patrons, a mix of black elites, Hollywood celebrities, and middle- and working-class folks from the surrounding neighborhood, were not accustomed to this kind of behavior. Club owner John T. McClain transformed this spacious room on West Washington Boulevard into the hippest spot in the city for modern jazz, momentarily shifting the center of gravity from the Sunset Strip to the "Westside" black community. On the heels of the demise of Central Avenue—the heart of black Los Angeles's jazz scene in the 40s and 50s—Washington between Crenshaw and LaBrea thrived; the Parisian Room, the Black Orchid (formerly the Hillcrest Club), and Tommy Tucker's Playroom were just a few of the night spots along the boulevard.[37] Thelonious loved the It Club in part because he dug the neighborhood. Anna Lou Smith lived just a few blocks away, and a neighboring beer and billiards joint, L.C.'s Hideaway, became his favorite refuge in between sets. Monk could hardly resist a good game of pool and he was usually welcomed there, although one night the owner had to ask him to leave after Monk broke several cue sticks in a fit of uncontrolled rage.[38]

Monk also dug John McClain, who was always patient with him. The slightly built, dapper McClain was a renowned promoter and local celebrity (reputed to have "introduced Ava Gardner to Negroes") who loved the music and musicians. He married pianist Dorothy Donegan and managed her career for a while, and when the talented

Phineas Newborn, Jr., moved to Los Angeles in 1960, the It Club not only became a frequent home for his piano trio but McClain moved Newborn into a house he owned behind the club when he began suffering from emotional problems.[39] McClain could afford to be generous and forgiving, since he had other sources of income; deemed "the Black Godfather," he happened to be one of the city's biggest drug dealers.[40]

Judging from the recordings Macero made at the It Club (October 31 and November 1), one would not have known Monk was on a downward emotional spiral. The band was on fire. Monk and Rouse are completely in sync, and Riley is unusually assertive in setting down a groove and driving both soloists—especially on "Misterioso." Their exploration of "Rhythm-a-ning," a song they must have played hundreds of times, is a veritable masterpiece. Monk tags on to the first phrase in the melody a kind of drunken flurry of descending notes, which Rouse then picks up and uses to build his solo.[41] Besides exhibiting a high level of originality and imagination, the band sounds as though it was having fun. Monk even strayed from his regular repertoire, calling the familiar standard "All the Things You Are," and the astonishingly difficult "Gallop's Gallop"—a tune that had been lying dormant for nearly a decade.[42]

During his stay in Los Angeles, Macero arranged for a couple of studio dates in order to complete a solo piano LP. These sessions were productive; in two days, Monk recorded sixteen good takes of ten songs, mostly old standards. Besides his usual chestnuts—"Sweet and Lovely," "I Should Care," "Everything Happens to Me," Monk delivered stunning renditions of "I'm Confessin'," "Dinah," and "I Hadn't Anyone Till You." He also included two original 12-bar blues—both probably made up in the studio. The medium-tempo "North of the Sunset" refers more to Sunset Boulevard than to the movement of celestial spheres, and "Monk's Point" is the pianist's homage to the bent note. These recordings reveal that, despite growing criticism that his quartet had become tedious and predictable, Thelonious Monk had not lost his chops. On the contrary, he had reinvented stride piano for the modern era.[43]

On November 3, the day after Monk's last studio session, the group flew back to San Francisco for a week-long engagement at the Jazz Workshop, and Macero followed in pursuit of more live recordings. What he and his engineer heard during the first two nights of their gig was not the same band. The group dragged, the musicians were out of sync, and Monk could not seem to make up his mind about what he wanted to do. During his solo on "Evidence," Monk suddenly started to play "Rhythm-a-ning," forcing Larry Gales and the rest of the band to shift gears midway into the song. Later in another set, he returns to "Evidence," but one chorus into Rouse's solo, Monk pushes him off the stand by playing over him. The confused Rouse stops abruptly a few bars into his second chorus, clearly confused over what had just happened. Similarly, the band launched into "Bright Mississippi"—a tune that generally lasts about ten minutes—but Monk abruptly ended it in less than three minutes.[44] What happened to the group those two nights remains a mystery, although the greater mystery is why Columbia released these recordings in the first place.

Thelonious and Nellie spent Thanksgiving week in Cincinnati, where he had a short engagement at the Penthouse, and returned home in December to begin a seven-week stay at the Village Gate.[45] Thelonious was glad to be home for the holidays, but the physical wear and tear of the road ultimately caught up with him; his gig at the Gate was cut short due to illness and he also had to cancel a two-week engagement at the Plugged Nickel in Chicago in early February.[46] Macero was not pleased about this, in part because he had planned to record Monk at the Gate and he needed him back in the studio to complete his solo LP. Despite four nights of live recordings from the It Club and the Jazz Workshop, Macero thought he needed "four additional selections to make a truly fantastic album."[47] And he needed a fantastic album because Columbia's executives found Monk's output and overall record sales disappointing.[48] Macero gently warned Monk that while "sales figures are quite good . . . we want to do better this year."[49]

In an effort to improve sales, they tried different marketing strategies. On the latest LP, *Monk*, Macero recruited pianist Bill Evans to write the liner notes. The bespectacled Evans was the industry's latest star and deemed something of an intellectual force in the jazz world. Indeed, his first draft of the notes was five times longer than what was printed, and it read like a master's thesis. The writing is pedantic in spots and the first half of the essay says little about Monk's music, but it served its purpose—to have a popular, respected, and articulate pianist legitimize Monk as a composer and musician.[50] Evans demonstrates a sophisticated knowledge of music, but betrays a surprising ignorance of Monk. He falls prey to the long-standing myth that Monk lacks exposure to the Western classical tradition or any music besides jazz and American popular music, but as a consequence "his ability to wipe away superficiality to get at and work with fundamental structure has resulted in a unique and astoundingly pure music."[51]

Columbia was willing to try almost anything to expand Monk's audience. They even considered producing a vocal album and sought out writers to put lyrics to Monk's music. Martin Williams proposed the idea, offered his own set of lyrics, and enlisted critic Joe Goldberg and composer/pianist/singer Margo Guryan to help with the task. Williams and Goldberg were not songwriters, and it shows, from their awkward, sophomoric efforts. Williams even borrowed an old blues lyric for "We See" ("I'm goin' in the subway/ Put my head on the track/ When that train comes in close/ I'll just pull my head right on back"). The only experienced lyricist in the trio was Margo Guryan, who at the time was employed by MJQ Music, the publishing company founded by John Lewis and Gunther Schuller. One of her many tasks, in fact, was to write lyrics for copyrights the company owned. She came up with lyrics for "Let's Cool One," "Worry Later," "Let's Call This," and "Nutty."[52] Although the project never saw the light of day, Guryan produced some clever and rhythmically incisive phrases that would have worked quite well with Monk's angular lines. For example, "Let's Cool One":

This has been a hot romance
Too hot to talk about
So let's not talk
Have another drink

It's a bit too warm to dance
So let's sit this one out
Go take a walk
Let me think.

Or "Worry Later," with its flurry of eighth notes:

If you wake up in the morning with a troubled mind
Don't worry now, worry later friend
If you stop to read the writing on the wall, you'll find
Your troubles gone–later on.

Macero's bosses liked the idea but chose a different direction, enlisting Jon Hendricks to write lyrics to "all of Monk's tunes" with the promise of a Monk–Hendricks LP.[53] This, too, floundered.

Thelonious wasn't so concerned about record sales. He made more money in 1964 than he had ever made, although given how hard he worked it is surprising how little income he took home. Whereas Monk's gross receipts reached $111,010, after salaries, expenses, and commissions he was left with $42,700, and tax bills amounting to $13,440.[54] Monk shelled out $13,000 in commissions alone, divided between his booking agent Jack Whittemore and Harry Colomby, whose relationship with the Monks cooled after Colomby had taken on a new client, a comedian named John Byner: "I got Byner on Ed Sullivan and Thelonious felt a little put out."[55]

Monk's decline was both physical and mental. Besides suffering from colds and occasional bouts of the flu that come with frequent travel and nightly performances, Monk continued to mix medications, such as Thorazine and "vitamin shots" with Benzedrine and a variety of other substances.[56] The combinations of drugs exacerbated what doctors would later determine to be a chemical imbalance. Consequently, his bipolar episodes became more frequent. According to his son, the beginning of 1965 marked a turning point: "I remember the first time I saw my father sort of get disconnected. I was home from school. I don't really remember what precipitated it. I just remember my mother waking me up in the middle of the night telling me that I had to run and get my uncle [Thomas]. All I knew was that he seemed to be acting very strange. He wasn't really talking. He was looking out the picture window and there was really nothing to see but the walls and the backyard. . . . So my uncle came over and stepped into the apartment and he looked at my father and he said, 'You OK Bubba?' And my father didn't say a word, just like he hadn't been saying a word. And then my uncle went home. He was useless." The episode shocked Toot, who really did not have a clue how bad things had gotten since he and Boo Boo went away to boarding school. And while Monk's bipolar condition manifested itself infrequently, the long-term effects on his physical well-being were becoming evident. "It wasn't until he started having these bipolar episodes that I saw any problems physically. Because he would walk himself to exhaustion, he might walk a sore into his foot. So when he was 'recovering,' this is the sort of thing he was recovering from."[57]

Recovering from whatever ailed Monk in late January forced him to cancel a studio session booked for February 17, but he was well enough to come in on the 23rd to work on the solo piano LP. The three-hour session yielded two numbers, "Ask Me Now" and another take of "Everything Happens to Me."[58] It was all he had time for, since the quartet had a short college tour at the end of February that took them to Brandeis and Howard Universities, a piano workshop at Hunter College (a repeat of the Newport Festival workshop), and a world tour lined up for most of March and April. Columbia's engineers taped Monk's Brandeis concert for the "On Tour" LP.[59] And two days before Monk left the country, Macero corralled him into 30th Street Studio one more time, in an effort to complete the solo LP. Monk brought his rhythm section along, however, to record a funky trio version of "Honeysuckle Rose," the Fats Waller classic that seeped into Monk's repertoire in California. Incredibly, Macero added an applause track and passed it off as "live at the Village Gate"![60]

Meanwhile, Monk and Nellie prepared for what was to be their longest international tour to date. Leaving on March 4 and returning on April 26, the tour took them to France, Germany, the Netherlands, England, Switzerland, Italy, Australia, New Zealand, the Philippines, and Hong Kong.[61] In Europe, Monk played to packed houses and was warmly received everywhere he went. The critics were not always so warm. The quartet's repertoire had not changed much since Monk's last tour a year earlier; the only significant difference was the addition of Larry Gales. Critics acknowledged Monk's importance and his genius, but they began to tire of the old routine. In Paris, the quartet performed four concerts at the Olympia Theatre (two on March 6 and two on Sunday, March 7), which meant some duplication was inevitable.[62] Critic Claude Lenissois was at two of the concerts and came away underwhelmed. Hoping Monk would "renew his style," he worried that the pianist had become complacent and the quartet, though quite good, had fallen into a kind of mechanical repetition.[63]

The English, on the other hand, praised Monk—a complete reversal from the Brits' response to his first tour. Gerald Lascelles found Monk's "simplicity" refreshing in an age when "most of his rivals . . . are wrapped in a mantle of complex exhibitionism almost totally unrelated to the forces which guide jazz separately from the well trodden path of classical music. His understanding of harmonics is unmatched in its concept, his technique is anything but deficient, and he constantly demonstrates his ability to transmit the true jazz pulse by the simple expedient of subtly timed runs."[64] Commenting on Monk's two concerts at Free Trade Hall in Manchester, Ian Breach noted that while the music remained essentially unchanged since his last concert four years earlier, the man on stage was quite different: "there was no burlesque, Monk got up from his piano and listened—solicitously, it seemed—to each solo, but these were taken in strict, almost staid order, with nothing to distract from their tight, methodic execution."[65] Sinclair Traill caught his two Festival Hall concerts in London, and while he complained about the routine and the all-too-frequent bass and drum solos, he appreciated Monk's sheer musicality—especially when he played unaccompanied. As a solo pianist he is "in his best angular vein, full of fascinating oblique chords . . . queer changing rhythms," and humor. It was his humor that the audience found most appealing and the critics seemed to miss, according to Traill. He concluded, "if Monk is the lonely man most critics make him out to be, I would wager his own private world is full of laughter."[66]

Traill might have lost the bet. Frustration and exhaustion better characterized Monk's mood during the European leg of the tour. Besides a few mishaps (Ben Riley's drums did not arrive in time for the Paris concert), Thelonious was simply not feeling well. And now that he was a bona-fide celebrity, well-meaning journalists invaded his "private world" in their quest to discover the real Thelonious. Monk and Nellie knew good press was essential so they gave generously of their time. In Paris, British writer Mike Hennessey spent nine hours hanging out with the Monks, much of it holed up in their room at the Prince de Galles hotel. And a day before Hennessey's visit, they entertained *Jazz Magazine*'s critic Jean-Louis Noames.[67] The interviews became tiresome after a while, in part because the writers frequently asked the same questions: What do you like to do? Where is modern music going? Are you writing new music? Why do you like to wear hats? Some questions Monk found annoying. When Hennessey asked about his alleged unreliability, he responded defensively, "This is the biggest bunch of lies. I suppose people just like to run their mouth off. You know, some people were billing me for their concerts without asking me to play. My name would bring the people in, then when I didn't turn up the promoters would say, 'That's Monk.'" Likewise, when the issue of his technique—or lack thereof—came up, he had this to say: "What they mean—the people who say that—is that their technique is limited—because they can't do what I do. I'll tell you one thing—my playing seems to work. I get good audiences, people seem to enjoy it."[68]

Sometimes he played into their expectations and assumptions. When Jean-Louis Noames asked if he read the newspaper and kept up with current affairs, Monk stated flatly that he never read anything. He watches television instead.[69] While he was a television junkie, his daughter Boo Boo described Monk as an "avid reader" who talked quite a bit about politics, history, and current events—often with a wry sense of humor: "Well, when reporters would talk to him, he wouldn't be bubbling over . . . but he could often be very talkative."[70] Similarly, Ben Riley found Monk to be "very worldly, knowledgeable. He kept up with all the world. It didn't look like he knew what was going on in the world [but] he could sit down and he could tell you about everything that happened internationally and everywhere else. He was on it, but he just never would say anything. Unless he was in a certain setting."[71]

One of his more revealing encounters occurred on March 14, when Valerie Wilmer and John "Hoppy" Hopkins showed up at their suite at London's Park Lane Hilton, rain-soaked and toting cameras and a portable Grundig tape recorder.[72] They were not your run-of-the-mill jazz photographers/journalists. Wilmer was only twenty-three, and yet had been writing for music magazines since she was a teenager. "Hoppy" was only twenty years old when he graduated from Cambridge University in 1960 with a master's degree in physics and mathematics. He gave up a promising career as a nuclear physicist to become a photographer. He and Wilmer met working for *Jazz News* and agreed that Thelonious Monk would make a good subject for the glossy men's magazine, *King*. Besides an interest in Monk, Wilmer and Hoppy had something else in common: They were budding activists passionately opposed to social injustice and war. Wilmer had a brief flirtation with the Young Communist League and increasingly became involved with antiracist, antiwar, and radical feminist organizations, and Hoppy emerged as a key figure in Britain's radical underground and the peace movement.[73] A month earlier, Hoppy had met and photographed Malcolm X during his short visit to England; on February 21, three weeks before Wilmer and Happy's meeting with Monk, Malcolm had been gunned down in Harlem's Audubon Ballroom.[74]

For Wilmer and Hoppy, politics clung to them like the rain. Although most of their queries focused on music and they shared many light-hearted exchanges, their concern for world events compelled them to ask questions of a more political nature, producing some moments of tension, misunderstanding, and revelation. At one point, Wilmer asks Thelonious if he's interested in what's going on in the world. He replied, "Well, I got a wife and two kids, you dig, to take care of. So I have to make some money and see that they eat and sleep. And me, too. Dig? It's not my business what's happening with his family. I have to take care of my family."[75] When Wilmer repeats the question with more precision, Monk becomes agitated and annoyed. "I don't go around looking. No! I'm interested in what's going on nowhere." The room is silent for a few seconds until Monk turns the table on his guests, blurting out, "Are you worrying about what's happening to everybody?"

> Wilmer: Not everybody, but some people. . . .
> Monk: Why you ask me that? Expect me to be worrying about what's happening to everybody. You not. You worrying about what's happening with everybody?
> Hoppy: Sometimes.
> Monk: You worrying about what's happening with the person around the corner? The person next door?
> Hoppy: Not everyone, but some.
> Monk: What if I asked you a stupid question like that? Something you don't do yourself?
> Wilmer: You can't care about every single person, but you can care about some people.
> Monk: But you asked me, do I care about what's happening to everybody around the corner. I don't be around the corner! Going to everybody's house, be looking to see what's happening. I'm not a policeman or a social worker. That's what your social workers should do.
> Hoppy: You're American. I'm English. I get bothered about things my government does.
> Monk: Well, I'm not in power. I'm not worrying about politics. You worry about the politics. Let the statesmen do that. That's their job. They get paid for it. So if you want to be a politician, you be one. Stop taking pictures. Be a politician.

The exchange was unsettling, difficult, and yet incredibly painful and transparent. Rather than shutting Monk down, their challenges opened him up. He spoke about his incarceration ("I know it's a drag to be in jail") and lamented the brutal behavior of police back home. "The police bothers you more in the United States than they do anywhere else. The police heckle the people more in the United States than they do anyplace else. You don't have as much trouble with the police in no other country like you do in the United States. The police just mess with you in the United States for nothing. They just bully people. They don't do that in no other country but the United States. They carry guns, too. And they shoot people for nothing."[76] Monk wasn't just speaking about himself. He was well aware of the rising incidents of police brutality in his own city, let alone other cities in the U.S. The previous summer Harlem exploded when a white patrolman killed an unarmed fifteen-year-old boy named James Powell. The riots spread to Brooklyn, and his own neighborhood in San Juan Hill became pretty tense. It was impossible for any New Yorker not to be affected by Powell's murder and its aftermath. And like most black Americans, Monk knew the problem wasn't limited to his beloved city. That same summer, incidents of police misconduct ignited riots in Rochester, Philadelphia, and Jersey City.[77]

While his anger over police violence was palpable, he nevertheless insisted that racism was not his concern and he had no desire to make his music a commentary on black oppression: "I never was interested in those Muslims. If you want to know, you should ask Art Blakey. I didn't have to change my name—it's always been weird enough! I haven't done one of these 'freedom' suites, and I don't intend to. I mean, I don't see the point. I'm not thinking that race thing now; it's not on my mind. Everybody's trying to get me to think it, though, but it doesn't bother me. It only bugs the people who are trying to get me to think it."[78]

In the end, the interview's most important revelation may have been the extent of Monk's exhaustion. "I don't sleep much," he wistfully admitted. "Wish I could. I haven't slept eight hours in a long time. . . . I've been kind of exhausted." His grueling schedule kept him from composing new music. "I don't get a chance to write . . . be working so much."[79] Signs of fatigue were evident to anyone who saw him on tour.[80] Indeed, immediately after Wilmer and Hoppy left the hotel, Monk had to get dressed and head over to the Marquee Club to tape the BBC television program "Jazz 625." Throughout the hour-long performance, Thelonious projects a rather vacant expression. He doesn't leave the piano and the energy he usually displays at the keyboard is absent. He and the quartet certainly play well, and Monk is not short of ideas, but he looks tired and terribly bored.[81]

Monk seemed to perk up once they left the gray skies of England for the beautiful resort town of San Remo, Italy, on the Mediterranean Sea. He played a lively set at the San Remo Jazz Festival, urged on by the presence of the legendary pianist Earl "Fatha" Hines,[82] and then enjoyed a three-day break before heading to the Pacific Rim. They spent six days touring southeastern Australia, which Monk and Nellie treated as a kind of adventure. Tour organizer and emcee Kym Bonython remembered it as a "financial disaster."[83] As soon as they arrived, Bonython had to fork over an excess weight fee for the Monks' luggage, which was loaded down with empty Coke bottles (Nellie insisted on redeeming the bottle deposits), fourteen suits, an iron and ironing board, and seventeen pairs of shoes. The Monks' luggage was the least of Bonython's problems. Because Sydney's Town Hall was unavailable, he booked a large dance hall, filled it with hundreds of rented folding chairs, and wrote row numbers on the floor with chalk. They numbered each seat with strips of paper, but fifteen minutes before the concert a gust of wind from an open door obliterated their efforts.[84] To make matters worse, most of the seats remained empty that night and the few reviews the concert got were less than enthusiastic.[85]

Immediately after the concert, the band was scheduled to play in Melbourne. Bonython assumed the Monks would be packed and ready to catch their flight, but when he arrived at their hotel room in Sydney he saw a "mountain of garments . . . heaped in the middle of the floor, as though suitcases had simply been upended and emptied out. Crowning this tangled heap a contraceptive device reposed coyly."[86] They had just enough time to gather a few belongings for the rest of the tour, and that meant keeping their suite an additional four days. Again, Bonython and his backers footed the bill. After Melbourne, they were supposed to continue west to Adelaide[87] for a concert at the Centennial Hall, but Dave Brubeck's quartet was also scheduled to perform in Adelaide the same night, and had no venue. Brubeck's drawing power won out, so Monk was re-routed to Newcastle, a coastal city about 100 miles north of Sydney, to play for a disappointing crowd of less than two hundred. To save money, they traveled by car. For most of the two-hour drive, Monk quietly gazed at the passing landscape. He finally broke his silence to ask, "Where the hell's all the fucking kangaroos?" According to Bonython, "Someone in New York had told him he should buy a kangaroo-skin coat in Australia, and he was becoming perturbed by the apparent dearth of marsupials. Later, we took him to a Sydney dealer where he bought no less than three kangaroo-skin coats."[88]

Nellie somehow found room for the new coats in their already overstuffed luggage, and they continued on to New Zealand, where the Chamber Music Federation arranged a two-week, ten-city tour.[89] The remaining concerts were canceled, but not until they had already arrived in Hong Kong. Perhaps as a gesture of apology, one of his hosts gave him a silk Chinese skullcap.[90] Before they left Hong Kong, Monk did a bit of shopping himself and picked up a beautiful black opal ring, which would become one of his prized possessions.[91]

While this was his hardest and longest tour to date, he had had a good experience overall. He told Russ Wilson, "The whole trip was a gas. We got a wonderful welcome everywhere we played."[92] However, he was less than pleased with the financial arrangements. Nellie complained that they had to shell out money to travel to Hong Kong but were never paid because of the concert's cancellation. Nellie also thought George Wein failed to pay Monk for the New Zealand concerts, so for months she badgered him, prompting Wein to ask Harry Colomby to "please inform her that no more money is due as far as I know and that any money she would receive now would come out of my pocket. I would appreciate it if she would let the matter drop."[93] She finally let the matter drop, but the incident jolted their relationship. From that point on, it changed the way Wein did business with Monk—or specifically with Nellie, who now handled his financial affairs. As Wein explained to Colomby, "We have never had any problem working together in the past but there still should be some written record if not a contract so we at least know how much money changes hands."[94]

The cancellations meant that Monk's group arrived in San Francisco a few days early. Jazz Workshop owner Art Auerbach arranged a weekend "preview" for the quartet beginning Friday, April 23, four days before their scheduled opening date, opposite the Mose Allison Trio. Showing no apparent signs of jet lag, Monk impressed Wilson with his "fast-paced" rendition of "Well, You Needn't" and his soulful reading of "Blue Monk," which "recalled the youthful days when he was accompanist for a faith healer." Especially noteworthy was the fact that Monk did not dance. The few times he got up from the piano he just "stood quietly waiting. There was no arm waving, no dancing."[95]

It was mid-May before Nellie and Thelonious could finally collapse in their own bed, though their respite was temporary. On May 24, Nica drove them to Buffalo for a week-long engagement at the Royal Arms.[96] They did make something of a vacation out of the trip by spending a day at Niagara Falls.[97] Upon their return, however, Monk learned that Denzil Best had died from injuries sustained from a bad fall on the streets of Manhattan. He was forty-eight. The circumstances surrounding his accident are hazy, but his health had been failing for some time. In 1957, he was diagnosed with a rare bone disease that caused calcium deposits to form in his wrists, thus severely limiting his ability to play.[98] Best's premature death shocked Monk. It was the first of many such losses he, and the jazz world, would endure over the next few years.

Except for the Pittsburgh Jazz Festival, Thelonious was off the entire month of June. Columbia finally sent his advance check for completing his "on tour" LP, now titled *Misterioso*,[99] and with the extra cash reserves Thelonious and Nellie did the unexpected: they moved. Harry Colomby had tried to get them to vacate their tiny apartment for some time, especially after the second fire. But Monk loved his neighborhood, and the Phipps Houses were still the best housing stock in the vicinity. That changed in late 1964 when the Lincoln Square Urban Renewal Project completed a massive, twenty-acre apartment complex called Lincoln Towers. Bounded by West End and Amsterdam Avenues, and running from 66th to 70th streets, the complex consisted of six twenty-eight-story rectangular buildings surrounded by abundant green space and, for some residents, spectacular views of the Hudson River.[100] Geraldine Smith's sister Millicent persuaded the Monks to move, which took some doing, given Thelonious's reluctance to leave West 63rd Street. That summer, the Monks migrated four city blocks and settled into 170 West End Avenue, apartment 18D.[101] The new space was nicer, larger, sunnier, and they had a terrace with a river view. The kitchen was semi-open with a passway, and both kids had their own rooms. The Baldwin grand—later replaced by a Steinway—found a grease-free location in the living room, and Nellie hired Bloomingdale's to decorate the newly constructed, box-like apartment. She hung a sign on the front door that read "T. Monk," and had someone stencil a couple of measures of Monk's music on a blank wall.[102] Thelonious liked his new digs, but he had no intention of leaving the neighborhood. They kept their apartment on West 63rd, and when Thelonious took his walks he headed south, down to Pat's Bar, his brother's place, and all of his old haunts.

But the kids were home for the summer, and their very presence was enough to make 170 West End feel like home. They accompanied their mother and father on several short trips, beginning with Newport on the Fourth of July, where Monk gave a commanding performance.[103] Their travels took them to Riverside, New Jersey, for his sell-out concert at the Barn Arts Center; the Berkshires, where he played the Music Barn; Chicago for the Down Beat Jazz Festival, where the quartet performed before a crowd of over 10,000 and Thelonious joined the Festival big band under the direction of Gary McFarland on an arrangement of "Straight, No Chaser"; Canada for the Montreal Jazz Festival; and Columbus, Ohio, for the Ohio Valley Jazz Festival.[104] Monk also had a couple of one-week stints at Lennie Sogoloff's popular club, Lennie's-on-the-Turnpike in West Peabody, Massachusetts.[105] These short trips became real family affairs. Ben Riley would also bring his wife and kids along. "[Monk's] children during the summer would be with my children. . . . We had like a family style, we would go on certain trips . . . with the band, we would all take our families with us."[106]

Toot and Boo Boo exhibited a more sustained interest in music that summer. Boo Boo continued to develop as a dancer, but she was also drawn to the piano. "She was the one who sat down at the piano," Toot confessed, "and learned to play 'Ruby, My Dear,' learned to play all of these things. . . . [S]he would ask him, 'Daddy, show me this.' And he would show it to her and she learned to do it—things that I never learned to do."[107] Monk also learned early on that his daughter was more interested in becoming a singer than following her father's footsteps. Not long after discovering Boo Boo's musical talents, he boasted to opera singer Dolores Wilson, "My daughter, she wants to be a star, a singer." When Wilson asked if she was taking voice lessons, Monk replied, "No, but she sings every song . . . every rock 'n' roll song that comes out. Plus, she digs other types of music too. She's not just a rock 'n' roll fan."[108]

Toot's passion was the drums—one he had been harboring since he saw Max Roach play with his father on the *Brilliant Corners* session. During his first year at Cherry Lawn, a classmate named Frank Serena gave Toot a pair of drumsticks, which he used to practice on his pillow.[109] "I didn't say a word to anybody, but when I came home the summer of my fifteenth year [1965], I said, 'You know, Dad, I think I want to play the drums.'"[110] Monk wasted no time. He called Art Blakey to help find a good drum kit. Blakey asked his son, Art Blakey, Jr., a drummer himself, who sold used Gretsch drums on the side, to give Toot his first set. Monk then sent Toot to Max Roach for some lessons. "He did not sit me down and say, 'This is how you play a paradiddle.' No, because it's all about hanging and digging the music, listening and learning. So basically I did everything with Max, from carrying drums to gigs to going to car shows. Of course, you know you got to study, you've got to practice, but what makes you a great jazz player is philosophy." Monk heard his son practice and kept tabs on him, but he essentially left him alone. Over the next four years "there wasn't one word on the subject of music between me and my father. Not one utterance."[111]

• • •

Between summer travels, the quartet returned to the Village Gate for three weeks in July and a week in August. For the first two weeks, they played opposite John Coltrane's quartet, and together they kept the house packed until closing time.[112] It was the best show in the city, in part because occasionally Coltrane joined his friend and mentor on the bandstand. Monk and 'Trane together again, especially as Coltrane's music moved further "out" in the realm of the avant-garde, thrilled audiences. But it challenged Monk's rhythm section. Ben Riley recalled, "[T]hey played all of those old things that 'Trane played with him, Shadow Wilson and Wilbur Ware at the old Five Spot. They would play 'Trinkle, Tinkle' and all of those songs."[113]

After the kids returned to school in September, Monk's schedule slowed considerably. The quartet spent a short week at the Cellar Door in D.C., where the *Washington Post* critic audaciously declared Monk to be "the greatest piano soloist since Tatum,"[114] and after Thanksgiving he returned to Lennie's-on-the-Turnpike for another week.[115] Health considerations and sheer exhaustion kept Monk home for much of the fall and early winter.[116] On Nellie's birthday (December 27), he appeared at the Village Gate for a benefit for WBAI, a Pacifica-owned radio station with radical leanings.[117] The following day, the quartet traveled to the Rhode Island School of Design in Providence for the only paying gig of the month, outside of Lennie's-on-the-Turnpike. For an afternoon concert they earned $1,650—about what Monk made working five nights at Lennie's.[118]

Monk may have needed a break, but it is unlikely that he deliberately limited his engagements. He needed money; he made less in 1965 than in the previous year, taking home only $38,796. And whatever savings the Monks had were meager; they reported interest earnings of $201.[119] But the worst financial setback came in mid-summer, when Columbia modified Monk's contract, reducing his advances from $10,000 per LP to $6,000. Business affairs decided to tighten the reins when Monk's unearned balance exceeded $40,000.[120] Most careful observers knew that Monk was floundering at Columbia, and they placed much of the blame on Teo Macero for lacking imagination. Unsolicited advice as to what to do with Monk came from all over the world. Henri Renaud proposed recording Monk with Kenny Clarke during his next European tour. In a fit of nostalgia, he suggested they might "play the tunes they used to play at Minton's."[121]

Macero preferred new music, and he gently nudged Monk to write some. It's not as if he hadn't been trying, but as he explained to Val Wilmer and "Hoppy" Hopkins in London, "You have to stay home and relax to write some music."[122] In December and early January he did stay home and composed "Green Chimneys" for Boo Boo, who was home for the holidays.[123] A swinging, twenty-four-bar vamp over descending chord progressions and a minor tonality, "Green Chimneys" was a labor of love. Its simplicity was deceptive; Monk took months to perfect it before he was willing to try it out in the studio. Composing had become more difficult, but so had everything else as he advanced in age. He confessed as much to Leonard Feather soon after he had written "Green Chimneys." When Feather asked Monk if he thought he was "playing more piano now than when you were 20?" Monk replied with an emphatic "No, I'm not." He looked back to Minton's Playhouse as his heyday, not only because he believed he played better but "things were being instigated in those years. I don't say I'm not play-ing anything now; it's just that there were all new ideas then, things that hadn't been thought of."[124] He had grown weary of the idea that he had to continually innovate, compose new music, lead jazz into the new horizon. "Why should I have to create something new? Let someone else create something new!" As he was about to leave, Monk got his revenge: he asked Feather, "How about you as a writer? Are you creating? Are you writing better than you did 20 years ago?"[125]

The issue clearly struck a nerve. For all the accolades and standing ovations that Monk received in Europe and at various concerts in the United States, he recognized a growing backlash against him. Although he rarely read his own press, he heard the com-plaints about his music becoming routine and knew his fans wanted something new. In the *Down Beat* Readers Poll, he held the number-two slot for best pianist behind his rival, Oscar Peterson, though Monk edged him out in the Critics Poll.[126] Some readers thought Monk was undeserving and his influence inflated. One irate reader "was dis-gusted to find people like Thelonious Monk stealing the show from people like Oscar Peterson. How an artist so hard to pin down or describe, like Monk, could take it away from great originals like Teddy Wilson is obviously a product of someone who was in a hurry or didn't stop to consider all that the old-timers have done for modern jazz."[127] What is ironic about this complaint is that Monk's own musical tastes had become fairly conservative. When Leonard Feather played Monk a record by pianist Andrew Hill during a "Blindfold Test," Monk responded by walking to the window, comment-ing on the view, and complimenting his host on his "crazy stereo system." Yet, Monk had been one of Hill's biggest influences, inspiring his tune "New Monastery."[128] Later, in a conversation with opera singer Dolores Wilson, he lamented the loss of melody and beauty in modern music, complaining that "what they call avant-garde" is ruining jazz. "[T]hey do anything, make any kind of noise. A lot of young musicians are doing that."[129] For Monk, melody was the song's essential quality. When Teo Macero, half-jokingly, suggested he record some "free form things," Monk took a moment to school his erstwhile producer: "I want it to be as easy as possible so people can dig it. And then, it should be good. A song is like that, it's easy."[130]

The second week of January he and Nellie escaped the New York winter for Califor-nia, where the quartet played two weeks at Shelly's Manne-Hole in Hollywood, two weeks at the Jazz Workshop in San Francisco, and a concert at Stanford University in between, where Monk shared the bill with Coltrane.[131] Thelonious never returned to the It Club, which had begun to flounder after the Watts riot of August 1965 and the subsequent imposition of martial law in neighboring communities. (The It Club tem-porarily closed a few months after the uprising, but its much anticipated reopening in October of 1967 was short-lived: the following month John T. McClain was arrested for receiving seventy kilos of marijuana with intent to sell.[132]) It must have been rather eerie to arrive in Los Angeles five months after one of the worst urban civil insurrections in American history, especially with the Harlem riot fresh in his mind. He and Nellie had heard the story of Leonard Deadwyler, a black man stopped by the LAPD for rushing his pregnant wife to the hospital and fatally shot in the head as he sat behind the wheel of the car. They knew the cops were cleared of all charges. And every newspaper in the country carried stories of subsequent arrests, rioting, looting, fires, and the governor's decision to dispatch the National Guard.[133] Shelly's Manne-Hole was far from the events in Watts, but it was also far from Monk's favorite pool hall, and far from the local black community who had patronized the It Club.

From sunny California they headed to the Windy City for a week at the Plugged Nickel, then on to the Boston Globe Jazz Festival before settling into a nine-day stay at the Village Vanguard, where Monk played opposite Coleman Hawkins.[134] He closed on March 6, and eleven days later he and Nellie were bound for Europe for a world tour terminating in Japan. The two-month tour Wein arranged proved fairly lucrative for Monk. On average he earned $1,000 per concert, with slightly larger fees in Paris and smaller fees in Switzerland since their dates fell over the Easter holiday.[135] They revisited some of the usual spots—Belgium, Italy, Denmark, England—but they also performed in several provincial towns in France, including Caen, Lyons, Nantes, and Amiens, made their first trip to Oslo, Norway, and crossed the so-called Iron Curtain into Warsaw, Poland.[136]

The tour got off to a bad start. The band arrived safely in Paris, but the big instruments did not. Gales and Riley had to perform at the historic Palais de Mutualité with rented bass and drums. Indeed, throughout the French leg of the tour, the quartet received lukewarm or bad reviews, in no small part due to the "poor quality of the instruments."[137] But Monk himself came under scrutiny, partly for sounding disconnected from his sidemen. One critic who attended the first concert at Palais de Mutualité even suggested that "Monk seems to be losing his touch."[138] The most common complaint against him was that nothing changed; he seemed stuck playing the same songs in the same format. After catching the quartet's concert at London's Royal Festival Hall, an exasperated British critic grumbled that it had become difficult "to find something new to say about the Thelonious Monk Quartet without nit picking and succumbing to a general feeling of crabby irritation."[139] Charles Fox was convinced that "the Quartet could play the whole lot in their sleep." Nostalgia was the only explanation for the crowd's warm response to Monk, because as far as Fox was concerned he had heard it all before. He left Festival Hall wondering "why Monk, one of the most original composers in jazz, doesn't seem to be composing anymore."[140] While it is true that his repertoire hardly changed, he did add his solo rendition of "Sweetheart of All My Dreams" as a closing number, and he came up with a radically different approach to "Blue Monk" that involved a boogie-woogie-style left hand—though he did not always pull it off successfully. At Free Trade Hall in Manchester, for example, he fumbled the introduction so badly that he had to start over twice.[141]

At the same time, critics treated the virtual disappearance of Monk's stage antics as a welcome change. In Amsterdam, Monk's midnight performance in the Concertgebouw was surprisingly subdued. Although the audience was comprised largely of young people, college students who were visibly attentive and focused, the Monk they had come to see was not the same man on stage. Critic A. D. Hogarth asked, "Where was the frantic search for him beforehand . . . Where were the fiendish dances . . . Where were the walk-offs . . . the trances . . . the overplaying time . . . the non-playing time? . . . Nowhere." Instead, what they got was "a polished professional." Hogarth attributed the change to money. Now that he had a name and could finally earn a living, eccentric behavior was unbecoming and unproductive. Besides, a younger generation of Europeans cares about the music "more than the Americans themselves."[142] And yet, what Hogarth interpreted as a newfound seriousness were signs of fatigue and illness. Monk wasn't through dancing.

Monk's quartet had its share of adoring crowds, especially in cities where he had never played before. In Warsaw, where they were guests of Pagart (the Polish Arts Agency), Monk gave two concerts before capacity crowds and taped a show for the state television network. The Polish jazz musicians came out in force, over 100 journalists showed up for a press conference, and the audiences treated Monk and his quartet like kings. A writer for the Polish music magazine *Ruch Muzyczny* hailed Monk as "the most original jazz pianist in the world." He praised him for his courage, for not being afraid to make mistakes, and for his vast knowledge of the keyboard. He also challenged the idea that jazz is supposed to always progress, suggesting instead that we pay attention to the "uniqueness" and "individuality" of each great artist. In the end, the writer left the concert hall with a "thirst for Monk's sensational way of playing jazz."[143]

Warsaw left a lasting impression on the Monks, as well. With nearly a week-long break before the next concert in Stockholm, Nellie, Monk, and the entire band decided to do a little sightseeing. They visited the historic Royal Castle (Zamek Królewski), the official home of Poland's monarchs since the thirteenth century. Everything was kept in pristine condition, and visitors were required to wear slippers over their shoes. When the tour reached one of the queen's bedrooms, with ceilings painted "like the Sistine Chapel" with cherubs and floating angels, Thelonious decided to slip under the velvet ropes and try the bed out. "I was downstairs," Ben Riley remembered, "when I heard Nellie screaming. I ran upstairs and saw Thelonious laying up in the queen's bed. And the guards and everybody is standing there like they don't know what to do. So I said, 'Thelonious, man, you got to get out of there, this is a national treasure. They're going to lock you up. What are you doing in the bed, man?' He's laying there with his arms crossed and says, 'I just wanted to see what the bitch saw.'"[144]

Fortunately, Monk wasn't locked up for his indiscretions and the band continued on to Stockholm, Helsinki, and Oslo, where they taped a half-hour television show and performed for a sold-out crowd at the University of Oslo.[145] That night, Jo Vogt— the wife of university president Hans Vogt and a prominent artist in her own right— jumped onstage and put a Peer Gynt–style hat on Monk's head. He later gave the hat to Nellie.[146] Monk also met Randi Hultin, a Norwegian critic who had befriended Bud Powell. She was anxious to learn of Bud's condition in the States. She knew he had barely escaped death the previous summer, after being hospitalized for five weeks with pneumonia and a severe case of jaundice, complicated by a relapse of tuberculosis.[147]

Thelonious let her know how bad things had gotten. "Bud is beautiful," he told her. "But he's not doing so well in America, he's sleeping in the gutter." She asked why he didn't help. "Monk gave no reply to this, but rather continued chattering away."[148] She probably never knew that Monk had been giving Bud money intermittently since he had first contracted tuberculosis. Or that he visited him at Cumberland Hospital in Brooklyn last July when the press wrote him off as virtually dead. In fact, he had been thinking about Powell quite a bit. In January, when he sat down with Leonard Feather for his "blindfold test," they listened to Powell's version of "Ruby, My Dear," recorded in Paris a little more than four years earlier.[149] When Feather asked if he thought Bud was "in his best form" when he made this recording, Monk replied wistfully, "No comment about him, or the piano . . . He's just tired, stopped playing, doesn't want to play no more. I don't know what's going through his mind. But you know how he's influenced all of the piano players."[150]

The quartet played its final European concert at Durham University in England on April 30, and then boarded a BOAC jet to Japan to begin a two-week tour that took them to Tokyo, Osaka, Kyoto, Kobe, and Fukuoka.[151] Much like their last trip in 1963, the Monks took some time to explore the country and the culture, thanks again to their gracious host, Reiko Hoshino, the celebrated owner of Kyoto's most popular jazz café.[152] Either through Ms. Hoshino or some musician acquaintances, Monk discovered a Japanese song titled "Kojo no Tsuki," which roughly translates as "The Moon Over the Desolate Castle." It was composed in 1901 by Rentaro Taki, one of Japan's legendary Meiji-era modernist composers. Then a graduate student and teacher at the Tokyo Music School, Taki had written "Kojo no Tsuki" in response to a school-wide contest. Consequently, the gifted young composer was selected to further his music studies in Leipzig, Germany, but within months of his arrival he fell ill and was forced to return home. He died tragically on June 29, 1903, while attending a cousin's funeral in Oita, Japan. He was twenty-three years old.[153] Taki's premature death and the song's haunting melody transformed "Kojo no Tsuki" into something of a national treasure, especially after poet Bansui Doi contributed lyrics.[154] When Monk heard it, he was drawn to its minor tonality, the medium tempo, and the harmonic movement—which vaguely resembles "Softly, As In a Morning Sunrise." He felt it swung naturally, and he loved the idea of playing music with which the Japanese could identify. "He was show business," Colomby explained. "I'm not sure if someone showed him the song or what, but he played ["Kojo no Tsuki"] and the people went crazy."[155]

By the time Monk returned to the states in mid-May, the tune that Columbia would rename "Japanese Folk Song" had become part of his repertoire. Finally, a new song, and one that sounded unlike anything they had heard from Monk. The first recorded evidence we have comes from the Newport Jazz Festival that summer. Anyone familiar with the melody must have marveled at how close Monk stayed to the original, how he maintained the song's somber mood throughout the statement of the theme, and how Rouse, in particular, played like a man possessed. The crowd really did go crazy.[156]

Monk experienced quite a bit of craziness upon his return home, not all of it good. No sooner had he and Nellie unpacked their bags in New York than they had to hop a plane to the Twin Cities for a concert at Carleton College and a week-long engagement at Davey Jones's Locker in Minneapolis.[157] The trip might have been uneventful, had it not been for an adoring fan at Davey Jones's who thought it would be cool to slip LSD in Monk's drink. "He couldn't calm down," Harry Colomby remembered. "He stopped playing and went out and was walking on cars. He had delusions and hallucinations. Had to be bedridden for weeks."[158] The following month, the quartet opened at the Vanguard for a three-and-a-half-month stay with sporadic breaks,[159] and a couple of weeks into the gig Thelonious had a relapse. Harry Colomby was there that night. "He didn't stop playing. He kept going around and around. After forty-five, fifty minutes into the opening tune I was like, 'wow, was that weird.' I finally had to take him home."[160]

Thelonious was not in the best physical or emotional state when he got the news that Bud Powell had been taken to Brooklyn's Kings County Hospital. He was suffering from a combination of tuberculosis, liver failure due to alcoholism, and malnutrition. Thelonious learned of Bud's condition while playing a gig at the Music Barn in the Berkshires, but he rushed back as soon as he could to see his old friend.[161] It would be the last time; Powell passed away the night of August 1.[162] When the *Amsterdam News* asked Monk for a comment, all he could say was, "The world has lost a great musician."[163] An understatement, to be sure. Monk loved Bud like a brother, and losing him at forty-one years of age was an emotional ordeal. Indeed, the third member of their trio, Elmo Hope, was so distraught he could not attend the funeral.[164] Monk and Nellie did attend. They followed the procession from the funeral home on Seventh Avenue to St. Charles Roman Catholic Church on West 143rd Street. As a few thousand mourners made their way through the streets of Harlem, the band played tunes dedicated to Powell, including "I'll Never Forget You," "I'll Be Seeing You," and "'Round Midnight."[165]

Thelonious pushed on. Besides working the Vanguard,[166] he did the annual summer concert circuit, performing at the Barn Arts Center in New Jersey,[167] and then the much larger Rheingold Music Festival at Central Park's Wollman Skating Rink. Over 4,000 adoring fans came out to hear Monk's quartet and the Bill Evans trio in Central Park, but anyone who had seen Monk before could not help but notice his subdued, disengaged performance. Critic Robert Shelton thought Monk appeared "uninvolved" but it didn't stop him from giving a good show: "even with his left hand, to be figurative, he had the audience in his palm."[168] He eventually snapped out of it; by the time the quartet performed at Syracuse University three days before his birthday, Thelonious was reportedly up and dancing again, to the crowd's delight.[169]

For Monk, the return of dancing and spinning about on stage wasn't just a sign that he was feeling better and digging the music. It was a matter of stagecraft, and as he got older he understood that spectacle sells and eccentricity makes good copy. During Monk's two-week stay at the Colonial Tavern in Toronto (he opened on Halloween), the local press focused on his strange behavior, his hats, and his unremitting lateness. His stage antics went over well with the Canadians. Besides dancing, he would stare at the wall while Rouse and the rhythm section played, and then suddenly turn toward the audience as if he was seeing them for the first time.[170] He told one journalist, "Yes, I'm eccentric musically. . . . If the music is eccentric, I have to be. Anybody talented in any way—they're called eccentric."[171] Another writer deemed him "the grand wizard of all the cultist hippies of the world." Monk did not like the word "cult" ("It sounds evil," he said), but he did admit, "I like to stand out, man. I'm not one of the crowd. If the crowd goes that way, man . . . I go the other way."[172]

During the day, curiosity-seekers and interviewers gathered at the Royal York Hotel to see Monk. Of the parade of characters who passed through their fourteenth floor suite, one guy showed up with a pretty blonde and her pet monkey; he wanted Monk to pose for a photo with a monkey. Monk could tolerate the eccentric label to a point, but when the press characterized him as aloof, difficult, or "arrogant," he became indignant. "You can write what you want to," he told one journalist, "I'm not arrogant. Do I seem to be? I never felt arrogant." To the contrary, he took requests from fans if he could remember the tune, he did not demand total attention or silence, and the sound of clinking glasses and waiters taking orders did not bother him. He wanted customers to buy drinks: "That's what pays us." He didn't mind being a spectacle, "as long as they come." His interlocutor was a little taken aback by his cold, business-like approach, but as Thelonious put it, "I have a wife and two kids."[173]

Two days after his return from Toronto, Monk returned to the studio to cut his ninth album for Columbia. The first day (November 14), they laid down three tracks of "new" music—a sluggish first attempt at Monk's new composition "Green Chimneys"; a gorgeous reading of Duke Ellington's "I Didn't Know About You" that featured Rouse as a soulful balladeer with flashes of Lester Young; and a solo piano rendition of Fanny Crosby and Phoebe Knapp's "This Is My Story, This Is My Song," known in most hymnals as "Blessed Assurance." In one slow, reverent chorus, Monk returned to his roots, perhaps invoking memories of his mother who first taught him the song. At the end of the day, only the Ellington piece was selected for the album. They returned to the studio the following evening, only to come away with one more usable track—a revisiting of "Locomotive," which Monk last recorded for Prestige twelve years earlier.[174] Macero hoped to complete the LP before the year ended, but Monk couldn't stick around for another recording session. A couple of days later, he and Nellie were off to Chicago for a concert at the University of Illinois–Chicago Circle, and a two-week stint at the Plugged Nickel.[175] The concert sold out and the quartet was well-received, but the pressure to produce new music was clearly wearing on Thelonious. The well of earlier compositions was beginning to run dry. When a *Chicago Tribune* writer asked if he was writing new music, he replied worriedly, "Not now in Chicago . . . but I've got to have some done when I get back to New York."[176]

He got back to New York the first week of December and enjoyed a short break before returning to work at the Village Vanguard.[177] It wasn't enough time to compose new music, but when he returned to the studio on January 10, he had enough material to complete the album. The band recorded a lively eleven-and-a-half-minute version of "Straight, No Chaser," a resurrected and slightly revised "We See" (from the same 1954 Prestige LP on which "Locomotive" appeared), and a nearly seventeen-minute version of "Kojo no Tsuki." He then capped the session with a humorous unaccompanied version of "Between the Devil and the Deep Blue Sea," with full tempo shifts and old "tinkler" clichés from the 1920s. Thelonious had fun with the tune, showing off his chops as a stride pianist and proving again that it is possible to play chorus after chorus of fresh improvisations without straying too far from the melody.[178]

Calling it *Straight, No Chaser*, Columbia rushed the LP to production. Because it was Thelonious's first studio album since the release of *Solo Monk* two years earlier, Macero and Bruce Lundvall, who ran Columbia merchandising, thought *Straight, No Chaser* "could use some extra publicity emphasis."[179] Monk was just happy to have another album out, although his somewhat paltry advance check—$6,000 minus union scale for his sidemen and related expenses—was yet another reminder how he had fallen a few notches in the corporate family.[180]

He still had to make money, and that meant hitting the road. In mid-January, the quartet played Washington University, St. Louis, the Boston Globe Jazz Festival, and then flew to Detroit for another George Wein production at Cobo Auditorium.[181] Billed as "Jazz in January—a Mid-Winter Jazz Festival," Wein gathered a star-studded show that included Sarah Vaughan, Dave Brubeck, the Modern Jazz Quartet, and Clark Terry, as well as Coltrane and Monk. The concert was scheduled for Sunday, January 22, but bad weather forced many airports to shut down, including Detroit Metro.[182] Nellie had the foresight to check the weather conditions and rerouted the band to Toledo. From there they drove to Detroit, arriving around midnight. The only other artists who made it were Sarah Vaughan (who performed with a local Detroit group) and John Coltrane, who had come a couple of days earlier with his new wife, pianist Alice (McLeod) Coltrane. (A native of Detroit, Alice arrived early to visit family.)[183] In an effort to salvage the evening, Wein asked Coltrane to sit in with Monk's quartet—a request he was more than happy to oblige. In Wein's view, what happened that night was magical. Coltrane played brilliantly, but in a more traditional vein. He "blew like he was glad to be back home. And I never saw Thelonious more enthusiastic; having Coltrane with the band seemed to make him feel years younger. The energy they exchanged was obvious; they were on the same wavelength. The people cheered the triumphant set, and the evening was saved."[184] After the concert, Wein tried to convince Coltrane to come back to his "roots," perhaps collaborate more often with Thelonious. He pondered the question for a moment and then replied, "You know George . . . sometimes I don't know exactly what to do—whether I should play in my older style or do what I'm doing now. But, for the moment, I have to continue in this direction."[185]

It turned out to be the last time these two giants played together. In six months, John Coltrane would be dead.

27

"Let Someone Else Create Something New!"

(1967–1969)

onk took nearly two months off before returning to the Vanguard in March.[1] His body desperately needed a break but he couldn't afford one. Despite being a busy year, 1966 had been a financial disaster: Thelonious took home only $17,735, thanks to Columbia's decision to reduce his advances and his diminished recording output.[2] Financially, he could barely keep it together. Besides two private school tuitions, he paid significantly higher rent on the Lincoln Towers apartment and continued to maintain the place on West 63rd. And then in the spring of 1967, they moved again within the Lincoln Towers complex, to a twentieth-floor apartment.[3]

To supplement his income, Thelonious occasionally took on paying students. One of his students in 1967 was Lem Martinez-Carroll, a rising junior at Northwestern University who happened to be home for the summer. Born in Harlem to Puerto Rican and African-American parents, Martinez-Carroll had some classical training and an abiding interest in jazz and gospel, but when he heard Monk perform solo piano, he decided he wanted to study with him. When Martinez-Carroll shyly broached the question, Monk replied, "'Yeah, I give some lessons. It's going to cost you.' Back then, I think it was $25 for a forty-five-minute lesson, which was real costly then." His teaching methods were somewhat unorthodox, but they were hardly strange. After the first lesson, Monk gave Martinez-Carroll a copy of a lead sheet for Charlie Parker's "Confirmation" and had him learn it in three different keys.[4] Monk did not speak much, choosing instead to teach by demonstration. This irritated Martinez-Carroll: "His style of teaching was abrasive. I'd be playing and he would take my hand off the keys. I'd look at him and he'd sort of brush me aside, sit down and say, 'No, that's not right. No, you're not doing it,' and play it correctly. It was frustrating for me because I was working from the genre of communication or something written and he was working from demonstration." Still, he recognized Monk's genius and recalled some astounding moments. "Once he demonstrated some gospel music for me. . . . His left foot was going and these octaves and the bass with these gospel chords. . . . I think he played 'Precious Lord, Take My Hand' and I almost imagined him getting ready to sing."[5] Martinez-Carroll ended the lessons in late August. "I told him I was going back to Illinois to college, and he asked me what school, so I said Northwestern. He didn't respond. So in a way, I was a little hurt. You know I'm a black dude attending a university and he never acknowledged it."[6]

Monk may have been thinking about his own son, who was just two years younger than Martinez-Carroll. Toot had just endured his most difficult year at Cherry Lawn, both academically and socially. The racial dynamics on campus changed slightly when the school recruited a few more black students through Project Upward Bound, a federal poverty program that afforded low-income youth an opportunity to attend elite schools.[7] The black students hung out together and Toot fell into the crowd, much to the discomfort of school director Ludwig C. Zuber, who accused the kids of self-segregation. Toot defended their choice: "I remember telling Mr. Zuber, 'What about five white kids? Is that a gang? Is that a band?'" The final straw came when Toot decided to grow an Afro. "They were livid. . . . You're talking about Black Power, and the Afro was the first symbol of that. . . . Zuber was so pissed that he suspended me. I knew he wasn't going to call Thelonious Monk and tell him that 'we are suspending your son from school because of his haircut,' especially when all the white kids were growing their hair long, you dig? So instead of sending me home, he gave me a ten-day suspension on campus doing manual labor. I had to dig out the foundation for the new school office building."[8]

Toot left Cherry Lawn in the spring of 1967, and on his own initiative transferred to Kingsley Hall, a boarding school in Great Barrington, Massachusetts, where, unbeknownst to his parents, he had to repeat tenth grade. During his year at Kingsley Hall, he joined the basketball team and learned about some of the other neighboring prep schools when they had away games. One school, in particular, Windsor Mountain in nearby Lenox, Massachusetts, caught his attention. Or more accuately, one girl caught his attention. Her name was Adrienne Belafonte, daughter of entertainer and activist Harry Belafonte. Toot promptly applied to Windsor Mountain. "Of course, I did not know that Adrienne Belafonte was a senior. So when I get there the next year, she's gone. Her little sister Shari was there, but she's twelve years old."[9] But Randy Weston's son, Azzedin, was also there, and Boo Boo joined him the same year, having graduated from Green Chimneys.

Perhaps the bigger crisis Monk faced was the loss of Harry Colomby. In July 1967, Colomby moved to Southern California. His client John Byner was doing well, and he believed the time was ripe to fulfill a lifelong dream to produce movies. And he wasn't making much money working for Monk. His commissions rarely topped $6,000 a year, and by the time he left teaching in 1967, he was earning about $17,000 annually.[10] Colomby's departure angered Thelonious, who had been feeling a little neglected for the past year or two. Colomby tried to ease the transition by passing the management duties to his brother Jules—a job he happily accepted.[11]

Meanwhile, Monk kept working—nightly at the Vanguard, a week at Lennie's-on-the-Turnpike, a concert at Stony Brook, New York, and down to Austin, Texas for the Longhorn Jazz Festival—where the band endured a horrible sound system and stifling heat in a poorly ventilated auditorium.[12] In May, Monk and the quartet returned to the

West Coast for ten days at Shelly's Manne-Hole, before heading south of the border for Mexico's first jazz festival. With the backing of American Airlines, George Wein put the package together and paid Monk a cool $4,000 for three days of work.[13] Billed with Dizzy Gillespie, Dave Brubeck, and the Newport All-Stars, Monk's quartet performed for near-capacity crowds at Mexico City's Palace of Fine Arts, the National Auditorium, and then drove out to Puebla for the second annual Festival de Puebla, dedicated primarily to classical music.[14] Not only was Monk's quartet well-received, he broke with his usual routine by sitting in with Gillespie's band and by playing a duet with Dave Brubeck. The idea was Teo Macero's, who had come down from New York to record Brubeck. Both artists were game, and with backing by Monk's rhythm section they took the stage together at Puebla's Reforma Auditorium and jammed on an improvised blues in E^b, based loosely on Ellington's "C Jam Blues." Thelonious took charge, with Brubeck responding to Monk's dissonant jabs. Their impromptu duet works up until the end, when Monk says "Let's go," and then plays the theme to signal the final cadence. Brubeck, in turn, mimics what Monk plays but neither Ben Riley nor Larry Gales seemed to have gotten the message. At that point, Monk gets up from the piano and can be heard saying to Brubeck, "You got it," and immediately walks offstage as the crowd applauds.[15] Brubeck recalls, "The rhythm section kept going after I felt Monk and I had finished, so I had to run after them and play an ending."[16]

Nellie, Monk, and the rest of the band extended their stay in Mexico a few days and turned the trip into a much-needed vacation. Residing at the elegant Alameda Hotel in Mexico City, the Monks went sightseeing with Rouse and his partner, Sandra Capello, who was traveling with the band for the first time. "We visited some of the ruins and the old churches. Thelonious seemed to be in a very good mood, though he hardly spoke."[17] When they returned to New York the third week of May, his mood shifted dramatically upon hearing the unexpected news that Elmo Hope was dead. His death was apparently preventable. Bertha Hope recalls what happened. "His left leg had been swelling for some time and I had been trying to get him to see a doctor. He had gone to Roosevelt Hospital before, because they had experience with addicts dealing with health problems, but Elmo did not want to go back there because he felt like he was part of an experiment. It was humiliating. So he went to St. Clare's, but they didn't have any idea how to deal with someone who was on methadone treatment. What they were doing put a bigger strain on his heart and I felt like I was constantly fighting with the staff. . . . I thought he was coming home. But then pneumonia set in and that caused cardiac arrest."[18] On May 19, 1967, forty-three-year-old Elmo Hope died at St. Clare's Hospital, the same hospital where Barbara Monk took her last breath.

It was almost too much for Monk to bear—first Bud, now Elmo. Then in July, John Coltrane joined the ancestors after losing a battle with liver cancer. He was only forty. "Coltrane's death seemed to be the straw that broke the camel's back," Toot recalled. "All of these deaths took the wind out of his sails, and he didn't seem to recover. I never saw my father get it back together after somebody died."[19] Perhaps it is fitting that the year 'Trane passed away, so too did the Five Spot. In 1967, the Termini Brothers finally gave up, turning one of the most important venues in jazz history into a pizza joint called "Izzy's Corner."[20] The only good death that year was the demise of the reviled cabaret card. Mayor John Lindsay killed it with a bill, ratified almost unanimously by the city council.[21] An end of an era, indeed.

Monk spent most of the summer between the Vanguard, the Village Gate, and the road, where the quartet was part of an extravagant package headlined by pop singer Dionne Warwick and others.[22] He suddenly found himself playing before stadium-sized audiences, not as the main attraction but frequently as the opening or closing act. In San Diego, for example, Monk's band did not come on until after midnight, and by that time half of the over 7,000 fans who piled into the International Sports Arena had already left. As Leonard Feather put it, "I wouldn't give a detergent a spot like that."[23] No matter where on the roster Monk appeared, however, accusations and complaints about Monk's "ennui" or the band's "predictable manner" prevailed.[24] He even dropped down in *Down Beat*'s International Critics Poll, falling from fourth the previous year to sixth, behind Earl Hines, Bill Evans, Oscar Peterson, Cecil Taylor, and Herbie Hancock.[25] George Wein attempted to break up the routine by inviting Monk alone to the Newport Jazz festival, to perform with Dizzy and Max Roach in an all-star ensemble designed to "depict the beginnings of bebop." Thelonious was reluctant but Wein implored Harry Colomby to persuade him otherwise: "It will not be a long set. They will probably just play about twenty or twenty-five minutes, and it should really be interesting. . . . [I]t is a very important favor to me that he does this."[26] Money was the deciding factor; Thelonious earned a grand for a half-hour gig.[27] The gathering fell far short of Whitney Balliett's expectations. No one impressed him save Monk, who was "stewing enjoyably in his own inexhaustible juices."[28]

While the critics demanded a new and fresh direction from Monk, his fans continued to deify him, the press persisted in making him a side show, and scholars found him worthy of serious interrogation. His name appeared in encyclopedias and college syllabi, and he was even the subject of an experimental film Doug Quackenbush made from stills he shot in 1964.[29] Between his failing health, exhaustion, and financial pressures, Monk struggled to keep all the attention in perspective. Family and close friends noticed disturbing changes in his behavior. "I remember visiting my uncle [Thelonious] at Lincoln Towers," Clifton Smith remembered, "and he was staring at me for a long time, and then he said 'Did you know that I was a genius?'" Clifton's response was rather noncommittal, so Monk angrily pressed him. "So you don't think I'm a genius, huh? . . . Let me tell you, motherfucker. How many geniuses do you know?"[30] His niece Evelyn tells a similar story, though from her perspective recognizing his fame was as much a source of panic as pride. "He was pacing back and forth for a long time, and then he suddenly blurts out, 'You know, I'm a living legend? I'm a fuckin' living legend!' He was alarmed. He had read it in an encyclopedia or something and it really moved him. . . . He talked about that for weeks and weeks. It took a while for him to digest that concept."[31]

Ironically, just as Monk struggled to "digest" his fame, Christian and Michael Blackwood approached him during the summer of 1967 to be the subject of a documentary film. The Blackwood brothers worked for a television station in Cologne, Germany, but their cinema vérité films of other artists aired across Europe. Once they got through to Thelonious and Nellie and assuaged whatever suspicions they may have harbored, Monk proved to be a willing subject—that is, whenever they were able to find him. Michael Blackwood explains: "It was really complicated to get in touch with Monk or Monk's people. . . . One day Nellie agreed to let us come over to shoot at his house. We set a time and then knocked on the door, but no one answered. We kept knocking because we could hear someone inside the apartment. Finally, we looked through the mail slot and saw Monk sitting down watching television. So we started to make some big racket and he finally came to the door. When he opened it he said simply, 'Oh, hello.'"[32] Once they got rolling, however, he turned out to be a compelling and camera-friendly subject.[33] They caught him at home and around his neighborhood, during a concert in Atlanta, a recording session at Columbia, and about three nights at the Vanguard. They also traveled with Monk and Nellie for ten days in Europe. And while he may not have self-consciously played to the camera, he *performed* nonetheless—holding forth in the kitchen of the Vanguard, spinning in circles at JFK Airport, strolling regally along Amsterdam Avenue while friends and admirers paid their respects. The final product were two highly acclaimed hour-long films, *Monk* and *Monk in Europe,* both broadcast on European television in 1968. These same films were also recut two decades later, providing the bulk of the footage for Charlotte Zwerin's documentary "Straight, No Chaser."[34]

Unbeknownst to the Blackwood brothers, Monk's two-week European tour[35] had all the makings of a compelling drama. It was Wein's sixth time presenting Monk to the Europeans, and the impresario was determined to break with routine. So in place of the quartet he proposed a nine-piece band, packaged with the Miles Davis quintet, Archie Shepp, and Sarah Vaughan. The European promoters loved the idea.[36] Joachim Berendt, organizer of the Berlin Jazz Festival, was so excited that he practically begged Teo Macero to record the band live in Germany.[37] But there was one problem: Monk wasn't interested. Robert Jones, Wein's colleague and road manager on the tour, remembers: "We had a lot of difficulty getting him to go. . . . He appeared to be somewhat frightened by the fact that he would be responsible for organizing the group. We were using Hall Overton's charts, for a group that was somewhat differently voiced. So I think he was a bit concerned about how this was going to work."[38] Eventually, he came around but insisted on choosing the band. He, Nellie, and Wein sat down together and came up with Phil Woods, trombonist Jimmy Cleveland, and Johnny Griffin, who had already moved to France. Wein wanted Clark Terry, but "Monk had some misgivings." Instead, Thelonious insisted on bringing Ray Copeland and agreed to include Terry on two numbers, "Blue Monk" and "Epistrophy." And, of course, he rounded out the band with his regular quartet.[39]

Thelonious was still reluctant to go when his niece, Jackie, asked to come along. He always had a special relationship with Jackie, given her passion for music, and she had long dreamed of going on tour with her uncle. A recent divorcée and mother of a five-year-old, she did not want to miss yet another opportunity. Monk agreed on the condition that she leave her daughter behind, though he was less than enthusiastic about going himself.[40] Hours before their departure, George and Joyce Wein and Nellie had to plead with Monk to leave the apartment, while Robert Jones, Jackie, and the rest of the band waited anxiously at JFK. Jones: "I am waiting at the door of the plane. We've now held the flight for about fifteen minutes. And Joyce and George drive up in their car on the tarmac and out come Nellie and Thelonious."[41] But Thelonious still wouldn't budge. Jackie recalled, "When they got there, Thelonious would not get on the plane. Everyone was trying to persuade him, Bob Jones, Nellie, and Nica who came to the airport to see them off."[42] Eventually, they convinced him to board the plane and took off before he could change his mind.

They were scheduled to land in London Friday morning, October 27, and perform that same night at Hammersmith Odeon, but none of the band members had seen the music, nor had they rehearsed as a unit. Monk had all the charts in a large, dark purple folder but was reluctant to share the music. He finally relented, designating Jackie the music's official caretaker.[43] She knew that some horn parts had to be transposed. "All night long on the plane, Phil, Ray and Jimmy wrote out and copied the various parts."[44] The next day, they had just enough time to shower, rest a couple of hours, and rehearse in the late afternoon. "These guys are trying to go through the tunes," Jones recalled, "Monk is sitting at the piano, with his head down like he's asleep. Finally, he goes to sit in the auditorium with Nellie to listen, about five rows back. Then he goes back to the piano. I think it was Phil or Johnny who said, 'Monk, what do we do here?' And he perked up. 'Naw, it should go like this.' He perked up a bit and they went through a couple of the tunes."[45]

Jones left the rehearsal fearing the worst. The concert was sold out and the audience was anxious to see Monk's first big band performance outside of the United States. When the quartet came out instead, the audience's disappointment was palpable. One angry critic went so far as to cast Rouse as "the world's first fully automated tenor saxophonist."[46] But once the larger ensemble took the stage for the second half of the concert, some magic happened. Jones: "Monk hits the first tune and it goes off unbelievably. The place leaped up. Suddenly, Monk was transfixed. It was really working, it was amazing." He danced. He smiled. He directed the band. "The place went bananas in the end," said Jones.[47] The band only played four tunes ("Evidence," "Oska T," "Blue Monk," and "Epistrophy"), and the ensemble passages were predictably rough for a band with one rehearsal, but they satisfied the audience, as well as a few skeptical critics.[48]

The London concert energized Monk. That night he and Jackie dropped in on Max Roach and Abbey Lincoln at Ronnie Scott's and an inspired Monk sat in with the band.[49] The next evening at Rotterdam's De Doelen Hall, the band and especially Monk gave a lively performance. He really stretched out on "Oska T" and an unusually swift version of "We See," and their rendition of "Blue Monk" practically brought down the house.[50] The band was still a bit ragged, but they were clearly coming together with every performance. By the time they reached Berlin on November 4, Monk wanted to add another tune to the big band's repertoire. Joachim Berendt found an arranger who had worked with the Clark-Boland big band, who did his best to reconstruct Hall Overton's arrangement of "I Mean You" from the record. They rehearsed long hours to get it right and premiered it at Baden-Baden two days later.[51] Berendt was pleased with the band's performance, but thoroughly disappointed with Columbia Records for their absence. Despite Teo Macero's initial enthusiasm for recording the big band in Europe, no one from Columbia followed through.[52]

The tour temporarily ignited Monk's creative juices, but the Blackwood brothers' roving camera also revealed signs of exhaustion, frustration, and fleeting moments of detachment.[53] Sometimes he is seen sitting or standing by the piano while the band plays, seemingly disengaged from the proceedings. Other times he appears disgruntled, as in his exchange on stage with Ray Copeland, which leads him to impatiently stop the band in its tracks.[54] And then he had to deal with a litany of dumb questions from the press:

> Journalist for Danish Television: What is more important in your work, playing the piano or composing?
> Monk: Doing both.
> Journalist: Mr. Monk, you always wear different hats and caps in your concerts. Do they have an influence in your music?
> Monk: [Laughing] No. [He then pauses and says with sudden and utmost seriousness] Maybe they do, I don't know.
> Journalist: Do you think the piano has enough keys, eighty-eight, or do you want more or less?
> Monk: I mean, it's hard work to play those eighty-eight.[55]

Hard, indeed. Monk did not always want to be there. He grew tired of the stage and the spotlight and the spectacle, and after the first couple of performances he pretty much stopped dancing altogether. In Copenhagen, Monk wandered off during intermission, prompting a frantic search through the concert hall at Tivoli Gardens. Robert Jones finally found him in one of the smaller rehearsal rooms playing hymns and old gospel songs on a raggedy, out-of-tune, upright piano. For a minute he was quite animated, explaining to Jones, "These pianos sound just like the ones I used to play."[56] He finished the tune but then it was back to work. When he wasn't working, according to Jackie, he chose to stay in his hotel room and rest. By the time they got to Stockholm, he became physically ill and vomited.[57]

Nellie was also showing signs of fatigue. Jimmy Cleveland did not think she ever rested. "She'd wipe his face, and she'd press his shirts, get his shirts from the laundry, and dress him, and make him eat, and tell him it's time to get out of bed, and it's time to get your shower, and it's time to get your clothes on, we got such and such time to get to the hall, we gotta do this, we gotta do that—and he needed that."[58] And she handled the money, travel arrangements, and, if she knew enough of the language, acted as interpreter. She worked so hard that she was usually too exhausted to attend the concert.[59] Nellie, now forty-six, was beginning to slow down just when Thelonious needed more attention and care. In what might be the most poignant moment in the Black-wood brothers' film, Nellie talks out loud as she walks around the hotel room helping Monk get dressed and out of bed. Complaining about missing one of the concerts, she muses, "You know, I really have to see some of those pictures they were taking. Because sometimes I'm flying around, I feel like a bird in the wings. And I wonder if I don't like it."[60]

Despite a packed itinerary, Monk and Nellie enjoyed some leisure time together, including a memorable excursion into East Berlin. Thelonious was anxious to go there after having seen televised images of East Germany. As with all travelers crossing into the German Democratic Republic, they had to declare whatever cash they had and pur-chase a minimum amount of East German marks, and whatever was not spent had to be given back. When they returned to Checkpoint Charlie (the entrance at the Berlin wall), Nellie balked at the idea of giving all the money back. Then the guards discovered Monk's prized $1,000 bill on a money clip. Luckily, the Blackwood brothers were part of the entourage. Michael Blackwood: "I had to explain to them in German that [the money] was a kind of good-luck charm. We explained that he was a cultural figure and he lives in his own world."[61] According to Jackie, Monk was quite animated over the prospect of losing his money. "He told them, 'You ain't taking my thousand dollars,' and they didn't. I think one of the guards also recognized him."[62]

They returned home on November 9 and took a couple of weeks off before heading to Chicago for a week-long gig at the Plugged Nickel and a three-week engagement at the Vanguard.[63] Monk used his free time to complete two new compositions. "Boo Boo's Birthday" is a loping, medium-tempo number with a tricky melody and a five-bar bridge. "Ugly Beauty," a medium-slow dirge in a minor key, was originally conceived in standard (4/4) time, but when Ben Riley played along for the first time he thought it worked better as a waltz. Monk agreed, giving birth to his first and only composition in 3/4 time.[64] Monk debuted "Ugly Beauty" in mid-November while taping a CBS television show called *Gateway*.[65] Anxious to put both tunes on vinyl, Macero arranged a couple of recording sessions in December. The first session on the 14th yielded an acceptable rendition of "Green Chimneys" and a fine version of "Ugly Beauty"— though it took five takes and an angry exchange when Monk found out Macero was letting them play without recording them.[66] When the quartet returned to the studio a week later, they left having recorded only one usable version of "Boo Boo's Birthday." Much of the time was devoted to simply learning the song—Rouse had to transpose the melody in the studio, and even Monk had difficulty with the melody. "It has a funny amount of bars," he confessed. "I'm just naïve like they are. I make up something and I don't even know what it is, so I look at it again myself. It's new to me!"[67] So new it took eleven takes to get it right.[68] Monk had hoped to do one more tune—his still unre-corded holiday song, "A Merrier Christmas." Macero had promised to record it the pre-vious year, but nothing came of it. Monk pressed the case, suggesting that it's appealing because it "has a Christmas sound. . . . I didn't do a way out, all kinda weird things, you know."[69] Unfortunately, Macero dropped the matter; Monk never recorded it.

Monk and Macero were under enormous pressure to complete another LP. So when

Charlie Rouse missed the next recording session on Valentine's Day 1968, because of his father's death, they proceeded without him.[70] The trio recorded a spirited version of "Thelonious," a slow, sexy take of Alan Rankin Jones's "Easy Street," and a new twelve-bar blues Monk called "Raise Four" because the intervals were based on the augmented fourth (or flatted fifth). On "In Walked Bud," however, they did add a fourth member to the band—vocalist Jon Hendricks, who later explained his presence on the date as pure serendipity. He happened to drop by the studio and Macero invited him to record. Hendricks recalls coming up with the lyrics on the spot, a tribute to Powell's bebop days, when his collaborators included Dizzy, Oscar Pettiford, Don Byas, and the like.[71] Perhaps they were written off the cuff, but three years earlier Columbia had commissioned him to write lyrics for "all of Monk's tunes," as the company contemplated featuring Hendricks on an all-Monk LP.[72] Like so many Columbia projects, it never came to fruition, but not because Monk objected. On the contrary, he once described Hendricks as "the only one I want to lyricize my music."[73] In the end, Monk was pleased with the lyrics and even happier to have completed another album. He needed that advance; in 1967 Thelonious took home only $18,324, and had to pay a big tax bill to boot.[74]

The marketing department really got behind this LP, which was titled *Underground*. The jazz market was shrinking and Monk's sales were steadily declining, so they decided to take a different tack: remake Monk into an icon for a younger generation. They hired John Berg and Dick Mantel to create a bizarre cover shot of Monk playing an old upright piano with a machine gun strapped to his back inside what is supposed to be a secluded haunt of the French underground.[75] The elaborate set included a couple of chickens, a cow, the accoutrements of war, bottles of vintage wine, a slim young model dressed in the uniform of the French Resistance (perhaps a younger version of Nica?), and a Nazi prisoner of war tied up in the corner. This spectacular photo punned on Monk's role in the jazz underground—though by then it was ancient history. It also tapped into contemporary images of revolutionary movements—the Black Panthers, the Revolutionary Youth Movement, etc.—but renders them benign by drawing on narratives of the "Good War" against fascism. The press release for *Underground* minces no words: "Now, in 1968, with rock music and psychedelia capturing the imagination of young America, Thelonious Monk has once again become an underground hero, this time as an oracle of the *new* underground."[76] Remarkably, the press release devoted more ink to the cover art than to the music itself, predicting that *Underground* would become "the most provocative and talked-about album cover in the history of the phonograph record."[77] Even Gil McKean's liner notes obsess over the image; he manufactures a fictional account of Monk as a WWII hero reliving his glory days ("With a cry of 'Take that, you honkie Kraut!' Capitaine Monk shot him cleanly and truly through the heart").[78]

A few days after the last recording session, Monk and the band took off for what had become an annual winter migration to California—a couple of weeks at San Francisco's Jazz Workshop, then downstate to Shelly's Manne-Hole.[79] For the first time in twenty years, Leonard Feather gave Monk an unflinchingly positive review, along with a mea culpa: "This writer was among those who mistakenly looked to him for the technical splendor one finds in a virtuoso instrumentalist."[80] Feather's assessment appeared in the wake of Ralph J. Gleason's adoring defense of Monk. Gleason dismisses complaints that Monk's music has grown stale and Charlie Rouse needs to go. His Jazz Workshop performances still possessed "all the mysterious combination of humor, lyricism, quaintness, and melancholy that has marked his work from the beginning." And like Feather, Gleason revealed a glimmer of nostalgia for the old days when jazz was jazz— not the angry soundtrack of revolution or rock fusion. "I find that I laugh a great deal when Monk is playing and it is a nice kind of laughter. It makes me feel good and it is a compliment to an old friend."[81]

But Columbia was less interested in reaching old friends with *Underground*. They wanted new friends and a bigger market share. Perhaps it is coincidence, but when *Underground* hit the stores in late April,[82] Thelonious just happened to be back in the Bay Area—the counter-cultural capital of the world. The quartet played the University of California, Berkeley, another week at the Jazz Workshop, and then three incredible nights at the Carousel Ballroom (it would later move and become the Fillmore West)— a San Francisco club better known for booking the Grateful Dead and Jefferson Airplane than jazz artists.[83] Monk played opposite the San Francisco–based rock group the Charlatans and Dr. John the Night Tripper (Mac Rebennack), whose synthesis of psychedelic rock and New Orleans rhythm-and-blues attracted a young audience.[84] Dr. John's piano playing impressed Thelonious almost as much as the group's name: "That name is a motherfucker!"[85] The feeling was mutual. The question, however, was whether the Night Tripper's followers felt the same way about the High Priest. Columbia's massive ad campaign tried to ensure they would, declaring "the beginning of a New Monk success. Because with great songs like 'Raise Four' and 'Easy Street'—plus another great cover photo that's just out of sight, the Rock generation will be clamoring for more and more Monk."[86]

That the "rock generation" did not run out to buy *Underground* surprised no one save Columbia's marketing department. They mistakenly believed that selling Monk, or jazz for that matter, was all about packaging and the music was secondary. (This is not to say that packaging doesn't matter; after all, *Underground* did win a Grammy for best album cover.) Monk fans and jazz lovers bought *Underground* not for the photo, but because he delivered four new compositions. And yet, while sales were respectable, the reviews were mixed. Martin Williams, perhaps Monk's most consistent champion in the world of American jazz criticism, was lukewarm toward the LP. He worried that "the younger Monk survived his years of neglect (and even ridicule) somewhat better and more productively than he is surviving success." Like so many of his colleagues, he slyly hinted at his own nostalgia for the bygone days by praising the latest Riverside reissues.[87] Whereas the old-guard critics pined for Monk to revisit the past, the folks at Columbia were slowly coming to the conclusion that he ought to follow Miles Davis's path and update his music for a hipper audience.

Thelonious had more pressing concerns than record sales. He wasn't feeling well. Leonard Feather noticed a change in Monk, a subdued quality to his performance—no dancing, no pacing, "no elbow-struck note clusters. He just sat there, the beard almost motionless, the expression impenetrable."[88] By the time he left L.A. for Chicago, he had withdrawn completely, forcing him to cut short his engagement at the Plugged Nickel and cancel a recording session for Columbia.[89] Simultaneously, Nellie came down with a severe case of the flu and was out of commission for three weeks. Her multiple jobs as wife, road manager, business manager, mother, caregiver, and accountant were clearly taking a toll on her health, well-being, and their general state of affairs. Crucial paperwork was neglected. Contracts and agreements remained in envelopes unsigned. The tax returns were exceedingly late.[90] And Nellie lacked the time and energy to see her husband perform. Nica had now assumed sole responsibility as his New York escort. Village Vanguard owner Max Gordon remembered Nica saying, "'I asked Nellie to come tonight. . . . But you know Nellie, always tired.'"[91]

In May, Nellie reached out to her niece Evelyn, who was now married with a five-year-old daughter and was eight months pregnant. She agreed to move her whole family in to the Monks' apartment in order to help care for her uncle and look after Boo Boo (and to a lesser degree, Toot, now seventeen and entering his senior year) while they were on tour over the summer. Evelyn had barely settled into Lincoln Towers when Thelonious faced one of the worst crises of his life. "Nellie was packing and Monk was sitting in the back room in one of those oval, low straw chairs," Evelyn recalled. "I walked in the room and noticed something kind of strange. I went back and said, 'Aunt Nellie, Thelonious doesn't look right.' She said, 'What's wrong with him? I'm trying to get these clothes packed and we need to get out of here in the morning.' Then I went back and was listening to see if I could hear him breathing, and he just was not sounding right. So I took the chair and pushed it forward. He just fell on the floor and didn't move. He was foaming at the mouth. I ran and got Nellie, but as soon as she saw him she started screaming, 'Don't cut out on me! Don't, don't pull a Bud Powell on me!'"[92] Fortunately, her sister Skippy was there, and she immediately ripped his shirt apart, cleared his nasal passages with her mouth, and kept him alive. An ambulance rushed him to the hospital where he lay in a coma for several days.

Family members on both the Monk and Smith sides kept vigil. "When he finally came to, there were tons of us sitting on the bed. We were all in there. After he came to, he started walking up and down saying, 'Y'all thought I kicked the bucket! Thought I was getting ready to split. Thought I was gonna cut out! Ain't that a bitch?' He was laughing. He was just glad to be alive."[93] No one knows what caused this episode, though most family members speculate that it might have been drug-related. He was still taking Thorazine for depression, vitamin shots from Dr. Robert Freymann, marijuana, and alcohol, and the substances in combination probably did more damage than any single drug. But a few things changed following this ominous incident. First, Thelonious began cutting down his alcohol consumption. Second, he no longer visited Dr. Freymann, though the New York State board for professional medical conduct made that decision for him when it suspended Freymann's medical license for administering narcotics to known addicts.[94] Finally, Nellie launched her own investigation into healthy alternatives. She discovered the healing qualities of natural carrot-based juices and tried to develop a regimen to improve her husband's health.[95]

No one from Columbia dropped by to see Thelonious, and in lieu of a get-well card he received an impatient phone call wondering why he had missed yet another recording date. Nellie explained that he had been hospitalized and was too ill to work. When Teo Macero asked the company to waive the studio charge, he got the memo back with a handwritten note from Roy Friedman in the business office stating, "I gave you a no-charge on a Monk session earlier this year. This one is charged."[96] It was deducted from his next check.

Thelonious could have used more than a couple of weeks' rest before going back on the road, but he had to make a living. As a musician, he had no medical insurance to pay for his hospital stay. The summer was particularly grueling because it was almost entirely taken up by a national tour sponsored by the Schlitz Brewing Company. The "Schlitz Salute to Jazz" covered twenty-one cities in nine weeks, and with Dionne Warwick as the headliner and Cannonball Adderley, Herbie Mann, Jimmy Smith, Gary Burton, Miriam Makeba, and Hugh Masekela on the roster, large crowds were guaranteed. By most estimates, the twenty-one performances reached some 55,000 people and generated about $850,000.[97] In between the tour, Monk's quartet made other appearances at jazz festivals in Toronto, Pittsburgh, and Hampton, Virginia.[98] He was well received most of the time, but many Monk fans found him disappointingly subdued, especially those who came to see hijinks. One writer left the Toronto Jazz Festival pleased with the music but still feeling a bit shortchanged: "His latest headgear was on the small side and he remained seated throughout a 60-minute set that began, of all things, a few minutes early. The only real eccentricity he allowed himself was a crashing elbow thrust as he closed the set."[99]

Throughout the tour, Thelonious and Nellie usually stayed in their hotel room, though occasionally Monk emerged to shoot pool with Jimmy Smith or if he detected a Ping-Pong table anywhere in the vicinity.[100] After a while, the concerts became routine and the coliseums and fairgrounds began to look alike. The first stop on the tour, Winston-Salem, may have held some significance. It was the first time Thelonious stepped foot in his birth state since he left as a four-year-old child. They only spent one night there, and Monk's nearest relatives were at least 150 miles away, but he also showed no signs of nostalgia or curiosity. For Monk, Winston-Salem was just another gig—the stop before Philadelphia.[101] A more memorable stop occurred outside the tour, at Jackie and Rachel Robinson's five-acre estate in Stamford, Connecticut. On Sunday, June 30, the former baseball hero-turned-leader held an "Afternoon of Jazz" benefit for the children of Martin Luther King, Jr., whose life had been snuffed out in April by an assassin's bullet. And just three weeks prior to the gathering, Robert Kennedy suffered a similar fate in Los Angeles. (Sadly, Robinson had buried his own mother in May.) Kennedy's assassination left a pall over the Stamford concert, as some 2,000 guests turned to the music of Monk, Duke Ellington, Dave Brubeck, Cannonball Adderley, Lionel Hampton, Billy Taylor, Marian McPartland, and Clark Terry to help renew their spirits, give them faith in a hopeful future.[102] But for most Americans, especially black Americans locked in the crumbling ghettoes, the spring and summer of 1968 was a period of rage and frustration. One hundred and twenty-six cities broke out in violence after King's death; Tommie Smith and John Carlos gave their iconic raised-fist salute at the Olympic Games in Mexico City, to symbolize black unity and protest black poverty; the streets outside the Democratic National Convention became a combat zone as antiwar protestors battled police in the streets of Chicago.

Thelonious was moved by these events. He still wondered about his contribution beyond playing benefits, though in 1967 a group of black artists affiliated with the Organization of Black American Culture had decided that he deserved a place alongside Malcolm X, Marcus Garvey, Stokely Carmichael, Billie Holiday, Muhammad Ali, John Coltrane, and W. E. B. DuBois, when they collectively created the "Wall of Respect," a mural celebrating black history located on Chicago's Southside.[103] But in 1968, Thelonious contributed directly to improving race relations during a tense situation—a contribution that Monk himself was probably unaware of.

The story begins in Palo Alto, California, an affluent, white college town in the shadows of Stanford University.[104] Across the Bayshore freeway from Palo Alto stood East Palo Alto—then a poor, predominantly black, "suburban ghetto." Given the high levels of poverty and unemployment, some likened it to another country. Inspired by African independence and rising black nationalist sentiment, some local activists proudly nicknamed the town "Nairobi." In 1966, the Nairobi Day School, an independent school committed to African-centered education, was founded, and two years later a campaign was launched to hold a referendum on making Nairobi the town's official name. The campaign was not antiwhite. On the contrary, supporters of the name change believed that if they could instill a sense of pride of place in the community, they could improve schools and neighborhoods, develop a stronger economy, and ultimately make Nairobi an attractive place for all families, irrespective of race. On April 3, the Municipal Council voted to hold a hearing on the name change; the next day, Dr. King was assassinated. Potential cooperation gave way to anger, as young people participated in sporadic looting and burning. The posters, ads, and black and orange bumper stickers urging "Yes on Nairobi" took on an aura of militancy.[105] As racial tensions rose, a group of Palo Alto liberals tried to attract middle-class blacks to integrate white residential neighborhoods.[106]

Enter Danny Scher, a sixteen-year-old Jewish kid born and raised in Palo Alto in an upper-middle-class family. A jazz fanatic, he was a rising junior at Palo Alto High School during the racially tense summer of 1968. Everyone knew Danny because a year earlier he single-handedly produced Palo Alto High School's first jazz concert, inviting none other than pianist Vince Guaraldi and the vocal group Lambert, Hendricks, and Ross. And every Wednesday during lunch, he hosted a jazz "radio show" on campus—though the "station" consisted of a mic, a few strategically placed speakers, and a turntable. On his own time, he had begun working for concert promoters in the Bay Area and got to know Darlene Chan, who had produced U.C. Berkeley's first series of jazz concerts and worked for critic Ralph J. Gleason. "My dream was to bring Thelonious

Monk and Duke Ellington to Palo Alto High School," Scher recalled. "Monk was my first choice, so I asked Darlene [Chan] how to get in touch with him, and she gave me Jules Colomby's number. I called Jules, said I wanted to book Monk at my high school. I think he said it would be about $500. Eventually, he sent me a contract, some pictures of Monk and copies of the *Underground* record. I had to have the school principal sign the contract."[107]

Since Monk already had a three-week engagement at the Both/And Club in San Francisco in late October, Scher secured the auditorium for Sunday afternoon, October 27, and booked two other bands—Jimmy Marks Afro Ensemble and Smoke, featuring Kenny Washington.[108] With Monk's quartet headlining and the proceeds dedicated to the International Club, Scher thought he'd have an instant sell-out. Not so. He had trouble moving the two-dollar tickets so he persuaded some of the proprietors on his newspaper route to buy ads in the program and place posters promoting the concert in their store windows. With ticket sales still slow, Scher decided to pitch the concert in East Palo Alto. "So now I'm putting up posters in East Palo Alto and the word on the street is, 'So Monk is coming to lily-white Palo Alto? We'll see it when we believe it.' The black guys I met were skeptical, so I told them to just show up in the school parking lot on Sunday, and if you see Monk buy a ticket."[109]

Now all he had to do was make sure Monk and the band got to the gig. A few days before the concert, Scher called Monk at his hotel just to remind him where he needed to be. Monk replied, "Well, I don't know anything about that." Turns out, he had never seen the contract, and the band had no way to get from San Francisco to Palo Alto and back in time for the first set. But Monk dug the kid's chutzpah and agreed to do it, especially after Scher volunteered his brother to shuttle the band back and forth.[110] Sunday afternoon, black and white kids from both Palo Altos gathered in the parking lot waiting to see if Monk would show. When the van pulled up and Monk, Charlie Rouse, Larry Gales, and Ben Riley stepped out, the crowd lined up to buy tickets. In the end, Monk's quartet gave the racially mixed, near-capacity audience an excellent show. They played for over an hour. Monk was called back by thunderous applause to play an encore—a solo piano rendition of "Sweetheart of All My Dreams"—and then graciously apologized for not playing another one: "I gotta play in the city tonight, dig?"[111] With that, Thelonious bid farewell, Danny paid his fee in cash, and his brother shuttled the band back to the Both/And Club with plenty of time to spare. A couple of days later, Jules called Danny asking for the money. "I told him I paid Monk. He asks, 'What about my commission?' I said, 'Well, Mr. Colomby, I never had a signed contract. So if you want your commission you should talk to Mr. Monk.'"[112] Scher would grow up to become one of the most successful concert promoters on the West Coast.

Neither Thelonious nor sixteen-year-old Danny Scher fully grasped what this concert meant for race relations in the area. For one beautiful afternoon, blacks and whites, P.A. and East P.A., buried the hatchet and gathered together to hear "Blue Monk," "Well, You Needn't," and "Don't Blame Me." Nine days later, the referendum on East Palo Alto becoming Nairobi was soundly defeated by a margin of more than two to one.[113]

. . .

Monk stayed out West for nearly six weeks, adding the Jazz Workshop and Shelly's Manne-Hole to his itinerary.[114] But he was also there for an important recording session. Teo Macero and others from A&R wanted to produce something radically different from the quartet and solo piano LPs he'd been putting out since he joined Columbia. Inspired by the previous year's European tour, Macero wanted to make a big-band record, but something extravagant and hip with crossover appeal. He wanted a bigger sound and fresh charts, fused with a little rock and a little R&B. Leonard Feather recommended hiring Oliver Nelson as the arranger—intuitively an obvious choice, if Columbia's main goal was to get a hit. In 1968, Nelson had the golden touch. A fine saxophone player and a band leader in his own right, he was better known for his compositions (e.g., "Stolen Moments," "Afro-American Sketches") and arrangements. In 1966, he won a Grammy for arranging Wes Montgomery's album, *Goin' Out of My Head*, and in 1967 won the *Down Beat* poll for best arranger. In the mid-1960s, he turned his attention to scoring for film and television and moved to Los Angeles, where he wrote background music for the hit television show *Ironside*. So many lucrative projects enabled Nelson and his wife, Audre, to purchase a lovely ten-room home in the View Park–Windsor Hills neighborhood of Los Angeles.[115]

Monk and Nelson agreed to the project, but the kind of collaborative working relationship Thelonious developed with Hall Overton never materialized. First, given Nelson's many obligations, he had little time to work on the music; Macero first approached him well into October with plans to record November 19 and 20.[116] Second, Monk and Nelson hardly interacted before the session. Harry Colomby, who was brought in as a kind of impromptu music director, accompanied Monk and Nellie to the Nelsons' palatial home and regarded their visit as a metaphor for their working relationship and artistic differences. "We go to Oliver Nelson's house and it's neat and pristine, everything in place. He's schooled, an academician, from a totally different world. And then here's Monk, smoking a cigarette, ashes defyng the law of gravity and he's nowhere near an ashtray. He's pacing and looking around and Nelson is like, 'Oh, my tapes!' He doesn't want ashes everywhere, and he especially doesn't want his house to go down in flames. The record came out sort of like his house: arranged so clean and neat."[117]

The only noteworthy collaboration was between Nelson and Macero, who not only helped select the band but slipped in three of his own compositions! Thelonious was taken out of the process, reduced to being the featured piano player and little more. And the band was big—three trumpets, five saxophones, three trombones, two drummers (alternating), bass, and guitar.[118] In Nelson's hands, Monk's music was flattened out, the jagged edges smoothed over, and the record as a whole was overproduced. On tunes such as "Little Rootie Tootie," "Trinkle Tinkle," and "Let's Cool One," the ensemble passages are overwrought, and when Monk isn't soloing his voice is practically drowned out. In order to simplify "Brilliant Corners," Nelson audaciously changed the melody, reducing the original A-section to the first four bars repeated and altering Monk's unique seven-bar bridge by adding an extra measure. The rhythm is machine-like and doesn't swing, partly because the drum parts were written out. Because Riley couldn't read the drum parts, on all but two songs Macero replaced Ben Riley with drummer John Guerin, a studio musician who began his career with Buddy DeFranco.[119] While Guerin was a fine drummer, Riley's absence changed the feel of the music. Nevertheless, Nelson scores a few successes. While his arrangement of "Straight, No Chaser" also strays from the original melody, it works and the ensemble (backed by Riley) seems to propel Monk forward rather than get in his way. The surprising innovation here is a four-bar tag where the rhythm shifts from 4/4 to 6/4 time. More importantly, nowhere on these tracks does Monk adjust to accommodate Nelson's artistic vision. On "Reflections," for example, his dissonant, authentic statement of the melody practically steamrolls over the saccharine flute and horn backing. Time after time, Monk makes sure his piano is the dominant voice.

Nelson's arrangements left much to be desired, but they were not as bad as Macero's compositions. All three were geared to the pop-and-rock market, right down to the under-three-minute format. "Consecutive Seconds" sounds as if it had been pulled from a British Mod movie soundtrack. A simple repeated phrase played over a go-go beat and blues changes, the song is an awkward vehicle for Monk, but he makes the best of it.[120] "Just a Glance at Love" is a pretty, very simple ballad in waltz time, clearly meant for popular consumption. Monk stays true to the melody and his dissonant sound, but Nelson's syrupy ensemble arrangement restores the tune to its intended realm of "easy listening." The final track, "Thelonious Rock (Teo's Tune)," was written expressly for the "turn on and tune out" generation. Mercifully, Monk sat out on this one and it was never released.[121]

Much to everyone's surprise, Monk was cooperative during these sessions and committed to making the best album possible. Saxophonist Gene Cipriano remembers, "The vibrations were right, the energy was great, and Monk was just wonderful!"[122] None of this surprised Harry, who enjoyed their brief reunion. In Monk's view, "It was a job, it was a gig. He hardly ever said, 'I don't like this.'"[123] Truth be told, his desire for a hit record never waned.

Macero needed a hit. Some Columbia execs considered Monk a liability and he hoped to prove them wrong. In an effort to save money, he completed the record under budget by canceling what was to be a third day of recording. But the costs still exceeded $6,000, with Oliver Nelson receiving a $2,300 arranger's fee, copying costs amounting to $400, and miscellaneous expenses (musicians' salaries, studio rental, travel) surpassing $4,000.[124] When Columbia released *Monk's Blues* in April of 1969,[125] the A&R and sales departments had high hopes. It was universally panned. Doug Ramsey derided Nelson's arrangements as "assembly line workmanship," and Martin Williams called them "alarmingly trite," "limp," and "hackneyed." He accused Nelson of ruining Monk's music with "professional slickness . . . a quality which Monk's music doesn't need and can't use," and he questioned the inclusion of Macero's compositions: "Does a major jazz composer need help writing a blues and a ballad?"[126]

Nelson took the heat for *Monk's Blues*, but privately Williams blamed Macero and Columbia Records. He tried to temper his criticism because he still believed he had some influence over Macero. A couple of weeks before publishing his withering *New York Times* review, Williams penned a letter to Macero proposing a reunion between Monk and Milt Jackson. "[S]ome of the best records in modern jazz were made by the two of them. Don't worry about repertory too much. But get a good polyrhythmic bass player and drummer—Ron [Carter] and Tony [Williams]? [Eddie] Gomez and [Jack] de Johnette?" He also recalled one night at the Five Spot when Monk expressed an interest in recording with Lionel Hampton. "It nearly came off. It still could."[127] Hollie West of the *Washington Post* echoed Williams, though she made her views public. She dismissed *Monk's Blues* as a "venture in arid territory," called for Rouse's resignation, and wanted Dizzy or Lionel Hampton to make a record with Monk. But she placed most of the blame on Columbia, especially Macero, for failing to show "much imagination in finding new contexts for his man."[128]

Macero heard the criticisms, but neither he nor his bosses were interested in nostalgic reunions. They wanted to expand Monk's audience, and that meant more rock, more pop, more R&B. In fact, just days before the release of *Monk's Blues*, Macero floated a plan for an LP with Monk and popular blues singer Taj Mahal. A long-time Monk fan, Taj Mahal had actually approached Harry Colomby about working with him, who in turn passed the idea on to Macero. Needless to say, Macero thought it was a "brilliant album concept." "In this way we could bring Monk into the current bag of soul/blues and Taj Mahal would have fabulous musical backing."[129] Although there is no evidence to suggest Monk opposed the collaboration, nothing ever came of it.

A few months later, Columbia's A&R department came up with another joint Monk project, this time with a hot new group called Blood, Sweat and Tears. A jazz-influenced rock group with strong instrumentals and a heavy brass sound, BS&T seemed like a likely choice for the kind of musical product Columbia was looking for. There was another incentive, however: The band's drummer was none other than the youngest Colomby brother, Bobby. Macero got A&R to authorize nearly $3,500 for the session and even asked the design department to come up with an album cover, "something psychedelic—way out."[130] But this idea, too, died on the vine, in part because Thelonious simply wasn't interested. He tolerated rock and roll, but he was never a fan. When asked about the music in an interview three years earlier, he replied, "Well, my wife tells me it gives her a stomach ache. It don't do that to me, I can listen to it, but as she explained it, it don't have that tone and it don't tell a story."[131] On another occasion, he was a bit more dismissive. "That's not lasting. That is not music. . . . And they're not musicians, either, most of them. But you take, like, Peter, Paul, and Mary. They're musicians, and what they're doing that'll last."[132] (Of course, it is no small matter that Peter, Paul, and Mary had hired Monk to open for them at the Hollywood Bowl!)

Irrespective of Monk's opinions on rock and roll, we must acknowledge that the initiative for the aborted project came straight from the company, not from any of the artists involved. "We would have been ecstatic to record with Monk if that's what he wanted," Bobby Colomby mused. "But this idea had nothing to do with the project I had in mind." Indeed, Bobby proposed an LP of Monk with strings, ballads only. "Not that boring crap. I wanted to use some real interesting score writers who understood his music, and it wouldn't sound like they were just doing his voicings for strings. . . . I wanted to create an environment rather than step all over what he's doing." Monk loved the idea and was anxious to proceed. But apparently it wasn't hip enough. Columbia killed it before Bobby Colomby could even come up with a budget.[133]

The day after the final *Monk's Blues* session, the quartet spent Thanksgiving week at the Jazz Workshop in San Francisco and then returned to New York . . . as a trio. Larry Gales jumped ship. He and his wife, Mabel Gales, had separated and he began seeing Rose Roberts, the pretty and talented pianist he had befriended when the quartet played the It Club. He decided to remain in L.A. with Rose. They married as soon as his divorce became final. Monk was disappointed, but he and Nellie gave their blessings and there were no hard feelings. "We went to see them at the Roosevelt Hotel where they were staying," Rose recalled, "and Nellie said, 'You guys make a nice couple.'"[134] Gales had no trouble finding work: he joined the Bobby Hutcherson–Harold Land quintet for a stint, and then worked with Erroll Garner at the Century Plaza Hotel's Hong Kong Bar.[135]

Back in New York, Monk hired bassist Walter Booker and started working at the Club Baron in Harlem.[136] A scion of an academic family, Booker grew up in Washington, D.C. and attended Howard University, where his father was the head of pharmacology. He attended medical school, but gave it all up for music. An original member of the JFK Quintet, he had worked with Donald Byrd, Sonny Rollins, Ray Bryant, Milt Jackson, Chick Corea, and on and off with Cannonball Adderley when Rouse recommended him to replace Larry Gales.[137]

As one might expect, Booker was "scared to death" his first few nights on the job. "The way he acted had me kind of uptight. I was already insecure." But in no time they grew close, and Monk would hang out with him on breaks and offer something akin to fatherly advice. "He saw me struggling with the music, so he pulled me aside and said, 'You don't have to try so hard. Just relax and play what you feel.'" The lessons were not limited to music. "One night, he saw me hittin' on some girl at the club or something. He said to me, 'Be sure that you want to have her for a girl or have her for a friend, because if you make love to a girl she ain't gonna be your friend. Because you can have a friend, like Nica's my friend, and I wouldn't touch her. She's the best friend I ever had.' I never forgot that."[138]

Life with Monk was peaceful for the first couple of weeks, but then he suffered another unexpected loss: Ben Riley quit after nearly five years and the split wasn't entirely amicable. With Monk's health failing, gigs were canceled. Riley could no longer afford the financial uncertainty. He not only left Monk but he chose to withdraw from the music scene altogether. He took a job at a Long Island school working in the audio-visual department, and he worked for the YMCA.[139] Monk was now faced with the unenviable task of hiring a new drummer. Mickey Roker tried out a couple of nights, then Art Blakey sat in one weekend, but once Roy Haynes became available the problem was solved. "When Roy joined the band," Walter Booker told me, "it was heaven. Roy knew all his music."[140] Monk's new band debuted at the Village Vanguard at the end of January 1969, and then performed in concert at the Fillmore East as a sextet with Ray Copeland and trombonist Bennie Green.[141] Monk wasn't feeling well that night, so "Nica gave him a whole bunch of uppers," Booker recalled. "He was up for days. We were supposed to go to Chicago and Monk was acting strange. Roy Haynes came all the way to the airport with us. He was waiting for Monk to ask him to go on the gig. Monk just ignored him the whole time. . . . Roy didn't want to go without being asked. He was really pissed."[142] Haynes gathered up his drums and took a cab back home, while the rest of the band looked on in confusion. Monk ended up hiring Wilbur Campbell to open at the Plugged Nickel.[143]

The situation grew worse. Nellie did not travel with Monk on this trip; instead she sent Nica. It is not clear what set him off—amphetamines, a post-manic crash, illicit drugs—but a week or so into the gig he had to be hospitalized. Nellie flew out to be with him and take him home. It was then that Monk was diagnosed with a biochemical imbalance.[144] Neither Nellie nor Nica fully understood what that meant, but it became clear that he needed different treatment. Thus began a long search for the right doctor, accompanied by a mountain of medical bills. Indeed, the health care needs of the entire household became a financial drain, especially with Monk's diminishing income. Just prior to Monk's hospitalization, Nellie needed major dental work—upper bridgework, gum surgery, extractions, root canals—which set them back $3,390.00.[145]

Monk was out of commission for nearly two months. Both Walter Booker and Roy Haynes moved on, leaving Thelonious without a rhythm section. When he and Rouse returned to work in May for a short stint at the Village Gate, he hired Victor Gaskin and Buster Smith, but with the next engagement over a month away he could not retain them.[146] And then Thelonious suffered another emotional setback when Coleman Hawkins, his mentor, friend, and hero, grew quite ill. He had a feeling that Hawk was also about to join the ancestors, so he went to visit him and insisted that Evelyn accompany him. "We had been up late playing Yahtzee," she recalled, "and Thelonious woke me up to go to Bean's house. I was tired and didn't want to go, but then he said, 'I gotta go see Bean. Bean's getting ready to split. So how would you feel if something happened to me and you deny me my last request? So how would you live with that shit for the rest of your life?' So we go and on the walk up there he gives me a history of his and Bean's relationship—how he never worked for anybody but Bean, and that Bean taught him to never compromise your music because if he did he wouldn't be who he is today." Nica was already there when they arrived, and so was Barry Harris. They stayed for a little while, exchanging few words as Thelonious paced nervously back and forth. Monk left with several LPs under his arm, parting gifts from Hawkins.[147] About a week later, on Friday, May 16, Hawkins was admitted to Wickersham Hospital on 58th and Lexington, diagnosed with bronchial pneumonia. Throughout the weekend he drifted in and out of a coma. When it was clear that the end was imminent, Nica and Monk spent all of Sunday with him, along with Eddie Locke, Barry Harris, the Reverend John Gensel, and family members.[148] His daughter Collette Hawkins was taken by Monk's reaction: "He was panting and he was repeating something like 'Bean is going to die.' He kept repeating it. . . . He would move side to side. He was just outside of his room going up and down, just outside the door. I felt so bad. He was so upset."[149] Hawkins died early Monday morning. "When he got back to the house, he paced for three days," recalled Evelyn. "He did not sleep, he hardly talked. Very rarely did Thelonious play records, especially someone else's music. But he played those albums Bean had given him for three days. I don't remember him saying a word during that time."[150]

Monk struggled to come to terms with Hawkins's death. He barely worked that summer, and in the eyes of friends and family he became tense and withdrawn. On Monday, July 7, he and Miles Davis got into a fight at the Schaefer Music Festival in Central Park. Monk's quartet, with Wilbur Ware and drummer Ed Blackwell, was part of a double-header, with Miles's group performing first.[151] Miles had begun experimenting with groove-based, free improvisation that borrowed heavily from rock, funk, even South Asian music. Thelonious reacted vehemently, furiously pacing backstage and mumbling to himself. When Miles got off the bandstand, Monk confronted him. "Why are you playing that bullshit for these people?" he asked. "They going out, they work all week, pay their money to see a show, and you all out there bullshittin'!" Miles angrily defended his music: "Man, Monk. You just don't know what we're doing, you're not hip to what we're doing!" Evelyn, who witnessed the entire exchange, thought they were about to come to blows. Miles didn't want to hear it, but Thelonious continued to elaborate. "So everybody's playing to the chord. You're just playing to the chord. I know what you doing. I don't care what you're playing. It's got to be pleasing to the ear. And that stuff you all's playing sounds like shit!"[152] Miles eventually walked away, but it didn't end there. When Monk's group took the stand, he was in for a rude awakening. "They played beautifully, and it did sound like music, pleasing to the ear. But he didn't get the kind of applause that he would normally get. And he certainly didn't get the reaction Miles got. It was awful."[153]

They made up a couple of weeks later, when Monk and Miles played opposite each other at the Village Gate,[154] but it became increasingly clear that "the people" dug Miles's new direction. Even longstanding Monk defender John S. Wilson favored Davis's fusion experiments to Monk's well-worn numbers. In reviewing their respective performances at the Holmdel (New Jersey) Jazz Festival, Wilson declared Miles "brilliant" and wrote of Monk that "time has apparently stood still. . . . [W]hat at once seemed odd and angular in his composition and performance has now become so familiar as to seem almost routine."[155] It wasn't always like this. At Monterey a couple of weeks later, it was Miles's group that was booed (with shouts of "We want some music!") and Monk, in concert with Bobby Bryant and the festival big band, that "brought the crowd to its cheering feet."[156]

Thelonious had more pressing problems than competing with the rock craze. Jules Colomby and Jack Whittemore failed to coordinate his schedule, resulting in double bookings and cancellations, and he was still working with half a band.[157] At Monterey he used drummer John Guerin, from the Oliver Nelson session, and twenty-one-year-old bassist Jiunie Booth.[158] When he went to Boston a few days later for a week-long engagement at the Jazz Workshop, he hired locals—veteran drummer Alan Dawson, a Berklee School of Music faculty member, and one of his prized students, a young bassist named Nate "Lloyd" Hygelund.[159] A white guy sporting a thick moustache and shoulder-length hair, he embodied the Sixties youth look. Monk kept Hygelund through the rest of the year, but he had yet to settle on a drummer (Dawson was a regular in Dave Brubeck's band). When they played the Cellar Door in Washington the week of October 6, Monk hired drummer Billy Kaye. (He also let the audience know that he turned fifty-two that week by playing "discordant versions of 'Happy Birthday' in each set."[160])

Monk returned from the road in mid-October determined to find a new drummer. He really had no choice, because he was scheduled to leave for another European tour at the end of the month. He scoured the city until he found his man—or boy. In a Harlem club he heard a skinny seventeen-year-old kid named Austin "Paris" Wright. He had an unorthodox way of holding his sticks and he sometimes swayed side to side when he played, but the boy could swing and that's what Monk was looking for. Thelonious did not hire Paris directly but instead called his father, Herman Wright, a bassist who had played with the likes of Yusef Lateef, Terry Gibbs, Dave Brubeck, and Sonny Stitt, to ask permission to take his son on the road. After all, Paris Wright was still in high school and the tour meant missing six weeks of school. His parents consented, but Thelonious, in his own fatherly way, encouraged Paris to continue his studies on the road. When Monk broke the news to his family, Toot was none too pleased. "He comes in the house and says, 'Oh man, I heard this badass young drummer tonight. This cat's got some fire. I'm really digging him. . . . I think I'm gonna take him to Europe with me.' Imagine how I'm feeling. I'm 18, he's 17, and I'm thinking, 'Damn, he's not taking me on the road.' I've been in the house practicing ten, fourteen hours a day, but then I wasn't out there playing. I think my dad sensed I was scared, so when he hired Paris that lit a fire under me."[161] Eventually, Paris and Toot met and they became the best of friends. Wright took him around Harlem to jam sessions, introduced him to a younger generation of musicians. "And the next thing I know I'm in this clique of badass young cats—Billy Gault, Carter Jefferson, Frank Mitchell, John Stubblefield, Jiunie Booth. It changed my life musically."[162]

Monk and Nellie left for London on October 29 and checked into the White House, Ltd. in Regent's Park, literally setting up camp there until December 1.[163] Monk's usually frenetic tour schedule was broken up by a three-week engagement at Ronnie Scott's club. After performing at Hammersmith Odeon as part of London's Jazz Expo '69, the quartet taped a television program at Ronnie Scott's. Both performances were marred by Monk's young rhythm section—particularly Wright, who barely had time to rehearse before arriving in Europe.[164] Thelonious granted Wright very few drum solos, as well. After taking a nearly four-minute solo on "Oska T" during the Ronnie Scott's Club taping, we hear very little solo work from Wright for the rest of the show.[165]

On November 6, Monk and Nellie hop a plane to Berlin for the "Berliner Jazztage" Festival, where he participated in a special seventieth birthday tribute to Duke Ellington. Several artists participated, including Miles Davis and Lionel Hampton, and Thelonious was one of six pianists brought on to perform solo pieces. Monk dug deep into his Duke bag and pulled three numbers from his 1955 Riverside LP—"Sophisticated Lady," "Caravan," and "Solitude"—and surprised the diehard Monk fans with a rendition of "Satin Doll." For someone who rarely played Duke's music, he exhibited an astonishing mastery over the material. His funky, rumbling, stride version of "Caravan" stole the show, producing enthusiastic applause and shouts of delight. The festival organizers decided to end his set with a piano duo opposite the stride master Joe Turner, backed by bassist Hans Rettenbacher and drummer Stu Martin. Some called it a cutting session, but their "Blues for Duke" is more of a homage to the song's namesake as well as a musical exercise in mutual admiration.[166]

The band reunited at Ronnie Scott's on the 10th of November, where they played every night for three weeks, giving them an opportunity to really gel. On December 1, they took off on a whirlwind tour of Germany, Italy, and France—eight cities in eight nights. By the time they performed in front of television cameras in Cologne, the group was more in sync and Wright and Hygelund were comfortable with the music. Monk also played faster than usual on tunes like "Straight, No Chaser" and "Bright Mississippi."[167] The repertoire was limited to tunes that had been in the book for some time, but Thelonious used the occasion of the tour to introduce a new standard: Richard A. Whiting, Newell Chase, and Leo Robin's gorgeous 1929 ballad "My Ideal." It happened to be a favorite of Coleman Hawkins, and both Ernie Henry and John Coltrane made lovely recordings of it.[168] Perhaps it was his tribute to his lost friends? Or maybe Hawk's recording of "My Ideal" was among the discs he gave Monk before he died?

The tour ended in Paris, with a concert at the Salle Pleyel, where Thelonious had played his first European concert to a rather hostile audience. Now, fifteen years later, he received a reception worthy of a star, and the entire concert was televised. No surprise that Monk and Rouse played well together; indeed, Rouse appeared so comfortable with the music he sometimes appeared vacant. Monk, too, also seemed to be on autopilot. What all the film evidence reveals is a fatigued Thelonious, stiff and diffident but thoroughly focused on playing his instrument. The days of dancing and stage antics are gone forever, but his music was still full of surprises. Paris Wright, on the other hand, was all there but visibly nervous. He handled himself well on "Bright Mississippi," "Light Blue," "Straight, No Chaser," and "I Mean You," but halfway through the concert Monk called Philly Joe Jones from backstage to sit in with the band. Jones had been living in Paris for nearly a year, working on and off with Archie Shepp and leading his own band. Jones looked terrible—he was gaunt, missing his front teeth, and appeared fragile—but he gave young Wright a drum clinic. On "Nutty" he provided a spark that had been missing throughout most of the concert. The band picks up the tempo and Monk comes alive, playing against Jones's polyrhythms.[169] The audience went wild for Philly Joe and responded favorably to the entire concert. So did most critics. *Jazz Hot*'s Natasha Arnoldi concluded, "Even if he hasn't played anything new in the last decade, it is more out of stubbornness than for lack of imagination. His impulsive creativity remains, and his alternate universe fascinates us with the infantile qualities, unpredictability and false naivete . . ."[170] The program closes with a strange interview conducted by bassist Jacques Hess, who seemed a little annoyed by Monk's brief answers.

Before Monk and Nellie returned, he agreed to participate in a remarkable television project produced by Bernard Lion and his old friend Henri Renaud. The half-hour *Jazz Portrait: Thelonious Monk* offered a rare glimpse of Monk sitting comfortably before a nine-foot Steinway, performing a variety of solo piano pieces between conversations with, and commentary by, Renaud. The setting is relaxed and Thelonious plays beautifully, putting all he has into "'Round Midnight," "Thelonious," "Crepuscule with Nellie," and "Nice Work." The performances are interspersed with photos of Monk and other musicians, insights into Monk's place in jazz history, and shots of Monk and Nellie at the airport and traveling by cab.[171] At one point, in the middle of one of Renaud's commentaries, the camera catches Thelonious smiling. He may not have understood most of Renaud's French, but he knew he was being treated with respect. It was a far cry from the world of Columbia Records, impatient critics, and fans clamoring for change.

The Monks were back home in time for the holidays and for the quartet to open at the Vanguard. In the end, Thelonious wasn't wild about his rhythm section, so he brought back his old friend Wilbur Ware and hired Ed Blackwell, a dynamic drummer originally from New Orleans who was a regular member of Ornette Coleman's band, but had also worked with Archie Shepp, and the late Eric Dolphy.[172] The band was ready, but Thelonious was not. He wasn't feeling well, and one night lashed out at Rouse when he was unable to play a song Monk requested. They argued right there on the bandstand. Wilbur Ware recalls, "Thelonious was kind of ill and he was saying things that really hurt Charles's feelings."[173] That was the last straw for Rouse. He knew Monk was sick, but could no longer handle his moodiness and strange behavior. It was wearing thin. He called Nellie the next night and gave notice.[174]

28

"What Do I Have to Do? Play Myself to Death?"

(1970–1971)

Anyone close to Monk could have seen it coming, and yet Rouse's departure was still something of a shock. For eleven years he was the group's loyal anchor. He knew the music, served as the band's unofficial musical director, remained a devoted friend, and rarely made demands on his boss. Monk never performed or recorded any of Rouse's compositions, though he granted him plenty of space to make his own LPs. Rouse's decision to leave wasn't impetuous; he had wanted to lead his own band and even pondered an acting career. He took acting classes with Uta Hagen at her renowned HB Studios on Bank Street, and in his spare time he took up fencing.[1] But music was his bread and butter. Six months after leaving Monk, he headed to Chicago for a long engagement at the North Park Apartment Hotel with fellow tenor player Booker Ervin, but when the latter died a few weeks later from kidney failure, Rouse joined Don Patterson's organ trio and remained in the Windy City a few weeks longer.[2] He subsequently returned to New York and formed his own quartet.

Although they parted ways professionally, the two men managed to salvage their friendship. Paul Jeffrey, who would later replace Rouse on tenor, tells a story that speaks volumes to the integrity of their bond. "Nellie and them, they didn't like Charlie Rouse towards the end after he left. So one day I was over Monk's house and they were talking about Rouse like a dog. Monk's not saying a word the whole time. Then suddenly Rouse knocks on the door and they let him in. Nellie asks, 'Oh, Rouse, do you want some tea?' And Monk waited until everybody greeted him. And do you know what Monk did? He tells Rouse, 'This one said you couldn't play shit. This one said that,' and so forth. He ran down everything they were saying, and then when he got done he said, 'But there are two things I don't do. I don't underpay nobody and I don't fire nobody.' So he made all of them look bad."[3]

With Rouse gone, Monk scrambled to find a saxophonist to finish out the week at the Vanguard. Ed Blackwell suggested Dewey Redman, a dynamic tenor player he had known from Ornette Coleman's band, but Redman turned down the offer once he learned that there would be no rehearsal. "You either knew his music or you didn't," Redman later explained. "I wasn't about to get up with Monk and just play changes, or treat his stuff Ornette's way, so I didn't really follow that up."[4] Wilbur Ware then suggested baritone saxophonist Laurdine "Pat" Patrick, a fellow Chicagoan trained by the legendary Captain Walter Dyett at DuSable High School. He grew up in a musical family, having studied piano, drums, and trumpet before switching to alto and then baritone saxophone. Patrick was best known for his work with Sun Ra and Mongo Santamaria, although he worked quite a bit with traveling artists who played Chicago's Regal Theater—notably Nat "King" Cole, Don Redmond, Illinois Jacquet, Cootie Williams, and a parade of singers. Patrick had played across many genres, from swing to Latin to avant-garde, and he was an excellent improviser.[5] Patrick was so anxious to play with Monk that he switched from baritone to tenor in order to make the gig. "I knew the problem that I'd be confronted with trying to transpose those things instantaneously on the spot, particularly with the maestro himself, you see. So, I guess just the plain desire to play with him got the better of my better judgment. So I went down and I didn't really expect to last more than the night, if that long, couple of sets or something. I really did it out of the sheer desire to simply want to play with him at least once, you know."[6] Monk liked what he heard and asked him to come back.

Yet, no sooner had he filled the saxophone slot than he lost his drummer. Monk replaced Ed Blackwell with William "Beaver" Harris, another avant-garde figure known for his work with Albert Ayler and Archie Shepp.[7] For a "free" drummer, he could swing with the best of them. And Monk liked that Harris had been a professional baseball player in the Negro Leagues. With Patrick and Harris, two emerging figures of the avant-garde, joining Monk's quartet, free-jazz devotees were abuzz with predictions that the High Priest might be moving in a radically different direction.[8] Instead, it was Monk who influenced his two younger sidemen. Patrick echoed the sentiments of virtually every musician who had worked with Monk when he described "how educational it was for me to be associated with him during that period."[9] Although many of their encounters were over drinks at Pat's bar on West 64th Street or just hanging around Monk's house, the times they sat down together at the piano revealed the depths of Monk's knowledge and skill. Once, while looking over a tune by Sonny Stitt, Thelonious "stumbled through the first chorus of it, you know, putting it together. And the second chorus he took off on one of the most amazing choruses I'd ever heard, I mean, reminiscent of Fats Waller or Art Tatum, I mean he just completely wiped it out, you know? And then . . . he went back into playing it like he couldn't determine what the chords were or anything. I mean just really putting it together. And I was wondering how could he in one instance play the heck out of it and in the next instance fumble with it like he wasn't familiar with it, you know? So that kind of wiped me out, you know, I never quite got over the shock of that."[10]

While it is impossible to fully explain the inconsistencies Patrick witnessed, Monk's health was in decline. Throughout the early part of 1970, he was constantly ill with colds and flu, and at fifty-two he began to feel the uncomfortable effects of an enlarged prostate. His emotional state was no better; he continued to take Thorazine sporadically, but his bouts of depression and manic episodes came with even greater frequency. That winter, Toot had to keep an eye on his father, who occasionally left the house dazed and underdressed. "I remember walking down from Lincoln Center . . . we walked from Lincoln Towers on 67th and West End all the way down to 63rd Street on West End in a blizzard. He had on his pajamas and his slippers. No coat or anything, just his hat."[11] During one particularly violent episode, Thelonious picked up a huge potted plant in the lobby of their building and rammed it through a plate-glass window. The Monks were charged for the damage and threatened with eviction.[12]

Improving Monk's health became Nellie and Nica's primary objective. Nica sought out doctors and willingly covered medical expenses beyond Monk's financial reach. Nellie turned to organic and holistic healing methods. She had become a devotee of juicing in an effort to deal with her own abdominal ulcers. "She had so many operations," Jackie explained, "and she was looking for an alternative. She wanted to heal instead of being constantly cut."[13] Nellie invested in two large juicers and kept a huge stock of fresh carrots, spinach, celery, and beets, which she would purchase at Hunt's Point produce market in the Bronx.[14] She put Thelonious on a regimen of juices to treat his enlarged prostate and related urinary tract problems. He tried the new regimen but was never consistent—though he did give up alcohol. So devoted was Nellie that she would bring her juicer to the Village Vanguard "and mix up health foods for him right there in the kitchen."[15]

Helping other musicians, friends, and family heal through juice therapy became Nellie's crusade. In the spring of 1970, she had even taken Nica on as a "patient" after she broke her finger and a couple of ribs in an accident that totaled her Bentley, and contracted hepatitis, she believed, from one of Dr. Freymann's needles ("I'm still getting vitamin shots"); and a bad case of cirrhosis of the liver forced her also to stop drinking.[16] But no matter how many sick folks Nellie restored, their neighbors did not appreciate the loud whirring of electric juicers at 3:00 or 4:00 a.m. Some Lincoln Towers residents campaigned to have the Monks evicted.[17]

The band was scheduled to begin a two-week engagement at Toronto's Colonial Tavern on February 2, but Monk's health delayed the opening by four days.[18] They made the gig, but for the duration of their stay he and Nellie remained holed up in their room at the King Edward Hotel. No one could get Monk out of his room, not even Duke Ellington, who happened to be in town to perform with the Toronto Symphony. Wilbur Ware recalls, "Duke was knocking on Monk's door. 'Hey, it's Duke.' Monk wouldn't answer him.'" When he did emerge from his room, however, he was delighted to see Duke and some members of his orchestra in the audience on closing night.[19]

Duke was impressed with Monk's new band, and he had good reason. Pat Patrick's private recordings made at the Jazz Workshop in Boston a couple of weeks later reveal a confident and swinging ensemble comfortable not only with Monk's repertoire but with the whole history of jazz. Patrick demonstrates strong blues chops on "Straight, No Chaser," but midway through his solo he takes his improvisation "outside" the changes and the melody, drifting into fairly radical harmonic territory. Similarly, Patrick takes off on "I Mean You" with a boppish solo, slips into echoes of Coleman Hawkins's improvisational style, and then goes "out" the standard harmony with a flurry of dissonant sixteenth notes. Beaver Harris played with little clutter and a driving rhythm that energized the band, Monk in particular. But when he soloed, he dispensed with tempo and time signatures and created abstract soundscapes using all components of his drum kit.[20] Monk granted Harris unusual freedom, as long as his experiments were limited to solos. But on the last day of the Jazz Workshop gig, Harris got a little too comfortable, a little too free. As Harris tells it, "I was working away, then all of a sudden something struck me, something told me to add something to the high priest of Jazz, free him up more. So I went out to Zildjian when we were in Boston and I brought some gongs back, cymbals and all. I told Nellie 'I'm gonna introduce the high priest of Jazz tonight with a big hit on the gong.' She said, 'Oh Beaver, I wouldn't do that if I was you, you better leave things as they are.' By that time I was drinking sloe gin, Patrick and Wilbur Ware were in the band, we were all together. Pat went out to pick up the cymbal and the gong with me, and brought 'em back to the Jazz Workshop and put this gong in the corner. Here comes Monk, tipping in the door, you know, and he's gettin' ready to come to the bandstand, I saw him, I'm drunk, the gin is rocking up on me ever faster, I said, 'Bam,' hit the gong like a baseball. Monk went straight to the bar and got a triple triple. Then he came up to the bandstand, sat down, started playing . . . playing for a while, then came my turn to take a solo. I played 'bap' (one beat) . . . 'bap bap' (two beats) . . . Monk played . . . I played 'bap' . . . Monk said 'Motherfucker, if you didn't feel like playing why didn't you stay at the hotel?'" [21] Wilbur Ware remembered, "Monk was very angry" with Harris, especially over the incident with the gong. The trip back to New York, Monk would not speak to Harris. Despite Monk's assertion that he "never fired nobody," he never called Harris back for the next date and wasted no time replacing him.[22]

When they opened at the Village Vanguard on March 5, Wilbur Ware suggested his fellow Chicagoan, Leroy Williams, to take over on drums. The thirty-two-year-old Williams had much in common with both Patrick and Ware. He was born to a musical family, having taken piano lessons from his mother and played drums in his grand-father's sanctified church. He, too, attended DuSable High School in order to study under Captain Walter Dyett, although Dyett insisted he study privately with drummer Oliver Coleman before joining the band. He played professionally around Chicago for several years before relocating to New York with Ware's encouragement.[23] Just prior to joining Monk, he had recorded with pianist Barry Harris.[24] Monk liked Williams enough to pay him a compliment after his first night at the Vanguard. "Leroy," he said, "you got good time. Most drummers don't have good time." But he also gave him some valuable advice. "The very first song we played, I was playing a whole lot of drums, pulling out all my tricks, you know, and when we finished Monk simply said to me, 'You have all night to play.' That's all he had to say."[25]

The band was supposed to open at the Frog and Nightgown in Raleigh, North Carolina, on March 30 for a six-day run,[26] but a case of pneumonia and a battery of tests kept Monk at Beth Israel Hospital for over a month.[27] By the time Thelonious was ready to make the North Carolina trip, Pat Patrick had taken a job in Puerto Rico. Wilbur Ware first called alto saxophonist Clarence "C" Sharpe, but when he couldn't make it Ware turned to his old friend, tenor saxophonist Paul Jeffrey.[28] Monk hired him without hearing him play a note, without a rehearsal, without acquainting Jeffrey with the music. Then again, Monk had known Jeffrey for years. Jeffrey was close to Charlie Rouse and had become a regular at Monk's gigs and an invited guest at a few rehearsals. At thirty-four, Jeffrey was a seasoned player who had toured with Dizzy Gillespie's big band.[29]

Jack Whittemore booked the band from May 15 through 23 at the Frog and Nightgown in Raleigh. Established in 1968 by a British scientist-turned-jazz drummer named Peter Ingram, the modest 125-seat club became a popular spot known for its mix-race clientele and a target for white supremacists, who had on occasion threatened the space and its owners with violence.[30] The local press made a big deal of the native son's return, though the buzz did not produce sizable crowds. On most nights, half the seats remained empty. With much fanfare, Ingram unveiled a "homecoming cake" with a fez perched on top emblazoned with the words "Welcome home to North Carolina." Monk dug the cake and graciously thanked everyone, announcing, "I'm from Rocky Mount,"[31] but neither Paul Jeffrey nor Leroy Williams remembers Thelonious speaking about North Carolina or traveling anywhere beyond the club and their hotel room at the Downtowner Motor Inn. "Every night after the gig we all took a cab back to the hotel and Monk and Nellie were the first ones out. They'd cut out to their room and we wouldn't see them until the next day. Wouldn't say a word."[32] None of the local Monk clan showed up to hear him, as far as we know, and Nellie recalled her husband having no interest in reaching out to lost relatives or discovering his roots.[33]

Monk's reaction should not surprise us. He rarely talked about North Carolina, and as an avid supporter of Southern civil rights struggles, his view of the region had been shaped immeasurably by stories of white racial violence. And on this trip, some of his fears and assumptions were confirmed. Four days before the band arrived, a twenty-three-year-old black man named Henry Marrow, Jr., was beaten and fatally shot in broad daylight by three white men in Oxford, just forty miles north of Raleigh. While patronizing a local grocery store owned by Robert Teel, Marrow allegedly propositioned Teel's teenage daughter-in-law. Larry Teel, the woman's husband, confronted Marrow and assaulted him with a wooden plank. In defense, Marrow threw gravel to ward off the blows and then drew a knife. Meanwhile, Robert Teel and his stepson, Roger Oakley, grabbed guns and the three men shot Marrow as he tried to flee. As he lay on the ground bleeding and onlookers ran for cover, the three men beat Marrow with the butts of their rifles and shot him in the head.[34] It was Emmett Till redux, except that Marrow was a husband, father, and veteran of the U.S. Army, and this was the era of *desegregation* and Vietnam. In response to Marrow's cold-blooded killing, black residents, many of whom were Vietnam veterans, rose up in rebellion and burned several white-owned businesses. Protests were held throughout the state. The Teels pleaded self-defense, claiming that the knife-wielding Marrow threatened their lives. As much as Thelonious and Nellie watched television, it is likely they knew about the tragedy in Oxford. They returned to New York before an all-white jury acquitted Marrow's accused killers.[35]

Whatever Monk thought about being "home" he kept to himself. He was there to do a gig, and even that he approached with nonchalance. Paul Jeffrey: "We get there and check into the hotel and I'm so nervous. I'm up [in the room] playing little songs that I know, and Monk's late for the gig. I'm waiting down there in the lobby for like half an hour and when Monk comes down we all jump in a cab; we go on out. So, I'm saying, oh, man, what is he going to play because Monk never says any tunes; he just starts playing. So he played, 'Blue Monk.' That's the first tune I ever played with him. I got through that. Then he played 'Hackensack.' That's like 'Lady Be Good.' Then the next tune was 'Bright Mississippi.' But then here's what he tells me. He says, you know, just play the rhythm that I play, you can play any note [laughing]. So I played that and then he played 'Epistrophy.' So I got through the first set."[36] For someone learning on the bandstand, he got through quite well. Homemade recordings made by Jeffrey reveal an energetic and swinging band despite the saxophonist's initial tentativeness. He makes up for his limited knowledge of the repertoire with assertive solos and a big sound, clearly influenced by John Coltrane and Dexter Gordon. Ware and Williams provide a formidable rhythmic foundation, but Monk is clearly in charge, rarely leaving the piano bench and leading the group with frequent interjections of the melody.[37]

While they never filled the club, Williams remembered, "the crowd was always receptive. We played a couple of matinees and there were even some children who came to hear us. Monk really got a kick out of this."[38] Not everyone was so enthusiastic. Local music critic Bill Morrison found the group formulaic, rigid, and disconnected from the audience. He wasn't impressed with Jeffrey, whom he criticized for playing "a flat horn intentionally" as a way to mirror Monk's piano. In fact, he suggested that the band stifled the pianist. "The combo's formula approach must inevitably restrict the star. Yet it was he we came to hear. And most frustrating were those flashes of solo piano that indicated if Monk were left alone with his keyboard, he might well produce music that could mesmerize."[39]

Never one to pay attention to reviews, Monk was pleased with his band and satisfied with Jeffrey's playing. Besides his work ethic and openness to new ideas, both Nellie and Monk appreciated Jeffrey's personality. Throughout the gig, he constantly tried to reach out to Monk, strike up a conversation, engage the man. "During intermission, Wilbur went one way, Leroy went the other way. So, I said, 'Doesn't anybody say anything to Monk?' . . . So I eased around there and said to Monk, 'You want a drink?' He replied, 'I don't drink.' I said, well, shit, I struck out there. Then he said, 'Maybe some orange juice.' And I knocked everybody over trying to get to that bar to get him this orange juice." It worked. Monk slowly opened up, talking about what was playing on the juke box and informing Jeffrey that he "invented the jazz waltz" when he recorded "Carolina Moon." Over time, Monk learned about Jeffrey—how he was born in Harlem but grew up on one of Father Divine's Peace Mission farms upstate, listened to classical music as a kid, and studied clarinet all through his matriculation at Ithaca College. He talked about knowing the late Scott LaFaro, the bass player Monk had adored, when they were both young clarinetists in the Ithaca College orchestra. And he hipped Monk to places he'd been and the people he'd played with, from blues singers Wynonie Harris,

Big Maybelle, and B.B. King, to Illinois Jacquet and Monk's old friend Sadik Hakim.[40]
Unfortunately, the trip ended on a sour note. When it was time to settle accounts, according to Nellie, Peter Ingram came up short. According to the contract, the band was supposed to receive $3,000 for the eight-day gig, minus Whittemore's ten-percent commission.[41] I don't know if Ingram simply didn't have the full $2,700 in cash to pay Monk, or if Nellie expected the entire $3,000 and believed Ingram was responsible for the commission, but all parties left on bad terms.[42] The next day, as protesters converged in Raleigh following a four-day, forty-one-mile march from Oxford led by Henry Marrow's pregnant widow, Willie Mae Marrow, Thelonious Monk left his birthplace for the last time.[43]

Back home, Monk had to hustle for work. Besides a short gig at the Vanguard the last week of May, the quartet played a concert in Chinatown in June, where they were the odd group alongside performances by the Chinese Music Ensemble of New York, the Taiwan Aborigine Dance Group, and the Lotus Sisters.[44] Monk's only other appearance that summer was a benefit organized by composer and activist Cal Massey on behalf of Harlem's St. Nicholas Park Renewal Corporation.[45] Monk rehired Pat Patrick on all of these dates, while Paul Jeffrey temporarily replaced Eddie "Lockjaw" Davis in Count Basie's band. But with so little work, Patrick had no choice but to quit the band. Once again, financial woes dogged Monk. He owed Columbia three LPs, but he had not made a single studio recording in almost two years, and Teo Macero was too busy producing other artists to record Monk live.[46] His contract was not up until September 1973, but as long as his lack of productivity was "due to Monk's illness or refusal to work," Columbia could drop him from the label without being vulnerable to breach of contract and Monk's claim to the $18,000 advance he would have earned for three albums.[47] Teo Macero begged corporate to keep him. He explained that illness kept Monk out of the studio, and he reminded his boss that, "Miles Davis didn't do anything really spectacular for three years and then came up with *BITCHES BREW*."[48] Macero's pleas were ignored. By the end of the year, Columbia quietly released Thelonious Monk from his contract. Their last release was *Thelonious Monk's Greatest Hits* in 1969. With Monk now declared a financial liability, the ad promoting the LP read as bitterly ironic: "If you dig the cat in the hat, you probably look upon all Monk music as great, because it's Monk and nobody comes close."[49]
Meanwhile, Monk and Nellie struggled to reconstruct his band. George Wein booked the quartet for a Japanese tour in October featuring Woody Herman's big band, Carmen McRae, and Baden Powell,[50] but because Japan imposed tighter guidelines barring convicted felons from obtaining visas, Wilbur Ware could not make the trip. Leroy Williams could have gone, but Nellie "told us, 'You can't have *anything* on your record if you want to go.' Well, I had a few traffic tickets so I thought they wouldn't let me in. Only later I found out that the rule only applied to felonies."[51] George Wein loaned Monk the rhythm section he had been using for the Newport Jazz Festival All-Stars—bassist Larry Ridley and drummer Lenny McBrowne.[52]
As soon as Paul Jeffrey returned from the road with Count Basie, he called Monk's

house. "I spoke to Nellie and she asked me, 'You got your passport? You want to go to Japan?' I said, 'Oh shit, yeah!' Like Pat Patrick before him, he also appealed to Monk for some one-on-one rehearsal time. Monk obliged and Jeffrey quickly discovered, as so many others before him, that learning from the High Priest was an adventure. Jeffrey would come by the apartment or meet at Nica's and Monk would teach him the melody of a song without giving him the chord progressions. "Monk said that sometimes when guys learn the chords they sound sadder." He'd have him play the melody over and over, ad infinitum. "Once you got the melody, Monk would say, 'Make a solo.' He'd lay across the bed and go to sleep. I'd be up there trying to play and shit. One time Monk acted like he was asleep. So I said, well, let me put my horn away. He waited until I just got ready to close the case and then he said, 'You tired of rehearsing?'"[53]

Much of the "rehearsal" time was spent walking around the old neighborhood, hanging out at Pat's Bar and greeting old friends on the street. Monk used the time to get to know his new protégé and train him in the art of musicianship. Among other things, he told Jeffrey, "You got to be clean [well-dressed] to work with me" and "you got to read music." With nineteen years separating the two men, Monk often treated Jeffrey in a fatherly manner. "He had the biggest heart, you know," Jeffrey recalled. "I was going over there just about every day and sometimes spent the night. He wanted to make sure I ate so he would take me to this Chinese restaurant in his neighborhood. . . . Even if I wasn't hungry he'd insist I eat. He'd say, 'Well, you're working, you're playing.' So I guess he remembered times when musicians didn't have nothing. But he would always do that. He'd say, 'Let's stop and get something to eat.' So the compassion that he had was like nobody I ever worked for."[54]

The band opened at Tokyo's Sankei Hall on October 1, and their performance was broadcast on Japanese television. "I think we only had a couple of rehearsals at Nica's before we left," Larry Ridley recalled, "so Lenny and I figured stuff out on the bandstand. Paul Jeffrey had some lead sheets and that was helpful, but I learned most of the tunes from hearing them and opening up my ears."[55] For the next two weeks, they traveled around the big island to cities Monk had played before—Sendai in the north, Osaka, Fukuoka, and Kyoto in the south.[56] But at least half of their concerts were held in Tokyo to sold-out, enthusiastic audiences. George Wein arranged for Monk to sit in with the New Herd, a Japanese big band known for its Dizzy Gillespie–style arrangements led by veteran clarinetist Toshiyuki Miyama.[57] Monk was open to collaborating, but the plan was almost derailed when Miyama sent over a young woman to "help" Thelonious with the score. He was insulted. "You think I can't read?" he asked her flatly before telling her to leave.[58]

The Japanese label Far East recorded their October 4 concert at Koseinenkin Hall. When they asked for permission to release an LP, Monk agreed despite his contractual obligations to Columbia. As he explained to Paul Jeffrey, "You might as well get paid for it, they tape everything you play anyway."[59] The recording gives no indication that the band had been hastily assembled. The quartet excited the crowd, which had a reciprocal effect on Monk's playing as well as his overall mood. He brought renewed energy to his solos, and his accompaniment provided a nervous, unsure Jeffrey with a melodic road map for his frenetic improvisations. Jeffrey grew tremendously since his North Carolina gig, though he still struggled with tunes like "Evidence." Ridley's bass playing was striking for its dissonance, frequent use of diminished scales, and sheer inventiveness. Because he and McBrowne had been working together fairly regularly, they established a good rapport and provided dynamic support for the soloists. And Thelonious granted the rhythm section generous solo space. The two closing numbers, an elaborate arrangement of " 'Round Midnight" and "Blue Monk," featured Monk with the New Herd. The latter was clearly arranged as a tribute to Monk and Art Blakey's 1957 collaboration because it included the exact ascending horn figure Monk tagged on to the turnaround of their version of "Blue Monk."[60]

Monk's spirits were high during the entire two-week tour. He and Nellie caught up with Japanese acquaintances, including Reiko Hoshino, who left her Kyoto jazz café to accompany Monk and Nellie on the tour. Larry Ridley had especially fond memories of the trip because Thelonious, whom he first met in 1958, had really opened up to him. He came away with an impression that belied the myths and media-generated stereotypes. "Thelonious was very astute about his music and contrary to that attempt to portray him as some people did as being weird or whatever, he was a very bright, brilliant person. . . . Like a lot of the older guys, he wasn't into playing a lot of notes or, even in conversation, using a lot of words. I remember telling Thelonious how I was sick of whites calling us 'boys' and stuff like that. He said, 'Ain't no drag, Larry, 'cause everybody wants to be young.' I said, hmm. Case closed. I mean, that was diametrically opposed to what I was even thinking about it. We were right in the Civil Rights period and we were very sensitive about what we were being called. And Thelonious just gave me a different way to think about it."[61]

The group left Japan for San Francisco on October 14 and opened the following night at the Jazz Workshop for what was to be a two-week engagement. Ridley couldn't make the gig, so Jules Colomby hired Los Angeles bassist Pat "Putter" Smith, a twenty-nine-year-old native Californian who was better known as the baby brother of Carson Smith, the bassist who backed Gerry Mulligan and Chet Baker's pianoless quartet.[62] The younger Smith had studied composition at Whittier College and he was known for having transcribed some of Monk's music. Smith was told, "there would be no rehearsal and there's 'no book' [set list of tunes]. I flew in and I got a pad at the Gates Hotel, which is in the Tenderloin district, very low area. I mean, the gig didn't pay much, you know, a couple hundred, I think, a week."[63] Smith had been making pretty good money as a studio musician backing popular artists like Cher and Johnny Mathis, but he never complained—a chance to work with Monk was priceless. Monk appreciated his playing and the two men got along famously, occasionally shooting pool between sets. "He didn't talk much at all. He had a tremendous sense of humor, but he gave off the sweetest, sweetest vibe, like a fountain of sweetness. But he was tremendously funny."[64] Smith remembered one night when Monk got up to dance for an entire tune—a rare spectacle during this period—and a woman near the stage shouted, "Monk, I paid good money to see you." Monk simply replied, "Are you blind?"[65] Overall, Monk seemed to be in a good mood. His old friend, critic Russ Wilson, showed up opening night and was impressed with the group. He praised Monk and all of his sidemen, characterizing the band as "a most felicitous meld."[66]

Then on Saturday, the 24th, Monk suffered a severe manic episode. Paul Jeffrey had never seen anything like it. "I had to check out of my room," he recalled, "and stay with them in their suite so I could walk with Monk because he'd stay up all night walking the street. He never went to bed. He would pace in the hotel lobby and kick over those sand-filled ashtrays. He was wreaking havoc and scaring people. . . . There was this old guy cleaning the pool. Monk went up behind him. The guy didn't see Monk until he was like five feet from him. The guy dropped that thing and made tracks, and Monk picked up net and started cleaning the pool."[67]

The hotel management called the police. Monk wasn't charged, but he was placed in a psychiatric ward for a couple of days. Jeffrey and Nellie remained with him the whole time—in fact, police permitted Jeffrey to stay in the "cell" with Monk until he was transferred to Langley Porter Psychiatric Hospital in San Francisco.[68] Fortunately, Langley Porter happened to have two African-American musicians on staff, a social worker named George Johnson who played piano and a newly minted M.D. named Eddie Henderson. Dr. Henderson was known in the jazz world as one of the rising young trumpeters in the Bay Area. He had just recorded with Herbie Hancock and begun juggling a career as a professional musician and full-time psychiatrist.[69] Henderson had not been on staff long when they admitted Monk. "No one knew who he was. I said, 'Wow, that's Monk!' . . . Nellie brought him in because he was more or less kind of catatonic. . . . He spoke in monosyllables, very abstract. The first thing I'm supposed to ask him, 'Why are you here?' That's the traditional thing that a resident says. So he shows me his MONK ring, turned it upside down, and it looked like K-n-o-w. He said, 'Monk, Know.' I knew what he meant but they had no idea of what he was talking about."[70]

The next morning, Henderson found one of his colleagues trying to engage Monk using the standard Rorschach or inkblot test. He wouldn't answer. When she tried the Thematic Apperception Test—a series of ambiguous pictures meant to prompt the subject to tell a story about what she or he sees—the situation went from bad to worse. Henderson recounts what happened: "She showed him a picture of a little boy sitting, grimacing, while his mother and father stand over him. He's like grimacing playing a violin, and the parents are saying, 'Well you better practice,' you know. So Monk looked at me and winked and said, 'Is this motherfucker crazy? I don't see nothing. It's just a picture.' So I fell out laughing. The psychologist kept insisting that he try to interpret the picture. So Monk finally said, deadpan serious, 'Okay, the little boy is really drugged.' 'Well, why, Mr. Monk?' the psychologist asked. Now I'm thinking, 'Oh no.' Monk replies with no expression whatsoever: 'Because his mother won't give him no more pussy.' The psychologist dropped the clipboard and that was the end of that interview.[71]

"That was his sense of humor," Henderson continued, "but the staff thought he was nuts. Besides being sarcastic, he just didn't want to relate on that stupid level." During his nearly two-month hospitalization, he participated in group therapy and was subjected to more tests and to electro-shock treatment in hopes that it would induce a grand mal seizure. Shock treatment apparently had no immediate positive effect. Henderson recalled, "He just gritted his teeth and said, 'Doc, get me out of this motherfucker.' He was a strong man."[72] He did suffer from the more common side effects—headaches, nausea, confusion, aching muscles, and limited memory loss. Eventually, the senior staff diagnosed him with "schizophrenia—unclassified type" and dramatically increased his daily dosage of Thorazine to 2,500 milligrams. (Fifty milligrams of the drug can sedate the average person.) When Jeffrey and Nellie visited Monk, they noticed a dramatic difference in his behavior. "Monk was moving like slow motion," Jeffrey noticed. "So I used to go up there every day and play ping pong, but for a while he couldn't play because of the Thorazine."[73]

Nellie panicked. No one could tell her when her husband might be released, so she made plans to stay. Besides, given the flood of complaints from management and neighbors regarding the noise and Monk's erratic behavior, she had had her fill of Lincoln Towers. She called her sister Skippy, who was now living in the Phipps Houses on West 64th Street, and asked her to move their entire household. It was a daunting task, but with her niece Jackie's help they packed up the Lincoln Towers apartment and found a Brooklyn moving company to put all of their things in storage.[74] In the meantime, Boo Boo joined Nellie in California to help care for her father and with the expectation that the Monks were permanently relocating to the West Coast. Less than a year out of high school, Boo Boo had begun to pursue a career in dance, having worked with the Chuck Davis Ethnic Dance Troupe and studied with dancer/choreographer Nina Garland at the Eubie Blake Theatrical Workshop.[75] She hoped California might offer some performance opportunities.

Meanwhile, Eddie Henderson and George Johnson looked after Monk and did what they could to shorten his stay at Langley. When Monk began playing the piano in the dayroom and dancing around in the hallway, "the staff thought he'd gone mad. They were ready to put him in Napa State Hospital for the mentally insane, but we told them, 'No, he's back to normal now. He's cool now.'" By early December, Henderson convinced the hospital to allow Monk out to play a week-long gig at the Both/And Club in San Francisco. Henderson agreed to chaperone him every night. Paul Jeffrey hired two prominent locals, drummer Clarence Becton and bassist James Leary. The first couple of nights were rough. Henderson wasn't the most aggressive chaperone: "I told him, 'No drugs, no alcohol,' but he just disregarded me and got a triple Jack Daniels on top of the 2,500 mg of Thorazine. . . . He just went up and played and pushed the piano keys down far enough not to make a sound. The band was really drugged, you know. You couldn't hear anything he was playing. He was making motions like he was playing and then he comes off [the bandstand] like he jumped in a pool, soaking wet. When I took him back to the hospital, he said, 'That was a good set, huh, doc?'"[76]

Nellie begged to differ, though for different reasons. She disliked Leary and reprimanded Jeffrey for hiring him. A couple of days later, she replaced Leary with Rafael Garrett.[77] Monk eventually found his bearings and midway through the run he began to sound like his old self. Critic Sammy Mitchell praised the music, but noticed the obvious effects of his illness. Monk was gaunt and "seemed introspectively deep in a nirvanic cocoon, occasionally emerging with a message sometimes cryptic but worth waiting for."[78] But he was well enough to be released and happy to be playing again. Despite being "off-form," Mitchell thought Monk "pulled a goodly quota of wily quips, subtle pokes and puns throughout the sets, pulling the tails of chords and putting a rueful grimace on runs. Shadowy at times, Monk was still substantial listening."[79]

Soon after closing the Both/And club, Monk, Nellie, and Boo Boo took off for Los Angeles, where Thelonious began a three-week engagement at the Manne-Hole four days after Christmas. Monk called back Putter Smith on bass and trusted Shelly Manne to find a drummer. Manne suggested eighteen-year-old Leon Ndugu Chancler for the coveted spot. "When I was sixteen, I used to stand in the alley outside the Manne-Hole to hear the music since I didn't have any money. Shelly would see me out there and let me in for the last set. Eventually, he let me sit in. My first paying gig there was with Gerald Wilson, whom I'd met when he was brought to Locke High School to conduct our band. When I got the job I was only a week out of school." Chancler also developed his chops as a member of Young Soul, an after-school program that trained black youth in the performing arts. In no time, he was gigging with Hugh Masekela, Willie Bobo, and sitting in with the likes of Donald Byrd and Herbie Hancock.[80]

Ndugu met Monk on the bandstand on opening night before a packed house—no rehearsal and no words from the leader. And yet, the young drummer felt comfortable. "Paul Jeffrey just told me to listen and follow Monk and that's what I did. I knew some of Monk's music from records. In fact, I had just joined the Columbia Record Club a few weeks before and gotten *Monk's Dream* so I was listening to that. So we weren't going beyond the things I already knew."[81] Leonard Feather was pleased to see Monk back on the scene and liked the band, though he found the drummer "occasionally a mite too intrusive." He parsed his words carefully, suggesting that while a new generation of jazz fans will find Monk's style "irresistible in its unorthodoxy," for veterans like himself "it will all have the air of *déjà entendu*."[82] Feather's bout of nostalgia for the good old days seemed to be wearing off.

While most of the audience followed Monk's every move, at least one patron was digging the hulking, bespectacled white guy hunched over the bass. "He was sort of looking at me from the audience in a way I would come to recognize," Putter Smith remembered. "He came up and asked me where the bathroom was, but he never introduced himself."[83] The patron turned out to be Guy Hamilton, director of the film *Goldfinger*. Three months later, Smith got a call from Universal Studios to read for the part of the notorious and quirky Mr. Charles Kidd, part of a duo of assassins in his latest James Bond film, *Diamonds Are Forever*. Smith got the gig but kept his night job. Monk, who had watched at least two of his sidemen (Frankie Dunlop and Charlie Rouse) pursue failed acting careers, couldn't help but be amused by Smith's good luck. Here was a soft-spoken, fairly conventional-looking white guy, with no desire to become an actor, landing a significant role in a huge Hollywood motion picture. Besides bit parts in a couple of movies and a television series, Smith's acting career suffered the same fate as Mr. Kidd—it went down in flames.[84]

Monk closed the Manne-Hole on January 17, and then took the band up north for a week at Mandrake's in Berkeley. The Mandrake's gig was especially memorable for Chancler. "The whole time I'm in the band, I'm talking to Nellie mostly. I'm talking to Boo Boo, getting to know her, but Monk really hasn't said more than two words to me. At Mandrake's he mumbled something about how he dug what I played. Then one night we all decided to go out and eat. We sit down and all of a sudden Thelonious starts to talk to me. The first thing he told me was that he had a son, around my age, that played drums. Now I was in shock. That was his introduction to conversation with me." This really warmed Chancler to Monk, whom he looked to with a kind of fatherly admiration. Indeed, he felt a very strong familial connection to the Monks. "I guess I reminded them a lot of Toot. So Nellie started talking to me. I was a kid, a meek little kid, and hungry for that connection. Nellie reminded me of one of my aunts on my mother's side."[85] And Chancler inspired Nellie and Boo Boo to begin lobbying Thelonious to put Toot in the drum chair. Monk didn't think he was ready. Besides, he hadn't seen or heard Toot in months. He just wanted to go back home.

Returning to New York wasn't part of the plan, but Monk insisted. Fortunately, Nellie had not given up their place in Lincoln Towers after all, but Thelonious was shocked to walk into a virtually empty apartment. "Monk kept asking, 'Where's my furniture?' and no one would answer. I remember one day we went down to Rouse's place—because Rouse lived underneath Monk, a couple of flights down. And Monk went into Rouse's house, knocked on the door, and Sandra opened the door. Monk went all through the house looking for his furniture. He was upset."[86] Nellie knew they eventually had to leave Lincoln Towers, so she kept most of their belongings in storage or at Skippy's place. Besides their bed, some cots, and Monk's piano, the apartment stayed bare for nearly a year.

Even before the Monks left California, Jules Colomby tried to resurrect Columbia's aborted collaboration between Monk and Blood, Sweat and Tears. He booked three nights at Lincoln Center's Philharmonic Hall (March 1–3) for the quartet to open for, and ultimately perform with, BS&T, to be followed by a four-city tour featuring both bands. Columbia planned to record the concert and prepared to deduct $5,258 from Monk's advance to cover the production costs (he was still under contract), but the deal was never consummated. I suspect that Monk was happy to share the marquee with BS&T but had no interest in performing with them.[87] Still, the show went on. Monk kept Paul Jeffrey and hired his old friends, Wilbur Ware and Philly Joe Jones. Bobby Colomby, BS&T's drummer, was beside himself. "I worshipped Philly Joe. When I saw him come into the hall during the sound check, I began playing some of his solos verbatim, but I don't acknowledge that he's there. I play about five of his solos from different recordings. . . . And each time he gets more upright and smiles and goes back to what he was doing. Finally at the very end I play one of his long solos, put the sticks down and say, 'All right, we'll all be here at seven o'clock. Okay? Let's get some rest.' And I walk past him and nonchalantly ask, 'Are you Philly Joe Jones?' He says, 'Uh-huh.' And then I say, 'Where did you cop all my licks?' He grabbed me and we hugged, and that night I never played so well in my life. I was walking on air. . . . The guys in the band were looking at me like, 'Wow, what the hell's up with you.' I could do anything. I could play anything. I was transformed."[88]

Bobby Colomby was perhaps the Monk quartet's most adoring fan during those three nights. While the audience appreciated the three old guys and the not-so-old saxophonist, they came to see BS&T. So did the press; they completely ignored Monk.[89] The same thing happened at the Coliseum in Washington, D.C.—5,000 fans waited respectfully for Monk's group to finish their set so that they could sit through the Tears' ninety-minute show. The reviewer for the *Washington Post* never mentioned Monk.[90] Wilbur Ware described the tour as "kind of weird. All these electronic Blood, Sweat & Tears and the Thelonious Monk acoustic quartet."[91] The tour's backers agreed, forcing Jules to cancel the remaining concerts—except for Quebec City and Syracuse University, where Monk's group performed alone.[92]

As soon as they came off the road in mid-March, Monk fell into a deep depression. He stopped speaking, barely ate, and appeared dazed and confused. He would not see a doctor, so Jeffrey persuaded an old college friend, Dr. Reese Markewich, to pay Monk a visit. A year out of medical school, specializing in psychiatry, Markewich had recently become a resident at Beth Israel Hospital. He also maintained a dual career as professional jazz pianist and flutist who gained some notoriety for organizing a city-wide, all-doctors jazz ensemble.[93] His prognosis wasn't good. He declared Monk catatonic and immediately checked him into Beth Israel for treatment and tests.[94]

Markewich kept him there nearly a month. Consequently, he missed gigs—including a week at the Village Vanguard—and lost precious income. Without Nica's help, he would not have been able to cover his mounting medical expenses. Family and friends paraded through the psychiatric ward to see Monk, but he remained uncommunicative. Photographer Doug Quackenbush, who dropped by a couple of times, observed: "Nellie would visit him every day and he wouldn't recognize her."[95] He didn't recognize anyone at first. Dr. Markewich and friends and family tried to vain to get him to play the piano in the day room, but he would not budge. Markewich finally drew him out by organizing a "talent show" for the psych patients. Paul Jeffrey and Toot were there. Jeffrey: "They had one [patient] down there with two or three fingers missing and he played some bullshit on the piano. They figured if Monk saw that, it might inspire him to play. So nobody knew whether Monk was going to go to the piano or not. So this little cat got out there and he did whatever the fuck he was doing, you know. And now it was Monk's turn. . . . So Monk went out there, sat down at the piano. First he didn't play anything. He sat there for a minute. And all of a sudden he started playing Rachmaninoff's 'Prelude in C-Sharp Minor.' Fucked everybody up."[96]

Thelonious was released in late April or early May. Dr. Markewich continued to care for him, making unofficial house calls and getting to know Nellie and the kids. Monk came to trust Markewich (though his distrust of hospitals never waned), but the doctor's genuine concern did not result in a more accurate diagnosis or treatment for his condition.[97] He did leave Beth Israel with a renewed desire to play, but in the interim he lost his rhythm section. Philly Joe and Ware formed their own quintet and played wherever they could, though both artists anticipated rejoining Monk when his health improved.[98] Nellie wasn't having it. She argued vociferously for Toot to take over the drum chair. Paul Jeffrey as well as most of the Smith cousins knew Nellie wanted Toot in the band. As Jackie explained, "Aunt Nellie promoted Toot with the same focus and determination that she invested in Thelonious." But she also mused that Boo Boo may have paid a price for her aunt's determination. "Boo Boo was very, very gifted. Besides dance, she had a beautiful voice and showed a lot of potential as a pianist. I was giving her [piano] lessons for a minute. . . . She wanted to be the best that she could be. Very likable, very social. She could have been more, but my aunt Nellie wanted to make another Thelonious with Toot, so Boo Boo was always in the shadow a little bit."[99]

Toot never wanted to be another Thelonious, but he wanted to be a musician. For the past five years, he had been practicing at home and taking little duo and trio dates with pianist Ran Blake—mostly house parties and university gigs.[100] Now at twenty-one, he was anxious for more serious challenges. Whether it was Nellie's admonitions, or the fact that Thelonious was home from the hospital and could hear what Toot was up to, or both, the elder Monk finally came around. "One day in May, my father just walked through the house and passed me sitting in his chair watching TV. He walked by and said 'You ready to play?' I started to look at him and I said, 'Yeah.' And he kept on walking. Two or three days later, we were on national television, and that's how it began. I mean, it was trial by fire."[101] The show was *Soul!*, an hour-long black arts and affairs program produced by the legendary Ellis Haizlip. *Soul!* enjoyed a national following and featured a wide range of performing artists, poets, and political figures.[102] Monk's quartet was slated to appear on a special show celebrating Malcolm X's birthday. Fortunately for Toot, the show wasn't live; it was taped on May 19 to be aired the next day.[103] Larry Ridley, the bassist on the date, remembered: "Toot was scared as hell. Naturally. I mean, to jump up in there and to be on the bandstand playing his father's music and playing with guys who were more established professionally."[104] Jackie Smith was there, too, though she thought everyone was a bit on edge. "Toot was nervous and Monk was fussing with Paul because he didn't come in at the right time. So Thelonious burst out, 'What do I have to do? Play myself to death?'"[105] Toot felt the strain as well, but not when he first arrived. On the contrary, he strolled into the WNET studios cocksure and confident. And then his dad threw him a curve. "Now keep in mind, I've been practicing in the same house with the man for five years, working on 'Evidence' and 'Rhythm-a-ning' and everything. So I'm ready to wail. I know we're going to hit something and swing to death. What does he do? Call 'Ba-Lue Bolivar Ba-lues-Are,' a *slow* blues I'm supposed to play with sticks, not brushes. So here I had geared myself for 'X' and he dropped 'Y' on me. I had to shift gears. Right then and there I realized, he wasn't jivin'."[106]

Toot passed his first test, and was now ready to hit the road. A few days later, the quartet began to play dates in Saginaw, Michigan, and Philadelphia, and then headed to the International Festival of Music in Mexico City.[107] Mexico provided Thelonious and Nellie with a much-needed mini-vacation. They stayed in a five-star hotel, dug local mariachi bands, and got box seats to the ballet. One of the highlights was a performance by a Brazilian samba band. Larry Ridley accompanied him and they were both blown away: "They were playing the real McCoy, not that commercial bossa nova. And we were both amazed at the way these guys could shift those rhythms and just move in and out of them. The music was so stirring . . . Brazilian thing, man, whew!"[108] The only down side was that Monk and Ridley contracted a bad case of dysentery. Nellie nursed Thelonious back to health with the juices, but in the process he had lost quite a bit of weight.[109]

Fortunately, Monk had nearly a month off before playing a week at the Vanguard in June and a week at the Cellar Door in Washington, D.C., in August.[110] Toot, whose style drew heavily from the polyrhythmic approach of Elvin Jones, played passionately, forcefully, and loudly. Like many young drummers he sometimes pushed the tempo, but his raw abilities were impressive. And what he lacked in experience he made up for in confidence. Still, Monk took him down a notch by refusing to grant him solos during the first couple of months. (By contrast, Larry Ridley was allowed to take lengthy solos.) Paul Jeffrey had the unenviable task of reining Toot in. "Monk told me not to give him any solos. So here I am on the bandstand, and when Monk finishes I got to come right in. Boo Boo got mad and would ask Monk why Toot didn't get any solos. But Monk had said that, because at that time he was still growing."[111] In retrospect, Toot realized that his father was right and he still had a lot to learn. Thelonious didn't mind mistakes, but he held his sidemen accountable for careless or thoughtless mistakes. Toot found out the hard way during his first engagement at the Vanguard: "The joint's packed and somewhere in the tune we're playing I dropped the ball. I turned the beat around. Now I recovered my butt off, and we continue and we finish, and it's Monk so everyone is cheering, saying yea, yea, yea. So we go off the bandstand and we're standing in the kitchen area and there's a whole lot of people. I'm standing against the wall in the Vanguard, these white folks are telling me I'm the greatest thing since roast beef and I'm sucking it up. All of a sudden, I feel this presence. It was my dad, and he leaned down in my ear, while I'm at the height of my ecstasy and he says, 'Stop fucking up the time, motherfucker.' And then he eased on away. The lesson was honesty. I hadn't said to him, when we finished, 'I'm sorry. I screwed up.' I tried to act like it didn't happen, or worse, because we had been so accepted, it didn't matter, which was the wrong attitude. From that day forward, accountability was serious."[112]

Being Monk's son certainly raised critics' and musicians' expectations—especially among the many drummers who wanted the gig. Toot not only had to endure accusations of nepotism but prove to the jazz world that he deserved to be there. "I would not have been there if Thelonious thought I couldn't handle it. And he had a history of turning musicians who are still learning and struggling into leaders of the pack. . . . I remember what Ben Riley sounded like when he got with Thelonious, and Frankie Dunlop and all those cats, and what they sounded like when they ended up with Thelonious. They were transformed. Coltrane sounded one way and was transformed. So was Rouse. Every single musician that ever played with Thelonious was transformed. So why wouldn't I be transformed? I just happened to be his son but I'm still flesh and blood."[113] But as his son, Toot carried all the baggage characteristic of father-son relationships—generational conflict, hunger for love and approval, struggle for identity.

Father and son were both fiercely opinionated, and now that Toot was an official member of the band, he was feeling his oats. A fascinating interview conducted in Mexico by Pearl Gonzalez captures a classic father-son tussle, while also revealing an impressive level of openness between the two men. Consider the following exchange when Gonzalez brings up the subject of religion:

> Me to Sr.: Do you think much about religion now?
> Monk, Sr.: At all times. You just know everybody goes for religion.
> Me to Sr.: How do you feel about *Jesus Christ Superstar*?
> Monk, Sr.: It's a gimmick.
> Monk, Jr.: It's gone too far for just a gimmick. I think it's healthy. The kids do not accept just anything. This is just another fight of the young.
> Me to Sr.: How do you feel about that?
> Monk, Sr.: No comment.
> Monk, Jr.: The people who are running the church are saying one thing and doing another. Why, the Catholic Church can pay off the national debt.
> Monk, Sr.: How do you know? Have you seen their books?
> Monk, Jr.: The Catholic Church owns everything inside the Catholic churches and all kinds of property.
> Monk, Sr.: This is a Catholic country, you know.
> Monk, Jr.: I can't help that. Look at Harlem. The church isn't helping the people. They throw people out. This is not an opinion, Dad, this a fact.
> Monk, Sr.: Well, I'm not a preacher.[114]

Sometimes their roles were reversed: Toot had to become his father's caretaker and protector. Besides having to keep him from wandering off or monitoring signs for possible manic behavior, Toot's job was to keep so-called fans and admirers from giving Monk drugs. "My mother told me I was responsible for keeping the drugs away from Thelonious. For a certain generation, that was a rite of passage, like bringing offerings to the king to be in his favor and shit. But those days were over for Thelonious. He couldn't handle getting high because it would throw his chemistry off, you dig? And it was his chemical balance that was precipitating his problem. So I had to do that the whole time I was on the road with Thelonious. I was running interference all the time."[115]

The quartet broke up temporarily in September so that Monk could go on a world tour with the Giants of Jazz, a kind of bebop revival group put together by George Wein. He wanted to resurrect his 1967 "Bebop All-Stars" idea but rather than limit the group to one performance he wanted to create a real band. Monk and Dizzy were always at the top of his list, as were Sonny Rollins, J. J. Johnson, Ray Brown, and Max Roach. The last four opted out due to scheduling or financial reasons, so Wein recruited alto saxophonist Sonny Stitt, trombonist Kai Winding, Al McKibbon, and Art Blakey.

In theory, there was to be no leader, everyone agreed to travel coach, and each member received a share of income from films or future recordings.[116] Monk was never enthusiastic about the group or the tour, but he needed money badly. What Monk's quartet could demand had not increased in years; he still drew between $2,000 and $2,500 a week for club engagements—minus his booking agent's 10 percent commission.[117] The two-month tour began in Australia, continued on to Japan and Israel, and hit all corners of Europe, ending in London on November 14.[118] The schedule was grueling; they performed in over thirty venues, sometimes giving two concerts a night. Paul Jeffrey counseled against Monk doing the tour. "He was very sick. He lost weight and his clothes didn't fit him. Then Nellie had him on the juices and the Baroness would come over every day and give him junk food, trying to get him to eat."[119] George Wein was well aware of Monk's condition, so he brought pianist Jaki Byard along as a possible backup.[120]

The Giants enjoyed enthusiastic crowds, generally positive reviews, and a relatively problem-free tour.[121] But even George Wein, the group's greatest champion, did not think the Giants of Jazz "cohered as a unit."[122] The initial Australian performances were a little rough but they retained some of the electricity of a classic jam session. But over time, especially once they hit Europe, spontaneity gave way to routine. They usually opened with a medium to uptempo blues such as Gillespie's "Blue 'n' Boogie" and/or "Wee" (aka "Allen's Alley") penned by Monk's old friend, the late Denzil Best. This was usually followed by "'Round Midnight" featuring Monk and Dizzy, Gillespie's "Tour de Force," a lovely rendition of "Everything Happens to Me" featuring Sonny Stitt, "Loverman" featuring trombonist Kai Winding, followed by three more Gillespie tunes: a rapid-fire "Woody 'n' You," a lengthy bass/trumpet duo on "Tin Tin Daeo," and for the finale, "A Night in Tunisia" showcasing Art Blakey.[123] Because they often played two shows a night, the repertoire ran a little deeper, but not much. For all intents and purposes, the Giants of Jazz evolved into the Dizzy Gillespie show. His tunes and musical conception dominated, and he became the unofficial emcee. Dizzy would later say that the role of leader in a band of leaders was thrust upon him. He did not want it and did not believe it was "good for any length of time because you fall into a groove where everybody looks at me in the band and says, 'What are we gonna play?' . . . I don't want to act like I want to be the leader of them, although all of them at one time or another have worked for me."[124]

Incidentally, Gillespie had been the last band leader Monk worked for—and that was back in 1946! Except for occasional guest spots, Monk had been calling the shots and the tunes for the last quarter-century. Now suddenly he was in a band playing surprisingly few of his own compositions. Besides "'Round Midnight," always a crowd favorite, the Giants sometimes launched into a rather old-fashioned arrangement of "Blue Monk." They initially included "I Mean You" and Monk's unaccompanied "Don't Blame Me," but both numbers were dropped after about a month into the tour.[125] George Wein assumed that fellow Giants, with the exception of Blakey and McKibbon, found Monk's music a tad too difficult. In fact, he was surprised to discover that "Dizzy did not know all of Monk's tunes the way Monk knew Dizzy's tunes."[126] Consequently, it was easier for Thelonious to adapt to Gillespie's repertoire—which he did. In fact, to Wein and members of the band, Monk's silence was interpreted as passivity. He said virtually nothing during rehearsals, never fought to include his own compositions, and elected not to solo on certain tunes. His lack of communication affected the music and frustrated Al McKibbon because it affected their ability to play together. "In about three months Monk said maybe two words, I mean, literally two words. He didn't say 'Good morning,' 'Goodnight,' 'What time,' nothing. He sent word back after the tour was over, the reason he couldn't communicate or play was that Art Blakey and I were so ugly."[127] Silence did not mean he was out of touch with reality. Jaki Byard remembered one incident in Perth when a fan tried to engage Monk in a conversation during lunch. After several exasperating attempts, the man implored, "'Please Monk, say something, you know, gee whiz, you're not talking.' So the guy went three or four times, so finally the guy said, 'Say *something*! Please!' So Monk looked up at him, and said 'Something.' And he continued to eat."[128]

The truth is, Monk did not look well. He was thinner than usual and constantly wore a vacant expression; the wispy white tuft of hair on his chin and balding head—he now performed hatless—made him look quite a bit older.[129] He and Nellie rarely left the hotel room and he practically lived in bed. According to McKibbon, "in Tokyo we were having suits made, because they do it so fast and all that. Monk had his measured lying in bed. He wouldn't get up for them."[130] But as soon as he hit the stage, he surpassed all expectations. Jaki Byard began to wonder why he was there. "In Perth, Monk sounded so . . . oh Jesus. I never heard anybody play so well. And everybody was saying, 'What's, what's happening with Monk?' I said, 'What do you mean, what's happening? He's playing his ass off! He's playing, he's sounding beautiful!'"[131] His solos were lyrical and vibrant, even on "Woody 'n' You," which the band played at breakneck speed—tempos Monk never liked. Even when he wasn't soloing, he revealed flashes of brilliance. Reminiscent of Minton's, Monk opened "Everything Happens to Me" with one of his jarring signature introductions before providing Sonny Stitt's nimble alto lines with startling harmonic and rhythmic support. Many critics agreed that Monk often stole the show. Dick Hughes, who reviewed the Sydney performance, ranked the Giants of Jazz concert among "the greatest experiences I've had in thirty years of listening to jazz," and Monk's solo on " 'Round Midnight" "the most impressive single contribution of the whole series—an inspired testimony to his genius."[132] The Paris concert prompted critic Alain Gerber to write, "To call Monk a genius that night is the least one could say. His improvisation of ' 'Round About Midnight' in the first concert was magnificent. I doubt he has ever played better in his life."[133] And Randi Hultin, who caught the Giants in Berlin, concurred, identifying " 'Round Midnight" as one of the evening's "highlights." "Monk," she observed, "from the first touch on the piano, was strong and in a good mood."[134] Strong indeed. Monk's Berlin performance is arguably the best on record with the Giants of Jazz. Blakey and Monk are on fire; the dynamism between them is reminiscent of 1947, as is Monk's playing, which is inventive and animated.[135]

The accolades Monk received caught Gillespie off guard, and by some accounts produced a little jealousy.[136] In Berlin Monk's introduction produced the longest ovation, and in Prague, the applause for " 'Round Midnight" went on so long that Thelonious took two bows. Dizzy just looked on rather awkwardly, and when they finished he said, "He deserves all of it. Give it to him, shoot it to him. The Master. How about another hand for the master, Mr. Monk."[137] Nearly two weeks later, at Tivoli Gardens in Copenhagen, Dizzy responded with a little biting humor and good-natured competitiveness. "I'm sure that Mr. Monk appreciates your generosity," he proclaimed. "We'd like to give you our interpretation of an original composition of *mine*."[138] He said "mine" with an exaggerated sense of rivalry that elicited laughter from the audience.

Following their final concert at London's Victoria Theater on November 14, British producer Alan Bates invited Monk to Chappell Studios in London to record a few sides for his Black Lion label. Since Monk had an extra day to spare (the band was not scheduled to leave until the 16th), he agreed and recruited Blakey and McKibbon to assist. Blakey remembered Monk being less than enthusiastic: "He just did it because they asked him to and I did it because I'd do anything they'd ask me to do with Monk."[139] Nevertheless, the impromptu session was extraordinary for several reasons. It was Monk's first studio date in three years, and it would prove to be his last as a leader. It also turned out to be his most productive session ever: In six hours, he recorded twenty different songs in thirty takes. Finally, the Black Lion session served as a personal and historical accounting. It was the old man's way of coming to terms with his *oeuvre,* taking stock of the past as he reflects on his musical legacy. After two long months of playing mainly Gillespie's repertoire and repeating the same show night after night, Thelonious was anxious to return to his own music. The atmosphere was fairly relaxed and he was surrounded by a small crowd of well-wishers, including his old friend the Ghanaian drummer Guy Warren.[140] Nellie and Thelonious had not seen Guy in over a decade, so the session provided a lovely reunion.

The first half of the session Monk played unaccompanied, opening with a haunting, nine-and-a-half-minute, improvised warm-up subsequently titled "Chordially." He followed with three takes of "Trinkle Tinkle," transforming the finger-twisting melody that John Coltrane ultimately mastered into a stride piece worthy of James P. Johnson. After the first take, however, Bates and everyone else in the control room kept hearing mysterious clicking and scratching noises. Nellie figured out that Monk's unmanicured nails were hitting the wooden cover behind the keys. So she borrowed a file from Al McKibbon's female companion and went to work on Monk's fingernails. By the next take, the clicking had stopped.[141]

The small audience, buttressed by the producer and young critic Alun Morgan and pianist Brian Priestley, served as a kind of peanut gallery, shouting requests and encouragement. Sometimes Monk tried to oblige, other times he was unresponsive. He traveled the length of his repertoire, from "Misterioso" and "Ruby, My Dear" to "Little Rootie Tootie" and "Jackie-ing." He took his time, never leaving that medium-slow tempo of which he was so fond. Choice standards also came out—"Nice Work if You Can Get It," "My Melancholy Baby," "Darn that Dream," and at least one song from the Giants' repertoire—"Loverman." He had a few memory lapses—part of a bridge here, a chord there—but he played with the mastery of a wizened old man. He even reached back to "Dreamland," that obscure melody he introduced at the Five Spot in 1958 but never recorded. And he invented a couple of spontaneous twelve-bar blues on the spot—the slow-swinging "Something in Blue" and the lively "Blue Sphere." In each case, he seemed to be channeling Willie "The Lion" Smith or Earl "Fatha" Hines.[142]

When Monk brought the rhythm section in for the second half of the session, things got interesting and tensions rose slightly. By this time everyone had an opinion about what Monk should play. Nellie asked for "Introspection" and proceeded to sing "part of the tune by way of encouragement," at which point McKibbon resisted: "There's a lot of changes in that goddamn thing, and I don't know them."[143] As an alternative, McKibbon wanted to play "Crepuscule with Nellie" but didn't know the changes. When he asked for some help, Monk just signified on him: "You played wrong notes up on the stage, you can play wrong notes with me!"[144] And he did. Four takes of "Crepuscule" (one unaccompanied) reveal McKibbon, barely audible, searching for the chords. It wasn't the only time; he can be heard struggling on several tunes—"Evidence," "Hackensack," "Criss Cross," and, yes, "Introspection." McKibbon found none of this amusing. "We went in the studio and there we are, what are we going to play next? No sound from Monk, nothing. They said, 'Okay, here we go. Watch the light. Okay, you're on.' And he started to play something and I just had to follow along. . . . So I told him, 'You know, what's going to happen now, we're going to play and I'm not going to play my best and when the critique comes out they're going to say, "It would've been a better recording had the bass player known the tunes."'"[145] Blakey knew the tunes, however, and he lit a fire under Monk. The rhythm kicked him into high gear and he played remarkably, particularly on "Nutty" and "Ruby, My Dear." Here the trio delivers near-flawless performances.[146]

The six-hour session was marred by one incident involving Bates and Guy Warren. "I asked His Grace, 'Why not play "Thelonious"?,'" Warren later recalled. "That's simple enough. So McKibbon says, 'No, it's not simple. The chord changes are not that simple!' So I said, at the head play no chords. So Alan Bates says to me, 'Why don't you shut up?'" Those were fighting words as far as Warren was concerned, but he stayed cool. "After the recording was over I said, 'Alan Bates, can I say something now you motherfucker. . . . I don't work for His Grace. I came here because he invited me to come. I'm his guest. And I don't work for you. Who the fuck are you?' So I tore him up."[147]

Monk took six days off after coming home and then began a two-week engagement at the Vanguard with the quartet—Toot, Paul Jeffrey, and now Al McKibbon. On December 9, the Giants of Jazz reunited to play a benefit concert at Boston Gardens to save the Newport Jazz Festival. The previous summer disgruntled white youths had rioted, destroying the fairgrounds and bringing the festival to a screeching halt. Wein lost a fortune and vowed to move the festival to New York City.[148] The fundraiser drew a crowd of 7,000 and many prominent names, from Dave Brubeck to Aretha Franklin. Fans of the Giants got a wonderful surprise when Charles Mingus came out in place of Al McKibbon.[149]

Monk returned from the tour thoroughly exhausted. He spoke to no one on the ride home from the airport and withdrew to his bed to relax. With no gigs lined up until the first of the year, he looked forward to the holidays and celebrating Nellie's fiftieth birthday. On the 27th, he treated her to a night at the Rainbow Grill at Rockefeller Center to hear Duke Ellington's Orchestra, though it was Duke who gave Thelonious a treat. As soon as they walked toward their table, Duke stopped the band mid-song and announced, "Ladies and gentlemen, the baddest left hand in the history of jazz just walked into the room, Mr. Thelonious Monk."[150] Monk smiled and shyly took a little bow, though deep down he was overcome with pride. In Monk's eyes, Duke was the real deal, a true Giant of Jazz and a living legend whose music and artistry spanned half a century. Nellie and Toot remembered Duke's one-sentence tribute as a high point during a difficult time in Monk's life.

A few days later, Thelonious reverted into a catatonic state and had to be hospitalized again.

29

"I Am Very Seriously Ill"

(1972–1982)

In January 1972, Thelonious checked into Gracie Square Hospital, a private, exclusive facility on East 76th Street specializing in short-term psychiatric care and substance abuse. Nica made the arrangements and footed the bill. She and Nellie agreed that he needed a radically different approach and diagnosis from what he had gotten at Beth Israel. Gracie Square was a leader in orthomolecular psychiatry, the idea that schizophrenia and manic depression are manifestations of chemical imbalances in the body, and thus could be treated by correcting imbalances or deficiencies on the molecular level based on one's individual biochemistry, by using natural substances such as vitamins, minerals, amino acids, essential fatty acids, as well as lithium.[1] Lithium salts were first introduced as an anti-psychotic drug in the late 1940s and took off in the early 1970s as the preferred treatment for mania and depression in bipolar disorder. By the time Monk entered Gracie Square, lithium was still relatively new in the United States—the Food and Drug Administration had approved it less than two years earlier.[2] Although many scientists worried about the drug's toxicity levels, lithium effectively alleviated the mood swings and excitability characteristic of bipolar disorder. This orthomolecular approach appealed to Nellie because of its emphasis on nutrients, diet, and supplements to restore chemical balance, and one of the attending physicians was Allan Cott, renowned for his use of fasting, diet, and vitamins to treat mood disorders.[3]

Gracie Square was attractive for another reason: his sister-in-law Geraldine Smith just happened to be working there on another floor. Geraldine's presence came as a bit of a surprise to the Monks because they had not been in touch. To say they were estranged would be an exaggeration, but over the past several years they saw each other less frequently. Geraldine's eldest daughter Jackie attributed the remoteness between them to Monk's success and hectic schedule. "We were used to having them over for the holidays and then we didn't see them as much. For Thelonious and Aunt Nellie, a wonderful thing was taking place; he was making money, making records, new friends. But something changed and they stopped coming around. It broke my heart."[4] Now, Monk had never been happier to see his sister-in-law. "When he came in, he was behaving very badly. In fact, for the first few days they had banned the family from coming to visit him. When he found out that I was there, he wanted me up there with him."[5] He had a private nurse, a large African-American man who sometimes had to physically subdue Thelonious, who was more belligerent than usual and had to be under constant observation the first few days, especially after he had set his bed on fire while smoking.[6] When word of the incident reached Geraldine, she went to investigate. "I walked into his room while his nurse was sitting there with him and Thelonious said, 'Don't you believe nothing that man says to you. I didn't set the bed on fire. But he stole my thousand-dollar bill. And he's trying to take my ring off my finger, too.'"[7] Over time, Geraldine became something of his second nurse and on subsequent stays she was assigned to him. She didn't mind; on the contrary, she found something quite serendipitous about the reunion, despite its challenges. After all, Monk was assigned to Room 517, the same number Sonny had been playing for years.[8]

Lithium takes a while to kick in—up to two or three weeks to reach a steady state. At first, it sedated him, but a couple of weeks into his stay he showed improvement. Once he was permitted to see visitors, he had many. Nellie, Nica, and Paul Jeffrey showed up every day, and Toot and Boo Boo came whenever they could. (Boo Boo was busy working as a principal dancer with Randy Weston's African Rhythms.[9]) Ellington's violinist, Ray Nance, happened to be a patient there, so many of his guests dropped in on Monk, and vice versa. (Ironically, Thelonious refused to speak to Nance during his stay.[10]) The list of well-wishers included Thomas and Marion, the whole Smith clan, Doug Quackenbush, Leroy Williams, Wilbur Ware, pianist Barry Harris, and the Reverend John Gensel, pastor of St. Peter's Lutheran Church in Manhattan—better known as the "jazz church." Monk said very little, though when he wasn't completely withdrawn he seemed grateful for the visits. Michael James, Ellington's nephew and a budding jazz critic, was moved by the sight of Monk sitting on the floor in front of a portable record player listening to the version of "Ruby, My Dear" he recorded with Coleman Hawkins.[11] He listened to that song over and over—was he perhaps reflecting on Hawk's death, or his own mortality, or just relishing the lush sound of Bean's horn doing justice to one of his great compositions?

Geraldine Smith concluded that the doctors at Gracie Square got it right with the lithium treatment, and both Nellie and Nica agreed. It stabilized his moods and virtually eliminated his manic episodes, as long as he took his meds, maintained his diet, and stayed away from narcotics. But there were negative side effects: fatigue, sleepiness, nausea, and increased thirst and urination—the latter was no fun, given his ongoing prostate problems. Quality of life issues notwithstanding, the drug may have affected his playing. Besides possibly producing "a fine tremor of the hands," lithium can cause memory impairment and cognitive slowing, and when taken at high levels can produce indifference, malaise, passivity, and decreased responsiveness to one's environment.[12] Consequently, by eliminating the cycles of hypomania, some researchers found that the drug may hamper creativity and reduce drive, although others have reported increased artistic productivity for bipolar patients on lithium.[13] While the research is inconclusive on the specific impact of the drug on creative drive, Monk showed signs of every one of these side effects through the remainder of his life.

Although he would return to Gracie Square a few times over the course of the next five years, Monk left the hospital in fairly good shape. Armed with a prescription for lithium to replace the Thorazine he had been taking, and buttressed by Nellie's all-natural concoctions, Thelonious was on the road to chemical balance and ready to play again. Those closest to him were charged with keeping him away from the junk food and the occasional line of cocaine (he wasn't about to give up reefer). Unfortunately, this was one challenge that he did not always overcome.

A few days after his release, Monk took his quartet, including Al McKibbon, to Los Angeles for a three-week stay at the Manne-Hole to begin on February 17.[14] Leonard Feather made his customary opening night pilgrimage, though he was far less sanguine than he had been in previous years. He bemoaned the fact that "for many years [Monk] has added little or nothing to his litany of songs," or his interpretations of them. He then heaped on the ultimate insult, arguing that the "full value" of "Ruby, My Dear" would have been better realized in Oscar Peterson's or Ben Webster's hands than in Monk's. Feather was unimpressed with Paul Jeffrey and thought McKibbon to be "a little stiff," but Toot he found "promising."[15] Whether or not Toot read his press, he was surely feeling his oats on this trip. From the very first night, tensions erupted between Toot and McKibbon, and Paul Jeffrey was caught in the middle. "Al didn't dig Toot. He said, 'What are we on the bandstand with this kid for?' And he would do little things to throw Toot off. . . . Later, we're sitting up there in the hotel room and Toot says to Monk, 'Daddy, you ought to fire Al McKibbon.' So Monk looks at me and says, 'What do you think?'"[16] Jeffrey did not have to decide because McKibbon quit on his own accord and sent Larry Gales in his place.

Gales finished out the Manne-Hole gig and played a date in San Diego, but when the quartet headed to Seattle for a one-nighter at the Fresh Air Club, he stayed behind. The club owner scoured the Pacific Northwest for a replacement and found a true jazz legend—Adolphus Alsbrook. The Kansas City–born Alsbrook was reputed to have been the only musician to quit Duke Ellington's band (he joined Duke's in 1939, only to be replaced by the legendary Jimmy Blanton). He was based in Minneapolis for many years, where he taught music at the university and anchored the local jazz scene there. Bassists Charles Mingus and Gene Ramey praised Alsbrook's skills, both as a player and an arranger.[17] "He had just gotten over a stroke when he worked with us, but he's still bad!" recalled Jeffrey. Toot disagreed. His opinion of Alsbrook was no different than his opinion of McKibbon, and he had no qualms about expressing it. After the gig, a journalist asked Jeffrey what he thought about Alsbrook. "I said, 'To me he's a legend.' He then tells me that he just spoke to Toot who said that the band would sound much better if Adolphus wasn't in it." Inevitably, Toot's criticisms got back to Alsbrook. What Toot did not know was that the seventy-year-old bassist was a judo expert. Jeffrey witnessed what happened next: "The dressing room was underneath the club and as we were packing up Adolphus calls Toot over. 'Man, come here. Just let me'—and he hit a pressure point and said, 'See if you can move.' And Toot couldn't move."[18] Slowly, he began to learn a couple of vital lessons:

Approach the music and fellow musicians with humility and don't underestimate the elders.

When Monk finally returned in March, he never had a chance to unpack. To the great relief of their neighbors in Lincoln Towers, the Monks moved to a twelfth-floor apartment at 473 West End Avenue. The prewar building located just south of 83rd Street lacked the picturesque view of the Hudson, but its spacious rooms, high ceilings, and elegant detail more than compensated. And the move finally allowed them to retrieve furniture that had been sitting in storage or at Skippy's apartment for the past year.[19] While Thelonious may have appreciated having furnishings again, the move was painful, since it put even greater distance between him and the old neighborhood.

He did not have much time to settle into his new digs. In April the quartet played a week at Lennie Sogoloff's new club, Lennie's–Village Green in Danvers, Massachusetts. Formerly Lennie's-on-the-Turnpike, the original spot burned down a year earlier.[20] The band was still without a permanent bass player, so Jules Colomby called his friend Ron McClure to see if he was interested. McClure, who taught at Berklee College of Music, not only jumped at the chance, he became somewhat of a local hero on campus.[21] Monk liked McClure enough to keep him for two more gigs—a week at the Village Vanguard and two weeks at the Aqua Lounge in Philadelphia. But he practically never spoke to him, and the baroness, who came to every performance, acted as if McClure did not exist. Hardly an ideal environment for the kind of master-apprentice mentoring the jazz world was known for. One of the few times Monk spoke, it was to level a complaint. In a fit of inspiration, McClure suddenly decided to play a bowed solo. After the set Monk politely asked his bassist to "leave the bow alone."

> McClure: Is there something you don't like about it?
> Monk: Uh, the sound.[22]

By the end of May, McClure had moved on and the Thelonious Monk quartet went back to being a threesome with a perennial want ad for a bassist.

Filling the bass chair ceased to become an urgent matter that summer, because George Wein decided to reconstitute the Giants of Jazz for a series of festivals all across the United States, followed by a European tour. Opening with the New Orleans Jazz and Heritage Fair, the festival circuit traveled to Oakland, Hampton Institute, Atlanta, New York City, Houston, Cincinnati, Monterey, and Philadelphia.[23] Wein took a page from the "Schlitz Salute to Jazz" tours, holding huge multiday concerts in stadiums and fairgrounds headlined by pop and R&B artists such as Aretha Franklin, Roberta Flack, and Ike and Tina Turner, as well as Nina Simone, B. B. King, Ray Charles, among others. The Giants of Jazz fell midway on the totem pole of popularity, functioning as a nostalgic throwback to the bop era. To some concertgoers they were the real deal, for others they represented a living museum, and for still others they were a chance to go to the concession stand.

No band member, except perhaps for Art Blakey, seemed gung-ho about another reunion, but it paid well in an era when commercial opportunities for jazz were disappearing. Monk earned roughly $2,000 per concert, and on the European leg of the tour they commanded anywhere between $10,000 and $15,000 a concert, or as much as $25,000 to $30,000 for two nightly shows.[24] The Giants' first outing in New Orleans disappointed critic Tom Bethell, who believed they were more interested in creating fireworks than making music. Except for Monk, "who . . . seemed alone to be attempting to convey a feeling of lyricism." The rest of the band "was dedicated to a cult of individualism which supposedly demonstrates itself in the attainment of great technical proficiency on one's instrument."[25] Nevertheless, the group was warmly received despite the Municipal Auditorium's horrible acoustics. Whatever press they may have gotten was overshadowed by Nina Simone's searing remarks from the stage about racism and her controversial effort to replace B. B. King's white pianist with a black one. She reminded everyone that the Sixties were not over.[26]

The remaining regional concerts were no different. The repertoire remained largely unchanged from the previous year, except now " 'Round Midnight" was the *only* Monk tune in the book. They added a few more tunes, including the ballads "I Can't Get Started" and "Stardust," Juan Tizol's "Perdido," and more Gillespie originals such as "And Then She Stopped" and "Kush."[27] The big test was New York: Wein's bold reinvention of the Newport Festival into a nine-day extravaganza spread all over the city. The Giants were scheduled to play twice—opening at the Philharmonic on Saturday, July 1, and nearly closing the festivities at Yankee Stadium exactly a week later, with a performance at the Houston Astrodome Jazz Festival sandwiched in between. For the opening, Max Roach and percussionist Big Black (Danny Ray) augmented the Giants' rhythm section on "A Night in Tunisia," setting up a drum duel between Blakey and Roach. All the fireworks produced few sparks; the Philharmonic concert received mixed and poor reviews. Don Heckman attributed what he thought was a poor performance to "the difficulties of getting highly inventive individuals to accept the discipline of an ensemble situation."[28] Leonard Feather praised Monk's handling of " 'Round Midnight," while dismissing him for being "weak as a rhythm functionary," and minced no words disparaging Max Roach's "excessive . . . applause-milking drum duel with Art Blakey."[29] Predictably, Feather noted that it was Dizzy who "dominated the group with a torrent of fiery, witty, febrile choruses." He was the star and, once again, the leader of the leaderless band. And yet, if audience response is any measure, then one might argue that Thelonious ultimately stole the show when he walked on stage alone and played a ninety-second, unaccompanied version of "I Love You, Sweetheart of All My Dreams." When it was over, an awestruck George Wein stood on stage, waited for the applause to die down, and simply said, "Wow! What can you say after that?"[30]

Monk didn't make it to Houston due to illness (probably fatigue), but he did join the Giants in Yankee Stadium the next day, despite pouring rain and an unexpectedly small crowd.[31] Because of temporary personnel changes, the last two stops on the U.S. tour produced some variation on what had become a routine performance. For Philadelphia's Quaker City Jazz Festival (September 22), Curtis Fuller replaced Kai Winding and Larry Ridley subbed for Al McKibbon.[32] The previous week at the Monterey Jazz Festival (September 16), Dizzy couldn't make it and Roy Eldridge and Clark

Terry filled in.[33] With Gillespie's absence, Monk seemed to have taken more of the spotlight. Before the Giants played a note, the audience reserved their loudest and longest ovation for Monk—who was introduced last.[34] On the opening number, "Blue 'n' Boogie," Sonny Stitt pays tribute to Monk by quoting "Rhythm-a-ning" in his solo, while Monk's own solo, full of dissonant block chords, seems to pay homage to Mary Lou Williams—the originator of "Rhythm-a-ning," who happened to be on the bill. He does wonders with "'Round Midnight," including a variation on Dizzy's famous introduction to the song. But overall, Monk seems uninspired. His solos wander a bit, lacking the structural coherence he was known for, and his accompaniment sounds mechanical. The one tune where Monk comes alive is "The Man I Love" featuring Roy Eldridge, who plays like a man possessed. His lyricism, energy, and sense of swing seem to have inspired Monk, who suddenly sounds like his old self—or rather, his young self. The crowd certainly agreed; their approval was deafening.[35]

The lithium treatment may have contributed to Monk's state of malaise and boredom heard on these recordings, but it probably had more to do with the setting. When Thelonious played the Vanguard that summer with his own quartet in between the Giants tour, he was alert and engaged.[36] A private tape from their June 15 gig reveals a more comfortable Monk and gives us a glimpse into the group's overall development a year after Toot joined the band. Both Toot and Jeffrey had grown more assertive in their attack, and with the addition of British-born Dave Holland, an incredibly strong bassist who had recently ended a two-year association with Miles Davis, the band's overall sound achieved a denser quality. Everyone plays with a level of ferocity uncharacteristic of Monk's previous bands, and Toot's powerful polyrhythms drive the ensemble. Monk comps continuously, never leaving the piano bench, and at times it's as if he is fighting to be heard over the rest of the band. And yet at no point does Monk sound bored or disengaged. His solos are substantial. On "Evidence" and "Rhythm-a-ning," he walks us through a quarter-century of Monkish phrases associated with those tunes. And on "Off Minor" and "Hackensack," he reminds his sidemen that the best improvisations build on the melody. Indeed, Toot follows his dad with one of his only drum solos of the night by pounding out the theme of "Hackensack" using every part of his drum kit. The band is still a bit rough around the edges; Toot occasionally pushes the tempo, as he does on "Straight, No Chaser," and Jeffrey leaves little or no space between phrases, filling every gap with trills, honks, long tones, and flurries of sixteenth notes. But Monk digs what he hears. All of Monk's solos play off the drummer, who in turn tries his best to follow his dad's instructions—to swing and swing some more.[37]

Despite Monk's disappointing experiences on the festival circuit, he had a pretty good summer. He suffered no mood swings and by some accounts he seemed a little more talkative. Joseph Wilson, a Columbia University student who was romantically involved with Boo Boo at the time, remembers having a couple of substantial conversations with her father during the course of the summer. Wilson impressed Monk. Here was this working-class kid, raised in a gang-infested neighborhood in Chicago, with a full scholarship to an Ivy League school and a commitment to social justice. At the time, he was affiliated with the youth wing of the Communist Party USA,[38] active in the W. E. B. DuBois Community Center in Harlem, and completely fearless. Indeed, he was first drawn to Boo Boo precisely because most men found her intimidating. "She had a majestic quality. That's what really attracted me, that and her stunning beauty. She was tall, about five foot, six, and usually wore heels. She struck me as not only attractive, but she seemed to be very aloof, distant. Boo Boo was a real challenge."[39] Monk appreciated the fact that Wilson wasn't intimidated or fawning all over him when they met. "Monk was actually pretty talkative. He asked me, 'What are you doing?' Then I got into the whole thing about how the masses have to take power, we have to redistribute the wealth, black people are catching hell. And he said, 'Well, I agree with that.' We spoke maybe for two hours, which was even more intense than the discussions I would have with Boo Boo. . . . He agreed with my analysis of the system. And he'd say things like, 'You a radical cat, yeah.' He was encouraging. He didn't have anything negative to say about it. He didn't come back and counter the arguments. He did ask me, 'How do you think all this is going to happen? Are there other people who think like you?' He never spoke about himself. He never revealed anything about his life or the family, but he was very interested in society and what young people were thinking."[40]

The quartet spent the first week of October at the Vanguard, with Reggie Workman holding down the bass chair, and then disbanded for a month while Monk took off for Europe with the Giants of Jazz. The schedule called for sixteen cities in twenty-two days, usually two concerts a night.[41] The road manager, a young Swiss man named Willie Leiser, did his best to hold everything together, but the trip was marred with problems from the beginning. In Paris, they were scheduled to play two shows six hours apart (6:30 p.m. and 12:30 a.m.); on the way to London, Blakey's cymbals were stolen; in Budapest half the entourage came down with a terrible virus.[42] (And Nellie tried her best to heal the sick with carrot juice.) American jazz critic Harriet Choice, traveling with the group, saw the effects of their grueling schedule and unfortunate luck on their performance: "They are tired and hungry, and their shows are hardly impressive."[43]

Sometimes problems became opportunities. When Dizzy Gillespie missed his flight to Vienna, tour mates Clark Terry and trumpeter Cat Anderson filled in. The next night in Cologne, Roy Haynes took over for Blakey, thus generating a different yet no less exciting rhythmic dynamic.[44] But much like the U.S. tour, critics and some fans grumbled that the thrill had gone. Reflecting on what many others were feeling, British writer Pete Gamble wrote, "Those of us who were lucky enough to catch the Giants last year must have left their recent performance . . . feeling a trifle disappointed. It was patently obvious that the important spark was missing, and that the rapport between musicians and audience engendered last year had waned."[45] There was, however, one patently obvious change: The band added more Monk tunes to the book, namely "Straight, No Chaser" and "Epistrophy." This seemed to stir Monk to greater heights, and reviewers took notice, since he was often singled out for praise.[46] The tour ultimately evolved into a celebration of Monk's work, culminating in a studio session Wein arranged in Berne, Switzerland, a few days before they were due back in the States.

It would be the last time Monk would set foot in a recording studio, and yet what they laid down that afternoon could have been called the story of Thelonious. Starting things off with a fifteen-minute version of "Straight, No Chaser," the band launched into an arrangement of "Thelonious" based on his 1947 Blue Note recording. Apparently arranged just for this session, the horns only play on the "head," leaving Monk free to noodle around with the descending chord changes he loved so much. The long whole-tone runs are absent, as are the sudden flights into stride piano, but what he might have lost in dexterity he made up for in sheer musicality. The standards selected were also Monk favorites—"Don't Blame Me," featuring Sonny Stitt, and an unusually fleet version of "Sweet and Lovely" featuring Kai Winding. Even Dizzy's feature, "I Waited for You," had a Monk connection—it was among the last songs they recorded together when Monk was a member of Gillespie's big band in 1946. Finally, the Giants sign off in Monk style with "Epistrophy," which Blakey accents in a bouncy, funky beat resembling Lee Morgan's "Sidewinder."[47] The entire LP is a loving tribute to Monk, and whatever tensions may have lingered between him and Dizzy evaporated that afternoon. The band is in sync, and the displays of virtuosity and individual prowess seem to give way to playfulness, humor, and deep listening.

The Giants played their last two concerts in Tel Aviv and Barcelona before returning on November 16. Monk flew directly to Chicago, where his quartet played two nights at the Brown Shoe, and then rushed back home for a gig at the Vanguard during Thanksgiving week. He opened to a full house of appreciative fans and critics, among them Tom Piazza, who described Monk's group (with Dave Holland on bass) as "his best in some time." He also noted that while his repertoire hasn't changed in years, he still delights audiences with his fresh interpretations, backed by a gang of younger players whose style can only be described as contemporary.[48] In other words, the old man wasn't dead just yet.

But death felt awfully close. On the fifth day of this run at the Vanguard, Thelonious got word that Hall Overton succumbed to cirrhosis of the liver. He was only fifty-two.[49] Monk knew he had been ill for some time, but Overton's death caught him off guard, since he had just seen him play at Bradley's piano bar two months earlier.[50] Either the night of his passing or the next night, Monk chose to play only standards. Barry Harris bore witness to this astonishing evening. "He didn't play like the sparing Monk . . . the spacious Monk. He played it more like the 'fluent' Monk, like Bud Powell would play."[51]

Exhausted from work and travel, Thelonious took December and part of January off. Nellie did not. As more and more friends and musicians sought her out for health advice and healing juices, she kept her machines running full pitch, sometimes through the wee hours of the morning. The apartment began to resemble a health food store. According to their niece Jackie, "The neighbors would complain because they had so much trash, since it would leave lots of pulp. And in the middle of the night, she would run two machines grinding up carrots and celery. It was so loud, it drove the neighbors crazy. One person, an attorney, threatened to sue."[52] Monk complained, too. He desired peace and quiet and he wanted all the health-seekers to go home. But there were other sources of tension between him and Nellie. They continued to struggle financially, but increasingly the burden of attending to Monk's business affairs fell on Nellie's shoulders. She was already his de facto personal manager and assistant road manager, administered his publishing, organized his tax records, and had assumed most of the duties for which Harry and later Jules Colomby were responsible. She was in way over her head. Their accountant, Morris Zuckerman, wrote many frustrating letters to Nellie pleading with her to sign a document, provide information—in short, take care of business. Their tax returns were perennially late, and in 1972 they were assessed an extra $1,000 for failing to file a New York State withholding tax statement.[53] A few months later, she almost lost some family belongings when a storage bill went unpaid for several months.[54] Furthermore, Nellie was bombarded with contracts as well as queries from record companies about reissues, royalties, permissions, among other things. The additional royalties were minuscule and came sporadically—when they came at all (some companies could not keep up with the Monks' recent moves).[55] Nellie worked to keep abreast of the paperwork, but she also needed time to make her juices and nurse others. Monk had become so dependent on Nellie that now he felt neglected.

The situation came to a head after the quartet returned to the Vanguard at the end of January. One night, Nica drove Thelonious and Paul Jeffrey home. When they arrived in front of Monk's apartment, he refused to leave. "He sat in the car," Paul Jeffrey explained. "I remember it was cold as a bitch. She kept turning the heat on and off because she couldn't keep the car running the whole time. So about six o'clock in the morning, I left. I got on the train and went to Coney Island."[56] She eventually persuaded Monk to go inside, but he didn't stay long. The next afternoon, Thelonious called Nica to come pick him up. There were no harsh words exchanged, no apparent anger—just a desire to move out. "I was there the day Nica came and got him," Jackie recalled. "She said, 'Come on Thelonious. Let's get the fuck out of here,' in her clipped British accent. I could still see her holding out her hand. They got on the elevator and that was it. He moved in with Nica and never came back."[57]

At first, Nellie was distraught. Despite all the stress she endured caring for Thelonious, she couldn't imagine living apart from her husband. They were best friends and she still adored him. She recruited Bertha Hope to help out: "Nellie sent me to Weehawken and said, 'Somebody's got to go over there and tell Thelonious to come back. See, I can even help him with the juices. I'm saving people. He doesn't understand. I'm helping people.' But Thelonious's position was, 'I'm not coming back until the juicer goes. When Nellie gets rid of the juicer and all those people she has that she's helping, I'll come back.'"[58] Once the initial panic faded, all parties came to agree that the move to Weehawken was a good idea. Nica had the space and resources Monk needed to become healthy again; not to mention it was an ideal location. Nellie, Toot, and Boo Boo thought moving him out of the city would make him less accessible, to the annoying fans and fellow musicians who wanted to get high with him.[59] And the move gave Nellie a much-needed respite. It freed her to advance her own knowledge of minerals, vitamins, and enzymes, eventually leading her to start a short-lived retail business.[60]

To call Monk's move a separation, however, would be a misnomer. Nica and Nellie's relationship was not harmed by the change; on the contrary, they teamed up rather well to provide the best care possible. Nica gave Monk the second floor, where he had a small bedroom, his own bathroom, and a large room with a panoramic view of the Hudson and a Steinway grand placed not far from his door. For the first couple of years, 63 Kingswood practically became Nellie's second home. Toot: "My mother used to come into New York and go back to New Jersey every night on the bus. She'd come into New York, take care of the banking business, whatever things she had to do, look out for her daughter and then get on the bus. She did that for a year."[61] Nica wasn't much of a cook, but she did have hired help, an older Englishwoman known affectionately as Miss D. Pianist Barry Harris also lived there, and although Harris and Monk rarely interacted, the family took comfort in knowing that Thelonious wouldn't be left alone. All in all, Nica provided a quiet, comfortable setting. If Monk had one grievance, it was the overwhelming feline presence—over sixty cats, by most accounts. Marion reported that when she came out to see her brother, Nica "had to keep them out of his room, he wouldn't allow them in his room. He didn't like them."[62]

Above all, the Weehawken house became a place for Monk to convalesce. Not long after the move, he confessed to Nica that he genuinely worried about his health. "We were driving home from New York, and he suddenly turned to me and said, 'I am very seriously ill.' This is the only thing Thelonious has ever been heard to say about being ill, at all. He never said it again."[63] Numerous physical ailments slowed him down considerably, from lung congestion and chronic fatigue to his ongoing prostate issues. He woke up every morning and got fully dressed, sometimes jacket and tie, and spent most of the day lying on his bed, watching television, or taking long walks around the neighborhood. Ironically, as the lithium brought his mood swings under control, he lost his desire to play. The medication certainly may have contributed to his feelings of listlessness, but his ongoing problems with incontinence made him reluctant to leave the house, let alone play in public.[64] He hardly worked in 1973. Besides a couple of nights at the Top of the Gate in February, and a week at the Half Note in June, he cancelled all of his club dates that year. He pulled out of performances with the Giants of Jazz in California and turned down the Newport in New York Jazz Festival. The people who showed up to hear Monk at Carnegie Hall on July 7 for the "So-Lo Piano Evening," dedicated to the music of Art Tatum, were disappointed when he did not show. Had they read the billing more closely, however, they would have realized that Monk was never included in the program. Rather, Thelonious Monk, *Jr.*, was scheduled to play that very night, but next door at the Carnegie Recital Hall with the jazz/funk band, Natural Essence.[65]

The elder Monk stopped working, for the most part, in 1973. Over the next three years he would come out occasionally for a concert, but he stopped playing clubs and would not leave New York. He paid an enormous financial cost for his inactivity. While Nellie struggled to turn her juice passion into a business, she continued to manage Monk's affairs and eke out a living on royalties and licensing fees. A flurry of reissues by Blue Note and Milestone (a division of Fantasy headed by Orrin Keepnews) helped out a little, but in the period from 1972 to the end of 1976, income from sales, fees, and BMI earnings amounted to less than $15,000 total.[66] But even in the world of reissues, record companies continued to deduct production costs. Milestone, for example, deducted $3,080 from Monk's royalties to pay for remastering.[67] Meanwhile, in 1974, Columbia Records tried to cash in by reissuing a two-LP set combining his big band concert recordings, supplemented with long, effusive notes by Leonard Feather. Titled *Who's Afraid of the Big Band Monk?* it is adorned with a horrible caricature of Monk as a grinning wolf, and if that wasn't insulting enough his name was frequently misspelled in their promotional materials.[68] Still, the LP sold fairly well and was selected as one of the top picks by *Billboard Magazine*; but it did not do much to put a dent in Monk's debt to the label. At the end of 1976, Monk owed Columbia $16,594.71.[69] Meanwhile, Nica continued to pay for Thelonious's upkeep and his mounting medical expenses. He spent much of his time in and out of hospitals—sometimes to run tests or adjust his medication, other times for prostate issues.

The precious few times Monk came out in public, it was always big, always memorable. He appeared only once in 1974, at Carnegie Hall—and he wasn't supposed to be there. George Wein had organized a tribute to Monk's music on April 6 to be performed by his latest creation: the New York Jazz Repertory Company. Wein had tried unsuccessfully to persuade Monk to perform again, so he had Paul Jeffrey put together a fifteen-piece band with strings and hired Barry Harris on piano. The concert reunited several Monk alumni—old and new. Budd Johnson, Julius Watkins, Eddie Bert, and Charlie Rouse were among the front line, while Toot occupied the drum chair. Nica practically had to drag Monk there; he had no desire to leave the house and no interest in hearing his music—especially played wrong. But when he walked into Carnegie Hall and saw the crowds and the stage and his old friends, something happened. Trumpeter Jimmy Owens, one of the musical directors of the Jazz Repertory Company, saw what transpired from the mezzanine. "I was able to look at the backstage door, and Barry was out on stage getting ready to play. Paul Jeffrey was about to count the song off, and who should walk out of the door but Monk. Everybody just went crazy. Monk sat down at the piano, just started to play. He didn't know the arrangements or anything."[70] The stunned crowd rose to their feet and gave Monk a long, thunderous, and, for some, tearful ovation before he played a single note.[71] The entire evening was electric. Critic Peter Keepnews (Orrin's son), who sensed that Monk's presence really did lift the bandstand, singled out Rouse for special praise, writing that he "may never have sounded more in tune with [Monk's] music than he did this night."[72] But Thelonious outshone everyone with his beautifully restrained solos and imaginative accompaniment. For Toot "it was an absolutely magical, magical evening."[73] For Martin Williams, seeing Monk that evening "provided one of the great moments in American music of my lifetime."[74] Afterward, Wein asked Monk if he would consider going back on the road. When Thelonious asked why, Wein replied, "The whole world wants you, Thelonious." He just smiled.[75]

In many ways, Wein was right. The serious jazz aficionados hungered for Monk's music, and the wave of reissues moved critics to call for his return to the stage and studio.[76] In the fall of 1975, his longtime friend Ran Blake organized a tribute concert for

Monk at the New England Conservatory in hopes of drawing him out.[77] But the world to which Wein referred was becoming smaller with each passing year. His own festival was proof; pop, R&B, rock, and even funk artists headlined the "jazz" festival circuit. In order to stay relevant, jazz musicians increasingly turned to electronic instruments, incorporated popular dance rhythms, fused jazz with rock and R&B. Willie "The Lion" died in 1973 with little fanfare. Duke left the following year. And Thelonious Monk ceased to be a household name.

Monk made his only 1975 appearance at Newport in New York in July. Philharmonic Hall was packed with young people, not to see Monk but to catch the Keith Jarrett Quartet and a popular group called Oregon—known for what later would be labeled "New Age" music. But the kids apparently dug him. The *Wall Street Journal* critic knew that half the room had never heard of Thelonious Monk, but once his quartet took off they "drew the loudest and most sustained applause."[78] John S. Wilson got a little nostalgic for the younger Monk when he noted the pianist's bare head, his polite stage manner, and the fact that "his craggy, angular style on the piano has smoothed out to more freely flowing lines."[79] Whitney Balliett echoed Wilson, lamenting how "his style, with its crabbed single note lines, crazy chords, and high, wicked humor, had inexplicably vanished. His playing resembled a gingerbread house stripped of it ornamentation."[80] Times had certainly changed. "Monk, once considered a radical innovator," Wilson declared, was now "the traditionalist centerpiece."[81]

In 1975, Nica and friends tried to motivate Monk by applying for a Guggenheim Fellowship on his behalf. Orrin Keepnews and Martin Williams wrote loving appraisals of Monk's importance to American culture. Williams minced no words, declaring Monk "the greatest living jazz composer. And that means, from my own point of view, that he is one of the great American composers of whatever category." Keepnews concurred: "As a performer, as an influence on countless younger artists during the past three decades, and as a composer he has been and continues to be of towering significance." But he also added that Monk needed money and that his recent illness had hindered his ability to work. A fellowship, he argued, could make it possible for him to begin composing again.[82] It worked; Thelonious Monk was among the 300 distinguished recipients.[83] The cash grant came in handy, helping to offset his mounting expenses, but it did not inspire him to write or play. Ironically, 1976, the year he was awarded the Guggenheim, was also the last year he performed in public.

On March 26, he played Carnegie Hall with a quintet consisting of Toot, Paul Jeffrey, Larry Ridley, and trumpeter Lonnie Hillyer. Monk had a lot to say that evening, pulling out tunes, such as "In Walked Bud" and "Reflections," that had gone unplayed for years. Audiences and critics cheered. Gary Giddins called Monk's solos "the pearls of the evening. . . . Monk plays the piano as purposefully as anyone ever has, and there is much emotion and beauty in his work."[84] Ira Gitler thought the band "did not really do his music justice," but Monk himself played with "crisp authority." He was especially taken with Monk's solo piano pieces, which Gitler found "redolent of his special, wistful, unsticky brand of what I like to call sentiment without sentimentality."[85]

Monk returned to Carnegie Hall three months later—Wednesday, June 30, to be exact—for what would be his final concert.[86] This time he appeared with his regular quartet and shared the bill with Dizzy Gillespie. It was as if the whole room knew this was Monk's last hurrah, for the hall was filled with old friends and family. Marion was there; so was Thomas and virtually all the nieces and nephews on the Monk side. The Smiths were out in force, including Skippy, who had recently been slowed down by illness. Just about every jazz musician who didn't work that night showed up to catch a glimpse of the High Priest. Monk received a standing ovation as soon as he walked on the stage, and every tune was met with enthusiastic shouts and applause. Monk tried valiantly to give the people a great show, but on this night he struggled. While he showed exuberance, he spent most of the set sounding as if he were fighting the piano. His left hand seemed to be pounding the keys rather than playing, and his right hand fumbled more than usual. He managed to produce fine solos on "We See" and "Ba-Lue Bolivar Ba-Lues-Are," but every note was hard fought. Whitney Balliett in *The New Yorker* found the whole thing painful. "His playing was mechanical and uncertain, and, astonishingly, his great Gothic style had fallen away."[87]

Later that week, he and Nica spent the Fourth of July at Bradley's, a popular piano bar in Greenwich Village, to hear Barry Harris. Monk felt like playing, so he commandeered the piano bench for several minutes and worked out on a few tunes, to the audience's delight.[88] Little did anyone know that when he ambled out the door in the wee hours of the morning, the humid air still thick with the smell and haze of fireworks, he was never coming back.

The second floor of Nica's home became Monk's permanent retreat. His daily routine rarely varied. He would wake up, shower, don some of his finest threads only to lie back in bed to nap, stare at the ceiling, or watch TV—he developed a fondness for game shows like *The Price Is Right*. He emerged from his lair to eat or take a walk in the neighborhood, but he ignored the Ping-Pong table and avoided the piano. Once in a blue moon, Nica and Nellie dragged him to the city to hear some music in Central Park[89] or to catch a performance by one of his kids, but he preferred the quiet comfort of 63 Kingswood Road and the convenience of having a bathroom just a few steps away.[90] "He's not unhappy, and his mind works very well," Nica told writer Whitney Balliett not long before he died. "He knows what is going on in the world, and I don't know how, because he doesn't read the newspapers and he only watches a little telly. He's withdrawn, that's all. It's as though he had gone into retreat. He takes walks several times a week, and Nellie comes over from New York almost every day to cook for him. . . . Monk isn't really interested in seeing anyone. The strange thing is he looks beautiful. He has never said that he won't play the piano again. He suddenly went into this, so maybe he'll suddenly come out."[91]

Nica and all of his closest friends and family did what they could to jolt him out of his state, and the consensus was that the piano was the key. Barry Harris practiced just outside his door, as did Joel Forrester and any other pianist who dropped by to pay respects.[92] Nica encouraged it, hoping it might draw Monk out of his room and back to the keyboard. If Thelonious dug it, he'd keep the door open; if he didn't, he would slam the door shut. Leroy Williams's recollections of Monk during the period are pretty typical. Because the piano was outside his room, he and Barry Harris would rehearse upstairs and he would have to pass by Monk's bed to get to the bathroom. "When I walked in the room there was Monk laying on the bed all dressed up, suit, tie and everything. He was just lying there, almost like he was in a casket or something. So I said, 'Damn, Monk, you looking pretty sharp lying there. Where you going?' Monk said, 'Man, I'm not going anywhere.' So he's still lying there and when I come back out I go to close the door and he said, 'Leave the door open, man. I want to hear what you all doing.'"[93]

Monk received stacks of letters and cards from around the world (which he stashed under his bed[94]), and a steady stream of visitors and well-wishers—Steve Lacy, Doug Quackenbush, Dizzy, Blakey, Rouse, Randy Weston, Eddie Locke, Ben Riley, John Ore, to name but a fraction. George Wein called frequently, offering Monk an obscene amount of money to come out and play.[95] Orrin Keepnews called once and offered to come by and "talk about the old days." Monk replied unequivocaly, "No, I wouldn't." It was almost like old times, except that this time Thelonious answered the phone.[96] He usually accepted visitors graciously, but said very little. He gave one- or two-word replies and often grew impatient when the question of him playing again came up. Paul Jeffrey, who had begun teaching at Columbia University and Rutgers after 1976, tried to inspire Monk by organizing a student ensemble to play his songs outside his window. "It was cold that day! We played all the Overton charts and we were outside freezing. Finally, the Baroness let us in and we continued in the room next to his. We played a whole concert for Monk. . . . He never came out, but he had to have heard it."[97]

Monk's refusal to play and his reluctance to leave his room were regarded by virtually everyone close to him as symptomatic of his mental illness. But as Nica said, his mind worked; he was alert, alive, and still incredibly witty. In March of 1976, Thelonious happened to be listening to a special broadcast by Columbia University's radio station, WKCR, dedicated to his music. A guest expert began droning on about how Monk created extraordinary music, in spite of "playing the wrong notes on the piano." Perturbed, Monk dialed the Columbia switchboard and left a message to "tell the guy on the air, 'The piano ain't got no wrong notes.'"[98]

So to label Monk's reclusive behavior as evidence of deep depression is a little too simple, especially since his mental and physical health improved dramatically during this period. By late 1977, Nica discovered a new physician—Dr. Carl Pfeiffer, the founder and director of the Brain Bio Center in Princeton, New Jersey.[99] A pioneer in the development of orthomolecular psychiatry, Pfeiffer and his staff offered a more effective treatment to rectify Monk's chemical imbalances, combining lithium salts, diet, vitamin and mineral supplements, and weekly shiatsu massage. Within two years he improved dramatically. As Nica reported to Mary Lou Williams, "T. is being as good as gold, keeping strictly to his diet, & taking all the pills prescribed for him every day. . . . (He is much stronger, & can do all kinds of exercises he couldn't before.) His doctor (who is in Princeton) is the greatest expert there IS on this 'biochemical imbalance' business, & T. is steadily getting better, though he still has a LONG way to go."[100]

If his health improved and his manic-depressive cycles were under control, why did he stop playing? Having spent the better part of fourteen years tracing Monk's every step, I was not surprised by his decision. In fact, I wondered why he did not retire earlier. Consider the final years of his working career: his record label dropped him, he could barely sustain a working band, the money was inadequate, he was practically reduced to opening for rock and R&B bands, he endured unremitting criticism for playing the same music, he lost all inspiration to compose, the lithium treatments deadened his senses and slowed his creative drive, and his ongoing battle with incontinence made performing an ordeal. And his old friends kept dying. Wilbur Ware split in 1979 at the age of 56, and Mary Lou Williams passed on two years later.[101] So why *should* he feel like playing? His siblings were among the few loved ones who understood and accepted his decision. During one of his many visits, Thomas asked, "'Brother, what should I tell everybody? They want to know why you don't want to play anymore? You want me to tell them you retired?' And he said, 'Yes, tell them I retired.'"[102] Marion would come over every so often and take walks with Thelonious. He made it clear to her that "he didn't feel like playing or appearing in front of the public."[103]

Nellie also accepted Monk's decision, and did what she could to comfort him during those final years. But she was also trying to start a life of her own in which her precious husband was not at the center. It wasn't easy. Her juice business failed as a retail venture, and with Monk's royalties her primary source of revenue, Nellie struggled to make ends meet. And the business of handling Monk's business overwhelmed her. She couldn't keep up with all the licensing requests, contracts, and inquiries from record companies. Desperate for help, she turned to Don Sickler, a trumpeter and arranger who ran Second Floor Music, a music publishing company, with his wife, Maureen. Don Sickler recalls, "Nellie came in, literally, with shopping bags of unissued licenses and everything else, and just dumped it all on the floor—this unbelievable mess. She hadn't signed anything, and she had no money to pay us. Essentially Maureen and I worked for them for free for several years, just trying to organize. It was just unbelievable. She was way over her head and was doing nothing. Issuing no licenses, issuing nothing. They had no money. They would make whatever comes to Thelonious from BMI and that was about it. And a lot of the songs were not even registered. Of the 70 songs of Monk there were probably 30 of them registered." Sickler immediately contracted Harry Fox, a mechanical collection agency, to begin collecting fees on behalf of the Monk estate.[104]

As Nellie struggled to put her finances together, in May of 1977, tragedy struck: her baby sister Skippy succumbed to cancer just days after her fifty-fourth birthday.[105] It was a devastating loss. Besides Thelonious, Skippy was Nellie's best friend. She had always been there for the Monks—she gave them shelter when they were burned out of their house, and she saved Thelonious's life once. And when she lost her residence, her job, even her son, Monk and Nellie were there for her. At this point, Nellie threw much of her energy into her children and taking care of her husband's business.

Toot and Boo Boo's musical careers began taking off in 1976. Tenor saxophonist Clifford Jordan recognized Boo Boo's talents and recruited her for a recording session in May for his LP *Remembering Me-Me*. She and Hank Diamond Smith were featured on "Powerful Paul Robeson," a beautiful, inspiring tone poem sung to an unbelievably intricate melody. She acquitted herself brilliantly with the kind of deep emotion that could have only been personal. In many ways, it was. Robeson, who had died four months earlier, was one of Thelonious's heroes. And like her dad, he spent his sunset years withdrawn and silent.[106] The lyrics could have described Monk: "His life was more than just a song . . . he sang true as he stood/beautiful."[107] When few people were paying attention to Boo Boo, Jordan stepped in and became something of a mentor, encouraging her to develop her voice.[108] Even her brother was initially unaware of her vocal work. He first heard her sing with Jordan's band in September at a free outdoor concert at Rockefeller Center. "One night in 1976 my mother said, 'Oh, I'm going to hear Boo Boo sing.' I said, 'Going to hear her sing? Sing what? With who?' I didn't know she sang. My mother said, 'Oh, well, I'm going down to hear her sing with Clifford Jordan.' I'm like, 'Singing! With Clifford Jordan?! What the hell? What the hell is going on?' But I was, at that point, twenty-six, deep into my young musician thing, she was twenty-three, just really getting to the age where maybe an older brother really starts paying attention to his younger sister again, because we're sort of moving into the peer zone. . . . I mean, she was completely off of my radar until my mother said that night, 'I'm going to hear Boo Boo.'"[109] She stole the show, singing Paul Robeson "with great feeling" and delighting the audience with her rendition of "Summertime" and "'Round Midnight."[110]

The person she most impressed, however, was her brother, who promptly drafted her into his own band, Cycles, which he had formed with former schoolmate Azzedin Weston. He had also been a percussionist for Natural Essence since 1973, a large R&B- and funk-influenced jazz ensemble organized by the Adderleys (Cannonball, Nat, and Nat, Jr.). Toot appreciated the band for its deep talent, heavy rhythmic drive, wide musical palette, and its lead female vocalist—the gifted Yvonne Fletcher. Fletcher, who was the same age as Boo Boo, was also an accomplished pianist and songwriter whose résumé included stints with Roberta Flack and jazz saxophonist Gene Ammons.[111] She was smart (at the time she was pursuing a degree in composition) . . . and she was gorgeous. Smitten, Toot eventually pursued Fletcher and eventually proposed marriage— though it wasn't his first proposal. Recognizing her enormous talent, Toot asked her to join Cycles and then, in 1977, formed the T. S. Monk Band with Fletcher and Boo Boo as the lead vocalists. Four years later, T. S. Monk rose to the top of the charts with their debut album *House of Music*, featuring their popular single, "Bon Bon Vie."[112] With "Bon Bon Vie," Toot and Boo Boo had finally fulfilled their father's elusive dream—to get a "hit."

The success of her children's musical careers, not to mention the prospect of a daughter-in-law, kept Nellie incredibly busy. So busy, in fact, that her trips to Wee-hawken grew less frequent. By 1979, Nellie's absence became a source of frustration for Nica. When Mary Lou Williams asked Nica to track down some publicity photos of Monk, she promised to get some from Nellie, "When (or *IF?) I see Nellie again (she has no telephone) . . . her visits are few and far between. . . ."[113] The time between visits certainly took its toll on Monk. For over four decades, Nellie had been his rock, his foundation, his sounding board. She picked up after him, dressed him, nursed him, and created the kind of environment that allowed him to work whenever he felt like it. Nica was there for him, but she was no substitute for Nellie. One day, about 1980 or '81, perhaps feeling a little romantic or nostalgic, he emerged from his room and sat down at the piano with Barry Harris. "He said, 'Let's play "My Ideal." ' So he started playing 'My Ideal.' He played a chorus; I played a chorus . . . I wish somebody had had a tape recorder because he made me play maybe a hundred choruses of 'My Ideal' and he played a hundred back and forth—non stop. . . . Well it could have been—I know it was over an hour but he made me just play that."[114] Monk knew the lyrics to every song he played, thus the simple words of hopeful, elusive love rang through his mind as he explored every dimension of J. Newell Chase's lovely ballad. And I bet Nellie was on his mind, too. After the final chorus, he got up from the piano and quietly retired to his room.

On Friday, February 5,1982, Barry Harris found Thelonious in his room unconscious and called an ambulance. The sixty-four-year old Monk had suffered a stroke, complicated by a bout of hepatitis. He was taken to Englewood Hospital, where he lay in a coma for twelve days. On February 17, at 8:10 a.m., Monk finally checked out. Nellie was there, holding him gently in her arms.[115]

POSTLUDE

You know what's the loudest noise in the world, man? The loudest noise in the world is silence.

Thelonious Monk

If the world had all but forgotten Thelonious Sphere Monk, no one told the over 1,000 people who tried to cram into St. Peter's Church on Lexington and 54th Street to attend his memorial service. On Monday morning, February 22, the musicians arrived in full force, and many contributed to what turned into a musical celebration of Monk's life and work. Monk's own recording of "Abide With Me" was selected for the processional, as the pallbearers carried him in and opened the casket to allow the world one last glimpse of the High Priest. For the next three hours he lay there, nattily attired, awash in his own music. Old friends, new friends, and young musicians who knew Thelonious only from records, played their last respects: Paul Jeffrey, Sadik Hakim, Muhal Richard Abrams, Tommy Flanagan, Max Roach, Ray Copeland, Walter Bishop, Jr., Sheila Jordan, John Ore, Gerry Mulligan, Frankie Dunlop, Eddie Bert, Ben Riley, Larry Ridley, Ahmed Abdul-Malik, Barry Harris, Lonnie Hillyer, Marian McPartland, Adam Makowicz, Ronnie Matthews, Randy Weston, and, of course, the Rutgers Jazz Ensemble. The right Reverend John Garcia Gensel presided, Ira Gitler eulogized, and George Wein and Walter Bishop, Jr., shared personal tributes.[1] Three generations of Monks and Smiths were on hand, as well as the Baroness and her daughters. Nellie and Nica sat and mourned together.

Following the benediction, the funeral caravan took the long route to Ferncliff Cemetery in Hartsdale, New York, traveling west on 52nd along what was once Swing Street, turning up West End Avenue, past the Phipps Houses on 63rd, and then on to Harlem to the old Cecil Hotel where Minton's used to be.[2] The trip proceeded without incident until they reached Hartsdale. Less than a mile from the cemetery gates, Nica's car, which was leading the caravan just behind the hearse, unexpectedly broke down. She was carrying the immediate family, including Nellie and her kids. Considering the prospects of divine intervention, Nellie asked, "What does it mean?" Boo Boo replied, with her father's legendary wit, "It means that everyone in the front get to the back, everyone in the back go to the front!"[3] Her words elicited gales of laughter, and yet they were profound, if not prophetic: "So the last shall be first, and the first last: for many be called, but few chosen."[4] This was Monk's life condensed to a parable—a life of constant struggle for work, for recognition, for respect as a pianist and composer. Not until the early 1960s had his fortunes shifted, and he moved from last to first, and not for long. The musical genius was again recast as the mad eccentric, who then became the boring old man, who subsequently metamorphosed into a relic of the past. Boo Boo vowed to change the order, to make her father first again and to remind the world of his enormous contribution to modern music. And she launched her crusade at the very moment when the T. S. Monk Band was riding on the crest of fame and potential fortune.[5]

First, Boo Boo formed an advisory board consisting of family members and close friends—most prominently choreographer/dancer Nina Garland, Monk's former drummer-turned-historian, Willie Jones, and New York Supreme Court Justice Bruce Wright. She envisioned several different projects to memorialize her father—each one linked Monk's musical legacy to the neighborhood in which he grew up. She wanted to save the Phipps Houses from being demolished. She was living in the very same apartment in which her father grew up, but the buildings were in shambles. Ever since the Phipps Foundation sold the buildings in 1961, the property had changed hands at least thirty times. By 1982, only 92 of the 346 apartments were legally occupied, as squatters and drug addicts took over. The then-current landlord planned to sell the land to developers, but Boo Boo and Toot, along with several residents, appealed to the Landmarks Preservation Commission to declare the Phipps Houses an historical landmark.[6] She also launched a campaign to rename that section of West 63rd Street "Thelonious Sphere Monk Circle."[7]

Boo Boo's most ambitious plan was to establish a scholarship program and a theatrical workshop in Monk's name, to be housed at Martin Luther King, Jr., High School on 65th and Amsterdam. To endow the workshop and scholarship, she conceived of an elaborate work of art and history that would take the forms of a documentary film, a staged musical production, and a photo exhibition that would tell the story of the San Juan Hill neighborhood through Monk's life and work. Calling it "Always Know, Two Is One: The Philosophy of Thelonious Sphere Monk," she hoped this ambitious work would draw links between black migration and settlement in the neighborhood, the struggle for civil and human rights and social justice, and the vision and music of Thelonious Monk. Most importantly, Boo Boo's dream was to establish a permanent foundation in her father's name that could support and oversee these specific projects while keeping Monk's legacy alive.[8]

She succeeded in getting at least one of her goals accomplished. On June 25, 1983, the Monk and Smith clans joined hundreds of fans and San Juan Hill residents for the unveiling of "Thelonious Sphere Monk Circle." Thelonious's brother, Reverend Thomas Monk, spoke, as did George Wein, Judge Bruce Wright, and journalist Marc Crawford. And, of course, there was music. Barry Harris played solo piano, followed by performances by Abbey Lincoln, Max Roach, Clark Terry, Frank Foster, Walter Davis, Jr., and Larry Ridley.[9]

Sadly, Boo Boo's triumph was marred by the recent news that she *and* Yvonne Fletcher, Toot's fiancée, had been diagnosed with breast cancer. The chances that these two young black women, friends, bandmates, not yet thirty years old, could be stricken with breast cancer simultaneously is astonishing. Boo Boo and Yvonne learned of their condition some time in the late winter or spring, but in lieu of chemotherapy or a mastectomy, they both opted to check into the Livingston-Wheeler Clinic in San Diego, California.[10] The clinic's founder, Dr. Virginia Livingston-Wheeler, held the unorthodox view that cancer was caused by a weakened immune system that enables the unchecked growth of particular bacteria. Thus she treated cancer by targeting the immune system with vaccines, antibiotics, megavitamins and nutritional supplements, digestive enzymes, enemas, and diet.[11] Although the clinic had treated nearly 10,000 patients by the time Boo Boo and Yvonne checked in, and many of her patients survived cancer, the Livingston-Wheeler methods were later questioned by the California State Health Department and the American Cancer Society.[12] A few months into their treatment, neither woman showed any improvement. On October 23, Yvonne Fletcher died in San Diego. She was one week away from her thirtieth birthday.[13] Boo Boo stayed in California and stuck with the treatments. Less than three months later, she too died.[14]

Nellie and Toot were devastated. Just two years after losing Thelonious, Nellie had to bury her baby daughter. And in a span of three months, Toot lost his only sibling *and* the woman he had intended to marry. He stopped playing music and went into seclusion for several months. When he emerged, he knew what he had to do: He threw himself into the work Boo Boo had left unfinished. With help and guidance from Nellie, several relatives, and longtime friends, Toot steered the Thelonious Monk Foundation from a fledgling family-run outfit to an internationally respected institution. In 1986, he and his board teamed up with Maria Fisher of the Beethoven Society of America and launched the Thelonious Monk Institute of Jazz to promote music education and to train and encourage new generations of jazz musicians.[15] The founding of the Monk Institute was a fitting tribute to an artist who was always willing to share his musical knowledge with others but expected originality in return. The work inspired Toot to not only return to music but to devote most of his energies to studying and performing his father's compositions.[16]

In more ways than one, Boo Boo's dream has been realized, and Nellie, who would pass in 2002, lived long enough to see it come to fruition. The music world accepts Thelonious Monk as an American master. He has been the subject of award-winning documentaries, scholarly studies, prime-time television tributes, and in 2006 was awarded a posthumous Pulitzer Prize for his contribution to jazz. His compositions constitute the core of jazz repertory and are performed by artists from many different genres. "'Round Midnight," "Straight, No Chaser," "Well, You Needn't," "Ruby, My Dear," among others, have become bona-fide jazz standards; no self-respecting jazz musician today can get a job or participate in a jam session without knowing these tunes.

Indeed, even as Monk prepared to meet his maker, his music was just beginning to experience a renaissance. On November 1, 1981, producer Verna Gillis gathered an array of musicians—from Steve Lacy and Barry Harris to trombonist Roswell Rudd and pianist Anthony Davis—at Columbia University's Wollman Auditorium for over four hours of "Interpretations of Monk."[17] And the day Monk died, Charlie Rouse was in the studio with former bandmate Ben Riley, pianist Kenny Baron, and bassist Buster Williams, launching a new band called Sphere. They recorded only Monk tunes that day, resulting in the landmark LP *Four in One*.[18] Soon CBS Records was digging through its vaults to issue Monk's unreleased Columbia recordings, and every label—legitimate and bootleg—scrambled to put out whatever Monk they had on hand. A new generation of musicians explored his compositions with fresh ears and built on Monk's idioms, his use of space, dissonance, rhythmic displacement, his angular lines and devotion to melody, to create new works of their own. Jason Moran, Geri Allen, Matthew Shipp, Vijay Iyer, Anthony Davis, Jessica Williams, Marcus Roberts, Danilo Perez, Gonzalo Rublcaba, and Fred Hersch are just a fraction of the post-Monk generation of pianists/composers whose ideas have been profoundly shaped by a serious engagement with Monk's music.[19]

Yet, for all the accolades and formal recognition, for all the efforts to canonize Monk and place his bust on the mantel alongside Bach and Beethoven, we must remember that Monk was essentially a rebel. To know the man and his music requires digging Monk—out of the golden dustbins of posterity, out of the protected cells of museums—and restoring him to a tradition of sonic disturbance that forced the entire world to take notice. He broke rules and created a body of work and a sound no one has been able to duplicate.

If I've learned anything from this fourteen-year adventure, it is that duplicating Monk's sound has never been the point. "Play yourself!" he'd say.[20] "Play yourself" lay at the core of Monk's philosophy; he understood it as art's universal injunction. He demanded originality in others and he embodied it in everything he did—in his piano technique, in his dress, in his language, his humor, in the way he danced, in the way he loved his family and raised his children, and above all in his compositions. Original did not mean being different for the hell of it. For Monk, to be original meant reaching higher than one's limits, striving for something startling and memorable, and never being afraid to make mistakes. Originality is not always mastery, nor does it always yield success. But it is very hard work.

You know, anybody can play a composition like ["Body and Soul"] and use far-out chords and make it sound wrong. It's making it sound right that's not easy.[21]

ACKNOWLEDGMENTS

In many ways, writing this book parallels Thelonious Monk's life—a long, arduous, rewarding journey with a gang of people generously helping along the way. This book was a community project, and the community of family, friends, musicians, activists, scholars, writers, and others runs deep. First and foremost, it was the late Marc Crawford, an extraordinary writer, jazz expert, mentor, and friend who encouraged me to write a book on Monk and put me in touch with Thelonious Monk, Jr. (Toot), and his lovely wife, Gale. Toot gave me something even more valuable—permission. He and Gale endured years of my pleading phone calls and faxes, as I tried to make the case that I was capable of taking on such a monumental figure. I only convinced him after Dr. Peter Grain, Gale's brother, invited me out to Toot's place and Toot granted me a hearing. I showed up that day over a decade ago, brimming with exuberance and toting four years of research stuffed in three large boxes and my computer hard drive. Six hours later, Toot and Peter were convinced they found their man, and I left feeling as though I knew nothing about Thelonious Monk. Thus began a wonderful and fruitful collaboration.

I did not want to write an authorized biography, and Toot agreed. He never told me what to write, or asked for the right to approve anything, or required early drafts. He wasn't interested in hagiography; he always expressed an enormous respect for careful scholarship, and in our many hours of conversation he never shied away from difficult questions. He only asked me to do two things: "Dig deep and tell the truth." I could not have dreamed of a better situation.

Toot, Gale, and Peter introduced me to Monk's kith and kin. Mrs. Nellie Monk, who passed away in 2002, showed me nothing but kindness and generosity. She shared her juices, her special remedies, and her heartfelt concern after a car struck me down in Newark, New Jersey. (Ironically, three minutes before it happened, I was on the phone with Nellie, having just returned from a particularly productive day of research at Rutgers's Institute for Jazz Studies.) She also shared many, many stories. Some stories she took to the grave with her, keeping her promise to her husband to preserve their privacy. It was one of the qualities about Nellie I have come to appreciate.

The rest of the family and close friends were equally generous with their time. I'm particularly indebted to Evelyn ("Weetee") Smith, Jackie Bonneau, Benetta ("Teeny") Bines, Thomas Monk, Jr., and Alonzo White, not only for sharing stories but also rare photographs, tapes, and various documents. They made phone calls, answered my persistent questions, and actively supported my efforts to the bitter end. Huge thanks to

Theolonious Monk, Charlotte Washington, Geraldine Smith, Clifton Smith, Judith Smith, Dr. Anna Lou Smith, Helen Graham, Nica Val-Hackett, Barbara Monk, Almetta Monk Revis (North Carolina), and the New Haven Monk clan—Olivia Monk, Pam Kelley Monk, Conley F. Monk, Jr., Marcella Monk Flake, and Evelyn Pue—for the valuable knowledge they passed on, and to Marcellus Green for making connections, digging through the storage facility with me, and sharing stories, photos, and scrapbooks.

Much gratitude to Mavis Swire, Alberta Saunders, and Theo Wilson for sharing their stories of San Juan Hill; to Toni and David Behm for graciously opening up their home and sharing their memories and precious collection of documents from the Five Spot left by Toni's dad, Joe Termini, and to Iggy Termini for his memories; to Mrs. Bernice Slaughter and her son, Ed Slaughter, Jr., for recounting Monk's adventures in the Pacific Northwest; to Valerie Wilmer for the gift of her taped interview with Thelonious Monk (with John "Hoppy" Hopkins), conducted, coincidentally, on my third birthday; and to Nadine and Shaun de Koenigswarter, for sharing rare documents, photos, and memories of the Baroness.

Of course, boundless gratitude to the musicians who shared their stories—some of whom have since joined the ancestors: David Amram, David Baker, Richard Duck Baker, Ran Blake, Walter Booker, Tyrone Brown, Jaki Byard, Leon Ndugu Chancler, Ornette Coleman, Bob Cranshaw, Richard Davis, William Edmonson, Morris Edwards, Rose Gales, Leonard Gaskin, Kofi Ghanaba, Johnny Griffin, Barry Harris, Roy Haynes, Albert "Tootie" Heath, Eddie Henderson, Jon Hendricks, Steve Lacy, Abbey Lincoln, Teo Macero, Wynton Marsalis, Jackie McLean, Rene McLean, Mischa Mengleberg, Larry Ridley, Ben Riley, Max Roach, Roswell Rudd, Idrees Sulieman, Sir Charles Thompson, Dr. Billy Taylor, Cecil Taylor, Butch Warren, and Leroy Williams. There are some musicians who deserve special mention: Bertha Hope, who granted many interviews, made phone calls on my behalf, and remained a champion of this project; Paul Jeffrey, who sat through what turned out to be a ten-hour conversation, capped off by Mr. Jeffrey treating *me* to dinner; Jimmy Owens, who not only offered recollections but gave me trumpet lessons back in 1969 (I was seven) and must bear some responsibility for my journey to Monk's music; Sathima Bea Benjamin, who taught me more about melody than she realizes; Eddie Locke, who not only told his stories with good humor, but gave me a dissertation of unsolicited (and useful!) advice, and graciously shared his beautiful photos of Thelonious Monk for this book. And, finally, Randy Weston—a giant among giants, Randy has encouraged me for over a decade and given me priceless insights into this magnificent music and its source.

Harry Colomby, Monk's manager, spent many patient hours with me searching his memory and files for anything and everything on his first client. His brother Bobby Colomby was equally generous. Monk's former road manager, Bob Jones, offered his stories as well as valuable documents from his own files. And many, many others shared memories and memorabilia: the late Prophet Jennings, Chris Albertson, Paul Bacon, Collette Hawkins, Teo Macero, Danny Scher, Sandra Capello, Robert Kraft, Alice Wright, Myra and Sam Ross, Jr., Herman Leonard, Michael Blackwood, Wren

Brown, the late Lem Martinez Carroll, Evelyn Colbert, Bevan Dufty, Margo Guryan and David Rosner, Lenore Gordon-Ferkin, Robin and Laura Dunlop (and Jacquelyn Modeste for the introduction), Freddie Robinson, Joseph Wilson, Bob Lemkowitz, Arthur Leibowitz, and Dr. Barry Zaret.

Thanks to my long-time editor, Bruce Nichols, who patiently shepherded this project through the first decade, offering suggestions and insights only a musician-editor could, and then passing it off to the capable Martin Beiser when Bruce decided to leave Free Press. Martin gently prodded me along and ignored my rants about needing two volumes. Instead, he calmly helped excise close to 70,000 words and made this a much better book. So did Eric Rayman, the renowned attorney and former magazine editor who read it for the legal department. The entire team at Simon & Schuster/Free Press treated me like royalty, and their excitement for *Thelonious Monk* was palpable. To my first agent, Denise Stinson, who sold the book, and my new agent, Tanya McKinnon, for her patience and encouragement; and finally, Deb Chasman and Tisha Hooks at Beacon Press, whose insight and support kept me focused.

My jazz people, my inner spheres, my sounding board: there would be no book without Columbia University's Center for Jazz Studies, then under the founding director, Robert O'Meally. He invited me to be the first Louis Armstrong Professor of Jazz Studies, giving me precious time to think about this book. Beyond the institutional support, Robert and his equally brilliant wife, dance scholar Jacqui Malone, have given me unyielding intellectual, moral, and spiritual guidance through my journey with Monk from its inception. So has Farah Jasmine Griffin, my intellectual soulmate. Her insights are all through the book, and she paved the way with her stunning meditation on Billie Holiday. Behind them and behind this book stands the entire Columbia University Jazz Studies Group: Dwight Andrews, Herman Beavers, Garnette Cordigan, Danny Dawson, Yulanda Denoon, Ann Douglass, Gerald Early, Brent Edwards, Krin Gabbard, Kevin Gaines, John Gennari, Maxine Gordon, Kyra Gaunt, William Harris, Vijay Iyer, Travis Jackson, Margo Jefferson, George Lewis, William Lowe, Timothy Mangin, Herbie Miller, Ingrid Monson, Fred Moten, Dawn Norfleet, Guy Ramsey, D. L. Smith, John Szwed, Jeff Taylor, Greg Thomas, W. S. Tkweme, the late Mark Tucker, Sherrie Tucker, Penny Von Eschen, Chris Washburne, and Salim Washington. Unfortunately, I don't have the space to delineate how each participant contributed to *Thelonious Monk*, but I can say it was paradigm shifting. I must also thank Monica Hairston, Nanette de Jong, Eric Porter, Nichole Rustin, Danny Widener, Karl Miller, Karen Sotiropolous—former students whose scholarship on music shaped this book immeasurably.

But this is just the tip of the iceberg. I've been thinking, talking about, and playing Monk's music for a good quarter century, and throughout I've been schooled by many of the greatest minds—poets and professors, composers and critics, friends and comrades. The list includes Amiri Baraka, T. J. Anderson and Lois Anderson, Jayne Cortez, Stanley Crouch, Angela Davis, Anthony Davis, Thulani Davis, Michael Dawson, Gina Dent, Graham Haynes, Geoffrey Jacques, Arthur Jafa, Keorapetse Kgositsile, Acklyn Lynch, Jason Moran, Lawrence "Butch" Morris, Tracie Morris, Franklin Rosemont,

Sonia Sanchez, Sekou Sundiata, Greg Tate, Quincy Troupe, Naomi Wallace, Cornel West, and Clark White. Ted Joans and Laura Corsiglia deserve special mention; our home was theirs whenever they were in New York, and often those visits turned into our very own "discourse on Thelonioulism." Thanks to George Lipsitz and Tricia Rose, my models for studying culture with an eye toward social justice; to Eric Wright, for our intermittent, twenty-five-year conversation about this music; to Michael and Marcia Dyson, for their insights, for shout outs, and unremitting love.

Thanks to Don and Maureen Sickler of Second Floor Music, not only for granting me permission to reprint some of the lyrics herein but also for schooling me on Monk's compositions and the secret world of music publishing. To Michael Cuscuna, for granting permission to reproduce some of Frank Wolff's photos as well as for his own pioneering research on Monk's Blue Note years. To Olga Quackenbush for graciously allowing me to include some of Doug Quackenbush's spectacular photographs and writings. To Bruce Lundvall, Bev McCord, and John Ray for their assistance gaining access to Blue Note's files. And to the great Marcel Fleiss, who kindly gave permission to reproduce two of his photos of Monk free of charge.

I'm grateful to the many research assistants I hired along the way, notably Adam Bush, Betsy Esch, Amy Jordan, Michael Heller, Liz Hinton, Mark Padoongpatt, Dan Prosterman, Kendra Tappin, Christine Jean-Louis, Kim Gilmore, Njoroge Njoroge, Russell Marlborough, Michael Kaye, Beth Coleman, Suzanne Lewis, Elleza Kelley, Harald Kisiedu, Rujeko Hockley, and especially Maxine Gordon, whose deep ties to the jazz world proved more valuable than tracking down articles. I also wish to thank Taylor Ho Bynum—a great musician in his own right—for interviewing Jaki Byard and helping out in many other ways, Lynda Wright for transcribing several interviews, and Carmela Kelly for genealogical assistance. Much gratitude to the many translators who stepped in—some working solely on a volunteer basis: Beth Coleman and Noubissie Thierry Kehou (French); Chris Kelley and Fujiko Kelley (Japanese); Virginia Kay (Italian); Andrzej M. Salski (Polish); Markus Wailand (Dutch); Harald Kisiedu (German); Yuko Miki (Portuguese).

To the archivists and individuals who shared private collections: special thanks to the Institute of Jazz Studies, Rutgers University, especially its eminent director, Dan Morgenstern, and its incredibly knowledgeable archivists, Ed Berger, Annie Kuebler, Vincent Pelote, and Tad Hershorn (who also shared draft chapters from his book on Norman Granz); Howard Dodson, James Briggs Murray, Diana Lachatanere, and the staff at the Schomburg Center for Research in Black Culture; George Boziwick, archivist for music division, New York Public Library, and his staff, Matt Snyder and Leslie Foss; Sam Perryman of the Library of Congress; Sam Stephenson of the Center for Documentary Studies for granting me access to the W. Eugene Smith tapes; the staff at the Tamiment Library at NYU, especially Andrew Lee and Jane Latour and the late Debra Bernhardt; Jeni Dahmus, archivist for the Juilliard School; Ms. Renee Leveen, Stuyvesant High School archivist; Ralph Scott, Special Collections, East Carolina University; Bruce Bastin, who shared documents from the Joe Davis Papers in his personal possession; Camille Billops and Richard Hatch of the Hatch-Billops collection; Toby

Byron, Avalon Archives, Ltd.; Victor Remer, the Children's Aid Society; Richard Wandel, Associate Archivist of the New York Philharmonic Archives; Lt. Jay Steinbrenner, City of Batavia Fire Department, for sharing valuable clippings; Ms. Lourdes Silva, Registrar Florida Memorial College, for finding Nellie Monk's college transcript; and, finally, to the various staff at the National Archives; Reuben Jackson and the staff at the Smithsonian Institution Jazz Archives, Museum of American History, Washington, D.C.; Columbia University Archives; CBS; Museum of Television and Motion Pictures; North Carolina State Archives, Records and Manuscript Division; Southern Historical Collection, University of North Carolina, Chapel Hill; several North Carolina county officials who helped me navigate various courthouse records; Beinecke Rare Book and Manuscript Library, Yale University; the Monterey Jazz Festival, Braun Music Library, Sound Archives, Stanford University; the New York City Municipal Archives; the WKCR archives at Columbia University, and its overseer, Phil Schaap; the Wagner Archives and Steinway Piano archives, both at LaGuardia Community College; the Centre d'Information du Jazz, Paris; the National Jazz Archive, Loughton Central Library, England; the National Sound Archive, the British Library; Wolfram Knauer of the Jazzinstitut Darmstadt.

The generosity shown me by most scholars, writers, and collectors has exceeded all expectations. I'm especially grateful to Ira Gitler, Eugene Holley, Jacques Ponzio, Lewis Porter, Peter Pullman, Chris Sheridan, Rob van der Bliek, Daniel Schafer, Lisa Hazirjian, and anonymous collectors for freely sharing insights, information, recordings, videos, and related material. I'm indebted to Antoine Sanfuentes of NBC for sharing his incredible interview with Butch Warren; Mark Naison and Brian Purnell for sharing rich materials on the history of the Bronx; and Mike Manners of the Cherry Lawn Alumni Association. Thanks to Peter Keepnews for giving me Paul Bacon's contact information, and to Orrin Keepnews for clarifying a few discographical questions—though to my regret he did not agree to be interviewed for this book.

I've enjoyed generous support for this project from the Center for Advanced Study in the Behavioral Sciences, Stanford University; Scholars-in-Residence Fellowship, Schomburg Center for Research in Black Culture; Montgomery Fellowship, Dartmouth College; as well as significant research support from the University of Michigan, New York University, Columbia University, and the University of Southern California. I am deeply indebted to my cofellows at the Schomburg (2000–2001), namely Genna Rae McNeil, Kali Gross, Jacqueline Goldsby, Kim Butler, and Cecilia Green, for making this a better book, and to Colin Palmer for his unparalleled commitment to the fellows program. My week-long stay at Brooklyn College, as the Robert L. Hess Scholar-in-Residence, also had a profound impact on this book. My colleagues there, Ellie Hisama, Salim Washington, Ray Allen, Jeff Taylor, as well as Rod and Melanie Bush, provided an engaging intellectual forum for my ideas, not to mention an opportunity to play Monk's music in front of an audience with a ten-piece band led by Salim! (To have the great trombonist, Frank Lacy, follow my solo on "Pannonica" was one of the greatest thrills of my life.) Henry Louis Gates, Jr., an unwavering champion of this project, kindly invited me to deliver the Nathan Huggins Lectures at Harvard.

Although those lectures are to be published soon, the critical engagement I enjoyed from colleagues at Harvard left a deep imprint on *Thelonious Monk*. Sam Floyd, director of the Center for Black Music Research, published my first piece on Monk in the *Black Music Research Journal*. Finally, Wynton Marsalis not only entrusted me with the immense task of teaching a course on Thelonious Monk at Jazz at Lincoln Center, but he generously spent a couple of hours of his time speaking with me about Monk's music. I'm grateful to Nyala Wright and my longtime friend Danielle Bias for coordinating my class at J@LC, and for their enthusiastic support for my work.

I've had many opportunities to share work-in-progress and receive critical feedback from colleagues all over the world. The list includes: Fine Arts Faculty Seminar, University of Melbourne, Australia; Postwar History Seminar, Princeton University; UCLA Oral History Program; Claremont Colleges; North Carolina Jazz Festival, University of North Carolina; W. E. B. DuBois Dialogue Series, Center for Black Literature and Culture, University of Pennsylvania; Department of Ethnic Studies and Department of Music, University of California at San Diego; University of California at Santa Cruz; Program in American Culture and the seminar in Comparative Studies in Social Transformation, University of Michigan; American Studies Forum, City University of New York; "Thermodynamic Reading," with pianist Craig Taborn, Tonic (Lower East Side, New York); History Department, Carnegie Mellon University; Symposium, Newport Jazz Festival, Newport, Rhode Island; W. E. B. DuBois Lecture, George Mason University; Institute for Studies in American Music, Brooklyn College; American Studies Center of the University of the Ryukyus, Okinawa, Japan; Studio Museum of Harlem; Russell B. Nye Lecture, Michigan State University; Addison Gayle Memorial Lecture, Baruch College, New York; Philosophy on Stage (performance/collaboration with Patrick Pulsinger), Vienna, Austria; University of North Carolina, Chapel Hill; Faculty Research Forum, Mt. Holyoke College; Reed College; Washington University in St. Louis; Northwestern University. Thanks to Beth Coleman, Arno Boehler and Susanne Granzer, Maurice Jackson, Simone W. Davis, Alva Stevenson, Daphne Brooks, Huey Copeland, Valerie Smith, Noliwe Rooks, Robert Reid-Pharr, David Stowe, Tuzyline Jita Allan, Genna Rae McNeil, Gerald Early, Iver Bernstein, Rafia Zafar, Sandra Jackson-Dumont, Lowery Sims, David Goodman, Shane White, Graham White, Kosuzu Abe and Katsuyuki Murata, Pancho Savery, Tyler Stovall, and Tukufu Zuberi. Special thanks to my old, old friend Sidney J. Lemelle, who brought me out to Claremont/Pomona a couple of times to talk about Monk and this incredible music.

I cannot reasonably name every friend, acquaintance, and colleague who helped sustain me on this journey or contributed a lead, a reference, some music, or simply a well-timed word of encouragement. Here is a partial list: Jane Andrias, her husband Richard, and their two amazing daughters, Eve and Kate; Wini Breines; Lisa Brock; Paul Buhle; MariJo Buhle; Janaki Bakhle; Nebby Crawford; Michaela Angela Davis; Nick Dirks; Sharon Fitzgerald; Ruth Wilson Gilmore and Craig Gilmore; Mawuko Ghanaba; Denise Greene and Emir Lewis; Delverlon Hall; Don Herzog; Tera Hunter; Jerma Jackson; Earl Lewis; Peter Linebaugh; Eric and Liann Hurst Mann; Manning Marable and Leith Mullings; Louis Massiah; Regina Morantz and Geoff Eley; Rene

Moreno; Jill Nelson; Stanley Nelson and Marcia Smith; Nell Irvin Painter; Mary Louise Patterson; Vijay Prashad; Barbara Ransby and Peter Sporn; Thelma Reyna; John Rockwell; David Roediger; Sherrie Russell-Brown; Jeffrey Sammons; George Sanchez; Julius Scott; Jack Stuart; Akinyele Umoja; Alan Wald; Francille and Ernie Wilson; James Williams; and Komozi Woodard.

Last but certainly not least, I thank my family: my late grandmother, Carmen Chambers; my siblings, Makani Themba-Nixon and her husband Ron Nixon; Meilan Carter and David Gilkey; Chris and Fujiko Kelley; Shannon Patrick Kelley; Benjamin Kelley; Craig Berrysmith; and all their children; my nieces and nephews, Miles and Laura Parish, Kamau Carter, and Brandon Kelley; and my extraordinary mother, Ananda Sattwa, who completed her doctorate the same year I finished *Thelonious Monk*. And I can never repay Paul Morehouse, for introducing me to this music in the first place. I'm especially indebted to Diedra Harris-Kelley, who saw this project grow from a faint idea to an actual manuscript. She was a constant cheerleader, occasional research assistant, critical reader, and artistic consultant. Much gratitude to Diedra's mother Annette Rohan and all her sisters—Dorothe, Dolores, Marie, Betsy (Gloria), Sheila, and especially Evelyn Jackson, who transcribed several of my taped interviews; Claudine Allison; Irie Harris and her son Idris; and Claudius Harris, Jr., and his children, Claudius, III, and Jamare.

Elleza Kelley, my brilliant daughter, not only labored one summer as my research assistant, but she continues to teach me how to be a better writer. Hard to believe that she was a few days old when I published my first book; now she is a college student whose literary and artistic talents are unmatched, as far as I'm concerned. When I grow up, I want to be like her.

To my new family: much gratitude to Tina Hamilton for being an endless font of support; to Heidi Hamilton and her kids, Omari and Kela, for their enthusiasm and good advice; to all the Bledsoes and the Blackwells for embracing me and Monk; and the late *Mr.* Ira Hamilton, who crossed over in January of 2007. Although Monk wasn't his "cup of tea," he appreciated the music and was a true jazz cat. And to my new son, Azizi Wilhite Hamilton, I thank him for his curiosity and wonder. The kid knows more about Thelonious Monk than most six-year-olds; he's the only kid in his first grade class who can play "Blue Monk" on the piano.

I save the last word for my heart, LisaGay Hamilton. For the past four years, she has been my Nellie, and her love and support has been unwavering as I struggled to complete those final chapters. With good humor and the patience of Job, she endured my endless Monk stories, frantic all-night writing sessions, papers and books scattered about the house, and a general grumpiness born of fatigue. But none of this repelled her; on the contrary, LisaGay read every page, asked the hard questions, helped me select photographs, suggested ways to make the story more cinematic, and always, always reminded me that every great work of art is an act of love.

APPENDIX A

A Technical Note on Monk's Music

Monk's unique sound has a lot to do with how he voiced his chords. As early as 1941, he was already experimenting with "open" voicings—i.e., sometimes playing just the root and seventh of a dominant or major seventh chord, eliminating the third and fifth. The impact on the ear is quite startling. A standard major seventh voicing with the root at the bottom—C–E–G–B—sounds consonant, but remove the E and G and suddenly you have a highly dissonant chord, because the two remaining notes are only a half-tone away from each other. Invert the chord and you have a minor second. Often he would eliminate the root altogether and just play the seventh or the ninth in the bass.[1]

Dizzy Gillespie gave Monk credit for introducing the half-diminished chord, a minor seventh chord with a diminished or "flat" fifth (e.g. C–E♭–G♭–B♭). Monk, however, called that example an E♭ minor sixth rather than a C half-diminished chord.[2] Whatever we call it, it became an essential element of Monk's harmonic language, partly because of the dissonance created by the C–G♭. That flatted fifth or "tritone" was critical to what would become his harmonic signature: descending chromatic chord changes. Pop songs and much of jazz up to that point built standard chord progressions around a cycle of fifths (e.g., the standard ii-V-I cadence, popular from the baroque era to Monk's day). Monk preferred to move chromatically, so in place of the V (dominant) chord he substituted a bii7. In the key of C, instead of G7, he would play D♭7. The cadence became Dm7–D♭7–Cmaj7. Three of the four voices moved in parallel, chromatically (e.g. the bass voice, D–D♭–C, and the alto, A–A♭–G). This is called "tritone substitution," because the new chord is a tritone distant from its predecessor. Monk did not "discover" tritone substitution, but his employment of descending chromatic chord progressions and the use of the dissonant tritone interval along with whole tone harmony became defining characteristics of Monk's sound.

And yet, Monk sometimes pared down his chord progressions—most commonly on the A-section of his own "Rhythm-a-ning" and other songs based on Gershwin's "I Got Rhythm." Typically, the eight-bar A-section called for chord changes every two beats and the first four bars (usually repeated or replaced with substitute chords) follow a I-VI-ii-V pattern (e.g., B♭maj7 Gm7 | Cm7 F7).[3] But Monk reduced all of that to a riff on one chord: B♭maj7 or B♭6. We hear evidence of this going back to his first record- ings at Minton's Playhouse, particularly on a tune Jerry Newman labeled "Monkin' the Blues."[4] It isn't a blues, and if it was a Monk original we will never know because the over nine-minute recording doesn't include the melody. Newman catches Monk in the middle of his solo at the beginning of the bridge. What Monk plays underneath Joe Guy owes a debt to Count Basie, who would play his own two- or three-note "shout choruses" behind his horns. The first of these phrases consists of two alternating notes F♯ to F, or the augmented fifth to the perfect fifth. Later in the song he creates a funky, bluesy little phrase alternating between D♭ and B♭—again reminiscent of Count Basie. By imposing a minor third interval over an implied major seventh chord, Monk not only evokes the blues but generates some dissonance.

APPENDIX B

Records and Tapes in Thelonious Monk's Personal Collection

Below is a selected list of recordings (LPs and reel-to-reel tapes) I found in a storage space holding some of Thelonious and Nellie's personal belongings. I cannot say when or how they obtained any of these recordings, but Nellie confirmed that they represented part of their personal collection. The fact that a substantial part of Monk's record collection was destroyed in the first fire, in 1956, explains why most of the recordings listed below were made in the late 1950s and 1960s.

LPs

Cannonball Adderley, *The Cannonball Adderley Sextet in New York* (Riverside RLP 404). Orrin wrote liner notes as he did for everything else he produced. The group included Nat Adderley, Yusef Lateef, Joe Zawinul, Sam Jones, and Louis Hayes. It was recorded in January 1962.

Gene Ammons, *The Happy Blues* (Prestige LP 7039). Recorded in 1956, the band included Art Farmer, Jackie McLean, Duke Jordan, Addison Farmer, Art Taylor, and the percussionist Candido.

Clifford Brown, *Memorial Album* (Blue Note BLP 1526). One side is from a 1953 date with Gigi Gryce, Charlie Rouse, John Lewis, Percy Heath, and Art Blakey. The other side consists of a studio date with Lou Donaldson, Elmo Hope, Percy Heath, and Philly Joe Jones, also recorded in 1953.

Nat King Cole, *Just One of Those Things* (Capitol W 903). Full orchestra conducted by Billy May.

John Coltrane, *Soultrane* (Prestige 7142). Recorded February 1958, Coltrane's band was comprised of Red Garland, Paul Chambers, and Art Taylor.

Xavier Cugat and the Waldorf Astoria Orchestra, *Rhumba with Cugat* (Columbia C-54). This is a four-disc set of 78 rpm recordings.

Billy Eckstine, *Billy's Best* (Mercury MG 20333). The album was terribly battered and evidently played often. It includes several standards Eckstine was known for, including "A Sunday Kind of Love," "Nobody's Heart," "Where Have You Been," and "Trust in Me," which Monk recorded with Clark Terry in 1958.

Billy Eckstine and Quincy Jones, *Billy Eckstine and Quincy Jones at Basin Street* (Mercury SR 60674). Included here is a medley of Ellington tunes and Duke himself wrote some brief notes on the back of the album praising Eckstine.

Ella Fitzgerald, *Ella Fitzgerald Sings the Cole Porter Song Book* (Verve MGV 4001–2). Recorded in 1956.

Dizzy Gillespie, *The Greatest of Dizzy Gillespie* (RCA Victor LPM 2398). Released in 1961, it includes Monk's "52nd Street Theme." Thelonious refers to this LP in his remarks at the New School for Social Research, June 22, 1963 (see Chapter 24).

Ahmad Jamal, *Ahmad Jamal* (Argo LP 636). Recorded in 1958, Ahmad Jamal's trio was made up of Vernell Fourier on drums and Israel Crosby on bass. Recorded live at the Spotlite Club in Washington, D.C.

Ahmad Jamal, *Portfolio of Ahmad Jamal* (Argo LP 2638).

Yusef Lateef, *Before Dawn: The Music of Yusef Lateef* (Verve, MGV 8217). Recorded in April 1957.

Sonny Rollins, *Tenor Madness* (Prestige LP 7047). A famous recording made in May 1956; Rollins and John Coltrane play together on the LP, backed by Red Garland, Paul Chambers, and Philly Joe Jones.

Sonny Rollins, *Sonny Rollins* (Blue Note BLP 1542). Recorded in December 1956, the personnel consisted of Donald Byrd, Wynton Kelly, Gene Ramey, and Max Roach.

Mort Sahl, *The Future Lies Ahead* (Verve, MG V-15002). Comedian, considered very political.

REEL-TO-REEL TAPES

Vladimir Horowitz, *Playing the Music of Chopin, Schumann, Rachmaninoff, Liszt* (Columbia Stereo Tape Masterworks, Stereo disc KS 6371).

David Oistrakh, Mstislav Rostropovich, Geroge Szell, and the Cleveland Orchestra, *Brahms: Double Concerto in A minor, Op. 102* (Angel M 36032).

Clifford Curzon with the London Symphony Orchestra, *Brahms Piano Concerto No. 1 in D minor, Op. 15* (London LCL 80126).

Karl Richter, conductor, Johann Sebastian Bach, *Mass in B-Minor* (AR 3177).

NOTES

Unless indicated otherwise, all interviews cited were conducted by author.

Prelude

1 Paul Bacon, "The High Priest of Be-bop: The Inimitiable Mr. Monk," *Record Changer* 8, no. 11 (November, 1949), 9.
2 Benetta Bines interview, January 30, 2004.
3 Nat Hentoff, *The Jazz Life* (New York: Da Capo Press, 1978, orig. 1961), 184.
4 Lewis H. Lapham, "Monk: High Priest of Jazz," *Saturday Evening Post* (April 11, 1964), 72.
5 André Hodeir, *Toward Jazz*, trans. Noel Burch (New York: Grove Press, 1962), 162.
6 John F. Mehegan, "Crepuscule with Monk," unpublished manuscript, December 1963, pp. 2–3, copy located in Monk vertical files, Institute for Jazz Studies, Rutgers University.
7 Bill Evans, liner notes to *Monk* (Columbia CS 9091).
8 Quoted in Valerie Wilmer, "Monk on Monk," *Down Beat* (June 3, 1965), 20.
9 Ben Riley interview with Quincy Troupe, Media Transcripts. Used by permission.
10 "Monk Rehearsal, 1963–64," CCP 103, W. Eugene Smith Loft Tape Collection, Center for Documentary Studies, Duke University.
11 Thelonious Monk rehearsal tape, circa 1960, Thelonious Monk Family Archives, in author's possession.
12 Frank London Brown, "More Man than Myth, Monk Has Emerged from the Shadows," *Down Beat* (October 30, 1958), 16.

1 "My Mother Didn't Want Me to Grow Up in North Carolina"

1 "Strictly Ad Libs," *Down Beat* (November 14, 1957), 10; Nellie Monk quoted in Valerie Wilmer, "Monk on Monk," *Down Beat* (June 3, 1965), 21.
2 Julius W. Monk, *Julius Monk's Baker's Dozen* (New York: Random House, 1964), p. xvi.
3 *Local 802 of AFM Directory* (Newark: International Press, 1947).
4 U.S. Census, *Population Schedule: 1930: Salisbury, Rowan, North Carolina*; ED: 36, p. 10 B; Julius Withers Monk to William James Monk, December 5, 1942, Archibald Monk Family Bible, North Carolina State Archives. Coincidentally, the *Chicago Defender's* "Onion for the Day" ran a humorous article—prompted by *TV Guide's* error mistaking Malcolm X for Elijah Muhammad's son—identifying celebrities with similar last names who could be mistaken as relatives. The list included "Julius and Thelonious Monk." Little did they know! *Chicago Defender*, May 27, 1964.
5 Franz Recum, "Monk Family Record—James Monk of Moore County - North Carolina," Compiled for Julius Withers Monk (typescript, 1943), expanded as Monk Family Record. Hereafter, Recum, "Monk Family Record."
6 Julius Monk to "Uncle William," December 5, 1942, Photostat copy in Recum, "Monk Family Record."
7 Monk, *Julius Monk's Baker's Dozens*, dust jacket copy.
8 See David Cecelski, *The Waterman's Song: Slavery and Freedom in Maritime North Carolina* (Chapel Hill: University of North Carolina Press, 2001); Marvin L. Michael Kay and Lorin Lee Cary, *Slavery in North Carolina, 1748–1775* (Chapel Hill: University of North Carolina Press, 1995); Walter E. Minchinton, "The Seabourne Slave Trade of North Carolina," *North Carolina Historical Review* 71 (January 1994), 1–61.
9 Monk Family, *Seventeenth Annual Family Reunion—August 30–September 1, 1996, Greenville, NC* (mimeograph in author's possession); Franz Recum, "Monk Family Record." According to the Monk family record lists, the number and age of Archibald Monk's slaves are based on the 1850 and 1860 Slave Schedule, but the document also includes the names of two, Channa and Isaac. According to the family tree compiled by Erich Jarvis, with assistance from several black Monks, Channa or Chaney was the daughter of John Jack Monk. Since she was born around 1812, only one person was old enough to have been her father and he was born around 1797. This would have been John Jack.
10 Aaron Hargrove Estate, Division of Negroes, May Term 1835, Estate Records, Sampson County, North Carolina, microfilm, North Carolina Division of Archives and History; "Deed of Gift, Aaron Hargrove to Harriet Monk," January 6, 1827, "Negro Girl by the name of Chaney about nine years of age," Sampson

County, NC Real Estate Conveyances, Book 21, pg. 611, microfilm, North Carolina Division of Archives and History.

11 Archibald Monk settled on a plantation owned by Squire John Ingram (who also presided over his marriage), but focused most of his attention on running the general store with his brother Cornelius, serving as postmaster for Newton Grove, practicing medicine, and seeking public office. Among other things, he was appointed Superintendent of Public Instruction for Sampson County and he served as a representative in North Carolina's House of Commons from 1830–1834. Franz Recum, "Monk Family Record"; Charles H. Bowman, "Archibald Monk: Public Servant of Sampson County," *North Carolina Historical Review* 47, no. 4 (October 1970), 339–369.

12 Monk Family, *Seventeenth Annual Family Reunion—August 30–September 1, 1996, Greenville, NC* (mimeograph in author's possession). No one knows much about Kaplin; apparently, he was lighter than Solomon and was able to pass for white. His name cannot be found in the Census. However, Solomon's name does appear in the 1880 Census in Sampson County and he is listed as "Mulatto." I don't think the story is apocryphal. U.S. Census, 1880, *Population Schedule: Sampson County, Westbrook*, ED 196.

13 See, Franz Recum, "Monk Family Record"; Charles H. Bowman, "Dr. John Carr Monk: Sampson County's Latter Day 'Cornelius,'" *North Carolina Historical Review* 50, no. 1 (January 1973), 52–72. Monk Family, *Seventeenth Annual Family Reunion—August 30–September 1, 1996, Greenville, NC* (mimeograph in author's possession).

14 U.S. Census, 1860, *Slave Schedule—Slave Inhabitants: Sampson County*, p. 49; Franz Recum, *Monk Family Record*.

15 Monk Family, *Seventeenth Annual Family Reunion—August 30–September 1, 1996, Greenville, NC* (mimeograph in author's possession); U.S. Census 1860, *Slave Schedule—Slave Inhabitants: Johnston County*, "Willis Cole Plantation," p. 213.

16 Williams S. Powell, *North Carolina Through Four Centuries* (Chapel Hill and London: University of North Carolina Press, 1989), 22–24; Theda Purdue, *Native Carolinians: The Indians of North Carolina* (Raleigh, NC: North Carolina Division of Archives and History, 2000); Marilyn Haas, *The Seneca and Tuscarora Indians* (Lanham, MD: The Scarecrow Press, 1994).

17 Monk Family, *Seventeenth Annual Family Reunion—August 30–September 1, 1996, Greenville, NC* (mimeograph in author's possession).

18 "Will of Willis Cole," Johnston County, State of North Carolina, 1832, Record of Wills, 1760–1859, Vol. 1, Johnston County, North Carolina Archives; U.S. Census 1860, *Slave Schedule—Slave Inhabitants: Johnston County*, "Willis Cole Plantation," p. 213; U.S. Census 1860, *Agriculture Schedule—Johnston County, Bentonville*, "Willis Cole plantation."

19 Richard Reid, "Raising the African Brigade: Early Black Recruitment in Civil War North Carolina," *North Carolina Historical Review* 71 (July 1993), 266–301. My understanding of emancipation and reconstruction is informed by W. E. B. DuBois, *Black Reconstruction in America: An Essay Toward a History of the Part Which Black Folk Played in the Attempt to Reconstruct Democracy in America, 1860–1880* (New York: Harcourt, Brace, 1935) and Stephen Hahn, *A Nation Under Our Feet: Black Political Struggles in the Rural South from Slavery to the Great Migration* (Cambridge, MA.: Harvard University Press, 2003).

20 Nathaniel Cheairs Hughes, Jr., *Bentonville: The Final Battle of Sherman and Johnston* (Chapel Hill and London: University of North Carolina Press, 1996), 43–46.

21 Roberta Sue Alexander, *North Carolina Faces the Freedmen: Race Relations During Presidential Reconstruction, 1865–1867* (Durham: Duke University Press, 1985), 1–12; Jeffrey J. Crow, *A History of African Americans in North Carolina* (Raleigh: Division of Archives and History, Department of Cultural Resources, 1992); Hahn, *A Nation Under Our Feet*, 116–159.

22 Alexander, *North Carolina Faces the Freedmen*, 49–50, 111–119.

23 U.S. Census, 1870, *Population Schedule—Sampson County, North Carolina, Westbrook Township*, p. 26

24 Jeffrey J. Crow, Paul D. Escott, and Flora J. Hatley, *A History of African Americans in North Carolina*, rev. ed. (Raleigh: Office of Archives and History, North Carolina Department of Cultural Resources, 2002), 90–93.

25 U.S. Census, 1870, *Population Schedule—Sampson County, North Carolina, Westbrook Township*, p. 26. Choosing a name after emancipation was an awesome responsibility that freed people took quite seriously. We need to remember that enslaved black people were not granted surnames. With freedom, most adopted their masters' surnames, though in some instances, they shed their master's name altogether, choosing names such as "Freeman," "Lincoln," "Washington," or names indicating their profession ("Green," "Bishop," etc.).

26 "Will of Blaney Williams," Sampson County, State of North Carolina, Record of Wills, Sampson County, Book 1, May Term of Court, 1852, page 414, microfilm.

27 "John Lucas of Eastern North Carolina Descendants and Related Families," Entries: 61464 www.ancestry .com; U.S. Census, 1880, *Population Schedule—Sampson County, North Carolina, Westbrook Township*, E.D. 196, p. 13; Division of the lands of John C. Monk, Deed, July 5, 1877 partitioned land among Anne E Monk, Flora H Monk and J Catherine Monk, Sampson County Record of Deeds, Book 46, pg. 200, North Carolina State Archives.

28 Their eldest child, Vera Elisa Cole, was born in 1878. She was followed by John Jack (b. 1880), Eulah (b. 1881), Alonzo (b. 1883, d. 1906), Lorenzo (b. 1886), Bertha (b. 1888), Thelonious (b. 1889), Theodoras or Theodore "Babe" (b. 1890), Squire Lee (b. 1894), and Hettie Fernandez (b. 1897). Monk Family, *Seventeenth Annual Family Reunion—August 30–September 1, 1996, Greenville, NC* (mimeograph in author's possession). Incidentally, Bertha is a male child. The family reunion document lists Theodore's birth year as 1891, but according to other sources such as his draft registration card, his birthdate is listed as December 10, 1890.

29 U.S. Census, 1900, *Population Schedule: Wayne County, ED, 104.*

30 Hahn, *A Nation Under Our Feet*, 436–37.

31 David S. Cecelski and Timothy B. Tyson, eds. *Democracy Betrayed: The Wilmington Race Riot and Its Legacy* (Chapel Hill: University of North Carolina Press, 1998); H. Leon Prather, Sr. *We Have Taken a City: Wilmington Racial Massacre and Coup of 1898* (Cranbury, N.J.: Associated University Press, Inc., 1984); The Wilmington Race Riot Commission, *1898 Wilmington Race Riot – Final Report, May 31, 2006*, http://www.ah.dcr .state.nc.us/1898%2Dwrrc; Herbert Shapiro, *White Violence and Black Response: From Reconstruction to Montgomery* (Amherst: University of Massachusetts Press, 1988).

32 Crow, Escott, and Hatley, *A History of African Americans in North Carolina*, 116–117; Anderson, *Race and Politics*, 296–312.

33 U.S. Census, 1900, *Population Schedule: Wayne County*, ED, 104. According to his children's birth certificates, Thelonious Monk could read and write and was recorded as having received "common school" education. See Marion Barbara Monk, Birth Certificate #75749 [original is 403], January 18, 1916 North Carolina State Board Of Health, Bureau Of Vital Statistics.

34 U.S. Census, 1900, *Population Schedule: Wayne County*, ED, 104.

35 U.S. Census, 1920, *Population Schedule, Johnston County, Bentonville*, ED 41, p. 6B

36 On the life of St. Tillo, see John J. Delaney, *Dictionary of Catholic Biography* (New York: Doubleday, 1961), 159. Sam Stephenson suggests that Hinton and Sarah may have derived the name from Reverend Fredricum Hillonious Wilkins, the distinguished pastor from Durham, North Carolina. "Thelonious Monk—Is This Home?" *Oxford American* 58 (2007), 114. While Thelonious is certainly a unique name—a name he proudly passed on to his more famous son—he was not the only one. I found at least four other people with the same name born between 1869 and 1911: Thelonius Melancon (white, male, b. 1869) of St. James, Louisiana; Thelonius Duncan (black, male, b. 1907) of Bamberg, South Carolina, and Thelonius Laws (white, male, b. 1911) of Somerset, Maine. [U.S. Census, 1920, *Population Schedule: Police Jury Ward 3, St James, Louisiana*; U.S. Census, 1930, *Population Schedule: Tampa, Hillsborough, Florida*; U.S. Census, 1930, *Population Schedule, Bamberg, Bamberg, South Carolina*; U.S. Census, 1920, *Population Schedule: Ripley, Somerset, Maine*.]

37 Eric Anderson, *Race and Politics in North Carolina, 1872–1901: The Black Second* (Baton Rouge: LSU Press, 1981), 4–6; Alan D. Watson, *Edgecombe County: A Brief History* (Raleigh: North Carolina Dept. of Cultural Resources, Division of Archives and HIstory, 1979), 78.

38 By the time Henry was born, Lucy Knight had already been married and widowed twice, first to Isaac Batts and then to David Barlow. See Cynthia, Herrin comp. *Edgecombe County, North Carolina, Vital Records, 1720–1880* (online database, www.ancestry.com); Tarboro, NC Genealogy and Library Association (comp.), *Early Families of Edgecombe Co North Carolina, Its Past and Present* (The Tarboro Society for Genealogy and Biography, 1881).

39 "Will of Peter Knight," 1809, Edgecombe Co. Will Abstracts 1793–1823, North Carolina State Archives, U.S. Census, 1860, *Slave Schedule: Edgecombe County, Deep Creek Township*, p. 164.

40 Since the plantation was owned by Peter Hedgepeth and Charity Braswell, Clara apparently could not decide if she was a Hedgepeth or a Braswell. On the marriage registry she is listed as Clara Braswell, but on her daughter's death certificate, she is recorded as Clara or Clearly Hedgepeth. See Cynthia Herrin comp. *Edgecombe County, North Carolina, Vital Records, 1720–1880* (online database, www.ancestry.com); Tarboro, NC Genealogy and Library Association (comp.), *Early Families of Edgecombe Co North Carolina, Its Past and Present* (The Tarboro Society for Genealogy and Biography, 1881); Standard Certificate of Death, Georgiana Williams, Filed November 1, 1921, North Carolina State Board of Health, copy in Edgecombe County Registrar of Deeds, Tarboro, NC.

41 Letter to Ruth, unsigned, March 18, 1966, Batts Family Papers, Manuscript Collections Special Collections Joyner Library East Carolina University.

42 Georgianna was the eldest of six children—three brothers (Blunt, b. 1869; Peter, b. 1874; and James, b. 1877), and two sisters (Emma, b. 1871 and Sena, b. 1876). U.S. Census, 1870, *Population Schedule: Edgecombe County—Deep Creek Township*; U.S. Census, 1880, *Population Schedule: Edgecombe County—Deep Creek Township*, ED 62.

43 U.S. Census 1880, *Population Schedule: Edgecombe County—Deep Creek Township*, ED 62.

44 U.S. Census, 1870, *Population Schedule: Edgecombe County—Deep Creek Township*. In 1860, John Knight owned 28 slaves. U.S. Census, 1860, *Slave Schedule: Edgecombe County*.

45 U.S. Census, 1870, *Population Schedule: Edgecombe County—Deep Creek Township*. On Speer Batts as a fiddler, see Marion White interview with Quincy Troupe, December 1, 1990, Media Transcripts Inc. For film *Thelonious Monk: American Composer*. Used by permission from Avalon Archives, Ltd.

46 Robert Hinton, *The Politics of Agricultural Labor: From Slavery to Freedom in a Cotton Culture, 1862–1902* (New York: Garland Publishing, 1997), 115. On the exodus of African-Americans, see Nell Irvin Painter, *The Exodusters: Black Migration to Kansas after Reconstruction* (New York: Knopf, 1977); Stephen Hahn, *A Nation Under Our Feet: Black Political Struggles in the Rural South from Slavery to the Great Migration* (Cambridge, MA: Harvard University Press, 2003), 317–363.

47 Joe A. Mobley, "In the Shadow of White Society: Princeville, a Black Town in North Carolina, 1865–1915," *North Carolina Historical Review* 63, no. 3 (July 1986), 340–384. "Freedom Hill" eventually was incorporated as Princeville, North Carolina's first independent black town.

48 According to the Census, they were unemployed for eight months out of the year. U.S. Census, 1880, *Population Schedule: Edgecombe County: Upper Conetoe Township*, p. 87C. Note that in the 1880 Census Speer's name is either misspelled or not fully legible, but he appears as "Spur Batts."

49 "Speen [sic] Batts and Georgeanna Knight," May 8, 1884, Marriage Register, Edgecombe County, Edgecombe County Courthouse, Tarboro. On the marriage register, Speer's age is listed as thirty, but the Census consistently places his birth at around 1856. I'm guessing that twenty-eight or twenty-nine is probably a more accurate figure.

50 I have not been able to figure out when Henry or Clara Knight died, but he is still living on the Batts plantation as late as June of 1897. He was called on to testify in a land dispute after the death of the owner, now Benjamin Batts, son of Isaac. "D.B. Batts vs. H. L. Staton," Case on Appeal, Superior Court, June Term 1897, Edgecombe County, North Carolina, typescript copy in Batts Family Papers.

51 Hinton, *The Politics of Agricultural Labor*, 127; Watson, *Edgecombe County*, 89.

52 Hinton, *The Politics of Agricultural Labor*, 119–125; E. Tunney Cobb, Jr., "Race Relations in Edgecombe County, North Carolina, 1700–1975" (B.A. Honors Thesis, UNC, 1975), pp. 35–45; Anderson, *Race and Politics*.

53 The birth certificates for Barbara's three children indicate their mother's birthplace as Hamilton Township, Martin County. Given that Barbara was born eight years after they married, it is likely that Georgianna had given birth before but lost her children, but we will never know since the state of North Carolina did not begin to maintain birth and death records until 1913.

54 "Rocky Mount Becomes Area's Largest City," *Rocky Mount Evening Telegram*, July 6, 1976; "Rocky Mount, The Railroad Town," *Rocky Mount Evening Telegram*, July 6, 1976; Lisa Hazirjian, "Negotiating Poverty: Economic Insecurity and the Politics of Working-Class Life in Rocky Mount, North Carolina, 1929–1969" (PhD diss., Duke University, 2003), 26. Hazirjian's dissertation is by far the best scholarly work on Rocky Mount's history.

55 Prior to meeting Thelonious, Georgianna briefly married a laborer named Alex Williams, though it is not clear how they met or where and when they actually wed. Tragically, Alex Williams died very soon after they settled down in Rocky Mount. In fact, Barbara is listed in the 1910 Census as "Barbara B. Williams" rather than Barbara Batts, the name she would consistently give as her maiden name. U.S. Census, 1910, *Population Schedule: North Carolina, Edgecombe County, Rocky Mount Township*, ED 26. Alex Williams is identified as her late husband on Georgianna's death certificate. Standard Certificate of Death, Georgiana Williams, Filed November 1, 1921, North Carolina State Board of Health, copy in Edgecombe County Registrar of Deeds, Tarboro, North Carolina.

56 Marion Monk's birth certificate indicates that both parents had formal schooling. North Carolina State Board Of Health, Bureau Of Vital Statistics, Certificate Of Birth: Marion Barbara Monk, Certificate #75749 [original is 403], January 18, 1916.

57 U.S. Census, 1910, *Population Schedule: North Carolina, Edgecombe County, Rocky Mount Township*, ED 26.

58 Booker T. Washington High School, Rocky Mount's first "colored" high school, wasn't built until 1924, and the first high school for black children in Edgecombe County was established in 1920. Oliver R. Pope, *Chalk Dust: An Autobiographical Account of a Dedicated Negro Teacher to Educate and Mold Young Lives* (New York: Pageant Press, 1967), 114–115; R. D. Armstrong, "Black Citizens Entering Mainstream of Area's Life," *Rocky Mount Evening Telegram*, July 6, 1976.

59 U.S. Census, 1910 *Population Schedule: North Carolina, Edgecombe County, Rocky Mount*, ED 26; Rocky Mount, N.C., *Directory, 1912–1913* (Rocky Mt. and Richmond, VA: Hill Directory Co., 1912), 45; Hazirjian, "Negotiating Poverty," 30. Initially, they lived at 570 Pennsylvania Avenue, but by the time of the 1912–13 city directory, they had moved a few doors down to 510 Pennsylvania Ave. By this time Barbara is using Batts instead of Williams, though the directory misspells her name "Betts."

60 Rocky Mount, N.C., *Directory, 1912–1913* (Rocky Mt. and Richmond, VA: Hill Directory Co., 1912), 26–27. Unfortunately, I could not determine to which church they belonged since most black Baptist church records from Rocky Mount for this period have been lost or destroyed. The most likely candidates were Little Hope Baptist Church on South Church, Primitive Baptist Church on Gay near Pearl, St. James Baptist Church on Thomas, or Mt. Zion Baptist Church on Pearl near Thomas.

61 Copy of Thelonious Monk, Sr., Draft registration card, State Archives, North Carolina, microfilm roll 1765640.

62 Hazirjian, "Negotiating Poverty," 36–38.

63 Olivia Monk, Pam Kelley Monk, Conley F. Monk, Jr., Marcella Monk Flake, Evelyn Pue, interview, August 6, 2007.

64 U.S. Census, 1910, *Population Schedule: North Carolina, Edgecombe County, Rocky Mount*, ED 26. Note: in the 1910 Census, Thelonious's name is spelled "Theolonious." On the 1914–15 City Directory, he appears as Cornelius. Rocky Mount, N.C., *Directory, 1912–1913* (Rocky Mt. and Richmond, VA: Hill Directory Co., 1912), 186; Rocky Mount, N.C., *Directory, 1914–1915* (Rocky Mt. and Richmond, VA: Hill Directory Co., 1915), 152.

65 Marriage License, North Carolina, Office Of Registrar Of Deeds, Edgecombe County, August 20, 1914; *Rocky Mount Directory: 1908–1909, Vol 1* (Hill Directory Co.: Rocky Mount, 1908), p. 129.

66 Monk's birth certificate and other documents refer to this block as Green Street, but the city directory and maps from the period identify it as Green Avenue or Greens Avenue. There is a Green Street in Rocky Mount, but it is in the north end of the city and is in Nash County. The Monks could not have lived on this street because it was all white and it was not in Edgecombe County (where all records show they resided). Besides, the census also reveals the neighboring streets, which clearly are adjacent to Green Avenue in Around the Y.

67 According to Marion's birth certificate, she was Barbara's second child, and the first was listed on her birth certificate as "born alive and now dead." North Carolina State Board Of Health, Bureau Of Vital Statistics, Certificate Of Birth: Marion Barbara Monk, Certificate #75749 [original is 403]. Such tragedy was not unusual. At the time, approximately 42% of all deaths in Edgecombe County were infants under two years old, or mothers during childbirth. The Edgecombe County Health Department was formed in 1916, in part to respond to the exceedingly high infant mortality rate in the county. For African-Americans, the situation was even worse. Black women had their babies at home and were attended to by midwives, in part because hospital care was generally unavailable. The Edgecombe General Hospital set aside a handful of beds for black patients, and no black doctors were on staff. Seriously ill patients often had to travel to Chapel Hill or Durham for medical

treatment. E. Tunney Cobb, Jr., "Race Relations in Edgecombe County, North Carolina, 1700–1975" (B.A. Honors Thesis, UNC, 1975), 49–50.

68 North Carolina State Board Of Health, Bureau Of Vital Statistics, Certificate Of Birth: Marion Barbara Monk, Certificate #75749 [original is 403], January 18, 1916. Their midwife, Lucy Cooper, born a slave in 1849, attended to all of Barbara's deliveries. She was also a neighbor and long-time acquaintance of the Monks; in 1910 she lived around the corner from their place on Dunn Street with her son, four grandchildren, and a boarder. On Lucy Cooper, see U.S. Census, 1920, *Population Schedule: North Carolina, Edgecombe County, Rocky Mount*, ED 19; U.S. Census, 1910, *Population Schedule: North Carolina, Edgecombe County, Rocky Mount*, ED 26; U.S. Census, 1900, *Population Schedule: North Carolina, Edgecombe County, Rocky Mount*, ED 13. In 1910, Cooper and her family lived on the corner of Dunn and South Street.

69 Copy of Thelonious Monk, Sr., Draft registration card, microfilm roll 1765640, Card #No. 613 Signed June 5, 1917, National Archives, Washington D.C.

70 I'm grateful to Jeffrey Sammons for pointing out reasons that black men might have wanted to be drafted or chose to enlist in the military. See also, Jeanette Keith, "The Politics of Southern Draft Resistance, 1917–1918: Class, Race, and Conscription in the Rural South," *Journal of American History* 87, no. 4 (March 2001), 1356– 58; Theodore Kornweibel, Jr., "Apathy and Dissent: Black America's Negative Responses to World War I," *South Atlantic Quarterly* 80 (Summer, 1980), 322–38.

71 North Carolina State Board Of Health, Bureau Of Vital Statistics, Certificate Of Birth: Thelonious Monk, Certificate #342, October 10, 1917. On Thelonious's birth certificate, Lucy Cooper's name is misspelled "Copper." It is correctly spelled on the other two Monk children's birth certificates, as well as in the census and city directories.

72 Rocky Mount *Evening Telegram*, October 10, 1917. City clean-up and maintenance crews spent much of the day repairing dirt roads that had been damaged by the storm. Rocky Mount *Telegram*, October 11, 1917.

73 North Carolina State Board Of Health, Bureau Of Vital Statistics, Certificate Of Birth: Thelonious Monk, Certificate #342, October 10, 1917. By the time Thelonious and Thomas were born, Lucy Cooper lived at 204 Bassett Street. *Rocky Mount City Directory*; U.S. Census, *Population Schedule, 1920: North Carolina, Edgecombe County, Rocky Mount*, ED 19.

74 Dr. Margaret Battle, "The Great Flu Epidemic of 1918," *Rocky Mount Telegram*, July 6, 1976.

75 North Carolina State Board of Health, Bureau of Vital Statistics, Certificate of Birth: Thomas William Monk, Certificate #5, January 11, 1920.

76 The new address and the boarders are recorded in the 1920 Census, which was taken in April of that year, four months after Thomas's birth. The names listed in the census schedule read Warnie and Annie Wares, but the writing is really illegible. We do know that Annie was 33 and her husband 43 years old at the time. U.S. Census, 1920, *Population Schedule: North Carolina, Edgecombe County, Rocky Mount*, ED 19.

77 Francois Postif, " 'Round 'Bout Sphere" *Jazz Hot* 186 (April 1963), 22. Monk said the same thing to Nat Hentoff, "Just Call Him Thelonious," *Down Beat* (July 25, 1956), 15.

78 Peter Keepnews, "Young Monk," in *The Thelonious Monk Reader*, ed. Rob van der Bliek (New York: Oxford University Press, 2001), 6. [Essay originally published in the *Village Voice*, August 8, 1989, pp. 18, 20–21.]

79 Standard Certificate of Death, Georgiana Williams, Filed November 1, 1921, North Carolina State Board of Health, copy in Edgecombe County Registrar of Deeds, Tarboro, North Carolina.

80 Hinton and Sarah and Lorenzo appear in the 1920 Census, although their ages are incorrect. Hinton is listed as a farmer but Lorenzo is shown as having no occupation, which leads me to believe that he might have been incapacitated in some way. U.S. Census, 1920, *Population Schedule: North Carolina, Johnston County, Township of Bentonville* (January 22, 1920); on the date of Hinton's death, see *Seventeenth Annual Family Reunion—August 30–September 1, 1996, Greenville, NC*.

81 Thanks to Roy L. Hudson of the National Railway Historical Society for helping me map out the Monks' train travel to New York.

2 "What Is Jazz? New York, Man!"

1 Marion White interview, with Quincy Troupe, December 1, 1990; on the streetcar routes, U.S. Works Progress Administration, City of NY, "Transportation Facilities, Public and Institutional Buildings," Area M-1, 1934.

2 On Louise E. Bryant, U.S. Census, 1920, *Population Schedule: Manhattan Borough*, ED 31-383.

3 Ibid.

4 Chicago, *Inter-Ocean* (February 5, 1905); Macon, Georgia *Telegraph* (February 1, 1905).

5 Phipps Community Development Corporation, *Phipps Houses Review* (brochure, n.d.); Gordon Heath, *Deep are the Roots: Memoirs of a Black Expatriate* (Amherst: University of Massachusetts Press, 1992), 9.

6 Marion White interview, with Quincy Troupe, December 1, 1990. The Henrietta School also launched an adult education program in 1909, in which they provided instruction in janitorial work, cooking, dressmaking, homemaking, etc. See Seth M. Scheiner, *Negro Mecca: A History of the Negro in New York City, 1865–1920* (New York: New York University Press, 1965), 147.

7 Marion White interview, with Quincy Troupe, December 1, 1990.

8 Mary White Ovington, *Half a Man: The Status of the Negro in New York* (New York: Schocken Books, 1969, orig. 1911), 40–41.

9 *The Columbus Hill Chronicle* 1, no. 1 (April 1915), 1–3; Ibid., 1, no. 2 (May 1915).

10 "Slums Must Go, Women Declare," *New York Times*, December 21, 1919.

11 Gilbert Osofsky, *Harlem: the Making of a Ghetto: Negro New York, 1890–1930* (New York: Harper Torchbooks,

1963), 113; see also, James Ford, *Slums and Housing, with Special Reference to New York City* (Westport: Negro Universities Press, orig. 1936), 328.

12 Ovington, *Half a Man*, 39. See also Ovington's essay, "Vacation Days on San Juan Hill—A New York Negro Colony," *Southern Workman* 38 (November 1909), 627–634.

13 "Black and White War in a Crowded District," *New York Times*, July 15, 1905; "Race Rioters at it Again," *New York Times*, July 18, 1905; "Mr. Devery on the Police," *New York Times*, July 27, 1905.

14 "Police Kill Negro in Race Riot; Seven Hurt," *New York Times*, May 27, 1917.

15 "Negro Guardsmen in San Juan Hill," *New York Times*, July 4, 1917; "Hayward Begins Inquiry Into Riot," *New York Times*, July 5, 1917.

16 Stephen L. Harris, *Harlem's Hell Fighters: The African-American 369th Infantry in World War I* (Washington, D.C.: Potomac Books, 2003); Reid Badger, *A Life in Ragtime: A Biography of James Reese Europe* (New York: Oxford University Press, 1995).

17 Scheiner, *Negro Mecca*, 19, 26–27.

18 Based on my analysis of the 1920 and 1930 U.S. Census *Population Schedule: Manhattan Borough*, ED 383, and the New York State Census, 1925, *New York County—Enumeration of Inhabitants, Assembly District 5, Election District 51*.

19 Interview with Alberta Saunders, April 1, 2004.

20 Mavis (Wilson) Swire interview, March 8, 2004. In 1930, Ms. Wilson lived at 224 West 64th St., and about three years later they moved to a nicer tenement on West 63rd across the street from the Phipps Houses. U.S. Census, 1930, *Population Schedule: Manhattan Borough*, ED 383.

21 Barry Farrell, "Loneliest Monk," *Time* 83 (February 28, 1964), 85.

22 Mavis Swire interview, March 8, 2004.

23 The black slang term "ofay" is pig latin for "foe."

24 Arthur Taylor, *Notes and Tones: Musician-to-Musician Interviews* (New York: Da Capo Press, 1993), 286.

25 Ibid., p. 286.

26 Interview with Alberta Saunders, April 1, 2004.

27 "City's Crime Spots Shown by Survey," *New York Times*, December 14, 1923.

28 "Negro's Wild Shots Wound 2, Cause Panic," *New York Times*, June 10, 1926.

29 James Weldon Johnson, *Black Manhattan* (New York: Knopf, 1930), 186–188; Arnold Shaw, *The Jazz Age: Popular Music in the 1920s* (New York: Oxford University Press, 1987), 89–92; Marshall Stearns and Jean Stearns, *Jazz Dance: The Story of American Vernacular Dance* (New York: Da Capo, 1994, orig. 1968), 132–137.

30 Herbert Gutman's statistical survey showed that the San Juan Hill neighborhood in New York had a disproportionately large community of black musicians and actors. See Gutman, *The Black Family in Slavery and Freedom, 1850–1925*, 507.

31 Mary White Ovington, *Half a Man: The Status of the Negro in New York* (New York: Schocken Books, 1969, orig. 1911), 125.

32 Geraldine Smith interview, February 12, 2004.

33 Greater New York Federation of Churches, *The Negro Churches of Manhattan (New York City): A Study Made in 1930* (New York: Greater New York Federation of Churches, 1930), 30; *Manhattan Address Directory, 1925, 1929, 1933–34*; *New York Times*, July 21, 1926; Thomas Monk, Jr., interview, February 16, 2004. Biographers in the past have mistakenly claimed that Barbara Monk attended St. Cyprian's Colored Episcopal Chapel, and others have insisted that she was a Methodist and raised her children as Methodists. Both assertions are wrong. She was a committed Baptist until around 1950, when she converted to the Jehovah's Witness faith.

34 Heath, *Deep are the Roots*, 65.

35 Greater New York Federation of Churches, *The Negro Churches of Manhattan*, 31.

36 Civil List, NYC Civil List, "Officials and Employees of the City of New York," *The City Record*, 1925, microfilm roll 16.

37 "Find City Schools Cold to Negroes," *New York Times*, April 30, 1915.

38 Morroe Berger, Edward Berger, and James Patrick, *Benny Carter: A Life in American Music*, vol. 1 (Metuchen, NJ: Scarecrow Press, 1982), 12.

39 Monk mentions Batavia in an interview with Lewis Lapham. See Lewis H. Lapham, "Monk: High Priest of Jazz," *Saturday Evening Post* 237 (April 11, 1964), 73.

40 "More Fresh Airs Arrived Today," *Batavia Daily News*, August 3, 1923.

41 Ibid.

42 "Children Will Return to New York Tomorrow," *Batavia Daily News*, August 16, 1923; "Colored Mascot Sorry to Leave," *Batavia Daily News*, August 17, 1923. All other biographers have mistakenly identified him as the mascot of Engine Company No. 40 located in the neighborhood, but my research into the FDNY archives reveals that he never served in such a role and they did not have a tradition of mascots. I believe writers simply took the information that he was a mascot for the fire department and looked for the closest fire station, not unlike the claim that his mother was a member of St. Cyprian's Chapel.

43 "Thelonius Monk Back with Kids," *Batavia Daily News*, July 25, 1924; "Past and Present," *Batavia Daily News*, July 26, 1924; "Fresh Air Children Going Home Friday," *Batavia Daily News*, August 6, 1924.

44 Jackie Bonneau interview, October 30, 2008.

45 Marion White interview, with Quincy Troupe, December 1, 1990.

46 Ibid.; *New York Times*, May 6, 1923, June 5, 1923, June 3, 1924, June 16, 1924, June 23, 1926.

47 Marion White interview, with Quincy Troupe, December 1, 1990.

48 The first evidence of Thelonious Monk, Sr.'s presence in New York is from the 1925 Census. New York State Census, 1925, *New York County—Enumeration of Inhabitants, Assembly District 5, Election District 51*, p. 490. He is still listed in the Rocky Mount city directory in 1924 as "T. Lonis Monk," but he does not appear in the

1925 directory. In fact, he does not show up again in the city directory until 1938, when the next directory appears. *Telephone Directory: Rocky Mount, Nashville, Spring Hope, Whitakers, and Enfield, NC* (New Bern, NC: Home telephone and telegraph, 1924), p. 25; *Rocky Mount, N.C., City Directory, 1925* (Rocky Mt. and Richmond, VA: Hill Directory Co., 1925); *Hill's Rocky Mount, N.C., City Directory, 1938* (Rocky Mt. and Richmond, VA: Hill Directory Co., 1940), 202.

49 Interviews with Thomas Monk, Jr., Theolonious Monk, Evelyn Smith, Benetta Bines, January 30, 2004; Marion White interview, with Quincy Troupe, December 1, 1990; Peter Keepnews, "Young Monk," 6; U.S. Census, 1930, *Population Schedule: Manhattan Borough*, ED 31-383. Barbara's occupation is listed as "cleaner children's court." Although she held a city job, the New York City Civil List did not include domestic and maintenance workers in most Manhattan city institutions. See NYC Civil List, "Officials and Employees of the City of New York," *The City Record,* Jan–June, 1930, microfilm, roll 9.

50 The make-up of 243 West 63rd Street is derived largely from a careful reconstruction of every household using the 1930 Census [see U.S. Census, 1930, *Population Schedule: Manhattan Borough*, ED 31-383.] See also, Nathaniel Shepard, Jr., "Neighborhood: San Juan Hill, 'Eden' to the Eyes of a Playwright," *New York Times,* April 12, 1976. On the response to Barbara Monk and her family by neighbors, see Marion White interview, with Quincy Troupe, December 1, 1990; Author interviews with Geraldine Smith, Edith Smith, Thomas Monk, Theolonious Monk.

51 One of these block parties took place on Monk's fourteenth birthday. "Party for Children Today," *New York Times,* October 10, 1931.

52 Copyright registration, Thelonious Monk and Denzil Best, "Bimsha Swing" (sometimes listed as "Bemsha Swing" or "Bemesha Swing"), Bayes Music, Registration Number: EU 297366, dated December 15, 1952, Library of Congress, Washington, D.C. Monk knew the meaning of Bimsha or Bemsha when he co-wrote the tune. As he said in an interview with Francois Postif, the word comes "from the Antilles." Francois Postif, "'Round 'Bout Sphere," *Jazz Hot* 186 (April 1963), 24.

53 Marion White interview, with Quincy Troupe, December 1, 1990.

54 Pearl Gonzalez, "Monk Talk," *Down Beat* (October 28, 1971), 12. In those days it was not unusual for a family relocating to give away their pianos, given the cost and difficulty of moving these "white elephants." Abandoned pianos were so common in San Juan Hill and Harlem that they became a fire hazard. Also, radios had begun to replace pianos as the more popular form of home entertainment. "Blocked Fire Exits Found by Thousand," *New York Times,* August 27, 1930. The first reference to the make of Monk's piano is from Herbie Nichols, who visited Monk frequently in the mid-1940s. Herbie Nichols, "The Jazz Pianist—Purist," *Rhythm* (July, 1946), 11.

55 Author interview with Thomas Monk, Theolonious Monk, Charlotte Washington; Marion White interview, with Quincy Troupe, December 1, 1990.

56 Marion White interview, with Quincy Troupe, December 1, 1990; Leslie Gourse, *Straight No Chaser: The Life and Genius of Thelonious Monk* (New York: Schirmer Books, 1997), 7.

57 When exactly Thelonious, Sr. left is still not clear. He does not appear anywhere on the 1930 Census, but a boarder by the name of "Claude Smith" shows up in the Monk household. He is listed as thirty-six years old from North Carolina and an employee of the Pennsylvania Railroad. Given that no one in the family remembers a boarder living with the Monks, it is possible that "Smith" could have been a pseudonym for Thelonious, Sr., who might have felt compelled for some reason to hide his true identity. I don't know why; perhaps he was in trouble with the law? Given that Barbara was employed full-time, it is unlikely that they were receiving relief and had to hide the fact that she was married. Or, the boarder might really be a railway worker named Claude Smith, but where would he sleep in an already overcrowded two-bedroom apartment? There is absolutely no evidence that Barbara Monk was involved with any other men besides her husband, and given her strong religious views she would not have been living with a man out of wedlock. U.S. Census, 1930, *Population Schedule: Manhattan Borough*, ED 31-383 (April 1930).

58 *Hill's Rocky Mount, N.C., City Directory, 1938* (Rocky Mt. and Richmond, VA: Hill Directory Co., 1938), p. 20; *Hill's Rocky Mount, N.C., City Directory, 1940* (Rocky Mt. and Richmond, VA: Hill Directory Co., 1940), p. 236; U.S. Census, 1930, *Population Schedule: North Carolina, Rocky Mount City*, ED 33-30. Neither Eulah nor Hettie lived with their respective husbands, and they both worked as domestics. The address of the property was now 124 Dunn Street instead of 112 because the numbers had been reconfigured as more homes were built on the block. (There was neither a 120 nor a 124 Dunn Street in the 1910 Census.) Family members confirmed that Theodore "Babe" owned the property, now listed as 124 Dunn Street. Olivia Monk, Pam Kelley Monk, Conley F. Monk, Jr., Marcella Monk Flake, Evelyn Pue, interview, August 6, 2007.

3 "I Always Did Want to Play Piano"

1 Les Tomkins interview with Thelonious Monk, 1965, http://www.jazzprofessional.com/interviews/Thelonius%20Monk.htm.

2 Grover Sales, "I Wanted to Make it Better: Monk at the Black Hawk," *Jazz: A Quarterly of American Music* 5 (1960), 34.

3 Marion White interview, with Quincy Troupe, December 1, 1990. He once told an interviewer, "I would have loved to play trombone." Jean-Louis Noames, "Monk Entre Deux Sommes," *Jazz Magazine* 124 (November 1965), 47.

4 Monk interview with Russ Wilson, KJAZ San Francisco, April 17, 1960, recording in author's possession.

5 "Overton, Monk at the New School," June 20, 1963, CCP 104 (Disc 4), W. Eugene Smith Tapes, Center for Documentary Studies, Duke University; Sales, "I Wanted to Make It Better," 34; Monk interview with Russ Wilson, KJAZ San Francisco, April 17, 1960.

6 Marion White interview, with Quincy Troupe, December 1, 1990; Les Tomkins interview with Thelonious Monk, 1965; See also Gonzalez, "Monk Talk," 12.
7 Barry Farrell, "Loneliest Monk," *Time* 83 (February 28, 1964), 85.
8 It has been difficult to reconstruct Simon Wolf's life, beyond what Gordon Heath has left us in his memoir. Nevertheless, there are documents that reveal his age, background, occupation and address (he generally lived on the Upper West Side, having moved between 111th and 114th Streets). Simon Wolf, World War I Draft Registration Card #31-9-168A, June 5, 1917; *Manhattan Address Directory, 1921*.
9 Gordon Heath, *Deep Are the Roots: Memoirs of a Black Expatriate* (Amherst: University of Massachusetts Press, 1992), 22; Interview With Gordon Heath, by Camille Billops, February 18, 1975, Hatch-Billops Collection. Heath recalled in the interview that Wolf studied with Mischa Elman, whom he identified as the first violinist for the New York Philharmonic, but Elman was never a regular member of the Philharmonic. In the book he simply identifies Wolf's teacher as the concert master but did not mention his name. Based on the evidence available, Wolf had already identified himself as a professional performer around the time of World War I, so it is likely that Alfred Megerlin was his teacher. I am grateful to Richard Wandel, Associate Archivist of the New York Philharmonic Archives, for helping me figure this out. (Wandel e-mail to author, March 22, 2004.)
10 Heath was born September 20, 1918.
11 Heath, *Deep are the Roots*, 23.
12 Ibid., p. 35.
13 Sales, "I Wanted to Make It Better," 34.
14 Morroe Berger, Edward Berger and James Patrick, *Benny Carter: A Life in American Music,* vol. 1 (Metuchen, NJ: Scarecrow Press, 1982), 14–16.
15 H. Flemming: "A Posthumous Salute to Freddie Johnson," *Coda*, 4, no. 9 (1962), 3.
16 Mark Tucker, *Ellington: The Early Years* (Urbana, IL: University of Illinois Press, 1991), 101; Edward Kennedy Ellington, *Music is My Mistress* (New York: Da Capo Press, 1973), 106; John Edward Hasse, *Beyond Category: The Life and Genius of Duke Ellington* (New York: Simon & Schuster, 1993), 75-79, 14-108, 140-42, 279; Draft Registration Card, William A. Procope, 3317, September 12, 1918; Berger, Berger and Patrick, *Benny Carter*, vol. 1, pp. 15–16.
17 U.S. Census, 1930, *Population Schedule, Manhattan Borough*, ED 383.
18 Alberta Saunders interview, February 10, 2004 and April 1, 2004.
19 U.S. Census 1920, *Population Schedule: Manhattan Borough*, ED 457, p. 457; New York State Census, 1925, *New York County—Enumeration of Inhabitants, Assembly District 5, Election District 51*, p. 286; U.S. Census, 1930, *Population Schedule: Manhattan Borough*, ED 374.
20 Alberta Saunders interview, February 10, 2004.
21 Gourse, *Straight, No Chaser*, 10. Gourse gives no citation for evidence that he studied under "Professor" Buster Archer, or that Monk substituted for him in his late teens. No surviving family member I spoke with remembers hearing about this, and there is no evidence that Barbara Monk continued to attend services at Union after they moved to 145th Street. Unfortunately, Union's archives were destroyed in two separate fires. Besides, even if he did take lessons from Archer, he could not have been older than twelve years old since Union Baptist Church had already relocated to Harlem from West 63rd Street by 1930. Greater New York Federation of Churches, *The Negro Churches of Manhattan*, 30; *Manhattan Address Directory, 1925, 1929, 1933–34*; *New York Times*, July 21, 1926.
22 Thomas Monk, Jr., interview, February 16, 2004.
23 *New York Times*, June 26, 1928; *The Children's Aid Society, Seventy-Sixth Annual Report, 1928*, p. 42. Thanks to Victor Remer, archivist at the Children's Aid Society, for access to these valuable reports. AICP stands for the Association for Improving the Condition of the Poor.
24 The Children's Aid Society, Seventy-Sixth Annual Report, 1928, p. 41; *New York Times*, May 1, 1930.
25 Mavis Swire interview, March 8, 2004; "When I Was a Little Girl at the 'Center,'" letter from Mavis Swire to Gil Snow, n.d., in Ms. Swire's possession.
26 Theo Wilson interview with Liz Hinton, October 29, 2004, New York City.
27 Mavis Swire interview, March 8, 2004; "When I Was a Little Girl at the 'Center,'" letter from Mavis Swire to Gil Snow, n.d., in Ms. Swire's possession.
28 "Negro Child Centre in 63rd St; Budget of the Columbus Hill Settlement, Endowed by Rockefeller, Is Exceeded." *New York Times*, May 1, 1930; "Columbus Hill Centre Will Reopen Soon; Closing is temporary for repairs, not permanent, due to lack of funds, officials say," *New York Times*, May 2, 1930.
29 Marion White interview, with Quincy Troupe, December 1, 1990.
30 Thomas Monk, Sr. interview with Phil Schaap, WKCR, Thelonious Monk Birthday Broadcast, 1984.
31 Assignment for Mr. Marks, March 3, 1933, Thelonious Monk Composition book, Spring 1933, Monk family papers. On the other hand, Monk's days at camp left him with a deep fascination with the country. In the same composition book three weeks earlier, he wrote that his favorite magazine was *Boys Life*, the official monthly of the Boy Scouts. Secretly, I think he wanted to be a Boy Scout himself. He liked, among other things, the "section . . . which teaches you necessary things while camping. Most boy scouts read them and I think it is a good magazine to read." Assignment for Mr. Marks, February 9, 1933, Thelonious Monk Composition Book, Spring 1933.
32 Thelonious mentions playing at the community center in Robert Kotlowitz, "After Hours: Monk Talk," *Harper's Magazine* 223 (November 15, 1961), 21.
33 Interview with Nellie Monk, February 8, 2002; on Taylor's address and family background, U.S. Census, 1930, *Population Schedule: Manhattan Borough*, ED 383.
34 Quoted in Peter Keepnews, "Young Monk," 8.
35 Correspondence from Jeni Dahmus, Archivist, The Juilliard School, November 10, 2000.

36 Nellie Monk interview, January 12, 2002.
37 "Student Cumulative Record, Board of Education, City of New York—Thelonious Monk," Files of Stuyvesant High School. The only school records available are from junior high and high school. I examined the original version of his report card, which is in the possession of Stuyvesant High School. Evidently, when students graduate from junior high to high school, their report card goes with them, which is why JHS 69 grades are listed alongside his Stuyvesant grades.
38 "Student Cumulative Record, Board of Education, City of New York—Thelonious Monk," Files of Stuyvesant High School.
39 Jackie Bonneau interview, October 30, 2008.
40 Files of Stuyvesant High School, "Student Cumulative Record, Board of Education, City of New York," Thelonious Monk; Conversation with Renee Leveen, administrator, Stuyvesant High School.
41 NYC Civil List, "Officials and Employees of the City of New York," *The City Record,* Jan–June, 1930, microfilm, roll 9; "Tenement 'Santa' Slain By Robbers," *New York Times,* August 26, 1935; "Narcotics Sold in the Street," *New York Times,* June 24, 1933; "Narcotics Raiders Bare 'Catacombs,'" *New York Times,* February 2, 1939.
42 This story is repeated in Gourse, *Straight, No Chaser,* 8.
43 Stuyvesant High School, *The Indicator: Class of January 1933* (New York, 1933); Stuyvesant High School, *The Indicator: Class of January 1934* (New York, 1934); Stuyvesant High School, *The Indicator: Class of June 1935* (New York, 1935). I'm grateful to Ms. Renee Leveen for granting me access to the original Stuyvesant yearbooks.
44 Files of Stuyvesant High School, "Student Cumulative Record, Board of Education, City of New York," Thelonious Monk.
45 Assignment for Mr. Marks, March 15, 1933, Thelonious Monk Composition Book, Spring 1933. The passage to which he refers appears in the opening paragraphs. Charles Dickens, *A Tale of Two Cities* (New York: Signet Classics, 1997), 14.
46 Assignment for Mr. Marks, March 13, 1933, Thelonious Monk Composition Book, Spring 1933.
47 Assignment for Mr. Marks, March 24, 1933, Thelonious Monk Composition Book, Spring 1933.
48 Thomas Monk, Sr. interview with Phil Schaap, WKCR, Thelonious Monk Birthday Broadcast, 1984; U.S. Census, 1930, *Population Schedule, Manhattan Borough,* E.D. 376.
49 Marion White interview, with Quincy Troupe, December 1, 1990.
50 Marv Goldberg, *More Than Words Can Say: The Ink Spots and Their Music* (Lanham, MD: Scarecrow Press, 1998); New York *Amsterdam News,* June 26, 1954. You can also hear Francis on The Ink Spots, *The Beautiful Music Company* (MCA MSD-35253 [1991]), and The Ink Spots, *Their Greatest and Finest Performances* (Reader's Digest Music MSD3-37113 [1997]).
51 Nellie Monk interview, January 12, 2002.
52 Ibid.; Geraldine Smith interview, February 12, 2004.
53 Department of Health, City of New York, Certificate of Death, Etta Smith, #7446, Municipal Archives. The Smiths lost another daughter, Rosa Smith, some time between late 1930 and 1932. She appears on the 1930 Census but by the time Etta died there are only three surviving siblings. U.S. Census, 1930, Population Schedule: Brooklyn Borough, ED 24-1559.
54 Department of Health, City of New York, Certificate of Death, Nellie Smith #17062; State of Florida, Certificate of Death, Elisha Bennett Smith, #12469; U.S. Census, 1880, *Population Schedule: Sumter, Georgia,* p. 124D.
55 Dr. Anna Lou Smith interview, April 7, 2004.
56 Ibid.; U.S. Census, 1880, *Population Schedule: Sumter, Georgia,* p. 124D; State of Florida, Certificate of Death, Elisha Bennett Smith, #12469; Interviews with Judith Smith, Evelyn Smith, Clifton Smith, and Benetta Bines, January 30, 2004. According to Nellie Smith's death certificate, she had resided in New York for ten years at the time of her death in 1936. Department of Health, City of New York, Certificate of Death, Nellie Smith #17062.
57 U.S. Census, 1930, *Population Schedule: Brooklyn Borough,* ED 24-1559; Interviews with Judith Smith, Evelyn Smith, Clifton Smith, and Benetta Bines, January 30, 2004; Department of Health, City of New York, Certificate of Death, Etta Smith, #7446, Municipal Archives.
58 Nellie Monk interview, January 12, 2002.
59 Brown, "More Man Than Myth," 45.
60 U.S. Census, 1930, *Population Schedule, Manhattan Borough,* ED 375; Geraldine Smith interview, February 12, 2004.
61 Geraldine Smith interview, February 12, 2004.
62 Ibid.
63 U.S. Census, *Population Schedule, Manhattan Borough, 1930,* ED 375; Interviews with Monk/Smith family, January 30, 2004. Brereton made several recordings with the Noble Sissle Orchestra, some of which appear on Sidney Bechet, *The Sidney Bechet Story* 4-CD Set (Proper Box 18 [2001]); Lena Horne, *Complete RCA-Victor Black & White Masters* (Jazz Factory 22827 [2002]); *Anthology of Big Band Swing 1930–1955* (Decca GRD2-629 [CD]). Also, he can be heard on Sarah Vaughan, *Sarah Vaughan Sings with John Kirby and his Orchestra* (Riverside RLP 2511 [1946]).
64 U.S. Census, 1930, *Population Schedule, Manhattan Borough,* ED 376; Marion White interview, with Quincy Troupe, December 1, 1990; Mavis Swire interview, March 8, 2004; Interviews with Monk/Smith family, January 30, 2004.
65 Les Tomkins interview with Thelonious Monk, 1965.
66 Nellie Monk, interview, January 12, 2002.

67   See *New York Age*, March 31, May 19, June 16, 1934; March 9, March 16, 1935. The histories of the Apollo all agree that Amateur Night began in 1934, but they do not make a distinction between the Monday night competitions and the Wednesday night "Amateur Hour." The black press, like the *New York Age*, reveal a more complicated story. Jack Schiffman, *Harlem Heyday: A Pictorial History of Modern Black Show Business and the Apollo Theatre* (Buffalo: Prometheus Books, 1984), 110; Ted Fox, *Showtime at the Apollo* (New York: Da Capo, 1993, orig. 1983).

68   Marion White interview, with Quincy Troupe, December 1, 1990.

69   Nellie Monk interview, January 12, 2002. Monk told writer Frank London Brown the same thing in 1959: his band kept winning "until the manager grew tired of paying the same *amateur* every week." Frank London Brown, "Magnificent Monk of Music," *Ebony* 14 (May 1959), 124.

70   *New York Age*, February 18, 1939; *New York Age*, July 29, 1939; see also, John H. Thompson, "Over 5,000 Amateurs have Appeared on the Apollo Theater's Amateur Hour in 7 years," *Amsterdam News*, June 15, 1940.

71   *Amsterdam News*, March 10, 1934.

72   Thomas Monk, Sr. interview with Phil Schaap, WKCR, Thelonious Monk Birthday Broadcast, 1984.

73   James M. Doran, *Herman Chittison: A Bio-Discography* (The International Association of Jazz Record Collectors: Monograph 2, 1993), 7–9. Monk could not have seen Chittison live again until 1940, when he finally returned to the states after a six-year residency in Europe. By 1942, Monk would have caught his hero on the weekly CBS series "Casey, Crime Photographer," also known as "Flashgun Casey." Chittison played "Ernie," the house pianist at the fictional "Blue Note Café," Casey's main haunt where the cases were often solved. Many young pianists listened to the show religiously just to catch a few bars of Chittison's piano. Horace Silver, who was eleven years younger than Thelonious, remembers: "I'd put my ear to the speaker so I could hear him more clearly. When he finished, I'd run downstairs to the kitchen where the piano was and try to copy some of what I had heard him play." See Horace Silver, *Let's Get to the Nitty Gritty: The Autobiography of Horace Silver*, ed. Phil Pastras (Los Angeles and Berkeley: University of California Press, 2006), 21; J. Randolph Cox and David S. Siegel, *Flashgun Casey, Crime Photographer: From the Pulps, to the Radio and Beyond* (Yorktown, NY: Book Hunter Press, 2005).

74   One can certainly hear this on recordings he made with singer Arita Day, recorded in Paris in 1934. *Herman Chittison, 1933–1941* (Classics 690).

75   U.S. Census, 1930, *Population Schedule: Manhattan Borough*, ED: 364; Thomas Monk, Jr. interview, February 16, 2004; Alberta Saunders interview, February 10, 2004; For a description of the Friday night dances at the Center, Mavis Swire interview, March 8, 2004; "When I Was a Little Girl at the 'Center,'" letter from Mavis Swire to Gil Snow, n.d., in Ms. Swire's possession.

76   Thomas Monk, Jr., interview, February 16, 2004.

77   Geraldine Smith interview, February 12, 2004.

78   Ibid.; Interviews with Monk/Smith family, January 30, 2004.

79   The Best family resided at 315 E. 100th St. His father worked as an elevator repair man for an apartment building. U.S. Census, 1930, *Manhattan Borough, Population Schedule:* ED 31-810. On Denzil Best's music background, Pat Harris, "None Better than Best with a Brush," *Down Beat* (April 20, 1951), 18; Burt Korall, *Drummin' Men: The Heartbeat of Jazz – The Bebop Years* (New York: Oxford University Press, 2002), 22–25; Ira Gitler, *Jazz Masters of the Forties* (New York: Da Capo Press, 1966), 190; "Drummer Denzil Best Dies of Skull Fracture," *Down Beat* (July 1, 1965), 14.

80   George Simon, "Bop's Dixie to Monk," *Metronome* (April 1948), 34; also reprinted in George Simon, *Simon Says: The Sights and Sounds of the Swing Era, 1935–1955* (New Rochelle, NY: Arlington House, 1971).

81   Hentoff, "The Private Word of Thelonious Monk," *Esquire* (April 1960), 134.

82   Files of Stuyvesant High School, "Student Cumulative Record, Board of Education, City of New York," Thelonious Monk.

83   *New York Times*, January 23, 1921; Harold G. Campbell, "High School Has a Boom," *New York Times*, September 24, 1933.

4   "We Played and She Healed"

1   Alonzo White interview, February 23, 2004; Marion White interview, with Quincy Troupe, December 1, 1990.

2   Thelonious Monk interview with Valerie Wilmer and John "Hoppy" Hopkins, March 14, 1965, cassette tape in author's possession. I am extremely grateful to Ms. Wilmer for sharing a copy of this incredible taped interview.

3   Peter Keepnews, "Young Monk," 9.

4   The only reference I've ever found for the evangelist's name comes from Leslie Gourse (*Straight, No Chaser*), but her source, an elderly man who did not know Monk when I spoke with him, is questionable. There is no evidence of a Reverend Graham on the circuit, or anyone who had the nickname Texas Warhorse. Nevertheless, without evidence to the contrary, I will use this name to identify her.

5   Monk interview with Valerie Wilmer, March 14, 1965.

6   Peter Keepnews, "Young Monk," 9.

7   Nat Hentoff, "Just Call Him Thelonious," *Down Beat* (July 25, 1956), 15. To *Time* magazine's Barry Farrell, he summed up his trip in five words: "we played and she healed." "The Loneliest Monk," *Time* 83 (February 28, 1964), 86.

8   Pearl Gonzalez, "Monk Talk," *Down Beat* (October 28, 1971), 12.

9   Monk interview with Valerie Wilmer and John Hopkins, March 14, 1965. An edited version of this quote appeared in Wilmer's article, "Monk on Monk," *Down Beat* (June 3, 1965), 20–22.

10 Tammy L. Kernodle, *Soul on Soul: The Life and Music of Mary Lou Williams* (Boston: Northeastern University Press, 2004), 182.
11 Charlotte Washington interview, April 5, 2004.
12 Monk interview with Valerie Wilmer and John Hopkins, March 14, 1965.
13 There are at least three denominations associated with the "sanctified" church: Holiness, Apostolic, and Pentecostal. The Holiness church have some identifiable African roots, but in its official capacity can be traced back at least to the 1880s. Unlike the Apostolic and Pentecostal churches, the Holiness church does not accept speaking in tongues as a doctrinal necessity, and in fact some Holiness churches reject it outright. Apostolics, on the other hand, reject Holiness and Pentecostal emphasis on the trinity, believing in the oneness of God as embodied in Jesus Christ. See, Cheryl J. Sanders, *Saints in Exile: The Holiness-Pentecostal Experience in African American Religion and Culture* (New York: Oxford University Press, 1996), 4–5; Hans Baer, *The Black Spiritual Movement: A Religious Response to Racism* (Knoxville, Tenn.: University of Tennessee Press, 1984). One of the most fascinating essays on the sanctified church remains Zora Neale Hurston, *The Sanctified Church* (Berkeley: Turtle Island, 1981).
14 Sanders, *Saints in Exile*, 7.
15 Geraldine Smith Interview, February 12, 2004.
16 Clarence Boyer, *The Golden Age of Gospel*, photos by Lloyd Yearwood (Urbana and Chicago: University of Illinois Press, 2000), 19. See also, James Daniel Tyus, "A Study of Four Religious Cults Operating Among Negroes" (M.A. Thesis, Howard University, 1938), copy in Dupree African American Pentecostal and Holiness Collection, 1876–1989, Schomburg Center for Black History and Culture, NYPL (Hereafter, Dupree Collection).
17 Jerma A. Jackson, *Singing in My Soul: Black Gospel Music in a Secular Age* (Chapel Hill: University of North Carolina Press, 2004), 27–33.
18 Jackson, *Singing in My Soul*, 36–39.
19 Meharry H. Lewis, *Mary Lena Lewis Tate: "A Street Called Straight" (Acts 9:11): The Ten Most Dynamic and Productive Black Female Holiness Preachers of the Twentieth Century* (Nashville: The New and Living Way Publishing Co., 2002), 3–5, 10.
20 Lewis, *Mary Lena Lewis Tate*, 19. Evangelists also take instruction from Luke 4:18, 19.
21 For descriptions of these Pentecostal revivals; beginning with the first revivals at the historic Azusa Mission in Los Angeles in 1906, see Wayne Warner, ed., *Touched by Fire: Eye-Witness Accounts of the Early 20th Century Pentecostal Revival* (Logos International: Plainfield, NJ, 1978); Boyer, *The Golden Age of Gospel*, 13–18; Lewis, *Mary Lena Lewis Tate*, 22.
22 There are many descriptions of Pentecostal services and revivals; my own description here derives largely from Boyer, *The Golden Age of Gospel*, 13–17; Warner, ed., *Touched by Fire*.
23 Wilmer, "Monk on Monk," 21.
24 Michael W. Harris, *The Rise of Gospel Blues: The Music of Thomas Andrew Dorsey in the Urban Church* (New York: Oxford University Press, 1992), 101–111; Jackson, *Singing in My Soul*, 49–65.
25 Harris, *Rise of the Gospel Blues*, 99. There has been much written on the rise of gospel music in the twentieth century. Some of the essential texts include, Anthony Heilbut, *The Gospel Sound: Good News and Bad Times* (Limelight Editions, 1997); Bernice Johnson Reagon, *We'll Understand It Better By And By: Pioneering African-American Gospel Composers* (Washington, D.C.: Smithsonian Institution, 1992).
26 Jackson, *Singing in My Soul*, 50.
27 Bernice Johnson Reagon, "Searching for Tindley," in *We'll Understand it Better By and By: Pioneering African American Gospel Composers*, 37–52; Horace Clarence Boyer, "Charles Albert Tindley," in *We'll Understand It Better By and By*, 53–78. See also Charles Tindley, *New Songs of Paradise* (Philadelphia: Paradise Publishers, 1916), copy in Box 15, Dupree Collection.
28 Monk uses this title when he introduces the song on a German television program in 1963. Thelonious Monk, "By and By, When the Morning Comes," SWF-TV Baden Baden, Germany, March 2, 1963, unreleased recording in author's possession. Incidentally, Monk's titling of the song generated a great deal of confusion for record producers and discographers unfamiliar with black sacred music. Tindley was not given composer's credit for the song. Instead, the song has been attributed to Richard Rodgers and Lorenz Hart, who had composed an entirely different tune called "Bye and Bye," a syrupy love song for the musical theater production of *Dearest Enemy*. The error is reproduced even in the most substantial discography to date, Chris Sheridan, *Brilliant Corners: A Bio-Discography of Thelonious Monk* (Westport and London: Greenwood Press, 2001), 95 and 121. *Dearest Enemy* premiered on Broadway in 1925 and was made into a film in 1955. See Richard Rodgers and Lorenz Hart, *Rodgers and Hart: A Musical Anthology* (Milwaukee, WI: Hal Leonard, 1984). A similar though less severe example of this problem is Columbia Records' decision to use Monk's title, "This Is My Story, This Is My Song," for his version of "Blessed Assurance." Once again, Monk called the song by the first line of the chorus (or the refrain). See Thelonious Monk, *Straight, No Chaser* (Columbia CL2651).
29 Clark Terry, *In Orbit* (Riverside RLP12-271).
30 Reagon, "Searching for Tindley," 51.
31 Sanders, *Saints in Exile*, 61–65; Sterling Stuckey, *Slave Culture: Nationalist Theory and the Foundations of Black America* (New York: Oxford University Press, 1987), 3–97, for the most substantive treatment of the ring shout.
32 Religious scholar Hugh Roberts goes so far as to suggest that Monk's dance was a form of sacred expression, an act of worship. He wrote: "even the improvisatory dance with shuffling feet and churning elbows that became one of Monk's trademarks . . . was part of his individuation and individual religious expression. Though he apparently used it to check out the rhythm of the music that was playing either audibly or in his inner ear, it was a holy dance—a dance to his individuational, musical objectification of God's will." Hugh J. Roberts, "Impro-

visation, Individuation, and Immanence: Thelonius [sic] Monk," *Black Sacred Music: A Journal of Theomusicology* 3, no. 2 (Fall 1989), 50–56.

33 Lewis, *Mary Lena Lewis Tate*, 22–23; see also, Boyer, *The Golden Age of Gospel*, 19.
34 Lewis, *Mary Lena Lewis Tate*, 24.
35 Mary Lou Williams, "Autobiographical Notebook, #2," manuscript, p. 173, Personal Papers, Mary Lou Williams Collection.
36 Mary Lou Williams, "Then Came Zombie Music," *Melody Maker* (May 8, 1954), 11; on the jazz scene in Kansas City, see Tammy L. Kernodle, *Soul on Soul: The Life and Music of Mary Lou Williams* (Boston: Northeastern University Press, 2004), 50–51; Linda Dahl, *Morning Glory: A Biography of Mary Lou Williams* (NY: Pantheon Books, 1999), 190; Nathan W. Pearson, Jr., *Goin' to Kansas City* (Urbana and Chicago: University of Illinois Press, 1987), 98–99.
37 Marcellus Green interview, November 11, 2003. I can't establish an exact date for Monk's gig with Andy Kirk, but Thelonious Monk, Jr., has also confirmed the story that Kirk hired Monk. Thelonious Monk, Jr., interview, April 4, 2005. Leslie Gourse also acknowledges Monk's brief stint with Andy Kirk, but she claims it was for the reopening of the Cotton Club. This is impossible because it reopened in 1936 and closed in 1940. Leslie Gourse, *Straight No Chaser*, 39.
38 Ad for Moten's band, *Kansas City Call*, June 14, 1935. See also, Pearson, Jr., *Goin' to Kansas City*; Frank Driggs and Chuck Haddix, *Kansas City Jazz: From Ragtime to Bebop—A History* (New York: Oxford University Press, 2005); Alyn Shipton, *A New History of Jazz* (New York and London: Continuum, 2001), 305–309.
39 Douglas Henry Daniels, *One-O'Clock Jump: The Unforgettable History of the Oklahoma City Blue Devils* (Boston: Beacon Press, 2006), 164–180; see also, Stanley Dance, *The World of Count Basie* (New York: Da Capo Press, 1980); Count Basie, *Good Morning Blues: The Autobiography of Count Basie, as told to Albert Murray* (New York: Random House, 1985).
40 Douglas Henry Daniels, *Lester Leaps In: The Life and Times of Lester 'Pres' Young* (Boston: Beacon Press, 2002), 188–89.
41 Quoted in Shipton, *A New History of Jazz*, 308.
42 Monk interview with Valerie Wilmer and John Hopkins, March 14, 1965.
43 Frank London Brown, "Magnificent Monk of Music," *Ebony* 14 (May 1959), 124.
44 Thomas Monk, Jr., Interview, February 16, 2004; Charlotte Washington Interview, April 5, 2004.
45 Thomas Monk, Jr., Interview, February 16, 2004.
46 Ibid.; Charlotte Washington Interview, April 5, 2004; Alonzo White interview, February 23, 2004.
47 Department of Health, City of New York, "Certificate of Death, Nellie Smith #17062," Municipal Archives, Manhattan.
48 Geraldine Smith interview, February 12, 2004.
49 Ibid.
50 Ibid.
51 Geraldine Smith interview, February 12, 2004; Anna Lou Smith, interview, April 7, 2004.
52 Thomas Monk, Sr. interview with Phil Schaap, WKCR, Thelonious Monk Birthday Broadcast, October 10, 1984; T. S. Monk, Jr., interview with Phil Schaap, October 10, 1994.

5 "Why Can't You Play Music Like the Ink Spots?"

1 Nellie Monk interview, January 12, 2002.
2 Charlotte Washington interview, April 5, 2004.
3 Mavis Swire interview, March 8, 2004.
4 Geraldine Smith interview, February 12, 2004.
5 Theolonious Monk, interview, January 30, 2004.
6 Thomas Monk, Jr., Interview, February 16, 2004; Alonzo White interview, February 23, 2004; Monk family group interview, January 30, 2004.
7 New York State Census, 1925, *New York County—Enumeration of Inhabitants, Assembly District 5, Election District 46*, p. 326; U.S. Census, 1930, *Population Schedule: Manhattan Borough*, 31-374 (April 1930); *New York City Directory, 1931–1932*. Below is a list of all the Richardson children and their ages according to the 1930 Census: Wilbert 13; Rubie 12; Linette 11; Rose 8; Archibald 6; Lunsford about 18 months.
8 Alonzo White interview, February 23, 2004.
9 Geraldine Smith interview, February 12, 2004; Nellie Monk interview, January 12, 2002.
10 Evelyn Smith interview, February 12, 2004.
11 Thomas Monk, Jr., interview, February 16, 2004.
12 Theolonious Monk Interview, January 30, 2004.
13 Nat Hentoff, "Just Call Him Thelonious," *Down Beat* (July 25, 1956), 15.
14 Orrin Keepnews, "Thelonious Monk's music may be first sign of be-bop's legitimacy," *Record Changer* (April 1948), 5, 20; also reprinted in Orrin Keepnews, *The View From Within*, 112.
15 Valerie Wilmer and John "Hoppy" Hopkins interview with Monk, March 14, 1965; Peter Keepnews, "Young Monk," 11.
16 Pianist and writer Herbie Nichols was the first to identify his Klein. Herbie Nichols, "The Jazz Pianist—Purist," *Rhythm* (July 1946), 11–12.
17 *International Musician* 37, no. 9 (March 1939), 20.
18 Emilie Elkin Khair, *Passion's Piano: the Eddie Heywood Story, Based on the Private Account of Evelyn Heywood About Her Beloved Music Man, Eddie* (Atlanta, GA: Care Publishing House, 1997).

19 Jean Clouzet and Michel Delorme, "L'amertume du prophète," *Jazz Magazine*, 9, no. 93 (April 1963), 38. Further evidence of Monk's relationship with Heywood as well as the older generation of stride pianists is a wonderful photograph of Monk, Art Tatum, and Eddie Heywood together shooting the breeze in *Rhythm* magazine. See John R. Gibson, "A Cavalcade of the Negro Dance Musician," *Rhythm* (July 1946), 22.

20 Billy Taylor interview, January 26, 2004. I can date Taylor's visit fairly accurately because Benny Goodman played at the World's Fair in September of 1939. Ross Firestone, *Swing, Swing, Swing: The Life and Times of Benny Goodman* (New York: W. W. Norton, 1994), 272.

21 Paul Matthews, "Billy Taylor Interview (Part 2)," *Cadence* (November 1995), 23.

22 Billy Taylor Interview, January 26, 2004.

23 Matthews, "Billy Taylor Interview," 24.

24 Billy Taylor Interview, January 26, 2004. He also tells a version of this story in Leslie Gourse, *Straight, No Chaser*, 16. Much is made of the "fact" that James P. Johnson lived in Thelonious Monk's neighborhood. However, he was not living there when Monk began playing music. In 1930, he lived in Queens on 108th Avenue, and by the time Monk appears on the scene he was firmly ensconced in Harlem, at 267 West 140th Street. See U.S. Census, 1930, *Population Schedule: Queens Borough*, ED 1161.

25 Matthews, "Billy Taylor Interview," 25.

26 Willie "The Lion" Smith, with George Hoefer, *Music on My Mind: The Memoirs of an American Pianist* (New York: Doubleday, 1964), 155.

27 Ibid., 253.

28 Teddy Wilson, with Arie Ligthart and Humphrey Van Loo, *Teddy Wilson Talks Jazz* (New York and London: Continuum, 2001), 114.

29 Those who have defended Monk from critics who assert that he has no "technique" tend to point to moments when he sounds like James P. Johnson or Art Tatum or Teddy Wilson. Examples abound, from Frank London Brown's 1958 interview (p. 15) to Gunther Schuller, "Thelonious Monk," *Jazz Review* (November 1958), 23, not to mention Mary Lou Williams's comment about Monk's technique in the previous chapter. (For an exhaustive list of examples and an excellent discussion of why proponents of Monk rely on these exceptional moments to prove he has technique, see David Kahn Feurzeig, "Making the Right Mistakes: James P. Johnson, Thelonious Monk, and the Trickster Aesthetic," [Ph.D. diss., Cornell University, 1997], 45–61.) In other words, it is when Monk sounds like someone else that he demonstrates "technique" and facility. If we buy this line of reasoning, then we might conclude that all he learned from the Harlem stride pianists was how to play like *them*, not techniques that might advance his own approach to the piano. I concur with musicologist David Feurzeig, who shows us that what we think of as Monk's "eccentric," unorthodox, and dissonant playing owes a great deal to James P. Johnson and company. Besides Monk's characteristic "bent notes" (which we hear on Johnson's recording of "Mule Walk"), Feurzeig identifies what he calls "trickster elements" in both of their music. These elements include "discontinuity, harmonic conflict, splattered notes, and a loping unevenness" (p. 61). Although it is beyond the scope of this book, Feurzeig makes a persuasive case for an affinity between Johnson and Monk, though he is skeptical of the idea that Monk spent any considerable time with Johnson.

30 U.S. Census, 1930, *Population Schedule: Manhattan Borough*, ED 581. On the history of the Kuna, see James Howe, *A People Who Would Not Kneel: Panama, the United States, and the San Blas Kuna* (Washington, D. C.: Smithsonian Institution Press, 1998).

31 George Hoefer, "Little Benny Harris," *Down Beat* (September 12, 1963), 38.

32 Quoted in Dick Hadlock, "Benny Harris and the Coming of Modern Jazz," *Metronome* 78, no. 10 (1961), 18.

33 Hoefer, "Little Benny Harris," 38.

34 Ibid.; Hadlock, "Benny Harris," 18–19; Leonard Feather, *Inside Be-bop* (New York: J. J. Robbins and Sons, 1948), 85.

35 Mike Hennessey, *Klook: The Story of Kenny Clarke* (Pittsburgh: University of Pittsburgh Press, 1990), 6–24; George Hoefer: "Klook: Kenny Clarke's Early Recordings," *Down Beat* (March 28, 1963), 23; Burt Korall, "View from the Seine," *Down Beat* (December 5,1963), 17; Shapiro and Hentoff, eds., *Hear Me Talkin' To Ya*, 347–48; Ira Gitler, *Jazz Masters of the Forties* (New York: Da Capo, 1983, 2nd ed.), 175–179.

36 Ira Gitler, *Swing to Bop: An Oral History of the Transition in Jazz in the 1940s* (New York: Oxford University Press, 1985), 52; James M. Doran and Barry Kernfeld, "White, Sonny," in *The New Grove Dictionary of Jazz*, 2nd ed., edited by Barry Kernfeld. *Grove Music Online. Oxford Music Online*, http://www.oxfordmusiconline .com/subscriber/article/grove/music/J481800 (accessed February 23, 2009). Leonard Feather identified White as Clarke's cousin, but I've not been able to confirm this and given the frequent errors in Feather's text, I'm a bit skeptical. (Feather, *Inside Be-Bop*, 8.) On White, see also Donald Clarke, *Wishing on the Moon: The Life and Times of Billie Holiday* (New York: Penguin Books, 1994), 171–72.

37 Marion White interview, with Quincy Troupe, December 1, 1990.

38 George Simon, "Bop's Dixie to Monk," *Metronome* (April 1948), 34; slso reprinted in George Simon, *Simon Says: The Sights and Sounds of the Swing Era, 1935–1955* (New Rochelle, NY: Arlington House, 1971). The official spelling of "Massapequa" has no "h" on the end, but it is frequently spelled "Massapequah."

39 On Jimmy Wright's recordings, see *Tom Lord Jazz Discography*, CD-Rom, Version 4.4.1. In 1939, he resided at 64 West 128th St. [See *Local 802 Directory*.]

40 Albert Vollmer, "Purnell, Keg," In *The New Grove Dictionary of Jazz*, 2nd ed., edited by Barry Kernfeld. *Grove Music Online. Oxford Music Online*, http://www.oxfordmusiconline.com/subscriber/article/grove/music/ J365600 (accessed February 24, 2009). Purnell lived at 55 West 110th in 1939, then moved to West 113th in 1941. [See *Local 802 Directory*.]

41 Minutes of Regular Membership Meeting, October 11, 1935, Records of AFM Local 802, microfilm, Tamiment Library.

42 Robin D. G. Kelley, "Without A Song: New York Musicians Strike Out Against Technology," in Dana Frank, Robin D. G. Kelley, and Howard Zinn, *Three Strikes: The Fighting Spirit of Labor's Last Century* (Boston: Beacon Press, 2001), 121–155. On the decline in record sales and overall conditions of the industry in the 1930s, see David W. Stowe, *Swing Changes: Big Band Jazz in New Deal America* (Cambridge, Mass.: Harvard University Press, 1994), 94–140; Shipton, *A New History of Jazz*, 318–319; Ted Gioa, *The History of Jazz* (New York: Oxford University Press, 1997), 136–37.

43 Kelley, "Without a Song," 138; *New York Times*, November 5, December 13 and 19, 1934.

44 David W. Stowe, *Swing Changes: Big Band Jazz in New Deal America* (Cambridge, Mass.: Harvard University Press, 1994), 122–23, 127; Samuel B. Charters and Leonard Kunstadt, *Jazz: A History of the New York Scene* (New York: Da Capo Press, 1981), 262–63.

45 Minutes of the Executive Board, February 4, 1947, Records of AFM Local 802. It should be noted that scale for dance bands in general was lower than scale for concert performers. In 1936 musicians in dance bands received a minimum of $42.00 for a seven-day work week consisting of five hour evenings and three matinees (a total of forty-four hours), concert performers earned $60.00 for six evenings for four-hour performances, or twenty-four hours of work. And they were entitled to an additional $10.00 for Sunday evening concerts. Not surprisingly, film studio musicians fetched the highest rates, earning $200.00 for a five-and-one-half-day work week not exceeding thirty-three hours. AFM Local 802, *Price List Governing Special and Regular Engagements of the Associated Musicians of Greater New York* (Newark, 1936), 44.

46 Kernodle, *Soul on Soul*, 76–77; Stowe, *Swing Changes*, 122–127.

47 Stowe, *Swing Changes*, 122.

48 Ibid., 129.

49 Simon, "Bop's Dixie to Monk," 34.

50 Red Callender and Elaine Cohen, *Unfinished Dream: The Musical World of Red Callender* (London and New York: Quartet Books, 1985), 40–41.

51 Dr. Anna Lou Smith, interview, April 7, 2004.

52 "Geraldine McMillan and James Smith," Marriage license, June 27, 1938, Vol. 6, no. 13432, Office of the City Clerk, Manhattan.

53 Geraldine Smith interview, February 12, 2004; Jackie Bonneau interview, October 30, 2008. Evidently, Geraldine was three months pregnant when she and Sonny married.

54 "Six Trade Schools Will Reopen Today," *New York Times*, January 7, 1935; "Trade School Chartered," *New York Times*, April 17, 1935; *New York Times*, September 18, 1938; *New York Times*, September 23, 1938; *New York Times*, January 4, 1940.

55 Geraldine Smith interview, February 12, 2004.

6 "They Weren't Giving Any Lectures"

1 This description of Minton's was constructed out of many different sources, all cited below. The reference to the bathroom door slamming, however, comes from George Hoefer, "Thelonious Monk in the '40s," *Down Beat* (October 25, 1962), 43–44. And one can hear Monk's name shouted, usually by musicians but perhaps by audiences, too, on some of the recordings made by Jerry Newman cited below.

2 Nat Hentoff, "Just Call Him Thelonious," *Down Beat* (July 25, 1956), 15–16; Neither Bud Powell, nor Charlie Parker, were on the scene then, and Mary Lou Williams doesn't settle in New York until 1943, months after Charlie Christian had already died of tuberculosis. And as for Dizzy, Monk's recollection is that the great bebop trumpeter appeared at Minton's "very rarely." Orrin Keepnews, "Thelonious Monk's Music," 5, 20, also reprinted in Keepnews, *The View From Within*, 112.

3 Ira Gitler, *Swing to Bop: An Oral History of the Transition in Jazz in the 1940s* (New York: Oxford University Press, 1985), 85.

4 Ralph Ellison, "The Golden Age, Time Past," in *Shadow and Act* (New York: Signet Books, 1964), 200.

5 U.S. Department of Interior, National Park Service, *Historic Preservation Certification Application: The Cecil Hotel, Location of Minton's Playhouse, Submitted by 106-10 W. 118th Street Low-Income Housing Partnership*, July 3, 1986; also author observations.

6 There is almost no biographical information on M. H. Minton. Using the 1920 census, I was able to establish his birthplace and birth year as well as his residence on West 140th Street in Harlem. He was married to Ella Minton but had no children. I found it particularly interesting that he was identified as "Mulatto" rather than Negro, which suggests he was light-skinned and, in some circumstances, might have been able to pass for white. U.S. Census, 1920, *Population Schedule: Manhattan Borough*, ED 1439.

7 Wilbur Sweatman, *Sweatman's Jazz Band* (Crescent 10058); Gunther Schuller, *Early Jazz: Its Roots and Musical Development* (New York: Oxford University Press, 1986), 260.

8 Percival Outram, "Activities Among Union Musicians," *New York Age*, January 28, 1933.

9 Willie "The Lion" Smith, *Music on My Mind*, 159.

10 Percival Outram, "Activities Among Union Musicians," *New York Age*, January 28, 1933.

11 Alan Groves and Alyn Shipton, *The Glass Enclosure: The Life of Bud Powell* (New York and London: Continuum, 2001), 25. Rex Stewart talks about Caldwell, but he never mentions him playing at Minton's. See Rex Stewart, with Claire P. Gordon, *Boy Meets Horn* (Ann Arbor: University of Michigan Press, 1991), 65–57, 72–75.

12 Minton's ad, *Amsterdam News*, December 21, 1940; U.S. Census, 1920, *Population Schedule: Manhattan Borough*, ED 1353; U.S. Census, 1930, *Population Schedule: Manhattan Borough*, ED 31-905. Garvin Bushell is among those listed as residents of the Hotel Grampion.

13 See advertisement in *Amsterdam News*, January 11, 1941. All other sources except for an early interview with Kenny Clarke place Hill's hiring in October of 1940, but I have found no evidence for this. He might have been in negotiations with Minton then, but he was still playing at the Savoy and Vanderburg was publicly identified as manager of Minton's Playhouse. See Burt Korall, "View from the Seine," *Down Beat* (December 5, 1963), 17; Nat Shapiro and Nat Hentoff, eds., *Hear Me Talkin' to Ya: The Story of Jazz As Told by the Men Who Made it* (New York: Dover, 1966, orig. 1955), 339.

14 "Teddy Hill Drawing 'em At Minton's," *Amsterdam News*, February 15, 1941.

15 Alyn Shipton, *Groovin' High* 36, 88; Shapiro and Hentoff, eds., *Hear Me Talkin' to Ya*, 348–49.

16 Mike Hennessey, *Klook: The Story of Kenny Clarke* (Pittsburgh: University of Pittsburgh Press, 1990), 17–24; Hoefer, "Klook,", 23; Korall, "View from the Seine," 17; Shapiro and Hentoff, eds., *Hear Me Talkin' To Ya*, 347–48' Ira Gitler, *Jazz Masters of the Forties* (New York: Da Capo Press, 1966).

17 Shipton, *Groovin' High*, 45, 87–88; DeVeaux, *The Birth of Bebop*, 219. It is worth noting that bassist John Simmons also included tenor saxophonist Kermit Scott as one of the original members. See "Interview with John Simmons, by Patricia Willard," Tapes 1–9, NEA Oral History Project, Washington, D. C. 1977, p. 53, Institute of Jazz Studies, Rutgers University.

18 U.S. Census, 1930, *Population Schedule: Manhattan Borough*, ED 31-902. He was born April 10, 1919 [Social Security Death Index]. By the time he started working at Minton's, he was living close by at 352 West 117th, apt. #54. See *Local 802 of AFM Directory* (Newark: International Press, 1941), 120. Fenton had just done a live radio broadcast for WNYC on February 15, 1941 with Young, Shad Collins (trumpet), John Collins (electric guitar), and Harold "Doc" West on drums. Lester Young, *Historical Prez - Lester Young 1940–44* (Everybody's EV-3002).

19 James Patrick, "Al Tinney, Monroe's Uptown House, and the Emergence of Modern Jazz in Harlem," *Annual Review of Jazz Studies* II (1983), 165.

20 The story that Clarke initially planned to hire Sonny White comes from Hennessey, *Klook*, 38. However, Hennessey claims that White turned him down because he was touring with Billie Holiday. He had already left Holiday by the time Clarke put the band together. What is more likely is that he was committed to Benny Carter's orchestra. For more on Sonny White, see Donald Clarke, *Wishing on the Moon: The Life and Times of Billie Holiday* (New York: Penguin Books, 1994), 171–72.

21 Les Tomkins interview with Thelonious Monk, 1965.

22 Hennessey, *Klook*, 14.

23 Ibid., 46–47.

24 Scale for a member of a dance band, working a seven-day schedule with Sunday matinees was $42.00 a week. Monk worked only six nights a week, so I am estimating what he might have received. AFM Local 802, *Price List Governing Special and Regular Engagements of the Associated Musicians of Greater New York* (Newark, 1936), 44.

25 Doug Long, "Duke Groner Interview," *Cadence* 9, no. 4 (April 1983), 18.

26 Paul Chevigny, *Gigs: Jazz and the Cabaret Laws in New York City* (New York and London: Routledge, 1991), 57–59; Maxwell T. Cohen, *The Police Card Discord* (Metuchen, NJ: Scarecrow Press, 1993). On the Waiters' Union strikes in 1940, see "Restaurant Strike Enters Second Year," *New York Times*, January 20, 1940; "Marathon Pickets Pass 700th Day at Chore with Café Fight as Far from Peace as Ever," *New York Times*, December 22, 1940; "Waiters to Cool Heels," *New York Times*, October 18, 1941; "AFL Urges Waiters to Fight Cabaret Tax," *New York Times*, May 13, 1944.

27 George Hoefer, "Thelonious Monk in the '40s," *Down Beat* (October 25, 1962), 43. While nearly all observers agree that not much dancing took place at Minton's, they differ on the extent to which audiences came to hear the music. Hoefer recalls, "No one sat and listened much, except on rare occasions when someone like Helen Humes sang a number with the band." (p. 43). Yet, Duke Groner tells us, "it wasn't noted for dancing, it was just for listening." Long, "Duke Groner Interview," 14.

28 Long, "Duke Groner Interview," 13; Reg Cooper, "Roche, Betty," in *The New Grove Dictionary of Jazz*, 2nd ed., edited by Barry Kernfeld. *Grove Music Online. Oxford Music Online*, http://www.oxfordmusiconline.com/sub scriber/article/grove/music/J383500 (accessed February 24, 2009); Ellington, *Music is My Mistress*, 222–223.

29 Charles Walton, "Bronzeville Conversation with Duke Groner," Oral Interview from Jazz Institute of Chicago, www. jazzinstituteofchicago.org; Long, "Duke Groner Interview," 13.

30 Long, "Duke Groner Interview," 13; DeVeaux, *Birth of Bebop*, 217–227; and especially the various recordings made by Jerry Newman. See below.

31 George Hoefer, "Thelonious Monk in the '40s," 43. Thelonious loved Laurence. When critic Stanley Dance asked him to name the greatest dancer he'd ever seen, he unequivocally answered "Baby Laurence." Then again, virtually every musician to whom he posed the same question gave the same reply. Laurence was universally revered by modern jazz musicians. See Stanley Dance, "Three Score: A Quiz for Jazz Musicians," *Metronome* (April 1961), 48. On Baby Laurence, see Jaqui Malone, *Steppin' on the Blues: The Visible Rhythms of African American Dance* (Urbana and Chicago: University of Illinois Press, 1996), 94–96; Marshall Stearns and Jean Stearns, *Jazz Dance: The Story of American Vernacular Dance* (New York: Da Capo Press, 1994, orig. 1968), 337.

32 Long, "Duke Groner Interview," 13. In Monk's words, "Monday used to be a night that nothing was happening, but they used to have 'Monday Night At Minton's,' as they called it. And generally, the show that was at the Apollo, they used to come in and eat and drink, and they'd have a party for them. That helped some, too. And all the different bands, and everybody, would always come in, and hear us play. And so it got around, about the way we were playing." Quoted from Les Tomkins interview with Thelonious Monk, 1965.

33 Gillespie, *To Be or Not to Bop*, 139–140.

34 Patrick, "Al Tinney," 177. Tinney remembers the union rep, Bob Roberts, coming to Monroe's fairly often, but because they were working past 4:00 a.m., they were facing other violations.

35 Alyn Shipton, *Groovin' High*, 87–88, 91–93; Gillespie, *To Be or Not to Bop*, 134, 136–37; Donald L. Maggin, *Dizzy: The Life and Times of John Birks Gillespie* (New York: HarperCollins, 2006), 115–126.

36 The use of "flatted fifths" (or augmented 4ths) and augmented and diminished 9ths.

37 Patrick, "Al Tinney, Monroe's Uptown House," 150–159. Specific personnel come from the original acetates of recordings made by Jerry Newman at Monroe's in 1941. He wrote the names down on the labels and these originals are in the possession of Bob Suneblick, who graciously passed this information to me.

38 Gillespie, *To Be or Not to Bop*, 140. Although Charlie Parker also established a presence at Monroe's, he didn't show up in earnest until 1943. In fact, according to Al Tinney, neither Parker nor Dizzy had any appreciable presence at Monroe's in those early days. Patrick, "Al Tinney," 159–160.

39 Shapiro and Hentoff, eds., *Hear Me Talkin' To Ya*, 15.

40 Hennessey, *Klook*, 43–44; see also Samuel B. Charters and Leonard Kunstadt, in their popular text *Jazz: A History of the New York Scene*; Gillespie, *To Be or Not to Bop*, 139–140; DeVeaux, *The Birth of Bebop*, 219; Gitler, ed., *Swing to Bop*, 75–108 passim. Given the recorded evidence from Minton's it seems as if Monk rarely played the blues. While he would go on to write a number of blues pieces ("Blue Monk," "Functional," "Ba-lue Bolivar Ba-Lues-Are," etc.), he only recorded two blues pieces during his first few recording sessions with Blue Note: "Misterioso" from July 2, 1948, and "Straight, No Chaser" (July 23, 1951).

41 Hentoff, "Just Call Him Thelonious," 15.

42 Sir Charles Thompson, interview, August 11, 2003.

43 Ira Peck, "The Piano Man Who Dug Be-bop," *PM* (February 22, 1948), p. M7.

44 Gillespie, *To Be or Not to Bop*, 262.

45 Korall, "View from the Seine," 17.

46 Gillespie, *To Be or Not to Bop*, 139.

47 Patrick, "Al Tinney," 158.

48 Shapiro and Hentoff, eds., *Hear Me Talkin' to Ya*, 342; Hoefer, "Thelonious Monk in the '40s," 43. Jerry Newman recalls seeing Monk working on the piano in the afternoon when he was setting up his sound equipment.

49 Long, "Duke Groner Interview," 15; Gillespie, *To Be or Not to Bop*, 134; Peck, "The Piano Man Who Dug Be-bop," M7.

50 See Chapter 17.

51 Marion White interview, with Quincy Troupe, December 1, 1990.

52 Bassist Red Callender remembers how hard he worked in New York: "By the time you get off you're exhausted. During our breaks we'd go out the back door to the alley, stand around drinking, smoking weed, chewing bennies—anything to keep going because the gig was so long." As a result of hanging outside in the cold while sweaty from the gig, he came down with pneumonia. Red Callender, *Unfinished Dream*, 54–55.

53 Peck, "The Piano Man Who Dug Be-bop," M7.

54 Sales, "'I Wanted to Make it Better,'" 36.

55 Nat Hentoff, *Jazz Life*, 188.

56 Scott DeVeaux, "'Nice Work if You Can Get It': Thelonious Monk and Popular Song," *Black Music Research Journal* 19, no. 2 (Fall 1999), 169–186.

57 Sales, "I Wanted to Make it Better," 35.

58 Leonard Feather, *Inside Be-Bop* (New York: J. J. Robbins and Sons, 1949), 7; Hennessey, *Klook*, 42.

59 The A section of their 32-bar composition is built on chromatic harmonic movement (C#7–D7 and D#7–E7).

60 All three definitions from *Webster's New International Dictionary of the English Language* (Springfield, MA: C.&G. Merriam Company, 1929), 739. According to critic George Simon in a profile on Monk published in 1948, "epistrophe" comes from "a botanical term that means 'the reversion of the abnormal to the normal.'" It's not clear where Simon got this definition, especially since the only botanical use of the term refers specifically to the "position assumed by the chloroplasts upon . . . the cell walls, upon exposure of the plant to diffuse daylight." Simon, "Bop's Dixie to Monk," 35.

61 *Webster's New International Dictionary of the English Language* (Springfield, MA.: C.&G. Merriam Company, 1929), 739.

62 In fact, when Clarke first recorded the song in 1946 with his own band, rather than improvise on the original chromatic progressions, the band reverts to "I Got Rhythm" changes in the A-section. It is a bit surprising given that the band comprised some of the finest modern jazz artists on the scene, including pianist Bud Powell, trumpeters Fats Navarro and Kenny Dorham, and saxophonist Sonny Stitt. Kenny Clarke, *Kenny Clarke: 1946–1948* (Classics CD 71171).

63 Certificate of Copyright Registration, "Epistrophy; Music by Kenneth Clarke Spearmen and T. Monk," E unp. No. 371980, Received June 2, 1941.

64 Certificate of Copyright Registration, "Harlem is Awful Messy; Words and Music by Oran Page, Joseph Guy, and Thelonious Monk (words and melody)," E unpub. No. 270021, Received September 16, 1941. Unfortunately, the original lead sheet has long been lost and there is no extant copy.

65 Long, "Duke Groner Interview," 17.

66 Hentoff, "Just Call Him Thelonious," 15.

67 Hennessey, *Klook*, 47.

68 Hentoff, "Just Call Him Thelonious," 15–16; see also, Les Tomkins interview with Thelonious Monk, 1965.

69 Hoefer, "Thelonious Monk in the '40s," 43; Liner notes, Charlie Christian, *Vox Presents Charlie Christian* (Vox VSP 302); Chris Sheridan, *Brilliant Corners*, 1–2; Liner notes, Harry Sweets Edison and Hot Lips Page, *Sweets, Lips and Lots of Jazz* (Xanadu 123); Liner notes, Thelonious Monk, *After Hours at Minton's* (Definitive Records, DRCD1197); See also, Ross Russell, *Bird Lives!: The High Life and Hard Times of Charlie Parker* (New York: Charter House, 1973), 136.

70 Once the war started, glass-based acetates replaced aluminum due to war rations, but all of his recordings of Monk at Minton's took place in the spring and summer of 1941, before Pearl Harbor.
71 Hoefer, "Thelonious Monk in the '40s," 43; Chris Sheridan, *Brilliant Corners*, 1–2.
72 Hoefer, "Thelonious Monk in the '40s," 43.
73 Les Tomkins interview with Thelonious Monk, 1965.
74 Bob Bernotas, "Johnny Griffin interview," www.melmartin.com/html_pages/Interviews/griffin.html
75 *Trumpet Battle at Minton's* (Xanadu 107); also available on Thelonious Monk, *After Hours at Minton's* (Definitive Records, DRCD1197).
76 "My Melancholy Baby" was composed by Ernie Burnett and George A. Norton, although there are other claimants to the melody and lyrics. See William Emmett Studwell, *The Popular Song Reader* (New York and London: The Haworth Press, 1994), 29.
77 "My Melancholy Baby," solo piano recorded in Paris, June 1938. Herman Chittison, *Herman Chittison, 1933–1941* (Classics 690).
78 First appeared on Joe Guy/Billie Holiday, *Harlem Odyssey* (Xanadu 112); also Thelonious Monk, *After Hours at Minton's* (Definitive Records, DRCD1197).
79 Willie "The Lion" Smith, *Music on My Mind*, 155.
80 Gillespie, *To Be or Not to Bop*, 207.
81 Pianist Cecil Taylor developed the notion of the piano as an "orchestral" instrument. For Taylor's ideas, see Cecil Taylor, "Sound Structure of Subculture Becoming Major Breath/Naked Fire Gesture," liner notes to *Unit Structures* (Blue Note CDP 7 84237 2); also quoted in Andrew W. Bartlett, "Cecil Taylor, Identity Energy, and the Avant-Garde African American Body," 279. Similar comments on Taylor's "comping" can be found in Robert Levin's liner notes to *Coltrane Time* (Blue Note CDP 7 84461 2); Jost, *Free Jazz*, 75.
82 Long, "Duke Groner Interview," 14
83 Don Byas, *Midnight at Minton's* (Onyx 208); Sheridan, *Brilliant Corners*, 7. Sheridan suggests that the date of the recording could have only been late May (May 20–21, 1941) because that was the only time Don Byas was in New York. Sheridan also lists Taps Miller as a regular drummer at Minton's, but from my research he was a singer, tap dancer, and trumpet player.
84 Les Tomkins interview with Thelonious Monk, 1965.
85 Newman quoted in Hoefer, "Thelonious Monk in the '40s," 44.
86 Herbert H. Nichols, "The Jazz Life," *New York Age*, July 5, 1941. Nichols knew the scene first-hand because he had become a regular at Monroe's Uptown House as early as 1938 and showed up frequently at Minton's just to hear Monk. A. B. Spellman, *Four Lives in the Bebop Business* (New York: Limelight Editions, 1985, orig. 1966), 157.
87 "A History of WKCR's Jazz Programming: An interview with Phil Schaap, conducted, transcribed, and edited by Evan Spring, October 5th, 1992," http://www.columbia.edu/cu/wkcr/jazz/schaap.html.
88 Unissued recording, WKCR archives, Columbia University.
89 Mary Lou Williams, *Mary Lou Williams Story 1930/1941* (EPM Musique, Jazz Archives No. 116 159002). These four bars were also recorded by pianist Al Haig as "Opus Caprice" and again by Sonny Stitt as "Symphony Hall Swing." See Hennessey, *Klook*, 48.
90 Marion White interview, with Quincy Troupe, December 1, 1990.
91 Peck, "The Piano Man Who Dug Be-bop," M7.
92 Hennessey, *Klook*, 48.
93 Gillespie, *To Be or Not to Bop*, 144. Duke Groner also talked about Monk's drinking. See Long, "Duke Groner Interview," 15. See also, Jacques Ponzio and Francis Postif, *Blue Monk: Portraits de Thelonious*, 59–62.
94 Peck, "The Piano Man," M7; Shapiro and Hentoff, *Hear Me Talkin' to Ya*, 341. By the time Monk submitted his Selective Service registration card in December of 1941, he reported that he was unemployed. Registration Card, Thelonious Monk, Order #3447, Selective Service Records, New York State.
95 Hoefer, "Thelonious Monk in the '40s," 43.

7 "Since You Went Away I Missed You"

1 Selective Service Classification Record, Local Board 23, Thelonious Sphere Monk, 3447, p. 109, Selective Service Records, New York State. He submitted his Selective Service registration card on October 18, 1940, received his questionnaire on October 6, 1941. On December 15 they sent out the first notice of his classification; I'm assuming he received it the next day since it came from the neighborhood.
2 Registration Card, Thelonious Monk, Order #3447, Selective Service Records, New York State.
3 Ibid.
4 Not only was the U.S. military still segregated, but blacks were deemed unfit for combat until 1944. See, Mary P. Motley, ed., *The Invisible Soldier: The Experience of the Black Soldier, World War II* (Detroit: Wayne State University Press, 1975); Bernard C. Nalty, *The Right to Fight: African-American Marines in World War II* (Washington, D.C., History and Museums Division, Headquarters, U.S. Marine Corps: Supt. of Docs., U.S. G.P.O., 1995); Neil A. Wynn, *The Afro-American and the Second World War* (New York: Holmes and Meier, 1975).
5 Cootie Williams and his Orchestra, "Fly right," first appeared on *Sounds of Harlem*, vol. 3 (Col C3L33).
6 Scott DeVeaux, "Bebop and the Recording Industry: The 1942 AFM Recording Ban Reconsidered," *Journal of the American Musicological Society*, 41, no. 1 (Spring 1988), 126–165; Anders S. Lunde, "The American Federation of Musicians and the Recording Ban," *The Public Opinion Quarterly* 12, No. 1 (Spring 1948), 45–56;

James P. Kraft, *Stage to Studio: Musicians and the Sound Revolution, 1890–1950* (Baltimore and London: Johns Hopkins University Press, 1996), 137–161.

7 Millinder was at the Savoy through most of July and the first half of August. "Where the Bands are Playing," *Down Beat* (July 1, 1942), 22; "Where the Bands are Playing," *Down Beat* (August 1, 1942), 22; "Where the Bands are Playing," *Down Beat* (August 15, 1942), 22.

8 Sales, "I Wanted to Make it Better," 34; on Gillespie with Millinder, see Shipton, *Groovin' High*, 103; Gillespie, *To Be or Not to Bop*, 162–163.

9 Fenton recorded with Millinder in July 1942. Lucky Millinder, *Apollo Jump* (Affinity 1004).

10 Frank Driggs and Barry Kernfeld, "Millinder, Lucky," In *The New Grove Dictionary of Jazz*, 2nd ed., edited by Barry Kernfeld. *Grove Music Online*. *Oxford Music Online*, http://www.oxfordmusiconline.com/subscriber/article/grove/music/J301700 (accessed January 17, 2009); Charles Garrod, *Lucky Millinder and His Orchestra* (Zephyrhills, FL: Joyce Record Club, 1994); "Lucky Millinder Dies," *Down Beat* (November 3, 1966), 11; Bob Rusch, "Al McKibbon Interview," transc. Kea D. Rusch, *Cadence* 13, no. 3 (March 1987), 15–16.

11 Jacques Ponzio and Francis Postif, *Blue Monk*, 70.

12 Minutes of the Trial Board, September 8, 1942, AFM Local 802, microfilm reel 5320, p. 268.

13 Ad, *Amsterdam News*, September 5, 1942.

14 Minutes of the Trial Board, September 8, 1942, AFM Local 802, microfilm reel 5320, p. 268.

15 Minutes of the Trial Board, October 27, 1942, AFM Local 802, microfilm reel 5320, pp. 320–321.

16 Ibid.

17 He can be heard with Al Sears on the compilation disc, *Ridin' the Riff* (Charly CRB 1128).

18 Minutes of the Trial Board, November 4, 1942, AFM Local 802, microfilm reel 5320, pp. 326–327.

19 Geraldine Smith interview, February 12, 2004; Nellie Monk interview, January 12, 2002; Alonzo White interview, February 23, 2004.

20 Thomas Monk, Jr., interview, February 16, 2004.

21 Before moving to Lyman Place, the Smiths lived briefly on Home Street, then Prospect Avenue. They were also the first black family to integrate Lyman Place, which had been predominantly Jewish. Geraldine Smith interview, February 12, 2004.

22 Geraldine Smith interview, February 12, 2004; ad in *New York Times*, April 25, 1943. On Bridgeport Brass during World War II, see www.heritageresearch.com/War%20Facilities; Oral histories in "Bridgeport Working: Voices from the 20th Century," http://www.bridgeporthistory.org.

23 Geraldine Smith interview, February 12, 2004; Dr. Anna Lou Smith interview, April 7, 2004.

24 Nellie Monk interview, January 12, 2002; Dr. Anna Lou Smith interview, April 7, 2004; Permanent Record: Miss Nellie Smith, Florida Normal and Industrial Institute, Smith; State of Florida, Certificate of Death, Elisha Bennett Smith, #12469.

25 Thomas Hunt and James C. Carper, eds., *Religious Higher Education in the United States: A Source Book* (New York: Garland, 1996), 362; "Brief History of Florida Memorial University," http://www.fmuniv.edu/About_Us/history.htm. Coincidentally, novelist and anthropologist Zora Neale Hurston had also arrived in St. Augustine around the same time as Nellie and took a summer teaching job at Florida Normal and Industrial College. Valerie Boyd, *Wrapped in Rainbows: The Life of Zora Neale Hurston* (New York: Scribner, 2003), 350–351.

26 Dr. Anna Lou Smith, interview in Los Angeles, April 7, 2004.

27 Thelonious met Bud at "a juice joint uptown," as he recalled. Hentoff, "Just Call Him Thelonious," 16.

28 U.S. Census, 1930, *Population Schedule, Manhattan Borough*, ED 31-1226 (April 18, 1930), sheet 18 B; Eugene Holley, Jr., "The Education of Bud Powell," *Village Voice* (June 28, 1994), 9; Groves and Shipton, *The Glass Enclosure*, 10–11.

29 William Powell quoted in Groves and Shipton, *The Glass Enclosure*, 10; Holley, Jr., "The Education of Bud Powell," 9.

30 Holley, Jr., "The Education of Bud Powell," 9; Groves and Shipton, *The Glass Enclosure*, 11; see also, Carl Smith, *Bouncing with Bud: All the Recordings of Bud Powell* (Brunswick, ME: Biddle Pub., 1997); Guthrie P. Ramsey, *In Walked Bud: Earl "Bud" Powell and the Modern Jazz Challenge* (forthcoming).

31 Michael C. Johanek and John L. Puckett, *Leonard Covello and the Making of Benjamin Franklin High School: Education as if Citizenship Mattered* (Philadelphia: Temple University Press, 2007), 136.

32 On Elmo Hope, see Ira Gitler liner notes, *Elmo Hope Trio* (Hi Fi Records 616); John Tynan, "Bitter Hope," *Down Beat* (January 4, 1961), 16; David H. Rosenthal, *Hard Bop: Jazz and Black Music, 1955–1965* (New York: Oxford University Press, 1992), 55; Stuart Broomer, "Elmo Hope Omission," *Coda* 271 (January-February, 1997), 36–37; Ira Gitler, *Masters of Bebop* (New York: Da Capo Press, 2001), 130–31; Bertha Hope interview, July 15, 2003.

33 "Another Youth Shot by Policeman," *Amsterdam News*, November 30, 1940; "Shot By Cop, May Not Live," *Pittsburgh Courier*, December 7, 1940; "Policeman Faces Lawsuit for Shooting Harlem Boy," *Amsterdam News*, January 18, 1941.

34 Ira Gitler liner notes, *Elmo Hope Trio* (Hi Fi Records 616); Tynan, "Bitter Hope," 16; Bertha Hope interview, July 15, 2003.

35 Marion White interview, with Quincy Troupe, December 1, 1990.

36 Elmo Hope enlisted on March 6, 1943, World War II Army Enlistment Records, 1938–1946, National Archives.

37 Paul Slaughter, "1970 Reflections," *Jazz Hot*, 306 (April 1982), 14.

38 Hentoff, "Just Call Him Thelonious," 16.

39 This story, related by Francis Paudras, contains the seeds of truth but some of the details are off. Clarke suggests that Oscar Pettiford was the bassist that night but he doesn't join the Minton's crew until spring of 1943, after

Clarke left Minton's. I'm also assuming that Powell's initial introduction at Minton's occurred before 1943. Paudras, *Dance of the Infidels*, 144.

40 Jean Clouzet and Michel Delorme, "L'amertume du prophète," *Jazz Magazine* 93, no. 9 (April 1963), 39.
41 Groves and Shipton, *The Glass Enclosure*, 11.
42 Clouzet and Delorme, "L'amertume du prophète," 39.
43 Mary Lou Williams, "Mad Monk," *Melody Maker* (May 22, 1954), 11; also, Mary Lou Williams, "Autobiographical Notebook, #2," p. 274, Mary Lou Williams Collection, Institute for Jazz Studies, Rutgers University.
44 Ponzio and Postif, *Blue Monk*, 53; Chan Parker, *My Life in E-Flat* (Columbia, SC: University of South Carolina Press, 1993), 14.
45 Malcolm X, *Autobiography*, 71; Gerald R. Gill, "Dissent, Discontent and Disinterest: Afro-American Opposition to the United States Wars of the Twentieth Century" (unpublished book manuscript, 1988), 166–67; Gitler, *Swing to Bop*, 115–16; Tyler, "Black Jive," 34–35. Sonny Rollins remembered musicians putting pinpricks in their arms to convince the induction officers that they were drug addicts and thus not fit to serve, though he himself was born too young to serve in the Second World War since he was born in 1930. Eric Nisenson, *Open Sky: Sonny Rollins and His World of Improvisation* (New York: St. Martin's Press, 2000), 25.
46 Gillespie, *To Be or Not to Bop*, 119–20.
47 Babs Gonzalez, *I Paid My Dues* (New York: Lancer Books, 1967), 29–30.
48 Gill, "Dissent, Discontent, and Disinterest," 164–68; George Q. Flynn, "Selective Service and American Blacks during World War II," *Journal of Negro History* 69 (Winter 1984), 14–25.
49 Selective Service Classification Record, Local Board 23, Thelonious Sphere Monk, 3447, p. 109, Selective Service Records, New York State.
50 Evelyn Smith interview, June 21, 2007.
51 Ellen Dwyer, "Psychiatry and Race During World War II," *Journal of the History of Medicine and Allied Sciences* 61, no. 2 (2006), 123–126.
52 Richard Dalfiume, *Fighting on Two Fronts: Desegregation of the Armed Forces, 1939–1953* (Columbia, MO: University of Missouri Press, 1969); Herbert Garfinkel, *When Negroes March: The March on Washington Movement in the Organizational Policies for FEPC* (Glencoe, IL.: Free Press, 1959); Lee Finkle, "The Conservative Aims of Militant Rhetoric: Black Protest During World War II," *Journal of American History* 60 (December 1973), 692–713; Neil A. Wynn, *The Afro-American and the Second World War*; Harvard Sitkoff, *A New Deal for Blacks: The Emergence of Civil Rights as a National Issue* (Oxford and New York: Oxford University Press, 1978), 298–325; Robert Korstad and Nelson Lichtenstein, "Opportunities Found and Lost: Labor, Radicals, and the Early Civil Rights Movement," *Journal of American History* 75 (December 1988), 786–811; Herbert Shapiro, *White Violence and Black Response: From Reconstruction to Montgomery* (Amherst, MA.: University of Massachusetts Press, 1988), 301–48; George Lipsitz, *A Rainbow at Midnight: Labor and Culture in the 1940s* (Urbana, IL: University of Illinois Press, 1994), 14–28; Nelson Lichtenstein, *Labor's War at Home: The CIO in World War II* (New York and Cambridge: Cambridge University Press, 1982), 124–26.
53 Paula F. Pfeffer, *A. Philip Randolph: Pioneer of the Civil Rights Movement* (Baton Rouge: Louisiana State University Press, 1996); Garfinkel, *When Negroes March*; Sitkoff, *A New Deal for Blacks*, 298–325.
54 A. Burran, "Urban Racial Violence in the South During World War II: A Comparative Overview," in Walter J. Fraser, Jr., and Winfred B. Moore, Jr., eds., *From the Old South to the New: Essays on the Transitional South* (Westport, CT: Greenwood Publishers, 1981), 167–77; Dominic J. Capeci, Jr., *Race Relations in Wartime Detroit: The Sojourner Truth Housing Controversy of 1942* (Philadelphia: Temple University Press, 1984) and *The Harlem Riot of 1943* (Philadelphia: Temple University Press, 1977).
55 Capeci, Jr., *Race Relations in Wartime Detroit*; Shapiro, *White Violence and Black Response*, 319, 327; Gail Williams O'Brien, *The Color of Law: Race, Violence and Justice in the Post-World War II South* (Chapel Hill, NC: University of North Carolina Press, 1999).
56 See Stuart Cosgrove, "The Zoot-Suit and Style Warfare," *History Workshop Journal* 18 (Autumn, 1984), 78–81; Bruce M. Tyler, "Black Jive and White Repression," *Journal of Ethnic Studies* 16, no. 4 (1989), 31–66; Steve Chibnall, "Whistle and Zoot: The Changing Meaning of a Suit of Clothes," *History Workshop*, 20 (Autumn 1985), 56–81. LeRoi Jones, *Blues People: Negro Music in White America* (New York: William Morrow, 1963), 202; Eric Lott, "Double V, Double-Time: Bebop's Politics of Style," *Callaloo* 11, no. 3 (1988), 598, 600; Ben Sidran, *Black Talk* (New York: Holt, Rinehart and Winston, 1971), 110–111.
57 Director of FBI to Legat, Tokyo (163–2971), cablegram, September 3, 1970, Thelonious Monk FBI File.
58 Jimmy Butts, "Harlem Speaks," *Jazz Record* (May 1, 1943), 6. In the previous issue, Butts announces Sonny White's induction and adds, "He was a favorite at Minton's Play house uptown. . . ." "Harlem Speaks," *Jazz Record* (April 1, 1943), 8.
59 Fenton enlisted on August 18, 1943, in Camden, N.J. See "Nicholas Fenton, U.S. Army World War II Enlistment Records, 1938–1946," National Archives and Records Administration, Record Group 64.
60 Gitler, *Jazz Masters of the 40s*, 150–55; Nat Hentoff, "An Oscar," *Down Beat* (March 21, 1957), 17; George Hoefer, "Oscar Pettiford," *Down Beat* (June 2, 1966), 25.
61 There are amateur recordings of these jam sessions made by Bob Redcross on February 15, 1943. They can be heard on *Birth of Bebop* (Stash ST 260) and on the CD boxed set, *Charlie Parker - Complete Collection* (Sound Hills SSCD-8017/34).
62 Les Tomkins interview with Thelonious Monk, 1965.
63 *New York Age*, May 1, 1943; Nat Brandt, *Harlem at War: The Black Experience in World War II* (Syracuse, NY: Syracuse University Press, 1996), 169–170; Capeci, *The Harlem Riot of 1943*, 17.
64 Capeci, *The Harlem Riot of 1943*; Brandt, *Harlem at War*, 183–207.
65 Nellie struggled in many of her classes. During the fall semester, she earned B's in accounting and physical education, a C in Bible lit, and took incompletes in business arithmetic, English composition, and shorthand.

By the spring semester, it appears as if she planned to remain in school and complete a degree, because she signed up for several general education classes—U.S. History, English composition (again), art, and reading. (At the time, Florida Normal granted a two-year degree but the administration was petitioning to make it an accredited four-year college.) But within a week she dropped these classes in favor of courses for which she had incompletes. She took the second half of accounting and earned a solid A, received a C in business arithmetic, and D's in both typing and shorthand. College Transcript, Permanent Record: Miss Nellie Smith, Florida Normal and Industrial Institute.

66 Dr. Anna Lou Smith, interview in Los Angeles, April 7, 2004.
67 Ibid.
68 Ibid.
69 Ibid.; State of Florida, Certificate of Death, Elisha Bennett Smith, #12469.
70 Plans were finalized in December of 1941 and construction began the following year. It was not completed until January 1, 1949. See Map of plan for Amsterdam Houses in "Findings of the State Commissioner of Housing in Re: A Low Rent Housing Project Located in the Borough of Manhattan" (December 1941); "Amendment to Loan & Subsidy Contract, Amsterdam Houses, NYS-5," BOX OO64C6, New York Housing Authority Papers, Wagner Archives. The plans for such a project date back to at least 1940. Simon Rosenzweig to Peter Grimm, July 19, 1940, BOX 0054C5, FOLDER #9, New York Housing Authority, Wagner Archives.
71 Geraldine Smith interview, February 12, 2004.
72 Certificate of Copyright Registration, "I Need You So: Music by Thelonious Monk, Lyrics by Thelma Elizabeth Murray," E unpub No. 348068, Received September 24, 1943.
73 Jackie Bonneau interview, June 17, 2005. Jackie not only got to know Ms. Murray late in her life, but she played me a tape of Murray at the piano playing and singing gospel music.
74 Certificate of Copyright Registration, "I Need You So: Music by Thelonious Monk, Lyrics by Thelma Elizabeth Murray," E unpub No. 348068, Received September 24, 1943; "I Need You So," Lead Sheet, submitted with Copyright Registration form. Used by permission of the Thelonious Monk estate.

8 "I'm Trying to See If It's a Hit"

1 Arnold Shaw, *Fifty-Second Street: The Street of Jazz* (New York: Da Capo Press, 1983, orig. 1971); Patrick Burke, *Come in and Hear the Truth: Jazz and Race on 52nd Street* (Chicago: University of Chicago Press, 2008), 156–79. The clubs on East 52nd retained an informal whites-only policy well into the 1940s, according to pianist Billy Taylor. See Gitler, *Swing to Bop*, 304.
2 Shaw, *Fifty-Second Street*, 256.
3 Burke, *Come In and Hear the Truth*, 178–79; Lewis A. Erenberg, *Swinging the Dream: Big Band Jazz and the Rebirth of American Culture* (Chicago: University of Chicago Press, 1998), 208; Shaw, *Fifty-Second Street*, 255–56, 257–58; Chan Parker, *My Life in E-Flat*, 14; Gitler, ed., *Swing to Bop*, 125, 304–309; W. O. Smith, *Sideman: The Long Gig of W.O. Smith* (Nashville: Rutledge Hill Press, 1991), 150–151; "Police 'Warn' 52nd Street Riot May Come from Mixing," *Amsterdam News*, July 22, 1944.
4 "Where to Go in New York," *Jazz Record* (July 1, 1943), 5.
5 Ibid., 5.
6 Charles Woideck, *Charlie Parker: His Music and Life* (Ann Arbor: University of Michigan Press, 1996), 18–19; Lawrence O. Koch, *Yardbird Suite: A Compendium of the Music and Life of Charlie Parker* (Boston: Northeastern University Press, 1999 rev. ed.), 29–32; Shipton, *Groovin' High*, 118–120.
7 Shipton, *Groovin' High*, 118–120.
8 Jimmy Butts, "Harlem Speaks," *Jazz Record* (December 1943), 7; Billy Taylor interview, January 26, 2004; Shipton, *Groovin' High*, 119. Thomas Fitterling misdates the gig as August of 1943, and identifies Monk as the regular pianist until he is replaced by George Wallington. Fitterling, *Thelonious Monk*, 35.
9 Quoted in Shipton, *Groovin' High*, 119.
10 Ibid. 119; Billy Taylor, interview, January 26, 2004.
11 Ponzio and Postif, *Blue Monk*, 131.
12 Gillespie, *To Be or Not to Bop*, 206–207.
13 Ibid., 206. See also, Pat Harris, "Oscar Pettiford Now on Cello Kick," *Down Beat* (December 29, 1950), 20.
14 Paul Matthews, "Billy Taylor Interview (Part 2)," *Cadence* (November 1995), 24.
15 Billy Taylor interview, January 26, 2004.
16 Kernodle, *Soul on Soul*, 86–91; Dahl, *Morning Glory*, 123–136.
17 Dahl, *Morning Glory*, 137–141; Dustin Prial, *The Producer: John Hammond and the Soul of America* (New York: Farrar, Straus and Giroux, 2006), 123–132; David W. Stowe, *Swing Changes: Big Band Jazz in New Deal America* (Cambridge, MA: Harvard University Press, 1994), 66–67.
18 Williams, "Mad Monk," 11.
19 "Autobiographical Notebooks, #3," p. 298, Mary Lou Williams Collection.
20 "Autobiographical Notebooks, #3," 298–99, Mary Lou Williams Collection. She tells a more dramatic and funnier version of the same story in her interview with John S. Wilson. In that version, Monk still had his tam on his head and upon her startled reaction he ran into the closet and "the clothes fell on him." I chose the less quoted and less comical version of the story since it was written much closer to the time the incident occurred, and it seems less embellished. See Mary Lou Williams, interview by John Wilson, July 26, 1977, Transcript, NEA/Institute of Jazz Studies.
21 "Autobiographical Notebooks, #2," p. 268, Mary Lou Williams Collection.

22 Williams quoting Monk in Kernodle, *Soul on Soul*, 114.

23 Mary Lou Williams, "Mad Monk," *Melody Maker* (May 22, 1954), 11.

24 Korall, *Drummin' Men*, 128–131; Leslie Gourse, *Art Blakey: Jazz Messenger* (New York: Schirmer Trade Books, 2002), 21–33; Joe Goldberg, *Jazz Masters of the 50s* (New York: Da Capo Press, 1988, orig. 1965), 45–47; Thomas Tolnay, "Art Blakey's Jazz Message," *Down Beat* (March 18, 1971), 14–15.

25 Wayne Enstice and Paul Rubin, *Jazz is Spoken Here: Conversations with 22 Musicians* (New York: Da Capo Press, 1994), 30; see also, "Art Blakey Interview: Part II" (taken and transcribed by Bob Rusch), *Cadence* 9 (September 1981), 12; Peter Danson, "Art Blakey: An Interview by Peter Danson," *Coda* 173 (1980), 15.

26 Linda Dahl, *Morning Glory*, 193.

27 Gunther Schuller, "Thelonious Monk—Reviews: Recordings," *Jazz Review* 1 (November, 1958), 23.

28 "Autobiographical Notebooks, #4," p. 469, Mary Lou Williams Collection; Dahl, *Morning Glory*, 193.

29 "Autobiographical Notebooks, #4," p. 468, Mary Lou Williams Collection.

30 Teddy McRae interview with Ron Welburn, Jazz Oral History Project, October 6 and 8, 1981, IJS, p. 629.

31 Lead sheet submitted with Certificate of Copyright Registration, "The Pump: Music by Teddy McRae and T. Monk," E unp. No. 363022, Received February 5, 1944. It is built on an ascending five-note phrase created from arpeggiated dominant seventh chords (A^b7–D^b7) that end on the sixth.

32 Benetta Bines and group family interview, January 30, 2004.

33 Monk and Smith group family interview, January 30, 2004.

34 Certificate of Copyright Registration, "The Pump: Music by Teddy McRae and T. Monk," E unp. No. 363022, Received February 5, 1944; Certificate of Copyright Registration, "You Need 'Na: Music by Teddy McRae and T. Monk," E unp. No. 363023, Received February 5, 1944.

35 Certificate of Copyright Registration, "Nameless: Music by Thelonious Monk," E unp. No. 371340, Received April 14, 1944.

36 A number of bands began using it to close their sets, much like "Epistrophy." Indeed, when Monk was playing in the Gillespie-Pettiford group at the Onyx Club, they were using it regularly under the title "Mop Mop." DeVeaux, *The Birth of Bebop*, 292.

37 Leonard Feather, *The Jazz Years: Earwitness to an Era* (New York: Da Capo Press, 1987), 105.

38 "Hall Overton, Monk at the New School" June 20, 1963 CCP 104 (Disc 4), W. Eugene Smith Tapes, Center for Creative Photography/Center for Documentary Studies, Duke University; on the date he composed it, see Simon, "Bop's Dixie to Monk," 35. His role in originating the term had been a pet peeve for Monk throughout 1963. In an interview with Francois Postif, he explained: "I remember it was when I first started writing my own compositions. I did a piece called 'Bip-Bop'—perhaps the word be-bop comes from there!" Postif, "'Round 'Bout Sphere," *Jazz Hot* (April 1963), 25. In the *Time* magazine profile, he told author Barry Farrell that the term "Bebop" is a corruption of his phrase, "Bip Bop," though he doesn't mention it as a song title. Barry Farrell, "Loneliest Monk," *Time* 83 (February 28, 1964), 86.

39 DeVeaux, *The Birth of Bebop*, 99; John Chilton, *The Song of the Hawk: The Life and Recordings of Coleman Hawkins* (Ann Arbor, MI: University of Michigan Press, 1990), 160–168.

40 Coleman Hawkins, *Coleman Hawkins—A Documentary: The Life And Times Of A Great Jazzman* (Riverside Records, RLP 12-117/118).

41 Chilton, *The Song of the Hawk*, 175–202.

42 Fletcher Henderson's 1933 recording of Hawkins's composition, "Queer Notions," was essentially a study in whole-tone scales. See Fletcher Henderson, *Study in Frustration: The Fletcher Henderson Story* (Columbia C4L19), disc 3.

43 Johnson quoted in Gitler, ed., *Swing to Bop*, 122.

44 Hawkins, *Coleman Hawkins—A Documentary*.

45 Shipton, *Groovin' High*, 124–126; Morgenstern, *Living with Jazz*, 318–320.

46 Collette Hawkins dates Monk's hire to December 1943, but all other evidence suggests that Thelonious did not begin to sit in until later in the winter. Collette Hawkins interview, November 5, 2004. It is possible that Monk was hanging around Hawkins and his group throughout this period since his gig at Kelly's Stable lasted throughout December, January, and February. See *Down Beat* (December 1, 1943), 18; *Down Beat* (January 1, 1944), 18; *Down Beat* (January 15, 1944), 18; *Jazz Record* (March 1944), 2.

47 Harris, "None Better than Best with a Brush," 18; Chilton, *The Song of the Hawk*, 212–213; Korall, *Drummin' Men*, 25. Chilton claims that Stan Levey was Hawkins's drummer before Denzil Best replaced him, but Levey himself doesn't say that. According to Levey's own recollections, he only sat in with Hawkins's band at the Down Beat Club (along with Charlie Parker) one night when Denzil Best was late. See Korall, *Drummin' Men*, 117.

48 Mary Louise Adams, "Almost Anything Can Happen: A Search for Sexual Discourse in Urban Spaces of 1940s Toronto," *Canadian Journal of Sociology* 19, no. 2 (Spring 1994), 220–222.

49 Selwyn Warner told John Chilton that "Monk did arrangements for the band; so too did Benny Harris and Denzil Best." Chilton, *The Song of the Hawk*, 213.

50 Hawkins, *Coleman Hawkins—A Documentary*.

51 Warner quoted in Chilton, *The Song of the Hawk*, 213.

52 Ibid., p. 213.

53 Hawkins only expressed a mild complaint that Benny would "fluff a few notes now and then," and even that was more a gesture of sympathy than criticism. Hawkins felt that Harris was blowing out his lip and he could not understand how that could happen to someone so young and talented. "When he was sixteen years old he was around here playing like a son of a gun." Hawkins, *Coleman Hawkins—A Documentary*.

54 "World's Greatest Saxophonist at Yacht Club Nitely," *Amsterdam News*, May 13, 1944. Sheridan and Chilton place the Toronto and Boston tours in May, but the *Amsterdam News* is clear that when Hawkins opened at the

Yacht Club on April 28, he had just returned from Toronto and Boston with the same band. They also insist that Monk opened at the Down Beat Club after it had changed hands and was renamed, but the contemporary evidence from the black newspapers suggest otherwise.

55 "World's Greatest Saxophonist at Yacht Club Nitely," *Amsterdam News*, May 13, 1944; *New York Age*, April 29, 1944.

56 "Open House Jam Session, starring Coleman Hawkins, Master of the Tenor Saxophone, Friday May 19—9-4, DownBeat Club," Handbill in author's possession; "Coleman Hawkins and Orchestra Feature New Composi-tions," *New York Age*, May 27, 1944.

57 Arnold Shaw, *Fifty-Second Street*, 180.

58 Hoefer, "Little Benny Harris," 13; Stan Levey's recollections in Korall, *Drummin' Men*, 25.

59 Bill Gottlieb, "Thelonius [sic] Monk—Genius of Bop," *Down Beat* (September 24, 1947), 2.

60 Background information on Coulsen's family (as well as the correct spelling of his name, which is often spelled "Coulson") has been culled from the 1930 Census manuscripts. See U.S. Census, 1930, *Population Schedule: Manhattan Borough*, ED 31-1040.

61 Gitler, ed., *Swing to Bop*, 79. Randy Weston also compared Coulsen with Miles Davis. Randy Weston lec-ture, Duke Ellington Society, New York Chapter, 1967. Audio tape, Schomburg Collection, New York Public Library.

62 Korall, *Drummin' Men*, 25.

63 Quoted in Leonard Feather, "Coleman Hawkins," in *The Jazz Makers: Essays on the Greats of Jazz*, eds. Nat Shapiro and Nat Hentoff (New York: Rinehart and Co.,1957), 172.

64 Randy Weston interview, February 22, 1999; Ira Gitler, "Randy Weston," *Down Beat* (February 27, 1964), 16–17, 36.

65 Spellman, *Four Lives in The Bebop Business*, 158–159.

66 Pettiford stayed on at the Onyx club after Dizzy left and hired Hartzfield, Guy and Johnston. Shaw, *Fifty-Second Street*, 270.

67 Herbert Nichols, "Jazz Milieu," *Music Dial* (August 1944). In an unpublished autobiographical essay quoted extensively in A. B. Spellman's book, Nichols mistakenly identifies the date of the *Music Dial* piece as 1946. (Spellman, *Four Lives*, 162.) He confused it with another piece he wrote on Monk in *Rhythm Magazine* in 1946, which I discuss below.

68 Nichols, "Jazz Milieu."

69 Ibid.

70 Evelyn Smith interview, July 6, 2005.

71 Geraldine Smith interview, February 12, 2004.

72 The Spotlite only lasted two years on the street. See Shaw, *Fifty-Second Street*, 329–330.

73 Smith played bass on the legendary "Body and Soul" recording of 1939.

74 W. O. Smith, *Sideman*, 147. The dates for the Spotlite gig are proposed by Sheridan, *Brilliant Corners*, 342.

75 W. O. Smith, *Sideman*, 147.

76 Ibid., p. 148.

77 On Washington, D. C.'s "Black Broadway," see "Historic U Street," http://www.gwu.edu/~jazz/venuesb.html.

78 Nap Turner quoted in "Jazzed in D.C.: Jazz Profiles from NPR," http://www.npr.org/programs/jazzprofiles/archive/jazzindc.html. Nap Turner insists that the event occurred at Keyes, but Rouse himself only identifies the Crystal Caverns as the venue for his first gig before leaving with the Eckstine band in 1944. Also, Rouse doesn't remember meeting Monk until he moved to New York, but given that Monk was a virtual unknown during his D.C. gig, he probably did not remember the meeting.

79 Peter Danson, "Interview: Charlie Rouse," *Coda Magazine* 187 (1982), 5–6; David A. Franklin, "Charlie Rouse Interview," *Cadence* 13, no. 6 (1987), 5–6; J. L. Ginibre, "La Longue Marche de Charlie," *Jazz Magazine* 105 (1964), 20–21.

80 *Amsterdam News*, September 9, 1944.

81 Leonard Feather, "Reynolds-Hawkins: Double Header in Harlem," *Metronome* (October 1944), 30.

82 At the Down Beat Club, they played opposite Billie Holiday and comedian Harry "The Hipster" Gibson, closing on New Year's Eve, 1944. Occasionally, the band did a few one-night stands and matinees in the area, including a huge dance at Hartford's Footguard Hall. *Jazz Record* (October 1944), 2; Chilton, *The Song of the Hawk*, 218.

83 Handwritten recording schedule, titles and matrix numbers, October 19, 1944, Joe Davis Papers, in posses-sion of Bruce Bastin. I'm grateful to Mr. Bastin for copying these rare documents and making them available to me. It indicates, among other things, that the session took place between 7 and 10 p.m. and that there were no additional takes. Davis also wrote down the titles and matrix numbers on the back of some of his own sheet music ("The Night You Said Goodbye"). "Drifting on a Reed" and "Flying Hawk" were released as 78s on Joe Davis 8250; "Recollections" and "On the Bean" (Joe Davis 8251).

84 Joe Davis to Coleman Hawkins, October 19, 1944, Letter of Agreement, Joe Davis Papers in Bruce Bastin's possession; Bruce Bastin, *Never Sell a Copyright: Joe Davis and his Role in the New York Music Scene, 1916–1978* (Chigwell, England: Storyville Publications, 1990), 131.

85 These sides have been re-released on several different labels and in different formats, notably as Bean and the Boys (Prestige PR 7824) and Coleman Hawkins, *Bean and Ben: Coleman Hawkins and Ben Webster, 1944–45* (HQ CD 04) [1990]. Scott DeVeaux provides an excellent transcription of Monk's solo on "On the Bean" in DeVeaux, *The Birth of Bebop*, 329.

86 It was first recorded August 22, 1944 and released on the Hit label (7119).

87 Powell quoted in Paudras, *Dance of the Infidels*, 123.

88 Ibid., 123; see also, Groves and Shipton, *The Glass Enclosure*, 15.

89 Interview with Cootie Williams, by Stanley Dance, May 1976, Smithsonian Institution, IJS, p. 247.
90 Certificate of Copyright Registration, "'Round About Midnight," Music by Thelonious Monk, Cootie Williams, Bernie Hanighen lyrics, publ. Advanced Music Corp, E pub. 127232, November 27, 1944. It was re-registered under a different title with lyrics. See Certificate of Copyright Registration, "Grand Finale," Music by Thelonious Monk, Cootie Williams, Bernie Hanighen lyrics, publ. Advanced Music Corp, E pub 130672, April 13, 1945.
91 A recorded broadcast exists. Ella sang with the Williams Orchestra at the Howard Theater in Washington, D.C., August 6, 1947. Williams plays "'Round Midnight" in a medley, but Ella doesn't sing.
92 Nellie Monk interview, January 12, 2002. According to Nellie, Williams only paid Monk $300 for "'Round Midnight." Interestingly, it would be five years before singer Jackie Paris made the first vocal recording of "'Round Midnight." Recorded November 12, 1949, it was first released on the National label (and later rereleased on a compilation LP called *Advance Guard of the 40s* (EmArcy 36016). He was accompanied by Eddie Shu on tenor, Dick Hyman (piano), John Collins (guitar), and bassist Tommy Potter. www.jackieparis .com/discography.
93 *Chicago Daily Tribune*, March 11, 1945.
94 Ad for Joe Davis 8250 in *Chicago Defender*, June 16, 1945.
95 Mary Lou Williams was listed as leader, but she used Hawkins's rhythm section of Eddie Robinson (bass) and Denzil Best (drums). She also hired Bill Coleman on trumpet, Claude Green on clarinet, and Joe Evans on alto. The recording was first released on Asch 552–3.
96 Collette Hawkins credits her father with composing the song. Interview, November 5, 2004. Linda Dahl insists that Mary Lou Williams originated the melody. Dahl, *Morning Glory*, 191–192. I think all three musicians treated the line as a riff rather than a fully-developed melodic statement, and thus it occupied a position in the "public domain," if you will. This may explain why no one seemed to complain when one of the others recorded the song under a different title. On the other hand, Williams might have felt silenced in the man's world of jazz, and more importantly, she respected and admired both men. Perhaps a formal complaint of theft on her part just wasn't worth the fallout.
97 It was an AFRS Jubilee transcription, Program no. 86. Carl A. Hällström and Bob Scherman, The AFRS Jubilee Transcription Series, http://home.swipnet.se/dooji/jubilee.htm; *Tom Lord Jazz Discography*. The original transcription version of "Mad Monk" was released on the Joyce Label LP 505.
98 Billy Taylor Interview, January 26, 2004.
99 He had Al Hall on bass and Jimmy Crawford on drums. It was first released as a ten-inch, *The Billy Taylor Trio/Quintet* (Savoy MG9035).
100 Billy Taylor Interview, January 26, 2004.
101 Chilton, *The Song of the Hawk*, 221; Sir Charles Thompson interview, August 11, 2003. On Thompson, see J. Chadwick, "Sir Charles Thompson," *Jazz Journal International* 41, no. 4 (1988), 8; "Sir Charles Thompson," in Stanley Dance, *The World of Count Basie* (New York: Da Capo Press, 1980), 333–338.
102 Chilton, *The Song of the Hawk*, 221–223; Tad Hershorn, *Verve: Norman Granz–The Conscience of Jazz* (forthcoming manuscript, Amistad Press, 2007), 15.

9 "Dizzy and Bird Did Nothing for Me Musically"

1 "Names Carry On With Big Jam Session in New York," *Pittsburgh Courier*, January 13, 1945.
2 McLean quoted in Spellman, *Four Lives in the Bebop Business*, 202.
3 The band debuted on April 29, 1945. *Amsterdam News*, April 28, 1945; Al Monroe, "Swinging the News," *Chicago Defender*, April 7, 1945. The common lore is that Thelonious led a trio with Max Roach and W. O. Smith to Philadelphia for a short engagement at some undetermined location in January 1945. The claim has been repeated continually because of what reportedly occurred on January 21, 1945. Bud Powell happened to be in Philadelphia, too, with Cootie Williams's Orchestra, and when he dropped in to hear Monk's trio, according to Francis Paudras, the police conducted a drug raid on the club and attempted to forcibly arrest Monk when he would not show his identification. Just then Powell intervened and shouted, "Stop that, man! You don't know what you're doing! The guy you're pushing around just happens to be the world's greatest pianist!" The officer then turned his attention on Powell and proceeded to beat him over the head with his billy club. Monk was supposedly taken into custody and held briefly for questioning while Bud was admitted to a hospital for treatment before being turned over to police. Paudras, *Dance of the Infidels*, 1–2, and it is repeated in every Monk biography: Ponzio and Postif, *Blue Monk*, 65; Fitterling, *Thelonious Monk*, 37; Gourse, *Straight, No Chaser*, 41. Even Sheridan's discography has Monk, Max Roach and W. O. Smith in Philadelphia in January 1945 at some unknown location. (Sheridan, *Brilliant Corners*, 345.) The only source apparently is Paudras. Alan Groves and Alyn Shipton question Paudras's account, suggesting that he conjoined two separate events. Groves and Shipton, *The Glass Enclosure*, 33–34. W. O. Smith, who allegedly was the bass player on the gig, only played with Monk once and that was at the Spotlite for one week in the summer of 1944. (See Chapter 8.) Most other accounts place the incident at Philadelphia's Broad Street Station, where Powell allegedly became loud after drinking too much. He was arrested for disorderly conduct but released to the custody of his mother, who was living at Willow Grove, Pennsylvania. A month later, Powell was committed to Pilgrim State Hospital, a mental institution on Long Island. Furthermore, I have searched through all possible sources, including the black press, and found no evidence of this particular incident or of Monk being in Philadelphia that week. And when I asked Max Roach about it, he knew of Bud's beating but said neither he nor Monk was there. Conversation with Max Roach, December 1996. Peter Pullman's forthcoming biography of Bud Powell should clarify what happened that night, but I do know Thelonious was not there.

4 "Old Faces Missing as Duke Repeats Concert," *Chicago Defender*, December 4, 1943; John Chilton, *Who's Who of Jazz* (New York: Da Capo, 1985), 363.

5 Ad, *Amsterdam News*, April 28, 1945; Shipton, *Groovin' High*, 142–44; Koch, *Yardbird Suite*, 62–64; Carl Woideck, *Charlie Parker: His Music and Life* (Ann Arbor: University of Michigan Press, 1996), 31.

6 Clouzet and Delorme, "L'Amertume du Prophète," 38–39. Of course, this is a translation from Monk's English to French back to English, thus in the process much of his unique language is lost. I'm grateful to Beth Coleman and Noubissie Thierry Kehou for their excellent translation work.

7 See, for example, Leonard Feather's interview, "Yardbird Flies Home," published in *Metronome* (August 1947), and John Fitch's 1953 radio interview for WHDH Boston, both of which are reprinted in Carl Wodieck, ed., *The Charlie Parker Companion: Six Decades of Commentary* (New York: Schirmer Books, 1998), 65, 113.

8 Jimmy Butts, "Where They're Playing," *Jazz Record* (August 1945), 13; Sheridan, *Brilliant Corners*, 346.

9 See ad from *Amsterdam News*, June 2, 1945. Sheridan, *Brilliant Corners*, 346, determined the date of August 30.

10 Bob Rusch, "Al McKibbon Interview," transc. Kea D. Rusch, *Cadence* (March 1987), 16–17.

11 Bastin, *Never Sell a Copyright*, 154.

12 Rusch, "Al McKibbon Interview," 17.

13 Miles Davis interview with Quincy Troupe, June 16, 1988, taped interview Quincy Troupe Collection, Schomburg Center for Research in Black Culture. And edited version of these same recollections, see Miles Davis, with Quincy Troupe, *Miles: The Autobiography* (New York: Simon & Schuster, 1989), 78–79.

14 Miles Davis interview with Quincy Troupe, June 16, 1988, taped interview Quincy Troupe Collection, Schomburg Center.

15 Ibid.

16 "Four Night Clubs Penalized," *New York Times*, November 5, 1945. Miles Davis remembers Bird taking the band to Minton's Playhouse after the police shut down the clubs. For him, the "drug and liquor license thing was only a cover, as far as a lot of black musicians were concerned, for the real reason, which was racism." Drug trafficking and prostitution existed around 52nd Street for years, but "when the music came downtown from uptown, the black hustlers around that scene came downtown with it, at least a whole lot of them did. And this didn't set too well with the white cops." Miles Davis, *Miles*, 72.

17 The tour was to be longer and include the South, but when Southern venues insisted on dividing audiences by race, Granz withdrew the offer.

   The date of the Philharmonic concert is not insignificant. For many years, historians, critics, and some musicians repeated the claim that Monk was supposed to be at a recording session for Savoy with Charlie Parker and Miles Davis on November 26, and that he simply skipped out—more evidence of Monk's unreliability. It was quite a session, considered among Bird's best recordings. If Monk was hired for the gig nobody told him. Works that repeat the myth include Ross Russell, *Bird Lives!*, 195; Ian Carr, *Miles Davis: The Definitive Biography* (New York: Thunder's Mouth Press, 1998), 24. Miles says in his memoir about the date, "Thelonious Monk and Bud Powell couldn't or wouldn't make it. . . ." Miles Davis, *Miles*, 75.

18 Dave Bittain, "Tatum Tops Philly Concert; Four Others Reviewed," *Metronome* (January 1946), 46.

19 Rusch, "Al McKibbon Interview," 20.

20 Hershorn, *Verve: Norman Granz*, chapter 6.

21 "Cheers, Moans at L.A. Concert," *Down Beat* (December 15, 1945), 2.

22 Ibid., p. 2; Hershorn, *Verve: Norman Granz*, chapter 7; Chilton, *The Song of the Hawk*, 234.

23 "Rhythm Round-Up," *Portland Observer*, December 10, 1945.

24 Hershorn, *Verve: Norman Granz*, chapter 7, pp. 17–19. Monk ended up staying at a large house owned by a black woman named Kitty White. She was known for renting rooms to traveling musicians. Bernice Slaughter and Ed Slaughter, Jr., interview, February 13, 2007.

25 *Portland Observer*, November 22, 1945; Concert handbill, reproduced in Robert Dietsche, *Jump Town: The Golden Years of Portland Jazz, 1942–1957* (Corvallis, OR: Oregon State University Press, 2005), 6.

26 *Portland Oregonian*, December 6, 1945.

27 Standifer quoted in Dietsche, *Jump Town*, 7; see also Paul de Barros, *Jackson Street After Hours: The Roots of Jazz in Seattle* (Seattle: Sasquatch Books, 1993), 189.

28 Dietsche, *Jump Town*, 2. Lucky Thompson wasn't there—he left the tour after the first concert. Ernest "Tom" Archia, a Texas-born tenor player known more for rhythm and blues, replaced him. On Tom Archia, see Robert L. Campbell, Leonard J. Bukowski, and Armin Büttner, "The Tom Archia Discography" (May 2007), http://hubcap.clemson.edu/~campber/archia.html.

29 "Rhythm Round-Up," *Portland Observer*, December 10, 1945.

30 Ibid.

31 Ibid.

32 Bernice Slaughter and Ed Slaughter, Jr., interview, February 13, 2007; Dietsche, *Jump Town*, 53.

33 Bernice Slaughter and Ed Slaughter, Jr., interview, February 13, 2007.

34 Ibid.

35 Ibid.

36 Hershorn, *Verve: Norman Granz*, 19.

37 *Jazz Record* (February 1946), 2; Chilton, *The Song of the Hawk*, 234–235.

38 Shipton, *Groovin' High*, 153–157; Gillespie, *To Be or Not to Bop*, 242–250.

39 The story of Gillespie's and Parker's California stay has been written about extensively, let alone debated. Some of the most obvious sources are Gillespie, *To Be or Not to Bop*, 248–250; but also see Robert Reisner, ed. *Bird: The Legend of Charlie Parker* (New York: Citadel Press, 1962); Russell, *Bird Lives!*.

40 The recording was first released on Dial 1001, but can be heard on Dizzy Gillespie, *Small Groups, 1945–1950: A Night in Tunisia* (Giants of Jazz, CD53122). Personnel: Dizzy Gillespie (tp,vcl) Lucky Thompson (ts,vcl) Milt Jackson (vib,vcl) Al Haig (p) Ray Brown (b) Stan Levey (d).

41 Feather, *The Jazz Years*, 104.

42 Hawkins quoted in Chilton, *The Song of the Hawk*, 235.

43 Gillespie, *To Be or Not to Bop*, 253.

44 Ibid., 254.

45 The band included Sonny Stitt and Howard Johnson on altos; Ray Abrams, James Moody, and Warren Luckey on tenors; Kenny Dorham, Dave Burns, Elmon Wright, and Talib Dawud were among the trumpet section, Ray Brown and Milt Jackson stayed on from the sextet. Max Roach initially occupied the drum chair before Kenny Clarke took over.

46 Shipton, *Groovin' High*, 181–183; Hennessey, *Klook*, 62–63; Kenny Clarke interview in Art Taylor, *Notes and Tones: Musician-to-Musician Interviews* (New York: Da Capo Press, 1993), 192.

47 Gillespie, *To Be or Not to Bop*, 252.

48 Fuller quoted in Gillespie, *To Be or Not to Bop*, 256.

49 Randy Weston recalls first hearing Monk play " 'Round Midnight" with Hawkins at the Down Beat Club, and Herbie Nichols made reference to Monk originals played by the band at the Spotlite. Randy Weston, interview, February 22, 1999; Herbie Nichols, "The Jazz Pianist–Purist," *Rhythm: Music and Theatrical Magazine* (July 1946), 12.

50 Lead sheet and Certificate of Copyright Registration, "Manhattan Moods: Melody by Thelonious Monk," Walter Gil Fuller Claimant, E unp. No. 444530, Received October 28, 1945.

51 Herbie Nichols's profile of Monk published in July 1946 refers specifically to "Ruby, My Dear." Nichols, "The Jazz Pianist," 12.

52 Lead sheet and Certificate of Copyright Registration, "Feeling That Way Now: Melody by Thelonious Monk," Walter Gil Fuller claimant, E unpub. 8741, Received February 26, 1946.

53 The first title is mentioned in Herbie Nichols, "The Jazz Pianist," 28; the second title comes from Steve Lacy interview, May 12, 1995, Paris, France. Lacy recalled Monk telling him that the song originally had lyrics, but I'm guessing that particular manuscript was burned in his first apartment fire in 1956. See Chapter 15.

54 Copy of original manuscript in Mary Lou Williams Collection, Rutgers University. I'm especially grateful to Annie Kuebler, the archivist in charge of Williams's papers, for helping me track down this music.

55 Lead sheet and Certificate of Copyright Registration, "Playhouse: Melody by Thelonious Monk," Walter Gil Fuller claimant, E unpub. 8742, Received February 26, 1946.

56 Chilton, *The Song of the Hawk*, 236.

57 Gillespie, *To Be or Not to Bop*, 252.

58 Ibid., 256.

59 Quoted in Shipton, *Groovin' High*, 185.

60 These recordings were first released as *Dizzy Gillespie '46 Live At The Spotlite* (Hi-Fly H 01), and re-released recently on a 2-CD set as Dizzy Gillespie Big Band, *Showtime at the Spotlight: 52nd Street, New York City, June 1946* (Uptown 2754).

61 See ads in the *Amsterdam News*, February 16, 23, March 2, 9, April 6, 13, 20, 27, May 4, 11, 18, 25, 1946.

62 On Ramey's distinguished career with Count Basie and Jay McShann, see Cameron Addis, "The 'Baptist Beat' in Modern Jazz: Texan Gene Ramey in Kansas City and New York," *Journal of Texas Music History* 4, no. 2 (Fall 2004), 8–16.

63 "Dizzy Gillespie Band Plays Apollo," *Amsterdam News*, June 29, 1946; "Dizzy, Thelma on Apollo Show," *Pittsburgh Courier*, June 29, 1946; ad in *New York Age*, June 29, 1946.

64 Quoted in Hennessey, *Klook*, 65–66.

65 Gillespie, *To Be or Not to Bop*, 256.

66 John Lewis inteview, by Marian McPartland—Piano Jazz (PBS), recorded October 30, 1978, Rodgers and Hammerstein Archives NYPL; Hennessey, *Klook*, 54–55; Shipton, *Groovin' High*, 189.

67 Gillespie, *To Be or Not to Bop*, 256.

68 Chico O'Farrill, who worked for Fuller, called it "ghost writing." Gitler, ed., *Swing to Bop*, 255. Gil Fuller had a history of questionable practices. As Ingrid Monson points out in her book (*Freedom Sounds: Civil Rights Call Out to Jazz and Africa* [New York: Oxford University Press, 2008], 39–40), in one incident he failed to pay Doc Cheatham, Maurio Bauza, and Frank Baristo for a recording session he put together for Mercury. After booking the studio, he literally slipped out the back door with the tapes. He was also expelled from Local 802 for bouncing checks.

69 Nichols, "The Jazz Pianist," 11–12, 28.

70 John R. Gibson, "A Cavalcade of the Negro Dance Musician," *Rhythm: Music and Theatrical Magazine* (July 1946), 22.

71 Nichols, "The Jazz Pianist," 11.

72 Ibid., p. 12.

73 Ibid., p. 12.

74 Geraldine Smith interview, February 12, 2004.

75 He eventually caught up on his dues and Local 802 reinstated him the first week of February 1947. Minutes of the Executive Board, AFM Local 802, February 6, 1947.

76 Mary Lou Williams, "Autobiographical Notebooks," #2, p. 271, Mary Lou Williams Papers.

77 Ira Gitler, "The Remarkable J. J. Johnson," *Down Beat* (May 11, 1961), 17; George Hoefer, "Early J. J.," *Down Beat* (January 28, 1965), 16; Joshua Berrett and Louis Bourgois, III, *The Musical World of J. J. Johnson* (Lanham, MD: Scarecrow Press, 1999).

78 Mary Lou Williams, "Autobiographical Notebooks," #2, p. 271.
79 Mary Lou Williams, "Mad Monk," *Melody Maker* (May 22, 1954), 11.
80 Ibid. p. 11.
81 Quoted in Eric Nisenson, *Open Sky: Sonny Rollins and His World of Improvisation* (New York: St. Martin's Press, 2000), 31.
82 Quoted in Ben Sidran, *Talking Jazz: An Oral History* (New York: Da Capo Press, 1995), 174–75. See also, George W. Goodman, "Sonny Rollins at Sixty-eight," *Atlantic Monthly* (July 1999), 84; Stanley Crouch, "The Colossus," *New Yorker* (May 9, 2005), 64–67.
83 Monk did not hire Rollins that year, in part because jobs were few and far between, but also because Rollins did not join the union until December of 1947. Minutes of the Executive Board, Local 802, December 2, 1947, microfilm reel 5276.
84 Spellman, *Four Lives in the Bebop Business*, 200.
85 Arthur Taylor interview, conducted by Warren Smith, July 26, 1994, Jazz Oral HIstory Project, Schomburg Center.
86 Randy Weston interview, July 30, 2003.
87 Both quotes from Ira Gitler, "Randy Weston," 16.
88 Randy Weston interview, July 30, 2003.
89 Arthur Taylor, *Notes and Tones*, 22.
90 Geraldine Smith interview, February 12, 2004.
91 Advertisement in *Amsterdam News,* April 12, 1947; and reproduced in Ken Vail, *Miles' Diary: The Life of Miles Davis, 1947–1961* (Sanctuary Publishing, 1997), 9; also posted on Jacques Ponzio's "Round About Monk" website, http://www.sojazz.org/monk/thelonious05.html.
92 Ernie Washington worked between swing and bebop artists, playing with Ben Webster, W. O. Smith, and early on with Dizzy Gillespie. Jimmy Butts, "Where They're Playing," *Jazz Record* (September 1945), 13; W. O. Smith, *Sideman*, 40, 42, 109.
93 Certificate of Copyright Registration, "What Now: Melody by Thelonious Monk," Walter Gil Fuller claimant, E unpub. 63809, Received February 21, 1947; Certificate of Copyright Registration, "I Mean You: Melody by Thelonious Monk," Walter Gil Fuller claimant, E unpub. 63802, Received February 21, 1947.
94 Geoffrey Wheeler, "The (American) Sonora Label and Jazz of the 1940s," *IAJRC Journal* 39, no. 3 (August 2006), 30. This version of "I Mean You" is available on Coleman Hawkins, *Bean and the Boys* (Prestige PRCD 24124-2).
95 Application for Registration of a Claim to Copyright in a Musical Composition, "I Mean You," Composer/Author - Thelonious Monk, Copyright Owner–Walter G. Fuller, Monogram Music Co., Application Received February 21, 1947, Registration Number R-570813. The lead sheet Monk submitted is nearly identical to what Hawkins played, except for one glaring omission: the first four bars of the bridge are missing. While it's possible Monk initially wrote it as a 28-bar song and his ex-boss contributed the four missing measures, this is an unlikely explanation. It was probably just a mistake in notating the music—one that Gil Fuller might have made.
96 *Vox presents Charlie Christian* (Vox VSP 302); Sheridan, *Brilliant Corners*, 5, 238.
97 Tinney quoted in Gitler, *Swing to Bop*, 120.
98 Quoted in Gillespie, *To Be or Not to Bop*, 219. Johnson tells a version of this story in Gitler, *Swing to Bop*, 120–121.
99 Gillespie, *To Be or Not to Bop*, 219.

10 "The George Washington of Bebop"

1 "William P. Gottlieb's Life and Work: A Brief Biography Based on Oral Histories," http://memory.loc.gov/ammem/wghtml/wgbio.html; see also, William P. Gottlieb, *The Golden Age of Jazz* (San Francisco: Pomegranate Artbooks, 1995).
2 See *Down Beat* (August 27, 1947), 2, 18; "Well, Be-Bop!" *Down Beat* (May 21, 1947), 15.
3 See for example, "Bebop and Old Masters," *New Republic* (June 30, 1947), 36; "The Jazz Beat: Memo on Bebop," *Saturday Review* (August 30, 1947), 18–19; "Be-Bop??!!—Man, We Called it Kloop-Mop!!" *Metronome* (April 1947), 21, 44–45; Gilbert McKean, "The Diz and the Bebop," *Esquire* (October 1947), 212–216; Jack Raes, "Que Pensez-Vous de Be-bop?" *Hot Club Magazine* (May 1947), 11, 13–14. For an historical accounting of the bebop debates, see Eric Porter, *What Is This Thing Called Jazz?: African American Musicians as Artists, Critics, and Activists* (Los Angeles and Berkeley: University of California Press, 2002), 54–100; Bernard Gendron, "'Moldy Figs' and Modernists: Jazz at War (1942–1946)," in *Jazz Among the Discourses,* ed. Krin Gabbard (Durham, NC: Duke University Press, 1995), 31–56.
4 Tadd Dameron, "The Case for Modern Music," *Record Changer* (February 1948), 5, 16; Mary Lou Williams, "Music and Progress," *Jazz Record* (November 1947), 23–24; Lennie Tristano, "What's Right with the Beboppers," *Metronome* (July 1947), 14, 31.
5 Bill Gottlieb, "Thelonious [sic] Monk—Genius of Bop: Elusive Pianist Finally Caught in Interview," *Down Beat* (September 24, 1947), 2.
6 The same issue of *Down Beat* that carried Gottlieb's profile on Monk also published his review (and photos) of the Thornhill band. Bill Gottlieb, "Thornhill, McKinley Are Superb; Auld's New 9 Piece Band Answer to Bad Biz," *Down Beat*, 3. Monk's praise for Thornhill is quoted below.
7 All of Gottlieb's photos can be viewed on "William Gottlieb: Photographs from the Golden Age of Jazz," http://memory.loc.gov/ammem/wghtml/wghome.html.
8 Gottlieb, "Thelonius [sic] Monk," 2.

9   Ibid., p. 2

10 Ibid., p. 2

11 Lorraine Gordon with Barry Singer, *Alive at the Village Vanguard: My Life in and Out of Jazz Time* (Milwaukee: Hal Leonard Corp., 2006), 63.

12 Descriptions of Monk's room from author interviews with Thomas Monk, Jr., Theolonious Monk, Alonzo White, and Charlotte Washington; Ira Peck, "The Piano Man who dug Be-bop," M7; "Creator of 'Be bop' Objects to Name and Changes in His Style," *Chicago Defender*, March 27, 1948.

13 Born in 1918 in Georgia as Isaac Abrams and raised in Newark, Ike was probably still a teenager when he adopted the name "Quebec." U.S. Census, 1930, *Population Schedule: Newark, New Jersey*, ED: 52. He knew his way around the music, having started his musical career as a pianist and dancer but picked up the tenor saxophone in 1940 as a member of the Barons of Rhythm. He played in a number of small bands around New York with Kenny Clarke, Benny Carter, Hot Lips Page, Frankie Newton, and the man whose tone he emulated—Coleman Hawkins. Claude Schlouch, *In Memory of Ike Quebec: A Discography* (Marseilles, France, 1983, rev. 3/1985); Michael Cuscuna, "Ike Quebec," *The Complete Blue Note Recordings of Ike Quebec and John Hardee* (Mosaic 107, 1984).

14 Richard Cook, *Blue Note Records: The Biography* (New York: Random House, 2003), 19–21; Michael Cuscuna and Michel Ruppli, comp., *The Blue Note Label: A Discography* (New York and Westport, CT: Greenwood Press, 2001), 9.

15 Gordon, *Alive at the Village Vanguard*, 63.

16 Gourse, *Straight, No Chaser*, 48.

17 Cook, *Blue Note Records*, 6–18; Michael Cuscuna and Michel Ruppli, comp., *The Blue Note Label: A Discography* (New York and Westport, CT: Greenwood Press, 2001), xi–xii, 8–16.

18 Gordon, *Alive at the Village Vanguard*, 33–36; "Lorraine Gordon: Administrator, Village Vanguard," interviewed by Ted Panken, March 23, 2002, *Artist and Influence*, vol. 21 (New York: Hatch-Billops Collection, 2002), 115–116.

19 Quoted in Cuscuna, *The Complete Blue Note Recordings of Thelonious Monk*, 3.

20 Cuscuna and Ruppli, comp., *The Blue Note Label*, 16–18.

21 Lorraine Gordon, *Alive at the Village Vanguard*, 68.

22 Greg Henderson, "Idrees Sulieman Interview," Transcribed by Bob Rusch, *Cadence* 5, no. 9 (September 1979), 3; "Jazz Encyclopedia Questionnaire: Idrees Sulieman," Vertical Files, Institute of Jazz Studies, Rutgers University.

23 Robert Dannin, *Black Pilgrimage to Islam* (New York: Oxford University Press, 2002), 35–38, 58–60; Richard Turner, "The Ahmadiyya Mission to Blacks in the United States in the 1920s," *Journal of Religious Thought* 44, no. 2 (Winter-Spring 1988), 50–66; Richard Turner, *Islam in the African American Experience* (Bloomington: University of Indiana Press, 1997).

24 "Moslem Musicians," *Ebony* (April 1953), 104–11; Claude Clegg, III, *An Original Man*; Art Taylor, *Notes and Tones*, 251; Mike Hennessey, "The Enduring Message of Abdullah ibn Buhaina," *Jazz Journal International* 30 (1977), 6; Porter, *What Is This Thing Called Jazz?*, 78–79.

25 "Moslem Musicians," 111.

26 Ibid., 108. Leslie Gourse, *Art Blakey: Jazz Messenger* (New York: Schirmer Trade Books, 2002), 40. She claims he converted to Islam after returning from two years in Africa in 1949, but earlier interviews indicated that he had already launched a Muslim Mission with Talib Dawud in 1947.

27 Porter, *What Is This Thing Called Jazz?*, 78; "Art Blakey Interview: Part I" (taken and transcribed by Bob Rusch), *Cadence* 7 (July 1981), 10–11. While the "seventeen" varied, original members included Sahib Shihab (Edmund Gregory) on alto; tenor players Musa Kaleem (Orlando Wright) and Sonny Rollins; Haleen Rasheed (Howard Bowe), trombone; trumpeters Kenny Dorham (another convert who had adopted the name Abdul Hamid), Ray Copeland, and Little Benny Harris; Cecil Payne (baritone sax); Bud Powell, Kenny Drew, and later Walter Bishop, Jr. (Ibrahim Ibn Ismail) held piano duties at different times; and Gary Mapp (bass). Steve Schwartz and Michael Fitzgerald, "Chronology of Art Blakey (and the Jazz Messengers)," http://www.jazzdiscography.com/Artists/Blakey/chron.htm; Henderson, "Idrees Sulieman Interview," 6. Gourse mistakenly claims the Messengers began in 1949, after Blakey allegedly returns from Africa, but clearly the group is advertised as the Messengers as early as January of 1948, and all other indications suggest they were in existence for much of 1947. Gourse, *Art Blakey*, 36–38.

28 Korall, *Drummin' Men*, 134–136; see also, "Art Blakey Interview: Part I," 8–11; "Art Blakey Interview: Part II" (taken and transcribed by Bob Rusch), *Cadence* 9 (September 1981), 12–13; Peter Danson, "Art Blakey: An Interview by Peter Danson," *Coda* 173 (1980), 15; Gourse, *Art Blakey*, 30–38.

29 For a fine analysis of Blakey's drumming, see Zita Carno, "Art Blakey," *Jazz Review* 3, no. 1 (January 1959), 6–10, and Korall, *Drummin' Men*, 134–140.

30 Quoted in Korall, *Drummin' Men*, 137.

31 Quoted in Michael Cuscuna, "Thelonious Monk—The Early Years," *The Complete Blue Note Recordings of Thelonious Monk* [Sleeve notes] (Santa Monica, CA: Mosaic Records, 1983), 3.

32 Alfred Lion quoted in Hentoff, *The Jazz Life*, 196.

33 All of these recordings can be heard on Thelonious Monk, *The Complete Blue Note Recordings* (Blue Note CD8 30363-2); for sequence and unissued takes, see Sheridan, *Brilliant Corners*, 17.

34 Bertha Hope showed me a manuscript of Elmo Hope's that resembled the A-section of "Off Minor," though the manuscript was not dated. Her discovery and her argument that Monk borrowed the melody from Elmo is persuasive, however. Bertha Hope interview, July 15, 2003.

35 Originally released on Roost 513, but can be heard on Bud Powell, *The Complete Blue Note and Roost Recordings* (Blue Note 1994).

36 Built on an AABA structure thirty-six measures long (he added four bars to the final A section), it contains

numerous examples of rhythmic displacement that gives a sense of shifting time signatures. It has no tonal center and is built on whole-tone harmony as well as chromatic motion, creating a kind of wandering chordal movement that resolves in the first A section in D Major, and the final A section in D^b Major.

37 Quoted in Richard Cook, *Blue Note Records*, 26.
38 A Harlemite of West Indian extraction, Taitt had worked in John Kirby's band with Clarence Brereton—Geraldine Smith's cousin from the neighborhood. It is likely that Brereton recommended Taitt to Monk. John Kirby, *John Kirby and His Orchestra, 1945–1946* (Classics). I determined Taitt's birth year and heritage from the U.S. Census, 1920, *Population Schedule: Manhattan Borough*, ED 819-839.
39 "Moslem Musicians," 104.
40 Dieter Salemann (assisted by Dieter Hartmann and Michael Vogler), *Edmund Gregory/Sahib Shihab: Solography, Discography, Band Routes, Engagements, in Chronological Order* (Basle, Switzerland, 1986); Roland Baggenaes, "Sahib Shihab," *Coda* 204 (1985), 6.
41 Sahib Shihab, "Jazz Encyclopedia Questionnaire," Request from Leonard Feather, Vertical File: Sahib Shihab, Institute of Jazz Studies, Rutgers University.
42 Nat Hentoff, *The Jazz Life*, 183.
43 Michael Cuscuna reviewed all of the recordings, including the rejected takes, and made the observation about Taitt's obsession with "Stranger in Paradise." Cuscuna, *The Complete Blue Note Recordings of Thelonious Monk*, 7.
44 Geraldine Smith interview, February 12, 2004.
45 *Amsterdam News*, January 24, 1948.
46 Ira Peck, who interviewed Thelonious at his house just two or three weeks after the January 25th gig, describes the new phonograph in his article, "The Piano Man," M7.
47 Paul Bacon interview, July 30, 2001.
48 Cuscuna, *The Complete Blue Note Recordings*, 3. I know what he wore because a photo of Monk on Fred Robbins's show, taken by Frank Wolff, was published in Nard Griffin, *To Be or Not to Bop* (New York: Leo Workman, 1948), 9.
49 "Thelonious Monk," (ca. early January, 1948), Blue Note Archives, Capitol Records. I'm grateful to Bruce Lundvall, Bev McCord and John Ray for their assistance gaining access to Blue Note's files. The release was also recently reprinted in Gordon, *Alive at the Village Vanguard*, 60.
50 Ibid.
51 Ibid.
52 Thelonious Monk press release (ca. February 1948), Blue Note Archives, Capitol Records; and quoted in Ira Peck, "The Piano Man," M7.
53 Lorraine Lion to George Hoefer, January 13, 1948, reprinted in Gordon, *Alive at the Village Vanguard*, 61. Note that the original letter was misdated 1947.
54 George Hoefer, "Pianist Monk Getting Long Awaited Break," *Down Beat* (February 11, 1948), 11.
55 Ibid., 11. And he made a couple of slips, like identifying Danny Quebec West and Ike Quebec as the same person, or attributing Dizzy Gillespie's composition "Emanon" to Monk. There is a possible explanation for Hoefer's error regarding the authorship of "Emanon." Recall that Monk's original title for "52nd Street Theme" was "Nameless," so it is easy to assume that "No Name" spelled backward is meant to be the same title, though the song is quite different. "Emanon" is a standard, fairly ordinary blues riff, uncharacteristic of anything Monk has ever written.
56 Ibid., 11.
57 Cuscuna, *The Complete Blue Note Recordings*, 3.
58 Hentoff, *The Jazz Life*, 184.
59 Gordon, *Alive at the Village Vanguard*, 66–67; on Ingersoll, see Roy Hoopes, *Ralph Ingersoll: A Biography* (New York: Atheneum, 1985).
60 In her memoir, Gordon refers to "Seymour Peck" when she actually meant Ira. Seymour was Ira's older brother and a more prominent literary figure on the New York scene. He also wrote for *PM* and became a major drama critic and editor for the *New York Times* Arts and Leisure section (after surviving a bout of Red-baiting during the McCarthy period). He was killed in a car accident in 1985. Ira Peck followed his older brother's path, writing drama, film, and television criticism for the *New York Times*, as well as juvenile biography and history for Scholastic. See Herbert Mitgang, "Seymour Peck: Times Editor for 32 Years, Killed in Crash," *New York Times*, January 2, 1985; "Ira Peck," *Contemporary Authors Online*, Gale, 2002, http://galenet.galegroup.com.
61 Gordon, *Alive at the Village Vanguard*, 66–67. Surprisingly, Peck never once mentions the fact that she is present during the interview.
62 Peck, "The Piano Man," 7.
63 Ibid., 7.
64 Ibid., 7.
65 Alonzo White, interview, February 23, 2004.
66 Peck, "The Piano Man," 7.
67 "Dizzy Writing Book on Be-Bop," *California Eagle*, February 5, 1948.
68 See for example Tera Hunter's brilliant book, *To 'Joy My Freedom: Southern Black Women's Lives and Labors after the Civil War* (Cambridge, MA: Harvard University Press, 1997).
69 Gordon, *Alive at the Village Vanguard*, 68; see also, Gourse, *Straight, No Chaser*, 55.
70 Jesse Hamlin, "A Life in Jazz," *Columbia College Today* (November 2004), www.college.columbia.edu/cct/nov04/features2.php; Keepnews, *The View from Within*, .
71 Quoted in Rob Tocalino, "Keepnews and Monk: A Shared Legacy," *8th Annual SF Spring Season—Official Program Book* (SFJazz, 2007), 7; see also, Keepnews, *The View from Within*, 108.
72 Orrin Keepnews, "Thelonious Monk's Music May Be First Sign of Bebop's Legitimacy," *Record Changer* 7, no. 4 (April 1948), 5; reprinted in Orrin Keepnews, *The View From Within*, 111.

73 Keepnews, "Thelonious Monk's Music," 20.
74 Ben Burns, Executive Editor of *Ebony* Magazine to Lorraine Lion, March 25, 1948, Blue Note Archives, Capitol Records.
75 Lorraine Lion, "Thelonious Monk Deserves Credit for Gifts to Jazz," *Pittsburgh Courier*, February 14, 1948.
76 Dan Burley, "Thelonious Monk and His Bebop," *Amsterdam News*, February 21, 1948.
77 "Creator of 'Be bop' Objects to Name and Changes in His Style," *Chicago Defender*, March 27, 1948.
78 Ibid.
79 "The News of Radio," *New York Times*, February 2, 1948; Sidney Lohman, "Radio Row: One Thing or Another," *New York Times*, February 8, 1948. They performed two standards: "Just You, Just Me," and "All the Things You Are," and Ike Quebec's "Suburban Eyes." The broadcast was released on Thelonious Monk and Art Tatum, *The Vibes are On* (Chazzer 2002).
80 The Executive Committee did not get around to approving Monk's contract with Minton's until May 6, 1948. Minutes of the Executive Board, June 3, 1948, AFM Local 802, reel 5276. This may mean the gig was later than March.
81 *New York Amsterdam News*, April 24, 1948.
82 Paul Bacon, "The High Priest of Be-bop: The Inimitiable Mr. Monk," *Record Changer* 8, no. 11 (November, 1949), 9–10.
83 *Down Beat* (February 25, 1948), 19.
84 *Metronome* (April 1948), 45–46.
85 *Down Beat* (April 21, 1948), 19.
86 *Billboard* (February 21, 1948), 117.
87 Paul Bacon interview, July 30, 2001.
88 See John Gennari, *Blowin' Hot and Cool: Jazz and Its Critics* (Chicago: University of Chicago Press, 2006).
89 Paul Bacon, " 'Round About Midnight,' 'Well, You Needn't,'" *Record Changer*, 7, no. 5 (May 1948), 18.
90 Cuscusna, *The Complete Blue Note Recordings*, 4.
91 Lorraine Gordon quoted in Gourse, *Straight, No Chaser*, 53.
92 Ibid., 53.
93 Amiri Baraka, *The Autobiography of LeRoi Jones/Amiri Baraka* (New York: Freundlich Books, 1984), 139.
94 Both Norman Lewis and Romare Bearden have talked about how modern jazz influenced abstract expressionism. For Lewis, 1948–1949 marked his embrace of a kind of bebop-influenced abstraction. See his "Jazz Band" (1948) and "Harlem at the Gate"(1949). See Romare Bearden and Harry Henderson, *A History of African American Artists from 1792 to the Present* (New York: Random House, 1993), 168–172. See also, Robin D. G. Kelley, "Breaking the Color Bind: A Decade of American Masters," catalogue essay for *African American Art: 20th Century Masterworks, X* (New York: Michael Rosenfeld Gallery, 2003).
95 Nard Griffin, *To Be or Not to Bop* (New York: Leo Workman, 1948), 5.
96 Ibid., 2.
97 Ray Nance quoted in Stanley Dance, *The World of Duke Ellington* (New York: Da Capo Press, 2000, orig., 1970), 139.
98 Shaw, *52nd Street*, 272; Shipton, *Groovin' High*, 208.
99 According to Chris Sheridan, Monk had two stints at the Roost—May 4–16 (or longer) and June 15–27. Sheridan, *Brilliant Corners*. 355–56. Local 802 approved Monk's contract with the Roost on June 3. Minutes of the Executive Board, June 3, 1948, AFM Local 802, reel 5276. Ira Gitler was a frequent patron and he was there the night Wardell Gray sat in with Monk. Ira Gitler interview, August 13, 2007.
100 "Interview with John Simmons," by Patricia Willard," Tapes 1–9, NEA Oral History Project, Washington, D.C., 1977, Institute of Jazz Studies, Rutgers University, pp. 58–59.
101 "Sydenham Seeks Aid to Bar Closing," *New York Times*, March 1, 1948; "Sydenham Gets $137,000," *New York Times*, March 8, 1948.
102 *Amsterdam News*, June 5, 1948; *New York Times*, June 7, 1948.
103 Director of FBI to Legat, Tokyo (163–2971), cablegram, September 3, 1970, Thelonious Monk FBI File.
104 The 1937 Marihuana Tax Act made possession or transfer of marijuana illegal throughout the United States, though exceptions were made for the pharmaceutical companies, who were required to pay an exorbitant excise tax. Several states had already outlawed marijuana use and possession, notably states in the Southwest where fear of the spread of marijuana was projected onto Mexican workers. Nevertheless, in New York and the rest of the country, the postwar period witnessed heightened policing of drug use and more draconian laws. African-Americans and Latinos, in general, and jazz musicians in particular, were often the target of raids, sting operations, and overall investigations. It is ironic that just four years before Monk's arrest, the LaGuardia Commission released a report challenging the federal bureau of narcotics' claims that marijuana is highly addictive, a source of crime and criminal activity, and is widespread. See H. Wayne Morgan, *Drugs in America: A Social History, 1800–1980* (Syracuse: Syracuse University Press, 1982), 140; Curtis Marez, *Drug Wars: The Political Economy of Narcotics* (Minneapolis: University of Minnesota Press, 2004), 131; La Guardia Commission, *The Marihuana Problem in the City of New York* (Metuchen, New Jersey: Scarecrow Reprint Corp.,1973).
105 He was charged under Section 422 of the *New York Public Health Law* (1941), p. 134, and Section 1751a of the *New York Penal Law* (1941), p. 153.
106 Nellie Monk interview, January 12, 2002; also, same story was repeated by Marcellus Green interview, December 31, 2003.
107 Arnold Shaw, *Fifty-Second Street*, 180.
108 The ban was called partly in response to the passage of the Taft-Hartley Act in 1947 banning closed shops, sympathy strikes, and secondary boycotts. It not only weakened the bargaining power of all organized labor, but a provision in the act outlawed the AFM's record-royalty fund. Any sort of industry paybacks to unions

that did not involve actual services was deemed illegal under Taft-Hartley. However, when the AFM's recording contracts expired on January 1, 1948, Petrillo announced the ban. This time the industry was in a strong position, having made and stockpiled many more records than it could release on the market at once. The ban lasted almost a full year, culminating in a small victory for the AFM. To replace the record-royalty fund, the industry agreed to establish a Music Performance Trust Fund that would finance free concerts and pay struggling musicians union scale.

109 This group can be heard on Milt Jackson/Sonny Stitt, *In the Beginning* (Galaxy XY 204).
110 "Interview with John Simmons, by Patricia Willard," Tapes 1–9, NEA Oral History Project; Johnny Simmen and Barry Kernfeld, "Simmons, John," in *The New Grove Dictionary of Jazz*, 2nd ed., edited by Barry Kernfeld. *Grove Music Online. Oxford Music Online*, http://www.oxfordmusiconline.com/subscriber/article/grove/music/J410000 (accessed February 24, 2009).
111 Korall, *Drummin' Men*, 59–69; Gitler, *Jazz Masters of the Forties*, 190.
112 All takes can be heard on *The Complete Blue Note Recordings of Thelonious Monk*.
113 "Interview with John Simmons, by Patricia Willard," Tapes 1–9, NEA Oral History Project, p. 60.
114 I must here acknowledge Milton Stewart, who suggests that Monk developed an "mbira" approach to the piano, in which the left and right hands play rhythmically separate melodies featuring alternating pitches in the middle and bass registers. It produces the effect of two independent instruments being played simultaneously. Milton Stewart, "Thelonious Monk: Bebop or Something Different?" *Jazz Research Papers* 5 (1985), 182–85.
115 Les Tomkins interview with Thelonious Monk, 1965.
116 Richard Boyer, "Profiles: Bop," *New Yorker* (July 3, 1948), 26.
117 Ibid., 29.
118 Ibid., 28.
119 Ibid., 29.
120 Ibid, 31.
121 Charlotte Washington interview, April 5, 2004.
122 *The Complete Dean Benedetti Recordings* (Mosaic MR10-129).
123 Subpeona for Alfred W. Lion, People of the State of New York vs. Thelonious Monk, called for trial on August 31, 1948, at 100 Centre Street at 10 AM, Blue Note Archives.

11 "It's a Drag to Be in Jail"

1 Department of Correction, City of New York, *Annual Report, 1948*, p. 44.
2 In 1948, the Tombs possessed 829 individual cells and another 106 single beds dormitory style, and thus at capacity could hold about 1,000 inmates. Since the late summer and early fall months (August, September, October) were the busiest months of the year, according to the Department of Correction annual report, we can guess that the Tombs was near capacity at the time of Monk's incarceration. The average population throughout the year was 813. Department of Correction, City of New York, *Annual Report, 1948*, pp. 42–43.
3 Geraldine Smith interview, February 12, 2004.
4 See Shaw, *52nd Street*, 256, 339 *passim*.; Morgan, *Drugs in America*, 140; Marez, *Drug Wars*, 131; Bonnie, Richard J., et al. *The Marijuana Conviction: A History of Marijuana Prohibition in the United States* (New York: Drug Policy Alliance, 1999); Barry Charles Wukasch, "Marijuana and the Law: An Analysis of Evolving Federal Drug Policy" (Ph.D. diss., University of Arizona, 1972).
5 Monk family interview, January 30, 2004. Both Judith and Evelyn Smith recalled simultaneously that "something happened in Mexico." Geraldine Smith also remembered, "They were out of town when they got married." Geraldine Smith interview, February 12, 2004. On the Monk side of the family, however, neither his niece Charlotte nor his nephew Alonzo recalls hearing about a marriage ceremony. "If they did [get married]," Charlotte explained, "it would have been Las Vegas or New York. But they never had a marriage ceremony." Charlotte Washington interview, April 5, 2004; Alonzo White interview, February 23, 2004.
6 It is indisputable from the flurry of press reports and profiles published about Monk, not to mention recollections of friends and acquaintances, that he was still single through the fall of 1947 and spring and summer of 1948. Nevertheless, the official date of their marriage is still subject to question and speculation, and the scenario I present here is based on all the sketchy evidence available. For one thing, there is no extant record of a marriage certificate. The issue came up after Monk's death in 1982 when Nellie's position as inheritor was called into question by the state of New York precisely because she could not produce a marriage license. In her affidavit, she testifies to having married Thelonious in September of 1947 and having signed a marriage certificate, but the minister who conducted the ceremony failed to file the documentation with the City Clerk of New York County. *Nellie Monk Affidavit, November 4, 1982, Proceeding for Letters of Administration, Estate of Thelonious Sphere Monk, Deceased, Surrogate Court of the State of New York, Case # 5484; Hudson H. Reid Affadavit*, ibid. It is possible they were married in September of 1947, but Thelonious was still living with his mother, and in every press interview the journalist and Monk himself made a point of his single status, and Lorraine Lion, who spent quite a bit of time with Monk, concurred. (Lorraine Gordon, *Alive at the Village Vanguard*, 67.) Monk was astonishingly honest about such things, so it seems unlikely he would marry and then lie about it. Finally, the fall 1948 date seems more realistic, given that the birth of their first child occurred a little over a year later, December 27, 1949. My own presentation of the sequence of events suggests they were married sometime in the first two weeks of October, prior to the Vanguard gig. However, it is equally probable that they were married later in the year, possibly before Nellie's birthday on December 27.
7 Jackie Bonneau interview, July 8, 2005. Marion White confirms that Thelonious and Nellie first lived together in the Bronx. Marion White interview, with Quincy Troupe, December 1, 1990.

8 Nellie Monk interview, January 12, 2002.

9 Quote from "Lorraine Gordon: Administrator, Village Vanguard," interviewed by Ted Panken, March 23, 2002, *Artist and Influence,* vol. 21 (New York: Hatch-Billops Collection, 2002), 117.

10 Lorraine Gordon recalls Monk's gig opening on September 14, but this is impossible since Monk was still in jail. Furthermore, Billy Taylor clearly remembers working at the Vanguard before Monk and Max Gordon holding him over just in case Monk's band failed to generate an audience. According to Local 802 records, Billy Taylor's contract with the Vanguard began October 1, 1948. Minutes of the Executive Board, October 6, 1948, AFM Local 802, reel 5276.

11 Lorraine Gordon remembered a slightly different line-up—a quintet with Idrees Sulieman with Blakey on drums. ("Lorraine Gordon: Administrator, Village Vanguard," interviewed by Ted Panken, March 23, 2002, *Artist and Influence* vol. 21 [New York: Hatch-Billops Collection, 2002], 117.) But Billy Taylor, who played opposite Monk that week, recalls a quartet with Denzil Best on drums and no trumpet. Billy Taylor interview, January 26, 2004. Of course, Sulieman might have sat in.

12 Gordon, *Alive at the Village Vanguard,* 96.

13 Ibid.

14 Billy Taylor Interview, January 26, 2004.

15 Lorraine Gordon, *Alive at the Village Vanguard,* 95–103.

16 Spellman, *Four Lives in the Bebop Business,* 198.

17 Ibid., 199.

18 Marion remembered that the one dish Monk cooked frequently was spaghetti. "Yeah, he could cook some mean spaghetti and meat ball. He used to cook that. That and a few other things, but that was his main dish, the spaghetti." Marion White interview, with Quincy Troupe, December 1, 1990.

19 Geraldine Smith and Evelyn Smith, interview, February 12, 2004.

20 Nat Hentoff, "The Private World of Thelonious Monk," *Esquire Magazine* (April 1960), 137.

21 Spellman, *Four Lives in the Bebop Business,* 198–99.

22 Frank Pelaez was actually born on Long Island and moved to San Juan Hill as a kid. U.S. Census, 1930, *Population Schedule: Islip, Suffolk County, New York,* ED 79. He composed and co-composed over twenty songs between 1948 and 1963. (See Library of Congress www.copyright.gov.)

23 See interview with Frank Paccione on Howard Mansfield's Thelonious Monk website, http://www.howardm.net/tsmonk/passions.php; see also, Sheridan, *Brilliant Corners,* 27–28.

24 David Hinckley, "Future of Radio," *New York Daily News,* March 17, 2004; Charles F. McGovern, *Sold American: Consumption and Citizenship, 1890–1945* (Chapel Hill: University of North Carolina Press, 2006), 53; http://www.swingmusic.net/.

25 Nor do we know the date of the recording. There has been a longstanding debate among Monk scholars about this date, initially placing the session in 1950 or later. But all of my evidence points to the winter of 1948–1949. Chris Sheridan independently has come up with 1948, based in part on the aural evidence of Rouse's playing and on Paccione's testimony on Howard Mansfield's website (http://www.howardm.net/tsmonk/passions.php). He also ventured some guesses as to personnel: Wesley Anderson, trumpet, William "Keter" Betts on bass, and possibly Jimmy Cobb on drums. (Sheridan, *Brilliant Corners,* 27.) He came up with these names based on who was playing with Rouse at the time, but I'm skeptical, since Monk put together the band, not Rouse, and he had many New York musicians to choose from. Michael Mattos and Jerry Smith seem to be the more likely candidates. Other possibilities are Gene Ramey or Al McKibbon (bass) and Denzil Best on drums, but none of these men have ever mentioned anything resembling this date.

26 "Frankie Passions," http://www.howardm.net/tsmonk/passions.php.

27 Both songs originally appeared on the Washington label (303 and 304) but were released on a compilation CD called *Cool Whalin'* (Spotlite [E]SPJ 135).

28 Quoted in "Frankie Passions," http://www.howardm.net/tsmonk/passions.php.

29 Johnny Griffin interview, February 2, 2004. See also, Mike Hennessey, *The Little Giant: The Story of Johnny Griffin* (London: Northway Publications, 2008), 6–42; Liner notes from *Elmo Hope Trio* (Hifirecords 616 [1959]); Arthur Taylor, *Notes and Tones,* 71.

30 Johnny Griffin interview, February 2, 2004. Two days earlier, Griffin and Hope had done a recording session for Joe Morris in New York, so there is no question as to whether or not they were in town. See *Tom Lord Discography,* session [M10371-4] Joe Morris.

31 Clifton Smith interview, July 27, 2004. Jackie MacLean also talked about Al Walker. See Spellman, *Four Lives in the Bebop Business,* 197.

32 Ponzio and Postif, *Blue Monk,* 110.

33 Gilbert Millstein, "The Twilight of a Zany Street," *New York Times,* January 1, 1950; "Trust Group Buys Sixth Ave. Corner," *New York Times,* February 28, 1950.

34 Sheridan, *Brilliant Corners,* 357.

35 For nearly all of Monk's sidemen, their first recording sessions took place in 1949, just weeks or months after they returned from their date at the Hotel Pershing. See *Tom Lord Discography.*

36 "Autographs by Frank L. Brown," *Amsterdam News,* May 9, 1959. According to the story, Brown "partially financed his education at Chicago's Roosevelt College by performing as vocalist with such outstanding groups as Thelonious Monk Quintette." He could have only performed with Monk during this gig because Brown had graduated from Roosevelt in 1951 and during the period of his matriculation, this was the only time Monk led a quintet in Chicago.

37 Jaki Byard interview with Taylor Ho Bynum, Hollis, New York, November 14, 1997, transcript in author's possession.

38 Noal Cohen and Michael Fitzgerald, *Rat Race Blues: The Musical Life of Gigi Gryce* (Berkeley, CA: Berkeley Hills Books, 2002), 29–52; Silver, *Let's Get to the Nitty Gritty*, 39.

39 Cohen and Fitzgerald, *Rat Race Blues*, 58.

40 Ibid., 59.

41 Paul Bacon review of "Epistrophy" and "In Walked Bud," *Record Changer* 7, no. 11 (November 1948), 19.

42 Paul Bacon review of "Ruby, My Dear" and "Evidence," *Record Changer* 8, no. 4 (April 1949), 28.

43 J. J. Finsterwald and J. F. Zbinden, "Thelonious Monk," *Jazz-Revue* 32 (April 1949), 36. I am tremendously grateful to Jacques Ponzio for generously sharing this document with me. He and François Postif also quote it in *Blue Monk*, 110–111.

44 *Down Beat* (October 20, 1948), 13.

45 *Down Beat* (March 25, 1949), 14.

46 Leonard Feather, *Inside Be-Bop* (New York: J. J. Robbins and Sons, 1949), 10.

47 Ibid., 10.

48 Ibid., 7–8.

49 Monk family interview, January 30, 2004; the same story is told in Leslie Gourse's book. See, Gourse, *Straight No Chaser*, 38.

50 Marion seems to think that Nellie had already delivered when they moved back in with Barbara, but Thelonious, Jr.'s birth certificate clearly states that they were already living at 243 W. 63rd. Certificate of Birth, Thelonious Monk, Jr., Certificate No. 156-49-151384.

51 State of New York Division of Housing, *Annual Report of the Commissioner of Housing to the Governor and Legislature, 1950*, 85.

52 Before the Amsterdam Houses were constructed, the area housed 2,913 people; after it was completed, the new structure accommodated 4,586 people. Ibid., p. 85.

53 T. S. Monk, interview, April 4, 2005. Alonzo White, Marion's son, recalls moving into the house in Queens in 1950. Alonzo White interview, February 23, 2004.

54 Evelyn Smith and Benetta Bines interview, July 6, 2005; Geraldine Smith interview, February 12, 2004.

55 Clifton Smith interview, July 27, 2004. Also, Evelyn Smith interview, July 6, 2005; Geraldine Smith interview, February 12, 2004.

56 Certificate of Birth, Thelonious Monk, Jr., Certificate No. 156-49-151384.

57 Judith Berdy and the Roosevelt Island Historical Society, *Roosevelt Island* (Charleston, SC: Arcadia, 2003), 9–21, 43–44, 71–72; "The Roosevelt Island Story," http://www.correctionhistory.org/rooseveltisland/index .html.

58 Weissman is listed as the attending physician at Thelonious, Jr.'s birth. On Weissman's distinguished career, see "Deaths: Weissman, Frederick, M.D.," *New York Times*, September 8, 2005; "Weissman Lecture in Analytical Chemistry," http://www.chem.scu.edu/about/named_seminars.asp.

59 To be precise, she walked to East 77th Street at the East River, where she hopped the trolley across the bridge. This was the only way to get to Welfare/Roosevelt Island at the time. There was a huge elevator that took pedestrians and vehicles from the Queensboro Bridge to the island. See Berdy, et. al., *Roosevelt Island*, 59.

60 Evelyn Smith interview, July 6, 2005; Geraldine Smith interview, September 16, 2007.

61 N.F. Vitalo vs. Thelonious Monk, AFM Local 802, Executive Board Minutes, February 2, 1950, reel 5278.

62 Geraldine Smith interview, February 12, 2004; Maely Danielle Dufty, "The Prophet's Exile to the Tombs— And Return," *New York Citizen Call*, July 2, 1960.

63 Jackie Bonneau interview, October 30, 2008.

64 Evelyn Smith interview, July 6, 2005.

65 Ibid.

66 Norman Granz from original liner notes, Charlie Parker and Dizzy Gillespie, *Bird and Diz* (Clef MGC-512), issued in 1954. The recordings were originally issued in 1951 under the Clef label as 78s: "Bloomdido"/"My Melancholy Baby" (Clef 11058); "Leap Frog"/"Relaxin with Lee" (Clef 11076); "An Oscar for Treadwell"/"Mohawk" (Clef 11082).

67 Phil Schaap, liner notes to ten-disc set, *The Complete Charlie Parker on Verve* (1988); Shipton, *Groovin' High*, 230; Lawrence O. Koch, *Yardbird Suite: A Compendium of the Music and Life of Charlie Parker* (Boston: Northeastern University Press, 1999, rev. ed.), 210–211.

68 Monk is granted very little solo space. He takes two choruses on the twelve-bar blues "Bloomdido" and half a chorus solo on "My Melancholy Baby," which sounds like a throwback to the days of Minton's Playhouse. Bloomdido, a twelve-bar blues named for Buffalo-based disc jockey Maury Bloom (not Bird's manager, Ted Blume, as is often claimed), and the only song done in one take. See Phil Schaap, *The Complete Charlie Parker on Verve* (1988); Koch, *Yardbird Suite*, 210.

69 For a different but useful analysis of these recordings, see Koch, *Yardbird Suite*, 210–213.

70 Nat Hentoff, "Granz Wouldn't Let Me Record with Parker, Says Roy Haynes," *Down Beat* (April 4, 1952), 7; Woideck, *Charlie Parker*, 196. The controversy surrounding Granz's hiring of Rich has been discussed in virtually all Bird studies. For a perspective sympathetic to Rich, see Mel Torme, *Traps, the Drum Wonder: The Life of Buddy Rich* (New York: Oxford University Press, 1991), 92.

71 Ted Hershorn, *Verve: Norman Granz*. Granz was committed to an integrated band and that's what he got, though he had other choices such as Stan Levey, a white drummer steeped in the bebop idiom.

72 The few sources that cite this story date it August 31, 1949, suggesting that it occurred on Birdland's opening night. (i.e., Fitterling, *Thelonious Monk*, and Ponzio and Postif, *Blue Monk*, 109). Besides the fact that Birdland did not actually open until December 15, 1949, Monk did not play at Birdland on opening night. (See "New Broadway Club in Grand Opening," *Amsterdam News*, December 17, 1949; Mike Waldman, "Birdland New Roost for Jazz Lovers on Gay White Way," *Pittsburgh Courier*, December 24, 1949. The first half of the

show was Dixieland, the second half was "modern," with Charlie Parker's group, Lennie Tristano sextet, Stan Getz, and Harry Belafonte.) It is true that Birdland management (Morris Levy and Oscar Goodstein) planned to open on September 8, but they could not get everything together in time. ("Birdland, New Bop Nitery, Sets Debut," *Pittsburgh Courier*, September 3, 1949; "Allan's Alley," *Amsterdam News*, September 10, 1949.)

73 Quoted and translated from Ponzio and Postif, *Blue Monk*, 110. The original source of the story comes from Sahib Shihab, who told the story to journalist and radio personality Yvan Amar on the radio show, "France Culture."
74 *Allegro*, January 1951.
75 Geraldine Smith interview, February 12, 2004.
76 Mary Ellen Moylan, "Harlem Jam Sessions," *New York Times*, April 22, 1951. Thelonious may have learned about Newman's intentions from the newspaper. Newman had become a key player in the world of independent record labels. See, Jerry Newman, "How a Small Company Works," *New York Times,* March 30, 1952. Russ Parmenter, "Business Booming, Say Record Makers," *New York Times*, November 21, 1954; "Collectors' Items," *New York Times*, February 24, 1952.
77 Agreement with Thelonious Monk and Alfred Lion, August 6, 1951, Blue Note Archives.
78 The title is a mathematical pun—there are four quarter notes per (one) measure, and when we divide each quarter note into four beats, the value of each beat is a sixteenth note. Four sixteenth notes to one quarter note; four quarter notes to one measure—hence the name "Four in One."
79 Agreement with Thelonious Monk and Alfred Lion, August 6, 1951, Blue Note Archives.
80 Ibid.
81 See Chapter 8.
82 Gitler, *Swing to Bop*, 120. Don Sickler, music publisher and trumpeter who knew Sulieman quite well, confirms the story of how "Eronel" was written. Don Sickler interview, September 9, 2003.
83 Lenore Gordon-Ferkin interview, August 6, 2003.
84 Ibid.
85 Contrary to jazz lore, however, he did not spell it backward because she was involved with a mobster. She had long divorced Baroni and had no ties to the Mafia. Lenore Gordon-Ferkin interview, August 6, 2003.
86 On the only extant recording of the tune by Miles Davis, he refuses to play the bridge and instead improvises over the B-section. Davis's interpretation of the song, which had been mistitled "Overturia," was caught on tape on June 30, 1950 live from Birdland. Miles Davis, *Hooray for Miles Davis–Vol. 2* (Session 102).
87 Gitler, *Swing to Bop*, 120. Leslie Gourse also quotes Sulieman, who suggests that the changed note was the third note of the song: "He played F sharp, and it should have been an E natural. A tone higher." (Gourse, *Straight, No Chaser*, 75.) But the aural evidence contradicts Sulieman's recollections. The first eight bars of Miles's version are practically identical, the only difference being phrasing. Trumpeter and music publisher, Don Sickler, has a more persuasive explanation of Monk's involvement with Eronel based on conversations Sickler had with Sulieman. Sickler insists that the A-section is Sulieman's and the bridge belongs to Hakim. Monk changed the fourth note in the A-section. Don Sickler interview, September 9, 2003.
88 Gitler, *Swing to Bop*, 120; Gourse, *Straight, No Chaser*, 76.
89 Charlotte Washington interview, April 5, 2004.
90 Thomas Monk, Jr. interview, February 16, 2004; see also, Carolyn Wah, "An Introduction to Research and Analysis of Jehovah's Witnesses: A View from the Watchtower," *Review of Religious Research* 43, no. 2 (2001), 4–5; *You Can Live Forever in Paradise on Earth* (Brooklyn: Watchtower Bible and Tract Society, 1989).
91 Jehovah's Witnesses reputation as conscientious objectors would have been known to Monk since their cases were fairly prominent in the press. "545 Urge Release of War Objectors," *New York Times*, November 24, 1947. The Jehovah's Witnesses also attracted many African Americans during the 1950s, despite some accusations of racial prejudice. Werner Cohn, "Jehovah's Witnesses and Racial Prejudice," *Crisis* (January 1956), 5–9; Marley Cole, "Jehovah's Witnesses Religion of Racial Integration," *Crisis* (April 1953), 205–211, 253–255.
92 Charlotte Washington interview, April 5, 2004.
93 The most thorough description of his arrest is Maely Danielle Dufty, "The Prophet's Exile to the Tombs—And Return," *New York Citizen Call*, July 2, 1960; see also, "Thelonious Monk," Docket # 7038, New York Felony Court Index Books, 1948–1956 (microfilm), NYC Municipal Archives; "Thelonius Monk Arrested on Drug Charge," *Melody Maker*, August 25, 1951; Director of FBI to Legat, Tokyo (163–2971), cablegram, September 3, 1970, Thelonious Monk FBI File.

12 "The 'Un' Years"

1 Dufty, "The Prophet's Exile to the Tombs."
2 Lewis H. Lapham, "Monk: High Priest of Jazz," *Saturday Evening Post* 237 (April 11, 1964), 74.
3 "Thelonious Monk," Docket # 7038, New York Felony Court Index Books, 1948–1956 (microfilm), NYC Municipal Archives; Director of FBI to Legat, Tokyo (163–2971), cablegram, September 3, 1970, Thelonious Monk FBI File; "Thelonious Monk Arrested on Drug Charge," *Melody Maker* (August 25, 1951).
4 Farrell, "Loneliest Monk," 86.
5 Paul Bacon interview, July 30, 2001.
6 Email correspondence from Supervisor Bevan Dufty to author, October 25, 2007.
7 Dufty, "The Prophet's Exile to the Tombs."
8 Ibid.
9 Receipt Books—Payment to Nellie Monk, September 15, 1951, for $25.00 for alterations on five gowns, Box 1, Series 6, Mary Lou Williams Collection, Rutgers University.

10 Department of Correction, City of New York, *Annual Report, 1951*, p. 2.

11 Charles R. Lucci, Secy of Local 802 AFM, to Thelonious Monk, September 6, 1951, Blue Note Archives.

12 It was issued around November of 1951 as Blue Note LP 5002, part of its "Modern Jazz Series." What would become volume 2 came out in the spring of 1952.

13 T. S. Monk interview, April 4, 2005; Hardie Gramatky, *Little Toot the Tugboat* (New York: G. P. Putnam, 1939). In 1954, Walt Disney spun off "Toot the Tugboat" as its own independent short cartoon.

14 Wilmer, "Monk on Monk," 21.

15 Monk hired Thompson both for his enormous talent and because he desperately needed the gig. As a result of a conflict Thompson had had with a club owner, "the word got around I was difficult, and from 1949 to 1954, I was never given a gig in a major jazz club in New York City." Monk understood the situation better than most. Nat Hentoff, "Lucky Thompson," *Down Beat* (April 4, 1956), 9; see also, Interview with Eli Lucky Thompson, by Daniel Brecker (Seattle on KCMU radio) www.melmartin.com/luck.ram; Christopher Kuhl, "Lucky Thompson Interview: Part II," *Cadence* (February, 1982), 11.

16 L. Tomkins, "The Lou Donaldson Story," *Crescendo International* 19, no. 11 (1981), 20; and no.12, p.16. The recordings with Jackson were released on Blue Note 1592, 1593, and 1594.

17 The melody is so full of intervallic leaps that the fact that it is based on "Tea for Two" is not so obvious, even among musicians. Steve Lacy interview, May 9, 1995; Max Harrison, "Mosaic Survey, Part I," *Jazz Forum* 96 (1985), 38.

18 Evelyn Smith and Binetta Bines interview, July 5, 2004.

19 Cuscuna, *Complete Blue Note Recordings*, 9.

20 Recorded at RCA Victor July 10, 1947. Perry Como, *Carolina Moon/Haunted Heart* (RCA Victor 20-2713).

21 Donaldson was born in Badin and Roach was from New Land. As Donaldson told Sam Stephenson in a recent interview, "We recorded 'Carolina Moon' as a tribute to our home state, with Max Roach on drums." Stephenson, "Thelonious Monk: Is This Home?," 58.

22 Surprisingly, Blue Note chose not to release "Sixteen" and "I'll Follow You" until 1985, on *More Genius Of Thelonious Monk* (Blue Note [J] BNJ 61011).

23 "CNA in Tribute to Jazz Pianist Mary Lou Williams Honored at Town Hall," *Amsterdam News*, June 21, 1952.

24 Nellie Monk conversation, November 9, 2001.

25 Kernodle, *Soul on Soul*, 171–175; Dahl, *Morning Glory*, 224–243.

26 Their association with Weinstock goes back to 1949, when he recorded J. J. Johnson's "Boppers" on his New Jazz label. Rollins and Dorham were in the band, along with John Lewis and Max Roach. [See, J. J. Johnson, *Spider's Webb* (New Jazz NJ 810)]. In January of 1951, Weinstock recorded both Rollins and Miles Davis as leaders for Prestige. See *Miles Davis And Horns* (Prestige PRLP 7025) and *Sonny Rollins With The Modern Jazz Quartet* (Prestige PRLP 7029). See entries for Sonny Rollins, 1949–1951, *Tom Lord Jazz Discography*; Ira Gitler interview, August 13, 2007.

27 Ira Gitler interview, August 13, 2007; M. Ruppli with B. Porter, *The Prestige Label: a Discography* (Westport, CT and London, 1980); Peter Keepnews, *Thelonious Monk: The Complete Prestige Recordings* (Liner Notes 3PRCD-4428-2: Prestige Records, 2000), 10–11.

28 Ira Gitler interview, August 13, 2007.

29 James Petrillo to Alfred W. Lion, October 3, 1952, Blue Note Archive, Capitol Records.

30 Randy Weston interview, July 30, 2003. The son of Bernice and Gary Mapp, Sr., a Barbadian subway porter who emigrated to the U.S. in 1923, the young Gary was born in Brooklyn January 9, 1926. Social Security Death Index, Gary Mapp, May 1987; U.S. Census, 1930, *Population Schedule: Kings County, Brooklyn*.

31 David Amram interview, July 15, 2003; Randy Weston interview, July 30, 2003.

32 Bob Weinstock quoted in Cohen and Fitzgerald, *Rat Race Blues*, 152–53.

33 Lead sheet submitted with Certificate of Copyright Registration, "The Pump: Music by Teddy McRae and T. Monk," E unp. No. 363022, Received February 5, 1944.

34 Lead sheet and Certificate of Copyright Registration, "Playhouse: Melody by Thelonious Monk," Walter Gil Fuller claimant, E unpub. 8742, Received February 26, 1946.

35 Ira Gitler interview, August 13, 2007. Peter Keepnews also recounts a version of this story in his liner notes, *Thelonious Monk: The Complete Prestige Recordings*, 16.

36 Sheridan, *Brilliant Corners*, 361.

37 Jon Pareles, "John S. Wilson, Jazz Critic, Is Dead at 89," *New York Times*, August 28, 2002.

38 John S. Wilson, "Some Jazz Piano Specialists," *New York Times*, October 26, 1952.

39 Ira Gitler interview, August 13, 2007.

40 Ibid.; and Keepnews liner notes, *The Complete Prestige Recordings*, 18.

41 Copyright registration, Thelonious Monk and Denzil Best, "Bimsha Swing" (sometimes listed as "Bemsha Swing" or "Bemesha Swing"), Bayes Music, Registration Number: EU 297366, dated December 15, 1952, Library of Congress, Washington, D.C. See also Chapter 3.

42 Ira Gitler, "Ira Gitler Interviews Thelonious Monk," *Metronome* 74 (March 1957), 20.

43 "Please, Mr. Sun" was a big hit that year and received much radio play. Johnny Ray's version reached #6 on the Billboard charts, followed by Perry Como's version which rose to #12. The Perry Como version was released in 1952 on 45 by RCA Victor. Perry Como, *Please Mr. Sun/Tulips And Heather* (RCA Victor 47-4453).

44 Sheridan, *Brilliant Corners*, 361.

45 *Pittsburgh Courier*, September 27, 1952; *Amsterdam News*, September 6, 1952.

46 Sheridan, *Brilliant Corners*, 363.

47 T. S. Monk interview, April 4, 2005.

48 Charlotte Washington interview, April 5, 2004.

49 Monk family interview; Alonzo White interview; Clifton Smith interview.

50 Prestige released the first six sides in 1953 in the following order: "Sweet and Lovely/Bye-ya" (Prestige 795); "Trinkle Tinkle/These Foolish Things" (Prestige 838); "Little Rootie Tootie/Monk's Dream" (Prestige 850).

51 Barry Ulanov, "Thelonious Monk Trio," *Metronome* (July 1953), 27.

52 Randy Weston interview, July 30, 2003.

53 K. Leander Williams, "Brooklyn New York," in *Lost Jazz Shrines* (The Lost Shrines Project, 1998), 12–16; Bilal Abdurahman, *In the Key of Me: The Bedford Stuyvesant Renaissance, 1940s–60s Revisited* (Brooklyn: Contemporary Visions, 1993); Randy Weston, interview, August 20, 2001; Bob Meyers interview, February 21, 2003; Freddie Robinson interview, January 9, 2002.

54 *Amsterdam News*, August 22, 1953; Brian Priestley, *Mingus: A Critical Biography* (New York: Da Capo Press, 1982), 54; Max Roach interview with Phil Schaap, WKCR, February 24 and March 13, 1981; Gene Santoro, *Myself When I Am Real: The Life and Music of Charles Mingus* (New York: Oxford University Press, 2000), 105–106.

55 Reisner, ed., *Bird*, 11–13, 24; on the no alcohol policy, see Allen Ginsberg, interview by Steve Silberman, December 16, 1996, http://www.levity.com/digaland/ginsberg96.html.

56 Certificate of Birth, Barbara Monk, Certificate No. 156-53-135326. Her middle name, Evelyn, is not listed on her birth certificate, but she had had that name since birth. See *Memorial Service for Barbara Evelyn Monk*, Program, January 17, 1984, in author's possession.

57 T. S. Monk, interview, April 4, 2005.

58 Ibid.

59 Evelyn Smith interview; Monk family interview; T. S. Monk interview; Charlotte Washington interview; Brown, "More Man than Myth," 13.

60 Quoted in Hentoff, "The Private World of Thelonious Monk," 137.

61 Hentoff, "The Private World of Thelonious Monk," 137.

62 Ira Gitler interview, August 13, 2007; Peter Keepnews, *The Complete Prestige Recordings*, 18–19.

63 Saxophonist Paul Jeffrey used to visit Watkins when he played with Les Jazz Modes, and sometimes they would play classical pieces together. "He'd play all of the horn parts in the classical repertoire, the higher parts and the lower parts. And tears would come to his eyes because he couldn't get a job working in any symphony orchestra." Paul Jeffrey interview, August 31, 2003.

64 John S. Wilson, "The Horn Nobody Wants," *Down Beat* (September 17, 1959), 37–38; and the excellent dissertation by Patrick Gregory Smith, "Julius Watkins and the Evolution of the Jazz French Horn" (Ph.D. dissertation, University of Florida, 2005), 31–42.

65 The MJQ, after all, was the label's latest sensation—with Milt Jackson, John Lewis on piano, and Kenny Clarke on drums. They first recorded with Prestige in 1952.

66 Randy Weston interview, February 22, 1999 and July 30, 2003; Marcellus Green interview, October 19, 2001.

67 Ben Ratliff, "At 75, a Drummer Whose Beat Is Always Modern," *New York Times*, June 4, 2000.

68 Ira Gitler interview, August 13, 2007.

69 See ads in *Amsterdam News*, August 15, 1953; August 22, 1953, September 5, 1953.

70 Henri Renaud, "Monk Jusqu' au bout Des Doigts," *Jazz Magazine* 520 (November 2001), 17; Renaud, "Un Revolutionnaire du Piano," *Jazz Hot* 393 (March 1982), 23; and quoted in Ponzio and Postif, *Blue Monk*, 131.

71 Randy Weston interview, July 30, 2003. French pianist/composer/critic Henri Renaud was also in attendance at Tony's that night and describes the events. Renaud, "Un Revolutionnaire du Piano," 23; and quoted in Ponzio and Postif, *Blue Monk*, 131.

72 Cohen and Fitzgerald, *Rat Race Blues*, 151; Renaud, "Un Revolutionnaire du Piano," 23; Sheridan, *Brilliant Corners*, 365.

73 Cohen and Fitzgerald, *Rat Race Blues*, 151; Renaud, "Un Revolutionnaire du Piano," 23.

74 Santoro, *Myself When I Am Real*, 106.

75 Theolonious Monk interview, January 30, 2004.

76 Gryce quoted in Cohen and Fitzgerald, *Rat Race Blues*, 151.

77 Santoro, *Myself When I Am Real*, 106. Santoro, and his informant Celia Mingus Zaentz, date the performance, and thus the incident, to the summer of 1953, but given the personnel it could have only happened during the Tony's gig because Gigi Gryce spent the previous summer as a regular member of Lionel Hampton's band. The alleged events that provoked Monk recounted in Santoro's book don't make sense; they seem both illogical and unlikely. He writes: "Onstage, Mingus wanted to play 'Memories of You.' He liked soloing on it but Monk said Davis didn't know the chords. Miles insisted he'd call out the changes on the bandstand, then deliberately mixed them up. [Oscar] Pettiford scolded him when the trumpeter came offstage. When they went back on, the pianist got his payback." (p. 106)

78 They arrived by ship six days before Christmas. Manifest of In-bound Passengers (Aliens), S.S. *Flanders*, December 19, 1953, www.ancestry.com; Henri Renaud, "Trois Mois à New York," *Jazz Hot* (October1954), 15–16. According to the Manifest, the Renauds were staying at 610 West 113th St. in Manhattan.

79 Renaud, "Un Revolutionnaire du Piano," 23.

80 Renaud, "Trois Mois à New York," 16.

81 Renaud, "Trois Mois à New York," 16; Henri Renaud, "Thelonious Monk," http://www.jazzmagazine.com/Interviews/Dauj/monk/monk.htm.

82 Advertisement in *New York Times*, February 26, 1954. On Gloria Davy, see Wallace McClain Cheatham, "African-American Women Singers at the Metropolitan Opera Before Leontyne Price," *Journal of Negro History* 84, no. 2 (Spring 1999), 167–181.

83 "Thelonious Monk [Review]," *Down Beat* (March 24, 1954), 15, 17.

84 C. Andrew Hovan, "Rudy Van Gelder—Interview," *All About Jazz* (January 30, 2004), allaboutjazz.com.

85 All of these recordings were released as *Thelonious Monk Quintet with Frank Foster* (Prestige PRLP 180), and can be heard on the *Complete Prestige Recordings of Thelonious Monk*.

86 Recorded December 15, 1944, it was first released on 78 on the Moe Asch label (Asch 552–3). It can be heard more readily on Folkways FA2966, Classics (F)1021 [CD].

87 Chilton, *The Song of the Hawk*, 224; Dahl, *Morning Glory*, 148–149. Collette Hawkins insists that her father had been playing "Rifftide" before he recorded with Mary Lou Williams, and that the song should have been listed as "Rifftide" instead of "Lady Be Good." Collette Hawkins interview, November 5, 2004.

88 Quoted in Ponzio and Postif, *Blue Monk*, 134; also, Henri Renaud, "Monk Jusqu' au bout des Doigts," 17.

89 The mainstream press actually misquoted Robeson, who purportedly said, "It is unthinkable that American Negroes would go to war on behalf of those who have oppressed us for generations against a country [the Soviet Union] which in one generation has raised our people to the full dignity of mankind." He actually said something quite different. After pointing out that American wealth had been built on the backs of black and white workers, he resolved that "we [the peace movement] shall not put up with any hysterical raving that urges us to make war on anyone. Our will to fight for peace is strong. We shall not make war on anyone. We shall not make war on the Soviet Union." Martin Duberman, *Paul Robeson* (New York: Knopf, 1988), 342, and on the revoking of his passport and the struggle to restore it, see pp. 381–449.

90 Martin Duberman mistakenly identifies May 24 as the date of the "Cultural Salute to Paul Robeson" (*Paul Robeson*, p. 425); Ingrid Monson, "Monk Meets SNCC," gives May 25, whereas Chris Sheridan actually pushes the date back to May 22, which suggests he confused the date of the newspaper in which the ad appeared with the date of the event. (See *Brilliant Corners*, 366.) One can see how easy it is to make such an error, especially since the advertisement in the *Amsterdam News* identifies the date as "Wednesday, May 28," which is impossible since the 28th was a Friday. Robeson's FBI file provides the most compelling evidence for the actual date being the 26th, in part because agents were there at the event. FBI HQ File: Paul Robeson, 100-25857, p. 51.

91 *Amsterdam News*, May 22, 1954.

92 Stanley Dance, "Three Score: A Quiz for Jazz Musicians," *Metronome* (April 1961), 48.

93 Duberman, *Paul Robeson*, 177.

94 Jean-Marie Ingrand, Monk's bass player and informal guide in Paris, had a vivid memory of the items in his suitcase. See Ponzio and Postif, *Blue Monk*, 138.

13   "France Libre!"

1 The plane employed for flight 076 was the F-BGNE, an Air France plane manufactured by Lockheed and known as LOCKHEED 1049C Super Constellation. General Declaration (In-Bound/Out-bound), Air France, Compagnie Nationale Air France, Flight #076/0530, May 30, 1954, Passenger and Crew Lists of Vessels Arriving at New York, New York, 1897–1957, Microfilm T715, Roll 8458, Records of the INS, National Archives, Washington, D.C. See also Claude Luisada, *Queen of the Skies: The Lockheed Constellation* (Raleigh, NC: Pentland Press, 2005).

2 See Chapter 7.

3 See for example, Eugene Weber, *The Hollow Years: France in the 1930s* (New York: W. W. Norton, 1994).

4 James M. Doran, *Herman Chittison: A Bio-Discography* (The International Association of Jazz Record Collectors: Monograph 2, 1993), 9.

5 Nicola Cooper, *France and Indochina: Colonial Encounters* (Oxford: Berg Publishers, 2001); Martin Windrow, *The Last Valley: Dien Bien Phu and the French Defeat in Vietnam* (New York: Da Capo, 2004).

6 Ponzio and Postif, *Blue Monk*, 137.

7 Dahl, *Morning Glory*, 235; Clarke, *Billie Holiday*, 68.

8 Quoted in Ponzio and Postif, *Blue Monk*, 135.

9 Ibid., p. 135.

10 Hentoff, "Just Call Him Thelonious," 16.

11 Jackie Bonneau interview, October 30, 2008.

12 Quoted in Raymond Horricks, "Thelonious Monk: Two Sides of an Enigmatic Musician," *Jazz Monthly* (April 1956), 8, also reprinted in Horricks's *These Jazzmen of Our Time* (London: Victor Golancz, 1959), as "Thelonious Monk: Portrait of the Artist as an Enigma." This description is drawn from several eyewitness accounts besides Horricks: Mike Nevard, "Mulligan, Monk—and then a French Surprise," *Melody Maker* (June 5, 1954), 9; "Le Troisième Salon Internationale Du Jazz," *Jazz Hot* (July-August,1954), 8–9; and Ingrand's account documented in Ponzio and Postif, *Blue Monk*, 136–37.

13 Quoted in Ponzio and Postif, *Blue Monk*, 137. Ingrand's account matches that of Horricks, "Thelonious Monk," 8.

14 Ibid., 137. Pochonnet met Mary Lou in November of 1953, played with her a few times, and not long after Monk returned to the United States they became lovers. Dahl, *Morning Glory*, 239.

15 Horricks, "Thelonious Monk," 8.

16 Nevard, "Mulligan, Monk," 9. Coincidentally, both Nevard and Horricks comment on Monk's foot movement, stating categorically that he's reaching for the pedal but keeps missing it. What neither Horricks nor Nevard realized is that he wasn't searching for the pedal. Having studied the instrument since he was at least eleven years old, he always knew the location of the pedals. They confused his tendency to move constantly and shuffle his feet in order to keep time with him reaching for the pedal.

17 "Le Troisième Salon Internationale Du Jazz," 8. Mulligan had Bob Brookmeyer on trombone, Red Mitchell bass, and Frank Isola drums. Raymond Horricks, *Gerry Mulligan's Ark* (London: Apollo Press Ltd., 1986), 43;

Jerome Klinkowitz, *Listen: Gerry Mulligan—An Aural Narrative in Jazz* (New York: Schirmer Books, 1991), 107–108. Mulligan's performance was initially released on the Vogue label as *Paris Concert* (Vogue 7381, 7383).

18 Horricks, *Gerry Mulligan's Ark*, 43.
19 Mae Mezzrow, an African-American woman, was the ex-wife of clarinetist/saxophonist Milton "Mezz" Mezzrow, author of the infamous memoir, *Really the Blues* (New York: Random House, 1946).
20 Christian Tarting, "Round About Monk—Douze Evidences et Reflections Sur Monk," *Jazz Magazine* 361 (May 1987), 19.
21 *Das Jazzbuch* (Fischer Taschenbuch,1953); it has since been translated into English as *The Jazz Book* and appeared in several editions, most recently by Lawrence Hill Books, 1992.
22 Joachim E. Berendt, "A Note on Thelonious Monk," *Jazz Monthly* (June 1956), 7.
23 Ibid., 7.
24 Ibid., 7. Berendt eventually understood that Monk was more interested in conversation than being interviewed: "I had no intention at the time of conducting an interview and I was concerned to get to know the man Monk. It is possible that this was the reason he accepted me."
25 Berendt, "A Note on Thelonious Monk," 7.
26 James Campbell, *Exiled in Paris: Richard Wright, James Baldwin, Samuel Beckett and Others* (Berkeley and Los Angeles: University of California Press, 2003), 88.
27 Horricks, *Gerry Mulligan's Ark*, 43.
28 "Le Troisième Salon Internationale Du Jazz," 9; Berendt, "A Note on Thelonious Monk," 7.
29 Horricks, "Thelonious Monk," 9.
30 Berendt, "A Note on Thelonious Monk," 7.
31 Nadine Koenigswarter, "Nica," in Pannonica de Koenigswarter, *Three Wishes: An Intimate Look at Jazz Greats* (New York: Abrams Image, 2008), 17. Nica tells the story of meeting Thelonious backstage in Charlotte Zwerin, *Straight, No Chaser*. What she did not mention in her interview is that while she was there she helped put together a benefit/memorial service for Garland Wilson. See Dahl, *Morning Glory*, 236.
32 Hentoff, "The Jazz Baroness," 101.
33 Max Gordon, *Live at the Village Vanguard*, 119.
34 David Kastin, "Nica's Story: The Life and Legend of the Jazz Baroness," *Popular Music and Society* 29, no. 3 (July 2006), 281; Nat Hentoff, "The Jazz Baroness," *Esquire* 65, no. 4 (October 1960), 99. On Nathaniel Charles Rothschild and the British wing of the Rothschild family, see Niall Ferguson, *The House of Rothschild, Volume II: The World's Banker, 1849–1999* (New York: Penguin, 1999), 444. Much has been written about Nica de Koenigswarter, most of it replete with errors, including the various biographies of Monk (i.e., Laurent de Wilde, Leslie Gourse, Thomas Fitterling, etc.) And nearly all the articles and books dealing with the Baroness draw heavily on Nat Hentoff's profile of her in *Esquire*, which her son Shaun de Koenigswarter suggests is still the most accurate source available on her. (Shaun de Koenigswarter to author, April 23, 2005.) Recently, renewed interest in the Baroness has generated more comprehensive accounts of her life. The best of these are Nadine Koenigswarter's wonderful introduction to Nica's collection of photos, published posthumously as *Three Wishes: An Intimate Look at Jazz Greats*, 14–25; David Kastin's excellent article, "Nica's Story" (cited above); and Hannah Rothschild's provocative documentary film, *The Jazz Baroness* (Clandestine Films, 2008). As of this writing, Rothschild had yet to secure a distributor, though she was kind enough to share a DVD copy of the film with me. For other sources besides those cited below, see Ebbe Traberg, "Nica o el Sueno de Nica," *Revista de Occidente* 93 (February 1989), 51–59; "L'Extraordinaire Destin de la Baronne du Jazz," *Le Journal du Dimanche* (December 18, 1988); Di Giuseppe Piacentino, "Nica, Bentley and Bebop," *Musica Jazz* (February 1989), 21–22; and Malcolm Forbes and Jeff Bloch, "Baroness Pannonica de Koenigswarter," in *Women Who Made a Difference* (New York: Simon & Schuster, 1990), 156–159.
35 Hannah Rothschild, *The Jazz Baroness* (Clandestine Films, 2008).
36 Nica's father suffered a terrible bout with Spanish influenza, leaving him with a severe neurological disorder which ultimately caused him to take his own life in 1923. Kastin, "Nica's Story," 282.
37 Hentoff, "The Jazz Baroness," 99.
38 Ibid., p. 100.
39 Shaun de Koenigswarter email to author, January 22, 2008.
40 She arrived in New York on September 24, 1935. List or Manifest of Alien Passengers for the United States, S.S. *Normandie,* September 19, 1935, Passenger and Crew Lists of Vessels Arriving at New York, New York, 1897–1957, Microfilm T715, roll 5710, Records of the INS, National Archives.
41 Jules was on the *Normandie*'s next outgoing trip from Le Havre to New York. List or Manifest of Alien Passengers for the United States, S.S. *Normandie,* October 2, 1935, Passenger and Crew Lists of Vessels Arriving at New York, New York, 1897–1957, Microfilm T715, roll 5717, Records of the INS, National Archives.
42 "Miss Rothschild Will Be Wed Here," *New York Times,* October 11, 1935; "Miss Rothschild Is Married Here," *New York Times,* October 16, 1935. They traveled west, leaving New York on October 19 and arriving in San Francisco on November 2. List or Manifest of Alien Passengers to the United States, October 19, 1935, S.S. *Virginia,* Passenger Lists of Vessels Arriving at San Francisco, 1893–1953. Micropublication M1410. RG 085. 429 rolls. National Archives, Washington, D.C.
43 Shaun de Koenigswarter email to author, January 22, 2008 ; "Jules de Koenigswarter," http://www.ordredela liberation.fr/fr_compagnon/525.html.
44 List or Manifest of Alien Passengers for the United States, S.S. M.V. *Britannic,* June 11, 1940, Passenger and Crew Lists of Vessels Arriving at New York, New York, 1897–1957, Microfilm T715, roll 6476, Records of the INS, National Archives. According to the manifest, she was accompanied by the children's "nurse," Sheila Trude.

45 Shaun de Koenigswarter email to author, January 22, 2008.

46 "Free French Organizing Units in U.S. and Other Countries," *Christian Science Monitor*, October 7, 1940; "France Forever Drive Launched," *Christian Science Monitor*, January 30, 1941; "France Depicted Ready to Resist," *New York Times*, December 18, 1940; "French Group Here Challenges Petain," *New York Times*, January 21, 1941. On Houdry, see Charles G. Moseley, "Eugene Houdry, Catalytic Cracking, and World War II Aviation Gasoline," *Journal of Chemical Education* 61 (August 1984), 65–66.

47 These were veritable "radio wars" between the Vichy regime, which broadcast their message from Dakar, and de Gaulle, whose base was Brazzaville. W. T. Arms, "Pick-Ups from Overseas," *New York Times*, February 9, 1941; W. T. Arms, "Short-Wave News from Overseas," *New York Times*, June 15, 1941.

48 List or Manifest of Alien Passengers, S.S. *Santa Paula*, December 3, 1941, Passenger and Crew Lists of Vessels Arriving at New York, New York, 1897–1957, Microfilm T715, roll 6606, Records of the INS, National Archives. She disembarked in New York on January 23, 1942.

49 "Torpedoes Miss U.S. Liner Twice, Navy Announces," *Chicago Tribune*, January 24, 1942; Shaun de Koenigswarter email to author, January 22, 2008.

50 Hannah Rothschild, *The Jazz Baroness*; Barry Singer, "The Baroness of Jazz," *New York Times*, October 17, 2008.

51 Hentoff, "The Jazz Baroness," 101.

52 Shaun de Koenigswarter email to author, January 22, 2008.

53 Ibid., 101; "Jules de Koenigswarter," http://www.ordredelaliberation.fr/fr_compagnon/525.html.

54 Quoted in Hentoff, "The Jazz Baroness," 101.

55 Hentoff, "The Jazz Baroness," 101; "Jules de Koenigswarter," http://www.ordredelaliberation.fr/fr_compagnon/525.html.

56 Nica quoted in Charlotte Zwerin, *Straight, No Chaser*.

57 Quoted in Ponzio and Postif, *Blue Monk*, 138.

58 "Le Troisième Salon Internationale Du Jazz," 9. Gerry Mulligan and Bob Brookmeyer also participated in the solo piano performances, and their group was featured during the second half of the concert.

59 Ponzio and Postif, *Blue Monk*, 139–40; Claude Carrière, "Thelonious Monk" Liner notes to *Thelonious Monk: Solo 1954* (Vogue 74321115022).

60 First released as *Thelonious Monk Piano Solo* (Swing M.33.342) as a 10-inch LP, it has been rereleased several times by the French Vogue label. (See Sheridan, *Brilliant Corners*, 322–323.) Another parallel with Herman Chittison is worth noting here: soon after he arrived in Paris in 1934, critic Hugues Panassie produced Chittison's first solo recordings! The sessions also occurred in the spring, early summer—May 22 and June 2, to be exact. Doran, *Herman Chittison*, 9.

61 Ponzio and Postif, *Blue Monk*, 141.

62 In a fascinating article, Milton L. Stewart suggests that Monk's approach to the piano resembles that of mbira ("thumb piano") players from Zimbabwe. Monk's left hand plays a rhythmically separate melody featuring alternating pitches in the middle and bass registers. Monk's playing here produces the effect of two independent instruments being played simultaneously. This is also characteristic of the playing of mbira players. Milton L. Stewart, "Thelonious Monk: Be-Bop or Something Different?" *Jazz Research Papers* 1, no. 5 (1985), 184.

63 Quoted in Ponzio and Postif, *Blue Monk*, 141.

64 Manifeste de Passagers/Passenger Manifest, Air France flight 29, June 10, 1954, Passenger and Crew Lists of Vessels Arriving at New York, New York, 1897–195 (National Archives Microfilm Publication T715, Roll 8463), Records of the INS, National Archives, Washington, D.C.

14 "Sometimes I Play Things I Never Heard Myself"

1 T. S. Monk interview, April 4, 2005.

2 Ibid.

3 Monk's approach mirrored poet Kahlil Gibran's oft-quoted injunction that your children "belong not to you/ You may give them your love but not your thoughts/For they have their own thoughts." Kahlil Gibran, *The Prophet* (New York: Alfred Knopf, 1923), 17–18.

4 Hentoff, "Just Call Him Thelonious," 16.

5 Farrell, "Loneliest Monk," 88.

6 T. S. Monk interview, April 4, 2005.

7 Ibid.

8 Barry Ulanov, "Review: Thelonious Monk Quintet," *Metronome* (September 1954), 26.

9 First released as *Thelonious Monk Plays* (Prestige LP 189).

10 Peter Keepnews, liner notes, *Thelonious Monk: The Complete Prestige Recordings*, 23. "Pastel Blue" was first released on Decca as John Kirby and his Onyx Club Boys, "Pastel Blue" (Decca 2367), but it can be heard on the CD *John Kirby, 1938–1939* (Classics 750). The band consisted of Charlie Shavers (tp) Buster Bailey (cl) Russell Procope (as) Billy Kyle (p arr) John Kirby (b) O'Neil Spencer (d).

11 When Stanley Dance asked Monk to "Name a record you play on that you especially like," Monk replied, "'Blue Monk,' with the trio." Stanley Dance, "Three Score: A Quiz for Jazz Musicians," *Metronome* (April 1961), 48.

12 Monk interview with Russ Wilson, KJAZ San Francisco, April 17, 1960, recording in author's possession; also, Ira Gitler interview, August 13, 2007.

13 Thomas S. Hischak, *The Tin Pan Alley Song Encyclopedia* (Westport, CT and London: Greenwood Press, 2002), 196–197.

14 *Amsterdam News*, September 25, 1954

15 Nisenson, *Open Sky*, 65.

16 These recordings were first released as a ten-inch, *Sonny Rollins* (Prestige PRLP 190), but later rereleased under Monk's name or with Monk and Sonny Rollins as co-leaders.

17 Reisner, ed., *Bird*, 15; Russell, *Bird Lives!*, 334–36.

18 See ads in *New York Times*, October 24, 1954: *Amsterdam News*, October 30, 1954.

19 Russell, *Bird Lives!*, 336; Leonard Feather, "Novelles d'Amerique," *Jazz Hot* (December 1954), 24.

20 Hentoff, "The Jazz Baroness," 101.

21 "Hall Overton of Juilliard Dead; Symphonic and Jazz Composer," *New York Times*, November 26, 1972; Oliver Daniel. "Overton, Hall." In *Grove Music Online. Oxford Music Online*, http://www.oxfordmusiconline .com/subscriber/article/grove/music/20614 (accessed February 24, 2009).

22 Harry Colomby interview, August 12, 2003.

23 *Jimmy Raney Plays* (Prestige PRLP 156) recorded April 23, 1953.

24 Paul H. Lang to Dr. John Krout, Vice President and Provost of the University, November 16, 1954, Columbia University Archives. Provost Krout seemed sympathetic to Lang's concerns, but he had a much bigger circus to deal with that fall as a result of another IAS program. Potter had invited Pete Seeger to perform American folk music, which generated a huge anti-Communist backlash. Potter, for his part, refused to take part in the Red-baiting and defended his choice to the bitter end. Seeger did perform at Columbia University on October 21, 1954. Dr. John Krout to Paul H. Lang, December 29, 1954; "Statement by Russell Potter," October 15, 1954; Robert Harron, Assistant to the President, to Russell Potter, Director of IAS, January 11, 1955, Russell Potter Correspondence, IAS Papers, Columbia University Archives.

25 "Music Notes," *New York Times*, September 17, 1954; Herbert Mitgang, "Cool Class at Columbia," *New York Times Magazine*, November 7, 1954.

26 Approximately a month or so before the class, Gross made several studio recordings with Jimmy Hamilton, Ernie Royal, and Lucky Thompson. He can be heard on *Jimmy Hamilton and the New York Jazz Quintet* (Fresh Sound FSCD 889677 [CD]) and Lucky Thompson, *Accent on Tenor* (Fresh Sound FSCD2001 [CD]).

27 Brendan Gill, "Magnetic Force," *The New Yorker* (December 25, 1954), 16–17; Langston Hughes, "Adventures in Jazz," handwritten notes, Box 481, Langston Hughes Papers, Beinecke Rare Book and Manuscript Library, Yale University. According to Hughes's notes, he participated on a Thursday night in October, which may mean that Gill was mistaken about the days the course met and the particular day Monk appeared, or Hughes might be mistaken.

28 Gill, "Magnetic Force," 17.

29 Hentoff, *Jazz Life*, 188. On the other hand, British critic Raymond Horricks, who was not there but might have heard the story from Gross, reports that Monk was asked to play the same "as they would have played in the swing era, prior to modern changes exerted upon them." According to Horricks, Monk unsuccessfully groped and fumbled for the chords. He then looked at the speaker and said, "Those simple chords ain't so easy to find now." I find this anecdote suspect, especially given alternative evidence, Horricks's distance from the event, and his reviews' general hostility toward Monk. Horricks, "Thelonious Monk: Two Sides of an Enigmatic Musician," 9.

30 Ira Gitler liner notes, *Miles Davis And The Modern Jazz Giants* (Prestige PRLP 7150); Gitler, "Ira Gitler Interviews Thelonious Monk," 30; John Szwed, *So What: The Life of Miles Davis* (New York: Simon & Schuster, 2002), 115. Poet Sasch Feinstein even wrote a poem about the date and the tensions between Monk and Miles entitled "Christmas Eve," in *Christmas Eve* (Bloomington, IN: The Bookcellar, 1994).

31 Miles Davis, with Quincy Troupe, *Miles: The Autobiography*, 187. In the interview with Quincy Troupe, Miles was even more concise: "I told him to lay out at the session. That didn't mean we were going to fight or anything. He used to do it himself. I just told him when to do it." Miles Davis, Interview with Quincy Troupe, February 16, 1988, Tape 13, Schomburg Collection. With less hindsight, Miles was not as generous about Monk's playing. In a 1958 blindfold test for *Down Beat* magazine, Leonard Feather had Miles listen to Sonny Rollins and Monk's Prestige recording of "The Way You Blow Tonight," to which Miles responded, "You know the way Monk plays—he never gives any support to a rhythm section. When I had him on my date, I had him lay out until the ensemble. I like to hear him play, but I can't stand him in a rhythm section unless it's one of his own songs." (Leonard Feather, "Blindfold Test: Miles Davis," *Down Beat* [August 7, 1958], 29.)

32 Gitler, "Ira Gitler Interviews Thelonious Monk," 30.

33 Grover Sales, "'I Wanted to Make it Better,'" 36–37.

34 Clouzet and Delorme, "L'amertume du prophète," 41.

35 Jack Chambers, *Milestones 1: The Music and Times of Miles Davis to 1960* (New York: William Morrow, 1983), 192; Ira Gitler interview, August 13, 2007.

36 See Chapter 14.

37 Clouzet and Delorme, "L'amertume du prophète," 39.

38 Gourse, *Straight, No Chaser*, 96.

39 Ira Gitler interview, August 13, 2007; Szwed, *So What*, 115; Chambers, *Milestones 1*, 192.

40 Van Gelder did exactly as Miles asked, including the exchange at the beginning of the track, though when these recordings were first released on 16 RPM LPs, only the second take of "The Man I Love" was included. *Miles Davis and The Modern Jazz Giants* (Prestige 7150). Also released under Esquire 32-100, and on CD on Original Jazz Classics OJC 2531-347-2.

41 The number of articles and books that speculate about this passage are too numerous to list here, but examples include Ian Carr, *Miles Davis*, 84; Chambers, *Milestones 1*, 193–196; Dick Katz, "Miles Davis," in Martin Williams, ed., *Jazz Panorama* (New York: Collier, 1964), 173; André Hodeir, "Outside the Capsule," in *The Worlds of Jazz* (New York: Grove Press, 1972), 79–99.

42 See Chapter 7.

43 Gitler liner notes to *Miles Davis and the Modern Jazz Giants.*

44 Clouzet and Delorme, "L'amertume du prophète," 41.

45 Clouzet and Delorme, "L'amertume du prophète," 41.

46 Rick Kennedy and Randy McNutt, *Little Labels–Big Sound: Small Record Companies and the Rise of American Music* (Bloomington, IN: Indiana University Press, 1999), 107–110; Jesse Hamlin, "A Life in Jazz," *Columbia College Today* (November 2004), www.college.columbia.edu/cct/nov04/features2.php; Keepnews, *The View from Within*, 120.

47 Kennedy and McNutt, *Little Labels–Big Sound*, 108–110.

48 These first two LPs were released as *Randy Weston Plays Cole Porter In A Modern Mood* (Riverside RLP 2508); *The Randy Weston Trio With Art Blakey* (Riverside RLP 2515). Initially, Orrin Keepnews and Bill Grauer wanted Weston to make a solo piano record while Weston wanted a trio. The duo was a compromise. Randy Weston interview, February 22, 1999; Gitler, "Randy Weston," 17.

49 Randy Weston interview, July 30, 2003. Chris Albertson, who joined the staff at Riverside in 1960, was clear on Weston's role in getting Grauer and Keepnews to hire Monk. "It was really Randy Weston who brought Monk to Riverside. Orrin takes credit for it, but it was really Randy Weston." Chris Albertson interview, July 11, 2003.

50 Randy Weston interview, July 30, 2003.

51 Keepnews, *The View from Within*, 121; Peter Keepnews, liner notes, *Thelonious Monk: The Complete Prestige Recordings*, 29.

52 Quoted in Goldberg, *Jazz Masters of the '50s*, 32.

53 Keepnews, *The View from Within*, 125.

54 The story of Bird's death has been told in dozens upon dozens of articles and books. For Nica's version of Parker's death, see Reisner, ed., *Bird*, 132–135; Russell, *Bird Lives!*, 348–358.

55 Jules remarried immediately after the divorce was final in 1955. His new bride was Madeline Le Forestier. She was listed officially as his wife on the passenger manifest when the couple traveled from New York to Paris in August of 1956. Air Passenger Manifest, Air France Flight 0700827, August 27, 1956, Passenger and Crew Lists of Vessels Arriving at New York, New York, 1897–1957, Microfilm T715, roll 8769, Records of the INS, National Archives.

56 "Musical Greats in Two Cities Pay Homage to Charlie Parker," *Pittsburgh Courier*, April 9, 1955.

57 Russell, *Bird Lives!*, 362–63; Chan Parker, *My Life in E-Flat*, 54. According to Mary Lou Williams, one of the organizers of the event, they took in $16,000, but some of the money went to Local 802 and some of it was simply stolen. See Williams's recollections in Gillespie, *To Be or Not to Bop*, 395.

58 Harvey Pekar, "Teo Macero: Tenor Player," *Jazz Journal*, 25, no. 8 (1972), 22; Gary Marmostein, *The Label: The Story of Columbia Records* (New York: Thunder's Mouth Press, 2007), 234–35.

59 Santoro, *Myself When I Am Real*, 107.

60 Ad in *Amsterdam News*, April 23, 1955.

61 Mingus quoted in Sue Mingus, ed., *Charles Mingus: More Than a Fake Book* (New York: Jazz Workshop, Inc., 1991), 75.

15   The Greta Garbo of Jazz

1 Quoted in Ben Alba, *Inventing Late Night: Steve Allen and the Original Tonight Show* (Amherst, NY: Prometheus Books, 2005), 93.

2 Ibid., 93–95.

3 Ibid., 98–101; Allen also wrote about the incident in "Talent Is Color-Blind," in *White on Black: The Views of Twenty-two White Americans on the Negro*, eds. Era Bell Thompson and Herbert Nipson (Chicago: Johnson Publishers, 1963), 78–80. This essay originally appeared in the September, 1955 issue of *Ebony* magazine.

4 "On Television," *New York Times*, June 10, 1955. The *Times* notice listed him as "Theolonious Monk."

5 Audio tape of the *Tonight Show*, June 10, 1955, in author's possession.

6 The entire exchange transcribed from audio tape of the *Tonight Show*, June 10, 1955, in author's possession.

7 Gordon Jack, "Eddie Bert [Interview]," *Jazz Journal International*, 52, no. 3 (March 1999), 8.

8 George Wein, with Nate Chinen, *Myself Among Others: A Life in Music* (New York: Da Capo Press, 2003), 458; Louis Lorillard, et. al., *Newport Jazz Festival 1955* (Jacques Willaumez Associates, 1955); Szwed, *So What?*, 118.

9 All of this is audible from the Voice of America (VOA) Broadcast, Newport All Stars, July 17, 1955, released on *Miles Davis: Misc. Davis, 1955–57* (Jazz Unlimited JUCD2050).

10 Wein, *Myself Among Others*, 458.

11 Miles Davis, with Quincy Troupe, *Miles*, 191.

12 *Miles Davis: Misc. Davis, 1955–57* (Jazz Unlimited JUCD2050). Wein agrees that Miles's performance was a triumph, but he attributes much of the positive response to his ability to overcome the inadequate sound system with a solid performance. "The clarity of his sound pierced the air over Newport's Freebody Park like nothing else we heard onstage that year. It was electrifying for the audience out on the grass, the musicians backstage, and the critics—some of whom had opined that Miles's career was already over." Wein, *Myself Among Others*, 458.

13 Wein, *Myself Among Others*, 459.

14 Miles Davis, with Quincy Troupe, *Miles*, 191–192; Szwed, *So What?*, 119.

15 Keepnews, *The View from Within*, 122–123; Orrin Keepnews liner notes, *Thelonious Monk Plays the Music of Duke Ellington* (Riverside RLP 12-201). When Riverside reissued the LP three years later, the title was streamlined to *Thelonious Monk Plays Duke Ellington*.

16 Mark Tucker, "Mainstreaming Monk: The Ellington Album," *Black Music Research Journal* 19, no. 2 (1999), 231–232.

17 Keepnews, *The View from Within*, 123.

18 Ibid., 122, 128. Keepnews' descriptions of each session were first published as "The Thelonious Monk Sessions," Liner notes, *Thelonious Monk: The Complete Riverside Recordings* (1986).

19 Keepnews, *The View from Within*, 123. Keepnews suggests in hindsight that Monk might have been transposing the music into a different key, and this is a reasonable assumption given aural evidence we have from homemade tapes in which he is working through a song (notably, "I'm Getting Sentimental Over You" discussed below). But Monk chose to play every song on the album in the key in which it was written, with one exception: "Solitude." He decided to play it in D♭, though originally written in E♭. Coincidentally, in 1957, when Ellington recorded a solo version of "Solitude," he played it in D♭. Duke Ellington, *Piano in the Foreground* (Columbia CK 87042).

20 Jeremy Yudkin, *The Lenox School of Jazz: A Vital Chapter in the History of American Music and Race Relations* (South Egremont, MA.: Farshaw Publishing, 2006), 16–33.

21 Randy Weston interview, July 30, 2003.

22 Published by Oxford University Press in 1956. On Stearns and the "Jazz Roundtables," see Gennari, *Blowin' Hot and Cool*, 144–153; Yudkin, *The Lenox School of Jazz*, 28–29; *Music Inn: A Documentary Film*, prod./dir. By Ben Barenholtz (Projectile Arts, 2007).

23 Stephanie Barber quoted in *Music Inn: A Documentary Film*.

24 The Music Barn's five-week summer festival of jazz and folk music was scheduled to coincide with the Boston Symphony Orchestra's residency at Tanglewood. "Berkshire Tempo to Add Jazz Beat," *New York Times*, April 28, 1955.

25 Quoted in Charles Edward Smith, "Madness Turned Out to be Musicianship," *Nugget* (October 1958), 68.

26 Weston quoted in *Music Inn: A Documentary Film*.

27 Milton R. Bass, "Thelonius Monk Disappoints in Music Barn," *Berkshire Eagle*, July 25, 1955.

28 *Thelonious Monk Plays The Music Of Duke Ellington* (Riverside RLP 12–201).

29 Schuller, "Thelonious Monk," 24; Max Harrison, "Thelonious Monk" in *Just Jazz 3*, eds. Sinclair Traill and Gerald Lascelles (London: Four Square Books, 1959), 19–20; Tucker, "Mainstreaming Monk," 235–40; Nat Hentoff, "Review of Thelonious Monk plays Duke Ellington," *Down Beat* (January 25, 1956), 23–24. Critics were divided, however, as the LP also earned its share of praise. See Bill Coss, "Review of Thelonious Monk plays Duke Ellington," *Metronome* (February 1956): 27; Gerald Lascelles, "Review of Thelonious Monk plays Duke Ellington," *Jazz Journal* 9, no. 10 (October 1956), 24.

30 The pre-eminent analysis of the Ellington album and Monk's resistance to it is the late Mark Tucker's excellent essay, "Mainstreaming Monk," 227–244. While this is a smart, incisive essay, I strongly disagree with Tucker's conclusion that Monk had little connection with or interest in Ellington, or that the recordings are restrained. Subtle, yes, but hardly restrained. The evidence of Monk's appreciation for Ellington, not to mention Ellington's admiration for Monk, is quite overwhelming and ought to be evident throughout my book.

31 T. S. Monk interview, April 4, 2005.

32 Gitler, "Ira Gitler Interviews Thelonious Monk," 20.

33 Joe Termini interviewed by Phil Schaap, WKCR, October 10, 1989.

34 Sales, "I Wanted to Make it Better," 37.

35 "Strictly Ad Lib," *Down Beat* (September 21, 1955), 39; Sheridan, *Brilliant Corners*, 369.

36 See Stephen J. Whitfield, *A Death in the Delta: The Story of Emmett Till* (Baltimore: The Johns Hopkins University Press, 1988); Mamie Till-Bradley, *Death of Innocence: The Story of the Hate Crime that Changed America* (New York: Random House, 2003).

37 Signal was a small label that initiated the "play-along" recordings—records packaged with sheet music and instructions for young musicians learning to play with a rhythm section. Cohen and Fitzgerald, *Rat Race Blues*, 158; http://www.jazzdiscography.com/Labels/signal.htm.

38 Harry Colomby interview, August 11, 2003.

39 Ira Gitler, liner notes *Nica's Tempo* (Savoy MG 12137).

40 Quoted in Cohen and Fitzgerald, *Rat Race Blues*, 173.

41 Quoted in Hentoff, "The Private World of Thelonious Monk," 137.

42 I'm grateful to dance historian Jacqui Malone for helping me figure this out. Until now, the meaning of "Shuffle Boil" has been a mystery to all Monk fans. See also Jacqui Malone, *Steppin' on the Blues: The Visible Rhythms of African American Dance* (Urbana: University of Illinois Press, 1996), 95, 109. On stop-time, or "disambiguation," see Samuel J. Floyd, *The Power of Black Music* (New York: Oxford University Press, 1995).

43 Gigi Gryce, *Nica's Tempo* (Signal S 1201), released later on the Savoy label (Savoy MG 12137).

44 On Kunstler's role in establishing Melotone Music, see Cohen and Fitzgerald, *Rat Race Blues*, 165. The year before Gryce retained him, Kunstler had published two small books for Oceana publishers, *The Law of Accidents* (1954) and *Corporate Tax Summary* (1954). See David J. Langum, *William M. Kunstler: The Most Hated Lawyer in America* (New York: NYU Press, 2000), 47.

45 Santoro, *Myself When I Am Real*, 117.

46 Kenny Mathieson, *Cookin': Hard Bop and Soul Jazz* (Edinburgh, UK: Canongate Books, 2002), 127–128; Chris Sheridan, *Dis Here: A Bio-Discography of Julian "Cannonball" Adderley* (Westport, CT: Greenwood Press, 2000).

47 "Strictly Ad Lib," *Down Beat* (November 30, 1955), 3; Santoro, *Myself When I Am Real*, 117; Priestley, *Mingus*, 65.

48 David Amram interview, July 15, 2003. In his memoir, he writes that he went to Monk's house first and then Monk paid him a visit, but his recollections in the interview were quite clear, insisting that it was the other way around. See David Amram, *Vibrations: A Memoir* (New York: Thunder's Mouth Press, 2001, orig. 1968), 224.

49 David Amram interview, July 15, 2003; Amram, *Vibrations,* 216–221. He discusses his arrival in New York Harbor in his memoir but never mentions the date. From the passenger manifest of the Groote Beer, the ship he arrived on from Rotterdam, I've determined the exact date to be September 10. David Amram, In-Bound Passenger List on 'Groote Beer,' September 10, 1955, Passenger and Crew Lists of Vessels Arriving at New York, New York, 1897–1957; Microfilm roll: *T715, 8633* (National Archives Microfilm); Records of the INS; National Archives, Washington, D.C.

50 David Amram interview, July 15, 2003.

51 Ibid.

52 Ibid.

53 Ibid.

54 Ibid.

55 Amram, *Vibrations,* 228–230.

56 He was billed as "Theolonius Monk, The Genius of Modern Jazz." *Chicago Defender,* December 3, 1955.

57 Griffin quoted in Mike Hennessey, *The Little Giant,* 73; see also Karl Seigfried, "'At Once Old-Timey and Avant-Garde': The Innovation and Influence of Wilbur Ware," (Ph.D. diss., University of Texas, Austin, 2002), 7; John Litweiler, "Remembering Wilbur Ware," *Down Beat* (December 1979), 27; Oral History Interview with Wilbur B. Ware Sr. by Gloria L. Ware, December 18, 1977 [transcript], Smithsonian Institution, Institute of Jazz Studies, p. 8; Dempsey Travis, *An Autobiography of Black Jazz* (Chicago: Urban Research Institute, Inc., 1983), 358–59.

58 Oral History Interview with Wilbur B. Ware Sr. by Gloria L. Ware, December 18, 1977 [transcript], Smithsonian Institution, Institute of Jazz Studies, pp. 5–9, quote on p. 9. See also Seigfried, "'At Once Old-Timey,'" 2–4; Orrin Keepnews, liner notes to Wilbur Ware Quintet, *The Chicago Sound* (Riverside RLP 12-252); Bill Crow, "Introducing Wilbur Ware," *Jazz Review* 2, no. 11 (1959), 14.

59 Hennessey, *The Little Giant,* 73.

60 Hentoff, "Just Call Him Thelonious," 16.

61 Segal quoted in Hennessey, *The Little Giant,* 73.

62 Hentoff, "Just Call Him Thelonious," 16

63 Hentoff, "Just Call Him Thelonious," 16; Kofi Ghanaba [Guy Warren] interview, August 13, 2004; Guy Warren, *I Have a Story to Tell* (Accra, Ghana: The Guinea Press, 1962), 79; Ed Veen, "Guy Warren Thrills Fans with N.T. Dance," *Gold Coast Sunday Mirror,* January 22, 1956. Guy Warren played in both events.

64 Monk was booked through the week before Bud Powell was scheduled to come in, on December 23. "Ivory Joe Hunter, Arnett Cobb, Chuck Berry on Tavern Parade," *Chicago Defender,* December 24, 1955.

16   "As Long as I Can Make a Living"

1 Both quotes from Charlotte Washington interview, April 5, 2004.

2 Ibid. Alonzo White and Thomas Monk, Jr., also remember the debate over Barbara's medical care.

3 Department of Health, City of New York, "Certificate of Death, Barbara Monk, #11105"; NYC Department of Health, *Deaths Reported in the City of New York, 1955,* 256.

4 Thomas Monk, Jr., interview, February 16, 2004. The details of the service are confirmed by Charlotte Washington interview, April 5, 2004; Alonzo White interview, December 16, 2007. The Smith side of the family thought Thelonious did not show up to the funeral at all [Jackie Bonneau interview, October 30, 2008], but all three Monk nephews agreed that he was there, just egregiously late.

5 Blakey recorded live there the following week. "Strictly Ad Lib," *Down Beat* (December 28, 1955), 5.

6 Harry Colomby interview, August 11, 2003.

7 Ibid.; Gourse, *Art Blakey: Jazz Messenger,* 56–57.

8 Harry Colomby interview, August 11, 2003.

9 Ibid.

10 Explaining business arrangements in the late 1950s, Nat Hentoff explained, "By union rule a manager gets a five per cent commssion. Usually, however, he has a personal contract with the player for an additional five per cent." Hentoff, *The Jazz Life,* 56.

11 Dr. Barry Zaret interview, August 19, 2007.

12 Arthur Lebowitz email correspondence, July 16 and 17, 2007.

13 Harry Colomby interview, August 11, 2003.

14 Ibid.

15 Ibid.

16 Ibid.

17 Their rent in the Phipps Houses might have been even less in 1956, but my estimate is based on the Monks' rent in 1963—$39.00 a month. Farrell, "Loneliest Monk," 88.

18 Jackie Bonneau interview, October 30, 2008.

19 Advertisement, *Los Angeles Times,* January 13, 1956.

20 Frank London Brown, "More Man than Myth, Monk Has Emerged from the Shadows," *Down Beat* (October 30, 1958), 14.

21 Judith Smith interview, January 30, 2004.

22 Evelyn Smith interview, February 12, 2004.

23 The piano (serial #349651) was delivered to Nica at 230 Central Park West. Steinway Piano Books, microfilm roll 7, Wagner Archives, LaGuardia Community College. In the film *Straight, No Chaser,* Nica states Monk accompanied her to pick out the piano.

24 Taylor Branch, *Parting the Waters: America in the King Years, 1954–1963* (New York: Simon & Schuster, 1988), 164–66; Stewart Burns, ed., *Daybreak of Freedom: The Montgomery Bus Boycott* (Chapel Hill, NC: University of North Carolina Press, 1997), 135; Jo Ann Gibson Robinson, *The Montgomery Bus Boycott and the Women Who Started It,* ed. David J. Garrow (Knoxville, TN: University of Tennessee Press, 1987), 130–133.

25 "Strictly Ad Lib," *Down Beat* (March 21, 1956), 6; *Down Beat* (April 4, 1956), 3; Amram, *Vibrations,* 234.

26 He basically plays the same arrangement he played in his 1948 performance of "Just You, Just Me" for the American Music Festival. See chapter 12.

27 Keepnews, *The View from Within,* 129. Interestingly, Keepnews's old employers, Simon & Schuster, published *The Rodgers and Hart Song Book.* Richard Rodgers, et. al., *The Rodgers and Hart Song Book: The Words and Music of Forty-Seven of Their Songs from Twenty-Two Shows and Two Movies* (New York: Simon & Schuster, 1951).

28 Keepnews, *The View from Within,* 130.

29 I have not been able to determine the exact date of the fire. The *New York Times* daily "Fire Record" makes no mention of a fire on West 63rd Street during this period and a request for information submitted to the NYFD yielded no information. As far as the fire department was concerned, the blaze at Monk's house was considered "trifling." However, by putting together evidence from oral histories and other documentary evidence, I've determined that the fire occurred a few days after the March 17 recording date and about a week before the Easter Jazz Festival. This would place the date somewhere between the 20th and 24th of March. Details of the events that follow are derived from the following sources: Monk family group interview, January 30, 2004; Geraldine Smith interview, February 8, 2004; Charlotte Washington interview, April 5, 2004; T.S. Monk, interview, April 5, 2005; Jackie Bonneau interview, October 30, 2008; Harry Colomby interview, August 11, 2003; David Amram interview, July 15, 2003; "Thelonious Monk Has a Fire," *Down Beat* (March 16, 1961), 11. And with regard to the loss of Keepnews's book, see Keepnews, *The View from Within,* 129.

30 Jackie Bonneau interview, June 17, 2005.

31 Thomas Monk Jr., interview, February 16, 2004.

32 Ibid. His sister, Charlotte Washington, tells essentially the same story. "The firemen broke through the place. You know how they smash everything. And he raced in there and said, 'You better not smash my piano!'" Charlotte Washington interview, April 5, 2004.

33 Alonzo White interview, February 23, 2004.

34 Harry Colomby interview, August 11, 2003.

35 Geraldine Smith interview, February 12, 2004.

36 David Amram interview, July 15, 2003.

37 Amram, *Vibrations,* 234.

38 Ibid., 234.

39 John S. Wilson, "Jazz Ensembles Sound Seasonal Note with an Easter Festival at Town Hall," *New York Times,* March 31, 1956.

40 Harry Colomby interview, August 11, 2003.

41 See Nick Catalano, *Clifford Brown: The Life and Art of the Legendary Jazz Trumpeter* (New York: Oxford University Press, 2000), esp. 183–185 for details on the accident.

42 Harry Colomby interview, August 11, 2003.

43 Alfred W. Lion to New York State Liquor Authority, April 30, 1956, Blue Note Archives, Capitol Records.

44 Raymond Horricks, "Thelonious Monk: Two Sides of an Enigmatic Musician," 10.

45 Hentoff, "Just Call Him Thelonious," 16.

46 Ibid., p. 16.

47 Ibid., p. 16.

48 Ibid., p. 16.

49 Colomby quoted in Frank London Brown, "More Man than Myth," 15.

50 Harry Colomby interview, August 11, 2003.

51 Helen Graham interview, January 30, 2004; Geraldine Smith interview, February 12, 2004; Jackie Bonneau interview, June 17, 2005.

52 Geraldine Smith interview, February 12, 2004.

53 Evelyn Smith interview, January 30, 2004.

54 Jackie Bonneau interview, June 17, 2005. These two characteristics led Jackie's junior high school class to select her as "Most Talented" and "Class Clown." *JHS 40 Yearbook, 1953,* p. 14.

55 Jackie Bonneau interview, June 17, 2005.

56 Monk family interview, January 30, 2004; Bertha Hope interview, July 15, 2003.

57 Hawes doesn't mention the month he first encountered Monk at the Embers, but we know he was still in L.A. in March and that his trio was recorded at the Embers on May 15, 1956, with Red Mitchell bass and Chuck Thompson on drums. The recording was released on *The Hampton Hawes Memorial Album* (Xanadu LP 161). By June 1, he was opening at Basin Street. "Ralph Cooper Presents," *Amsterdam News,* May 5, 1956; Ad, *Amsterdam News,* June 9 and 16, 1956.

58 Hampton Hawes, with Don Asher, *Raise Up Off Me* (New York: Da Capo Press, 1979), 84.

59 Ibid., 85.

60 Hawes, *Raise Up Off Me,* 107.

61 Jack Cooke, "Fading Flowers: a Note on Ernie Henry," *Jazz Monthly*, 7, no. 5 (1961), 9; Dieter Salemann, Dieter Hartmann, Michel Vogler, *Ernie Henry: Solography, Discography, Band Routes, Engagements in Chronological Order* (Basle, 1988).

62 Randy Weston interview, July 30, 2003.

63 *Down Beat* reported that "Thelonious Monk is rehearsing with altoist Ernie Henry." *Down Beat* (August 8, 1956), 5.

64 Harry Colomby interview, August 11, 2003.

65 Derek Ansell, "The Forgotten Ones: Ernie Henry," *Jazz Journal International* 40, no.9 (1987), 21; Randy Weston interview, July 30, 2003; Keepnews, *The View from Within*, 131; Keepnews liner notes for Ernie Henry, *Presenting Ernie Henry* (Riv RLP12-222).

66 Ernie Henry, *Presenting Ernie Henry* (Riv RLP12-222). He also recorded with trombonist Matthew Gee for Riverside around the same time.

67 Oral History Interview with Wilbur B. Ware Sr. by Gloria L. Ware, December 18, 1977, 64–66; Litweiler, "Remembering Wilbur Ware," 82.

68 Gene Feehan, "Jazz Unlimited: New Club is Formed," *Metronome* (November 1956), 17, 41; see also, Cohen and Fitzgerald, *Rat Race Blues*, 206.

69 Oral History Interview with Wilbur B. Ware Sr. by Gloria L. Ware, December 18, 1977, 66–69; Seigfried, "'At Once Old Timey,'" 105. After the Ernie Henry and Matthew Gee sessions in August of 1956, Riverside used Ware on only two other sessions (Zoot Sims in December and Kenny Drew in March and April) before Monk hired Ware in the spring of 1957.

70 Vail, *Miles' Diary*, 83.

71 Szwed, *So What*, 125.

72 Lewis Porter, *John Coltrane: His Life and Music* (Ann Arbor: Univ. of Mich. Press, 1998), 63–97.

73 Released on Miles Davis, *'Round About Midnight* (Columbia CK 85201).

74 Porter, *John Coltrane*, 104.

75 Thelonious Monk interview, January 30, 2004; Helen Graham interview, January 30, 2004.

76 David Amram interview, July 15, 2003.

77 Thelonious's introduction and the song can be heard on the soundtrack to Charlotte Zwerin's film *Straight, No Chaser*, released on CD as *Straight, No Chaser* (Columbia CK45358). Sheridan asserts that this recording was made at Monk's home, but that's impossible since he did not have a piano in his apartment throughout the fall of 1956.

78 Hentoff, "The Jazz Baroness," 101.

79 Keepnews, *The View Within*, 131.

80 Jack Cooke believes this to be the case. See Cooke, "Fading Flowers," 10.

81 Keepnews, *The View Within*, 132.

82 Harry Colomby interview, August 11, 2003.

83 Quoted in Nisenson, *Open Sky*, 99.

84 Max Roach conveyed a completely different story in *Du* magazine a few years ago. He tells us that Monk would not give anyone the music in hopes that the band might learn it by ear. But there was more to it: "The sidemen were only paid the minimum union [wage] based on a six-hour day. When finally the producer got tired of our messing up the tune, Monk took out the music and handed it out to us, and we managed to play that difficult tune without problems. Monk had had the music ready to hand out at any moment. . . . He just wanted us to be paid as long as possible." Peter Ruedi, "Just Play These Goddam Drums!," *DU* 12 (December1996), 32–33, 36–39, 42–43, 46, 48. This sounds unlikely for many reasons. It assumes that Monk knew they would fail, and thus prolong the studio time. And it assumes the four-hour-long, grueling experience actually generated more income for the band when it really didn't. What might be true, however, is Roach's claim that in the end Monk relented and shared the music.

85 Keepnews, *The View from Within*, 132.

86 Chambers, *Milestones 1*, 250; Vail, *Miles's Diary*, 86–87.

87 Nat Hentoff, "Paul Chambers," *Jazz Hot*, 109 (April1956), 14–15; Barbara Gardner, "Paul Chambers: Youngest Old Man in Jazz," *Down Beat* (July 21, 1960), 31. In 1956 he recorded two albums as a leader, *Chambers' Music* (Jazz West LP7) and *Whims of Chambers* (Blue Note BLP 1534).

88 Quoted in Frank London Brown, "More Man than Myth," 45. Nellie refers to his gig in Philadelphia, which had to have been this one. Monk played at the Blue Note again in February of 1957, but Nellie did not come and he did not engage the audience. See Chapter 18.

89 Porter, *John Coltrane*, 104.

90 Shipton, *Groovin' High*, 290; Dieter Salemann, Dieter Hartmann, Michel Vogler, *Ernie Henry*.

91 T. S. Monk interview, April 4, 2005.

92 Keepnews, *The View from Within*, 132–33.

93 Ibid., 133.

94 T. S. Monk interview, April 4, 2005.

95 Nica recorded Monk on her reel-to-reel on December 10, 1956. Reel #19, The Pannonica Collection (1956–1970), reel description.

96 Harry Colomby interview, August 11, 2003; Evelyn Smith interview, July 6, 2005; Gitler, "Ira Gitler Interviews Thelonious Monk," 37.

97 Harry Colomby interview, August 11, 2003. The precise date of the accident has been difficult to determine. Colomby thought it might have taken place in February of 1957, but the best evidence we have is Monk's interview with Ira Gitler, which took place in January of 1957—the date confirmed by Gitler himself in an interview with me (August 13, 2007). The best clues are in the interview—he mentions having just been released

from the hospital (he had spent about three weeks at Bellevue—see chapter 17); he mentions having just gotten a new Steinway for Christmas, and he expressed concern that the Mad Bomber (George Metesky) was on the loose—he was arrested on January 21, 1957. [Gitler, "Ira Gitler Interviews Thelonious Monk," 30, 37.] So the accident would have to have taken place around the third week of December, 1956.

17 "People Have Tried to Put Me Off As Being Crazy"

1 Frederick L. Covan, MD, with Carol Kahn, *Crazy All the Time: On the Psych Ward of Bellevue Hospital* (New York: Ballantine Books, 1994), 3.
2 "Hospitals of City New Space Goal," *New York Times*, January 15, 1957; "Wagner to Check Bellevue Charge," *New York Times*, May 8, 1957.
3 Harry Colomby interview, August 11, 2003; Nellie Monk interview, January 12, 2002.
4 A year later Nellie told writer Frank London Brown, "[Thelonious] doesn't suffer on the surface. . . . Not even when he was sick in hospital. He's like a rock." Brown, "More Man than Myth," 15.
5 Harry Colomby interview, August 11, 2003; Nellie Monk interview, January 12, 2002.
6 See Santoro, *Myself When I Am Real*, 143; Paudras, *Dance of the Infidels*, 351; Ellis Amburn, *Subterranean Kerouac: The Hidden Life of Jack Kerouac* (New York: St. Martin's Press, 1998); Jonah Raskin, *American Scream: Allen Ginsberg's 'Howl' and the Making of the Beat Generation* (Berkeley and Los Angeles: University of California Press, 2004).
7 Patricia D. Barry, *Mental Health and Mental Illness* (New York: J. B. Lippincott Co., 1990, Fifth Edition), 260–69; Kay Redfield Jamison, *Touched with Fire* (New York: The Free Press, 1993), 12–30. Thelonious's excessive drinking was likely a byproduct of the illness. Studies show that people suffering from bipolar disorder are not only prone to high rates of alcohol and substance abuse, but alcohol and drugs tend to worsen the clinical course of manic depression, making it more difficult to treat. Bipolar disorder complicated by alcoholism leads to increased hospitalizations and speeds up the onset of the disease. [Susan C. Sonne, Kathleen T. Brady, "Bipolar Disorder and Alcoholism," *Alcohol Research & Health*, 26 (2002), 103–108; Jamison, *Touched by Fire*, 37–39.] To complicate matters, amphetamines such as benzedrine—Monk's drug of choice—are not only addictive but can actually produce "a toxic psychosis that is clinically indistinguishable from paranoid schizophrenia." Quote in Patricia D. Barry, *Mental Health and Mental Illness* (New York: J. B. Lippincott Co., 1990, Fifth Edition), 234.
8 Hentoff, *The Jazz Life*, 187–88.
9 Quoted in Jean Bach, *A Great Day in Harlem* (Home Vision Entertainment, 2005, 1994), Disc Two, Bonus material.
10 There is an extensive literature suggesting that bipolar disorder is conducive to creativity, and that many if not most significant artists in all genres suffer from some form of manic depression. While this may be true, the scholarship on the subject tends to be impressionistic, inconclusive, and limited primarily to white men. The literature is voluminous and the association with genius and "madness," or at least melancholia, can be traced back to Aristotle. In the twentieth century, the link between artistic genius and manic depression, in particular, was made even more explicit. See Ernst Kretschmer, *The Psychology of Men of Genius*. Translated by R. B. Cattell (New York: Harcourt, Brace and Co., 1931); Lord Russell Brain, *Some Reflections on Genius* (New York: Pitman Medical Publishing Co., 1960); H. Akiskal and K. Akiskal, "Reassessing the Prevalence of Bipolar Disorders: Clinical Significance and Artistic Creativity," *Psychiatry and Psychobiology* 3 (1988), 295–365; N. C. Andreasen, "Creativity and Mental Illness: Prevalence Rates in Writers and Their First Degree Relatives," *American Journal of Psychiatry* 144 (1987), 1288–1292; D. Jablow Hershman and Julian Lieb, M.D., *Manic Depression and Creativity* (Amherst, NY: Prometheus Books, 1998); and of course, Jamison's popular *Touched with Fire*. Yet, as popular as these claims may be, there is a significant and persuasive body of scholarship questioning the link between mental illness and artistic temperament. See Albert Rothenberg, *Creativity and Madness: New Findings and Old Stereotypes* (Baltimore: Johns Hopkins University Press, 1990); George Becker, *The Mad Genius Controversy: A Study in the Sociology of Deviance* (Beverly Hills, CA: Sage Publications, 1978); Arnold M. Ludwig, *The Price of Greatness: Resolving the Creativity and Madness Controversy* (New York: The Guilford Press, 1995); and the important work by Judith Schlesinger, whose forthcoming book, *Dangerous Joy: The Mad Musician and Other Creative Myths*, not only deals specifically with jazz musicians but challenges assertions that highly creative people are prone to mental disorder. See her essays, "Issues in Creativity and Madness Part One: Ancient Questions, Modern Answers," *Ethical Human Sciences and Services* 4, 1 (2002), 73–76, and "Issues in Creativity and Madness. Part two: Eternal flames," *Ethical Human Sciences and Services* 4, 2 (2002), 139–142.
11 He was committed on August 16, 1941. North Carolina State Board of Health, Certificate of Death: Thelonious Monk. Registrar's Certificate No. 521.
12 Olivia Monk, Pam Kelley Monk, Marcella Monk Flake, interview, August 6, 2007. He also went by Theodoras.
13 Olivia Monk interview, August 6, 2007. Olivia Monk was married to Conley Monk, son of Theodore "Babe" Monk.
14 Ibid.
15 A. M. Rivera, Jr. "Negro Mentally Ill in N.C. Need Much Better Care," *Pittsburgh Courier*, August 27, 1949.
16 Ibid. The conditions were allegedly worse prior to a 1937 investigation, resulting in significant reforms. Maurice H. Greenhill, "The Present Status of Mental Health in North Carolina," *North Carolina Medical Journal*, 5 (January 1945), 10, 12; Karen Kruse Thomas, "The Hill-Burton Act and Civil Rights: Expanding Hospital Care for Black Southerners, 1939–1960," *Journal of Southern History* 72, no. 4 (November 2006), 843. However, when Rivera conducted his own investigation in 1949, he produced a damning report.

17 Rivera, "New State Mental Hospital." M. M. Vitols's publications include, M. M. Vitols, "The Significance of the Higher Incidence of Schizophrenia in the Negro Race in North Carolina," *North Carolina Medical Journal* 22 (April 1961), 147–58; M. M. Vitols, H. G. Waters, and M. H. Keeler, "Hallucinations and Delusions in White and Negro Schizophrenics," *American Journal of Psychiatry* 120 (November 1963), 472–476; M. H. Keeler and M. M. Vitols, "Migration and Schizophrenia in North Carolina Negroes," *American Journal of Orthopsychiatry* 33 (April 1963), 554–7; A. J. Prange and M. M. Vitols, "Jokes Among Southern Negroes: The Revelation of Conflict," *Journal of Nervous Mental Disorders* 136 (February 1963),162–7; A. J. Prange and M. M. Vitols, "Cultural Aspects of the Relatively Low Incidence of Depression in Southern Negroes," *International Journal of Social Psychiatry* 8(1962), 104–12.

18 North Carolina State Board of Health, Certificate of Death, Theodoras Babe Monk, December 6, 1949.

19 Olivia Monk, Pam Kelley Monk, Conley F. Monk, Jr., Marcella Monk Flake, Evelyn Pue, interview, August 6, 2007. As one can imagine, the death of Theodore "Babe" Monk has been a source of immense family controversy and division, especially since the much-coveted land ended up in the hands of Mamie Lofton Monk and Leroy and Isabella Cole.

20 Olivia Monk interview, August 6, 2007.

21 Harry Colomby interview, August 11, 2003; he tells a similar story to Leslie Gourse, *Straight, No Chaser*, 116.

22 Ira Gitler interview, August 13, 2007.

23 Gitler, "Ira Gitler Interviews Thelonious Monk," 30.

24 Interview with Albert "Tootie" Heath, January 22, 2008.

25 Ibid. On Saturday night, February 9, part of the gig was broadcast on local radio. See Sheridan, *Brilliant Corners*, 63.

26 Monk family interview, January 30, 2004. See also the photograph of Monk at his piano in Lewis Lapham's profile. Since it was taken in 1964, it is not the same piano, but the configuration is the same. Lewis H. Lapham, "Monk: High Priest of Jazz," *Saturday Evening Post* 237 (April 11, 1964), 72.

27 Homemade tape in author's possession, ca. 1957.

28 T. S. Monk, interview, April 4, 2005.

29 Original recording in author's possession. This particular recording was released on Thelonious Records as *Thelonious Monk Transforms "I'm Getting Sentimental Over You" Solo Piano and Concert Performance* (TMTS).

30 Kastin, "Nica's Story," 283; Evelyn Smith interview, February 12, 2004. Nica was notorious for street racing with this car. See Hawes, *Raise Up Off Me*, 87.

31 "Coltrane Learns Monk's Mood at Algonquin," Reel #14, The Pannonica Collection (1956–1970). These tapes are in the possession of pianist Barry Harris. The handwritten reel description in author's possession. Coltrane also tells the story of how he asked Thelonious to teach him "Monk's Mood." "John Coltrane interview by August Blume, June 15, 1958, Baltimore," Audio copy on http://www.melmartin.com/html_pages/interviews.html. Although a transcript of the interview originally appeared as August Blume, "An Interview with John Coltrane," *Jazz Review* 2, no. 1 (1959): 25, I chose to transcribe directly from the recording.

32 "John Coltrane interview by August Blume, June 15, 1958, Baltimore."

33 "'Round Midnight" [in Progress], *Complete Riverside Recordings*.

34 Recorded on April 14, 1957, "Reflections" and "Misterioso" were first released on Sonny Rollins, *Sonny Rollins, Vol. 2* (Blue Note 1558). Eric Nisenson suggests that it was Monk who dropped by and Silver had been hired for the date. (*Open Sky*, 112–113.) Silver's memoir does not indicate one way or another, and he devotes one sentence to the session. Rollins states that "Monk was originally supposed to be there and Horace also came by or was there or was invited or something." Silver, *Let's Get to the Nitty Gritty*, 84; Sidran, *Talking Jazz*, 174. The most plausible explanation is that they both were hired for the date, but Rollins wanted Monk to play on his own tunes.

35 Keepnews, *The View from Within*, 124; *Down Beat* (August 16, 1962).

36 I discuss Monk's connection to the Harlem stride pianists in Chapter 6.

37 Quoted in Thomas, *Chasin' the 'Trane*, 85. The story of Davis punching Coltrane is legendary and has been told repeatedly. Besides J. C. Thomas, with whom the story apparently originates, see, Porter, *John Coltrane*, 104–105; Szwed, *So What*, 140; Chambers, *Milestones 1*, 257. It is repeated in Miles's memoir with Quincy Troupe (*Miles*, 207), but he places the event in October 1956, not April 1957. Perhaps Miles's version is correct, though most of the evidence points to his April engagement at the Bohemia. Moreover, Miles never mentions the incident in the many hours of taped interviews Quincy Troupe donated to the Schomburg Library. These tapes were the basis for the memoir.

38 David Amram interview, July 15, 2003. The gig had been booked already in January because Colomby mentions it during Gitler's interview with Monk. Gitler, "Ira Gitler Interviews Thelonious Monk," 30.

39 David Amram interview, July 15, 2003.

40 Ibid.

41 Harry Colomby interview, August 11, 2003.

42 "Two Bass Hit!," *Jazz Journal International* 30, no. 11 (November 1977), 12, and see Alan Groves, "The Loneliest Monk," 12.

43 Oral History Interview with Wilbur B. Ware Sr. by Gloria L. Ware, December 18, 1977, p. 80. Blakey's version is slightly different: "Halfway through one number we heard this great thump and looked round to see the bass player slumped on the floor dead drunk with the bass on top of him." Hennessey, "The Enduring Jazz Message of Abdullah ibn Buhaina," 9.

44 "Two Bass Hit!," 12.

45 Ibid.

46 Geraldine Smith interview, February 12, 2004.

47 Harry Colomby interview, August 11, 2003.

48 See Reel #21, The Pannonica Collection (1956–1970), reel description.

49 Geraldine Smith interview, February 12, 2004; Harry Colomby interview, August 11, 2003. Nat Hentoff reported that Monk spent a month working on the "inside" to "Crepuscule with Nellie" (Hentoff, "The Private World of Thelonious Monk," 137), whereas Lewis Lapham later suggested it took three months. Lapham, "Monk: High Priest of Jazz," 74. See also Goldberg, *Jazz Masters of the 50s*, 38.

50 Hyperthyroidism occurs when the thyroid gland is overactive, causing the body to metabolize at a faster rate and producing a greater demand for oxygen, nutrients, and other material. See, Kenneth Ain, *The Complete Thyroid Book* (New York: McGraw-Hill, 2005); Jay K. Harness, Lit Fung, Norman W. Thompson, Richard E. Burney, and Michael K. McLeod, "Total thyroidectomy: Complications and technique," *World Journal of Surgery* 10, no. 5 (October 1986), 781–785; P. Ruggieri, *A Simple Guide to Thyroid Disorders: From Diagnosis to Treatment* (Omaha, NE: Addicus Books, 2003); Irving B. Rosen, "A Historical Note on Thyroid Disease and its Surgical Treatment" (April 2006), http://www.thryvors.org/pdf/Rosen_Apr_06.pdf. Although there were other methods to treat thyroid conditions—medications, radioactive iodine—it appears that a complete thyroidectomy was the most popular in the late 1950s, as evidenced by an article published in *Science News Letter* just two months before Nellie's surgery. "Overactive Thyroid is Best Treated by Removal," *Science News Letter* (March 2, 1957), 133. Although Geraldine Smith, then a nurse, seems to remember Nellie suffering from hyperthyroidism, her low-grade fever may have indicated hypothyroidism, or the slowing down of the thyroid gland. Hypothyroidism could affect some endocrine control of body temperature, which means running a low-grade fever. See Elbert T. Phelps, "Fever—Its Causes and Effects," *American Journal of Nursing* 56, no. 3 (March 1956), 319.

51 David Dean Brockman and Roy M. Whitman, "Post-Thyroidectomy Psychoses," *Journal of Nervous and Mental Disease* 116 (1952), 340–345; Leslie S. Libow and Jack Durrell, "Clinical Studies on the Relationship Between Psychosis and the Regulation of Thyroid Gland Activity," *Psychosomatic Medicine* 27 (July-August, 1965), 377–382.

52 Geraldine Smith interview, February 12, 2004.

53 Chilton, *The Song of the Hawk*, 292.

54 Keepnews, *The View from Within*, 134–135. The first takes of "Crepuscule with Nellie" are on *The Complete Riverside Recordings of Thelonious Monk*.

55 Keepnews, *The View from Within*, 135; Cohen and Fitzgerald, *Rat Race Blues*, 226–227. It appeared as part of a compilation album billed as the "East Coast All-Stars." East Coast All-Stars, *Blues for Tomorrow* (Riverside RLP 243).

56 Henry Francis Lyte, *Abide with Me* (Boston: Lee and Shepard Publishers, 1878), 1–2. "Abide with Me" can be found in virtually any hymn book.

57 This story was told by Gigi Gryce. Quoted in Hentoff, *The Jazz Life*, 183.

58 Ibid.

59 Blakey quoted in Thomas, *Chasin' the Trane*, 90.

60 He did record both songs in Paris in 1954 for his first solo LP. See chapter 13.

61 J. C. Thomas, *Chasin' the Trane*, 82.

62 Keepnews remembered it this way and Alonzo White, Monk's nephew, was in the studio that night and confirms the story. (Alonzo White interview, February 23, 2004.) See also, Porter, *John Coltrane*, 109.

63 Nat Hentoff, "Review *Brilliant Corners*," *Down Beat* (June 13, 1957), 28; *Metronome* 74, no. 7 (June 1957), 26.

64 Brown, "More Man than Myth," 14.

65 Paul Bacon interview, July 30, 2001.

66 Ibid.

67 Brown, "More Man than Myth," 15.

18 "My Time for Fame Will Come"

1 Farrell, "Loneliest Monk," 86; Hentoff, "The Private World of Thelonious Monk," 137; Harry Colomby interview, August 11, 2003. All of the press accounts credit the Baroness with getting Monk's cabaret card back, but Colomby doesn't remember Nica playing any significant role in the process. On the contrary, he was worried that her involvement might send the wrong signal to the police and the state liquor authority, given her reputation for hanging out with jazz musicians. On the other hand, the idea that she hired a lawyer who was able to get a hearing with an inspector—apparently a requirement for restoring one's card—seems plausible. Paul Chevigny and Maxwell T. Cohen, the leading crusader against the cabaret identification cards, pointed out that in cases where an applicant is denied a card, he or she can hire a lawyer and get a hearing. Chevigny, *Gigs*, 60.

2 Joe Termini interviewed by Phil Schaap, WKCR, October 10, 1989.

3 His card number is listed in the late Joe Termini's Cabaret notebooks from the Five Spot, in the possession of his daughter, Toni Behm. I'm eternally grateful to Toni for giving me access to these precious volumes.

4 Associated Musicians of Greater New York, Local 802, Contract, June 3, 1958; Personnel Roster, Five Spot Cabaret Books, 1957, Joseph Termini Personal Papers. The Terminis did not have the original 1957 contract, but the terms are the same.

5 Thelonious was so committed to making his gig that he missed out on an opportunity to go to Hollywood to appear on the television program *Stars of Jazz* with Art Blakey and the Jazz Messengers on July 29, 1957. They performed three Monk compositions, "Blue Monk," "I Mean You," and "Evidence," with Sam Dockery subbing on piano. The recordings were released on Art Blakey, *Sessions Live* (Calliope CAL 3008).

6   Several others have also taken credit for bringing Monk to the Five Spot. Larry Rivers claims he hounded the Terminis to hire Monk until they finally relented. But Rivers, whose account is questionable on many fronts, also claims Monk was the first black musician to perform there and that he suggested Monk because "jazz is black." He makes no mention of Taylor's 1956 date. Larry Rivers, with Arnold Weinstein, *What Did I Do?: The Unauthorized Autobiography of Larry Rivers* (New York: HarperCollins, 1992), 341–42. Randy Weston, who played there in April, made a strong case for bringing Thelonious, just as he lobbied Grauer and Keepnews to sign him to Riverside. Randy Weston interview, July 30, 2003.

7   Salvatore Termini Draft Registration Card, Serial U 3003, United States, Selective Service System. *Selective Service Registration Cards, World War II: Fourth Registration*. National Archives; U.S. Census, *Fifteenth Census of the United States, 1930: Population Schedule, Manhattan Borough,* ED 118; Toni Behm interview, March 15, 2008; Joe Termini resume, n.d., in possession of Toni and David Behm; John S. Wilson, "'Village' Becomes Focal Center for Modern Jazz," *New York Times*, October 27, 1960; Burt Glinn, "New York's Spreading Upper Bohemia," *Esquire* 284 (July 1957), 50.

8   The notorious gangster Harry Rich (aka Arthur Clayton) lived in an apartment at 5 Cooper Square. In 1934, he earned the distinction of becoming the first organized crime figure arrested under New Jersey's new "public enemy" law. "First Gangster Convicted Under New Jersey's New Law," *New York Times*, June 28, 1934. He was involved in an armed robbery at the Newark Farmer's Market.

9   U.S. Census, 1930, *Population Schedule, Manhattan Borough,* ED 118. Their children were John (age 19), Katherine (14), Ignacio or "Iggy" (11), Joe (6), and Antoinette (3). Their eldest son, Frank, no longer lived at home, which at the time was 11 Stanton Street. Salvatore immigrated in 1906; his wife Angelina arrived in 1904.

10 Salvatore Termini Draft Registration Card, Serial U 3003, United States, Selective Service System. *Selective Service Registration Cards, World War II: Fourth Registration*. National Archives. In the 1940s, they moved to 122 Bay Street in the Red Hook section of Brooklyn. Bureau of the Census,1930, *Population Schedule: Manhattan Borough, ED 118.*

11 Iggy ended up using "Ignazio" because few people could pronounce Ignatze. Iggy Termini interview, March 8, 2008.

12 "Ignazio Termini," "Joseph Termini," World War II Army Enlistment Records, National Archives and Records Administration, Record Group 64; Iggy Termini interview, March 8, 2008. Frank went on to earn a law degree and briefly took on the lion's share of the administrative responsibilities for the Bowery Café. Both Joe and Iggy were decorated for their combat duty. Iggy was assigned to a B-26 bomber unit in the Pacific theater, mainly China, India and Burma, while Joe's B-17 bomber unit was stationed in Africa.

13 Iggy Termini interview, March 8, 2008.

14 Lawrence Stelter, *By the El: Third Avenue and its El at Mid-Century* (New York: Stelterfoto LLC, 2007); Ralph Katz, "Last Train Rumbles on Third Ave. 'El'," *New York Times*, May 13, 1955; Harrison E. Salisbury, "Cars are Packed for Last 'El' Trip," *New York Times*, May 13, 1955; Charles G. Bennett, "3rd Ave. Must Pay for Lights and Air," *New York Times*, June 2, 1955; "3rd Ave. to Emerge Broad and Beautiful," *New York Times*, August 3, 1955. The demolition of the downtown sections of the El was complete by December of 1955. In the planned redevelopment, however, many of the flop houses were razed without provisions for alternative shelters for homeless men. See, "Big Rise Is Feared in Vagrant Cases," *New York Times*, October 20, 1955.

15 Wilson, "'Village' Becomes Focal Center for Modern Jazz"; Gene Balliett, "Busman's Holiday," *Cincinnati Inquirer*, October 28, 1958.

16 "Thursday Jazz Piano," radio show, October, 1998, Joe Termini interview by Henry Wales. Audio copy in author's possession, courtesy of Toni Behm.

17 Personnel Roster, Five Spot Cabaret Books, 1956. Some of the first wave of musicians include Raymond Charles, Jay Chasen, and Mike Dacek.

18 David Amram interview, July 15, 2003; Amram, *Vibrations*, 261; Wilson, "'Village' Becomes Focal Center for Modern Jazz."

19 Marika Herskovic, *American Abstract Expressionism of the 1950s: An Illustrated Survey* (New York School Press, 2003); Marika Herskovic, *New York School Abstract Expressionists Artists Choice by Artists* (New York School Press, 2000).

20 Glinn, "New York's Spreading Upper Bohemia," 50; On Herman Cherry, see H.H. Aranson, *60 American Painters, 1960* (Minneapolis: Walker Arts Center, 1961), 78; "Herman Cherry, Artist, Is Dead; an Abstract Painter and Poet," *New York Times*, April 14, 1992.

21 Michael Magee, "Tribes of New York: Frank O'Hara, Amiri Baraka, and the Poetics of the Five Spot," *Contemporary Literature*, Vol. 42, No. 4 (Winter, 2001), 694–726; Larry Rivers, *What Did I Do?*, 341–42; Amram, *Vibrations*, 262; Dan Wakefield, *New York in the Fifties* (New York: Houghton Mifflin, 1992), 306–311; Ted Joans interview, December 15, 1995.

22 Larry Rivers played a competent saxophone; Howard Kanovitz began as a jazz trombone player before turning to the canvas; and writer Mike Zwerin was a seasoned practitioner of the bass trumpet and trombone, having recorded with Miles Davis and others. Larry Rivers, *What Did I Do?*, 340–41; Mike Zwerin, "Larry Rivers: A Look into Two Camps of the Painter-Jazzman," *Down Beat* (August 11, 1966), 20–21; Jorn Merkert, "*Between Worlds, Howard Kanovitz, Painter of Contradiction*," *Howard Kanovitz* (Berlin: Akademie der Kunste, 1979), translated from German and posted on http://www.howardkanovitz.com.

23 Helen Tworkov quoted in Wakefield, *New York in the Fifties*, 307.

24 LeRoi Jones/Amiri Baraka, *The Autobiography*, 124–133; see also, Michael Magee, "Tribes of New York," 694–726.

25 Ted Joans interview, December 15, 1995.

26 LeRoi Jones/Amiri Baraka, *The Autobiography*, 133. Baraka tells a version of Ted Joans's story in his memoir, but uses the pseudonym Tim Poston. See also Hettie Jones, *How I Became Hettie Jones*, 36.

27 LeRoi Jones/Amiri Baraka, *The Autobiography*, 133.

28 See Robin D. G. Kelley, "Dig They Freedom: Meditations on History and the Black Avant-Garde," *Lenox Avenue: A Journal of Interartistic Inquiry* 3 (1997), 13–27; see also Lorenzo Thomas, "Alea's Children: The Avant-Garde on the Lower East Side, 1960–1970," *African American Review* 27, no. 4 (1993), 573–78; Calvin Hernton, "Umbra: A Personal Recounting," *African American Review* 27, no. 4 (1993), 579–83; Rashidah Ismaili-Abu-Bakr, "Slightly Autobiographical: The 1960s on the Lower East Side," *African American Review* 27, no. 4 (1993), 585–89; Sarah E. Wright, "The Lower East Side: A Rebirth of World Vision," *African American Review* 27, no. 4 (1993), 593–96; Hettie Jones, *How I Became Hettie Jones* (New York: E.P. Dutton, 1990); Jon Panish, *The Color of Jazz: Race and Representation in Postwar American Culture* (Jackson: University Press of Mississippi, 1997), 23–41. Many of these artists actually lived in the same neighborhoods in the East Village and the Lower East Side. As John Szwed points out in his biography of Sun Ra, many of the leading figures associated with the jazz avant-garde lived around Third Street, including Archie Shepp, Ornette Coleman, Giuseppi Logan, Sonny Simmons, Burton Greene, Henry Grimes, Charles Tyler, Charles Moffett, Sunny Murray, James Jackson, and Cecil Taylor. Szwed, *Space is the Place: The Lives and Times of Sun Ra* (New York: Pantheon, 1997), 195.

29 David Amram interview, July 15, 2003; Personnel Roster, Five Spot Cabaret Books, 1956.

30 For background on Cecil Taylor, see Spellman, *Four Lives in the Bebop Business*, 3–76; Wilmer, *As Serious as Your Life*, 45–59; Goldberg, *Jazz Masters of the Fifties*, 213–227; Bill Coss, "Cecil Taylor's Struggle for Existence; Portrait of the Artist as a Coiled Spring," *Down Beat* (October 26, 1961), 19–21; "Cecil Taylor: The Space of 61 Years Danced Through," *Village Voice* (June 26, 1990).

31 David Amram interview, July 15, 2003.

32 Spellman, *Four Lives in the Bebop Business*, 67.

33 David Amram interview, July 15, 2003; Amram, *Vibrations*, 261–62.

34 Spellman, *Four Lives in the Bebop Business*, 67–68.

35 This same band had just recorded Taylor's first LP, *Jazz Advance* (Transition TRLP 19) a couple of months earlier.

36 See also Steve Lacy interview, May 12, 1995; "Jazz and Sculpture: Interview by Alain Krili," in Jason Weiss, ed., *Steve Lacy: Conversations* (Durham, NC: Duke University Press, 2006), 160.

37 Personnel Roster, Five Spot Cabaret Books, 1957; David Amram interview, July 15, 2003; Amram, *Vibrations*, 262. Williams was a black Canadian out of the "Bud Powell school" of piano who was better-known for being the son of a prominent Harlem chemist than for being a musician. See Jesse H. Walker, "Theatricals," *Amsterdam News*, April 13, 1957.

38 Reil Lazarus, "Bassist John Ore," *All About Jazz* (March 15, 2004) www.allaboutjazz.com. According to Termini's cabaret books, Ore was hired on February 9th. Personnel Roster, Five Spot Cabaret Books, 1957.

39 David Amram interview, July 15, 2003; Amram, *Vibrations*, 262–63.

40 Personnel Roster, Five Spot Cabaret Books, 1957; Randy Weston interview, July 30, 2003; David Amram interview, July 15, 2003. According to the Cabaret books, Mal Waldron and Freddie Redd alternated a couple of Monday nights (May 20 and 27), but through June and early July they had longer gigs—two weeks each. From June 20 to July 3, Waldron's group expanded to a quartet with Art Farmer. There was quite a bit of shuffling going on with regard to rhythm sections, but generally Williams retained Ahmed Abdul-Malik and Al Harewood (who played with Randy Weston); Redd used Wilbur Ware and Wilbur Campbell, and Waldron generally hired bassist Julian Euell, drummer Williams James and others. Personnel Roster, Five Spot Cabaret Books, 1957.

41 Glinn, "New York's Spreading Upper Bohemia," 46–52.

42 David Amram interview, July 15, 2003.

43 LeRoi Jones/Amiri Baraka, *The Autobiography*, 175.

44 *Thelonious Monk Trio* (Prestige LP 7027); *Monk* (Prestige LP 7053); and under Sonny Rollins' name, *Sonny Rollins: Moving Out* (Prestige LP 7058); Thelonious Monk, *Genius of Modern Music, vol. 1* (Blue Note 1510); Thelonious Monk, *Genius of Modern Music, vol. 2* (Blue Note 1511); and sessions with Milt Jackson, once again released under Jackson's name as *Milt Jackson* (Blue Note 1509). Both labels advertised the discs and the Blue Note albums sold well enough to yield Monk $170 in royalties after the first year. Francis Wolff to Morris Zuckerman, November 21, 1961, Blue Note Archives, Capitol Records.

45 Nat Hentoff, "Review *Brilliant Corners*," *Down Beat* (June 13, 1957), 28.

46 *Metronome* 74, no. 7 (June 1957), 26.

47 Personnel Roster, Five Spot Cabaret Books, 1957. We now know that *Down Beat*'s announcement that Monk's group opened on July 19, after Payne and Jordan left is mistaken. "Strictly Ad Lib," *Down Beat* (July 25, 1957), 8. But other sources that identify Frankie Dunlop as the drummer, or that have the group beginning on the 18th of July, are also mistaken. The Cabaret Books kept by Joe Termini are clear evidence of who played when. Mack Simpkins was an unknown quantity at the time, but he did go on to work with Shirley Scott and Stanley Turrentine.

48 David Amram interview, July 15, 2003

49 Hentoff, "The Private World of Thelonious Monk," 137.

50 Harry Colomby interview, August 11, 2003.

51 Personnel Roster, Five Spot Cabaret Books, 1957.

52 On Dunlop's background, Scott K. Fish, "Frankie Dunlop: Making it Swing," *Modern Drummer*, 9, no. 8 (1985), 22–25; Ira Gitler, "Monk's Drummer: Frankie Dunlop," *Down Beat* (January 16, 1964), 16; Laura Dunlop interview, March 1, 2008.

53 Dunlop quoted in Fish, "Frankie Dunlop: Making it Swing," 84; Gitler, "Monk's Drummer: Frankie Dunlop," 16. Although Dunlop remembered working about two or three weeks, he actually began on the 16th and tech-

nically stayed on until July 21, but he was replaced by Shadow Wilson on the 18th. Joe Termini kept him on just so he could get paid. Personnel Roster, Five Spot Cabaret Books, 1957.

54 He was listed in the cabaret book as "R. Vandella Wilson." Personnel Roster, Five Spot Cabaret Books, 1957. His middle name "Vandella" was confirmed by his army records. "Rossiere Vandella Wilson," enlistment date May 28, 1944, U.S. World War II Army Enlistment Records, 1938–1946, National Archives.

55 Harry Colomby interview, March 24, 2008; see also Korall, *Drummin' Men*, 68–69.

56 Joe Termini Interviewed by Phil Schaap, WKCR, October 10, 1989.

57 Ibid.

58 Dom Cerulli, "Thelonious Monk Quartet," *Down Beat* (September 5, 1957), 33.

59 LeRoi Jones, "The Acceptance of Monk," *Down Beat* (February 27, 1964), 21; also reprinted in Amiri Baraka, *Black Music* (New York: Quill, 1967), 26–34.

60 Coltrane quoted in Hentoff, "The Private World of Thelonious Monk," 133.

61 Private recording, Thelonious Monk Estate.

62 Cerulli, "Thelonious Monk Quartet," 33.

63 In 1958, Nellie told writer Frank London Brown, "last year he did a dance . . . during the solos." Brown, "More Man than Myth," 45.

64 John Coltrane interview by August Blume, June 15, 1958.

65 Ibid.

66 Ibid.

67 Oral History Interview with Wilbur B. Ware Sr. by Gloria L. Ware, December 18, 1977, p. 29. Other works that explore Coltrane and Ware's incredible rapport during the Five Spot engagement include Martin Williams, "What Kind of Composer Was Thelonious Monk?" *The Musical Quarterly* 76 (Fall 1992), 439; J. C. Thomas, *Chasin' the Trane*, 88; Porter, *John Coltrane*, 111, 112.

68 Andrew W. Bartlett's remarkable essay, "Cecil Taylor, Identity Energy, and the Avant-Garde African American Body," *Perspectives of New Music* 33 (winter-summer, 1995), 274–293, reminds us of the importance of the body in public performance in late 50s, early 60s bohemian cultural politics. See also, Sally Banes's *Greenwich Village 1963: Avant-Garde Performance and the Effervescent Body* (Durham, NC: Duke University Press, 1993). Bartlett points to the extraordinary political importance the white avant-garde invested in the body, particularly in its performance of pleasure and excess. In this context, it is easy to see how Monk's spontaneous dance, combined with his drinking during and between sets, might be attractive to the generation Banes writes about.

69 Monk family interview, January 30, 2004.

70 Hentoff, "The Private World of Thelonious Monk," 137.

71 Peter Danson, "Interview: Charlie Rouse," *Coda Magazine* 187 (1982), 7–8.

72 Ben Riley interview with Quincy Troupe, Media Transcripts, Inc., p. 12. Monk's bassist Ahmed Abdul-Malik says much the same thing. Ahmed Abdul-Malik Interview with Ed Berger, "Jazz from the Archives," WBGO, recorded January 30, 1984 (tape at IJS).

73 Quoted in Wilmer, "Monk on Monk," 22; Monk interview with Valerie Wilmer and John Hopkins, March 14, 1965.

74 David Amram interview, July 15, 2003. The fact that Monk linked dancing to sacred traditions is significant. Historian Sterling Stuckey, who saw Thelonious perform in person, described Monk's movement as a variation on the "ring shout," a West African derived dance form in which men and women move in a circle counterclockwise, shuffling their feet and gesticulating with their arms. It was a group dance that demanded individual improvisation, and it was deeply sacred. Sterling Stuckey, *Slave Culture: Nationalist Theory and the Foundations of Black America* (New York: Oxford University Press, 1987), 96. See also Chapter 5, and Hugh J. Roberts, "Improvisation, Individuation, and Immanence," 50–56.

75 Jack Kerouac, *The Subterraneans* (New York: Grove Press, 1994, orig. 1958), 84. I have to thank my daughter, Elleza, for insisting I read *The Subterraneans*.

76 Farrell, "Loneliest Monk," 84. For an excellent bird's-eye view of the Beats and jazz in the 1950s, see Ted Joans's entertaining essay, "Bird and the Beats," *Coda* (June 1981), 14–15.

77 Norman Mailer, "The White Negro," *Dissent* (November 1957), 276–93; Panish, *The Color of Jazz*, 56–66; and on the crisis of masculinity in the 1950s, see Barbara Ehrenreich, *The Hearts of Men: American Dreams and the Flight from Commitment* (London: Routledge, 1983); Andrew Ross, *No Respect: Intellectuals and Popular Culture* (London and New York: Routledge, 1989), 65–101.

78 At least this is precisely how Steve Lacy described Monk's music in the pages of *Jazz Review*. He not only said that Monk's music possessed, among other things, a "balanced virility" but in the context of a discussion about Sonny Rollins observed "[Rollins's] masculinity and authority can only be matched in jazz by that of Thelonious Monk." In the liner notes to his first all-Monk album *Reflections* (1958), penned by critic Ira Gitler, Lacy also characterized Monk's music as "masculine." Gitler concurred, calling Lacy's remark "an interesting and pointed observation in the light of the numerous effeminate jazz offerings we have heard in the past five years. The inner strength of songs like *Ask Me Now* and *Reflections* demonstrates that it is not slow tempos and lower decibels which necessarily indicate an effeminate performance." "Introducing Steve Lacy," in Martin Williams, ed., *Jazz Panorama* (New York: Collier Books, 1964), 269, 271; Gitler liner notes on *Reflections: Steve Lacy Plays Thelonious Monk* (Prestige 8206). For an extended discussion of gender and masculinity, in particular, in Monk's music, see my essay, "New Monastery: Monk and the Jazz Avant-Garde," *Black Music Research Journal* 19, no. 2 (Fall, 1999), 135–168.

79 Albert Goldman, "Man, You Gotta Dig that Cat, Thelonius [sic] The Thinker, The Skull, the Long Medulla," *New Leader* (October 19, 1959), 27.

80 "Strictly Ad Lib," *Down Beat* (December 12, 1957), 12.

81 Goldberg, *Jazz Masters of the 50s*, 35.

82 Jones, *How I Became Hettie Jones*, 34.

83 Ted Joans interview, December 15, 1995.

84 J. C. Thomas, *Chasin' the Trane*, 88.

85 Ted Joans interview, December 15, 1995.

86 Joe Termini interviewed by Phil Schaap, WKCR, October 10, 1989.

87 Monk was supposed to "hit" around 9:15 and play until 3:00 a.m., but he usually showed up around 11:00 or sometimes even midnight. Joe Termini interviewed by Phil Schaap, WKCR, October 10, 1989. Monk's hours are clearly established on the Local 802 contract. Although we don't have a contract from 1957, we do have one for his second gig in the summer of 1958, and according to Iggy Termini the terms were the same. See Associated Musicians of Greater New York, Local 802, Contract, June 3, 1958.

88 Joe Termini interviewed by Phil Schaap, WKCR, October 10, 1989.

89 Harry Colomby interview, August 12, 2003.

90 T. S. Monk interview, April 4, 2005.

91 Bob Lemkowitz interview, July 15, 2003.

92 Ibid. Mr. Lemkowitz kindly shared a photograph of all of these items with me.

93 Bob Lemkowitz interview, July 15, 2003.

94 Marcel Romano, "De Saint-Germain des Pres au New York: Au Five Spot," *Jazz Hot* 125 (October 1957), 24.

95 Evelyn Smith interview, February 12, 2004.

96 Every niece and nephew I spoke to, as well as Toot, said the same thing.

97 Charlotte Washington interview, April 4, 2004. Robert A. Perlongo observed Monk falling asleep at the piano, as well. See Perlongo, "A Night of Thelonious," *Metronome* (August 1959), 18–19.

98 "Strictly Ad Lib," *Down Beat* (September 5, 1957), 8. Miles was there from July 8 to August 11. Vail, *Miles' Diary*, 102–103.

99 First released on LP as *Thelonious Monk with John Coltrane* (Jazzland JLP 946).

100 Gerry Mulligan, *Mulligan Meets Monk* (Riverside RLP 12-247); Keepnews, *The View From Within*, 136; Horricks, *Gerry Mulligan's Ark*, 43–44; Jerome Klinkowitz, *Listen: Gerry Mulligan*, 107–108.

101 They were off the night before, August 12. That night Cecil Payne led a sextet at the Five Spot and the gig was recorded and released as *A Night at the Five Spot* (Signal S1204).

102 Harry Colomby interview, August 11, 2003.

103 Oral History interview with Wilbur B. Ware Sr. by Gloria L. Ware, December 18, 1977, p. 79.

104 Personnel Roster, Five Spot Cabaret Books, 1957; "Strictly Ad Lib," *Down Beat* (October 3, 1957), 14; Ahmed Abdul-Malik Interview with Ed Berger, "Jazz from the Archives," WBGO, recorded Jan. 30, 1984 (tape at IJS).

105 U.S. Census, 1930, *Population Schedule, Kings County, Brooklyn*, ED 24-571. According to the union directory, in 1948 Abdul-Malik went by Jonathan Timm and lived at 687 Halsey Street, apt. 33, Brooklyn. The following year's directory, 1949, he is listed as "Ahmad H. Abdul-Malik," still living on Halsey Street. *Local 802 of AFM Directory* (Newark: International Press, 1948), 125.

106 "Abdul-Malik, Âhmed," Questionnaire for Leonard Feather's Encyclopedia of Jazz, 1959, typescript, Institute for Jazz Studies, Rutgers; Ahmed Abdul-Malik Interview with Ed Berger, "Jazz from the Archives," WBGO, recorded Jan. 30, 1984. During the second half of 1956, Abdul-Malik was Weston's regular bass player and he appeared on two LPs recorded that fall, namely *Jazz a la Bohemia* (Riverside RLP 12-232) and *The Modern Art of Jazz* (Dawn DLP 1116).

107 Randy Weston interview, August 20, 2001.

108 Ahmed Abdul-Malik Interview with Ed Berger, "Jazz from the Archives," WBGO, recorded Jan. 30, 1984. For more on Ahmed Abdul-Malik, see my forthcoming book *Speaking in Tongues: Jazz and Modern Africa* (Cambridge: Harvard University Press).

109 Bill Coss, "The Philosophy of Ahmed Abdul-Malik," *Down Beat* (July 4, 1963), 14. His group consisted of Naim Karacand (violin), Jack Ghanaim (kanoon), Mike Hamway (darabeka—a metal vase with skin stretched across top), Bilal Abdurrahman (duf—large tambourine, without cymbals; and reed instruments).

110 Ahmed Abdul-Malik Interview with Ed Berger, "Jazz from the Archives," WBGO, recorded Jan. 30, 1984.

111 John S. Wilson, "Jazz Calms Down," *New York Times*, August 25, 1957.

112 A group led by Lou Donaldson and Donald Byrd substituted for Monk while he was on vacation. Shadow Wilson missed the first week, so Philly Joe Jones stepped in until September 12. Personnel Roster, Five Spot Cabaret Books, 1957.

113 "Strictly Ad Lib," *Down Beat* (November 14, 1957), 10.

114 The gig was announced in "Strictly Ad Lib," *Down Beat* (October 3, 1957), 62.

115 "Notables Support Benefit Concert," *New York Times*, October 2, 1955; "Opera Benefit October 25," *New York Times*, August 15, 1956.

116 "Strictly Ad Lib," *Down Beat* (December 26, 1957), 6; Whitney Balliett, "Jazz," *The New Yorker* (December 7, 1957), 208; "Center Plans Benefit," *New York Times*, November 3, 1957; "Benefit Jazz Concerts," *New York Times,* November 29, 1957; John S. Wilson, "Jazz Is Presented at Carnegie Hall," *New York Times*, November 30, 1957.

117 Whitney Balliett, "Jazz," *The New Yorker* (December 7, 1957), 208; John S. Wilson, "Jazz is Presented at Carnegie Hall," *New York Times*, November 30, 1957.

118 See liner notes to Thelonious Monk, *Thelonious Monk Quartet with John Coltrane at Carnegie Hall* (Blue Note 35173).

119 Jack Gould, "TV: Accent Was on Jazz," *New York Times*, December 9, 1957.

120 Hentoff, "The Private World of Thelonious Monk," 134.

121 First released in 1958 on Count Basie, et. al., *The Sound of Jazz* (Columbia CL1098).

122 Brown, "More Man than Myth," 14.

123 Harry Colomby interview, August 12, 2003.
124 *New York Times*, December 8, 1957.
125 On a few occasions Philly Joe Jones and Kenny Dennis subbed for Wilson. Personnel Roster, Five Spot Cabaret Books, 1957.
126 Nat Adderley sat in on December 20. Personnel Roster, Five Spot Cabaret Books, 1957.
127 Thomas Monk, Jr. interview, January 30, 2004.
128 Personnel Roster, Five Spot Cabaret Books, 1957. According to *Down Beat,* Oscar Pettiford's quintet joined Thelonious Monk's group for New Year's Eve, but the personnel rosters kept by Joe Termini indicate clearly that Monk's last night was the 26th. It is possible that Monk's band played with Pettiford's but without Monk. "Strictly Ad Lib," *Down Beat* (February 6, 1958), 8.
129 The ring begins to appear in photos of Monk in 1958. All of his family members have talked about this ring and how precious it was to him, and he tells the story of its origins in an interview with Pearl Gonzalez. See Gonzalez, "Monk Talk," *Down Beat* (October 28, 1971), 113.
130 Derek Ansell, "The Forgotten Ones: Ernie Henry," *Jazz Journal International* 40, no.9 (1987), 21; Jack Cooke: "Fading Flowers: a Note on Ernie Henry," *Jazz Monthly*, 7, no. 5 (1961), 9

19 "The Police Just Mess With You . . . For Nothing"

1 Josef von Sternberg, *Fun in a Chinese Laundry* (London: Secker and Warburg, 1965); John Baxter, *The Cinema of Josef Von Sternberg* (London: A. Zwimmer, 1971).
2 Thomas Hines, *Richard Neutra and the Search for Modern Architecture* (New York: Oxford University Press, 1982).
3 Hentoff, "The Jazz Baroness," 108; Kastin, "Nica's Story," 289.
4 Quoted in Pannonica de Koenigswarter, *Three Wishes*, 31–32.
5 Hentoff, "The Jazz Baroness," 99; Dore Ashton, "Art: Face of New York," *New York Times*, June 20, 1958.
6 Keepnews, *The View from Within*, 137; see also "Strictly Ad Lib," *Down Beat* (April 3, 1958), 8 for rumors on the session.
7 The one usable take wasn't released until after Monk died. It first appeared on Thelonious Monk, *Blues Five Spot* on Keepnews's Milestones label (M-9124).
8 "Strictly Ad Lib," *Down Beat* (April 17, 1958), 61. At the same time, Coltrane frequented Nica's place throughout April and May and rehearsed with Monk and Wilbur Ware, despite having already joined Miles Davis. "Rehearsal at Mad Pad with Coltrane, and Wilbur Ware and Monk," April 1958, Reel #49, The Pannonica Collection, 1956–1970.
9 Sheridan has Monk there for two weeks (*Brilliant Corners*, 378), but the Vanguard advertised Monk's second opening on May 6. *New York Times*, May 6, 1958; see also, *New York Times*, May 11, 1958.
10 *Village Voice*, April 2, 1958; "Strictly Ad Lib," *Down Beat* (May 1, 1958), 8; Strictly Ad Lib," *Down Beat* (June 12, 1958), 8. A band made up of Stan Getz, Bob Brookmeyer, Jerry Segal, Knobby Totah, and Wynton Kelly substituted for Monk the night of April 1st. "Strictly Ad Lib," *Down Beat* (May 15, 1958), 8.
11 Max Gordon, *Live at the Village Vanguard*, 99. Later in the year, Monk told writer Frank London Brown that he generally refused to do matinees. Brown, "More Man than Myth,"15.
12 It worked out well because on a few Sunday nights, customers had the privilege of hearing Langston Hughes read his poetry with a jazz combo. *New York Times*, May 11, 1958; Jesse H. Walker, "Theatricals," *Amsterdam News*, May 10, 1958.
13 T. S. Monk interview, April 4, 2005.
14 Harry Colomby interview, August 11, 2003.
15 Ibid.
16 Keepnews, *The View from Within*, 125.
17 "Strictly Ad Lib," *Down Beat* (June 26, 1958), 8.
18 Wilbur Ware was slated for the session but never showed up.
19 Clark Terry Interview with Steve Voce, part II, Jazz Institute of Chicago, www.jazzinstituteofchicago.org. Originally published in *Jazz Journal* (1985).
20 Clark Terry, *In Orbit* (Riverside RLP 12-271).
21 John S. Wilson, "Jazz Musicians Kick Over Old Traces on LP," *New York Times*, October 19, 1958.
22 Clark Terry Interview with Steve Voce, part II.
23 Associated Musicians of Greater New York, Local 802, Contract, June 3, 1958, copy in David and Toni Behm's possession.
24 Ad, *Village Voice*, July 23, 1958; Joe Termini resume (undated), in possession of Toni Behm; Iggy Termini interview, March 5, 2008.
25 Personnel Roster, Five Spot Cabaret Books, 1958. According to Johnny Griffin, Monk had tried several times to hire Art Blakey in place of Haynes, but I've not found any other corroborating evidence. Johnny Griffin interview, February 2, 2004; Hennessey, *The Little Giant*, 81.
26 "Strictly Ad Lib," *Down Beat* (July 24, 1958), 52; Personnel Roster, Five Spot Cabaret Books, 1958. On a typical night, by the beginning of the second set "there were no empty tables . . . and there were clusters of standees along the length of the bar. Robert A. Perlongo, "A Night of Thelonious," *Metronome* (August 1959), 19.
27 Johnny Griffin interview, February 2, 2004. He tells the same story in Jean Bach, *A Great Day in Harlem* (Home Vision Entertainment, 2005, 1994), supplemental DVD.
28 Griffin quoted in Ben Sidran, *Talking Jazz*, 201–202.
29 Ibid., 202.

30 Robert Perlongo witnessed the band play "A Night in Tunisia" during one of his visits to the Five Spot that summer of 1958. See Perlongo, "A Night of Thelonious," 19.

31 "Dreamland" has been mislabeled and misrepresented many times. Sheridan confuses it with the E. Ray Goetz and John Ringling North composition of the same title, and when it was released on the Black Lion label in 1971, it was listed as "Meet Me Tonight in Dreamland," the 1904 composition by Leo Friedman and Beth Slater Wilson. But I have reviewed both songs, along with dozens of other songs with the title "Dreamland" (Harry L. Newman's "Take Me Back to Dreamland," Harold Arlen's "Hit the Road to Dreamland," Francis Paul, "Dreamland," *ad nauseam.*) None of these songs bear any resemblance to what Monk played on those two occasions. After ten years of searching, querying, and digging, I have come to the same conclusion that Jacques Ponzio and François Postif have come to: it is a Monk original. Perhaps it is a sketch of a song never quite finished.

32 "Strictly Ad Lib," *Down Beat* (October 2, 1958), 10; Keepnews, *The View from Within*, 138–139.

33 Released in 1984 as *Blues Five Spot* (Milestone M-9124)

34 Kofi Ghanaba [Guy Warren] interview, August 13, 2004.

35 "Jazz Star from Africa Shines on Radio Airer," *Chicago Defender*, October 16, 1956; Al Monroe, "So They Say," *Chicago Defender*, March 12, 1956; Baker E. Morten, "African Drummer Beats His Way to Music Fame," *Chicago Defender,* March 2, 1957. He recorded the album with the Gene Esposito band and it was released as *Africa Speaks, America Answers* (Decca 8446). For more on Warren, see my forthcoming book, *Speaking in Tongues: Jazz and Modern Africa* (Harvard University Press).

36 Warren's biography is drawn from Kofi Ghanaba [Guy Warren] interview, August 13, 2004; Warren, *I Have a Story to Tell*, 13–17.

37 Guy Warren, *Themes for African Drums* (RCA/Victor LSP 1864).

38 Liner notes, *Themes for African Drums*; Kofi Ghanaba [Guy Warren] interview, August 13, 2004.

39 Kofi Ghanaba [Guy Warren] interview, August 13, 2004.

40 It was recorded on October 22, 1959, and released on Thelonious Monk, *Alone in San Francisco* (Riverside RLP 12-312).

41 Kofi Ghanaba [Guy Warren] interview, August 15, 2004.

42 Ibid.

43 T. S. Monk interview, April 4, 2005.

44 Ads and press releases, *Village Voice*, June 18, 1958; *Chicago Defender*, July 5, 1958; Michael Jackson, "Backstage with Henry Grimes," *Down Beat* (July 2005), 14; Bob Reisner, "The Newport Scene," *Village Voice* (July 23, 1958), 7. On Monk's repertoire that afternoon, see Sheridan, *Brilliant Corners*, 84.

45 Anita O'Day, with George Eells, *High Times, Hard Times* (New York: Limelight Editions, 1989), 243–44; Wein, *Myself Among Others*, 189; Scott Saul, *Freedom Is, Freedom Ain't: Jazz and the Making of the Sixties* (Cambridge and London: Harvard University Press, 2003), 113–117.

46 Saul, *Freedom Is, Freedom Ain't*, 114–117; Brook Cormer, "Reminiscing About 'Jazz on a Summer's Day,' " *American Cinematographer,* 79, no. 1 (January 1998), 20, 22; Wein, *Myself Among Others*, 189. The boat race apparently did not take place during Monk's performance, but was added later for effect. On the America's Cup, see Leonard O. Warner, "Rhode Island's Specials—Yachting and Jazz," *New York Times*, June 8, 1958.

47 All of the artists in the film were paid less than $1,000, except for Louis Armstrong. Joe Glaser, Armstrong's agent, demanded $25,000 for his client. Cormer, "Reminiscing About 'Jazz on a Summer's Day,' " 22.

48 See ads in *Amsterdam News*, August 2, 1958; "If You Can't Dig, Don't Read This," in *Amsterdam News*, August 2, 1958; *New York Times*, August 3, 10, and 21, 1958; *Village Voice*, August 20, 1958.

49 John S. Wilson, "Jazz: Playing It Safe," *New York Times*, August 25, 1958.

50 "International Jazz Critics Poll," *Down Beat* (August 21, 1958), 13. He did well in the Readers' Poll as well, placing second behind Garner and just ahead of Peterson. *Down Beat Music '59: Fourth Annual Yearbook* (1959), 97.

51 Altschuler quoted in Jean Bach, *A Great Day in Harlem* (Home Vision Entertainment, 2005, 1994).

52 Jean Bach, *A Great Day in Harlem.*

53 Ibid.

54 Harry Colomby interview, August 12, 2003.

55 "Strictly Ad Lib," *Down Beat* (October 2, 1958), 51; "Strictly Ad Lib," *Down Beat* (October 30, 1958), 6; "Monk et les liaisons dangereuses," *Jazz Magazine* 52, no. 5 (October 1959), 20.

56 Marcel Romano, "De Saint-Germain des Pres au New York: Au Five Spot," *Jazz Hot* 125 (October 1957), 24.

57 Szwed, *So What*, 151–56.

58 "Strictly Ad Lib," *Down Beat* (August 21, 1958), 6.

59 "Ivan Black, 75, a Publicity Agent." *New York Times*, March 27, 1979.

60 Frank London Brown, *Trumbull Park* (Chicago: Henry Regnery, 1959); Les Brownlee, "Frank London Brown—Courageous Author," *Sepia* (June 1960), 26–30; "Ex-Trumbull Resident Pens Short Story," *Chicago Defender*, May 2, 1957. On the integration of the Trumbull Park Homes, see Arnold R. Hirsch, "Massive Resistance in the Urban North: Trumbull Park, Chicago, 1953–1966," *Journal of American History* 82, no. 2 (September 1955), 522–550; Adam Green, *Selling the Race: Culture, Community, and Black Chicago, 1940–1955* (Chicago: University of Chicago Press, 2007), 184–192. Stephen Grant Meyer, *As Long as They Don't Move Next Door: Segregation and Racial Conflict in American Neighborhoods* (Lantham, MD: Rowman and Littlefield, 2001), 121.

61 "Personality Spotlight," *Chicago Defender*, December 19, 1959; Sterling Stuckey, "Frank London Brown: A Remembrance," in Abraham Chapman, ed., *Black Voices: An Anthology of Afro-American Literature* (New York: New American Library, 1968), 669–676 (quote from p. 670); Mary Helen Washington, "Desegregating the 1950s: The Case of Frank London Brown," *Japanese Journal of American Studies* 10 (1999), 22. *Trumbull Park*

was reprinted by Northeastern University Press in 2005, and it includes an excellent foreword by Mary Helen Washington. Sterling Stuckey's moving memoir of Brown was also published as the introduction to *The Myth Maker* (Chicago: Path Press, 1969), 1–11.

62 Quoted in Brownlee, "Frank London Brown—Courageous Author," 30.

63 Frank London Brown to Ivan Black, August 13, 1958, Box 7, Ivan Black Papers, JPB 06-20, Music Division, The New York Public Library for the Performing Arts. (Hereafter Ivan Black Papers.)

64 See *Chicago Defender*, June 16 and 23, July 14, 1958; Lee Blackwell, "Off the Record," *Chicago Defender*, August 14, 1958 and October 13, 1958; Frank London Brown to Ivan Black, August 13, 1958, Box 7, Ivan Black Papers; Evelyn Colbert interview, January 26, 2009.

65 Brown, "More Man than Myth," 14; Evelyn Colbert interview, January 26, 2009.

66 Brown, "More Man than Myth," 15.

67 Ibid., 45. He later recanted the quote in an interview for the French jazz magazine *Jazz Hot*. François Postif, "'Round 'Bout Sphere," *Jazz Hot* (April 1963), 41.

68 Paul Bacon interview, July 30, 2001.

69 Ibid.; Chris Albertson interview, July 11, 2003; *Philadelphia Bulletin*, August 31, 1959; Jesse H. Walker, "Theatricals," *Amsterdam News*, July 25, 1959.

70 In the liner notes for the re-issue of *Monk Plays Ellington*, Keepnews was clear that the redesign was inspired by the fact that Monk's audience "has clearly become many times broader than it was when this album was first issued."

71 Paul Bacon interview, July 30, 2001

72 Ibid.

73 Sam Hunter and John Jacobus, *Modern Art* (New York: Prentice Hall and Harry N. Abrams, 1992, 3rd Ed.), 165. Frank London Brown described Monk's music as "mathematical." He wrote that Monk's "facility with mathematical problems has been a guide in the study of basic musical problems of harmony, rhythm, and melody." Brown, "More Man than Myth," 15.

74 Perlongo, "A Night of Thelonious," 19.

75 Personnel Roster, Five Spot Cabaret Books, 1958; Coltrane quoted in Porter, *John Coltrane*, 136. These recordings were released by Blue Note in 1993 as Thelonious Monk, *Live at the Five Spot: Discovery!* (Blue Note CDP7-99786-2).

76 Coltrane is listed as a frequent visitor on the reel list for The Pannonica Collection, 1956–1970. Monk family members confirm Coltrane's jam sessions with Monk at Nica's house.

77 Porter, *John Coltrane*, 136.

78 Johnny Griffin interview, February 2, 2004.

79 Ibid.; "Strictly Ad Lib," *Down Beat* (October 30, 1958), 39. Even before Rollins joined Monk, rumors were flying that the two were about to go on tour together. *Down Beat* reported, "Sonny Rollins is scheduled to go to England and the continent in October, for a three- to five-week tour, with Thelonious Monk, Johnny Griffin, and a bass man and drummer to be named." "Strictly Ad Lib," *Down Beat* (August 21, 1958), 6.

80 Rollins was with Monk from September 19 to October 1, 1958. Personnel Roster, Five Spot Cabaret Books, 1958. The concert took place on Saturday, September 20. Ad, *Amsterdam News*, September 20, 1958. As a result of the concert, Monk missed the first set at the Five Spot; pianist Myke Schiffer sat in for Thelonious during the first set. "Strictly Ad Lib," *Down Beat* (October 30, 1958), 39. On the Bel Canto Foundation, see Dahl, *Morning Glory*, 265–76; Kernodle, *Soul on Soul*, 190–199.

81 Danson, "Interview: Charlie Rouse," 6; David A. Franklin, "Charlie Rouse Interview," *Cadence* 13, no. 6 (1987), 7; see also, "Strictly Ad Lib," *Down Beat* (November 13, 1958), 54.

82 Nellie Monk interview January 12, 2002. This story was confirmed for me by Herbie Hancock. (Conversation with Herbie Hancock, Washington, D.C.)

83 David Amram interview, July 15, 2003.

84 See Danson, "Interview: Charlie Rouse," 5–6; DeMicheal, "Charlie Rouse," 17–18; Franklin, "Charlie Rouse Interview," 5–6; J. L. Ginibre, "La Longue Marche de Charlie," *Jazz Magazine* 105 (1964), 20–21; Jef Langford, "Monk's Horns," Part II *Jazz Journal* (January1971), 7; Peter Keepnews, "Rouse and Nica," *Down Beat* (April 1989), 59–60.

85 Sandra Capello interview, July 19, 2003; T. S. Monk interview, April 4, 2005. Rouse never denied his addiction. See, Eric C. Schneider, *Smack: Heroin and the American City* (University of Pennsylvania Press, 2008), 29; Ira Gitler, ed., *Swing to Bop*, 281.

86 Paul Jeffrey interview, August 31, 2003; T. S. Monk, interview, April 4, 2005. Orelia first managed Les Jazz Modes, but then took on Rouse as an individual client. "Les Modes Quintet Masters Refreshing New Jazz Sound," *Pittsburgh Courier*, May 31, 1958; "Izzy Rowe's Notebook," *Pittsburgh Courier*, September 29, 1956. On Princess Orelia Benskina, see "Orelia Benskina." *Marquis Who's Who*™, 2008. Reproduced in *Biography Resource Center*. Farmington Hills, Mich.: Gale, 2008. http://galenet.galegroup.com/servlet/BioRC; John O. Perpener, *African-American Concert Dance: The Harlem Renaissance and Beyond* (Urbana: University of Illinois Press, 2001), 125. Known as Margarita Orelia Benskina, she would go on to a distinguished career as a poet, scholar, socialite and Harlem celebrity. Her volumes of poetry include *I Have Loved You Already* (Hicksville, NY: Exposition, 1976); *I Thank You Father* (Hicksville, NY: Exposition, 1976); *No Longer Defeated and Other Poems* (New York: Carlton Press, 1972). She passed away in 2002.

87 U.S. Census, 1920, *Population Schedule, Kingston Ward 4, Lenoir, North Carolina*, ED 60. Both of his parents were literate.

88 U.S. Census, 1930, *Population Schedule, Washington, D.C.*, ED 234. They lived at 401 M Street near 4th Street, worth $8,000 in 1930. Mary and Williams were eighteen and twenty-two, respectively, when they were married. Also, the 1930 Census states that Mary was born in West Virginia and both children, Charles and his

older sister, were born in D.C. Rouse himself says he was born in West Virginia, however. Danson, "Interview: Charlie Rouse," 5.

89   Danson, "Interview: Charlie Rouse," 5.
90   Ibid., 5; Franklin, "Charlie Rouse Interview," 5–6.
91   The first rehearsal tapes Nica made with Rouse and Monk begin on October 2, though this is not to say they did not rehearse before then. Reel #1—October 2, 1958, Reel #56—October 1958, The Pannonica Collection, 1956–1970, Reel list.
92   Franklin, "Charlie Rouse Interview," 7; see also Humphrey Lyttelton, "Monk is Fantastic," *Melody Maker* (June 17, 1961), 5.
93   Ibid., 7.
94   Ibid., 8.
95   Danson, "Interview: Charlie Rouse," p. 6.
96   DeMicheal, "Charlie Rouse," 18.
97   Thelonious Records released these tapes on CD as Thelonious Monk, *Live in New York: Vols. 1 and 2* (Thelonious Records TMNY).
98   Franklin, "Charlie Rouse Interview," 8.
99   Nica de Koenigswarter quoted in Gordon, *Live at the Village Vanguard*, 119–120. Nica remembers it being "blistering hot," but the highs between New York and Baltimore were between 55 and 60, perhaps a little warm for October but hardly "blistering hot." "Weather Reports Throughout Nation and Abroad," *New York Times*, October 15, 1958.
100 Superior Court of Delaware, New Castle County, The STATE of Delaware v. Nica DE KOENIGSWARTER, also known as Kathleen de Koenigswarter. Jan. 19, 1962, 177 A.2d 344 (Del. Super. 1962); Baker E. Morten, "Nabbed in Motel with Baroness Koenigswarter," *Baltimore Afro-American*, October 25, 1958; "Baroness, Jazz Pianist in a Jam—with Cops," *New York Post*, October 16, 1958; On the Park Plaza Motel, see "Route 40 Scrapbook," http://route40.net/scrapbook/de/page03.shtml.
101 Quoted in Gordon, *Live at the Village Vanguard*, 120; Lapham, "Monk: High Priest of Jazz," 74.
102 One columnist for the *Baltimore Afro-American* compared the response to racial mixing in Delaware with that of Mississippi. Baker E. Morten, "Monk's Mysterious Arrest in Delaware," *Baltimore Afro-American*, October 25, 1958.
103 "Baroness, Jazz Pianist in a Jam—with Cops."
104 Superior Court of Delaware, New Castle County, The STATE of Delaware v. Nica DE KOENIGSWARTER; Baker E. Morten, "Nabbed in Motel with Baroness Koenigswarter"; "Baroness, Jazz Pianist in a Jam—with Cops."
105 Quoted in Gordon, *Live at the Village Vanguard*, 120.
106 Superior Court of Delaware, New Castle County, The STATE of Delaware v. Nica DE KOENIGSWARTER.
107 Quoted in Gordon, *Live at the Village Vanguard*, 120.
108 Superior Court of Delaware, New Castle County, The STATE of Delaware v. Nica DE KOENIGSWARTER; "Baroness, Jazz Pianist in a Jam—with Cops."
109 Lapham, "Monk: High Priest of Jazz," 74.
110 "Baroness, Jazz Pianist in a Jam—with Cops"; Director of FBI to Legat, Tokyo (163–2971), cablegram, September 3, 1970, Thelonious Monk FBI File; Hentoff, "The Private World of Thelonious Monk," 134; Baker E. Morten, "Nabbed in Motel with Baroness Koenigswarter."
111 Nica told Max Gordon that they, in fact, did make the gig (Gordon, *Live at the Village Vanguard*, 120), but the press reports at the time state unequivocably that the engagement had to be postponed. "Collapses on Way to Court," *Amsterdam News*, October 25, 1958
112 "Baroness, Jazz Pianist in a Jam—with Cops."
113 "Collapses on Way to Court"; Irma Lawson, "Stormy Hearing for Pianist Monk," *Baltimore Afro-American*, November 1, 1958.
114 On Nix, see Jeanne D. Nutter, *Delaware* (Mt. Pleasant, SC: Arcadia Publishing, 2000), 120.
115 Irma Lawson, "Stormy Hearing for Pianist Monk."
116 "Monk Fined for Using His Hands," *Amsterdam News*, November 29, 1958.
117 Irma Lawson, "Stormy Hearing for Pianist Monk"; Superior Court of Delaware, New Castle County, The STATE of Delaware v. Nica DE KOENIGSWARTER; Hentoff, "The Private World of Thelonious Monk," 134.
118 Eric Larrabee, "Jazz Notes," *Harpers* (January 1959), 97.
119 Brown, "More Man than Myth," 14–15; *Down Beat Music '59: Fourth Annual Yearbook* (1959), 21. In the wake of Brown's article, several essays came out referring to Brown's interview. See for example, Charles Edward Smith, "The Mad Monk," *Nugget* (October 1958), 53, 68, 70; Gene Balliet, "Busman's Holiday," *Cincinnati Inquirer*, October 27, 1958.
120 Copy in author's possession. Registered with Library of Congress October 2, 1958, It was released in October of 1958 and included three songs: "Ba-Lue Bolivar Ba-Lues-Are," "Brilliant Corners," and "Functional."
121 Gunther Schuller, "Thelonious Monk: Review," *Jazz Review* 1 (November, 1958), 22–27, quote on p. 27. There were several essays that followed celebrating Monk's work and newfound importance. See, for example, G. Coulter, "Clark Terry with Thelonious Monk: In Orbit," *Jazz Review* 2 (Jan. 1959): 37–38; J. McKinney, "Giants in Jazz," *Music USA* 76 (January 1959), 21.
122 Curiously, Charlie Rouse did not lose his cabaret card. He continued to work on and off at the Five Spot in the months of November and December. Personnel Roster, Five Spot Cabaret Books, 1958.
123 T. S. Monk interview, April 4, 2005.
124 *Amsterdam News*, November 8, 1958.

125 John S. Wilson, "Music: Jazz Concert," *New York Times*, November 29, 1958.
126 Stephen Fleischman, *A Red in the House: The Unauthorized Memoir of S. E. Fleischman* (New York: Universe Inc., 2004), 31–43, 52–58. The best historical overview of the show can be found in Richard C. Bartone, "*The Twentieth Century* (CBS, 1957–1966) Television Series: A History and Analysis" (Ph.D. dissertation, New York University, 1985).
127 "Generation without a Cause: Part I—Self-Portrait," *The Twentieth Century* (CBS), aired March 1, 1959. Copy of episode in author's possession, courtesy of CBS.
128 Joe Termini remembered that they shot the segment around 8:00 a.m., but his recollections of who filled the space differed. He remembered having to stop passers-by and offering them a dollar "and you get all the beer you can drink" in order to create an audience. Perhaps a few members of the audience came that route, but it is clear from the footage that the same young people sitting in the Five Spot are the same people who appear on campus at Rutgers. Joe Termini interviewed by Phil Schaap, WKCR, October 10, 1989.
129 Harry Colomby interview, March 30, 2008.
130 Discerning viewers might have noticed four black men and one black woman seated in a distant corner behind the bass player. They appear for a split-second as the camera covers the bandstand from another angle, but otherwise remain beyond the camera's frame.
131 "Generation without a Cause: Part I—Self-Portrait," *The Twentieth Century* (CBS), aired March 1, 1959.

20 "Make Sure Them Tempos Are Right"

1 Hentoff, "Just Call Him Thelonious," 16.
2 Gitler, "Ira Gitler Interviews Thelonious Monk," 20.
3 The exact address was 821 Sixth Avenue.
4 David X. Young claims that he rented three floors, made some minor improvements, and sublet two of the floors to Overton and Cary. Sam Stephenson, Eugene Smith's biographer, discovered that all three men moved in at the same time and rented directly from the owner, Al Esformes. On Young, see "DXY on DXY," http://www.davidxyoung.com/artist/dxy/index.html; David Szpunar and Melanie Dante, "'There Are Pictures in Your Paintings!': An Interview with David X. Young," http://www.black-dahlia.org/dxy.html.
5 Jim Hughes, *Shadow and Substance: The Life and Work of an American Photographer* (New York: McGraw-Hill Publishers, 1989), 369–70; Sam Stephenson, "Nights of Incandescence," *DoubleTake Magazine*, 18 (Fall 1999), 48–49. For the definitive history of the loft, see Sam Stephenson, *The Jazz Loft Project: Photographs and Tapes of W. Eugene Smith from 821 Sixth Avenue, 1957–1965* (New York: Random House, 2009).
6 Harry Colomby interview, August 12, 2003.
7 Quoted in Stephenson, "Nights of Incandescence," 48.
8 Young also recorded some of these impromptu jam sessions, some of which were released as the two-CD set, *David X. Young's Jazz Loft, 1954–1965* (Jazz Magnet B00004YL9T).
9 Overton had been subletting the space to artist Harold Feinstein before Smith moved in. Jim Hughes, *Shadow and Substance*, 376.
10 See Sam Stephenson's introduction to *Dream Street: W. Eugene Smith's Pittsburgh Project* (New York: W.W. Norton, 2003); Stephenson, *The Jazz Loft Project*. See also Jim Hughes, *Shadow and Substance*, 371–388.
11 Virtually all of these precious tapes have been preserved by Sam Stephenson and the Jazz Loft Project, housed at the Center for Documentary Studies, Duke University. I'm grateful to Sam for granting me early access to these materials, which I will refer to as the Eugene Smith Collection.
12 CCP 28 (Disc 1): "Thelonious and Hall," "More of Thelonious and Hall (Some of Hall playing fragments, still preliminary searchings and rehearsals)," Eugene Smith Collection.
13 Monk quoted in "CCP 30 (Disc 1): Monk, Hall Rehearsal Tapes, 1959," Eugene Smith Collection.
14 One can hear this process on most of the tapes with just Monk and Overton (and often Jules Colomby can be heard in the background). See especially, "CCP 30 (Discs 1 and 2): Monk, Hall Rehearsal Tapes, 1959," "CCP 112 Monk and Overton, 1959," and "CCP 24: 'Little Rootie Tootie'—Mostly Dialogue & Search," Eugene Smith Collection, Duke University.
15 CCP 24: "Little Rootie Tootie" "Mostly Dialogue & Search," Eugene Smith Collection.
16 CCP 24: "Little Rootie Tootie" "Mostly Dialogue & Search," Eugene Smith Collection.
17 CCP 30 (Disc 1): Monk, Hall Rehearsal Tapes, 1959, Eugene Smith Collection.
18 CCP 112 Monk and Overton, 1959, Eugene Smith Collection.
19 CCP 30 (Disc 1): Monk, Hall Rehearsal Tapes, 1959, Eugene Smith Collection.
20 CCP 24: "Little Rootie Tootie" "Mostly Dialogue & Search," Eugene Smith Collection.
21 Gunther Schuller criticized the ensemble for being "too bottom-heavy." Schuller, "Thelonious Monk at Town Hall," *Jazz Review* 2 (June 1959), 7.
22 David Amram interview, July 15, 2003.
23 Quoted in Dan Gilgoff, "Brother from Another Planet," *Washington City Paper* 20, no. 5 (February 4–10, 2000), http://www.washingtoncitypaper.com. Northern is better known as Brother Ah. He went on to a distinguished career in both the jazz and classical world, playing with the likes of John Coltrane, Gil Evans Orchestra, and Sun Ra. He later joined the faculties at Dartmouth College and Brown University.
24 Brother Ah interview by Sam Stephenson, June 29, 2008. Used by Permission.
25 CCP 112 Monk and Overton, 1959, Eugene Smith Collection.
26 Ad, *Chicago Defender*, January 31, 1959; "Jazz Concert," *Chicago Tribune*, February 1, 1959; "Jazznotes," *Down Beat* (February 19, 1959), 47.
27 Frank London Brown, "Magnificent Monk of Music," 121.

28 Evelyn Colbert interview, January 26, 2009.
29 Arthur Taylor interview, conducted by Warren Smith, July 26, 1994, Jazz Oral History Project, Schomburg Center for Research in Black Culture.
30 Paul B. Matthews, "Eddie Bert: Interview, Part 2," trans. Susan F. Matthews, *Cadence* (February 1992), 15.
31 Brother Ah interview with Sam Stephenson, June 29, 2008.
32 Quoted in Sidran, ed., *Jazz Talk*, 214.
33 CCP 39 (Disc 2): "Thelonious Monk in Early Rehearsals . . . Made at Hall's, 1959," Eugene Smith Collection.
34 CCP 37: "Thelonious Monk, February 27, 1959," Eugene Smith Collection. Nat Hentoff, who was at this rehearsal, recounted the same exchange from memory, though he never mentions the trumpet player by name. According to Hentoff, Monk said, "If you know the melody . . . you can make a better solo and you won't sound as if you're just running changes." Quoted in Hentoff, *The Jazz Life*, 201–202.
35 CCP 31 (Disc 1): February 27, 1959, "Rootie Tootie, etc." and CCP 32 (Disc 1): "February 27, 1959" "Thelonious Monk Rehearsals at Hall's," Eugene Smith Collection.
36 Brother Ah, interview with Sam Stephenson. He tells the same story in Dan Gilgoff, "Brother from Another Planet," http://www.washingtoncitypaper.com.
37 Matthews, "Eddie Bert Interview, Part 2," 15.
38 Bob Rolontz, "Much Town Hall—Too Little Monk," *Billboard* 71, no. 10 (March 9, 1959), 16.
39 Rolontz, "Much Town Hall—Too Little Monk," 16. See also Orrin Keepnews liner notes, *The Thelonious Monk Orchestra at Town Hall* (RLP 12–300).
40 Three of the five recordings were released on Thelonious Monk, *San Francisco Holiday* (Milestone 9199) and all recordings are available on *The Complete Riverside Recordings of Thelonious Monk*.
41 Keepnews, *The View from Within*, 139.
42 Whitney Balliet, "A Celebration for Monk," *New Yorker* (March 7, 1959), 156.
43 John S. Wilson, "Thelonious Monk Plays His Own Works," *New York Times*, March 2, 1959.
44 All quotes and references from the segment are taken directly from "Generation without a Cause: Part I—Self-Portrait," *The Twentieth Century* (CBS), aired March 1, 1959. Copy of episode in author's possession, courtesy of CBS.
45 The first march took place on October 25, 1958, and a follow-up march was already in the works when "Generation without a Cause" aired. The second march occurred on April 18, 1959. See, "Set D.C. Youth March October 25," *Chicago Defender*, October 20, 1958; "Negro, White Youths March in D.C. Today," *Atlanta Daily World*, October 25, 1958; "Harry Belafonte, Jack Robinson Lead Integrated Schools March," *Washington Post*, October 26, 1958; Evelyn Cunningham, "10,000 Jam Capitol for Youth March," *Pittsburgh Courier*, November 1, 1958; "Ike Plays Golf; Youth for Integration Rebuffed," *Chicago Defender*, October 27, 1958; "State 'Day' Proclaimed," *New York Times*, October 26, 1958; Clayborne Carson, et. al., ed., *The Papers of Martin Luther King, Jr. – Volume 5: Threshold of a New Decade, January 1959–December 1960* (Los Angeles and Berkeley: University of California Press, 1992), 14–18.
46 Wilson, "Thelonious Monk Plays His Own Works."
47 Rolontz, "Much Town Hall—Too Little Monk," 16.
48 Robert A. Perlongo, "Tristano and Monk," *Metronome* (April 1959), 33.
49 Balliet, "A Celebration for Monk," 154.
50 Ibid., 155.
51 Schuller, "Thelonious Monk at Town Hall," 6.
52 T. S. Monk interview, April 4, 2005; Pepper Adams says the same thing, see Sidran, ed., *Jazz Talk*, 214–215.
53 Harry Colomby interview, August 12, 2003; Bar-Thel Music was officially incorporated on April 3, 1959. Thelonious Monk and Nellie Monk, federal tax returns, 1972, in author's possession; Press release, "Thelonious Monk Joins BMI," from New Department of BMI, Vertical Files, Institute for Jazz Studies; "Thelonius [sic] Monk Hits Jackpot with Records," *Chicago Defender*, May 23, 1959; "Strictly Ad Lib," *Down Beat* (June 25, 1959), 49. As compensation for administering Bar-Thel Music, Colomby took 20 percent of the proceeds, though he told me that he returned most of his share to the estate.
54 "Jazz Star Miles Davis Shares With Ruth Brown at Apollo Theater," *New York Age*, March 14, 1959.
55 Schiffman quoted in Ted Fox, *Showtime at the Apollo* (New York: Da Capo Press, 1993), 271.
56 Fox, *Showtime at the Apollo*, 271; "House Reviews," *Variety* 214 (March 18, 1959), 87; Harry Colomby interview, August 11, 2003.
57 John S. Wilson, "Concert at Town Hall," *New York Times*, March 30, 1959. They performed two shows that night. Ad, *Village Voice*, March 4, 1959; "Strictly Ad Lib," *Down Beat* (April 16, 1959), 56.
58 Hentoff, "The Private World of Thelonious Monk," 134.
59 Wein, *Myself Among Others*, 218.
60 Conversation with Ananda Sattwa, n.d.
61 (Quote) Wein, *Myself Among Others*, 218; Hentoff, "The Private World of Thelonious Monk," 134.
62 Hentoff, "The Private World of Thelonious Monk," 134.
63 "Castro Departs to Joy of Police," *New York Times*, April 26, 1959; "Students Impress Castro," *New York Times*, April 27, 1959.
64 Harry Colomby interview, August 11, 2003; Hentoff, "The Private World of Thelonious Monk," 134; Wein, *Myself Among Others*, 218; Farrell, "Loneliest Monk," 85
65 "Grafton State Hospital," http://www.1856.org/grafton/grafton.html. In 1945, Grafton State Hospital counted 1,730, with a total staff of 250 with 241 vacancies, but the number of patients began to decline slowly by the late 1950s. My figure of 1,500, therefore, is purely an estimate.
66 Nellie Monk interview, January 12, 2002; Harry Colomby interview, August 11, 2003; Hentoff, "The Private World of Thelonious Monk," 134; Wein, *Myself Among Others*, 218; Farrell, "Loneliest Monk," 85.

67 See Michael J. Gitlin, M.D., *The Psychotherapists Guide to Psychopharmacology* (New York: Free Press, 1990), 75, 130, 287–88, 290–94; Wes Lindamood, "Thorazine," *Chemical and Engineering News*, 83, no. 25 (June 20, 2005), http://pubs.acs.org/cen/coverstory/83/8325/8325thorazine.html; "Thorazine Side Effects," http://www.drugs.com/sfx/thorazine-side-effects.html. Nellie Monk and her cousin, Dr. Anna Lou Smith, noticed most, if not all, of these side effects in Monk. Nellie Monk interview, January 12, 2002; Anna Lou Smith interview, April 7, 2004.

68 Clifton Smith interview, July 27, 2004. Monk's reliance on Chapstick was confirmed by virtually all of my interviews with family members, though they did not know the chapped lips were a side effect of the Thorazine.

69 See Wes Lindamood, "Thorazine"; "Thorazine Side Effects," http://www.drugs.com/sfx/thorazine-side-effects .html. Smith remembers clearly that Monk was on Thorazine when he and Nellie visited Los Angeles in October of 1959. This kind of involuntary movement is also known as tardive dyskinesia.

70 Harry Colomby interview, August 11, 2003.

71 Robert Freymann, *What's So Bad About Feeling Good?* (New York: Playboy Paperbacks, 1981).

72 Boyce Rensberger, "Two Doctors Here Known to Users as Source of Amphetamines," *New York Times*, March 25, 1973.

73 T. S. Monk, interview, April 4, 2005.

74 R. Rondanelli, *Clinical Pharmacology of Drug Interaction* (Pavia, Italy: PICCIN, 1988), 696.

75 Geraldine Smith interview, February 12, 2004; T. S. Monk, interview, April 4, 2005; Evelyn Smith interview, July 5, 2005.

76 "Strictly Ad Lib," *Down Beat* (May 28, 1959), 45; "Thelonious, Dinah, Her Sons at the Apollo," *Amsterdam News*, June 6, 1959. Sheridan has Monk's quartet at Hank's for two weeks, but the only notice for the gig appeared in *Down Beat* and it indicates that the club will be offering "two weeks of jazz nightly with Thelonious Monk, the Duke Ellington orchestra, Maynard Ferguson's band, Buddy Rich's big band, and Lionel Hampton, all following each other." In other words, they appeared on successive days within a two-week period rather than one two-week show with all of these bands on the same bill. Therefore, Monk's group might have played two or three days at most. On the Apollo engagement, Monk's group was there from June 5–11.

77 His last studio date was as a sideman with Clark Terry in May of 1958. The last studio album he had made was with Gerry Mulligan, recorded in August of 1957.

78 According to Keepnews, Monk believed Thad was "seriously underappreciated." Orrin Keepnews liner notes, *Thelonious Monk, Five by Five* (RLP 12-305).

79 Tony Gieske, "Accent on Jazz," *Washington Post*, September 13, 1959.

80 A Lydian mode runs from the fourth degree of the major scale to an octave above, so for B♭ Lydian, the notes are: B♭–C–D–E–F–G–A–B♭. The anchoring chord for Monk is B♭ maj. 7 #11. On Monk's use of Lydian harmony, see Lawrence Koch, "Thelonious Monk: Compositional Techniques," *Annual Review of Jazz Studies* 2 (1983), 67.

81 Jackie Bonneau interview, January 30, 2004.

82 Art Taylor once said that his solo on "Jackie-ing" was his most famous drum solo, but besides the introduction he really doesn't solo on this recording. Arthur Taylor interview, conducted by Warren Smith Jazz, July 26, 1994, Oral History Project, Schomburg.

83 "Thelonious Monk en Europe," *Jazz Hot* 12 (April 1959), 7; "Jazz et Cinema," *Jazz Hot* 143 (May 1959), 5.

84 "Set Swing Concert at the Sutherland Tonite," *Chicago Defender*, June 23, 1959.

85 Ad, *Chicago Defender*, June 16, 1959; "Thelonious Monk Sutherland Ace," *Chicago Defender*, June 10, 1959; "Thelonious Monk Hits Stand at Sutherland," *Chicago Defender*, June 18, 1959, and June 23, 1959; Ad, *Chicago Defender*, June 23, 1959.

86 Charles Walton, "Jazz in the Sutherland Lounge," http://www.hydeparkhistory.org/herald/SutherlandLounge .pdf

87 Harry Colomby interview, August 12, 2003. Colomby told me of the incident and the weather somewhat supports his account. During the final week of the gig, Chicago was hot and very muggy, scattered rain, mid-90s by day. On the other hand, at night the temperature dropped to the upper 70s, low 80s, which suggests that there may be more to the story than just the weather. "Official Weather Report," *Chicago Tribune*, June 27, 28, 1959.

88 "Band, Pianist are Added to Jazz Festival," *Newport Daily News*, June 11, 1959.

89 Dan Morgenstern, "Newport '59," *Jazz Journal* 12 (August 1959), 4.

90 Charlotte Washington interview, April, 2004.

91 Wein, *Myself Among Others*, 190.

92 The remaining numbers were "Well, You Needn't," and Rhythm-a-ning." Unreleased recording in author's possession.

93 Dan Morgenstern, "Newport '59," 4.

94 Wilson died on July 11, 1959. Korall, *Drummin' Men*, 69. It should be noted that heroin users are prone to tuberculosis and fungal infections, including cryptococcal meningitis. John C. M. Brust, "Opiate Addiction and Toxicity," *Handbook of Clinical Neurology*, eds. P. J. Vinken, G. W. Bruyn, vol. 21, no. 65: *Intoxications of the Nervous System: Part II*, ed., F. A. de Wolff (Amsterdam: Elsevier Health Sciences, 1994), 355.

95 David Amram interview, July 15, 2003.

96 John Tynan, "Blakey: The Message Still Carries," *Down Beat* (June 21, 1962), 20; Art Blakey, *Les Liaisons Dangereuses-Film Soundtrack: Art Blakey and the Jazz Messengers* (EmArcy 848245-2 [CD]). The Jazz Messengers, which included Barney Wilen, recorded their contribution to the soundtrack on July 28 and 29, 1959, just a day after Monk's group. Some of Duke Jordan's songs include "Prelude in Blue," "Valmontana" nos. 1 and 2, "No Hay Problem," and "Weehawken Mad Pad," clearly dedicated to Nica's house where the band rehearsed along with Monk's quartet.

97 "Annette Stroyberg," *The Times*, December 17, 2005, http://www.timesonline.co.uk/tol/comment/obit uaries/article7669 95.ece; See also Roger Vadim, *Bardot, Deneuve, Fonda* (New York: Simon & Schuster, 1986).

98 "Monk et les liaisons dangereuses," *Jazz Magazine* 52, no. 5 (October 1959), 23–24. For Nica, it must have been strange to see her friend Boris Vian in the small role of Prévan, a prolific writer and well-known French jazz critic. Exactly a month earlier, the thirty-nine-year-old Vian died of a heart attack at a screening of the film version of his 1946 novel, *I Shall Spit on Your Graves* [*J'irai cracher sur vos tombes*]. On Boris Vian, see Mike Zwerin, ed. and trans., *Round About Close to Midnight: The Jazz Writings of Boris Vian* (London and New York: Quartet Books, 1988), vii-x; Boris Vian, *Chroniques de Jazz* (Paris: French and European Publications, 1971); Alfred Cismaru, *Boris Vian* (New York: Twayne Publishers, 1974).

99 The same quintet led by Kenny Clarke had just recorded the soundtrack for "Un Temoin Dans La Ville" in April, and the same group (sans Clarke) had a short engagement at the Club Saint Germain during the same month. See *Un Temoin Dans La Ville: Film Soundtrack* (Fontana (F)660226HR); Barney Wilen Quintet, *Barney* (RCA (F)430.053); Hennessey, *Klook*, 131–32. Oddly, in the cameo appearance Clarke's group is actually pantomiming the recording Blakey and the Jazz Messengers made in New York.

100 "Monk et les liaisons dangereuses," 20–23.

101 These may not have been Romano's exact words, but this is the story he conveyed to *Jazz Magazine*—add, too, that this is translated from French. "Monk et les liaisons dangereuses," 24.

102 There are a couple of tapes listed as rehearsals for "Les Liaisons Dangereuses" from Reel #6, The Pannonica Collection (1956–1970), reel description.

103 Hennessey, *Klook*, 131.

104 Unfortunately, for years this song has been misidentified as either an "untitled blues" or Richard Rodgers and Lorenz Hart's "Bye and Bye" from the musical *Dearest Enemy*. See footnote 28 of Chapter 4 for an accounting of the error.

105 "1,000 Students to Take Part in U of I Summer Program," *Chicago Tribune*, May 31, 1959; Wein, *Myself Among Others*, 202–203.

106 Len Lyons, "Lyons Den," *Chicago Defender*, August 17, 1959; *New York Post*, August 11, 1959.

107 Ad, from the *Christian Science Monitor*, July 29, 1959.

108 "The Night Monk Forgot the Music," *Amsterdam News*, August 13, 1960.

109 John S. Wilson, "Jazz: Changing Pattern," *New York Times*, August 24, 1959.

110 "Strictly Ad Lib," *Down Beat* (October 29, 1959), 47; ad, *Washington Post*, August 31, 1959.

111 Tony Gieske, "Accent on Jazz," *Washington Post*, September 13, 1959; Nellie Monk interview, January 12, 2002.

112 "Newport Jazz Festival to be Introduced Here," *Chicago Defender*, August 11, 1959; *Chicago Tribune*, September 9, 1959; "Newport Jazz Festival Stars Hit Chicago," *Chicago Defender*, September 12, 1959; John S. Wilson, "Music: English Jazz," *New York Times*, September 18, 1959. By some accounts, the tour was supposed to travel to fifteen cities, though I have only been able to confirm nine. The other cities mentioned include Buffalo, Cleveland, Cincinnati, and Columbus. "Newport Jazz at Mosque," *Pittsburgh Courier*, September 19, 1959; "Theolonious Monk (sic) on Jazz Tour," *Atlanta Daily World*, September 6, 1959.

113 Joy Tunstall, "A Little Bit About Everything," *Pittsburgh Courier*, October 24, 1959. According to Tunstall, Monk missed a plane, but Humphrey Lyttelton reports that the tour traveled by bus. The story is a little more complicated. George Shearing had had a dispute with Town Hall's stage manager after he brought the curtain down on Shearing because they were running overtime. Shearing threatened to quit the tour and gave his sidemen notice, and some of the headliners considered following his lead. He was persuaded to change his mind the next day, but by then he had missed the bus to Pittsburgh. He chartered a plane and offered to take other musicians with him. Tunstall is referring to Shearing's chartered plane, though it is worth noting that the flight still did not make it in time for the gig. *Pittsburgh Courier*, September 26, 1959; Dorothy Kilgallen, "Around New York," *Mansfield News-Journal*, September 26, 1959; "Strictly Ad Lib," *Down Beat* (October 29, 1959), 48.

114 Tony Gieske, "Newport Jazz Stars Shine in D.C. Concert," *Washington Post*, September 20, 1959.

115 Joy Tunstall, "A Little Bit About Everything," *Pittsburgh Courier*, October 24, 1959.

116 Humphrey Lyttelton, "Monk . . . Genius in a Straw Hat," *Melody Maker* 34 (October 10, 1959), 13.

117 Humphrey Lyttelton, "That Hat Again," *Melody Maker* 34 (October 17, 1959), 3.

118 Lyttelton, "Monk . . . Genius in a Straw Hat," 13.

119 Barbara Gardner, "Along Came Jones," *Down Beat* (March 10, 1966), 15. When Nica asked Jones to name his three wishes, he responded: "Two of my wishes were already carried out: to play with Thelonious Monk and Dizzy Gillespie." Quoted in Pannonica de Koenigswarter, *Three Wishes*, 183.

120 Chris Sheridan suggests that Sam Jones and Art Taylor left Monk after the Hollywood Bowl gig in October, but both men were already recording with other artists during Monk's engagement at Club 12 in Detroit. Jones appears on Blue Mitchell, *Blue Soul* (Riv RLP12-309), recorded in New York, September 24, 1959; Taylor on Lem Winchester, *Winchester Special* (New Jazz LP8223), recorded at Van Gelder's studio on September 25, 1959. Finally, Prophet Jennings confirms that Jones and Taylor had just left before Monk opened at Club 12. Prophet Jennings interview, May 12, 2005, and see below.

121 Prophet Jennings interview, May 12, 2005.

122 Lars Bjorn with Jim Gallert, *Before Motown: A History of Jazz in Detroit, 1920–1960* (Ann Arbor, MI: University of Michigan Press, 2001), 112.

123 Stanley Dance asked Monk in 1961 to name his biggest "headache" on the job. Monk: "Trying to get proprietors to have a good piano in tune on the stand." Stanley Dance, "Three Score: A Quiz for Jazz Musicians," *Metronome* (April 1961), 48.

124 Joy Tunstall, "A Little Bit About Everything," *Pittsburgh Courier*, October 24, 1959. The story was also reported in *Down Beat*, but because it was taken from the *Pittsburgh Courier*, the writer assumed Club 12 was in Pittsburgh—an error that has been repeated many times, most recently in Sheridan's *Brilliant Corners*, 386. "Strictly Ad Lib," *Down Beat* (November 26, 1959), 66. Joy Tunstall was the Detroit correspondent for the *Courier*.

125 Both quotes from Prophet Jennings interview, May 12, 2005.

126 "Jazz Festival at Bowl Tonight," *Los Angeles Times*, October 2, 1959.

127 "Thelonius Monk Makes Debut Here at Jazz Festival," *Los Angeles Sentinel*, September 17, 1959.

128 Monk quoted in Gover Sales, "I Wanted to Make It Better," 36.

129 Don Alpert, "Bowl Goes Hip for Jazz Fete," *Los Angeles Times*, September 27, 1959; A. S. Doc Young, "L.A. Goes 'Major League' with First Jazz Festival," *Los Angeles Sentinel*, October 1, 1959.

130 Hope was working mainly with bassist Curtis Counce, drummer Lenny McBrowne, and saxophonist Harold Land. Harold Land Quintet, *The Fox* (Hi-Fi Jazz J612); Lenny McBrowne, *Lenny McBrowne and the Four Souls* (Pacific Jazz PJ1).

131 Gover Sales, "I Wanted to Make It Better," 33. Butler and Hope play together on Harold Land, *The Fox* (see above). On Frank Butler, see Valerie Wilmer, "What the Butler Plays," *Melody Maker* (September 4, 1976), 35.

132 Dr. Anna Lou Smith, interview, April 7, 2004.

133 Ibid.

134 John Tynan, "The Bowl Fest," *Down Beat* (November 12, 1959), 18.

135 Stanley Robertson, "Are Negroes Becoming 'Jazz Bums'?" *Los Angeles Sentinel*, October 15, 1959.

136 Mimi Clar, "Both Jazz Concerts Dull; Programming Bad," *Los Angeles Times*, October 5, 1959.

137 Robertson, "Are Negroes Becoming 'Jazz Bums'?"

138 Harry Colomby interview, August 11, 2003; Arrested for Assault to Do Bodily Harm, October 3, 1959, Los Angeles. No Disposition. Director of FBI to Legat, Tokyo (163-2971), cablegram, September 3, 1970, Thelonious Monk FBI File. I do not know where the Monks stayed during this trip. Colomby thought it was Gene Autry's Continental Hotel, where they stayed during their 1964 visit (see Chapter 26), but that hotel wasn't built until spring of 1963.

139 Dr. Anna Lou Smith, interview in Los Angeles, April 7, 2004.

140 Ibid.

141 Bertha Hope interview, June 30, 2003, July 15, 2003. Rollins was at the Hillcrest Club the third week of October, and Elmo Hope had become a fairly regular participant in the club's Tuesday night jam sessions. Ads, *Los Angeles Sentinel*, October 16 and 23, 1958.

142 Elmo Hope, *Elmo Hope Trio* (Hi Fi Jazz J(S)616). He had recorded "B's-a-Plenty" and "Minor Bertha" on this LP, which he made with Jimmy Bond (bass) and Frank Butler (drums).

143 *Oakland Tribune*, October 18 and 20, 1959.

144 Nellie Monk interview, January 12, 2002; Photographer Doug Quackenbush, who spent quite a bit of time with Nellie, recounts the same story in his personal notes. See "Doug Quackenbush Typed Notes," n.d., in author's possession.

145 Gover Sales, "I Wanted to Make It Better," 33; Hentoff, "Jazz Baroness," 102.

146 Gover Sales, "I Wanted to Make It Better," 32.

147 Ibid., 31.

148 Ibid., 37.

149 *Something Else !!!: The Music of Ornette Coleman* (Contemporary M3551) was completed in Los Angeles in March of 1958, and had Walter Norris on piano, Don Payne bass, and Billy Higgins on drums. Ornette Coleman, *Tomorrow is the Question!* (Contemporary M3569), was completed a year later, March 1959, and included drummer Shelly Manne and bassists Red Mitchell (on three tunes) and Percy Heath. Finally, *The Shape of Jazz to Come* (Atlantic Atl LP1317) and *Change of the Century* (Atlantic Atl LP 1327) were recorded in May and October of 1959, respectively, with the group that had, for the time being, become his regular ensemble: Charlie Haden (b) Billy Higgins (d).

150 Martin Williams, "Letter from Lenox," *Jazz Review* (October, 1959), 29–32.

151 John Litweiler, *Ornette Coleman: A Harmolodic Life* (New York: William Morrow, 1992), 70; see also Peter Niklas Wilson, *Ornette Coleman: His Life and Music* (Berkeley, CA: Berkeley Hills Books, 1999), 24; Spellman, *Four Lives in the Bebop Business*, 80–81.

152 Helen McNamara, "This Jazz Hero Can Do No Wrong," *Toronto Telegram*, May 8, 1959.

153 Julian Cannonball Adderley, *The Cannonball Adderley Quintet in San Francisco* (Riverside RLP 12-311). Although Keepnews states that Monk opened the week after the Adderley recording dates, they actually took place the same week. Monk opened on the 19th and Addereley's quintet was recorded on the 18th and 20th of October. Keepnews, *The View from Within*, 141.

154 Thelonious Monk, *Thelonious Alone in San Francisco* (Riverside RLP 12-312).

155 See Chapter 19.

21   "Hell, I Did That Twenty-Five Years Ago"

1 Ad, *Washington Post*, November 19 and 20, 1959.

2 George Hoefer, "Caught in the Act," *Down Beat* (January 7, 1960), 40–41; also quoted in virtually everything written on Coleman, including Litweiler, *Ornette Coleman*, 78; Spellman, *Four Lives in the Bebop Business*, 81–82; Iain Anderson, *This is Our Music: Free Jazz, The Sixties, and American Culture* (Philadelphia: University of Pennsylvania Press, 2007), 58–60.

3 Bob Reisner, "Jazz," *Village Voice*, November 25, 1959, 2.
4 There has been much written on Coleman, whose work is much too complicated to address here. See, for example, Wilson, *Ornette Coleman*; Litweiler, *Ornette Coleman*; Nat Hentoff, *The Jazz Life*, 222–248; Iain Anderson, *This Is Our Music*, 58–72; David Lee, *The Battle of the Five Spot: Ornette Coleman and the New York Jazz Field* (Toronto: Mercury Press, 2006); Valerie Wilmer, *As Serious as Your Life: The Story of the New Jazz* (Westport, CT: Lawrence Hill and Co., 1980, orig. 1977), 60–74; Steven Block, "Pitch-Class Transformation in Free Jazz," *Music Theory Spectrum* 12, no. 2 (Fall 1990), 181–202 and "Organized Sound: Pitch-Class Relations in the Music of Ornette Coleman," *Annual Review of Jazz Studies* 6 (1993), 229–252; Ornette Coleman, "Prime Time for Harmolodics," *Down Beat* (July 1983), 54.
5 Initially, Coleman's group was billed opposite Art Farmer and Benny Golson's "Jazztet," but the Terminis quickly moved them to their latest venture called the Jazz Gallery a few blocks away on St. Marks Place. *Village Voice*, November 18, 1959, December 16, 1959.
6 Mingus quoted in Wayne Enstice and Paul Rubin, *Jazz is Spoken Here: Conversations with 22 Musicians* (New York: Da Capo Press, 1994), 216.
7 John S. Wilson, "Program of Jazz Is Offered Here," *New York Times*, November 30, 1959.
8 Whitney Balliett, "Jazz Concerts: Historic," *The New Yorker* (December 5, 1959), 150–152.
9 Morgenstern, "Newport '59," 2.
10 Quoted in André Hodeir, *Toward Jazz*, tran. by Noel Burch (New York: Da Capo Press, 1986, orig. 1962), 159. The article appeared as a two-part series in *Jazz Hot* 142 and 143.
11 Hentoff, "The Jazz Baroness," 102; Hentoff, *Listen to the Stories*, 74.
12 A sly tribute to Thelonious, the title also referenced the famous legend of a monk and a nun who fell in love, escaped from the cloisters in order to pursue their carnal desires, and were turned to stone in a lover's embrace.
13 Hentoff, *The Jazz Life*, 241; also quoted in Spellman, *Four Lives in the Bebop Business*, 120.
14 Don Cherry and John Coltrane, *The Avant-Garde* (Atlantic Records Atl LP1451).
15 Sidran, ed., *Talking Jazz*, 409.
16 Steven Block, "Organized Sound," 229–252; see also Spellman, *Four Lives in the Bebop Business*, 84–104; Wilson, *Ornette Coleman*, 7–23; Litweiler, *Ornette Coleman*, 21–40.
17 Spellman, *Four Lives in the Bebop Business*, 70–71. Critic Michel-Claude Jalard linked Monk, Cecil Taylor, and Duke Ellington together precisely because of their strong use of the left hand, though he argues they do not use it to the same effect. See Jalard, "Trois Apôtres du Discontu," *Jazz Magazine* 6, no. 65 (December 1960), 42–46, 63.
18 "Monk composes Christmas Carol," December 21, 1959, Reel #18, The Pannonica Collection (1956–1970), reel description. He never recorded the song himself, but the music and lyrics by Monk were published in Don Sickler, ed., *The Thelonious Monk Fake Book* (Milwaukee: Hal Leonard, 2002).
19 "Thelonious Plays the New Year (1960) in Round Midnight, December 31, 1959," Reel #3, The Pannonica Collection (1956–1970), reel description.
20 "Thelonious Composes Classified Information," Reel #3, "Monk rehearsing 'Worry Later' [aka 'San Francisco Holiday'] at Mad Pad, Jan. 2, 1960," Reel #62, The Pannonica Collection (1956–1970), reel description.
21 Harry Colomby interview, August 11, 2003. Though just a few years out of Ithaca Conservatory, LaFaro had an impressive resume, having played with Chet Baker, Sonny Rollins, Stan Kenton, Hampton Hawes, Victor Feldman, Cal Tjader, Benny Goodman, to name a few. Martin Williams, "Introducing Scott LaFaro," *Jazz Review* 3 (August 1960), 16; "A Light Gone Out," *Down Beat* (August 17, 1961), 13.
22 Peter Pettinger, *Bill Evans: How My Heart Sings* (New Haven, CT: Yale University Press, 1998), 90–93; Tony Scott, *Sung Heroes* (Sunnyside (F)SSC1015). Two weeks before the Storyville gig, they recorded Evans's historic trio LP *Portrait in Jazz* for Riverside Records (Riv RLP-315).
23 John McLellan, "Le Jazz Hot Is Often Cool," *The Boston Traveler*, January 21, 1960. He mistakenly identified Paul Motian as "Pete Modrian."
24 Williams, "Introducing Scott LaFaro," 16.
25 Chuck Braman, "Paul Motian: Method Of A Master (Part 1 and 2)," 1996, www.chuckbraman.com/Writing/WritingFilesDrumming/.
26 Dufty, "The Prophet's Exile to the Tombs." Gollay built a reputation representing artists and estate issues—his clients included Willem de Kooning and Franz Kline. "Benjamin Gollay," *New York Times*, July 3, 1983.
27 *Chicago Defender*, March 9, 1960; "Television Programs," *New York Times*, March 13, 1960.
28 See Theodore Mann, *Journeys in the Night: Creating a New American Theater with Circle in the Square: A Memoir* (New York: Applause, 2007).
29 Dan Ouellette, *Ron Carter: Finding the Right Notes* (New York: Artistshare, 2008), 83.
30 John S. Wilson, "Concert Is Offered by Thelonious Monk," *New York Times*, February 9, 1960.
31 Whitney Balliett, "Jazz Concerts," *New Yorker* (February 20, 1960), 137, 135.
32 Dan Morgenstern, "An Evening with Monk," *Jazz Journal* 13 (May 1960), 2–4, 9.
33 It was later renamed Pep's Music Lounge or simply Pep's Lounge. Catalano, *Clifford Brown*, 31; Christine Bird, *The Da Capo Jazz and Blues Lover's Guide to the United States* (New York: Da Capo Press, 2001), 185; and on Gerson, see John L. Smith, *Running Scared: The Life and Treacherous Times of a Las Vegas Casino King* (New York: Thunder's Mouth Press, 2001), 39.
34 Oulette, *Ron Carter*, 83.
35 "Strictly Ad Lib," *Down Beat* (March 31, 1960), 38. Nat Adderley compared Wright to Max Roach. "Oral history interview with Nat Adderley, 2 April 1993," conducted by Jimmy Owens [Videorecording], Schomburg Collection, New York Public Library. On Wright, see "Wright, Specs." In *The New Grove Dictionary of Jazz*, 2nd ed., edited by Barry Kernfeld. *Grove Music Online. Oxford Music Online*, http://www.oxfordmusiconline.com/subscriber/article/grove/music/J492300 (accessed May 25, 2008).

36 Harry Colomby interview, August 11, 2003. Ironically, Wright was a panelist for a roundtable discussion on jazz musicians and narcotics held at the Newport Jazz Festival in 1957. George E. Pitts, "Narcotics Discussion Is Key Phase of Festival," *Pittsburgh Courier*, July 20, 1957.
37 Lars Bjorn with Jim Gallert, *Before Motown*, 113.
38 Riel Lazarus, "Bassist John Ore," *All About Jazz* (March 15, 2004), www.allaboutjazz.com. The tape of that rehearsal was recorded on Reel #9, The Pannonica Collection (1956–1970), reel description.
39 Harry Colomby interview, August 11, 2003.
40 "Wright, Specs." In *The New Grove Dictionary of Jazz*, 2nd ed., edited by Barry Kernfeld. *Grove Music Online*. *Oxford Music Online*, http://www.oxfordmusiconline.com/subscriber/article/grove/music/J492300 (accessed May 25, 2008).
41 "Weather," *Chicago Tribune*, March 8, 9, 11, 1960; "Auto Output Rise Due: Weather May Cut Goal," *New York Times*, March 10, 1960.
42 Sheridan, *Brilliant Corners*, 99.
43 Ad, *New York Times*, March 13, 1960; *Amsterdam News*, March 19, 1960; Nina Simone, with Stephen Cleary, *I Put A Spell on You: The Autobiography of Nina Simone* (New York: Da Capo Press, 2003, orig. 1992), 66–68.
44 John S. Wilson, "Troubles Beset a Jazz Concert," *New York Times*, March 28, 1960.
45 Ibid.
46 Litweiler, *Ornette Coleman*, 81. The band opened at the Five Spot on April 5th. The night before, Higgins played a concert with Coleman at the Circle in the Square Theater. John S. Wilson, "Ornette Coleman Heard in Concert," *New York Times*, April 5, 1960.
47 "Wednesday the 23rd of March 1960 (3 pm)," handwritten note, attached to letter Nica to Mary Lou Williams, February 20, 1967, Personal Correspondence, Box 4, Mary Lou Williams Papers. Ellipses in the original, reproduced in the same format.
48 Her attorneys were John J. Morris, Jr., and Arthur J. Sullivan, of Morris, James, Hitchens & Williams, Wilmington, and Thomas A. Wadden, Jr., and Robert L. Weinberg, of Williams & Stein, Washington, D.C.
49 "Baroness Sentenced," *New York Times*, April 22, 1960; Jesse H. Walker, "Theatricals," *Amsterdam News*, April 30, 1960; Dufty, "The Prophet's Exile to the Tombs"; 1960; Superior Court of Delaware, New Castle County. The STATE of Delaware v. Nica DE KOENIGSWARTER; Nica de Koenigswarter, *Three Wishes*, 17.
50 Russ Wilson, "Thelonious Monk's Comedy of Errors," *Oakland Tribune*, April 14, 1960.
51 Ibid. Guaraldi is best known for writing music for Charles Schultz's "Peanuts" cartoons.
52 Ibid.
53 "Strictly Ad Lib," *Down Beat* (June 9, 1960), 50.
54 Valerie Wilmer, "A Lesson in Lovemaking," in *Jazz People* (New York: Da Capo, 1977), 61.
55 Monk interview with Russ Wilson, KJAZ San Francisco, April 17, 1960, recording in author's possession.
56 Keepnews, *The View from Within*, 142–43.
57 Ibid., 143.
58 The album was first released as *Thelonious Monk Quartet Plus Two at the Blackhawk* (Riverside RLP 12-323).
59 John S. Wilson, "'Village' Becomes Focal Center for Modern Jazz"; Ivan Black, "A Note on the Jazz Gallery," n.d. Box 9, Ivan Black Papers.
60 Dufty, "The Prophet's Exile to the Tombs"; "Cabaret Permit Reinstated," *Pittsburgh Courier*, June 25, 1960; Edward Kosner, "Thelonious Monk Gets a Key to the City," *New York Post*, June 15, 1960.
61 Schuller, "Thelonious Monk: Review," 24–25.
62 John S. Wilson, "Music: A Third Stream of Sound," *New York Times*, May 17, 1960. Schuller also debuted his "Variants on a Theme by John Lewis (Django)," the same night. In December he recorded both pieces with most of the same personnel. Gunther Schuller, *Jazz Abstractions* (Atlantic Atl LP1365). Personnel: Eric Dolphy (as,fl,b-cl) Ornette Coleman (as) Robert Di Domenica (fl) Eddie Costa (vib) Charles Libove, Roland Vamos (vln) Harry Zaratzian (viola) Joseph Tekula (cello) Bill Evans (p) Jim Hall (g) Scott LaFaro, George Duvivier (b) Sticks Evans (d) Gunther Schuller (arr, cond). Schuller also published the score. See, *Variants on a theme of Thelonious Monk* (Newton Centre, MA: Margun Music, 1983).
63 Richard Jennings and UN Staff Recreation Council Jazz Society, *Twenty-Five Years of the UNSRC Jazz Society, April 1959–April 1985: Special Issue of "The World of Jazz"* (New York: United Nations, 1985), 3–9.
64 Lindesay Parrott, "U.N. Council Bids Hammarskjöld Act on South Africa," *New York Times*, April 2, 1960; Bruce W. Munn, "U.N. Group Acts on 'Mass Killings' in Africa," *Chicago Defender*, April 2, 1960; Leonard Ingalls, "More Disorders Hit South Africa," *New York Times*, April 3, 1960; Philip Frankel, *An Ordinary Atrocity: Sharpeville and its Massacre* (New Haven: Yale University Press, 2001); United Nations, *The United Nations and Apartheid, 1948–1994* (New York: United Nations Publications, 1994); Tom Lodge, *Black Politics in South Africa since 1945* (London: Longman, 1983).
65 Max Roach began his project as a collaboration with singer/composer Oscar Brown, Jr., but Brown split citing creative differences. Roach recorded *We Insist–Freedom Now Suite* (Candid CJM 8002) on August 31 and September 6, 1960. For an excellent discussion of its genesis, see Ingrid Monson, *Freedom Sounds*, 152–175; Scott Saul, *Freedom Is, Freedom Ain't*, 90–96. Weston would record *Uhuru Afrika* (Roulette R65001) in November of 1960. Incidentally, Max Roach appears on Weston's *Uhuru Afrika*.
66 John Henrik Clarke, "The New Afro-American Nationalism," *Freedomways* 1, no. 3 (Fall 1961), 285–95; Rod Bush, *We Are Not What We Seem: Black Nationalism and Class Struggle in the American Century* (New York: NYU Press, 1999), 184; Peniel Joseph, *Waiting 'Til the Midnight Hour: A Narrative History of Black Power in America* (New York: Macmillan, 2006), 39; Adelaide Cromwell Hill and Martin Kilson, eds., *Apropos of Africa: Sentiments of Negro American Leaders on Africa from the 1800s to the 1950s* (London: Frank Cass and Co., 1969), 9.
67 Jennings, et. al., *Twenty-Five Years of the UNSRC Jazz Society*, 31; "U.N. Cats Dig Jazz," *New York Times*, June 12, 1960.

68 "Sculpture and Jazz: Interview by Alain Kirli," in Jason Weiss, ed., *Steve Lacy: Conversations*, 161; also he tells the same story in "In the Old Days: Interview by Lee Friedlander and Maria Frielander," Ibid., 198.

69 Jennings, et. al., *Twenty-Five Years of the UNSRC Jazz Society*, 31; "U.N. Cats Dig Jazz," *New York Times*, June 12, 1960. Monk's performance at the U.N. attracted some followers, including three Nigerian officials who went to the Jazz Gallery to hear him later in the summer. Jesse H. Walker, "Theatricals," *Amsterdam News*, September 10, 1960.

70 Jennings, et. al., *Twenty-Five Years of the UNSRC Jazz Society*, 31.

71 Personnel Roster, Five Spot Cabaret Books, 1960.

72 Kirk Silsbee, "Thelonious: Exploring the Monk Canon," *L.A. Reader* (February 20, 1987), 8.

73 Quoted in "Sculpture and Jazz: Interview by Alain Kirli," in Jason Weiss, ed., *Steve Lacy: Conversations*, 161.

74 Lacy's biographical information is derived from the following sources: Steve Lacy Interview, May 12, 1995; several interviews in Jason Weiss, ed., *Steve Lacy: Conversations*, 3–6, 43–45, 193–196, passim.; Bobbie Lacy, "Introducing Steve Lacy," in Martin Williams, ed., *Jazz Panorama* (New York: Collier Books, 1964), 268–72; Raymond Gervais and Yves Bouliane, "Interview with Steve Lacy," translated by Effie Mihopolous, *Brilliant Corners: A Magazine of the Arts* 5 (Spring 1977), 77–112; Ira Gitler, "Focus on Steve Lacy," *Down Beat* (March 2, 1961), 15 and 46; Gerard Rouy, "Lacy: 'Thelonious Monk et Moi,'" *Jazz Magazine* 368 (February 1988), 32–33.

75 They recorded "Bemsha Swing" on Taylor's *Jazz Advance* (Transition TRLP 19). Buell Neidlinger and Dennis Charles, members of Taylor's quartet when he played at the Five Spot, rounded out the rhythm section. See Chapter 18.

76 Gitler liner notes on *Reflections: Steve Lacy Plays Thelonious Monk* (New Jazz/Prestige NJLP 8206).

77 A. Down Katz, "The Cats and Chicks Dug Thelonious Monk's Homecoming the Most!" *Pittsburgh Courier*, June 25, 1960.

78 Ads, *Village Voice*, June 16 and 30, 1960. Coltrane was held over, having played opposite Dizzy Gillespie's quintet the week before. *Village Voice*, June 1, 1960.

79 Quoted (by way of Monk's press agent Mildred Fields) in A. Down Katz, "The Cats and Chicks Dug Thelonious Monk's Homecoming the Most!"; see also Kosner, "Thelonious Monk Gets a Key to the City"; Dufty, "The Prophet's Exile to the Tombs"; "Cabaret Permit Reinstated," *Pittsburgh Courier*, June 25, 1960.

80 Personnel Roster, Five Spot Cabaret Books, 1960.

81 "In Search of the Way: Interview by Jason Weiss," in Jason Weiss, ed., *Steve Lacy: Conversations* (Durham, NC: Duke University Press, 2006), 97.

82 Steve Lacy interview, May 12, 1995, Paris, France.

83 Quoted from Lacy's "Foreword" to Fitterling, *Thelonious Monk*, 13–14. He repeats versions of this advice in other interviews, with me as well as published interviews, e.g., "In Search of the Way: Interview by Jason Weiss," in Jason Weiss, ed., *Steve Lacy*, 98. A two-page document surfaced after Lacy's death that first alleged to be in Monk's hand and then later claimed to be pages from a notebook Steve Lacy kept in 1960. It repeats much of what Monk taught Lacy as well as a few choice "Monkisms" (quotes), but I question its authenticity. The handwriting does not appear to be Lacy's but rather a poor attempt at a forgery, and it seems unlikely that a man who published just about everything would not have published or mentioned such a document. If it is authentic—and I am unwilling to categorically say it is not—it appears as if it was written long after 1960, perhaps in preparation for the Foreword he wrote for Fitterling's discography. Either way, it is fascinating. There are a few choice lines that did not appear to make it into Fitterling's foreword: "Stay in *shape*! Sometimes a musician waits for a gig, when it comes, he's out of shape and can't make it." "Don't sound *anybody* for a gig, just be *on the scene*." "These pieces were written so as to have something to play, and to get cats *interested* enough to come to *rehearsal*." "You've got it! If you don't want to play, tell a joke or dance, but in any case, *you got it*! (to a drummer who didn't want to solo)." Quoted in "T. Monk's Advice (1960)" in author's possession.

84 Steve Lacy interview, May 12, 1995.

85 "In the Old Days: Interview by Lee Friedlander and Maria Frielander," in Jason Weiss, ed., *Steve Lacy: Conversations*, 193–194.

86 He is heard on "Evidence," "Straight, No Chaser," and a snippet of "Rhythm-a-ning," in which his solo competes with announcements by Louis Armstrong and emcee Mitch Miller. "Thelonious Monk quartet at the Quaker City Jazz Festival, August 26, 1960," private recording in author's possession. The date of the performance is usually listed as August 27, but Monk was clearly scheduled to play Friday night, August 26. See Ad, "1st Quaker City Jazz Festival," *Washington Post*, August 7, 1960.

87 "In Person," *Down Beat* (July 7, 1960), 45; "In Person," *Down Beat* (July 21, 1960), 69; "In Person," *Down Beat* (August 4, 1960), 48; "In Person," *Down Beat* (August 18, 1960), 46.

88 Harry Colomby interview, July 5, 2007.

89 "Miles and Monk in Apollo Show," *Amsterdam News*, July 23, 1960; Jesse H. Walker, "Theatricals," *Amsterdam News*, July 30, 1960.

90 Ad, *Amsterdam News*, August 13, 1960; Sheridan, *Brilliant Corners*, 392. The concert was rained out on Friday night, August 19. The change did not affect Monk's performance since he was always scheduled to appear on Saturday night, August 20. Instead, the acts scheduled for Friday night were moved to Saturday afternoon. "Jazz Festival Postponed," *New York Times*, August 20, 1960.

91 Wein, *Myself Among Others*, 195–196; Burt Goldblatt, *The Newport Jazz Festival: The Illustrated History* (New York: Dial Press, 1977), 80–85; Thomasina Norford, "Newport Freezes Jazz Festival," *Amsterdam News*, July 9, 1960.

92 Quoted in Bob Reisner, "The Newport Blues," *Village Voice* (July 7, 1960), 2.

93 Reisner, "The Newport Blues," 2; Jesse H. Walker, "Theatricals," *Amsterdam News*, July 2, 1960; see also, Saul, *Freedom Is, Freedom Ain't*, 124–128; Wein, *Myself Among Others*, 194–196.

94 "Minutes of NY CORE Membership Meeting of 20 July 1960," p. 2, CORE Papers, microfilm; Jesse H. Walker, "Theatricals," *Amsterdam News*, July 30, 1960. See also Ingrid Monson, *Freedom Sounds*, 163–64.

95 Monson, *Freedom Sounds*, 165; Ronald D. Cohen, *Rainbow Quest: The Folk Music Revival and American Society, 1940–1970* (Amherst, MA: University of Massachusetts Press, 2002), 138.

96 August Meier and Elliot Rudwick, *CORE: A Study in the Civil Rights Movement, 1942–1968* (New York: Oxford University Press, 1973), 101–107; Clayborne Carson, *In Struggle: SNCC and the Black Awakening of the 1960s* (Cambridge, MA: Harvard University Press, 1981), 9–19.

97 As Ingrid Monson points out, Local 802 rules required that musicians be paid something for benefits. The general rule was that the venue must hire the minimum number of musicians mandated at scale and then, upon union approval, any additional musicians could work on a volunteer basis. In many cases, however, musicians who were paid scale would give their earnings to the sponsoring organization. Monson, *Freedom Sounds*, 164. However, I have found exceptions in Local 802 records where the union granted Monk's entire band permission to play without remuneration—one being his performance for the U.N. Correspondents Association dinner. "Executive Board Minutes," *Allegro* 36, no. 12 (November, 1961), 7.

98 Hubert Robertson, Jr., a founder of Woodsmen Enterprises, organized the concert. Some of the other participants included Art Taylor, Donald Byrd, and Curtis Fuller. Morton Fega emceed the event. "Jazz Concert," *Amsterdam News*, September 3, 1960; *Amsterdam News*, September 16, 1960. On neighborhood transition and the role of the Bedford YMCA, see "Launch Drive to Give YM New Look," *Amsterdam News*, November 28, 1959; George Barner, "Youth Served and Taught to Serve at Bedford YMCA," *Amsterdam News*, March 28, 1959; "First Negro Exec at Bedford YMCA," *Amsterdam News*, June 20, 1959; "Introducing Russell Service, New Ex. Director of Bedford YMCA, is Man of Service," *Amsterdam News*, December 26, 1959.

99 *Music '67: Down Beat* (1967), 45; "Sinatra Gets Recording Prize," *New York Times*, October 24, 1960.

100 Haynes worked with Eric Dolphy, Oliver Nelson, Etta Jones, Randy Weston, and made his own album as a leader during the sixteen-week engagement at the Jazz Gallery.

101 In interviews Dunlop said he began working with Monk in 1961, but he's clearly a member of the band when they open at the Jazz Gallery on November 15, 1960. See Personnel Roster, Jazz Gallery, 1960.

102 Ira Gitler, "Monk's Drummer," 17; Fish, "Frankie Dunlop," 25, 84–85; Cohen and Fitzgerald, *Rat Race Blues*, 296–97.

103 Quoted in Fish, "Frankie Dunlop," 86–87.

104 Ibid., 87.

105 Ibid., 87.

106 Personnel Roster Jazz Gallery, 1960; "In Person," *Down Beat* (October 13, 1960), 50; "In Person," *Down Beat* (November 24, 1960), 46; "In Person," *Down Beat* (December 22, 1960), 60; "In Person," *Down Beat* (January 5, 1961), 46.

107 The LP was recorded in two sessions, December 20 and 21, 1960, and released as *Yeah!: Charlie Rouse Quartet* (Epic LA16012).

108 Charlie Rouse, *Takin' Care of Business!: Charlie Rouse Quintet* (Jazzland JLP19). They recorded the LP on May 11, 1960.

109 T. S. Monk interview, April 4, 2005.

110 Chris Albertson interview, July 11, 2003.

111 Randy Weston interview, July 30, 2003.

112 Albertson worked for CBS in Philadelphia and then for Philly's all-jazz station, WHAT. John Szwed, then a young critic, met Albertson while doing a story on the station for *Jazz Review*. His glowing review of Albertson's abilities and knowledge as a DJ attracted Nat Hentoff's attention, who then convinced Bill Grauer to give him a job. Chris Albertson interview, July 11, 2003.

113 Chris Albertson interview, July 11, 2003.

114 Harry Colomby interview, August 11, 2003. I don't know what Keepnews's opinion on all of this is, since he would not grant me an interview or allow me to see any company records he may still have in his possession.

115 Harry Colomby interview, August 11, 2003.

116 Monk quoted in Jean Clouzet and Michel Delorme, "L'amertume du prophète," *Jazz Magazine* 9 (April 1963), 40.

117 Chris Albertson interview, July 11, 2003; see also, Rick Kennedy and Randy McNutt, *Little Labels–Big Sound: Small Record Companies and the Rise of American Music* (Bloomington, IN: Indiana University Press, 1999), 120.

118 Ran Blake interview, March 22, 2005.

119 "1,000 Are Trapped on Belt Parkway," *New York Times*, February 5, 1961; McCandlish Phillips, "-2 Cold in City Sets 18-year Low," *New York Times*, February 3, 1961; "Snow Coats City and Most of East; Cold Sets Record," *New York Times*, February 4, 1961; "Currier and Ives Snowfall Bids for Place in Weather History," *New York Times*, February 6, 1961.

120 "Thelonious Monk Has a Fire," *Down Beat* 28, no. 6 (March 16, 1961), 11.

121 T. S. Monk, interview, April 4, 2005.

22 "Bebopens Oversteprast"

1 "Thelonious Monk Has a Fire," *Down Beat* (March 16, 1961), 11; T. S. Monk interview, April 4, 2005.

2 Ran Blake interview, March 22, 2005.

3 Ibid.; *Down Beat* (April 13, 1961), 45.

4 Ran Blake interview, March 22, 2005.

5 Geraldine Smith interview, February 12, 2004.
6 T. S. Monk, interview, April 4, 2005; Clifton Smith interview; Evelyn Smith interview; Conversation with Nica Val-Hackett.
7 Johnny Griffin interview, February 2, 2004. The album was recorded on February 7, 1961 and released as *Lookin' at Monk! Johnny Griffin and Eddie 'Lockjaw' Davis Quintet Playing the Music of Thelonious Monk* (Jazzland JL39). Had Monk showed up at Plaza Sound Studios that day, he would have heard an outstanding young rhythm section—bassist Larry Gales and drummer Ben Riley—both of whom would join Monk's band in a few years.
8 Nat Hentoff, Liner notes for Abbey Lincoln, *Straight Ahead* (Candid CJM8015).
9 Ibid.
10 Ran Blake interview, March 22, 2005.
11 Nat Hentoff, Liner notes for Abbey Lincoln, *Straight Ahead*.
12 Conversation with Abbey Lincoln, Jazz Studies Group, Columbia University, November 6, 1999. She tells this story elsewhere; see, for example, Lisa Jones, "Late Bloomer in her Prime," *New York Times*, August 4, 1991; Nate Chinen, "Abbey Lincoln's Emancipation Proclamation," *New York Times*, May 20, 2007. Fred Moten, who was also at the meeting with Abbey Lincoln in 1999, really explored the depths of Monk's "advice" to Lincoln in his brilliant book, *In the Break: The Aesthetics of the Black Radical Tradition* (Minneapolis: University of Minnesota Press, 2003), 23.
13 John S. Wilson, " Thelonious Monk Quartet Gives Brief Jazz Concert at Museum," *New York Times*, February 24, 1961.
14 Quoted in "Strictly Ad Lib," *Down Beat* (April 13, 1961), 45.
15 Birdhouse's no-alcohol policy wasn't by choice. Located at 1205 N. Dearborn, the club was located in a neighborhood not zoned to permit the sale of alcohol. Just a week before Monk was scheduled to open, the owners appealed to the city to grant the club an exception or alter the zoning requirements in the area. "Zoners to Air Liquor Plea of Birdhouse," *Chicago Tribune*, March 5, 1961.
16 "Strictly Ad Lib," *Down Beat* (April 27, 1961), 70.
17 Gabriel Favoino, "The Jazz Beat – T. Monk, Architect," *Chicago Sun-Times*, March 18, 1961.
18 Ibid.
19 Wein, *Myself Among Others*, 219. Monk said the same thing in a 1965 interview: "You get paid for one night at a concert as much as you do for a whole week in a club." Mike Hennessey, "Monk's Moods," *Melody Maker* (March 20, 1965), 9.
20 The festival did take place in 1961, but under a new producing group calling itself "Music at Newport, Inc." (Sid Bernstein and John Drew). The police stepped up security, enforced ordinances against public drinking, and increased their numbers—funded in part by a donation of $10,000 from Music at Newport, Inc. The headliners included Cannonball Adderley, Carmen McRae, and Dave Brubeck, but they only attracted about 11,000 patrons. Philip Benjamin, "11,000 in Newport at Jazz Festival," *New York Times*, July 1, 1961; "Newport Jazz Fete Proceeding Calmly," *New York Times*, July 3, 1961. Oddly, neither George Wein's memoir nor official Festival Productions literature acknowledges the 1961 Festival. The official line is that it was cancelled. Wein, *Myself Among Others*, 231–32; Charles Avenengo, "Newport Jazz Festival Golden Jubilee," http://www.newportharborguide.org/art_jazz_festival.htm.
21 Wein, *Myself Among Others*, 128–130, 225.
22 The other band members were trumpeter Ruby Braff, Pee Wee Russell on clarinet, trombonist Vic Dickinson, bassist Jimmy Woode, and drummer "Buzzy" Drootin.
23 "Strictly Ad Lib," *Down Beat* (April 27, 1961), 68.
24 Groves and Shipton, *Glass Enclosure*, 70. Part of Powell's performance at the Essen Jazz Festival that year can be heard on Bud Powell, *Bud Powell in Europe* (Duke (It)D-1012). Clarke had moved to Paris in 1949, lived there two years, and returned again in 1956. Hennessey, *Klook*, 78–80, 125–126.
25 On Powell's condition and living circumstances during this period, see Paudras, *Dance of the Infidels*, 78–91. Bud and Buttercup were never legally married, but they lived together in common law for many years, had a son together (Earl John Powell), and she used Powell's last name. "Earl John Powell – Affidavit," Surrogates Court, County of Kings, Proceeding for Letters of Administration. Estate of Earl Bud Powell, File No. 7370/1968.
26 Marion White interview, with Quincy Troupe, December 1, 1990; T. S. Monk, interview, April 4, 2005; and on young Johnny's tantrums and attitude toward his father, Randi Hultin, *Born Under the Sign of Jazz* (London: Sanctuary Publishing, LTD, 1998), 199–200. Earl John Powell was born November 24, 1955. "Earl John Powell – Affidavit," Surrogates Court, County of Kings, Proceeding for Letters of Administration. Estate of Earl Bud Powell, File No. 7370/1968.
27 This is not the place to sort out the complex relationship between Bud Powell, Buttercup, Oscar Goodstein, Francis Paudras, and others. I eagerly await Peter Pullman's biography of Powell to do so. Meanwhile, I've seen much of the correspondence between various parties attached to the Estate proceedings for Powell's son (he made the entire file available to Nellie) and I've spoken to various members of the Monk family, including Nellie, about the situation. Suffice it to say, there is more to the story than Paudras's account reveals. Goodstein was hardly a saint, and his correspondence demanding his commission fees and placing conditions on loans suggests that he had more than Powell's interest in mind.
28 Anton Eop, "The Monk Myth Continued," *Melody Maker* (August 19, 1961).
29 Video tape of April 15, 1961, recording in author's possession. It aired on AVRO-TV in August of that year.
30 Thelonious Monk, VARA Radio Broadcast, Amsterdam, April 15, 1961, in author's possession. Most of this concert is available on Thelonious Monk Quartet, *The First European Concert '61: 'Concertgebouw,' Amsterdam, Holland, April 15, 1961* (Magnetic Records MRCD 120).

31 Fortunately, much of the 1961 tour was well documented through radio broadcasts and private bootleg recordings. Monk's Paris and Milan concerts (April 18 and 21, respectively) are available in their entirety on *The Complete Riverside Recordings*; Monk Quartet at Town Hall, Manchester, May 6, 1961 (in author's possession); *Monk in Bern, May 10, 1961* (Magnetic Records MRCD 126); *Stockholm Live* (Thelonious Records TR-1008); *Monk in Copenhagen* (Storyville STCD8283), as well as radio broadcasts from Berlin (ARD Broadcast, May 21, 1961) and Essen, Germany (NDR Broadcast, April 14, 1961).

32 Groves and Shipton, *The Glass Enclosure*, 7–8.

33 "Jazz a la carte," *Jazz Hot* (April 1961), 28–29.

34 Jean Tronchot, "Trop Courte Prestation du Quartette de Monk," *Jazz Hot* 165 (May 1961), 20.

35 Tronchot, "Trop Courte Prestation du Quartette de Monk," 20–21.

36 The concert was recorded for radio by ORTF, and released by Riverside records. See below.

37 Paudras, *Dance of the Infidels*, 79. Paudras wrote that the concert took place in June but he is mistaken.

38 Tronchot, "Trop Courte Prestation du Quartette de Monk," 20–21.

39 Nellie Monk interview, January 12, 2002; Alonzo White interview, February 23, 2004.

40 Robert Reisner, Liner notes *Monk in France* (Riverside RLP (9)491).

41 "Le Jazz-Club du Sud-Est Presente . . . Le Quartet de Thelonious Monk," (flyer in author's possession). Saxophonist Barney Wilen was also on the bill.

42 See Dominic Thomas, *Black France: Colonialism, Immigration and Transnationalism* (Bloomington, IN: Indiana University Press, 2007), 235–38. On the Marseille Network's opposition to the Algerian War in 1961, see Martin Evans, *Memory of Resistance: French Opposition to the Algerian War, 1954–1962* (Oxford: Berg Publishers, 1997), 209–211.

43 No tape exists of their televised performance, nor is there any official record of which I am aware, but critic/musician Arrigo Polillo was at the studio when Monk's group was taped. See Polillo, "Thelonious e Bud Insieme," *Musica Jazz* 17 (June 1961), 12.

44 Sheridan, *Brilliant Corners*, 106–107.

45 Quoted in Paudras, *Dance of the Infidels*, 79. Much of Powell's performance was recorded and released on Bud Powell Trio, *Pianology* (Moon (It)MCD055-2).

46 Arrigo Arrigoni, "Il Piano Dopo Monk," *Musica Jazz* 17 (May 1961): 17–18.

47 Arrigo Polillo, "Thelonious e Bud Insieme," *Musica Jazz* 17 (June 1961), 12.

48 Ibid., p. 12.

49 Ibid., p. 13.

50 Ibid., p. 13.

51 Danson, "Interview: Charlie Rouse," 7.

52 Jackie Bonneau interview, October 30, 2008. On pêche Melba or peach Melba and its history, see "peach Melba." *Encyclopædia Britannica*. 2008. Encyclopædia Britannica Online. 08 December 2008 <http://www.britannica.com/EBchecked/topic/447801/peach-Melba>.

53 Wein, *Myself Among Others*, 224; Robert Reisner, Liner Notes, *Monk in Italy* (Riverside RLP (9) 443); Nellie Monk interview, January 12, 2002.

54 Wein, *Myself Among Others*, 219.

55 Alonzo White interview, February 23, 2004.

56 Michael Gibson, "Modern Jazz Piano," *Jazz Journal* 13 (February 1960), 9.

57 Bob Dawbarn, "The Greatest Show in Jazz," *Melody Maker* (May 10, 1961), 3. Critic Mark Gardner, who said he was there for "Monk's first tour of England," tells a completely different story. He played a "couple hour-long sets during which he was very close to his best," adding that there "was no eccentricity from Monk on this occasion. He was totally involved with playing, and those who came to gawp at his much-publicised shuffling and unpredictable antics were the only disappointed customers present." But his account is a little suspect because he mistakenly identifies Ben Riley and Larry Gayles [sic] in the rhythm section. He also claims they returned in 1963, the same group, and the concert was a "disaster." "They were late on, Monk kept walking on and off stage, prancing about, distracting the audience when Rouse was soloing." However, Monk doesn't return to England until 1965. I can only surmise that Gardner was there in 1961 and just got his story reversed. Mark Gardner, Liner Notes, Thelonious Monk Quartet, *Thelonious Monk: Live at the Village Gate* (Xanadu CD PR9).

58 Reprinted in Eric Hobsbawm, *The Jazz Scene* (New York: Pantheon, 1993), 277. When he published the review, he was using the pen name "Francis Newton," named after Frankie Newton, an African-American trumpeter whom Hobsbawm admired. Coincidentally, like Hobsbawm, Newton was also a Communist, not to mention a very good friend of George Wein. On Hobsbawm's Communist Party activities as well as his jazz writing under the name Francis Newton, see Eric Hobsbawm, *Interesting Times: A Twentieth Century Life* (New York: Random House, 2002), 111–113, 118–125, 134–136, 216–218, 225–227, 394–398. On Frankie Newton's Communist participation, see Wein, *Myself Among Others*, 46.

59 Max Jones, "Monk Talks to MM," *Melody Maker* (May 6, 1961).

60 Ronald Atkins, "Thelonious Monk," *Jazz Monthly* 7 (July 1961), 15–16; See also, Max Harrison, "Concert Reviews," *Jazz Journal* 14 (June 1961), 9–10; "Seven Dates for Blakey and Monk," *Melody Maker* (March 25, 1961); "Monk Leaves after Mixed Receptions," *Melody Maker* (May 13, 1961).

61 "Monk Leaves after Mixed Receptions," *Melody Maker* (May 13, 1961).

62 The tape of this concert was released as Miles Davis Quintet, *Manchester Concert: Complete 1960 Live at the Free Trade Hall* (Lone Hill LHJ 10212).

63 Thelonious Monk at Free Trade Hall, May 6, 1961, private recording in author's possession. I'm only describing the first set, in which he played "I'm Getting Sentimental Over You," "Jackie-ing," "Crepuscule with Nellie," "Blue Monk," "Rhythm-a-ning," "Body and Soul," and a drum solo. The second set was equally slim—

"Ba-lue Bolivar Ba-lues-Are," "April in Paris," "Bemsha Swing," " Crepuscule with Nellie," "Rhythm-a-ning," "Body and Soul," and a long bass solo.

64 Ian Breach, "Thelonious Monk at the Free Trade Hall, Manchester," *Manchester Guardian*, March 22, 1965.

65 Harold Jackson, "Jazz Without Distraction," *Manchester Guardian*, June 13, 1961.

66 Wein, *Myself Among Others*, 220.

67 Ibid., p. 220. It's also possible that Wein had the city wrong. We do not have aural evidence of the other concerts, so the events he describes might have occurred in Birmingham or Liverpool or Bristol.

68 They played "Sweet Georgia Brown" at the Paris concert on April 22, the night Monk's quartet played in Bologna. Throughout the tour it was one of their regular numbers. George Wein and the Newport Jazz Festival All-Stars, *Midnight Concert in Paris* (Smash (F)27023).

69 It's also one of the most complete recordings we have of any concert, so the comparison may not be entirely fair. It was first released as *Thelonious Monk Quartet Live in Stockholm, 1961* (Dragon DRLP 151/152), and recently re-released as Thelonious Monk, *Stockholm Live* (Thelonious Records TR-1008).

70 Erik Wiedemann, "Thelonious Monk: Bebopens Overstreprast," *Orkester Journalen* 20 (April 1952), 12–13; Claes Dahlgren, C. "Glimtar om Glimtar," *Orkester Journalen* 22 (December 1954), 23; J.G. Jepsen, "Jazzens Instrumentalister: Pianot," *Orkester Journalen* 23 (September 1955), 13; Claes Dahlgren, "Monk Komiker I Town Hall," *Orkester Journalen* 24 (May 1956), 6–7.

71 "En Lektion I Jazz – Recension av Thelonioius Monks konserter I form av ett delvis redigerat bandat samtal mellan Bertil Sundin och Lars Werner," *Orkester Journalen* 29 (June 1961), 9. Also quoted in Ake Karlsson, Liner notes, *Thelonious Monk Quartet Live in Stockholm, 1961* (Dragon DRLP 151/152).

72 Quoted in Ake Karlsson, Line notes, *Thelonious Monk Quartet Live in Stockholm, 1961* (Dragon DRLP 151/152).

73 Ibid.

23 "Maybe I'm a Major Influence"

1 *New York Times*, May 22, 1961. The weather report is from the same issue.

2 On the history of the Freedom Rides in 1961, see Raymond Arsenault, *Freedom Riders: 1961 and the Struggle for Racial Justice* (New York: Oxford University Press, 2006). The firebombing of one of the buses in Alabama and the riders' arrests later in Mississippi became international news—prompting Art Blakey to record his album *The Freedom Rider* on May 27, very soon after his own band returned from Europe. See Art Blakey and the Jazz Messengers, *The Freedom Rider* (Blue Note BLP 4156); Gourse, *Art Blakey*, 82.

3 King quoted in *New York Times*, May 22, 1961.

4 Bertha Hope interview, June 30, July 15, 2003.

5 Bertha Hope interview, July 15, 2003.

6 Ibid.

7 Interviews with Bertha Hope, Evelyn Smith, Clifton Smith, Geraldine Smith.

8 T. S. Monk, interview, April 4, 2005.

9 On the Personnel Roster for the Five Spot, Sonny Clark frequently listed his address as 63 Kingswood Rd., Weehawken, NJ.

10 The song was recorded at Rudy Van Gelder's studio on October 26, 1961. Clark copyrighted it as "Five Will Get You Ten" three weeks later. The other musicians on the date were Tommy Turrentine (trumpet), Butch Warren (bass), and Billy Higgins (drums). Jackie McLean, *A Fickle Sonance* (Blue Note BLP 4089); Application for Registration of a Claim to Copyright, "Five Will Get You Ten," Sonny Clark, Groove Music, November 15, 1961, Registration No. Eu 695464; T. S. Monk interview, October 10, 2001.

11 I know this from the documentation on Nica's collection of home tapes. He was there on May 25 (playing "Body and Soul" and other things), on May 27, where he is documented in a "Conversation Piece" between "T. Nellie, Nica," and again on May 29 in a jam session. And these are only the days on which he was recorded. See Reels #60 and #67, The Pannonica Collection (1956–1970), reel description.

12 Williams arranged it for a recording session she did in 1946 with a trio consisting of June Rotenberg (bass) and Bridget O'Flynn (drums). Thanks to archivist Ann Kuebler for helping me locate the arrangement (titled simply "Chillun") in Mary Lou Williams's papers at the Institute for Jazz Studies. The recording is available on Mary Lou Williams, *The Chronological Mary Lou Williams, 1945–1957* (Classics Records 1050).

13 Reel #60, May 25, 1961, The Pannonica Collection (1956–1970), reel description. Recording in author's possession.

14 "Mary Lou Williams Back from Retirement," *Amsterdam News*, October 7, 1961. See also, Kernodle, *Soul on Soul*, 199.

15 Humphrey Lyttelton, "Monk—Joker or Genius?" *Melody Maker* (April 29, 1961), 5.

16 Jesse H. Walker, "Theatricals," *Amsterdam News*, May 27, 1961. Taylor was leading a trio at the Five Spot at the time. Personnel Roster, Five Spot Café, Cabaret Books, 1961; Ad, *Village Voice*, May 4, 1961.

17 New York *Daily News*, June 1, 1961; *East Side News*, June 2, 1961.

18 Leonard Harris, "Worth Waiting for Monk at Jazz Gallery," *New York World-Telegram and Sun*, June 5, 1961.

19 Quoted in Spellman, *Four Lives in the Bebop Business*, 10–11. There is no way to confirm if the Terminis fired Taylor because of this remark, or even if they fired him at all. The Cabaret books suggest that they may have already lined up a new act and that his contract had ended. His trio was making only $500 a week that year.

20 "Philly Joe Jones Joins Monk," *Amsterdam News*, June 24, 1961. Besides Hope, Jones had Freddie Hubbard (trumpet), Phil Lassiter (alto sax), and Larry Ridley (bass).

21 Appropriately named *Homecoming* (Riverside RLP 12-381), the complete LP was recorded on June 22 and 29, 1961. The sextet was comprised of Blue Mitchell (trumpet), Frank Foster and Jimmy Heath (tenors), Percy Heath (bass), and Philly Joe Jones. For the session on June 29 he only used a trio. Some have speculated that Monk helped arrange the session for Elmo Hope, but this is unlikely. For one thing, Monk's relationship with Riverside had completely deteriorated by now and negotiations had already begun to move him to another label. Second, Hope was already a Riverside recording artist; he made an album for Riverside in L.A. a year earlier.

22 Harry Colomby interview, August 12, 2003.

23 "Strictly Ad Lib," *Down Beat* (August 17, 1961), 10; Jesse H. Walker, "Theatricals," *Amsterdam News*, July 15, 1961; Personnel Roster, Jazz Gallery Cabaret Books, 1961.

24 *Down Beat* (August 3, 1961), 19; Eugene Archer, "France Will Lift Film's Export Ban," *New York Times*, August 2, 1961.

25 Benetta Bines interview, January 30, 2004; Monk/Smith group interview, January 30, 2004.

26 Geraldine Smith interview, February 12, 2004.

27 Evelyn Smith interview, January 30, 2004.

28 Benetta Bines interview, January 30, 2004.

29 Evelyn Smith interview, January 30, 2004.

30 Rouse recorded a session on July 13 with pianist Gildo Mahones, Reggie Workman on bass, and drummer Art Taylor. The LP, which included tracks with Seldon Powell, was released as *We Paid Our Dues* (Epic LA16018). Ore recorded with Sun Ra later in the fall of 1961. He played on at least one track on the LP, *Bad and Beautiful: Mr. Sun Ra and his Arkestra* (Saturn 532).

31 "Where & When," *Down Beat* (September 28, 1961), 74; "Where & When," *Down Beat* (October 12, 1961), 44; also see Ad, *Chicago Tribune*, October 20, 1961.

32 Al Monroe, "So They Say," *Chicago Defender*, October 12, 1961.

33 Sterling Stuckey, "Frank London Brown: A Remembrance," in Brown, *The Myth Maker* (Chicago: Path Press, 1969), 3.

34 Frank London Brown, *The Myth Maker*, 100–101. The book was published posthumously.

35 "The Departed," *Negro Digest* 8 (September 1962), 50; Gwendolyn Brooks, "Of Frank London Brown: A Tenant of the World," *Negro Digest* 8 (September 1962), 44.

36 "Where & When," *Down Beat* (November 9, 1961), 44.

37 "Village Vanguard," *Variety* 224 (November 15, 1961), 58.

38 Dorothy Kilgallen, "Kim Fought that Fire with a Flair," *Washington Post*, November 15, 1961.

39 "Where & When," *Down Beat* (December 7, 1961), 54; "Where & When," *Down Beat* (December 21, 1961), 62; On Clara Ward, see Willa Ward-Royster, *"How I Got Over": Clara Ward and the World-Famous Ward Singers* (Philadelphia: Temple University Press, 1997).

40 Of course, to make Dorothy Kilgallen's column was a big deal (see above), but part of what made Monk good gossip copy was hanging out with the baroness. The *New York Daily News* mentioned Nica and Monk on occasion, like the time Nica was described as "Thelonious Monk's most avid follower, drives to the Five Spot these nights in her Bentley or Rolls from her mansion in Weehawken." *New York Daily News*, July 11, 1963. Or the rumor that Nica was looking to sell her infamous car for $19,000: When Monk heard this he replied, "For $19,000 I can buy a house with four bedrooms, two bathrooms, living room, kitchen and garage." Nica's comeback: "Of course you can . . . but where will it take you?" *New York Daily News*, December 31, 1963.

41 Robert Kotlowitz, "After Hours: Monk Talk," *Harper's Magazine* 223 (November 15, 1961), 21–23.

42 Benny Goodman, with Leslie Lieber, "Benny Goodman Picks the 60 Greatest Jazz Records of All Time," *Los Angeles Times*, November 12, 1961.

43 "Strictly Ad Lib," *Down Beat* (January 4, 1962), 10. It should be noted that Monk also agreed to play without remuneration. "Executive Board Minutes," *Allegro* 36, no. 12 (November 1961), 7

44 Ad, *Amsterdam News*, December 30, 1961. They shared the bill with John Coltrane, Sonny Rollins, and Nina Simone.

45 Kotlowitz, "After Hours: Monk Talk," 23.

46 Harold C. Schonberg, *The Great Pianists: From Mozart to the Present* (New York: Simon & Schuster, 1987), 456; Donal Henahan, "The Perils of Celebrity," *New York Times*, July 13, 1980; "Jose Iturbi." *Dictionary of American Biography, Supplement 10: 1976–1980* (New York: Charles Scribner's Sons, 1995), reproduced in *Biography Resource Center* (Farmington Hills, Mich.: Gale, 2008), http://galenet.galegroup.com/servlet/BioRC; and the wonderful documentary, *The Art of Jose Iturbi* (Video Artists International, 2005).

47 Stanley Dance, "Three Score: A Quiz for Jazz Musicians," *Metronome* (April 1961), 48.

48 Ibid., 48.

49 Zuckerman squeezed a little bit of money out of Blue Note Records. The year before, Monk's royalties for *Genius of Modern Music* amounted to $286.70. Morris Zuckerman to Blue Note Records, November 19, 1961; Francis Wolff to Morris Zuckerman, November 21, 1961, Blue Note Archives.

50 Harry Colomby interview, August 12, 2003.

51 Gary Marmostein, *The Label: The Story of Columbia Records* (New York: Thunder's Mouth Press, 2007), 234–35.

52 Teo Macero to Walter Dean, May 1, 1961, memo re: Carmen McRae and Thelonious Monk, Box 30, Teo Macero Collection, JPB-00-8 Music Division, New York Public Library for the Performing Arts. Hereafter, Ted Macero Collection.

53 Marmostein, *The Label*, 253–54.

54 Walter L. Dean to Clive Davis, July 18, 1961, Box 30, Teo Macero Collection.

55 Walter Dean to Teo Macero, September 29, 1961, Box 30, Teo Macero Collection.

56 "Columbia Records Elects," *New York Times*, January 5, 1962.

57 Walter L. Dean to Dave Kapralik, July 25, 1962, Memo Re: Thelonious Monk; "Artist Contract Card–Columbia Records," page 1, Box 30, Teo Macero Collection.

58 Clive J. Davis to Teo Macero, August 10, 1961, Walter Dean to Teo Macero, September 29, 1961, Walter L. Dean to Dave Kapralik, July 25, 1962 Memo Re: Thelonious Monk, Box 30, Teo Macero Collection.

59 Keepnews, *The View from Within*, 125.

60 (Riverside RLP [9[460/1]. These recordings were later released as separate LPs, *Thelonious Monk in Italy* (Riverside RLP [9]443) and *Thelonious Monk in France* (Riverside RLP [9]490).

61 From the Library of Congress, I obtained the applications from Bar-Thel Music for "Registration of a Claim to Copyright," all dated April 2, 1962, for the following songs: "Ask Me Now"; "Ba-lue Bolivar Ba-lues-Are"; "Bluehawk"; "Blue Monk"; "Brilliant Corners"; "Bye-Ya"; "Crepuscule with Nellie"; "Criss Cross"; "Eronel"; "Evidence"; "Four in One." Among these tunes was the controversial "Eronel," which was originally written by Sadik Hakim and Idrees Sulieman, but because Colomby was unfamiliar with the circumstances behind this song he went ahead and listed Monk as the sole composer. This error on Colomby's part would simply add fuel to a longstanding dispute over the authorship of the tune. See Chapter 12.

62 Harry Colomby interview, August 11, 2003. He said the same thing to Leslie Gourse. See Gourse, *Straight, No Chaser*, 185.

63 Ibid., p. 185.

64 Thelonious and Nellie Monk, U.S. Individual Income Tax Return, 1963, in author's possession.

65 Superior Court of Delaware, New Castle County, The STATE of Delaware v Nica DE KOENIGSWARTER.

66 Gordon, *Live at the Village Vanguard*, 120.

67 "Apollo on Jan. 26: Big Names Are Slated for Job Benefit Headed by Archie Moore," *Pittsburgh Courier*, January 27, 1962; "Strictly Ad Lib," *Down Beat* (April 12, 1962), 43.

68 At the time of the gala (which coincided with the NALC's national executive board meeting), Randolph was embroiled in a dispute with the AFL-CIO leadership over its failure to address racism within its own ranks. "Randolph Calls NALC Bd. to NYC," *Pittsburgh Courier*, January 13, 1962; "Labor's Dispute Over Civil Rights Flares Anew," *New York Times*, December 13, 1961; "King Finds Labor Lagging on Rights," *New York Times*, December 12, 1961. On Randolph's history, see Jervis Anderson, *A. Philip Randolph: A Biographical Portrait* (Berkeley and Los Angeles: University of California Press, 1986); Paula Pfeffer, *A. Philip Randolph, Pioneer of the Civil Rights Movement* (Baton Rouge: Louisiana State University Press, 1996); Andrew E. Kersten, *A. Philip Randolph: A Life in the Vanguard* (Rowan and Littlefield, 2006).

69 See "Biography," *Guide to Ivan Black Papers, 1887–1979 [Bulk dates 1937–1978]*, JPB 06-20, NYPL.

70 Ad, *New York Times*, February 18, 1962; *Amsterdam News*, February 17, 1962. Franklin was booked for a week and then the following weekend he played opposite Tiny Grimes trio, followed by singer Dakota Staton the weekend of March 9. Ads, *Amsterdam News*, March 3, 1962; *Village Voice*, March 8, 1962; *New York Times*, March 8 and 9, 1962. For much of the gig, his quartet was the only act listed.

71 Ad, *Los Angeles Sentinel*, April 26, 1962.

72 Mimi Clar, "Thelonious Monk: Living His Own Legend," *Los Angeles Times*, September 6, 1964.

73 David Amram interview, July 15, 2003.

74 Ibid.

75 Dr. Anna Lou Smith interview, April 7, 2004; "Norwalk Center to be Dedicated," *Los Angeles Times*, May 20, 1962.

76 Dr. Anna Lou Smith interview, April 7, 2004.

77 Wally Guenther, "Night Life: Kitty Quits Circuit, Goes on Own," *Los Angeles Times*, April 29, 1962; *Los Angeles Sentinel*, May 3, 1962. Gillespie had a three-week engagement at the Summit.

78 Clar, "Thelonious Monk: Living His Own Legend."

79 "Penthouse Jazz Party on May 20," *Amsterdam News*, May 19, 1962; "Strictly Ad Lib," *Down Beat* (June 21, 1962), 44. The other artists on the bill included Erskine Hawkins, Benny Golson, Art Farmer, Kenny Dorham, and Pete LaRoca.

80 Jesse H. Walker, "Theatricals," *Amsterdam News*, November 15, 1958; "Jazz Arts Society Sets First Concert," *Amsterdam News*, November 19, 1960; John S. Wilson, "Adderley and Handy are Heard at Debut of Jazz Arts Society," *New York Times*, December 5, 1960; "Jazz Arts Society Concert at Hunter," *Amsterdam News*, December 10, 1960; "Teenagers Hear Jazz Arts Society Program," *Amsterdam News*, March 25, 1961.

81 "First International Jazz Festival," *Washington Post*, May 27, 1962. See, especially, Penny M. Von Eschen, *Satchmo Blows Up the World: Jazz Ambassadors Play the Cold War* (Cambridge, MA: Harvard University Press, 2004). It is no coincidence that during the same week of the International Jazz Festival, Benny Goodman led the first American jazz tour of Russia. See Teddy Wilson, *Teddy Wilson Talks Jazz*, 61–70; "Muscovites Swing to Goodman Jazz," *Washington Post*, June 1, 1962.

82 Ad, "Jazz at the Coliseum," n.d., Claude Barnett Papers, American Negro Press, Reel 6; "International Show Jumps with Jazzfest," *Los Angeles Sentinel*, May 10, 1962; "Uncle Sam's Jazzfest set to Roll 'People to People,'" *Pittsburgh Courier*, May 19, 1962; Phil Casey, "Crowd was 'With It' – at a Distance," *Washington Post*, June 1, 1962; "Jazz Fete is Missed by Kennedy," *Washington Post*, June 2, 1962; Tony Gieske, "Red Combo Blows Hot Festival Notes," *Washington Post*, June 2, 1962.

83 Dan Morgenstern, "Jazz Goes to Washington," *Musical America* 82 (July 1962), 18, and reprinted in Morgenstern, *Living With Jazz: A Reader* (New York: Pantheon Books, 2004), 498–502; Pete Welding, "First International Jazz Festival (Report from Washington)," *Down Beat* (July 19, 1962), 20–21, 60.

84 Tony Gieske, "Duke to Be Star of Jazz Festival," *Washington Post*, April 15, 1962; Paul Hume, "Duke Ellington Livens Up Spiritless Jazz Festival," *Washington Post*, June 2, 1962.

85 The only evidence of a Monk-Hall collaboration on a piece for the Ellington Orchestra appeared as a brief notice in *Down Beat*: "Thelonious Monk will write, and Hall Overton will orchestrate, a special piece for the Duke Ellington Orchestra . . ." "Strictly Ad Lib," *Down Beat* (June 21, 1962), 10.
86 See Chapter 8; David Hajdu, *Lush Life: A Biography of Billy Strayhorn* (New York: North Point Press,1996), 74.
87 The original lead sheets and drafts of the arrangements survive in the Duke Ellington Collection at the Smithsonian. Unfortunately, they are not dated but it appears from other evidence that they were completed in June. "Frère Monk" in Box 125 and "M.D." ["Monk's Dream"] in Box 211, Music Series, Duke Ellington Papers, Collection 301, Smithsonian Museum of American History.
   I find it puzzling that virtually all Ellington and Strayhorn biographers skip over these arrangements or Monk's appearance with the Ellington Orchestra. David Hajdu never mentions it and Walter van de Leur only references the title, "Frère Monk." Walter van de Leur, *Something to Live For: The Music of Billy Strayhorn* (New York: Oxford University Press, 2002), 115. Mark Tucker is one of the few to discuss these two pieces, though he devotes just a few sentences to the entire Monk-Ellington collaboration. Mark Tucker, "Mainstreaming Monk: The Ellington Album," *Black Music Research Journal* 19, no. 2 (1999), 228, also reprinted in Robert G. O'Meally, Brent Hayes Edwards, Farah Jasmine Griffin, eds., *Uptown Conversations: The New Jazz Studies* (New York: Columbia University Press, 2004), 151.
88 Advertisement and "Afro-Latin Jazz at Apollo," *Amsterdam News*, June 23, 1962; "Notebook: 1/5/62 to 12/25/62," Box 3, Frank Schiffman Apollo Theater Collection, Smithsonian Institution.
89 "Pickets March, Tensions Mount on West 125th Street," *Amsterdam News*, June 30, 1962. The picketing worked. Singer offered to either partner with, or sell to, black investors in order to end the standoff. Schiffman also offered to cancel the lease if it would ease racial tensions. Nevertheless, the picketers' were roundly criticized by other black leaders—notably A. Philip Randolph and Jackie Robinson. "Harlem Business Yields in Dispute," *New York Times*, July 13, 1962.
90 "Notebook: 1/5/62 to 12/25/62," Box 3, Frank Schiffman Apollo Theater Collection, Smithsonian Institution.
91 "Village Vanguard: Thelonious Monk, Clark Terry–Bob Brookmeyer, 6/26–7/1," Press Release, Box 25, Ivan Black Papers; "Where & When," *Down Beat* (July 5, 1962), 46; "Where & When," *Down Beat* (May 24, 1962), 54; "Strictly Ad Lib," *Down Beat* (June 7, 1962), 10.
92 The entire program was broadcast by Voice of America and is available on *Duke Ellington, Newport Jazz Festival, 1962* (Toshiba EMI (Jap)TOLW3162).
93 Ellington eventually recorded both songs in the studio a few months later, without Monk, although they were not issued until the 1980s. Duke Ellington and his Orchestra, *The Private Collection: Vol. 3 – Studio Sessions, New York, 1962* (Saja 7 91043 2).
94 John S. Wilson, "Newport Jazz Festival Ends on a Calm and Orderly Note," *New York Times*, July 9, 1962.
95 Wein, *Myself Among Others*, 235.
96 Bill Coss, "Newport Jazz Festival Report: Good Music, Good Times, and Even a Profit," *Down Beat* (August 16, 1962), 17.
97 Ibid., p. 17.
98 See Thomasina Norford, "Rousing Jazz Revival at Newport," *Amsterdam News*, July 14, 1962; Wein, *Myself Among Others*, 235; Wilson, "Newport Jazz Festival Ends."
99 "Where & When," *Down Beat* (May 24, 1962), 54; "Strictly Ad Lib," *Down Beat* (June 7, 1962), 10.
100 "Strictly Ad Lib," *Down Beat* (October 11, 1962), 12.
101 Don Schlitten, who released these tapes on his Xanadu label, originally dated them November 12, 1963. [Liner notes, *Thelonious Monk Live at the Village Gate* (Xanadu 202) and later on CD (Xanadu FDCD 5161).] This isn't possible, since Monk was at the Five Spot then, with different personnel. Chris Sheridan then claimed the recording was made November 12, 1962 (*Brilliant Corners*, 118), but this, too, is impossible since Monk's engagement at the Gate ended the first week of September. The weekend of November 11–12, the line-up at the Gate consisted of Larry Adler, Paul Draper, and Nina Simone. [See ads, *New York Times*, November 9 and 12, 1962.]
102 Edward "Chip" Monck would achieve fame as the MC and lighting director of the 1969 Woodstock Festival. Bob Spitz, *Barefoot in Babylon: The Creation of the Woodstock Music Festival, 1969* (Ann Arbor: University of Michigan Press, 1979).
103 "Cabaret Tonight," *New York Times*, July 31, 1962; *Amsterdam News*, August 4 and 11, 1962; "Where & When," *Down Beat* (August 2, 1962), 46; "Where & When," *Down Beat* (August 30, 1962), 46; "Where & When," *Down Beat* (September 13, 1962), 46; *New York Post*, July 30, 1962. Hawkins's quintet recorded at the Village Gate on August 13 and 15, while Monk's band was still there. Coleman Hawkins, *Hawkins! Alive! At the Village Gate* (Verve 829260-2 [CD]). On the 13th, Hawkins led his quartet with Tommy Flanagan (p) Major Holley (b) Eddie Locke (d), but on the 15th he added Roy Eldridge and Johnny Hodges.
104 John Chilton, *The Song of the Hawk*, 367.
105 Eddie Locke interview, August 31, 2001.
106 "Big Benefit at Apollo August 11," *Amsterdam News*, July 28, 1962; Ad, *Amsterdam News*, August 11, 1962. Some of the participants included Tony Bennett, Art Blakey, "Moms" Mabley, Gerry Mulligan, Lambert, Hendricks and Bavan, Max Roach, and Billy Taylor.
107 T. S. Monk interview, April 4, 2005.
108 According to Peter W. Cookson, Jr., and Caroline Hodges Persell, "Progressive schools tend to draw children of affluent, liberal, professional families, including those who are successful in the arts. Progressive schools have not traditionally sought to prepare students for excercising power, but rather encourage them to develop their individual intellectual and creative potentials." *Preparing for Power: America's Elite Boarding Schools* (New York: Basic Books, 1985), 41. Cherry Lawn no longer exists and thus its records are not available. I'm grateful to

Mike Manners of the Cherry Lawn Alumni Association for providing valuable information about the school, including the tuition in the early to mid-1960s. Email from Mike Manners, Cherry Lawn Alumni Association, to author, August 6, 2008.

109 T. S. Monk, April 4, 2005; Harry Colomby, August 12, 2003; evidence on the social origins of the students derive from examining the yearbooks (*Cherry Pit*) from 1963–1968. I'm grateful to the Cherry Lawn Alumni Association, and especially Mike Manners, for making the yearbooks available. Thelonious Monk, Jr., first appears in *Cherry Pit 1963*, p. 46, with the eighth grade class.

110 On the history of these settlements, which date back to the 18th century, see Linda Baulsir and Irwin Miller, *The Jewish Communities of Greater Stamford* (Charleston, SC: Arcadia Publishing, 2002).

111 See photo of Toot with the entire eighth grade class, which consisted of seventeen students. *Cherry Pit 1963 [Yearbook]* (South Norwalk, CT: T. O'Toole and Sons, 1963), 46. Andy Adler is the only student not pictured, and he was not black. Of the twenty-eight students who made up the graduating class of 1963, only one was African-American—Jane Laster from Teaneck, N.J. (pp. 64, 72.)

112 *Cherry Pit 1963* [Yearbook], 55.

113 Peter Adelman, "The Case for Rebellion," Ibid., p. 40.

114 T. S. Monk, interview, April 4, 2005.

115 Ibid. Ronnie Greenberg was an eleventh grader when Toot entered school. *Cherry Pit 1963*, p. 49.

116 T. S. Monk, interview, April 4, 2005. As it turned out, the two boys were practically neighbors; the Libermans lived on 79th and West End. "Student Directory," *Cherry Pit 1963*, p. 72.

117 Sam Ross, Jr., and Myra Ross, interview, August 14, 2008; "Green Chimneys Farm," http://www.historicpatterson.org/Exhibits/ExhGreenChimneys.php; "A History of Green Chimneys," http://www.greenchimneys.org/; Email from Sam Ross, founder and managing director of Green Chimneys, to author, August 4, 2008. See also the arresting documentary film, *Green Chimneys,* for a more recent view of the campus and the school's mission. Now it is a nonprofit social service organization helping children with special needs, particularly poor children in the foster care system with behavioral and emotional problems. Neil P. Parent, Constance Marks, and James Miller, *Green Chimneys* (DVD Cinequest).

118 Sam Ross, Jr., and Myra Ross, interview, August 14, 2008.

119 Ibid.

120 "Thelonious Cathouse, September 17, 1962, New Tune called 'Everything Begins Here & Everything Ends Here,'" Reel # 59, The Pannonica Collection (1956–1970), reel description.

24 "Everything Begins Here and Everything Ends Here"

1 Jim Cogan and William Clark, *Temples of Sound: Inside the Great Recording Studios* (San Francisco: Chronicle Books, 2003), 183–186; Dave Simons, *Studio Stories: How the Great New York Records Were Made—from Miles to Madonna, Sinatra to the Ramones* (San Francisco: Backbeat Books, 2004), 26–27; Ashley Kahn, *Kind of Blue: The Making of the Miles Davis Masterpiece* (New York: Da Capo Press, 2000), 75–76.

2 Artist Contract Card–Columbia Records, Box 30, Teo Macero Collection. The piano tuner was Gene Manfrini, and he received anywhere between $25 and $90 for tuning during the years Monk was with Columbia. And his costs were always deducted from Monk's advances.

3 Simons, *Studio Stories,* 26–29.

4 "Strictly Ad Lib," *Down Beat* (February 28, 1963), 12.

5 Nat Shapiro to George T. Wein, January 18, 1963, Box 30, Teo Macero Collection.

6 Nica de Koenigswarter to Teo Macero, April 2, 1963, Box 30, Teo Macero Collection.

7 Martin Williams to Teo Macero, October 19, 1962, Teo Macero to Martin Williams, November 29, 1962, Box 30, Teo Macero Collection.

8 Teo Macero to Irving Townsend, November 23, 1962, Box 30, Teo Macero Collection.

9 Released on *Monk's Dream* (Columbia CL 1965).

10 All three versions are on Thelonious Monk, *Monk Alone: The Complete Columbia Solo Studio Recordings of Thelonious Monk (1962–1968)* (Columbia C2K 65495). The remake of take 2, recorded on November 1, was selected for *Monk's Dream.*

11 Evidently, he named it well after the studio session because "Sweet Georgia Brown" is crossed out on the Tape Identification sheet and "Bright Mississippi" written over it. See, Tape Identification Data, Job. No. 78233, and Artist Contract Card, Columbia Records, page 2, Box 30, Teo Macero Collection. It was released on *Monk's Dream* (Columbia CL1965).

12 The alternate version was released in 1979 on *Always Know* (Columbia JG35720), and now available on CD.

13 He and Nellie bought the reel-to-reel version of Vladimir Horowitz, *Chopin, Schumann, Rachmaninoff, Liszt* (Columbia Stereo Tape Masterworks Stereo disc KS 6371). See Appendix, "Records and Tapes in Thelonious Monk's Collection." It is tempting to think that Columbia gave Monk a promotional copy, but he never removed the Sam Goody price tag!

14 Although it appears to be apocryphal, a story has been circulating for many years among jazz musicians whereby Horowitz played his variation of "Tea for Two" for Art Tatum, whom he admired very much, and then when Tatum responded in kind with *his* variation, Horowitz was astounded. He asked Tatum, "How long did it take for you to make that up?" Tatum replied, "I don't know, how long was it?" Horowitz found it amazing that he could improvise such an elaborate variation of the theme, and legend has it, he never played "Tea for Two" in public again. What is true is that the only recording we have of Horowitz playing "Tea for Two" took place that November 1962, and it was clearly not intended for release. See "Recorded Horowitz: An Index of Released & Unreleased Recordings," Prepared and Compiled by Christian Johansson, http://web.telia.com/~u85420275/

chronological.htm These recordings (sans "Tea for Two") are available on Vladimir Horowitz, *The Complete Masterworks Recordings, Volume I: The Studio Recordings 1962–1963* (Sony Classical: S2K 53457)

15   Artist Contract Card, Columbia Records, page 2, Box 30, Teo Macero Collection.

16   Thelonious Monk, U.S. Individual Income Tax Return, 1964, Item 25 – Other Business Expense, in author's possession. Colomby thought he had gotten at least half off the regular price, but ads in the *New York Times* reveal that the regular price for the top of the line Grand M was $3,365.00, and had he waited for the spring sale he could have gotten the same piano (though a floor model) for $1,965.00! See ad, *New York Times*, May 17, 1963; Harry Colomby interview, August 11, 2003.

17   Thelonious and Nellie Monk, U.S. Individual Income Tax Return, 1963.

18   Macero to Dave Kapralik, January 22, 1963, Box 30, Teo Macero Collection.

19   James Forman, *The Making of Black Revolutionaries* (Seattle: University of Washington Press, 1997, orig. 1972), 293; Taylor Branch, *Parting the Waters: America in the King Years, 1954–1963* (New York: Simon & Schuster, 1988), 713.

20   Alfredo Graham, "Shelley Winters Dubs Race Bigotry Nonsense," *Pittsburgh Courier*, January 26, 1963; Carson, *In Struggle*, 45–86; Barbara Ransby, *Ella Baker and the Black Freedom Movement: A Radical Democratic Vision* (Chapel Hill, NC: University of North Carolina Press, 2005), 281–313.

21   "A Salute to Southern Students," February 1, 1963, SNCC Papers, microfilm reel 45; 2110 Alfredo Graham, "Shelley Winters Dubs Race Bigotry Nonsense," *Pittsburgh Courier*, January 26, 1963; "Fri. Concert to Aid Students," *Amsterdam News*, February 2, 1963; and for an overview of the event, see Monson, *Freedom Sounds*, 199–201.

22   Alice Wright interview, August 28, 2000; Forman, *The Making of Black Revolutionaries*, 292–93.

23   "Entertainers contacted," n.d., SNCC Papers, microfilm reel 27. Musicians preferred Monday night benefits since it was traditionally their off night. "A Salute" fell on a Friday, February 1.

24   "A Salute to Southern Students," February 1, 1963, SNCC Papers, microfilm reel 45; " Salute to Southern Students," Press Release, n.d., Box 33, Ivan Black Papers; Graham, "Shelley Winters Dubs Race Bigotry Nonsense"; "Fri. Concert to Aid Students," *Amsterdam News*, February 2, 1963; "'Salute to Southern Students' Slated for Carnegie Hall, Feb. 1," *Atlanta Daily World*, January 31, 1963.

25   Alice Wright interview, August 28, 2000.

26   Joanne Grant, *Ella Baker: Freedom Bound* (New York: John Wiley and Sons, 1999), 154.

27   John Henry Faulk, celebrated storyteller and radio host who was perhaps best known for winning a libel suit against radio and television networks after he had been blacklisted during the McCarthy era. See, Michael C. Burton, *John Henry Faulk: The Making of a Liberated Mind: A Biography* (Austin: Eakin Press, 1993); John Henry Faulk, *Fear on Trial* (New York: Simon & Schuster, 1964).

28   "'Freedom Singers' Here to Raise Funds for Miss. Vote Victims," *Chicago Defender*, January 19, 1963; Forman, *The Making of Black Revolutionaries*, 297; Alice Wright interview, August 28, 2000; Laureen Gunther, "Carnegie Hall Show—The Students Took Over from Featured Artists," *Amsterdam News*, February 9, 1963.

29   Laureen Gunther, "Carnegie Hall Show."

30   Alice Wright interview, August 28, 2000.

31   Quoted in Monson, *Freedom Sounds*, 201.

32   SNCC Press Release, "Jazz Greats in SNCC Concert at Carnegie Hall, November 23," n.d., Box 33, Ivan Black Papers.

33   Michael James, "Sonny Clark," *Jazz Monthly* 9, no. 3 (1963), 5; Jesse H. Walker, "Theatricals," *Amsterdam News*, February 2, 1963; Claude Schlouch, *In Memory of Ike Quebec: a Discography* (Marseilles, France, 1983, rev. 3/1985); Cook, *Blue Note Records*, 143.

34   Nellie and Toot both told me that Monk gave Sonny Clark money and that he had stayed at their place at least once (Nellie Monk interview, January 12, 2002; T. S. Monk interview, October 10, 2001), and this is consistent with Hampton Hawes's account of his dealings with Monk when he and Sonny Clark were strung out together. Monk loaned Hawes money and tried to help him straighten up. Hawes, *Raise Up Off Me*, 104–107.

35   Freymann, *What's So Bad About Feeling Good?*, 69–73.

36   "Clark Benefit This Monday," *Amsterdam News*, February 2, 1963; "Strictly Ad Lib," *Down Beat* (March 28, 1963), 54. The benefit was originally scheduled for January 28 but was postponed. "Sonny Clark Benefit Mon.," *Amsterdam News*, January 26, 1963.

37   Cherry Hospital was finally integrated in 1964.

38   North Carolina State Board of Health, Certificate of Death: Thelonious Monk. Registrar's Certificate No. 521. Olivia and Conley Monk were never contacted after Thelonious, Sr., died, despite the fact that the hospital had their forwarding address. Olivia Monk, Pam Kelley Monk, Conley F. Monk, Jr., Marcella Monk Flake, Evelyn Pue, interview, August 6, 2007.

39   See Chapter 11.

40   Monk's dislike for Goodstein was well known in the family and among musicians. See Marcellus Green interview, October 19, 2001; Nellie Monk interview, January 12, 2002; T. S. Monk interview, October 10, 2001. An example of Goodstein's vindictiveness is evident in a letter he wrote to Bud Powell and Buttercup a few months after they moved to Paris. Angered partly over commission fees Powell allegedly owed him, he wrote: "And if you are smart you will start figuring out how much you owe me to date and start paying because some day you will return to the United States and find out what a difficult spot you are in if you try to cross me." Oscar Goodstein to Bud and Buttercup, October 22, 1959, copy in Surrogates Court, County of Kings, Proceeding for Letters of Administration. Estate of Earl Bud Powell, File No. 7370/1968.

41   Goodstein would close the club the following year and declare bankruptcy. He had already begun to move away from an all-jazz policy. When Birdland finally closed in June of 1964, he was over $100,000 in debt. "Bankruptcy Proceedings," *New York Times*, June 20, 1964.

42 Five tunes from the three broadcasts were released on Thelonious Monk, *Spastic and Personal* (Alto AL725).

43 Matthews, "Mr 1-2-5 Street," *Amsterdam News*, February 23, 1963; Bob Hunter, "New Comic Has Flip Tongue, Fly Style," *Chicago Defender*, February 27, 1963. Monk and Wilson shared the bill just a few months earlier at the Apollo. "Apollo Extends Another Show," *Amsterdam News*, June 16, 1962.

44 "Thelonious Monk at Queensborough," *New York Post*, February 7, 1963.

45 Sheridan (*Brilliant Corners*, 120–121) gives slightly different dates for all of these sessions, but I am going by the Artist Job Sheets in Teo Macero's papers. They list the date, time, and songs recorded. "Artist Job Sheet," February 25, 1963, Box 30, Teo Macero Collection. "Tea for Two," Home recording in author's possession, ca. February 1963.

46 "Five Spot Café Opens in New Location," *East Side News*, January 25, 1963; (Quote) Martin T. Williams, "A Night at the Five Spot," *Jazz Changes* (New York: Oxford University Press, 1992), 91–94. The essay first appeared in *Down Beat* (February 13, 1964), 20–22, but all page numbers refer to Williams' book.

47 LeRoi Jones, "The Acceptance of Monk," 21.

48 "Strictly Ad Lib," *Down Beat* (April 25, 1963), 14.

49 Contract between Joseph Termini and Thelonious Monk, February 22, 1963, New York, Joseph Termini Papers, courtesy of Toni Behm.

50 Harry Colomby interview, August 12, 2003; "Thelonious Monk in Philharmonic Hall Concert, Fri. November 29," press release, 11/22/1963. Handwritten over the release is the explanation for the postponement—Kennedy's assassination. BOX 25, Ivan Black Papers.

51 Wein, *Myself Among Others*, 226.

52 "Strictly Ad Lib," *Down Beat* (May 23, 1963), 44; Lennart Ostberg, "Monk I Hogform," *Orkester Journalen* 31 (March 1963), 14; Ole Just Astrup, "Musikerna Kring Monk," *Orkester Journalen* 31 (July-August 1963), 10–11; Farrell, "Loneliest Monk," 84. Farrell writes as if he went on tour with Thelonious. He did not. These stories he obtained through various interviews with Monk, Nellie, and others on the tour. He also collapses two different tours since he placed Thelonious in cities like Milan in March of 1963 when he played there in 1961 and February 1964.

53 Postif, "'Round 'Bout Sphere," 25, 29.

54 Farrell, "Loneliest Monk," 84. It should be noted, however, that the German cities they played were also part of the U.S. occupation and thus had an established jazz tradition.

55 "Strictly Ad Lib," *Down Beat* (July 4, 1963), 44.

56 Thelonious Monk, "By and By, When the Morning Comes," SWF-TV Baden Baden, Germany, March 2, 1963, unreleased recording in author's possession.

57 Liner notes, Thelonious Monk, *Monk's Dream* (Columbia CL1965). A copy of the original draft, which had been cut substantially for publication, has been preserved in Teo Macero's Collection. In the first draft of Macero's own essay, he compares Monk and Picasso to great effect. See "Monk's Dream" notes, Box 30, Teo Macero Collection.

58 See for example, "Une Retrospective Monkienne," *Jazz Hot* 185 (March 1963), 6; J. Bens, "Monk l'Explorateur," *Jazz Magazine* 9 (April 1963), 37–38; Ostberg, "Monk I Hogform," 14; Jack Cooke, "Better Times Ahead," *Jazz Monthly* 8 (January 1963), 3–5.

59 Postif, "'Round 'Bout Sphere," 25. Postif actually reconstructs the interview from notes and memory because after he finished taping, Thelonious asked to hear it back on the tape recorder they had just purchased in Hamburg. Then he put the tape in his pocket to "borrow" it for a while, promising to send it back. As Postif explained, he cabled him several times and got no response, nor did he ever get his tape back. Ibid., p. 41.

60 Postif, "'Round 'Bout Sphere," 25, 29 and 41.

61 Monk quoted in Clouzet and Delorme, "L'amertume du prophète," 38.

62 Ibid., p. 38.

63 I quote portions of this interview in other parts of the book, notably in Chapter 9.

64 Clouzet and Delorme, "L'amertume du prophète," 39–40.

65 Ibid., pp. 40–41.

66 Artist Job Sheet, 3/29/63, Box 30, Teo Macero Collection.

67 Nine tracks were included on the second LP: "Hackensack"; "Rhythm-A-Ning"; "Tea for Two (trio)"; "Criss-Cross"; "Eronel"; "Don't Blame Me (solo)"; "Think of One"; "Crepuscule with Nellie"; "Pannonica." Thelonious Monk, *Criss Cross* (Columbia CL 2038).

68 Nica de Koenigswarter to Teo Macero, April 2, 1963, Box 30, Teo Macero Collection.

69 Ibid.

70 Peter Welding review, *Downbeat* (March 14, 1963); Martin Williams, "Thelonious Monk: Arrival Without Departure," *Saturday Review* 46 (April 13, 1963), 32–33, 37, quote on p. 32.

71 Jesse H. Walker, "Theatricals," *Amsterdam News*, April 6, 1963; "Strictly Ad Lib," *Down Beat* (May 23, 1963), 12. Monk was the second featured artist in the series. The inaugural workshop took place on March 31, 1963, with Charles Mingus, Donald Byrd, Clifford Jordan and Willie Jones.

72 On Reverend Callender, see "It's Callender vs. Crawford in NAACP," *Amsterdam News*, November 30, 1957; James Booker, "Addicts form Club to 'Kick Dope Habit,'" *Amsterdam News*, March 22, 1958; "Wagner Agrees to Back Harlem Youth Program," *Amsterdam News*, November 11, 1961; "Churches Honored at New YWCA," *Amsterdam News*, December 8, 1962; "Rev. Eugene Callender Honored on 50th Anniversary of his Ministry," *Amsterdam News*, October 26, 2000; Noel A. Cazenave, *Impossible Democracy: The Unlikely Success of the War on Poverty Community Action Programs* (Albany: SUNY Press, 2007), 113.

73 Fred H. Russell, "Gossip of the Rialto," *Bridgeport Sunday Post*, April 21, 1963; "This Week With the Arts," *Bridgeport Sunday Post*, April 28, 1963.

74 T. S. Monk, interview, April 4, 2005. Monk made sure he stayed on good terms with the school. He even had Columbia send Cherry Lawn his entire catalogue of LPs (billed to Thelonious Monk, of course!). Teo Macero to Don Curry, May 10, 1966, Box 30, Teo Macero Collection.

75 Paul Slaughter, "Les Tenoirs de Thelonious," *Jazz Hot* (April 1982), 17; "Charlie Rouse: Monk, un Classique Moderne," *Jazz Hot* 186 (April 1963), 6–8.

76 Donald Byrd, *Royal Flush* (Blue Note BLP 4101); Jackie McLean, *A Fickle Sonance* (Blue Note BLP 4089); Dexter Gordon, *Go!* (Blue Note 84112); Sonny Clark, *Leapin' & Lopin': Sonny Clark All Stars* (Blue Note BLP 4091); Elmo Hope, *High Hope* (Beacon LP 401); Slaughter, "Les Tenoirs," 17; Erik R. Quick, "Butch Warren," *All About Jazz* (July 21, 2006), http://www.allaboutjazz.com/php/article.php?id=22403; Edward "Butch" Warren, NBC interview with Antoine Sanfuentes, 2008, used by permission. See also the excellent segment on Warren produced by Antoine Sanfuentes for MSNBC, http://www.msnbc.msn.com/id/24864395.

77 Edward "Butch" Warren, NBC interview with Antoine Sanfuentes, 2008, used by permission.

78 Recording in author's possession, courtesy of the Thelonious Monk Estate.

79 Edward "Butch" Warren, NBC interview with Antoine Sanfuentes, 2008, used by permission. Warren remembers only working with Monk one night before leaving for Japan, but this is impossible, given how difficult it was to obtain a visa. George Wein says that it took months to get the appropriate work visas since every traveler had to go to the consulate directly. Wein recalls finally arranging a date when Monk, Nellie, and the band could meet at the consulate but when they got there it was closed in observance of Emperor Akihito's birthday (which, incidentally, was December 23). Wein, *Myself Among Others*, 224–225.

80 David Amram interview, July 15, 2003.

81 E. Taylor Atkins, *Blue Nippon: Authenticating Jazz in Japan* (Durham, NC: Duke University Press, 2001), 209. In 1960, even *Down Beat* launched a Japanese edition of its magazine. "Shinu, Shinu, Shinu," *Time* (September 12, 1960), 60.

82 "Jazz Records Best Twenty in Critics Choice," *Swing Journal* (January 1959), 64–66. Translated from the Japanese by Chris and Fujiko Kelley. I am grateful to both for all of the Japanese translations in this book.

83 Jiro Kubota, "Monk," *Swing Journal* (November 1958), 92–93; Yui Shoichi, "Brilliant Corners," *Swing Journal* (December 1958), 95.

84 Jinichi Uekusa, "Blakey and Monk Together are the Greatest," *Swing Journal* (October 1958), 86–87, 97; Jinichi Uekusa, "A Guide to Understanding Thelonious Monk," *Swing Journal* (June 1960), 20–24.

85 The Tokyo-born pianist played Hawaiian music until the mid-1950s when he switched to jazz and joined Shin Matsumoto's Ichiban Octet and later replaced Akiyoshi Toshiko in the Cozy Quartet led by alto saxophonist Watanabe Sadao. Yozo Iwanami and Kazunori Sugiyama, "Yagi, Masao." In *The New Grove Dictionary of Jazz*, 2nd ed., edited by Barry Kernfeld. *Grove Music Online. Oxford Music Online*, http://www.oxfordmusiconline.com/subscriber/article/grove/music/J493400 (accessed July 18, 2008); Akiyoshi Toshiko founded the Cozy Quartet, but when she left in 1956 to study at the Berklee College of Music, alto saxophonist Watanabe Sadao took over as leader. See Lem Lyons, *The Great Jazz Pianists, Speaking of their Lives and Music* (New York, 1983), 249–56.

86 *Masao Yagi Plays Thelonious Monk* (King (Jap)SKK-3014). Besides the songs mentioned, the LP includes "Misterioso," "Straight, No Chaser," and "Blue Monk."

87 Other members of the quintet were trumpeter Nakano Akira, saxophonist Watanabe Sadao, and drummer Tabata Teiichi.

88 This dilemma is at the heart of E. Taylor Atkins' book, *Blue Nippon*, although he doesn't deal specifically with Yagi Masao's exploration of Thelonious Monk. As he demonstrates, it was immediately following the "rainichi" rush that Japanese jazz musicians began pushing for a distinctive national style as opposed to an American derivative.

89 "Strictly Ad Lib," *Down Beat* (June 20, 1963), 12; "Strictly Ad Lib," *Down Beat* (July 4, 1963), 44; "Strictly Ad Lib," *Down Beat* (July 18, 1963), 44; *New York Post*, May 28, 1963; *New York Journal-American*, May 28, 1963; *Chicago Defender*, May 20, 1963. Jimmy Rushing, former Count Basie vocalist, was backed by a rhythm section made up of George Wein, Butch Warren, and Frankie Dunlop.

90 Kiyoshi Koyama, Liner notes to Thelonious Monk Quartet, *Monk in Tokyo* (Columbia C2K 63538); *Chicago Defender*, May 20, 1963; Sheridan, *Brilliant Corners*, 407.

91 Thelonious Monk Quartet, *Monk in Tokyo* (Columbia C2K 63538).

92 *Thelonious Monk in Japan—1963* (Toshiba/EMI TOLW-3123).

93 He is wearing the jacket in the photo published in Lewis Lapham's article, "Monk: High Priest of Jazz," *Saturday Evening Post* 237 (April 11, 1964), 72. The two dolls also appear in the photo on a glass case behind the piano. I found the jacket in Monk's storage facility and had it repaired, so I can attest to the quality of the piece. It looks as if it might have been handmade, and the label indicates 100% silk.

94 See Dianne McWhorter, *Carry Me Home: Birmingham Alabama—The Climactic Battle of the Civil Rights Revolution* (New York: Simon & Schuster, 2001), 365–410; Glenn T. Eskew, *But for Birmingham: The Local and National Movements in the Civil Rights Struggle* (Chapel Hill, NC: University of North Carolina Press, 1997), 299–332; Taylor Branch, *Parting the Waters*, 793–802; Anthony Lewis, "U.S. Sends Troops into Alabama After Riots Sweep Birmingham," *New York Times*, May 13, 1963; Hedrick Smith, "Stores Hit by Riots Still Smolder As Birmingham Removes Debris," *New York Times*, May 14, 1963. The English-language daily *Japan Times* carried front page articles about the Birmingham confrontation nearly every day the first week of Monk's tour.

95 Ivan Black, "Thelonious Comes Home and Opens New Five-Spot Café," May 25, 1963, Box 25, Ivan Black Papers; "Strictly Ad Lib," *Down Beat* (July 18, 1963), 6; Jonny Bowden, "The Beat," *The Queen's Voice*, July 19, 1963.

96 He opened on May 28. Associated Musicians of Greater New York, Local 802, Contract, May 27, 1963, copy in Joseph Termini Papers.

97   *New York Daily News*, July 31, 1963.
98   "Strictly Ad Lib," *Down Beat* (August 15, 1963), 10; also, Jesse H. Walker, "Theatricals," *Amsterdam News*, July 13, 1963.
99   Banes, *Greenwich Village 1963*.
100 Robert Sylvester, "Dream Street," *New York Daily News*, June 9, 1963.
101 John S. Wilson, "Concerts Stress Teaching of Jazz," *New York Times*, June 3, 1963; John S. Wilson, "A Village Affair," *New York Times*, June 9, 1963; George F. Brown, "New York Day and Nite," *Pittsburgh Courier*, June 22, 1963; "Strictly Ad Lib," *Down Beat* (June 20, 1963), 12.
102 John S. Wilson, "Jazz Event Centers on Thelonious Monk," *New York Times*, June 24, 1963.
103 "Overton, Monk at the New School," June 20, 1963 [sic], CCP 104 (Disc 4), Eugene Smith Tapes. The date on the tape was wrong. It should have read June 22. Besides the fact that all press reports as well as the poster advertising the event give the date as the 22nd, but Monk was in Cleveland playing a concert on the 20th of June.
104 "Overton, Monk at the New School" June 20, 1963 [sic], CCP 104 (Disc 4), Eugene Smith Tapes.
105 Ibid.
106 Ibid.
107 Wilson, "Jazz Event Centers on Thelonious Monk."
108 "Strictly Ad Lib," *Down Beat* (July 4, 1963), 10 and 43.
109 Robert Hilbert, *Pee Wee Russell: The Life of a Jazzman* (New York: Oxford University Press, 1993), 252; Wein, *Myself Among Others*, 222.
110 Hilbert, *Pee Wee Russell*, 243, 249–52.
111 Ibid., 254.
112 Ibid., 253.
113 John S. Wilson, "New Jazz Faces Seen At Newport," *New York Times*, July 6, 1963.
114 Wein, *Myself Among Others*, 222.
115 *Miles and Monk at Newport* (Columbia CL 2178).
116 Memo from Maida Schwartz and Stan Rublowsky, March 16, 1964, Box 7, Teo Macero Collection.
117 Harry Colomby interview, August 12, 2003.
118 Ibid.; see also Gourse, *Straight, No Chaser*, 200.
119 Bernhard M. Auer, "A Letter from the Publisher," *Time* (February 28, 1964), 15.
120 The piece, "The Top U.S. Orchestras," appeared in *Time* (February 22, 1963), 65.
121 Farrell related this story to Harry Colomby, whom he subsequently befriended. Colomby interview, August 12, 2003.
122 Barry Farrell, "The Beautiful Persons," *Time* (June 28, 1963), 33.
123 Auer, "A Letter from the Publisher," 15.
124 Stephen Hawk, ed., *How I Got to Be This Hip: The Collected Works of One of America's Preeminent Journalists* (New York: Washington Square Press, 1999), x–xi, 57.
125 From John Gregory Dunne, "Introduction" to Hawk, ed., *How I Got to Be This Hip*, x; also reprinted in John Gregory Dunne, *Regards: The Selected Non-Fiction of John Gregory Dunne* (New York: Thunder's Mouth Press, 2005), 367–72.
126 "More Top Names for Big Benefit," *Amsterdam News*, August 10, 1963; "'March' Gala Has $250,000 Talent," *Amsterdam News*, August 24, 1963.
127 Harry Colomby interview, August 11, 2003.
128 Ronnie died on September 8, 1963. "Ronald Newkirk, Death Certificate #9841," NYC Department of Health, *Deaths Reported in the City of New York, 1963*, p. 286.
129 T. S. Monk, interview, April 4, 2005.
130 Clifton Smith interview, July 27, 2004.
131 Theolonious Monk interview, January 30, 2004.
132 Jackie Bonneau interview, October 30, 2008.
133 Benetta Bines, Monk family interview, January 30, 2004.
134 T. S. Monk, interview, April 4, 2005.
135 See McWhorter, *Carry Me Home*; Eskew, *But for Birmingham*.

25   "That's a Drag Picture They're Paintin' of Me"

1   Both Martin Williams and Amiri Baraka give nearly identical descriptions of Monk's routine at the Five Spot, based on their attendance during the fall of 1963. *Down Beat* published their accounts within a couple of weeks of one another; Martin T. Williams, "A Night at the Five Spot," 91; LeRoi Jones, "The Acceptance of Monk," 20–22.
2   LeRoi Jones, "The Acceptance of Monk," 21, 22.
3   Edward "Butch" Warren, NBC interview with Antoine Sanfuentes, 2008, used by permission.
4   Jesse H. Walker, "Theatricals," *Amsterdam News*, July 13 and 27, and November 30, 1963.
5   Sandra Capello interview, July 19, 2003; Paul Jeffrey interview, August 31, 2003. That Rouse used heroin and broke the habit in the early 1960s is confirmed by Capello; Nellie Monk (interview January 12, 2002); Marcellus Green (interview); Alonzo White (interview, February 23, 2004). See also Chapter 19.
6   Auer, "A Letter from the Publisher," 15.
7   "Strictly Ad Lib," *Down Beat* (November 7, 1963), 10, 46; "Line Up Jazz Festival for Monterey, Calif.," *Chicago Defender*, August 26, 1963; "Thelonious Monk Added to Jazz at Monterey," *Los Angeles Sentinel*, September

19, 1963; *Sixth Annual Monterey Jazz Festival, September 20–21–22, 1963* [Program], p. 14, copy in Stanford University, Archives of Recorded Sound, Braun Music Center.

8 Thelonious Monk, *Thelonious Monk Quartet—Live at Monterey Jazz Festival, 1963: Vol. 1 and 2* (Storyville STCD 8255/6). John Ore is mistakenly listed as the bassist on this recording.

9 *Monterey Jazz Festival: Seventh Year, September 19–20–21, 1964* [Program], p. 19.

10 Farrell, "The Loneliest Monk," 87. Powell's bills for November 19 through December 31 alone added up to 3,819 francs. See "Relève [Statement]," Bud Powell, December 31, 1963, Sanatorium Universitaire Jacques Arnaud, copy in Surrogates Court, County of Kings, Proceeding for Letters of Administration, Estate of Earl Bud Powell, Deceased, File No. 7370/1968.

11 Oscar Goodstein to Bud Powell, October 26, 1963, copy of letter in Surrogates Court, County of Kings, Proceeding for Letters of Administration, Estate of Earl Bud Powell, Deceased, File No. 7370/1968. The featured artists included Horace Silver, Terry Gibbs, Mary Lou Williams, and Clark Terry. *Amsterdam News*, October 26, 1963. See also, Paudras, *Dance of the Infidels*, 186–194; Groves and Shipton, *The Glass Enclosure*, 84–86.

12 "CORE Repeats Jazz Concert," *Amsterdam News*, October 26, 1963. The benefit was scheduled virtually the same time as the Bud Powell benefit. Other performers included, Al Cohn–Zoot Sims Quintet, Bill Evans, Freddie Redd Quintet, George Russell Sextet, vocalist Shelia Jordan. Ira Gitler was the emcee.

13 Flyer for Bronx Cocktail Sip, Papers of Congress of Racial Equality [microfilm], Addendum, subgroup F., Reel 18, Series 2.

14 "Strictly Ad Lib," *Down Beat* (September 26, 1963), 10; "Strictly Ad Lib," *Down Beat* (December 5, 1963), 12; *Philharmonic Hall: Lincoln Center for the Performing Arts, 1963–1964* [Program], p. A; Memo from Morton M. Drosnes to Ed Beulike, December 2, 1963, Box 30, Teo Macero Collection, NYPL.

15 "Strictly Ad Lib," *Down Beat* (December 5, 1963), 12; Dizzy Reece interview with Ed Berger, January 23 and 30, 2005, WBGO, Jazz From the Archives.

16 See "Gene Allen," in Gordon Jack, ed., *Fifties Jazz Talk: An Oral Retrospective* (Metutchen, NJ: Scarecrow Press, 2004), 1–8.

17 Peter Bart, "Advertising: Impact on Industry Continues," *New York Times*, November 26, 1963.; "Carnegie Hall (Unaware) Plugs Philharmonic Hall Concert," press release from Ivan Black, New York, December 29, 1963, Box 25, Ivan Black Papers. The fact that Monk's story did not appear in the next few issues led the black press to speculate that *Time* killed the article. See, Louise Davis Stone, "The Jazz Bit," *Chicago Defender*, December 28, 1963; "Monk Off Cover," *Amsterdam News*, December 7, 1963; Whitelaw McBride, "People in the News," *Pittsburgh Courier*, December 7, 1963.

18 "Monk Rehearsal at Hall's. Day of Storm," December 23, 1963, CCP 115 (Disc 1), Eugene Smith Tapes.

19 "Monk Rehearsal at Hall's. Day of Storm," December 23, 1963, CCP 115 (Disc 2), Eugene Smith Tapes.

20 "Carnegie Hall (Unaware) Plugs Philharmonic Hall Concert," press release from Ivan Black, New York, December 29, 1963, Box 25, Ivan Black Papers.

21 John S. Wilson, "Thelonious Monk, Unworldly from Way Back," *New York Times*, December 29, 1963.

22 *Philharmonic Hall: Lincoln Center for the Performing Arts, 1963–1964* [Program], p. A.

23 Virtually every recording of "Oska T." was for big band. After the Philharmonic concert, he did not play it again until he toured Europe with a big band in 1967, and the only other time it popped up was in 1969 when he performed it with a quartet.

24 Larry Langman and David Ebner, comp., *Hollywood's Image of the South: A Century of Southern Films* (Westport, CT: Greenwood Press, 2001), 205.

25 When the LP was originally released as *Thelonious Monk Big Band and Quartet in Concert* (Columbia CL 2164), "Bye-Ya," "Misterioso," and "Light Blue" were not included, and Macero edited out Dunlop's drum solos. The entire unedited concert is available on two CDs as *Monk Big Band and Quartet in Concert* (Columbia C2K57636).

26 The plaque, which the family possesses, recognizes "Mr. Thelonius Monk" [sic] and is dated November 29, 1963.

27 Robert Shelton, "Thelonious Monk at Philharmonic," *New York Times*, December 31, 1963; Ira Gitler, "Caught in the Act," *Down Beat* (February 27, 1964), 34–35; Mark Humphrey liner notes to *Monk Big Band and Quartet in Concert* (Columbia C2K57636).

28 George T. Simon, "Philharmonic Hall Set a-Swinging with Monk," *New York Herald-Tribune*, December 31, 1963. There were some outlyers, like the critic for *The Villager* who would have preferred to hear what "a jazz arranger like Oliver Nelson or Gil Evans" might have done with Monk's music. "Thelonious Monk in Philharmonic Hall," *The Villager*, January 9, 1964.

29 Thelonious and Nellie Monk, New York State Income Tax Resident Return, 1963; U.S. Individual Income Tax Return, 1963; "Thelonious Monk Statement of Income and Expenses, 1963," in author's possession.

30 Barry Farrell claimed that Monk earned $50,000 in 1963. Farrell, "Loneliest Monk," 84.

31 Artist Contract Card, Columbia Records, page 3, Box 30, Teo Macero Collection. Upon completing the LP, the remaining advance less these charges amounted to $3,607.20.

32 Artist Contract Card, Columbia Records, page 5–7, Box 30, Teo Macero Collection. In fact, the following modification was written on his contract card: "No $10,000 album payment for Newport Jazz Fest. Album unless we release 2 LP sides of your performances in such an album."

33 Artist Contract Card, Columbia Records, pp., 1–8, Box 30, Teo Macero Collection.

34 "Modification on Artist Contract Card," January 1, 1964, Box 30, Teo Macero Collection.

35 Jesse H. Walker, "Theatricals," *Amsterdam News*, January 25, 1964; "Strictly Ad Lib," *Down Beat* (February 27, 1964), 10; Associated Musicians of Greater New York, Local 802, Contract, May 27, 1963, copy in Joseph Termini Papers. Joe Termini expected Monk to return in May.

36 Thelonious Monk interview, Paris, February 23, 1964, audio recording in author's possession.

37 Robin and Laura Dunlop interview, February 12, 2008; Slaughter, "Les Tenoirs de Thelonious," 17; "Charlie Rouse: Monk, un Classique Moderne," *Jazz Hot* 186 (April 1963): 6–8; Ad, New York *Amsterdam News,* May 1, 1965. Jazz Pantomime comes from John Alden Carpenter, "Krazy Kat: A Jazz Pantomime," see John Edward Hasse, ed., *Jazz: The First Century* (New York: HarperCollins, 2000), 40.
38 Ben Riley interview with Quincy Troupe, Media Transcripts, Inc., p. 2, Used by Permission; Ken Micallef, "Ben Riley: Power of the Lion, Patience of the Ages," *Modern Drummer* 292 (February 2005), 82.
39 Micallef, "Ben Riley," 82.
40 Peter Danson, "Interview: Charlie Rouse," *Coda Magazine* 187 (1982), 7.
41 Artist Job Sheet, recording session January 29, 1964, Box 30, Teo Macero Collection.
42 Artist Job Sheet, recording session January 30, 1964, Box 30, Teo Macero Collection. Both of these takes of "Shuffle Boil" and "Epistrophy" did not see the light of day until 1979, when Columbia released the two-disc compilation, *Always Know* (Col JG35720). Clearly, they were not acceptable to Monk.
43 Sir Charles Thompson interview, August 11, 2003. Phil Schaap told Coleman Hawkins's daughter, Collette, that Monk wrote "Stuffy" originally, but I have found no evidence to support or deny the claim. Monk never attempted to copyright it. Collette is convinced that "Stuffy" belongs to her father. Collette Hawkins, Interview, November 5, 2004.
44 Released on Thelonious Monk, *It's Monk Time* (Columbia CL 2184).
45 Macero booked the studio from 2:30–5:30 and from 7:30 to 10:30. Artist Job Sheet, recording session, February 10, 1964, Box 30, Teo Macero Collection.
46 Memo from Joe Paz to Teo Macero, April 14, 1964, Box 30, Teo Macero Collection.
47 Quoted in Micallef, "Ben Riley," 82. He tells the same story in Ben Riley interview with Quincy Troupe, Media Transcripts, Inc., p. 3.
48 Don Williamson, "An Interview with Ben Riley," *All About Jazz* (December 1999), www.allaboutjazz.com/iviews/briley.htm; Leslie Gourse, "Ben Riley: Around Sphere [Interview]," *Jazz Hot* 523 (September 1995), 34; Ben Riley interview, June 9, 2004.
49 Ben Riley interview, June 9, 2004; Williamson, "An Interview with Ben Riley." Ben Riley interview with Quincy Troupe, Media Transcripts, Inc., p. 13.
50 Riley quoted in Rich Thompson, "Ben Riley's Comping on 'Bemsha Swing'—A Drum Transcription," *Down Beat* (November 1991), 61–62. Thompson's excellent transcription and commentary illustrates Riley's conversational style.
51 Micallef, "Ben Riley," 82; Ben Riley interview with Quincy Troupe, Media Transcripts, Inc., p. 8.
52 Micallef, "Ben Riley," 82; also Ben Riley interview, June 9, 2004.
53 Monk introduced a drum solo at every concert, though the first recording we have is from Copenhagen on February 21. Concert recording, Danmarks Radio Broadcast, Copenhagen, February 21, 1964. In Zurich, he simply said, "Thank you, ladies and gentlemen. Ben Riley, the drummer got it!" Concert recording, Volkshaus, Zurich, February 26, 1964, in author's possession.
54 Williamson, "An Interview with Ben Riley."
55 Ben Riley interview with Quincy Troupe, Media Transcripts, Inc., p. 6.
56 *Thelonious Monk Live in Paris, 1964: Alhambra Vol. 1* (France's Concert FCD 135).
57 Thelonious Monk interview with Michel Delorme, Paris, February 23, 1964, audio tape in author's possession.
58 Ibid.
59 *Thelonious Monk Live in Paris, 1964* (France's Concert FCD 132).
60 Michel-Claude Jalard, "Thelonious Monk a l'heure du simulacra," *Jazz Magazine* (April 1964), 26–31.
61 Paudras, *Dance of the Infidels,* 212.
62 Or perhaps the date of the recording Paudras made is wrong. Paudras dates it February 16, 1964, the night Monk opened in Amsterdam and a full week before playing Paris. The tape, which includes Powell's declaration that Monk "is my best friend," sounds like something he would have done after the first Paris concert. Besides, there are many similarities between Powell's choices and Monk's repertoire—"Stuffy Turkey" being the most obvious. But this is all just speculation. The recording was released by Paudras as *Earl "Bud" Powell—Tribute to Thelonious, '64* (Mythic Sound MS6007-2 [CD]).
63 Paudras, *Dance of the Infidels,* 213.
64 Pablo Ruggeri to Michael Vermette, November 13, 1963, Memo from Teo Macero to Michael Vermette, December 4, 1963, Box 30, Teo Macero Collection.
65 Giancarlo Testoni and Arrigo Polillo, "Incontro con Thelonious Monk," *Musica Jazz,* 20 (March 1964), 8–10.
66 Abdullah Ibrahim, "Monk in Harlem: A Short Brief on Some Aspects of the Music of Thelonious Monk," *DU: The Magazine of Culture,* 3 (March 1994), 80. The story was also recounted to me by Sathima Bea Benjamin in an interview with me, May 31, 2005.
67 See especially, Jurgen Arndt, *Thelonious Monk und der Free Jazz* (Akademische Druck—u. Verlagsanstalt: Graz, Austria, 2002), 133–150; and my forthcoming book, *Speaking in Tongues: Jazz and Modern Africa* (Cambridge, MA: Harvard University Press).
68 Quoted in liner notes by Donald McCrae, Abdullah Ibrahim, *Blues for a Hip King* (Kaz CD 104). He also identified Monk as his greatest influence. Jack Lind, "Dollar Brand," *Down Beat* (November 21, 1963), 34.
69 Dollar Brand Trio, *Dollar Brand Plays Sphere Jazz* (Gallo Continental (SA)ZB8047). It came out on an obscure South African label, but was later released on CD as *Blues for a Hip King* (Kaz (E)LP104). Lars Rasmussen, ed., *Abdullah Ibrahim: A Discography—Second Edition* (Copenhagen: The Booktrader, 2000), 17–19.
70 Dollar Brand, *Duke Ellington Presents The Dollar Brand Trio* (Reprise R96111). I don't know if Monk ever heard the LP and if so what he thought about it, but he probably would have criticized his version of "Brilliant Corners" for playing D instead of $D^\flat$ in the second half of the second measure, and for slightly altering the

turnaround. He plays beautifully and the arrangement fits within Monk's style—with carefully placed drum fills, and all the instruments playing the melody in unison, including the bass and drums. On "Ubu Suku," I've also obtained a copy of the lead sheet from the Ruth Ellington Collection, Box 47, Smithsonian Institution.

71 Farrell, "Loneliest Monk," 85.
72 Ibid., 87.
73 Ibid., 87.
74 "Crow Jim," *Time* (October 19, 1962), 58–60. In March of 1962, for example, critic Ira Gitler published a highly defensive critique of black protest politics in jazz in the guise of a review of Abbey Lincoln's album *Straight Ahead*. Gitler disparaged her militant politics, criticized the fact that there were no white musicians on the date, and called her "misguided and naive" for her support of African nationalism. Given the politically charged atmosphere, Gitler believed this album and the current trends in jazz were precursors to a powerful black separatist movement. He warned, "We don't need the Elijah Muhammed [sic] type thinking in jazz." Ira Gitler, "Racial Prejudice in Jazz," *Down Beat* (May 24, 1962), 24. The controversy led to a panel discussion titled "Racial Prejudice in Jazz," the results of which were printed in *Down Beat*. The participants included Gitler, Lincoln, Nat Hentoff, Max Roach, and *Down Beat* editor Don DeMichael. The exchange turned quite nasty with Gitler defending his review (and the fact that he never interviewed Lincoln but based his critique on Hentoff's liner notes) and DeMichael raising the issue of "Crow Jim"—that white musicians were being discriminated against. Of course, white critics nervous about the presence of black nationalist sentiment in jazz directed most of their criticism at artists identified with the avant-garde. See for example, Ira Gitler, "Chords and Discords: To Hentoff from Gitler," *Down Beat* (September 9, 1965), 8; Nat Hentoff, "New Jazz—Black, Angry, and Hard to Understand," *New York Times Magazine* (December 25, 1966), 36–39; series of exchanges on "Jazz and Revolutionary Black Nationalism" in *Jazz* (from April 1966 to July 1967); LeRoi Jones, "White Critics, Black Musicians, New Music," *African Revolution* 1,no. 6 (October 1963), 143–152; and for excellent overviews of these debates and the broader context, see Monson, *Freedom Sounds*, 238–266; Eric Porter, *What is This Thing Called Jazz?*, 149–90; Farah Jasmine Griffin, *If You Can't Be Free, Be A Mystery: In Search of Billie Holiday* (New York: Free Press, 2001), 161–191.
75 Letters from Pat Pannell and E. T. Shineman, "Letters," *Time Magazine* (March 6, 1964), 6–8.
76 Ralph J. Gleason, "Monk Puts on a Magazine," *San Francisco Chronicle*, March 2, 1964.
77 Leonard Feather, "Feather's Nest," *Down Beat* (April 23, 1964), 39. Amiri Baraka's essay on Monk is often lumped in the category of responses to the *Time* magazine article, but this really misrepresents what the article sets out to do. He does ask why Monk, why now, but he wrote it before he'd even had a chance to see the *Time* profile. Indeed, it appeared in *Down Beat* the day before the *Time* cover story. Jones, "The Acceptance of Monk," 20–22.
78 Clebert Ford, "Black Nationalism and the Arts," *Liberator* 4, no. 2 (February 1964), 15; Theodore H. Pontiflet, "The American Way," *Liberator* 4, no. 6 (June 1964), 8–9. Nor was Jones worried about Monk selling out, even if he did express concerns about his music standing still.
79 Ralph de Toledano, "Thelonious Monk and Some Others," *National Review* (October 19, 1965), 940–941. A few years later, writer Glen Elder used Monk in a different way to lament the infusion of politics in jazz, particularly black nationalism. Attacking Baraka's critique of Monk's acceptance in 1964, Elder (mis)interpreted the critique as a racially motivated defense against "mainstreaming" jazz. In other words, he asserted his right to "own" jazz as a "mainstream" white man (as if "dues-paying" black artists actually owned the structures through which this music was produced and distributed!). See Glen Elder, "Well, You Needn't," *Journal of Popular Culture* 4, no. 4 (1971), 850–62.
80 Toledano, "Thelonious Monk and Some Others," 942. The idea that jazz needs to be danceable has been a common theme in De Toledano's writing for a very long time. Ralph De Toledano, "Directions of Jazz," in De Toledano, ed., *Frontiers of Jazz* (New York: Oliver Durrell, Inc., 1947), 71.
81 Memo from Mr. Vermette to ALL AFFILIATES, March 2, 1964, Box 30, Teo Macero Collection.
82 T. S. Monk interview, April 4, 2005.
83 "Letters," *Time* (March 6, 1964), 6–8.
84 "For Immediate Release," January 27, 1964, and various undated clippings from *Danbury News-Times* and Mt. Kisco, New York, *The Patent Trader*, from Personal Files of Sam B. Ross, Jr., Green Chimneys School. I'm enormously grateful to Sam and Myra Ross for generously making these files available to me.
85 The press release from Green Chimneys was published in the *Danbury News-Times* unchanged. "For Immediate Release," March 16, 1964, "Monk Fan Seeks Player's Autograph," *Danbury News-Times*, n.d. (March or early April, 1964), from Personal Files of Sam Ross, Jr., Green Chimneys School.
86 Mimeographed flyer; Samuel B. Ross, Jr., Headmaster, form letter, n.d.; *Green Chimneys News*, 14, no. 3 (March 1964), personal files of Sam B. Ross, Green Chimneys School; "Thelonious Monk Concert Set Tonight," *Bridgeport Post*, April 14, 1964.
87 Dan Hall, "Monk Plays a Little Bit of Everything," *Danbury News-Times*, April 17, 1964.
88 Ibid.
89 Ben Riley interview with Quincy Troupe, Media Transcripts, Inc., p. 23.
90 Lapham, "Monk: High Priest of Jazz," 73.
91 Ibid., 74.
92 Ibid., 73–74.
93 Ibid., 72.
94 Ibid.
95 Warren Gerard, "The Monk: 'Everybody's Different, Man!'," *Toronto Globe and Mail*, November 5, 1966.
96 And the second song so named: In 1961 Miles Davis composed and recorded a Spanish-tinged melody he called "Teo," also produced by Macero.

97 Apparently unaware that the music had been destroyed, at a later rehearsal Overton tells Thad Jones that "Monk lost the score and I had to do it all over again." "Monk Rehearsal at Hall's for Carnegie Concert," June 4, 1964, CCP 107 (Disk 2), Eugene Smith Tapes. Martin Williams attended this rehearsal and either taped the proceedings himself or took Eugene Smith's tape and transcribed it for his article, "Rehearsing with Monk," *Down Beat* (July 30, 1964), 14–16. In the transcription, Williams makes a number of small edits (i.e., he has Overton saying "misplaced" instead of "lost"). I prefer the original language, so all quotes from this rehearsal come from my transcriptions.

98 "Strictly Ad Lib," *Down Beat* (April 9, 1964), 12; "Strictly Ad Lib," *Down Beat* (April 23, 1964), 10, 43.

99 Chris Welles, "Rewarding Workouts by Monk and Mingus," *Life* (April 10, 1964), 15.

100 Memo from Joe Paz to Teo Macero, April 14, 1964, Artist Contract Card, Columbia Records, page 10, Box 30, Teo Macero Collection.

101 "Where & When," *Down Beat* (May 7, 1964), 43; "Strictly Ad Lib," *Down Beat* (June 4, 1964), 8.

102 Quotes from Patrick Scott, "Monk's Piano Chases the Gathering Chaos," *Toronto Globe and Mail*, April 27, 1964; see also Ralph Thomas, "Fans Too Much Jazz for Monk," *Toronto Daily Star*, April 27, 1964. He concurred, dismissing Thompson's band as "cluttered" and "routine."

103 Helen McNamara, "Monk Show Flies Low," *Toronto Telegram*, April 27, 1964.

104 "Where & When," *Down Beat* (May 7, 1964), 44, 46; John Pagones, "Celebrity Room Turns to 'Names,'" *Washington Post*, May 3, 1964.

105 Bob Scott, "Grammy Prizes Awarded at Dinner Here," *Los Angeles Times*, May 13, 1964; Russ Wilson, "World of Jazz," *Oakland Tribune*, May 29, 1964.

106 Ad, Long Beach *Press-Telegram*, May 3, 10, 22, 1964; Ad, Long Beach *Independent*, May 13, 1964; "Strictly Ad Lib," *Down Beat* (July 30, 1964), 45.

107 Bobby Timmons, *Holiday Soul* (Prestige PR 7414), recorded November 24, 1964.

108 Edward "Butch" Warren, NBC interview with Antoine Sanfuentes, 2008, used by permission; Erik R. Quick, "Butch Warren," *All About Jazz* (July 21, 2006), http://www.allaboutjazz.com/php/article.php?id=22403.

109 Richard Davis interview, July 24, 2003. Davis was all set to play, but he never received a follow-up phone call. Though he was young at the time, he had an outstanding reputation as a versatile bassist, having recorded with artists ranging from Andrew Hill and Eric Dolphy to Sarah Vaughan and Johnny Hodges.

110 "Monk Rehearsal at Hall's for Carnegie Concert," June 4, 1964, CCP 107 (Disk 2), Eugene Smith Tapes. See also Williams, "Rehearsing with Monk," 14–16.

111 "Monk Rehearsal at Hall's for Carnegie Hall Concert," June 6, 1963, CCP 108, "Last Monk Rehearsal Before '64 Carnegie Hall," CCP 110 (Disc 1). Eugene Smith Tapes.

112 "Monk to Appear at Carnegie," *Amsterdam News*, June 6, 1964; Dan Morgenstern, "Caught in the Act: Thelonious Monk, New York City, Carnegie Hall," *Down Beat* (July 30, 1964), 17.

113 Morgenstern, "Caught in the Act," 17.

114 John S. Wilson, "Monk's Jazz Group Heard at Carnegie," *New York Times*, June 8, 1964.

115 Morgenstern, "Caught in the Act," 17.

116 "Strictly Ad Lib," *Down Beat* (August 27, 1964), 44; "Jazz Concerts at Guthrie Theater," *Albert Lea Sunday Tribune*, May 24, 1964; Hazel Garland, "Mary Lou Williams Spearheads Drive To Bring Jazz Festival to Pittsburgh," *Pittsburgh Courier*, April 18, 1964; Hazel Garland, "Interest Mounts in First Pittsburgh Jazz Festival," *Pittsburgh Courier*, May 30, 1964. Monk played Minneapolis on June 14, not the 21st as reported in Sheridan, *Brilliant Corners*, 416. For most of these gigs, Monk "borrowed" Horace Silver's regular bassist, Gene Taylor.

117 Bob Cranshaw interview, August 2, 2008; Lawrence Koch and Barry Kernfeld. "Cranshaw, Bob." In *The New Grove Dictionary of Jazz*, 2nd ed., edited by Barry Kernfeld. *Grove Music Online. Oxford Music Online*, http://www.oxfordmusiconline.com/subscriber/article/grove/music/J105200 (accessed August 2, 2008).

118 Bob Cranshaw interview, August 2, 2008.

119 Their set, which consisted of "Bemsha Swing," "Straight, No Chaser," and "Rhythm-a-ning" was broadcast on Voice of America and a recording of at least one track ("Bemsha Swing") survives. See Sheridan, *Brilliant Corners*, 143.

120 "Jazz Officials Eying Sky, Gate Hopefully," *Newport Daily News*, July 3, 1964; Don DeMichael, "Newport Report," *Down Beat* (August 13, 1964); John S. Wilson, "Brubeck Plays in Piano Session on 3d Day of Newport Festival," *New York Times*, July 5, 1964.

121 "Auto Crash Kills Meade Lux Lewis," *Pittsburgh Courier*, June 20, 1964.

122 "Where & When," *Down Beat* (June 4, 1964), 42, 44; Claudia Cassidy, "On the Aisle," *Chicago Tribune*, April 17, 1964; Ad, *Chicago Tribune*, June 14, 1964; "Musical Forecast," *Chicago Defender*, August 1, 1964.

123 Bob Cranshaw interview, August 2, 2008.

124 "Strictly Ad Lib," *Down Beat* (August 27, 1964), 43; "Where & When," *Down Beat* (August 27, 1964), 46.

125 Recordings of all three tunes can be heard on *Archie Shepp with the New York Contemporary Five* (Storyville STCD 8209 [CD]). The CD is a reissue of recording made at the Jazzhus Montmartre, Copenhagen, November 11, 1963.

126 On Moore, see Wilmer, *As Serious As Your Life*, 165; Steve Lacy interview, May 12, 1995; also, Robin D. G. Kelley, "New Monastery: Monk and the Jazz Avant-Garde," *Black Music Research Journal* 19, no. 2 (Fall, 1999), 135–168.

127 Leonard Harris, "Monk Thrills Village Gate Jazz Fans," *New York World-Telegram*, August 6, 1964; Jo McDonald, "Mongo, Flip, and Monk," *The Villager*, August 6, 1964. Indeed, only Jo McDonald named the whole band, and she merely repeated Ivan Black's press release (written and circulated before Moore was hired), identifying Bob Cranshaw on bass. *Down Beat* took note of Moore's hiring, but not much else. "Strictly Ad Lib," *Down Beat* (September 24, 1964), 42.

128 Jo McDonald, "Mongo, Flip, and Monk."

129 Doug Quackenbush unpublished typed notes, ca. 1996, pp. 1–11 (quote page 11), in author's possession.

130 Ibid., pp. 11–12. Quackenbush dates the Music Inn gig August 8, but he was off by one day. See "Strictly Ad Lib," *Down Beat* (July 16, 1964), 47; "Music in New York and Out of Town," *New York Times*, August 9, 1964.

131 Doug Quackenbush unpublished typed notes, ca. 1996, pp. 13–14.

132 Ibid., p. 14.

133 Doug Quackenbush unpublished typed notes, ca. 1996, p. 20. Most of Nica's photos have not been exhibited and are in the hands of the family.

134 Doug Quackenbush unpublished typed notes, ca. 1996, p. 18.

135 "Festival Reports," *Down Beat* (October 8, 1964), and Sheridan, *Brilliant Corners*, 144. Both sources mistakenly identify Alvin Jackson as Oliver Jackson, another Detroiter but a drummer.

136 (Jazzland JL39)

137 Charlie Rouse, *Bossa Nova Bacchanal* (Blue Note BLP4119), which was recorded November 26, 1962.

138 Rose Gales interview, August 25, 2008; Harry Colomby interview, August 11, 2003; "Bronx Groups," http://www.harmonytrain.com/Artists/bronx-2.htm. The other three members of the Twilighters were Bill Lindsay, John E. Johnson, and Donald Redd.

139 Harry Colomby interview, August 11, 2003; Ben Riley interview, June 9, 2004; Rose Gales interview, August 25, 2008. Besides a long stint with Lockjaw and Griffin, his employers included J. C. Heard, Buddy Tate, Bennie Green, Junior Mance, Herbie Mann, singer Joe Williams, Sonny Stitt, and Mary Lou Williams. Gary Carner and Barry Kernfeld. "Gales, Larry." In *The New Grove Dictionary of Jazz*, 2nd ed., edited by Barry Kernfeld. *Grove Music Online. Oxford Music Online*, http://www.oxfordmusiconline.com/subscriber/article/grove/music/J161900 (accessed August 4, 2008).

26 "Sometimes I Don't Feel Like Talking"

1 My description of opening night is derived from Paudras, *Dance of the Infidels*, 259–63; Dan Morgenstern, "Caught in the Act," *Down Beat* (October 2, 1964), reprinted in Morgenstern, *Living with Jazz*, 445–46; "Bud's OK," *Time* (September 4, 1964), 78; Robert Shelton, "Jazz: Bud Powell Returns to Birdland," *New York Times*, September 5, 1964; Ira Gitler, *The Masters of Bebop: A Listener's Guide* (New York: Da Capo Press, 2001), 128. I suspect the *Time* magazine piece was written by Barry Farrell since he had become the music editor, but the piece was run without a byline.

2 Most of the letters from Goodstein to Bud and Buttercup made reference to all the money Powell owed, and to Buttercup's squandering of his income. See letters dated October 22, 1959, August 8, 1960, August 31, 1960, September 16, 1960, September 29, 1962, December 14, 1962, copies in Surrogates Court, County of Kings, Proceeding for Letters of Administration, Estate of Earl Bud Powell, Deceased, File No. 7370/1968.

3 Shelton, "Jazz: Bud Powell Returns to Birdland"; [quote] "Bud's OK," 78.

4 Paudras, *Dance of the Infidels*, 259, 262; Morgenstern, *Living with Jazz*, 445.

5 Doug Quackenbush unpublished typed notes, ca. 1996, p. 17. Quackenbush provides the only account we have of the Montreal trip. Nica decided to tag along this time, which must have made Thelonious and Nellie happy. She not only booked a huge suite for the three of them, but her fluency in French came in handy. Since Quackenbush had no money, Nellie let him sleep on the couch in the suite's sitting room.

6 Paudras, *Dance of the Infidels*, 274–75.

7 After J. C. Moses replaced Horace Arnold on drums, Powell played even more Monk compositions. On one of Paudras's recordings, Powell played "Off Minor," "Well, You Needn't," "Hackensack," "Straight, No Chaser," "Bemsha Swing," and "I Mean You." Bud Powell, *Bud Powell Trio* (Mythic Sound (It)MS6007-1).

8 "Strictly Ad Lib," *Down Beat* (October 22, 1964), 13. Technically, they were booked from September 10–27, and returned October 6–10.

9 Paudras, *Dance of the Infidels*, 286, 290.

10 Harry Colomby interview, August 11, 2003.

11 See Tom Lord, *The Jazz Discography* [CD], "Steve Swallow" recording sessions from 1961–1964.

12 "The Monk Returns to Monterey," *Los Angeles Sentinel*, September 10, 1964; *Monterey Jazz Festival: Seventh Year, September 19–20–21 (sic), 1964* [Program], p. 19; Art Seidenbaum, "Jazz Rebels Find Cause, Applause at Monterey's Three-Day Festival," *Los Angeles Times*, September 21, 1964.

13 Buddy Collette, with Steve Isoardi, *Jazz Generations: A Life in American Music and Society* (London and New York: Continuum, 2000), 167–168.

14 Unreleased concert recordings of Monterey Jazz Festival, 1964, Tapes 54 and 55, Recorded September 20, 1964, Sunday afternoon, Monterey Archives Stanford.

15 Ibid.

16 Art Seidenbaum, "Jazz Rebels Find Cause, Applause at Monterey's Three-Day Festival," *Los Angeles Times*, September 21, 1964.

17 "Monterey and All that Jazz," *Ebony* (December 1964), 60.

18 Les Carter, "For Listeners Only," *Los Angeles Sentinel*, September 24, 1964.

19 Eunice Pye, "Monterey Is a Jazz Lover's Dream," *Los Angeles Sentinel*, October 1, 1964.

20 "The Penn Sate (University) Jazz Club presented two concerts by pianist Thelonious Monk October 3," noted in "Strictly Ad Lib," *Down Beat* (November 5, 1964), 33. An earlier notice mistakenly announced that Monk was "booked to play at Brandeis University on October 3." "Strictly Ad Lib," *Down Beat* (October 22, 1964), 44. It is repeated in Sheridan, *Brilliant Corners*, 418.

21 Doug Quackenbush unpublished typed notes, ca. 1996, p. 18.

22 Artist Job Sheets, recording sessions for *Monk.* and *Solo Monk*, recordings made October 6, 7, 8, 1964, Box 30, Teo Macero Papers; Thelonious Monk, *Monk.* (Columbia CL2291).

23 It was also given the title "The Children's Marching Song" after Mitch Miller and his Orchestra recorded it in 1958, but this is not the original title. The nursery rhyme originated in Europe and has no known author.

24 Teo Macero to Thelonious Monk, December 2, 1964; Teo Macero to Thelonious Monk, December 30, 1964, Box 30, Teo Macero Collection.

25 Artist Contract Card–Columbia Records, page 11, Box 30, Teo Macero Collection.

26 Paudras, *Dance of the Infidels*, 293–334; Groves and Shipton, *The Glass Enclosure*, 90–92.

27 Monk reported that the person driving them to the airport had gotten into an accident and as a result they missed their plane. I have not been able to corroborate this story, and it seems unlikely. My guess is that he simply did not want to go. Russ Wilson, "Thelonious Monk's Meeting Gets Off to a Sorry Start," *Oakland Tribune*, October 17, 1964.

28 Ibid.

29 Ibid.

30 "Thelonious Monk Debuts at UCLA," *Los Angeles Sentinel*, October 8, 1964; (Quote) Mimi Clar, "A Piano Excursion with Thelonious Monk," *Los Angeles Times*, October 19, 1964.

31 Ad, *Los Angeles Times*, October 11, 1964; "Jazzman Monk Plans VMT Show," *Oxnard Press-Courier*, October 13, 1964; Ads for It Club, *Los Angeles Times*, October 16, 18, 23, 30, 1964.

32 The 300-room hotel opened in May of 1963. "May Opening Planned for Sunset Strip Hotel," *Los Angeles Times*, April 21, 1963.

33 Ben Riley interview with Quincy Troupe, Media Transcripts, Inc.

34 Harry Colomby interview, August 12, 2003.

35 Hawes, *Raise Up Off Me*, 130.

36 Rose Gales interview, August 25, 2008.

37 Conversation with Wren T. Brown, September 17, 2008; Troy Brown, Jr., interview, October 4, 2008; "It Club for Jazz Lovers," *Los Angeles Sentinel*, January 17, 1963; ads throughout *Los Angeles Sentinel*, 1960–64. See also Horace Tapscott, with Steve Isoardi, *Songs of the Unsung: The Musical and Social Journey of Horace Tapscott* (Durham, NC: Duke University Press, 2001), 70; Roy Porter, with David Keller, *There and Back* (New York: Continuum International Publishing, 1995), 99.

38 Ben Riley thought Monk was going to get shot over this. Ben Riley interview, June 9, 2004.

39 Tapscott, *Songs of the Unsung*, 70; and on Newborn, see Calvin Newborn, *As Quiet as It's Kept: The Genius of Phineas Newborn, Jr.* (Memphis: Phineas Newborn, Jr. Family Foundation, 1996); Paul Rinzler and Barry Kernfeld, "Newborn, Phineas," in *The New Grove Dictionary of Jazz*, 2nd ed., edited by Barry Kernfeld. *Grove Music Online. Oxford Music Online*, http://www.oxfordmusiconline.com/subscriber/article/grove/music/J325700 (accessed September 19, 2008). On Newborn being billed at the It Club, see, *Los Angeles Sentinel*, January 3 and June 6, 1963.

40 Troy Brown, Jr., interview, October 4, 2008; Touré, *Never Drank the Kool-Aid: Essays* (New York: Macmillan, 2006), 67–68.

41 Thelonious Monk, *Live at the It Club—Complete* (Columbia C2K65288). When Columbia released some of these recordings, Macero meticulously removed all the drum solos.

42 Ibid.

43 Some of these recordings were first released on *Solo Monk* (Columbia CL 2348), but all are now available on *Monk Alone: The Complete Columbia Solo Studio Recordings, 1962–1968* (Columbia C2K65495).

44 Thelonious Monk, *Live at the Jazz Workshop—Complete* (Columbia C2K65189).

45 "Where & When," *Down Beat* (November 5, 1964), 46; "Where & When," *Down Beat* (December 31, 1964), 46; Ad, *Village Voice*, December 17, 1964; "Jesse H. Walker, "Theatricals," *Amsterdam News*, January 16, 1965; "Strictly Ad Lib," *Down Beat* (January 14, 1965), 37; "Strictly Ad Lib," *Down Beat* (January 28, 1965), 40; Ivan Black, "Clancy Brothers, Thelonious, and Letta M'Bulo for Holidays," press release, n.d., Box 25, Ivan Black Papers. At the Gate, Monk's quartet played opposite Mongo Santamaria, South African singer Letta M'bulo, and the Irish folk group the Clancy Brothers.

46 "Strictly Ad Lib," *Down Beat* (February 11, 1965), 16; "Strictly Ad Lib," *Down Beat* (March 25, 1965), 40; "Strictly Ad Lib," *Down Beat* (February 10, 1966), 16. Herbie Mann's sextet substituted for Monk's group at the Village Gate.

47 Teo Macero to Thelonious Monk, December 30, 1964, (Quote) Teo Macero to Thelonious Monk, December 2, 1964, Box 30, Teo Macero Collection.

48 Teo Macero to Thelonious Monk, December 2, 1964, Box 30, Teo Macero Collection.

49 Ibid.

50 Evans had developed a reputation for writing notes, both for his own LPs and for others. See Peter Pettinger, *Bill Evans: How My Heart Sings* (New Haven: Yale University Press, 1998), 171.

51 Bill Evans original liner notes, typescript, n.d., Box 30, Teo Macero Collection.

52 Martin Williams to Teo Macero, February 8, 1964, Box 30, Teo Macero Collection; Margo Guryan Rosner interview, August 22, 2008; Margo Guryan Rosner email to author, August 1, 2008. All of these lyrics were compiled and passed on to Teo Macero. Williams contributed lyrics for "Brake's Sake" and "We See"; Joe Goldberg for "Straight, No Chaser," "Ask Me Now," "Crepuscule with Nellie."

53 Memo from Irving Townsend to Teo Macero, November 24, 1964, Box 30, Teo Macero Collection.

54 Thelonious and Nellie Monk, U.S. Individual Income Tax Return, 1964; New York State Income Tax Resident, 1964. Federal and state tax owed came out to $10,332 and $3,108, respectively.

55 Harry Colomby interview, August 11, 2003.

56 Howard Johnson recalled an incident in the dressing room of the Village Gate in the summer of 1965, when Monk offered Charles Mingus some drugs: "So he opened his cigar box. It had a variety of pills of all kinds, colors, sizes. Monk grabbed a handful of pills and threw them in his mouth, whatever they were. He didn't even

look, and said, 'Yeah, go ahead, Ming.' Mingus was looking at the box and trying to figure out what he wanted. And Monk said, 'Come on, go ahead.' . . . So he grabbed a handful and threw them in his mouth. Later he whispered to me, 'Gee, I don't know what that shit was.'" Santoro, *Myself When I Am Real*, 249.

57 T. S. Monk interview, April 4, 2005.

58 Teo Macero to Thelonious Monk, February 12, 1965, Artist Job Sheet, February 23, 1965, Box 30, Teo Macero Collection.

59 Whitney Balliett, "Jazz Concerts," *New Yorker* (March 13, 1965), 191; "Strictly Ad Lib," *Down Beat* (April 22, 1965), 49; "Jazz Piano Workshop–Hunter College Assembly Hall, Fri. Feb. 26, 8:30 PM," flyer in author's possession; "Strictly Ad Lib," *Down Beat* (March 11, 1965), 39; ad, *Village Voice*, February 11, 1965; John S. Wilson, "Jazz Pianists Join and Show Styles," *New York Times*, February 27, 1965; Thelonious Monk, *Misterioso—Recorded on Tour* (Columbia CL 2416).

60 According to the Artist Job Sheet, March 2, 1965, this recording of "Honeysuckle Rose" was made in the studio, not in a club. Teo Macero confirmed that he had added an applause track because he did not know when he'd be able to record Monk live again. Teo Macero phone conversation with author, October 28, 2002. Chris Sheridan also insists that the applause track was added. See Sheridan, *Brilliant Corners*, 156.

61 Memo from Jack Tessler to West, Mikulski, et. al., February 25, 1965, Box 30, Teo Macero Collection; "Strictly Ad Lib," *Down Beat* (January 28, 1965), 12; "Strictly Ad Lib," *Down Beat* (April 22, 1965), 16; Conrad Clark, "Monk, Satch Make it Big On Continent," *Pittsburgh Courier*, April 3, 1965. The memo from Tessler is the only accurate listing of Monk's itinerary. Published sources contain several errors.

62 "Nouvelles," *Jazz Hot* (March 1965), 63; *Jazz Magazine* (March 1965), 13.

63 Claude Lenissois, "Monk Toujours," *Jazz Hot* (April 1965), 3, 5.

64 Gerald Lascelles, "Thelonious Monk: Portrait of the Hat," *Jazz Journal* 18 (April 1965), 11.

65 Ian Breach, "Thelonious Monk at the Free Trade Hall, Manchester," *Manchester Guardian*, March 22, 1965.

66 Sinclair Traill, "Thelonious Monk at the Festival Hall," *Jazz Journal* (April 1965),12.

67 Mike Hennessey, "Monk's Moods," *Melody Maker* (March 20, 1965), 9; Jean-Louis Noames, "Monk Entre Deux Sommes," *Jazz Magazine* 124 (November 1965), 46–49.

68 Hennessey, "Monk's Moods," 9.

69 Noames, "Monk Entre Deux Sommes," 48.

70 Boo Boo Monk, quoted in J. R. Mitchell, "Thelonious Monk: The High Priest of Bop" (unpublished manuscript in author's possession), 33.

71 Ben Riley interview with Quincy Troupe, Media Transcripts, Inc., p. 14. Used by Permission.

72 Valerie Wilmer, *Mama Said There'd Be Days Like This: My Life in the Jazz World* (London: The Women's Press, 1989), 134.

73 Ibid., 28–134 *passim.*; Valerie Wilmer interview, January 12, 2005; see John Hopkins website, http://www .hoppy.be.

74 See especially, "The Malcolm X Project at Columbia University," http://www.columbia.edu/cu/ccbh/mxp/; Steve Clark, ed., *Malcolm X, February 1965: The Final Speeches* (New York: Pathfinder Press, 1992), 46–71; George Breitman, ed., *Malcolm X Speaks* (New York: Grove Press, 1994), 194–226; "Malcolm X Barred From France," *London Times* (February 10, 1965),11. Later that year, Hoppy would join with Malcom's friend and comrade, Michael de Freitas (better known as Michael X) and set up the London Free School in Notting Hill, a countercultural activists space. See John Williams, *Michael X: A Life in Black and White* (London: Century, 2007).

75 Unless otherwise indicated, all quotes from the Wilmer/Hopkins interview are taken directly from my transcription of the cassette, which Val Wilmer shared with me. Monk interview with Valerie Wilmer and John Hopkins, March 14, 1965, audio cassette, used by permission.

76 Monk interview with Valerie Wilmer and John Hopkins, March 14, 1965.

77 Janet L. Abu-Lughod, *Race, Space, and Riots in Chicago, New York, and Los Angeles* (New York: Oxford University Press, 2007), 159–188; Thomas J. Sugrue, *Sweet Land of Liberty: The Forgotten Struggle for Civil Rights in the North* (New York: Random House, 2008), 313–355; Robin D. G. Kelley and Earl Lewis, eds., *To Make Our World Anew: A History of African Americans* (New York: Oxford University Press, 2000), 523.

78 Valerie Wilmer, "Monk on Monk," *Down Beat* (June 3, 1965), 22. Interestingly, Monk does not say this on the tape recording, which suggests that he may have made this statement the next day when they interviewed him in Birmingham. A taped record of that conversation does not exist. Incidentally, when Hennessey asked Monk if he had had any run-ins with racism, he responded, "Not really. But then I don't let things bug me." Mike Hennessey, "Monk's Moods," 9.

79 Monk interview with Valerie Wilmer and John Hopkins, March 14, 1965.

80 Sinclair Traill observed that during the Festival Hall concert Monk "looked tired." (Traill, "Thelonious Monk at the Festival Hall," 12.) Monk also told Jean-Louis Noames, "What's terrible is not being able to find time to sleep," adding that in an ideal world, he would prefer "to sleep and play at the same time, but that's impossible." (Noames, "Monk Entre Deux Sommes," 48.)

81 *Jazz 625 - Giants of Jazz Golden Era - Thelonious Monk: Recorded at the Marquee Club in London—March 14, 1965. Vols. 1 and 2* (PNV 1035 and 1036). Parts of this video are available from other distributors: *Thelonious Monk: Monk in Europe* (Green Line Video 18); and as a bonus DVD on Thelonious Monk, *Monk 'Round the World* (Thelonious Records TMF 9323-9).

82 "Strictly Ad Lib," *Down Beat* (April 22, 1965), 16.

83 Kym Bonython, *Ladies' Legs and Lemonade* (Adelaide: Rigby Ltd., 1979), 162.

84 Ibid., 161.

85 Merv Acheson, Review, *Music Maker* (June 1965); Bill Thorpe, "Twist and Stomp, Thelonious Monk, and Sergeant Pepper's Lonely Hearts Club Band: Recollections of Rock, Pop, and Jazz in Sydney 1959–1967," *Everyday Wonders: Journal of Australian Studies* 58 (1997), 182.

86 Bonython, *Ladies' Legs*, 162.
87 Memo from Jack Tessler to West, Mikulski, et. al., February 25, 1965, Box 30, Teo Macero Collection.
88 Bonython, *Ladies' Legs*, 162.
89 Memo from Jack Tessler to West, Mikulski, et. al., February 25, 1965, Box 30, Teo Macero Collection.
90 Russ Wilson, "Thelonious Monk Previews Combo," *Oakland Tribune*, April 27, 1965. Besides Hong Kong, a concert in Manila was also canceled. They arrived in Honolulu on April 21 and then continued on to San Francisco. Memo from Jack Tessler to West, Mikulski, et. al., February 25, 1965, Box 30, Teo Macero Collection.
91 Pearl Gonzalez, "Monk Talk," *Down Beat* (October 28, 1971), 12.
92 Wilson, "Thelonious Monk Previews Combo."
93 George Wein to Harry Colomby, September 14, 1965, Robert Jones Personal Papers.
94 George Wein to Harry Colomby, September 23, 1965, Robert Jones Personal Papers.
95 Wilson, "Thelonious Monk Previews Combo."
96 "Strictly Ad Lib," *Down Beat* (July 15, 1965), 42.
97 Postcard, Nica to Mary Lou Williams, June 2, 1965, Box 8, Mary Lou Williams Collection.
98 "Denzil Best, Drummer, Dies After Sudden Fall," *Amsterdam News*, June 5, 1965; "Drummer Denzil Best Dies of Skull Facture," *Down Beat* (July 1, 1965), 14; Korall, *Drummin' Men*, 22–25.
99 Memorandum from Teo Macero to Bob Ciotti, April 13, 1965, Box 30, Teo Macero Collection.
100 Columbia University School of Architecture, *Lincoln Square: Preserving the Modern Architecture of Slum Clearance, Urban Renewal, and their Architectural Aftermath*, http://www.arch.columbia.edu/hp/studio /2006–2007/pdf/Lincoln %20Square.pdf. S. J. Kessler and Sons won the contract to design these very basic, simple, box-like high-rise apartments. It is worth noting that the architect of choice was none other than I. M. Pei, who came up with the idea of a cluster of buildings of varied sizes—he wanted to break the monolithic grid that had come to dominate modern urban residential buildings. But the financiers wouldn't go for it. Cary Reich, *Financier—The Biography of Andre Meyer: A Story of Money, Power, and the Reshaping of American Business* (New York: John Wiley and Sons, 1998), 137–139.
101 The change of address is evident from their 1965 returns as well as correspondence sent to Monk from Columbia Records. Thelonious and Nellie Monk, U.S. Individual Income Tax Return, 1965.
102 Evelyn Smith, Benetta Bines, T. S. Monk, Jackie Bonneau, Clifton Smith, interviews, January 30, 2004; Marion Prilook, "An Interview with the Monk," *Danbury News-Times*, March 19, 1966.
103 A recording of Monk's performance at the 1965 Newport Jazz Festival is available on *Monk at Newport, 1963 & 1965* (Columbia 63905). George Wein had moved the festival from Freebody Park to a 35-acre field north of the city that was used to dry fish nets. When there was no breeze, the odor was overwhelming. Robert Flynn, "Jazz Bash Set for Field of Fish Nets," *Los Angeles Times*, June 21, 1965.
104 "Strictly Ad Lib," *Down Beat* (August 26, 1965), 16 and 43; "Music Barn to Open with Jazz on Sunday," *North Adams Transcript*, July 2, 1965; and ads, *North Adams Transcript*, July 23, 29, 1965; Milton Bass, "The Lively Arts," *Berkshire Eagle*, August 12, 1965; George T. Wein to Harry Colomby, February 28, 1965, Robert Jones Personal Papers; Ad, *Chicago Tribune*, July 4, 1965; "Top Names on Down Beat Festival," *Chicago Tribune*, August 8, 1965; Thomas Willis, "Chicago's Summer Music Program," *Chicago Tribune*, May 30, 1965; "Downbeat Jazz Festival Plays Soldier's Field," *Chicago Defender*, July 10, 1965; Lee Ivory, "My Son, The Jazz Dancer or Thelonious Monk Rides Again," *Chicago Defender*, September 4, 1965; "Strictly Ad Lib," *Down Beat* (October 7, 1965), 41; Elyria, OH, *Chronicle Telegram*, August 6, 1965; "For Music," Elyria, OH, *Chronicle Telegram*, August 27, 1965; "What's Your Pleasure?" *Mansfield News Journal*, August 29, 1965.
105 "Strictly Ad Lib," *Down Beat* (September 23, 1965), 49.
106 Ben Riley interview with Quincy Troupe, Media Transcripts, Inc.
107 T. S. Monk, interview, April 4, 2005.
108 "Encounter: Monk and Dolores Wilson," *Toronto Telegram*, November 12, 1966.
109 See *Cherry Pit, 1964*, p. 70.
110 T. S. Monk interview, April 4, 2005.
111 Ibid.
112 Ivan Black, "Village Gate's Summer Jazz Festival Stars Monk, Coltrane, Mingus, et. al.," press release, June 28, 1965, and Flyer, n.d., Box 9, Ivan Black Papers; "Summer Festival at the Gate," *Amsterdam News*, July 3, 1965; "Where & When," *Down Beat* (July 15, 1965), 45; "Strictly Ad Lib," *Down Beat* (July 29, 1965), 10; "Where & When," *Down Beat* (July 29, 1965), 45; Ad, *Village Voice*, July 8 and 15, 1965; Ad *Village Voice*, August 12, 1965; "Strictly Ad Lib," *Down Beat* (August 12, 1965), 13.
113 Williamson, "An Interview with Ben Riley."
114 John Pagones, "Cugat Brings Rhythm to Blue Room," *Washington Post*, October 22, 1965.
115 "Strictly Ad Lib," *Down Beat* (January 27, 1966), 42.
116 Monk did come out in mid-December to play a memorial benefit at the Five Spot for tenor saxophonist Frank Haynes, who died of cancer at the age of thirty-three. Monk knew and respected Haynes, who had worked with Kenny Dorham, Walter Bishop, Jr., and most recently Randy Weston. "Memorial Jazz for Haynes," *Amsterdam News*, December 11, 1965.
117 "Jazz Benefit for WBAI at the Village Gate," flyer, n.d., Box 9, Ivan Black Papers; Ad *Village Voice*, December 16, 1965. The event took place from 9 p.m. to 4 a.m., and included such luminaries as Clark Terry, Joe Williams, Sonny Rollins, Charles Davis, Jimmy Rushing, King Curtis, Jim Hall, Kenny Dorham, Randy Weston, Betty Carter, among others. Dan Morgenstern, Ira Gitler, Don Schlitten, Chris Albertson, and Dave Lambert emceed the event. For an account of WBAI's history, see Steve Post, *Playing in the FM Band: A Personal Account of Free Radio* (New York: Viking Press, 1974).

118 George Wein to Harry Colomby, December 28, 1965, Robert Jones Personal Papers. As late as 1972, Lennie Sogoloff paid Monk's quartet $1,800 for five days (after Jack Whittemore's fee had been deducted). See AFM Contract, Thelonious Monk Local 802, Lennie Sogoloff, March 20, 1972, in author's possession.

119 Thelonious and Nellie Monk, U.S. Individual Income Tax Return, 1965.

120 Artist Contract Card, Columbia Records, page 1, John Donahue to Clive Davis, July 29, 1965, Box 30, Teo Macero Collection. As of June 30, 1965, Monk's unearned balance was $42,538.26.

121 Henri Renaud to Teo Macero, January 26, 1966, Box 30, Teo Macero Collection.

122 Monk interview with Valerie Wilmer and John Hopkins, March 14, 1965.

123 Leonard Feather, "Thelonious and the March of Time," *New York Post*, February 6, 1966; Marion Prilook, "An Interview with the Monk," *Danbury News-Times*, March 19, 1966.

124 Feather, "Thelonious and the March of Time."

125 Ibid.

126 "Reader's Poll," *Down Beat* (December 30, 1965), 19–25.

127 Letter from Randy Bloch, Sherman Oaks, Calif., "Chords and Discords: A Forum For Readers," *Down Beat* (September 23, 1965), 12.

128 Leonard Feather, "Blindfold Test, T. Monk," *Down Beat* (April 21, 1966), 39. Incidentally, "New Monastery," which got its name after Frank Wolff of Blue Note remarked that the tune reminded him of "something Thelonious Monk wrote long ago," happened to be one of the cuts on *Point of Departure,* the LP Feather played for Monk. Andrew Hill, *Point of Departure* (Blue Note CDP 7 84167 2). For a detailed discussion of Monk's influence on Andrew Hill, see my "New Monastery: Monk and the Jazz Avant-Garde," 135–168.

129 "Encounter: Monk and Dolores Wilson," *Toronto Telegram*, November 12, 1966.

130 Monk quoted in the film *Monk* by Christian and Michael Blackwood (Michael Blackwood Productions, 1968).

131 "Strictly Ad Lib," *Down Beat* (March 10, 1966), 13; "Changing Manne-Hole Scene," *Los Angeles Times*, January 9, 1966; Leonard Feather, "Stanford—College of Musical Knowledge," *Los Angeles Times*, January 30, 1966; Russ Wilson, "World of Jazz," *Oakland Tribune*, January 16, 1966.

132 The It Club remained closed for about eighteen months, reopening in mid-October, 1967 with Art Blakey's group. Eunice Pye, "Tripping Around Town," *Los Angeles Sentinel*, October 12, 1967; "Local Jazz Clubs Going Full Blast," *Los Angeles Times*, October 21, 1967. The details of McClain's arrest, the result of an elaborate sting operation, are detailed in his appeal. 417 F.2d 489, *John T. McCLAIN, Appellant, v. UNITED STATES of America,* Appellee. No. 23335. United States Court of Appeals Ninth Circuit. September 18, 1969. He was originally indicted on November 28, 1967. All of his appeals failed. McClain's drug-dealing activities are also briefly discussed in Toure, *Never Drank the Kool-Aid,* 67–68.

133 See Gerald Horne, *Fire This Time: The Watts Uprising and the 1960s* (Charlottesville: University of Virginia Press, 1995); Janet L. Abu-Lughod, *Race, Space, and Riots,*197–226.

134 "Strictly Ad Lib," *Down Beat* (February 10, 1966), 16; Louis P. Dumetz, "'Monk' At Plugged Nickel," *Chicago Defender*, February 9, 1966; "Strictly Ad Lib," *Down Beat* (March 10, 1966), 10, 42; "Hawkins, Monk to Play Jazz at Vanguard," *Amsterdam News*, February 26, 1966; ad, *Village Vanguard*, February 24, 1966.

135 In Switzerland, Wein could only get $750 a night, but in Paris proper he was guaranteed $1,200 a night. George Wein to Harry Colomby, September 23, 1965, Robert Jones Personal Papers.

136 "Monk, Too, To Swing At," *Chicago Defender*, April 19, 1966; "Strictly Ad Lib," *Down Beat*, (May 19, 1966), 53; "Nouvelles," *Jazz Hot* (March 1966), 12.

137 Pierre Lattes, "Monk à Paris—Quelle Palette," *Jazz Hot* (May 1966), 5–6.

138 M. B., "Monk à la Mutualité," *Jazz Magazine* (May 1966), 17.

139 Christopher Bird, "Monk Is Now Instant Creation Twice Nightly," *Melody Maker* (April 30, 1966), 6.

140 Charles Fox, "Thelonious Monk at Royal Festival Hall," *Manchester Guardian*, April 25, 1966.

141 Private recording in author's possession, Free Trade Hall, Manchester, April 29, 1966.

142 A. David Hogarth, "Monk: In Europe," *Jazz Journal* (June 1966), 23.

143 B. P. J., "Thelonious Monk," *Ruch Muzyczny* 10 (1966), 9–10. I am grateful to Andrzej M. Salski for translating this article from the Polish.

144 Ben Riley interview, June 9, 2004; Gourse, *Straight, No Chaser*, 228; Larry Ridley interview, September 7, 2001.

145 "Strictly Ad Lib," *Down Beat* (February 24, 1966), 43; Hultin, *Born Under the Sign of Jazz*, 213–14. The television show, called "Tema Med Variasjoner," or "Theme and Variation," is available on video under the title *Monk in Oslo.*

146 Randi Hultin, *Born Under the Sign of Jazz*, 214.

147 "Top Pianist Critical in Cumberland Hospital," *Amsterdam News*, July 10, 1965; "Jazzman Bud Powell Critical in New York," *Chicago Defender*, July 10, 1965; "Bud Powell Still Listed as Critical," *Amsterdam News*, July 17, 1965; "Bud Powell Near Death in Hospital," *Pittsburgh Courier*, July 24, 1965.

148 Hultin, *Born Under the Sign of Jazz*, 213.

149 Feather put on "Ruby, My Dear" from the LP *The Giants of Jazz* (Columbia CL1970).

150 Feather, "Blindfold Test, T. Monk," 39.

151 *Japan Times*, May 5, 1966.

152 The Monk family has photos of Reiko Hoshino and Thelonious together in Japan. On Ms. Hoshino and her role as host to jazz musicians, see Leonard Feather, *The Jazz Years: Earwitness to an Era* (New York: Da Capo, 1987), 227.

153 Peter Burt, *The Music of Toru Takemitsu* (London and Cambridge: Cambridge University Press, 2005), 12.

154 Ibid.,12; "Kojo no Tsuki," http://www.ne.jp/asahi/minako/watanabe/moon.htm. Indeed, it had become so identified with Japanese nationalism that Allied forces banned the song during the immediate postwar occupation. "Allies Ban Sweet Songs in Japan, Considered Dangerous," *New York Times*, November 21, 1945.

155 Harry Colomby interview, March 30, 2008.

156 Recording of "Japanese Folk Song," live at Newport Jazz Festival, July 4, 1966, in author's possession.

157 "Strictly Ad Lib," *Down Beat* (July 14, 1966), 69.

158 Nellie Monk interview, January 12, 2002; Harry Colomby interview, August 12, 2003; Gourse, *Straight, No Chaser*, 225.

159 Monk stayed at the Vanguard on and off until September 18. "Strictly Ad Lib," *Down Beat* (July 28, 1966), 12; "Strictly Ad Lib," *Down Beat* (September 8, 1966), 15; "Where & When," *Down Beat* (June 30, 1966), 48; Ad, *Village Voice*, September 6, 1966; "Where & When," *Down Beat* (September 22, 1966), 53.

160 Harry Colomby interview, August 12, 2003.

161 Monk's quartet played at the Music Barn on July 24. "Strictly Ad Lib," *Down Beat* (August 11, 1966), 13; "Folk Minstrel at Music Barn," *North Adams Transcript*, July 22, 1966.

162 "Bud Powell, Influential Jazz Pianist, Dies at 41," *New York Times*, August 2, 1966; Groves and Shipton, *The Glass Enclosure*, 93. Francis Paudras incorrectly claims he was hospitalized at Cumberland early July and then transferred. Paudras, *Dance of the Infidels*, 349–50.

163 "Dizzy and Local 802 to Bury Bud Powell," *Amsterdam News*, August 6, 1966.

164 Bertha Hope interview, July 15, 2003.

165 Homer Bigart, "Bud Powell Given Jazzman Funeral," *New York Times*, August 9, 1966; "Sextet Plays at Funeral for Jazz's Powell," *Chicago Tribune*, August 9, 1966; "Jazz Sextet Leads March at Bud Powell's Funeral," *Washington Post*, August 10, 1966; Groves and Shipton, *The Glass Enclosure*, 93.

166 Ad, *Village Voice*, July 28 and August 4, 1966; Ad, *Amsterdam News*, September 17, 1966. He played opposite Bill Evans and later Jackie McLean.

167 "Strictly Ad Lib," *Down Beat* (September 8, 1966), 42.

168 Robert Shelton, "Park Shows Given by Monk and Evans," *New York Times*, August 23, 1966.

169 Ad, *Syracuse Herald-Journal*, October 7, 1966; Earl George, "Thelonious Monk Concert is Explosive," *Syracuse Herald-Journal*, October 10, 1966.

170 Patrick Scott, "Thelonious, Musak or Pumpkins?" *Toronto Globe and Mail*, November 1, 1966; Warren Gerard, "The Monk: 'Everybody's Different, Man!'," *Toronto Globe and Mail*, November 5, 1966.

171 Charles Gerein, "The Monk-Like Mr. Monk," *Toronto Daily Star*, November 5, 1966.

172 Ibid.; Warrren Gerard, "The Monk."

173 Gerein, "The Monk-Like Mr. Monk."

174 "Green Chimneys" was later released on the CD reissue of Thelonious Monk, *Straight, No Chaser* (Columbia CK64886). "This Is My Story, This Is My Song" was also not released until 1979, first appearing on the compilation 2-LP set, *Always Know* (Columbia JG35720).

175 "Strictly Ad Lib," *Down Beat* (November 3, 1966), 13; "Strictly Ad Lib," *Down Beat* (November 17, 1966), 15; "Where & When," *Down Beat* (November 17, 1966), 54; "Strictly Ad Lib," *Down Beat* (December 1, 1966), 15; "Where & When," *Down Beat* (December 1, 1966), 44.

176 Susan Nelson, "Monk Is as Unique as His Music," *Chicago Tribune*, November 25, 1966.

177 "Strictly Ad Lib," *Down Beat* (January 26, 1967), 13; Ad, *Village Voice*, December 29, 1966.

178 Thelonious Monk, *Straight, No Chaser* (Columbia CL2651).

179 Teo Macero and Bruce Lundvall, "Popular Album Exploitation Plan," n. d., Box 30, Teo Macero Collection.

180 Although the LP was completed in January, it took six weeks for Columbia to cut him a check. Teo Macero to Bob Ciotti, February 27, 1967, Box 30, Teo Macero Collection.

181 "Strictly Ad Lib," *Down Beat* (February 23, 1967), 41; "Monk to Open Star-Studded Boston Globe Concert," Boston, *Bay State Banner*, January, 21, 1967; Ad, *Michigan Chronicle*, January 14, 1967.

182 Most sources, up until now, mistakenly date the concert February of 1966. The original source of the error is Wein himself, who is quoted in J. C. Thomas, *Coltrane: Chasin' the Trane*, 206. Wein repeats the error in his own memoir, *Myself Among Others*. But besides the ads in the Michigan Chronicle dating the concert January 22, 1967, we also have an audio tape of a talk Wein delivered to the Duke Ellington Society literally the day after the concert. The talk is dated January 23, 1967. George Wein talk, Duke Ellington Society, New York, January 23, 1967, audio tape, NYPL.

183 George Wein talk, Duke Ellington Society, New York, January 23, 1967; Wein, *Myself Among Others*, 263. Alice [McLeod], Coltrane's wife of a year and the band's pianist since 1965, was a Detroit native and was visiting family at the time.

184 Wein, *Myself Among Others*, 263. In Wein's talk to the Duke Ellington Society, he said pretty much the same thing, though it was all so fresh in his mind. His enthusiasm was contagious. "I had never heard Thelonious play better," he told the crowd. And Coltrane sounded "almost like Bud Freeman." The context, of course, was Wein's general frustration with Coltrane's new direction, which he vehemently disliked. He told the group, "Before, he was way out. Now he's downright out of sight." George Wein talk, Duke Ellington Society, New York, January 23, 1967.

185 Wein, *Myself Among Others*, 263.

27 "Let Someone Else Create Something New!"

1 "Strictly Ad Lib," *Down Beat* (April 20, 1967), 16; Ad, *Village Voice*, March 23, 1967; "Where & When," *Down Beat* (April 20, 1967), 51.

2 Thelonious and Nellie Monk, New York State Tax Resident Return, 1966. This figure includes his BMI Foreign Royalties for 1966, which earned an impressive $1,851.76—indicating that Monk sold well overseas. See BMI Foreign Royalty Statement, Thelonious S. Monk and Mr. Harry Colomby, Date issued 1966, Monk family papers.

3 Their new address was 165 West End Avenue, apartment 20-D. Thelonious and Nellie Monk, New York State Tax Resident Return, 1967; Teo Macero to Bob Ciotti, April 3, 1968, Box 30, Teo Macero Collection.
4 Lem Martinez-Carroll interview, July 2, 2003. I found the original lead sheet, written in Monk's hand, among his papers. At the bottom someone scrawled the names and addresses of two people—perhaps other students: Lisle Parris and "Nick." Manuscript in possession of the Thelonious Monk Estate.
5 Lem Martinez-Carroll interview, July 2, 2003.
6 Ibid.
7 "Poor Attend Private School," *New York Times*, June 27, 1966.
8 T. S. Monk interview, April 4, 2005.
9 Ibid.
10 Harry Colomby interview, August 12, 2003.
11 Ibid.; Bobby Colomby interview, August 14, 2003.
12 "Strictly Ad Lib," *Down Beat* (April 20, 1967), 46; "Strictly Ad Lib," *Down Beat* (June 15, 1967), 50; "Strictly Ad Lib," *Down Beat* (October 17, 1968), 46; "With K.D. in Texas," *Down Beat* (June 15, 1967); Emily Lamon, "Jazz Ambassadors Head for Austin," *Corpus Christi Caller-Times*, April 9, 1967; George T. Wein to Harry Colomby, January 24, 1967; George T. Wein to Harry Colomby, March 7, 1967, Robert Jones Personal Papers.
13 George T. Wein to Harry Colomby, January 24, 1967, George T. Wein to Harry Colomby, March 7, 1967, George T. Wein to Harry Colomby, March 28, 1967, Robert Jones Personal Papers.
14 Howard B. Woods, "Mexico Fans Love Jazz Played the U.S. Way," *Pittsburgh Courier*, May 27, 1967; "Newport Jazz Festival Set for Mexico," *Pittsburgh Courier*, May 13, 1967; Roderick Nordell, "No Blues for El Jazz in Puebla," *Christian Science Monitor*, May 17, 1967; Roderick Nordell, "Jazz Comes to Mexico," *Christian Science Monitor*, June 2, 1967.
15 Dave Brubeck, *Summit Sessions* (Columbia C 30522); Martin A. Totusek, "Dave Brubeck Interview," *Cadence* 20, no. 12 (December 1994), 9; Nordell, "No Blues for El Jazz in Puebla."
16 Totusek, "Dave Brubeck Interview," 9; Nordell, "No Blues for El Jazz in Puebla."
17 Sandra Capello interview, July 19, 2003.
18 Bertha Hope interview, July 15, 2003.
19 T. S. Monk interview, January 30, 2004.
20 Iggy Termini interview, March 8, 2008; John S. Wilson, "Jazz: A Club Reappears," *New York Times*, December 19, 1972.
21 Paul Chevigny, *Gigs: Jazz and the Cabaret Laws in New York City* (New York and London: Routledge, 1991), 67.
22 "Where & When," *Down Beat* (June 15, 1967), 54; "Strictly Ad Lib," *Down Beat* (June 29, 1967), 16; "Where & When," *Down Beat* (June 29, 1967), 59; "Strictly Ad Lib," *Down Beat* (September 21, 1967), 16; Ad, *Village Voice*, August 3, 1967; *The Villager*, August 3, 1967; Ivan Black, "Thelonious Monk and Ornette Coleman into Village Gate," press release, n.d., Box 9, Ivan Black Papers. In October, the quartet played Detroit's Masonic Temple on a bill that headlined Gloria Lynne and Hugh Masekela. "Strictly Ad Lib," *Down Beat* (November 30, 1967), 44.
23 Leonard Feather, "Jazz Salute Draws 7,100 in San Diego," *Los Angeles Times*, July 30, 1968.
24 Ibid.; Helen McNamara, "Nonconformist of Accomplishment," *Toronto Telegram*, August 22, 1967.
25 "International Jazz Critics Poll," *Down Beat* (August 25, 1966), 17; "International Jazz Critics Poll 1967," *Down Beat* (August 24, 1967), 17.
26 George T. Wein to Harry Colomby, March 7, 1967, Robert Jones Personal Papers.
27 Ibid.
28 Whitney Balliett, "Musical Events: Newport Notes," *New Yorker* (July 22, 1967), 74.
29 "Strictly Ad Lib," *Down Beat* (November 16, 1967), 14. The film, set to Monk's music, was supposed to premiere at the Museum of Modern Art in 1967, but Quackenbush was forced to cancel two hours before because the equipment failed to produce a sufficiently bright image when projected from a distance. It was not shown publicly until 1981. Doug Quackenbush unpublished typed notes, p. 20.
30 Clifton Smith interview, January 30, 2004.
31 Evelyn Smith interview, January 30, 2004.
32 Michael Blackwood interview, February 13, 2004.
33 Ibid.
34 Christian and Michael Blackwood, *Monk* (Michael Blackwood Productions, 1968); Christian and Michael Blackwood, *Monk in Europe* (Michael Blackwood Productions, 1968).
35 The tour opened in London on October 27 and passed through the Netherlands, Sweden, Denmark, France, Germany, and Switzerland. Italy and Spain were on the original itinerary, but concerts there were canceled at the last minute. George Wein to Jimmy Cleveland, July 29, 1967, Robert Jones Personal Papers.
36 George Wein to Jimmy Cleveland, July 29, 1967, Robert Jones Personal Papers; Robert Jones interview, June 15, 2007.
37 Joachim E. Berendt to Teo Macero, September 13, 1967, Box 30, Teo Macero Collection.
38 Robert Jones interview, June 15, 2007. Jackie remembered how reluctant Monk was to go. Jackie Bonneau interview, June 17, 2005.
39 Robert Jones interview, June 15, 2007; George Wein to Jimmy Cleveland, July 29, 1967, Robert Jones Personal Papers.
40 Jackie Bonneau interview, June 17, 2005.
41 Robert Jones interview, June 15, 2007.
42 Jackie Bonneau interview, October 30, 2008.

43 Ibid.
44 Quote Ibid.; Bob Rusch, transc. by Kea D. Strate, "Jimmy Cleveland Interview – Part Two," *Cadence* 17, no. 2 (February 1991), 16.
45 Robert Jones interview, June 15, 2007; Bob Rusch, "Jimmy Cleveland Interview – Part Two," 16–17.
46 Michael Shera, "Monk: Mann," *Jazz Journal* (December 1967),10.
47 Robert Jones interview, June 15, 2007.
48 Valerie Wilmer, "London Lowdown," *Down Beat* (December 28, 1967); Shera, "Monk: Mann," 10–11.
49 Jackie Bonneau interview, October 30, 2008. Max Roach had been at Ronnie Scott's for nearly six weeks when Monk arrived. "Roach Opens at Ronnie's With Abbey," *Melody Maker* (September 16,1967), 2; "Roach Missing at Scott Club Opening Night," *Melody Maker* (September 23, 1967), 4; Frank King, "Max Roach Reviewed," *Crescendo* 6, no. 3 (October 1967), 12; Barry McRae, "Jazz in Britain: Max Roach," *Jazz Journal* 20, no. 11 (November 1967), 17.
50 Unreleased recording in author's possession.
51 Robert Jones interview, June 15, 2007. The rehearsal and the performance are captured on *Monk in Europe* (1968).
52 On Berendt's letter suggesting that Columbia record the band in Berlin, Macero wrote boldly "Great Idea." Joachim E. Berendt to Teo Macero, September 13, 1967, Box 30, Teo Macero Collection. Radio broadcasts of the band occurred in Rotterdam, Stockholm, Copenhagen, Paris, and Berlin.
53 *Monk in Europe* (1968).
54 Ibid.
55 Ibid.
56 Robert Jones interview, June 15, 2007.
57 Jackie Bonneau interview, October 30, 2008.
58 Bob Rusch, "Jimmy Cleveland Interview – Part Two," 16.
59 Jackie Bonneau interview, June 17, 2005.
60 *Monk in Europe* (1968). The same scene is included in *Straight, No Chaser,* but for some reason Charlotte Zwerin decided to replace Nellie's words with a soundtrack of Monk playing "I Should Care." Needless to say, the substitution completely changes the meaning of the scene.
61 Michael Blackwood interview, February 13, 2004.
62 Jackie Bonneau interview, October 30, 2008. Robert Jones tells a slightly different story. He remembers an argument between Thelonious and Nellie over Nellie's reluctance to give back the money she did not spend. "'It's not your money,' Thelonious said. The East German guard didn't understand. Finally Thelonious took this wad of money and threw it on the counter. 'Fuck it, count the money,' he said. The guard was laughing. Another guard came in and knew Monk, the piano player, and told the first guard. Nellie put all the money in her bag. Monk said, 'You may think that's your money, but when I get in the car again, I'm taking it back.'" Quoted in Gourse, *Straight, No Chaser,* 244; Robert Jones interview, June 15, 2007. I cannot corroborate the story, especially since both Jackie Bonneau and Michael Blackwood tell an identical story about the $1,000 bill.
63 "Strictly Ad Lib," *Down Beat* (February 22, 1968), 14.
64 Ben Riley interview, March 1, 2005.
65 "Strictly Ad Lib," *Down Beat* (April 4, 1968), 15. The program was taped on November 14 and aired on February 24, 1968. Hall Overton participated, providing expert commentary on Monk's music. "What's On TV?" *Amsterdam News,* February 24, 1968.
66 Session Data Sheet, Columbia Records, 12/14/67, Job #20696, Box 30, Teo Macero Collection. The scene is documented in Christian and Michael Blackwood, *Monk* (Michael Blackwood Productions, 1968), as well as Charlotte Zwerin's *Straight, No Chaser.*
67 Quoted in *Monk* (1968). Jackie Bonneau, Monk's niece, was also in the studio during the session. She appears in the film sitting on a stool, though is often mistaken for Monk's daughter.
68 Session Data Sheet, Columbia Records, 12/21/67, Job # 20730, Box 30, Teo Macero Collection.
69 *Monk* (1968).
70 Danson, "Interview: Charlie Rouse," 7. Charlie Rouse tells a different story. When Rouse didn't show, Teo Macero was upset and thought the session was going to be a bust. But then suddenly, in walked Jon Hendricks and the rest is history. Rouse claimed he came late and he finished the session, but he does not appear on any tune during the session. Moreover, as we have seen in Chapter 26, Columbia had asked Hendricks to write lyrics for all of Monk's music.
71 Conversation with Jon Hendricks, Jazz Study Group, "Rhythm-a-ning: Symposium on Jazz Culture," May 2000; Peter Keepnews liner notes, reissue, Thelonious Monk, *Underground* (Columbia CK63535).
72 Memo from Irving Townsend to Teo Macero, November 24, 1964, Box 30, Teo Macero Collection.
73 This quote has circulated widely but it's not clear where it originated. Denis Naranjo, "Hendricks Soars Vocally at the Bird of Paradise," *Michigan Daily,* September 14, 2001. M. Joyce and K. Joyce, "Jon Hendricks: Interview," *Cadence,* 9, no. 1 (1983), 13.
74 Thelonious and Nellie Monk, New York State Tax Resident Return, 1967.
75 Marmostein, *The Label: The Story of Columbia Records,* 350.
76 Columbia Records PRESS RELEASE "Thelonious Monk in the Underground," n.d., Box 30, Teo Macero Collection.
77 Ibid.
78 Gil McKean liner notes, Thelonious Monk, *Underground* (Columbia CS9632).
79 "Where & When," *Down Beat* (February 22, 1968), 46; John L. Scott, "Jerry Vale Sings in Westside Room," *Los Angeles Times,* March 2, 1968.

80 Leonard Feather, "Thelonious Monk at the Manne-Hole," *Los Angeles Times*, March 9, 1968.
81 Ralph J. Gleason, "Thelonious Monk—A Great Artist," *New York Post*, March 5, 1968.
82 The official release date for *Underground* was April 22, 1968. Artist Contract Card–Columbia Records, p. 20, Box 30, Teo Macero Collection.
83 "Where & When," *Down Beat* (March 7, 1968), 44; "Where & When," *Down Beat* (March 21, 1968), 54; "Where & When," *Down Beat* (April 18, 1968), 54. On April 19, the day before the Berkeley concert, Monk's quartet performed at Brooklyn Academy for over 2,000 people. John S. Wilson, "Jazz a Challenge in Brooklyn Bill," *New York Times*, April 20, 1968.
84 "Thelonious Monk, Dr. John the Night Tripper, The Charlatans at the Carousel Ballroom–May 3, 4, 5, 1968" [poster in author's possession]. On the Carousel Ballroom's distinguished history, see "The Virtual Museum of the City of San Francisco," http://www.sfmuseum.org/hist1/rock.html.
85 Robert Jones interview, June 15, 2007; also quoted in Gourse, *Straight, No Chaser*, 240.
86 See enclosure, Teo Macero to Thelonious Monk, June 17, 1968, Box 30, Teo Macero Collection.
87 Martin Williams, "How Underground Is Monk?" *New York Times*, July 21, 1968.
88 Feather, "Thelonious Monk at the Manne-Hole."
89 "Strictly Ad Lib," *Down Beat* (March 21, 1968), 52; Telegram to Mr. Thelonious Monk from Teo Macero, May 3, 1968, Box 30, Teo Macero Collection.
90 "Application for Extension of Time to File, U.S. Individual Income Tax Return," April 11, 1968. In their letter requesting an extension to file (clearly drafted by their accountant Morris Zuckerman but signed by Thelonious), Nellie's three-week illness is to blame for their tardiness. She is also described in the letter as Monk's "personal and business manager."
91 Max Gordon, *Live at the Village Vanguard*, 117.
92 Evelyn Smith interview, July 6, 2005.
93 Evelyn Smith and Benetta Bines interviewed by author, July 6, 2005; also, Geraldine Smith and Evelyn Smith interview, February 12, 2004.
94 Boyce Rensberger, "Two Doctors Here Known to Users as Source of Amphetamines," *New York Times*, March 25, 1973. Freymann was also charged with "procuring and conducting abortions" and investigated after one of his patients, Erica Mann, died under his care.
95 Nellie Monk interview, January 12, 2002; Ran Blake interview, March 22, 2005. Monk family interview, January 30, 2004.
96 Teo Macero to Roy Friedman, June 3, 1968, Box 30, Teo Macero Collection.
97 Press Release, Schlitz Salute to Jazz '68, "Jazz Festival Success Assured," n.d., Robert Jones personal papers; "Schlitz Salute a Hit: '69 Expansion Planned," *Down Beat* (October 17, 1968), 13; Robert Jones interview, June 15, 2007.
98 Hazel Garland, "Pittsburgh CYO Slates 'Jazz Festival' in June," *Chicago Defender*, February 20, 1968; "Strictly Ad Lib," *Down Beat* (April 4, 1968), 49.
99 John Norris, "Monk Brings Real Jazz to the Jazz Festival," *Toronto Daily Star*, June 8, 1968.
100 Robert Jones interview, June 15, 2007.
101 Ibid.; Press Release, Schlitz Salute to Jazz '68, "Jazz Festival Success Assured," n.d., Robert Jones Personal Papers.
102 "Jackie Robinson Hosts 'Jazz Greats' Today," *Bridgeport Sunday Post*, June 30, 1968; Arnold Rampersad, *Jackie Robinson: A Biography* (New York: Knopf, 1997), 429. All in all, they raised about $30,000 for Coretta Scott King and her four children.
103 Robert S. Browne, "The Case for Two Americas–One Black, One White," *New York Times*, August 11, 1968; Jeff Donaldson, "The Rise, Fall, and Legacy of the Wall of Respect Movement," *International Review of African American Art* 15 no. 1 (1991), 22–26; Justin Gershwin, "The Magical Revolution: Frank Smith and the Rise of AfriCobra," http://www.subbasementartiststudios.com/themagicalrevolutionessay.html.
104 Before Monk returned to California, he spent most of September and part of October at the Blue Coronet in Brooklyn, Count Basie's Lounge, the Village Vanguard, the Village Gate, and briefly in Boston at Paul's Mall. "Strictly Ad Lib," *Down Beat* (October 17, 1968), 14; "Strictly Ad Lib," *Down Beat* (October 31, 1968), 12; "Strictly Ad Lib," *Down Beat* (November 14, 1968), 43; "Strictly Ad Lib," *Down Beat* (November 28, 1968), 13.
105 "Racial Violence Hits Cities Across Nation," *Los Angeles Times*, April 6, 1968; Daryl Lembke, "East Palo Alto to Vote on Becoming Nairobi," *Los Angeles Times*, November 3, 1968.
106 "Palo Alto Residents Seek Negro Neighbors," *Los Angeles Times*, April 28, 1968.
107 Danny Scher interview, January 18, 2008.
108 "*Benefit Concert—International Club Present Thelonious Monk Quartet,*" Program, Palo Alto High School, October 27, 1968; *The Madrono*, Palo Alto High School Yearbook (1969), copies in Danny Scher's possession.
109 Danny Scher interview, January 18, 2008
110 Ibid.
111 Tape of concert in Danny Scher's possession. The concert was actually recorded by an African-American janitor who worked at Palo Alto High School. He not only shared the tape of the concert with Danny but also made arrangements to tune the piano. Danny Scher interview, January 18, 2008.
112 Danny Scher interview, January 18, 2008.
113 "New Name Defeated for East Palo Alto," *New York Times*, November 6, 1968; "East Palo Alto to Keep Name," *Los Angeles Times*, November 6, 1968; "No Change in Name," *Amsterdam News*, November 9, 1968; Earl Caldwell, "Renaming of Town Divides Negroes on Coast," *New York Times*, December 26, 1968.
114 Leonard Feather, "Monk Quartet at the Manne-Hole," *Los Angeles Times*, November 15, 1968.
115 Phyl Garland, "The Many Bags of Oliver Nelson," *Ebony* 24 (November 1968), 109–110; also see Richard Williams, "Straight Ahead—The Early Work of Oliver Nelson & Eric Dolphy," *Jazz Journal* 20, no. 7 (July

1967), 4–6, 40; William L. Fowler, "Oliver Nelson: New Hope for the Abstract Truth," *Down Beat* (April 24, 1975), 10–11, 43; Leonard Feather, *The Pleasures of Jazz* (New York: Horizon, 1976), 187–192; John McDonough, "Oliver Nelson—Black, Brown and Beautiful," *Down Beat* (November 1989), 36–37; Richard Palmer, "The Nelson Touch," *Jazz Journal* 43, no. 9 (September 1990), 10–12.

116 Artist Contract Card, Columbia Records, page 20, Box 30, Teo Macero Collection. The idea for the LP originated in October, and as of October 7 an arranger had not been chosen. Jack Gold to Teo Macero, October 7, 1968, Box 30, Teo Macero Collection.

117 Harry Colomby interview, August 12, 2003.

118 Monk's regular quartet was part of the band. The other instrumentalists were Ernie Small, Thomas Scott, Gene Cipriano, and Ernie Watts (saxophones); Bobby Bryant, Frederick Hill, Conte Candoli (trumpets); Bob Brookmeyer, Billy Byers, and Mike Wimberley (trombones); Howard Roberts (guitar); John Guerin (drums).

119 "John Guerin (October 31, 1939–January 5, 2004)," http://johnguerin.com/home.htm; Ben Riley interview, March 1, 2005.

120 Besides listening to the recording, I was privileged to see a copy of the original lead sheet. Teo Macero, "Consecutive Seconds," Lead Sheet, n.d., Box 30, Teo Macero Collection.

121 Session Data Sheet, Columbia Records, 11/20/68, Box 30, Teo Macero Collection; John Snyder, "Producer's Note," Thelonious Sphere Monk, *Monk's Blues* (Columbia CK53581); Sheridan, *Brilliant Corners*, 190.

122 Quoted in Mark Humphrey, liner notes, Thelonious Sphere Monk, *Monk's Blues* (Columbia CK53581).

123 Harry Colomby interview, August 12, 2003.

124 A&R Recording Authorization, November 11, 1968, Artist Contract Card, Columbia Records, page 22, Box 30, Teo Macero Collection. Columbia initially authorized a budget of $8,155.

125 The original working title was "Blue Sphere," but they changed the name just prior to its release. Memo from Teo Macero to John Lemmermeyer, February 13, 1969, Box 30, Teo Macero Collection.

126 "Doug Ramsey's Jazz Review," typescript of broadcast on WDSU-FM, New Orleans, broadcast on 9/20/1969, Box 30, Teo Macero Collection; Martin Williams, "Jazz Musicians with Big Bands," *New York Times*, June 29, 1969. See also Jef Langford, "Monk's Horns," part III, p. 4; Barry McRae, "Review," *Jazz Journal* 22, no. 11 (November 1969).

127 Martin Williams to Teo Macero, June 10, 1969, Box 30, Teo Macero Collection.

128 Hollie I. West, "Monk: In Need of a New Life," *Washington Post*, July 20, 1969.

129 Teo Macero to Jimmy Wisner, April 4, 1969, Box 30, Teo Macero Collection; Harry Colomby interview, August 11, 2003. On Taj Mahal's love of jazz and especially Monk, see Art Tipaldi, *Children of the Blues: 49 Musicians Shaping a New Blues Tradition* (San Francisco, CA: Backbeat Books, 2002), 179–185.

130 Harry Colomby interview, August 11, 2003; Bobby Colomby interview, August 14, 2003; A&R Recording Authorization, September 10, 1969; Teo Macero to John Berg, Lee Trippett, September 11, 1969, Box 30, Teo Macero Collection.

131 "Encounter: Monk and Dolores Wilson," *Toronto Telegram*, November 12, 1966.

132 "An Interview with the Monk."

133 Bobby Colomby interview, August 14, 2003.

134 Rose Gales interview, August 25, 2008; on Gales's divorce from Mabel Gaut, see State of California, "California Divorce Index," Dissolution Case number 759833, Center for Health Statistics, California Department of Health Services, Sacramento, California.

135 John L. Scott, "Erroll Garner at the Century Plaza," *Los Angeles Times*, March 8, 1969; "Erroll's a Pearl," *Los Angeles Sentinel*, May 13, 1969; Creig Lewis, "James Brown Brings Show to the Loop," *Chicago Defender*, May 27, 1969.

136 Walter Booker interview, February 24, 2005. Flora Purim confirms both Monk's and Booker's presence at the Club Baron that winter, although her recollections are off by a year: "The first person I met on the second day of my arrival was Thelonious Monk. I went to the Harlem and was attempting to get into a club called Club Baron, and the doorman was giving me a hard time. . . . I could barely speak English; my English was broken and I had an accent. Thelonious scolded the doorman and extended his hand to me. . . . After the show, we went to Walter Booker's house where all the musicians that played in every other jazz club in the city converged to hang out and play music all night long." "Flora Purim—Queen of Brazilian Jazz: Artist Interview by: Beatrice S. Richardson," http://www.jazzreview.com/articleprint.cfm?ID=1202.

137 Walter Booker interview, February 24, 2005.

138 Ibid.

139 Conversation with Ben Riley, March 1, 2005; Gourse, "Ben Riley: Around Sphere [Interview]," 34.

140 Walter Booker interview, February 24, 2005.

141 Whitney Balliett, "Jazz: New York News," *New Yorker* (March 15, 1969), 172; John S. Wilson, "Newport All-Stars Headline Program of New Jazz Series," *New York Times*, March 3, 1969.

142 Walter Booker interview, February 24, 2005.

143 Ibid. The band opened March 4. Ad, *Chicago Defender*, March 1, 1969.

144 Walter Booker was no doctor, but he had spent a year in medical school and had an opportunity to speak with staff during Monk's hospitalization in Chicago. He distinctly recalls this diagnosis and, in hindsight, concluded that the mixture of drugs Thelonious used exacerbated his condition. Walter Booker interview, February 24, 2005.

145 Statement for Professional Services, Marcus Weldon Moore, DDS to Nellie Monk, December 5, 1968 [Receipt], Monk family papers.

146 *New York Daily News*, May 8, 1969; Ivan Black, "Dizzy, Thelonious and Horace in Gate Gala," Press Release, n.d., Box 25, Ivan Black Papers.

147 Evelyn Smith interview, January 30, 2004 and July 6, 2005.

148 Chilton, *The Song of the Hawk*, 387–88; Eddie Locke interview, August 31, 2001; Collette Hawkins interview, November 5, 2004.
149 Collette Hawkins interview, November 5, 2004.
150 Evelyn Smith interview, January 30, 2004 and July 6, 2005.
151 Ad, *New York Times*, July 6, 1969. A month earlier, Monk and Miles played opposite each other at the Morgan State Jazz Festival, but they did not perform the same day. "Jazz Festival in Baltimore," *Gettysburg Times*, May 22, 1969.
152 Evelyn Smith interview, January 30, 2004.
153 Ibid.
154 "Strictly Ad Lib," *Down Beat* (October 2, 1969), 38; Ivan Black, "Miles Davis & Thelonious Monk into Art D'Lugoff's Village Gate," Press Release, n.d., Box 25, Ivan Black Papers.
155 John S. Wilson, "Jazzmen of 1950s Play in Holmdel," *New York Times*, September 8, 1969.
156 Stanley G. Robertson, "L. A. Confidential," *Los Angeles Sentinel*, October 2, 1969; Leonard Feather, "Monterey Jazz Fest Amplifies Rock Aspects," *Los Angeles Times*, September 22, 1969.
157 Monk was booked at Baker's Keyboard in Detroit the same days he was scheduled to appear at the Fresno Jazz Festival (September 13–15, 1969). Monk had to postpone Baker's until October. "Thelonious Monk," *Fresno Bee*, August 17, 1969.
158 "Thelonious Monk Added to Monterey Jazz Fete," *Chicago Defender*, August 18, 1969; Robertson, "L. A. Confidential"; "Monterey Jazz Fest Amplifies Rock Aspects"; Ponzio and Postif, *Blue Monk*, 338–339. Before working with Monk, the Buffalo-born Booth had played with Art Blakey, Eddie Harris, Freddie Hubbard, and Sonny Simmons. Gary W. Kennedy, "Booth, Jiunie," In *The New Grove Dictionary of Jazz*, 2nd ed., edited by Barry Kernfeld. *Grove Music Online. Oxford Music Online*, http://www.oxfordmusiconline.com/subscriber/article/grove/music/J522400 (accessed September 14, 2008).
159 Bill Bennett and Barry Kernfeld. "Dawson, Alan." In *The New Grove Dictionary of Jazz*, 2nd ed., edited by Barry Kernfeld. *Grove Music Online. Oxford Music Online*, http://www.oxfordmusiconline.com/subscriber/article/grove/music/J115000 (accessed September 14, 2008); Ponzio and Postif, *Blue Monk*, 339–40. Hygelund appears on a compilation album of Berklee students, recorded circa 1965, *Jazz In The Classroom Vol. X: A Tribute To Charlie Mariano* (Berklee Records BLP-10), as well as a 1968 unreleased recording of a recital at Berklee by the Ray Santisi septet. *Tom Lord Jazz Discography* [Session S 1104–4].
160 Hollie I. West, "Thelonious Monk at the Cellar Door," *Washington Post*, October 8, 1969.
161 T. S. Monk interview, April 4, 2005.
162 Ibid.
163 Account bill, White House (Regent's Park) LTD, December 1, 1969, Thelonious Monk Family Papers.
164 Ponzio and Postif, *Blue Monk*, 340.
165 Audio tape of BBC-TV, *Jazz Scene at Ronnie Scott's*, November 3, 1969, in author's possession.
166 Television broadcast in author's possession; see also Ponzio and Postif, *Blue Monk*, 340–41.
167 WDR-TV recording, Cologne, Germany, December 3, 1969, audio tape in author's possession.
168 Coleman Hawkins's 1943 recording of "My Ideal" was originally issued as a 78 on the Commodore label (Commodore 548), but it has since been reissued on several compilations, including Coleman Hawkins and Frank Wess, *The Commodore Years: The Tenor Sax* (Atlantic SD2-306). Ernie Henry, *Seven Standards and a Blues* (Riverside RLP 12-248); John Coltrane Quintet, *Standard Coltrane* (Prestige LP7353).
169 Natasha Arnoldi, "Thelonious Monk à Pleyel: 15 Decembre 1969," *Jazz Hot* 257 (January 1970), 7; *Thelonious Monk–in Paris—Recorded at the Salle Pleyel, December 15, 1969* (Pioneer LDC-PILS-1103).
170 Arnoldi, "Thelonious Monk à Pleyel," 7.
171 Bernard Lion and Henri Renaud, *Jazz Portrait: Thelonious Monk* (Pioneer PIL-J-1125); see also Ponzio and Postif, *Blue Monk*, 343. The date given for the taping is December 25, but this is incorrect since Renaud himself admitted that it took place before Christmas. See Sheridan, *Brilliant Corners*, 198.
172 Oral History Interview with Wilbur B. Ware Sr. by Gloria L. Ware, December 18, 1977, Smithsonian Institution; Val Wilmer, "Ed Blackwell: Well-tempered Drummer," *Down Beat* (October 3, 1968), 18; Robert Palmer: "Ed Blackwell, Crescent City Thumper," *Down Beat*, (June 16, 1977), 17; Scott K. Fish, "Ed Blackwell: Singin' on the Set," *Modern Drummer* (November 1981), 14.
173 Oral History Interview with Wilbur B. Ware Sr. by Gloria L. Ware, December 18, 1977, p. 13; also, Paul Jeffrey interview, August 31, 2003.
174 Oral History Interview with Wilbur B. Ware Sr. by Gloria L. Ware, December 18, 1977, p. 13; Sandra Capello interview, July 19, 2003; Paul Jeffrey blames Sandra Capello for Rouse leaving, suggesting that she had wanted him to go out on his own for some time. Paul Jeffrey interview, August 31, 2003.

28 "What Do I Have to Do? Play Myself to Death?"

1 Sandra Capello interview, July 19, 2003.
2 Harriet Choice, "The Jazz Sound," *Chicago Tribune*, June 12, 1970; Harriet Choice, "Jazz by Choice," *Chicago Tribune*, September 18, 1970.
3 Paul Jeffrey interview, August 31, 2003.
4 Howard Mandel, "Dewey Redman: Nobody's Foil," *Down Beat* (February, 1983), 18.
5 Oral History Interview with Wilbur B. Ware Sr. by Gloria L. Ware, December 18, 1977, pp. 38–39; Pat Patrick, interviewed by Phil Schaap, WKCR, March 16, 1976; Szwed, *Space is the Place*, 87–88; Maurice Cullaz, "Pat Patrick," *Jazz Hot*, no. 330 (1976), 34. His son, Deval Patrick, went on to be the first African American elected governor of Massachusetts.

6 Pat Patrick, interviewed by Phil Schaap, WKCR, March 16, 1976.

7 Gene Feehan, "Black Baseball to Black Music." *Downbeat* (March 15, 1973), 18–21; Ed Hazell, "Portraits: Beaver Harris," *Modern Drummer* (November 1989), 51–52.

8 Wilmer, *As Serious as Your Life*, 85, 187; Jef Langford, "Monk's Horns," Part I, *Jazz Journal* (November 1970), 2; Jeff Langford, "Monk's Horns," Part III *Jazz Journal* (February 1971), 4.

9 Pat Patrick, interviewed by Phil Schaap, WKCR, March 16, 1976.

10 Ibid.

11 T. S. Monk interview, April 4, 2005.

12 Jackie Bonneau interview, October 30, 2008.

13 Ibid.

14 Doug Quackenbush was among several friends who volunteered to drive Nellie to Hunt's Point at 5:00 a.m. to purchase fresh produce. Doug Quackenbush unpublished typed notes, ca. 1996.

15 Quote from Lorraine Gordon, *Alive at the Village Vanguard*, 224; on Nellie and juicing, see interviews with Jackie Bonneau, Evelyn Smith, T. S. Monk, Binetta Bines; Leroy Williams interview, June 24, 2003; Paul Jeffrey interview, August 31, 2003.

16 Nica to Mary Lou Williams, April 21, 1970, Personal Correspondence, Box 4, Mary Lou Williams Collection.

17 Jackie Bonneau interview, October 30, 2008.

18 Ponzio and Postif, *Blue Monk*, 346; Sheridan, *Brilliant Corners*, 450.

19 Oral History Interview with Wilbur B. Ware Sr. by Gloria L. Ware, December 18, 1977, pp. 39–41.

20 Audio tape, Jazz Workshop, February 24, 1970, in author's possession. Patrick played these two cuts during a Monk birthday broadcast at WKCR hosted by Phil Schaap.

21 Bob Rusch, "Beaver Harris: Stories–Part Three," interview transcribed by Kathy Joyce, *Cadence* 9, no. 4 (April 1983), 20.

22 Oral History Interview with Wilbur B. Ware Sr. by Gloria L. Ware, December 18, 1977, 42–43; Rusch, "Beaver Harris: Stories," 20.

23 Leroy Williams interview, June 24, 2003.

24 Barry Harris Trio, *Magnificent!* (Prestige PR7733). The recording was made in New York, November 25, 1969.

25 Leroy Williams interview, June 24, 2003.

26 AFM Local 802 Contract, Thelonious Monk at Frog and Nightgown, February 24, 1970. Copy courtesy of Sam Stephenson.

27 Nica to Mary Lou Williams, April 21, 1970, Personal Correspondence, Box 4, Mary Lou Williams Collection. Nica's letter does not say what Monk was hospitalized for, but as late at April 21, five weeks after he was admitted, she wrote: "Thelonious has been very sick . . . He is MUCH better, now, and should be out of the hospital any day."

28 Oral History Interview with Wilbur B. Ware Sr. by Gloria L. Ware, December 18, 1977, p. 43; Paul Jeffrey interview, August 31, 2003.

29 Paul Jeffrey interview, August 31, 2003.

30 Sam Stephenson, "Thelonious Monk–Is This Home?" *Oxford American* 58 (2007), 112–114

31 *Raleigh News and Observer*, May 15, 1970; Leroy Williams interview, June 24, 2003; Sam Stephenson, "Thelonious Monk–Is This Home?" 116.

32 Leroy Williams interview, June 24, 2003.

33 Nellie Monk interview, January 12, 2002.

34 Timothy Tyson, *Blood Done Sign My Name: A True Story* (New York: Crown, 2004), 118–145; "N.C. Negro Describes Execution," *Washington Post*, May 15, 1970; "Tension Racks Oxford," *Chicago Defender*, May 14, 1970; "Ben Chavis," in Bud Schultz, ed., *It Did Happen Here: Recollections of Political Repression in America* (Los Angeles and Berkeley: University of California Press, 1989), 198–199.

35 Tyson, *Blood Done Sign My Name*, 220–246; "Father, Son Acquitted in Negro's Death," *Atlanta Daily World*, August 4, 1970.

36 Paul Jeffrey interview, August 31, 2003.

37 Recordings in Paul Jeffrey's possession.

38 Leroy Williams interview, June 24, 2003.

39 Bill Morrison, "Monk and His Piano—Too Much Anticipation," *Raleigh News and Observer*, May 19, 1970.

40 Paul Jeffrey interview, August 31, 2003.

41 AFM Local 802 Contract, Thelonious Monk at Frog and Nightgown, April 17, 1970; Jack Whittemore to Peter Ingram, May 6, 1970, copies courtesy of Sam Stephenson.

42 Paul Jeffrey interview, August 31, 2003; Leroy Williams interview, June 24, 2003.

43 Tyson, *Blood Done Sign My Name*; 155–159; *Burlington Times-News*, May 26, 1970.

44 Ad, *New York Times*, June 25, 1970; Oral History Interview with Wilbur B. Ware Sr. by Gloria L. Ware, December 18, 1977, 43; Leroy Williams interview, June 24, 2003; Pat Patrick, interviewed by Phil Schaap, WKCR, March 16, 1976.

45 "Black Is – Featuring Freddie Hubbard Quintet, Thelonious Monk, McCoy Tyner Quintet, August 14, 1970," flyer in author's possession; Ad, *Amsterdam News*, August 8, 1970.

46 By 1969, Macero was producing pop music, Dave Brubeck, the demanding Miles Davis, Andre Kostelanetz, and handling the Ed Sullivan line of products. Marmostein, *The Label: The Story of Columbia Records*, 383.

47 Dennis Katz to Jack Gold, memo July 9, 1970, Dennis Katz to Jack Gold, memo, July 21, 1970, Box 30, Teo Macero Collection.

48 Teo Macero to Jack Gold, July 10, 1970, Box 30, Teo Macero Collection.

49 Advertisement for "Greatest Hits,"; Memo from Teo Macero to John Lemmermeyer and Russ Payne, November 19, 1968, Box 30, Teo Macero Collection.

50 *Newport Jazz Festival in Jappan [sic], '70 Oct. 1–13* (Program, Morioka Printing Co., Ltd., 1970), program in Monk family papers. Most of the text is in Japanese. I'm grateful to Chris and Fujiko Kelley for translating this material for me.

51 Leroy Williams interview, June 24, 2003.

52 Larry Ridley interview, September 7, 2001; Paul Jeffrey interview, August 31, 2003. Both men had toured Japan in June and recorded with Kohsuke Mine and Attila Zoller during their brief stay; Kohsuke Mine, *Morning Tide* (Philips (Jap)FX8508); Attila Zoller Trio, *Guitar Genius in Japan* (Over Seas (Jap)UPS81).

53 Paul Jeffrey interview, August 31, 2003.

54 Ibid.

55 Larry Ridley interview, September 7, 2001.

56 "Legat Tokyo (163–2971) to Director, FBI, August 27, 1970 re: Japanese Immigration Bureau Name Check Requests," and "Visa Application, July 17, 1970," both documents in FBI/FOIA file Subject: Thelonious Monk.

57 The personnel on the recording were Koji Hatori, Bunji Murata, Kenichi Sano, Kunio Fujisaki (tp), Teruhiko Kataoka, Masamichi Uetaka, Seiichi Tokura, Takeshi Aoki (tb), Hiroshi Takami, Shinji Nakayama (as), Kosuke Ichihara, Shoji Maeda (ts), Shunzo Sunahara (bar), Masahiko Satoh, Yoshinobu Imashiro (p), Kozaburo Yamaki (g), Masao Kunisada (b), Teiichi Tabata (d), Toshiyuki Miyama (cond). Thelonious Monk Quartet, *Thelonious Monk in Tokyo* (Far East ETJ-60006). On Miyama, see Atkins, *Blue Nippon,* 156–176; Yozo Iwanami and Kazunori Sugiyama, "Miyama, Toshiyuki." In *The New Grove Dictionary of Jazz,* 2nd ed., edited by Barry Kernfeld. *Grove Music Online. Oxford Music Online,* http://www.oxfordmusiconline.com/subscriber/article/grove/music/J304700 (accessed November 30, 2008).

58 Paul Jeffrey interview, August 31, 2003.

59 Ibid.

60 Thelonious Monk Quartet, *Thelonious Monk in Tokyo* (Far East ETJ-60006).

61 Larry Ridley interview, September 7, 2001.

62 Russ Wilson, "Thelonious Monk Opens at S.F.," *Oakland Tribune,* October 16, 1970; "Beyond Central: Putter Smith Interviewed by Alex Cline [July 30–September 10, 2003]," UCLA Oral History Project (2007), transcription. Used by permission, UCLA Oral History Project.

63 "Putter Smith Interviewed by Alex Cline," 173.

64 Ibid., p. 176.

65 Ibid., p. 177; the story is also repeated in Gourse, *Straight, No Chaser,* 262.

66 Wilson, "Thelonious Monk Opens at S. F."

67 Paul Jeffrey interview, August 31, 2003.

68 Ibid.

69 In 1970, he appeared on Herbie Hancock's *Mwandishi* (Warner Bros WS1898). It was Henderson's first recording session.

70 Eddie Henderson interview, January 11, 2004.

71 Ibid.

72 Ibid.; also, Paul Jeffrey interview, August 31, 2003.

73 Paul Jeffrey interview, August 31, 2003.

74 Jackie Bonneau interview, October 30, 2008.

75 Memorial Service for Barbara Evelyn Monk, Program, January 17, 1984, in author's possession; "Eubie Blake Now 89; In Show Biz 72 Years," *Amsterdam News,* February 12, 1972.

76 Eddie Henderson interview, January 11, 2004. Paul Jeffrey interview, August 31, 2003.

77 Paul Jeffrey interview, August 31, 2003.

78 Sammy Mitchell, "Caught in the Act," *Down Beat* (March 4, 1971), 31.

79 Ibid., p. 31.

80 Leon Ndugu Chancler, interview, September 30, 2008. In an article about Young Soul, Chancler is described as one of its outstanding graduates who went on to play with Hugh Masekela and Monk, but he is not mentioned by name. Erwin Washington, "Group with Plenty of Soul," *Los Angeles Times,* June 16, 1971.

81 Leon Ndugu Chancler interview, September 30, 2008.

82 Leonard Feather, "Thelonious Monk Spins Original Tunes," *Los Angeles Times,* January 8, 1971.

83 Quoted in "Putter Smith Jazz Wolverine," *All About Jazz,* May 12, 2008, http://www.allaboutjazz.com/php/news.php?id=18383.

84 As Smith tells it, "An agent signed me and nothing ever happened. It was about a year of nothing, absolutely nothing." Ten years later, a friend of his became an agent and tried to resurrect his acting career. "So for about a year I went out on interviews and I did about ten small jobs, and then he got enough money to buy himself a Roto-Rooter franchise in Las Vegas, and so now he's cleaning toilets in Las Vegas, which is a step up. [laughs] . . . So I thought, well, that's a perfect end to my acting career." "Putter Smith Interviewed by Alex Cline," 186–87. He appeared in the films *Love Thy Neighbor* (1984), *In the Mood* (1987) and *Win, Place, or Steal* (1975). See Putter Smith, http://www.imdb.com/name/nm0809623/.

85 Leon Ndugu Chancler interview, September 30, 2008.

86 Paul Jeffrey interview, August 31, 2003.

87 A&R Recording Authorization Form, February 12, 1971, Memo from Dennis Katz to Mallory Rintoul, March 18, 1971, Box 30, Teo Macero Collection.

88 Bobby Colomby interview, August 14, 2003.

89 James Lichtenberg, "Making Rock Respectable," *New York Times,* February 28, 1971.

90 Tom Zito, "Blood, Sweat and Tears: No Spontaneity," *Washington Post,* March 8, 1971. The review ranged from lukewarm to negative. Zito took BS&T to task for their lack of spontaneity and overly slick performance style. "Instead of feeding off each other, it's almost as if all the musicians are being controlled by a central computer."

91 Oral History Interview with Wilbur B. Ware Sr. by Gloria L. Ware, December 18, 1977, p. 47.

92 Paul Jeffrey interview, August 31, 2003; Oral History Interview with Wilbur B. Ware Sr. by Gloria L. Ware, December 18, 1977, p. 47.

93 John S. Wilson, "The 'Jazz Doctors' Prescribe Music as the Best Therapy," *New York Times*, October 10, 1971; John S. Wilson, "Jazz at Noon—Anyone Can Have Lunch With Jam," *New York Times*, May 25, 1975. Dr. Markewich recorded as a leader in 1957, while he was still in college at Cornell University. The LP is Reese Markewich Quintet, *New Designs in Jazz* (Modern Age MA134). Personnel were Markewich (piano and flute), Nick Brignola (alto and baritone sax), Jesse Avery (tenor), Steve Fillo (bass), and Ronnie Zito (drums). He also published books and articles about jazz throughout the 1970s and '80s. Perhaps his best known book is *The New Expanded Bibliography of Jazz Compositions Based on the Chord Progressions of Standard Tunes* (New York: Reese Markewich, 1974). On Reese Markewich's biography, "Maurice Elish Markewich." *Marquis Who's Who ™*. Marquis Who's Who, 2008, Reproduced in *Biography Resource Center*. (Farmington Hills, MI.: Gale, 2008), http:// galenet.galegroup.com/servlet/BioRC. I spoke with Dr. Markewich on November 30, 2008, but he was restricted by Beth Israel from sharing any information pertaining to Thelonious Monk's case—medical or otherwise.

94 Paul Jeffrey interview, August 31, 2003.

95 Doug Quackenbush unpublished typed notes, ca. 1996, pp. 23–24.

96 Paul Jeffrey interview, August 31, 2003.

97 T. S. Monk, interview, April 4, 2005; Paul Jeffrey interview, August 31, 2003.

98 The Philly Joe Jones Quintet included Nico Brunick on piano, Tommy Turrentine on trumpet, Monty Walters on alto. Their gigs were limited to the Sunday jazz concerts held at the Jazz Center on West 57th Street and short-term gigs. Jones told critic John S. Wilson that the group was temporary and he planned to work with Red Garland. John S. Wilson, "Joe Jones, Drummer, and Quintet Fill in at Jazz Interactions," *New York Times*, May 18, 1971. Paul Jeffrey, on the other hand, insists that Philly Joe planned to come back but Nellie blocked him. "Philly Joe said something to me just before he died. He said, imagine putting your kid in my place. I didn't know what he was talking about because I didn't connect the two. And I'm trying to say, what is he talking about? He was talking about Toot [replacing him]. He said, 'But I left him in the hot seat.' But that was Philly Joe's feeling about that. And I didn't know that it had bothered him all them years." Paul Jeffrey interview, August 31, 2003.

99 Jackie Bonneau interview, October 30, 2008.

100 T. S. Monk interview, April 4, 2005; Ran Blake interview, March 22, 2005.

101 T. S. Monk interview, April 4, 2005.

102 C. Gerald Fraser, "Ellis Haizlip, Producer, 61, Dies; Mentor to Many Black Performers," *New York Times*, January 30, 1991. Also, I'm grateful to Louis Massiah and Gayle Wald for their extensive research on Ellis Haizlip and *Soul!*

103 "Week's T.V. Highlites," *Los Angeles Sentinel*, May 20, 1971; *Bridgeport Telegram*, May 20, 1971; *Oneonta Star*, May 20, 1971; Lumberton, NC, *Robesonian*, May 20, 1971. In New York City it aired twice, once on Thursday, May 20 and then Sunday, May 23. ["What's On TV?" *Amsterdam News*, May 22, 1971.] In addition to Monk's set, the show featured poetry readings by Frank Adu, Anna Maria Horsford, Peter Bailey, W. Adell Stevenson, and Imam Tawfig, and performances by the George Faison Dance Experience.

104 Larry Ridley interview, September 7, 2001.

105 Jackie Bonneau interview, October 30, 2008.

106 T. S. Monk, interview, April 4, 2005.

107 Paul Jeffrey interview, August 31, 2003; T. S. Monk interview, April 4, 2005; Jackie Bonneau interview, October 30, 2008; Bill Lane, "People, Places, and Situwayshuns," *Los Angeles Sentinel*, April 22, 1971; Pearl Gonzalez, "Monk Talk," *Down Beat* (October 28, 1971), 12–13.

108 Larry Ridley interview, September 7, 2001.

109 Ibid.; Paul Jeffrey interview, August 31, 2003; Gourse, *Straight, No Chaser*, 275.

110 The gig at the Cellar Door, August 9–14, was due to a last-minute cancellation by Miles Davis who was scheduled to play. Hollie I. West, "Movies on Billie Holiday," *Washington Post*, July 30, 1971; Ad, *Washington Post*, August 3, 1971.

111 Paul Jeffrey interview, August 31, 2003.

112 T. S. Monk interview, April 4, 2005.

113 Ibid.

114 Gonzalez, "Monk Talk," 12–13.

115 T. S. Monk interview, April 4, 2005.

116 George Wein, *Myself Among Others*, 226–27; and original liner notes by George Wein, *Giants of Jazz* (Atlantic SD2-905). Paul Jeffrey tells a different story. Roach reportedly organized some of the other musicians so they could hold out for a better contract, but then he alleged that Dizzy "went behind everybody's back, from what I understand, and got his price." The other musicians followed suit, including Monk—though Nellie negotiated with Wein on his behalf. Paul Jeffrey interview, August 31, 2003.

117 For a five-night engagement at Lennie's–Village Green, Monk earned $2,000 minus ten percent for his booking agent, Jack Whittemore, leaving him $1,800 to divide between him and his sidemen. He paid his sidemen $250 each, leaving Monk with $800 for himself. AFM Contract, Thelonious Monk Local 802, Lennie Sogoloff, March 20, 1972, in author's possession.

118 *The Jazz Weekend* (Program, Victoria Theater, 1971), in author's possession; original liner notes by George Wein, *Giants of Jazz* (Atlantic SD2-905); Shipton, *Groovin' High*, 336; Sheridan, *Brilliant Corners*, 457–58; Wein, *Myself Among Others*, 227.

119 Paul Jeffrey interview, August 31, 2003. Jeffrey even implied that Monk exhibited some suicidal tendencies during this period, though it may have also been expressions of his humor. Jeffrey: "I remember, I was driving

in the tunnel and it was two-way traffic, and Monk said, 'Crash.' I was fighting with Monk over the wheel. I don't know how I got out of there, big as Monk was, but he grabbed the steering wheel and was trying to crash the car. You know, when he'd go out, he'd got out. So he'd laugh, you know." Paul Jeffrey interview, August 31, 2003. In what may have been another telling sign, Monk told interviewer Pearl Gonzalez that the purpose of life is "To die." Gonzalez responded, "But between birth and death, there's a lot to do." To which Monk replied, "You asked a question, that's the answer." Gonzalez then noted that he said these words while staring out of a twelfth-floor window. Gonzalez, "Monk Talk," 13.

120 Jaki Byard interview with Taylor Ho Bynum, November 14, 1997, transcript in author's possession.
121 See also, Alain Gerber, "Giants of Jazz," *Jazz Magazine* (December 1971), 22–31; Randi Hultin, "Caught in the Act," *Down Beat* (January 20, 1972), 32; Barry McRae, *Dizzy Gillespie: His Life and Times* (Tunbridge Wells: Spellmount, 1988), 98; Shipton, *Groovin' High*, 337–38. The only major problem they encountered was in Japan, where Sonny Stitt was denied entrance into the country because of prior drug convictions. In 1948–49, he served time in federal prison in Lexington, Kentucky, for drug dealing. Sleepy Matsumoto substituted for Stitt, whom the Japanese refused to pay for the two weeks he was absent. The Giants decided to share their earnings from the next performance with Stitt so he wouldn't lose money. George Wein and Hideki Sato, Liner notes to *Giants of Jazz in Berlin* (EmArcy 834 567–2); Wein, *Myself Among Others*, 227. On Stitt's drug conviction, see Kenny Mathieson, *Giants of Bebop*, 102.
122 Wein, *Myself Among Others*, 227.
123 My comments are based on radio and television broadcasts, as well as bootleg and authorized recordings of the Giants of Jazz tours in my possession. I'm grateful to T. S. Monk, Peter Grain, Lewis Porter, and various collectors for making these recordings available to me. Below is a near-complete list: ABC Radio concert recording, Melbourne, Australia, September 24–25, 1971; RAI recording, Conservatorio Giuseppe Verdi, Milan, Italy, Wednesday, October 20, 1971, released on CD as *The Bop Fathers 1* (Jazz View COD026); *The Bop Fathers 2* (Jazz View COD027); ORTF "Jazz s'il vous plaît" and "Jazz sur scene" radio recordings, Theatre National Populaire, Paris, Friday, October 22, 1971; Television Broadcast in author's possession, Concert Lucerna Hall, Prague, Saturday, October 30, 1971; NOS radio recording, De Doelen, Rotterdam, Netherlands, October 31, 1971; JRT radio recording, Belgrade, Yugoslavia, November 2, 1971, released as *Giants of Jazz and The Dizzy Gillespie Quintet—Live* (Jazz Door JD1277); Berliner Jazztage concert recording, Philharmonie, Berlin, November 4, 1971, authorized and produced by George Wein, released as *Giants of Jazz in Berlin* (EmArcy 834 567–2); SDR "Treffpunkt Jazz" recording, Congresshalle, Boblingen, Germany, November 7, 1971; Television Broadcast, Tivoli Gardens, Copenhagen, Tuesday, November 9, 1971 (in author's possession); and the 2-LP concert recording from the Victoria Theater in London, November 14, 1971: *The Giants of Jazz* (Atlantic SD 2-905).
124 Gillespie, *To Be or Not to Bop*, 488–89.
125 According to the recorded evidence, it appears that both songs were dropped after the Paris performance on October 22. ABC Radio concert recording, Melbourne, Australia, September 24–25, 1971; RAI recording, Conservatorio Giuseppe Verdi, Milan, Italy, Wednesday, October 20, 1971, released on CD as *The Bop Fathers 1* (Jazz View COD026); *The Bop Fathers 2* (Jazz View COD027); ORTF "Jazz s'il vous plaît" and "Jazz sur scene" radio recordings, Theatre National Populaire, Paris, Friday, October 22, 1971.
126 Wein, *Myself Among Others*, 227; (Quote) George Wein and Hideki Sato, Liner notes to *Giants of Jazz in Berlin*.
127 Bob Rusch, "Al McKibbon Interview," transc. Kea D. Rusch, *Cadence* (March 1987), 18.
128 Jaki Byard interview with Taylor Ho Bynum, November 14, 1997.
129 His physical condition is evident in television broadcasts in my possession. Television Broadcast, Concert Lucerna Hall, Prague, Saturday October 30, 1971; Television Broadcast, Tivoli Gardens, Copenhagen, Tuesday, November 9, 1971.
130 Rusch, "Al McKibbon Interview," 19.
131 Jaki Byard interview with Taylor Ho Bynum, November 14, 1997.
132 Dick Hughes, "Caught in the Act," *Down Beat* (December 9, 1971), 27–28.
133 Alain Gerber, "Giants of Jazz," *Jazz Magazine* (December 1971), 22–24.
134 Randi Hultin, "Caught in the Act," *Down Beat* (January 20, 1972), 32.
135 *Giants of Jazz in Berlin* (EmArcy 834 567–2).
136 George Wein observed, "I remember noticing Dizzy's astonishment at the recognition and applause that Thelonious's tunes evoked." Wein, *Myself Among Others*, 227.
137 Television Broadcast in author's possession, Concert Lucerna Hall, Prague, Saturday, October 30, 1971.
138 Television Broadcast, Tivoli Gardens, Copenhagen, Tuesday, November 9, 1971.
139 John Litweiler, "Bu's Delights and Laments," *Down Beat* (March 25, 1976), 15.
140 Guy Warren interview, August 12, 2004; Brian Priestley, "Monk in the Studio," *Melody Maker* (July 22, 1972), 30.
141 Guy Warren interview, August 12, 2004; Alun Morgan Liner notes, *Thelonious Monk—The London Collection: Volume One* (Black Lion BLCD760101).
142 *Thelonious Monk—The London Collection: Volume One* (Black Lion BLCD760101); *Thelonious Monk—The London Collection: Volume Three* (Black Lion BLCD760142).
143 Priestley, "Monk in the Studio," 30.
144 Ibid., 30.
145 Rusch, "Al McKibbon Interview," 19.
146 *Thelonious Monk—The London Collection: Volume Three* (Black Lion BLCD760142); *Thelonious Monk—The London Collection: Volume Two* (Black Lion BLCD760116).
147 Guy Warren interview, August 12, 2004.
148 Wein, *Myself Among Others*, 304–12.

149 "Stars to Lend Hand in Benefit to Aid Newport Jazz Festival," *Pittsburgh Courier*, December 4, 1971; "Newport Salute Set for Boston Garden," *Hartford Courant*, December 9, 1971; Victor E. Sasson, "Thousands Hail Newport Event at Monumental Jazz Session," *Hartford Courant*, December 12, 1971; Roderick Nordell, "A Jazz Galaxy's Six Hour 'Salute to Newport,' " *Christian Science Monitor*, December 27, 1971; "Stars Turn Out For Newport," San Francisco *Sun Reporter*, February 5, 1972.

150 T. S. Monk, interview, April 4, 2005. Toot was there, too; he celebrated his 22nd birthday that night. The Duke Ellington Orchestra began a three-week engagement at the Rainbow Grill on December 13, 1971. "Arts Roundup," *Amsterdam News*, December 11, 1971; John S. Wilson, "Ellington Back with 9 Jazzmen; Pianist is at Rainbow Grill after his Soviet Tour," *New York Times*, December 16, 1971.

29 "I Am Very Seriously Ill"

1 One of the foundational texts for orthomolecular psychiatry is David R. Hawkins and Linus Pauling, *Orthomolecular Psychiatry: Treatment of Schizophrenia* (San Francisco: W. H. Freeman, 1973); see also, Eric R. Braverman, *The Healing Nutrients Within: Facts, Findings, and New Research on Amino Acids* (New Canaan,CT: Keats Pub., 1997); Carl Pfeiffer, *Nutrition and Mental Illness: An Orthomolecular Approach to Balancing Body Chemistry* (Rochester, VT: Healing Arts Press, 1988); Carl Pfeiffer, *Mental and Elemental Nutrients: A Physician's Guide to Nutrition and Health Care*, (New Canaan, CT: Keats Pub. 1976); and articles in the *Journal of Orthomolecular Medicine* launched in 1972 as *Orthomolecular Psychiatry*.

2 Elliot S. Valenstein, *Blaming the Brain: The Truth About Drugs and Mental Health* (New York: Free Press, 1998), 42–52; Mogens Schou, *Lithium Treatment of Mood Disorders: A Practical Guide* (Basel, Switzerland: S. Karger Pub., 2004); Johan Schioldann, "Mogens Abelin Schou (1918–2005)–Half a Century with Lithium," *History of Psychiatry* 17, no. 2 (2006), 247–252; Samuel Gershon and Baron Shopsin, eds., *Lithium. Its Role in Psychiatric Research and Treatment* (New York: Plenum Press, 1976).

3 Sally Quinn, "Most Widespread Illness," *Washington Post*, April 4, 1970; Lynn Lilliston, "Megavitamin Controversy: Part II; Schizophrenia–The Key Target Response In Schizophrenics Rewarding Results In Schizophrenics," *Los Angeles Times*, November 27, 1972.

4 Jackie Bonneau interview, October 30, 2008.

5 Geraldine Smith interview, February 12, 2004.

6 Ibid.; T. S. Monk, interview April 4, 2005.

7 Geraldine Smith interview, February 12, 2004.

8 Ibid.

9 On Sunday afternoon, January 23, Boo Boo performed with Weston at the Harlem Music Center on St. Nicholas Avenue. Press Release, Harlem Music Center, n.d., Box 5, Joseph Black Papers, Schomburg Library, Special Collections; "Strictly Ad Lib," *Down Beat* (March 2, 1972), 11. The following month they performed at the North Park Hotel in Chicago. "Randy Weston Plays Jazz at North Park," *Chicago Defender*, February 19, 1972.

10 Paul Jeffrey interview, August 31, 2003; Gourse, *Straight, No Chaser*, 280.

11 Gourse, *Straight, No Chaser*, 280.

12 (Quote) Pfeiffer, *Nutrition and Mental Illness:* 70; Kay Redfield Jamison, *Touched with Fire*, 240–246.

13 See, for example, P. Polatin and R. R. Fieve, "Patient Rejection of Lithium Carbonate Prophylaxis," *Journal of the American Medical Assocation* 218 (1971), 864–866; Mogens Schou, "Artistic Productivity and Lithium Prophylaxis in Manic-depressive Illness," *British Journal of Psychiatry* 135 (August 1979), 97–103; Jamison, *Touched with Fire*, 240–47.

14 "Strictly Ad Lib," *Down Beat* (March 30, 1972), 36.

15 Leonard Feather, "Thelonious Monk at Shelly's Manne-Hole," *Los Angeles Times*, February 19, 1972. Colman Andrews's assessment of the band was far more charitable, but he echoed Feather's point about repetition: "If he sounds less than shocking (less than exciting, for that matter) today, it's only because he's been playing pretty much the same thing for a very long time. To see and hear Monk in 1972 is not a thrilling, convention-shattering experience. It's more like paying homage to a legitimate, living American musical tradition." Colman Andrews, "Two Evenings at the Manne-Hole," *The Staff*, March 10, 1972.

16 Paul Jeffrey interview, August 31, 2003.

17 Paul de Barros, *Jackson Street After Hours*, 95; Charles Mingus, *Beneath the Underdog: His World as Composed by Charles Mingus,* ed. Nel King (New York: Knopf, 1971), 156.

18 Paul Jeffrey interview, August 31, 2003.

19 Jackie Bonneau interview, October 30, 2008. They moved on March 9. Receipt, Same Day Moving & Storage Co., Inc., March 9, 1972, Thelonious Monk Personal Papers.

20 AFM Contract, Thelonious Monk Local 802, Lennie Sogoloff, March 20, 1972, in author's possession; Matt Robinson, "Years After Hosting Jazz Legends, Lennie's on the Campus," *Boston Globe*, September 23, 2006.

21 Jeremiah Rickert, "Ron McClure Interview, November 1, 1998," www.rdrop.com/users/rickert/mcclure.htm; Gourse, *Straight, No Chaser*, 281–82.

22 Quoted in Gourse, *Straight, No Chaser*, 283.

23 "Wein Schedules Five Major U.S. Festivals," *Down Beat* (June 8, 1972), 9; Harriet Choice, "The Best of an Era Blowing Together," *Chicago Tribune*, May 7, 1972; *Oakland Tribune*, June 10, 1972; *San Mateo Times*, May 12, 1972; *Hayward Daily Review*, June 2, 1972; *San Mateo Times*, June 17, 1972; "Lineup for Bay Area Jazz Fest," *Los Angeles Times*, May 12, 1972; "Annual Hampton Jazz Fest Set for June Weekend," *Amsterdam News*, June 17, 1972; "Atlanta Jazz Festival to Feature the Nation's Best," *Atlanta Daily World*, June 1, 1972;

Ad, *Atlanta Daily World*, June 4, 1972; "Jazz Artist Slated to Appear at Festival," *Atlanta Daily World*, June 22, 1972; Murray Schumach, "City Feels Vibrations as 9-Day Jazz Festival Begins," *New York Times*, July 2, 1972; Hollie I. West, "Here's Newport in New York," *Washington Post*, June 11, 1972; Leonard Feather, "Jazz Festival in New Setting," *Los Angeles Times*, July 3, 1972; *San Antonio Express and News*, July 2, 1972; Ad, *Amsterdam News*, June 17, 1972; "Jazz Schedules," *New York Times*, July 8, 1972; John S. Wilson, "Jazz Sessions Prove an Attraction for the Purists," *New York Times*, July 10, 1972; Hollie I. West, "Newport Jazz: A Rousing Welcome," *Washington Post*, July 3, 1972; "Giants Set for Festival," *Chicago Defender*, June 17, 1972; "11th Annual Ohio Jazz Festival Feature Great Musicians," *Chicago Defender*, July 15, 1972; Leonard Feather, "Jazz Reigns in Monterey," *Los Angeles Times*, September 18, 1972.

24 Giants of Jazz Itineraries, 1972, Robert Jones Personal Papers. Of course, compensation varied; sometimes they earned less for a shorter set.

25 Tom Bethell, "Jazzfest Number Five," *Jazz Journal* (June 1972), 6.

26 Harriet Choice, "The Best of an Era Blowing Together," *Chicago Tribune*, May 7, 1972.

27 Voice of America Broadcast, "Newport in New York" Concert, Philharmonic Hall, July 1, 1972, in author's possession, courtesy of Brent Edwards; Broadcast "Newport in New York," Yankee Stadium, New York, July 8, 1972, in author's possession; Don Heckman, "An All-Star Night at Philharmonic Hall," *New York Times*, July 2, 1972. See also Sheridan, *Brilliant Corners*, 216–217.

28 Don Heckman, "An All-Star Night at Philharmonic Hall," *New York Times*, July 2, 1972.

29 Leonard Feather, "Jazz Festival in New Setting," *Los Angeles Times*, July 3, 1972. Hollie West came to the opposite conclusion. She thought the drum duel was the highlight of the evening. Hollie I. West, "Newport Jazz: A Rousing Welcome," *Washington Post*, July 3, 1972.

30 Recording in author's possession, courtesy of Brent Edwards.

31 The Houston concert was scheduled for July 7, the night before the New York event. Herbie Mann's pianist subbed for him. Lyle Jones, "Caught in the Act," *Down Beat* (October 27, 1972), 31.

32 Larry Ridley interview, September 7, 2001.

33 Leonard Feather, "Jazz Reigns in Monterey," *Los Angeles Times*, September 18, 1972.

34 Voice of America Broadcast, Tape 217, September 16, 1972, Monterey Jazz Festival, Braun Music Library, Sound Archives, Stanford University.

35 Ibid.

36 The quartet played the Vanguard June 13–18 and August 1–6. "Strictly Ad Lib," *Down Beat* (July 20, 1972), 12; Sheridan, *Brilliant Corners*, 461–62.

37 Thelonious Monk Quartet at the Village Vanguard, June 15, 1972, recording in author's possession, courtesy of Jacques Ponzio.

38 Wilson was a member of the Young Workers Liberation League. Formed in 1970, it was an outgrowth of the Young Communist League and the W. E. B. DuBois Clubs in the 1960s.

39 Joseph Wilson interview, July 1, 2003.

40 Ibid.

41 Here is the official itinerary:

October 25—Brussels; Palais des Beaux Arts
October 27—Paris, Olympia Theater
October 28—London; Odeon Theater, Hammersmith
October 29—Rotterdam; De Doelen
October 30—Budapest; Erkel Theatre
October 31—Aarhus (Denmark) Performed at Royal Hotel
November 1—Helsinki
November 3—Bucharest [Cancelled, went to Berlin instead and played the Berliner Jazztage]
November 4—Vienna; Stadthalle Vienna
November 6—Venice, Teatro la Fenice
November 7—Belgrade; Dom Sindikata Hall
November 8—Frankfurt, performed at Jahrhundert Haller
November 11—Bologne; performed at Teatro Communale
November 15—Sochaux, performed at Maison Des Arts et Des Loisirs
November 16—Barcelona; Palacio de la Musica
Source: Giants of Jazz Itineraries, 1972, Robert Jones Personal Papers

42 Harriet Choice, "European Trip a Test for the Pros," *Chicago Tribune*, November 12, 1972.

43 Ibid.

44 ORF Recording, Stadthalle, Vienna, November 4, 1972; Private Recording, Cologne, Germany, November 5, 1972; Sheridan, *Brilliant Corners*, 220. Haynes and Terry were traveling with the Jimmy Smith Jam Session and Anderson was with Charles Mingus's group.

45 Peter Gamble, "The Giants of Jazz," *Jazz Journal* (December 1972), 26.

46 Choice, "European Trip a Test for the Pros"; Michael James, "Art Blakey and Thelonious Monk [Review]," *Jazz & Blues* 2 (February 1973), 11; *Down Beat* (April 26, 1973), 22; *Jazz Hot* (October 1972), 25; *Melody Maker* (November 18, 1972), 46; *Jazz & Blues* 2 (January 1973), 30–31.

47 Giants of Jazz, *Giants of Jazz* (Concord GW 3004). On Monk in Dizzy's big band, see Chapter 10. The recording of "I Waited for You" was recorded on *Dizzy Gillespie '46 Live At The Spotlite* (Hi-Fly H 01), and rereleased on CD as Dizzy Gillespie, Big Band, *Showtime at the Spotlight: 52nd Street, New York City, June 1946* (Uptown 2754).

48 Tom Piazza, "Caught in the Act: Thelonious Monk," *Down Beat* (December 1972), 26.

49 "Hall Overton of Juilliard Dead; Symphonic and Jazz Composer," *New York Times*, November 26, 1972.

50 In an interview with Sam Stephenson, the conductor Dennis Russell Davies had seen Monk at Overton's gig in September, and between sets the two men interacted in a very warm and friendly manner. E-mail correspondence from Sam Stephenson to author, January 14, 2004.

51 Barry Harris interview with Phil Schaap, October 9, 1996, WKCR Broadcast. In another interview, he described Monk's playing as "real fluid like maybe Bud Powell would play, Art Tatum would play." Barry Harris interview with Quincy Troupe, November 30, 1990. Media Transcripts Inc., for film "Thelonious Monk: American Composer." Used by permission from Avalon Archives, Ltd.

52 Jackie Bonneau interview, October 30, 2008.

53 Morris Zuckerman to Nellie Monk, May 15, 1973; Corporate Tax Return, Bar-Thel Music, 1972; Federal Tax Return, Bar-Thel Music, 1972; New York State Department of Taxation and Finance to Monk Thelenious [sic]/Zuckerman, October 6, 1972, Monk family papers. Zuckerman grew quite frustrated with Nellie over time, in part because he had worked for a few years without receiving compensation, until he decided to draw it himself from their revenue. Zuckerman to Nellie Monk, February 24, 1974, Monk family papers.

54 Flatbush Moving Van Co., Inc. "Sale Notice" January 5, 1973, Lot no: 3383-A, Nellie Monk & Evelyn Newkirk, Monk family papers. She made the payment just before the contents of the space were to be auctioned off.

55 Between 1971–72, for example, Monk received royalty checks amounting to less than $1,700 for reissues of his 1952–54 sessions. Artist Royalty Card, Thelonious Monk, Prestige, March 1, 1971–December 31, 1972. His royalties from Consolidated Music during the same period came to $338.59. Music Sales Royalty Statement: Thelonious Monk, Period Ending June 30, 1972. Monk Family Papers.

56 Paul Jeffrey interview, August 31, 2003.

57 Jackie Bonneau interview, October 30, 2008.

58 Bertha Hope interview, July 15, 2003.

59 T. S. Monk interview, April 4, 2005.

60 Interviews with Jackie Bonneau, Evelyn Smith, Binetta Bines, Bertha Hope, T. S. Monk.

61 T. S. Monk interview, April 4, 2005. Nellie did not drive, but family and friends often drove her to Nica's, including Doug Quackenbush and long-time family friend Marcellus Green. Marcellus Green interview, June 27, 2002; Doug Quackenbush unpublished typed notes, ca. 1996, pp. 22–23.

62 Marion White interview, with Quincy Troupe, December 1, 1990.

63 Nica de Koenigswarter quoted in Charlotte Zwerin, *Straight, No Chaser.*

64 T. S. Monk interview, April 4, 2005.

65 I think the rumor began in *Down Beat*, but it has been repeated many times, recently in Sheridan, *Brilliant Corners*, 223. (Sheridan also mistakenly asserts that Monk played Carnegie Hall on June 6 of the same year. He did not.) The pianists billed for the So-Lo Piano evening were Bill Evans, Earl Hines, Art Hodes, Ellis Larkins, Dave McKenna, Jimmy Rowles, George Shearing, Billy Taylor, Eubie Blake, and Brooks Kerr. "Jazz Events," *New York Times*, July 7, 1973. On Toot's performance with Natural Essence that same night, see Rudy Johnson, "The Accent is on Rhythm," *New York Times*, July 7, 1973.

66 Music Sales Corp., Royalty Statement: Thelonious Monk, Period Ending, June 30, 1974; Music Sales Corp., Royalty Statement: Thelonious Monk, Period Ending, December 31, 1974; Music Sales Corp., Royalty Statement: Thelonious Monk, Period Ending, June 30, 1975; United Artists Music, Statement of Publisher Royalties, Bar-Thel Music Corp, Period Ending December 30, 1976; United Artists Music, Statement of Publisher Royalties, Bar-Thel Music Corp, Period Ending September 30, 1976; Artist Royalty Card, Thelonious Monk, Fantasy Records, December 31, 1972–December 31, 1975; BMI Contract, Modification of Agreement, June 24, 1976; Stanley Catron to Thelonious Monk, September 13, 1976. Copies of all statements in Monk Family Papers. In spite of Keepnews's role in producing these re-issues, Fantasy Records payments were delayed for three years because they sent the checks to the wrong address. In August of 1975, Monk received a check for $4,579.97 for back royalties. H.M. Wolstencroft, Castle Bank Trust, LTD to Thelonious Monk, August 1975; Malcolm Burnstein to Mrs. Nellie Monk, December 8, 1975.

67 Artist Royalty Card, Thelonious Monk, Fantasy Records, 12/31/1972–12/31/1975.

68 Thelonious Monk, *Who's Afraid of the Big Band Monk?* (Columbia KG32892); A&R album release info.; Artist job sheet; Promotional flyers, n.d., Box 30, Teo Macero Collection.

69 *Billboard Magazine* (September 7, 1974), 48; CBS Records Earnings Summary, "Thelonious Monk," Period Ending December 31, 1976, Monk Family Papers.

70 Jimmy Owens interview, April 5, 2005; also, Paul Jeffrey interview, August 31, 2003; T. S. Monk interview, April 4, 2005; Matthews, "Eddie Bert Interview," 16; Wein, *Myself Among Others*, 228.

71 Martin Williams confidential letter to Guggenheim Fellowship re: Thelonious Monk, November 25, 1975, Monk Family Papers; Wein, *Myself Among Others*, 228; T. S. Monk, interview, April 4, 2005; Jackie Bonneau interview, October 30, 2008; Evelyn Smith interview.

72 Peter Keepnews, "Thelonious Monk: Caught," *Down Beat* (July 1974), 37.

73 T. S. Monk, interview, April 4, 2005.

74 Martin Williams confidential letter to Guggenheim Fellowship re: Thelonious Monk, November 25, 1975, Monk Family Papers.

75 Wein, *Myself Among Others*, 228.

76 See for example, Alan Rosenthal, "The Music of Thelonious Monk," *Nation* (September 21, 1974), 247–250; Alan Goodman, "Thelonious Gestalt: Monk Disrobed," *Crawdaddy* (November 1976), 72; Alan Groves, "The Loneliest Monk," *Jazz Journal International* 30 (November 1977), 10–13.

77 Ran Blake interview, March 22, 2005; Marianne Votta, Public Affairs New England Conservatory to Thelonious Monk, October 23, 1975, Monk Family Papers.

78 Edwin McDowell, "Ten Days When Jazz Was King," *Wall Street Journal*, July 8, 1975.
79 John S. Wilson, "Full House for Thelonious Monk," *New York Times*, July 5, 1975.
80 Whitney Balliett, "Jazz," *New Yorker* (July 19, 1976), 85.
81 Wilson, "Full House for Thelonious Monk."
82 Martin Williams confidential letter to Guggenheim Fellowship re: Thelonious Monk, November 25, 1975, Orrin Keepnews, Confidential Report on Candidate for Fellowship, November 21, 1975, Monk Family Papers.
83 "Grants Awarded by Guggenheim," *New York Times*, April 4, 1976.
84 Gary Giddins, "Rabbi Monk Reasserts His Mastery," *Village Voice* (April 12, 1976), 99; John S. Wilson, "Thelonious Monk Is in Fine Fettle with a Quintet," *New York Times*, March 28, 1976.
85 Ira Gitler, "Thelonious Monk Returns to Carnegie Hall," *Radio Free Jazz* 17 (May 1976), 10.
86 Monk was scheduled to make a brief appearance at Radio City Music Hall the following night for "A Salute to Reverend John G. Gensel," but he never made it. "Jazz Events," *New York Times*, June 30, 1976; C. Gerald Fraser, "Jazz Minister's Flock to Honor Him Tonight," *New York Times*, July 1, 1976; Chuck Berg, "Newport, '76," *Down Beat* (September 9, 1976), 40.
87 Whitney Balliett, "Comment," *New Yorker* (March 1, 1982), 37. John S. Wilson came away with a more positive take, concluding that Monk's solos were interesting and that his style "is so personal that no other jazz pianist even approaches it." John S. Wilson, "Monk and Gillespie Share Bill at Carnegie," *New York Times*, July 2, 1976.
88 Lee Jeske, "Thelonious Monk, 1917–1982," *Down Beat* (May 1982), 11. Barry Harris's trio had a regular gig that summer at Bradley's. "Arts and Leisure Guide," *New York Times*, July 25, 1976.
89 Johnny Griffin once ran into Monk, supposedly in Central Park, when Griffin and Illinois Jacquet were playing together. If this happened, it would have been 1979, since they did work together as part of Wein's Kool Jazz Festival. Ad, *New York Times*, May 20, 1979.
90 This description is based on many interviews with family and friends who visited.
91 Nica de Koenigswarter quoted in Whitney Balliett, "Comment," *New Yorker* (March 1, 1982), 37.
92 Barry Harris interviews; Gourse, *Straight, No Chaser*, 292–93.
93 Leroy Williams interview, June 24, 2003.
94 Robert Kraft, a talented young musician/composer, sent Monk Christmas and birthday cards every year beginning in 1974. After Monk died, Nica found them among the stacks of his correspondence under his bed. Robert Kraft interview, June 6, 2007.
95 T. S. Monk, interview, April 4, 2005.
96 Keepnews, *The View from Within*, 126.
97 Paul Jeffrey interview, August 31, 2003.
98 "A History of WKCR's Jazz Programming: An interview with Phil Schaap, conducted, transcribed, and edited by Evan Spring," October 5, 1992, http://www.columbia.edu/cu/wkcr/jazz/schaap.html.
99 Nica to Mary Lou Williams, November 3, 1977, Box 8, Mary Lou Williams Collection. Nica never mentions him by name, but evidence from her letters and oral testimony from Toot and others indicate that she is referring to Dr. Pfeiffer and the Brain Bio Center (which is not affiliated with Princeton University). Coincidentally, Nica found the Brain Bio Center just after it had been revealed that Dr. Pfeiffer participated in experiments in behavior control for the CIA from 1955–1964. Under CIA financing and direction, he and other researchers administered LSD to prisoners, reportedly with the consent of the subjects. "Carl C. Pfeiffer, Pharmacologist, Dies at 80," *New York Times*, November 23, 1988.
100 Nica to Mary Lou Williams, February 15, 1979, Personal Correspondence, Box 4, Mary Lou Williams Collection.
101 "Wilbur Ware, Bassist, 56, Dies," *New York Times*, September 13, 1979; John S. Wilson, "Mary Lou Williams, a Jazz Great, Dies," *New York Times*, May 30, 1981.
102 Thomas Monk, Sr. interview with Phil Schaap, WKCR, Thelonious Monk Birthday Broadcast, 1984.
103 Marion White interview, with Quincy Troupe, December 1, 1990.
104 Don Sickler interview, September 9, 2003.
105 Social Security Death Index, "Evelyn Newkirk," 4 May 1923 to May 1977; Evelyn Smith and Benetta Bines interview.
106 Robeson died January 23, 1976. On his final years, see Duberman, *Paul Robeson*, 539–550.
107 Clifford Jordan, *Remembering Me-Me* (Muse MR5105). It is worth noting that the bassist on the date was none other than Wilbur Ware.
108 Evelyn Smith and Benetta Bines interviewed by author, July 6, 2005.
109 T. S. Monk interview, April 4, 2005.
110 Jon Sanders, "Jazz Rocks Rockefeller Center," *Amsterdam News*, September 4, 1976.
111 Flyer for Cycles, "Jazz/Funk/Concert/Party," Sun Drop Lounge, Jan. 29, 1977, Press Kit, "Natural Essence," Atlantic Records, n.d., in author's possession.
112 T. S. Monk Band, *House of Music* (Mirage); T. S. Monk interview, April 4, 2005; "T. S. Monk–Beautiful Day Productions," Press Release, in author's possession; Gene Gillis, "Turntable Talk," *Amsterdam News*, January 3, 1981; Stephen Holden, "T. S. Monk in Showcase Led by Thelonious Monk, Jr.," *New York Times*, April 9, 1981; Geoffrey Himes, "Up From Disco," *Washington Post*, February 11, 1982; "T. S. Monk's House of Music," *Pittsburgh Courier*, May 23, 1981.
113 Nica to Mary Lou Williams, February 15, 1979, Personal Correspondence, Box 4, Mary Lou Williams Collection.
114 Barry Harris interview with Quincy Troupe, November 30, 1990. He tells the same story in Barry Harris interview with Phil Schaap, October 9, 1996, WKCR broadcast.

115 Certificate of Death, 568–3450, "Thelonious Sphere Monk," February 17, 1982; "Jazz Pianist Monk, 61, Suffers Stroke," *Los Angeles Times*, February 9, 1982; "Personalities," *Washington Post*, February 9, 1982; John S. Wilson, "Thelonious Monk, Created Wry Jazz Melodies and New Harmonies," *New York Times*, February 18, 1982; Jerry Belcher, "Jazz Great Thelonious Monk Dies," *Los Angeles Times*, February 18, 1982; Sam Sutherland, "Thelonious Monk Dies; Sowed Seeds of Bebop," *Billboard* (February 27, 1982); Brian Case, "Monk's Dream," *Melody Maker* (February 27, 1982), 18; Robert Palmer, "Thelonious Monk: 1917–1982," *Rolling Stone* (April 1, 1982); Ronald Atkins, "Jagged Edged Genius," *The Guardian* (London). February 18, 1982; Richard Harrington, "Thelonious Monk, 63, Jazz Pianist, Composer Dies," *Washington Post*, Feburary 18, 1982; Orrin Keepnews, "The Monk of Jazz: Memories of Thelonious," *Washington, Post*, February 18, 1982.

Postlude

1 *Thelonious Sphere Monk, October 10. 1917–February 17, 1982* (Funeral Program, 1982); Ira Gitler, "Playing Tribute to Monk," *Jazz Times* (April 1982), 9; Ted Joans, "The Funeral of Thelonious Monk," *Coda* 183 (April 1982), 33; John S. Wilson, "Friends Pay Tribute to Monk with His Music," *New York Times*, February 23, 1982; Paul Morris, "Theatrical Briefs," *Amsterdam News*, February 27, 1982.
2 Gitler, "Playing Tribute to Monk," 9.
3 Jackie Bonneau interview, October 30, 2008.
4 Matthew 20:16.
5 While my discussion is limited to Boo Boo's efforts to preserve and expand her father's legacy, it is important to acknowledge the many tributes for Monk immediately after he died. Dan Morgenstern organized one of the first, held at Carnegie Hall on July 1, 1982. It involved over two dozen musicians, including Max Roach, Walter Bishop, Jr., Clifford Jordan, Paul Jeffrey, Teo Macero, Teddy Charles, Frankie Dunlop, Percy Heath, Barry Harris, Charlie Rouse, Sweets Edison, Al Grey, Buddy Tate, Al Cohn, Hank Jones, Max Roach, Dizzy Gillespie, Stan Getz, McCoy Tyner, Shelly Manne, Clark Terry, Jimmy Owens, Eddie Bert, Cecil Payne, Freddie Hubbard, Wynton Marsalis, Herbie Hancock, and Tony Williams. "Musicians for Monk–Musicians' Fund Benefit," n.d., vertical files, IJS.
6 Paul La Rosa, "The Battle to Save Phipps Houses," *New York Daily News*, December 31, 1982.
7 With the expansion of the Amsterdam Houses, West 63rd Street was turned into a cul-de-sac, blocking automobile access between West End and Amsterdam.
8 Thelonious Sphere Monk Foundation, application for Incorporation, New York State Education Department, July 20, 1984; "A Memorandum of Understanding, to Carlos V. Morales from Boo Boo Monk, Thomas Monk, Nina Garland, and Willie Jones, October 29, 1982"; "Outline of a Documentary Entitled ALWAYS KNOW, TWO IS ONE: The Philosophy of Thelonious Sphere Monk," pp. 4–6; Lynda Simmons, President of Phipps Houses to Ms. Barbara Monk, January 14, 1983, all documents in Monk Family Papers.
9 Memorandum From Barbara Monk to George Wein, June 7, 1983, Monk Family Papers; Maurice Carroll, "Strokes of a Koch Pen Yield Laws Broad and Narrow," *New York Times*, July 7, 1983; *Amsterdam News*, July 2, 1983.
10 Health Insurance Claim Form: Boo Boo Monk, June 30, 1983, Monk Family Papers.
11 See Virginia Wuerthele Caspe Livingston, *Cancer, A New Breakthrough* (Los Angeles: Nash Publishing Corp, 1972); Virginia Livingston-Wheeler and Edmond G. Addeo, *The Conquest of Cancer: Vaccines and Diet* (New York: Franklin Watts, 1984). Despite the searing critique by the American Cancer Society, Dr. Livingston-Wheeler was beloved by many of her patients and a few eminent doctors who subscribed to her ideas. See Ralph W. Moss, "Virginia Livingston, 84," *The Cancer Chronicles* 6 (Autumn 1990), http://www.ralphmoss.com/livingston.html; Alan Cantwell, M.D., "Virginia Livingston, M.D.: Cancer Quack or Medical Genius?" http://www.rense.com/general72/cancer.htm.
12 "Unproven Methods of Cancer Management: Livingston-Wheeler Therapy," *CA: A Cancer Journal of Clinicians* 40, no. 2 (March/April 1990), 103–108.
13 "Obituary," *New York Times*, October 27, 1983; State of California Department of Health Services, *California Death Index, 1940–1997*.
14 State of California Department of Health Services, *California Death Index, 1940–1997*; *Memorial Service for Barbara Evelyn Monk*, Program, January 17, 1984, in author's possession. Boo Boo died on January 10, 1984; her memorial service was held at Riverside Church.
15 Willie Jones, "Report from the Monk Cultural Center Committee, October 14, 1986," "Memorandum Regarding the Location of Thelonious Sphere Monk Center for Jazz Studies, October 18, 1986," "Thelonious Sphere Monk Center for Jazz Studies," n.d., all in Monk Family Papers; Geoff Mayfield, "N.C. Benefit Honors Monk," *Billboard* (May 13, 1989), 27; Peter Keepnews, "Blue Notes: The funding Search is on for D.C.'s Monk Center," *Billboard* (February 21, 1987), 29; W. Royal Stokes, "Monk Center for Arts: Closer to Reality," *Jazztimes* (December 1986), 8–9; T. Wilborn, "Monk Conservatory Announced," *Down Beat* 55 (October 1988), 13.
16 Beginning in 1991, Toot formed a sextet and included several Monk tunes in its repertoire. The band cut three LP's, *Take One* (Blue Note CDP7-99614-2); *Changing of the Guard* (Blue Note CDP7-89050-2); and *The Charm* (Blue Note CDP7-89575-2). His focus on Monk culminated in his Grammy-award winning LP *Monk on Monk* (N2K Encoded Music).
17 The concerts were recorded and released on four discs as, *Interpretations of Monk*, Vol. I (Koch CD-7838) and Vol. II (Koch CD-7839). The other performers were Mal Waldron, Muhal Richard Abrams, Don Cherry, Charlie Rouse, Richard Davis, Ben Riley, and Ed Blackwell.

18 Sphere, *Four in One* (Elektra Musician 60166-1). "Sphere" was never intended to be a Monk tribute group. The name was coincidental—Kenny Baron came up with it as a way to symbolize the band's closeness, then Ben Riley reminded them that "Sphere" was Monk's middle name. They planned to dedicate their first album to Monk because he was so sick. David A. Franklin, "Charlie Rouse Interview," *Cadence* 13, no. 6 (1987), 10.

19 For a brilliant examination of Monk's impact on contemporary jazz, see Gabriel Solis, *Monk's Music: Thelonious Monk and Jazz History in the Making* (Los Angeles and Berkeley: University of California Press, 2008).

20 Farrell, "Loneliest Monk," 86.

21 Max Jones, "Monk Talks to MM," *Melody Maker* (May 6, 1961).

Appendix A

1 My descriptions of Monk's harmonic and rhythmic approach to the piano derive partly from my own transcriptions and analysis, but owe a great debt to the following sources: Ran Blake, "The Monk Piano Style," *Keyboard* (July 1982), 26–30; Lawrence Koch, "Thelonious Monk: Compositional Techniques," *Annual Review of Jazz Studies* 2 (1983), 67–80; Mark S. Haywood, "Rhythmic Readings in Thelonious Monk," *Annual Review of Jazz Studies* 7 (1994–95), 25–45; Gabriel Solis, *Monk's Music: Thelonious Monk and Jazz History in the Making* (Los Angeles and Berkeley: University of California Press, 2008); Eddie S. Meadows, *Bebop to Cool: Context, Ideology, and Musical Identity* (London and Westport, CT: Praeger Publishers, 2003), 219–240; James Kurzdorfer, "Outrageous Clusters: Dissonant Semitonal Cells in the Music of Thelonious Monk," *Annual Review of Jazz Studies* 8 (1996), 181–201; Charles Blancq, "Standard Tune Transformation: A Retrospective Look at Thelonious Monk," *Jazz Research Papers* 3 (1983), 17–19; David Kahn Feurzeig, "Making the Right Mistakes: James P. Johnson, Thelonious Monk and the Trickster Aesthetic" (Ph.D. diss., Cornell University, 1997); Laila Rose Kteily-O'Sullivan, "Klangfarben, Rhythmic Displacement, and Economy of Means: A Theoretical Study of the Works of Thelonious Monk" (M.M. Thesis, University of North Texas, 1990).

2 Gillespie, *To Be or Not to Bop*, 135.

3 The most common progressions for the A-section of "I Got Rhythm" usually called for the following changes: B♭ Gm7 | Cm7 F7 | Dm7 G7 | Cm7 F7 | Fm7 B♭7 | E♭7 A♭7 | Dm7 G7 | Cm7 F7 B♭.

4 Joe Guy/Billie Holiday, *Harlem Odyssey* (Xanadu 112). The title, "Monkin' the Blues" was written on the original acetate, but when the song was issued on Xanadu, the title was changed to "Rhythm Riff." On the latest reissue, Thelonious Monk, *After Hours at Minton's* (Definitive Records, DRCD1197), it was simply called "I Got Rhythm," See Sheridan, *Brilliant Corners*, 8.

ORIGINAL COMPOSITIONS
BY THELONIOUS MONK

Ask Me Now—First recorded July 23, 1951 (Blue Note 1591), it is considered one of Monk's most beautiful ballads.

Ba-lue Bolivar Ba-lues-Are (aka **Bolivar Blues**)—First recorded October 9, 1956 (Riverside LP12-226) The title refers to the Hotel Bolivar in Manhattan, then the home of the Baroness Nica de Koenigswarter.

Bemsha Swing—Co-written with Denzil Best, it was originally titled "Bimsha Swing" as a tribute to Best's native land of Barbardos. Bimsha is the phonetic pronunciation of "Bimshire," and Barbados's nickname was "Little Bimshire." Monk first recorded it on December 18, 1952 (Prestige LP7027).

Bip Bop (see **52nd Street Theme**)

Bluehawk—This solo piano blues was only recorded once, on October 22, 1959, in San Francisco (Riverside RLP12-312).

Blue Monk—Monk recorded "Blue Monk" more than any other composition besides "'Round Midnight." His first recording dates back to September 22, 1954 (Prestige PRLP 189 LP7027).

Blues Five Spot (aka **Five Spot Blues**)—First recorded July 9, 1958 (Milestone M-9124, Riverside RIV-4005/5), the title refers to the Five Spot Café, where Monk was playing when he recorded this song for the first time.

Blue Sphere—A medium-tempo, classic twelve-bar blues for solo piano, "Blue Sphere" was recorded only once, on November 15, 1971, during a session in London (Black Lion BLP30119).

Bolivar Blues (see **Ba-lue Bolivar Ba-lues-Are**).

Boo Boo's Birthday—Recorded only once, on December 21, 1967 (Columbia CS9632), Monk wrote this song for his daughter.

Brake's Sake—First recorded on October 15, 1955 (Signal S1201), with a quartet led by alto saxophonist Gigi Gryce.

Bright Mississippi—First recorded on May 10, 1961 (Ingo 8) at a concert in Berne, Switzerland. It is a completely original melody based loosely on the chord changes of "Sweet Georgia Brown."

Brilliant Corners—First recorded on October 15, 1956 (Riverside RLP12-226), this composition proved notoriously difficult for Monk's band. After twenty-five attempts, the final recorded version consisted of parts of various takes spliced together. It was recorded only one other time, on November 20, 1968, with Oliver Nelson's Orchestra (Columbia CS9806).

Bye-Ya—First recorded on October 15, 1952, for *Thelonious Monk Trio* (Prestige LP 7027).

Children's Song (aka **That Old Man**)—Recorded once on October 7, 1964, for *Monk* (Columbia CS 9091), it is a Monkishly altered version of the traditional ditty "This Old Man," also known as "The Children's Marching Song."

Chordially—Recorded only once in London on November 15, 1971 (Black Lion CD760142), it is not a composition, per se, but a very musical and coherent improvised warm-up exercise on solo piano. It was not released on the original LP because it was not considered to be a song.

Coming on the Hudson—First recorded on February 25, 1958, at a session led by Johnny Griffin. The only useable take wasn't released until after Monk died on Thelonious Monk, *Blues Five Spot* (Milestones M-9124). The first released version, however, was recorded live five months later after Griffin had joined Monk's band. It appeared on *Thelonious in Action* (Riverside RLP 1190).

Crepuscule with Nellie—First recorded on June 25, 1957, although the first released take was recorded the following day (*Monk's Music* [Riverside RLP12-242]), this beautiful ballad is unusual in that it is his only composition played straight through without improvisation.

Criss Cross—First recorded on July 23, 1951 (Blue Note 1590, 1509), critic and composer Gunther Schuller called it "*the* Monk masterpiece of this period." So, enthused with "Criss Cross," Schuller used it as the basis for his tribute to Monk titled "Variants on a Theme of Thelonious Monk" (1960).

Dreamland—The first recorded evidence of this old-fashioned ballad comes from a live recording at the Five Spot on July 9, 1958. Monk never copyrighted it, rarely performed it, and only recorded it once in the studio, thirteen years later. He only played it unaccompanied. Monk wasn't satisfied with the 1958 recording and refused to grant Riverside permission to release it. Orrin Keepnews eventually put it out after after Monk died on *Blues Five Spot* (Milestone M-9124).

Epistrophy—One of Monk's earliest compositions, it was co-written with drummer Kenny Clarke and went by various names; Clarke called it **Fly Right** or **Fly Rite**, it was also called **Iambic Pentameter**, and known, too, as simply "The Theme," since it was used by Minton's house band to open and close a set. It was first recorded by the Minton's house band on June 7, 1941, but the first version by Monk appeared on his early Blue Note recordings (July 2, 1948, Blue Note 548, 1510).

Eronel—Initially composed by pianist Sadik Hakim (Argonne Thornton) and trumpeter Idrees Sulieman. Monk made a small alteration to the song, recorded it on July 23, 1951 (Blue Note 1590, 1509), and ended up taking sole composer's credit. Many years later, T. S. Monk restored the names of both Hakim and Sulieman as original co-authors.

Evidence—First recorded on July 2, 1948 (Blue Note 549, 1509), it went by various names, notably "Justice" and "We Named It Justice." It puns off the song on which it was loosely based, "Just You, Just Me" (by Jesse Greer and Raymond Klages). "Just Us" became "Justice" and ultimately "Evidence."

Feeling That Way Now (see **Monk's Mood**)

52nd Street Theme (aka **Bip Bop** and **Nameless**)—Monk originally copyrighted the song in 1944 as "Nameless," although the title he eventually settled on was "Bip Bop." It became popular on 52nd Street as a closing theme song for many groups. Music journalist and producer Leonard Feather is responsible for the title for which it has come to be known, "52nd Street Theme." Ironically, Thelonious never recorded the song.

Five Spot Blues (see **Blues Five Spot**)

Five Will Get You Ten (see **Two Timer**)

Fly Right (see **Epistrophy**)

Four in One—First recorded on July 23, 1951 (Blue Note 1589), "Four in One" was known to have a particularly treacherous melody built on sixteenth note phrases (hence the name—a quarter note [one beat] divided into sixteenth notes [four beats]).

Friday the Thirteenth—First recorded for Prestige [PRLP 7075] on Friday, November 13, 1953, it refers not only to the date but the turn of events the day of the session—tenor saxophonist Sonny Rollins was delayed because of a car accident and trumpeter Ray Copeland called in sick.

Functional—There are actually two different versions of the blues given the title "Functional," which was probably just a name made up on the spot. Both takes were recorded the same day, April 16, 1957, and never recorded again. The master take was released on *Thelonious Himself* (Riverside RLP 12-235).

Gallop's Gallop—First recorded on October 15, 1955, with Gigi Gryce as leader. It was released on Gryce's LP, *Nica's Tempo* (Savoy MG 12137).

Green Chimneys—Another one of Monk's later compositions, it was first recorded on November 14, 1966, although this particular take was not released until 1996. The take that was released initially was recorded a year later, on December 14, 1967, for *Underground* (Columbia CS 9632). "Green Chimneys" is named after the school Barbara Monk attended at the time—a progressive private boarding school located in Putnam County, New York.

Hackensack—First recorded on May 11, 1954 (*Monk* [Prestige PRLP 7053]), it was also the first day Monk recorded in Rudy Van Gelder's famous studio in Hackensack, New Jersey. Part of the melody for "Hackensack" was borrowed from an arrangement of "Lady Be Good" Mary Lou Williams did for Coleman Hawkins.

Harlem Is Awful Messy—Co-written with Oran "Hot Lips" Page and Joe Guy, this jump tune (apparently with lyrics) was never recorded, but copyrighted by the trio on September 16, 1941. Unfortunately, the original lead sheet was lost.

Hornin' In—Recorded only one time (four takes), on May 30, 1952, during his last session for Blue Note as a leader. It first appeared on Blue Note 1603.

Humph—Another early classic, "Humph" was recorded only once (three takes) during Monk's first recording session as a leader (October 15, 1947). It first appeared on Blue Note 560.

I Mean You (aka **Stickball**)—First recorded in December of 1946 by Coleman Hawkins. It would be another year and a half before Monk recorded "I Mean You" (July 2, 1948 [Blue Note 1564, 1510]).

Iambic Pentameter (see **Epistrophy**)

Introspection (aka **Playhouse**)—Originally titled "Playhouse" as a tribute to Minton's, this song was first recorded for Blue Note on October 24, 1947, but was not released until 1956.

In Walked Bud—First recorded on November 21, 1947 (Blue Note 548), it was written for Monk's very good friend, pianist Bud Powell. It is based on the chord changes for Irving Berlin's "Blue Skies."

Jackie-ing—First recorded on June 4, 1959 (*5 by Monk by 5* [Riverside RLP12-305]), Monk named this song after his niece, Jackie Smith. After 1960, "Jackie-ing" became a regular part of the Monk quartet's live repertoire.

Let's Call This—First recorded on November 13, 1953 and released on *Monk* (Prestige PRLP 7053), he only recorded it one other time: live at the Blackhawk in San Francisco on April 29, 1960 (Riverside RLP12-323).

Let's Cool One—First recorded on May 30, 1952 (Blue Note 1602, 1511).

Light Blue—The first recorded evidence of this tune comes from a radio broadcast from Pep's Music Lounge in Philadelphia, where Monk led a trio on February 9, 1957, but the first released version was also live, this time at the Five Spot Café on August 7, 1958. It is not a blues but rather a sixteen-bar theme played at a slow, plodding tempo built on descending chord progressions.

Little Rootie Tootie—A version of the melody was first copyrighted as "The Pump" in 1944 but was not recorded until October 15, 1952 (Prestige PRLP 7027). By this time, Monk had revised and renamed it "Little Rootie Tootie" in tribute to his son, Thelonious, Jr., who was two years old at the time. He earned the nickname "Toot" after "Little Toot the Tugboat" from a favorite Walt Disney cartoon based on a children's book of the same name; young Thelonious learned to whistle like "Little Toot" before he learned to talk. The song has also been associated with the sound of the railroad, a common motif in blues and jazz since the early part of the century. (See **Locomotive**)

Locomotive—First recorded on May 11, 1954 (Prestige PRLP 7053), it is definitely in the tradition of "train" recordings going back to Count Basie, Ellington, and the train-whistle guitar blues of the early part of the twentieth century. Built on an odd 20-bar chorus and played as a medium-slow tempo, rhythmically and melodically it captures the motion of the old steam engines steadily chugging down the railroad line. Monk made only one other recording of "Locomotive" . . . twelve years later (Columbia CL2651).

Manganese (see **We See**)

Manhattan Moods (see **Ruby, My Dear**)

A Merrier Christmas—Monk composed the song during the Christmas holiday, 1959. Aside from a homemade tape, he never recorded it or performed it in public, but a copy of the original manuscript survived. The music and lyrics by Monk were published in Don Sickler, ed., *The Thelonious Monk Fake Book* (Milwaukee: Hal Leonard, 2002).

Misterioso (sometimes spelled **Mysterioso**)—was the first original twelve-bar blues Monk recorded (July 2, 1948 [Blue Note 1510]). Its distinctive melody is built on even eighth notes of ascending and descending parallel sixths.

Monk's Dream—First recorded on October 15, 1952 (*Thelonious Monk Trio* [Prestige PRLP 7027]), like "Bye-Ya," this is another strongly Caribbean "flavored" composition.

Monk's Mood—One of Monk's early ballads, he gave it several different titles before settling on "Monk's Mood," (i.e., **That's the Way I Feel Now, Feeling that Way Now, Why Do You Evade the Facts,** and **Be Merrier Sarah**). He had originally conceived of the song with lyrics. Monk first recorded "Monk's Mood" on November 21, 1947 (Blue Note 1565).

Monk's Point—Recorded only twice, once as a solo piano piece (November 2, 1964 [Columbia CL2349]) and again with Oliver Nelson's Orchestra (November 19, 1968 [Columbia CS9806]), it is a fairly straightforward, twelve-bar blues in B$^\flat$ full of Monk's signature "minor seconds" in the melody.

Nameless (see **52nd Street Theme**)

North of the Sunset—Recorded only once on October 31, 1964 (*Solo Monk* [Columbia CS 9149]), it is a twelve-bar blues whose melody is very close to **Monk's Point**.

Nutty—First recorded on September 22, 1954 (*Thelonious Monk/Sonny Rollins* [Prestige PRLP 7075]), "Nutty" was among Monk's more popular tunes. Perhaps the most famous recording of it is with John Coltrane, July 1957 (Jazzland JLP[9]46).

Off Minor (aka **What Now**)—Was actually debuted in January of 1947, by Bud Powell, *not* by Monk. Monk first recorded it on October 24, 1947 (Blue Note BLP 1510). Also, Dizzy Gillespie's big band had intended on using it in their book. It stands among Monk's more frequently recorded tunes. It is so named probably because it is written in G minor but never resolves on the tonic.

Oska T—First recorded on December 30, 1963, during Monk's famous Town Hall concert (Columbia CS 8964), there are many different stories in circulation explaining this title. The most common is that it is Monk's impersonation of a bourgeois Englishman saying "ask for tea" or "ask for T."

Pannonica—First released recording was made on October 9, 1956 (*Brilliant Corners* [Riverside RLP12-226]). The song was written for the Baroness Pannonica de Koenigswarter, whom Monk had met in Paris in June of 1954. This first recorded version of "Pannonica" is significant in that Monk plays both piano and celeste.

Played Twice—First recorded on June 1, 1959 (*5 by Monk by 5* [Riverside RLP12-305]), the title refers to the structure of the song itself. It is a rhythmically complex, sixteen-bar AABC theme based on a series of repeated phrases or "echoes" that fall in different places in the meter.

Playhouse (see **Introspection**)

Portrait of an Eremite (see **Reflections**)

Raise Four—Recorded only once, on Valentine's Day, 1968 (*Underground* [Columbia CS 9632]), Monk probably wrote this in the studio. Reminiscent of **North of the Sunset** and **Monk's Point**, **Raise Four** is a basic twelve-bar blues, but built on Monk's signature harmonies—the augmented or "raised" fourth, also known as the "flatted fifth" or the tritone.

Reflections—First recorded on December 18, 1952 (Prestige LP 7027), it was not issued until 1956. Although it is often thought of as a ballad, Monk originally played it at medium tempo. He recorded it unaccompanied in Paris in 1954 (Vogue 500-104), as **Portrait of an Eremite**, a title given by French producer André Francis because Monk either did not title it or Francis misunderstood him. Eremite or *ermite*, in French, means hermit.

Rhythm-a-ning—One of Monk's most recorded and performed songs, it doesn't actually get put on vinyl by Monk under this title until May 15, 1957, at a recording session led by drummer Art Blakey (Atlantic 1278). Monk certainly made the melody his own, but he borrowed the A-section from Mary Lou Williams's arrangement of "Walking and Swinging," recorded in 1936. The title references the fact that it is based on the chord changes to Gershwin's "I Got Rhythm," popularly known in the bebop world as "rhythm changes."

Round Lights—Recorded once on October 21, 1959, in San Francisco (Riverside RLP12-312), "Round Lights" is a slow, twelve-bar blues for solo piano.

'Round Midnight (aka **'Round About Midnight** and **Grand Finale**)—Certainly the most recorded Thelonious Monk song of all time, Monk was *not* the first to record it. Cootie Williams's Orchestra recorded it in 1944 and used it as its theme song. Williams also took co-composer credit for "'Round Midnight" despite not having contributed anything to the score besides an interlude no one uses. Bernie Hanighen added lyrics and suddenly Monk was forced to share composer credit (and royalties) with two other people. Monk first recorded it as a leader on November 21, 1947 (Blue Note 543).

Ruby, My Dear (aka **Manhattan Moods**)—A beautiful ballad and one of Monk's best-known compositions, it was written originally for his then-girlfriend, Rubie Richardson.

San Francisco Holiday (aka **Worry Later**)—First recorded on April 28, 1960, at the Blackhawk in San Francisco (Riverside RLP12-323), Monk had given it the title "Worry Later" initially as a response to Orrin Keepnews's question as to what to call it. Eventually, he settled on "San Francisco Holiday" since his children accompanied him on the trip, turning an out-of-town gig into a family vacation.

Shuffle Boil—First recorded with the Gigi Gryce quartet on October 15, 1955 (Signal S1201), the song was then resurrected in 1964 and, for about a year, became part of the band's repertoire.

Sixteen—Recorded only once (two takes), at the Blue Note session of May 30, 1952, but it was not released until many years later, when Blue Note decided to issue Monk's complete recordings.

Skippy—Named after Nellie's sister, this song was recorded only once, on May 30, 1952 (Blue Note 1602, 1511).

Something in Blue—Recorded in London on November 15, 1971 (Black Lion BLP 30119), another classic, slow, solo blues played in Monk's unorthodox stride piano style.

Straight, No Chaser—Recorded July 23, 1951 (Blue Note 1589, 1511), it was only the second blues Monk recorded—**Misterioso** being the first.

Stuffy Turkey—First recorded on January 30, 1964 (Columbia CL2184), it is Monk's rendering of Coleman Hawkins's and Sir Charles Thompson's tune "Stuffy."

Teo—First recorded on March 9, 1964 (Columbia CL2291), **Teo** was written for Monk's producer at the time, Teo Macero. It is loosely based on Eddie Durham's "Topsy."

Thelonious—First recorded on October 15, 1947 (Blue Note 542), it is a brilliant example of Monk's use of ostinato (a short phrase repeated throughout a composition). Based on the reiteration of a single note (B^b) played over descending chord progressions, the song has an unusual thirty-six-bar AABA structure: the second and last A-sections are ten measures long rather than the customary eight measures.

Think of One—First recorded on November 13, 1953 and released on *Monk* (Prestige PRLP 7053). It shares many features with **Thelonious**—notably, Monk's use of ostinato. It is based on one note repeated over a stop-time rhythm in the A-section, which releases to a swinging bridge.

Trinkle Tinkle—First recorded in a trio setting on December 18, 1952 (Prestige PRLP 7027), the best known version of "Trinkle Tinkle" was made with John Coltrane in July of 1957 (Jazzland JLP[9]46).

Two Timer (aka **Five Will Get You Ten**)—Monk himself never recorded this composition, which he apparently wrote in the late 1950s. Unbeknownst to Monk, pianist Sonny Clark recorded it in a session led by alto saxophonist Jackie McLean in October 1961 as **Five Will Get You Ten**. Clark also took composer's credit for the song. The first to record **Two Timer** under its original title was T. S. Monk, who had discovered the original manuscript among his father's papers. His version appears on *Monk on Monk* (N2KE – 10017).

Ugly Beauty—The first known recording took place on November 14, 1967, for a taped television broadcast. Exactly one month later, Monk's quartet made their only studio recording of this song (*Underground* [Columbia CS 9632]). "Ugly Beauty" is significant in that it is Monk's only composed waltz.

Well, You Needn't—First recorded for Blue Note (549) on October 24, 1947, but an early version was copyrighted in 1944 under the title, "You Need' Na."

We See (aka **Manganese**)—First recorded on May 11, 1954 (Prestige PRLP 7053), it was named for Monk's niece "Weetee" but the title was lost in translation. It was mistitled **Manganese** when Monk recorded it in France in 1954. His producer, André Francis, came up with the title as a French-speaking pun on "Monk at Ease." And, of course, it refers to the mineral.

Who Knows—Yet another Blue Note–era tune recorded once and disbanded, **Who Knows** required eight takes when it was recorded in an October 21, 1947 session (Blue Note 1565, BNJ61011).

Work—Recorded only once, in a trio setting on September 22, 1954 (Prestige PRLP 7075), "Work" has one of those intricate melodies similar to "Trinkle Tinkle" and "Gallop's Gallop."

SELECTED RECORDINGS BY THELONIOUS MONK

The following list is not comprehensive. Rather, it is a representative example of Monk's entire body of work for readers who may want to pursue a deeper examination of the music. I have provided session details and other discographical information for all of Monk's recordings in the footnotes to this book, but in most cases list the original release rather than subsequent CD issues. For the most complete and accurate sessionography, see my website, http://monkbook .com. The site contains material related to Monk that could not be included in this book. The list below also excludes bootleg discs made from unauthorized concert recordings and radio broadcasts. For the most exhaustive discography of Monk's work, see Chris Sheridan, *Brilliant Corners: A Bio-Discography of Thelonious Monk* (Westport and London: Greenwood Press, 2001), or consult the following websites: Jacques Ponzio's "Round About Monk" website, www.sojazz.org/monk/thelonious05.html; Howard Mansfield's Thelonious Monk website, www.howardm.net/tsmonk; or the official Thelonious Monk site, www.monkzone.com.

The Early Thelonious Monk (Moon CD 086-2)

The Complete Blue Note Recordings (Blue Note 30363 4-CD boxed set)

Charlie Parker, Dizzy Gillespie, Thelonious Monk, *Bird & Diz* (Verve CD 314 521 436-2)

Solo 1954 (Vogue 111502)

Thelonious Monk—The Complete Prestige Recordings (Prestige 4428-2 3-CD boxed set)

Gigi Gryce, *Nica's Tempo* (Savoy MG 12137)

The Complete Riverside Recordings (Riverside RCD-022-2 15-CD set)

    Or the following individual Riverside releases:

    Thelonious Monk plays Duke Ellington (Riverside CD OJC 2531-24-4)

    The Unique Thelonious (CD OJC 2531-64-4)

    Brilliant Corners (CD OJC-026-2)

    Thelonious Himself (CD OJC 2531-254-2)

    Monk's Music (CD OJC-084-2)

    Thelonious Monk with John Coltrane (CD OJC 2531-039-4)

Gerry Mulligan and Thelonious Monk, *Mulligan Meets Monk* (CD OJC 2531-301-2)

Clark Terry Quintet, with Thelonious Monk, In Orbit (CD OJC 2531-302-4)

Thelonious Monk Quartet—Thelonious in Action (CD OJC-103-2)

Thelonious Monk Quartet—Misterioso (CD OJC-206-2)

The Thelonious Monk Orchestra at Town Hall (CD OJC 135-4)

5 by Monk by 5 (CD OJC-362-2)

Thelonious Alone in San Francisco (CD OJC 2531-231-2)

Thelonious Monk Quartet Plus Two at the Blackhawk (CD OJC 2531-305-2)

Thelonious Monk Quartet—Monk in France (CD OJC-670-2)

Thelonious Monk Quartet—Monk in Italy (CD OJC-488-2)

Art Blakey's Jazz Messengers with Thelonious Monk (Rhino R2 75598)

Thelonious Monk Quartet with John Coltrane at Carnegie Hall (Blue Note 35173)

Monk's Dream (Columbia CK 40786)

Criss-Cross (Columbia CK 48823)

It's Monk's Time (Columbia CK 468405)

Monk. (Columbia CK 468407)

Monk at Newport, 1963 & 1965 (Columbia C2K 63905)

Straight, No Chaser (Columbia CK 64886)

Underground (Columbia CK 40785)

Big Band and Quartet in Concert (Complete) (Columbia C2K 57636)

Monk in Tokyo (Columbia C2K 63538)

Straight, No Chaser Soundtrack (Columbia CK 45358)

Thelonious Monk—The Columbia Years (1962-1968) (Columbia C3K 64887)

Always Know (Columbia CD 469185-2)

Live At The Jazz Workshop Complete (Columbia C2K 65189)

Live At The It Club Complete (Columbia C2K 65288)

Monk Alone—The Complete Columbia Piano Solo Recordings (Columbia C2K 65495)

The Giants of Jazz (George Wein Collection) (Concord Jazz GW-3004)

Giants of Jazz in Berlin '71 (EmArcy 834567)

The Complete Vogue and Black Lion Recordings (Mosaic MR4-112 3-CD boxed set)

SELECTED DOCUMENTARIES AND VIDEOS OF THELONIOUS MONK

Robert Herridge, *The Sound of Jazz* (1957)

Bert Stern, *Jazz on A Summer's Day* (1958)

Roger Vadim (dir.), *Les liaisons dangereuses, 1960* (Fox Lorber DVD 2003)

Thelonious Monk in Japan—1963 (Toshiba / EMI TOLW-3123)

Thelonious Monk—"Japan–Europe 1961-1963" (Green Line Video 2)

Thelonious Monk: Monk in Europe (Green Line Video 18)

Jazz 625 - Giants of Jazz Golden Era - Thelonious Monk: Recorded at the Marquee Club in London - March 14, 1965. Vols. 1 and 2 (PNV 1035 and 1036). Also available as a bonus DVD on Thelonious Monk, *Monk 'Round the World* (Thelonious Records TMF 9323-9)

Monk in Oslo (1966) (Rhapsody films – 9024)

Christian and Michael Blackwood, *Monk* (Michael Blackwood Productions, 1968)

Christian and Michael Blackwood, *Monk in Europe* (Michael Blackwood Productions, 1968)

Thelonious Monk Solo '69 [Paris, December 1969] (Pioneer PILJ-1125 Laserdisc)

Thelonious Monk Quartet [Concert, Salle Pleyel, Paris, Monday December 15, 1969] (Pioneer PA92-473 and PILJ-1103)

Stephen Rice, Paul C. Matthews, and John Goodhue, *Music in Monk Time* (Songfilms—Jazz/Tribute/VA104)

Charlotte Zwerin and Bruce Ricker, *Straight, No Chaser: Thelonious Monk* (Warner Home Video 11896)

Toby Byron, *Thelonious Monk: American Composer* (BMG 80065-3)

Jean Bach, *A Great Day In Harlem* (ABC Video 41110)

Michael Stokes, *Celebrating a Jazz Master* (Thelonious Monk Institute of Jazz, 1986)

INDEX

ABOUT THE AUTHOR

Robin D. G. Kelley is Professor of History and American Studies at the University of Southern California. His books include *Race Rebels: Culture, Politics, and the Black Working Class* and *Freedom Dreams: The Black Radical Imagination*. He has written on music for the *New York Times*, the *Village Voice, Jazz Times, Lenox Avenue, The Nation*, and other publications, and in 2005 was nominated for a Jazz Journalist Association Award. He lives with his family and his Baldwin baby grand in Los Angeles.